Handbook of
SMALL GROUP RESEARCH

Handbook of
SMALL GROUP RESEARCH
Second Edition

A. Paul Hare

THE FREE PRESS
A Division of Macmillan Publishing Co., Inc.
NEW YORK

Collier Macmillan Publishers
LONDON

The Free Press
A Division of Macmillan Publishing Co., Inc.
866 Third Avenue, New York, N.Y. 10022

Collier Macmillan Canada, Ltd.

Library of Congress Catalog Card Number: 75–28569

Printed in the United States of America

printing number
    3 4 5 6 7 8 9 10

Library of Congress Cataloging in Publication Data

Hare, Alexander Paul
    Handbook of small group research.

    Bibliography: p.
    Includes index.
    1. Small groups. 2. Small groups--Research.
3. Small groups--Bibliography. I. Title.
HM133.H36 1976   301.18'5'018   75-28569
ISBN 0-02-913841-8

CONTENTS

Appendixes

Bibliography

Indexes

FIGURES

TABLES

PREFACE

THE GOAL OF THIS SECOND EDITION of my *Handbook of Small Group Research* is the same goal I had in 1962 when the first edition was published. Then I proposed to make "a first excursion through the literature in order to make available to students, researchers, and practitioners a catalogue of the field together with some suggestions of principles by which it may be organized." Now I have made a second excursion, using essentially the same approach.

There are some differences. (1) The "exhibits" which summarized research related to some major generalizations about group dynamics have been dropped, since the fact that several investigators can replicate the same finding is no longer news. There are now many more generalizations supported by many more replications. (2) The former chapter on interaction and decision process has now been split into three by adding separate chapters on group development and social perception. (3) The appendix giving a brief description of factor analysis has been dropped on the assumption that this statistical technique is now used more widely and the description, along with that of other statistical techniques referred to in this volume, is available in many standard statistics texts. (4) Appendixes giving suggestions for laboratory experiments, on the history of small group research, and on sensitivity training and other applications have been added. (5) Some hypotheses derived from functional theory are presented in the first chapter and applied at various points in the text where they seemed appropriate. And (6) there are now 6,037 references, compared with 1,385 in the earlier edition. As a result of the growth of research in the field over the past 15 years fewer articles are described in detail, most references are covered by a sentence or part of a sentence, and many articles are cited only by major emphasis. Thus the material in the text ranges from theoretical interpretations of a small number of studies, through brief summaries without any particular theoretical orientation, to lists of articles in the form of a topical bibliography.

This book is still intended primarily as a reference work rather than a college text, although the first edition was used as a text with advanced courses. The material covered includes research on the small group under controlled conditions as well as studies of interpersonal behavior in small groups in less formal, social situations. However, the field is not so broad as social psychology; such subjects as individual motivation, socialization, psycholinguistics, and mass phenomena are not included.

Since 1953 I have had a continuing interest in assembling and codifying the results of research on social interaction. This interest has led to a number of bibliographies, review articles, and books. Chief among them are "Bibliography of Small Group Research from 1900 through 1953" (Strodtbeck and Hare, 1954), *Small Groups: Studies in Social Interaction* (Hare, Borgatta, and Bales, 1955; rev. ed., 1965), *Handbook of Small Group Research* (Hare, 1962), and "Bibliography of Small Group Research: 1959–1969" (Hare, 1972a).

The present canvass of the literature includes all the references from the 1962 edition and the 1972 bibliography and extends the survey through all the relevant journals available in the University of Cape Town library as of December 1974. In the course of this review of the literature, two sets of abstracts have been checked completely under the listing "Small Groups" or comparable headings: *Psychological Abstracts* from the first volume in 1927 through volume 52 (1, 2, 4, 6), 1974, and *Sociological Abstracts* from the first volume in 1953 through volume 22 (1, 3), 1974. For the 1962 edition the *Annual Review of Psychology* and the following journals, which publish most of the articles on social interaction in small groups, were examined issue by issue from 1950 through February 1959: *American Journal of Sociology, American Psychologist, American Sociological Review, British Journal of Sociology, Current Sociology, Human Organization, Human Relations, Journal of Abnormal and Social Psychology, Journal of Applied Psychology, Journal of Consulting Psychology, Journal of Educational Psychology, Journal of Educational Sociology, Journal of Personality, Journal of Psychology, Journal of Social Psychology, Journal of Social Issues, Psychological Bulletin, Psychological Reports, Social Forces, Social Research, Sociology and Social Research,* and *Sociometry.* From March 1959 through December 1974 the same set of journals was checked with the exception of *Current Sociology, Human Organization, Journal of Educational Psychology, Journal of Educational Sociology,* and *Sociology and Social Research,* which were not available in the University of Cape Town library, and with the addition of *Behavioral Science, Journal of Abnormal Psychology, Journal of Applied Behavioral Science, Journal of Conflict Resolution, Journal of Experimental Social Psychology, Journal of Personality and Social Psychology, Proceedings of Annual Conventions of the American Psychological Association, Psychological Review, Small Group Behavior,* and *Sociological Inquiry.*

The present review focuses on the content of the research findings, with only a brief outline of the methods of research given in appendix 3. For summaries of current research techniques for the study of social interaction in small groups, the reader will find the following sources helpful: books on method, such as Jahoda, Deutsch, and Cook's *Research Methods in Social Relations* (1951) and Festinger and Katz's *Research Methods in the Behavioral Sciences* (1953); chapters in Lindzey's *Handbook of Social Psychology* (1954); and Lindzey and Aronson's *Handbook of Social Psychology* (1968).

As before, I have read a lot and learned a lot. I guess that I have rejected two articles as not relevant for every one that I have referred to in this volume. As you will see, much more work is needed before this mass of research is brought together into a single theoretical formulation. That task remains for some future time and probably for some other author.

ACKNOWLEDGMENTS

I AM STILL IN DEBT TO Professor Robert F. Bales of Harvard University, whose interest in the study of small groups provided both inspiration and guidance for the first edition of this handbook. Over the years since I left Harvard I have continued to use his category system for interaction process analysis and more recently his three-dimensional view of interaction, until I branched out and added a fourth dimension. I have also faithfully made duplicate copies of each new addition to his course description and reading list for use with "self-analytic groups." These groups have provided insights into group dynamics well beyond those obtainable through laboratory observation.

A more recent colleague, Dr. Andrew Effrat, now at the University of Toronto, introduced me to the AGIL functional categories and the intricacies of Parsonian theory. He proposed the LAIG theory of group development, which has helped me to understand development in small groups, mass rallies and protests, and other forms of collective behavior. In the earlier edition of this book the conceptual scheme was influenced by the three-dimensional analysis of Dr. William C. Schutz. I have Andy to thank for leading me into the fourth dimension.

Dr. Gerd Wiendieck, a colleague in the Department of Sociology at the University of Cape Town, read the manuscript in draft form and made many helpful suggestions for clarifications and additions.

I am also indebted to the authors and publishers who made it possible to include tables, charts, and other materials from previously published sources. Specific credits are given in the text.

On the task side of the ledger, Jill Curling combined expert typing with a determination to see that every jot and tittle was correctly placed. Thanks to her, most of the citations given in the text should match the references in the bibliography. Ramela Bhaga also pitched in at various points, pasting abstracts on cards, reading proof, duplicating pages, and doing with a smile whatever had to be done. Henry Goodman prepared the cards for the author index so that we could make sure that there was a reference for every citation and a citation for every reference.

On the editorial side, I wish to thank certain members of the staff of The Free Press for their help at various stages of manuscript preparation and book production. Charles Smith made the initial arrangements which have brought the second edition into being. Hunt Cole copy edited the text manuscript. Claude Conyers, as editorial supervisor, gave most careful attention to the many details that needed to be checked to bring consistency and style to the text. One need not have much understanding of role theory to know that he has turned in an outstanding performance. Paul van der Bijl, of Collier Macmillan South Africa (Pty.) Ltd., was also helpful in ensuring the rapid and safe transfer of manuscript and proofs to and from New York to Cape Town via Johannesburg.

On the social-emotional side, my wife June did her best to keep me in touch with the real world by using her charms to lure me away, occasionally, from the boxes of cards with notes about other people's research, with which I had apparently become obsessed.

INTRODUCTION

THE THREE PARTS of this book present essentially the same material organized in three different ways: first, by considering the central tendencies of the interaction process and group structure; second, by emphasizing the deviations from typical patterns that may result from variations in such factors as members' personalities, group size, and leadership; and third, by reviewing differences in productivity related to variations in group process and structure.

In chapter 1, the elements of social interaction are introduced. These concepts are elaborated in later chapters as parts of the conceptual scheme are discussed in detail. Since the basic problem in social psychology is *social control,* chapter 2 includes a review of research on the process through which culture develops, persists, and changes. Chapter 3 considers the interaction process as group members solve problems through discussion. This emphasis is continued in chapter 4 with a description of the phases a group passes through in its development during the course of a single meeting and over a series of meetings. An analysis of some of the details of social perception is included in chapter 5, since the observation of social objects is an important phase in the cycle of the social act. Part 1 of the text concludes with two chapters on aspects of group structure: the role system of the group and the network of interpersonal choice.

Part 2 reviews some of the factors which can be varied to produce changes in group norms, the interaction process, the role system, and the pattern of interpersonal choice. These factors are the personalities of members, social characteristics of members, group size, task, communication network, and leadership.

Part 3 is a summary of the literature from the point of view of productivity. Here the questions considered are "When is a group more productive than an individual?" and "What are the characteristics of the most productive groups, given the central tendencies described in part 1 and the variations producible by manipulating the factors described in part 2?"

The four appendixes provide specialized information for persons involved in teaching, research, or applications. Appendix 1 includes several small group experiments which may be used as classroom demonstrations. Appendix 2 reviews the history of small group research, with special attention to the period before the 1960s. Appendix 3 provides an outline of the most commonly used research methods. Finally, appendix 4 gives an overview of the application of group dynamics in sensitivity training and related areas together with a list of references to recent research.

In most chapters at least one relevant piece of research has been reported in some detail to allow the reader to evaluate its results in the context of the complete research design. Whenever possible, "classic" pieces of small group research have been used for this purpose. In some cases excerpts from these classics are quoted directly with minor changes in wording. In others there has been considerable editing to shorten the article while maintaining many of the author's original phrases. In general, tables or original data have not been given except to illustrate the findings in these key pieces of research.

One of the major problems in reviewing the literature is that of finding the least number of generalizations under which to subsume results of research. The present scheme is not a *theory* in any formal sense. Although some attempt is made to indicate what appear to be some of the basic elements in the interaction process and some of the relationships among these elements, the whole set of elements and generalizations has not been tied to a single, integrated framework. In many instances terms are used as the authors originally defined them. As a result, various meanings have been attached to the same term and various terms appear with substantially the same meaning.

Handbook of
SMALL GROUP RESEARCH

Part 1

GROUP PROCESS AND STRUCTURE

Chapter 1

ELEMENTS OF
SOCIAL INTERACTION

THE OBJECTIVE OF THE review of the literature on social interaction in small groups which led to the present volume has been to develop the broad outlines of a conceptual scheme for the analysis of human interaction. In reviewing the research published over the past years it became apparent that each social scientist was reporting some part of the social act which seemed important to him and which should be included in an overall theory of human interaction. Many of these previous researchers seemed to be talking about the same thing. The only problem was that they talked about it from different points of view and with different vocabularies. In the present review, some of the concepts are used in familiar ways, whereas others have been broadened to include several more specific concepts. The generalizations are made at a rather gross level, leaving the more subtle aspects of social interaction to be specified by future research.

Elements in the Interaction Process

The major elements appearing in most category systems for the analysis of social interaction are given in figure 1. Although the present focus is on the prediction of the interactive behavior of individuals in small groups, it is assumed that the same elements would appear in a theory which attempted to describe interaction of individuals in larger social units such as communities or nations. In the conceptual scheme to be developed here, *social interaction* is seen as a compromise between the inputs from man's *biological nature* and *personality,* on the one hand, and *role, culture,* and *environment,* on the other. Here *environment* refers to the natural and man-made nonhuman elements which form the situation in which the interaction occurs. To predict some aspects of social interaction, we need know only how an individual's biological nature typically responds to his environment. For some predictions, particularly with a clinical population, personality may be the dominant element in the system. However, we can predict many of the details of everyday life if we know only the patterns of behavior which are typical of the group or groups to which a person belongs.

SPECIAL NOTE: This chapter is based on "The Dimensions of Social Interaction" (Hare, 1960b) but has been extensively revised and updated.

Figure 1. Elements of Social Interaction

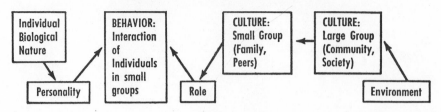

Man's *biological nature* and his *environment* represent a different order of data than the other elements of the system since they can be measured independently of the social behavior which one wishes to predict. However, the social nature of the individual and the social nature of the group are both abstractions from inter-active behavior. Those tendencies to behave which are consistent for an individual as he moves from group to group are called *personality*. The expectations shared by group members about the behavior associated with some position in a group, no matter what individual fills the position, are called *role*.[1] The same individual usually plays roles in a number of groups at the same time; some of these groups are small and some large. For example, an individual who is a student may also be a son, a husband, a club man, and a citizen. Although there are many occasions when he acts in only one role, there are enough instances of conflicting expecta-tions, particularly between small and large groups, to justify the designation of multiple group membership as a primary element in the conceptual scheme. The terms *small* and *large* are used here in a relative sense. Except for the group of two, a group may be broken down into subsystems. For groups of any size there is always some larger group to which an individual may also belong.

The sum of the expectations for the roles of all members of a group plus the expectations for behavior of members in general is the *culture* of a group. The culture includes patterns of behavior which are transmitted from one generation to the next. These patterns include ways of thinking, ways of acting, and ways of feeling.

The Small Group

There is no definite cutting point in the continuum between a collection of individuals, such as one might find waiting for a bus on a corner, and a fully organized "group." There is also no definite cutting point between the small, intimate, face-to-face group and the large, formal group. For a collection of indi-viduals to be considered a group there must be some *interaction*. In addition to the *interaction* of the members, four features of group life typically emerge as a *collection of individuals* develops into a *group* (Znaniecki, 1939; Sherif, 1954a):

---

1. Although a number of authors use the concept of role in a similar fashion, to refer to the "expectations" for behavior, others use it in a more general sense to refer to everything asso-ciated with a position in a group. When role is used in this general way the emphasis is on the *behavior* of the person playing the *role* rather than on the "expectations" for behavior. The term is actually used in both senses throughout the text. In the interest of having a con-ceptual scheme composed of nonoverlapping concepts, I have used *role* to mean "expectations," but in the interest of reviewing the literature without doing too much violence to the authors' original intentions, I have also used the term in the more general sense.

1. The members share one or more *motives* or *goals* which determine the direction in which the group will move.
2. The members develop a set of *norms,* which set the boundaries within which interpersonal relations may be established and activity carried on.
3. If interaction continues, a set of *roles* becomes stabilized and the new group becomes differentiated from other groups.
4. A *network of interpersonal attraction* develops on the basis of the "likes" and "dislikes" of members for one another.

There are then, in sum, five characteristics which differentiate the *group* from a *collection of individuals.* The members of the group are in *interaction* with one another. They share a common *goal* and set of *norms,* which give direction and limits to their activity. They also develop a set of *roles* and a *network of interpersonal attraction,* which serve to differentiate them from other groups.

Small groups include all those having from two up to about twenty members. However, even larger groups may be considered "small" if face-to-face interaction is possible, and collections of fewer than twenty individuals may actually include several smaller groups. The most commonly used definition of a small group is that given by Bales (1950b, p. 33):

A small group is defined as any number of persons engaged in interaction with each other in a single face-to-face meeting or a series of meetings, in which each member receives some impression or perception of each other member distinct enough so that he can, either at the time or in later questioning, give some reaction to each of the others as an individual person, even though it be only to recall that the other person was present.

Process, Structure, and Change

The relationship of the elements in social interaction may be examined from three points of view: process, structure, and change. When the focus is on *process,* we analyze the act-by-act sequence of events as it unfolds over time. This is a longitudinal approach. The same data may be used to describe the *structure* of the group where the focus is on the relations among elements in the system at a given time. This is the cross-sectional approach. The analysis of *social change* typically focuses on changes in the *structure* of a group over time.

These three themes of process, structure, and change appear at many points throughout the volume. In part 1, they form the basic framework around which the material is organized. Process is reviewed in chapter 3, two aspects of structure (roles and interpersonal choice) in chapters 6 and 7, and change in chapter 2.

The Form and Content of Social Behavior

With this general outline of the elements in an interactional system and some notion of the characteristics of a small group, we can now look a little more closely at the *behavior* of individuals in interaction. Observers of social behavior tend to break behavior down into three different categories. In some cases the focus is on *inter*personal behavior, such as cooperative problem-solving. In other cases it is on *intra*personal behavior, as evidenced in tension or anxiety. In still other cases the focus is on aspects of *individual performance,* which may characterize an individual whether he is alone or in a group. In this text, intrapersonal behavior and individual performance will be combined, leaving two very general categories—*interpersonal behavior* and *personal behavior.*

Although many different category systems can be used in describing interpersonal behavior, the categories of interaction given in figure 2 appear to represent the major "dimensions" of observed behavior. The categories are given here in simplified form and will be elaborated at later points in the text, particularly in chapter 8 on personality.

The form of interaction is less specific than content and is more easily recorded. As one approaches a group from the "outside," the first aspect of interaction which becomes apparent is the communication network (i.e., who speaks to whom), and next the amount of interaction carried by each of the communication channels. For a closer analysis of *what* is going on in the group, one needs some content categories. Here the most frequent division is between content directed primarily towards the solution of task problems *versus* content directed primarily towards the solution of social-emotional problems. Within the social-emotional area, the categories of control and affection represent the predominant types of behavior, whereas in the task area there is less consensus on the "typical" problem-solving categories. The minimum set of categories would probably parallel the steps in the scientific method, namely of observation, hypothesis formation, and the testing of hypotheses.

Each of the major categories in figure 2 can be defined as follows:

FORM
>   *Communication network.* The channels of communication between group members.
>   *Interaction rate.* The frequency of interactions, sometimes represented by the number of contributions, sometimes by the relationship between the number and duration of contributions, i.e., action and silence, and sometimes by the number of contributions times the average duration of each, i.e., total talking time.

CONTENT
>   *Task behavior.* Interaction directed toward the completion of group or individual tasks. The minimum number of categories would include observing, hypothesizing, and formulating action.
>   *Social-emotional behavior.* Interaction directed primarily toward the relationships between group members that form the basis for problem-solving. The minimum number of categories would include control and affection.

Each of these categories can be used at the level of personality, behavior, and role. At the personality level they represent *tendencies to act,* and at the level of role they represent *expectations for behavior.*

Output and Input: Form

The description of the behavior of an individual from the interactional point of view includes not only how he acts toward others (output), but also how others respond to him (input). For this reason, the minimum number of actors involved is two, the minimum number of acts is two (one action and one reaction), and the

Figure 2. Paradigm for the Analysis of Interaction

Form	Communication network
	Interaction rate
Content	Task behavior a. observe b. hypothesize c. propose action
	Social-emotional behavior a. control b. affection

minimum number of time periods in which interaction occurs is two (Bales and Slater, 1955).

The output and input characteristics for both form and content of interaction can be considered with varying degrees of complexity. For the communication network, one could record simply the total number of channels for outgoing messages and incoming messages. At the other extreme one could specify the extent to which each channel from a subject to every other member of the group is open for output or input. Similarly, the interaction rate can be described simply as the total number of acts an individual gives and the total number he receives, or the output and input rate could be given for each channel in the communication network.

Although it is possible to differentiate output from input for the communication network, particularly experiments where the communication network is the major variable, the correlation between output and input for a given channel is very high. The person who speaks most often in a group is usually the one who is spoken to most often. In those cases where the correlation is high, specification of the input characteristics may add little to the description of the interaction process.

This type of reduction in the number of experimental "variables" occurs over and over again in those experiments which use comprehensive category systems for recording the interaction process. Since relatively few categories of behavior are appropriate in any given situation, most of the interaction tends to take place within two or three categories. As a result, the remaining categories are either correlated with these or appear too infrequently to yield reliable measures.

Output and Input: Content

For the analysis of behavior where one may wish to consider several categories of content simultaneously, the characteristics of an individual's interaction for either output or input may be described by a set of *interaction profiles* similar to those used by Bales (1950b). If only one dimension or area of content is to be considered at a time, a graphic plot may be used to advantage, with one axis representing output and the other input (see figure 3). The explicit recognition of the distinction between input and output may help clarify some theoretical issues, especially in the construction of typologies.

In the description of behavior tendencies in the area of control, for example,

Figure 3. Representation of Input and Output in a Two-dimensional Plot

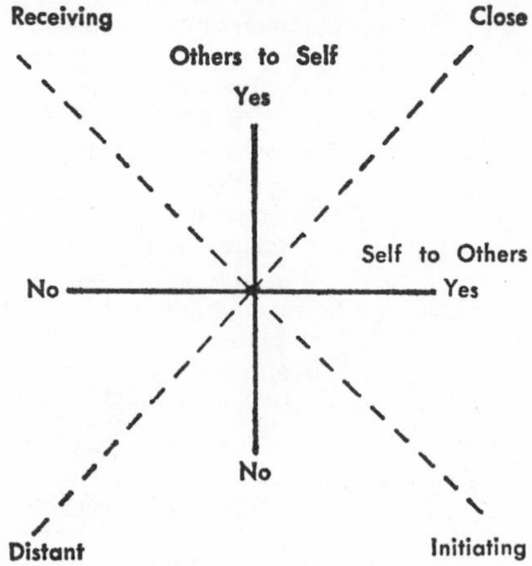

the vertical axis might represent the behavior desired from others ranging from yes, he wants to be controlled by others, to no, he does not want to be controlled by others. The horizontal axis could then represent the desired behavior toward others ranging from yes, he wants to control others, to no, he does not want to control others.

The individual who wants strongly to control and to be controlled may be called *authoritarian*. On the other hand, the individual who wants neither to control nor to be controlled may be said to desire a situation in which there is distance between group members. In the extreme, this kind of independence may be called *anarchism*.

On the opposite diagonal are individuals who vary from wanting to control but not be controlled, the *dominators,* to those who want to be controlled but do not want to conrol, the *submitters*. In the center are those individuals who want both to control and to be controlled in a moderate degree, a type of behavior which tends to be called *democratic*. All other combinations of tendencies to give or receive control can be represented as points in this two-dimensional space.

In the description of *personality,* the two axes in figure 3 would represent the tendencies to give and receive, which the individual brings to the situation. In the description of *role,* the axes would represent expected behavior, the duties (output) and the rights (input) associated with each role. The expectations for behavior would vary along each axis from behavior which is required to that which is prohibited.

Personal Behavior

In addition to the interpersonal categories, there are dimensions of *personal* behavior, which also play a part in the activity of a group. The personal categories include those dimensions usually associated with personality such as intelligence, social sensitivity, and adjustment, as well as aspects of the individual's biological nature such as age, sex, and physical strength. These categories like the previously discussed interpersonal categories can also be used to describe "tendencies" within the individual and "expectations" for the role he is to perform.

Although the mean or average behavior in each category is stressed in the present formulation, this should not obscure the fact that the mean may not be as important for the prediction of behavior in a particular instance as some measure of the extent of variation and the conditions under, which the variation occurs.

Predicting Behavior from Personality and Role

To predict an individual's behavior in one of the form or content areas, one could first indicate on the plane a point representing the tendency in the personality (see figure 4) and also a point representing the expected behavior called for by the individual's role in the group. The actual behavior would then lie somewhere along the line between the personality and the role.

In a ceremony, such as a marriage, the actual behavior would be very close to the role. At the other extreme, when role is not well defined, for example, the role for a patient in a mental hospital ward, the behavior would be close to the tendencies in personality. Since in many personalities and in many roles one of the content areas may be more salient than the others, an individual's behavior may be predominantly in *one* of the content areas.

Variations in Interaction Rate

The characteristic of an individual's interactive behavior most frequently reported in the literature is his interaction rate. An individual's interaction rate can vary while the content of interaction remains relatively stable. In most situations the interaction rate of a single group member is related to the rates of the other members of the group as well as to his own personality.

An increase in the interaction rate of an individual may be associated with activity in any one of the content areas. In some experiments, an increase in interaction has been found to be associated with attempts to control a deviant member

Figure 4. The Relationship between Personality, Behavior, and Role in One Content Category

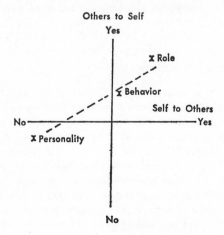

(Schachter, 1951). In other research, a high interaction rate is correlated with task success (Strodtbeck, 1954a). In still other studies, as for example in the observation of working girls doing piecework which does not require control, the interaction rate is highly correlated with affection (Homans, 1950).

Choice Behavior and Cohesiveness

The criteria which individuals use in making interpersonal choices may fall into any of the content areas. However, in social research, subjects are often asked to designate group members whom they would like to work with (a criterion which appears to combine task ability and control), and whom they would like to play with (a criterion which appears to be primarily affection). Since individuals who desire to be close to people will choose others who prefer closeness, it is generally true that "birds of a feather flock together." However, individuals who like to initiate tend to choose those who like to receive, so that it is also true that "opposites attract."

Groups containing a large number of mutual choices on either a "work" or "play" criterion are often said to be highly "cohesive" in that they will "stick together" longer than groups in which there are few mutual choices. Although groups are often referred to as being highly "cohesive" without specifying the basis on which the choices were made, the criterion is important. Subjects who have chosen each other because they like to work with each other should be more productive than those who have chosen each other because they like to play together, provided, of course, that the task calls for the type of control relationships which they prefer. A group composed of anarchists who had chosen each other could not be expected to do well on a task requiring authoritarian relationships.

The importance of the criterion on which choice is based is not always evident in the literature since many subjects will make the same choices regardless of the criterion which the experimenter suggests. In some cases, the multiple choice is justified since there are "great men" who are actually high on all criteria (Borgatta, Couch, and Bales, 1954), but in other cases it appears that the subject has his own preferred criterion for choice and will use the same one no matter what the experimenter suggests (E. G. French, 1956). That is, a subject with a salient need for affection would always choose others whom he expected to satisfy his affectional need whether the situation called for affection, or some other predominant category of behavior.

Formal and Informal Structure

Since expectations for behavior tend to vary in the extent to which they are "formally" defined by group members, it is often useful to differentiate the *formal* role structure of the group from the *informal* role structure. Of the two types of structure, the formal structure is usually more visible since it is often recorded in the group's table of organization. In the *informal* structure, such positions as "best-liked" or "scapegoat" can be identified through the use of "sociometric" tests on which group members indicate their choices or rejections of other group members. The direction of interpersonal choice may also be inferred from behavioral indices, such as frequency of association, or the content category which dominates the interaction with a given individual.

Within the role structure, the various positions may be ordered in a hierarchy according to their relative evaluation. Some investigators treat the role structure of the group (either formal or informal) as if it consisted of only a single *hierarchy* in which each role included expectations for behavior in all categories. Other investigators treat the structure as if it were composed of several *hierarchies,* each composed of roles represented by some dominant category of interaction; for example, "task ability" or "likeability." In the latter formulation, an individual can be said to have a high status in one hierarchy and a low status in another.

Four Problems for Groups

Another way of looking at social behavior is to consider the goal to which the behavior is directed. The categories in figure 2 suggest the range of observable variation in the social behavior of two or more individuals working together on a common task, but they do not specify the types of tasks which groups may have as a central focus or the direction the interaction process may take. If one assumes that human behavior is directed primarily toward the solution of problems, particularly the problem of survival, then all human behavior in groups can be described in relation to the solution of four types of problems represented by the four cells in figure 5.

Two of these problems are at the group level, and two are at the individual level. At the group level, the first problem is that of the task, the solution of a publicly stated problem of the group. Second is the solution of group problems in the social-emotional area. These problems often take the form of a "hidden agenda" dealing with shared anxieties which are not explicitly stated and dealing with the establishment of the group structure. The third type of problem is the task for the individual, a publicly stated individual goal. The fourth type consists of the individual's social-emotional problems, his efforts to deal with his own problems of membership and self-integration.

Although these four types of problems are present in all groups, some groups emphasize one type rather than another. For example, a typical action group, such as an industrial team, sees problem-solving of the first type as its goal. Some seminars in group dynamics emphasize a goal of the second type, an awareness of the social-emotional problems of the group. A goal of type three is typically the

Figure 5. Four Problems for Groups

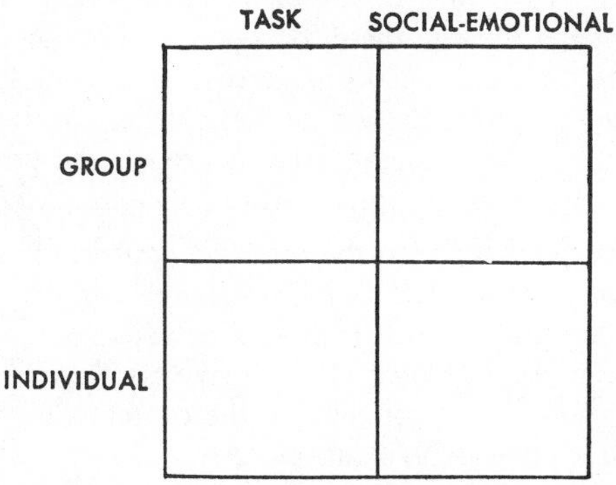

goal of most educational enterprises, while the fourth goal of individual social adjustment is the concern of group therapy (Thelen, 1954). In some analyses of group problems, only those of types one, two, and four are emphasized (Harnack, 1953).

This table of four types of goals, two for the group and two for the individual, can be expanded to a table of eight if one considers each of these problems first in relation to the group being studied and then in relation to other groups. That is, the success of the resolution of the publicly stated problem of the small group can be evaluated in its own terms or in terms which are relative to the solutions contributed by other groups. The structure of the group can be examined from a position internal to it, or one can relate the structure of the small group to that of the larger society. The individual's goals can be evaluated from within the group or from the outside, and so on. For example, at the individual level, the task goal might be to gain good grades in a particular class, but in the larger social system, to earn a college degree. Or, at the individual social-emotional level, the individual may want to satisfy only some of his needs in one group, because other needs are satisfied in other groups to which he belongs.

These four types of problems for individuals and groups usually have a priority for the individual member in the reverse order in which they have been presented. That is, the individual views as most important a problem of type four, then three, two, and one. Usually the individual has more energy to devote to his individual task after he has satisfied his own social-emotional needs. In turn, a satisfactory solution to the problems of group structure facilitates the solution of the group task.

Norms and Social Control

Individuals and groups form and conform to norms to achieve goals. Since goal achievement for a group depends upon concerted action, some consensus on acceptable task and social-emotional behavior must be attained before the members of a group can act together. For this reason even competition requires a minimum of cooperation in establishing and maintaining the rules of the contest. The goal which is achieved through conformity may be at any one or any combination of the four levels of group task, group structure, individual task, and individual integration.

The Functional Needs of Groups

Up to this point my review of the elements of social interaction is the same as in the 1962 edition. Although these concepts still provide an introduction to the field, I have since found that a more detailed understanding of functional theory has been useful in the interpretation of some parts of the literature, especially when considering the basic problems faced by groups, the process of social control, and the phases in group development. The following brief overview, including some examples of applications, has been extracted and adapted from Hare (1973a).[2]

When a set of people come together for some purpose or with some goal in mind they form a group. Some of these groups are small. In such a group the members can

2. A. Paul Hare, "Group Decision by Consensus: Reaching Unity in the Society of Friends," *Sociological Inquiry* 43, 1 (1973): 77–80. Reprinted by permission of the publisher.

meet face to face. Some groups can be very large. In the largest groups, whole societies, the members may all be aware that they are part of the same tribe or nation but may never meet more than a fraction of the total group in their lifetime. All of these groups, if they are to survive, must meet four basic needs: (L) the members must share some common identity and have some commitment to the values of the group, (A) they must have or be able to generate the skills and resources necessary to reach the group goal, (I) they must have rules which allow them to coordinate their activity and enough feeling of solidarity to stay together to complete the task, and finally (G) they must be able to exercise enough control over their membership to be effective in reaching their common goal.

This Four Functions (or AGIL) scheme for the analysis of groups has been developed in large part by Talcott Parsons and his colleagues to provide a comprehensive theory for the study of social groups.[3] The four categories of the AGIL scheme—Adaptation, Goal attainment, Integration and Latent pattern maintenance and tension management (or simply pattern maintenance)—were derived empirically from an analysis of small groups, psychotherapy, and the economic factors in production. However, they may also be derived by cross cutting two major continua of problems confronting any goal-directed action system. The first continuum concerns whether the problem is primarily *internal* to the system or primarily *external*. The second continuum concerns whether the structure or processes are primarily oriented toward *instrumental activities* (such as developing, gathering, preparing, or generalizing means or facilities) or toward *consummatory* ones (such as using, applying, or consuming the resources). This results in a two by two table (see figure 6).

In a large social system the four categories, AGIL, are represented by the economic, political, legal, and familial and religious substructures. For each of these substructures there is a generalized medium of exchange (money, power, influence, and commitments), a value principle which guides action in this area (utility, effectiveness, solidarity, and integrity), and a standard of coordination for activity in this area (solvency, success, consensus, and pattern consistency). A summary of these concepts is given in figure 7.

Thus an activity which seems to be primarily economic, such as raising money to be used for the general purposes of a group, where the focus is on utility with concern for solvency, would be classified as the *A* or *Adaptive* sector. In contrast, an activity which seemed religious or familial, which had to do with forming basic commitments to the group, was concerned with its integrity, and was related to the consistency of its pattern of activity over time would be classified in the *L* or *Pattern-maintenance* sector. In a

Figure 6. Paradigm of Functional Problems

		Action Direction	
		Instrumental	Consummatory
Boundary reference	External	Adaptation	Goal attainment
	Internal	Pattern maintenance	Integration

Source: A. Paul Hare, "Group Decision by Consensus," *Sociological Inquiry* 43 (1973). Reprinted by permission of the editor for Alpha Kappa Delta.

3. A summary appears in Parsons (1961) and in Effrat (1968) and other articles in a special issue of *Sociological Inquiry.*

Figure 7. Substructures, Generalized Media of Exchange, Value Principles, and Standards of Coordination for Four Functional Problems

	Instrumental	Consummatory
External	(1) Adaptation (2) Economic (3) Money (4) Utility (5) Solvency	(1) Goal attainment (2) Political (3) Power (4) Effectiveness (5) Success
Internal	(1) Pattern maintenance (2) Familial and Religious (3) Commitments (4) Integrity (5) Pattern consistency	(1) Integration (2) Legal (3) Influence (4) Solidarity (5) Consensus

Key: (1) the functional problem
(2) the substructure at the social system level
(3) the generalized medium of exchange
(4) the value principle
(5) the coordinative standard

Source: A. Paul Hare, "Group Decision by Consensus," *Sociological Inquiry* 43 (1973). Reprinted by permission of the editor for Alpha Kappa Delta.

Figure 8. Toward Operationalizing the AGIL Scheme

L PHASE + Seeks or provides basic categories or ultimate values
Asks for or seeks to define:
basic purpose or identity of group
fundamental meaning of "all this"
general orientation
basic obligations
− Seeks to deny, take away, or inhibit the development and recognition of values.

I PHASE + Seeks or provides solidarity or norms (as primary mechanisms of conflict management)
Asks for or seeks to define:
how the group can get along better, promote harmony, or decrease conflict
what the specific norms governing relations should be
− Seeks to deny, inhibit, or prevent the formation of norms and movement toward group solidarity

G PHASE + Seeks or provides relatively specific direction, goal-definition, or problem solutions relevant to the group's goals.
Asks for or seeks to define:
relatively specific group goals (be careful to distinguish from values and norms)
decisions which in effect are attainment of group goals
− Seeks to prevent or inhibit movement toward the group's goals

A PHASE + Seeks or provides facilities for goal attainment
Asks for or seeks to define:
how to get or increase (especially to generalize) resources, relevant information, or facts
− Seeks to deny, inhibit, or prevent the provision of facilities and relevant information

Source: A. Paul Hare, "Group Decision by Consensus," *Sociological Inquiry* 43 (1973). Reprinted by permission of the editor for Alpha Kappa Delta.

similar way other activities of a group would be classified as related to the other two functions: *Integration* or *Goal attainment*.

A further indication of the content of the acts which are related to each sector is given in figure 8, a step toward operationalizing the AGIL scheme.

The Cybernetic Hierarchy of Control

The "cybernetic hierarchy of control" is a concept which can be applied to both physical and social systems. The basic idea is that a unit containing information will be able to control a unit containing raw energy. Thus a thermostat which processes information will control a furnace which produces heat or a computer will control the sequence of activities on an industrial production line. In the case of groups the highly generalized normative elements of the system generally guide and control the more specific aspects of action. Thus the area of pattern maintenance controls the integrative area, which in turn provides more control than the goal-attainment area. The adaptive area ranks lowest in its influence on the other parts of the system.

Each of the four functional areas which have been discussed up to this point are actually substructures within the *social system level* of the total system of human action. There are four major system levels which fit the same fourfold paradigm which has been identified before. (See figure 9.) The four system levels are cultural, social, personality, and organismic. They are also related to each other in the cybernetic hierarchy of control. That is, in the total action system, the values represented by the culture are more controlling than the norms of the social system, which are in turn more controlling than the personality of the individual. Finally personality characteristics play a more dominant and controlling role in social interaction than the biological traits and processes of the physical organism.

Group Development

At the social system level, which is the focus of our analysis of groups, groups seem to develop through a sequence of stages in the order L-A-I-G. In a learning group, such as a classroom group, the sequence of events seems to be as follows: first, the work of the group requires that the purpose of the group be defined (L), second, that new skills be acquired (A), third, that the group be reorganized so that the members can try out the new skills without being too dependent on the leader (I), and fourth, that the group members work at the task (G). Finally there is a terminal phase in which the group returns to L to redefine the relationships between the members and the group as the group is disbanded. The amount of time the group spends in each phase is determined by the activity of the leader (his direction or non-direction) and by the

Figure 9. Four Subsystems of the Total Action System Classified by Functional Sector

	Instrumental	Consummatory
External	Organismic level	Personality level
Internal	Cultural level	Social system level

Source: A. Paul Hare, "Group Decision by Consensus," *Sociological Inquiry* 43 (1943). Reprinted by permission of the editor for Alpha Kappa Delta.

skill and emotional strengths of the members. Presumably the leader is "ready" for each stage at the outset since he has been through the stages before. However, members come to the group with different degrees of problem-solving skills or preferences for different emotional modalities. Subgroups tend to form on the basis of these skills or emotional modalities. If the subgroup with the appropriate skills and emotional state for each stage is large enough it can carry the whole group through that phase. If not enough members of the group are ready for a particular stage, more intervention by the leader may be necessary. Some groups may never progress beyond the early stages.

We might suppose that groups would develop through the four stages in the order of the cybernetic hierarchy of control. Indeed, at one point in the development of the functional approach Parsons and Bales suggested that problem-solving groups go through a sequence of stages in the order A-G-I-L, while learning groups or therapy groups develop in the order L-I-G-A (Parsons, Bales, and Shils, 1953). However, these models were based on somewhat different definitions of the basic categories than those used in the present analysis. What seems to be happening is that the members of a group "test the limits" in the different functional areas as they try to determine whether or not they can form a fully functioning group. It is not difficult to see that a group must begin with a basic purpose (L) and end with the enactment of that purpose (G), but whether A should come before I or vice versa may not be immediately clear. The dramatic example of a trip to the moon might help. Once there is an idea of the possibility of the trip, one can imagine different types of group organization (I) which would be best. However, these plans are limited by the availability of a rocket big enough to lift a group to the moon. If only a small rocket is available, the effort becomes an individual task rather than a group task. If it is to be a group task, the presence of two, three, or more astronauts is again determined by the size of the rocket. Thus, although in the cybernetic hierarchy of control the rocket represents the raw energy and is at the bottom of the hierarchy, there can be no movement without it. Further in this case, and in general, the availability and complexity of equipment may determine whether or not a single individual can achieve a goal or whether a group is required. Thus the developing group starts at the top of the hierarchy with L, then checks out the lowest point, A, to see if the game can proceed (if no one brings a ball, we can't play). Once resources are assured, the group moves back up to the next highest level (I) to the roles of the group members, before proceeding to carry out the actual work of the group (G).

Summary

The goal of this chapter has been to develop the outlines of a conceptual scheme for the analysis of human interaction in small groups. The major elements in the scheme are man's biological nature and personality, which influence his interaction from the "inside" and his roles in the small and large group, and environment, which influence his interaction from the "outside." Interactive behavior is thus seen as a compromise between the needs of the individual and the demands of the situation.

Although there is no definite upper limit to the size of a "small" group, a group is usually defined as "small" if each member has the opportunity for face-to-face interaction with all others. The process by which a collection of individuals becomes a group includes the evolution of a set of goals and norms, the development of a role system, and the establishment of a network of affective ties. The relationship of the elements affecting the interaction of group members may be examined from the point of view of process, structure, or change.

Behavior, personality, and role each have both interpersonal and personal aspects. The interpersonal categories include, under form, communication network and interaction rate, and, under content, task behavior and social-emotional behavior. Both input and output characteristics in each category would be included in a complete description of the interaction process. Because of the limitations set by role expectations, the interaction rate of an individual may be correlated with behavior in one of the content areas.

Interpersonal choices, which represent a frequently studied aspect of social interaction, may be based on criteria which fall into any of the interpersonal categories. The criteria actually used by an individual will vary with his personality and the situation in which the choice is made.

In many groups, there is an informal structure which is indicated by the network of interpersonal choice as well as a formal structure which may be represented by an organizational chart. Within each structure, the roles tend to be ordered according to their relative evaluation into one or more hierarchies.

Group members have four types of problems to solve, two at the group level and two at the individual level. At each level there are both task problems and social integration problems. The individual must usually satisfy his own needs and reach his own goal before he is willing to give time to the organization of the group and the accomplishment of the group task. Conformity to norms is necessary to solve problems at all levels.

Functional theory suggests that groups must meet four basic needs in order to survive: (L) the members must share a common identity and have a commitment to the values of the group, (A) they must have or be able to generate the skills and resources necessary to reach the group goal, (I) they must have rules which allow them to coordinate their activity and enough feeling of solidarity to stay together to complete the task, and finally (G) they must provide enough leadership and control to be effective in reaching their goal. Groups usually develop through the four phases in the order L-A-I-G with a terminal phase of L. The power of each of these areas in providing control over group members tends to follow the cybernetic hierarchy of control with the areas of high information controlling the areas of high energy in the order L-I-G-A. In the total action system the L, I, G, and A sectors are represented by the four levels: cultural, social system, personality, and organismic.

The approach to the analysis of interaction in small groups outlined in this chapter is suggested as a framework for organizing ideas. The elements included in the theory have been found to be important sources of variation in social behavior in a variety of situations. However, the prediction of behavior in any specific situation may require knowledge of only a few of these elements or, on the other hand, an elaboration and differentiation of these concepts well beyond the present level of analysis.

Additional References

The texts and edited works which cover the major contributions to the study of small groups include Homans, 1950; Klein, 1956; Bonner, 1959; Olmsted, 1959; Stogdill, 1959; Thibaut and Kelley, 1959; Bion, 1961; Klein, 1961; Golembiewski, 1962; Berne, 1963; Berkowitz, 1964–1968; Hare, Borgatta, and

Bales, 1965; McGrath and Altman, 1966; T. M. Mills, 1967; Cartwright and Zander, 1968; Lindzey and Aronson, 1968; Sills, 1968; Bales, 1970a; Mills and Rosenberg, 1970; Shaw, 1971; Knowles and Knowles, 1972; Napier and Gershenfeld, 1973; Ofshe, 1973; Homans, 1974; Crosbie, 1975.

Books which are more specialized in that they refer to only part of the field or more general in that they refer to subject matter which is only partly relevant to small groups include Coyle, 1930, 1937; Benne and Muntyan, 1951; Guetzkow, 1951; Kozman, 1951; Stirn, 1952; Swanson, Newcomb, and Hartley, 1952; Parsons, Bales, and Shils, 1953; Argyle, 1957b; Gittler, 1957; Schaffner, 1957; Heider, 1958; Maccoby, Newcomb, and Hartley, 1958; Lifton, 1961; Newcomb, 1961; Verba, 1961; King, 1962; Goffman, 1963; Berne, 1964; Hopkins, 1964; Mills, 1964; Shepherd, 1964; Barber, 1966; Slater, 1966; Mann, Gibbard, and Hartman, 1967; Argyle, 1969; Borgatta, 1969; J. H. Davis, 1969a; Goffman, 1969; Luft, 1970; Shaw and Costanzo, 1970; Ward, 1970; Argyle and Lee, 1972; Scharmann, 1972; Sudnow, 1972; Secord and Backman, 1974; Tubbs and Moss, 1974.

Articles which provide theoretical statements, reviews of the literature, or bibliographies include Lasswell, 1939; Wirth, 1939; Znaniecki, 1939; Homans, 1947; Cattell, 1948; Loomis and Beegle, 1948; Bruner, 1950; James, 1950; Cattell, 1951a, 1951b; Hill, 1951; Katz, 1951; M. B. Smith, 1952; Benne and Levit, 1953; Carter, 1953; Horwitz, 1953; Horowitz and Perlmutter, 1953; Newcomb, 1953b; Bogardus, 1954; Crutchfield, 1954; Maas, 1954a; Strodtbeck, 1954b; Strodtbeck and Hare, 1954; Argyle, 1955; Brown and Brown, 1955; Coser, 1955; Deets, 1955–1956; Dodd, 1955; Festinger, 1955; Stirn, 1955; R. L. French, 1955; Israel, 1956; Strodtbeck, 1956; Cartwright, 1957; Corsini and Putzey, 1957; Criswell and Petrullo, 1957; McGrath, 1957; Sherif, 1957; Bales, 1959; M. L. Borgatta, 1958; Hare, 1958; Heyns, 1958; Dupuis, 1959; Gilchrist, 1959; Jackson, 1959a; Raven, 1959b; Borgatta, 1960b, 1960c; de Montmollin, 1960; Keltner, 1960; Riecken, 1960; Terauds, Altman, and McGrath, 1960; Atoji, 1961; Borgatta and Simpson, 1961; Keltner, 1961; Meister, 1961; Shaw, 1961b; Anger, 1962; March, 1962; Matejko, 1962; Hare, 1963; Irle, 1963; McGrath, 1963a, 1963b; Hare, 1964; Moreno, 1964; Sherwood, 1964; Steiner, 1964; Cloyd, 1965; DeLamater, McClintock, and Becker, 1965; Hoffman and Arsenian, 1965; Jones and Davis, 1965; Raven, 1965; Anger, 1966; Gerard and Miller, 1967; Gouldner, Goode, and Bettelheim, 1967; Allport, 1968; Aronson and Carlsmith, 1968; Collins and Raven, 1968; Deutsch, 1968a, 1968b; Effrat, 1968; Homans, 1968; Ingils, 1968; Parsons, 1968a, 1968b; Swanson, 1968; Burnstein, 1969b; Rice, 1969; Bales, 1970b; C. Couch, 1970; Pentony, 1970; Stirn, 1970; Irle, 1971; Kolominskiy, 1971; Leik and Curry, 1971; Weschsler, 1971; Blomfield, 1972; Cowell, 1972; Gillespie, 1972; Hare, 1972a; Kolominskiy, 1972; Sader, 1972; Abraham, 1973; Betz, 1973; Runcie, 1973; Helmreich, Bakeman, and Scherwitz, 1973; Steiner, 1974; Swanson, 1974; Anger and Nachreiner, 1975.

Chapter 2

NORMS AND
SOCIAL CONTROL

THE FRAMEWORK FOR THE analysis of social interaction outlined in chapter 1 indicated that the interaction process was the result of a compromise between the needs of group members (biological nature and personality) and the demands of the situation (role expectations and environment). The present chapter analyzes the process by which the group brings pressure to bear on its members to conform to group norms. In laboratory experiments on conformity, the extent of group influence on an individual's judgment is found to be a function of the *object* to be judged, the *subject* who is making the judgment, and the *situation* in which he finds himself. The study of the process of *social control* is a basic problem for social psychology, since it is only with some type of social control that individuals can carry out concerted action and thus become a group.

Formation of Norms

Group members tend to form and conform to norms. Norms are rules of behavior, proper ways of acting, which have been accepted as legitimate by members of a group. Norms specify the kinds of behavior that are expected of group members. These rules or standards of behavior to which members are expected to conform are for the most part derived from the goals which a group has set for itself. Given a set of goals, norms define the kind of behavior which is necessary for or consistent with the realization of those goals (Bates and Cloyd, 1956). When the *norms* refer to the expectations for a single individual they constitute the individual's *role*. The norms are then, in effect, the expectations for the role of an "undifferentiated group member." Each person has within him a set of norms and goals which are a composite of his own idiosyncratic ideals, the expectations of the group in which he is participating at the moment, and the expectations of other groups of which he is also a member.

The shared expectations developed in the current group are added to the prior ones as group members go through the process of culture building. Especially in the early meetings of a group, much of the members' attention is taken up with decisions about rules for appropriate behavior. This process may not be recognized

19

by the group members until the group bogs down on some simple issue, such as the length of time for a coffee break. It is only when they are faced with the problem of allotting time (a scarce commodity) for particular activities that the members discover that they have not reached a consensus on such basic issues as the relative importance of the needs of the task *versus* the needs of the individual members. The concern over *norms* and *goals* is the old problem of the *means* and the *ends,* and there is no basis for *organized* interaction in a group until some agreement is reached about each of these kinds of expectations.

When the individual's norms and goals are in accord with those of the group, his behavior will meet approval. However, if the group finds that the behavior of one deviates from the group norms, the individual has four choices: *to conform, to change the norms, to remain a deviant,* or *to leave the group.* Of course, he may also be removed from the group without his consent. The literature on the formation of norms and social control in the small group deals with the first three types of behavior, *conformity, change,* and *pressures on the deviant.* Current research with leaderless groups has little to say about the choice to leave the group, since most of these experimental groups are disbanded after only a few meetings. The problem of withdrawal of a group member is a real one for the group therapist, however, since the antisocial person may be just the type that he is trying to reach through this kind of therapy.

Social Control

The process by which the individual manipulates the behavior of others or by which group members bring pressure on the individual is the process of *social control.* Through social control, behavior is confined to acceptable limits, limits which maximize the possibilities of survival for the individual in the group. Social control can be thought of as *formal,* the rules and regulations imposed by a large organization, or *informal,* the social pressure of the small intimate group. Although there are many instances in which social control is forcibly applied by others, in most cases social control is *self-control.* This is the self-control which takes place during the initial phase of the social act when the individual modifies his behavior as a result of his anticipation of the response of the other person. If the individual is at all effective in his social relationships, the process of social control will be over before his overt act. Since the absolute degree of conformity to a group norm is a function of the initial distance from the norm, individuals who show the greatest deviation can also show the greatest amount of change toward conformity (Goldberg, 1954; Rule, 1964; Rule and Renner, 1965, 1968; Nemeth and Markowski, 1972).

This process of modification of behavior may range from an individual's conscious attempts to conform to norms to the unconscious acceptance of group or individual directives. The latter case is exemplified by the psychological experiments in "operant conditioning." In these experiments, subjects are "conditioned" to carry out sequences of behavior, such as taking the top off a fountain pen and putting it back, by continually "rewarding" bits of behavior, until the final sequence of behavior which the experimenter desires is produced (Verplanck, 1956).

The Autokinetic Effect and Group Norms

Sherif uses the autokinetic effect to demonstrate the relations between individual and group norms (Sherif, 1935, 1936; Sherif and Sherif, 1956; Sherif, 1961).

Each subject is placed in a dark room and asked to judge how far a dot of light moves. The light actually does not move but only appears to. Under these conditions, each subject develops a range in which he makes his estimates. When these same individuals are placed together in groups of two and three members, their judgments converge in a group standard or norm. If the subjects make their first judgments in a group, their judgments tend to converge even more rapidly. The group norm persists for the individual member when he faces the same stimulus alone at a later time.

The same experimental results have been obtained by others using slightly different experimental designs, e.g., in groups in which all responses other than that of the subject are tape-recorded (Schonbar, 1954; Blake and Brehm, 1954; Linton, 1954; Rohrer et al., 1954; Olmstead and Blake, 1955; Downing, 1958), and are predictable enough to be used as a classroom demonstration (Ray, 1951). Additional variations on the Sherif experiment include Endler, 1960; Jacobs and Campbell, 1961; Whittaker, 1964; Beach and Lloyd, 1965; Pollis and Montgomery, 1966, 1968; Stone, 1973; Martin, Williams, and Gray, 1974.

Effects of Group Opinion on Judging Line Lengths

A second example of the experimental work which has been undertaken to operationalize certain pertinent concepts and problems regarding conformity to or independence from group standards of judgment will be described in more detail.[1] Solomon Asch, a psychologist of the Gestalt tradition, designed an ingenious study to yield objective measures of conformity of an individual's psycho-physical judgments when confronted by an incorrect majority opinion (Asch, 1951, 1952, 1955, 1956).

In this experiment, a number of persons are instructed by the experimenter to unanimously give incorrect judgments in what is ostensibly an exepriment in visual perception. The stimulus materials are two sets of white cards. One set consists of cards, each of which displays a single black line (the standard). Each card of the other set bears three lines, one being the same length as the standard, the other two being easily recognizable departures from this length. These cards are illustrated in figure 10. The task is to match the correct line of the three with the standard. All judgments are expressed orally. In the experiment proper, a single "naive" subject is placed in a group of "coached subjects," the total number varying in different experiments from seven to nine. The behavior of the "coached subjects" and the manner of assembling for the experiment give no indication of the collusion between group and experimenter. The naive subject is seated at the end (or in some cases next to the end) of the line of subjects. The experimenter shows a pair of cards and one by one the subjects state their opinions of the line which matches the standard. A series of eighteen trials consists of twelve critical trials, in which the coached members unanimously give incorrect responses, and six neutral trials, in which the coached members give correct responses. The performance in the experimental groups may be compared with a control series in

1. In each chapter one or two studies will be presented in enough detail to give the reader some feeling for the theory, the method, and the results of the research. Those parts of the study which are not relevant for the particular chapter in which the study is reported have generally been omitted. Most of these studies are the "classics" in the field, early pieces of research which provided the stimulus for rapid growth of the field. A list of books and articles in this category which were published from 1931 appears in Strodtbeck and Hare (1954, pp. 111–112).

Figure 10. A Pair of Stimulus Cards

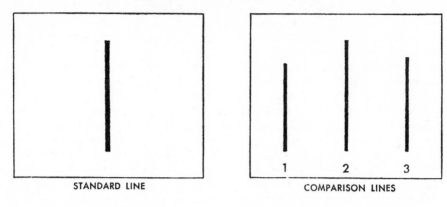

STANDARD LINE   COMPARISON LINES

which all members of the group are "naive" and uninstructed and merely write their judgments down on paper, trial by trial.

Using this basic experimental design, 123 college students were placed in the minority situation described above. When a subject was faced with an incorrect majority opinion, there was a significant increase in his errors, always in the direction of the majority. Nearly 37 percent of the subjects' responses were in error, as compared with almost no error in the control groups. Thus, influence of group opinion on the individual was in many cases sufficient to dissuade him from responding in terms of his immediate sense impressions, which were clearly in contradiction to the group. However, in most instances a different judgment by the majority was not enough to make the individual conform.

The percentage of the 123 subjects who made correct judgments on each of the twelve critical trials is indicated in figure 11 by a solid line. The accuracy of subjects who are not under group pressure is indicated by a dotted line. The largest percentage of correct judgments was made on the first critical trial (over 80 percent), while the smallest percentage of correct judgments was made on the fourth trial (less than 50 percent).

More information about the subjects who yielded and those who did not was obtained in the interviews which were conducted with the subjects immediately after the experiment. Asch interpreted his interviews as indicating three types of independent subjects and three types of yielding subjects. Among independent subjects he found independence accompanied by confidence. This type of individual was aware of majority opinion, but did not allow it to shake his reliance on the evidence of his eyes. A different type was the withdrawn individual, who seemed to be more oriented in terms of "explicit principles concerning the necessity of being an individual." His third type was described as independent, but felt anxious and uncomfortable over the public declaration of minority judgments. He would rather be with the majority but was unwilling to join them at the cost of discarding his sensory impressions, which were in this instance so clear.

The subjects who yielded on more than half of the critical trials were cate-

Figure 11. Percentage of Correct Estimates for Critical Trials

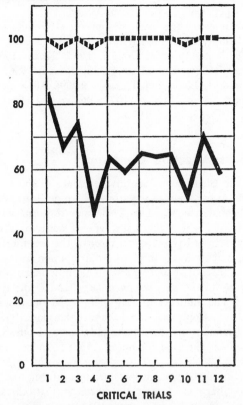

CORRECT ESTIMATES (Per Cent)

CRITICAL TRIALS

gorized by Asch into those who distorted their perception, those who distorted their judgment (decided they was inaccurate and the group was accurate), and those who distorted their action, yielding overtly only because of a great need not to appear deviant in the group.

It is evident that this experiment must be evaluated in terms of the restrictions under which it was performed. The discrepancy between majority opinion and immediately present sensory information was quite marked and the problem for judgment was clearly defined. The types of yielders derived from the interviews may, therefore, not obtain when individuals are judging psycho-physical or nonphysical problems in which the discrepancy is not as marked and the problem not as clearly delimited. Another feature of the experiment is that interaction between members was not permitted. The process by which discrepancies are detected between majority and minority opinions, and the complexities of adjustment, accommodation, and conflict between such positions when they are detected, are not explored in this research design. Finally it may be noted that, in part, the classification of yielders is based on differences in personality, such as the need to join the majority. In order to investigate the relationship between personality structure and conformity, as studied in this experiment, some objective assessment of relevant aspects of personality would be necessary.

Additional research using the Asch design or a modification developed by Crutchfield includes Rhine, 1960; Endler, 1961; Malof and Lott, 1962; Back et al., 1963; Rosenhan, De Wilde, and McDougal, 1963; Khan, 1965; Wrench and Endicott, 1965; Hicks, Monty, and Myers, 1966; Nurmi, 1966; Pollis and Cammalleri, 1968; Mertesdorf, Lück, and Timaeus, 1969; Allen and Levine, 1971a, 1971b; Wolosin, Sherman, and Mynatt, 1972; Endler and Hartley, 1973; Nosanchuk and Lightstone, 1974; Vidmar, 1974.

General Conditions Affecting Conformity

The experiments by Sherif and Asch give evidence of the general tendency to conform to norms, but other types of experiments are needed to suggest the conditions which affect the extent to which a person may conform. Although all of the physical and social factors which affect any type of behavior also have a bearing on conformity, a few factors have received most of the attention in the literature. An individual is more likely to conform to group opinion in the following cases: when the *object to be judged is ambiguous,* if he must make his *opinion public,* if the *majority holding a contrary opinion is large,* and if the *group is especially friendly or close-knit.* The influence of each of these factors is subject to the individual's awareness that his opinions are deviant (Mausner, 1955). If individuals make judgments and remain unaware of the judgments of others, no tendency towards conformity can be expected (Jenness, 1932b). In one experiment which provides an example of the effects of *not* applying social influence, individuals who were *not* members of groups, under no pressure to conform, told to use their own judgment, certain that they were correct, and uncertain that others were correct did not conform to norms (Deutsch and Gerard, 1955).

Homans (1958) has suggested that conformity can be seen as a case of the economic principle: that the individual tries to maximize his reward and minimize his cost in any transaction. Thus the individual will conform to group opinion if the cost of deviation is high and the rewards (e.g., liking) for conformity are high, or any other combination of reward and cost which yields some profit. The individual would be least likely to conform when the cost exceeds the reward. Thus we find some individuals using conformity as an ingratiation tactic (Jones and Jones, 1964; Jones, 1965; Kauffman and Steiner, 1968).

Generalizations derived from research on conformity are organized in this chapter under three headings: the *object* about which a judgment is to be made, the *subject* who is making the judgment, and the *situation* in which the group has the primary influence.

Conformity and the Object

Individuals are called upon to make judgments about two general classes of objects: those which are unambiguous, such as the length of a line or the number of dots on a card, and those which are ambiguous, such as the merit of a painting. In addition to real ambiguity there are also objects for which there is actually an objective standard of judgment although they are perceived as ambiguous by the subjects. Generally, *the greater the ambiguity of the object, the greater will be the influence of other group members in determining the judgment of the subject* (Berenda, 1950; Crutchfield, 1955; Blake, Helson, and Mouton, 1957; Wiener, Carpenter, and Carpenter, 1957; Blau, 1960b; Weiner and McGinnies, 1961; Graham, 1962; Jamous, 1962; Seaborne, 1962; Luchins and Luchins, 1963b, 1963c, 1963d; London and Lim, 1964; McDavid and Sistrunk, 1964; Chipman, 1966; Wheeler and Arrowood, 1966; Timaeus, 1967; Latané and Darley, 1968; Myers and Arenson, 1968; Leppaluoto, 1972; Bruehl and Solar, 1973; Mills and Kimble, 1973; Keating and Brock, 1974).

The relative influence of *perceived ambiguity* is illustrated by a series of studies in which pairs of individuals are asked to identify the objects in drawings which become progressively more or less ambiguous as the experiment progresses. When the drawing is complete in all its details the partner's opinion has no influence (Luchins, 1945, 1955; Luchins and Luchins, 1955b). Even though the object is ambiguous or hard to judge, subjects who are correct when there is an objective standard are less likely to be influenced by others in the group (Thorndike, 1938b; Luchins, 1955).

When the phenomenon is actually *ambiguous*, the subject cannot be objectively "correct" in his judgment, but the extent to which he is *certain* of his judgment will have a similar effect on his conformity. The autokinetic situation can be used as an example, although not a pure one since the light objectively *does not move,* but only appears to move. There is no fixed standard for the length of the *apparent movement.* In one experiment individuals alone and in pairs were examined for fluctuation in judgments under three conditions of uncertainty. The greater the uncertainty, the greater was the individual's fluctuation in judgment and the more important was the group interaction (of the pairs) in reducing the range of fluctuation (Sherif and Harvey, 1952). A similar effect of the uncertainty of the subject has been noted with different kinds of stimulus objects (Boomer, 1959; Di Vesta, 1959; Flament, 1959; Dauler, 1966; Julian, Regula, and Hollander, 1968; London, Meldman, and Lanckton, 1970a, 1970b; London, McSeveney, and Tropper, 1971).

When the object is *unambiguous* group opinion has little impact on individual judgment. In one experiment 60 pairs of children of ages 10 to 12 measured objects such as lines, parallelograms, and blocks with two different rulers. In each case the child using a linear ruler, who was told he was correct, announced his judgment first. Following this, the child using a metric ruler announced his judgment. There was little tendency for the second child to conform (Luchins and Luchins, 1956). If the subject is particularly suggestible, however, or the situation is more coercive, as in the Asch experiment (1955), some conformity will take place even with an objective standard.

Conformity when judging an ambiguous object can be reduced to zero if the experimenter tells the subjects that the autokinetic effect is simply an illusion (Alexander, Zuker, and Brody, 1970) or that the other persons in the experiment have been instructed to give incorrect judgments (Horowitz and Rothschild, 1970). The subject may see through the experiment and know that he is being tricked, (Allen, 1966; Glinski, Glinski, and Slatin, 1970; Gallo, Smith, and Mumford, 1973) or be suspicious that some deception is involved (Stricker, Messick, and Jackson, 1967; Martin, 1970; Adair, 1972; Geller and Endler, 1973; Wagner and Shaw, 1973); in either case he will probably not conform to the bogus norms.

Since the *social value* of any object is always ambiguous in the sense that it varies from group to group and is a product of group interaction, the individual is forced to compare himself with a group on many issues. Although some have posited the existence of a *drive* to determine the correctness of opinion (Festinger, 1954, 1957), the present theory suggests that this *drive* may be accounted for by an action system in which an individual attempts to learn which response will follow from any given behavior, where the nature of the response is relative to the deviation of the behavior from the norm, so that he can predict the consequence of his act (Kelly, 1955, p. 49).

Conformity and the Subject

The individual *brings with him into the judgment situation certain tendencies to conform or not conform which may be related to his personality* (Crutchfield, 1955), *his skill or previous success with the task, and prejudgments about the phenomena which are "anchored" in some other group.* An example of *personality* as a variable occurs in an experiment in which 64 subjects with all combinations of two personality traits, anxiety and neuroticism, were given social approval or disapproval of their opinions in a five-to-seven-minute discussion with two role players. All of the subjects participated more when approved. The high-neurotic subjects were more rigid in holding their opinions when under disapproval, especially when they were also high-anxious (Cervin, 1955a, 1956). However, no differences in behavior between emotionally stable and unstable subjects were observed in a similar situation when the subjects were praised rather than subjected to disapproval (Cervin, 1955b).

A similar relationship between nonconformity and high neuroticism was found in a hospital study in which neurotic patients from a psychiatric ward conformed less in an experiment using autokinetic effect than patients from the medical wards (Levine et al., 1954).

Subjects are also more likely to conform if they are high in anxiety (Mangan, Quartermain, and Vaughan, 1959, 1960; Walters, Marshall, and Shooter, 1960; Steiner and Vannoy, 1966; Meunier and Rule, 1967; Rule and Sandilands, 1969), low in self-esteem (Hovland and Janis, 1959; Appley and Moeller, 1963; Rosenberg, 1963; League and Jackson, 1964; Macbride and Tuddenham, 1965; Gergen and Bauer, 1967; Costanzo, 1970), and of low intelligence (Lucito, 1964; Streufert, 1966; Long, 1970; Nurmi, 1970).

In general any personality trait which tends to make the subject "field-dependent" so that he looks to others for confirmation of opinions will increase his conformity (cf. McDavid, 1959; Feldman and Goldfried, 1962; Breger, 1963; Bass and Dunteman, 1964; Anderson and McGuire, 1965; Goldman, Haberlein, and Feder, 1965; Sistrunk and McDavid, 1965; Willis, 1965c; Blackman, Goldstein, and Mandell, 1966; Breger and Ruiz, 1966; Davis and Phares, 1967; Mausner and Graham, 1970; Cull, 1971; Herrmann, 1971; Khol and Nickols, 1971; Trickett, 1971; Hajek and Kratochvil, 1973; Toder and Marcia, 1973; Cooper and Scalise, 1974; Hamid and Flay, 1974). Similar results are obtained when subjects are in a "state" of fear or anxiety, or are otherwise aroused (Walters and Quinn, 1960; Darley, 1966; Horwitz et al., 1966; Sears, 1967; Corfield, 1969; Mertesdorf, Lück, and Timaeus, 1969; Mintz and Mills, 1971; Horowitz, 1972; Cantor, Mody, and Zillmann, 1974; Giesen and Hendrick, 1974).

Some studies report that subjects who receive high scores on the F scale of "authoritarianism" conform more than low-F subjects (Wells, Weinert, and Rubel, 1956; Berkowitz and Lundy, 1957; Nadler, 1959; Birney and Houston, 1961; Gorfein, 1961; Rokeach, 1961; Vidulich and Kaiman, 1961; McGee, 1962a, 1962b; Solomon, 1963; Steiner and Johnson, 1963; C. E. Smith, 1964; Vaughan and White, 1966; Kirtley, 1968; Centers, Shomer, and Rodrigues, 1970; Marquis, 1973; Saiyadain and Summers, 1973). However, other research with the F scale suggests that a subject who receives a high score may simply be one who is willing to agree with a number of fairly extreme statements such as "Prison is too good for sex criminals, they should be publicly whipped or worse," or one who gives answers which he believes to be socially desirable (Cronbach, 1946; Owens, 1947; Cronbach, 1950; Leavitt et al., 1955; Shelley, 1956; Chapman and Campbell, 1957b; Chapman and Bock, 1958; Chapman and Campbell, 1959; Couch and Keniston, 1960; Gage and Chatterjee, 1960; Hare, 1960a; Small and Campbell, 1960; Couch and Keniston, 1961; Edwards, 1961; Edwards and Walker, 1961a, 1961b; Lichtenstein, Quinn, and Hover, 1961; Peabody, 1961; Taylor, 1961a, 1961b; Mahler, 1962; Solomon and Klein, 1963; Berkowitz and Wolkon, 1964; Samelson, 1964; Hare and Peabody, 1971). Unfortunately for research, many subjects who answer "agree" to the F Scale items in the form in which they are usually given also answer "agree" to similar items in which the meaning has been reversed. Thus a subject who scores as a high authoritarian on one test scores as a low authoritarian on the next (Bass, 1955, 1957; Jackson and Messick, 1957; Jackson, Messick, and Solley, 1957; Messick and Jackson, 1957; Rabinowitz, 1957; Christie, Havel, and Seidenberg, 1958; Kerlinger, 1958; Hare, 1960a). The F Scale may then simply be another measure of submissiveness like scales for ascendance-submission, social desirability, or acquiesence, or a rating made from the content of stories told in response to pictures of the Thematic Apperception Test. Subjects who are rated as submissive or dependent in these tests or who describe themselves as submissive are found to submit more frequently to majority opinion (Barron, 1952; Helson et al., 1956; Kagan and Mussen, 1956; Gage, Leavitt, and Stone, 1957; Foster, 1961; Frye and Bass, 1963; Back and Davis, 1965; Loomis and Spilka, 1972). Apparently, whatever the device for measuring a subject's tendency to conform, whether it be a paper-and-pencil test as in the case of the F Scale, a measure of conventionality derived by comparison of a subject with the mean response of his group (Beloff, 1958), or a test of the Asch type (Rosner, 1957), subjects who conform in one situation will probably conform in another. (See also Block and Block, 1952.)

Other related characteristics of conforming individuals appear to be a high need to be approved by others (Tuddenham, 1959; Di Vesta and Cox, 1960; Wilson, 1960; Strickland and Crowne, 1962; Harvey, 1964; Hollander, Julian, and Haaland, 1965; Srivastava, 1968; Crawford and Haaland, 1972), a low need to be outstanding as an individual (Moeller and Applezweig, 1957; Krebs, 1958; Schroder and Hunt, 1958), and a feeling that parental figures are harsh, punitive, restrictive, and rejecting (Mussen and Kagan, 1958). Sex also appears to be a factor, since women have been found to yield more to a bogus group norm than men (Tuddenham, 1958a; Tuddenham, McBride, and Zahn, 1958; Steiner, 1960; Tuddenham, 1961a; Allen and Crutchfield, 1963; Reitan and Shaw, 1964; Lietaer, 1965–1966; Wittaker, 1965; Endler, 1966; Neuringer and Wandke, 1966; Phelps and Meyer, 1966; Vaughan and Taylor, 1966; F. W. Schneider, 1970; K. H. Smith, 1970; Ryckman and Rodda, 1972; Johnson and MacDonnell, 1974). For children the influence of peers is less as the children grow older (Hunt and Synnerdahl,

1959; Iscoe, Williams and Harvey, 1964; Query, 1968; Janney et al., 1969; Allen and Newtson, 1972; Strassberg and Wiggen, 1973). At any age, persons who are first born in their family generally conform more (Becker and Carroll, 1962; Sampson, 1962; Stotland and Cottrell, 1962; Becker, Lerner, and Carroll, 1964; Arrowood and Amoroso, 1965; Becker, Lerner, and Carroll, 1966; Sampson and Hancock, 1967; Bragg and Allen, 1970). Cultural background has also been reported as a significant factor in either conformity or anticonformity, that is, a tendency to be individualistic by moving away from the majority position (cf. Willis and Hollander, 1964; Stricker, Messick, and Jackson, 1970). American students showed a greater tendency toward anticonformity than Chinese students from Taiwan (Meade and Barnard, 1973). One-third of the student subjects in an Asch-type experiment in Japan gave anticonformity responses (Frager, 1970). Children in East Africa are more compliant than American children (Munroe and Munroe, 1972). For other cultural variations see Berry, 1967; Fthenakis, 1967.

The fact that self-confident subjects will resist pressures to conform (Hochbaum, 1954; Coleman, Blake, and Mouton, 1958) has already been indicated in the discussion of the effects of the ambiguity of the stimulus. This self-confidence can result from skills which the subject brings with him or it can be built up experimentally by allowing the subject to experience success in a series of individual trials before he is placed in a group (Kelman, 1950; Mausner, 1954b; Kelley and Lamb, 1957; Mausner and Bloch, 1957; Samelson, 1957; Goldberg and Lubin, 1958; Harvey and Rutherford, 1958; Croner and Willis, 1961; Julian and Steiner, 1961; K. H. Smith, 1961; Crowne and Shephard, 1963; de Montmollin, 1965, 1966a; London, Meldman, and Lanckton, 1970a, 1970b; Ettinger et al., 1971; Endler, 1973; Endler and Hartley, 1973; Geller, Endler, and Wiesenthal, 1973; Misra, 1973; Wiesenthal, Endler, and Geller, 1973). On the other hand, if the subject does not possess the necessary skills or characteristics which would make it possible for him to conform, he may fall behind, like the new recruit in a long infantry march, and remain a deviant (Levi, Torrance, and Pletts, 1954).

An individual may also be a nonconformist in one group if his opinions are well "anchored" in another group. The family, for example, is one of the principal reference groups for many subjects (Rosen, 1955b). The general tendency for individuals to have particular reference groups in mind is usually discussed in relation to large aggregates such as religious groups, political parties, or nations. In most of the experiments on face-to-face groups, the extent of "anchorage" of opinions is left as an unspecified part of the variance in conformity. In a study which exemplifies the "anchorage" of opinions in large aggregates, highschool and college students who were members of a church expressed attitudes which were farther from the norms of their church when they were influenced by contrary norms, an indication that influence was possible. But, in addition, the highschool students were less influenced if they were first reminded of their church affiliation, thus making the reference group more prominent in the mind at the time that they were asked to make a series of judgments (Hovland, Janis, and Kelley, 1953; Kelley, 1955).

In another study, opinions were first "anchored" in an *ad hoc* experimental group which served in later discussion as a reference group. When individuals' opinions on a fictitious labor-management dispute were discussed in three-man laboratory groups, subjects who were told that they would get along extremely well with each other made more attempts to influence each other than did subjects who were told that they would not do well together. When challenged by a role player about the opinion formed in the *ad hoc* "reference group" a week later, members of "high attraction" groups who were in initial agreement on their opinions were less likely to change them than those who were in initial disagreement. Members of "low attraction" groups did not show the same trend, presumably because their opinions were not well "anchored" (Gerard, 1954). The influence of the anchorage of opinions has also been reported with other kinds of judgmental tasks (Madden, 1960; Blake and Mouton, 1961a; B. P. Cohen, 1962; Hood and Sherif, 1962; Mouton and Blake, 1962; Gorfein, 1964a; Sherif and Sherif, 1964; Atkins and Bieri, 1968; Diab, 1968; Pollis, 1968; C. Sherif et al., 1973).

A reference for an opinion need not be a whole group, it may be a single person whose opinion is highly valued. The presence of a highly valued person within a group may give the group members the appearance of consensus or agreement with each other, when in fact the members are similar only in that they agree with the central person. When his opinion shifts all other opinions will also shift.

Conformity and the Situation

The relevant aspects of the situation are those which have to do with the subject's "commitment" to the group. *The subject is more apt to conform if his alternative is to go on record as a deviant in a group to which he is highly attracted and whose influential members disagree with him* (Festinger and Aronson, 1960).

Opinions given in public are often different from those expressed privately. Generally, the views expressed in public or with a possibility of being made public are more conforming (Schank, 1932; Festinger, 1947, 1950a, 1950b; Gorden, 1952; Kelley and Volkhart, 1952; Hovland, Janis, and Kelley, 1953; Mouton, Blake, and Olmstead, 1956; Argyle, 1957a; Raven, 1959a; Cervin et al., 1961; Gerard, 1964; Savell and Healey, 1969, Rokeach and Cochrane, 1972), although this is not always the case (Bennett, 1955), since the first persons to vote publicly are often the ones who are the most confident of their opinions (Terman, 1904; Gurnee, 1937a; Thorndike, 1938b; Carment, 1961). Some of these early responders will influence later responses. In such a case, the opinions of the first to answer will turn out to represent majority opinion because they had a part in its formation. Other individuals, equally confident of their opinion, will turn out to be deviants. In either event, if a person expresses his opinion (or intended course of action) publicly, he is more likely to follow up the opinion with appropriate behavior than if the opinion is given privately, especially if the group restraints against giving an opinion are high (Schachter and Hall, 1952). In addition, if a group member is allowed to make his point in a group discussion, even if he does not win others over to his opinion, he will be more satisfied with the discussion and more likely to accept the final group judgment (Preston and Heintz, 1949; Bovard, 1951a; Hare, 1952).

Since deviant opinions are generally suppressed once the group norm is known, the *apparent conformity* of the members to the norms may be increased (Wheeler and Jordan, 1929). This apparent conformity, which is based on public compliance without private acceptance, occurs when the individual is restrained from leaving the situation or when there is a threat of punishment for noncompliance. That is, where pressure is exerted on a person to express an opinion different from the one he privately affirms, there is a tendency for him to change his overt opinion (Janis and King, 1953; Kelman, 1950). Public compliance with private acceptance occurs if the individual desires to remain in the existing relationship with those who are attempting to influence him (cf. Festinger, 1953a).

In work groups or living groups, members who are highly attracted to the group either for its prestige, its productivity, or the friendship of its members will conform more to the standards of the group than will members who place a low value on these criteria (Festinger, Schachter, and Back, 1950; Back, 1951; Festinger, 1951b; Schachter et al., 1951; Moreno, 1953; Kelley and Shapiro, 1954; Rasmussen and Zander, 1954; Thrasher, 1954; Thibaut and Strickland, 1956; Berkowitz, 1957a; Brehm and Festinger, 1957; Siegel and Siegel, 1957; Kidd, 1958; Jackson and Saltzstein, 1958; Steiner and Peters, 1958; Lott and Lott, 1961; Turk, Hartley, and Shaw, 1962; Kiesler, 1963; Carment, Schwartz, and Miles, 1964; Kinoshita, 1964; Patterson and Anderson, 1964; Kiesler and de Salvo, 1967; Back et al., 1969; Lott and Lott, 1969; Mehrabian and Williams, 1969; Mehrabian and Ksionsky, 1970; Jovick, 1972). However, some experiments which have been designed to test this proposition have failed to confirm it (Downing, 1958; Fauquier and Vinacke, 1964; Harper and Tuddenham, 1964; Moran, 1965; Rotter, 1967). The attraction to the group may be increased if members first have to undergo a severe initiation (Aronson and Mills, 1959; Festinger and Aronson, 1960). Even though the group members are not friends initially, if they anticipate that they will work together at a later time the effect is the same (Gerard and Rotter, 1961; Schopler and Bateson, 1962; Gerard and Mathewson, 1966; Lewis, Langan, and Hollander, 1972; Pallak et al., 1972; Hautaluoma and Spungin, 1974).

One explanation for the relationship between attraction to a group or an individual and conformity is that people prefer to have interpersonal relationships that have a cognitive balance. Thus if a person likes someone, he achieves balance if he also likes what his friend likes. An imbalanced state would exist if he liked something that his friend did not like, or disliked something that his friend liked. As a result people tend to conform to the opinions of their friends (Berkowitz, 1957b; Tagiuri and Kogan, 1960; Feather, 1964; Sampson and Insko, 1964; McLeod, Price, and Harburg, 1966; Feather, 1967b; Feather and Armstrong, 1967; Sigall and Aronson, 1967; Rodrigues, 1968; Crockett, 1969; Mills, 1971) and to like people who conform to their opinions (Streufert, 1965; Kiesler, Kiesler, and Pallak, 1967; Lombardo, Weiss, and Buchanan, 1972).

In a panel study of 2,500 ninth- and tenth-grade students from 15 highschool grades, the students who were chosen as "liked" were more often conforming in their behavior than those who were disliked. The authors suggest that the high-status members may be surrounded by conformity-approving relationships (with those who like them) and deviance-disapproving relationships (with those who dislike them). These networks may be more effective for social control than the networks of low-status members, which tend to be made up exclusively of deviance-disapproving relationships (Riley and Cohn, 1958). However, in some *ad hoc experimental groups,* the amount of convergence on a norm (such as the number of dots in a square) may not be correlated with the amount of liking of the members for the group (Bovard, 1953), or of the group for a particular member (Dittes and Kelley, 1956).

The relation between friendship and conformity is evident in the Relay Assembly Test Room study which was part of the Western Electric researches (Mayo, 1933; Turner, 1933; Whitehead, 1938; Roethlisberger and Dickson, 1939). To study the effects of food, rest periods, and other situational factors on productivity, six female workers were placed in a special test room. Two pairs of girls had known each other before the study began. Over the two years of the experiment other friendships were formed. As time went on, high correlations between the fluctuations of the output rates of several of the girls began to appear in the data, especially between girls who were friends and sat next to each other. This happened in spite of the fact that the girls were making telephone assemblies so fast that their conformity could hardly have been the result of conscious effort. However, when the seating arrangement was changed so that friends no longer sat next to each other, the high correlations disappeared for a time, reappearing gradually as new friendships were formed.

Although this group had only five members, it does illustrate the point that behavior, in this case the output of relay assemblies, may be highly correlated with the norms of some *subgroup,* here the pair, whatever may be its relation to the norms of the group as a whole. This effect is also evident in boy gangs, which would be rated as highly cohesive subgroups of a larger society from whose norms they consciously deviate (Sherif and Cantril, 1947).

Friendship within the group increases conformity only if the norm or standard has been set by the group itself. If the standard is set by some agent outside the group such as an experimenter or other authority, then conformity to this standard may occur only when the members are not well known to each other, so that each member can assume that his opinion will not be recognized and recalled by other group members and that he will not be held accountable for his opinion (Festinger, Pepitone, and Newcomb, 1952).

The size of the majority whose opinions oppose those of the individual is directly related to the amount of influence on his opinion (Thorndike, 1938b; Bennett, 1955; Luchins and Luchins, 1955a; Kelley and Woodruff, 1956; Rosenberg, 1961; Rath and Misra, 1963; Edmonds, 1964; Frye, Spruill, and Stritch, 1964; Stone, 1967; Gerard, Wilhelmy, and Conolley, 1968; Feldman and Scheibe, 1972). Subjects in some experiments are found to be more anxious as measured by their galvanic skin response when disagreeing with the majority (C. E. Smith, 1936; Hoffman, 1957; Lawson and Stagner, 1957). The influence is greatest when the subject perceives near unanimity of opinion in the group. For example, in an experiment in which the major elements of the early Lewin experiment (1943) were combined in various ways, an attempt was made to influence groups of eight to sixteen college students to volunteer for social science experiments. Group discussion and lecture methods were each compared with control groups under different conditions of decision, public or private commitment, and degree of consensus. Neither did discussion, lecture, and control groups differ in number of volunteers, nor did public commitment increase the probability of executing the decision. However, if the *majority* of the subjects in a group decided to volunteer and *each subject perceived that the majority was in favor,* then he probability of actually acting on the decision was greater (Bennett, 1955).

A number of experiments which illustrate these phenomena have been performed by Asch (1952, 1955). In his original experiment described earlier in this chapter, the naive subject was confronted with a unanimous majority opinion which did not agree with his perceptual experience. Under this kind of group pressure one-third of the naive subjects distorted their judgments in the direction of that given by the majority.

In a variation of the same experiment the naive subject was given a "partner" who gave the true estimate of the line length. The effect of this alliance was to reduce the number of times that the subject would conform with the majority. However, if the partner changed over to the majority opinion in the middle of the experiment, the majority's influence was again felt with full force. On the other hand, if the partner began with the majority and joined the naive subject halfway through the experiment, the subject was encouraged to become independent of the majority.

In one series Asch varied the size of the opposition from one to fifteen persons. The results, which are given in figure 12, showed a clear trend. When a subject was confronted by a single individual who contradicted his answers, he continued to answer independently and correctly on nearly all trials. When the opposition was increased to two, the presure became substantial. Minority subjects now accepted the wrong answer 13.6 percent of the time. Under the pressure of a majority of three, the subjects' errors jumped to 31.8 percent. However, further increases in the size of the majority only increased the tendency to conform to majority opinion by a relatively small percentage. Asch concluded that when a naive subject was confronted with the contradictory opinion of only one or two persons he remained relatively independent. But when three persons were in opposition, the full effect of the majority was felt and no further significant differences appeared with majorities as large as fifteen.

Other experiments confirm the hypothesis that having even one person support the subject increases the number of times he will hold out against a majority (Mouton, Blake, and Olmstead, 1956; Brodbeck, 1956; Hardy, 1957; Gorfein, 1964b; Allen and Levine, 1968, 1969, 1971a; Bragg, 1971; Bragg and Dooley,

Figure 12. Percentage of Errors with Majorities of One to Fifteen Opponents

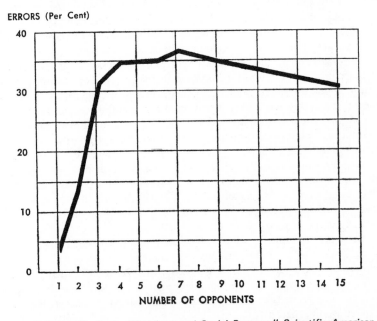

ERRORS (Per Cent)

NUMBER OF OPPONENTS

1972; Darley et al., 1974; Kimball and Hollander, 1974). The support will be especially effective if it comes from the leader or a high-prestige person (Maier and Solem, 1952; Jones, Wells, and Torrey, 1958). As group size increases, there is an increase in the opportunities to form subgroup coalitions representing minority opinions (Hare, 1952).

It is the *relative* size of the majority rather than the *absolute* size which is important, since in a group of two the "majority" influence may be exerted by only one person (Grosser, Polansky, and Lippitt, 1951; Fisher and Lubin, 1958). The amount of influence of this majority of one is in turn related to the characteristics of the two persons composing the group. In one experiment with groups of two the pressure to conform was higher if it came from a highly emotional partner (i.e., one who received a high score on a test of emotional responsiveness), unless the subject himself was also highly emotional (Cervin, 1957).

Seeing one person comply with a suggestion or initiate an activity is also enough to increase the probability of compliance (Rosenbaum and Blake, 1955; Rosenbaum, 1956; Luchins and Luchins, 1961b, 1961c, 1961d; Berger, 1971; Stephenson and Fielding, 1971; Dannick, 1973; Craig, Best, and Reith, 1974). Some subjects were *asked* by an experimenter whether or not they wished to volunteer for an experiment after they had seen (1) someone asked who refused, (2) someone asked who complied, or (3) no one else asked. In the cases in which the subject had seen another person volunteer to participate in the experiment, the probability was greater that he would also volunteer. An important difference between this and other studies was that the subjects were *asked to conform*. A similar effect was observed in an experiment in which subjects tolerated a more intensive electric shock when they believed that a partner was receiving the same treatment (Seidman et al., 1957).

The majority of the studies on the influence of group norms on individual judgment deal only with the results of the subject's internal struggle to reconcile his own opinion with the weight of the contrary opinion. If one wishes to maximize conformity, then direct appeals to change opinion and coercion must be added to the types of "pressures toward uniformity" discussed up to this point. The influence of the direct appeal will be discussed in a section on changing the norms, but the effects of coercion are not treated in detail since everyday examples of police and military action give evidence of its effectiveness.

The influence of "majority" opinion, of course, extends beyond the small face-to-face group. In a number of early studies (Dashiell, 1935) individuals were given information about the majority opinions of such large groups as the student body of a high school or a college, or all adults in general. In all of these studies there were shifts in the direction of greater conformity with majority opinion even though the opinions communicated to the subject were those of broad classes of people which might not coincide with any to which the subject belonged.

The size of the majority is related to the amount of influence on a subject only if the members of the majority have equal or higher status than the subject. If a minority or a subgroup of equal size has high status through power, popularity, or expert knowledge, then the minority view will prevail. Subjects who are aware of the opinions of a person with high power, such as a teacher in a classroom of students, the group leader, or the experimenter, will limit the range of their opinions and conform more to the opinions of high-status person (Berenda, 1950; Ziller, 1955; Barilari et al., 1958; Wolf and Zolman, 1959; von Cranach, 1960; Luchins and Luchins, 1961a, 1961b, 1961c, 1963a; Knapp and Knapp, 1966; Vidulich and Bayley, 1966; Schulman, 1967; Critchlow, Herrup, and Dabbs, 1968;

Moore and Krupat, 1971; Endler and Marino, 1972; Keasey and Tomlinson-Keasey, 1973; Neely, Heckel, and Leichtman, 1973). A newcomer to a group may have relatively little power to influence group opinion or activity (Philips, Shenker, and Revits, 1951), whereas the behavior of the popular child in camp is "contagious" in that it is copied by other campers (Polansky, Lippitt, and Redl, 1950a; Lippitt, Polansky, and Rosen, 1952).

A member who is an expert, either because he has demonstrated his skill in the past or because he appears at the moment to have the ability to make correct decisions, will have more influence than one who is not as successful (Sherif, 1935; Mausner, 1953, 1954a; Luchins and Luchins, 1955b; Torrance, 1959; Ziller and Behringer, 1959; Chalmers, Horne, and Rosenbaum, 1963; Vidulich and Stabene, 1965; Willis, 1965b; Feshbach, 1967; Poitou, 1969; Crano, 1970; Mills and Harvey, 1972; Crisci and Kassinove, 1973; Richardson et al., 1973; Ross, 1973). The expert will tend to have more influence in the absence of any apparent homogeneity of opinion in the group (Gerard, 1953) and under conditions which allow him to defend his position with rational arguments (Cole, 1954).

If the whole group is successful in the decision task then the whole group becomes the "expert." In one experiment, some three-man groups "succeeded" on a series of collaborative tasks and others "failed." When the members of the successful groups were then asked to estimate the number of flickers of a light during a five-second time interval, they conformed more to a fictitious "average judgment" for their group than did members of unsuccessful groups. Presumably their previous success "reinforced" their confidence in their group's opinion (Kidd and Campbell, 1955).

Leaders Also Conform

Group leaders who would be expected to have the greatest power to bring about a change in the group norms also find it difficult to resist their influence once the norms are established (Pellegrin, 1953; Harvey and Consalvi, 1960; Schmitt, 1967; MacNeil and Pace, 1973). Sherif (1935) noted that, in cases where one person took the initiative in an initially leaderless group, the group norm which was then established would reflect his judgment. However, if the same member changed his individual norm after the group norm was established, he was no longer followed. Further evidence for this hypothesis is found in a study of nursery school children (Merei, 1949). Some of the children in the nursery school who were relatively docile and ineffectual in the open playroom were formed into separate groups and placed in a room by themselves with a new set of toys. In time, each new group developed its own set of rules, habits, and traditions of play. After the new set of norms had developed, a child was added to each group who had been unusually influential and powerful in the initial nursery-wide situation. The success of these old "leaders" in maintaining their dominant position in the new group varied; however, not even the most successful and adept leaders were able to abolish the new norms.

We see then that group leaders conform to the norms, but for different reasons than the followers. Where the follower may conform because he is coerced by majority opinion, the leader's opinion may be close to that of the group because he played a major part in the formation of group opinion (Jackson, 1944; Hare, 1952; Talland, 1954). Since his influence over the group is usually measured by the number of members who agree with his opinion, it is often difficult to tell whether he is the most "conforming" or the most "influential" (Simpson, 1938). On the other hand, the leader may be accorded more freedom to deviate from the norms than other members who are less secure of their status in the group (Hughes, 1946; Hollander, 1958, 1960a, 1960b, 1961a, 1961b; Wiggins, Dill, and Schwartz, 1965; Wahrman and Pugh, 1972). Leaders, as well as others who appear to conform, are often the most popular members of the group (Newcomb, 1943; French, 1951.) To be popular, the individual must be careful to conform only to the behavioral norms of the small group. If the individual conforms more to the norms of the larger organization, he may be classed as an overconformist (e.g., teacher's pet) and thus be less popular than a person who is willing to deviate when it will serve the group's interest.

Additional studies of aspects of the relationship between leadership and conformity include Borgatta, Cottrell, and Wilker, 1959; Harvey, 1960; Oerter, 1963; Gergen and Taylor, 1969; Shichor, 1970; Wright and Worthy, 1971; Wahrman, 1972.

Cognitive Consequences of Forced Compliance

As a test of part of Festinger's (1957; see also Aronson, 1969) theory of cognitive dissonance Festinger and Carlsmith (1959) conducted an experiment to test the hypothesis that after a subject has been forced to say or do something in public which is contrary to his private opinion, he will tend to change his private opinion. They outline their reasoning as follows:

Let us consider a person who privately holds opinion "X" but has, as a result of pressure brought to bear on him, publicly stated that he believes "not X."

1. This person has two cognitions which, psychologically, do not fit together: one of these is the knowledge that he believes "X," the other the knowledge that he has publicly stated that he believes "not X." If no factors other than his private opinion are considered, it would follow, at least in our culture, that if he believes "X" he would publicly state "X." Hence, his cognition of his private belief is dissonant with his cognition concerning his actual public statement.

2. Similarly, the knowledge that he has said "not X" is consonant with (does fit together with) those cognitive elements corresponding to the reasons, pressures, promises of rewards and/or threats of punishment which induced him to say "not X."

3. In evaluating the total magnitude of dissonance, one must take account of both dissonance and consonances. Let us think of the sum of all the dissonances involving some particular cognition as "D" and the sum of all the consonances as "C." Then we might think of the total magnitude of dissonance as being a function of "D" divided by "D" plus "C."

Let us then see what can be said about the total magnitude of dissonance in a person created by the knowledge that he said "not X" and really believes "X." With everything else held constant, this total magnitude of dissonance would decrease as the number and importance of the pressures which induced him to say "not X" increased.

Thus, if the overt behavior was brought about by, say, offers of reward or threats of punishment, the magnitude of dissonance is maximal if these promised rewards or threatened punishments were just barely sufficient to induce the person to say "not X." From this point on, as the promised rewards or threatened punishment become larger, the magnitude of dissonance becomes smaller.

4. One way in which the dissonance can be reduced is for the person to change his private opinion so as to bring it into correspondence with what he has said. One would consequently expect to observe such opinion change after a person has been

forced or induced to say something contrary to his private opinion. Furthermore, since the pressure to reduce dissonance will be a function of the magnitude of the dissonance, the observed opinion change should be greatest when the pressure used to elicit the overt behavior is just sufficient to do it.[2]

For their experiment Festinger and Carlsmith used 71 male university students who were required to spend a certain number of hours as experimental subjects (*Ss*) as part of their introductory psychology course. The description of the experiment is included here in some detail, since it provided the stimulus for a number of subsequent research projects and represents a "classic" design for social-psychological laboratory experiments.

The students were told that a sample of students would be interviewed after having served as subjects. They were urged to cooperate in the interviews by being completely frank and honest.

When the *S* arrived for the experiment on "Measures of Performance" he had to wait for a few minutes in the secretary's office. The experimenter (*E*) then came in, introduced himself to the *S* and, together, they walked into the laboratory room where the *E* said:

> This experiment usually takes a little over an hour but, of course, we had to schedule it for two hours. Since we have that extra time, the introductory psychology people asked if they could interview some of our subjects. [Offhand and conversationally.] Did they announce that in class? I gather that they're interviewing some people who have been in experiments. I don't know much about it. Anyhow, they may want to interview you when you're through here.

With no further introduction or explanation the *S* was shown the first task, which involved putting 12 spools onto a tray, emptying the tray, refilling it with spools, and so on. He was told to use one hand and to work at his own speed. He did this for one-half hour. The *E* then removed the tray and spools and placed in front of the *S* a board containing 48 square pegs. His task was to turn each peg a quarter turn clockwise, then another quarter turn, and so on. He was told again to use one hand and to work at his own speed. The *S* worked at this task for another half hour.

While the *S* was working on these tasks, the *E* sat, with a stop watch in his hand, busily making notations on a sheet of paper. He did so in order to make it convincing that this was what the *E* was interested in and that these tasks, and how the *S* worked on them, was the total experiment. From our point of view the experiment had hardly started. The hour which the *S* spent working on the repetitive, monotonous tasks was intended to provide, for each *S* uniformly, an experience about which he would have a somewhat negative opinion.

After the half hour on the second task was over, the *E* conspicuously set the stop watch back to zero, put it away, pushed his chair back, lit a cigarette, and said:

> O.K. Well, that's all we have in the experiment itself. I'd like to explain what this has been all about so you'll have some idea of why you were doing this. [*E* pauses.] Well, the way the experiment is set up is this. There are actually two groups in the experiment. In one, the group you were in, we bring the subject in and give him essentially no introduction to the experiment. That is, all we tell him is what he needs to know in order to do the tasks, and he has no idea of what the experiment is all about, or what it's going to be like, or anything like that. But in the other group, we have a student that we've hired that works for us regularly, and what I do is take him into the next room where the subject is waiting—the same room you were waiting in before—and I introduce him as if he had just finished being a subject in the experiment. That is, I say: "This is so-and-so, who's

2. Leon Festinger and James M. Carlsmith, "Cognitive Consequences of Forced Compliance," *Journal of Abnormal and Social Psychology* 58 (1959): 203–204. Copyright 1959 by the American Psychological Association. Reprinted by permission of the authors and the publisher.

just finished the experiment, and I've asked him to tell you a little of what it's about before you start." The fellow who works for us then, in convesation with the next subject, makes these points: [The E then produced a sheet headed "For Group B" which had written on it: It was very enjoyable, I had a lot of fun, I enjoyed myself, it was very interesting, it was intriguing, it was exciting. The E showed this to the S and then proceeded with his false explanation of the purpose of the experiment.] Now, of course, we have this student do this, because if the experimenter does it, it doesn't look as realistic, and what we're interested in doing is comparing how these two groups do on the experiment—the one with this previous expectation about the experiment, and the other, like yourself, with essentially none.

Up to this point the procedure was identical for S's in all conditions. From this point on they diverged somewhat. Three conditions were run, Control, One Dollar, and Twenty Dollars, as follows:

Control Condition

The E continued:

Is that fairly clear? [Pause.] Look, that fellow [looks at watch] I was telling you about from the introductory psychology class said he would get here a couple of minutes from now. Would you mind waiting to see if he wants to talk to you? Fine. Why don't we go into the other room to wait? [The E left the S in the secretary's office for four minutes. He then returned and said:] O.K. Let's check and see if he does want to talk to you.

One and Twenty Dollar Conditions

The E continued:

Is that fairly clear how it is set up and what we're trying to do? [Pause.] Now, I also have a sort of strange thing to ask you. The thing is this. [Long pause, some confusion and uncertainty in the following, with a degree of embarrassment on the part of the E. The manner of the E contrasted strongly with the perceding unhesitant and assured false explanation of the experiment. The point was to make it seem to the S that this was the first time the E had done this and that he felt unsure of himself.] The fellow who normally does this for us couldn't do it today—he just phoned in, and something or other came up for him—so we've been looking around for someone that we could hire to do it for us. You see, we've got another subject waiting [looks at watch] who is supposed to be in that other condition. Now Professor ———, who is in charge of this experiment, suggested that perhaps we could take a chance on your doing it for us. I'll tell you what we had in mind: the thing is, if you could do it for us now, then of course you would know how to do it, and if something like this should ever come up again, that is, the regular fellow couldn't make it, and we had a subject scheduled, it would be very reassuring to us to know that we had somebody else we could call on who knew how to do it. So, if you would be willing to do this for us, we'd like to hire you to do it now and then be on call in the future, if something like this should ever happen again. We can pay you a dollar (twenty dollars) for doing this for us, for doing it now and then being on call. Do you think you could do that for us?

If the S hesitated, the E said things like, "It will only take a few minutes," "The regular person is pretty reliable; this is the first time he has missed," or "If we needed you we could phone you a day or two in advance; if you couldn't make it, of course, we wouldn't expect you to come." After the S agreed to do it, the E gave him the previously mentioned sheet of paper headed "For Group B" and asked him to read it through again. The E then paid the S one dollar (twenty dollars), made out a handwritten receipt form, and asked the S to sign it. He then said:

O.K., the way we'll do it is this. As I said, the next subject should be here by now. I think the next one is a girl. I'll take you into the next room and introduce you to her, saying that you've just finished the experiment and that we've asked you to tell her a little about it. And what we want you to do is just sit down and get into a conversation with her and try to get across the points on that sheet of paper. I'll leave you alone and come back after a couple of minutes. O.K.?

The *E* then took the *S* into the secretary's office where he had previously waited and where the next *S* was waiting. (The secretary had left the office.) He introduced the girl and the *S* to one another saying that the *S* had just finished the experiment and would tell her somehing about it. He then left saying he would return in a couple of minutes. The girl, an undergraduate hired for this role, said little until the *S* made some positive remarks about the experiment and then said that she was surprised because a friend of hers had taken the experiment the week before and had told her that it was boring and that she ought to try to get out of it. Most *S*s responded by saying something like "Oh, no, it's really very interesting. I'm sure you'll enjoy it." The girl, after this listened quietly, accepting and agreeing to everything the *S* told her. The discussion between the *S* and the girl was recorded on a hidden tape-recorder.

After two minutes the *E* returned, asked the girl to go into the experimental room, thanked the *S* for talking to the girl, wrote down his phone number to continue the fiction that we might call on him again in the future and then said: "Look, could we check and see if that fellow from introductory psychology wants to talk to you?"

From this point on, the procedure for all three conditions was once more identical. As the *E* and the *S* started to walk to the office where the interviewer was, the *E* said: "Thanks very much for working on those tasks for us. I hope you did enjoy it. Most of our subjects tell us afterward that they found it quite interesting. You get a chance to see how you react to the tasks and so forth." This short persuasive communication was made in all conditions in exactly the same way. The reason for doing it, theoretically, was to make it easier for anyone who wanted to persuade himself that the tasks had been, indeed, enjoyable.

When they arrived at the interviewer's office, the *E* asked the interviewer whether or not he wanted to talk to the *S*. The interviewer said yes, the *E* shook hands with the *S*, said good-bye, and left. The interviewer, of course, was always kept in complete ignorance of which condition the *S* was in. The interview consisted of four questions, on which the *S* was first encouraged to talk about the matter and was then asked to rate his opinion or reaction on an 11-point scale.[3]

After the experiment each subject was "debriefed" by way of an explanation of the true purpose of the experiment. The subjects who received money were asked to return it, which they did. The data for 11 of the 71 subjects were discarded because the subjects were suspicious or failed to follow instructions, leaving 20 subjects for each experimental condition.

The results of the experiment are given in table 1. The average ratings on the question "Were the tasks interesting and enjoyable?" are presented in the first row of figures. These results are the ones most directly relevant to the specific dissonance which was experimentally created. It will be recalled that the tasks were purposely arranged to be rather boring and monotonous. Indeed, in the Control condition the average rating was $-.45$, somewhat on the negative side of the neutral point.

In the other two conditions, however, the *S*s told someone that these tasks were interesting and enjoyable. They could, of course, most directly reduce the resulting dissonance by persuading themselves that the tasks were indeed interesting and enjoyable. In the One Dollar condition, since the magnitude of dissonance was high, the pressure to reduce this dissonance would also be high. In this condition the average rating was $+1.35$, considerably on the positive side and significantly different from the Control condition at the .02 level ($t = 2.48$).

3. Ibid., pp. 204–206.

Table 1. Average Ratings on Interview Questions for Each Condition

Question on Interview	EXPERIMENTAL CONDITION		
	Control (N = 20)	One Dollar (N = 20)	Twenty Dollars (N = 20)
How enjoyable tasks were (rated from −5 to +5)	−.45	+1.35	−.05
How much they learned (rated from 0 to 10)	3.08	2.80	3.15
Scientific importance (rated from 0 to 10)	5.60	6.45	5.18
Participate in similar exp. (rated from −5 to +5)	−.62	+1.20	−.25

Source: Leon Festinger and James M. Carlsmith, "Cognitive Consequences of Forced Compliance," *Journal of Abnormal and Social Psychology* 58 (1959): 204. Copyright 1959 by the American Psychological Association. Reprinted by permission of the authors and the publisher.

In the Twenty Dollar condition, where less dissonance was created experimentally because of the greater importance of the consonant relations, there is correspondingly less evidence of dissonance reduction. The average rating in this condition is only −.05, slightly and not significantly higher than in the Control condition. The difference between the One Dollar and Twenty Dollar conditions is significant at the .03 level ($t = 2.22$). In short, when an S was induced, by offer of reward, to say something contrary to his private opinion, this private opinion tended to change so as to correspond more closely with what he had said. The greater the reward offered (beyond what was necessary to elicit the behavior), the smaller was the effect.

In their article Festinger and Carlsmith go on to discuss the other results given in table 1 which they feel are consistent with their hypothesis and alternative hypothesis which they feel would not account for the results.

Further evidence and analysis have confirmed the effect of dissonance reduction on attitude change with adults and children (Cohen, Brehm, and Latané, 1959; Zajonc, 1960; Zimbardo, 1960; Brehm and Cohen, 1962; Brehm and Sensenig, 1966; Carlsmith, Collins, and Helmreich, 1966; Mills, 1967; Hollander and Wiesenthal, 1969; Collins and Hoyt, 1972; Crawford, 1972; Goethals and Cooper, 1972; Calder, Ross, and Insko, 1973; Frey, Irle, and Kumpf, 1973; Gold, Ryckman, and Rodda, 1973; Lepper, 1973; Schlenker and Schlenker, 1973; Sheras, Cooper, and Zanna, 1973; Touhey, 1973b; Zanna, Lepper, and Abelson, 1973; Cooper and Goethals, 1974; Green, 1974; Kaplan and Baron, 1974; Trope, 1974; Wiesenthal, 1974; Wilhelmy and Duncan, 1974). However, the theory of cognitive dissonance has been criticized both on methodological and on theoretical grounds (Chapanis and Chapanis, 1964; Bem, 1965; Elms and Janis, 1965; Rosenberg, 1965; Wallace, 1966; Bem, 1967a, 1967b; Kelley, 1967; Bem and McConnell, 1970; Bem, 1972; Liebhart, 1972a). It has also been argued that additional variables like "self-concept" and "utility" have to be brought into the theoretical system to allow for more adequate predictions of dissonance effects (Aronson, 1973). In fact, dissonance is not always perceived as a cognitively uncomfortable situation producing a drive toward dissonance reduction; occasionally dissonance is even sought and enjoyed (Zajonc, 1968).

Of course the effect of dissonance will not occur if the subject does not see the need to restore balance in his cognitive field. For example, if a subject is led to believe that a speech he has delivered which is contrary to his own attitude has actually convinced a colleague to take a new position, the subject will change his own attitude only if he likes the colleague. This restores the balance between liking the colleague and agreeing with the colleague's attitude. If the subject convinces a colleague whom he does not like, there is no need to restore balance (Cooper, Zanna, and Goethals, 1974). Or, in another variation, if a subject who was committed to persuading his partner of the worth of his own position on an attitudinal issue and found, contrary to expectation, that the partner took the counter position more strongly despite persuasion, he would become more extreme in his own position than before. This has been called the "boomerang effect" (A. R. Cohen, 1962; Numakami, 1972).

Another experiment indicated that attitude change is not the only way to reduce dissonance in this type of situation. Fifty male and fifty female subjects were placed in an experimental situation in which they found their judgments contradicted by a respected associate of the same sex. They were free to resolve the dissonance by (1) conforming to the contrary judgments of the associate, (2) rejecting the associate as one who was less competent than he or she had seemed, (3) underrecalling the disagreements, or (4) devaluating the importance of the topics about which the disagreements had occurred. Given this choice, female subjects made less use of rejection than did male subjects and were more inclined to tolerate the conflict. Other findings suggest that the subjects were inclined to employ the four responses as alternative means of reducing dissonance rather than as supplementary means (Steiner and Rogers, 1963; see also Gormly, Gormly, and Johnson, 1972).

A Shocking Experiment

In 1963 Stanley Milgram published an article describing a procedure for the study of destructive obedience in the laboratory. He was motivated by the same concern that was shared by Sherif, Asch, Lewin, and the other social psychologists who had performed experiments on conformity 20 years earlier, at the time of World War II. Given that obedience is a basic element in the structure of social life and that some system of authority is a requirement for all communal living, how is it that the tendency to obey can override training in ethics, sympathy, and moral conduct? In particular, how was it possible for some persons in Germany in 1933–1945 to obey orders to kill millions of people?

Milgram devised a procedure for studying obedience which consisted of ordering a naive subject to administer electric shock to a victim. A simulated shock generator was used, with 30 clearly marked voltage levels that ranged from 15 to 450 volts. The instrument bore verbal designations that ranged from "Slight Shock" to "Danger: Severe Shock." The responses of the victim, who was a trained confederate of the experimenter, were standardized. The orders to administer shocks were given to the naive subject in the context of a "learning experiment" ostensibly set up to study the effects of punishment on memory. As the experiment proceeded, the naive subject was commanded to administer increasingly more intense shocks to the victim, even to the point of reaching the level marked "Danger: Severe Shock." Internal resistances became stronger, and at a certain point the subject refused to go on with the experiment. Behavior prior to this rupture was considered "obedience," in that the subject complied with the commands of the experimenter. The point of rupture was the act of disobedience. A quantitative value was assigned to the subject's performance based on the maximum intensity shock he was willing to administer before he refused to participate further. Thus for any particular subject and for any particular experimental condition the degree of obedience was specified with a numerical value. The crux of the study was to systematically vary the factors believed to alter the degree of obedience to the experimental commands.

The subjects were 40 males between the ages of 20 and 50. They answered a newspaper advertisement which led them to believe that they would participate in a study of memory and learning. A wide range of occupations was represented in the sample including postal clerks, highschool teachers, salesmen, engineers, and laborers. They were paid $4.50 for their participation in the experiment.

Milgram describes the procedure and results as follows.[4]

Procedure

One naive subject and one victim (an accomplice) performed in each experiment. A pretext had to be devised that would justify the administration of electric shock by the naive subject. This was effectively accomplished by the cover story. After a general introduction on the presumed relation between punishment and learning, subjects were told:

> But actually, we know *very little* about the effect of punishment on learning, because almost no truly scientific studies have been made of it in human beings.
>
> For instance, we don't know how *much* punishment is best for learning—and we don't know how much difference it makes as to who is giving the punishment, whether an adult learns best from a younger or an older person than himself—or many things of that sort.
>
> So in this study we are bringing together a number of adults of different occupations and ages. And we're asking some of them to be teachers and some of them to be learners.
>
> We want to find out just what effect different people have on each other as teachers and learners, and also what effect *punishment* will have on learning in this situation.
>
> Therefore, I'm going to ask one of you to be the teacher here tonight and the other one to be the learner.
>
> Does either of you have a preference?

Subjects then drew slips of paper from a hat to determine who would be the teacher and who would be the learner in the experiment. The drawing was rigged so that the naive subject was always the teacher and the accomplice always the learner. (Both slips contained the word "Teacher.") Immediately after the drawing, the teacher and learner were taken to an adjacent room and the learner was strapped into an "electric chair" apparatus.

The experimenter explained that the straps were to prevent excessive movement while the learner was being shocked. The effect was to make it impossible for him to escape from the situation. An electrode was attached to the learner's wrist, and electrode paste was applied "to avoid blisters and burns." Subjects were told that the electrode was attached to the shock generator in the adjoining room.

In order to improve credibility the experimenter declared, in response to a question by the learner: "Although the shocks can be extremely painful, they cause no permanent tissue damage."

Learning task. The lesson administered by the subject was a paired-associate learning task. The subject read a series of word pairs to the learner, and then read the first word of the pair along with four terms. The learner was to indicate which of the four terms had originally been paired with the first word. He communicated his answer by

4. Stanley Milgram, "Behavioral Study of Obedience," *Journal of Abnormal and Social Psychology* 67 (1963): 373–378. Copyright 1963 by the American Psychological Association. Reprinted by permission of the author and the publisher.

by pressing one of four numbered quadrants in an answerbox located atop the shock generator.

Shock generator. The instrument panel consists of 30 lever switches set in a horizontal line. Each switch is clearly labeled with a voltage designation that ranges from 15 to 450 volts. There is a 15-volt increment from one switch to the next going from left to right. In addition, the following verbal designations are clearly indicated for groups of four switches going from left to right: Slight Shock, Moderate Shock, Strong Shock, Very Strong Shock, Intense Shock, Extreme Intensity Shock, Danger: Severe Shock. (Two switches after this last designation are simply marked XXX.)

Upon depressing a switch: a pilot light corresponding to each switch is illuminated in bright red; an electric buzzing is heard; an electric blue light, labeled "voltage energizer," flashes; the dial on the voltage meter swings to the right; various relay clicks are sounded.

The upper left-hand corner of the generator is labeled Shock Generator, Type ZLB, Dyson Instrument Company, Waltham, Mass. Output 15 Volts–450 Volts.

Details of the instrument were carefully handled to insure an appearance of authenticity. The panel was engraved by precision industrial engravers, and all components were of high quality. No subject in the experiment suspected that the instrument was merely a simulated shock generator.

Sample shock. Each naive subject is given a sample shock on the shock generator, prior to beginning his run as teacher. This shock is always 45 volts, and is applied by pressing the third switch of the generator. The shock is applied to the wrist of the naive subject, and has its source in a 45-volt battery wired into the generator. This further convinces the subject of the authenticity of the generator.

Shock instruction. The subject is told to administer a shock to the learner each time he gives a wrong response. Moreover—and this is the key command—the subject is instructed to "move one level higher on the shock generator each time the learner flashes a wrong answer." He is also instructed to announce the voltage level before administering a shock. This serves to continually remind subjects of the increasing intensity of shocks administered to the learner.

Preliminary and regular run. Pretests revealed that the procedure of reading words and administering shocks requires some practice before it can be handled smoothly. Therefore, immediately preceding the regular run, the teacher is given a preliminary series of 10 words to read to the learner. There are 3 neutral words in the practice series (i.e., words that the learner answers correctly), so that shocks are administered for 7 of the words, with the maximum shock at 105 volts (moderate shock). Almost all subjects master the procedure by the time the preliminary run is over.

Subjects are then presented with a second list, and are told that the procedure is the same as for the first list; the experimenter adds, however:

> When you get to the bottom of the list, repeat it over again, and continue giving shocks, until the learner has learned all the pairs correctly.

The experimenter instructs the subject to

> start from 15 volts and increase the shock level one step each time the learner gives a wrong answer.

Feedback from the victim. In all conditions the learner gives a predetermined set of responses to the word pair test, based on a schedule of approximately three wrong answers to one correct answer. In the present experimental condition no vocal response or other sign of protest is heard from the learner until Shock Level 300 is reached. When the 300-volt shock is administered, the learner pounds on the wall of the room in which he is bound to the electric chair. The pounding can be heard by the subject. From this point on, the learner's answers no longer appear on the four-way panel.

At this juncture, subjects ordinarily turn to the experimenter for guidance. The experimenter instructs the subject to treat the absence of a response as a wrong answer, and to shock the subject according to the usual schedule. He advises the subjects to allow 5–10 seconds before considering no response as a wrong answer, and to increase the shock level one step each time the learner fails to respond correctly. The learner's pounding is repeated after the 315-volt shock is administered; afterwards he is not heard from, nor do his answers reappear on the four-way signal box.˙

Experimenter feedback. At various points in the experiment the subject may turn to the experimenter for advice on whether he should continue to administer shocks. Or he may indicate that he does not wish to go on. It was important to standardize the experimenter's responses to these inquiries and reactions.

If the subject indicated his unwillingness to go on, the experimenter responded with a sequence of "prods," using as many as necessary to bring the subject into line.

> Prod 1: Please continue, *or* Please go on.
> Prod 2: The experiment requires that you continue.
> Prod 3: It is absolutely essential that you continue.
> Prod 4: You have no other choice, you *must* go on.

The prods were always made in sequence: Only if Prod 1 had been unsuccessful could Prod 2 be used. If the subject refused to obey the experimenter after Prod 4, the experiment was terminated. The experimenter's tone of voice was at all times firm, but not impolite. The sequence was begun anew on each occasion that the subject balked or showed reluctance to follow orders.

Special prods. If the subject asked if the learner was liable to suffer permanent physical injury, the experimenter said:

> Although the shocks may be painful, there is no permanent tissue damage, so please go on. [Followed by Prods 2, 3, and 4 if necessary.]

If the subject said that the learner did not want to go on, the experimenter replied:

> Whether the learner likes it or not, you must go on until he has learned all the word pairs correctly. So please go on. [Followed by Prods 2, 3, and 4 if necessary.]

Dependent Measures

The primary dependent measure for any subject is the maximum shock he administers before he refuses to go any further. In principle this may vary from 0 (for a subject who refuses to administer even the first shock) to 30 (for a subject who administers the highest shock on the generator). A subject who breaks off the experiment at any point prior to administering the thirtieth shock level is termed a *defiant* subject. One who complies with experimental commands fully, and proceeds to administer all shock levels commanded, is termed an *obedient* subject.

Further records. With few exceptions, experimental sessions were recorded on magnetic tape. Occasional photographs were taken through one-way mirrors. Notes were kept in any unusual behavior occurring during the course of the experiments. On occasion, additional observers were directed to write objective descriptions of the subjects' behavior. The latency and duration of shocks were measured by accurate timing devices.

Interview and dehoax. Following the experiment, projective measures, and attitude scales were employed. After the interview, procedures were undertaken to assure that the subject would leave the laboratory in a state of well being. A friendly reconciliation was arranged between the subject and the victim, and an effort was made to reduce any tensions that arose as a result of the experiment.

Results

Preliminary Notions

Before giving an account of the experimental results, it is instructive to consider how persons predict others will perform when commanded to administer powerful shocks to another person. Fourteen Yale seniors, all psychology majors, were provided with a detailed description of the experimental situation. They were asked to reflect carefully on it, and to predict the behavior of 100 hypothetical subjects. More specifically, they were instructed to plot the distribution of obedience of "100 Americans of diverse occupations, and ranging in age from 20 to 50 years," who were placed in the experimental situation.

There was considerable agreement among the respondents on the expected behavior of hypothetical subjects. All respondents predicted that only an insignificant minority would go through to the end of the shock series. (The estimates ranged from 0 to 3%; i.e., the most "pessimistic" member of the class predicted that of 100 persons, 3 would continue through to the most potent shock available on the shock generator—450 volts.) The class mean was 1.2%. The question was also posed informally to colleagues of the author, and the most general feeling was that few if any subjects would go beyond the designation Very Strong Shock.

Result of Experiment I

Subjects accept situation. With few exceptions subjects were convinced of the reality of the experiment situation, that they were administering shocks to another person, and the most potent shocks were extremely painful. In the post-experimental interview subjects were asked: "How painful to the learner were the last few shocks that you administered to him?" Subjects were instructed to indicate their answers on a printed 14-point scale ranging from "Not at all painful" to "Extremely painful." The modal response was 14 (Extremely painful) with the mean at 13.42.

Signs of extreme tension. Many subjects showed signs of nervousness in the experimental situation, and especially upon administering the more powerful shocks. In a large number of cases the degree of tension reached extremes that are rarely seen in sociopsychological laboratory studies. Subjects were observed to sweat, tremble, stutter, bite their lips, groan, and dig their fingernails into their flesh. These were characteristic rather than exceptional responses to the experiment.

One sign of tension was the regular occurrence of nervous laughing fits. Fourteen of the 40 subjects showed definite signs of nervous laughter and smiling. The laughter seemed entirely out of place, even bizarre. Full-blown, uncontrollable seizures were observed for 3 subjects. On one occasion we observed a seizure so violently convulsive that it was necessary to call a halt to the experiment. The subject, a 46-year-old encyclopedia salesman, was seriously embarrassed by his untoward and uncontrollable behavior. In the post-experimental interviews subjects took pains to point out that they were not sadistic types, and that the laughter did not mean they enjoyed shocking the victim.

Distribution of scores. It had been conjectured that persons would not, in general, agree to administer shocks beyond the level designated as Very Strong Shock. The distribution of maximum shocks for this experiment is shown in table 2. The obtained distribution of scores deviates radically from the prediction.

Upon command of the experimenter, each of the 40 subjects went beyond the expected breakoff point. No subject stopped prior to administering Shock Level 20. (At this level—300 volts—the victim kicks on the wall and no longer provides answers to the teacher's multiple-choice questions.)

Of the 40 subjects, 5 refused to obey the experimental commands beyond the 300-volt level. Four more subjects administered one further shock, and then refused to go on. Two broke off at the 330-volt level, and 1 each at 345, 360, and 375 volts. Thus a total of 14 subjects defied the experimenter. It is instructive to reprint their remarks at the point of defiance, as transcribed from the tape recordings:

[0124] I think he's trying to communicate, he's knocking.... Well it's not fair to shock the guy ... these are terrific volts. I don't think this is very humane.... Oh, I can't go on with this; no, this isn't right. It's a hell of an experiment. The guy is suffering in there. No, I don't want to go on. This is crazy. [Subject refused to administer more shocks.]

[0123] He's banging in there. I'm gonna chicken out. I'd like to continue, but I can't do that to a man. . . . I'm sorry I can't do that to a man. I'll hurt his heart. You take your check. . . . No really, I couldn't do it.

These subjects were frequently in a highly agitated and even angered state. Sometimes, verbal protest was at a minimum, and the subject simply got up from his chair in front of the shock generator, and indicated that he wished to leave the laboratory.

Table 2. Distribution of Breakoff Points

Verbal designation and voltage indication	Number of subjects for whom this was maximum shock
Slight Shock	
15	0
30	0
45	0
60	0
Moderate Shock	
75	0
90	0
105	0
120	0
Strong Shock	
135	0
150	0
165	0
180	0
Very Strong Shock	
195	0
210	0
225	0
240	0
Intense Shock	
255	0
270	0
285	0
300	5
Extreme Intensity Shock	
315	4
330	2
345	1
360	1
Danger: Severe Shock	
375	1
390	0
405	0
420	0
XXX	
435	0
450	26

Source: Stanley Milgram, "Behavioral Study of Obedience," *Journal of Abnormal and Social Psychology* 67 (1963). Copyright 1963 by the American Psychological Association. Reprinted by permission of the author and the publisher.

Of the 40 subjects, 26 obeyed the orders of the experimenter to the end, proceeding to punish the victim until they reached the most potent shock available on the shock generator. At that point, the experimenter called a halt to the session. (The maximum shock is labeled 450 volts, and is two steps beyond the designation: Danger: Severe Shock.) Although obedient subjects continued to administer shocks, they often did so under extreme stress. Some expressed reluctance to administer shocks beyond the 300-volt level, and displayed fears similar to those who defied the experimenter; yet they obeyed.

After the maximum shocks had been delivered, and the experimenter called a halt to the proceedings, many obedient subjects heaved sighs of relief, mopped their brows, rubbed their fingers over their eyes, or nervously fumbled cigarettes. Some shook their heads, apparently in regret. Some subjects had remained calm throughout the experiment, and displayed only minimal signs of tension from beginning to end.

Discussion

The experiment yielded two findings that were surprising. The first finding concerns the sheer strength of obedient tendencies manifested in this situation. Subjects have learned from childhood that it is a fundamental breach of moral conduct to hurt another person against his will. Yet, 26 subjects abandon this tenet in following the instructions of an authority who has no special powers to enforce his commands. To disobey would bring no material loss to the subject; no punishment would ensue. It is clear from the remarks and outward behavior of many participants that in punishing the victim they are often acting against their own values. Subjects often expressed deep disapproval of shocking a man in the face of his objections, and others denounced it as stupid and senseless. Yet the majority complied with the experimental commands. This outcome was surprising from two perspectives: first, from the standpoint of predictions made in the questionnaire described earlier. (Here, however, it is possible that the remoteness of the respondents from the actual situation, and the difficulty of conveying to them the concrete details of the experiment, could account for the serious underestimation of obedience.)

But the results were also unexpected to persons who observed the experiment in progress, through one-way mirrors. Observers often uttered expressions of disbelief upon seeing a subject administer more powerful shocks to the victim. These persons had a full acquaintance with the details of the situation, and yet systematically underestimated the amount of obedience that subjects would display.

The second unanticipated effect was the extraordinary tension generated by the procedures. One might suppose that a subject would simply break off or continue as his conscience dictated. Yet, this is very far from what happened. There were striking reactions of tension and emotional strain. One observer related:

> I observed a mature and initially poised businessman enter the laboratory smiling and confident. Within 20 minutes he was reduced to a twitching, stuttering wreck, who was rapidly approaching a point of nervous collapse. He constantly pulled on his earlobe, and twisted his hands. At one point he pushed his fist into his forehead and muttered: "Oh God, let's stop it." And yet he continued to respond to every word of the experimenter, and obeyed to the end.

Any understanding of the phenomenon of obedience must rest on an analysis of the particular conditions in which it occurs. The following features of the experiment go some distance in explaining the high amount of obedience observed in the situation.

1.   The experiment is sponsored by and takes place on the grounds of an institution of unimpeachable reputation, Yale University. It may be reasonably presumed that the personnel are competent and reputable. The importance of this background authority is now being studied by conducting a series of experiments outside of New Haven, and without any visible ties to the university.

2.   The experiment is, on the face of it, designed to attain a worthy purpose—advancement of knowledge about learning and memory. Obedience occurs not as an instrumental element in a situation that the subject construes as significant, and meaningful. He may not be able to see its full significance, but he may properly assume that the experimenter does.

3.   The subject perceives that the victim has voluntarily submitted to the authority system of the experimenter. He is not (at first) an unwilling captive impressed for involuntary service. He has taken the trouble to come to the laboratory presumably to aid the experimental research. That he later becomes an involuntary subject does not alter the fact that, initially, he consented to participate without qualification. Thus he has in some degree incurred an obligation toward the experimenter.

4.   The subject, too, has entered the experiment voluntarily, and perceives himself under obligation to aid the experimenter. He has made a commitment, and to disrupt the experiment is a repudiation of this initial promise of aid.

5.   Certain features of the procedure strengthen the subject's sense of obligation to the experimenter. For one, he has been paid for coming to the laboratory. In part this is canceled out by the experimenter's statement:

> Of course, as in all experiments, the money is yours simply for coming to the laboratory. From this point on, no matter what happens, the money is yours.

6.   From the subject's standpoint, the fact that he is the teacher and the other man the learner is purely a chance consequence (it is determined by drawing lots) and he, the subject, ran the same risk as the other man in being assigned the role of learner. Since the assignment of positions in the experiment was achieved by fair means, the learner is deprived of any basis of complaint on this count. (A similar situation obtains in Army units, in which—in the absence of volunteers—a particularly dangerous mission may be assigned by drawing lots, and the unlucky soldier is expected to bear his misfortune with sportsmanship.)

7.   There is, at best, ambiguity with regard to the prerogatives of a psychologist and the corresponding rights of his subject. There is a vagueness of expectation concerning what a psychologist may require of his subject, and when he is overstepping acceptable limits. Moreover, the experiment occurs in a closed setting, and thus provides no opportunity for the subject to remove these ambiguities by discussion with others. There are few standards that seem directly applicable to the situation, which is a novel one for most subjects.

8.   The subjects are assured that the shocks administered to the subject are "painful but not dangerous." Thus they assume that the discomfort caused the victim is momentary, while the scientific gains resulting from the experiment are enduring.

9.   Through Shock Level 20 the victim continues to provide answers on the signal box. The subject may construe this as a sign that the victim is still willing to "play the game." It is only after Shock Level 20 that the victim repudiates the rules completely, refusing to answer further.

These features help to explain the high amount of obedience obtained in this experiment. Many of the arguments raised need not remain matters of speculation, but can be reduced to testable propositions to be confirmed or disproved by further experiments.

The following feaures of the experiment concern the nature of the conflict which the subject faces.

10.   The subject is placed in a position in which he must respond to the competing demands of two persons: the experimenter and the victim. The conflict must be resolved by meeting the demands of one or the other; satisfaction of the victim and the experimenter are mutually exclusive. Moreover, the resolution must take the form of a highly visible action, that of continuing to shock the victim or breaking off the experiment. Thus the subject is forced into a public conflict that does not permit any completely satisfactory solution.

11. While the demands of the experimenter carry the weight of scientific authority, the demands of the victim spring from his personal experience of pain and suffering. The two claims need not be regarded as equally pressing and legitimate. The experimenter seeks an abstract scientific datum; the victim cries out for relief from physical suffering caused by the subject's actions.

12. The experiment gives the subject little time for reflection. The conflict comes on rapidly. It is only minutes after the subject has been seated before the shock generator that the victim begins his protests. Moreover, the subject perceives that he has gone through but two-thirds of the shock levels at the time the subject's first protests are heard. Thus he understands that the conflict will have a persistent aspect to it, and may well become more intense as increasingly more powerful shocks are required. The rapidity with which the conflict descends on the subject, and his realization that it is predictably recurrent may well be sources of tension to him.

13. At a more general level, the conflict stems from the opposition of two deeply ingrained behavior dispositions: first, the disposition not to harm other people, and second, the tendency to obey those whom we perceive to be legitimate authorities.

Shocking and Other Aggressive Acts

Milgram's research set off a wave of experiments which sought to discover conditions which would either increase or decrease the likelihood of a person delivering shocks to a victim at the suggestion of an experimenter. Some experiments are close to the original (Milgram, 1965b, 1966; Sheridan and King, 1972; Schuck and Pisor, 1974), while others report variations which result from characteristics of the person giving the shocks, the person receiving the shocks, or other influences in the situation.

As in other studies of conforming behavior, female subjects are less likely to give shocks or be aggressive in other ways (Landau, Packer, and Levy, 1973; McGuire, 1973; Miller and Miller, 1973; Kilham and Mann, 1974; A. G. Miller et al., 1974). Persons who are low in guilt feelings (Knott, 1970; Gentry, Harburg, and Hauenstein, 1973; Knott, Lasater, and Shuman, 1974), low in anxiety (Ancoma and Pareyson, 1971–1972), or high in prejudice (Genthner and Taylor, 1973) are more likely to give shocks.

Subjects who are in an aroused state after hearing a sexually exciting story, riding a bicycle, or having to wait for another person to arrive are more likely to show aggressive feelings through shocks (Geen, Rakosky, and Pigg, 1972; O'Neal and Kaufman, 1972; Zillman, Katcher, and Milavsky, 1972; Buss, Plomin, and Carver, 1973), although sexual arousal may also have the opposite effect (Baron and Bell, 1973; Geen and Pigg, 1973). The arousal is especially likely to result in aggression if the subject has seen an aggressive model in the laboratory or in a film (Berkowitz, 1970; Baron, 1971c; Zillman, 1971; Atkins et al., 1972; Dove and McReynolds, 1972; Geen and Stonner, 1972; Leyens, 1972; Meyer, 1972a, 1972b; Berkowitz and Alioto, 1973; Doob and Kirshenbaum, 1973; Geen and Stonner, 1973; Harrell, 1973; Harris, 1973; Kniveton, 1973a, 1973b; Kniveton and Stephenson, 1973; Leyens and Picus, 1973; Scharff and Schlottmann, 1973; Schwanenberg, 1973; Wilkins, Scharff, and Schlottmann, 1974). In a number of these studies the films used were ordinary commercial films of war or athletic events. However, having weapons present in the room did not seem to stimulate aggression; rather, aggression was inhibited (Ellis, Weinir, and Miller, 1971). Nor did firing guns at targets seem to have any effect (Buss, Booker, and Buss, 1972).

One study reversed the sequence by showing the film after the aggression. Subjects were asked to shock another person (a confederate), then they saw a brutal boxing film. Among the subjects who had not been reminded of the movie's fictitiousness, the subjects who heard the confederate respond to shocks with expressions of suffering rated the film less violent than those who had shocked the confederate without any indication that he was suffering. When reminded that the film was fictitious, subjects who had shocked and heard the confederate rated the film as more violent than those who had not heard. The authors conclude that a violent act on film reminds the subject of his own aggression and thereby intensifies his anxiety. Thus reappraising the film, and his own act, as being less violent would mitigate the anxiety. When the subjects are told the film is fictitious, they have less need to appraise the film as nonviolent (Geen, Stonner, and Kelley, 1974).

As in the Festinger and Carlsmith experiment on cognitive dissonance (1959), subjects seem to be using a form of social exchange in which equity is achieved if relationships are balanced. Thus subjects respond favorably to others whom they like (Schlenker, Brown, and Tedeschi, 1971), because they are similar (Pigg and Geen, 1971; Farina et al., 1972), because they are cooperative or conciliatory (Goldman, Kretschmann, and Westergard, 1972; Gaebelein, 1973a), because they already seem to be suffering (Farina, Sherman, and Allen, 1968; Geen, 1970; Baron, 1971a, 1971b; Levitt and Viney, 1973; Baron, 1974a), because they are disadvantaged (Doob, 1970; Drost and Knott, 1971; Chase and Mills, 1973), or because they are female (Larsen et al., 1972). Generally subjects respond to aggression with aggression (Williams, 1968; Merrick and Taylor, 1970; Helm, Bonoma, and Tedeschi, 1971; Hendrick and Taylor, 1971; Knott and Drost, 1971; McDaniel, O'Neal, and Fox, 1971; Pallak and Heller, 1971; Rule and Hewitt, 1971; Taylor and Pisano, 1971; Dengerink and Levendusky, 1972; Foa, Turner, and Foa, 1972; Gentry, 1972; Konečni and Doob, 1972; Rywick and Gaffney, 1972; Albert, 1973; Bandura, 1973; Baron, 1973b; Dertke et al., 1973; Greenwell and Dengerink, 1973; Hart, 1973; Hepburn, 1973; Kane, Doerge, and Tedeschi, 1973; Legant and Mettee, 1973; O'Leary and Dengerink, 1973; Pitkanen, 1973; Donnenwerth and Foa, 1974; Fenigstein and Buss, 1974; Gaebelein and Hay, 1974; Thompson and Kolstoe, 1974; Worchel, 1974).

Additional ways in which the subject can achieve balance include compensating for the aggressive act by complying with a later request for help (Berscheid, Walster, and Barcley, 1969; Brock, 1969; Carlsmith and Gross, 1969) or by devaluing the victim as if he deserved the punishment (Berscheid, Boye, and Walster, 1968; Lerner, 1971; Mills and Egger, 1972; Katz, Glass, and Cohen, 1973; Aderman, Brehm, and Katz, 1974; Sorrentino and Boutilier, 1974). If the victim seems to benefit from the shocks (Baron and Eggleston, 1972; Brown, Schlenker, and Tedeschi, 1972; Cherry, Mitchell, and Nelson, 1973; Savitsky et al., 1974) or if the subject is rewarded (Parke, Ewall, and Slaby, 1972; Lange and Van de Nes, 1973), the subject will continue to be aggressive.

If other persons appear to be taking part in the experiment, then the subject is more likely to obey the experimenter and give the shocks if others (actually confederates) also conform (Milgram, 1964; Baron and Lawton, 1972; Powers and Geen, 1972) or censure the subject if he does not conform (Borden and Taylor, 1973; Donnerstein and Donnerstein, 1973). He is less likely to obey if others do not obey (Milgram, 1965a; Waldman and Baron, 1971; Gaebelein, 1973b) or might censure him if he does (Baron, 1971f, 1972b). A model has a similar effect on the victim, who will tolerate more shock if others appear to do so (Strassberg and Klinger, 1972; Craig and Neidermayer, 1974).

The effects of other variables, such as eye contact, room temperature, or a dangerous shock machine, suggest that the more a subject identifies with the victim, the less likely he is to be aggressive (Haas, 1969; Lanzetta and Kleck, 1970; Penner and Hawkins, 1971; Pisano and Taylor, 1971; Baron, 1972a; Cohen and Murray, 1972; Diener et al., 1973; Ellsworth and Carlsmith, 1973; Geer and Jarmecky, 1973; Ulehla and Adams, 1973).

Additional articles reporting research on aggression which cover aspects of the object of the aggression, the subject, or the situation include Berkowitz, 1960; de Charms and Wilkins, 1963; Kaufmann and Feshback, 1963; Glass, 1964; Wiggins, 1965; Grebstein, 1967; Miller and Levy, 1967; Wheeler and Levine, 1967; Craig and Crockett, 1968; Hicks and Lathrop, 1968; Baker and Schaie, 1969; Berkowitz, Lepinski, and Angulo, 1969; Lidman, 1969; Rosen and Helgerson, 1969; Stone and Hokanson, 1969; Tedeschi and Bonoma, 1969; Baron, 1971d; Graf and Green, 1971 Zabrack and Miller, 1972; Brown, 1973; Gentry, Harburg, and Hauenstein, 1973; Green and Murray, 1973; Harrell and Schmitt, 1973; Harris, Liguori, and Joniak, 1973; Baron, 1974b; Baron and Ball, 1974; Carver, 1974; Harris and Huang, 1974; Henry, Rousseau, and Schlottmann, 1974; Krupat, 1974; Scheier, Fenigstein, and Buss, 1974; Tedeschi, Smith, and Brown, 1974; Turner and Simons, 1974.

Norms of the Primary Group

Some indication of the relative influence of the norms of a small primary group, such as a family or peer group, and of a large secondary group, such as a religious or occupational group, has already been given in the discussion of the anchorage of opinions in reference groups. In general, the norms of the *primary group* are more important for the individual than those of the *secondary group* (Baur, 1960; Bates and Babchuk, 1961; Dentler, 1961; Iwao, 1963; Lana, 1964).

Disasters, such as floods and tornadoes, which affect a whole community bring out ordinarily latent conflicts between loyalties to primary and secondary groups. Under these conditions the loyalty to the primary group is usually the most demanding, but if a person is trained as a disaster worker or is responsible for the work of a large organization, he may stay by his post (Killian, 1952).

In another example, the food preferences of a sample of urban children were found to be closer to those of their small peer group than to the larger religious organization which specified certain food taboos (Rosen, 1955a).

Conflicts in group norms have been most apparent over the years in industry, where the systematic attempts on the part of management to overcome "soldiering" or "gold-bricking" among the workers go back at least to Taylor's first efforts at "Scientific Management," when he persuaded men in a steel mill to shovel coal from coal cars individually rather than in groups. Once freed from the influence of the group norm, his workers were able to earn 60 percent more wages ($1.85 per day, rather than the prevailing $1.15) and were no more fatigued than when working at the old pace (Taylor, 1903, 1911). This same tendency for the informal group to depress the output rates has been noted in the Western Electric Researches (Mayo, 1933; Whitehead, 1938; Roethlisberger and Dickson, 1939; Homans, 1946) and in other industrial studies (Wyatt, Frost, and Stock, 1934).

Race relations is another area in which informal groups are able to enforce norms which are not in line with those leading to maximum efficiency of the larger organization. Hughes (1946) describes a plant in which three-man teams who worked closely together were nearly all members of the same ethnic group, as well as being related in other ways. When management attempted to introduce workers from a second ethnic group into these teams, the workers who were "old-timers" forced them to quit by obvious forms of pressure. However, a three-man team composed of members of the second ethnic group was able to stay on the job, although not fully accepted by the other workers. In another part of the same plant women from the second group were partially accepted by other women workers in a situation in which each worker could work independently. However, the workers in the second ethnic group did not conform to the informal production norms, since they were not members of the informal cliques.

Similar findings have been duplicated in the laboratory, where highly cohesive groups produce substantially less than those with lower cohesiveness when the group standard is for lower production (Schachter et al., 1951, Seashore, 1954), and overachievers tend to modify their goals to conform to the group norm (Hilgard, Sait, and Margaret, 1940).

The norms of the primary group are not always in conflict with those of the secondary group. They may provide informal social control which is more effective than the formal control of the larger organization in fulfilling the goal of the organization (Gross, 1953). Several examples of this come from experiences in armies during World War II where soldiers in both the American army and the German Wehrmacht derived their motivation to fight from their loyalty to their military primary group rather than from their acceptance of strategic or political goals (Dicks, 1944; Shils and Janowitz, 1948; Stouffer et al., 1949; Shils, 1950). The success in ending segregation in the American armed services during the same war has also been attributed to the fact that blacks became co-members of primary groups with white soldiers and thus shared common loyalties (Mandelbaum, 1952).

As a follow-up of the war experience, one test of the hypothesis that primary group affiliation is related to institutional group morale was made with a sample of students from a large university. In this instance, the number and strength of the ties in a friendship group did not appear to be related to "institutional morale," as measured by the extent of the desire to remain in college if the subject was not doing well academically (Zenter, 1955).

Pressures on the Deviant

Since individuals generally perceive their opinions as being closer to group norms than they actually are (Travers, 1941; Wallen, 1943; Gorden, 1952), the deviant, who tends to be marginal to the group and less informed about group decisions, may not be aware of the norms or of the extent of his deviation (Newcomb, 1943; Festinger, Schachter, and Back, 1950; Chowdhry and Newcomb, 1952). Under these conditions, his own attempts at *self-control* may not bring him close enough to the group standard to satisfy the other group members. Since the group members cannot tolerate deviation without being forced to reexamine their concept of reality (Festinger, 1954), they will make overt attempts to secure the conformity of the deviant.

Conformity can be expected to be greater when the limits of the group's tolerance and the penalties for deviation are clearly specified (Riecken, 1952). In groups which are of primary importance for the members, punishment may take violent forms. Present-day examples are found in industry where new workers are punished for rate-busting (Taylor, 1911; Hughes, 1946), or for holding unpopular ideologies.

Interaction with the deviant increases when the group first recognizes his deviance, but falls off if he begins to conform or if other members feel that he is a lost cause (Festinger and Thibaut, 1951; Schachter, 1951; Festinger et al., 1952; Israel, 1956; Berkowitz and Howard, 1959; Sampson and Brandon, 1964; Allen, 1965a). In one study of highschool students in clubs, the amount of pressure on the deviant was also related to the attractiveness of the club for the other members. The more highly the club was rated by its members, the greater was the pressure exerted towards the deviant (Emerson, 1954). Rejection of the deviant appears to be an almost universal phenomenon as experimental evidence from a number of different cultures has indicated (Schachter et al., 1954; Israel, 1956); however, an exception is found in a study which was made in England. There the presence of the deviant, persisting quietly and unaggressively with his own choice, seems to have reinforced the strength of other individual opinions. Other group members appeared to reason "If he won't give up his choice, why should I?" (De Monchaux and Shimmin, 1955). In some cases the persistent deviant can win over other members of the group (Harnack, 1963; Grove, 1965). In addition to punitive control of the deviant, the group exerts positive control by giving more support to the opinions of well-liked members (Horowitz, Lyons, and Perlmutter, 1951) and support to the deviant if he eventually conforms (Doise and Moscovici, 1969–1970; Levine, Saxe, and Harris, 1973) rather than leaves the group (Singer, Radloff, and Wark, 1963).

An analysis of deviant behavior in a series of therapy groups provides a further example of some of the processes underlying deviance and conformity (Stock, Whitman, and Lieberman, 1958). In these groups, a person was seen as a deviant if he interfered with the group's solution to some focal conflict, causing the other members to reexperience the tensions and anxieties which were present before the solution was reached. When a deviant appeared, the other group members would either exert influence on the deviant to conform, reinterpret the deviant's behavior so that it no longer threatened the group's solution to the conflict, or modify the solution to include the deviant behavior. The individual who was most likely to become a deviant was the one who tried to force his habitual solutions to emotional problems on the group.

Small groups as well as large groups will reject deviant members if the group can survive more effectively without them than with them. However, members whose deviance in one area is counterbalanced by skills in another area which the group needs may be retained by the group at the expense of a change in group norms (Hollander, 1958). When the deviance is attributed to the situation, members may have an "inclusive" reaction to deviance by an attempt to control interaction through intense interaction pressure accompanied by relatively low attitudinal hostility, which has the effect of including the deviant in the group. When the deviance is attributed to the character of the deviant, members may have an "exclusive" reaction to deviance and reject the deviant as an outsider and have low levels of interaction and high covert hostility (Orcutt, 1973). The reactions to deviance will be influenced by the status of the deviant member and the strength of the expectations for conformity (Zeisel, 1963; Spitzer, 1964; Berkowitz, 1965; Norrison and Carment, 1968; Wahrman, 1970; Frank and Wolman, 1973).

Changing the Norms

Since norms are formed through group interaction, they can also be changed through group interaction (Lippitt, Watson, and Westley, 1958). Although some patterns of behavior, such as fads of dress, speech, and mannerisms, change through contagion (Polansky, Lippitt, and Redl, 1950a), group discussion is generally found to result in more change than other forms of persuasion, such as lectures or directives. In one industrial plant twenty-nine supervisors were divided into three groups of nine, nine, and eleven members. The first group was given a one-and-one-half-hour lecture on the technique and theory of "merit rating," and questions were answered. The second group held a discussion of the problem of rating the job rather than the man, and decided how it would solve the problem. The third group was a control group which was given no instruction. The purpose of the lecture and the discussion was to reduce the tendency of the supervisors to rate certain workers highly simply because they held highly skilled jobs. A comparison of the average "before" and "after" merit ratings by individuals in each of the three groups indicated that there was some reduction of ratings in the lecture group, a greater reduction in the discussion group, and no change in the control group (Levine and Butler, 1952).

A second example of behavior change is found in the "action research" of Lewin and his colleagues during World War II. They were seeking the best way to convince housewives to buy low-priority foods which they were not accustomed to eating (Lewin, 1943; Willerman, 1943; Guthe, 1945; Lewin, 1947a, 1947c; Radke and Klisurich, 1947; Lewin, 1951). As in the industrial study mentioned above, Lewin (1947b) brought together key persons or "gate-keepers," who exert the major influence on some small group to which they belong. In the case of food habits, the housewife is the "gate-keeper" who exerts the major influence on the family diet. More housewives changed their behavior and attitudes about various types of foods after participating in a group discussion than after hearing a lecture on the value of eating these same new foods. Once the new group standard had been formed through group discussion, it was easier for the housewives to change their behavior to conform to the new standard.

In addition to these two examples, other studies report changes in pattern over a wide range of behavior (Cartwright, 1951):[5] community problems are solved (Williams, 1947; Jaques, 1948; Dean and Rosen, 1955), alcoholics cured (Bales, 1945), productivity raised (Kelley and Ware, 1947; Lewin, 1948, pp. 125–141; Coch and French, 1948; Jenkins, 1948; French, 1950; Lawrence and Smith, 1955; Trist and Murray, 1960; Maier and Hoffman, 1964; Bronzo, 1968), group skills improved (Bradford and French, 1948; Lippitt, 1949; Coffey et al., 1950), attitudes changed (McKeachie, 1954a; Lawler, 1955; Kipnis, 1958; Miller and Biggs, 1958; Mitnick and McGinnies, 1958; Flanders and Havumaki, 1960a; Hawkins and Meyer, 1965; Cook, 1967; Hofstetter, 1972; Woods, 1972), and personality patterns changed (Slavson, 1947; Burchard, Michaels, and Kotkov, 1948; Foulkes, 1950; Kotkov, 1950; Jones and Peters, 1952; Schneider, 1955; Corsini and Putzey, 1957; Kelman and Parloff, 1957; Briskin, 1958; Foulds, 1972b; Leith and Uhlemann, 1972; Nobler, 1972). Changes in pattern which are associated with applications of group dynamics are discussed in appendix 4.

5. In some of these cases where the small group discussion is used to change indirectly the norms of a larger group to which the members also belong, the members of the small group are only brought together for one discussion.

When discussion groups are compared with each other in their effectiveness in bringing about change in opinion, the groups in which the opportunities for discussion are maximized are found to be the most effective. The amount of participation is usually controlled through some "democratic" leader who urges all members to take part in the discussion (Preston and Heintz, 1949; Maier and Solem, 1952; Hare, 1953). The discussion leader will tend to have more success in changing opinions if he is the "natural" group leader rather than a leader who has joined the group only for this purpose (Torrance and Mason, 1956).

There is evidence that the important element in change is not so much having a chance to discuss the problem as it is in providing an effective method for breaking down the old value system before adopting a new one (Alpert and Smith, 1949), an emotional as well as an intellectual process. As the process of change takes place, group members tend to show the greatest resistance to change just before they yield to the new set of values (Redl, 1948). An intensified version of this technique of breaking down old values was developed in China after the Korean War as part of the Chinese political reeducation program (Lifton, 1956; Schein, 1956; Biderman, 1959; Schein, 1960; Lifton, 1961; Schein, Schneier, and Barker 1961). On the other hand, if the change of "opinion" involves only learning new information without a change in commitment to a new norm, then information from an expert, teacher, or book may be as effective as group discussion (Robinson, 1941). If also the task of the group is simply to discuss the merits and demerits of an issue and not to form a new policy for handling the issue, no change in attitude may result (Timmons, 1939). Resistance to changes in norms is based on the strength of the initial patterns. The patterns are more easily maintained in the absence of all the *conditions for change* previously described.

Additional research on the relationship between group discussion and attitude change includes Mann and Borgatta, 1959; McGinnies and Altman, 1959; Mann, 1960; Mann and Mann, 1960; March and Feigenbaum, 1960; Steiner and Field, 1960; Cohn, Yee, and Brown, 1961; Jordan, 1966; Muney and Deutsch, 1968; Coons, McEachern, and Annis, 1970; Kahn and Alexander, 1971; Scioli, 1971; Triandis and Malpass, 1971; Cialdini et al., 1973.

A Functional Interpretation of Pressures to Conform

In the mid-1950s both Jahoda (1956) and Kelman (1958) outlined theories of conformity which illustrate an application of the cybernetic hierarchy of control in functional theory, although neither seemed to be aware of the similarity at the time. Johoda's paper provides an example of four types of conformity which turn out to match A, G, I, and L.

At the time of Jahoda's research, civil liberties, especially centering on the loyalty oath, were a dominant issue in universities in the United States. Although Jahoda had conducted several surveys about this issue, she does not cite her own research evidence, but rather makes up an incident which she feels illustrates all the processes of conformity which are involved. She notes that any similarity with actual events is purely coincidental.

A college president together with a faculty committee of four persons considers applicants for a new appointment. The best qualified man is one who is known to be a socialist. Each of the four faculty members initially favors his appointment. The president recommends rejection because of the candidate's unsuitable political views. He adds that such an appoinment would furthermore seriously offend a benefactor of the college who is about to make a substantial gift to it. As it happens, in this fictitious example, all four members of the faculty go along with the president's recommendation and reject the candidate.[6]

Since each of the faculty members went along with the president's recommendation, we might suppose that they were all equally conforming. However, Jahoda suggests that we use our imagination to hold confidential conversations with each of them after the event. They turn out to have four different stories:

Faculty member A says: "I feel awful. I still believe that we should not have considered the candidate's political views. But I couldn't stand up to the President. I admit I acted out of fear. The question of my promotion will come up next week."

Faculty member B says: "We had an interesting meeting. Originally I was quite opposed to the notion of considering a candidate's political views. But I changed my mind. The President made a very good argument against the inappropriateness of socialism for our country. He really convinced me of the mistake of deliberately exposing our students to an unrealistic idealist."

Faculty member C says: "I go to these meetings solely because I have been appointed to the committee. I really am not very much interested in these matters. But it is nice to sit together with the President and my colleagues. It makes me feel good to have close friendly contact with them. And if a group of nice people agree, I am the last to make difficulties. I think we did the right thing today."

Faculty member D says: "This was a really difficult decision for me. I still believe in academic freedom. But the argument that convinced me was that I know the college depends on getting that gift. After all you can fight for academic freedom only if you have a college that can pay its expenses. I decided to reject the candidate because the President was right when he said we would never get that gift otherwise." [7]

Jahoda then suggests that these four types can be explained by two underlying dimensions: first, whether the subject was moved by the argument or by pressure, and second, whether his belief was changed or unchanged as a result. This cross classification is presented in figure 13.

Figure 13. Four Processes of Conformism

	Belief changed	Belief unchanged
Argument	Consentience (Faculty member B)	Convergence (Faculty member D)
Pressure (unrelated to issue)	Conformance (Faculty member C)	Compliance (Faculty member A)

Source: Marie Jahoda, "Psychological Issues in Civil Liberties," *American Psychologist* 11 (1956): 236. Copyright 1956 by the American Psychological Association. Reprinted by permission of the author and the publisher.

6. Marie Jahoda, "Psychological Issues in Civil Liberties," *American Psychologist* 11 (1956): 236. Copyright 1956 by the American Psychological Association. Reprinted by permission of the author and the publisher.
7. Ibid., pp. 233–237.

The four types fit the AGIL scheme directly as we rotate figure 13 counter-clockwise one position: the process of convergence is related to adaptation (A) since it is based on facts, compliance to goal attainment (G) since it is based on the power of an authority, conformance to integration (I) since it is based on friendship ties, and consentience to pattern maintenance (L) since it is based on adherence to basic values. Following the cybernetic hierarchy of control we would expect conformity pressures of type L to be the most powerful, then I, then G, and last of all A.

Although Jahoda does not discuss these types in connection with the cybernetic hierarchy of control, her further examples and illustrations suggest reasons why the hierarchy of control might function as it does. Let us consider what it would take to change the minds of the four faculty members after their meeting with the president. The person who was convinced by the facts (A) should be the easiest to influence. Give him a new set of facts and he should reach a different decision. Next would come the person who complied through threat of loss of promotion (G). If he was actually promoted, or if in some other way the threat could be removed, he should be free to change. More difficult to change would be the person who enjoyed being with a friendly group (I). Even in another situation, this group might remain as a positive reference group and provide an anchorage for his opinions. If he were placed in a new group, the new group would have to appear more salient to him if he were to change. Finally the most difficult to change would be the person who has actually taken over the beliefs of the president (L). Since he now considers the beliefs his, it becomes a matter of his own integrity to maintain them.

Kelman (1958) identified only three processes, which he called compliance (G), identification (I), and interalization (L). A separate "A" process was not described. He defines his processes in terms similar to Jahoda's. He then continues by offering some hypotheses concerning the conditions under which each type of behavior is performed. The hypotheses are as follows:

1. When an individual adopts an induced response through compliance, he tends to perform it only under conditions of surveillance by the influencing agent.
2. When an individual adopts an induced response through identification, he tends to perform it only under conditions of salience of his relationship to the agent.
3. When an individual adopts an induced response through internalization, he tends to perform it under conditions of relevance of the issue, regardless of surveillance or salience.

These propositions of Kelman's add something to our understanding of how the cybernetic hierarchy of control actually works. It is not that information is more controlling than energy in some abstract way, but that the information, in the form of values, is carried within the individual while the factors which depend on energy are external. Beginning at the top, the values (L) are the most powerful, since once they are internalized, the individual carries them with him. Next come the norms representing reciprocal role relationships (I). Once adopted through identification, they can be called up whenever the other person is present or when-ever the relationship is "salient" for some other reason. Next in order comes the response to the power of a task supervisor (G), since it will only be effective while the supervisor is present. Last would be the power of money or another energy source as a means of influence in the adaptive area. Although Kelman does not include this type of influence in his experiment, it should have the least power because money only insures a response at the moment it is exchanged. Once the deal is closed, the vote is purchased, or whatever form of influence was sought is obtained, the money has no continuing influence. For the next round, more money must be produced if the influence is to be maintained. In a similar way, other sources of high energy tend to be consumed in use.

Unfortunately few experiments consider more than one variable at a time, so that it is difficult to find evidence to support the hypothesis that four types of influence on conformity are ordered according to the L, I, G, A hierarchy. Kelman's (1958) experiment demonstrates that variables of the L, I, and G types have an influence on attitude change (see also Leet-Pellegrini and Rubin, 1974), and experiments by Kiesler and colleagues give evidence that commitment to continue in a group (L) is a more powerful influence on conformity than attraction to the group (I) (Kiesler and Corbin, 1965; Kiesler, Zanna, and de Salvo, 1966; Kiesler, 1969, 1971).

Asch's experiment (1955) on judging lengths of lines provide the best illustration of the cybernetic hierarchy. He showed that individuals could be influenced by a coached majority giving incorrect answers, but that this effect would be countered by having at least one person agree with the subject. Further, the majority would have some influence no matter how extreme its opinion appeared to be. However, over 60 percent of the subjects held out against the majority. Many of these subjects said that they typically held out for their own opinions or that they considered the judgments an individual task. These results illustrate the hypothesis that a variable related to pattern maintenance (defining the task as one of individual judgment) was more powerful than an integrative variable (having a partner). The integrative variable was in turn more powerful than a goal-attainment variable (majority pressure). Finally, the adaptive variable (modifying the length of the line) was the least powerful.

The results of the Milgram experiments were similar. Although the effect of the shocks was unambiguous (A), the authority of the experimenter was much more powerful as an influence (G). This power could in turn be modified if one other subject appeared to defy the experimenter (I). Finally, the value the subject placed on not harming another human was the most effective deterrent (L).

Summary

Group members tend to form and conform to norms. The *norms* are the group standards which set limits for present behavior, while *goals* are standards to be achieved. There is no basis for *organized* interaction until group members reach some agreement about each of these kinds of expectations. If a group member finds that his behavior deviates from the group norms, he has four choices: to conform, to change the norms, to remain a deviant, or to leave the group.

Both formal and informal social pressures are brought to bear on deviant members. The informal pressure to conform is illustrated by the experiments of Sherif and Asch, which demonstrate that knowledge of the majority opinion on some issue is enough to lead some individuals to conform publicly to a judgment which differs from the one they privately hold. Results of more formal pressure, especially from an authority, are illustrated by the experiments of Festinger and Carlsmith and Milgram.

The factors which influence the general tendency to conform to group opinion are found in the *object* about which the judgment is to be made, in the *subject* who is making the judgment, and in the *situation*. The subject will conform more to group opinion when the object to be judged is ambiguous, if he must make his opinion public, if the majority holding a contrary opinion is large, and if membership in the group is highly valued. A minority view will prevail if the minority has high status, through power, popularity, or expert knowledge. The group leader is an example of a high-status member whose opinions are influential in the formation of group opinion. Although he may be allowed more freedom to deviate than other group members, the leader must also conform to the norms once they are formed if he is to maintain his leadership.

Since the norms of the intimate primary group are usually more important to the individual than the norms of the larger secondary group, the norms of a large organization may be changed by first bringing about change in the smaller informal groups through group discussion.

There appear to be four major types of conformity: convergence, based on a similar interpretation of facts (A); compliance, based on the influence of someone with authority (G); conformance, based on attraction to a reference group (I); and consentience, based on internalized values (L). According to the cybernetic hierarchy of control the most powerful pressure to conform should be L, followed by I, G, and A.

Additional References

Books and articles which provide an overview of issues related to conformity in small groups or related areas include Blake and Mouton, 1957; de Montmollin, 1958; Hollander, 1959; Hovland, 1959; Jahoda, 1959; Asch, 1961; Bass, 1961a; Berg, 1961; Berg and Bass, 1961; Campbell, 1961; Pepinsky, 1961; Willis, 1961; Allport, 1962; Willis, 1963; McGuire, 1964; Walters and Parke, 1964; Allen, 1965b; Willis, 1965a; B. Smith, 1966; Hollander and Willis, 1967; Flanders, 1968; Luchins and Luchins, 1971; Tedeschi, 1972.

Articles which deal with methodological issues related to the study of conformity include Di Vesta and Merwin, 1960; Kassarjian and Kassarjian, 1962; R. A. Jones et al., 1968; Chudnovskii, 1971; Bale, 1972; Page, 1972b; Rhine, 1973.

Articles which present mathematical models of aspects of the process of conformity include B. P. Cohen, 1958; Cervin and Henderson, 1961; Suppes and Krasne, 1961; Camilleri and Berger, 1967; Witt and Sen, 1972.

Finally, articles which elaborate or modify some of the generalizations in this chapter but did not fit easily into the present outline include Cartwright and Lippit, 1957; Lambert, 1957; Flament, 1958a, 1958b; Foa, 1958a; Tuddenham, 1958b; Tuddenham and McBride, 1959; Videbeck and Bates, 1959; Wiener, 1959; French, Morrison, and Levinger, 1960; Gnagey, 1960; Strickland, Jones and Smith, 1960; Zipf, 1960; Zolman, Wolf, and Fisher, 1960; Bachrach, Candland, and Gibson, 1961; Raven and Fishbein, 1961; Shaw, 1961a; Shaw and Penrod, 1962b; Suppes and Schlag-Rey, 1962; Bryant, Dobbins, and Bass, 1963; Miller and Tiffany, 1963; Turk, 1963a; Vaughan and Mangan, 1963; Faucheux and Thibaut, 1964; Frye and Stritch, 1964; Garai, 1964; Katz, Libby, and Strodtbeck, 1964; Linde and Patterson, 1964; Schmitt, 1964; Brock, 1965; Endler, 1965; Zander and Curtis,

1965; Goodkin, 1966; Luchins and Luchins, 1966; Wright, 1966; Wyer, 1966; Zeff and Iverson, 1966; Barocas and Gorlow, 1967; Carter, Hill, and McLemore, 1967; Endler and Hoy, 1967; Faucheux and Moscovici, 1967; Nahemow and Bennett, 1967; Peterson, Saltzstein, and Ebbe, 1967; Pollis, 1967; Steiner, Anderson, and Hays, 1967; Allen and Bragg, 1968; Bossman, 1968; Costanzo, Reitan, and Shaw, 1968; Haaland, 1968; S. C. Jones, 1968c; Luchins and Luchins, 1968; Mudd, 1968; Summers, 1968; Schwartz, 1968a; Yin and Saltzstein, 1968; Dabbs, 1969; Horowitz, 1969; Moscovici, Lage, and Naffrechoux, 1969; Sereno and Mortensen, 1969; Sistrunk, 1969; Albert and Dabbs, 1970; Jastrebske and Rule, 1970; Julian and Kimball, 1970; Gilmore, 1971; Montgomery, 1971; Moscovici and Neve, 1971; Endler, Wiesenthal, and Geller, 1972; Hass and Linder, 1972; Jones and Tager, 1972; Scherer, Rosenthal, and Koivumaki, 1972; Sistrunk, Clement, and Ulman, 1972; Smith and Savell, 1972; Upmeyer and Schreiber, 1972; Zillman, 1972; Dutton, 1973; Goethals and Nelson, 1973; Heller, Pallak, and Picek, 1973; Kane and Tedeschi, 1973; Macaranas and Savell, 1973; Nemeth and Wachtler, 1973, Rosnow et al., 1973; Sistrunk, 1973; Terry, Carey, and Hutson, 1973; Walker, 1973; Buby and Penner, 1974; Cooper, Darley and Henderson, 1974; Cupchik and Leventhal, 1974; Delin and Poo-Kong, 1974; Moriarity, 1974; Munson and Kiesler, 1974; Steele and Ostrom, 1974; Taylor and Huesmann, 1974; Wahrman and Pugh, 1974.

Chapter 3

INTERACTION AND DECISION PROCESS

To PROVIDE SOME BACKGROUND in the methodology of research on social inter-action, some examples of category systems which are in current use will be dis-cussed in this chapter. These category systems are used to analyze the process of interaction as it occurs in a small discussion group during a single meeting and as it changes from meeting to meeting. The major emphasis in research has been on the problem the group faces in establishing an equilibrium between the time spent on the task and the time spent on the social-emotional problems of maintain-ing the group structure. The other two types of problems which were referred to in chapter 1, namely, the progress toward each individual's private goal and the solu-tion of each individual's social-emotional problems, are covered in the literature on group therapy, sensitivity training, and other forms of applied group dynamics. An introduction to this literature is given in appendix 4.

Although there has been some attempt to study the characteristic modes of interaction *between* small groups of persons, the primary focus in the social-psycho-logical literature has been on *within-group* or *between-person* interaction. The term *interaction* refers to all words, symbols, and gestures with which persons respond to each other; however, in most research only verbal behavior is recorded, while some research focuses exclusively on nonverbal behavior. Communication is important for humans because it enables two or more persons to maintain simul-taneous orientation toward each other and toward other subjects (Newcomb, 1953a).

Every word or gesture carries with it at least two kinds of information: task and social-emotional. First, it has implications for the task of the group (or the individual); that is, it affects the decision-making process. Second, it has implica-tions for the relative evaluation of members as well as the emotional attachments among members. Although these two types of implications of any individual act are always present and it is difficult to talk about one without talking about the other, the *decision-making* aspect of interaction will be emphasized in this chapter, and interaction in relation to the development of a differentiated internal structure in chapter 7.

Category Systems

Before one is able to indicate the implications of a particular act for the task and social-emotional life of the group, it is necessary to develop a category system or method of content analysis which allows one to break the interaction process into small units and to assign each unit to one of the categories. The number of different kinds of acts included in the category system depends on the theoretical orientation of the observer. Some category systems divide all interaction into two types, action and silence (Chapple, 1942), some use more than 100 types (Ruesch and Prestwood, 1950). Some systems record only one type of verbal content, such as personal pronouns (Conrad and Conrad, 1956), others are used to rate words, gestures, and any other form of bodily activity which indicates the individual's mental state (Freedman et al., 1951). (For an outline of the research methods used to study small groups see appendix 3.)

Reliability

A recurring problem in the use of category systems is that of interobserver reliability. Since most of the systems attempt to describe all behavior, an observer's decision to place an act in one of several categories is not an independent event. That is, if there are three categories in a system and one decides to call an act *category 1*, then it cannot also be *category 2* or *3*. Therefore, a *high* frequency of acts in *category 1* results automatically in *low* frequencies in the other two categories, making it difficult to apply statistical tests.

Despite these difficulties, the reliability of trained observer judgments is usually sufficient to encourage the use of interaction categories. In one report on consistency, judgments of an individual's interpersonal behavior were made on the basis of interaction in three-man groups during a 15-minute discussion. The membership of the three-man groups was reconstituted between sessions, the observers were different, and the task was different. In this experiment the reliability in several categories was substantial (Blake, Mouton, and Fruchter, 1954).

Scoring the Unit Act

The category system developed by Bales (1950b) is an example of the most common method of coding interaction. Bales takes as his unit act a bit of behavior (usually verbal) which can provide enough of a stimulus to elicit a meaningful response from another person. In practice, this is usually a sentence. Each sentence or comparable act is given only one score to indicate the element of task behavior or social-emotional behavior which appears to the observer to dominate the act. For example, if a group member says "Let us all get back to work" and laughs as he finishes his remark, his statement would be scored as *giving a suggestion* and the laughter which occurs after the statement is completed would be given a separate score as *showing tension* or *tension release,* depending upon the nature of the laugh. The fact that the subject may laugh while he is making the suggestion would not be scored, since the observer is trained to record only the dominant characteristic of the act.

In contrast to Bales's approach, the category system suggested by Bion (Bion,

1948–1952, 1961; Rioch, 1970) and developed by Thelen (Thelen et al., 1954; Thelen, 1956; Stock and Thelen, 1958) is based on the assumption that every statement contains some element of work as well as some element of emotion. The observer's job is to score the amount of each in each act. In the Bion-Thelen formulation, work is scored at four levels ranging from very little help to remarks which integrate the present group activity with universal goals. The basic emotional states in a group are seen as fight or flight, pairing among group members, and dependency on the leader. Using the Bion-Thelen category system, the statement "Let us all get back to work," accompanied by laughter, would be scored as *work at level three* and *flight,* if the laughter seemed to indicate that the subject was a bit hesitant about his suggestion and was laughing to indicate that it should not be taken too seriously or that he was about to withdraw it.

Both the Bion-Thelen and the Bales categories cross-cut the set of content areas suggested in chapter 1 in different ways. In the Bion-Thelen system the work category is equivalent to the task area, while dependency represents an aspect of control and pairing an aspect of affection. The fight or flight category is a mixture of hostility and withdrawal from the communication network. Within the Bales system of twelve categories the six categories representing asking for and giving suggestions, opinions, and information appear to be primarily in the task area, while showing solidarity and antagonism are in the social-emotional area. Agreeing and disagreeing appear to be on the border between tasks and social-emotional behavior. Showing tension and tension release seem to refer more to personal than interpersonal behavior.

Bales's Categories for Interaction Process Analysis

Since the categories for interaction process analysis developed by Bales have been used by a number of investigators in research on behavior in small groups, his system will be treated in some detail at this point. In this system each act is scored in one of twelve categories. These categories are listed in table 3 together with the interaction profiles for a sample of laboratory groups (Talland, 1955) and psychiatric interviews (Hare et al., 1960). The profiles represent average percentages of the total number of acts for a single group meeting which fall into each of the twelve categories.

In table 3 the first three categories, "shows solidarity," "shows tension release," and "shows agreement," are *positive reactions* which, coupled with the three *negative reactions,* "shows disagreement," "shows tension," and "shows antagonism," constitute *social-emotional* behavior. The six categories describing *task* behavior also are grouped in sets of three. "Gives suggestion," "gives opinion," and "gives information" are *problem-solving attempts,* and "asks for information," "asks for opinion," and "asks for suggestion" are *questions.*

The principal categories of activity in the laboratory discussion groups in this sample are giving opinion and giving information, which account for approximately 48 percent of the acts. In the psychiatric interview these same two categories account for 74 percent of the acts. These differences in interaction pattern reflect the difference in the group task. The laboraory groups must discuss a human-relations problem and reach a solution within 40 minutes. This is a task which requires a wider range of behavior than the psychiatric interview, in which the

Table 3. Interaction Profiles for Laboratory Groups and Psychiatric Interviews

Category	PERCENTAGE OF ACTS	
	Laboratory Groups	Standardized Psychiatric Interview
1. Shows Solidarity: jokes, raises other's status, gives help, reward	3.4	0.1
2. Shows Tension Release: laughs, shows satisfaction	6.0	0.5
3. Shows Agreement: pasive acceptance, understands, concurs, complies	16.5	0.9
4. Gives Suggestion: direction, implying autonomy for other	8.0	0.5
5. Gives Opinion: evaluation, analysis, expresses feeling, wish	30.1	16.7
6. Gives Information: orientation, repeats, clarifies, confirms	17.9	56.9
7. Asks for Information: orientation, repetition, confirmation	3.5	12.9
8. Asks for Opinion: evaluation, analysis, expression of feeling	2.4	2.8
9. Asks for Suggestion: direction, possible ways of action	1.1	0.0
10. Shows Disagreement: passive rejection, formality, withholds help	7.8	0.6
11. Shows Tension: asks for help, withdraws "out of field"	2.7	6.1
12. Shows Antagonism: deflates other's status, defends or asserts self	0.7	1.8

Source: Combined data, adapted from Talland (1955) and Hare et al. (1960).

primary purpose is to encourage the patient to give personal information which can be evaluated by the psychiatrist.

Some Variations in the Interaction Profile

If one varies the task, the personalities or other social characteristics of the members, or the size of the group, a different balance of task and social-emotional behavior will result. To make it possible to use the interaction profile of a group as a diagnostic tool, Bales and Hare brought together interaction profiles from 21 different studies (Bales and Hare, 1965). A summary profile for each type of group is given in table 4.

Each profile in table 4 is shown as a column of percentage rates in each category on the base of the total number of acts observed in the given study. To use the set of profiles diagnostically, a new profile could be compared in turn with each of the 21 until one was found which closely matched, but this would be a laborious procedure. To simplify the task, a set of cutting points was computed representing points above and below the mean for the average profile. This makes it possible to identify cases of unusually high or low rates in each of the 12 interaction categories. As an indication of some of the sources and effects of variation in the interaction profile, several of Bales and Hare's descriptions are quoted.

Table 4. A Reference Population of Interaction Profiles

Interaction process analysis category	1. Standard case discussion, Harvard, 1955–1958*	2. Social conversation, Slater and Bales, 1957	3. Discussion of self-ratings, Couch, 1960	4. Planning role playing, Borgatta and Bales, 1953a	5. Projective stories, Mills, 1951	6. Playing board game, Olmsted, 1952	7. Subjects under lysergic acid, Slater, Morimoto, and Hyde, 1958	8. Subjects under lysergic acid, Lennard et al., 1956	9. Drinking brandy and beer, Takala et al., 1957	10. Therapy groups, Psathas, 1960	11. Prison therapy groups, Winter, 1952	12. Paranoid and depressed patients, Roberts and Strodtbeck, 1953	13. Therapy groups, Evans, 1950	14. Psychiatric-stress interview, Hare et al., 1960	15. Jury deliberation, Strodtbeck and Mann, 1956	16. Husbands and wives, Strodtbeck, 1950	17. Husbands and wives, Quade, 1955	18. Labor-mediation sessions, Landsberger, 1955	19. Boy leaders, Hare, 1957	20. Children's doll play, Gruber, 1952	21. Group-process discussion, Borgatta et al., 1958
1. Shows solidarity	3.5	8.8	5.4	2.3	0.8	2.0	9.5	3.0	0.3	3.4	2.1	1.8	2.1	0.1	1.2	2.0	0.6	2.4	4.3	2.5	4.3
2. Shows tension release	7.0	17.7	12.7	6.0	7.3	6.1	30.4	13.8	9.7	7.4	3.4	3.5	5.6	0.5	3.0	5.0	5.3	1.2	6.2	7.5	12.2
3. Shows agreement	16.9	9.0	9.5	9.3	18.4	13.7	10.5	7.9	6.7	16.3	5.6	8.0	5.8	0.9	17.9	17.0	9.7	10.5	4.7	5.0	21.5
4. Gives suggestion	8.0	0	2.2	5.8	25.2	20.2	7.1	3.5	3.7	0.7	2.0	1.8	1.1	0.5	4.0	6.0	14.5	3.0	16.3	9.0	3.1
5. Gives opinion	33.4	17.4	26.0	27.3	17.5	25.7	16.7	32.5	32.7	26.2	29.8	19.5	19.8	16.7	26.1	22.0	19.2	24.5	7.7	3.5	22.8
6. Gives information	15.5	28.7	20.2	33.8	14.5	14.2	13.6	21.0	23.9	29.8	33.2	35.8	42.2	56.9	38.3	29.0	29.0	32.7	34.2	37.0	19.7
7. Asks for information	2.3	11.0	7.1	6.8	3.6	3.0	3.2	4.7	1.8	5.1	3.0	8.4	2.9	12.9	4.6	6.0	8.2	7.3	9.7	8.0	4.0
8. Asks for opinion	2.2	1.8	4.0	1.9	2.2	3.8	1.2	7.9	1.0	3.7	9.3	3.6	7.3	2.8	1.9	4.0	4.5	2.2	0.5	1.0	1.9
9. Asks for suggestion	0.7	0	0.4	0.7	2.2	1.8	0.6	1.0	0.3	0	0.3	0.1	1.1	0	0.2	1.0	1.5	0.3	0.1	0	0.4
10. Shows disagreement	7.9	2.1	5.4	0.9	6.4	7.7	5.3	2.4	14.3	3.7	7.0	2.6	4.7	0.6	2.0	5.0	3.1	7.5	4.4	3.0	3.4
11. Shows tension	2.0	3.0	6.7	5.1	1.5	1.0	2.0	1.0	0.2	2.7	1.8	6.0	4.6	6.1	0.6	1.0	2.2	1.7	2.5	15.5	4.8
12. Shows antagonism	0.5	0	0.5	0.1	0.4	0.2	0.4	1.3	5.4	0.8	2.4	7.9	2.7	1.8	0.2	2.0	2.0	4.7	9.2	6.5	1.6

*Bales and Slater (1955) and additional unpublished data.

Source: Robert F. Bales and A. Paul Hare, "Diagnostic Use of the Interaction Profile," *Journal of Social Psychology* 67 (1965): 240. Copyright © 1965 by The Journal Press. Reprinted by permission of my co-author and the publisher.

Profile 1: Standard Case Discussion (Harvard, 1955–1958)

Although the figures differ slightly from those presented earlier in this chapter for a smaller sample of groups, the task is the same.

Profile 7: Slater et al.'s Four-Man Groups under the Influence of LSD

Twenty-four male subjects, all college students, are formed into six four-man groups (Slater, Morimoto, and Hyde, 1958). Each group meets twice, once in a control meeting under normal conditions and once for a period of one and one-half hours following the administration of lysergic acid diethylamide (LSD). Three of the groups receive LSD prior to their first meeting; three, prior to their second meeting. For each meeting the subjects are brought into a small room and told to sit around a rectangular table. An observer with an interaction recorder is seated at another table opposite the subjects. The subjects are then instructed to read a case study of a human-relations problem in an administrative situation, discuss it, and within 40 minutes reach a group decision as to how the problem should be handled (Bales's standard task). The profile given in table 4 represents the average interaction patterns for the six groups under the influence of LSD.

In these groups the rates of showing of solidarity and tension release are extremely high. Both percentage values are more than 1.96 standard deviations above the mean. Slater reports that even subjects with depressed or withdrawn reactions participate in this apparent hilarity, however involuntary their participation may seem. The task-oriented parts of the profile are similar to those of other groups on the Standard Case Discussion, except for the rate of giving opinion, which is less than half as high as for normal groups on this task. The additional fact that asking for opinion is below the cutting point seems to indicate a marked drop in concern for logical analysis or consensual evaluation in these groups. In general the subjects seem to be using the group situation to relieve individual tensions rather than to meet the demands of the task.[1]

Profile 9: Takala et al.'s Groups Drinking Brandy and Beer

The subjects are employees of the Finnish government chosen from volunteers in consultation with the company's doctor and the supervisor concerned (Takala et al., 1957). They meet in eight groups of four to six members immediately after work in a room suitably prepared with tables and tablecloths. Each group discusses a series of three topics during a five-hour testing period. A 15-to-20-minute sample of interaction is observed for each topic. During one session brandy is served; during another, beer. The profile in table 4 is a combination of the observations under both the brandy and beer conditions.

The authors note that their Finnish groups not under the influence of alcohol are different from ordinary American laboratory groups. The low frequencies of showing solidarity and tension and asking for information and opinion may be attributable to cultural differences rather than intoxication. The rate of giving opinion, which is high according to American standards, is nevertheless lower than in the Finnish normal groups; thus the effect of alcohol in these groups is to depress the rates of activity in the task categories and increase the amount of disagreement and antagonism.

Perhaps the most salient aspects of this profile are the high rates of showing disagreement and antagonism and the low rate of showing tension. These are effects one would plausibly expect from the action of alcohol. The low rate of showing solidarity may not be characteristic of the action of alcohol under other conditions. A more usual pattern may be an early increase in solidarity later followed by an increase in antago-

---

1. Robert F. Bales and A. Paul Hare, "Diagnostic Use of the Interaction Profile," *Journal of Social Psychology* 67 (1965): 247–248. Reprinted by permission of my co-author and the publisher.

nism. The study showed that the groups drinking beer tended to be more positive than those drinking brandy.[2]

Profile 15: Strodtbeck and Mann's Jury Deliberations

The participants in these mock-jury deliberations are drawn from the regular jury pools of the Chicago and St. Louis courts (Strodtbeck and Mann, 1956). The jurors listen to a recorded trial. They then deliberate and return their verdict—under the customary discipline of bailiffs of the court. The deliberations are recorded with two microphones to facilitate binaural identification of individual participants. The recordings are fully transcribed, and these protocols are in turn scored in terms of interaction-process categories. The scoring is done by an assistant who listens again to the recording and has available the indications of nonverbal gestures made·by the original observer. The level of interscorer reliability is checked before the scoring begins and rechecked periodically while scoring is in process.

The protocols utilized in computing the summary profile shown are the final 12 of a set of 30 in which jurors considered an auto negligence case. Seventeen of 144 jurors originated less than five acts each and have been dropped from the tabulations.

In the task area this summary profile does not differ from the average of the 21 profiles. However, the jurors show more agreement and less tension and antagonism than the average group. A higher-than-average amount of agreement is also found in other types of discussion groups in which the group members are required to reach consensus on an issue.[3]

Profile 16: Strodtbeck's Husbands and Wives

Each of 10 couples from three cultures, Navaho, Texan, and Mormon, are asked to discuss the differences in their ratings of some mutual friends (Strodtbeck, 1950). Each couple is asked to pick three reference families with whom they are well acquainted. The husband and wife are then separated and requested to designate which of the three families appears most satisfactory with respect to each of a series of 26 conditions, such as "Which family has the happiest children?" "Which family is the most religious?" "Which family is the most ambitious?" After both husband and wife have individually marked their choices, they are requested to reconcile their differences and and indicate a final "best" choice from the standpoint of their family. The discussions are recorded in the field by portable sound equipment powered from a truck. The recordings are then transcribed and, in the case of the Navaho, translated into English before being scored.

Although Strodtbeck found differences in interaction profiles between cultures and between the most-talking and least-talking spouse in each culture, the only category in which the summary profile for all 30 couples is distinguished from the others in table 4 is a high rate of agreement. This seems to reflect the fact that the task called for reaching agreement on a number of judgements.[4]

Profile 19: Hare's Boy Leaders

Twelve third-grade boys who have been identified by their teachers as leaders on the school playground are observed at play with their friends in their home neighborhoods after school (Hare, 1957). Six of the boys have been selected because they are group oriented; the other six, because they are self oriented. Two observers score interaction in the field. Each observer scores only one boy at a time, recording all of his acts directed to others and all acts directed to him by other group members. When possible, each observer makes half of the observations on each subject.

The average observation period in the neighborhood is four sessions for a total of 75 minutes (218 acts). Interaction with parents or observers is not recorded; only

2. Ibid., pp. 248–249.
3. Ibid., p. 252.
4. Ibid., pp. 252–253.

the interaction with other children is included in the profiles. Nonverbal interaction called for by the rules of the game is also omitted.

This average profile for boys' leaders and their peers is similar in several repects to that of Gruber's children playing with dolls. Both show a marked contrast with the Harvard-laboratory discussion groups. For the children, agreement and giving opinion are low; asking for information is high. The tendencies are just the opposite of those in the problem-solving groups. Rather than to deliberate and attempt to reach consensus on issues, these boy leaders and their followers interact very directively, with high rates of giving suggestions and showing antagonism.[5]

Action and Reaction

So far, only the total interaction profile of a group has been considered. However, the central concern in the observation of interaction is more often the typical patterns of action and reaction which constitute the group process. These act-to-act sequences change over the period of a meeting and over a series of meetings. In generalizing from these patterns, the reader should keep in mind the fact that most of the observations of interaction are made on initially leaderless groups of college students, usually males, who do not know each other before the experiment begins and are brought together for the first time in the laboratory to solve a series of human-relations or construction problems. Any generalizations emerging from these experiments would therefore be more applicable to *ad hoc* committees composed of persons of equal social rank than to groups, such as the family, which have been organized for a long period of time and contain a definite structure. In general, each of the factors discussed in part 2, such as personalities of members, group size, or task, may modify the central tendencies of interaction in some important respect. Unless otherwise noted, the setting for the interaction described is usually the small-task-oriented group without a formal leader.

An analysis of the typical actions and reactions in a small discussion group (Bales, 1950, 1954, 1955), as given in figure 14, shows that about half (56 percent) of the acts during a group session are problem-solving attempts, whereas the remaining 44 percent are distributed among positive reactions, negative reactions, and questions. In this two-sided process, the reactions act as a constant feedback on the acceptability of the problem-solving attempts. A typical interchange between two group members is illustrated by the following example (Bales, 1955):

Member 1:   I wonder if we have the same fact about the problem? (*Asks for opinion.*) Perhaps we should take some time at the beginning to find out." (*Gives suggestion.*)

Member 2: Yes. (*Shows agreement.*) We may be able to fill in some gaps in our information. (*Gives opinion.*) Let's go around the table and each tell what the report said in his case. (*Gives suggestion.*)

As in this example, a speaker's first remark is likely to be a reaction, and if he continues speaking, the probability is very high that his second act will be a problem-solving attempt. Figure 15 sums up this finding statistically: about 50 percent of the time a member's first remark in a series is a reaction; if he continues, about 80 percent of the succeeding comments or other offerings are classed as attempts to solve the problem.

5. Ibid., pp. 254–255.

Figure 14. Interaction Profile for a Small Discussion Group

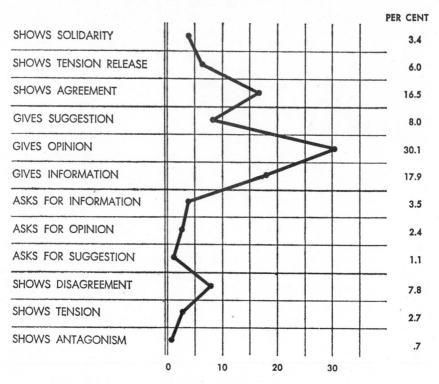

	PER CENT
SHOWS SOLIDARITY	3.4
SHOWS TENSION RELEASE	6.0
SHOWS AGREEMENT	16.5
GIVES SUGGESTION	8.0
GIVES OPINION	30.1
GIVES INFORMATION	17.9
ASKS FOR INFORMATION	3.5
ASKS FOR OPINION	2.4
ASKS FOR SUGGESTION	1.1
SHOWS DISAGREEMENT	7.8
SHOWS TENSION	2.7
SHOWS ANTAGONISM	.7

Note: This profile is the same as that in table 3.
Source: Robert F. Bales, "How People Interact in Conferences," *Scientific American* 192 (March 1955): 33. Copyright © 1955 by Scientific American, Inc. All rights reserved. Reprinted by permission of the author and W. H. Freeman & Co.

There are about twice as many positive as negative reactions. This indicates that the members share a common definition of the situation and can make problem-solving attempts which will be in line with the group's goals most of the time.

Although an action is usually followed immediately by the "appropriate" reaction, the reaction may be stored (remembered) and appear at a later time in its original or perhaps a disguised form. This delayed reaction would be especially evident if the interaction was interrupted either through outside forces or because the individual felt that his reaction would be inadvisable at that time. The effect of the interruption by an outside force is evident in a communication experiment in which, following an act of hostility on the part of a paid participant, some subjects were allowed to communicate back to him immediately whereas others were not. Subjects who were allowed to react immediately showed more postexperimental friendliness to the hostile paid participant than those who were forced to store their negative feelings until the opportunity for reaction arose (Thibaut and Coules, 1952).

Figure 15. A Comparison of a Speaker's First Act with His Following Act

	PER CENT ▬	▮▮▮▮
SHOWS SOLIDARITY	3.8	4.1
SHOWS TENSION RELEASE	1.6	8.0
SHOWS AGREEMENT	2.0	26.3
GIVES SUGGESTION	10.0	5.9
GIVES OPINION	39.5	22.3
GIVES INFORMATION	31.4	15.4
ASKS FOR INFORMATION	3.4	3.4
ASKS FOR OPINION	3.4	2.1
ASKS FOR SUGGESTION	1.4	.9
SHOWS DISAGREEMENT	1.4	8.7
SHOWS TENSION	1.4	1.8
SHOWS ANTAGONISM	.7	1.1

▮▮▮▮ FIRST ACT IN A SEQUENCE
▬▬ NEXT ACT

0   10   20   30

Source: Robert F. Bales, "How People Interact in Conferences," *Scientific American* 192 (March 1955): 33. Copyright © 1955 by Scientific American, Inc. All rights reserved. Reprinted by permission of the author and W. H. Freeman & Co.

Four Dimensions of Interpersonal Behavior

Although the category systems proposed by Bales and Bion-Thelen had the virtue of being comprehensive in that anything that was said or done in a group could be classified in one of the categories, a search continued for the minimum number of categories or dimensions that was necessary to describe interpersonal behavior. The following account has been updated and modified from Hare (1972b).[6]

From the earliest use of category systems to describe interpersonal behavior in the late 1920s (cf. Goodenough, 1928; Thomas, 1929) to the present day, some of the category systems designed for the study of interaction in groups have turned out in practice to have too many categories for useful analysis. Part of this may simply reflect the difficulty in obtaining enough data for reliable measures for each cell in a multi-category matrix; however, it may also be true that interpersonal interacion is played

6. A. Paul Hare, "Four Dimensions of Interpersonal Behavior," *Psychological Reports* 30 (1972): 499–512. Reprinted by permission of the publisher.

out on a fairly limited set of underlying themes or dimensions. In the early 1950s a number of social psychologists concentrated on the search for the minimum number of dimensions, especially in the area of personality test data (cf. chapter 8, "Personality"). This type of search was only made possible on any scale with the development of large electronic computers which could handle the hundreds of test items or behavior scores which formed the basic data for factor analysis. The earliest of these studies were done with desk calculators, a task requiring so much time and energy that the entire tables of correlations and factor matrices would be published in the journals in recognition of the heroic achievement.

Chapple's One-dimensional Approach

Some of the earliest category systems which were developed to observe children at play on the school playground or at work in the classroom were not designed to cover all possible forms of behavior nor to represent basic dimensions of interaction. However, one of these, which has been used widely with adults, is based on a single dimension of interaction. Chapple's scheme had only two categories: action and silence (Chapple, 1940, 1942, 1953). He usually observed only two persons at one time, in an interview situation, recording the frequency and duration of their speeches and silences on a machine which he called the Interaction Chronograph. The stability of an individual's pattern and related personality correlates were recorded for a variety of types of subjects by Matarazzo et al., (see, for example, Matarazzo, Saslow, et al., 1958; Guze and Mensh, 1959; Kanfer et al., 1960; Matarazzo and Saslow, 1961; Phillips et al., 1961; Matarazzo, Wiens, and Saslow, 1964). Although Chapple generated a number of measures from various combinations of his chronograph measures, a factor analysis indicated that there was still only one basic dimension being measured, namely, action and silence (Matarazzo, Saslow, and Hare, 1958).

More recently Hayes et al., using more elaborate recording equipment for larger discussion groups, show that persons with high talking rates are typically described as hostile, arrogant, and aggressive, while those with low talking rates are described as inhibited, shy, and meek.[7] (See also Hayes and Sievers, 1972). Chapple-like measures of frequency and duration of interaction can also be derived from Bales's categories by counting the number of times an individual begins to speak and the number of acts per speech (Hare et al., 1960).

Couch and Carter's Three Dimensions

Couch and Carter performed one of the first factor-analytic studies of behavior ratings from small laboratory groups (Couch and Carter, 1952; Carter, 1954). They observed college undergraduates in groups of four and eight members with three kinds of tasks: reasoning, mechanical assembly, and discussion. As a result of a factor analysis of 19 observers' ratings they identified three factors: individual prominence, group goal facilitation, and group sociability (see figure 16). We would expect Couch and Carter's first factor to be correlated with Chapple's dimension of talk-silence, since "individual prominence" is essentially a measure of dominance versus submission. (See also Longabaugh, 1966.)

Leary's Interpersonal Diagnosis of Personality

The next important research in this area was that of Leary and his colleagues, summarized in Leary's book *Interpersonal Diagnosis of Personality* (1957). The book was written primarily for the psychologist in a clinical setting. Based on experience in psychological clinics and with psychological tests, Leary showed how 16 psycholo-

---

7. Leo Meltzer and Donald P. Hayes, "Conversational Behavior" (Unpublished manuscript, Department of Social Psychology, Cornell University, 1968).

gical categories of interpersonal behavior could be arranged in a circle and described in turn as combinations of two principal axes: dominance-submission (vertical dimension) and positive-negative, or love-hate (horizontal dimension reading from right to left). Leary's basic chart relating the 16 categories to the two dimensions is given in figure 17. He suggested that personality was an interpersonal phenomenon,

Figure 16. Behavior Traits Associated with Couch and Carter's Three Factors of Interpersonal Behavior

I. *Individual prominence*	II. *Group goal facilitation*	III. *Group sociability*
Authoritarianism	Efficiency	Sociability
Aggressiveness	Cooperation	Adaptability
Confidence	Adaptability	Pointed toward
Leadership	Pointed toward	group acceptance
Striving for recognition	group solution	

Source: A. Paul Hare, "Four Dimensions of Interpersonal Behavior," *Psychological Reports* 30 (1972): 499–512. Reprinted by permission of the publisher.

Figure 17. Leary's Classification of Interpersonal Behavior into 16 Mechanisms or Reflexes

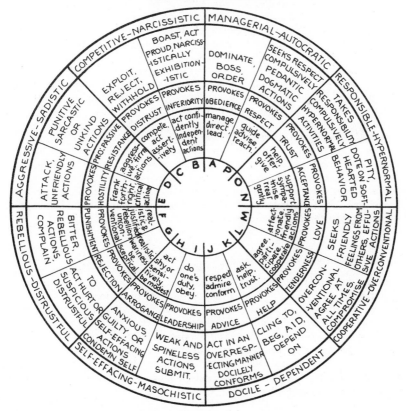

Source: Timothy Leary, *Interpersonal Diagnosis of Personality* (New York: Ronald Press, 1957), p. 65. Copyright © 1957, The Ronald Press Company, New York. Reprinted by permission of the publisher.

that actions on the part of one subject would tend to "pull" certain reactions on the part of another. For example, dominating behavior would tend to "pull" submission, and vice versa, whereas positive behavior would pull positive and negative would pull negative. Combinations of these behaviors would pull the expected combination in return. Thus bitter rebellious behavior (negative and submissive) would pull punitive rejection and superiority from others. (See also Lorr and McNair, 1963, 1965; Shannon and Guerney, 1973; Benjamin, 1974.)

Couch's Psychological Determinants of Interpersonal Behavior

The most intensive analysis of interpersonal behavior to date is reported by Couch in his dissertation "Psychological Determinants of Interpersonal Behavior" (1960). His study is based on observations of 12 groups of five undergraduates each, working on a variety of tasks over five meetings. In connection with the experiment each subject was given a long battery of psychological tests and some subjects were interviewed in depth. The thesis includes a series of factor analyses of different domains of interpersonal behavior: overt behavior, perception, personality characteristics, concealment defenses, apperceptions, and behavior received. Of these domains, that of overt behavior is the most relevant for the present analysis.

The variables in the domain of overt behavior included Bales's Interaction Process Analysis categories (Bales, 1950b) for initiated behavior both in raw form and in percentage form plus the total IPA acts initiated (25 variables, actually scored by Bales); five variables representing a Value Content Analysis scheme, then being developed at Harvard by Kassebaum (1958); and 25 variables representing raw rates and standard scores for a "Kaiser-Harvard" system developed by Couch.[8] Four of Couch's 12 categories are dominant-positive, dominant-negative, submissive-positive, and submissive-negative.

The 55 measures of initiated behavior were intercorrelated and the resulting matrix factor analyzed by the Complete Centroid method. Six factors were extracted from the matrix of intercorrelations. Each of them is listed in figure 18 together with a brief description of some of the associated variables.

It is perhaps not surprising that Couch finds factors similar to those of Leary and his own previous work with Carter in his more intensive research, since he had these studies in mind while making his factor rotations. Again, we see the three factors of dominance-submission, positive-negative, and task-oriented-joking playing the dominant part in explaining interpersonal behavior. Next we will look at the work of Borgatta, who also tried to expand Bales's basic set of categories in search of more dimensions, before considering the current work of Bales, who bases his own three-dimensional analysis directly on the research by Couch.

Borgatta's Interaction Process Scores

Borgatta subdivided and reorganized Bales's 12 categories into a set of 18 categories (Borgatta, 1962, p. 279). This was done to meet the objections by some social psychologists that the Bales categories blurred too many distinctions and lumped together too many modalities into a single category (Weick, 1968, p. 398). On the one hand Borgatta sought to permit greater discrimination of intensity by splitting some of the crucial categories in Bales's system into two categories, one for a minimum response and the other for an active response. On the other hand, he made further differentiations in those categories which combined many possible shades of meaning, for example, "gives opinion." (See figure 19.)

8. The word *Kaiser* referred to the Kaiser Clinic in California, where Leary and his colleagues had done much of their work, since part of Couch's scheme was based on Leary's two dimensions.

Figure 18. Couch's Six Factors of Interpersonal Behavior

I. *Interpersonal dominance*

This first factor which accounts for almost three times as much variation in behavior as any of the other factors is most clearly associated with the total interaction for each of the three category systems (Bales, Value Content, and Kaiser-Harvard). This indicates a diffuse pattern of high participation in the group. Since the person who talks a lot is usually taking the initiative away from others in his group, he is aggressively achieving a position of individual prominence.

II. *Interpersonal affect*

This factor is represented by a cluster of traits rather than by any one specific indicator. Behavior along this dimension ranges from "Shows antagonism" and "Dominant-negative" on the negative side to "Shows agreement" and "Asks for opinion" on the positive side. All of this behavior represents different manifestations of an affiliative attitude or positive affect toward others.

III. *Social expressivity vs Task serious*

For this factor "Shows solidarity" stands out as a relatively pure indicator of this behavioral tendency. On the positive side it also includes "Shows tension release" and on the negative side "Gives opinion" and "Asks for opinion." Thus on one end of the factor we find behavior which represents socially-oriented participation with joking, and on the other, a seriousness of purpose in working on the group task.

IV. *Influence attempts*

This factor represents another form of dominance. Instead of a high rate of manifest activity (as in Factor I), there is an intellectual assertiveness centered around the attempt to influence other people to one's own value-determined viewpoint or conception of group goals. The behaviors most highly correlated with the factor are "Attempts to influence" and "Supports self."

V. *Surface acquiescence*

This factor has some conceptual similarity to Factor II since it does have a high correlation with "Shows agreement." However the other behaviors associated with it are not the same. The negative end is represented by "Shows tension" and Different interpretation." The dimension ranges from surface agreement with others to manifest resistance.

VI. *Conventional behavior*

The last factor is rather weak and Couch only offers an interpretation of it with some reluctance. The highest positive correlation is with "authoritarian" statements while the negative end is represented by a cluster of traits which suggests a rather withdrawn pattern of behavior, perhaps with the overtone of a reluctance to participate in conventionally expected ways.

Source: A. Paul Hare, "Four Dimensions of Interpersonal Behavior," *Psychological Reports* 30 (1972): 499–512. Reprinted by permission of the publisher.

Figure 19. Borgatta's Interaction Process Scores (IPS)

1 Common social acknowledgments (1a)
2 Shows solidarity through raising the status of others (1b)
3 Shows tension release, laughs (2)
4 Acknowledges, understands, recognizes (3a)
5 Shows agreement, concurrence, compliance (3b)
6 Gives a procedural suggestion (4a)
7 Suggests a solution (4b)
8 Gives opinion, evaluation, analysis, expresses feelings or wish (5a)
9 Self-analysis and self-questioning behavior (5b)
10 Reference to the external situation as redirected aggression (5c)
11 Gives orientation, information, passes communication (6a)
12 Draws attention, repeats, clarifies (6b)
13 Asks for opinion, evaluation, analysis, expression of feelings (8)
14 Disagrees, maintains a contrary position (10)
15 Shows tension, asks for help by virtue of personal inadequacy (11a)
16 Shows tension increase (11b)
17 Shows antagonism, hostility, is demanding (12a)
18 Ego defensiveness (12b)

Source: Edgar F. Borgatta, "A Systematic Study of Interaction Process Scores, Peer and Self-assessments, Personality and Other Variables," *Genetic Psychology Monographs* 65 (1962): 279. Copyright © 1962 by The Journal Press. Reprinted by permission of the author and the publisher.

Shortly after expanding the system, Borgatta found that assessments of social interaction could be made using peer ratings with only six categories (Borgatta, 1963a, p. 32). (See figure 20.) A factor analysis showed that these six categories could be represented by two dimensions: assertiveness (talking, activity, visibility) and sociability (being liked, pleasant, friendly). (See figure 21.) These are the same as Couch and Carter's factor I, individual prominence, and II, group sociability.

Borgatta's instructions to observers for using the system (Borgatta and Crowther, 1965) suggest that the observer record who speaks to whom and also use subscores to indicate whether an act may be group-oriented (task-determining acts or group maintaining acts) and whether the action includes excessive emotionality (tension displayed or unpredictable behavior). The effect is to introduce the second dimension of Couch and Carter: group goal facilitation (third dimension of Couch, 1960). Thus Borgatta ends his analysis with a position similar to that of Carter and Couch, that there are at least three dimensions which can be described with approximately six categories (one for each end of each dimension).

Figure 20. Borgatta's Categories for Peer Ratings

Assertive actions
1. Neutral assertions or communications (continuation, explanation, etc.)
2. Assertions or dominant acts (draws attention, asserts, initiates conversation, etc.)
3. Antagonistic acts (rejects other, rejects other's position implying rejection of other, is self-assertive or ego-defensive, etc.)

Withdrawal
4. Withdrawal acts (leaves field, fails to respond when the situation demands, etc.)

Supportive actions
5. Supportive acts (acknowledges, responds, etc.)
6. Assertive supportive acts (status raising, implies initiative beyond mere responsiveness, etc.)

Source: Edgar F. Borgatta, "A New Systematic Interaction Observation System," *Journal of Psychological Studies* 14 (1963): 32. Reprinted by permission of the author.

Figure 21. Reference Points for Borgatta's Behavior Scores System

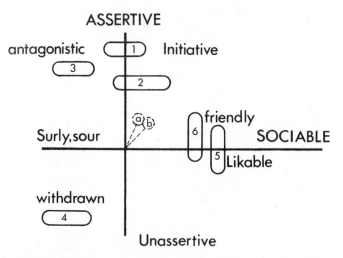

Source: Edgar F. Borgatta, "A New Systematic Interaction Observation System," *Journal of Psychological Studies* 14 (1963). Reprinted by permission of the author.

Bales's Three Dimensions of Social Evaluation

Following a current trend in social psychology, Bales has come out from behind the one-way mirror and has given up the observer's role. He now takes his place inside the classroom as a trainer in a self-analytic group. His primary concern is no longer to provide a set of categories for professional social scientists to use in their laboratory studies of groups, rather it is to provide the group member with a way of evaluating his own behavior and that of his peers. Bales's *Analysis of Interpersonal Behavior* (1970a), unlike his first book, *Interaction Process Analysis* (1950b), is written for the participant rather than the observer. Using Couch's thesis as a primary source of data, Bales gives in considerable detail a three-dimensional scheme for social evaluation. He also gives a brief account of the theory in an article, "Interaction Process Analysis" (Bales, 1968), in the *International Encyclopedia of the Social Sciences.* (*See also* Sbandi and Vogl, 1973.)

The three dimensions are called:

    I. Upward-downward (dominance versus submission)
    II. Positive-negative
    III. Forward-backward (task-oriented and conforming versus deviant)

Each of the original 12 categories in the IPA scheme can be used as a measure of some combination of the three dimensions (see figure 22), although the 12-category system has been modified slightly in the new book to give an even better fit with Bales's current approach. In addition, Bales has developed a 26-item check list which can be used by group members to rate themselves or others and translate their ratings into a summary position in the three-dimensional space. After completing the ratings, the summary judgment may be checked against one of the 26 profiles which indicate behavior expected for persons with any given combination of the three dimensions.

In sum, Bales's description of the correlates for the three dimensions of interpersonal behavior is the most complete to date and provides a rich source of hypotheses for further research. Bales stopped at three dimensions for much the same reason that Chapple stopped at one and Leary at two. Given the measures he had and the behavior he wished to predict, he seemed to have accounted for as much of the variance as he could. Three dimensions have the further advantage that they can be visualized in relation to the three-dimensional physical space in which the subject moves. As we move out of the realm of three dimensions we make life more difficult for the human being, but not yet too difficult for the computer, as evidenced by the larger number of factors proposed by Couch and others. The question is, then, would it be useful theoretically and practically to add a fourth, fifth, or larger number of dimensions to Bales's three?

The Fourth Dimension

For our evidence for the fourth dimension, we turn to the same source which has provided the best evidence for the first three dimensions, Couch's thesis (1960). As a final *tour de force,* Couch performed a factor analysis of 300 variables drawn from all of the domains which he had investigated in his research. Altogether about 600 variables had been involved in the various factor analyses.[9]

9. This seemed to be too many variables to consider at one time, so Couch decided to use factorial measures for some of his clusters of variables and not to include other variables in both "raw sum" and "standard score" form. This reduced the interdomain matrix to 300 variables in the following categories: (1) manifest behavior initiated, (2) perception by external observers, (3) perceptions by participating members, (4) Q-sort descriptions by members, (5) self-perceptions, (6) self Q-sort descriptions, (7) apperception of situational press, (8) apperceptive "appearance," (9) perception of group, (10) behavioral press, (11) selected personality measures, (12) concealment defense measures, and (13) major personality dimensions.

Figure 22. Bales's Key for Interpretation of High and Low Rates of the Interaction Profile[a]

Interaction Category	Interaction Initiated Directional components[b] indicated if the rate of initiation is:		Interaction Received Directional components[b] indicated if the rate of receiving is:	
1. Shows solidarity	Low = DF	High = UB	Low = NF	High = PB
2. Shows tension release	Low = U	High = D	Low = DPF	High = UNB
3. Agrees	Low = NB	High = PF	Low = UB	High = DF
4. Gives suggestion	Low = O	High = O	Low = DN	High = UP
5. Gives opinion	Low = DPB	High = UNF	Low = DNB	High = UPF
6. Gives orientation	Low = U	High = D	Low = N	High = P
7. Asks for orientation	Low = DN	High = UP	Low = UPF	High = DNB
8. Asks for opinion	Low = N	High = P	Low = UP	High = DN
9. Asks for suggestion	Low = O	High = O	Low = B	High = F
10. Disagrees	Low = P	High = N	Low = DPB	High = UNF
11. Shows tension	Low = UF	High = DB	Low = PB	High = NF
12. Shows antagonism	Low = DP	High = UN	Low = DPB	High = UNF

a. High and low rates of interaction in all categories of interaction initiated and received by an individual may be combined to predict the attitudes other members may have toward that individual, that is, where they place him in the three-dimensional evaluative space. The combination is performed by addition of the directional components. [Rates are considered high if they are above the median for the 21 profiles in table 4. Rates are low if they are below the median.]

b. A directional component is an indicator of a direction of movement in the three-dimensional evaluative space. The dimensions and directions are:

Dimension I	Dimension II	Dimension III
U = Upward	P = Positive	F = Forward
D = Downward	N = Negative	B = Backward

No movement in any direction is indicated by O. Directional components are considered to be algebraically additive as they are in three-dimensional physical space. U and D are of opposite sign and cancel each other. The same is true of P and N, and again of F and B. Thus, U + U = 2U, but U + D = 0, and similarly for the other dimensions. The prediction of actual movement is obtained by summing all components to a single resultant direction. A resultant direction may name one, two, or three components, such as: U, UP, UPF. Thus U + P + F = UPF. Personality and role traits related to each resultant direction are known.

Note: The directional components indicated are based on factor loadings reported in Couch (1960). Unfortunately, the components shown for categories 1 and 2 are not characteristic, since in the source study jokes were scored in category 1 instead of 2.

Source: Robert F. Bales, "Interaction Process Analysis," in *International Encyclopedia of the Social Sciences,* ed. D. L. Sills (New York: Macmillan and Free Press, 1968) 7: 468. Copyright © 1968 by Crowell Collier and Macmillan, Inc. Reprinted by permission of the author and the publisher.

Over one-third of the 300 variables used in the final analysis (110 variables) were categories of manifest behavior initiated and received (called behavioral press) in the Bales, Value Content, and Kaiser-Harvard systems. This in itself would tend to weight the resulting factors in the direction of the behavioral categories. In addition, Couch consciously used the six factors in the behavior domain as guides for his analysis of the combined domain matrix (Couch, 1960, p. 495). Using the Thurstone Complete Centroid method he again extracted six factors. The first two factors were left in their "centroid" positions since these positions indicated interdomain dimensions which were very similar to the first two factors of interpersonal behavior. The remaining factors were rotated so that the initiated-behavior variables served to create dimensions as similar as possible to the other factors of interpersonal behavior.

As in so many studies of interpersonal behavior, the first factor (interpersonal dominance) explains two to four times as much of the variation in the matrix of correlations as any other factor. The amount of variation explained is indicated by the sum of the squared "loadings" for that factor. A "loading" is a number which ranges from -1.00 to $+1.00$ which represents the correlation between a variable and a factor. For example, the loading for the total IPA initiated (Bales's categories) on factor I is .91, which indicates that total talk has a high positive association with interpersonal dominance. As an indication of the importance of each of the six interdomain factors in explaining behavior, the sums of the squared loadings are given in table 5. Here we see that factor I accounts for almost twice as much of the variance as factor II, and factor II in turn almost twice as much variance as factor III. Factors IV, V, and VI are about equal, so that if we were selecting a fourth dimension using this criterion alone, we could not make a strong case for selecting one rather than the other.

On both theoretical and empirical grounds the best conceptualization of the fourth dimension would appear to be Couch's "conventional versus unconventional behavior." Couch himself notes that this dimension was rather inappropriately labeled, since it did not emerge clearly in the analysis of manifest behavior (Couch, 1960, p. 536). Couch indicates that the factor is much better defined by measures of the perception of individuals than it is by manifest behavior, since the category systems were not oriented to this aspect of interpersonal behavior. The external-observer variable "authoritarian values" provides a stable reference point for an interpretation of this dimension. The observers also see individuals who are high on the dimension of conforming as "self-confident," "extroverted," lacking "individualistic values," and not attracting "personal admiration" or "liking." The group members agree that these high individuals seem to have authoritarian values and lack individualism, but they also perceive them as rather anxious and lacking in self-confidence and understanding. Group members do not show personal liking for this type of individual. The personality variable with the highest negative loading is "ascension" (fantasies of being an all-controlling person), indicating that conforming is associated with a constriction of an active fantasy life.

Table 5. Sums of Squared Factor Loadings for Six Factors for Couch's Combined Interdomain Analysis

Factor	Sum of Squared Factor Loadings
I Interpersonal dominance	46.10
II Interpersonal affect	25.81
III Social expressivity	13.79
IV Influence attempts	12.16
V Surface acquiescence	11.84
VI Conventional behavior	11.35

Source: A. Paul Hare, "Four Dimensions of Interpersonal Behavior," *Psychological Reports* 30 (1972): 499–512. Reprinted by permission of the publisher.

In sum, this factor is reflected primarily in the quality of the content of an individual's behavior indicating a degree of conformity to traditional norms that is maintained in interpersonal interaction.

In his own interpretation of Couch's material, Bales considered using conforming as a fourth factor but decided instead to combine this factor with Couch's factor III. Thus Bales's factor III (forward versus backward) is in effect a fusion of the negative end of Couch's II (social expressivity versus task seriousness) and factor VI (conventional versus unconventional behavior). *Forward* for Bales is then task-oriented and conforming, while *backward* is socially expressive and nonconforming.

Parsons, Couch, Bales, and Bion

By introducing a fourth dimension there is the possibility of a better fit between the theoretical systems proposed by Parsons, Couch, Bales, and Bion than there was with three or fewer factors. An indication of the relationship between the systems is given in figure 23. This figure is similar to the periodic table in chemistry in that it shows categories which have already been "discovered," but in addition it indicates where missing categories need to be developed to fill out the system. The Parsonian dimensions (L—Latent pattern maintenance, I—Integration, G—Goal attainment, and A—Adaptation) have been described in chapter 1, figure 8. A paper by Hare and Effrat (1969) demonstrates the relationship between these categories and those of Bales (see also Parsons, Bales and Shils, 1953). This comparison is based on a content and process analysis of the text of the novel *Lord of the Flies*. Bion's categories are described by Stock and Thelen (1958). (See figure 24.) The relationship between Bion's categories and the others is also based on my analysis of *Lord of the Flies* and my experience as a member of the team, headed by Thelen, who first used the categories for systematic observation.

In figure 23, column 2, Couch's dimensions are given as they were previously described. In column 3, Bales's categories are given with their current definition. However, categories 2 and 11 appear twice since Bales did not distinguish between the aspects of these categories which would appear on the third and the fourth dimension. The expressive end of the third dimension (A) is represented by the joking in category 2 and the laughter in category 11. The positive end of the fourth dimension

Figure 23. Parsons, Couch, Bales, and Bion in Four Dimensions

	Parsons	Couch	Bales	Bion
L	+ Basic Obligations	IV Conforming	2. Fantasy	Dependency
	− (Individual Orienta- tion)	Nonconforming	11. Tension	Flight
I	+ Get Along Better	II Positive	1. Friendly	Pairing
	− (Promote Dis- tance)	Negative	12. Unfriendly	Fight
G	+ Makes Decisions	I Dominant	Total IPA 4. Gives Suggestion	Work Level 3, 4
	− (Individual Goal)	Submissive	9. Asks for sugges- tion	Dependency
A	+ Information or Facts	III Task Serious	5. Gives opinion 6. Gives informa- tion	Work Level 2
	− (Withholds or avoids giving relevant facts)	Social Expressivity	2. Jokes 11. Laughs	Flight

Source: A. Paul Hare, "Four Dimensions of Interpersonal Behavior," *Psychological Reports* 30 (1972): 499–512. Reprinted by permission of the publisher.

Figure 24. Bion's Category System as Developed by Stock, Thelen, and Others

a. The quality of work expressed: every statement receives one of four work ratings:

   1—level work is personally need-oriented and unrelated to the group work.

   2—level work is maintaining or routine in character. It may involve attempting to define a task, searching for methodology, clarifying already established plans, and the like.

   3—level work is group-focused work that introduces some new ingredient; active problem solving.

   4—level work is highly creative, insightful, and integrative. It often interprets what has been going on in the group and brings together in a meaningful way a series of experiences.

b. The character of the emotionality expressed: a statement may contain no detectable affect. If it does, the affect is placed in one of the following emotional categories:

   Fight (F): expressions of hostility and aggression.

   Flight (Fl): expressions of avoidance of the problem or withdrawal from participation.

   Pairing (P): expressions of warmth, intimacy, and supportiveness.

   Dependency (D): expressions of reliance on some person or thing external to the membership.

   E: This category is reserved for the relatively few statements in which some affect is clearly present but is too confused or diffuse to be placed in any one or any combination of the above categories.

Source: Dorothy Stock and H. A. Thelen, *Emotional Dynamics and Group Culture* (New York: New York University Press, 1958), p. 193. Reprinted by special permission of the NTL Institute for Applied Behavioral Science, Arlington, Virginia.

(L) is represented by the fantasies in category 2 which serve to define the basic values and obligations of group members, while the negative end is represented by the tension in category 11 which indicates withdrawal from the field or other forms of idiosyncratic behavior. In a similar way, in column 4, Bion's category "flight" appears in two places, once in the third dimension (A), where it indicates expressive behavior, and once in the fourth dimension (L), where it represents withdrawal.

To provide a more complete description of interaction in small groups two category systems can be used concurrently, one for process and the other for content. A set of categories for the analysis of content, based on AGIL, has been suggested in chapter 1. A set of categories for the analysis of process, based on the work of Bales, Couch, and others reviewed here, would include these dimensions:

   I. Dominant versus submissive

   II. Positive versus negative

   III. Serious versus expressive

   IV. Conforming versus nonconforming

Some indications of the kinds of behaviors which would be included in each dimension are given in figure 25.

Bales has also found that descriptions of both process and content are desirable, since he supplemented his descriptions of group process with indications of content (cf. Bales and Strodtbeck, 1951; Heinicke and Bales, 1953). However, Bales never proposed a formal set of content categories of his own. Instead he indicated the probable relationships between his categories and those of Parsons in *Working Papers in a Theory of Action* (Parsons, Bales, and Shils, 1953).

Additional articles which report dimensions similar to these four include Borgatta, 1960a; Cloyd, 1964b; Park, 1967; Lorr and Suziedelis, 1969; Lorr,

Figure 25. Interaction Process Analysis, Four Dimensions

I Dominant vs Submissive	
Dominant:	Assuming autocratic control or seeking status in the group by making direct suggestions or by giving opinions which serve to guide group activity. (Also measured by total talking rate.)
Submissive:	Showing dependence by asking for help, showing anxiety, shame and guilt, or frustration, laughing at the jokes of a dominant person.
II Positive vs Negative	
Positive:	Seeming friendly by showing affection, agreement, or by asking for information or opinion in an encouraging way.
Negative:	Seeming unfriendly by disagreeing, showing antagonism, or diffuse aggression.
III Serious vs Expressive	
Serious:	Giving information or opinions which indicate serious involvement in the task. Routine agreement.
Expressive:	Giving support to others regardless of task performance or showing tension release through joking or other evidence of flight from the task.
IV Conforming vs Nonconforming	
Conforming:	Seeking to be guided by the group norms by asking for information or suggestions. Making jokes or dramatic statements which reveal the basic nature of the group.
Nonconforming:	Showing tension which indicates withdrawal from the field. Describing fantasies which reveal individual goals rather than group goals. Resisting pressure to conform.

Source: A. Paul Hare, "Four Dimensions of Interpersonal Behavior," *Psychological Reports* 30 (1972): 499–512. Reprinted by permission of the publisher.

Suziedelis, and Kinnane, 1969; Osgood, 1970; Reed, 1972; Blunden, Spring, and Greenberg, 1974.

Group Differences in Task and Social-Emotional Activity

In groups of long standing, the leadership style, the social class or personalties of the members, or other factors may produce characteristic differences between groups in their patterns of task and social-emotional activity. Some indication of the nature of these differences has been given in the comparison of interaction profiles of groups with different tasks and member composition. Other studies report that the type of task (producion, discussion, problem-solving) may account for 60 percent of the distribution of group activity (Morris, 1966), although there is still consistency of behavior since some aspects of problem-solving are similar regardless of the setting (Mann, 1961). For children, groups assembled for meals and structured or unstructured games show different patterns of behavior (Raush, Dittman, and Taylor, 1959; Raush, Farbman, and Llewellyn, 1960; Raush, 1965). The effect of leader style is evident when "democratic" leaders who act positively toward their group members and set a standard for cooperative activity between members tend to receive positive reactions, while leaders who are "authoritarian" provoke negative reactions and intermember hostility (Lewin, Lippitt, and White, 1939).

An example of the influence of social class is found in a study of ten adolescent clubs, five with members from the lower class and five with members from the middle class. The lower-class members were more aggressive with each other and collaborated more with the adult leader, whereas the middle-class members directed more collaborative and aggressive acts to the club president who was a peer (Maas, 1954b).

Group differences which result from the personalities of members are best illustrated by studies which contrast groups of mental patients where extremes of activity in the task area (compulsiveness) and the social-emotional area (hysteria) as well as extremes of inactivity (withdrawal) have been observed (Rowland, 1938; Chapple and Lindemann, 1942; Roberts and Strodtbeck, 1953). Even with relatively "normal college students, pairs of subjects whose common psychosexual disturbance has been aroused by reading materials, and who *project* as a defense mechanism, tend to perceive their interaction as more negative than pairs of subjects who utilize other defenses, are less aroused, or us differing defenses (Cohen, 1956).

It is also possible to alter the characteristic task or social-emotional activity by stimulating one category of act. For this purpose, less global methods than changing the leadership style or the group composition can be used. For example, subjects in paired interaction increased their rate of giving opinion when the experimenter reinforced their opinions by repetition or agreement (Verplanck, 1955). Subsequent research has confirmed the fact that either the total interaction rate or the frequency of some particular category of behavior can be increased by positive reinforcement or decreased by negative reinforcement (Cieutat, 1959; Rosenberg, 1959; Oakes, Droge, and August, 1960; Deutsch, 1961; Rickard and Timmons, 1961; Salzberg, 1961; Cieutat, 1962; Hall, 1962; Oakes, 1962a, 1962b; Heckel, 1963; Kanfer, Bass, and Guyett, 1963; Aiken, 1965; Bavelas et al., 1965; McClintock, 1965; Simkins and West, 1965; D'Zurilla, 1966; Simkins and West, 1966; M. K. Wagner, 1966; Davis, 1967; Sarbin and Allen, 1968a; Marlatt, 1970; Simkins, 1971; Weiss et al., 1971; Baron, Jackson, and Fish, 1972; David, 1972; Helm, Brown, and Tedeschi, 1972; Page, 1972a; Crawford, 1974).

One type of behavior which traditionally received negative reinforcement was the transmission of bad news. Apparently the same feelings about bad news which once led kings to kill messengers bearing bad tidings still hold some force, for subjects in a variety of experimental situations are found to be reluctant to transmit bad news and much more likely to disclose good news (Becker and Brock, 1966; Rosen and Tesser, 1970; Eagly and Acksen, 1971; Rosen and Tesser, 1972; Tesser and Rosen, 1972; Tesser, Rosen, and Batchelor, 1972a, 1972b; Tesser, Rosen, and Conlee, 1972; Conlee and Tesser, 1973; Rosen et al., 1973; Tesser and Conlee, 1973; Wilson, 1973; Johnson, Conlee, and Tesser, 1974).

In addition to differences in content of interaction between groups, norms are also established within groups which tend to regulate the frequency and duration of member interaction (Talland, 1957a) and the channels through which communications are allowed to travel.

The principal content category associated with a high interaction rate varies from group to group and over time within the same group depending upon the problem the group faces at the moment. In some types of groups a high interaction rate is associated with the expression of both positive and negative feeling in the area of affection (Blake, 1953; Festinger and Hutte, 1954; Homans, 1954), in other groups, a high interaction rate is associated with control as members try to bring a deviant into line (Festinger et al., 1952), and in still other groups a high interaction rate is associated with leadership and task behavior (Stephan and Mishler, 1952).

Further differences between groups in task and social-emotional activity are described in part 2, where these and other examples are given in more detail.

Individual Interaction Characteristics

Perhaps the most consistent finding in all of the research on social interaction is that *some people talk more than others.* The person who initiates the most action tends to receive more than anyone else and to address more of his remarks to the group as a whole than to specific individuals (Bales, 1951b; Bales et al., 1951; Keller, 1951; Stephen and Mishler, 1952). In one experiment, low-ranking persons sent more messages up the line to high-status persons even when the high-status persons were not initiating most of the activity (Kelley, 1951).

Since relative rate and direction of interaction are such basic dimensions of individual and group activity, they are perhaps the first things to be affected by any changes in the group. As the size of the group is increased from three to twelve members, the differences between the relative interaction rates of members tend to disappear, while the difference between the leader and the average member becomes more apparent (Bales et al., 1951; Stephan, 1952; Stephan and Mishler, 1952). The rate of interaction for any one member is inversely related to the rates of the other members composing the group (Borgatta and Bales, 1953b) and directly related to the freedom to participate allowed by the communication net (Bavelas, 1950). An individual's communication rate can be increased by removing the high interactors from the group (Stephan and Mishler, 1952), by having the leader encourage equal participation (Bovard, 1951a), or by placing him in a favorable position in the communication net, which may mean simply having him sit at the head of the table (Strodtbeck and Hook, 1961). A number of mathematical models have been derived to represent the distribution of participation in discussion groups (Horvath, 1965; Leik, 1967; Horvath, 1969; Kadane and Lewis, 1969; Kadane, Lewis and Ramage, 1969a, 1969b; Lewis, 1971).

Previous experience and training can also affect the participation rate of the group member. In a therapeutic setting, therapists who had been psychoanalyzed were found to be more active with their patients than therapists who had not been psychoanalyzed (Strupp, 1955c).

Not only the form of an individual's interaction pattern but also the content is predetermined in part by his role and his personality. Again to take an example from the therapeutic interview, therapists who had been trained to be "nondirective" were found to "reflect" more of the patient's statements and to show less inclination to set therapeutic goals than analytically oriented therapists (Strupp, 1955a; Strupp, 1958). In a similar comparison of social workers with psychiatrists, the social workers were found to reassure the patients more, whereas inexperienced psychiatrists explored more of the patient's problems but did not interpret as much. However, in both professions differences in content which were related to level of training were greater than differences between professions (Strupp, 1955b). The inexperienced therapists who were less certain of their role tended to be more limited in their range of behavior.

Some indication of the effect of personality type on interaction content is evident in a study in which 75 college students judged the amount of aggression in the "tone of voice" of a sample of 30 Air Corps officers who had either high or low blood pressure and related personality characteristics. The judges found that aggression was more apparent in the tone of voice of the officers with high blood pressure (Starkweather, 1956).

In another study of the content of a problem-solving discussion held by six pairs of men, the subjects judged to be "emotionally mature" made more statements which had mutual satisfaction as their aim, while the immature subjects made more statements for self-gratification (Lichtenberg, 1955). Further examples of differences in individual interaction characteristics which are associated with different group roles and different personality types are given in chapters 6 and 8.

Nonverbal Behavior

Early research on interaction tended to combine all verbal and nonverbal cues for the classification of social interaction. More recently some research has focused on the nonverbal aspects of behavior. Since nonverbal behavior may be less consciously controlled, it may contradict as well as amplify verbal behavior. Often research does not distinguish between nonverbal behaviors which a subject emits unconsciously, although they give information to others, and nonverbal signals which are consciously used in lieu of verbal communication or to supplement it (Wiener et al., 1972).

The dimensions of nonverbal behavior are not surprisingly similar to those of verbal behavior. In some research the dimensions identified are clearly the same as those described earlier in this chapter; in others the authors present slightly different summations of traits. Mehrabian, for example, identifies three dimensions: (1) evaluation, (2) potency or status, and (3) responsiveness. Increases in positive *evaluation* are denoted by immediate positions and postures (e.g., a closer position, more forward lean, more eye contact, and more direct orientation); increases in *potency or status* are denoted by greater degrees of postural relaxation; and increases in *responsiveness* by greater activity, e.g., facial activity, speech intonation, or speech rate (Mehrabian, 1970a, 1971a; Mehrabian and Ksionzky, 1972a).

The principals of social exchange operate with nonverbal behavior as they do with verbal behavior. If an interviewer emits positive cues by facing the subject, leaning forward, maintaining eye contact, and smiling appropriately, then the subject will tend to respond by maintaining eye contact and smiling in return (Gatton and Tyler, 1974). If a subject seeks approval, he will offer smiles and positive head nods (Rosenfeld, 1966a, 1966b).

The forms of nonverbal behavior tend to be consistent over time for the same subject (Patterson, 1973b), but may vary across cultures (Morsbach, 1973). It has been suggested that behavior patterns such as smiling, nodding, and a very brief lift of the eyebrows, particularly prominent in flirting behavior, appear to be genetically fixed and are used in comparable situations of social contact in various cultures (Eibl-Eibesfeldt, 1968). Other general works on nonverbal behavior include Hall, 1959; Rolla and Rolla, 1964; Hall, 1966; Argyle, 1972; Myers and Myers, 1972; Ruesch and Kees, 1972; Speer, 1972b.

Studies with a more specific focus which illustrates the importance of understanding "body language" include Knapp, 1964a, 1964b; Mehrabian, 1968a, 1968b; O'Toole and Dubin, 1968; Mehrabian, 1969; E. W., Smith, 1972; Zavala and Paley, 1972.

Some studies of nonverbal communication focus primarily on one aspect of communication—the use of the face, the eyes, the hands, or the voice. There appears to be a fairly reliable set of cues for recognizing facial expressions that are pleasant, unpleasant, irritated, etc. (Gubar, 1966; Shapiro, 1968a; Hoshino, 1969; Saral, 1972; Watson, 1972; Schiff, 1973; Shoemaker, South, and Lowe, 1973), even in drawings of faces which provide minimal cues (Cuceloglu, 1972; Simpson and Crandall, 1972). However, one study reports that the states of happiness, love, fear, and determination were more often accurately recognized than disgust, contempt, and suffering (Thompson and Meltzer, 1964). It helps the judgment if the observer knows more about the subject or the situation (Shapiro, 1968b; Tewes, 1973). This would have the effect of reducing the ambiguity of the stimulus, since information about the subject or the situation provide cues concerning the expected emotional state. When subjects are asked to reproduce emotional states through facial expressions, women do better than men (Buck et al., 1969, 1972; Buck, Miller, and Caul, 1974), and persons who are very anxious or emotionally aroused do least well (Draughon, 1973; Schiffenbauer, 1974a). Mixed messages—for example, giving criticisms with a smile—can affect children differently from adults (Bugental, Kaswan, and Love, 1970). Since it is easier to control expression in the face than the body (Ekman and Friesen, 1974), cues from the body may give a more reliable picture of feelings than the face (Shapiro, 1972).

The amount of eye contact a person receives from another will affect his attitudes and emotional responses (LeCompte and Rosenfeld, 1971; Nichols and Champness, 1971; Breed and Porter, 1972; Ellsworth, Carlsmith, and Henson, 1972; Ellsworth and Ludwig, 1972; Hobson et al., 1973). As a behavior trait, eye contact patterns for a subject tend to be stable (Daniell and Lewis, 1972). Generally people look more at others they like (Ellsworth and Carlsmith, 1968; Kendon and Cook, 1969; Modigliani, 1971; Schneider et al., 1971; Scherwitz and Helmreich, 1973; Griffitt, May, and Veitch, 1974) or from whom they seek approval (Efran and Broughton, 1966; Pellegrini, Hicks, and Gordon, 1970). If subjects are sad, they look away (Exline et al., 1968; Fromme and Schmidt, 1972). Women tend to look more and be more observant of eye contact than men (Exline, 1963; Argyle and Dean, 1965; Argyle, Lalljee, and Cook, 1968; Kleck and Nuessle, 1968; Libby, 1970; Aiello, 1972; Gitter, Mostofsky, and Guichard, 1972; Kleinke et al., 1973; Thayer and Schiff, 1974). Extroverts and those concerned with others also look more (Rutter, Morley, and Graham, 1972; Libby and Yaklevich, 1973; Nevill, 1974).

Some authors have suggested that the immediacy behaviors, which include physical distance, eye contact, body orientation, and body lean, are critical in the nonverbal communication of interpersonal attitudes. They all appear to combine to produce a single message. Thus any substantial change in one of the behaviors would require a reciprocal change in one or more of the other behaviors. For example, if a subject stands close there is less need to have a large amount of eye contact (Goldberg, Kiesler, and Collins, 1969; Patterson, 1973a). On the other hand, some studies report a positive association between eye contact and intimate positions (Breed, 1972; Scherer and Schiff, 1973), while still other studies try to sort out the apparent conflict in the two sets of findings (White, Hegarty, and Beasley, 1970; Vine, 1971; Kleinke, 1972).

Lower-satus persons are more likely to look at and up to persons of higher status, especially if the higher-status persons show approval (Efran, 1968; Strongman and Champness, 1968; Burroughs, Schultz, and Autrey, 1973; Fugita, 1974). In any event people speak more to people they look at (McDowell, 1973).

A dimensional analysis of manual expression reveals four factors which are quite similar to those of the more inclusive category systems. Subjects were shown 36 photographs on an adjective checklist. The four factors which emerged were designated (1) activation—active versus passive, (2) evaluation—good versus bad, (3) dynamism—shy versus brave, slow versus fast, and weak versus strong, and (4) control—deliberate versus impulsive, and controlled versus uncontrolled (Gitin, 1970).

As with other nonverbal behaviors, hand movements vary with personality (N. Freedman et al., 1972). When persons are showing overt hostility, they tend to use more large gestures which parallel their speech; when they are showing covert hostility, they engage in smaller, body-focused movements, such as playing with their fingers or clothing (N. Freedman et al., 1973). In a courtroom nonverbal behavior of witnesses was observed which included movements of the head, arms, feet, and legs, as well as the hands. It was noted that the witnesses decreased their large movements during cross-examination as compared with direct (friendly) questioning (Means and Weiss, 1971). Not surprisingly, students use more hand signals to give directions on campus when they are face to face with the person seeking help than when the directions are given over an intercom (Cohen and Harrison, 1973).

Voice is used to signal affection as persons speak more often and for longer periods of time to those they prefer (Mehrabian, 1971b; Word, Zanna, and Cooper, 1974). In contrast, tension is reflected in longer pauses in speech (Dittmann and Llewellyn, 1969). Although all persons in one experiment tended to speak louder when they were farther away from another person, males spoke even louder than females. The intensity of the voice was decreased when talking to another person of the same sex, possibly as an indication of greater affiliation (Markel, Prebor, and Brandt, 1972). A person's use of his voice tends to reflect his personality (Brown, Strong, et al., 1973), although culture is also an important variable (Scherer, 1971, 1972).

Vocal variations (as well as eye movements and gestures) can be used as "addressor regulators." These are cues which are emitted by the speaker which appear (1) to serve as cues for the addressee that encoding is occurring and continuing, (2) to check whether listening and decoding are occurring, and (3) to indicate when the addressee is to speak (Wiener et al., 1972). Speakers also indicate when it is time to take turns in speaking (Wainerman, 1969; Duncan, 1970, 1972), when they do not want to be interrupted, usually by raising the voice (Meltzer, Morris, and Hayes, 1971; Morris, 1971), and when it is time to leave (Knapp et al., 1973).

Touching, as a form of nonverbal behavior, appears to be the privilege of high status as indicated by age, sex, race, or socioeconomic class. Persons of higher status tend to initiate touching (Henley, 1973). Touch also indicates intimacy and solidarity (Silverman, Pressman, and Bartel, 1973) and may reduce stress in interpersonal relations (Geis and Viksne, 1972).

Summary

The observation and analysis of the interaction process usually depends upon a category system which allows the observer to code each act in one of a limited set of content areas. Current usage of category systems is represented by the work of Thelen, who gives a double score to each unit act by noting the amount of task and social-emotional behavior it contains, and by Bales, who scores each act on its predominant content. The Bales system has 12 categories which are subdivisions of four general types of acts: positive reactions, negative reactions, problem-solving attempts, and questions.

Some variations in the interaction profile are observed in groups with different tasks or member composition. In contrast to the typical laboratory group where the emphasis is on problem-solving attempts, showing solidarity and tension release are high in groups whose members have taken lysergic acid, and showing disagreement and antagonism are relatively high in groups whose members have been drinking beer or brandy. Jurors deciding a court case and husbands and wives who are asked to reconcile differences in opinion show high amounts of agreement since the task requires it, and schoolboy leaders give suggestions and show antagonism since no consensus is needed.

In the typical interaction pattern of a small leaderless group, there is a balance between action and reaction. About half of the acts during a group session are problem-solving attempts, while the remaining half are distributed among positive reactions, negative reactions, and questions. This balance between task and social-emotional activity will vary with the nature of the task and the characteristics of the members.

Four dimensions of interpersonal behavior have been identified which account for most of the variance in the process of social interaction. Chapple based his work on the first dimension; dominant versus submissive. Leary found that the relationships between 16 types of interpersonal behavior could be understood by adding a second dimension of positive versus negative. Bales has shown that the addition of a third dimension, combining task-oriented and conforming behavior, can illuminate the relationships between 26 modes of interpersonal behavior. Using Couch's data and analysis, a fourth dimension can be added by separating the two dimensions which were fused by Bales. Thus the third dimension is serious versus expressive and the fourth dimension is conforming versus nonconforming. The use of four dimensions for the description of interaction process provides a complementary system to the four functional categories developed by Parsons.

Groups may differ in their behavior on each of the four dimensions depending upon the group task and the characteristics of the members. Any category of action can be increased if it is positively reinforced, or decreased if it is negatively rein-forced, as is the case with the transmission of bad news. The person who initiates most of the interaction in a group tends to receive more than the others and to address more of his remarks to the group as a whole.

Nonverbal behaviors, which include physical disance, eye contact, body orienta-tion, and body lean, usually reinforce the messages which are transmitted through verbal communication. Since nonverbal behavior may be less consciously controlled, it may contradict as well as amplify verbal behavior. As with other forms of be-havior, variations in nonverbal behavior are associated with different personality and social characteristics.

Additional References

Additional articles which cover various aspects of the interaction and decision process include Bruun, 1959; Mumford, 1959; Palmore, Lennard, and Hendin, 1959; Gruen and Bierman, 1960; Reisman, Potter, and Watson, 1960; Stone, 1960; Bernstein and Lennard, 1961; Shaw, 1963; Borgatta, 1964; Matarazzo et al., 1964; Bonny et al., 1965; Leik, 1965a; Bouillut and Moscovici, 1967; Jakobovits and

Hogenraad, 1967; Alkire et al., 1968; Feldstein, 1968; Furuhata, 1968; Emerson, 1968; Hayes, Meltzer, and Lundberg, 1968; Denner, 1969; O'Leary and Goldman, 1969; Rosenfeld and Sullwold, 1969; Cannavale, Scarr, and Pepitone, 1970; Prock and Weick, 1970; Welkowitz and Feldstein, 1970; Scheiblechner, 1971; Siegman, Blass, and Pope, 1971; Weick and Gilfillan, 1971; Hayes and Meltzer, 1972; Insko, Rall, and Schopler, 1972; Jackson et al., 1972; Maslach, 1972; Mugny, Pierrehumbert, and Zubel, 1972–1973; Reynolds and Fisek, 1972; Siegman and Pope, 1972; Weiss, Williams, and Miller, 1972; Willard and Strodtbeck, 1972; Anthony, 1973; Bikson and Goodchilds, 1973; Brown, Amoroso, et al., 1973; Crawford, Williams, and Haaland, 1973; Lalljee and Cook, 1973; Newtson, 1973; Traylor, 1973; Welkowitz and Kuc, 1973; Bordow, 1974; Carter, 1974; Duncan and Niederehe, 1974; Maslach, 1974; O'Reilly and Roberts, 1974.

Chapter 4

GROUP DEVELOPMENT

ALTHOUGH SOME INTEREST in the stages of group development can be traced in the writings of behavioral scientists in the 1920s, 1930s, and 1940s (see Coyle, 1930), the first studies which caught the attenion of a number of group observers, leaders, and therapists were the works of Bales (1950b) and Bion in 1948–1952 (see Bion, 1961). Their work, along with that of about 50 others, was summarized by Tuckman (1965) in the first major review of studies of group development. He reviewed studies drawn from four somewhat distinct fields: therapy groups, training groups (i.e., educational groups conducted with a nondirective leader in group dynamics tradition), natural groups, and laboratory groups. From these various studies, he abstracted a theory of four stages of group development.

After Tuckman began his review, studies were published by Dunphy (1964), Mills (1964), Slater (1966), and Mann, Gibbard, and Hartman (1967). They used observations of a version of the training group developed at Harvard University (Social Relations 120) to generate theories of development which combined elements of Bales and Bion, as well as other themes.

The theories of group development of most of the major authors have been associated with category systems for the observation of interpersonal behavior which could be used to test or illustrate the theories. Over the same period of time that theories of development were being proposed, some of the same authors, as well as others, were making refinements in various category systems with the intention of discovering the smallest number of dimensions which would be necessary to describe most of the variance in interpersonal behavior. This work resulted in the proposal for using the four dimensions described in chapter 3.

Bales's Observations of Group Activity

Bales had first described his system of 12 categories in detail in his book *Interaction Process Analysis: A Method for the Study of Small Groups* in 1950.[1] From his observations of groups up to that time he already had some notion of the

SPECIAL NOTE: This chapter has been adapted from my "Theories of Group Development and Categories for Interaction Analysis," *Small Group Behavior* 4, 3 (August 1973): 259–304, and is reprinted by permission of the publisher, Sage Publications, Inc.

1. An extensive revision of this system is given in Bales (1970) but the new version has not yet been used for the direct observation of groups.

phase movements which would appear in a single problem-solving session and also in a series of meetings of the same group over a period of time.

Phase Movements

In phrases similar to those of Dewey (1933), Bales (1950b, p. 49) described group activity as moving toward a goal:

With regard to time involvement, the total process of action as a system of acts is conceived as proceeding from a beginning toward an end, from a felt need of a problem toward a solution, from a state of tension toward tension reduction, from a state of heightened motivation toward motivation reduction, or in an instrumently oriented and meaningful way which may be described in terms similar to these.

In sum, he felt that the order of problems a group would face in reaching a decision would be communication (about the nature of the problem to be solved), evaluation, control (of overt action), decision, and tension reduction (Bales, 1950b, p. 60). The relationships between these five problems and the four functional problems faced by all groups (adaptation, goal attainment, integration, and latent pattern maintenance and tension management) are discussed briefly in this early work. The relationships were made much more explicit in work by Parsons, Bales, and Shils (1953).

As a general trend over time, Bales (1950b, pp. 175–176) saw groups becoming more formal and less solidary.

[There is a] balance of conflicting tendencies, fluctuating according to more or less temporary changes in the relative urgency of functional problems of instrumentation, adaptation, integration, and emotional expression [which] probably shows a trend toward greater specificity of functional social roles, a greater differentiation of property rights, a greater formality of authority, a greater differentiation of strata, and a lesser overall solidarity.

These same trends would tend to appear as the group increased in size, added new members, or became more heterogeneous or complex.

The year after Bales published his category system, Bales and Strodtbeck published the first evidence of trends within a single meeting using this new system.

The balance between task and social-emotional activity appears over the course of a whole meeting. However, when problem-solving discussion meetings are divided into three time periods, the predominant type of activity shifts from one phase to another in a manner which reflects the stages in the group's progress toward a decision (Bales and Strodtbeck, 1951; Plank, 1951; Bales, 1952; Landsberger, 1955b). These shifts are illustrated in figure 26. The rate of acts of information decreases steadily from initial to final phase, while the rate of acts of suggestion rises. Acts of opinion increase in the middle phase and then fall off again. Both positive and negative reactions increase in rate from the initial to the final phase, with the positive reactions increasing more rapidly in the final phase. In phase one, the group members are collecting information, in phase two, evaluating the information, and in phase three, pressing for a decision with a concomitant increase in support of some members and rejection of others.

The increase in positive and negative reactions may be connected mainly with the social-emotional problems of the group process. Since the ratio of negative to positive reactions tends to be higher in response to suggestions than to factual

Figure 26. Phase Movements in Group Progress toward a Decision

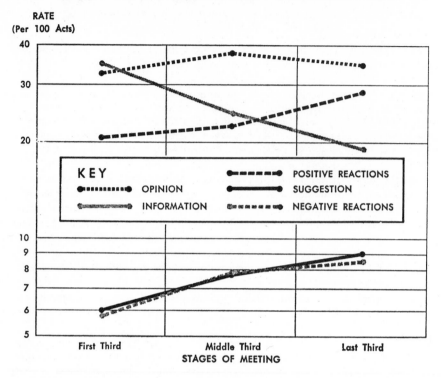

statements, the *decision point* is the critical bottleneck in the process. Once the decision point has been passed, the rates of negative reaction usually fall off and the rates of positive reaction rise sharply. Joking and laughter, indicating solidarity and tension release, become more frequent. With the problems of the task settled for the time being by the decision, the group apparently turns its attention to the emotional states of the individuals and their social relationships.

The tendency of negative reactions to increase from phase to phase also appears when subjects react negatively to the attempts of leaders or counselors to control future action (Lippitt, 1940; Rogers, 1941). Evidence that the nature and duration of the phases which may appear are directly related to the task of the group is found in a study of therapy groups in which the Bales categories for interaction process analysis were used (Talland, 1955). In these groups, the phases described above did not appear, nor was there any tendency to establish equilibrium, since the group did not have to reach a decision and the therapist's job was to keep the level of emotional involvement sufficiently high so that the patients would talk about their problems.

In contrast to Talland, Psathas (1960b) did find some evidence for phase movement and equilibrium tendencies within therapy groups. He did so, however, by combining the data for meetings at the beginning, middle, and end of a nine-month period of treatment. In the two therapy groups, he observed that the movement of acts from beginning, through middle, to end of the nine months of therapy was similar to the pattern Bales and Strodtbeck reported for a single problem-solving session. He notes that Talland observed only the beginning of therapy and suggests that the "task" of therapy takes place over a longer period of time than the single 50-minute session.

Meeting-to-Meeting Trends

In addition to shifts or phase movements in activity within a single meeting, Bales found that patterns of activity in groups also change from meeting to meeting. In a series of four meetings, members of initially leaderless groups gradually spent less time in task behavior and more time in positive social-emotional behavior as the series progressed from the first to the last meeting. Negative social-emotional behavior rose briefly in the second meeting during the "status struggle" in which the hierarchy was established (Heinicke and Bales, 1953). In table 6, these ten-

Table 6. Mean Percentage of Group Interaction in Various Categories and Combinations of Categories in Successive Sessions for Groups with High Status Consensus

Categories	Weekly Sessions				Level of Significance for Total Trend
	1	2	3	4	
A. Positive reactions					
1 + 2 shows solidarity and tension release	6.1	7.4	15.2	18.4	a
3 shows agreement	17.7	16.4	14.7	12.6	
B. Attempted answers					
4 gives suggestion	9.0	10.2	9.1	9.0	
5 gives opinion	27.2	27.4	23.7	23.3	
6 gives information	16.8	12.1	13.8	12.6	
C. Questions					
7 + 8 + 9 asks for information, opinion, and suggestion	4.2	3.4	2.9	3.5	
D. Negative reactions					
10 shows disagreement	12.8	17.8	11.4	11.2	
11 shows tension	0.18	0.49	0.45	0.47	
12 shows antagonism	0.06	0.20	0.01	0.44	
Subtotals for four classes of categories					
A. Positive reactions	24.6	24.2	30.3	31.1	
B. Attempted answers	53.9	50.2	47.6	45.4	
C. Questions	4.2	3.4	2.9	3.5	
D. Negative reactions	13.3	18.7	11.9	12.6	
A-D (positive reactions minus negative reactions)	10.5 a	2.7 b	16.2	17.5	b

a. The difference between two numbers is significant at the 0.01 level.

b. The difference between two numbers is significant at the 0.05 level.

Source: Christopher M. Heinicke and Robert F. Bales, "Developmental Trends in the Structure of Small Groups," *Sociometry* 16 (1953): 24. Reprinted by permission of the authors and the publisher. (Note: Volumes 1–18 of *Sociometry* were edited by J. L. Moreno and published by Beacon House, Inc.)

dencies in *ad hoc* groups with *high* status consensus over four meetings are indicated by decreasing rates of activity in the task-oriented categories (giving information, opinion, and suggestion) and rising rates in the social-emotional categories.
Negative reactions are low in the first meeting, show a sharp rise during the
second, and then drop off again.

There are two different trends within the area of positive reactions. Overt
showing of agreement shows a steady downward trend, which is counteracted by a
sharp rise in showing solidarity and tension release through joking and laughing,
especially in the final session. In other words, there is a marked shift from the
more neutral and tentative task-oriented agreement to the more emoional positive
reactions as the meetings progress.

Although groups with *low* consensus on the relative status of members go
through a similar period of social-emotional conflict, in general the trends within
each of the categories are not as sharply focused as they are in the *high* status
consensus groups. As a result of their continued attention to "social-emotional"
problems, the low status consensus groups tend to be less efficient and less satisfied
with their group and with their group's solution to the problem. Phase movements
similar to those in the high status consensus groups have also been noted in discussion groups over a longer series of meetings (Theodorson, 1953).

If the members of the group have the experience of taking part in a series of
meetings, each with a different set of group members, then the effect is the same
as if the group is meeting for the first time. Although the task and other aspects
of the situation remain the same, the individuals must take time to get to know
the other group members at the beginning of each meeting. Group structure is not
given a chance to develop, and the status struggle usually reflected in the interaction
pattern of the second meeting does not take place (Borgatta and Bales, 1953a).

Phase Movement and Trends in Psychotherapy

A modification of the Bales categories was used in an analysis of communication between psychotherapists and their patients (Lennard et al., 1960). This study
provides another example of phase movement within a session and trends between sessions. Tape recordings were made of eight therapies (four therapists with
two patients each) for a period of eight months. One hundred twenty of the five
hundred recorded sessions were then subjected to content analysis. Previous to and
concurrent with the therapy each patient and therapist responded to eight questionnaires and interviews. For the content analysis, six sets of categories were used
covering type of content, grammatical form, affective content, interaction process,
and role-system reference.

A major theme throughout the study was the analysis of the process through
which the patient learns his patient role with the possibility of later transferring
what he has learned about role patterns in therapy to other significant role relationships. The "socialization" of the patient in his role appears to be more of a
conscious effort at the beginning of the therapy. As therapy progresses the amount
of discussion about therapy itself and about the reciprocal therapist-patient roles
tends to decrease. There is a similar decrease within each session. At the same
time, there is an increase in the amount of communication about affect as the
patient learns to put his thoughts and feelings into words. The therapist and
patient establish rather stable "norms" for their interaction rate with the patient
talking most of the time. However, in a given hour, if he patient talks less, the

therapist will talk more. When patient and therapist differ initially in their expectations about the activity of the therapist, the therapist spends more time in the socialization process.

The Equilibrium Problem

One way of looking at the status struggle in laboratory groups that takes place in the second session is to note that while group members are in this type of social-emotional activity they have less time and energy available for the task. In industry, for example, the most productive teams were found to spend less time on "within" team interaction (Horsfall and Arensberg, 1949). In another study, when carpenters and bricklayers who were accustomed to being assigned to work teams each day by their foremen where given a chance to choose the men they would prefer to work with, they showed marked differences in performance when compared with teams composed in the usual way (Van Zelst, 1952). In the groups of buddies, job satisfaction increased, labor and material costs dropped, and labor turnover decreased practically to zero. These effects presumably occurred because the "buddies" did not have to spend as much time in the solution of status problems.

This tendency of the group to swing back and forth between attempts to complete the task and attempts to maintain the group and to satisfy the needs of its members has been identified by Bales as the *equilibrium problem* (Bales, 1953). Pendulum-like swings in activity occur as members become more absorbed in the task and neglect individual member needs and then lose sight of the task as they turn their attention to group solidarity. In an extreme case, members of three-man groups who were drugged by an "anxiety-reducing medication" (a mixture of Seconal and Benzedrine) showed little anxiety, were elated, unassertive, and happy, but carried out little task-related behavior (Lanzetta et al., 1956).

Bion's Concepts of Work and Emotionality in Groups

At about the same time that Bales began his systematic observations of groups in the United States, Bion was conducting group therapy with neurotic patients in England. As a result of his "experiences in groups," he wrote a set of discursive articles over the period 1948–1952 in which he described the ways in which the members of his groups reacted to his leadership and to each other. The articles were later collected and published as a book (Bion, 1961).

In the summer of 1951, after all but the final review article by Bion had appeared, Thelen and his colleagues decided to develop Bion's concepts into a systematic set of observation categories similar to those of Bales.[2] The first groups to be observed using the new system were training groups a the National Training Laboratory at Bethel, Maine. The results of this research are reported by Stock and Thelen (1958, pp. 12–15).

In brief, Bion felt that the emotional aspects of group operation could be described in terms of three rather comprehensively defined emotional states which he called "cultures." These are dependency (when group members see to be dependent on the leader or some external standard for direction), pairing (when group

2. Thelen's colleagues were Saul Ben-Zeev, Paul Hare, Ida Heinz, William Hill, Joseph McPherson, Robert Rogers, and Dorothy Stock.

members turn to each other in pairs for more intimate emotional response), and fight-flight (when group members act as if their purpose is to avoid some threat by fighting or running away from it).

In addition, the group is continuously "at work" on some problem. At specific times, the particular emotional states associated with the work activity may be dependency, pairing, or fight-flight. The ongoing process of a group can be described in terms of successive shifts from one of these work-emotionality states or cultures to another.

Each individual in the group can be seen as having a "valency" for each emotional state. Individuals with high or low valencies on a particular emotional state will tend to combine with others in the group to develop, maintain, or move away from the various work-emotionality cultures.

In generating a set of observational categories from Bion's theory Thelen and his colleagues distinguished between four levels of work ranging from activity which was personally need-oriented and unrelated to group work which was highly creative, insightful, and integrative. They also separated "fight" from "flight" and added an "E" category for statements which had some emotion that was too confused or diffuse to be classified. In practice, they would distinguish between a lot of emotion in a statement (noted for example as "F" for strong fight) and a little emotion in a statement (noted for example as "f" for fight). In contrast to Bales, who gave only one score to each "act" for its dominant process category, Thelen et al. would score each act twice: once for the amount of work being performed and again for the amount and type of emotion represented. Their scoring system was given in detail in chapter 3.

Although this scoring system could be used with units of interaction as small as those used by Bales, Thelen et al. used larger units for some of their research. One procedure was to identify "natural units" of group interaction. This meant identifying points in the group discussion where a shift could be detected in the particular subgroup which was actively participating. This method was based on the theoretical assumption that, because of their individual valency patterns, different members "carry" different kinds of work-emotionality operations in a group. Consequently, when there was a definable shift in participation pattern, it was likely to reflect a shift in the amount of work and emotionality being expressed and in the character of the content. Using this scheme, protocols of group meetings would be divided into from four to twenty natural units of interaction ranging in length from three to eighteen minutes (Stock and Thelen, 1958, p. 194).

Although Stock and Thelen describe the ways in which several groups move through sequences of work and emotion over a period of time, they did not see any one sequence of development which seemed to predominate. They hoped that eventually "it may be possible to identify a fairly limited number of developmental patterns" (Stock and Thelen, 1958, p. 206).

Bion also was more interested in the swing back and forth between the various emotional states in combination with work than he was in a specific theory of group development. However, Dunphy (1964) observed that Bion's scheme does contain a sequential analysis of group development. In the first stage, the group members are dependent on the leader. Next, they begin to attack him (fight) followed by scapegoating a rival leader (flight from the group leader). Next, they pass through the stage of pairing and finally develop into a work group with relatively little emotionality (Dunphy, 1964, pp. 21–22).

Bennis and Shepard's Theory of Group Development

In 1956, Bennis and Shepard presented the first detailed theory of group development related to training groups (Bennis and Shepard, 1956). They based their theory on their own experience with training groups in workshops and educational settings and the theoretical insights of Freud (1922), Schutz (1955), and Bion (1961). Freud had stressed the ties each group member forms with the group leader, Schutz had noted two major orientations in groups, one toward authority and the other toward personal intimacy wih other members, and Bion had also noted that groups combine these orientations in states of "dependency," "fight-flight," and "pairing."

The core of the theory of group development for Bennis and Shepard "is that the principal obstacles to the development of valid communication are to be found in the orientations toward authority and intimacy that members bring to the group" (Bennis and Shepard, 1956, p. 417). As members joining a new group, they face two areas of internal uncertainty: they are concerned about dependence (how they will relate to authority) and interdependence (how they will work out the personal relations with their peers).

The development of a training group (in this case, one that meets for 17 weeks) is seen as passing through two phases, each with three subphases. Each of the main types of activity for each phase and subphase is given in tables 7 and 8. For each subphase, there is a brief description of the dominant (1) emotional modality, (2) content themes, (3) roles, (4) group structure, (5) group activity, (6) behavior which facilitates group movement, and (7) defenses. In the first phase, the members are concerned with dependence and power relations. In the first subphase, the members act as if they were in an ordinary discussion group and avoid the task of training by talking about outside issues. They seem dependent on the leader for direction. In the second subphase, the most assertive counterdependent members attack the leader and search for an effective way of organizing the group. In the third subphase the members assert their independence of the leader, become very involved in the work of the group, and take over the leadership roles formerly perceived as held by the trainer.

In Phase II (table 8), the members deal with the problem of interdependence and their personal relations with one another. They begin Subphase 4 in a period of enchantment. This is a high point of group morale, with much joking, laughing, and good fellowship. With such a good group, the members feel that no further analysis is required. Next, in Subphase 5, the members become disenchanted. They wonder how close or distant they should be. They wonder, as they did in Subphase 1, what the goals of the group are. Their disparagement of the group and its activities shows itself in tardiness and absenteeism. Finally, in Subphase 6, provided that the group has developed through the previous five subphases, group members deal with each other with understanding and acceptance. Members gradually withdraw their personal involvement in the group and sum up the progress of the group as the course ends.

In their summary of these phases of development, Bennis and Shepard observe that the evolution from Phase I to Phase II represents a change in emphasis not only from power to affection but also from role to personality. Phase I activity generally centers on broad role distinctions such as class, ethnic background, and professional interests. Phase II activity involves a deeper concern with personality modalities, such as reaction to failure, warmth, retaliation, and anxiety. This

Table 7. Phase I. Dependence—Power Relations[a]

	Subphase 1 Dependence-Submission	Subphase 2 Counterdependence	Subphase 3 Resolution
1. Emotional Modality	Dependence-fight.	Counterdependence-fight. Off-target fighting among members. Distrust of staff member. Ambivalence.	Pairing. Intense involvement in group task.
2. Content Themes	Discussion of interpersonal problems external to training groups.	Discussion of group organization; i.e., what degree of structuring devices is needed for "effective" group behavior?	Discussion and definition of trainer role.
3. Dominant Roles (central persons)	Assertive, aggressive members with rich previous organizational or social science experience.	Most assertive counterdependent and dependent members. Withdrawal of less assertive independents and dependents.	Assertive independents.
4. Group Structure	Organized mainly into multi-sub-groups based on members' past experiences.	Two tight subcliques consisting of leaders and members, of counterdependents and dependents.	Group unifies in pursuit of goal and develops internal authority system.
5. Group Activity	Self-oriented behavior reminiscent of most new social gatherings.	Search for consensus mechanism: voting, setting up chairman, search for "valid" content subjects.	Group members take over leadership roles formerly perceived as held by trainer.
6. Group movement facilitated by:	Staff member abnegation of traditional role of structuring situation, setting up rules of fair play, regulation of participation.	Disenthrallment with staff member coupled with absorption of uncertainty by most assertive counterdependent and dependent individuals. Subgroups form to ward off anxiety.	Revolt by assertive independents (catalysts) who fuse subgroups into unity by initiating and engineering trainer exit (barometric event).
7. Main Defenses	Projection. Denigration of authority.		Group moves into Phase II.

a. Course terminates at the end of 17 weeks. It is not uncommon for groups to remain throughout the course in this phase.

Source: Warren G. Bennis and H. A. Shepard, "A Theory of Group Development," *Human Relations* 9 (1956). Reprinted by permission of the Plenum Publishing Corporation.

Table 8. Phase II. Interdependence—Personal Relations

	Subphase 4 Enchantment	Subphase 5 Disenchantment	Subphase 6 Consensual Validation
Emotional Modality	Pairing-flight. Group becomes a respected icon beyond further analysis.	Fight-flight. Anxiety reactions. Distrust and suspicion of various group members.	Pairing, understanding, acceptance.
Content Themes	Discussion of "group history" and generally salutary aspects of course, group, and membership.	Revival of content themes used in Subphase I: What is a group? What are we doing here? What are the goals of the group? What do I have to give up—personally—to belong to this group? (How much intimacy and affection are required?) Invasion of privacy vs "group giving." Setting up proper codes of social behavior.	Course grading system. Discussion and assessment of member roles.
Dominant Roles (central persons)	General distribution of participation for first time. Overpersonals have salience.	Most assertive counterpersonal and overpersonal individuals, with counterpersonals especially salient.	Assertive independents.
Group Structure	Solidarity, fusion. High degree of camaraderie and suggestibility. Le Bon's description of "group mind" would apply here.	Restructuring of membership into two competing predominant subgroups made up of individuals who share similar attitudes concerning degree of intimacy required in social interaction, i.e., the counter-personal and overpersonal groups. The personal individuals remain uncommitted but act according to needs of situation.	Diminishing of ties based on personal orientation. Group structure now presumably appropriate to needs of situation based on predominantly substantive rather than emotional orientations. Consensus significantly easier on important issues.

Table 8 (continued)

	Subphase 4 Enchantment	Subphase 5 Disenchantment	Subphase 6 Consensual Validation
Group Activity	Laughter, joking, humor. Planning out-of-class activities such as parties. The institutionalization of happiness to be accomplished by "fun" activities. High rate of interaction and participation.	Disparagement of group in a variety of ways: high rate of absenteeism, tardiness, balkiness in initiating total group interaction, frequent statements concerning worthlessness of group, denial of importance of group. Occasional member asking for individual help finally rejected by the group.'	Communication to others of self-system of interpersonal relations; i.e., making conscious to self, and others aware of, conceptual system one uses to predict consequences of personal behavior. Acceptance of group on reality terms.
Group movement facilitated by:	Independence and achievement attained by trainer rejection and its concomitant, deriving consensually some effective means for authority and control. (Subphase 3 rebellion bridges gap between Subphases 2 and 4.)	Disenchantment of group as a result of *fantasied expectations of group life.* The perceived threat to self-esteem that further group involvement signifies creates schism of group according to amount of affection and intimacy desired. The counterpersonal and overpersonal assertive individuals alleviate source of anxiety by disparaging or abnegating further group involvement. Subgroups form to ward off anxiety.	The external realities, group termination and the prescribed need for a course grading system, comprise the barometric event. Led by the personal individuals, the group tests reality and reduces autistic convictions concerning group involvement.
Main Defences	Denial, isolation, intellectualization, and alienation.		

Source: Warren G. Bennis and H. A. Shepard, "A Theory of Group Development," *Human Relations* 9 (1956). Reprinted by permission of the Plenum Publishing Corporation.

presents an interesting contrast, for the *group* in Phase I emerged out of a heterogeneous collectivity of individuals, whereas the *individual* in Phase II emerges out of the group.

Schutz's Three-dimensional Theory of Interpersonal Behavior

In his book on fundamental interpersonal relations orientation (FIRO for short), Schutz (1958a) present a number of postulates concerning interpersonal behavior together with evidence from his own research to support each of the postulates. The first of these (p. 13) is:

Postulate 1: The Postulate of Interpersonal Needs
(a) Every individual has three interpersonal needs; inclusion, control, and affection.
(b) Inclusion, control, and affection constitute a sufficient set of areas of interpersonal behavior for the prediction and explanation of interpersonal phenomena.

In brief, Schutz suggests that each individual has a need to be included and to include others in groups. This need may be found at any point along a continuum from wanting to be the focus of attention in the center of a group to wanting to be completely withdrawn and isolated. The individual also has a need in the area of control which can represent any combination of wanting to control others or to be controlled by them. Finally, each individual has a need for affection which can represent any combination of liking for other people and a desire to be liked in return.

Most of Schutz's book is devoted to showing how these needs can be measured and how they affect the interaction of individuals who find themselves working in groups composed of "compatible" or "incompatible" members. However, he also suggests a sequence of events in the development of groups which he sees as paralleling the sequence of events in the development of the child in the family. He acknowledges that the theory is strongly influenced by the Bennis and Shepard theory described above. The theory is set forward as a postulate:

Postulate 4: The Postulate of Group Development
The formation and development of two or more people into an interpersonal relation (that is, a group) always follows the same sequence (Schutz, 1958a, p. 168):

Principle of group integration. For the time period starting with the group's beginning until three intervals before the group's termination, the predominant area of interaction begins with inclusion, is followed by control, and finally, by affection. This cycle may recur.
Principle of group resolution. The last three intervals prior to a group's anticipated termination follow the opposite sequence in that the predominant area of interpersonal behavior is first affection, then control, and finally inclusion.

The control and affection stages of Schutz are essentially the same as the dependence and interdependence phases of Bennis and Shepard. They are also related to the dependent and pairing modalities of Bion. The problems of inclusion were not stressed by Bennis and Shepard, in part because the determination of who is to be included or excluded from the group has already taken place by the time the "training" begins.

Dunphy (1964), in his case of two training groups, gives an example of the impact that problems of inclusion can have on a group. In this case, so many students had registered for the training group with the senior instructor that on the first day of class he had to ask half of those present to leave and take part in a group to be led by a less experienced trainer. Since no one volunteered to leave, he went around the room, pointing to each person in turn and saying "you stay" or "you go." Many times in the life of the groups, this incident was referred to, with the ones who stayed calling themselves the "chosen people."

Schutz's theory is different from those which precede it, in that he poses a definite set of recurring cycles and also in that he suggests a reversal of the order of events as the group nears termination. First, group members break their ties of affection, then they cease to control one another, and finally they give up their attendance and sense of identity with the group.

Tuckman's Four Stages in Group Development

As I have indicated earlier, Tuckman's summary of the literature on group development covers almost all the research on group development up to the time his study was published, including the theories which have been presented here in some detail, as well as many more, especially derived from work with therapy groups, which have not been mentioned. His review can therefore be taken as representative of the current state of theory about group development.

Tuckman first abstracted his theory from some 26 studies of development in therapy groups. The task in these groups was to help individuals deal with personal problems. The groups typically contained from five to fifteen members and a therapist and existed for a period of three months or more. The developmental data for groups of this type consist of the observations of the therapist and those professional observers who may be present, usually as trainees. The data are highly anecdotal in nature and reflect the clinical biases of the observers. The accounts are usually formulated after the fact and based on the observation of a single group. Tuckman then went on to show how this same theory might be applied to training groups and later to laboratory groups and those observed in natural settings.

Each of the four major stages in group development which Tuckman describes are divided into two aspects: (1) *group structure,* where he describes patterns of interpersonal relationships—that is, the way in which members act and relate to one another as persons; and (2) *task behavior,* where he describes the nature of the work being done by the group. This distinction between task and social-emotional behavior had earlier been proposed by Bales (1953) and others. The four stages in group structure are, briefly, testing and dependence, intragroup conflict, development of group cohesion, and functional role-relatedness. The four stages of task activity are orientation and testing, emotional response to task demands, discussing oneself and other group members, and emergence of insight. Each of these stages as it applies to a therapy group can be summarized as follows:

STAGE 1

Group structure: Testing and dependence. An attempt by group members to discover what behaviors are acceptable in the group, based on the reactions of the therapist. Members look to the therapist for guidance and support in this new and unstructured situation. (With antisocial individuals, there may be a prestage of resistance, silence, and hostility.)

Task activity: Orientation and testing. At this stage, the group members make indirect attempts to discover the nature and boundaries of the task. These attempts are evident in the following kinds of activity:

1. Discussion of irrelevant and partially relevant issues
2. Discussion of peripheral problems
3. Discussion of immediate behavior problems
4. Discussion of symptoms
5. Griping about the institutional environment
6. Intellectualization

Also, group members make more direct attempts at orientation toward the task as illustrated in:

1. Search for the meaning of therapy
2. Attempts to define the situation
3. Attempts to establish a proper therapeutic relationship with the therapist through the development of rapport and confidence
4. Mutual exchange of information
5. Attempts to overcome suspicion and fear of the new situation

STAGE 2

Group structure: Intragroup conflict. Group members now become hostile toward one another and toward the therapist as a means of expressing their individuality and resisting the formation of group structure.

Task activity: Emotional response to task demands. Emotionality is expressed by the group members as a form of resisting the techniques of therapy or of sensitivity training groups which require that they "expose" themselves. They also challenge the validity and usefulness of the training.

STAGE 3

Group structure: Development of group cohesion. Group members accept the group and accept the idiosyncracies of fellow members. Harmony is of the maximum importance, and task conflicts are avoided to ensure harmony.

Task activity: Discussing oneself and other group members. The self and other personal characteristics are discussed. Information is acted on in such a way that alternative interpretations of the information can be made. The openness of members to each other is characteristic.

STAGE 4

Group structure: Functional role-relatedness. The group members work together on the task with a minimum of emotional interaction. This is made possible by the fact that the group as a social entity has developed to the point where it can support rather than hinder the task processes through the use of function-oriented roles.

Task activity: Emergence of insight. Group members show insight into their own problems, an understanding of their own abnormal behavior, and, in many cases, modifications of their behavior in desired directions.

Tuckman sees these stages in group development as parallel to those in individual development—namely, dependence, affection, and maturity. In his formulation the stage of dependence precedes that of intermember conflict, whereas in the Slater formulation (which will be discussed below) the stage of dependence follows the stage of intermember conflict.

In his summary of groups, Tuckman considers groups that have met for only a few meetings as well as those who have met for a longer period of time, although he recognizes that there could well be a difference between the phases over a single meeting and those of longer duration.

Certainly duration of group life would be expected to influence amount and rate of development. The laboratory groups, such as those run for a few hours by Bales and Strodtbeck (1951), followed essentially the same course of development as did therapy groups run for a period of a year. The relatively short life of the laboratory group imposes the requirement that the problem-solving stage be reached quickly, while no such imposition exists for the long-lived therapy group. Consequently, the former groups are forced to develop at a rapid rate. The possibility of such rapid development is aided by the impersonal and concrete nature of the laboratory task. Orientation is still required due to the newness of the task, but is minimized by task rules, players' manuals, and the like, that help to orient group members.[3]

Training Groups at Harvard

During the years 1964 through 1967, four major studies of group development were published, all based on observation and experience with a version of the training group which had been developed at Harvard University. These training groups were conducted as part of a course in the Department of Social Relations (Social Relations 120). For a number of years, Bales had been the director of the course, and these authors had worked with him as trainers in sections of the course. The class format at this time was a combination of the "case analysis" approach, developed at the Harvard Business School, and discussions of the group's own process following the group dynamics tradition, developed at the National Training Laboratory at Bethel, Maine. Usually a class of about 25 students and an instructor would meet three times a week for one hour throughout the nine-month academic year around a circular table in a conference room. At one end of the room was a one-way mirror with a hidden observation booth. The group sessions were recorded on tape. Three of the authors used category systems for an analysis of the content and process of interaction in the groups; the other relied on anecdotal evidence taken from the group transcripts.

Dunphy's Study of Social Change

Dunphy's (1964) study of social change in self-analytic groups is based on an analysis of two of the Harvard Social Relations 120 groups. One with 23 students was led by Bales and the other with 26 students was led by Dunphy. Both groups met at the same hour, three times a week for a full academic year.

The data for the study consisted of weekly reports of group interaction written by the group members. Each report, approximately 250 words in length, was

3. Bruce W. Tuckman, "Developmental Sequence in Small Groups," *Psychological Bulletin* 63 (1965): 397. Copyright 1965 by the American Psychological Association. Reprinted by permission of the author and the publisher.

punched on IBM cards for analysis by computer using the *General Inquirer* system of content analysis (Stone et al., 1966). As the actual verbatim reports are read into the computer, the program removes cerain regular word endings, and each word is looked up in a dicionary, which is stored in the computer. If a word is found in the dictionary, the defining tags which indicate its membership in one or more categories in the dictionary are automatically assigned to the sentence. Later, a "tag tally" program counts how many times each of the tags has been used. The observer then notes the differences in the frequencies with which certain of the tags have been used during the various phases of the group's development and uses this information as a basis for his theory of development. The tags consist of 55 first-order tags which are discrete, independent variables such as self, small-group, food, affection, and work, and 28 second-order tags which are not independent variables. Several of the second-order tags—such as academic, political, higher-status, and male-theme—could be used to define a single word (Dunphy, 1964, pp. 83–98).

In his summary of the major shifts in themes in the two groups over the year, Dunphy notes that at first the individual member differentiates himself ("self"), the instructor, and other members who are able to gain the attention of the group ("leaders") from an undifferentiated collection of others ("people"). At this time, there is little coordination of group activity. After a short period of trying to maintain traditional patterns for discussion groups, action takes on a strongly manipulative character. The men become particularly active with behavior directed toward the satisfaction of aggressive and sexual drives. Emotional involvement with the group is avoided as each person throws up a barrier around his ego for its protection.

In the first part of the second semester, there is a change in this pattern. Ego boundaries are undermined, and there is more involvement with the group. Students feel lost in the group. There is increased effort toward the realization of group goals with a primary concern with personal involvement with others and affection. Toward the end of the group, the group seems to develop its own human qualities. There is a sense of group identity as members develop a set of symbols for communication and a set of norms. "The earlier defense of non-involvement which found its active expression in aggression, gives way to the deeper defense of resistance and denial, actively expressed in avoidance" (Dunphy, 1964, p. 165). Then, as the group ends, there is a concern for the loss of the group and for its relative state of unity and achievement.

In addition to these general trends, Dunphy also reported some intergroup differences related to differences between the status and style of the leaders. However, his main analysis follows the pattern suggested by Tuckman, with more explicit emphasis on the problems the group faces at its termination. For a later comparison with a functional analysis of group development, we note that Dunphy, like Bennis and Shepard, gives evidence that the "group" under study is at first a collection of individuals and only becomes a "group" after the members have met together in interaction for a period of time.

Mills's Analysis of Group Transformation

Mills (1964) sums up some of the observations which he and others have made of the Social Relations 120 training groups at Harvard. He then presents his analysis of a training group he conducted, using a new system for group analysis called "sign process analysis." His title, *Group Transformation,* is taken from the fact that, by taking a comparatively passive role in the group, the instructor forces the group members to work out their own method of learning, thus undergoing a "transformation." Mills felt that previous accounts of training groups had not sufficiently stressed three processes (1964, pp. 67–69):

1. The process of forming indigenous norms. To do this, members first have to give up their preconceived normative notions, create a state of normlessness, and then select new norms and refashion them through experience.
2. The process of *partial* consumption of new knowledge about human behavior. Mills stresses the word "partial" since he feels that so little is actually known about human behavior that group members cannot help but be dissatisfied with the group's achievements.
3. The process of group termination. The fact that anticipating the group death and handling its reality is an important issue to those who commit themselves to the group.

By adding these emphases to the type of analysis of group development represented by Tuckman, Mills proposes five principal periods in the life of a training group (1964, pp. 70–80):

1. The encounter (similar to Schutz's inclusion)
2. Testing boundaries and modeling roles (Tuckman's Stage 1)
3. Negotiating an indigenous normative system
4. Production (Tuckman's Stage 4)
5. Separation (Schutz's final period of inclusion)

Mills builds his actual case analysis on his category system "sign process analysis" (SPA) which he proposed for the systematic collection of group process data. An observer, or in this case a person listening to a tape recording of the group, records the principal object and the secondary object in each simple sentence and whether the "sign" that links the two objects is positive, neutral, or negative. For example, the sentence "She greeted him warmly" links the principal object "she" with the secondary object "him" with a positive valuation.

Mills suggests that objects be distinguished according to their locus (internal or external to the group), sociological status (superior or subordinate), sex, social versus nonsocial nature, and, finally, individual versus collective nature. This gives 11 categories for each object. Since each type of principal object can be linked with each of the 11 categories of secondary objects, plus a separate category when the principal object appears alone, a matrix of 11-by-12 cells represents all possible relationships. Further, within each cell, valuations may be positive, neutral, or negative, yielding a grand total of 396 possibilities for classifying each assertion made in the group.

The principal difficulty is that an observer can seldom accumulate enough data from a single group to analyze who-to-whom interaction within a single meeting or trends through several meetings. In this case, Mills observed his group for 68 meetings over an eight-month period, recording over 34,000 statements. In summarizing his data, however, he found it necessary to combine several categories, leaving a matrix of 90 cells rather than 396. Even then, 6 cells are empty, and 24 contain fewer than 10 entries. About one-third of the entries fall into 2 of the neutral cells, leaving only about half the entries for the positive and negative indices on which Milis bases most of this analysis. Fortunately, his analysis of group development does not depend entirely on the usefulness of his category system.

Slater's Microcosm

Slater (1966) covers a wide range of material as he discusses parallels in the stages of the evolution of consciousness and its correlates at the psychological level, the social-psychological level, group level, and societal level. His principal thesis is that many of the concerns which societies and groups have dealt with over time are re-enacted as new groups are formed and developed. His description of the processes in small training groups follows the same overall pattern that Tuckman describes. The first period includes the anxiety of members over their lack of differentiation from each other and their frustration with the passive leader. Next, members go on to attack the group leader. As they try to incorporate his mana, which represents his learning, they often have symbolic feasts. At the time of the revolt, the female group members experience almost no guilt, whereas the male members evidence a great deal (Slater, 1966, p. 119). Following the revolt, there is a period of high group morale as members come close to each other and feel a spirit of equalitarianism.

The underlying theme in development is a continuing increase of consciousness of self and differentiation from others. "Prior to the group revolt," Slater (1966, p. 146) suggests, "three entities are bound together: the person of the group leader, the group deity (i.e., the object of the worshipful attitude, the dependence needs, or whatever of the group members), and a set of abstract skills, qualities, or powers which are desired by the members."

"The symbolic ideas of communal killing and communal devouring express the fact that before a group can become united around a set of principals, it must (a) rid itself of the fantasy of a living omnipotent protector, (b) separate the valued principals from their living vehicle, and (c) make them available to all on an equal basis" (Slater, 1966, p. 147).

In a summary of his ideas, Slater indicates that there are really three different stages in the structural development of the member-member-leader triangle. In the first stage as a result of normal social training, there is generalized inhibition of hostile sentiments. However, the group members have throughout their lives found that the expression of hostility toward their peers has been sanctioned less rigidly than manifest hostility toward authority, so that there is a certain amount of displacement from the authority to their peers. As the revolt builds, this process is increasingly reversed and, finally, a successful revolt depends on near unanimity of animosity toward the leader. Following the revolt, this demand for unanimity of feeling continues, and there is an intense taboo on intermember conflict. Gradually, however, this restriction is relaxed, and there is again a great deal of hostility expressed between individual members. This coincides with the more or less universal acceptance of the usual training group value on free and candid expression of feelings in interpersonal relationships (Slater, 1966, p. 150).

The major difference between Slater's and Tuckman's theories lies in the sequence of modalities described by Bion as fight-flight, dependency, and pairing. Tuckman describes the group as going through the dependency mode first, then fight-flight, and finally pairing, whereas Slater feels that fight-flight precedes dependency, although he agrees that the final stage is pairing.[4] He feels that the stages in this order reflect the major concern of the group members towards differentiation. When they first enter the group and find themselves essentially undifferentiated from each other, they attempt to fight or fly. Thus, by setting themselves off from each other, they gain some minimum of differentiation. This might be seen as comparable to the stage in the development of the child when he takes a negative stance toward his mother, who in this case is represented by the group. In the next stage, the group members begin their attack on the leader and first suggest that they are very dependent upon him. This gives them some feeling of differentiation by identifying with the leader. Presumably, this reflects a second stage in child development, where the child looks to the father, who is at least different from the mother (group). Finally, having overthrown the leader and absorbed his mana, the group members become anxious about being too differentiated from each other and losing something of the group feeling. They therefore begin to establish subgroups and close interpersonalities through pairing.

Mann's Analysis of Member-Leader Relationships

In developing his category system for the analysis of member-leader relationships in training groups, Mann combined categories from Bales, Bion, and others, but his final result comes closer to Bion's scheme. He is primarily concerned with the way the members of a training group relate to the leader. This can occur at four levels, ranging from a direct expression of feeling toward the leader to remarks in which the reference to the member may be disguised or symbolized although the reference to the leader may be direct. The first problem for the scorer using this system is to note the level at which the inference about content is being made. The four levels are as follows:

Level One: Both members and leader are referred to directly.
Level Two: Member referred to directly, but leader symbolized by equivalent within the group.
Level Three: Member referred to directly, but leader symbolized by equivalent outside group.
Level Four: Member symbolized by equivalent inside or outside the group, leader referred to either directly or symbolically.[5]

Once the scorer has noted the level of inference, he selects the appropriate content category from the list given in table 9. The content categories of the member-to-leader scoring system can be looked at as three separate systems which are used simultaneously. Eight of the sixteen categories describe the affective

4. In a personal communication, Slater qualifies my statement that fight-flight precedes dependency in his model, with the following observation: "This would only be true for a totally independent society. In a group which forms in the midst of a society like ours, the fight-flight stage is more a matter of fantasy than behavior. Empirically, open inter-member conflict is more likely to occur after the dependency stage, as a function less of the fight-flight modality than of the long-delayed confrontation of realistic differences. The problem is that the same behavior may mean different things. Fight-flight conflict is too abrupt, sporatic, and explosive to get defined as an empirical stage, partly because cultural defenses available to all members can be used as a substitute during the early life of the group."
5. Richard D. Mann, Graham S. Gibbard, and John J. Hartman, Interpersonal Styles and Group Development (New York: John Wiley & Sons, 1967), p. 40. Reprinted by permission of the publisher.

Table 9. Mann's Member-to-Leader Scoring System Categories

Area	Subarea	Category
Impulse	Hostility	1. Moving against 2. Resisting 3. Withdrawing 4. Guilt inducing
	Affection	5. Making reparation 6. Identifying 7. Accepting 8. Moving toward
Authority relations		9. Showing dependency 10. Showing independence 11. Showing counterdependency
Ego state	Anxiety	12. Expressing anxiety 13. Denying anxiety 14. Expressing self-esteem
	Depression	15. Expressing depression 16. Denying depression

Source: Richard D. Mann, Graham S. Gibbard, and John J. Hartman, *Interpersonal Styles and Group Development* (New York: John Wiley & Sons, 1967), p. 42. Reprinted by permission of the publisher.

response a member may have to the leader; three of the categories describe feelings which are activated by the leader's status in the authority structure of the group; and five of the categories describe how the member feels about himself in relation to the leader. These three approaches to the member's feelings are referred to by Mann as areas of (1) impulse, (2) authority relations, and (3) ego state.

The impulse is divided in turn into two subareas—hostility and affection— and the ego state area divided into the subareas of anxiety and depression. The authority relations area is also considered one of the five subareas. These five areas are important in one of the scoring conventions which Mann proposes. Each act may be scored in as many subareas as seems appropriate, but no more than one category within a subarea may be used. Also, self-esteem is never double-scored with an anxiety or depression category. Thus "expressing self-esteem" is considered a category, but not a subarea within the ego state area. Examples of each of the 16 categories are given in some detail in the text (Mann, Gibbard, and Hartman, 1967, pp. 41–60). For some of the categories, Mann has been guided by definitions of similar categories used by Bales: for example, "moving against" for Mann is similar to "showing antagonism" for Bales, "resisting" similar to "disagrees," "accepting" similar to "agrees," and "moving toward" similar to "shows solidarity."

Mann's unit of analysis is more global than that of both Bales (1950b) and Mills (1964), who used the simple sentence as the prototypic act in an effort to isolate the most rudimentary element of interaction. In contrast, Mann is attempting to infer the member's feelings from statements which range from the direct to the symbolic. In many cases, the scorer can only discern the latent, leader-relevant feelings by examining the recurrent shadings of many phrases and sentences. For this reason, he defines an *act* as a single speech or burst of sentences within which the expressed feelings are uniform. One of two events signals the end of an act: (1) the speaker is interrupted by another member or by the leader; or (2) the speaker shifts from expressing one set of feelings to expressing feelings which call for a different array of scored categories.

The length of an act in this scoring system can vary from a single word to a speech extending over almost a page of double-spaced typescript. Whereas Bales typically records around 1,000 acts per hour using the smallest unit which would be coherent, Mann's scoring system averages 200 acts per hour (Mann, Gibbard, and Hartmann, 1967, pp. 60–61). Mann's system could still result in a larger number of scored units than the Bion system as it was proposed by Stock and Thelen (1958, p. 194), who might include several different speakers in the same unit if the emotional content of the act remained the same.

The behavior of the leader is also scored using the 16 categories, although the observer does not ask what feeling he is expressing toward the members. Instead, Mann records the leader's reflection of members' feelings back to the group.

The 16 categories and four levels of inference were applied to the interaction in four classroom groups conducted at the Harvard Summer School in the years 1961–1963. They were all sections of the Social Relations 120 course. Before carrying out his analysis of the process of development in the four groups Mann subjected the 20 dimensions to the statistical method of factor analysis to see if a smaller number of underlying dimensions could be used to describe the behavior. That is, he wished to know if the various categories fell into a smaller number of clusters. For this purpose, he converted the amount of behavior in each category for each member of the groups in each session to percentages. This unit of one member for one session he called a *performance*. A performance was only included in the analysis if he had recorded at least 20 acts to the group member for that session. This gave him a sample of 430 performances. As a result of the factor analysis, Mann identified six basic factors.

These six factors, together with the behaviors which represent the positive and negative end of each factor, are given in table 10. In parentheses next to each factor name is included the Bion category which seems to come closest to the predominant factor content (Mann, Gibbard, and Hartman, 1967, pp. 68–70).

Before using these six factors in the description of group development, Mann added a description of the conceptual framework which emerged from his clinical study of the groups. He saw four themes which occurred with considerable regularity: nurturance, control, sexuality, and competence (Mann, Gibbard, and Hartman, 1967, p. 73). His theory of group development in its simplest form is that groups pass through phases of development in this same order. That is, group members begin in a dependent stage concerned with problems of nurturance, then move to a struggle with the leader as they work on problems of control, then to more concern with intermember relations and the problem of sexuality, and finally arrive at a stage of mature work which they do with competence. In general, these phases are similar to the four phases described by Tuckman (1965).

Using examples from the transcripts of group meetings and graphs showing the trends in activity on each of the six factors over the life of the four training groups, Mann goes on to show the relationships between the four themes, the six factors, and other theories of group development. In brief, the primary factor associated with the first theme of nurturance is Factor II: relations with the leader as an authority figure. The principal Bion category associated with the theme is "dependency." The second theme, control, is associated with Factor III: relations

Table 10. Mann's Factor Patterns for Member Performances

Factor I: Relations with the leader as analyst (work)
      I+: Enactment
      I—: Dependent complaining

Factor II: Relations with the leader as authority figure (dependency)
      II+: Rebellion
      II—: Loyalty

Factor III: Relations with the leader as manipulator (fight-flight)
      III+: Counterdependent flight
      III—: Resistant complaining

Factor IV: Relations with the leader as audience (pairing)
      IV+: Relating to the leader as colleague
      IV—: Concern with inner distress

Factor V: The effect of the leader on the ego state of the member
      V+: Anxiety
      V—: Depression

Factor VI: Commitment to the member-leader relationship
      VI+: Emotional involvement
      VI—: Emotional neutrality

Source: Richard D. Mann, Graham S. Gibbard, and John J. Hartman, *Interpersonal Styles and Group Development* (New York: John Wiley & Sons, 1967), p. 187. Reprinted by permission of the publisher.

with the leader as manipulator and with Bion's category "fight-flight." The third theme, sexuality, is associated with Factor IV: relations with the leader as audience and Bion's category "pairing." Finally, the fourth theme, competence, is associated with Factor I: relations with the leader as analyst and Bion's category "work." Thus, after beginning with Bales's twelve categories and amplifying them with four more interpersonal categories and four levels of inference, Mann finds that four themes are sufficient to account for most of the process of group development. These themes are quite similar to those proposed by Bion. In his final analysis, Mann does add a fifth phase to emphasize a type of activity which he feels previous observers have overlooked. Just after the period of initial complaining and nurturance, group members appear to take over the group for a brief period of work at the task of group and case analysis. Since the group has not yet worked out its basic problems, this period of work cannot be sustained. For this reason, Mann calls this period one of "premature enactment." In his final presentation of a theory of group development (table 11) Mann places the themes of control and sexuality in the middle phase of "confrontation" and, like Mills, stresses a final phase of "separation and terminal review."

A Functional Analysis of Group Development

Mann's account of group development is not only the most recent of these analyses of group development but also the most comprehensive (Mann, Gibbard, and Hartman, 1967). However, Mann's theory can in turn be described in terms of a functional theory of groups developed primarily by Parsons (Parsons, Bales, and Shils, 1953; Parsons, 1961). This approach begins with an analysis of the four basic problems which every social system must solve in order to survive. These problems are latent pattern maintenance and tension management (L),

Table 11. Mann's Subgroup Characteristics by Phase

Phase	Dominant Subgroups	Deviant Subgroups
Initial complaining	Dependent complaining Loyal compliance Counterdependent heroics Self-sufficiency	Enactment in the service of autonomy
Premature enactment	"The sensitive ones" Withdrawal and denial "The accepting enactors" "The heroic enactors"	Disappointment and resentment
Confrontation	Rebellion and complaining (including "the spokesmen") Independence Anxiety and withdrawal	"The heroes"
Internalization	Enactment and work	"The scapegoats"
Separation and terminal review	Depression and manic denial Personal involvement Complaining abdication of responsibility	

Source: Richard D. Mann, Graham S. Gibbard, and John J. Hartman, *Interpersonal Styles and Group Development* (New York: John Wiley & Sons, 1967), p. 187. Reprinted by permission of the publisher.

adaptation (A), integration (I), and goal attainment (G). (See summary of theory in chapter 1.)

A category system based on the AGIL scheme is given in chapter 1, which makes it possible to analyze the content of the activity of a social system to determine the functional nature of each unit of activity and to test hypotheses about the "typical" sequence of development of the system. This developmental sequence of L-A-I-G with a terminal stage of L is similar in many respects to the previous analyses of group development based on data from therapy groups, self-analytic groups, classroom groups, and work groups described earlier (Bennis and Shepard, 1956; Schutz, 1958a; Mills, 1964; Tuckman, 1965; Mann, 1967).

As indicated in chapter 1, when the AGIL categories are applied to the description of a learning group such as a classroom group, the forces at work seem to be as follows: the work of the group requires that the purpose of the group be defined (L), that new skills be acquired (A), that the group be reorganized so that the members can try out the new skills without being too dependent on the leader (I), and that the group's members work at the task (G). Finally, there is a terminal phase in which the group returns to L to redefine the relationships between the members and the group as the group is disbanded. The amount of time the group spends in each phase is determined by the activity of the leader (his direction or nondirection) and by the skills and emotional strengths of the members. Presumably, the leader is "ready" for each stage at the outset, since he has been through the stages before. However, members come to the group with different degrees of problem-solving skills or preferences for different emotional modalities (for example, a preference for fight-flight, pairing, or dependency; Bion, 1961). Subgroups tend to form on the basis of skills or emotional modalities. If the subgroup with the appropriate skills and emotional state for each stage is large enough, it can carry the whole group through that phase (Bennis and

Shepard, 1956; Mann, Gibbard, and Hartman, 1967). If not enough members of the group are ready for a particular stage, more intervention by the leader may be necessary. Some groups may never progress beyond the early stages.

The assumption that the group moves from phase to phase when a subgroup or leader is able to carry the movement needs to be documented by further research, since previous observers do not discuss the *process* of development in any detail; rather they simply *observe* that one phase follows another. A typical comment is that of Schutz (1958a, p. 171) concerning the affection phase: "Finally, following a satisfactory resolution of these problems of control, problems of affection become focal." Schutz does not tell us how the problems of control become resolved or by what process the group moves to the next phase. However, it may not require as much justification to assert that a group will face special problems at the beginning and at the end of its life. For example, at the beginning of the training group, when the leader fails to assert himself, Bennis and Shepard (1956, p. 420) observe, "The ambiguity of the situation at this stage quickly becomes intolerable for some." Or Mills (1964, p. 78), describing the termination of a group, says, "The fact of separation forces a complex set of demands and issues."

Finally, with the L-A-I-G sequence in mind, we can go back to Mann's description of group development to observe the fit between his phases and the four functional categories. His first stage of "initial complaining" is primarily the L stage as group members seek a definition of the situation. The second stage of "premature enactment" reflects the members' first attempts to use their new skills in the analysis of interpersonal behavior (A phase). The enactment is "premature" because members have not yet reorganized themselves in a way that frees them from dependence on the trainer. This is done in the next phase of "confrontation" (I). The next-to-last phase of "internalization" is G as members carry out the work of group analysis. This is followed in Mann's scheme by a final phase of "separation and terminal review" which brings the group again to L.

Summary

One of the first to describe the stages in group development for laboratory groups was Bales, who noted that the dominant content of interaction changes within a single meeting as a group moves from phase to phase in the discussion, and between meetings over a series of meetings. In the first phase of a discussion, the group members are collecting information, in the second phase, evaluating the information, and in the final phase, pressing for a decision. Over a series of four meetings, members gradually spend less time in task behavior and more time in positive social-emotional behavior. Negative social-emotional behavior rises briefly in the second meeting during the "status struggle" in which members establish the hierarchy. In their attempts to solve problems in both task and social-emotional areas, groups face an *equilibrium problem*. If they become too absorbed in the task, they will neglect group or individual needs, and if they pay too much attention to group structure and member satisfaction, productivity will decline.

Further contributions to the theory of group development have been made by Bion, who identified three emotional modalities (fight-flight, pairing, and dependency) which seemed to underly the work of a group, Bennis and Shepard who identified six stages as group members dealt with the problems of dependence and independence, Shutz, who saw three stages of inclusion, control, and affection, and

Tuckman, who summarized the literature, primarily with therapy groups, to abstract four stages of dependence, conflict, cohesion, and functional role-relatedness.

After Tuckman's review Dunphy, Mills, Slater, and Mann added detailed observations for "self-analytic" groups. Their work suggests four stages of development and one of termination which in turn can be seen in terms of functional theory: (L) defining the situation, (A) developing and using new skills, (I) developing roles appropriate for the task, and (G) carrying out the work of the group. The final stage is a return to L to redefine the relationships of the members now that the group has terminated.

Additional References

Subsequent research on group development tends to confirm the developmental sequence presented here. In the following list of additional articles, most of those published before 1965 were used as a basis for Tuckman's (1965) review: Barron and Krulee, 1948; Powdermaker and Frank, 1948; Abrahams, 1949; Stoute, 1950; Mann, 1953; Ostlund, 1953; Bach, 1954; Rotter, 1954; Levy, 1955; Corsini, 1957; Tulane Studies in Social Welfare, 1957; Bradford and Mallinson, 1958; Schlindler, 1958; Philp and Dunphy, 1959; Psathas, 1960a; Olmsted, 1962; Smith, Bassin, and Froehlich, 1962; Thelen and Dickerman, 1962; Theodorson, 1962; Jordan, Jensen, and Terebinsky, 1963; Kaplan and Roman, 1963; Bradford, 1964a, 1964b; Chatterjee, 1965; Emerson, 1966a, 1966b; Psathas and Hardert, 1966; W. M. Smith, 1966; Hare, 1967, 1968b; Marwell, 1968; Stone, 1969; Culbert, 1970; Doll and Gunderson, 1970; Morris, 1970; Whittaker, 1970; Levine, 1971; Lundgren, 1971; Mattmüller-Frick, 1971; Merei, 1971; Runkel et al., 1971; Franck, 1972; Liebowitz, 1972; Schönpflug, 1972; Gibbard and Hartman, 1973b; Hill and Gruner, 1973; Krain, 1973; Tucker, 1973; Kingdon, 1974.

Chapter 5

SOCIAL PERCEPTION

THIS CHAPTER GIVES AN overview of research on the initial phase of the social act. This includes a description of the individual's *perceptions* of himself and others, and the part these perceptions play in the imagined interaction between self and others through which the individual *pretests* his behavior. The pretest phase tends to occur between the steps of hypothesizing and proposing action.

The Initial Phase of the Act

Before the individual acts, he first imagines himself carrying out the act, then imagines the response of another person to his action. If the imagined response is desired, he will proceed with the overt act, but if the imagined response is not desired, he will modify his intended action before actually carrying it out (Cooley, 1909; Cottrell, 1942; Mead, 1950; Blumer, 1953; Turner, 1956). In either event, the actual behavior of the other person serves as a check on his perceptions. The perceptions of the "self" and "other person" are then modified to correspond to the new evidence presented by actual behavior (Sullivan, 1938, 1954).

Group members are generally aware of their behavior and of the effect that it is having on other group members (Crowell, Katcher, and Miyamoto, 1955). Behavior is apt to be least self-conscious in a small group in which the individual is highly involved (Goffman, 1957) and most self-conscious in larger groups which provide some time for reflection between acts.

Books and articles which provide reviews of the factors involved in person perception or suggest general models include Steiner, 1959; Sherif and Hovland, 1961; Hammond, Wilkins, and Todd, 1966; Tagiuri, 1968; Frijda, 1969; Stotland, 1969; Cook, 1971; Bodalev et al., 1972; Boyd and Perry, 1972; Brandt and Brandt, 1972; P. B. Smith, 1972.

First Impressions

Although the perception of another person usually changes as new information is gathered about him, one's first impression of a person may color all subsequent information. In laboratory experiments and in classroom settings, the effect of the first impression has been demonstrated by presenting a list of adjectives which

113

presumably describe a person with the word *warm* as the key adjective for half of the subjects and the word *cold* as the key adjective for the other half.

In one laboratory experiment, groups of students were given two lists of discrete qualities said to belong to a person. The first list was *intelligent, skillful, industrious, warm, determined, practical,* and *cautious.* The second list was identical with the first, except that the word *warm* was replaced by the word *cold.* The subjects were then instructed to write personality sketches of these two persons and to select from a checklist of pairs of opposite traits the terms that best fitted the impression they had formed. The reactions to the two lists of persons differed markedly. The "warm" person was perceived as wise, humorous, popular, and imaginative, whereas the "cold" person was perceived less favorably in some, but not all, of these traits (Asch, 1946).

In a classroom experiment, students in three sections of a college course in psychology were introduced to a new instructor who was to take over the class. They were told that research was being conducted to find out how they reacted to different teachers. Appended to the description of the research was a short "personality sketch" of the new instructor, allegedly obtained from a person who knew him well. The sketches given to each student were identical, except that on half of the sheets he was described as "rather cold," while on the other half the phrase "very warm" was substituted. After the class meeting, the students were asked to write a free description of the instructor and to rate him on 15 rating scales. Differences in the briefing as to the warmth or coldness of the instructor were found to influence student judgment, since the instructor received more favorable ratings when he was expected to be warm than when he was expected to be cold. The "warm" instructor was described as more informal, sociable, popular, humorous, and humane (Kelley, 1950).

In similar experiments the subjects made less extreme ratings on the warm-cold dimension when they anticipated future interaction with the stimulus person than when they did not (Bond and Dutton, 1973); however, the context in which the central (warm-cold) trait is presented plays a part (Bell and Stanfield, 1973). The actual behavior with a person who was expected to be "cold" may be the reverse of what one would expect if the subjects overcompensate and talk more in order to complete a discussion task (Bond, 1972).

Another example of the influence of first impressions is found in the research on group "cohesiveness" (Schachter et al., 1951) in which subjects were told that they were either similar to each other in interests and personality, and would get along well together, or that they were mismatched, and would probably not do very well together. After a short period of interaction during which the subjects solved some problems together, the subjects who had been told that they *would* like each other reported that they *did* like each other better than those who had been told that they would not be attracted to each other.

The importance of any particular trait in forming a first impression depends on the context in which it is presented. The order of presentation, contrast with other traits, and desirability of other traits all play a part (Anderson and Barrios, 1961; Blake, Heslin, and Rotton, 1970; Takahashi, 1971; Eswara, 1972; Louis-Guerin, 1972–1973; Rosenthal, Rogers, and Durning, 1972; Gollob and Lugg, 1973; Anderson and Lopes, 1974; Bryson, 1974; Hamilton and Zanna, 1974; Leach, 1974; Wyer, 1974). Generally it is reported that negative traits are given more weight than positive traits (Weinstein and Crowdus, 1968; Bryson, 1972; Hamilton and Zanna, 1972; Richey, Richey, and Thieman, 1972; Beigel, 1973; Kaplan, 1973;

Levin et al., 1973; Richardson, 1973; Wyer, 1973; Hodges, 1974; Singh et al., 1974). A number of experiments have been designed to determine the nature of the rule which subjects seem to follow in combining a series of traits into a weighted average (Hendrick, 1968; Himmelfarb, 1969; Rosnow, Wainer, and Arms, 1970; Takahashi, 1970; Ohashi et al., 1971; Byrne et al., 1973a, 1973b; Davis and Ostrom, 1973; Gollob and Fischer, 1973; Kaplan and Anderson, 1973a, 1973b; Leon, Oden, and Anderson, 1973; Hamilton and Fallot, 1974). Some evidence suggests that new or inconsistent information is given more weight (Lay, 1972; Gollob, Rossman, and Abelson, 1973), while other evidence suggests that differential weighting is given to new information after formation of a first impression. When highly polarized stimuli are added to a polarized stimulus, the impression of a person becomes more evaluatively polarized, and when information of less polarity is added, the impression becomes less polarized. However, the less polarized information is given less weight (Himmelfarb, 1973).

It is helpful in sorting out the differences in person perception to note that some traits are primarily descriptive, denoting actual behaviors, while others are more evaluative, implying that the activity is good or bad (Felipe, 1970; Peabody, 1970a; Rosenberg and Olshan, 1970; Rosenthal and Kaplan, 1973). For example, in the Philippines, persons of Chinese ancestry are described by Chinese and non-Chinese alike as more saving with money than the average Filipino. However, the Chinese evaluate themselves as thrifty and others as squanderers, while others describe the Chinese as stingy and themselves as generous.

As with other types of social judgments, people with different cognitive styles make different types of judgments. Women are found to seek more information than men and make more complex judgments (Nidorf and Crockett, 1964; Nidorf, 1968). Subjects who tend to make complex judgments are more positive in their evaluation (Fertig and Mayo, 1969; Nottingham, 1970; Frauenfelder, 1974). However, strong reactors tend to use less information and form more stable first impressions of others (Ehrlich, 1969; Johnson and Ewens, 1971; Reid and Ware, 1972).

The Group Basis of Perception

Individuals are continually making observations, sometimes about things, sometimes about people. The *perceptions* which remain the same over a long period of time are here called *attitudes*. The concept of attitude has been used historically in a number of different ways, and the present definition is one of several current meanings (Allport, 1954). Put another way, the attitudes which are transmitted from one generation to the next play a major role in defining the categories in which persons will be socially perceived. The individual's perception, at any given time, is a function of the *attitudes* of the society transmitted in culture, the more transient *perceptions* of the small group involved in the action of the moment, and an idiosyncratic component which results from the personality of the perceiver and the perceived and other unique situational factors. The fundamental part of the individual's perceptual base is, however, to be found in his assessment of the perceptions of his group (Cartwright, 1952; Zander, 1958; Tuddenham, 1961b; Backman, Secord, and Peirce, 1963; Mannheim, 1966; Walum, 1968). Although the influence of the group on individual judgment has already been discussed in detail in chapter 2, some further indication of the influence of the group upon judgments of the self and others will be given here.

The self-concepts of men living in a dormitory in four-man living units have been found to be influenced by others' perceptions of them over a period of months of living together (Manis, 1955). In another study the ways in which individuals rated themselves on four personality traits in 10 college classroom and fraternity groups of 8 to 48 persons were analyzed. The subjects' self-perceptions were compared with the actual feelings of others in the group about these traits, with their perceptions of others' attitudes, and with their perception of the attitudes of the *members of most groups* or a *generalized other*. The self-perceptions were found to be related to the actual attitudes of others in the group. However, the self-perceptions were even more related to the subjects' perceptions of others' attitudes, and most closely related to the subjects' estimates of the generalized attitude (Miyamoto and Dornbusch, 1956).

The group's percepion of an individual will have more influence on his self-perception when he is highly attracted to the group and when the other group members place a high value on his participation (Festinger, Torrey, and Willerman, 1954; Stotland et al., 1957; Zander, Stotland, and Wolfe, 1960). Under these conditions the individual will pay more attention to the opinions of the group, and the group members in turn will be more explicit in their valuation of the individual. If a person is uncertain about his judgments and anxious about the consequences of an incorrect judgment, he will often seek out others to have some basis for social comparison (Festinger, 1954; Gerard and Rabbie, 1961; Brickman and Berman, 1971; Gruder, 1971a; Evans and Bonder, 1973; Liebling and Shaver, 1973; Samuel, 1973; Wuebben, 1973; Evans, 1974; Jones and Regan, 1974).

The group basis of the perception of others is also evident in the research on attitudes toward different classifications of people. The concept of *stereotype* is used to refer to the group prejudgment of a class of persons which so colors the "first impression" that the individual characteristics which do not fit the stereotype are suppressed (Cronbach, 1955; Felker, 1972; see also Gitter, Black, and Mostofsky, 1972a; Gitter, Kozel, and Mostofsky, 1972). Further research on the group basis of perception includes Herman and Schild, 1961; Silver and Mood, 1971; Wilson and Benner, 1971; Izzett and Leginski, 1972; Saltzstein, Klausner, and Schiavo, 1974.

Further research relating to membership in a social category formed by age, sex, race, or role, either on the part of the perceiver or the perceived, includes Steinmann, Fox, and Farkas, 1968; Black, 1969; Johnson and Ewens, 1969; Heslin and Collins, 1970; Canon and Mathews, 1971; Soares and Soares, 1971; Bankart, 1972; Crandall, 1972; Gitter, Black, and Mostofsky, 1972b; Hogan and Loadholt, 1972; Koenig, 1972; Messick and Reeder, 1972; Touhey, 1972b; Aboud, Taylor, and Doumani, 1973; Combest, Kasten, and Shaffer, 1973; Friedland, Crockett, and Laird, 1973; Hanno and Jones, 1973; Jellison and Davis, 1973; Kaplan and Goldman, 1973; Maddock and Kenny, 1973; McCall and Rae, 1973; Stewart, Tutton, and Steele, 1973; Tarantino, 1973; Calder, 1974; Quereshi, Leggio, and Widlak, 1974; Switkin and Gynther, 1974; Triandis, Weldon, and Feldman, 1974.

Perceptual Accuracy

Individuals differ in their ability to perceive accurately the characteristics of others. Some of the factors relevant to this differential perception are found in the age, sex, and personality of the perceiver, in the characteristics of the perceived, and in the content area in which the predictions are to be made (Bender and

Hastorf, 1950; Bruner and Tagiuri, 1954; Taft, 1955; Tagiuri and Petrullo, 1958; Cline and Richards, 1960, 1961; Vingoe, 1973).

To measure the *ability* to perceive accurately, one must first rule out the accuracy which could be expected if only chance factors were operating (Tagiuri, Bruner, and Kogan, 1955), and then, since the subject may *project* his own values on the other person (Murtstein, 1957; Alfert, 1958; Hrabal, 1967; Ex and Schouten, 1968; Ford and Singer, 1968), as is the case where students are found to project their own values on their chosen faculty members (Precker, 1953), one must rule out the apparent accuracy which is due only to the fact that the *subject* and the *object* are similar (Lindgren and Robinson, 1953; Gage and Cronbach, 1955; Halpern, 1955; Hastorf, Bender, and Weintraub, 1955; Gage, Leavitt, and Stone, 1956; Runkel, 1956; Suchman, 1956; Triandis, 1960b). In addition to these difficulties in dealing with data on social perception, there are a variety of technical problems which can occur in the collection and analysis of data which make this type of analysis "a breeding ground for artifacts" (Cronbach, 1958).

Social perceptions, like other forms of judgment, are more accurate when the object being judged is less ambiguous. Thus increasing the information available about the person to be judged or including redundant information tends to result in greater perceptual accuracy (Pyron, 1965; Blanchard and Ganam, 1969; Squier, 1971; Cline, Atzet, and Holmes, 1972; Obitz and Oziel, 1972; Perry and Boyd, 1972, 1974a, 1974b; Lay, Burron, and Jackson, 1973; Sloan and Ostrom, 1974).

Perceptual accuracy apparently increases with age, at least among children, since eleven-year-olds show greater perceptive ability than seven-year-olds (Dymond, Hughes, and Raabe, 1952). Sex is also a factor, since the general notion in the folklore that women are more intuitive (perceptive) than men is borne out by some experimental results (Exline, 1957; Olesker and Balter, 1972; Haan and Livson, 1973). Close friends, who might be expected to know more about each other, do indeed make more accurate perceptual judgments (Taft, 1966; Hjelle, 1968). (See also next section on perception of friends.)

When the relationship between empathic ability and personality is explored through direct and projective tests, high-empathy persons appear to be outgoing, optimistic, warm, emotionally secure, and interested in others. Low empathy is associated with rigidity, introversion, emotionality, self-centeredness, and interpersonal incompetence (Dymond, 1949, 1950; Chance, 1958; Berlew, 1961; Jacoby, 1969, 1971; Vesprani, 1969; Pierce, 1971; Kohn and Mercer, 1973). Within a clinical population, mental patients who have "improved" as a result of hospitalization also appear to be more accurate in their descriptions of interpersonal relations than those who have not "improved" (Kalis and Bennett, 1957). In another study of patients in group therapy, the perceptions of eight patients regarding part of the interaction during a therapy session were compared with the perceptions of their therapist. The patients were found to vary widely in their perceptions of the same incident, each having his own point of view. The therapist tended to see the events in longer time perspective, while the patients were more apt to use ego-defense responses or selective inattention to defend against some aspect of the situation (Stock and Whitman, 1957).

Further evidence of the relationship between personality and perception comes from a series of experiments with college-age subjects who were classified on the single personality dimension of authoritarianism. In one experiment, the individuals who were rated as high authoritarians on a personality test were paired with low authoritarians for a 20-minute general discussion. In a second experiment, high authoritarians were paired with high, and low with low. After the discussion, the high authoritarians rated their partners as high on authoritarianism whether they were high or low, while the low authoritarians thought all their partners were either middle or high. Apparently the highs thought that everyone was just as high as they were, whereas the lows thought that no one could be as low as they (Scodel and Mussen, 1953; Crockett and Meidinger, 1956; Scodel and Freedman, 1956; see also Kates, 1959; Schulberg, 1961). High authoritarians were even found to rate the attitude of a "typical student" as also being high without any intervening interaction (Rabinowitz, 1956). This finding suggests that 20 minutes of interaction did little to alter the highs' original perception that most people were authoritarian. Similar results have been obtained for persons with a high need for affiliation, who tend to emphasize the affiliative characteristics of others (Kaplan, 1971; Solar and Mehrabian, 1973).

Other types of distortions of perception which are related to personality factors are those which result from being overanxious to see others' behavior as related to a particular goal the individuals may have, or being unwilling to accept indications of hostility from another person who may be thwarting the goal (Pepitone, 1950). There are also general tendencies in individuals to either overestimate or underestimate the position of themselves or others in the hierarchies based on interpersonal choice (Schiff, 1954).

Additional studies which relate aspects of personality to perceptual accuracy include Altrocchi, 1961; Jones and Shrauger, 1968; Halverson, 1970; Adams-Webber, Schwenker, and Barbeau, 1972; Kuusinen and Nystedt, 1972; Wilkins, Epting, and Van de Riet, 1972.

If individuals have similar feelings for each other their perceptions will tend to be more accurate because otherwise they may mask their feelings to avoid conflict (Tagiuri, Blake, and Bruner, 1953; Taylor, 1957; Tagiuri, Bruner, and Blake, 1958). An individual may also attempt to mask his feelings if he does not trust another group member. In one study 244 pairs drawn from a population of 330 professional scientists engaged in laboratory research were compared on their attitudes about the long-run consequences of a new research program, their attitudes of trust toward each other, their reports as to whether they had ever discussed the new program, and their estimate of each other's attitudes about the issue. If a scientist did not trust another scientist, he tended to conceal his own attitudes about an issue so that the accuracy of the other's perception was impaired (Mellinger, 1956).

The effect of training upon the accuracy and variability of interpersonal perception has been studied by Crow (1957). In his experiment, 72 senior medical students were divided into an experimental group who received training in physician-patient relationships and a control group who did not receive such training. At the beginning, during, and at the end of their senior year, the students estimated the real status and self-ratings of patients presented in sound-film interviews. Actual self-ratings and relevant personality test scores (MMPI) were available for these patients as criteria. As a result of the training, the members of the experimental group became *less* accurate and increased their variability of estimates significantly more. A possible explanation offered is that training programs may decrease accuracy when they increase the trainees' responsiveness to individual differences. This hypothesis is in line with the results of a similar experiment with medical students in which a "response set" to "stereotype" others was found to be more stable than differential accuracy from test to retest. Here it appeared that consistency in perception was largely due to consistency in response set (Crow and Hammond, 1957).

Because of the tendency of individuals to predict that others will fit a "stereotype," some further refinement in data analysis must be introduced if one wishes to know when a subject has been accurate simply because the other person fits the "stereotype" (Jackson, 1972). One solution is to note the "accurately shifted items" and the "inaccurately shifted items" which are different from the responses one would expect on a test of social perception if only stereotyped responses were given. In this way measures of two kinds of accuracy in predicting another's responses would be derived: (1) a measure of how well the subjects could distinguish the characteristics of an individual from those of the average members of the group, and (2) how misled the subject was by individual cues (Stone, Gage, and Leavitt, 1957).

When individuals form social perceptions either alone or in the presence of others, or when individuals are compared with groups in the accuracy of their impressions, the results are similar to those one would expect with any individual or group task (see chapter 14). The most accurate individuals make more correct judgments when they are not distracted by the presence of others and when the tendency to be influenced by group norms does not lead to inaccuracies (Fancher, 1969; Moscovici, Zavalloni, and Louis-Guerin, 1972; Moscovici, Zavalloni, and Weinberger, 1972).

Additional research on factors related to the accuracy of interpersonal judgments includes Lundy, 1959; Rodgers, 1959; Borgatta, 1960d; Purcell, Modrick, and Yamahiro, 1960; Gerard, 1961a; Stotland, Zander, and Natsoulas, 1961; Marwell, 1963; Waisman, 1964; Dornbusch et al., 1965; Davis, Kalb, and Hornseth, 1966; Powell and Wilson, 1969; Meltzer and Russo, 1970; Budman, 1972; Terry and Snider, 1972; Adams-Webber, 1973; Bledsoe and Wiggins, 1973; Borman and Graham, 1973; Gerard et al., 1973.

Perception of Friends

In general, if one subject likes another, he tends to think that his liking is returned (Tagiuri, 1957), and if he likes two other subjects, he will perceive them as liking each other (Kogan and Tagiuri, 1958a). If he is with someone who is attractive, he will perceive himself as being also liked. Each of these perceptions of liking suggests that subjects assume that a "balance" in relationships will be maintained. (See chapter 7 for an outline of balance theory.) For example, a study of the effects of person perception on having a physically attractive partner reports that a male college student is rated most favorably if he is thought to be the boyfriend of an attractive girl. In addition, male students guess that they will be rated more favorably with an attractive girlfriend (Sigall and Landy, 1973).

Group members who have many friends in the group are generally more accurate in their perception of the informal group structure and of the characteristics of others in the group than are individuals who are relatively isolated (Dymond et al., 1952; Gronlund, 1955a). Accuracy of perception of the informal hierarchies on the part of well-liked members of the group may result from the fact that when friendship choices are openly reciprocated the place of the self in a hierarchy is more evident (Tagiuri, 1952; Tagiuri, Kogan, and Bruner, 1955; Tagiuri and Kogan, 1957; Foa, 1958b; Kogan and Tagiuri, 1958b). The isolated person who may like others but is less sure of the extent to which his liking is returned may not be as accurate in his judgment.

Pairs of friends tend to be more accurate in the perception of each other's personalities than pairs of nonfriends, partly as a result of increased knowledge of the other person from continued social interaction (Bieri, 1953; Suchman, 1956; Taylor, 1957; Vernon and Stewart, 1957) and partly as a result of a tendency to project one's own values on a friend (Fiedler, Warrington, and Blaisdell, 1952; Davitz, 1955). In addition, subjects perceive that their friends have more accurate perceptions of them than those with whom they interact less frequently (Backman and Secord, 1962).

This tendency of subjects to describe others whom they like best as more similar to themselves than those they like least (Lundy et al., 1955; Peri, 1966; Loprieno, Emili, and Esposito, 1967) presumably reflects some of the common interests which brought the pair together as friends in the first place. People like others who are similar (Byrne, 1961a; Kaufmann and Zener, 1967; see chapter 7). Marital happiness for 20 university student couples, for example, was found to be positively associated with similarity of self-perception of mates (Corsini, 1956). Further evidence of the relation between similarity of values and perception of friends is found in a study in which each of 90 college women classified 100 self-referent statements in a "Q-Sort" for her self-concept, ideal self-concept, and her perception of her first- and second-best friend. The perception of each friend's personality was more similar to the ideal self-concept of the subject ($r = .42$) than to her self-concept ($r = .33$). Here the ideal self appeared to be a composite of traits valued both in the self and others (McKenna, Hoffstaetter, and O'Connor, 1956). Although it would be desirable to know the points of similarity and dissimilarity of friends' self-concepts and perceptions in each of the interpersonal and personal categories, it is not possible to carry the analysis much further from the published results of research, since few authors using a 50-to-100 item checklist give any indication of the items the list contains.

Additional studies on aspects of the relationship between interpersonal attraction and perception include Chance and Meaders, 1960; Holmes and Berkowitz, 1961; Levy, 1964; Mirels and Mills, 1964; Brewer and Brewer, 1968; Sappenfield, 1969; Hendrick and Page, 1970; De la Haye, 1972-1973; J. Hewitt, 1972; Kaplan, 1972b; Murstein and Beck, 1972; Soucar and DuCette, 1972; Adams-Webber and Benjafield, 1973.

Self-Perception[1]

Three components of the social self have been identified by Ziller (1973). He suggests that the first component consists of the relationships with significant others. Feelings of self-esteem are associated with this component. The second

---

1. Scientific interest in the field of self-perception stems from two main sources, the study of small groups and the study of cognitive processes. These two approaches are not in conflict; they basically follow different aspects, and so far they are not yet integrated into a coherent theoretical model of self-perception. The cognitive approach explores the more formal characteristics of individual information handling as determinants for the formation of cognitions about oneself. This approach leads to formulations which stand in contrast to other cognitive theories, in particular to Festinger's "theory of cognitive dissonance" (see Bem, 1965, 1967a, 1972; Bem and McConnell, 1970). The group dynamic approach to self-perception, which is of greater relevance to our topic here, follows the general and more content-oriented question of how self-perception is formed and modified under social influence.

component consists of relationships with significant categories of others, with associated feelings of social interest. The third component consists of relationships to significant groups of others, with associated feelings of marginality. Ziller reports that subjects with high self-esteem are more consistent in social participation across tasks and less neurotic. (See also Mussen and Porter, 1959; Coombs, 1969; Jacobs, Berscheid, and Walster, 1971; Richmond, Mason, and Padgett, 1972; S. C. Jones, 1973; P. H. Baron, 1974.) Subjects high on social interest have learned to expect positive reinforcement from significant others, and subjects who feel that they are marginal will avoid categorization or will take a neutral position between opposing groups. Other authors have suggested somewhat different categories for describing the components of the self (cf. Verhofstad, 1962a).

Persons who perceive themselves in the same way that they are perceived by others in their group are likely to be satisfied with the relationship (Doherty and Secord, 1971), while those who are unable to predict how they will be rated by other members of their group tend to be isolated from the group (Goslin, 1962). In discussion groups, high participators have been found to be more accurate in perceiving their position in the dominance hierarchy, whereas low participators were more accurate in perceiving their position in the liking hierarchy (Pleck, 1972).

However a person perceives himself, he is likely to try to project an image which will be acceptable to the other members of his group. Thus his self-presentation can vary from one situation to the next, and the perceptions which others have of him in each situation will vary accordingly. In one study business executives were asked to fill out a value inventory twice, first describing themselves in the standard manner and then repeating the procedure answering the items so as to portray the values they expressed in their work settings (Tagiuri and Barnett, 1968). The results indicated that an executive may behave at work so as to fit the expectations others may hold for him, either because he believes they expect him to or because he wants them to behave toward him in certain ways. The others in turn perceive him as he presents himself. Similar effects of "self-monitoring" behavior have been observed in other experimental settings, especially where the outcome of the interaction was related to the success or failure of the subject (S. C. Jones, 1968b; Schneider, 1969; Weiler and Weinstein, 1972; Snyder, 1974).

It has been suggested that the manipulation of self-presentation also extends to taking psychological tests (Cowan, 1969). For example, the "Machiavellian" is described as a cynical opportunist, manipulating and exploiting others. It may be that the low scorer on the "Mach" scale is the manipulator, for he is the individual sensitive to appropriate kinds of behavior in an experimental situation and is more skillful in presenting himself favorably. This approach to test interpretation is a reminder that taking a psychological test is also an instance of interpersonal behavior. A subject who can present himself favorably on a test may also be able to present himself favorably in other situations. This hypothesis is similar to that derived from the analysis of tests of conformity (see chapter 2), where it is found that subjects who are "yea-sayers" in that they will agree with almost any test item will also agree in other situations. Unfortunately the experimenter is left with the task of distinguishing "honest" scores on tests from those which are the result of controlled self-presentation. For example, in one study it was expected that subjects with low self-esteem scores should show an increase in liking for someone who evaluated them positively and a decrease in liking for someone who evaluated them negatively (Hewitt and Goldman, 1974). When the expected correlation did not appear, the authors looked again at the test scores. Some of the subjects with high self-esteem scores had patterns of behavior which were similar to the low scorers. They also had high scores on another test which revealed the fact that they were probably not answering the self-esteem test in an honest manner but were presenting themselves in an overly favorable light. Thus studies which report a curvilinear relationship between a measure of self-esteem and some other variable may not have sorted out the extremely high scores which are the result of a manipulated self-presentation (cf. Reese, 1961; Berger, 1973).

Self-presentation can be controlled by the amount of personal material which is disclosed to other persons. The amount of self-disclosure seems to follow the norm of reciprocity in interpersonal exchange (cf. Ehrlich and Graeven, 1971; Kahn and Rudestam, 1971; Kangas, 1971; Savicki, 1972; Certner, 1973; Derlega, Harris, and Chaikin, 1973; Pearce and Sharp, 1973; Chaikin and Derlega, 1974a). In a review of the literature Altman (1973) notes that people will reveal more or less personal information to each other depending on (1) the stage of the relationship, with more information exchanged in later stages (cf. D. A. Taylor, 1968; Jones and Gordon, 1972), (2) the level of intimacy, with more exchange among friends (cf. Cozby, 1972; Panyard, 1973; Pearce and Wiebe, 1973), (3) the degree of commitment to the relationship, and (4) personal and group composition factors. A number of experiments have been performed which support generalizations related to each of these factors, some using a "Self-disclosure Scale" developed by Jourard (1964, 1971). These studies include Altman and Haythorn, 1965; Levin and Gergen, 1969; Pedersen and Higbee, 1969; Berger and Anchor, 1970; Brein and Ryback, 1970; DeLeon, DeLeon, and Sheflin, 1970; Jourard and Resnick, 1970; Hood and Back, 1971; Janofsky, 1971; Levy and Atkins, 1971; Vondracek and Marshall, 1971; Bath and Daly, 1972; Jackson and Pepinsky, 1972; Johnson and Noonan, 1972; Lawless and Nowicki, 1972; MacDonald, Games, and Mink, 1972; MacDonald, Kessel, and Fuller, 1972; Pasternack and Van Landingham, 1972; Wiebe and Williams, 1972; Derlega, Walmer, and Furman, 1973; Knecht, Lippman, and Swap, 1973; Ryckman, Sherman, and Burgess, 1973; Sermat and Smyth, 1973; Sousa-Poza, Shulman, and Rohrberg, 1973; Taylor, Wheeler and Altman, 1973; Truax, Altmann, and Whittmer, 1973; Woodyard and Hines, 1973; Allen, 1974; Chaikin and Derlega, 1947b; Davis and Skinner, 1974; Doster and Brooks, 1974; Ellison and Firestone, 1974.

Although a subject may control the first impression he makes by revealing only selected aspects of his personality, eventually he has to act in the new situation and his actions will be evaluated by those who observe him. In general subjects will change their self-perceptions to bring them into line with the evaluations they perceive. Although subjects prefer to be evaluated positively, whatever their performance, a credible judge is liked better than a noncredible one. The research supporting these hypotheses concerning the relationship between self-perception and evaluations by others includes Deutsch and Solomon, 1959; Jones et al., 1959; Videbeck, 1960; Gerard, 1961b; Hicks, 1962; Maehr, Mensing, and Nafzger, 1962; Pilisuk, 1962; Gergen, 1965; Gergen and Wishnov, 1965; Sherwood, 1965, 1967; Johnson and Steiner, 1968; S. C. Jones, 1968a; Mettee, 1971b; Skolnick, 1971; Dutton, 1972; Eiser and Smith, 1972; Levine, Ranelli, and Valle, 1974.

Attribution of Causality

Another aspect of the initial phase of the act is the attribution of causality. When people are trying to explain behavioral events, they make inferences about the cause of the event. Kelly (1967, 1971) has sugegsted that the average individual is similar to the scientist in that both look for covariation between events when inferring cause-effect relations (cf. Gurwitz, 1973).

In a review of the literature on the attribution of intent Maselli and Altrocchi (1969) conclude that the conditions which facilitate the attribution of intent include personalism, hedonic relevance, power, intimacy, and ascription of responsibility. Attribution of intent is alternatively described as a logical process of inference from cues or as a more intuitive process based on personal knowledge of one's own intentions. Attribution of intent often contributes to a perception of the social world as more predictable and to the enactment of socially appropriate behavior, but it can also lead to behavior which is destructive to the self or others.

In a theoretical note Fishbein and Ajzen (1973) argue that research on factors influencing the attribution of responsibility has resulted in inconsistent and inconclusive findings because researchers have not sufficiently distinguished the factors of association, commission, foreseeability, justification, and intentionality. They also suggest that two dimensions must be controlled: (1) the developmental or response level, and (2) the contextual level.

When the same behavior is considered by the actor and an observer, the actor is more likely to attribute the cause of the behavior to himself, while the observer is more likely to attribute it to the situation. This is especially true if the behavior has a good outcome. If the outcome is bad, the actor is more willing to ascribe the cause to factors in the situation. For example, Kruglanski and Cohen (1973) tested the hypothesis that an actor's freedom, inferred from his act by an observer, is a function of the degree to which the act is attributed to the actor's person (rather than to the external environment). One hundred twenty-eight male 18- and 19-year-old Israeli Air Force candidates received information about a target person's predispositions and about his behavior in a specific situation, answered questions as to this person's perceived freedom, and attributed responsibility for the behavior depicted. The target person was described as writing an essay on cooperation or competition in response to a request by a social worker. Consistent with the hypothesis, greater freedom and responsibility were attributed to the target person when the act was consistent with his presumed predispositions. When the act was inconsistent with the target person's predispositions, greater freedom was assumed when it was also incongruent with the situational demands. Manipulated rationality of the act did not affect perceived freedom, but was positively related to attributed responsibility. Other studies indicate that if a group member is thought to be responsible for a negative event, his continued presence in the group will be disruptive (Shaw and Breed, 1970, 1971). Additional research comparing the perceptions of actors and observers or considering the attribution of responsibility to either the actor or the situation include Shaw, Floyd, and Gwin, 1971; Zander, Fuller, and Armstrong, 1972; Bowerman, 1973b; Deci, Benware, and Landy, 1973; Duval and Wicklund, 1973; Jones and Aronson, 1973; A. G. Miller et al., 1973; Nelson, 1973; Nisbett et al., 1973; Ruble, 1973; Storms, 1973; Williams, 1973; Wortman, Costanzo, and Witt, 1973; Harvey et al., 1974; Regan, Straus, and Fazio, 1974; Worchel et al., 1974.

When an accident occurs, observers are more likely to attribute responsibility to the actor if the accident is severe than if it is a "happy accident" which has a fortunate outcome. Observers are also likely to use "defensive" attributions to ward off future blame or harm. (See Vidmar and Crinklaw, 1974, for a review of research.) One example of the research on accidents is the study by Chaikin and Darley (1973) entitled "Victim or Perpetrator?: Defensive Attribution of Responsibility and the Need for Order and Justice." The authors presented a video-tape of a two-person experimental group working on a task to 40 male under-graduates. On the tape, an accident occurred, initiated by one person, which had negative consequences for the other person. Stacks of blocks were knocked over, thus spoiling a decoding task. The experimental instructions made the conse-quences either mild or severe. Cross-cutting this variable, either the victim or the perpetrator was made situationally relevant for the witnessing subject. The wit-ness was told that he would later work on the same experimental task and take either the role of the accident perpetrator or the victim. The results of the experi-ment indicated that perpetrator-relevant subjects attributed the causes for the ac-cident to avoid future blame for themselves, while victim-relevant subjects acted to avoid future harm. The more severe the consequences, the less responsibility attributed to chance. Perpetrator-relevant subjects, but not victim-relevant subjects, derogated the victim of a severe accident. The authors suggest that these findings are relevant to the hypotheses of "defensive attribution" and a "just world." Addi-tional research concerning accidents and attribution includes Shaw and Skolnick, 1970; McKillip and Posavac, 1972; McMartin and Shaw, 1972; Shaw, 1972a; Schiavo, 1973; Wortman and Linder, 1973; Sosis, 1974; Worchel and Andreoli, 1974.

If a person seeks help, the responsibility the observer attributes to him for his condition is relevant to whether or not help will be given. If, for example, a help-less person seems to be getting what he deserves, then an observer is less likely to render aid. The research on helping behavior is reviewed in chapter 11. Some articles which focus on the role of the attribution process in mediating helping behavior include Horowitz, 1968b; Schopler and Thompson, 1968; Thompson, Stroebe, and Schopler, 1971; Grant, 1973.

Additional studies on various aspects of attribution theory include Eiser and Stroebe, 1972; Goethals, 1972; Kilty, 1972; Schopler and Layton, 1972; Touhey, 1972c; Zuckerman, 1972; Albert, 1973; Allen, 1973; Blumstein, 1973b; Busse and Love, 1973; Chaikin and Cooper, 1973; Peevers and Secord, 1973; Reisman and Schopler, 1973; Rule and Duker, 1973; Zemore and Greenough, 1973; Ajzen and Fishbein, 1974; Costanzo, Grumet, and Brehm, 1974; Hochberg and Galper, 1974; Newtson, 1974; Zadny and Gerard, 1974.

Changing Perception through Interaction

Evidence for both the consistency and change of perception as a result of in-teraction between two individuals has been presented in the literature (Cronbach, 1955). On the one hand, research on the importance of "first impressions" indi-cates that judgments of persons once formed are slow to change; on the other hand, research on friendship suggests that the longer two individuals know each other and the more intimate their interaction, the greater will be the accuracy of their interpersonal perceptions (Bieri, 1953). When changes in perception do occur, it is quite likely that the subjects are trying to restore some "balance" in their perceptual field by reducing some form of "cognitive dissonance" (cf. Davis and Jones, 1960).

Since individuals may or may not increase their perceptual accuracy as a result of interaction, further evidence must be presented to enable one to predict the conditions under which increased accuracy of perception occurs. It might be expected, for example, that persons with high test scores on insight or empathy would increase their accuracy more than those with low scores. However, in one study, after 30 minutes of interaction in 12-man, leaderless discussion groups, subjects with high empathy scores were not able to estimate the way in which one member's personality traits would be viewed by the other members any more effectively than low scorers (Bell and Stolper, 1955).

Whether or not the subject focuses attention on himself or the other person does seem to make a difference, since in one experiment paired interaction increased the accuracy of a member's prediction of another's values if he focused attention on the other person, but changed the prediction toward his own values and away from those of his partner when he focused attention on himself (Lundy, 1956a). It appears that any form of interaction which requires the subject to actively focus on the other person, including reversing roles with him, is likely to increase perceptual accuracy (Johnson, 1970; Summers, Taliaferro, and Fletcher, 1970; Dowdle, 1973). This fact may help explain why subjects who cooperate in a group or who have a high interaction rate perceive more similarity between themselves and the other members after the group activity than subjects who are in competition or had a lower interaction rate (Rosenbaum, 1959; Stotland, Cottrell, and Laing, 1960).

Apparently close contact on a work basis does not increase the accuracy of perception to the same extent as interaction on a basis of friendship. For example, a female psychologist was asked to describe, using a "Q-Sort," her typical interactive behavior with her professional associates at work and with some friends known in other situations. Her descriptions were then compared with the descriptions of the same interactions by each of the other persons involved. Her descriptions of interactions with friends known off the job were found to agree more with their own descriptions than did her descriptions of interactions with professional associates (Block and Bennett, 1955). In another example of the relation between intimacy and perception, married couples were found to make more accurate predictions of each other's responses than couples who were dating (Kirkpatrick and Hobart, 1954). When changes in accuracy of perception do occur as a result of increased communication or intimacy between the members of a pair, the changes can be expected to be more pronounced if the members initially have the same underlying attitudes (Runkel, 1956).

In addition to changing his perception as a result of increased knowledge of the typical behavior of the other person, the subject also changes his perceptions as a result of his own reactions to the other person. For example, in discussion groups, members who were seen as being influential were assigned desirable personality traits (Perlmutter, 1954), presumably because the group members wished to feel that they were being influenced by worthy persons.

In a similar fashion, a subject in a hypothetical interpersonal situation (i.e., one in which he was asked to give the most probable responses of an actor in a series of fictitious incidents in which the actor was criticized) was more likely to change his negative reaction to a positive one following a criticism if he was then told that the criticism was intended for his own good (Pepitone and Sherberg, 1957).

On the other hand, if one member fails to contribute to the group task or makes things more difficult for the other members, he may then be perceived as having less desirable personality traits (Harvey, Kelley, and Shapiro, 1957; Jones and de Charms, 1957; Steiner and Dodge, 1957). The perception of certain behavior as undesirable can, in turn, become more favorable if the original behavior is compared with behavior which is even more undesirable (E. Cohen, 1957a).

Initial perceptions can also change as a result of the ways in which other members appear to be affected by the subject. Subjects who "won over" two role players to their point of view after a discussion thought that the role player who was presumed to have the higher status was probably convinced by the logic of their arguments, while a role player with lower status than the subject was presumed to have been coerced into changing his opinion (Thibaut and Riecken, 1955b).

Once an individual has established himself in a high-status position, his performance may be overvalued by other group members when his group is in competition with another group. In one experiment, college women who were members of 16 campus cliques containing a total of 74 individuals were selected from a larger population because they represented four pairs of friendly and four pairs of antagonistic groups. Members of each group were first asked to list city names while listening to a distracting tape recording, and then to estimate the number of names written by each subject as her list was flashed on a screen. This task was performed once while only members of the same clique were present, and once in the presence of a friendly or antagonistic clique. In each case, subjects overestimated the performances of the members of their own clique. The performances of members with high leadership status were overestimated more than those of members with low leadership status. This was especially true in the presence of an antagonistic outgroup. Furthermore, the performance of the antagonistic outgroup was greatly underestimated (Harvey, 1956).

Group experiences which are specially designed to provide "sensitivity training" are found to facilitate personal growth, which in turn results in changes in the perception of oneself and others. As a result of encounter experiences subjects are generally found to be more positive about themselves and others (Burke and Bennis, 1961; Foulds, 1971b, 1973; Hewitt and Kraft, 1973; Jacobs et al., 1973a; see also appendix 4).

Perception and Adjustment

Although it might be supposed that the person with the greatest insight should be able to make the best adjustment to the group, the evidence to support this generalization is not clear. Some studies suggest a positive relationship between adjustment and the ability to estimate one's own position as seen by the group (Green, 1948), as well as the tendency to be more accurate in the perception of others (Gage, 1953; Baker and Sarbin, 1956; Bach, 1973). Other studies report no correlation between insight and effectiveness in interpersonal relations (Lemann and Solomon, 1952; Gage and Exline, 1953).

These conflicting findings may indicate that insight or accuracy of perception is a necessary but not sufficient condition for effectiveness, since some deviant members may be well aware of their position in the group and yet be unable to get along well with the other group members. Steiner (1955) has suggested that accurate social perception should promote "interpersonal competence" and group efficiency if (1) the group members are motivated to cooperate, (2) the accurately perceived qualities are relevant to the activities of the group, (3) members are free to alter their own behaviors in response to their perceptions of other members, (4) the behavioral changes which are a consequence of accurate social perception are the kinds which produce a more thoroughly integrated system.

Whenever any one or more of these conditions is not met, accurate social perception will not affect adjustment to the group.

In cases in which perceptual accuracy and level of adjustment are related, changes in the individual's level of adjustment brought about by therapy can be expected to change his perceptions (and vice versa; Butler, 1952). For example, 21 patients who received counseling were given projective tests before and after therapy. In these tests the patients' own self-descriptions were found to be less loaded with feeling after therapy (Dymond, Seeman, and Grummon, 1956).

Leader's Perception

The same factors which affect the perceptions of the average group member also operate on the perceptions of the leader. In addition, since the leader is in the center of the communication net and is usually selected or arises because of his ability to put himself in the place of others (Mead, 1950; Bell and Hall, 1954), his perceptions of others tend to be more accurate than those of the average member (Trapp, 1955), although it has been suggested that some of this apparent superiority may be a statistical artifact (Campbell, 1955). As evidence of the superior perceptual accuracy of leaders, school teachers were found to perceive accurately the choice structure of their classes (Gronlund, 1956a), and teachers who were the most accurate in perceiving the structure of the classroom also perceived accurately the structure of their own peer group of teachers (Gronlund, 1956b). The leader, on the other hand, may be more favorable in his self-perceptions than he appears to other members of the group (Gebel, 1954).

As a result of his favored position, the leader is usually superior to nonleaders and isolates in his ability to judge group opinion on issues which are relevant to the group's activity (Chowdhry and Newcomb, 1952; Exline, 1960b). However, if all members of the group actually share the same opinion on an issue and there is a high rate of interaction among group members, the difference in perception between leaders and nonleaders may not appear (Hites and Campbell, 1950). Further, with groups of children in a summer camp, no relationship between leadership and ability to predict attitudes of others was found (Cohn, Fisher, and Brown, 1961).

The importance of being in the center of the communication net for accurate perception is demonstrated by evidence from studies in which communication between all members is maximized either because the groups are small (Travers, 1941) or because the members have known each other longer. In these cases, all members may be able to predict group opinion or group structure more accurately than members of groups with less effective communication (Greer, Galanter, and Nordlie, 1954), although one study of highschool students in discussion groups of 14 to 16 members revealed that estimates of group opinion on certain issues were no more accurate after discussion than they were without discussion (Stone and Kamiya, 1957).

In the previous discussion of perceptual accuracy and adjustment, the average individual's social adjustment was not found to be clearly related to his perceptual ability. Nevertheless, leaders who are more discriminating in their social perception are apparently better able to organize group activity. The most preferred co-worker chosen by members of winning highschool basketball teams and highly rated college surveying teams was found to be the one who in turn perceived his preferred and rejected co-workers as differing and perceived little similarity between himself and his co-workers (Fiedler, Hartmann, and Rudin, 1952; Fiedler, 1953a, 1954a). Since subjects tend to perceive those they like as similar to themselves, Fiedler concludes that the member who differentiates in his perceptions of other group members is also the one who maintains enough emotional distance from others and has enough task orientation to make him an effective team leader (Fiedler, 1953b, 1958). Similar findings have been reported with bomber crews and tank crews in the armed forces (Fiedler, 1954b, 1955, 1960).[2] An elaboration of this model to include situational determinants is discussed in chapter 13 on leadership.

This positive association between the ability to influence and perceptual accuracy is also evident in the study of a 17-man training group. Members whose perceptions were accurate in that their judgments of the power of others agreed with the average group judgment were considered effective by observers and valuable and powerful by the other group members (Smith, Jaffe, & Livingston, 1955).

The results of any attempt to change the perceptions of leaders can be expected to vary with the personality of the leader and the situation in which he finds himself. In one experiment, 22 leaders of youth groups were given a course designed to increase their perceptions of causal factors in behavior. By the end of the course, leaders who tended to project blame on others and who led informal groups, and leaders who tended to blame themselves and who led formal, clearly structured groups, showed changes in the expected direction by being more aware of causal factors in behavior. However, leaders with the opposite type of group placement (i.e., extrapunitive leaders in formal groups and intrapunitive leaders in informal groups) showed some undesirable changes in modes of perceiving members' behavior. These undesirable changes consisted of either an increase or no change in the number of perceptions distorted by judgments of blame and a decrease or no change in perceptions which were accompanied by questions about the cause of the behavior (Maas, 1950).

Additional research comparing perceptions of low- and high-status persons includes Gallo and McClintock, 1962; Sabath, 1964; Frey and Newtson, 1973; Rump and Delin, 1973.

From Perception to Action

After the individual has *observed* the elements in the situation and perceived the similarities and differences in the other group members, he next formulates some *hypotheses* about behavior appropriate to the situation. After pretesting the hypotheses in imagined behavior, he *proposes action*. Since only the action which follows the final step in the social act is open to public observation, the existence of the other steps is generally inferred. Responses to a person who appears to deviate from the group norm differ from responses to those who appear to conform (Schachter, 1951). Forms of address and behavior which are used for social

2. Steiner and McDiarmid (1957) suggest that Fiedler's Assumed Similarity Score can be broken into two components: (1) the perceived discrepancy between the overall "goodness" of the traits possessed by the two co-workers, and (2) the perceived dissimilarity between the patterns of traits possessed by the two co-workers. Foa (1958c) notes that variables such as assumed similarity, empathy, and conformity will be correlated if they are composed of similar "facets," e.g., actor, observer, level, and alias.

equals differ from those used with inferiors and superiors (Maas, 1954b; Zander and Cohen, 1955). Women talk to women about things different from those that men talk to men about (Landis and Burtt, 1924).

A further example of differences in the content of interaction which may follow from differences in the social characteristics of the members of the interacting pair is found in an analysis of the paired interaction of teachers and children, parents and teachers, and parents and children. Teachers were most interested in friendliness in all the relationships. Power and control were paramount in both the teacher-student and parent-child relations, while parents, teachers, and children all shared an interest in extracurricular activities. However, these similarities and differences in interaction content were generally not perceived by the subjects (Jenkins and Lippitt, 1951).

Many more examples of this type appear in chapters 8 and 9 on personality and social characteristics.

Clear, organized perceptions seem to provide a basis for more assertive action. In an experimental study, discussion groups composed of five to eight subjects who perceived clear boundaries for objects on Rorschach cards were compared with groups composed of subjects who did not perceive clear boundaries. The subjects who were found to be high in boundary perception were also found to be more assertive, more self-initiating, and more achievement-oriented, and to talk more in the leaderless discussion groups. In the groups composed of subjects who saw fewer clearly defined objects, the interaction rate was slower. The members tended to sit back and wait for the emergence of a leader who would then organize things for them (Cleveland and Fisher, 1957).

On the basis of the initial definition of the situation the individual member may also posit a goal for interaction which influences his behavior for several acts. This initial goal will be held for a period of time even in the face of evidence that the goal is unobtainable. For example, one can infer that in the experiment performed by Asch (1952) the subject first organizes his behavior to conform to the goal set by the experimenter, to make correct visual judgments. The subject then finds that this goal is untenable if he is to maintain his perception of himself as an adequate (and conforming) group member and so posits a new goal of taking the group judgment into account.

The goal for interaction has the greatest effect when the subject is "self-conscious" and rehearses each act carefully before carrying it out. The goal changes more rapidly when he acts "off the top of his head" and responds more directly to present stimuli. The goal is much more likely to persist if it is shared with other group members and becomes a group norm.

The goal of behavior in a group can be primarily individual in response to some self-oriented need (Fouriezos et al., 1950), a goal for which members compete with each other, or a goal which can only be reached through mutual cooperation. In each case the individual would be sensitive to different aspects of the behavior of the other group members, such as emotional rather than task response, if the goal is self-oriented, behavior that would block efforts to reach the goal if he is in competition, or behavior that moves the whole group toward the goal if he is cooperating.

The relative importance of social goals and individual physical needs is illustrated by a study of frustration in adult subjects. Experimenters were more successful in frustrating subjects by preventing them from fulfilling group expectations and goals than by depriving them of food (Lindzey and Riecken, 1951).

Summary

The "first impression" which one member forms of another is found to be an important factor in *perception*, since it tends to color subsequent perceptions of behavior. However, the more intimate the interaction becomes, the more accurate will the perception of others be; e.g., friends are more accurate in their perceptions of each other than nonfriends.

Groups provide a basis for perception by providing a set of *attitudes* which are passed on to their members. The attitudes which are most resistant to change are *stereotypes*, group prejudgments of classes of persons.

Group leaders tend to be more accurate in their perceptions of other members and of the structure and norms of the group. The accuracy of other members is increased if they can share the leaders' central position in the communication net or if the group is very homogeneous in traits or opinions. The average member's perceptual accuracy is not clearly related to his adjustment in the group.

An individual who perceives himself as others do is likely to be satisfied with his relationships, especially if he has high self-esteem. In a new group he will usually try to project an image that will be acceptable to the other members of the group and will reveal more or less personal information depending upon the level of his involvement in the relationship.

In the attribution of causality for a behavioral event a subject is more likely to attribute the cause to himself if there is a good outcome, while an observer is more likely to attribute the cause to the situation. However, if a severe accident occurs the observers are more likely to attribute it to the actor and a "happy accident" to the situation. Persons seeking help are given less if they are judged to be responsible for their condition.

Additional References

Some articles which discuss methodological problems in person perception include Bass and Fiedler, 1961; Beach and Wertheimer, 1961; O'Connor, 1963; Todd and Rappoport, 1964; Fancher, 1969.

Finally, articles on aspects of person perception which do not fit easily under any of the topics considered in this chapter include Fiedler, Hutchins, and Dodge, 1959; Mann and Mann, 1959a; Altman and McGinnies, 1960; Iwashita, 1961; Jones, Davis, and Gergen, 1961; Fishbein, 1963; Heiss, 1963; Smith, Pedersen, and Lewis, 1966; Tuckman, 1966; Bem, 1967b; Fox, 1967; Kerckhoff and Bean, 1967; De Soto, Henley, and London, 1968; Ferneau, 1968; Hayes, Meltzer, and Bouma, 1968; Miller, 1968; O'Neal and Mills, 1969; Thayer and Schiff, 1969; Welkowitz and Feldstein, 1969; Lumsden, 1970; Mills and O'Neal, 1971; Brown, Strong, and Rencher, 1972; Gerard et al., 1972; Jones and Young, 1972; Woodyard, 1972; D'Augelli, 1973b; Dmitruk, Collins, and Clinger, 1973; Jacobs et al., 1973b; Kenny and Fletcher, 1973; Misovich, Colby, and Welch, 1973; Pellegrini, 1973; Peterson, 1973; Sewell, 1973; Archer, 1974; Canter, West, and Wools, 1974; Edwards and McWilliams, 1974; Lemon and Warren, 1974; Lindskold et al., 1974; Orpen and Bush, 1974; Schiffenbauer, 1974b; Warr, 1974.

Chapter 6

ROLES

As GROUPS GROW IN size and complexity, individuals tend to specialize in some aspect of the interaction process. The expectations for behavior in these specialities are represented by the roles of the group members. The development of the informal structure and some of the problems which arise from conflicting role expectations are considered in more detail in this chapter.

Role: A Set of Expectations

There is a role which goes with the informal position of the best-liked person in a group just as there is a role which goes with the formal position of foreman of a shop crew. In each case the term *role* refers to the set of expectations which group members share concerning the behavior of a person who occupies a given position in the group (F. L. Bates, 1956; Bates and Cloyd, 1956; Gross, Mason, and McEachern, 1958; Levinson, 1959; Southall, 1959).[1] The actual behavior of a person occupying a position in a group remains as something to be understood in terms of the expectations which are imposed from without and the tendencies of his personality which express themselves from within.

Roles in discussion groups which are the focus of much of the research on groups are usually not fixed. Any aspect of an individual's behavior that is initially an expression of his personality can come to be expected by other group members and thus become part of his role. In general the dimensions of role are the same as the dimensions of interaction and personality (see chapters 3 and 8).

Some evidence that behavior in a roles does not always agree with the expectations for that role is reported in two studies of the relationship between the ideologies of aircraft commanders and educational administrators and their actual behavior (Halpin, 1955a, 1955b). In these studies the "ideology" of the subject represents his perception of the expectations for his role, since each subject had been asked to indicate how he believed he should behave as a leader. Ratings of the actual behavior of the aircraft commanders and administrators were made by their subordinates.

In one study, the behavior of commanders of 10- to 11-man aircraft crews in the categories of "initiating group structure" and "consideration" as rated by mem-

1. Although some authors use the term *role* to refer to the behavior which an individual directs toward fulfilling expectations (Newcomb, 1950; Sarbin, 1954), in this text the term *role* is used to refer only to the expectations associated with a position in a group.

bers of their crews was found to be lower on the average than the "'ideology" of the commanders. Thus it is apparent that the commanders did not live up to the expectations for their roles. In addition, the ideology of the commanders was not correlated with their rated performance, an indication that knowledge of expectations alone may not be enough to predict behavior. In the other study, the educational administrators showed greater "consideration" and less "initiating structure" than aircraft commanders in both ideology and behavior, an indication of differences in the expectations for the two roles. As before, however, there was only a low correlation between real and ideal behavior.

The expectations for a role may be formalized in laws, such as those which outline the rights and duties of the President of the United States; they may be less formal but generally agreed-on regulations, such as Robert's Rules of Order, which outline appropriate behavior for a good committee chairman; or they may exist in a group without any overt awareness on the part of the members. However, moving down toward the informal end of the scale, one would eventually reach a point where the concept of role would not be useful. In a case where a person actually carried out the same type of behavior meeting after meeting but where the other group members did not have any expectations about this person because of his regular behavior, the term *role* would not be applied.

Individuals vary in their ability to play a given role (Sarbin and Jones, 1955). The expectations for a role are met most easily by the individual whose personality fits the role (Rapoport and Rosow, 1957). The first person to occupy a new position in a group has the opportunity to create a role which is most compatible with his own personality. If his personality traits are somewhat unique, the group may never by able to fill the role satisfactorily again after he leaves the group.

Some of the consequences for a group if a member does not fulfill his role expectations are illustrated in a study of the effects of clear and unclear role expectations on group productivity and defensiveness. College students played the game of Twenty Questions in groups of five members. Each group contained two confederates who remained silent throughout the game. When the silence on the part of these two members was unanticipated, the productivity and satisfaction of the other participants decreased and their defensiveness increased. However, the groups did better if the silent subjects announced that they would remain silent before the experiment began, thus altering the expectations for their roles in the group (E. E. Smith, 1957).

Additional articles which provide a review of role theory, suggest mathematical models, or give case materials which illustrate general propositions include Borgatta, 1960b; Znamierowski, 1960; Anderson, 1962; Arsenian, Semrad, and Shapiro, 1962; Gruen, 1962; Oeser and Harary, 1962; Ramsoy, 1963; Oeser and Harary, 1964; Jackson and McGehee, 1965; Oeser and O'Brien, 1967; Stebbins, 1967; Hage and Marwell, 1968; Sarbin and Allen, 1968b; Sampson, 1969; Marwell and Hage, 1970; Zurcher, 1970; Janoušek, 1971; Miller, 1971; Szmatka, 1974.

A Paradigm for Role Analysis

The content of role expectations can be visualized along the two axes in figure 27. The behavior expected from others to the self and by the self to others can, in each case, extend from that which is *required* to that which is *prohibited*.[2] As

2. The *rights* and *duties* of the person occupying the position are often stressed in the literature (Sarbin, 1954). In the present formulation, the *rights* include those behaviors which others

Figure 27. Paradigm for Role Analysis in the Control Area

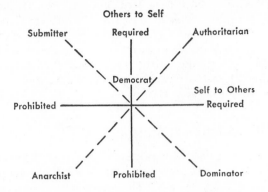

indicated in chapter 1, these expectations include both the form and content of interaction. To some extent there are also expectations for the personal characteristics of the individual who will fill the role.

The central tendency of the expectations for a role in each area could be indicated by a point to which behavior in that area is required or prohibited along each axis. Some typical roles in the control area would be those of the "authoritarian" who is required to control and be controlled, the "anarchist" who neither controls nor is controlled, the "dominator" who is required to control and cannot be controlled, and the "submitter" who is required to be controlled but cannot control. The "democrat" would appear in the middle of the figure as one who is required to control or be controlled as the occasion demands.

In addition to these expectations for the content of interaction, a role can be seen as also including expectations for the frequency and duration (i.e., pattern) of interaction and the communication network involved for both output and input in each of the content areas. To continue the example in the control area, the expectations for the behavior of self to others would include a specified degree of control, carried out with a given frequency and duration, to specified group members. In the same way the control of the self by others would have a given interaction pattern, emanating from given members of the group.

Although this method of delineating the expectations for a role may prove too complex to be used in its complete form, it may prove relevant for some research problems. For example, one might wish to distinguish a role which required an individual to interact in a controlling way frequently but for a short duration, from one in which the individual was expected to act with the same degree of control infrequently but over a longer period of time. Or, in another case, two roles might be equal in power and similar in interaction pattern, and yet different in that an individual in one role might control only one other person, while in the other role he might control a dozen persons. Similar variations might occur in the interaction patterns and communication networks which govern the control of the self by others.

are expected to direct toward the individual, and the *duties* include those behaviors which the individual is expected to direct toward others. Roles tend to be reciprocal, so that the "rights" of one role are the "duties" of another (F. L. Bates, 1957).

The concept of role as it is used in the literature does not generally involve all of the aspects of behavior which have been suggested here. Rather, each author tends to limit his description of role to some aspects which are particularly relevant to his experiment. In some cases the subject's position in a communication network (e.g., central person, member, or isolate) is seen as the most important aspect of the role, in others his position in the typical interaction or pattern (e.g., the person who talks most), and in others his position in the content area (e.g., task leader versus social-emotional leader).

Development of the Informal Structure

Perhaps the clearest distinction between a *collection* of individuals of the sort one might find sitting in the last seven seats on a commuter train and a bona fide group is that the group has a structure.[3] The collection of people on the train may have common activities, such as reading the paper or getting off at the same station, but this activity would be described as elementary collective behavior and not as evidence of a functioning group.

The studies which deal with the development of the informal structure in the group tend to focus on the network of positions, rather than on the roles or expectations for behavior which go with the positions. In many of these studies the researcher is concerned with development of the simplest type of network, the straight-line hierarchy, in which a subject's position is operationally defined by the sum of the ratings he receives on some criterion. In laboratory experiments, when the experimenter leaves the members to their own devices in developing a structure, the group is referred to as an "initially leaderless group." In other cases, roles are assigned by the experimenter before the group begins its task or are developed in response to the leader's style. In most large organizations and in many types of small group, a formal structure, a set of "official" positions, incorporates the accepted division of labor for the group's task. Other "unofficial" positions make up the informal structure.

All aspects of the work situation, including the formal structure, influence the development of the informal structure (Roesthlisberger and Dickson, 1939). In some groups the formal structure and informal structure may be the same. This would be especially true in clubs which developed first on an informal basis and were later formalized. In either case, the structure tends to develop around the leader (Freud, 1949), or some other type of central person, such as the tyrant, idol, or scapegoat (Redl, 1942). The relationship of the group structure to the type of central person will be discussed in chapter 13.

The attempts of children to establish a hierarchy (Hanfmann, 1935) are perhaps more apparent than those of college-age students, who characteristically wait until the second meeting of a laboratory discussion group before launching their struggle for status.[4] The greater the agreement among members concerning

3. Blau (1957) sees the "structure" of a group as the network of interpersonal choice. He defines the "structural dimension" as "a network of social relations between individuals which finds expression in their interaction." The expectations for behavior appear in what he refers to as the "organizational dimension," which includes "relationships between personnel, policies, supervisory practices, and interaction among workers."

4. Some authors use the term *status* to refer to the rank of a group member on some criterion. Although *status* is often synonymous with *position* in everyday usage, the term seems to be associated with a less well-defined set of expectations than the term *position*. In the text the original author's usage has usually been adopted.

the potential status of individuals in an initially leaderless group, the less time it will take to solve the status problem. Some groups never solve the problem to everyone's satisfaction, i.e., never develop perfect consensus with respect to the ranking system. Groups with low status consensus go throught repeated crises. After they have passed through such crises, the men who come out on top in the groups where their status is recognized spend less and less time in interaction in attempts to gain and maintain a position of high rank.

Over a series of meetings in five-man discussion groups where agreement on status was high, the top three men shifted positions, while the men who ranked fourth and fifth in status tended to maintain their positions. In other words, once a man found himself in fourth or fifth position, he was likely to stay there. However, in the five-man groups which were low in their initial status consensus, there were more shifts in position over time and the shifts involved men at all levels in the hierarchy (Heinicke and Bales, 1953).

These shifts of position are most evident in experimental groups or in groups in which the informal structure is not reinforced by a formal structure. If the power differences between members are obvious and firmly fixed from the start, the positions of the top men are less likely to be challenged by those down the line (Crockett, 1955). However, poker players try to bluff and beat the strongest player (Riddle, 1925), and players in a three-man game in which members are given an initially unequal point advantage tend to break up into a coalition of the two low-point men trying to unseat the high-point man (Hoffman, Festinger, and Lawrence, 1954). This tendency for the two-man coalition to attack the high-power person or to withstand attack from a low-power person is seen as a basic structural type in the three-person group (Simmel, 1902; Mills, 1953).

In most discussion groups in which members have approximately equal amounts of information and no one holds more cards or points at the outset, the leadership rank is established by the relative amount of talking of each member. The person who talks the most generally wins most of the decisions and becomes the leader (Bales, 1953; Strodtbeck, 1954a; March, 1956; Shaw, and Gilchrist, 1956; Bass et al., 1958; Riecken, 1958; Kirscht, Lodahl, and Haire, 1959).

Street Corner Society

Whyte's study of gangs of corner boys in an Italian urban area of Boston provides many examples of the development and maintenance of an informal structure in a group (1943). In the final chapter of his book, Whyte summarizes his impressions of the typical gang structure,[5] with illustrations taken from his study of a gang called the "Nortons," led by "Doc":

The corner-gang structure arises out of the habitual association of the members over a long period of time. The nuclei of most gangs can be traced back to early boyhood, when living close together provided the first opportunities for social contacts. School years modified the original pattern somewhat, but I know of no corner gangs which arose through classroom or school-playground association. The gangs grew up

---

5. William F. Whyte, *Street Corner Society: The Social Structure of an Italian Slum* (Chicago: University of Chicago Press, 1943), pp. 255–263. Copyright 1943 by The University of Chicago. All rights reserved. Reprinted by permission of the author and the publisher.

on the corner and remained there with remarkable persistence from early boyhood until the members reached their late twenties or thirties. In the course of years some groups were broken up by the movement of families away from Cornerville, and the remaining members merged with gangs on nearby corners; but frequently movement out of the district does not take the corner boy away from his corner. On any evening on almost any corner one finds corner boys who have come in from other parts of the city or from suburbs to be with their old friends. The residence of the corner boy may also change within the district, but nearly always he retains his allegiance to his original corner.

Home plays a very small role in the group activities of the corner boy. Except when he eats, sleeps, or is sick, he is rarely at home, and his friends always go to his corner first when they want to find him. Even the corner boy's name indicates the dominant importance of the gang in his activities. It is possible to associate with a group of men for months and never discover the family names of more than a few of them. Most are known by nicknames attached to them by the group. Furthermore, it is easy to overlook the distinction between married and single men. The married man regularly sets aside one evening a week to take out his wife. There are other occasions when they go out together and entertain together, and some corner boys devote more attention to their wives than others, but, married or single, the corner boy can be found on his corner almost every night of the week.

His social activities away from the corner are organized with similar regularity. Many corner gangs set aside the same night each week for some special activity, such as bowling. With the Nortons this habit was so strong that it persisted for some of the members long after the original group had broken up.

Most groups have a regular evening meeting-place aside from the corner. Nearly every night at about the same time the gang gathers for "coffee-and" in its favorite cafeteria or for beer in the corner tavern. When some other activity occupies the evening, the boys meet at the cafeteria or tavern before returning to the corner or going home. Positions at the tables are fixed by custom. Night after night each group gathers around the same tables. The right to these positions is recognized by other Cornerville groups. When strangers are found at the accustomed places, the necessity of finding other chairs is a matter of some annoyance, especially if no nearby location is available. However, most groups gather after nine in the evening when few are present except the regular customers who are familiar with the established procedure.

The life of the corner boy proceeds along regular and narrowly circumscribed channels. As Doc said to me: "Fellows around here don't know what to do except within a radius of about three hundred yards. That's the truth, Bill. They come home from work, hang on the corner, go up to eat, back on the corner, up a show, and they come back to hang on the corner. If they're not on the corner, it's likely the boys there will know where you can find them. Most of them stick to one corner. It's only rarely that a fellow will change his corner."

The stable composition of the group and the lack of social assurance on the part of its members contribute toward producing a very high rate of social interaction within the group. The group structure is a product of these interactions (see figure 28).

Out of such interaction there arises a system of mutual obligations which is fundamental to group cohesion. If the men are to carry on their activities as a unit, there are many occasions when they must do favors for one another. The code of the corner boy requires him to help his friends when he can and to refrain from doing anything to harm them. When life in the group runs smoothly, the obligations binding members to one another are not explicitly recognized. Once Doc asked me to do something for him, and I said that I welcomed the chance to reciprocate. He objected: "I don't want it that way. I want you to do this for me because you're my friend. That's all."

Figure 28. The Nortons, Spring and Summer, 1937

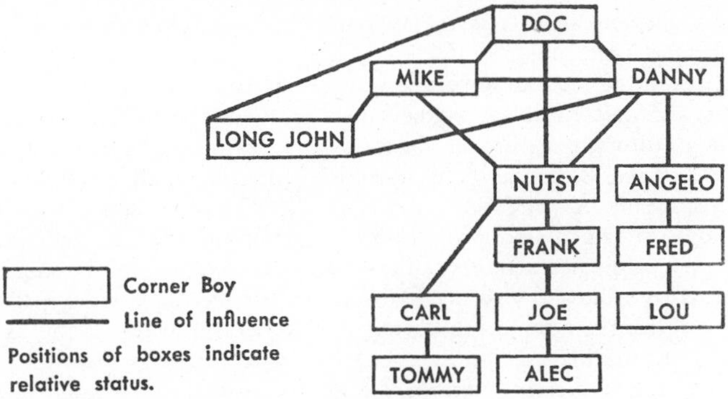

Corner Boy
Line of Influence
Positions of boxes indicate
relative status.

It is only when the relationship breaks down that the underlying obligations are brought to light. While Alec and Frank were friends, I never heard either one of them discuss the services he was performing for the other, but when they had a falling-out over the group activities with the Aphrodite Club, each man complained to Doc that the other was not acting as he should in view of the services that had been done him. In other words, actions which were performed explicitly for the sake of friendship were revealed as being part of a system of mutual obligations.

Not all the corner boys live up to their obligations equally well, and this factor partly accounts for the differentiation in status among them. The man with a low status may violate his obligations without much change in his position. His fellows know that he has failed to discharge certain obligations in the past, and his position reflects his past performances. On the other hand, the leader is depended upon by all the members to meet his personal obligations. He cannot fail to do so without causing confusion and endangering his position.

The relationship of status to the system of mutual obligations is most clearly revealed when one observes the use of money.

Doc did not hesitate to accept money from Danny, but he avoided taking any from the followers. The leader spends more money on his followers than they on him. The farther down in the structure one looks, the fewer are the financial relations which tend to obligate the leader to a follower. This does not mean that the leader has more money than others or even that he necessarily spends more—though he must always be a free spender. It means that the financial relations must be explained in social terms. Unconsciously, and in some cases consciously, the leader refrains from putting himself under obligations to those with low status in the group.

The leader does not deal with his followers as an undifferentiated group. Doc explained: "On any corner you would find not only a leader but probably a couple of lieutenants. They could be leaders themselves, but they let the man lead them. You would say, 'They let him lead because they like the way he does things.' Sure, but he leans upon them for his authority. Many times you find fellows on a corner that stay in the background until some situation comes up, and then they will take over and call the shots. Things like that can change fast sometimes."

The leader mobilizes the group by dealing first with his lieutenants.

The leadership is changed not through an uprising of the bottom men but by a shift in the relations between men at the top of the structure. When a gang breaks into two parts, the explanation is to be found in a conflict between the leader and one of his former lieutenants.

This discussion should not give the impression that the leader is the only man who proposes a course of action. Other men frequently have ideas, but their suggestions must go through the proper channels if they are to go into effect.

The actions of the leader can be characterized in terms of the origination of action in pair and set events. A pair event is one which takes place between two people. A set event is one in which one man originates action for two or more others. The leader frequently originates action for the group without waiting for the suggestions of his followers. A follower may originate action for the leader in a pair event, but he does not originate action for the leader and other followers at the same time— that is, he does not originate action in a set event which includes the leader. Of course, when the leader is not present, parts of the group are mobilized when men lower in the structure originate action in set events. It is through observation of such set events when the top men are not present that it is possible to determine the relative positions of the men who are neither leaders nor lieutenants.

Each member of the corner gang has his own position in the gang structure. Although the positions may remain unchanged over long periods of time, they should not be conceived in static terms. To have a position means that the individual has a customary way of interacting with other members of the group. When the pattern of interactions changes, the positions change. The positions of the members are inter-dependent, and one position cannot change without causing some adjustments in the other positions. Since the group is organized around the men with the top positions, some of the men with low standing may change positions or drop out without up-setting the balance of the group. For example, when Lou Danaro and Fred Mackey stopped participating in the activities of the Nortons, those activities continued to be organized in much the same manner as before, but when Doc and Danny dropped out, the Nortons disintegrated, and the patterns of interaction had to be reorganized along different lines.

Fluctuations in Organization

Since groups which are well organized are usually the most productive (French, 1941; Darley, Gross, and Martin, 1952), any movement of members from one position to another within the role structure or any discrepancies in the criteria for establishing status in the group, such as age and pay, result in more activity in the social-emotional area in an attempt to re-establish the structure or resolve the differences with a consequent decrease in productivity (Adams, 1953; Heinicke and Bales, 1953; Bales and Slater, 1955; Shepherd and Weschler, 1955; Bales and Slater, 1957; Wheeler, 1957).

Permanent and Temporary Groups

Where the status of members is fixed by the formal structure, as in the air corps, the authority of the formal leader will probably go unchallenged, even in groups composed only for the purpose of an experiment. In assessing the influence of a formal structure on the interaction process within a group, it is important to distinguish between status relations which are ascribed and status relations which have been developed through some considerable previous interaction. It is likely that the clarity with which a structure is perceived, as well as the degree of influence it can exert over the group's activity, will be related to the length of time during which the structure has developed. Torrance, in a study of some consequences of power differences on decision-making in "permanent" and "temporary" three-person groups (1954a), demonstrates differing effects of the same official position when groups whose members had been a unit for several months are compared with *ad hoc* groups formed for research purposes. The crews in both instances were B26 bomber crews consisting of a pilot, navigator, and gunner. Both pilot, who was also aircraft commander, and navigator were commissioned officers, while the gunner was an enlisted man. Each of 62 permanent and 32 temporary (composed for experiment) crews was given four problems which required a group decision.

The first problem was the Maier Horse-Trading Problem. "A man bought a horse for $60 and sold it for $70. Then he bought it back for $80 and sold it for $90. How much money does he make in the horse-trading business? Each individual was asked to write on a slip of paper his solution without conferring with anyone. Crew members were then asked to confer to reach a crew decision.

The second problem required the subjects to estimate the number of dots on a 16″ x 21″ card with 3155 black dots scattered evenly but not geometrically over a white background. The card was exposed for fifteen seconds, and then each subject was asked to write his individual estimate on a slip of paper. They were then asked to confer to decide upon the best estimate. Finally, each man was asked to write on a slip of paper the number of dots he personally *really* thought were there.

The sketch of the conference group in the Michigan Group Projective Sketches was used in the third problem. Subjects were instructed to write within a five-minute limit a story about the picture. After the individual stories had been collected, the subjects were asked to agree upon and write, within a ten-minute limit, a crew story about the same sketch.

The fourth problem was a survival situation in which the crew had been downed in enemy territory. After two days, one of the members of the crew had been slowing down the attempts to reach safe territory, estimated to be about 40 miles away. He developed severe blisters on his feet and felt he was nearing exhaustion. He does not believe he can continue and urges the other two men to go ahead without him. The crew was instructed to designate one member to act as the man who insists on giving up, and to make its decision as it would be in an actual situation.

After the four decision-making problems, a very brief questionnaire regarding their reactions to the fourth decision-making problem was administered, along with a question concerning their attitude toward being transferred to another crew.[6]

The resulting data may be examined for two sources of influence on final group decisions: (1) differences among the three positions in the group, (2) differences between temporary and permanent groups. With respect to the Horse-Trading Problem, in the permanent groups 31 percent of the pilots, 50 percent of the navigators, and 29 percent of the gunners had recorded correct answers individually. Pilots were most successful and gunners least successful in getting the crew

6. E. Paul Torrance, "Some Consequences of Power Differences on Decision Making in Permanent and Temporary Three-Man Groups," *Research Studies, Washington State College* 22 (1954a): 130–140.

Table 12. Consequences of Power Differences on
Influence on Decision Concerning Story about
Conference Group

Degree of Influence	PERCENTAGES		
	Pilots	Navigators	Gunners
Strong influence	58.7	37.7	0
Some influence	23.4	26.9	23.2
Little or no influence	17.0	34.6	78.6

Source: Torrance (1954a).

to accept their answers as the group decision. In temporary crews, any members who had the correct answer was likely to influence the group regardless of his position, thus indicating a lessened effect of position on decision-making in groups where the positions had not been operative over a considerable period of time.

Results from the dot test display no differences which are significantly different from chance, though the tendency is in the direction of less influence from the gunner.

The conference group story, possibly because of the difference in task (in the direction of more ambiguous criteria of performance), yields clearer results. Since individuals wrote their stories about the conference group sketch before the crew story, Torrance developed an index of influence for each person.

In each case, the five most salient aspects of each story were identified and then the individual stories checked for the presence of these same five aspects. If all five aspects were common to the crew and individual stories, a score of 5 was assigned; if four aspects were common, a score of 4 was given, etc. If four or five aspects were common, it was considered that the individual exerted a strong influence on the crew's decision. If three elements were common, the individual was considered to have exerted "some influence." Less than three common aspects was considered as evidence of little or no influence.[7]

The results of the conference group story task shown in table 12 indicate that the members of permanent crews influenced the crew's decision according to the power structure (differences significant at better than the 5 percent level of confidence.)

For various reasons the survival problem does not permit straightforward comparison with the other three problems. First, there is no record of individual positions held prior to group discussions. Second, the measure of influence is not direct. Third, member self-ratings which were not a feature of the other three tasks are employed.

In his report of the findings on a postdiscussion questionnaire for the survival problem, Torrance concluded that in permanent groups, according to self-reports, the pilots and gunners made less effort to influence the crew's decision ($P. < .01$) and did not feel that they influenced the decision greatly. None of the gunners felt that he greatly influenced the decision.

A comparison of permanent with temporary groups via content analysis of their discussions of the survival problem showed temporary groups more frequently made a series of decisions which required testing and modification, rather than

7. Ibid., p. 134.

single decisions which would be final. More of the permanent crews decided to retain the disabled member under any circumstances. Although the *esprit de corps* was higher in permanent crews (93.7 percent of permanent crews were concerned with keeping the crew together, compared with 71.8 percent of temporary crews), the temporary crews manifested less rigid, more pragmatically directed thinking in these problem sessions.

The evidence from each of the four problem-solving tasks supports the generalization that individuals with high formal rank in a group will have more influence on a group decision than those with low rank. This tendency was more evident in permanent three-man crews than it was in crews composed of members who had been brought together temporarily for the purpose of the experiment.

Structure in Therapy Groups

The therapy group is a good example of a simple group structure. The formal structure of the therapy group, like that of the classroom, is given in the simplest possible terms. There are only two formal positions, leader and follower. The members of the therapy group are brought together to discuss their common emotional problems under the guidance of a clinician. Members of groups with this simple structural type are related to each other primarily because they are all related in the same way to the leader. Little formal role differentiation is expected of the members.

During the first few meetings the therapy group passes through the phases of being an assemblage of patients waiting for the therapist to initiate action, a participating audience, and finally an interacting group (Luchins, 1947). Since the therapist's position as leader is secured by the formal structure, a member with inclinations for power can only hope to play the informal role of the "doctor's assistant" (Frank et al., 1952; Margolin, 1952) or the role of leader of the subgroup which resists suggestions made by the therapist (Bion, 1951; Herbert and Trist, 1953).

In one study of therapy groups, each member's rank in the group on a task-effectiveness criterion was found to be almost identical with his rank based on a social-emotional criterion (Talland, 1957b). This overlap apparently occurred because the task of the group was to handle social-emotional problems of the members. As a result, the person who made the most contributions and was seen as the leader was also the best-liked person because his activity was instrumental in helping other members with their problems. (See also Krieger and Kogan, 1964.) A similar overlap in the task and social-emotional hierarchies has been observed in other types of discussion groups which also serve the purpose of meeting members' social-emotional needs (Theodorson, 1957).

Differentiation in Hierarchies

Although the hierarchies of task and social-emotional positions may at first appear undifferentiated, there is a tendency, particularly in large groups, for them to separate as the group grows older. In the initially leaderless group the most apparent differentiation of informal roles is the gradual development of a *task leader* and a best-liked person or *social-emotional leader* (Benne and Sheats, 1948; Norfleet, 1948; James, 1956; Grusky, 1957; Verhofstad, 1962c; Torrance and

Aliotti, 1965; Burke, 1967, 1968; Berger and Fisek, 1970; Fisek and Ofshe, 1970; Bonacich and Lewis, 1973), although the same person can play both role since the roles are not incompatible (Lewis, 1972), and some overlap may be integrative for the group (Landecker, 1970).

In a series of four meetings of groups which met to discuss human-relations problems (Bales, 1953), the member most chosen as "liked" was usually also chosen for "best ideas" and "guidance" in the first meeting; however, this coincidence of choice became less likely in later meetings. In fact, when observations for all four meetings were summarized, the member who ranked highest on "guidance" and "best ideas" and who initiated most of the activity in the group was found to be the member who was *disliked* most (i.e., received the most negative votes) and ranked only third on *liked* choices. The second or third man on "guidance" and "best ideas" was usually best liked.

When the same person is capable of playing both the *task* and *social-emotional leader* roles, he usually favors being best liked and gives up the task leader role. In 10 cases where the same person played both roles in the first meeting of an initially leaderless group, the "best ideas" role was dropped nine times in favor of the "liked" role. In the remaining case, the person dropped both roles (Bales, 1953). This same trend has been noted in groups over a longer series of meetings. In one case, a high correlation of .70 between choices on the criterion of productivity (task) and choices for spending leisure times (best liked) obtained at the end of the first day of a series of group meetings declined to around .55 by the end of the third week (Lippitt, 1948).

Investigation of an established group will usually uncover similar differences between choices on a task and social-emotional basis (Jennings, 1947a, 1947b; Coffey, 1952), where the top man in either category may be regarded as a *leader* if he initiates most of the activity in his specialty. However, high rank in these two categories is not always correlated with all criteria for leadership (Gibb, 1950).

In a study of four work groups in a large welfare agency, a group perceiving its environment as bland or friendly developed a pyramidal structure with a task leader, a social worker with skills, at the vertex. In contrast a group interpreting its environment as threatening clustered about a social-emotional leader, who was sympathetic, who became the hub of a wheel-like structure. Distinctive norms and patterns of interaction developed in the two groups (Marcus, 1960).

Since the roles which develop in a group do so in response to the requirements of the task and the particular constellation of individuals who compose the group, the specific content of any role may be expected to vary primarily with the group's task and secondarily with the characteristics of the members. In groups which have a life which is longer than any of the individual members, the task requirements would be less variable than the social-emotional requirements.

Culture and Role Differentiation

In the typical middle-class family in the United States and Great Britain the father is the task leader and the mother the social-emotional leader (Bott, 1955; Parsons, Bales, et al., 1955; Bott, 1956, 1957; Kenkel, 1957, Wolfe, 1959; Kenkel, 1961; Leik, 1963; Levinger, 1964; Hansen, 1965; Aldous and Straus, 1966; Schuham, 1972), but this is not always the case in other cultures or even within

Table 13. Decisions Won, by Spouse and Culture			
CULTURE	NO. OF COUPLES	DECISION WON BY:	
		Husband	Wife
Navaho	10	34	46
Texan	10	39	33
Mormon	10	42	29

Table 14. Decisions Won and Talking Time for 34 Married Couples		
SPOUSE WHO TALKED MOST	SPOUSE WHO WON MOST	
	Husband	Wife
Husband	14	5
Wife	5	10

Source: Fred L. Strodtbeck, "Husband-Wife Interaction over Revealed Differences," *American Sociological Review* 16 (1951). Reprinted by permission of the author and the American Sociological Association.

all subcultures to be found in the United States. Strodtbeck (1951) observed husband-wife interaction in three subcultures in the southwestern United States and found differences in the amount of activity and power of the husband and wife in each of the cultures. Married pairs of Mormons, Texans, and Navaho were asked to make independent evaluations of other families in their neighborhood and then to reconcile through discussion any differences in their evaluations. Among the Mormons, a patriarchal group, the husbands won most of the decisions (table 13), and among the Navaho, a matriarchy, the wives won the most. The husbands and wives were about equal for the Texans, who are the most equalitarian, although the husbands won slightly more decisions. No matter what the culture, the spouse who did most of the talking won most of the decisions (table 14).

Cliques and Cabals

Another example of group structure which emphasizes the subgroups within the informal structure is taken from a factory study. Burns (1955) differentiates "cliques," which allow men who are partial failures some protection and a chance to withdraw from the institution, and "cabals," which offer the possibility of "illegitimate" control to members who wish to move up in the organization.

The "cliques" were formed by groups of older men whose conversation reflected a tendency to withdraw from the situation as far as they could. Their lack of acceptance of the changes in the engineering firm for which they worked, their position in the age-grade hierarchy, and their previous experience and qualifications led them into positions whose functions were well defined but were not the key production positions. Their positions were also out of the main line of career opportunities, so that they had, to this extent, resigned from the race. Their cliques had a specifically protective, reassuring purpose. They reassured themselves by being critical of certain features of the organization. They complained that the factory's chief product was scrap, that the place was full of youngsters from universities who knew nothing about industry and yet told experienced craftsmen what to do, and that the craftsmen who were made lab technicians were spoiled for good work thereafter. This older group thought of their jobs in contractual terms, as employees in a firm in which they were prepared to do certain specified work and to undertake specific duties in return for a salary, rather than in terms of responsibility shared with colleagues in a professional group for the discharge of a whole task that the whole firm set.

In contrast, the "cabals" were formed by younger men in the factory. These men were executives who were well satisfied with the positions, were well placed in the age-grade system, and had developed their careers during the years that they had been members of the firm. A member of a "cabal" identified himself and his interests much more with the firm but did not on this account accept the "ways of doing things" which were criticized by members of the older groups, but rather discussed them as features of policy emanating from this or that person and subject to improvement or change if sufficient pressure or persuasion were applied. Thus, the needs for reassurance about possible failure and the need to improve the chances of success by "illegitimate" means (i.e., means that were infractions of the rules and order prevailing in that particular milieu) were met through membership in "cliques," which appeared to offer compensation to the older workers, and "cabals," which provided improved chances of success to the younger generation.

Patterns of Role Differentiation [8]

Natural groups which have been in existence for some time will probably have a greater degree of role differentiation than laboratory groups (Sherwood and Walker, 1960), unless the group organization allows only one leader who is expected to perform all functions. Thus in some industrial and governmental conference groups a "sharing" of leadership is resisted by the members (Berkowitz, 1953). Over the life of a group there may be more differentiation in roles when functional problems of the group become more acute, for example, when the group is under stress or the task is complex (Bales, 1953). Similarly, members in cooperative groups are more apt to be differentiated in their functions than members who are competing (Homans, 1961, p. 135).

The small military unit or industrial work team is perhaps the best example of the simplest form of role differentiation. In each case one or two members may have clearly defined functions with little overlap in their "expectations," while the remainder of the members play undifferentiated roles of "soldier" or "worker." In discussion groups (and especially in laboratory groups) it is not always clear whether a single person plays one role or many roles, or whether these roles are assumed at the same or at different times.

In some research all members are viewed as specializing in some content area, with those with the highest interaction rates identified as the leaders (Heinicke and Bales, 1953; Grusky, 1957). In other research some individuals may be described as playing a variety of roles and others none (J. A. Davis et al., 1961; Cloyd, 1964b). In either case the authors are not usually concerned with the rights and duties associated with each role. They rather use the term *expectations* in the sense that group members can predict or "expect" that a group member will act in a given way on the basis of past performance. There is no sense that the member is "obliged" to act in this way to fulfill a function in the group or that he is entitled to any special privileges for performing this function.

In some research, the evidence that a person is playing a given role is that other members associate a certain set of behavioral characteristics with him; these behavioral characteristics are presented as a cluster without any special rationale concerning their interconnection (Bates and Cloyd, 1956; J. A. Davis, 1961; Cloyd, 1964b). In other research a person is described as playing a role because he has been nominated as a frequent contributor of some specified type of behavior, for example, giving information or giving opinion (Bales, 1958; Borg, 1960). An even less functionalist view is taken in research in which some members are described as

8. This and the following five sections have been adapted and updated from Hare (1968c). A few points made elsewhere in this chapter are repeated here for continuity. Cf. A. Paul Hare, "Groups: Role Structure," in *International Encyclopedia of the Social Sciences*, ed. D. L. Sills (New York: Macmillan and Free Press, 1968), 6: 283–288. Copyright © 1968 by Crowell Collier and Macmillan, Inc. Reprinted by permission of the publisher.

playing individual or self-oriented roles that presumably are extraneous to the group task (Benne and Sheats, 1948). Another variation on the use of the term *role* is for the experimenter to describe someone as playing a role such as "newcomer" (Mills et al., 1957) or "doctor's assistant" (Margolin, 1952) without actually assessing the perceptions of the other members.

Most of the research on small groups has so far not used a definition of role as a set of rights and duties, but rather as a description of recurring patterns of behavior. But the former, more limited definition of role still appears to be theoretically useful even though it is not widely used. For instance, in those studies that report the interaction in initially "leaderless" groups, the expectations for the average member are probably most clearly related to the directions given by the experimenter at the beginning of the session. Often, indeed, the experimenter will test to see if the subjects have been as friendly or as competitive as he directed them to be, but he will not refer to these instructions as "role expectations" (Olmsted, 1954).

The power of an experimenter's instruction is evident in an experiment in which one member in each of several discussion groups was given more information about the task than the other members. In some of these groups the experimenter announced, "Some of you may have more information than others." In other groups he gave the impression that all members were equally informed. It was observed that group members reacted negatively to the best-informed man unless they had been led to "expect" that he would play a different role (Shaw and Penrod, 1962a).

Although early research on groups, especially with children, often described "individual" or "self-oriented" roles as if the only role of some individuals was to satisfy their own needs in the group (Benne and Sheats, 1948), later formulations by Redl, (1942), Bion, (1961), and Stock and Thelen, (1958) suggest that all roles in the group serve some function. However, some of these roles, particularly the ones that allow members to deal with emotional themes, may not be recognized as part of the "official" group structure. For example, in a training group composed of teachers who were being led by Bion's methods of "interpretive group discussion," the group members persisted, without success, in trying to induce the leader to act as a therapist. Finally six members did not appear at the scheduled group session and a spokesman for the absentees sent in a paper on truancy to be discussed by the remaining members. Thus, by taking the "role" of absent members, some of the group acted out the group's need for flight from the task (Herbert and Trist, 1953).

Task versus Social-Emotional Roles

The most common division of roles that has been described in small discussion and work groups, as well as in families viewed as small groups, is specialization in the task and social-emotional areas (Bales and Slater, 1955; Bales, 1958). This has been shown most clearly in small laboratory groups in which members have a high degree of consensus at the end of a meeting on the relative amount of interaction in each of these areas exhibited by group members. These groups appear to recognize two kinds of role specialists: one an "idea man" who concentrates on the task and plays a more aggressive role, the other a "best-liked" man who concentrates on social-emotional problems of group process and member satisfaction, giving emotional rewards, and playing a more passive role. However, in groups similar to these in which there is less consensus on the status of members, a third type of person appears to be present, one who talks a great deal but who is not well liked or highly rated on his task ability. He has been referred to as a "deviant." In addition, researchers have found a more passive task specialist and a "popular" person (Slater, 1955).

The so-called deviant who overtalks is probably expressing the group's anxiety about the discussion task. To please the experimenter, the group allows a member to fill the time with "discussion" even though he may not be the most effective at the task. This tendency to have a high or low interaction rate has often been reported as the first of three factors or dimensions that may be used to describe behavior, the other two being task behavior and sociability (Carter, 1954).

In families, the father has been identified as the task specialist, the mother as the social-emotional specialist (Parsons, Bales, et al., 1955). A similar dichotomy has been reported among caseworkers in a welfare agency where some colleagues were respected and sought out for consultation on cases and others were attractive because of their sociable companionship (Blau, 1962). However, a study of therapy groups reported that the distinction was not evident in this setting, since the "task" of the group was to deal with social-emotional problems (Talland, 1957).

When the same individual is required to play the role of both the task and the social-emotional leader, he may find some aspects of the roles incompatible and thus experience "role conflict" (Seeman, 1953). Officers in small military units, for example, may be required to consider the personal problems of their men as well as to be task leaders. The second role requires distance, since some assignments must be made without regard to personal feelings, yet the first role requires closeness and intimacy (Hutchins and Fiedler, 1960).

The Joker

In addition to these two roles, a third role has been identified in some groups which actually has a long history in many cultures. This is the role of the clown or the joker. Just as the English court jester's costume set him apart from the group, so the joker tends to take a somewhat marginal position with regard to the task. He tends to look at things differently, providing both a source of humor and of new ideas. Under the cover of wit he is able to introduce ideas that the group might otherwise find unacceptable.

In its literary form, comedy has been described as "an escape not from truth but from despair; a narrow escape into faith" (Fry, 1950, p. 27). One must be able to grasp the tragic nature of life before one can go on to grasp its comic nature. Thus the comic person in a play or in a real-life small group is often one who gives special insight into the problem. This is evident from a study of a series of "great-books" discussion groups where the joking role was most highly correlated with the role of providing "fuel" for the discussions in the form of new ideas and opinions (J. A. Davis et al., 1961). In a study of laboratory discussion groups the following cluster of behavioral characteristics was identified as composing a role: "jokes and makes humorous remarks, is liberal, challenges other's opinions, gets off the subject, is egotistical, is cynical, and interrupts others" (Cloyd, 1964a). Generally members of groups with jokers (wits) like the group better and do better work (Goodchilds and Smith, 1964). However, within the dimension of "joking versus task serious behavior" there may be different styles to wit. Thus sarcastic wit may be perceived as powerful but unpopular in a group, while clowning wit may be seen as popular but powerless (Goodchilds, 1959).

Further research on the place of wit and humor in groups includes Goodchilds, 1959; Malpass and Fitzpatrick, 1959; O'Connell, 1960; Smith and Goodchilds, 1963; Young and Frye, 1966; F. B. Miller, 1967; Treadwell, 1967; Berlyne, 1968; Malefijt, 1968; Davis and Farina, 1970; Zillmann and Cantor, 1972.

The Member

The fact that simple membership in a group carries with it a set of rights and duties is evident in the group's concern for the "silent member." Although silence may be functional if it means that more able persons are being allowed to solve problems (Homans, 1961, p. 136), group members are usually dissatisfied with a member's performance if he does not participate. This dissatisfaction may be reduced if it is made clear at the outset that certain members will not participate at all (E. E. Smith, 1957).

On the other hand the group will be more concerned if a member appears indifferent and neglectful in his role (Rosenthal and Cofer, 1948).

Another type of member role that has received some attention in the literature is that of the "newcomer" (Ziller and Behringer, 1961; Ziller, 1962). Group members will have an easier time assimilating the newcomer if they have been told to expect change (Ziller, Behringer, and Jansen, 1961), provided that the newcomer is not seen as too different from other group members (Ziller, Behringer, and Goodchilds, 1960) and that group members have already had a pleasant time with each other (Heiss, 1963). In any event there will probably be a minimal alteration in the role patterns of the old members at first (Mills et al., 1957).

Other Roles

Other roles may be found in groups with special tasks. In therapy groups a "doctor's assistant" may fill the group's need to keep the discussion going when the therapist is is playing a rather passive role, and a "help-rejecting complainer" may give the group case material to discuss (Frank et al., 1952; Margolin, 1952). Somewhat similar to the "doctor's assistant" may be the "feeder-to-leaders" identified in a sociometric study of a home for girls (Jennings, 1947a). These were girls who would have their ideas accepted after they had been endorsed by highly chosen leaders, although they were not highly chosen themselves.

The classic study of authoritarian and democratic group atmospheres by Lewin, Lippitt, and White does not focus on role differentiation; however, two types of roles are mentioned in addition to the leaders. In the "democratic" groups the authors describe two boys who are allies of the adult leaders, and in the "autocratic" groups they describe a scapegoat who receives the aggression of the group (White and Lippitt, 1960, pp. 160–186). Thrasher (1927) in his study of gangs in Chicago gives a longer list of special roles, to which he gives such names as brains of gang, funny boy, sissy, show-off, and goat. Redl (1942) lists 10 types of roles of central persons, which may be grouped into three categories: identification objects, objects of drives, and ego supports.

In addition to roles which may arise naturally in groups, some authors have suggested certain roles which should be introduced if a group is to operate with maximum efficiency. For example, Jenkins (1948) suggests that effective discussion requires attention to such mechanics of operation as awareness of direction, goal, and rate of progress. He proposes that groups appoint a "group productivity observer" who will report at the end of each meeting.

Where role differentiation occurs in a group, individuals accustomed to playing the same roles in other groups will probably continue to play them in the new situation (Strodtbeck and Mann, 1956; J. A. Davis et al., 1961; Lagrou, 1968; Freese and Cohen, 1973). In addition, differences in age, sex, social class, and occupation between members will result in role differentiation in small discussion groups even when these differences are not related to the task at hand (Maas, 1954b; Torrance, 1954a).

Eight Roles in Discussion Groups

From the review of the literature presented above it is evident that a variety of roles reported may be small or large depending upon the level of analysis, the task, the group size, and the length of time the members have been together. Although the dichotomy of task versus social-emotional roles is adequate to describe the basic differentiation in some groups, in others there are probably more distinct roles that have been grouped under these two more general headings. A framework for the description of more distinct and independent roles is provided by Couch's (1960; see chapter 3) factor analysis of categories of interaction in five-man laboratory discussion groups. He finds that interpersonal behavior can be described by the following independent dimensions: dominance versus submission, positive versus negative, serious versus expressive, and conforming versus nonconforming.

If we assume that behavior at the extremes of each dimension may identify a role, we find a rather good fit with six role patterns identified by Cloyd (1964b) without reference to any particular dimensions and wihout actually assigning them names.

At the dominance end of Couch's first factor we find a set of behaviors similar to a cluster identified by Cloyd that includes "aggressive, self-confident, and gets things started." This role might be called the "high talker." At the submissive end of Couch's first factor is Cloyd's cluster of traits: "modest, shy, and ill at ease." This role might be called the "silent member."

In a similar way one could match dimensions and clusters of traits to identify a "supporter" who is friendly and objective, a "critic" who is idealistic and argumentative, a "serious worker" who is dependable and constructive, and a "joker" who makes humorous remarks and challenges others' opinions. Cloyd does not provide examples that would fit the last of Couch's dimensions; however, the last dimension suggests the roles of "conformist" and "nonconformist."

These four dimensions of interaction which are represented by eight roles are in turn related to the four functional problems. The roles of high talker and silent member are primarily related to goal attainment, supporter and critic to integration, serious worker and joker to adaptation, and conformist and nonconformist to pattern maintenance.

Role Collision, Incompatibility, and Confusion

There is usually agreement among group members concerning some specific attributes of a member's role (especially in highly cohesive groups; Hall, 1955), but there are also areas in which the expectations for role behavior are contradictory or ill-defined. The clash of expectations concerning some aspects of a role have usually been called "role conflict." These conflicts can arise in a number of different ways. The term *role collision* will be used to indicate the type of conflict which may occur if two different individuals in a group hold roles which overlap in some respect. In a hospital, for example, two doctors are often called in to treat the same patient. Each is expected to prescribe treatment for the patient, but unless the doctors coordinate their behavior the patient's wounds may be bound up one day and left open the next, depending upon which of the doctors last visited the ward.

Another example of role collision may occur in the family, where the father and mother roles may collide in some areas but not in others. While the father may carry out the principal economic activities and the mother the household tasks, their roles may collide in the area of child rearing, where both play a part. Tension in that area may be indicated by an increase in the number of disagreements on who is to perform an activity and who is the source of authority (Herbst, 1952).

A second type of role problem is that of *role incompatibility,* in which an individual is forced to meet expectations for different roles which are incompatible (Simmel, 1955, p. 155; Gross, McEachern, and Mason, 1958). This phenomenon appeared in a small group of clothing salesmen where the expectations of "friend" were incompatible with those of "competitor" (Wispe, 1955). It also appears in groups in which the same person plays both task and social-emotional leader roles. If a follower does not know whether the leader is going to be a hard taskmaster or a warm counselor at a given time, it is hard to react properly (Sampson, 1963b). Similar conflicts can arise from incongruencies in sex, skill, and leadership roles (Brandon, 1965).

Usually the problem of incompatibility is solved on a time basis: one role is allowed to "cool off" while the individual "warms up" to the next role (Yablonsky, 1953). The most common source of conflict for a man is between his roles at work and at home. This conflict may be solved by spending a limited number of hours in each place. During a busy season at the office, however, he may have to work late, making it impossible for him to fulfill all his obligations as a husband-father. Since a doctor, for example, may be called away from his family at any time in an emergency, this conflict continually recurs. To solve the problem, the doctor's family may decide that when the conflict arises, the role of doctor has precedence over the role of father, but this does nothing to reduce the *number* of occasions of conflict.

The incidence of role incompatibility among married persons is related to their ratings of self-happiness. Women report fewer conflicts and rate themselves higher on happiness than men (Ort, 1950).

A third problem is that of *role confusion*. There are usually some inconsistent expectations concerning the behavior appropriate to any role. These incompatible expectations arise from three sources: (1) within the group there is agreement on the expected behavior, but there are expectations which are difficult to satisfy at the same time; (2) within the group there is disagreement regarding role defini-tion; (3) other groups of which the individual is a member may disagree regard-ing the nature of his role (Seeman, 1953).

An example of the first subtype of *role confusion* is the problem of male cooks or countermen in the restaurant industry. These men have relatively high status within the industry and should be the ones to initiate activity, yet they must take orders from female waitresses who have low status in the hierarchy (Whyte, 1949). This situation produces interpersonal friction, which is often avoided by various devices which make it unnecessary for a counterman to respond each time a waitress brings an order.

The second subtype of *role confusion* involves significant disagreement within the group regarding role definition. In a school study, teachers were asked 10 forced-choice questions concerning the role of an "ideal superintendent." One ques-tion asked, "Should an ideal superintendent invite staff members to his home for social occasions?" and a second, "Should an ideal superintendent feel free to dis-cuss his personal problems with the teachers?" Simple yes and no answers were the forced-choice alternatives provided. In both cases, the split in opinion among the teachers was close to a 60-to-40 division, so that any move on the part of the superintendent to become intimate with the teachers would result in approval from some of his teachers and disapproval from others (Seeman, 1953).

Similar problems arise for children faced with conflicting suggestions from adults (Meyers, 1944) and shop stewards who can take an "'active" part in pro-moting the interests of the workers only at the risk of antagonizing the foremen who expect them to be "passive" (Jacobson, Charters, and Lieberman, 1951).

In an office of a department store we find an example of the third subtype of *role confusion*. Here the informal group rated one office job as having higher status than the other, while the management gave equal pay for both jobs. When an individual was shifted from the job which the informal group designated as high-status to the low-status job, he was dissatisfied, since the rights and privi-leges accorded to the two positions by management and the informal group were not the same (Homans, 1953).

This subtype of role confusion is also apparent where conflicting expectations are held by two family groups about "traditional" and "companionship" forms of marriage (Motz, 1952). The parents of one member of a newly married pair might expect the marriage to be formed on the "traditional" lines of the dominant male, while the other set of parents expect a "companionship" arrangement in which the husband and wife would share equally in decisions. In this case the confusion arises from conflicting definitions held by members outside the group in which conflict takes place.

Although role collision, incompatibility, or confusion may be found in the social structure at many points, not all individuals may experience stress in coping with the problems which arise in these situations. In the same way, not all persons will find stressful problems which may occur in *role transition,* when the individual gives up one role to take another, as is the case with a new job or marriage. There is some evidence that certain types of personalities find these "hazardous situations" especially stressful. In a study of the stresses involved in the conflict of officer and instructor roles in the air corps, a "conflict-prone personality" was identified, a man who tended to be feminine, nervous, introverted, depressed, cycloid, authoritarian, and extrapunitive (Getzels and Guba, 1955). Such a person found it especially difficult in his relations with enlisted men to reconcile the social distance required of the officer with the equalitarian behavior expected of the instructor.

Three similar types of role problems have been identified in the clinical analysis of family case-study material. In general, contradictions in the role expectations for a family member tend to make that individual more self-aware and on guard, forcing him constantly to make decisions about his role behavior. This type of family situation appears to foster more disturbed children (Spiegel, 1957).

For related explanations of the nature of role conflict see Ehrlich, Rinehart, and Howell, 1962; Kimberly and Crosbie, 1967; and McCranie and Kimberly, 1973.

Additional studies related to roles and role differentiation include Argyle, 1952b; Turk, 1963b; Weinstein and Deutschberger, 1963; Collins et al., 1964; Burke, 1969.

Summary

The term *role* refers primarily to the set of expectations which group members share concerning the behavior of a person who occupies a position in a group. The expectations for a given role are met most easily by the individual whose personality most nearly fits the role. The expectations for a role for any content category of behavior may be visualized as falling somewhere in a space defined by two axes. One axis represents the behavior which the individual is expected to direct toward others and the other axis represents the behavior which others are expected to direct toward him. In both cases this behavior ranges from that which is required to that which is prohibited. In addition to the specification of expected role content, the expected communication network and interaction rate may be viewed with various degrees of complexity.

Groups tend to have an informal structure, as well as a formal structure. The ease with which the informal structure is developed and maintained depends upon the relevant characteristics of the group members and the extent to which the formal structure is well defined. If individuals differ significantly in their characteristics, the *informal* structure will develop rapidly and remain relatively stable over time, since attempts of low-ranking members to displace those of higher ranks will fail. If fluctuations occur among the individuals who fill positions in the informal structure, members' energies may be diverted from productivity as they attempt to reestablish the structure. Whyte describes the development and maintenance of the informal structure of a group of "corner boys" in his account of "street corner society."

In newly formed leaderless groups without a formal structure, members tend to assume the same positions which they hold in other groups of long standing. Thus the influence of air corps pilots, navigators, and gunners in "temporary" problem-solving groups is related to the relative power they hold in their own "permanent" crews.

The simplest type of formal structure is found in the therapy group where there are only two formal roles, leader and follower. Within the informal structure, however, there may be role specialization.

Although task and social-emotional hierarchies may at first be undifferentiated, there is a tendency for them to separate as a group develops or grows larger. The age, sex, and social characteristics required for the positions in each of the hierarchies may be determined by the culture of the society in which the group develops. In the family, for example, the role of task leader may be played by the father, by the mother, or shared, depending upon the culture.

In an industrial setting, two types of informal groups were identified: *cliques,* which had a social-emotional orientation allowing partial failures a chance to withdraw from the institution, and *cabals,* which had a task orientation offering the possibility of illegitimate control to members who wished to move up in the organization.

Although special roles develop in small groups which reflect some aspects of the group task, eight role types tend to reoccur. The roles include clusters of traits that are found at the extremes of each of the four dimensions of social interaction (dominance versus submission, positive versus negative, serious versus expressive, and conforming versus nonconforming). Names suggested for the eight roles are high talker, silent member, supporter, critic, serious worker, joker, conformist, and nonconformist.

Three types of problems occur as a result of conflicting role expectations. In *role collision* two different individuals have roles which are in conflict in some respect; in *role incompatibility* the same individual plays roles which have contradictory expectations; and in *role confusion* there is a lack of agreement among group members about the expectations for a given role.

Chapter 7

INTERPERSONAL CHOICE

INDIVIDUALS INDICATE THEIR interpersonal choices in a variety of ways: through frequency of association through formal elections, and through ratings of other group members elicited by observers and experimenters. Ratings of the last type, popularized by Moreno, have been called "sociometric" ratings. Sociometric ratings are based on a variety of criteria which may fall into any of the content areas described in chapter 1.

Although an analysis of "sociograms," which depict the patterns of interpersonal choice, is useful in identifying the position of an individual in the informal structure of a group, it does not reveal the behavior which is associated with the position. The ratings on several criteria are often combined; thus, individuals are identified as "overchosen" or "underchosen" in the informal structure without reference to the particular position which they hold. Although the "overchosen" members tend to be those who prefer close relationships with others, they are not necessarily the informal leaders.

The sociometric test has been used widely in studies of children in school populations. Here the principal problem for research has often been to determine the basis of friendship between pairs of children. The friendship bonds between individuals tend to be influenced by the following factors: (1) proximity, and similarities in (2) biological traits, (3) personality characteristics, (4) common or reciprocal roles, and (5) common values.

Sociometric ratings are often used to derive measures of morale or cohesiveness, since individuals who are highly attracted to a group tend to be the most productive if the norms of the group specify high productivity. A measure of cohesiveness may then be used to predict productivity.

Books and articles which give a general overview of sociometry and interpersonal attraction include Glanzer and Glaser, 1959; Moreno et al., 1960; Albert and Brigante, 1962; Bjerstedt, 1963; Mucchielli, 1963; Adams, 1967; Lindzey and Byrne, 1968; Northway, 1968; Sherif and Sherif, 1968; Bramel, 1969; Byrne, 1969; Hunyady, 1970; Sutherland, 1972; Byrne and Griffitt, 1973; M. S. Davis, 1973; Rubin, 1973; S. C. Jones, 1974.

The Sociogram

The term *sociometric* is usually used to designate the interpersonal choices which group members have revealed to an observer or experimenter, although the term has also been used to include a variety of forms of social measurement

152

(Bjerstedt, 1956a). Sociometry was introduced by Moreno (1953), who has suggested six rules to be followed in using the sociometric test:

1. The limits of the group in which the test is given should be indicated.
2. There should be unlimited choices of other persons.
3. Individuals should be asked to choose and reject other group members with a specific criterion or activity in mind.
4. The results of the sociometric tests should be used to restructure the group; that is, the group should be reorganized by placing people together who have chosen each other as liked.
5. The opinions should be given in private.
6. Questions should be phrased in ways that members can understand.

In practice, these six rules are followed in only about 25 percent of all "sociometric" studies (Lindzey and Borgatta, 1954). The most frequent deviations from the rules are the limitation on choices, usually to about three, and the omission of the action step of actual reorganization of the group in line with the results of the test.

Although interpersonal liking is usually determined by asking group members "sociometric" questions which can be simple or complex (Tagiuri, 1952; Weschler, Tannenbaum, and Talbot, 1952; Eng, 1954; Barr, 1955), other behavioral indices may be used such as time spent together (Moreno, Jennings, and Sargent, 1940; Fischer, 1953), visiting patterns, or work exchange (Loomis, 1941). The interpersonal choice data are then analyzed visually by using "sociograms" in which individuals are represented as circles and their choices as arrows pointing from one to the other (Borgatta, 1951a), or mathematically through matrix algebra (Ross and Harary, 1952). Further details concerning the use of the test are given in the methodological note which appears as an appendix to this volume.

One of Moreno's sociometric diagrams or "sociograms" is reproduced in figure 29. Here he has plotted the pattern of interpersonal choice in one of the cottage families in a school for delinquent girls which provided the population for an early sociometric study made in collaboration with Jennings (1950a).

The circles in the diagram represent the girls in the cottage and the lines between them represent their choices of the five other girls from the cottage they most wanted to live with. Although it was not done for this group, the subjects are also often asked whom they would reject. The rejections may then be plotted on the same or a different sociogram. The arrowhead on a line indicates the direction of choice. If two persons choose each other, the arrows are joined in a straight line with a dash across the center.

After the choices of each girl in cottage C3 have been plotted, the resulting choice pattern indicates the following characteristics of the 23 girls:

Type	Number	Identification
Isolated	5	BA, GM, RA, LY, TS,
Unchosen	5	CM, JM, GL, RC, BN,
Mutual attractions (pairs)	6	AE-HF, AE-PC, PC-PP,
		PC-YA, PC-KR, UT-SY,
Chains	1	HF-AE-PC-KR-PP
Triangles	0	
Stars	1	LT (*Note:* LT is an "isolated star," as she chooses no one in return)

Figure 29. Pattern of Interpersonal Choice in a Cottage Family

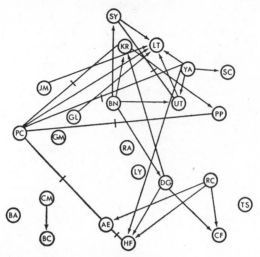

Source: Jacob L. Moreno, *Who Shall Survive?*, rev. ed. (Beacon, N.Y.: Beacon House, 1953), p. 267. Reprinted by permission of the publisher.

Moreno describes this group as one with an extroverted group organization. Its special features are a large number of nonparticipating individuals, low group cohesion, and low differentiation between underchosen and overchosen members.

Choice Criteria

The criterion used in Moreno's study of the cottage (i.e., choice of roommates) is similar to the criterion of "Whom would you choose as a friend?" which is used in many studies. Both criteria are rather general, but both would appear to lie primarily within the *social-emotional* area. A typical criterion in the task area is "Whom would you choose to work with?"

Subjects tend to make fewer choices on a friendship criterion than on a work criterion (Jennings, 1947b, Gibb, 1950). However, correlations are high between choices based on each of these criteria (Bjerstedt, 1956b; Hollander, 1956), since there are some "great men" (Borgatta, Couch, and Bales, 1954) who actually have desirable traits in all areas, and there are some subjects who will choose on a criterion which is important to them regardless of the experimenter's request. As a result there is little difference in choice no matter what criterion is proposed (Hoffman, 1962; P. B. Smith, 1963; Petersen, Komorita, and Quay, 1964). Subjects who value task performance will choose others who are effective in the task (Turk, 1961a, 1961b; Gustafson, 1973), and those who value social or emotional traits will choose on that basis (Eisenstadt, 1970). In general, social traits (e.g., warm, hostile, generous) are more important than nonsocial traits (e.g., happy, intelligent, hard-working) in determining attraction (Diggins, 1974).

An example of choice based on the subject's own criterion rather than that of the experimenter is found in an experiment by E. G. French (1956) using 137 air corps personnel in their seventh week of training. The men were given a test designed to measure both achievement and affiliation motivation. They were then divided into groups of four to work on "important concept formation test." The groups were so constructed that three of the subjects had previously rated each other as "liked" and the fourth member as "not liked." All subjects first worked individually on a sorting task in which the disliked member was made to succeed and the other members to fail. The subjects were then asked to make one or two choices for a work partner to repeat the same task in pairs. On this sociometric test the subjects who were high in achievement and low in affiliation motivation made significantly more single choices of the unliked members who appeared to be successful, while the subjects who were high in affiliation and low in achievement made significantly more choices of the two friends. Those who were high in both motivations made significantly more double choices involving both a friend and the successful person, while the subjects who were low in both motivations predominantly chose a friend.

In this study the use of the sociometric test meets all the criteria suggested by Moreno, since a specific work criterion is used and the group is restructured on the basis of the choices; it is evident, however, that some subjects tend to disregard the criterion and choose on the basis of their predominant interpersonal need. An additional finding that the subjects in this experiment with high need for achievement differed from those with high need for affiliation in the extent to which they made "dislike" ratings in the first place suggests that the two types of individuals also have a different basis for choice on the more general criterion of "friend."

Different choice criteria also influence the form and content of interaction. In a study by Back (1951; see chapter 9 for more detail), the "cohesiveness" of two-man groups was manipulated by telling some pairs that they would or would not like each other, others that they would or would not receive a prize for the best group performance, and still others that they would or would not serve as a model of a highly productive group. Back found that when cohesiveness was based on personal attraction, group members tended to make the discussion into a long pleasant conversation; when it was based on task performance, the members tried to finish quickly and efficiently; and when it was based on group prestige, the members acted cautiously so that they would not endanger their status.

In another example, caseworkers in a welfare agency were asked to choose whom they would "respect as a colleague" and to whom they were "attracted as a sociable companion." Persons high on choices of respect were sought for consultation about casework matters, while those who were high on attraction were looked to for informal interaction (Blau, 1962).

Even though sociometric choices do vary to some extent with the criterion, the experimenter often pools the ratings made on several criteria so that the distinctions are lost (Jennings, 1943; Bassett, 1944). Most of the literature on interpersonal choice is summarized in this chapter without regard to specific criteria, although it is possible, in some cases, to illustrate the variations in the behavior of a subject which are associated with his choices based on different criteria.

Reciprocal Choice

When an investigator asks the subjects to rate all other members of the group using some criterion of choice, the data include not only those choices which the individuals have consciously made before the experimenter arrives on the scene but also those choices which have only been made for the purpose of the questionnaire, which played no major part in the development of the social structure. An individual who is ranked low by another individual may, therefore, be someone who is disliked, or someone who is relatively unknown to the first person. When group members are relative strangers, mutual choices may occur simply by chance (Deutschberger, 1947). In general, however, choices are not random, since in every group some persons are more chosen and some less than would be expected if only chance factors were operating (Moreno and Jennings, 1938; Barker, 1942; Bronfenbrenner, 1943, 1944). A number of mathematical models which may be used to determine the extent to which the choice pattern deviates from chance have also been reported in the literature (Leeman, 1952; Nehnevajsa, 1955a, 1955b).

Almost any indication of positive choice will be reciprocated, including simple agreement, using a person's name, touching, giving positive evaluations, helping, or rewarding in various ways (Backman and Secord, 1959; Flament and Apfelbaum, 1966; Moran, 1966; Jones and Pines, 1968; Landy and Aronson, 1968; Blumberg, 1969; Hewitt, 1969; Hewitt and Chung, 1969; Lott et al., 1969; Sigall and Aronson, 1969; Blake and Tesser, 1970; Ettinger, Nowicki, and Nelson, 1970; Lott et al., 1970; Lowe and Goldstein, 1970; Nemeth, 1970b; Dutton and Arrowood, 1971; Hewitt, 1971; Holstein, Goldstein, and Bem, 1971; Jones and Panitch, 1971; Posavac, 1971; Schopler and Compere, 1971; Jones and Wein, 1972; Kleinke, Staneski, and Weaver, 1972; McGinley and McGinley, 1972; Arrowood and Short, 1973; Johnson, Gormly, and Gormly, 1973; Jones, Knurek, and Regan, 1973; Lamberth, Gouaux, and Padd, 1973; Breed and Ricci, 1973; Brown, Helm, and Tedeschi, 1973; Potter, 1973; Smith and Campbell, 1973; Stapleton, Nacci, and Tedeschi, 1973; Walster et al., 1973). Reciprocation of choice will not appear, however, unless a sociometric question is asked which makes reciprocation of choice possible (Criswell, 1949; Katz and Powell, 1955). For example, mutual choices would not be expected if subjects were asked to nominate the best potential leaders in the group. Mutual choice would be expected with a criterion of "sit next to" or "room with."

As with other forms of interaction, reciprocal choice can be shown to be another instance of the subject's attempt to achieve "balance" in social exchange. An example of a balanced state is when person P and other O like each other and both like some other object or person (X). Most research assumes that each of the relationships between P, O, and X have equal weight and that a person will prefer a balanced to an unbalanced state. However, it has been noted that the bond between persons P and O may take precedence over the bond between P and X. For example, if P likes O but dislikes X and O also dislikes X (see figure 30, structure A), the structure has the same degree of balance as if P dislikes O but likes X and O dislikes X (see figure 30, structure B). In this case subjects are found to prefer A to B. Apparently in the B case, since P dislikes O, he has no interest in his attitude toward X (Crano and Cooper, 1973).

A number of studies report variations on the theme of balanced states of structures of interpersonal relations, especially in comparison with mathematical models. The reports which are more relevant for the analysis of interpersonal choice include Davol, 1959; A. J. Smith, 1960b; Shrader and Lewit, 1962; Broxton, 1963; J. A. Davis, 1963; Fathi, 1965; Feather, 1965; Price, Harburg, and McLeod, 1965; Rodrigues, 1965; Feather, 1966; Morrissette, Janke, and Baker, 1966; Price, Har-

Figure 30. Two Equally Balanced Structures

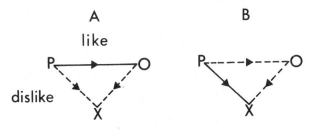

burg, and Newcomb, 1966; Feather, 1967a; Rodrigues, 1967; Taylor, 1967; Zajonc and Sherman, 1967; Berscheid, Boye, and Darley, 1968; Aderman, 1969; Horsfall and Henley, 1969; Nahinsky, 1969; Cartwright and Harary, 1970; Curry and Emerson, 1970; Johnsen, 1970; Wyer and Lyon, 1970; Gardiner, 1972; Gutman and Knox, 1972; Miller and Geller, 1972; Burgess and Willis, 1973; Delia and Crockett, 1973; Stephan, 1973; Crockett, 1974; Gutman, Knox, and Storm, 1974; Insko, Songer, and McGarvey, 1974; Willis and Burgess, 1974.

Subgroups

The pattern of interpersonal choices may reveal the presence of an *informal structure,* although sociometricians do not generally distinguish the choices which a person might receive because of his position in the *formal* structure from those choices which he might receive because of his position in the *informal* structure. In any case, the interpersonal choices indicate only the position which a person holds in in the structure without describing the role which is associated with that position. Thus an analysis of the sociometric data may reveal only the presence of *subgroups* within the larger group.

Since subgroups tend to form around different member characteristics or interests, they often serve different functions in the larger group. For example, on an open psychiatric ward informal patient groups were identified by observational and sociometric techniques. The structures of these groups were studied in relationship to those of more formal patient groups. Two subgroups were observed; one was the *leadership clique,* which functioned as a governing, staff-value-supporting, and quasi-socializing agency, and the other was the *dissident clique,* which permitted withdrawal of about-to-be discharged patients from institutional values and also undermined the values (Bloom, Boyd, and Kaplan, 1962). Additional examples have been recorded for hospital patients (Smith and Thrasher, 1963), school children (R. Nash, 1973), adolescent peer groups (Dunphy, 1963), college freshmen (Glick and Jackson, 1970), and merchant seamen (Herbst, 1971). A bibliography of related studies has been prepared by Hart (Hart, 1961).

The tendency for the group to split into subgroups becomes marked as the group size increases (Homans, 1950; Hare, 1953). The typical sociometric chart of interpersonal choices shows a series of interlocking subgroups as the informal group structure. So characteristic is the tendency for members of groups to form subgroups on some choice basis (Roethlisberger and Dickson, 1939; Klein, 1956), that, even when the subgroups are imposed by some outside condition, the amount of friendly interaction within the subgroups increases and the number of social isolates in the group decreases (Moreno and Jennings, 1944; Thibaut, 1950). The straight-line hierarchy is perhaps only characteristic of the group of two, as is the case in the two-boy gangs where it has been observed that "Gerry is running Alfred now" (Thrasher, 1927).

The relative nature of positions in an informal structure is evidenced by the fact that if "overchosen" or central members and "underchosen" or fringe members are separated from each other into new groups, a new informal structure will form in each group in which some members will again be "overchosen" and others "underchosen" (Powell et al., 1956).

Groups in Harmony and Tension

In a series of studies in a summer camp for boys, Sherif and his colleagues experimentally demonstrated that an *increase* in hostility toward some outgroup is usually associated with an *increase* in affection for members of the ingroup (Sherif, 1956).[1] Sherif chose to study groups of the informal type, where group organization and attitudes would evolve naturally and spontaneously, without formal direction or external pressures. For this purpose 11- and 12-year-old boys were selected as subjects. These were normal boys of homogeneous background who were picked by a long and thorough procedure, which involved interviews with each boy's family, teachers, and school officials, an analysis of school and medical records and scores on personality tests, and observations of behavior in class and on the playground. By these means, the authors assured themselves that their sample included boys who were all healthy, socially well adjusted, somewhat above average in intelligence, and from stable, white, Protestant, middle-class homes.

The boys thus selected spent three weeks in an isolated summer camp. Sherif continues:

None of the boys was aware that he was part of an experiment on group relations. The investigators appeared as a regular camp staff—camp directors, counselors, and so on. The boys met one another for the first time in buses that took them to camp, and so far as they knew it was a normal summer of camping. To keep the situation as lifelike as possible we conducted all our experiments within the framework of regular camp activities and games. We set up projects which were so interesting and attractive that the boys plunged into them enthusiastically without suspecting that they might be test situations. Unobtrusively, we made records of their behavior, even using "candid" cameras and microphones when feasible.[2]

Producing Intergroup Tensions

The first of the camps was conducted in the hills of northern Connecticut in the summer of 1949. Here Sherif and his staff began by observing how the boys

1. In a letter to me, Sherif stressed the fact that this account is a composite picture of a series of three different experiments using different (but comparable) subjects. More detailed accounts of these experiments appear in Rohrer and Sherif, 1951; Sherif and Sherif, 1953; Sherif, White, and Harvey, 1955; Sherif and Sherif, 1956; and Sherif, 1958.
2. Muzafer Sherif, "Experiments in Group Conflict," *Scientific American* 195 (November 1956): 54–55. Copyright © 1956 by Scientific American, Inc. All rights reserved. Reprinted by permission of the author and W. H. Freeman & Co. The selections from Sherif's article reprinted here are expanded and updated in chapters 5 and 10 of Carolyn Sherif, *Orientation in Social Psychology* (New York: Harper & Row, 1976).

became a coherent group. When the boys arrived, they were all housed at first in one large bunkhouse. As was to be expected, they quickly formed particular friendships and chose buddies. The boys had been deliberately put together for this reason, so that changes in their affectional relationships could be observed later when the boys were separated into different groups which were not formed on the basis of personal attraction. After a few days, the boys were divided into two groups, the Red Devils and the Bulldogs, each in its own cabin. Before doing this, each boy was informally asked who his best friends were, then "best friends" were placed in different groups as far as possible. The pain of separation was assuaged by allowing each group to go at once on a hike and camp-out.

Each of the two newly formed groups soon acquired an informal and spontaneous kind of organization as some members came to be looked upon as leaders, duties were divided among members, unwritten norms of behavior were adopted, and an *esprit de corps* developed (see figures 31 and 32).

One boy excelled in cooking. Another led in athletics. Others, though not outstanding in any one skill could be counted on to pitch in and do their level best in anything the group attempted. One or two seemed to disrupt activities, to start teasing at the wrong moment or offer suggestions. A few boys consistently had good suggestions and showed ability to coordinate the efforts of others in carrying them through. Within a few days one person had proved himself more resourceful and skillful than the rest. Thus, rather quickly, a leader and lieutenants emerged. Some boys sifted toward the bottom of the heap, while others jockeyed for higher positions.[3]

These developments were watched closely. Each boy's relative position in his group was rated not only on the basis of observations but also by informal sounding of the boys' opinions as to who got things started, who got things done, and who could be counted on to support group activities.

Figure 31. Percentage of Ingroup Friendship Choices of Bulldogs and Red Devils

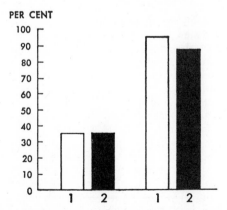

Source: Muzafer Sherif, "Experiments in Group Conflict," *Scientific American* 195 (November 1956): 56. Copyright © 1956 by Scientific American, Inc. All rights reserved. Reprinted by permission of the author and W. H. Freeman & Co.

3. Ibid., pp. 55–56.

Figure 32. Friendship Choices of Bulldogs and Red Devils

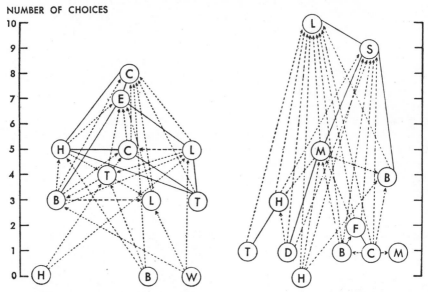

As the group became an organization, the boys coined nicknames. The big, blond, hardy leader of one group was dubbed "Baby Face" by his admiring followers. A boy with a rather long head became "Lemon Head." Each group developed its own jargon, special jokes, secrets and special ways of performing tasks. One group, after killing a snake near a place where it had gone to swim, named the place "Moccasin Creek" and thereafter preferred this swimming hole to any other, though there were better ones nearby.

Wayward members who failed to do things "right" or who did not contribute their bit to the common effort, found themselves receiving the "silent treatment," ridicule or even threats. Each group selected symbols and a name, and they had these put on their caps and T-shirts. The 1954 camp was conducted in Oklahoma, near a famous hideaway of Jesse James called Robber's Cave. The two groups of boys at this camp named themselves the Rattlers and the Eagles.

Our conclusions at every phase of the study were based on a variety of observations, rather than on any single method. For example [in the 1953 experiment, reported in Sherif, White, and Harvey (1955)] we devised a game to test the boys' evaluations of one another. Before an important baseball game, we set up a target board for the boys to throw at on the pretense of making practice for the game more interesting. There were no marks on the front of the board for the boys to judge objectively how close the ball came to a bull's-eye, but, unknown to them, the board was wired to flashing lights behind so that an observer could see exactly where the ball hit. We found that the boys consistently overestimated the performances by the most highly regarded members of their group and underestimated the scores of those of low social standing.

The attitudes of group members were even more dramatically illustrated during a cook-out in the woods. The staff supplied the boys with unprepared food and let them cook it themselves. One boy promptly started to build a fire, asking for help in getting wood. Another attacked the raw hamburger to make patties. Others prepared a place to put buns, relishes and the like. Two mixed soft drinks from flavoring and sugar. One boy who stood around without helping was told by the others to "get to it." Shortly the fire was blazing and the cook had hamburgers sizzling. Two boys distributed them as rapidly as they became edible. Soon it was time for the watermelon. A low-ranking member of the group took a knife and started toward the melon. Some of the boys protested. The most highly regarded boy in the group took over the knife, saying, "You guys who yell the loudest get yours last."

When the two groups in the camp had developed group organization and spirit, we proceeded to the experimental studies of intergroup relations. The groups had had no previous encounters; indeed, in the 1954 camp at Robber's Cave the two groups came in separate buses and were kept apart while each acquired a group feeling.

Our working hypothesis was that when two groups have conflicting aims—i.e., when one can achieve its ends only at the expense of the other—their members will become hostile to each other even though the groups are composed of normal, well-adjusted individuals. . . . To produce friction between the groups of boys we arranged a tournament of games: baseball, touch football, a tug-of-war, a treasure hunt, and so on. The tournament started in a spirit of good sportsmanship. But as it progressed good feeling soon evaporated. The members of each group began to call their rivals "stinkers," "sneaks" and "cheaters." They refused to have anything more to do with individuals in the opposing group. The boys in the 1949 camp turned against buddies whom they had chosen as "best friends" [on a sociometric test] when they first arrived at the camp. A large proportion of the boys in each group gave negative ratings to all the boys in the other. The rival groups made threatening posters and planned raids, collecting secret hoards of green apples for ammunition. In the Robber's Cave camp the Eagles, after a defeat in a tournament game, burned a banner left behind by the Rattlers; the next morning the Rattlers seized the Eagles' flag when they arrived on the athletic field. From that time on name-calling, scuffles, and raids were the rule of the day.

Within each group, of course, solidarity increased. There were changes: one group deposed its leader because he could not "take it" in the contests with the adversary; another group overnight made something of a hero of a big boy who had previously been regarded as a bully. But morale and cooperativeness within the group became stronger. It is noteworthy that this heightening of cooperativeness and generally democratic behavior did not carry over to the group's relations with other groups.

Restoring Intergroup Harmony

We now turned to the other side of the problem: How can two groups in conflict be brought into harmony? We first undertook to test the theory that pleasant social contacts between members of conflicting groups would reduce friction between them. In the 1954 camp we brought the hostile Rattler and Eagles together for social events: going to the movies, eating in the same dining room and so on. But far from reducing conflict, these situations only served as opportunities for the rival groups to berate and attack each other. In the dining-hall line they shoved each other aside, and the group that lost the contest for the head of the line shouted "Ladies first!" at the winner. They threw paper, food and vile names at each other at the tables. An Eagle bumped by a Rattler was admonished by his fellow Eagles to brush "the dirt" off his clothes.

We then returned to the corollary of our assumption about the creation of conflict. Just as competition generates friction, working in a common endeavor should promote harmony. It seemed to us, . . . that where harmony between groups is established, the most decisive factor is the existence of "superordinate" goals which have a compelling appeal for both which neither could achieve without the other. To test

Figure 33. Intergroup Friendship   Figure 34. Negative Ratings of Opposing
Choices of Rattlers and Eagles   Group Members for Rattlers and Eagles

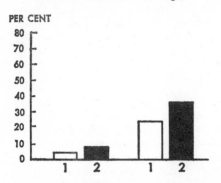
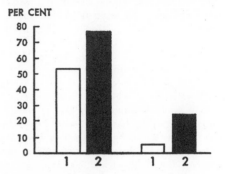

Source: Muzafer Sherif, "Experiments in Group Conflict," *Scientific American* 195 (November 1956): 57, 58. Copyright © 1956 by Scientific American, Inc. All rights reserved. Reprinted by permission of the author and W. H. Freeman & Co.

this hypothesis experimentally, we created a series of urgent, and natural, situations which challenged the boys.

One was a breakdown in the water supply. Water came to the camp in pipes from a tank about a mile away. We arranged to interrupt it and then called the boys together to inform them of the crisis. Both groups promptly volunteered to search the water line for the trouble. They worked together harmoniously, and before the end of the afternoon they had located and corrected the difficulty.

A similar opportunity offered itself when the boys requested a movie. We told them that the camp could not afford to rent one. The two groups then got together, figured out how much each group would have to contribute, chose the film by a vote and enjoyed the showing together.

One day the two groups went on an outing at a lake some distance away. A large truck was to go to town for food. But when everyone was hungry and ready to eat, it developed that the truck would not start (we had taken care of that). The boys got a rope—the same rope they had used in their acrimonious tug-of-war—and all pulled together to start the truck.

These joint efforts did not immediately dispel hostility. At first the groups returned to the old bickering and name-calling as soon as the job in hand was finished. But gradually the series of cooperative acts reduced friction and conflict. The members of the two groups began to feel more friendly to each other. For example, a Rattler whom the Eagles disliked for his sharp tongue and skill in defeating them became a "good egg." The boys stopped shoving in the meal line. They no longer called each other names, and sat together at the table. New friendships developed between individuals in the two groups.

In the end the groups were actively seeking opportunities to mingle, to entertain and "treat" each other. They decided to hold a joint campfire. They took turns presenting skits and songs. Members of both groups requested that they go home together on the same bus, rather than on the separate buses in which they had come. On the way the bus stopped for refreshments. One group still had five dollars which they had won as a prize in a contest. They decided to spend this sum on refreshments. On their own initiative they invited their former rivals to be their guests for malted milks.

Our interviews with the boys confirmed this change. From choosing their "best friends" almost exclusively in their own group, many of them shifted to listing boys in the other group as best friends (see figure 33).

They were glad to have a second chance to rate boys in the other group, some of them remarking that they had changed their minds since the first rating made after the tournament. Indeed they had. The new ratings were largely favorable (see figure 34).[4]

Consistency of the Informal Structure

Since the formal structure of a group is usually instituted or altered in a way which is obvious to everyone, including the investigator, little attention has been given to the consistency of the formal structure in the literature. On the informal side, the persistence of the structure based on interpersonal choice is usually studied by administering sociometric tests at several points in a group's life. A number of investigators find high correlations between successive tests, indicating that the informal structure persists or becomes more apparent over a period of time (Jennings, 1937; Newstetter, Feldstein, and Newcomb, 1938; Criswell, 1939; Zeleny, 1939b; Jennings, 1942; Williams and Leavitt, 1947; Jennings, 1950a; Byrd, 1951; Gronlund, 1955b; Klein, 1956; Davis and Warnath, 1957; Bjerstedt, 1958; Newcomb, 1963; Nelson, 1964c; Fjeld, 1965; Horrocks and Benimoff, 1966; Shubkin, Karpov, and Kochetov, 1968; Griffitt and Nelson, 1970; Singh, 1971).

The reliabilities of sociometric tests used in 53 studies have been analyzed in detail by Mouton, Blake, and Fruchter (1955a). They conclude that there is enough evidence to justify the hypotheses that the consistency of sociometric choices between test and retest will be greater under the following conditions:

1. The time interval between test and retest is short.
2. The subjects are adults or near adults.
3. The subjects have known each other for a long time before the first test.
4. The criterion of choice by which judgments are made is relevant to the activity of the group.
5. A large number of discriminations is required by the technique of choosing.
6. The group from which the choices are made is large.

Once social structures are formed, it is easier for subject to learn them if the structures are balanced and complete (Mosher, 1967; Van Kreveld and Poitou, 1972; Innes, 1973; Yang and Yang, 1973) provided that the subject's emotional state does not interfere with judgment (Reker, 1974).

Bases of Friendship

Most people choose each other for a variety of reasons. The generalization that "birds of a feather flock together" is supported by most of the studies of friendship, although there is also evidence that "opposites attract." To sort out the conditions under which one or the other of these generalizations will hold, it is helpful to have some theory. Once more AGIL comes to our aid to provide a preliminary ordering to the voluminous literature on friendship. The first factor in friendship formation is *proximity,* since persons who never meet never become part of the same social system and therefore have no opportunity to form interpersonal relations. Once two persons are part of the same system, they may be attracted to each

4. Ibid., pp. 56–58.

other because of biological traits (A), personality characteristics (G), common or reciprocal roles (I), or common values (L). We would expect that the strongest interpersonal bonds would include all four system levels.

The evidence for the importance of proximity is as follows: persons who live near each other (Hunt and Solomon, 1942; Danielsson, 1949; Lundberg, Hertzler, and Dickson, 1949; Festinger, Schachter, and Back, 1950; Festinger, 1951a; Willerman and Swanson, 1952; Blake et al., 1956; Loether, 1960; Barnlund and Harland, 1963; Priest and Sawyer, 1967; Athanasiou and Yoshioka, 1973; Martin, 1974) or are near to each other on the job (James, 1951b; Kipnis, 1957) or in school (Maisonneuve, Palmade, and Fourment, 1952; Byrne and Buehler, 1955; Heber and Heber, 1957; Byrne, 1961b) become friends more often than persons who live or work farther apart. Once acquainted, persons who are attracted to each other seek each other out at lunch or other places of possible contact and so increase the "chance" of being together (Hughes, 1946). Friendship groups continue longest if the members have a work relationship with each other (Gross, 1956)).

Once two persons are part of the same social system, they may form a friendship on the basis of similar biological traits such as athletic ability or physical attractiveness, although physically attractive persons tend to be highly chosen by everyone (Byrne, London, and Reeves, 1968; Byrne, Ervin, and Lamberth, 1970; Kiesler and Baral, 1970; Aronson and Aronson, 1971; Berman and Brickman, 1971; Stroebe et al., 1971; Cavior and Boblett, 1972; Murstein, 1972; Poe and Mills, 1972; Curran, 1973a; Huston, 1973; Insko et al., 1973; Dion and Berscheid, 1974; Lerner and Moore, 1974).

Even more likely is that they will have personality characteristics which are compatible in some way. Individuals with the same personality type tend to choose each other (Maisonneuve, 1954; Bennis and Peabody, 1962; Hoffman and Maier, 1966; Byrne, Griffitt, and Stefaniak, 1967), and marriage partners with similar personality traits are found to be more satisfied with their spouses (Burchinal, Hawkes, and Gardner, 1957).

Persons are also found to choose others whom they describe as having traits similar to their own positive traits (Thompson and Nishimura, 1952; Lundy, 1958) and to reject others whom they describe as having traits similar to their own negative traits (Lundy, 1956b). However, not all studies agree on the similarities in the personalities of friends, and some studies report no significant correlations (Pintner, Forlano, and Freedman, 1937; Zimmer, 1956; Hoffman, 1958). In one study of married couples, assertive persons were found to marry receptive persons. Other personality needs such as abasement, achievement, approach, and autonomy were found to be generally complementary (Winch, Ktsanes, and Ktsanes, 1954, 1955; Winch, 1955, 1957). This somewhat conflicting evidence may only mean that friends are similar on some but not all of their personality characteristics (Bowerman and Day, 1956; Rosow, 1957).

It is also possible that "congruence" of personality traits is more important than similarity. Two personality needs are "congruent" if they allow reciprocation; that is, dominant persons will choose those who are submissive, while those who prefer close interpersonal warmth will choose others who are similar in this trait rather than those who prefer distance (Secord and Backman, 1964). (See the discussion of Leary's 16 interpersonal categories in chapter 3 and that of the research by Lemann and Solomon later in this chapter).

Additional articles on the issue of similarity versus complementarity in personality traits of friends include Richardson, 1939; Thorpe, 1955; Ramey, 1958;

Winch, 1958; Hilkevitch, 1960; Izard, 1960a, 1960b; Reilly, Commins, and Stefic, 1960; Beier, Rossi, and Garfield, 1961; Mehlman, 1962; Banta and Hetherington, 1963; Izard, 1963a, 1963b; Alexander, 1964; Rychlak, 1965; Griffitt, 1966; Hoffman and Maier, 1966; Byrne, Griffitt, and Stefaniak, 1967; Streufert, Bushinsky, and Castore, 1967; Alexander and Campbell, 1968; Meyer and Barbour, 1968; Novak and Lerner, 1968; Wright, 1968; Byrne and Griffitt, 1969; Jellison and Zeisset, 1969; Reitz and Robinson, 1969; Rosenfeld and Nauman, 1969; Murstein, 1970; Palmer and Byrne, 1970; Peabody, 1970b; Pierce, 1970; Stalling, 1970; Tomekovic, 1970; Wiener, 1970; Banikiotes, Russell, and Linden, 1971; Centers and Granville, 1971; Hendrick and Brown, 1971; Mann, 1971; Phares and Wilson, 1971; Silverman and Shrauger, 1971; Barton and Cattell, 1972; Shepherd, 1972; Curran, 1973b; Dion and Dion, 1973; Duck, 1973a, 1973b; Johnston and Centers, 1973; Markey, 1973; Seyfried and Hendrick, 1973a; Singh, 1973; Ajzen, 1974; Posavac and Pasko, 1974.

Moving up to the social system level, we find that friendships are formed on the basis of common roles such as those based on age, sex, and group position (Furfey, 1927; Parten, 1933b; Smith, 1944; Faunce and Beegle, 1948; James, 1951b; Triandis, Vassiliou, and Thomanek, 1966; Kiesler and Goldberg, 1968; Peters and Kennedy, 1970; Graham, 1971; Duck, 1972; Duck and Spencer, 1972; King and Easthope, 1973; R. A. Lewis, 1973a). Congruence also functions here. It has been reported that men like women (Seyfried and Hendrick, 1973b) and the research on mate selection suggests that women may also like men regardless of their other social characteristics.

Of course age and sex are also associated with biological traits, personality characteristics, and value systems, but with the advent of the various liberation movements in the 1970s it became apparent that social characteristics traditionally associated with age and sex (and also race) were not firmly fixed, but were roles which could be learned. As long as these role distinctions exist, it will not be surprising to find that interpersonal attraction will be influenced by traditional norms (cf. research on attraction between blacks and whites: Mann, 1959; Byrne and McGraw, 1964; Smith, Williams, and Willis, 1967; Hendrick and Hawkins, 1969; Richardson and Emerson, 1970; Boyanowsky, 1971; Hendrick, Bixenstine, and Hawkins, 1971; Mezei, 1971; Parrott and Coleman, 1971; Penner, 1971; Green, 1972; Hendrick, Stikes, and Murray, 1972; Savell and Luttrell, 1972; Weitz, 1972; Hendrick and Rumenik, 1973; Hendrick et al., 1973; Koulack and Cumming, 1973; Larsen et al., 1973; Moss and Andrasik, 1973; Sherif, 1973; Silverman, 1974).

Finally, at the cultural level, a friendship is more likely to continue if the individuals have *common interests* or *values* (Winslow, 1937; Richardson, 1940; Newcomb, 1943; Precker, 1952; Gross, 1954; Newcomb, 1956, 1960). For instance, in a study of the Supreme Court as a small group, three cliques were identified. The membership in these cliques appeared to be related to the ideology of the judges (Snyder, 1958). In student veteran families, the number of family friends increases with the length of residence in the community and the number of children in the family (Hare and Hare, 1948). Being an "old-timer" at camp or in the factory provides the type of common experience upon which friendship is based (Hunt and Solomon, 1942; Rich, 1952), and religion, ethnic group, and social class may provide a *common value orientation* (Hollingshead, 1949; Goodnow and Tagiuri, 1952; Dahlke, 1953; Oppenheim, 1955; Berkun and Meeland, 1958; Mann, 1958). In addition to providing a common value orientation, social class often serves the additional function of restricting the contacts of members of a given class to others within the same class (Rowland, 1939). The gross effects of class differences on behavior are seldom apparent in small group research, since the school populations which provide the subjects for most of the experiments present a sample of a very limited range of the total society.

More recent studies which have explored the relationship between attitude similarity and interpersonal attractiveness include Lerner and Becker, 1962; Byrne and Nelson, 1965; Aronson and Worchel, 1966; Byrne and Griffitt, 1966; Marsden, 1966; Clore and Baldridge, 1968; Byrne et al., 1969; McGrew, 1969; Gouaux and Lamberth, 1970; Kaplan and Olczak, 1970; Perloe, 1970; Rake, 1970; Banikiotes, 1971; Batchelor and Tesser, 1971; Bloom, 1971; Byrne et al., 1971; Franklin, 1971; Gormly, Gormly, and Johnson, 1971; Jackson and Mascaro, 1971; Kaplan and Olczak, 1971; Lamberth and Byrne, 1971; Mascaro and Jackson, 1971; Nelson and Meadow, 1971; Tesser, 1971; Frisch and Zedeck, 1972; Good and Good, 1972a, 1972b, 1972c; Gouaux, Lamberth, and Friedrich, 1972; Hodges and Byrne, 1972; Johnson and Tesser, 1972; Kaplan, 1972a; Levinger, 1972; A. G. Miller, 1972; Tesser, 1972; Touhey, 1972a; Wright and Wright, 1972; Bergeron and Zanna, 1973; Bleda, Bell, and Byrne, 1973; Bleda and Castore, 1973; Hautaluoma and Scott, 1973; Mascaro and Graves, 1973; R. Nash, 1973; Posavac and McKillip, 1973; Scott, 1973; Touhey, 1973a; Veitch and Griffitt, 1973; Griffitt and Veitch, 1974; Hendrick and Seyfried, 1974; Insko and Wetzel, 1974; Layton and Insko, 1974; Manis, Cornell, and Moore, 1974.

In addition to the research mentioned above on friendship formation, some studies provide a general overview or do not fall easily into one of the categories already discussed. (See Zander and Havelin, 1960; Wilson and Miller, 1961; Nowak, 1963; von Sivers, 1963; Rapoport and Rapoport, 1964; Chambliss, 1965; Miller et al., 1966; Darley and Berscheid, 1967; Jellison and Mills, 1967; Lerner, Dillehay, and Sherer, 1967; Fiebert and Fiebert, 1969; Goldstein and Rosenfeld, 1969; Rosenblood and Goldstein, 1969; Tesser, 1969; Wright, 1969; Bhojak and Mehta, 1970; Bowditch and King, 1970; Levinger, Senn, and Jorgensen, 1970; Mascaro, 1970; Rubin, 1970; Byrne, 1971; Taylor and Mettee, 1971; Zellner and Levinger, 1971; Bull et al., 1972; Driscoll, Davis and Lipetz, 1972; Schmidt and Levin, 1972; Vockell and Asher, 1972; Bonacich and Lewis, 1973; R. A. Lewis, 1973b; Saegert, Swap and Zajonc, 1973; Sutherland and Insko, 1973; Wakil, 1973b; Black and Angelis, 1974; Layton and Insko, 1974.) Bibliographies on friendship have been published by Coelho (1959) and Gratton (1970).

One way to look at the formation of friendship bonds between members is to consider the exchanges which are being made or which can be called upon within the friendship pair. Friends try to keep their relationships balanced by exchanging affection (I) or respect (L) for other valued forms of behavoir such as information (A) or power (G) (Blau, 1960a, 1962; J. A. Davis, 1963; Newcomb, 1963; Feather, 1967a). Thus submissive persons choose those who will provide direction (Secord and Backman, 1964), or a person will increase his liking for another if he anticipates cooperation in a mutual task (Darley and Berscheid, 1967). These types of exchanges may be more obvious among pairs of friends, but some form of exchange appears to be basic to all human interaction.

Overchosen and Underchosen Members

Certain types of personalities appear to be more "popular" since persons with these characteristics are chosen more often on sociometric tests. Specifically, girls in one college who were rated as generous, enthusiastic, and affectionate were chosen more often than those who were rated as stingy, apathetic, and cold (Lemann and Solomon, 1952), and girls with scores near the median on dominance, security, and femininity were the most chosen in another college (Lindzey and Urdan, 1954). These same personality characteristics (with the exception of femininity) have been found to be associated with popularity in a summer camp for boys (Hunt and Solomon, 1942). In general, persons who are high on socially desirable traits tend to be overchosen (Lansing, 1957; Fishman, 1966; Horrocks and Benimoff, 1967; Smith and Olson, 1970; Walster, 1970; Crandall, 1971; Larsen, 1971; Codol, 1972–1973; Lemineur and Meurice, 1972; Leonard, 1973). Popularity appears to be related to the extent to which a person exemplifies the group ideal (McCandless, 1942; French and Mensh, 1948; Bates, 1952; Stevens, 1953). If a person is popular, he may be receiving votes from some who are not like him in personality as well as some who are since friendship involves two-way or reciprocated choices, whereas popularity involves only one-way choices (Backman and Secord, 1964; Berscheid et al., 1971).

In many cases, the "popular" person may represent the "ideal" or "norm" of the group simply because the indications of what is "ideal" and who is "popular" are derived from the same source. That is, the observer asks group members on one occasion to indicate their preferred personality traits. The average rating on a trait then becomes a "norm." At another time the observer asks who is preferred for work or play. Since the majority of the group, who represent the norm, will tend to choose others like themselves, the result will be that the individuals receiving the most choices will also represent the norm. This may explain the finding that the attractiveness of certain personality types, as rated by members of the group, may be different than when rated by an outside judge or observer (Rosemary Lippitt, 1941). The use of the same population to derive measures of "normal" and "popular" may also account for the "accuracy" of perception of popular members. When college subjects in a class of 48 were divided into five work groups, the popular members were found to be more "accurate" than the task leaders in their "perception" of the popularity of others and certain group dimensions (those suggested by Hemphill, 1956). Here "accuracy" was measured by agreement with the group as a whole (Bugental and Lehner, 1958).

The individuals in the group who receive the most choices from all the group members also choose each other (Potashin, 1946; Weber, 1950; Lemann and Solomon, 1952; Roistacher, 1974). These "overchosen" members also make more positive choices (French and Chadwick, 1956) have patterns of choice and rejection which differ from "isolates" (Jennings, 1941), and are highly chosen by members of other subgroups within the same social system (Festinger, Schachter, and Back, 1950).

Part of the correlation between choices inside and outside of a given small group may be accounted for by the finding that status differences from large organizations carry over into *ad hoc* training groups so that individuals who have high "outside" status are chosen in the *ad hoc* group over those with low "outside" status (Horwitz, Exline, and Lee, 1953; Lammers, 1967).

In small discussion groups, these overchosen members also reveal a pattern of interaction which one would associate with leadership, especially if they rank high on both a control and an affection criterion (Borgatta and Bales, 1956).

Apparently, being well liked does not make a person especially friendly to those less popular, even though they may be friendly to him (Newstetter, 1937). This is probably a reflection of the fact that high-status persons (upper social class or college class) are chosen in preference to those of lower rank and receive more communications because the low-ranking members would like to move up in the hierarchy (Dodd, 1935; Lundberg and Steele, 1938; Vreeland, 1942; Kelley, 1951). Although more recent research has confirmed the fact that persons choose upward in the hierarchy, the reasons for this are not always given (Tagiuri, Kogan, and Long, 1959; Larsen and Larsen, 1969; Jones and Shrauger, 1970; Mehrabian, 1970b; Greenberger and Sorensen, 1971; Anderson, Linder, and Lopes, 1973). Future research will probably reveal the fact that we are looking at one half of an exchange between the low-status and the high-status person. The low-status person is giving liking in return for something of value from the high-status person.

This same tendency to choose upward is also found when status differences are developed in the course of group interaction rather than ascribed to members before they join the group. For example, when a number of subjects were given intellectual tasks which appeared the same and some subjects were made to fail and some succeed, most of the subjects chose as a partner for a second similar task a person who had been successful on the first task. For the second part of the experiment pairs of subjects were composed of those who had chosen each other and those who had not. Again success was given to some, failure to others for both types of pairs. Finally, when each subject was asked to choose a partner for a second time, he again chose a person who had been initially successful or one with whom he had previously worked (Gilchrist, 1952). In a similar experiment, the successful partner was also chosen when the subject was allowed free choice (Shaw and Gilchrist, 1955). Other studies confirm the relationship between attraction and task success (Flanders and Havumaki, 1960b; Kleiner, 1960; Lerner, 1965; Senn, 1971).

When an opinion is presented in a group discussion, an individual tends to think that the group members he likes agree with his judgment and that those he dislikes disagree (Horowitz, Lyons, and Perlmutter, 1951). This effect, combined with the tendency of low-status persons to choose upward in the hierarchy, probably results in an overestimation by a low-status member of the backing he is receiving from the more "weighty" members of the group. For example, in a rural high school more of the lower-rank students (lower class and younger) tended to overestimate the number of their acquaintances, although the relationship was not statistically significant (Buck, 1952). Somewhat contradictory findings are reported in a study of therapy groups in England (Talland, 1958). There, men overestimated their rank received on leadership and popularity rankings, whereas women underestimated their rank.

Attempts at friendliness from low- to high-status persons will tend to subside if the low-status persons see no chance of improving their position. Friendliness of the high-status persons toward the lows will diminish if the high-status persons are worried about maintaining their positions at the top (Kelley, 1951).

In one study of schoolboys, the number of *negative* choices a boy received was found to be most predictive of his behavior. The largest number of negative choices was received by boys who tended to be the scapegoats. The boys who were rejected most often were either truants who had few friends or delinquents who had many enemies (Croft and Grygier, 1956). In general, individuals who are emotionally disturbed will initiate fewer positive relationships (McMillan and Silverberg, 1955), and therefore receive fewer positive choices in return. It is also possible to have central members who are poorly adjusted if they derive their "popularity" from a set of neurotic relationships with other group members (Scheidlinger, 1952).

Choices along the Close-Distant and Initiate-Receive Axes

The study by Lemann and Solomon (1952) is reported in sufficient detail to permit analysis of choices along the close-distant and initiate-receive axes of personality. In this study, six personality traits were compared for popular and unpopular members of three women's dormitories in an urban college. The scales, which were all bipolar, were divided into two sets: "alpha" scales in which the ratings ran from good to bad (generous-stingy, affectionate-cold, enthusiastic-apathetic), and "beta" scales in which the ratings ran from bad to good to bad (dominating-submissive, shy-bold, stubborn-yielding). In general, Lemann and Solomon found that overchosen and underchosen members were different on the alpha scales but not on the beta scales.

When these scales are considered in the light of the first two dimensions of interpersonal behavior, the alpha scales appear to represent the positive-negative dimension, while the beta scales represent the dominant-submissive dimension (see figure 35). As a result, the finding that choices are related to differences in alpha scale characteristics but not beta scale characteristics supports the hypothesis that individuals who want close relationships will not choose those who prefer distant relationships but that those who prefer to initiate may choose those who like to receive. This hypothesis receives further support from the fact that both high-status (close) individuals and low-status (distant) individuals chose those of similar status and rejected those at the opposite pole more often than could be expected by chance.

The finding that the girls who received the largest number of choices were generous, enthusiastic, and affectionate suggests that individuals who prefer close relationships tend to have more friends that those who prefer to keep their distance, since a close orientation encourages friendship.

Since there was no positive correlation between being dominating, bold, or stubborn and receiving many sociometric choices, there must have been passive as well as active members among the "sociometric stars." This confirms Gibb's (1950) observation that not all "stars" are leaders and not all active individuals are "stars." The amount of initiating behavior of a member was, however, related to her "noticeability." The noticeability score was computed by adding all choices and

Figure 35. Lemann and Solomon's Alpha and Beta Scales and the Output and Input Axes

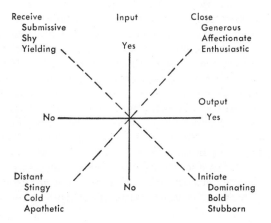

rejections for each subject. Girls who were high on noticeability were also more dominating, bold, and stubborn.

Popularity and Skill

High choice status has also been found to be positively related to skill in recreational groups, such as bowling teams (Whyte, 1943), and also to combat effectiveness (Baier, 1947; Williams and Leavitt, 1947), individual productivity in work groups (Blau, 1954b; Jackson, 1959b), and influence in laboratory groups of children (Gardner, 1956) and in other laboratory and field settings (Fishbein, 1965; Mikula and Walter, 1969; D. W. Johnson and Johnson, 1972; Spence and Helmreich, 1972; Harvey and Kelley, 1973; S. B. Kiesler, 1973b).

Popularity shows a negative correlation with accident-proneness, sickness, and disciplinary offenses (Mouton, Blake, and Fruchter, 1955b). However, the positive relation between skill and popularity in industry may not be evident in cases in which choice status in the group depends more upon the extent to which a person conforms to the production standards set by the informal group than to the overall production level of the whole industry (French and Zander, 1949).

If a person seems flawless, he may not be as attractive as one who has some fault. Great Chinese artists of the past were presumably aware of this when they would leave one obvious flaw in each painting so that the viewers would see that they too were human. Several experiments have explored the hypothesis that "to err is humanizing." Subjects are asked to make judgments about a highly competent person being interviewed. In one version the same person spills a cup of coffee part way through the interview. The person who blunders is judged to be more attractive (Helmreich, Aronson, and LeFan, 1970; Deaux, 1972).

The individual's perception of his skill may not be accurate. In one study of informal groups which were competing at dart throwing, the high-status members tended to overestimate their own performance (Harvey, 1953). Other group members also tend to overestimate the skill of well-liked members (Sherif, White, and Harvey, 1955; Nunn, 1971).

Morale and Cohesiveness

As well as being an indication of the informal structure of a group, interpersonal choices can also be used to form an index of morale or cohesiveness. Groups are said to have high morale or to be cohesive if members are highly attracted to the group. The terms *morale* and *cohesiveness* have generally been used interchangeably. Some authors form an index of the ratio of ingroup to outgroup sociometric choices which they call an "index of morale" (Zeleny, 1939b), others call a similar index an "index of cohesiveness" (Martin, Darley, and Gross, 1952), and still others call it an "index of cohesiveness-morale" (Fessenden, 1953).

The term *cohesiveness* is generally favored by those whose work follows the pattern set by Lewin (Schachter et al., 1951; Gross and Martin, 1952; Schachter, 1952; Cartwright and Zander, 1953; Libo, 1953; Keedy, 1956; Eisman, 1959; Ramuz-Nienhuis and Van Bergen, 1960; Lott, 1961; Gruen, 1965; de Montmollin, 1966b; Enoch and McLemore, 1967; Cartwright, 1968; R. A. Feldman, 1968). They use an index of attractiveness to the group which is based on any one or a combination of choices in the task or social-emotional areas. One should be cautious, however, about combining the results of studies which use different socio-metric criteria for their indices. Attraction based on "likability," for example, may lead to different forms of interaction than attraction based on "task ability." If the group members come together with work as the primary goal, they will probably spend little time on the social activity which would be characteristic of a group formed on an affectional basis.

Where a distinction is made between cohesiveness and morale, cohesiveness is used more to represent the "desire to belong to a group," wheras morale includes an emphasis on a "disposition to act toward a goal" (Albert, 1953; see also Hagstrom and Selvin, 1965). In one methodological study of the concept of morale, for example, the concept was defined as "an average feeling of contentment or satisfaction about the major aspects of the work situation" (Campbell and Tyler, 1957).

An index of the attractiveness of the group for its members is often desired, since the extent of the attractivesness is also found to be related to significance of the group as a reference group for judgments about the self and others, as indicated in chapters 2 and 5. Once an individual has dropped out of a group which has lost its attraction for him (Sagi, Olmsted, and Atelsek, 1955), the group will no longer be important as a positive reference group.

A group will tend to become cohesive if it is formally well organized, the members are individually motivated to do the task and are attracted to each other, and the group is successful (French, 1941; Deutscher and Deutscher, 1955; Pepitone and Kleiner, 1957; Deutsch, 1959; Dittes, 1959; Wolman, 1960; Myers, 1962; Shaw and Shaw, 1962; Snoek, 1962; Endleman, 1963; Heslin and Dunphy, 1964; Frye, 1966; C. Wagner, 1966; Gartner and Iverson, 1967; Lott, Lott, and Matthews, 1969; Samuels and O'Rourke, 1969; Dayhaw and McInnis, 1970; Good and Nelson, 1971, 1973). For example, some college rooming houses for girls contained girls who were very satisfied with their dormitory life. The houses with the largest number of satisfied girls (i.e., houses which were cohesive) were the ones which started with some core of members who had known each other before, which lost fewest members over time, and whose members developed more new friends within the house than outside it (Darley, Gross, and Martin, 1951). At the other end of the continuum, in a school for delinquent girls, it was observed that cottages with a low percentage of choices made within the cottage were marked by a high degree of deviant behavior and low interest in controlling this behavior (Moreno, 1953). The relative number of within-group choices as an index of cohesiveness is less appropriate for children, since the number and strength of interpersonal relationships is correlated with age. Very young children make few choices either in or out of a group (Parten, 1932; Harrocks and Buker, 1951).

In industrial plants where the personal bonds are well established and newly recruited members are easily incorporated, there is less labor turnover than in plants which are similar in geographic location, technology, and labor force, but where the bonds between members are weak and no informal group standards are enforced (Fox and Scott, 1943; Mayo and Lombard, 1944). Absenteeism and turnover are especially high among the new workers in such plants. High ingroup choice is also related to effective performance on field problems by infantry rifle squads (Goodacre, 1951). However, a cohesive group may be less productive if the members have agreed on a lower production rate in opposition to the norms of the larger organization (Cartwright and Robertson, 1961; Warwick, 1964; Lott and Lott, 1965).

In an extensive study of group cohesiveness in industrial workgroups, data were drawn from 228 workgroups ranging in size from five to fifty members in a machine factory. The results indicated that members of high-cohesive work groups exhibited less anxiety than members of low-cohesive work groups. In the high-cohesive groups there was also less variation in productivity among the members, although the high-cohesive groups differed more frequently and in greater amounts from the plant norm of productivity than did the low-cohesive groups. The amount of cohesiveness in a group was positively related to the degree of prestige which the members of the group attributed to their own jobs, the opportunities for interaction as measured by the size of the group (i.e., the larger the group, the fewer opportunities for interaction), and the length of time members had been together on the job (Seashore, 1954).

Anxiety and Affiliation

Most of the early investigators of interpersonal choice focused on the results of the choice and not on the emotional state or the situation of the chooser at the time the choice was made. Schachter's research on the psychology of affiliation (1959) led to a series of experiments on the effects of different types of emotional arousal on the tendency to seek affiliation with others. Schachter had been studying the consequences of isolation. Some subjects who were isolated appear to be quite anxious. To test the hypothesis that an increase in a subject's anxiety would lead to an increase in affiliative tendencies, Schachter conducted the following experiment.[5]

Experimental Procedure

There were two experimental conditions, one of high anxiety and one of low anxiety. Anxiety was manipulated in the following fashion. In the high-anxiety condition, the subjects, all college girls, strangers to one another, entered a room to find facing them a gentleman of serious mien, horn-rimmed glasses, dressed in a white laboratory coat, stethoscope dribbling out of his pocket, behind him an array of formidable electrical junk. After a few preliminaries, the experimenter began:

> Allow me to introduce myself, I am Dr. Gregor Zilstein of the Medical School's Departments of Neurology and Psychiatry. I have asked you all to come today in order to serve as subjects in an experiment concerned with the effects of electrical shock.

Zilstein paused ominously, then continued with a seven- or eight-minute recital of the importance of research in this area, citing electroshock therapy, the increasing number of accidents due to electricity, and so on. He concluded in this vein:

> What we will ask each you to do is very simple. We would like to give each of you a series of electric shocks. Now, I feel I must be completely honest with you and tell you exactly what you are in for. These shocks will hurt, they will be painful. As you can guess, if, in research of this sort, we're to learn anything at all that will really help humanity, it is necessary that our shocks be intense. What we will do is put an electrode on your hand, hook you into apparatus such as this [Zilstein points to the electrical-looking gadgetry behind him], give you a series of electric shocks, and take various measures such as your pulse rate, blood pressure, and so on. Again, I do want to be honest with you and tell you that these shocks will be quite painful but, of course, they will do not permanent damage.

5. Stanley Schachter, *The Psychology of Affiliation* (Stanford, Calif.: Stanford University Press, 1959), pp. 12–19. © 1959 by the Board of Trustees of the Leland Stanford Junior University. Reprinted by permission of the author and the publishers.

In the low-anxiety condition, the setting and costume were precisely the same except that there was no electrical apparatus in the room. After introducing himself, Zilstein proceeded:

> I have asked you all to come today in order to serve as subjects in an experiment concerned with the effects of electric shock. I hasten to add, do not let the word "shock" trouble you; I am sure that you will enjoy the experiment.

Then precisely the same recital on the importance of the research, concluding with:

> What we will ask each one of you to do is very simple. We would like to give each of you a series of very mild electric shocks. I assure you that what you will feel wil' not in any way be painful. It will resemble more a tickle or a tingle than anything unpleasant. We will put an electrode on your hand, give you a series of very mild shocks and measure such things as your pulse rate and blood pressure, measures with which I'm sure you are all familiar from visits to your family doctor.

From this point on, the experimental procedures in the two conditions were identical. In order to get a first measurement of the effectiveness of the anxiety manipulation, the experimenter continued:

> Before we begin, I'd like to have you tell us how you feel about taking part in this experiment and being shocked. We need this information in order to fully understand your reactions in the shocking apparatus. I ask you therefore to be as honest as possible in answering and describe your feelings as accurately as possible.

He then passed out a sheet headed, "How do you feel about being shocked?" and asked the subjects to check th appropriate point on a five-point scale ranging from "I dislike the idea very much" to "I enjoy the idea very much."

This done, the experimenter continued:

> Before we begin with the shocking proper there will be about a ten-minute delay while we get this room in order. We have several pieces of equipment to bring in and get set up. With this many people in the room, this would be very difficult to do, so we will have to ask you to be kind enough to leave the room.
>
> Here is what we will ask you to do for this ten-minute period of waiting. We have on this floor a number of additional rooms, so that each of you, if you would like, can wait alone in your own room. These rooms are comfortable and spacious; they all have armchairs, and there are books and magazines in each room. It did occur to us, however, that some of you might want to wait for these ten minutes together with some of the other girls here. If you would prefer this, of course, just let us know. We'll take one of the empty classrooms on this floor and you can wait together with some of the other girls there.

The experimenter then passed out a sheet on which the subjects could indicate their preference. This sheet read as follows:

> Please indicate below whether you prefer waiting your turn to be shocked alone or in the company of others.
> —————I prefer being alone.
> —————I prefer being with others.
> —————I really don't care.

In order to get a measure of the intensity of the subjects' desires to be alone or together, the experimenter continued:

> With a group this size and with the number of additional rooms we have, it's not always possible to give each girl exactly what she'd like. So be perfectly honest and let us know how much you'd like to be alone or together with other girls. Let us know just how you feel, and we'll use that information to come as close as possible to putting you into the arrangement of your choice.

The experimenter then passed out the following scale:

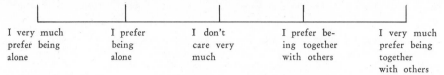

| I very much prefer being alone | I prefer being alone | I don't care very much | I prefer being together with others | I very much prefer being together with others |

To get a final measure of the effectiveness of the anxiety manipulation, the experimenter continued:

> It has, of course, occurred to us that some of you may not wish to take part in this experiment. Now, we would find it perfectly understandable if some of you should feel that you do not want to be a subject in an experiment in which you will be shocked. If this is the case just let us know. I'll pass out this sheet on which you may indicate whether or not you want to go on. If you do wish to be a subject, check "yes"; if you do not wish to take part, check "no" and you may leave. Of course, if you check "no" we cannot give you credit in your psychology classes for having taken part in this experiment.

After the subjects had marked their sheets, the experiment was over and the experimenter took off his white coat and explained in detail the purpose of the experiment and the reasons for the various deceptions practiced. The cooperation of the subjects was of course enlisted in not talking about the experiment to other students.

In summary, in this experimental set-up, anxiety has been manipulated by varying the fear of being shocked. The affiliative tendency is measured by the subject's preference for "Alone," "Together," or "Don't care" and by the expressed intensity of this preference.

Subjects

The subjects in this study were all girls, students in Introductory Psychology courses at the University of Minnesota. At the beginning of each semester, students in these classes may sign up for a subject pool. More than 90 percent of the students usually do so, for they receive one additional point on their final examination for each experimental hour they serve. This fact should be kept in mind when considering the proportion of subjects who refused to continue in the experiment.

The experimental sessions were run with groups of five to eight girls at a time, for a total of 32 subjects in the high-anxiety condition and 30 subjects in the low-anxiety condition. A deliberate attempt was made to insure that the subjects did not know one another before coming to the experiment. Despite our best efforts, 16 percent of the subjects had known one another beforehand. Data for these subjects were discarded, for it seemed clear that previous friendship would thoroughly confound the meaning of a choice of "Together" or "Alone." It should be noted, however, that though in both conditions such girls chose "Together" considerably more often than did girls who had not known one another before the experiment, the between-condition differences were in the same direction for both groups of subjects.

On this same point, an attempt was made to prevent the subjects from talking to one another while waiting for the experiment to begin, for again its felt that an interesting conversation or a particularly friendly girl might confound the choice of "Together" or "Alone." As each subject entered the experimental room, she was handed a multipaged questionnaire labeled "Biographical Inventory" and asked to begin filling it out. This device worked well and effectively prevented any chatter until all the subjects could begin his monologue.

Results

Table 15 presents data permitting evaluation of the effectiveness of the manipulation of anxiety. The column labeled "Anx" presents the mean score, by condition, of responses to the question "How do you feel about being shocked?" The greater the score, the greater the anxiety; a score greater than 3 indicates dislike. Clearly there are large and significant differences between the two conditions.

The results of the second measure of anxiety, a subject's willingness to continue in the experiment when given the opportunity to drop out, are presented in the column labeled "% S's refusing to continue." This is, perhaps, the best single indicator of the effectiveness of the manipulation, for it is a reality-bound measure. Again it is clear that the manipulation of anxiety has been successful. Some 19 percent of subjects in the low-anxiety condition were willing to go through with the experiment.

The effect of anxiety on the affiliative tendency may be noted in table 16, where, for each condition, the number of subjects choosing "Together," "Alone," or "Don't Care" is tabulated. It is evident that there is a strong positive relationship between anxiety and the index of affiliative tendency, the proportion of subjects choosing the "Together" alternative. Some 63 percent of subjects in the high-anxiety condition wanted to be together with other subjects while they waited to be shocked. In the low-anixety condition only 33 percent of the subjects wished to be together.

The column labeled "Overall Intensity" in table 16 presents the mean score for all subjects, in each condition, of responses to the scale designed to measure the intensity of the desire to be alone or together with others. The point "I don't care very much" is scored as zero. The two points on this scale indicating a preference for being together with other subjects are scored as $+1$ and $+2$ respectively. The points indicating a preference for being alone are scored as -1 and -2. The mean scores

Table 15. Effectiveness of Anxiety Manipulation

	N	Anx	% S's refusing to continue
High Anxiety	32	3.69	18.8
Low Anxiety	30	2.48	0
		$t = 5.22$	Exact $p = .03$
		$p < .001$	

Source: Stanley Schachter, *The Psychology of Affiliation* (Stanford, Calif.: Stanford University Press, 1959). © 1959 by the Board of Trustees of the Leland Stanford Junior University. Reprinted by permission of the author and the publishers.

Table 16. Relationship of Anxiety to Affiliative Tendency

	No. Choosing			Overall Intensity
	Together	Don't Care	Alone	
High Anxiety	20	9	3	+.88
Low Anxiety	10	18	2	+.35
	χ^2 Tog vs DC + A $= 5.27$			$t = 2.83$
	$.02 < p < .05$			$p < .01$

Source: Stanley Schachter, *The Psychology of Affiliation* (Stanford, Calif.: Stanford University Press, 1959). © 1959 by the Board of Trustees of the Leland Stanford Junior University. Reprinted by permission of the author and the publishers.

of this scale provide the best overall index of the magnitude of affiliative desires, for this score combines choice and intensity of choice. Also, this index incorporates the relatively milder preferences of subjects who chose the "Don't Care" alternative, for 30 percent of these subjects did express some preference on this scale. Again it is clear that affiliative desires increase with anxiety. The mean intensity score for high-anxiety subjects is +.88 and for low-anixety subjects is +.35.

Schachter concluded that his expectations about the relationship between anxiety and affiliation were "confirmed, but confirmed, in truth, in a blaze of ambiguity." He felt that he still needed to be clearer about various aspects of the relationship. Subsequent research by Schachter and others spelled out more of the details. When it was appropriate to be with others, subjects were more likely to choose to be with others if the others were also anxious (or fearful) about the same thing, thus providing an opportunity for "social comparison" of their feelings (Mattsson, 1960; Radloff, 1961; Zimbardo and Formica, 1963; Navar and Helmreich, 1971; Mills and Mintz, 1972; Firestone, Kaplan, and Russell, 1973; Lynch et al., 1973; Teichman, 1973). First-born or only children are more likely to want to affiliate (Wrightsman, 1960; Greenberg, 1967), but highly anxious persons or introverts are more likely to want to keep to themselves (Shapiro and Alexander, 1969; Teichman, 1974). Some subjects who are afraid may prefer a group with an older leader present to one composed entirely of peers (Helmreich and Collins, 1967).

Variations on this experiment in which subjects are aroused by hunger, sexual stimuli, danger, or negative evaluations produce similar results in that subjects seek out others or show a greater attraction to strangers (Weller, 1963; Rosenfeld and Franklin, 1966; Stapert and Clore, 1969; Gouaux, 1971; Mettee, Taylor, and Fisher, 1971; Walster and Berscheid, 1971; Buck and Parke, 1972; Dabbs and Helmreich, 1972; La Gaipa, 1972; R. E. Smith, 1972; Dutton and Aron, 1974).

Summary

Evidence of the direction of interpersonal choice may be drawn from observations of behavior, from the results of formal elections, or from the group member's private expression of opinion on a sociometric test. The rules which govern a sociometric test, as it has been developed by Moreno, are that there shall be private expression of unlimited choices and rejections for a specific activity made with reference to a clearly defined group. As a result of the test, the group should be reorganized by allowing persons who have chosen each other to do such things as sit together, work together, or play together, depending upon the criterion of the test. The use of the test is illustrated by a sociogram of the pattern of interpersonal choice in a cottage family in a school for delinquent girls. Here "stars," "isolates," and other constellations of choice can be differentiated.

Correlations are often high between choices based on a variety of criteria. This result occurs because there are actually some individuals who, as "great men," actually have desirable traits in all areas, and there are some subjects who will choose others on the basis of their own preferred criterion regardless of the criterion the experimenter suggests. Because the correlations between choices based on different criteria tend to be significant, many experimenters pool the ratings made on several criteria so that the distinctions are lost.

Any indication of positive choice will tend to be reciprocated. If two subjects like each other and each in turn likes a third person or object, the relationships are in "balance." If a combination of positive and negative choices does not result in a balanced state, subjects will usually try to restore balance to the relationships.

There is a tendency for a group to split into subgroups as the group increases in size. The subgroups may have different task or social-emotional functions. Sherif's experiments have demonstrated that an increase in tension between groups (or subgroups) may increase the cohesiveness within each group (or subgroup). Harmony may be restored if the subgroups join in working for superordinate goals.

The stability of the informal structure, as revealed by a sociometric test, is greater in groups of adults who have known each other for a long time. The consistency of choice is also greater if the time between test and retest is short, if the criterion of choice is relevant to the group activity, if a large number of choice discriminations are required, and if the group from which choices are made is large.

Individuals vary in the intimacy of their interpersonal relations; interaction with an "acquaintance" is less intimate than that with a "friend." Five factors which influence the degree of intimacy in a friendship are (1) proximity, (2) biological traits, (3) personality characteristics, (4) common or reciprocal roles, and (5) common values.

Popular individuals choose each other and are highly chosen by members of other groups. Although the popular person is usually one who desires to be close to people, he is not necessarily an active person. Not all sociometric "stars" are leaders, and not all active persons are "stars."

If members are highly attracted to their group, their group is said to have high morale or to be cohesive. A cohesive group is usually more productive, unless the group members have agreed on a lower production rate in opposition to the norms of a larger organization.

Schachter's experiment on anxiety and affiliation led to a series of experiments which report that when it is appropriate to be with others, subjects are more likely to choose to be with others if the others are also anxious (or fearful) about the same thing, thus providing an opportunity for "social comparison" of feelings. The choice of others is more likely to occur if subjects are aroused and less likely if they are highly anxious or introverted.

Additional References

Additional research on aspects of interpersonal attraction which are not closely related to the topics covered in this chapter includes Carlson, 1960; Exline, 1960a; Lott and Lott, 1960; Maucorps and Bassoul, 1960; Berkowitz and Macaulay, 1961; Dodd and Garabedian, 1961; Gumpert, Thibaut, and Shuford, 1961; Goldstone et al., 1963; Marston and Levine, 1964; Kaplan et al., 1965; Smart, 1965; Wilson, 1965; Julian, Bishop, and Fiedler, 1966; Marwell, 1966; Spaulding, 1966; Walster et al., 1966; Lott, Lott, and Matthews, 1969; Wheeler et al., 1969; Lott et al., 1970; de Montmollin, 1971; Griffitt, Byrne, and Bond, 1971; Mehrabian and Ksionzky, 1971; Mettee, 1971a; J. A. Armentrout, 1972; Bayes, 1972; Benlifer and Kiesler, 1972; Blumberg, 1972; Bridgeman, 1972; Brown, Shaw, and Kirkland, 1972; Centers, 1972; Christian, 1972; Curran, 1972; Dickenberger and Grabitz-Gniech, 1972; Donnay, 1972; Eiser and Taylor, 1972; Kanin and Davidson, 1972; Lerner and Agar, 1972; Michener and Schwertfeger, 1972; Peele and Morse, 1972;

Tognoli and Keisner, 1972; Wyer, 1972; Brickman and Horn, 1973; Dion and Mathewson, 1973; Gatton and Nelson, 1973; Good and Good, 1973; Grundy and Wilson, 1973; Leinhardt, 1973; Lombardo, Weiss, and Stich, 1973; Ross and Walters, 1973; Sadler and Tesser, 1973; Spivey and Wilson, 1973; Wakil, 1973a; Wiggins, Itkin, and Clore, 1973; Anthony, 1974; Bleda, 1974; Kleinke, Meeker, and La Fong, 1974; Nowicki, Nelson, and Ettinger, 1974; Reisman and Yamokoski, 1974; Schettino and Baldwin, 1974; Sherman, Sprafkin, and Higgins, 1974; Sote and Good, 1974.

Part 2

INTERACTION
VARIABLES

In the description of the central tendencies of group process and structure in part 1, some of the variations which could be expected from groups of different member composition or different organizational characteristics were mentioned. In part 2, the effects of six major "variables" on the interaction process are considered in more detail. Three of these variables are aspects of the composition of the group and three are aspects of the group organization.

Some of the chapters in this part, such as those on group size or communication network, deal with one fairly well-defined variable. Other chapters, such as those on social characteristics and task, actually combine several more specific variables. Whether a variable has been treated by itself or in the company of others has been largely determined by the quantity of appropriate research in that area. Since leadership is the hardy perennial among research topics, it would be difficult to discuss it in less than a chapter. On the other hand, there has not been enough research to date on the effects of age and sex differences on decision-making to warrant a separate chapter.

The variable most directly related to the individual is personality. To vary the personality composition of the group, the experimenter must have information about each individual member. The social characteristics, such as age and sex, are more easily varied, since members can be selected from classes of individuals which are more easily identified than personality types. The third composition variable, group size, requires only adding or subtracting individuals without regard to personality or social characteristics.

The most inclusive way in which to specify the general outlines of group organization is to designate the task of the group. More specific restrictions are placed on the group organization by variations in the communication network, and the group's leadership.

SPECIAL NOTE: An early version of some of the material in chapters 8, 10, 11, and 12 was published in Bales, Hare, and Borgatta (1957).

Chapter 8

PERSONALITY

THE FIRST OF SIX "factors" which can be "controlled" by the experimenter to create variations in the typical interaction patterns of groups is group composition according to variations in members' personalities. Research on the effects of variations of personality composition on group behavior provides a link between individual and group psychology. It is especially important since the categories which are used throughout this text to describe social interaction were derived in part from factor-analytic studies of personality traits.

Although one may wish to summarize those individual behavior tendencies which remain constant, no matter what the situation, under the concept "personality," the basic tendencies of the individual are never seen in their raw form (Murphy and Murphy, 1935; Murphy, 1937). All intended behavior is modified to some extent before it becomes overt, so that the relative strength of the basic tendencies can only be inferred by considering the force exerted in the situation to modify them. There are, however, individuals in clinical populations who are relatively insensitive to the pressures of the situation, so that their own central tendencies in behavior are dominant. But even, in these cases, it would seem that an individual cannot remain a social being, a person, and stand wholly apart from social pressure (cf. Falk, 1969). For reviews of the literature on personality and social interaction see Marlowe and Gergen, 1968; Schutz, 1968.

Predicting Interaction from Personality

Although predictions from personality data to social interaction can take a number of forms (Bales, 1956), the most common method might be called the simple, unconditional prediction. Its logical form may be represented by the following statement:

1. Persons of type X (as measured by a personality test) tend to behave in way W in interpersonal relations.

An example would be the prediction that persons who have a high score on the "Manic" scale of a personality test will tend to talk a lot in an interpersonal situation. There is no attempt to predict differentially either according to the other characteristics of the subject or according to the characteristics of the other participants.

A second method which introduces more conditions takes the following form:

2. Persons of type X (as measured by a personality test) tend to behave in way W toward persons of type Y (as measured by a personality test) in interpersonal situations.

As an example, persons who like close personal relations with others would be expected to be incompatible with persons who wish to keep everyone at a distance, and therefore less productive when placed in a work group.

A third type of approach takes still more complications into account. The predictions take the following form:

3. Persons of type X (as measured by a personality test) tend to behave in way W toward persons of type Y (as measured by a personality test), provided the person of type Y has a given social position within the group (as measured by the way persons Z behave toward Y).

An example would be the prediction that persons who tend toward values of equalitarianism, love, and integrity of subjective experience tend to form alliances with rebellious, alienated persons and to protect them as long as they are in the position of underdogs and are under attack by group members.

Predictions of each of these three types have been made and tested in the experimental literature on behavior in small groups. Some studies deal with the central tendencies of certain personality types in different situations, some with the effect of one personality type on another in leaderless group activity in which personality is the dominant variable, and some with the behavior of an individual in a specified role. The list of basic personality dimensions described in studies of each type is usually a long one which varies from experimenter to experimenter. However, factor-analytic studies of personality have indicated some of the independent dimensions which may be enough to account for the major variations in personality.

Factor-Analytic Studies of Personality and Behavior

In chapter 3 we noted the contribution of the statistical techniques of factor analysis in the search for the basic dimensions of interpersonal behavior. Over the years first one, then two, then three and four dimensions or factors were identified. There has been a parallel search for the minimum number of personality dimensions which would be needed to predict interpersonal behavior. Often the two explorations have been conducted by the same people. Authors who have made primary contributions to this area, including some whose contribution was clinical rather than statistical, are Champney, 1941; Baldwin, Kallhorn, and Breese, 1945; Horney, 1945; Fromm, 1947; Bion, 1949a, 1949b; Roff, 1949; Freud, 1950; Freedman et al., 1951; Tyler, 1951; Wheeler, Little, and Lehner, 1951; Couch and Carter, 1952; Sakoda, 1952; Lorr and Jenkins, 1953; Carter, 1954; Williams and Lawrence, 1954; Sewell, Mussen, and Harris, 1955; Cattell, 1956; Giedt, 1956; Mitchell, 1956; Leary, 1957; Karson and Pool, 1958; Schutz, 1958a, 1958b; Kassebaum, Couch, and Slater, 1959; Harvey, Hunt, and Schroder, 1961; Schroder and Harvey, 1963; Borgatta, 1964b; Heslin, 1964; Stimpson and Bass, 1964; Loehlin, 1965; Ring, Braginsky, and Braginsky, 1966; Ring et al., 1967; Rosenberg, Nelson, and Vivekananthan, 1968; Lorr and Suziedelis, 1969; Hall and Williams, 1971.

Although the studies listed above report many different factors depending on the population studied and the interest of the investigator, a typical list of factors is the one given by Mann (1959) after reviewing the research on the relation between personality and group behavior. He found that the seven personality factors which were reported most often were intelligence, adjustment (anxiety), extroversion-introversion, dominance, masculinity-feminity, radicalism-conservatism, and interpersonal sensitivity. Since personality measures representing these seven factors are commonly used, they provide a convenient way to summarize the literature. However if one wishes to predict behavior along the four dimensions described in chapter 3, then it is simpler if the comparable personality dimensions are measured directly. In that case at least four dimensions derived from the work of Couch (1960) would be included, namely (1) dominant-submissive, (2) positive-negative, (3) serious-expressive, and (4) conforming-nonconforming.

Some of the factors on Mann's list are actually rotations of those on Couch's list. For example, Couch suggests that the four factors of anxiety, extroversion-introversion, aggression (related to Mann's dominance), and radicalism-conservatism can be represented in a two-dimensional space where dominant-submissive is the vertical axis and negative-positive is the horizontal axis. Anxiety is scored as lower left, i.e., submissive and negative; extroversion as upper right, i.e., dominant and positive; aggression as upper left, i.e., dominant and negative; and conservatism as lower right, i.e., positive and submissive. Using the four factors from Mann's list scored in this way, Couch reports significant correlations of about .33 with behavior in small laboratory groups.

Thus if one wishes to study the major dimensions of personality in a small group context, measures of the four dimensions representing tendencies toward dominant, positive, serious, and conforming behavior (or some variation of these dimensions) could be used as well as additional dimensions such as intelligence, masculinity-feminity, and interpersonal sensitivity should these measures prove to be independent of the others and relevant for the research.

Dominant-Submissive Dimension

Over the years more research has focused on the personality dimension of dominant-submissive than on any of the other personality traits. One line of investigation developed by Chapple and others is to use an interview rather than a paper-and-pencil test to assess a subject's interaction rate as a measure of his tendency to be dominant or submissive (Chapple, 1942; Chapple and Coon, 1942, pp. 47–50; Matarazzo, Saslow, and Hare, 1958). During a 30-minute interview, a record is made of the duration of the subject's actions, which are primarily verbal, and of the duration of his silences.

In the standard interview as Chapple has designed it, the half-hour interview is divided into five periods. In periods 1, 3, and 5, the interviewer responds with a five-second utterance to each action of the subject within one second after the subject has finished speaking. Periods 2 and 4 are periods of stress for the subject. In period 2, the interviewer applies a silence stress by failing to respond to the subject for 15 seconds after the subject has finished speaking. If the subject speaks again during the 15 seconds, a new period of silence begins. In period 4, the interviewer applies an interrupting stress by interrupting the subject each time he speaks.

The interaction rate of a sample of hospital patients interviewed by a doctor using this "standard" interview technique was found to be consistent between a first and second interview by the same doctor and between a first interview by one doctor and a second interview by another doctor. Patients with low intelligence were found to have short actions and long silences (Saslow, Matarazzo and Guze, 1955; Matarazzo, Saslow, and Guze, 1956; Matarazzo, Saslow and Matarazzo, 1956; Saslow, Goodrich, and Stein, 1956; Matarazzo, Saslow, et al., 1958; Saslow et al., 1957; Phillips et al., 1957; Matarazzo et al., 1958; Hare et al., 1960).

Using the same category on a doctor-patient interview with patients in a psychiartic ward, characteristic patterns were found for varying diagnoses as well as specific differences between individuals (Chapple and Lindemann, 1942).

In a series of conversations long silences (as compared with short silences, short actions and long actions) were found to be the most characteristic indices of the individual's conversation activity (Goldman-Eisler, 1951).

Some studies in which a number of personality or behavioral ratings are made report frequencies of interaction initiated as the dominant variable because of its high correlation with such variables as the amount of action directed toward the individual in response to his activity (Bales et al., 1951; Stephan and Mishler, 1952) and the observer's rating of the desirability of the subject as a job candidate (Bass, 1951).

Each individual who is a prospective member of a group may usefully be regarded as having, in addition to his characteristic rate of interaction,[1] a characteristic upper bound (or relative limit on the variability of his performance), with a tendency to increase his rate of initiation in a given group in the direction of the upper bound as a function of the opportunity afforded by the rates and bounds of the other participants (Borgatta and Bales, 1953b). The rate actually achieved by a given person is an inverse function of the characteristic rates of his coparticipators. The total rate achieved by a given group is a positive function of the summed characteristic rates of the participants, but it is also a positive function of the differentiation of the characteristic rates. Why the latter should be the case is not immediately clear. For both individuals and groups, qualitative differences in interaction are associated with differences in gross interaction rates. For individual persons, specialization on the side of activities characteristic of task leadership is generally associated with high gross interaction rate. Persons with relatively lower rates tend to assume roles of supporting, modifying, qualifying, or rejecting. Persons with the lowest rates may be excluded or may withdraw; they tend to show high rates of tension, and may not contribute substantially either to the task or to the support of coparticipators.

When personality tests are used to provide a prediction of interpersonal behavior in groups, those scales which measure tendencies to be dominant, aggressive, and outgoing are positively correlated with high participation, while scales measuring depression and anxiety are associated with low participation (Lerea and Goldberg, 1961; Gold, DeLeon, and Swensen, 1966; Stern and Grosz, 1966; Aronson and Weintraub, 1967; Sales, 1971; Wagoner and Grosz, 1971; Moerk, 1972; Leader, 1973). Measures of self-esteem and integration of body image are similar in that persons with high self-esteem tend to play a dominant part in groups while persons of low self-esteem are less willing to participate in discussions (Cleveland and Morton, 1962; Efran and Boylin, 1967; Frankel, 1969; Archibald and Cohen, 1971; Crandall, 1973).

1. In experiments using the Bales categories, interaction *rate* usually refers to an individual's total number of acts. The total number of acts is equal to the number of *contributions* times the *duration*, measured in Bales acts, of each utterance. The interaction *rate* is usually highly correlated with the number of *contributions*. Contributions and duration, however, tend to be uncorrelated (Hare et al., 1960).

Positive-Negative Dimension

On the positive-negative dimension those personality scales which provide measure of tendencies to be extroverted, trusting, and affiliative will predict warm, personal, cooperative behavior in groups, with the opposite effects for high negative scores. Persons with high positive scores are more willing to disclose information about themselves. (See Glad, Smith, and Glad, 1957; Exline, 1962a, 1962b; Borgatta, 1963b; Harrison and Lubin, 1965; McLaughlin and Hewitt, 1972; Cozby, 1973b; Schlenker, Helm, and Tedeschi, 1973.)

In therapy groups positive-negative behavior represents an important dimension. Individuals who are affectionate or hostile to the group think that they arouse the same feelings in others and assume that the feelings are reciprocated (Taylor, 1954, 1955). Another study with a laboratory population provides more evidence of the results of the projection of feelings in the affection area. In small groups of four to six members, subjects who were high on affiliation motivation but who *feared rejection* by group members tended to "compete" with them in anticipation of the feared rejection. As a result, the high-affiliation subjects were found to be more productive in competitive tasks and less productive in cooperative tasks (de Charms, 1957).

Serious-Expressive Dimension

Both Couch (1960, p. 525) and Bales (1970a, pp. 279, 309), who provide analyses of a set of small group data which includes a wide range of personality and behavioral measures, report that few personality traits, as they are currently measured, are directly correlated with this dimension of personality and interpersonal behavior. Behaviorally the serious person is one who gives information and opinions or routine agreement which indicates serious involvement in the task. The expressive person is one who shows tension release through joking or other evidence of flight from the task and who gives support to others regardless of task performance (Hare, 1972b). In Couch's study serious behavior was positively correlated with intelligence and anxiety and negatively correlated with impulsivity. Thus it appears that although high intelligence is associated with dominant behavior and anxiety with submissive behavior, the combination of high intelligence and high anxiety produces a person who is very task-oriented and serious.

Conforming-Nonconforming Dimension

The most commonly used measure of a tendency to conform is the F (Fascist) Scale, which was developed to measure authoritarianism. A subject's score on this scale was found to be related to his perception of others in an experiment in which subjects rated their partners on "authoritarianism" after a 20-minute period of interaction. A high rating on "authoritarianism" was an indication that the subject liked to have a rigid set of rules, was uncritically submissive to those in power, was ready to punish anyone who deviated from the rules, and had a preoccupation with power (Adorno et al., 1950). A subject who was himself high on authoritarianism thought that his partner was also high whether he was high or low, while a subject who was low on authoritarianism thought that all of his partners were middle or high (Scodel and Freedman, 1956). Further research has confirmed the tendency of authoritarians to value a centralized group structure and to be punitive with deviants (Vroom, 1959; De Soto, Kuethe, and Wunderlich, 1960; Friedell, 1968; Gladstone, 1969; Aronoff and Messe, 1971).

Subjects who desire a controlling authority structure were found to be the most suggestible in the experimental situation in which groups of subjects make estimates of the distance a dot of light appears to move (Kelman, 1950), as well as in other experimental situations (Block and Block, 1952). An authoritarian attitude among naval recruits was also found to be negatively related to popularity, although differences in military rank were much more of a determining factor in sociometric choices received. High-ranking members of military units received the most choices (Masling, Greer, and Gilmore, 1955).

One of the difficulties in using personality tests to measure "authoritarianism" has been referred to in chapter 2. Most of the studies of authoritarianism as a personality trait use the F Scale developed by Adorno et al. (1950) as their principal personality test. The number of items used in the scale varies from study to study, but the content of the items remains fairly close to those developed in the original study of the authoritarian personality (Titus and Hollander, 1957; Christie and Cook, 1958). The following four items are typical:

Obedience and respect for authority are the most important virtues children should learn.
What the youth needs most is strict discipline, rugged determination, and the will to work and fight for family and country.
Sex crimes, such as rape and attacks on children, deserve more than mere imprisonment; such criminals ought to be publicly whipped, or worse.
People can be divided into two distinct classes: the weak and the strong.

Subjects are usually asked to indicate the extent of their agreement with each item, from "strongly agree" to "strongly disagree." Unfortunately, for the use of this particular type of test, there are some subjects who are so "agreeable" that they will also answer "agree" to a reversed F Scale in which similar items with meaning reversed are presented (Bass, 1955; Jackson and Messick, 1957; Jackson, Messick, and Solley, 1957; Rabinowitz, 1957; Chapman and Bock, 1958; Couch and Keniston, 1960; Hare, 1961). Because of this tendency which some subjects have to agree with opinions presented on a personality questionnaire, many currently used personality scales may also be measures of a tendency to conform to an opinion which they assume to be that of the majority.

Additional research which fails to find some expected correlations between personality measures and interpersonal behavior or gives evidence of personality traits which do not fit easily into the four-dimensional scheme includes Holmes, 1967; Finch, Rickard, and Wilson, 1970; Streufert and Castore, 1971; Vraa, 1971; D. Hewitt, 1972; Moerk, 1972; Vraa and Gerszewski, 1972; Braun and Daigle, 1973; Brenner and Hjelmquist, 1973.

The Consistency of Individual Behavior

For any given personality type, the simplest prediction is that the person will act in the same way in all situations. The extent to which the subject exhibits the same tendencies to act in a variety of groups, or in standardized settings, such as a paper-and-pencil test or role playing, is a measure of the *stability* or *consistency* of personality.

There are significant tendencies toward stability or consistency in both quality and quantity of interaction initiated and received by the individual in both "actual" and role-playing situations, although certain qualities are more stable than others (Borgatta and Bales, 1953b). In general, the stability for all qualities of interaction over a series of sessions is dependably greater when the individual participates with the same individuals than when the individual participates with different ones, although consistency is shown in either event. Using an index based on interaction rate, sociometric popularity, leadership rating, and intelligence, "great men" can be identified in the first session who have simultaneously high scores on all four of these variables (Borgatta, Couch, and Bales, 1954). These "great men" often maintain their status in subsequent sessions in which they participate with different persons, and have, according to indirect measures, a significant influence on the satisfaction and effective functioning of the group.

Another study of the consistency of individual behavior which supports the hypothesis that the basic tendencies which make up the personality are derived from early experiences in the family was based on the direct observation of mother-child relationships. The child was left alone in a playroom for two half-hour play periods with the mother and for two additional half-hour sessions with a woman who was previously unknown to the child. Thirty-four mothers and their preschool children (17 boys and 17 girls) served as subjects. Consistency in behavior was found for the mothers and for the children over the two sessions. By the second session with the neutral adult, each child would tend to stimulate his typical interaction pattern with his mother (Bishop, 1951).

A number of additional studies report consistency of behavior between a test situation and observed behavior (Washburn, 1932; Swanson, 1951b; Borgatta, 1955; Lipsitt and Vallance, 1955; Tear and Guthrie, 1955). Although it is evident that the variety of behaviors which have been predicted from paper-and-pencil or projective tests generally support the hypothesis of an underlying consistency in behavior, the evidence is not all positive. For example, one study reports that the expression in a discussion group of such "self-oriented needs" as dependency, status, dominance, aggression, and catharsis can be predicted from a battery of tests including the Rorschach (Fouriezos, Hutt, and Guetzkow, 1950), whereas another study reports little or no relation between Rorschach scores and behavior as scored by Bales's categories for interaction process analysis (Borgatta and Eschenbach, 1955).

Behavior Contingent upon the Personalities of Self and Others

A study which illustrates the increase in predictability obtained with pre-measures of the personality and social characteristics of the subjects as well as the other group members was made using 20 five-man groups of college students including both men and women (Breer, 1960). Before the experiment each subject was given the Leary Interpersonal Checklist, the Thurstone Test of Mental Alertness, the Bales-Couch Value Profile, and an information sheet asking for age, sex, and social-class background. Individuals were also rated on physical attractiveness.

Each group met for 90 minutes and was given the task of guessing an unnamed student's responses to the Bales-Couch Value Profile. The subjects were given the answers to five itmes from the Value Profile on which to base their initial guess. After each guess the true answer was revealed. An observer made an act-by-act recording of the meeting using the eight major categories of the Leary two-dimensional grid: ascendant-neutral, ascendant-affectionate, affectionate-neutral, submissive-affectionate, and so on around the grid. An index of how ascendantly man one behaved toward man two was computed by taking the absolute number of ascendant acts initiated, subtracting the number of submissive acts initiated, and dividing the difference by the total number of acts initiated. A similar procedure was used for the affection-hostility dimension.

For the prediction of how ascendantly a subject would behave toward some other particular person in the group, an index based on those attributes of the other person thought to correlate positively with his ascendance (intelligence, age, sex, social class, and pretested dominance) was subtracted from an ascendance index based on measures of the subject. This was done on the assumption that the more ascendantly the other person behaved toward the subject, the less ascendantly the subject would behave in return. For the prediction of affectionate behavior, the index also included the characteristics of the other three group members.

A prediction based on preinteraction measures of the subject and the other person was found to be superior to one based on attributes of the subject alone. The results were most striking in the case of ascendance-submission. Combining measures of both the subject and the other person, it proved possible to account for some 37 percent of the variance in the subject's ascendance toward the other person ($r = .62$). With preinteraction ascendance for subjects alone, the correlation was .51; with preinteraction measures of others alone, the correlation was .46. Thus it was possible to account for approximately 21 percent of the variance in the subjects' behavior toward others solely on the basis of what was known about the others.

The relationship between prediction and behavior for the affection-hostility dimension was not as marked. The correlation between affection predicted and affection observed was .33. The relative failure to predict differences along this dimension was attributed to the limited number of affectionate or hostile acts in a situation strongly oriented to logical problem-solving activity.

As a part of his research Breer developed a "Conditional Personality Test" (CPT) designed to measure how a subject would respond in interaction with another person of given social characteristics. A modification of this test was used by Hare (1971b) in several different cultures. When the test is administered, the subjects are given, in turn, four descriptions of persons—one who is dominant, one who is positive, one who is submissive, and one who is negative. After reading each description, they are asked to indicate on a seven-point scale how "quiet or active" they would be and how "critical or agreeable" they would be if each kind of person were in a group with them. Further, each subject is asked how he would act if the other person were older or younger than himself or more or less intelligent. This version of the test or a longer version was given to Peace Corps volunteers in the Philippines and to university students taking part in a communication network experiment in the United States, Nigeria, and the Philippines.

Across cultures, regardless of the types of personality being described, subjects were more active when they were responding to a younger person and to a person of less intelligence. Also subjects were more agreeable with dominant and positive persons if they were older or had higher intelligence. However, if a person was submissive, subjects were more agreeable if the other person was younger or had less intelligence. There was no significant pattern in agreeable responses to negative persons, although the agreeable responses to negative persons were lower than for any other type. Thus negative behavior seemed to pull a negative response, regardless of age or intelligence.

With the Peace Corps sample, where it was possible to test the difference in the response of male and female subjects to male and female persons, no consistent significant differences appeared. Males and females responded in the same way to the four personality types, and the sex of the stimulus person did not make a difference. In general, subjects responded more actively to submissive persons than to dominant persons, and more agreeably to positive persons than to negative persons. However, there was considerable variability in the "active" ratings from sample to sample, with American subjects making more discriminations than the Nigerian subjects. The Nigerians were about equally active with dominant, positive, and negative persons, while the American subjects were least active with dominant and negative persons. The Philippine subjects had a pattern which was closest to the United States subjects. No consistent significant correlations were found across cultures between CPT ratings and social-background variables or behavior in the communication network experiment.

The results give support to Leary's theory that, in general, dominant behavior pulls submissive behavior (and vice versa), positive pulls positive, and negative pulls negative. It is clear that social variables, such as age and intelligence, must be specified, since these reactions of the subjects are related to the expected behavior of another person according to his social status. In addition, dominance-submission shows the greatest variability across cultures.

Some formal models to be used in making conditional predictions concerning behavior patterns have been suggested by Scheiblechner (1972).

Personality and Compatibility

Some personality differences, such as those between individuals with high and low interaction rates, may still allow the individuals to work together productively in a group, since each type of person can select a role which fits his personality. This does not appear to be the case, however, with differences on the dimension of affection. Two experiments in this area have been carried out by Schutz. In the first experiment, with naval trainees as subjects, some five-man groups were composed of members who were "personal," that is, who preferred close, intimate relations with others. Other groups, matched for intelligence, were composed of men who were "personal" as well as men who were "counterpersonal," that is, who preferred to keep others at a distance. Each group performed a number of tasks requiring cooperation under time pressure, and finally met groups of the opposite type in a series of "playoffs." The "compatible" groups whose members were either all "personal" or all "counterpersonal" were judged to be more productive, since they made the highest team scores and won more of the playoffs. Presumably the basic differences in orientation of the "incompatible" groups, whose members were a mixture of personal and counterpersonal, prevented the members from reaching agreement on the basis for establishing intermember relations with a consequent loss in efficiency (Schutz, 1955). In similar experiments with male college students as subjects and with outpatient psychotherapy groups, similar findings were reported (Schutz, 1958a; Yalom and Rand, 1966).

Evidence that individuals with certain types of personalities tend to choose each other to form "compatible" pairs and friendship groups of larger sizes is presented in chapter 7. A compatibility experiment by Schutz (1958a) is reported in detail in chapter 15.

Personality and Role

More specific predictions can be made about the behavior of an individual with given personality types if something is known about the expectations for behavior in the particular situation in which he will find himself. Sometimes these expectations are indicated only in a general way, sometimes the role of the individual is specified, and sometimes the role of the person with whom the individual will interact is specified.

Individuals will find it easier to fit a role which matches their personality characteristics or participate effectively in an area of group activity which uses their special skills (Watson, 1971). This is illustrated by a role-playing experiment in which three groups were arranged. In each group one person played an assertive role, one a nonassertive role, and one an emotional role (Borgatta, 1961). Before the experiment each subject was ranked on assertiveness and on emotionality. Then assertive, nonassertive, and emotional subjects were systematically rotated through each role. The subjects were found to be better at playing roles which were congruent with their personalities.

Another experiment used different communication networks for a decision-making task (Shaw, 1959a). In one network, messages could only be passed to a person in the center of the network, while in the other network messages could be passed between all members. Subjects who were high on authoritarianism were found to be relatively more efficient in the centralized group structure.

Since a role specified by the group may be composed of expectations for behavior which are modeled after the behavior of some former group member, there is probably someone in each society who is ideally suited to each role. A role could probably be found in which the behavior of the most extreme personality type would be appropriate. On the average, however, each individual has some range of role adaptability, such that a variety of roles can be learned if they are not represented exactly by the particular combination of basic tendencies which the individual brings to the situation. Because of this adaptability or because of an underlying similarity in all personality types (since no one is ever so far out toward one pole of a dimension that he does not have some tendency to behave in the opposite way), some sets of expectations will elicit similar behavior regardless of personality type.

In addition to personality, the individual's previous experience in the role is a factor which influences his ability to play the role. Experience with the role can be introduced by either selecting an individual with prior experience or providing training in a test situation which will prepare him for the role. The effect of prior experience is evident in an experiment in which subjects were asked to play the role of a salesman while observers made judgments of their rigidity in the role. Two situations, one anxiety-inducing and one neutral, were used. The role-playing behavior was not correlated with the results of a paper-and-pencil test of rigidity under either condition. However, individuals with experience in selling showed less rigidity (Moldawsky, 1951). The effects of training are evident in a range of studies from those which introduce formal training for a specific role, such as that of a foreman in industry, to therapeutic methods with an individual alone or in a group which prepare him for a more general member role.[2]

In general the group's *expectations* for a given individual are revealed in the *behavior* of group members toward him. It is through the behavior of the other group members in response to an individual's act that the expectations of the group become known. Although the other group members may explicitly state their common expectations for the role of leader or follower, the individual's usual indication that he is still within the limits of the role comes from the approval or disapproval of the others. The problems which occur when role expectations are not uniform are discussed in chapter 6 in relation to role collision, incompatibility, and confusion.

An example of the ways in which individuals with different personality traits react to approval and disapproval is found in an experiment in which 64 college-age subjects who represented the four combinations of two personality variables, anxiety and neuroticism, as measured by a paper-and-pencil test were given social approval or disapproval of their opinions in a five-to seven-minute discussion with two role players. All subjects participated more when approved of, an indication that when the subjects felt that the other group members valued their contributions they would respond in a uniform way. The same experiment, however, also provides evidence of the differential response of certain personality types to the same action on the part of other group members. The high-neurotic subjects were more rigid in holding their opinions when under disapproval, especially when they were also high-anxious (Cervin, 1956).

Thus far the individual's personality has been considered in relation to his own role. The way in which he responds to the personality of another member is also related to the role the other person is playing. High-authoritarian subjects were found to accept a high-status person who was hostile but to reject a low-status person with the same personality characteristic (Thibaut and Riecken, 1955a). Another set of experiments involving the variables of high and low authoritarianism and high and low status was carried out by Haythorn and his associates. These experiments will be treated in detail as an example of the relative influence of personality and role.

Authoritarian and Equalitarian Personalities in Groups

In a complex research design Haythorn, Couch, Haefner, Langham, and Carter investigated several aspects of leadership and membership behavior related to authoritarianism. Because of the complex design, not all of the details of their experiment will be described (Haythorn et al., 1956a, 1956b).

The first problem area under investigation concerned behavioral differences in groups whose members were all high or low on the Authoritarian Personality (F) Scale. Several hypotheses were advanced at the outset. It was expected that authoritarian (F+) persons would behave more aggressively, would be less effective in

2. See, for example, Chittenden (1942) in which 10 experimental and 10 control groups of pre-school children were used as subjects. Highly dominating children were trained through doll play with an adult. The effect of the training was to reduce domination and increase coopera-tion. Maas, Varon, and Rosenthal (1951) studied the results of group therapy on schizo-phrenic patients from the wards of a mental hospital. After the therapy, patients made more purposeful acts and engaged in more verbal relationships.

dealing with the group's problem, would be more concerned with the status hierarchy, would strive more for individual prominence, would be less concerned with asking for other people's opinions and more likely to support each other in discussions, than would be the more equalitarian (F—) subjects. It was also hypothesized that leaders emerging in the F+ groups would be more autocratic, less sensitive to others, and generally less effective than equalitarian leaders.

To test these hypotheses, 32 high-F and 32 low-F persons were selected from a sample of some 350 college men who had taken the F Scale and other screening tests; they were composed into four-man groups, each group being made up of uniformly high- and low-F persons. Their task was to construct a dramatic skit and tape-record their finished product.

While the group was at work at this, observers behind one-way glass categorized the behavior as it occurred, using a stenotype system of interaction recording devised by Carter (Carter, 1951). A scorer was relieved by a colleague every 30 minutes. Each observer rated the subjects on 16 behavioral traits: individual prominence, friendliness, security, influence, equalitarianism, striving for group approval, submissiveness, striving for goal achievement, self-isolating behavior, effective intelligence, sensitivity to others, leadership, aggressiveness, autocratic behavior, social ability, and nonadaptability. These trait ratings had an average inter-observer reliability of .75 with a range of .30 to .90. At the end of each session, all observers filled out reaction sheets on which they made ratings of the group. There were 37 items, such as "the atmosphere in the group was pleasant and cordial" and "at least one member was sort of left out of things." Observers rated the group on these items using a seven-point scale, and achieved satisfactory reliability. In addition to these observer data, the subjects also answered some standard sociometric questions about liking, disliking, and satisfaction. While they were making ratings, the observers did not know the F type of group.

The various questions raised in the beginning of the study were tested by t-tests for the significance of differences between mean values for F+ and F— groups on each variable. The groups were found to differ in general in the expected directions. Low-F subjects were rated higher on effective intelligence and demonstrated more leadership behavior. In addition they had tendencies, although not statistically significant, for greater sensitivity to others, equalitarian behavior, more goal striving, and greater security in the experimental situation. All differences in trait-rated behavior between F+ and F— groups are given in table 17.

In examining the person with the highest average rank on leadership based on the rankings of the subjects within each group, the experimenters concluded that persons who emerge as leaders in groups composed of equalitarian individuals behave differently from those who emerge in groups composed of authoritarian individuals. Leaders in F— groups were significantly more sensitive to others, showed more leadership, contributed more to moving their groups toward the group goal, showed greater effective intelligence, showed less concern with solidifying attitudes from other group members, and were more submissive in their attitudes toward other group members. Only three significant mispredictions occurred in the recorded observations of the subjects' behavior, namely, in the findings that F— subjects supported their own proposals more, initiated more activities, and gave more opinions than did F+. In the predicted direction were the findings that F— subjects gave more acts of positive effect, asked for group evaluation more frequently, were less likely to engage in overtly directive acts, and were more often engaged in diagnosing and clarifying action.

Table 17. Differences in Rated Behavior between High F and Low F Groups

TRAIT NAMES	GROUP MEANS		
	(N=8)	(N=8)	
	F+ Groups	F− Groups	t
I. Individual prominence	3.58	3.56	0.08(F+)
II. Friendliness	3.68	3.79	0.51(F−)
III. Security	4.35	4.56	1.29(F−)
IV. Influence	4.33	4.33	0.00
V. Equalitarianism	3.35	3.87	1.26(F−)
VI. Striving for group approval	3.15	3.03	0.63(F+)
VII. Submissiveness	2.97	3.06	0.48(F−)
VIII. Striving for goal achievement	4.08	4.41	1.41(F−)
IX. Self-isolating	2.33	2.23	0.50(F+)
X. Effective intelligence	3.63	4.24	2.60(F−)†
XI. Sensitivity	3.16	3.70	1.38(F−)
XII. Leadership	3.39	3.77	2.02(F−)*
XIII. Aggressiveness	2.65	2.41	0.59(F+)
XIV. Autocratic	2.68	2.45	0.60(F+)
XV. Social ability	3.67	3.69	0.10(F−)
XVI. Nonadaptability	2.42	2.46	0.12(F−)

*Significant at .10 level   †Significant at .05 level

Source: William Haythorn et al., "The Behavior of Authoritarian and Equalitarian Personalities in Groups," *Human Relations* 9 (1956): 62. Reprinted by permission of the Plenum Publishing Corporation.

In table 18 are reproduced the results of postmeeting questionnaires. It will be noted that F+ subjects were more dissatisfied with their goal progress than were F− subjects and were more apt to rate their groups as lacking cooperation. F+ subjects also described their groups as having fewer differences of opinion and less competition among members. Both observers and subjects agreed on the direction of the differences for indices in table 18 which are significant.

After the groups were observed in the manner described above, the same subjects were observed with appointed leaders. Half of the new groups had leaders whose F scores were similar to those of their followers, and the other half of the groups had leaders whose F scores were different from those of their followers. This arrangement permitted comparisons of the following order: (1) F+ and F− leaders, (2) F+ and F− followers, (3) followers with F+ and F− leaders, (4) leaders with F+ and F− followers, and (5) followers with leaders whose F scores were similar and dissimilar to the followers. In other characteristics of observing and rating, these groups were conducted in the manner described for the first series.

The results of the trait ratings of the appointed leaders are summarized in table 19.

Inspection of column g of this table reveals that leaders, irrespective of their classifications, achieved greater individual prominence and acted more aggressively and more autocratically with F+ followers. This the authors believe is due to the tendency for high-F followers to seek and accept more autocratic direction. F+ leaders, disregarding classification of followers (column b), were rated as striving less for group approval, being less equalitarian and more autocratic, demonstrating less effective intelligence, and less sensitivity to others. In the first experiment, F+ and F− leaders differed significantly on the rating of striving for group ap-

Table 18. Differences between High F and Low F Groups on Subjects' Postmeeting Reaction Sheet Indices

INDEX NAMES	Ss PMRS GROUP MEANS		
	(N=8) F+ Groups	(N=8) F− Groups	t
I. Dissatisfaction with goal programs	3.29	2.69	1.93(F+)*
II. Degree of equal participation	4.02	4.27	0.92(F−)
III. Degree of personality conflict	2.34	2.56	0.93(F−)
IV. Degree of informal friendliness	5.39	5.18	0.66(F+)
V. Definiteness of leadership	4.26	4.04	0.80(F+)
VI. Striving for equal participation	5.80	5.50	1.15(F+)
VII. Satisfaction with leadership	5.56	5.38	0.81(F+)
VIII. Degree of conflict within group	2.99	3.38	1.42(F−)
IX. Competence of members	5.56	5.61	0.26(F−)
X. Morale	5.80	5.76	0.12(F+)
XI. Group productivity	6.62	6.41	0.55(F+)
XIV. Motivation toward group goal	4.53	4.84	0.71(F−)
XV. Formation of cliques	2.09	2.16	0.21(F−)
XXI. Differences of opinion	3.73	4.59	3.633(F−)‡
XXII. Competition among members	2.31	2.78	3.524(F−)‡
XXIII. Lack of co-operation	2.84	2.12	2.175(F+)†

*Significant at .10 level   †Significant at .05 level   ‡Significant at .01 level
Source: William Haythorn et al., "The Behavior of Authoritarian and Equalitarian Personalities in Groups," *Human Relations* 9 (1956): 70. Reprinted by permission of the Plenum Publishing Corporation.

proval in the *emergent* session, with the F+ being rated higher. Yet when appointed as leaders (in the second session), these same subjects differed significantly *in the opposite direction,* with the F− leaders showing more striving for group approval. Presumably the F+ leaders no longer felt it necessary to strive for group approval when they held the "official" leader's position.

Leaders of subjects with F scores similar to their own were seen as less submissive and more aggressive and autocratic as compared to leaders of subjects with dissimilar scores (table 19, column *i*). Analysis of the observer's rating of followers on the same variables yields results similar to the analysis of ratings of leaders.

In the categorization of the interaction by the stenotype system, there were no statistically significant differences in the acts of any of the category indices between followers with F+ and F− leaders. For F− followers, disregarding the nature of their leaders, however, there were more requests for group evaluation, democratic behavior, and acts of a diagnosing or clarifying character, and less withdrawal, tension release, and out-of-field behavior.

Other findings of interest are that leaders with F+ followers were rated higher on autocratic behavior, that subjects and observers both rated groups with F+ followers as having more definite leadership, and that F+ followers rated their groups as being more dominated by the appointed leader. The hypothesis that followers are more secure in homogeneous groups was supported by the difference in rating of security by the observers. Followers in the homogenous groups were also rated as striving for goal achievement more than in heterogeneous groups. A result not anticipated was that followers in the heterogeneous groups showed self-

Table 19. Trait-rating Results for Leaders in Appointed Leadership Session

ANALYSIS OF VARIANCE		LEADER MEAN					EFFECT ON LEADERS OF:		
		F+ Leaders			F− Leaders		F+ vs. F− Followers	Leader's Personality	Group's Composition
Trait Names	Sessions	(F+ F)‡	(F− F)‡	(F+ F)	(F− F)	s^2w	F	F	F
	(a)	(b)	(c)	(d)	(e)	(f)	(g)	(h)	(i)
1. Individual prominence	II	4.76	3.19	4.08	4.13	0.16	14.574(F+)†	0.028(F−)	1.097(Homo)
	III	4.51	3.08	4.28	3.52	0.77	6.298(F+)*	0.056(F−)	0.572(Homo)
5. Equalitarianism	II	3.56	4.76	5.29	4.82	0.70	0.747(F−)	4.569(F−)	3.954(Hetero)
	III	3.27	4.04	4.89	5.48	1.00	1.837(F−)	9.350(F−)*	0.033(Hetero)
6. Striving for group approval	II	3.89	3.62	4.49	4.26	0.25	1.039(F+)	6.264(F−)*	0.008(Homo)
	III	4.12	3.31	4.42	4.24	0.72	1.360(F+)	2.068(F−)	0.567(Homo)
7. Submissiveness	II	3.03	3.28	3.43	2.75	0.59	0.325(F+)	0.026(F+)	1.462(Hetero)
	III	2.57	3.77	3.34	3.07	0.41	2.100(F−)	0.011(F−)	5.165(Hetero)*
9. Agressiveness	II	2.98	1.78	1.92	2.49	0.39	1.013(F+)	0.329(F+)	8.037(Homo)*
	III	2.95	1.63	1.96	1.34	0.51	7.441(F+)*	3.223(F+)	0.964(Homo)
10. Autocratic	II	3.64	1.99	2.21	2.61	0.56	2.773(F+)	1.150(F+)	7.459(Homo)*
	III	3.56	1.98	2.20	1.64	0.43	10.821(F+)*	6.877(F+)*	2.471(Homo)
11. Effective intelligence	II	4.32	4.46	5.23	4.92	0.31	0.095(F+)	5.963(F−)*	0.653(Hetero)
	III	4.21	3.90	4.96	5.42	0.53	0.038(F−)	9.759(F−)†	1.099(Homo)
12. Sensitivity	II	3.27	4.26	4.89	4.47	0.77	0.423(F−)	4.361(F−)	2.607(Hetero)
	III	3.28	3.85	4.80	5.39	0.83	1.616(F−)	11.304(F−)†	0.001(Homo)
15. Nonadaptability	II	2.01	1.38	1.31	1.70	0.14	0.407(F+)	1.055(F+)	7.469(Homo)*
	III	1.45	1.75	1.45	1.08	0.60	0.008(F+)	0.759(F+)	0.759(Hetero)

*P (.05) 4.75: df 1/12

†(.01) 9.33

‡(F+ F), (F− F), refers to the personality of followers [(F+ Followers) (F− Followers)].

Note: In session II, three members who had been together during session I were placed together with an alien member who was appointed leader. In session III, two of the original session I members were reassembled with the member who had been withdrawn during session II. In addition, an alien member was introduced as the leader of that session.

Source: William Haythorn et al., "The Effects of Varying Combinations of Authoritarian and Equalitarian Leaders and Followers," *Journal of Abnormal and Social Psychology* 53 (1956): 213. Copyright 1956 by the American Psychological Association. Reprinted by permission of the publisher.

ratings higher on satisfaction with their appointed leaders. No satisfactory explanation was provided for this result.

In the summary, the authors are satisfied that most of their expectations were confirmed by the data reported, although not always to a statistically significant degree. Two of the five comparisons possible (concerning F+ and F— leaders and F+ and F— followers) were straightforward predictions from individual attitude and personality measurements. The other three, they point out, were concerned with combinatorial results which indicate the extent to which the interpersonal climate in a group affects the behavior of designated individuals, i.e., the degree to which the behavior of leaders is a function of the personality attributes of those who are led. The converse of this statement is also supported concerning follower behavior. This study is, then, further evidence that personality and group structure should be assessed in relational or combinatorial terms.[3]

Some Effects of Combinations of Personalities

In the initial stages of group formation we may expect the characteristics of the group to be strongly conditioned by the personalities of the members. Some personality variables (as measured by Cattell's 16-Factor Personality Test) act in a more or less additive or subtractive way, so that the group *mean* on the personality variable is the best predictive measure of externally defined characteristics of the group. Other variables seem to act on some kind of principle of compatibility (or incompatibility), so that the particular *combination* of values among the members is the best predictive measure (Cattell and Wispe, 1948; Cattell, Saunders, and Stice, 1953). Cases in which the combination of values is important include not only those in which high or low variance on a single variable predicts something about the performance of the group but also those in which the combination of two or more different types of personality has some predictable effect.

High group *means* on personality characteristics of adventuresomeness, vigor, dominance, purposefulness, orderliness, willed application, and freedom from anxiety are associated with a congruent kind of group performance, i.e., high performance on tasks requiring vigorous coordinated action and a preference for such tasks over discussion.

High group *means* on personality characteristics of paranoid suspiciousness, nervous tension, emotional immaturity, worrying suspicious anxiety, and lack of self-sufficiency are associated with low observer ratings on degree of leadership, orderliness, we-feeling, level of motivation, degree of group organization and interdependence, and with high ratings on frustration. It is notable, however, that subject ratings do not coincide with those of observers, indicating that defense mechanisms must be taken into account in evaluating subjects' own estimates of the characteristics and performance of their group.

There is some evidence that high *variances* among members on personality traits of surgery (liking for carefree bustle and excitement) and radicalism (liking for intellectual and "rational" examination of issues of convention and authority) and high variance on degree of internalization of social norms, along with high

3. Not all researchers have been as successful. Chapman and Campbell (1957a) found that they could not predict group performance on a guessing game and ball-and-spiral task from individual F Scale scores. In another study, a checklist designed to indicate the extent to which subjects were *superior-oriented* (i.e., sought control from an authority) did not predict their reactions to inadequate leadership (Campbell and Mehra, 1958).

mean friendliness, intelligence, and general level of radicalism, are associated with a high level of accuracy on tasks requiring a judgment of facts from inferential grounds. The personality characteristic of surgency is related to a preference for this kind of verbal task, but observers report that groups with high means on this variable suffer from a lack of freedom in the group atmosphere (possibly as a reaction to a verbal free-for-all).

High variances on personality measures of tough- versus tender-mindedness, "Bohemian aggressiveness," and paranoid suspiciousness are associated with dislike for a task of resolving opinion and attitude differences, slowness in ranking attitude preferences, and a feeling by members that other members hinder group progress. Of these traits, two are similar to what are probably major factorial dimensions of the attitude universe (see Eysenck, 1954): tender- versus tough-mindedness and "Bohemian aggressiveness." Variance on these traits would be expected perhaps to lead to conflict of values. The other trait in this cluster is paranoid suspiciousness. Apparently what is involved here is an incompatibility of defensive mechanisms for dealing with threat induced by value conflict.

Finally, on the personality variable of emotional maturity (general freedom from defensive mechanisms), *low variance* or uniformity is found to be associated with a certain optimism and confidence in level of aspiration. This seems reasonable in cases where the mean level of emotional maturity is high, but its implications are not clear where the general level is low.

It is important to note that in the research of Cattell, Saunders, and Stice (1953) some characteristics of the groups are not significantly related to any of the personality measures included in their experiment. Some of these, such as performance on and preference for different tasks (card sorting, construction, planning, resolution of interests), may be more or less directly related to measures of personality characteristics not included in the tests. However, certain others may arise from small, accidental differences in group experience which have the peculiarity of exaggerating themselves by a feedback mechanism or which for some reason produce relatively large results. Hence one could include a group elation factor, possibly as a success-failure consequence, and a factor related to high general evaluation of the integration of the group by the members (intrinsic group synergy). Factors might also be added which are related to observer ratings of a high degree of group organization and a concern with procedure, a pattern of low absolute but realistic level of aspiration, and a low general level of planning and verbal communication. All of these factors appear to be the result of a complicated synthesis of many small intangible causes, amplified into a general tangible effect through the interaction process. One might expect each of these factors to be found in the content of developing group norms and subject to normative control.

Using Cattell's personality test in a different way, results were obtained which generally confirm those reported above (Haythorn, 1953). In laboratory discussion groups, measured personality traits of members involving emotional maturity, friendly cooperativeness, trustfulness and adaptability, adventuresomeness, willed application, and freedom from anxiety were positively related to smooth and effective group functioning as judged by observers of the group. Conversely, the characteristics of paranoid suspiciousness, eccentricity, and coolness to others were found to be negatively related to smooth functioning as seen by the observers. In this study, observers also rated the behavior of individuals, and group members rated the characteristics of their group. Observer ratings on variables of individual behavior conceptualized as "facilitating the achievement of the group goal," such as cooperativeness, efficiency, and insight, tended to predict the ratings subjects gave their groups on such variables as morale, cooperativeness, productivity, motivation, and interest in job completion. Observer ratings of variables of individual behavior designated as "striving for individual prominence," such as aggressiveness, initiative, confidence, authoritarianism, interest in individual solution, and attempts at leadership, were negatively related to members' own ratings of the cohesiveness and friendliness of their group. Finally, observers' ratings of a third group of variables conceptualized as "social behavior" were related to members' own ratings of their group as noncompetitive, friendly, and talkative. In general, subjects chose as co-workers and nominated as best in leadership those members who seemed to "facilitate" group functioning, and rejected those who hindered smooth functioning.

Subsequent research on the effects of combinations of personalities on group performance confirms the findings of Cattell and Haythorn. High scores on intelligence or some measure of ability to deal with complex materials is especially important if group members are to combine effectively. The more recent research includes Hoffman, 1959; Tuckman, 1964; Lucas, 1965; Zander and Wulff, 1966; Conway, 1967; Carrera and Cohen, 1968; Dubno, 1968; Haythorn, 1968; Kennedy, 1971b; Lambert, 1971.

Defense Mechanisms

An experiment by Cohen (1956) illustrates some aspects of the relation between defense mechanisms (i.e., unconscious ways of dealing with anxiety) and interpersonal behavior. Forty-four college students were given written tests to determine the area of their primary psychosexual disturbances and their preferred denfense mechanisms. They were then paired in terms of defense, psychosexual dimension, and intensity of disturbance. No two subjects were paired if they had indicated one another as friends in a preliminary sociometric questionnaire. The basic pairs were of three kinds: pairs of projectors, pairs with similar defenses other than projection, and pairs where defenses were dissimilar. The members of each pair were then asked to read some short stories which would arouse their common area of disturbance, to make individual judgments about the motives of the actors in the stories, and to arrive at a common decision about the motives through group discussion.

The pairs of subjects who used *projection* (i.e., the tendency to attribute to someone else the impulses which the subject finds unacceptable to himself) as a defense perceived their own interaction as more hostile than pairs of subjects who utilized other defenses. These negative effects were obtained only when two projectors were paired. When projectors discussed the stories with persons using other defenses, they were no different in their perception of hostility from any other pairs having dissimilar defenses. The negative feeling was also less marked if only one of the partners was highly disturbed.

When pairs with similar defense preference were compared with other similar pairs on the extent to which they experienced their own interaction as negative, the rank order from most negative to most positive was projection, regression, reaction formation, and avoidance. A similar ordering from negative to positive for the psychosexual conflicts was sibling rivalry, castration anxiety, oral sadism, anal expulsiveness, and oedipal intensity.

Summary

Predictions about the interaction process which are based on the personality composition of a group can be simple in that they only consider the central tendencies of individuals of a given type no matter what situation they are in, or they can include estimates of the modifications of central tendencies which result from the presence of other personality types or of persons playing specific roles.

The seven personality factors which are reported most often in small group research are intelligence, adjustment (anxiety), extroversion-introversion, dominance, masculinity-feminity, radicalism-conservatism, and interpersonal sensitivity. Most of these factors in turn can be seen as variations of four dimensions representing tendencies toward dominant, positive, serious, and conforming behavior.

A dominant personality trait is associated with a high rate of interaction in a group and a specialization in task leadership. A submissive trait is associated with behavior which is supporting, modifying, qualifying, or rejecting. A positive trait is associated with warm, personal, and cooperative behavior and willingness to disclose personal information about oneself. Although few personality traits are directly correlated with the behavioral dimension of serious-expressive, the combination of high intelligence and high anxiety produces a person who is very task-oriented and serious. Conformity versus nonconformity is the most frequently measured personality dimension. Subjects who accept a controlling authority structure (i.e., have high scores on the authoritarian scale) are more suggestible and conforming.

The consistency of an individual's behavior increases with the similarity in the two situations in which he is being observed. The correlations between personality traits and interpersonal behavior can be substantially increased if the characteristics of the other group members are considered.

Groups composed of individuals who are compatible in that they all prefer close intimate relations are more productive than groups in which some individuals are "personal" and some are "counterpersonal." Individuals will also be more effective when playing a role which is similar to their personality type.

In an experiment in which subjects who were high and low in authoritarianism were observed in separate groups as they worked on a task involving group discussion, the low-authoritarian subjects were rated higher on effective intelligence and demonstrated more leadership behavior. The leaders who emerged in the leaderless group sessions differed according to the type of group. Leaders in the low-authoritarian groups were more equalitarian in their leadership behavior. The members in the high-authoritarian groups reported that their meetings showed little progress and were less cooperative. But they also reported fewer differences of opinion and less competition. In later sessions, the groups were assigned leaders who were either similar or dissimilar in their personality type. The leader's behavior varied with his own personality type and with the type of persons he was leading. The presence of an F+ leader or of F+ followers increased the amount of autocratic behavior.

Other research with leaderless groups indicates that the characteristic patterns of group interaction tend to be strongly influenced by the personalities of the members in the initial stages of group formation. As in the experiments with compatible groups, a high group mean on a personality trait usually results in a similar type of behavior for the group, while high variance on other traits may produce more effective groups if the task calls for variability in individual performance, or conflict if the task calls for similarity of individual performance.

Chapter 9

SOCIAL CHARACTERISTICS

IT IS POSSIBLE TO control the pattern and outcome of interaction by selecting members with certain combinations of social characteristics. Some of these characteristics, such as age, sex, physical attractiveness, and physical handicaps are easily identified, and others, such as social class, ethnicity, friendship group, and birth order, can be discovered with relatively little investigation. Since these characteristics of group members are so easily controlled, they have usually been "held constant" in experimental studies of interaction by selecting groups of persons who are of college age, male, middle-class, and unacquainted prior to the experiment. For this reason, the data on the effects of some social characteristics of members on interaction in small groups reported here are drawn largely from the child-study literature, which is based more on field than experimental studies.

As children grow older they play less by themselves and more with others, so that their group skills increase. By adulthood the children have learned roles which are appropriate for their sex in their own culture. These roles vary by social class, ethnic group, and birth order. Society also provides role expectations for persons who are physically attractive or have handicaps. Whether children or adults, popular persons tend to have similar behavioral characteristics, and groups of friends behave differently from groups of nonfriends. Although the roles associated with different social characteristics are learned in the larger society, they tend to carry over into small decision-making groups, where they affect the distribution of participation, influence, and prestige among members (Bechtel and Rosenfeld, 1966; Moore, 1968; Freese, 1974). These effects are independent of any prior cultural belief in the relevance of the status characteristics to the task (Berger, Cohen, and Zelditch, 1972).

Age

Age as a variable appears almost entirely in the child-study literature, which describes the number and intensity of social relationships characteristic of children in different age groups. The major generalization regarding the relation between age and social interaction is represented by the work of Piaget (1932), who observed that very young children move through phases of isolated or egocentric

200

play, parallel play, and cooperative or competitive play as they mature from the ages of about two to seven years. The size of the group in which the children play increases with age (Green, 1933b; Parten, 1933b).

In experiments where children of different ages were observed playing in pairs, quantitative scores for friendliness were higher than those for unfriendliness (Mengert, 1931). Competition and rivalry developed gradually and began to dominate the interaction at age four or five, although this was not true for all children of a given age (Greenberg, 1932; Leuba, 1933). Preschool children, ages two through four, showed an increase in the number of social contacts with increasing age (Beaver, 1932). The number of individual children with whom they had contact decreased as they grew older, although there was an increase in the intimacy of the contacts which remained (Green, 1933a; Bernhardt et al., 1937; Harrocks and Thompson, 1946). The older children can form more intimate relationships because of maturation and also because they have known the other children in the group over a longer period of time (Salusky, 1930; Hagman, 1933; Clampitt and Charles, 1956). Older children also are more adept at problem-solving in groups (de Montmollin, 1959; A. J. Smith, 1960a; Voicu, 1971), and their groups show more differentiation in status and power (H. W. Smith, 1973).

Jersild and Fite (1939) used the method of direct observation supplemented by other data to study group trends and individual patterns of adjustment in the behavior of 18 two-and-a-half- to four-year-old nursery school children at the beginning of the school year and again (16 cases) in the spring. Children who had previously attended nursery school showed about twice as much social participation as did "new" children during the first weeks of school, but the "new" children began to make rapid gains at once, and by spring the two groups were equal. The higher "social contact" scores of the "old" children in the fall were in a large measure due to special companionships carried over from the previous year.

In one study of some consequences of age heterogeneity in adult decision-making groups, the effect of age on participation was found to be related to the sex of the group members. Twelve male and twelve female three-person groups were composed of teachers whose ages ranged from 21 to 63 years. Half of the groups in each set were heterogeneous with respect to age, containing three members who were approximately 20, 30, and 40 years of age. Each group had two tasks: one the discussion of the number of dots on a card and the other a judgment problem. All groups were observed using the Bales category system. In both male and female groups, the amount of participation was found to be related to age. However, in the male groups the older teachers talked the most, while in the female group the younger teachers talked the most. No differences were found in the Bales profiles (Ziller and Exline, 1958).

Sex

In addition to differences in physical ability, which are primarily biological in origin, males and females also differ, as a result of socialization, in typical ways of solving problems and in their efficiency in different types of tasks (Mukerji, 1940; de Montmollin, 1955b; Cattell and Lawson, 1962). In their earliest school years, girls assume adult female roles as they "play house" in the doll corner, while boys build machines with their blocks (Hartley, Frank, and Goldenson, 1952). In later years, in free discussion the content of their discussion differs. In one study of 500 conversations overheard on the college campus, in streetcars, hotel lobbies, barbershops, churches, and other public places, men were found to talk most of business and money, while women talked mostly of men and clothes (Landis and Burtt, 1924). In committee work, females are quicker and more accurate with personal interesting tasks (e.g., interpreting photographs portraying emotions) while males are superior on more abstract multiple-choice problems (South, 1927). Women tend to recognize this difference (Carey, 1958). In mixed committees, men tend to initiate activity and women tend to react to it (Strodtbeck and Mann, 1956; Strodtbeck, James and Hawkins, 1957), with men playing a more instrumental and women a more expressive role (Borgatta and Stimson, 1963; Heilbrun, 1968). A one-sex committee is usually more efficient than a mixed one, since less time is spent in social-emotional activity (South, 1927).

Further evidence of the importance of knowing the sex composition of the group in order to predict behavior comes from a study of kindergarten children in an experimental play situation. The boys were more dominating with other boys than the girls were with other girls, and the teachers were generally more dominating with the children than the children were with each other (Anderson, 1939). In another study boys tended to receive more disapproval from the teacher than girls received (Meyer and Thompson, 1956).

The fact that the typical sex role is determined to a large extent by culture is evident in Strodtbeck's study (1951) described in chapter 6, in which revealed differences in judgments between husband and wives in three cultures indicated that the amount of activity and power as defined by the culture was related to the way differences were settled. Husband-wife differences similar to those reported by Stroudtbeck were also found among undergraduate married couples (Kenkel, 1957). The husbands did most of the talking and had the most influence on decisions, while the wives tended to play a more social-emotional role. Couples who are dating show the same patterns (Heiss, 1962; Shaw and Sadler, 1965; Lowe and Murphy, 1972).

Another experimenter recorded husband-wife interaction as they discussed the "revealed differences" in their opinions on a series of political questions. The questions involved labor, foreign, and local issues. In this sample of eight couples, the wives were all members of a women's nonpartisan political organization. In addition to doing most of the talking (55 percent), the husbands differed from their wives in the proportion of their acts which were scored as giving information, opinions, and suggestions. The proportion of the husbands' activity in these categories was highest for the labor issues, next highest for the foreign-affairs issues, and lowest for the local issues. When asked to rank the issues in the order in which they were appropriate for discussion by women's political groups, the husbands and wives generally agreed that the local issues were most appropriate, foreign next, and labor least (March, 1953).

In addition to differences between males and females in their own roles, differences are also found in the ability of each of the sexes to take the role of the other sex. In a study in which 16 college students were tested in groups of four for the quality of performance in roleplaying of four situations, each subject was asked to perform the roles of the other group members. The men were better in their performance of the roles of other men than they were of women in the group, and the same was true for the women. However, the men appeared to be more perceptive of the roles of the women than women of the roles of the men (Brown, 1952).[1]

Experiments with three-person groups using a simple competitive negotiable game (and similar games with groups of other sizes) have consistently revealed a significant difference in the strategy followed by men and women. The male strategy is more exploitative. It is characterized by an orientation toward winning. Bargaining is directed toward the maximization of advantages accruing to the individual player. The female strategy is more accommodative. It is oriented toward the social situation. Bargaining is directed toward reaching agreements mutually satisfactory to the three players. Distinctive features of the accommodative strategy include a high frequency of triple alliances, a preference for 50-50 deals, and an avoidance of direct competition. Bargaining often resembles a discussion rather than a competition (Vinacke, 1959; Sidowski and Smith, 1961; Uesugi and Vinacke, 1963; Weinstein, Wiley, and DeVaughn, 1966; Marwell, Schmitt, and Shotola, 1970; Wiley, 1973; House, 1974).

Men also take the initiative in the large society, where men are more likely to join voluntary groups, especially those which are instrumental rather than expressive (Booth, 1972; Tiger, 1972). Anthropological evidence suggests that in many cultures men have a propensity to form stronger and more enduring ties with each other than women do with other women (Tiger, 1969).

Additional research related to sex roles includes Leventhal, Shemberg, and Van Schoelandt, 1968; Maier, 1970; Joesting and Joesting, 1972; Galejs, 1974.

Sex Roles in Jury Deliberations

In the study conducted by Strodtbeck and Mann (1956) the data employed arise from mock jury deliberations conducted in connection with the Law and Behavioral Science research of the Law School, University of Chicago. The participants in these deliberations are jurors drawn by lot from the regular jury pools of the Chicago and St. Louis courts. The jurors listen to a recorded trial, deliberate, and return their verdict—all under the customary discipline of bailiffs of the court. The deliberations are recorded with two microphones to facilitate binaural identification of the individual participants. The recordings are fully transcribed and these protocols are in turn scored in terms of interaction process categories. The scoring is done by an assistant who listens again to the recording and has available the indications of non-verbal gestures made by the original observer. The level of inter-scorer reliability is checked before the scoring begins and rechecked periodically while scoring is in process.

In table 20, percentage profiles for 127 jurors split into inactive and active males, inactive and active females are presented. The data in this form show women to exceed men in the three Positive Reactions categories and to be exceeded by men in the three Attempted Answers categories. This finding strongly confirms the hypothesis that there is a continuance in jury deliberations of sex role specialization observed in adult family behavior.

[Analysis of all the data of the experiment] suggests that men *pro-act*, that is, they initiate relatively long bursts of action directed at the solution of the task problem, and women tend more to *react* to the contributions of others. These important differ-

---

1. In an analysis of some of the determinants of role-taking accuracy, Powell & LaFave (1958) suggest that accuracy depends on such situational factors as (1) type and circumstance of interaction, (2) motivational relevance of the situation, (3) acting ability of the other subject, and (4) attitudinal consistency of the other subject.

Table 20. Interaction Profile by Sex and Activity

Categories	MALE		FEMALE	
	Inactive	Active	Inactive	Active
A. Positive reactions				
1. Shows solidarity	1.14	1.03	1.39	1.45
2. Shows tension release	1.75	1.50	8.49	2.91
3. Shows agreement	10.50	8.26	16.98	20.59
B. Attempted answers				
4. Gives suggestions	3.50	3.54	2.31	1.52
5. Gives opinion	25.44	19.42	22.07	18.07
6. Gives information	41.59	48.49	35.96	34.95
C. Questions				
7. Asks for information	4.85	5.09	6.33	6.76
8. Asks for opinion	1.08	2.65	.77	1.26
9. Asks for suggestion	.00	.08	.00	.03
D. Negative reactions				
10. Shows disagreement	6.46	4.99	3.70	9.31
11. Shows tension	1.82	2.61	1.54	2.36
12. Shows antagonism	1.88	2.36	.46	.77
Total	100.01	100.02	100.00	99.98
Base frequencies	1486	12413	648	3093
Jurors	41	45	23	18

Source: Fred L. Strodtbeck and R. D. Mann, "Sex Role Differentiation in Jury Deliberations," *Sociometry* 19 (1956). Reprinted by permission of the authors and the American Sociological Association.

ences, which may be read from the interaction profiles, coexist with similarities arising from the information-exchanging, consensus-seeking nature of the deliberation problem. By and large, the jurors' interaction profiles are quite similar. In the face of this similarity the direction of attention of the differences associated with sex roles should not be permitted to obscure the determinative influences of the problem situation.

It should perhaps be stressed that the acts involved in the task and social-emotional distinctions are included in the repertoire of all persons. When taken in isolation, these acts do not suggest male or female behavior; it is only in the statistical analysis of aggregates of acts that the sex-typed connotation emerges. Among the various subjects, there are many individual instances in which men are more social-emotional than women, and vice versa. The twelve juries reported upon contained from one to six women, however, in the aggregate profiles there were no discernible trends associated with the increased number of women in the group.[2]

Sex of Audience and Recall

An experiment by Grace (1951) indicates that even the order of recall of a set of objects is related to the anticipated sex of the future audience, and provides some evidence for the hypothesis stated in chapter 2 that the social act typically involves some modification of behavior to fit the expectations of the other group members. Grace varied the extent to which subjects would anticipate that a future audience would be a woman by asking a number of undergraduates, both men and women, to look at some objects on a table and then to report what they had seen

2. Fred L. Strodtbeck and Richard D. Mann, "Sex Role Differentiation in Jury Deliberations," *Sociometry* 19 (1956): 4–10. Reprinted by permission of the authors and the publisher.

to a person in the next room. Some subjects were told nothing about the person, some were told that they would report to a woman, and some were reminded several times that they would report to a woman. In each case the person actually was a woman who asked the subjects to name all of the objects on the table. Some of the objects were masculine, e.g., a supporter; some were feminine, e.g., a brassiere; and the remainder were neutral, e.g., sunglasses. Anticipation of the type of audience had no effect on the frequency with which the various items were recalled, but it did effect the order of recall. Subjects who were reminded that the audience would be a woman recalled the female items earlier than they did when they were told only once or not at all. Since the actual audience was the same for all subjects, the difference is probably not due to restraints operating in the face-to-face situation, but to the effect of the anticipated audience on learning and recalling the items so that certain ones were more readily recalled than others.

Later experiments by Grace (1952a, 1952b) did not wholly confirm these results. In fact, in one experiment the males recalled male items earlier when reporting to a female audience. Grace concludes that "the strongest effect on the content of communication is achieved when the communicator and the audience are of the same background, and the communicator is definitely and deliberately briefed about the audience" (1952b, p. 95).

Physical Attractiveness

Some of the implications of being physically attractive have been noted in chapter 7 in the discussion of interpersonal choice. Good looks are associated with popularity (Dion, Berscheid, and Walster, 1972). In terms of exchange, physical attractiveness appears to be an asset which can be bestowed by associating with someone. The behavior of the attractive person is enhanced so that behavior which would ordinarily take on a negative value is found to be acceptable (Landy and Sigall, 1974).

One study suggests that a physical attractiveness stereotype may be present at an early level of development in children. To test the hypothesis that adults display differential treatment toward attractive and unattractive children in circumstances in which their behavior is identical, an experiment was conducted in which 243 female college undergraduates read a description of a transgression committed by a seven-year-old and viewed a photograph of the child involved. A research design was used which varied the attractiveness of the child, the severity of the transgression, the sex of the child, and the type of transgression in a $2 \times 2 \times 2 \times 2$ design. Support was found for the hypothesis that (1) the severe transgression of an attractive child is less likely to be seen as reflecting an enduring disposition toward antisocial behavior than that of an unattractive child, and (2) the transgression itself tends to be evaluated less negatively when committed by an attractive child (Dion, 1972). The physical attractiveness of a criminal defendant is also found to affect a juridic judgment (J. I. Shaw, 1972a; Sigall and Ostrove, 1973), and the physical attractiveness of inept or unwilling workers affects the amount of coercive power used by their supervisors (Goodstadt and Hjelle, 1973b).

Male experimental subjects work harder for an attractive female experimenter than an unattractive one. In an experiment a physically demanding task was assigned to 44 male undergraduates to be performed before another male. A female experimenter who made up to look either attractive or unattractive then evaluated the performance. The men worked harder for the attractive experimenter, especially when she gave a negative evaluation on the first round (Sigall, Page, and Brown, 1971).

Physical Handicaps

Persons without physical handicaps feel uncomfortable in the presence of handicapped persons. They often attempt to restore a balance in the relationship by being more agreeable or changing their opinions in the direction of the disabled persons (Kleck, 1966, 1968; Kleck et al., 1968; Kleck, 1969; Clore and Jeffery, 1972; Comer and Piliavin, 1972; Zych and Bolton, 1972). In a typical experiment subjects are interviewed by an experimenter who either appears to be normal, or sits in a wheel chair, or seems to have a leg amputated. Subjects interviewed by the "handicapped" experimenter show less variability in their behavior, terminate the interaction sooner, and express opinions less representative of their own beliefs (Kleck, Ono, and Hastorf, 1966).

In another experimental variation, this time in the field, a man with an eye patch asks housewives to fill out a questionnaire or, as an alternative, have a 15- to 20-minute interview. A similar request is made of another sample of housewives by a man without an eye patch. More housewives choose to send in a questionnaire when the request is made by the interviewer with the eye patch, presumably to ward off the embarassment of dealing with someone who is stigmatized (Doob and Ecker, 1970). As in other forms of social interaction, sex differences are reported, with women being more considerate of the handicapped (Titley and Viney, 1969).

Persons who are handicapped try to restore balance to the situation. Interviews with blind, crippled, and facially disfigured young to middle-aged adults in a metropolitan area indicate that some socially skilled handicapped persons use a variety of strategies to put normals "at their ease" (Davis, 1964). However, subjects playing the role of handicapped persons are not always so successful (Farina, Allen, and Saul, 1968).

Social Class

Differences in interaction pattern which are related to social class are found in membership roles of lower-class and middle-class adolescent clubs (Maas, 1954b). The lower-class member directed more collaborative interaction to the adult leader than did the middle-class member to his leader, the middle-class member directed more collaborative and aggressive interactions to the club president (who was his peer), and the lower-class member was more aggressive with other members. Lower-class gang boys are more tolerant in their attitude toward deviant behaviors than middle-class nongang boys (Gordon et al., 1963).

Within adult discussion groups the members with higher social-economic status tend to participate more. In jury deliberations the jurors who were higher in social-economic status were found to talk more and to have more influence on other members, and were perceived by fellow jurors as more competent for the jury task (Strodtbeck, James, and Hawkins, 1957). In community groups in which members discussed a mental health film, the members who participated more often were of higher social class, had high status within the group, and were familiar with the topic (McGinnies and Vaughan, 1957).

Ethnic Group

The influence of ethnic group in determining the typical interaction pattern of a group member is evident in Strodtbeck's study of husband-wife interaction in three cultures which was referred to above (1951). Marked cultural differences in the interaction of members of discussion groups are also reported in an analysis of committee-member behavior with different national and ethnic groups (Gyr, 1951; Stimson, 1960; Crowther, 1962; Maier and Hoffman, 1962; Rossel, 1970; Ogawa, 1971; Ogawa and Welden, 1972) and in interaction patterns in families (Roberts, 1951). However, despite differences cross-cultural communication may be possible (Simard and Taylor, 1973), especially if the leader is trained to recognize cultural differences (Mitchell and Foa, 1969).

Ethnic group affiliation is important in determining the lines along which sub-groups will form, since members of the same ethnic group will tend to interact more with each other than with other group members. In a study of the role of group belongingness when voting for a leader (Festinger, 1947), girls from two religious groups tended to vote for members of their own group when the religion of the nominees for the leader position was identified. The trend was more apparent in a large group of 48 subjects than in a smaller group. Subgroup formation along ethnic lines is also evident in seating patterns (Parker, 1968).

In another study four-man groups were composed of college students representing two different ethnic groups. The groups met for a total of over 12 hours, performing a variety of tasks. In each group the two members of the ethnic group with higher status tended to talk more to each other than to the two members from the group with lower status. The lower-status members also talked more to the high-status members than they did to each other (Katz, Goldston, and Benjamin, 1958).

In general, lower-status members talk less and have less influence in group discussion unless they are especially reinforced (Katz and Benjamin, 1960; Ziller, Behringer, and Goodchilds, 1960; Katz and Cohen, 1962; E. G. Cohen, 1972). As a result of the fact that the group may not find a way to use the contributions of low-status members and that subjects may feel inhibited when dealing with other ethnic groups, productivity will generally be lower in ethnically mixed groups than in homogeneous groups (Harrison, Messe, and Stollak, 1971). However, a threat shared by the members of a mixed group may increase ingroup solidarity (Burnstein and McRae, 1962).

Friendship

Since friendship is based upon common social characteristics, persons who choose each other for friends may well be of the same age, sex, social class, and ethnic group. For this reason friendship is not as "independent" a variable as the other characteristics. The association between the number of friends and age, for example, has already been noted. In general, friends tend to be more homogeneous in their behavior patterns than nonfriends, they communicate to each other more (Philp, 1940), and they are more productive, unless they spend too much time in social-emotional activity or conspire to slow down on the job. They also conform more to self-originated norms and show more resistance to change from the outside.

Friendship is used as an experimental variable in two ways. First, one may select the popular individuals from several groups and place them together in a new group. Second, one can select from a larger group a small group of mutual friends.

Similarities among Friends and Popular Members

Friends are generally found to be similar in intelligence and temperament (Richardson, 1939), although no relationship between these two variables and friendship is reported in at least one study (Bonney, 1946). Friends tend to have congruent personality traits (see chapter 7). If the individuals studied are friends and are also among the *most chosen* members of the group, then the differences between friends and nonfriends are more apparent. Overchosen children are more apt to be high interactors, more cooperative, least hostile to members of competing groups, superior in emotional and physical adjustment, and more representative of the group norms (Hardy, 1937; Hunt and Solomon, 1942; Sherif, 1951; Bates, 1952; Bonney, Hoblit, and Dreyer, 1953; Bonney and Powell, 1952; Dahlke, 1953).

Similar differences between popular and unpopular members have also been observed for adult groups. (Cf. Lansing, 1957; Fishman, 1966; Horrocks and Benimoff, 1967; Smith and Olson, 1970; Walster, 1970; Crandall, 1971; Larsen, 1971; Codol, 1972–1973; Lemineur and Meurice, 1972; Leonard, 1973.) In industry, for example, overchosen members may be more satisfied with their jobs (Speroff, 1955). If a sample population for an industrial study is limited to friends, a further bias will be introduced in that pairs of friends are usually individuals who are near each other functionally and spatially, and are of the same sex (J. James, 1951b).

The effects of selecting popular individuals have been summarized in a review of 43 sociometric studies (Mouton, Blake, and Fruchter, 1955b). A positive relation has been found between sociometric choices received by an individual and productivity, combat effectiveness, training ability, and leadership, and a negative relation between popularity and accident-proneness, sickness, and disciplinary offenses.

Some of the differences between the behavior of well-liked or "overchosen" individuals and that of other group members are illustrated by a study of a peer group of 16 government agents (Blau, 1954b). Although the men in this group were supposed to work as individual inspectors and to consult only with the supervisor if they needed help with a case, in practice they formed an informal hierarchy based on a member's willingness to cooperate and skill in handling cases. Men at the top of the hierarchy were well liked because they would give advice to those farther down who were less skilled and needed help with their cases. In this way the men with less skill could avoid having their deficiencies come to the attention of the supervisor. In addition to the differences in skill and willingness to cooperate, high-status members received more contacts from within the group, made more contacts with outsiders, and were less concerned about the opinions of their secretaries than the low-status members.

Members who are "overchosen" and "underchosen" in a large group will form new hierarchies when separated into two new groups so that in the group of former "overchosen" individuals some are now relatively "underchosen," and in the group of formerly "underchosen" individuals some are now relatively "overchosen" (Powell et al., 1956).

It is evident that the extent to which popular or "overchosen" members differ from the average of the population as a whole depends upon the characteristics of the subgroup of the total population from which they are drawn. To draw on an example from college life, the least active and least popular of the campus leaders in extracurricular activities may still be more active and more popular than the average undergraduate.

Friendship and Productivity

Pairs of close friends were found to be more efficient in the solution of problems than pairs of strangers (Husband, 1940). This effect also occurs in larger groups. Ratings of proficiency for 12 six-man reconnaissance units from the same army regiment were highly correlated (+.77) with the proportion of intraunit friendship choices (Goodacre, 1951). Part of this effect may be due to higher "morale" or "attractiveness" of the groups containing the most friends, but it is also probably due to the increased ease of *communication,* since several studies on circulation of rumors support the assumption that friendship acts to reduce barriers in communication (Festinger et al., 1948; Festinger et al., 1950).

If too much time is spent by the friends in social-emotional activity, the productivity of the group will go down (Bos, 1937; Horsfall and Arensberg, 1949). A slowdown may also occur if the group members conspire to lower the output. The efforts of the group to impose a slowdown will be more effective if the group members are highly congenial (Schachter et al., 1951).

Having a friendly person to work with also appears to increase individual productivity. In an experiment with three-year-old children, intelligence tests were administered by a teacher who had previously acted friendly with some and distant with others. The children to whom she had been friendly performed better on the tests (Sacks, 1952).

Influence of Friends

In addition to increasing the quantity of interaction, friendship also influences the quality of interaction. Children who were paired with friends in a frustrating situation showed more cooperation and, incidentally, more aggression toward the experimenter than pairs of acquaintances (Wright, 1943). A similar effect was observed with previously unacquainted pairs of college students who had been insulted by the experimenter. Pairs of students who had been told they would get along well with each other reacted with more hostility to the experimenter and the experiment and were less restrained in their interaction than pairs of equally unacquainted students who were told they would probably *not* get along well together (Pepitone and Reichling, 1955). The tendency for friends to be more cooperative has also been observed in adult groups in which an inverse relation was found between the degree to which a person strove for individual prominence and the amount of friendliness displayed in the groups of which he was a member (Haythorn, 1953).

Persons who are attracted to each other have more influence on each other, since individuals are more willing to agree with the opinions of others whom they like (Festinger, Schachter, and Back, 1950). In a study made at a summer workshop, the friendship pattern of a group of 20 persons was first determined by sociometric methods. Then, after each group discussion, the investigators presented to the group three statements made during the discussion together with the name of the person who had made each statement. Each group member indicated on a questionnaire his perception of which other members agreed or disagreed with each of the assertions and his own agreement or disagreement. The data indicated that members agreed with a statement more if they liked the person who made it, and that they perceived other persons whom they liked agreeing more with statements they made (Horowitz, Lyons, and Perlmutter, 1951). A tendency for members to talk most to those they like best or like least and least to those to whom they are indifferent was reported in a study carried out in two different cultures (Festinger and Hutte, 1954).

Friendship, unlike age and sex, is a variable which may be affected by experimental manipulation when some other factor is actually the focus of the investigation. For example, in one experiment teams were composed of ten- to twelve-year-old boys in such a way that at the outset of the experiment each group member found approximately half of his sociometric choices in his own group and the remaining half on the opposing team. When these groups were observed under frustration, the number of friendship choices within the groups at least persisted or improved for unsuccessful low-status and consistently high-status groups (Thibaut, 1950). (Here group status was manipulated by the experimenter, who assigned different values to the tasks the groups performed.)

Influence through Social Communication

Back (1951) demonstrates some of the effects of "cohesiveness" on influence and productivity. He also provides evidence for the assumption, discussed in chapter 7, that the criterion used to determine "cohesiveness" will affect the form and content of the interaction process. The main purpose of the experiment was to measure the effects of strength of cohesiveness on pressure toward uniformity within pairs of subjects and the consequences of this effect. Cohesiveness, which was defined as "the resultant of forces which are acting on the members to stay in the group," was varied in three ways by telling the members that they would or would not (1) like each other (a variable related to integration in the AGIL scheme), (2) receive a prize for the best group performance (a variable related to goal-attainment), or (3) serve as a model for a highly productive group (a variable related to latent pattern maintenance). These three types of cohesiveness based on personal attraction, group goal, and group prestige were compared with a control group which received a negative treatment in which all forces to belong to the group were minimized.

Seventy pairs of college students who had not known each other previously and were of the same sex took part in the experiment. The pairs were divided by type of "treatment" into seven sets. After the subjects in each pair were introduced to each other, they were taken to separate rooms, where each was instructed to write a preliminary story about a set of three pictures. They were then brought together and asked to discuss the story. Each was then asked to write a final story. Although the subjects thought that the sets of picures were identical, there were actually slight differences which led to different interpretations. The subjects were also given the special instructions appropriate to their experimental conditions.

The amount of influence of one partner on another was measured by the num-

Table 21. Changes Influenced by the Partner

Group	Personal attraction	Task direction	Group prestige	Negative
Low cohesive	7.9	8.9	6.7	8.5
High cohesive	10.5	11.0	8.3	

F = Var.: strength/Var.: within cells = 3.13; df = 1 and 54; p < .11

Source: Kurt W. Back, "Influence through Social Communication," *Journal of Abnormal and Social Psychology* 46 (1951): 22. Copyright 1951 by the American Psychological Association. Reprinted by permission of the author and the publisher.

ber of changes in a subject's story which tended toward the position the partner had shown in either his first or final story. The actual discussion was recorded by two observers who used a set of 20 categories to identify influence attempts, reactions to attempted influence, and other types of behavior. After the discussion, each observer characterized the pair as "active" or "withdrawing," and each subject indicated the extent to which he was attracted to his partner.

The results of the experiment showed that, within this setting, certain effects could be expected to follow an increase of cohesiveness, independent of the basis of the cohesiveness. "In the high cohesive groups the members made more attempts to reach an agreement. Both the ratings of the total discussion and direct observation showed more serious effort to enter the discussion in highly cohesive groups. The subjects' own statements also confirmed the high pressures in these groups" (Back, 1951, p. 22).

Attempted influence appeared to be more a question of personal preference in the low cohesive groups, while it was almost a necessary result of the pressures toward uniformity in the high cohesive groups. In the high cohesive groups, acceptance of the experimental situation, interest in the problem itself, and a desire to help the experimenter combined to motivate the subjects to make something of the discussion.

In the highly cohesive groups the discussion was more effective in that it produced influence, that is, group members changed more toward the partners' positions than they did in the less cohesive groups (see table 21). In the highly cohesive groups the change was quite unevenly distributed between the members, while in the less cohesive groups the change was more evenly distributed. On the average, one member of the highly cohesive groups changed more than either member of the less cohesive groups; and the other member of the highly cohesive group was nearly the same as one member of the less cohesive group.[3]

The differences among the ways in which cohesiveness was produced also led to differences in patterns of communication and influence.

If cohesiveness was based on personal attraction, group members wanted to transform the discussion into a longish, pleasant conversation. The discussion was taken as a personal effort, and rejection of persuasion tended to be resented.

If cohesiveness was based on the performance of a task, group members wanted to complete the activity quickly and efficiently; they spent just the time necessary for performance of the task (see table 22) and they tried to use this time for the per-

3. Kurt W. Back, "Influence through Social Communication," *Journal of Abnormal and Social Psychology* 46 (1951): 22–23. Copyright 1951 by the American Psychological Association. Reprinted by permission of the author and the publisher.

Table 22. Time of Discussion (Seconds)

Group	Personal attraction	Task direction	Group prestige	Negative
Low cohesive	412.5	415.5	307.0	330.0
High cohesive	449.0	321.5	362.5	

t not significant $t = 2.91$ $t = 3.65$
                     $p < .01$ $p < .01$

Source: Kurt W. Back, "Influence through Social Communication," *Journal of Abnormal and Social Psychology* 46 (1951): 23. Copyright 1951 by the American Psychological Association. Reprinted by permission of the author and the publisher.

formance of the task only. They tended to participate in the discussion only as much as they thought it valuable to achieve their purposes.

If cohesiveness was based on group prestige [the assumption that the group would serve as a model for other groups], group members tried to risk as little as possible to endanger their status: they acted cautiously, concentrated on their own actions, and adjusted to their partners as the social environment. One partner would easily assume a dominant role, and the submissive member was influenced more, without their actually trying to establish this relationship.

Finally, with cohesiveness at a minimum, the members of the pair acted independently and with little consideration for each other. As the subject did not try to adjust to the other member of the pair, each member was concerned only with his own discussion. Influence, accordingly, did not depend on the action of the partner but on the interest of the member himself in entering the group activity.[4]

Summarizing these results in AGIL terms, we see that the pairs who were given directions stressing goal attainment (i.e., producing the best group performance) were in fact the most efficient. When the directions stressed integration (they would like each other) or pattern maintenance (they would serve as a model group), then the pair was diverted from goal attainment to work on these higher-order problems.

Birth Order

First-born and only children tend to be given a more responsible place in the family and thus exhibit more of the characteristics of the task leader, in contrast to later-borns, who have more of the characteristics of the social-emotional leader. First-borns are more likely to be seen as powerful, and to be more authoritarian, more anxious, more affiliative, and more responsive to cues from others but less empathic than later-borns (Stotland and Walsh, 1963; Weller, 1964; Weiss, 1966; Sutton-Smith and Rosenberg, 1968; Tomeh, 1970; Hardy, 1973; McGhee, 1973; Vernon, 1974). In a college sample first-born chose more popular students and exhibited a greater similarity in sociometric choice than did later-borns (Schachter, 1964). However in a highschool sample first-borns were found to choose relatively less popular students (Alexander, 1966). The difference is presumably explained by the fact that later-born students who go to college are more popular in high school than first-born students who go to college, although more first-born persons go to college.

4. Ibid., p. 23.

Summary

Some social characteristics such as age, sex, physical attractiveness, and physical handicaps are easily identified, and others, such as social class, ethnicity, friendship group, and birth order, can be discovered with relatively little investigation. The effects of age on interaction patterns are evident as children develop through preschool age. During these years they pass through phases of egocentric play, parallel play, and group play. When they reach the third stage, they first make many social contacts and then, in latency and adolescence, restrict their contacts to a more intimate few. By adulthood boys and girls have assumed typical sex roles which usually require more activity in the social-emotional area for the women and more activity in the task area for the men.

This sex role differentiation is evident in mock jury deliberations, where men tend to initiate relatively long bursts of activity directed at the solution of task problems and women tend to react to the contribution of others. The sex of an anticipated audience is found to influence the order in which certain sex-linked objects are recalled.

Physical attractiveness has a positive value and is associated with popularity. In contrast, physical handicaps are a social liability, since the presence of a physically handicapped person makes those without handicaps feel uncomfortable. Handicapped persons try to restore "balance" to the situation by using a variety of strategies to put normals "at their ease."

Adolescents from different social classes are found to differ in their patterns of relationship to authority. Upper-class adults tend to participate more and have more influence in discussion groups.

Members of the same ethnic group can be expected to have similar patterns of behavior and to choose each other as subgroups from within the larger group. Lower-status members in a group usually talk less and have less influence on discussion. Friendship, whatever its basis, produces marked differences in interaction. Groups of friends usually have higher morale, exert more influence on each other, and are more productive. Popular individuals, whether grouped with their friends or considered as individuals, are found to be more productive, better students, and less subject to accidents, illness, and disciplinary offenses.

Differences in interaction also appear between groups of "friends" if members in each group are attracted to each other for different reasons. In an experiment in which the basis for "cohesiveness" between members of a pair was varied, it was found that the members tried to turn the task into a social occasion if they were told that they would "like each other," that they completed the activity quickly and efficiently if they were working for a prize, and that they acted more cautiously when their group was to serve as a model.

First-born and only children, who tend to be given a more responsible place in the family, exhibit more of the characteristics of a task leader, while later-born children have more of the characteristics of a social-emotional leader.

Chapter 10

GROUP SIZE

THERE IS NO EXACT specification of how large a group may be before one no longer feels it appropriate to call it a small group. An attempt to name some exact number would actually be misleading. The usefulness of the designation presumably rests on the fact that size is a limiting condition on the amount and quality of communication that can take place among members as individual persons, and hence tends to affect the character of interpersonal orientations that members develop toward each other (Krech and Crutchfield, 1948, p. 371). But other conditions may also be limiting in the same way. For example, the characteristics of the members and the time available may have a similar limiting effect. Consequently, the effects of size should be considered in conjunction with other relevant variables.

Some of the effects of increasing size will be considered as they relate to the form and content of interaction. Since the number of potential relationships between group members increases rapidly as a group grows larger, the larger group tends to break into subgroups with a more rigid hierarchy of positions. When the time for discussion is limited, the average member has fewer chances to speak and intermember communication becomes difficult. Morale declines, since the former intimate contact between members is no longer possible. Although the larger group has in its membership a greater variety of resources for problem-solving, the average contribution of each member diminishes and it becomes more difficult to reach consensus on a group solution. The pair and the three-person group have special characteristics of intimacy and of power structure which give each group some unique aspects. Although the optimum size for a group varies with the task of the group, a five-man group is found to have some advantages for problems which can be solved by group discussion. (See Thomas and Fink, 1963.)

Natural Groups

In terms of effective participation in group activity, it may be that certain group sizes are more "natural" and occur more frequently than others under particular conditions. Age seems to be a variable which is related to size in this way. It appears that the increasing maturity associated with age permits effective participation in larger groups. Preschool children tend to play first individually, although in parallel, then in pairs, then in larger groups. (Piaget, 1932; Green, 1933b; Parten, 1933b).

214

Another variable which appears to be associated with "natural" sizes is the rural-urban continuum. Rural highschool youth form cliques of about three persons, while town youth are more likely to form cliques of four to five persons (Hollingshead, 1949). The smaller size of the rural cliques seems to result primarily from the fact that the rural youth live farther apart.

Frequency and duration of contact between members is to some extent conditioned, as well as the converse (Tannenbaum, 1962). Among college students, as the size of the group increased, frequency, duration, and intimacy of contact decreased (Fischer, 1953). In two studies of the frequency of occurrence of small groups of different sizes, data were collected by observation and from records of the sizes of groups formed by pedestrians, shoppers, play groups, work groups, and congressional committees. The frequency of occurrence of groups of different sizes was found to be a negative function of size. The function described appears smooth, and the mean size for both counts was close to 2.4 (J. James, 1951a, 1953; see also Coleman and James, 1961). Observers have also reported on the relationship between the size of a stimulus crowd, standing on a busy city street looking up at a buliding, and the response of 1,424 passersby. As the size of the stimulus crowd was increased, a greater proportion of the passersby adopted the behavior of the crowd (Milgram, Bickman, and Berkowitz, 1969). There seems to be a tendency for face-to-face groups to gravitate to the smallest size, two. In another study of boys' gangs, the two- or three-boy relationship was often found to be more important to the individual boy than the relationship to the larger gang (Thrasher, 1927).

The Size of the Gang

Thrasher (1927) found in his study of adolescent gangs that the necessities of maintaining face-to-face relationships set definitie limits to the magnitude to which the gang could grow. The size of one group, for example, was determined by the number of boys readily able to meet together on the street or within the limited space of their hangout. The gang did not usually grow to such proportions as to be unwieldy in collective enterprises or to make intimate contacts and controls difficult. Ordinarily, if all members were present, what was said by one of the group could be heard by all. Otherwise, common experience became more difficult and the group tended to split and form more than one gang. The number of "fringers" and hangers-on upon whom the gang could count for backing, however, might be larger, especially if it had developed a good athletic team.

Greater growth was accomplished only through modifications of structure, such as those resulting from conventionalization. When a gang became conventionalized, assuming, for example, the form of a club, it might possibly grow to large proportions. The original gang, however, now became an "inner circle," remaining the active nucleus in such cases. The additional members might develop their own cliques within the larger whole or maintain merely a more or less formal relationship to the organization. In many cases such a club was the result of the combination of two or more gangs.

Table 23 includes only some of the gang clubs; these varied in number of members ordinarily from 20 or 25 to 75 or 100; only a few of the more prosperous clubs exceeded 100 members. It will be seen that 806 of these gangs had memberships of 50 or under; these were largely of the unconventionalized type. Most

Table 23. Approximate Number of Members
in 895 Gangs

No. of Members		No. of Gangs	Percentage of Total
From 3 to 5 (inclusive)		37	4.1
From 6 to 10		198	22.1
From 11 to 15		191	21.5
From 16 to 20		149	16.7
From 21 to 25		79	8.8
From 26 to 30		46	5.1
From 31 to 40		55	6.1
From 41 to 50		51	5.7
From 51 to 75		26	2.9
From 76 to 100		25	2.8
From 101 to 200		25	2.8
From 201 to 500		11	1.2
From 501 to 2,000		2	.2
Total gangs		895	100.0

Source: Frederic M. Thrasher, *The Gang* (Chicago: University of Chicago Press, 1927). Copyright 1927 and 1936 by The University of Chicago Press. All rights reserved. Reprinted by permission of the publisher.

of the remaining 89 had membership ranging from 51 to 2,000, though not all of them had been conventionalized.

Size and Satisfaction

Students in large discussion groups are usually found to be less satisfied than those in smaller groups, although the instructors may prefer the larger groups (Schellenberg, 1959).

The importance of the individual's relationship with a small group as a factor contributing to his satisfaction with the task is further indicated by evidence that infantrymen in the American army who were sent into the front lines as replacements in a group of four buddies who had mutually chosen each other as well liked had higher "morale" than men sent as individual replacements (Chesler, Van Steenberg, and Brueckel, 1955). When coal miners in Great Britain, who were accustomed to working in three-man teams, were shifted to groups of 40 to 50 men (the "longwall" method of coal mining), they became highly dissatisfied with the work (Trist and Bamforth, 1951). Another study suggests that because experiences in larger groups are less satisfying (in this case groups of 15 compared with groups of 5), the members are more likely to take a radical stance and endorse change in the larger society (Lundgren and Bogart, 1974).

In general, as the size of the group decreases, the strength of the affectional ties between members increases (Coyle, 1930; Kinney, 1953), with the dyad allowing the possibilities for the greatest degree of intimacy (Wolff, 1950).

Favorableness of ingroup evaluations is found to vary directly with the distinctiveness of ingroup membership, i.e., as the ingroup's relative size decreases (Gerard and Hoyt, 1974). In an experiment ingroups of various sizes were created with 56 university students. Each student then wrote a short essay and evaluated essays ostensibly written by two others, one of whom "happened" to be an ingroup member, the other an outgroup member. The result was that the smaller the ingroup, the more favorable were evaluations of the ingroup writer relative to the outgroup writer.

The Emergence of Leadership

As size increases, it presumably becomes more difficult for each member to keep each other group member in mind as a separate, differentiated person. Experiments on estimating the number of dots in a visual field with very short time exposures indicate individual subjects can report the exact number up to and including seven with great confidence and practically no error, but above that number confidence and accuracy drop (Taves, 1941). When report time is allowed to vary, time required increases as a function of number of dots on the card, up to six or seven dots, and then flattens abruptly and remains about flat, suggesting that the estimation is being done by a different psychological procedure that somehow does not involve a separate discrimination of each dot (Kaufman et al., 1949; Jensen, Reese, and Reese, 1950). Observers rating group members face a problem not unlike that of the dot estimators in the sense that they can pay attention to only a limited number of persons at a given time. Observers reach maximum agreement on leadership assessment at size six, as compared with sizes two, four, eight, and twelve (Bass and Norton, 1951). It may be that leadership tends not to emerge so clearly in the even sizes below six, and that above that size the observer may begin to run into cognitive difficulties. The coincidence of these findings suggests that the ability of the observing individual to perceive, keep track of, and judge each member separately in a social interaction situation may not extend much beyond the size of six or seven. If this is true, one would expect members of groups larger than that size to think of other members in terms of subgroups, or "classes" of some kind, and to deal with members of subgroups other than their own by more stereotyped methods of response.

The Increasing Number of Relationships

Possibly a more relevant way of viewing size as a variable is to consider the number of possible relationships in the group by pairs and larger subgroups rather than the number of persons. As the number of individuals increases, the number of possible relationships increases much more rapidly than size.

The number of potential symmetrical relationships between individuals is given by the formula:

$$x = \frac{n^2 - n}{2}$$

where $x =$ the number of symmetrical relationships, $n =$ the number of individuals. For example, if there are three members in the group, there are $(9 - 3)/2$, or three, potential symmetrical relationships with the group. If the group is increased to six members, there are $(36 - 6)/2$, or fifteen, relationships (Bossard, 1945). However, since the relationships between subgroups, as well as those between individuals, are usually important in the analysis of a group, a better approximation of the number of potential relationships between individuals, between subgroups, and between an individual and a subgroup is given by the formula $x = \frac{1}{2}(3^n - 2^{n+1} + 1)$.

Using the family as an illustration, the relationship between two brothers would be an example of a relationship at the individual level, between parents and children an example of the subgroup level, and between grandfather and grandchildren an example of the individual and subgroup level. The rapid increase in the potential number of relationships is indicated in table 24. The addition of an in-law to a household of five members which includes mother, father, and three children means that 211 potential relationships have been added (Kephart, 1950). However, in a discussion group only a few of the potential relationships are actually manifest. As a result, the percentage of the total possible relationships which are enacted is found to have a negative correlation with group size (Castore, 1962; Becker et al., 1973).

The word *symmetrical* has been used to qualify the type of relationships referred to in these formulas, since the formulas are based on a global use of the term *relationship* to refer to the sum of all forms of mutual association which might take place between two persons. The bond between two persons can be thought of as the sum of a number of relationships which are usually neither totally present nor fully absent, but present in some degree. If one takes as an example a relationship like *love*, and assumes that the relationship can either be present or absent for each pair of individuals (or a pair of subgroups, or an individual and a subgroup), then there are two ways to fill each of the symmetrical relationships represented by the second formula. The number of different *sets* of potential relationships would actually be 2^x, where x is given by the second formula. For the group of five the number is 2 to the ninetieth power, which is already a very large number (R. L. Davis, 1954).

It may be expected, then, that when there is a desire for intimate and highly developed relationships or need for fine coordination, there will also be a tendency toward the restriction of size. It is worth noting in this connection that the appearance of a leader can permit a reduction of the psychological complication of the group to a series of pair relationships of each member with the leader for certain purposes of coordination. The development of leadership is possibly in part an alternative to an actual reduction in size.

A number of investigators associate the emergence of leadership with increas-

Table 24. Increase in Potential Relationships (x) with an Increase in Group Size (n)

Size of Group	Number of Relationships
2	1
3	6
4	25
5	90
6	301
7	966

Source: William M. Kephart, "A Quantitative Analysis of Intragroup Relationships," *American Journal of Sociology* 60 (1950). Copyright 1950 by The University of Chicago. Reprinted by permission of the publisher, The University of Chicago Press.

ing size of the group. In the restaurant industry, increasing size of the restaurant staff is related to increasing difficulty in coordinating activities (Whyte, 1949). On the basis of a large questionnaire study, leader behavior in many different types of groups was found to differ as size increased (especially above size 31). The demands upon the leader role, moreover, became more numerous and exacting, and member tolerance for leader-centered direction of group activities became greater (Hemphill, 1950). In initially leaderless groups, correlations between observer ratings of members on "initiative," "insight," "leadership behavior," and also "authoritarianism" are greater in groups of size eight than those of size four (Carter et al., 1951b). A similar increase in correlation between prediction of leadership skill made from TAT analysis and the amount of change toward consensus in group discussion is found when size five is compared with size twelve (Hare, 1952), since the larger groups "demand more skill from the leader." In a study of adjustment over time in a group of machine shop workers, a fluctuation in the underlying emotional tone was observed from an initial period of aggression and withdrawal to a period of dependency on the leader and then back to aggression and withdrawal, as size was increased (Rice, 1951). Members of larger groups tend to form subgroups with spokesmen for their opinions (Homans, 1950; Hare, 1952).

Time for Communication

The time available per member for overt communication during a meeting of any given length decreases as the group size increases. Thus each member has a more complicated set of social relationships to maintain and more restricted resources with which to do it (Huff and Piantianida, 1968). In the larger groups a few members do most of the talking (Hawkins, 1962; Zimet and Schneider, 1969). Members of discussion groups are aware of this, and report that they have fewer chances to speak in groups of size twelve as compared with size five (Hare, 1952). In addition, an increased proportion of the members report feelings of threat and inhibition of impulses to participate as size is increased (J. R. Gibb, 1951). As the size of kindergarten groups is increased from 14 to 46, not only do the average number of remarks per child and the percentage of the total number of children who participate decrease, but also the total amount of discussion decreases (Dawe, 1934). Thus the effect of increasing size appears to involve not only a mechanical constriction of time per member but also a feeling of threat or inhibition. In experiments with three-and-a-half-year-old children, the combination of one adult observer and two children results in a higher rate of talking and more "friendly intercourse" than the combination of observer with either one or three children (Williams and Mattson, 1942). Here size is interpreted as a factor of significance in the development of language skills. Such an interpretation may be derivatively correct if size is, as it appears to be, a factor which limits the character of performance of members of the group.

Not only does the average amount of participation per member diminish as group size is increased, but the distribution of participation also varies (Bales et al., 1961; Hamblin and Miller, 1961; Reynolds, 1971; see figure 36). Generally, in discussion groups of sizes three to eight, all members address some remarks to the group as a whole, but typically only one member, the top participator, addresses more to the group as a whole than to specific other members. As group size increases, a larger and larger proportion of the participators have total amounts of

Figure 36. Rank-ordered Series of Total Acts Initiated, Compared with Harmonic Distribution, for Groups of Three to Eight (n = Persons in Group, s = Sessions, N = Hundreds of Acts)

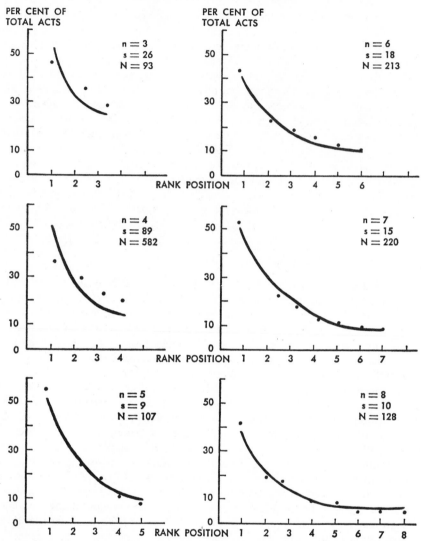

Source: Robert F. Bales et al., "Channels of Communication in Small Groups," *American Sociological Review* 16 (1951). Reprinted by permission of the authors and the American Sociological Association.

participation under their "equal" share, that is, under the mean for the group. At the same time, at least where a participating leader is appointed, the gap between the top participator and the others tends to grow proportionately greater as size increases. When the designated leader of a group is excluded, the gradient of total acts initiated by the remainder of the members tends to follow a simple curve that flattens as the size of the group increases (Stephan and Mishler, 1952). In one experiment involving a group four males, each individual had sufficient latitude or space for interaction, and thus the basic abilities of each individual could be expressed; in a group of eight, however, only the more forceful individuals were able to express their abilitities and ideas, since the amount of freedom in the situation was not sufficient to accommodate all the group members (Carter et al., 1951b).

Increased Resources versus Diminishing Returns

While size may be viewed as a limiting condition in certain respects, increasing size is obviously not in every respect a constricting factor. Many abilities or resources needed in task performance tend to have an additive character. They may include such things as the number of items of information which can be absorbed and recalled, the number of critical judgments available to correct errors of information and inference, the number of ideas or suggestions available for solution of problems, and the range of values that are likely to be brought to bear, as well as the range of technical skills, abilities, and amount of muscular power that are available to implement decisions. (See Steiner, 1966.) For example, in a word-building task, the number of words built in a given time increased as the group size was increased from three to ten (Watson, 1928; see also Neumann, 1969).

Group members are interested in who the additional members, newcomers, will be (Ziller and Behringer, 1965) and will probably accept them more readily if the group is not doing well, since they may be seen as an additional resource (Ziller and Behringer, 1960).

However, the familiar phenomenon of "diminishing returns" tends to set in at some point. The addition of a person to a group of a given size may not represent a unit addition to task ability (cf. Smith and Murdoch, 1970). The tendency for difficulty of coordination to increase with size is one factor that may lead to diminishing net returns, but there are other factors also. In audience-like groups of eight sizes ranging from 1 to 96 persons (J. R. Gibb, 1951), the absolute number of volunteered ideas for the solution of a problem produced within a set time follows a negatively accelerated increasing function. The negative acceleration might possibly be due to some limit to the number of solutions available and reluctance to repeat, or to the increasing difficulty faced by the experimenter in recording all suggestions as they occur. However, the proportion of subjects who report feelings of threat or inhibition of their impulses to participate increases with size. In the same experiment, the design includes a situation which increases feelings of threat by creating a more formal procedure. This situation also leads to a reduction in the number of ideas proposed. One infers then that increased feeling of threat may reduce participation as size increases, and thus create an obstacle to the completion of the task.

On a task requiring physical pulling power, a four-man group was the most efficient (Moede, 1927). Above that size the pulling power per member decreased by 10 percent with each additional member. One would suppose that difficulty of coordination may be an interference factor in this case (Ingham et al., 1974). Since an inverse relation between output per man and size of work group was also found in motor-car factories, it is possible that the formation of norms restricting output and the strength of the group sanctions may be additional factors which produce interference (Marriott, 1949).

On a concept formation task ("Twenty Questions"), groups of two persons obtained the answer in shorter time, used fewer questions, and failed less often at the task than did individuals (Taylor and Faust, 1952). Groups of four failed least often, but were not otherwise superior to groups of two. Here we see, apparently, a gain from having available a larger pool of questions to ask and a gain from the exercise of critical judgment in eliminating poor ideas or testing closure on the solution, but both sources of gain are subject to diminishing returns. The number of man-minutes required per problem increases with size. This, of course, is typically the case. However, for many practical purposes, where the task is one in which some absolute level of effectiveness must be obtained in a set time to avoid complete failure, the lowered efficiency per unit of time per man may be a secondary consideration.

A number of early experiments include the finding that groups have a lower probability of failure or a greater probability of accuracy in problem-solving than individuals, since the groups have greater resources for ideas and error checking (South, 1927; Shaw, 1932; Dashiell, 1935; Ziller, 1957b). Later experiments show that larger groups are more accurate than smaller groups (Porter, 1963; Holloman and Hendrick, 1971; Waag and Halcomb, 1972). However, the only clearly demonstrated gain so far is essentially of a statistical sort: "four judgments are better than one for the same nonsocial reason that four thermometers are better than one." The group effect is essentially a trend toward homogeneity or reduction of variance (Zajonc, 1962b). "In a secondary way this usually increases the accuracy of individual judgments, or the size of the majority vote, but it does not by itself increase the accuracy of group judgment" (Johnson, 1955, p. 471). If the true value of the variable being judged is bracketed by the range of individual judgments, and if the errors are only of a random kind, the tendency to converge toward a group norm of judgments will increase the accuracy of the average individual judgment. If the true value is outside the range of judgments, the average error of the judgments will not be changed by the convergence effect.

The greater variety of opinion available as size increases may give some advantage of critical power, but has its price in the greater difficulty of reaching consensus, unless there is a clear majority (Godwin and Restle, 1974). The difficulty is apparently most marked when the task is primarily one of modifying opinion, in the absence of any clear objective criteria for judgment. For example, groups of six took longer on tasks of this sort than groups of three (South, 1927), and groups of twelve took longer on a group decision than groups of five (Hare, 1952). On the other hand, if the task is a technical one with clear criteria of correct performance and requires some absolute level of intelligence, speed, or the like, the larger group may have a higher probability of containing some member who can obtain an answer easily acceptable to the others once it is presented (Frank and Anderson, 1971; Goldman, 1971). On "abstract" tasks, groups of six were faster than groups of three, possibly for this reason (South, 1927). If quantity rather than quality of ideas produced is the criterion for productivity, then larger groups are also more productive, but simply pooling the ideas of the number of individuals may be even better (Bouchard and Hare, 1970).

Interaction and Consensus in Different-sized Groups

In the experiment designed by Hare (1952) which illustrates some of the difficulties in reaching consensus in larger discussion groups, some 150 Boy Scouts took part in small discussion groups. In a summer camp, nine groups of five boys and nine groups of twelve boys played a "camping game." First, the boys were told a story about a camping trip which ended in misfortune so that it was necessary for each boy to find his way back to civilization alone. Then the boys individually ranked 10 pieces of camping equipment in the order of their importance for such a trip. The items of camping equipment were pack, cook kit, sleeping bag, flashlight, waterproof match box, axe, compass, first-aid kit, scout knife, and canteen. Each group was then asked to rank the pieces of equipment in the order of their importance. After the discussion, the boys as individuals again ranked the 10 pieces of equipment. This was followed by a short questionnaire to record observations about the discussion. Some time after the game, the leader was interviewed and given a Thematic Apperception Test.

Measurement of Consensus

The amount of consensus in the group was measured by having each individual rank the 10 pieces of camping equipment before discussion, the group rank the equipment during discussion, and the individual again rank it after discussion. The rank orders of equipment before discussion for each of the followers in a group were combined by using the statistic r_{av}, average correlation of all rank orders. The $\bar{r}_{av}$ was also computed for each group after discussion. The mean correlation ($\bar{r}_{av}$) before discussion for all groups of the same size represented the average amount of agreement among Boy Scouts about the importance of camping equipment, and the $\bar{r}_{av}$ after discussion represented the point to which consensus was increased as a result of the discussion.

Because an increase in consensus could not be made without some change in individual opinions, another statistic (the rank-order correlation, r') was used to describe the amount of consistency in each individual as well as his change of opinion in the direction of the group decision. Three rank-order correlations were computed for each individual: the individual's first ranking of the 10 items of equipment was correlated with the ranking arrived at by the whole group after discussion (r'_{12}), the group ranking was correlated with the final individual ranking (r'_{23}), and the first individual ranking was correlated with the final ranking (r'_{13}).

A high correlation for r'_{12} indicated that the group discussion was close to that which the individual selected at first, and that he may have influenced the group. A low correlation for r'_{12} combined with a high r'_{23} indicated that, although the individual originally had ideas which were different, he had been won over to the group decision. Finally, a high correlation for r'_{13} indicated that the individual had not changed his opinion as a result of the discussion.

The Questionnaire

The questionnaire was designed to reveal some characteristics of the nature of interaction during discussion. Among the factors about which information was sought were the role of persons other than the leader, the importance of enough time for discussion, the amount of participation of the members and their feelings of satisfaction or dissatisfaction, and the breaking of the groups into smaller factions with individual spokesmen.

Leader Skill

An attempt was made to control and measure leadership by the use of specific directions for the leader during the game, and a projective test later to indicate his potential leadership skill.

The leaders were chosen, on the basis of recommendations by their camp counselors, as boys who had had leadership experience, held positions of responsibility in their troop, or were recognized as leaders by their peers. Before the group discussion, they were taken aside and given instructions as participatory leaders. These instructions emphasized that the leader was to participate himself, to see that every member had a chance to speak, to keep the discussion moving so that a ranking could be obtained in 20 minutes. Thus the leader was thought of as an agent who helped to facilitate the interaction of group members. To check this, he was observed during the game and questioned on his methods in a post-experiment interview.

On the basis of a Thematic Apperception Test administered to all leaders, the leaders were classified in three groups, representing a rough differentiation between their leadership potentials. These classifications of skills were:

1. Type A (good leaders)—above average leaders; boys who seemed to be able to handle others of their age reasonably well and who desired to the status of leader
2. Type B (average leaders)—boys not very different from other Boy Scouts who were able to exercise authority in well-structured situations where there was no great opposition from the followers
3. Type C (poor leaders)—boys who were either so maladjusted or so constricted and passive that they could be expected to have trouble even in a well-structured and supervised situation

Results

Three of the hypotheses which found support in this research are restated below, together with the data which are related to them.

As the size of a discussion group is increased from five to twelve members, the amount of consensus resulting from group discussion will decrease.

This major hypothesis was substantiated by the $\bar{r}_{av}$'s for each set of groups before and after discussion. The average amount of agreement before discussion was almost the same for both groups, about .37 (table 25), since the followers in the different-sized groups came from the same population with regard to their initial opinions about camping equipment. The average amount of agreement after discussion increased to .88 for the groups of five and .67 for the groups of twelve, a significant increase ($p. < .05$) in both cases. Furthermore, the average amount of change in consensus for the small groups (.50) was significantly larger than the average amount of change in the large groups (.30).

This relationship is also evident in the r' data (table 26), where the followers showed less agreement with the group decision (r'_{23}) in the large groups.

Table 25. Means of the Average Correlation of All Rank Orders before and after Discussion of the Followers in Groups of 5 and 12

Group size	Number of groups	$\bar{r}_{av}$ before	$\bar{r}_{av}$ after	Difference
5	9	.38	.88	.50
12	9	.37	.67	.30

Source: A. Paul Hare, "A Study of Interaction and Consensus in Different-sized Groups," *American Sociological Review* 17 (1952). Reprinted by permission of the American Sociological Association.

Table 26. Average Rank-Order Correlation Coefficients for Leaders and Followers in Groups of 5 and 12

	Number of groups	r'_{12}	r'_{23}	r'_{13}
Leaders				
Groups of 5	9	.85	.98	.91
Groups of 12	9	.64	.91	.78
Followers				
Groups of 5	36	.59	.97	.60
Groups of 12	99	.56	.88	.70

Source: A. Paul Hare, "A Study of Interaction and Consensus in Different-sized Groups," *American Sociological Review* 17 (1952). Reprinted by permission of the American Sociological Association.

Within groups of the same size, the amount of change in consensus will be related to the leader's skill.

A second hypothesis was only partially verified, since the measure of the leader's skill derived from the TAT stories had no predictive value in estimating the amount of change in consensus in the small groups; in fact, there was a negative relationship which approached but did not reach significance (table 27). When the twelve-man groups were considered separately, however, there was a significant positive correlation between the measure of leader skill and the amount of change in consensus.

The leader in the group of five will have more influence on the group decision than the leader in the group of twelve.

The data confirmed the hypothesis that the leaders in the small groups will have more influence. The three rank-order correlations for the leaders in the groups of five were all significantly higher than the corresponding correlations for the leaders in the groups of twelve (table 26), indicating that the average leader in the group of five agreed with the group more before and after discussion and was more consistent with himself than was the average leader in the group of twelve. These higher correlations indicate that the group ranking was close to the leader's original ideas in the smaller groups.

The postmeeting questionnaire provided evidence that the followers in the large groups felt that they had too little time for discussion and that the lack of

Table 27. Average Change in r_{av} by Leader Skill

Leader Skill	Number of Groups	Average Change in r_{av}
Groups of 5		
Good	3	.39
Average	4	.52
Poor	2	.62
Groups of 12		
Good	4	.41
Average	3	.24
Poor	2	.14

Source: A. Paul Hare, "A Study of Interaction and Consensus in Different-sized Groups," *American Sociological Review* 17 (1952). Reprinted by permission of the American Sociological Association.

opportunity to participate led to dissatisfaction with the discussion. The followers in the large group also tended to feel that their opinions were not important.

In this experiment a change in group size resulted in a change in the *control* area, since the larger groups apparently placed more demands on the skill of the leader, and a change in *interaction rate,* since the amount of time available for participation was restricted in the larger groups.

Changes in the Content of Interaction

The frequency with which certain categories of acts appear tends to vary with group size. In groups of sizes two to seven engaged in a group decision problem, where the criteria of the goodness of the solution depended upon the values of the members (Bales and Borgatta, 1955), the rate of giving information and suggestion increased as size increased, while the rate of asking for opinion, giving opinion, and showing agreement decreased. These changes are consistent with the hypothesis, that as size increases, there is a tendency toward a more mechanical method of introducing information (by round-robin procedure, for example), a less sensitive exploration of the point of view of the other, and a more direct attempt to control others and reach solution whether or not all group members indicate agreement. All these effects are reasonably associated with the increasing constriction of time available per person. Rates of showing tension tended to decrease, but joking and laughter increased, which may indicate a tendency for less direct involvement of members in task success and for tension to be displaced into humor, rather than to be reduced directly through serious attempts to resolve opinion differences. In this sense, it is suggested that unresolved differences appear to be more tolerable in larger groups, and they may be handled by compartmentalization and other similar devices rather than by resolution.

The Dyad

In addition to these effects of size which show an increasing or decreasing trend, groups of two appear to show unique characteristics (Becker and Useem, 1942; Rustin, 1971). They tend to have high rates of showing tension, consistently avoid disagreement and antagonism, have high rates of asking for opinion, but avoid giving opinion, and concentrate rather on exchange of information and agreement (or acknowledgment) (Bales and Borgatta, 1955; Borgatta and Guerrin, 1960; O'Dell, 1968). This pattern of rates is consistent with an interpretation that in groups of two a delicate balance of power exists when, as in *ad hoc* experimental groups, there are few group norms regarded as binding except those to which both members currently assent. In such a case there is no "public opinion," no majority to which either can appeal. Either member can prevent task completion by disagreement or withdrawal. Both members have to proceed within certain limits to avoid this reaction on the part of the other. If they are similar in their cognitive styles, their communication will be more effective (Triandis, 1960a).

The task of building a common set of norms in this situation is apparently an anxiety-provoking prospect, and tends to be avoided or in part glossed over by agreement on more specific and superficial matters. In a loose interpretation, the two-man group may be viewed as having built into it an implicit agreement that the two members will stay within spheres on which they can agree. In spite of the delicate balance of power, however, there is a strong tendency for two asymmetric roles to develop, that is, for the members to specialize in different types of overt behavior. The differences appear in practically all categories of behavior. Apparently there is a tendency for one member to gravitate toward a more active role and exercise the power of initiative, while the other tends toward a more passive role and holds the power of veto. In this context, it is difficult to ascribe power or leadership to either role, for the passive person may be construed as defining the permissive range of the active person. In the sense that the group cooperates toward the achievement of a given task, leadership associated with proper completion of the group task certainly may be associated with both the initiating and control functions.

In a study of husband-wife pairs in three cultures, the norms in each culture defining the expected power of wife versus husband enable prediction of the tendency of one spouse or the other to take the more active role, and the tendency to win more decisions (Strodtbeck, 1951). A direct relation exists between the amount of participation and number of decisions won. The more influential spouse tends more frequently to ask questions, give opinions, and make rewarding remarks, while the less influential takes a more reactive role with more acts of agreement, disagreement, and antagonism.

Above size two there are significant differences between groups with an even or odd number of members (Bales and Borgatta, 1955). Groups of even size (four and six) have higher rates of showing disagreement and antagonism, and lower rates of asking for suggestion and possibly in showing agreement, than groups of odd size (three, five, and seven). These effects are attributed to the fact that in even sizes, a division of the group into two subparts of equal size is possible. Thus in cases of disagreement in even-size groups the probability of a majority and a minority is lower than in odd sizes, and this in turn may increase the probability that disagreements will remain deadlocked between two subgroups.

The Triad

The power of majority over minority is especially marked in groups of size three, since in this size any minority must be that of a single person, who is thus left isolated without the support of any other group member, at least with respect to the immediate discussion.

On the other hand, the three-person situation is the one in which an individual (or nation) has the opportunity to control through the technique of "divide and conquer" (von Wiese and Becker, 1932; Simmel [in Wolff, 1950]). If the power distribution in the group is unequal, these observations may not hold, since the most powerful member may prevail (Caplow, 1956), or, as in one experiment, the weakest person may initiate a coalition with the strongest (Vinacke and Arkoff, 1957; see also Gamson, 1961a).

In laboratory discussion groups of three persons (Mills, 1953, 1956; Robson, 1971) a relationship in which the two top participators disagreed with each other and sought the support of the third, low member was unstable through time within a meeting and tended to change toward the end of the meeting to a supporting coalition between the two higher participators with the low man excluded. In laboratory groups such as these, any pattern, once clearly formed, tends to be preserved with minimal alteration when a fourth member (a newcomer) is added to the group (Mills et al., 1957).

Many laboratory studies of coalitions have been conducted in which three players are given unequal resources—for example, $A > B > C$, but $A < (B + C)$ —and then asked to bargain over a number of trials. Komorita and Chertkoff (1973) have summarized the major results in a bargaining theory of coalition formation. They define coalition formation as a situation in which a subset of a group agrees to cooperate in the joint use of resources so as to maximize reward. The group members try to make the best deal. For any new situation they would make the following predictions: (1) on the initial trial, the coalition that mutually maximizes $\hat{E}$ (most probable expected outcome) will predominate, and their average outcome will be the maximum $\hat{E}$ values; (2) in subsequent encounters, various coalitions can be expected to form, but the outcomes for the coalition members should converge to an agreement that minimizes temptation to defect; (3) for an indefinite number of trials, the outcomes will converge to the solution which is best for all; and (4) if a stable coalition develops, it is most likely to be the one which minimizes the temptation to join other coalitions. For examples of laboratory studies see Caplow, 1959; Chaney and Vinacke, 1960; Kelley and Arrowood, 1960; Stryker and Psathas, 1960; Aubert, 1961; Bond and Vinacke, 1961; M. L. Borgatta, 1961; Gamson, 1961b; Turk and Turk, 1962; Borgatta and Borgatta, 1963; Gamson, 1964; Psathas and Stryker, 1965; Trost, 1965; Chertkoff, 1966; Vinacke et al., 1966; Chertkoff, 1967; Caplow, 1968; E. W. Kelley, 1968; Mazur, 1968; Strickland and Lacome, 1968; Nitz and Phillips, 1969; R. J. Ofshe and S. L. Ofshe, 1969; Willis, 1969; S. L. Ofshe and R. J. Ofshe, 1970; R. J. Ofshe and S. L. Ofshe, 1970; Raven and Shaw, 1970; Caldwell, 1971; Chertkoff, 1971; Michener and Lawler, 1971; Wilke and Mulder, 1971; Michener and Lyons, 1972; Michener and Zeller, 1972; Shinotsuka, 1972; Wahba, 1972a, 1972b, 1972c; Wahba and Lirtzman, 1972; Ashour, 1973; Burhans, 1973; Crosbie and Kullberg, 1973; M. B. Walker, 1973; Wilke, Meertens, and Steur, 1973; Chertkoff and Braden, 1974; Laing and Morrison, 1974. Similar findings are reported for groups larger than three, although the process of forming coalitions is more complex (Willis, 1962; Emerson, 1964; Schubert, 1964; Shears, 1967; Vitz and Kite, 1970; Cole, 1971; Hinckley, 1972; Lindsay, 1972; Rohde, 1972; Buckley and Westen, 1973; Komorita, 1974).

In more permanent groups of three (father, mother, and son), no one person was singled out for exclusion in a series of decisions (Strodtbeck, 1954a). It may be inferred that the power of a coalition of two in a three-person group to force a decision is considerable and is so employed with reference to particular disagreements. Indeed it may be so powerful that members tend to switch coalitions from one disagreement to another simply to maintain solidarity and avoid the permanent exclusion of one member. The overt interaction activity should, however, be considered as only one possible indicator of the existence of coalitions. If the coalition pattern in interaction is defined only by the amount of support that is overtly demonstrated between pairs, one may overlook the fact that where a coalition exists there may be no need for the supporters to demonstrate to each other their agreement. In another study on coalitions, a third member was forced to change his behavior pattern completely by two role players who first allowed him to form a coalition with one of them and then combined against him. He changed his opinion less often than his behavior, and he tended to retain his liking for the original partner in spite of the overt desertion (Mills, 1954). Another complicating consideration is the fact that as one disagrees, one must also support, or the situation may deteriorate. In terms of interaction scoring, responses in the active support categories vary directly with those in the negative categories.

In general, these data suggest that the problem of deadlock is most severe in the two-person group, but in this case each person is also without support in a deadlock, and if the group is to remain in existence, each person must respond to the emergency signs of the other. The level of tension may be high, but the hostility must be controlled, since each person *must* face the other. In the four-person group, on the other hand, in a deadlock situation each person may have a supporter, and the deadlock may continue with each person still having available a source of support and gratification. In the three-person group the problem of the overpowerful majority is emphasized. At least some of the idiosyncrasies of two-, three-, and four-man groups may thus be viewed as special cases of the odd and even effects, and these in turn, may be seen as results of the power of perceived consensus among a majority in persuading the minority (or single person) to change its views, or at least not to oppose outwardly the resolution of the disagreement.

The Optimum Size

A final comment may be made on the relation of size to member satisfaction. In one study, members of smaller (five-man) groups were more satisfied with the discussion than members of twelve-man groups (Hare, 1952), and in another sample of discussion groups the optimal size appeared to be five (Bales, 1954; Slater, 1958; see also Hackman and Vidmar, 1970). Below this size, members complain that the group is too small, although amount of talking time available to each increases. This may be a reflection of the strains associated with the face-to-face relationship which have been noted above in the description of the two-, three-, and four-man groups, and the odd and even effects. Above the size of five, members complain that the group is too large, and this may be due to the restriction on the amount of participation. Size five combines the characteristics that (1) a strict deadlock is not possible with an odd number of members; (2) the group tends to split into a majority of three and a minority of two, so that being in a minority does not isolate the individual, but allows him sources of gratification; and (3) the group appears to be large enough for the members to shift roles easily and for any individual to withdraw from an awkward position without necessarily having the issue resolved.

Crowding

When a group is too large for the space it is given to occupy, members may feel "crowded" as they respond to the increased density and visual exposure (Baxter and Deanovich, 1970; Loo, 1972; Stokols, 1972; Zlutnick and Altman, 1972; Kutner, 1973). It is clear that the absolute size of the group is not the main factor, since "three's a crowd" under some circumstances, especially if the three persons are isolated in a small compact space as they are in space exploration or in some forms of military missions, real or simulated (Smith and Haythorn, 1972). Even two can be too many if the first person has chosen to be alone (Kelvin, 1973). For example, students studying alone in the library resent it when an "intruder" sits beside them at the study table (Patterson, Mullens, and Romano, 1971). However, as with the earlier "together and apart" experiments, for some types of individual tasks the presence of many other people in the room performing the same task may have no noticeable effect (Freedman, Klevansky, and Ehrlich, 1971).

Given the same number of people, subjects are more likely to feel crowded in a small room than in a large room (Stokols et al., 1973). In a large room with a high density of others a person is more apt to feel crowded if he sees all the others than if the shape of the room or objects in the room block some people from view (Daves and Swaffer, 1971; Desor, 1972).

Sex seems to make a difference, since females find smaller rooms more comfortable and are more likely to engage in intimate, positive conversations, while males prefer larger rooms (J. L. Freedman, 1971; J. L. Freedman et al., 1972; Ross et al., 1973).

A series of field experiments have demonstrated that people will usually avoid crowded situations if they are given a chance. When an experimenter stood close beside a pedestrian waiting for a traffic light to change or at a bus stop, the pedestrian would move away, especially if the experimenter was a man (Dabbs, 1972). When a bogus phone repairman entered a room at a university, subjects would also move away unless they felt at home in the room (Edney, 1972). If two persons were standing, talking, in a hall at a university, few students would walk between them (Cheyne and Efran, 1972; Efran and Cheyne, 1973), especially if the persons were of higher status (Knowles, 1973). If forced to intrude, they would be unhappy about it (Efran and Cheyne, 1974).

When persons have no choice but to work or live in crowded conditions, they try to change to less crowded conditions when it is possible. Thus students at larger, and presumably more crowded, universities are observed to gather in smaller groups at lunch break than students at smaller universities (Tucker and Friedman, 1972). Within the university students who live in corridor-design dormitories (an overloaded social environment) indicate that they feel more crowded than students who live in suite-design dorms (Baum and Valins, 1973; Valins and Baum, 1973; see also Eoyang, 1974). Students sharing double rooms with twin beds are found to change roommates more often than those with bunk beds, presumably because of the greater privacy of the bunk bed (Rohner, 1974). However, when the couple living in the small room are married, they may find ways to overcome the handicap of limited space (MacDonald and Oden, 1973).

Raising the temperature of the room has an effect similar to that of adding more people. The effect can be amplified by making the room both hot and crowded. Under these conditions people tend to react more negatively to each other (Griffitt, 1970; Griffitt and Veitch, 1971) although, perhaps fortunately, hot crowded rooms appear to have no effect on one's ability to make moral judgments (Arbuthnot and Andrasik, 1973).

Summary

Although the size of the "natural" group varies with the age and other social characteristics of the population, casual work or play groups most often have only two or three members, while the modal size for an adolescent gang is about ten members. Members are generally less satisfied with the group if the size is increased. Observers find it easier to identify leaders in discussion groups of about six members than either smaller or larger groups.

As each additional member joins a group, the number of potential relationships between individuals and subgroups increases rapidly, thus placing more demands on the leader in coordinating group activity. The time available to each member for communication decreases, an increased proportion of the members feel threatened and inhibited, and the gap between the top participator and the others tends to grow proportionately greater as size increases.

With the addition of members, the resources of the group are increased so that a variety of problems may be solved more efficiently, although after some point, depending upon the task, the addition of new member brings diminishing returns. The time for task completion is reduced at the expense of lowered efficiency per unit of time per man, and the range of ideas available is increased at the expense of greater difficulty in reaching consensus in the absence of any clear-cut criteria for judgment.

The quality of the interaction process for a group decision problem changes with increasing group size as groups use more mechanical methods of introducing information, are less sensitive in the exploration of differing points of view, and make more direct attempts to reach a solution whether or not all members agree. The interaction pattern in a group of two has unique characteristics which suggest a delicate balance of power in making decisions. Above size two, there are differences between groups with even and odd numbers of members. Probably as a result of a split into two opposing subgroups of equal size, there is more disagreement and antagonism in the even-sized groups. Laboratory groups of size three characteristically form a coalition of two, leaving one member isolated; however, the same tendency is not observed in family groups of mother, father, and son. When coalitions do form between members of unequal power, a pair will join forces to maximize their reward and minimize the temptation to form a different coalition.

The optimum size for a small discussion group may be five members, since members are generally less satisfied with smaller or larger groups. In smaller groups members may be forced to be too prominent, and in larger groups they may not have the opportunity to speak. In the group of five, strict deadlocks can be avoided and members can shift roles swiftly.

If the number of persons in a group is too large for the space it is given to occupy, subjects are more likely to feel crowded in small rooms where everyone can be seen. However, women find the smaller rooms more comfortable and intimate. When possible, people will avoid crowded situations.

Chapter 11

TASK

THE TASK OF A GROUP or of an individual can be described in terms of six variables, each of which partially determines the way in which the task will be accomplished. The specification of each of these six variables is implicit in the directions for any task, although it is not always made explicit (Schutz, 1952b):

1. The kind of task (goal)
2. The criteria for task completion
3. The rules (or roles) which must be followed
4. The method of imposing the rules
5. The amount of stress on the members
6. The consequences of failure or success

Although the "task" of the group is usually thought of as the stated objective of the group's activity, all but the most casual groups usually deal with tasks or problems at four levels simultaneously (see chapter 1). Two of these types of problems are at the group level and two at the individual level. At the group level, the first problem is the publicly stated problem of the group. At the second level, members deal with the establishment and maintenance of a group structure which is appropriate for the group task. At the third level is the publicly stated goal for each individual, and at the fourth level are the problems of individual social-emotional adjustment.

In chapter 1 it was also suggested that generally problems of individual adjustment had to be solved before energy was available to solve problems at a higher level. In addition, the four types of tasks can be expanded to eight types if problems of relating the small group to the larger society are added at each level.

Since an adequate solution for the publicly stated objective of the group or individual is often reached only at the expense of the social-emotional goals of the group or particular individuals, the interaction pattern in groups which focus on one set of problems usually differs from the pattern of a group which focuses on the other set. This "equilibrium problem" was discussed in chapter 4. These differences are evident in groups which have been instructed to concentrate on either "task" or "social-emotional" problems (Olmstead, 1954) and in groups which have been selected because they are task-oriented (socio-groups) versus those which are social-emotional-oriented (psyche-groups) (Jennings, 1947a, 1947b; Coffey, 1952).

However, most of the laboratory research on "task" deals primarily with the level of the publicly stated problem of the group.

Once a group has been formed to deal with problems at one of the four levels, the members will resist a change to activity at another level. For example, in small therapy groups, when members were asked to rate the value of the topics discussed, those topics which caused disturbance and those which could be discussed only in the permissive therapeutic group were judged to be of greatest importance (Talland and Clark, 1954).

The typical steps in task solution are described in chapter 15, where various types of groups are compared in their effectiveness in carrying out these steps and in their productivity on each of the four levels of group problems.

The group task, as compared with the communication net (chapter 12) and leadership (chapter 13), is the most global way of specifying the situation in which interaction will take place. The *communication net* emphasizes the form of interaction, *leadership* emphasizes the roles of members and the method of social control; the *task* emphasizes the *goal* of interaction as well as the other five variables.

The task, in a sense, requires the minimum amount of intervention by an outside agent, since once the group has accepted a task it can complete the task outside the range of continuing influence of an experimenter or observer. When a particular communication net is introduced, however, the group must accept a set of restrictions on the form that its interaction may take, and when a leader is introduced the group must accept a new number or a new set of behaviors from an old member.

The Kind of Task

The kind of task a group is given is broadly defined by the goal to be reached and the outlines of the path the group should follow in reaching the goal. Some of the effects of differences in the clarity of the group path and the group goal upon the individual and his relationship to the group are illustrated by an experiment in which each subject was given the task of cutting out geometrical figures, presumably to be used by the other members of his group in constructing some three-dimensional objects. While the subject was involved in his paper cutting he was permitted to hear, over a loudspeaker, a tape recording of what the "others" were doing with the pieces he had provided. One half of the subjects were given, through the recorded discussion, a clear picture of the goal the others were working toward and what they were doing to achieve it. The recording heard by the other half of the subjects presented the group task as quite vague and ambiguous. As a result of the manipulation, the subject in the clearly defined situation became more group-oriented in his behavior and feelings, and experienced less hostility. He also tended to be more inducible by the "others." That is, he responded more readily and favorably to their requests, in the form of fictitious notes delivered by a messenger (Raven and Rietsema, 1957).

Since the task is, in the most pertinent sense, what the group members subjectively define it to be as they respond to the *situation* in which they find themselves, all the internal features of the social system are likely sooner or later to become relevant to task specification. The task should not be narrowly viewed in terms of what the experimenter intends, or what some objective sense of the situation apparently demands.

In its broadest sense, then, the definition of the task is the definition of the situation, and differences in behavior which appear between "situations" are the most general indication of differences in tasks. Several studies of children provide evidence of situational differences in behavior.

Children from a public nursery school, when paired in an experimental play situation, had a higher rate of interaction and were more accepting and less dominating in their behavior than children from an orphanage nursery school (Anderson, 1937b). Although the differences in domination could be the result of differences in home background of the children, in the two situations, they appear to be the result of the situation, since within the orphanage population, children attending nursery school were more dominating than those not attending school (Anderson, 1937a).

In another study of children, two-year-old children watched each other more and accepted suggestions more when playing with clay than when playing with blocks. Clay seemed to elicit more imitation and sociable cooperative behavior (Updegraff and Herbst, 1933). Dramatic play appeared to release tensions in children more than other types of play (Hartley, Frank, and Goldenson, 1952).

Several authors have provided typologies for the classification of group tasks. These include Roby and Lanzetta, 1958; Watson, 1958; Rapoport, 1959; Roby, 1962; Altman, 1966a, 1966b; Zagona, Willis, and MacKinnon, 1966; Hackman, 1968; Frederiksen, 1972.

Situational Differences in Leader Behavior

In a study of situational differences in behavior, public grade school boys were found to be more aggressive on the school playground than in the neighborhood (Hare, 1957). Twelve nine-year-old boys who were leaders on the school playground were selected from the third grades of four New England public schools. During the winter and spring of the school year, the boys were observed on the playground during a free play period and in the neighborhood after school using the set of categories for interaction process analysis developed by Bales (1950b).

In field observation, interaction was scored rather than taken down verbatim and individual activity apart from the group was not scored. An observer scored only one boy at a time, recording all of his acts directed to others and all acts directed to him by other group members. The average observation period on the school playground was four sessions for a total of 47 minutes (204 acts), and in the neighborhood was four sessions for a total of 75 minutes (360 acts). Interaction with teachers, parents, or observers was not recorded.

Several significant differences ($p. < .05$) in the percentages of activity in the 12 behavior categories appeared between the two situations (see table 28). Giving and asking for information were both greater in the neighborhood, and showing antagonism was greater on the playground. Differences in giving suggestion, showing disagreement, and showing tension approached significance ($p. < .10$) with more suggestions and tensions on the playground and more disagreement in the neighborhood.

Differences in input (acts by group members directed toward the leaders) were in the same direction. Significantly more information was given and asked for by members in the neighborhood, and more antagonism was shown on the playground.

The higher amount of information in the neighborhood probably resulted from the fact that the children spent more time in making up games, while the increase

Table 28. Mean Percentage Interaction Output and Input of 12 Boy
Leaders for Playground and Neighborhood*

| | OUTPUT | | INPUT | |
	Playground	Neighborhood	Playground	Neighborhood
1. Shows solidarity	5.0†	3.5	8.4	4.6
2. Shows tension release	7.4	7.4	1.4	4.5
3. Shows agreement	2.9	4.0	7.8	4.7
4. Gives suggestion	19.5	15.7	11.2	15.1
5. Gives opinion	7.2	7.3	8.0	7.2
6. Gives information	18.2	31.8	11.5	32.3
7. Asks for information	1.4	8.8	2.4	9.6
8. Asks for opinion	0	0.2	0	0.5
9. Asks for suggestion	0	0.1	0	0.1
10. Shows disagreement	2.2	4.1	4.4	4.6
11. Shows tension	7.1	3.7	0.9	0.9
12. Shows antagonism	19.8	8.2	24.1	8.6

*Average number of acts per boy is 149 on the playground and 218 in the neighborhood
for output, and 55 on the playground and 142 in the neighborhood for input.

†The raw percentage was converted by the arc sine transformation for calculation and re-
converted for the table. For this reason the sum of the percentages for each column
does not equal exactly 100.

Source: A. Paul Hare, "Situational Differences in Leader Behavior," *Journal of Abnormal and Social Psychology* 55 (1957). Copyright 1957 by the American Psychological Association. Reprinted by permission of the publisher.

in suggestion, tension, and antagonism on the playground reflected a more competitive situation in which the individual had to assert himself to maintain his
status in a large group composed of children his own age playing games with
established rules.

Intellectual and Manual Tasks

When variations in tasks which had been given some experimental groups were
analyzed by Carter, Haythorn, Shriver, and Lanzetta (1951), two principal types
of tasks were evident. Some required intellectual skills, and some required manual
skills. In one study differences between intellectual tasks, clerical tasks, and mechanical assembly tasks were shown to affect leadership behavior. In general, the
subjects who took the lead in the intellectual task also influenced their partners in
the clerical tasks. The mechanical assembly task gave only low correlations with
the other two problem-solving situations (Carter and Nixon, 1949a). In a similar
study a factor analysis of the leadership ratings received by subjects in six types of
tasks (reasoning, intellectual construction, clerical, discussion, motor cooperation,
and mechanical assembly) indicated two major factors which have been called
"intellectual leadership" and "doing-things-with-one's-hands leadership" (Carter,
Haythorn, and Howell, 1950). In another factor analysis of ratings of performance
made in the OSS assessment program, two similar factors were attributed to situations or tasks that called for verbal intelligence versus those that called for active
intelligence. It seems likely that, from the point of view of abilities required, the
same abilities that can be differentiated from each other by individual testing will
also be useful in the description of group tasks.

The sequence of events required to reach the goal in problem-solving groups varies between problems which range in substance from stories about group projection sketches (Henry and Guetzkow, 1951) and chess, to group decision and planning problems with various degrees of reality (Bales and Strodtbeck, 1951).

Additional studies which give evidence of characteristic forms of interpersonal behavior with a variety of tasks include Goldman, Bolen, and Martin, 1961; Calabria, 1963; Breer and Locke, 1965; Shaw and Blum, 1965; Nagata, 1966; Weiner, 1966; Vos and Brinkman, 1967; Kent and McGrath, 1969; S. R. Wilson, 1969; O'Brien, 1970; Swinth and Tuggle, 1971; Gergen, Gergen, and Barton, 1973; Trickett and Moos, 1973; Weinstein, and Holzbach, 1973; Weissbach, 1973; Price and Bouffard, 1974.

Consistency of Behavior for Different Tasks

The consistency of some aspects of individual behavior has already been indicated in chapter 8 on personality. Since the central tendencies of the group members are modified by the expectations for the task, consistent behavior from one task to another could be anticipated under two conditions:

1. The tasks, such as projective tests, require little modification of individual central tendencies.
2. The tasks, such as group discussions, require standard behavioral responses but differ only slightly in discussion content. Examples of the second type of consistency are found in the stability of leadership which exists when the task of holding a leaderless group discussion is varied by changing the discussion topic and the composition of group members (Bass and Wurster, 1953b; Blake, Mouton, and Fruchter, 1954), and when the problem for group solution remains the same but the method of problem presentation is varied (Lorge et al., 1955a, 1955b).

The Criteria for Task Completion

The criterion for task completion may be either an "objectively correct" answer or an answer which is simply a matter of group consensus. A considerable body of theory centering around motivations to compare oneself with others and to communicate with those more deviant in an effort to achieve uniformity has been developed (Festinger, 1954). These motivations are strongest in situations where the main criterion of correctness is agreement with "social reality"—that is, consensus. In general, it is more difficult to achieve consensus when the problem strongly involves values members are likely to hold individually in advance that are different or believed to be different (South, 1927; Festinger and Thibaut, 1951). Although a variety of group tasks is used for the diagnosis of interaction, the type of task on which a number of the current observations of interaction process are made is a case-discussion problem with instructions that require assembly of information initially distributed among members, interpretation and evaluation of the information, and eventual group decision on a concrete and detailed plan of action (Bales, 1955). Several phases of a typical planning-execution cycle are thus included, but not the actual execution of a plan and re-evaluation of results. This task lies somewhere between a highly projective and highly realistic one.

Rules and Roles

The rules for the task can vary in their explicitness from those which allow no freedom for individual choice to those in which the roles which the members are to follow are left unstated and the members are free to make up their own rules. The most common tasks used in the experimental laboratories leave all of these aspects unspecified. Some tasks may not require interaction but may be best performed by an individual working alone. When rules are made a major part of the task, the most common contrast is between *cooperation* and *competition.*

Most of the "together and apart" experiments in which individuals work on the same types of tasks, both as individuals and in groups, are designed to reveal which tasks are completed more efficiently by individuals and which by cooperating with other members of a group. Many examples of this type of research appear in chapter 14 on individual and group productivity. In one typical experiment, 40 subjects worked alone and 80 subjects worked in pairs on three types of tasks: a word puzzle, a jigsaw puzzle, and five arithmetic problems. The time taken to complete each task was the measure of performance. Paired subjects were significantly faster than individual subjects except on the arithmetic problems, where no differences were observed (Husband, 1940). The differences in performance between tasks are presumably due to the fact that a division of labor was not efficient for the solution of the arithmetic problems. When a division of labor is required and the life of the group is relatively long, subgroups will tend to form among the members who play similar roles (Horsfall and Arensberg, 1949; Homans, 1950).

The rules should be appropriate for the goal if the group is to perform efficiently (Steiner and Dodge, 1956). Experiments which introduce a variety of task goals with a fixed communication net provide examples of some inefficient rules. Controlled communication channels in three-man groups were used with three kinds of tasks: (1) a simple reassembling of a list of standard words, (2) construction of a sentence, the words of which had been distributed among the group members, and (3) anagram formation. The relative efficiency of a given communication network depended upon the kind of problem the group was trying to solve. While the communication network was an important variable in the reassembly and construction problems, it had little effect on anagram formation. The reassembly task was the most efficiently solved in groups where all members could talk and listen to all other members. The sentence construction problem, however, was solved most efficiently in a group which had a man in a central coordinating position (Heise and Miller, 1951).

The rules for attaining the goal can be seen as including specifications or expectations for the average behavior and acceptable variations of behavior in each of the categories of form and content outlined in chapter 1. When viewed in this manner, certain variations in the major "factors" described in part 2 appear to produce the same results. Groups composed of individuals who are competing in their tasks, large groups, groups in which all communications are channeled through one person in the center of the net, and groups with an authoritarian leader tend to be similar. In all of these groups, the expected amount of interaction between members is low, the amount of interaction received by the leader or central person is high, the expected differentiation in authority is high (in competition each individual attempts to exert the most control), and the expected amount of affection between members is low. This particular combination of characteristics tends to result in high productivity with low member satisfaction.

Cooperation versus Competition

In groups which are motivated to cooperate, the members all work toward a group goal which depends on interdependent activity on the part of the members, while in competition an individual's reward depends upon his own achievement, which can usually be maximized only at the expense of other group members (May and Doob, 1937; Vogler, 1968, 1969).

In general, group members who have been motivated to cooperate show more positive responses to each other, are more favorable in their perceptions, are more involved in the task, and have greater satisfaction with the task (Stendler, Damrin, and Haines, 1951; Grossack, 1954; Gottheil, 1955; Harnack, 1955; Phillips and D'Amico, 1956; Thomas, 1957; Mann and Mann, 1959b; Church, 1962; Crombag, 1966; Haines and McKeachie, 1967; Julian and Perry, 1967; Wheeler and Ryan, 1973). However, when the primary motive in competition is to compare one's abilities with others, then competition increases satisfaction (Cherrington, 1973). As a result of their cooperative effort, the members are less likely to work at cross purposes (Mintz, 1951; Schultz, 1965; Kruglanski, 1969; Gross et al., 1972), are more efficient and productive (Deutsch, 1949b; Smith, Madden, and Sobol, 1957; Shaw, 1958b, 1959b; Lambert, 1960; Raven and Eachus, 1963; Crawford and Sidowski, 1964; Zander and Wolfe, 1964; Furuhata, 1965; Dunn and Goldman, 1966; Haines and McKeachie, 1967; Laughlin and Doherty, 1967; K. H. Smith, 1972b; Wolf, 1972–1973; Workie, 1974), especially members who might not do as well without help (Zajonc, 1962a; Crannell, Switzer, and Morrissette, 1965; Goldman, 1965), and are better able to recall meaningful material (Yuker, 1955; Gurnee, 1968) and their own contributions (Smith, Madden, and Sobol, 1957). While competition makes the average group less productive, it may spur an individual on to more productivity (Blau, 1954; Rychlak, 1960).

The effects of cooperation may be minimized if the group members are not highly attracted to the group or to its goals (Dashiell, 1935). In one study of school children, cooperation of individuals who had volunteered to be members of a team resulted in greater efficiency than work in competition, while cooperation within an arbitrary group, chosen by the experimenter, resulted in lower efficiency (Maller, 1929). The effects of cooperation will also be minimal if the task does not lend itself to a division of labor (Hammond and Goldman, 1961; Cottrell, 1963; Raven and Eachus, 1963; Jones and Vroom, 1964; Bruning and Mettee, 1966; Bruning, Sommer, and Jones, 1966; Julian and Perry, 1967), or if the rewards for the individual for cooperating are less than those for competing (Rosenberg, 1960; Miller and Hamblin, 1963; W. P. Smith, 1968b; Samuels, 1970; Weinstein and Holzbach, 1972).

With a task like reading or substituting items in a text, individual motivation to do better than oneself on the next trial and also to surpass a paired competitor actually resulted in more improvement than motivation for the group (pair) to surpass another group. The motivation to have a winning team, presumably implying some cooperation, resulted in only slightly better performance than asking the subject to "try to improve" when he was working alone (Sims, 1928). In another study of "cooperation" with children, the tasks of carrying marbles and buckets of sand were primarily individual tasks. Also the instructions to work for a group reward would actually have resulted in less reward per member than work for an individual reward. "Collective or group remuneration" in this case meant that the toys which were given as prizes were not allowed to be taken home, as they could be in the competitive groups), but everyone would have to enjoy them as a collective possession. As a result "individual renumeration" stimulated greater efficiency than "group remuneration" (Sorokin et al., 1930). Usually cooperation within a group will increase if the group has to compete against another group (Sherif et al., 1961; Vinacke, 1964; Kalin and Marlowe, 1968; Blake and Mouton, 1974).

Additional studies on cooperation and competition explore the effects of various member characteristics on group activity. These studies include Banghart, 1959; Kelley and Ring, 1961; Smelser, 1961; Whitmyre, Diggory, and Cohen, 1961; Cohen and Lindsley, 1964; O'Connell, 1965; Rappoport, 1965; Ryan and Lakie, 1965; S. A. Smith, 1965, Crowne, 1966; Myers, 1966; Kaufmann, 1967; Schmitt and Marwell, 1968; Sinha, 1968; Weick and Penner, 1969; Brehmer and Hammond, 1970; Codol, 1970; Dustin and Davis, 1970; Dustin and Polihronakis, 1970; Eifermann, 1970; Lewis and Sample, 1970; Crawford and Haaland, 1971; Deaux and Coppess, 1971; D. P. Armentrout, 1972; Karabenick, 1972; Shapira and Lomranz, 1972; Thompson, 1972; Wankel, 1972; Faroqi, 1973; Kelly, Rawson, and Terry, 1973; Mithaug, 1973; Roby and Rubin, 1973; Wish, Kaplan, and Deutsch, 1973; Wolosin, Sherman, and Till, 1973; Jellison and Ickes, 1974; Mettee and Riskind, 1974; Silverthorne, Chelune, and Imada, 1974.

Effects of Cooperation and Competition upon Group Process

Deutsch's (1949b) experimental study of the effects of cooperation and competition upon group process illustrates the differences between cooperative and competitive groups which can be expected, if other variables like group organization and motivation are controlled. In his study, 10 experimental groups were established. Each group was composed of five students in an introductory psychology class who were participating in the experiment as a substitute for the regular class sections. Each group met once a week for a three-hour session for five consecutive weeks. During the first week the 10 groups were observed and rated as they discussed a human-relations problem. The ratings of the discussion productivity were then used to pair off equated groups. For the five pairs, one group was assigned by a random procedure to the cooperative treatment, while the other was given the competitive treatment.

The "cooperative situation" was produced by instructions that the group as a whole would be rated in comparison with the efforts of four other similarly constituted groups; the grade or reward that each member received would be the same and would be determined by the relative position of his group in contrast with the four other similar groups. The "competitive" situation was produced by instructions which stated that each member would be rated in comparison with the efforts of the other four members composing his group and that the grade or reward that each would receive would be different and would be determined by the relative contributions of each to the solution of the problem.

Apart from the differences in instructions, all groups were exposed to similar routines during their three-hour meetings. The first part of the meeting was spent solving a Sunday-supplement-type puzzle, the second part of the meeting was spent discussing and writing some recommendations for a human-relations problem, and in the third part of the meeting the instructor-experimenter informally lectured on psychology.

Three of four observers were present during the first two parts of any meeting. Each observer filled out Overall Rating Scales at the end of the meeting in addition to collecting other data. Information was also collected from subjects, who filled out a questionnaire every meeting after the human-relations problem and supplied additional data at the end of the experiment.

Instruments Used by the Observers

Two major tasks, among others, were assigned to the different observers. The first job of the observer was to categorize each participation of the members on a Functions Observation Sheet in terms of the following: (1) who spoke (or gestured), (2) to whom the remark was addressed, (3) the intent of the participant, and (4) the length of the participation. Deutsch used the utterance to define a unit of participation, with the exception that if more than one function distinctly occurred in any utterance, two or more categorizations would be made. To provide the possibility of cross-analysis with other instruments, a new functions sheet was used for each five-minute period. To facilitate the tabulation, no attempt was made to retain the sequence of utterances or to record who spoke to whom.

The categories used in the Functions Observation Sheet were divided into three broad groupings:

1. *Task functions,* which included participations which were directed toward the task with which the group was confronted. These functions had as their immediate purpose the facilitation of problem solution. Included in this grouping were such functions as initiator-contributor, information giver, position stater, elaborator, coordinator, orientor, evaluator-critic, energizer, and information seeker.

2. *Group functions,* which included participations which were directed toward the functioning of the group. They had for their immediate purpose the maintenance, strengthening, regualtion, or perpetuation of the group. Included here were such functions as encourager-rewarder, harmonizer-mediator, good group member, gatekeeper, standardsetter, follower, and group observer.

3. *Individual functions,* which included participations which were directed toward the satisfaction of the participant's individual needs. They had as their immediate objective an individual goal which was neither task- nor group-relevant. The goal was individual in the sense that the satisfaction aimed at by the participant could not be participated in by the others, either at all or in the same way. Such functions included playboy, sympathy seeker, aggressor, dominator, blocker, recognition seeker, self-defender, and self-observer.

An observer, using this instrument, was trained for approximately 30 hours before observing the experimental group meetings.

The observers also used a series of nine-point rating scales covering such things as group discussion productivity, group orientation, self-centeredness, involvement, communication difficulties, attentiveness, and acceptance-rejection.

In considering the various ratings, Deutsch noted that it was impossible to maintain any absolute standards. The ratings more or less presumed a standard of judgment based on experience with groups of introductory psychology students. Thus the emphasis throughout the analysis of the results is primarily on the direction of the obtained differences rather than on size of differences between the two types of groups.

Instruments Used by the Subjects
The subjects filled out two types of questionnaires:

1. *The Weekly Questionnaire,* which was used used at each meeting after the discussion of the human-relations problems. The items on the questionnaire consisted for the most part of rating scales which roughly paralleled those in the observers' Overall Rating Scales. In addition, the questionnaire included scales such as attentiveness, communication difficulties, and acceptance-rejection; the subjects also rated interest, group feeling, amount of group cooperation, group productivity, individual productivity, and anticipated reactions of the others to their own contributions.
2. *The Postexperimental Questionnaire,* which was given one week after the last experimental group meeting. The questionnaire attempted to get at such things as (a) when first and last names were learned, (b) amount and kinds of social activities mutually engaged in by group members outside of the class hours, (c) reactions to the small group meetings, the instructor, and the course, (d) the importance of different factors in motivating the subject to achieve during the solution of the problems, (e) reactions to the grading system, and (f) reactions to being observed.

The data collected from observers and subjects in the experimental groups allowed Deutsch to test a number of hypotheses derived from a theory of cooperation and competition which he had presented in an earlier article (1949a). As an example of his work the data relevant to four of his major hypotheses are presented here. All of his findings are summarized at the end of the following account of his research.

Perceived Interdependence
Deutsch had hypothesized that members of the groups in the cooperative situation would perceive themselves to be more cooperative than would members of the groups in the competitive situation. Data relevant to this hypothesis are given in table 29. Group-centeredness (we-feeling) was rated by the observers to be considerably higher in the cooperative groups for both the puzzles and the human-relations problems. The subjects' ratings in the weekly questionnaire pertaining to the human-relations problems gave the same results. Cooperating members gave themselves credit for more "group feeling" than did competing members. These differences with respect to group-centeredness and group feeling were significant at the 1 percent level for both the puzzles and human-relations problems.

A related hypothesis that competing members will see themselves to be more competitive than will cooperating members is partly supported by the same evidence. The competitive group members were rated to be more self-centered by the observers. Likewise, competing members rated themselves as being more self-

Table 29. Differences between Cooperative and Competitive Groups in Perceived Cooperation and Competition

VARIABLE	PROBLEM TYPE	TOTAL	
		M diff	p
Group-centeredness (A)	H.R.	+2.98	.001
Group-centeredness (A)	P	+2.54	.001
Group feeling (C)	H.R.	+1.20	.01
Competitiveness (C)	H.R.	−0.37	*
Desire to excel others (D)	H.R.	−2.30	.03
Desire to excel others (D)	P	−2.20	.01

*The differences for three of the pairs are in the same direction as the total difference; these differences have p values of .01, .01, and .13 respectively. The differences for the other pairs are in an opposite direction; these differences have p values of .14 and .23.

Key: P = puzzles; H.R. = human-relations problems; (A), (B), (C), or (D) = the measuring instrument. (A) refers to the *Overall Rating Scales*, (B) to the *Functions Observations Sheet*, (C) to the *Weekly Questionnaire* filled out by subjects, and (D) to the *Postexperimental Questionnaire*. Total M diff = average of the differences (cooperative minus competitive) between each of the five paired groups for each of the five experimental weeks. A plus sign indicates that the cooperative groups had more of the variable than did the competitive groups. Total p = the p value obtained by combining the p values for each of the five pairs. A combined value is given only when the direction of the differences for all five pairs is the same as the total mean difference.

Source: Morton Deutsch, "An Experimental Study of the Effects of Cooperation and Competition upon Group Process," *Human Relations* 2 (1949). Reprinted by permission of the author and the Plenum Publishing Corporation.

oriented than did cooperating members. Perceived competition, however, seemed to Deutsch to include, in addition, to self-centeredness," the notion of "I" versus "the others." To measure this component, the subjects were asked in reference to the human-relations problem, "How competitive with the other members of your group did you feel you were during the discussion?"

The results obtained in response to this question were not so conclusive, although they tended to support the hypothesis (see table 29, data on competitiveness). Deutsch suggested that the lack of clean-cut results might be a reflection of the differing interpretations placed on the word *competitiveness* by cooperating members. This interpretation was supported by the fact that when the question was phrased, "How much did you desire to excel others?" on the Postexperimental Questionnaire, significant differences were obtained in the predicted direction (i.e., the members of competitive groups reported more desire to excel others).

In sum, the data tended to support the prediction that perceived cooperation would be greater among members in the cooperating situation and that perceived competition would be greater among members in the competitive situation.

Coordination of Efforts

Another hypothesis asserted that there would be a greater degree of coordination of efforts and that coordination would occur more frequently among cooperative members than among competitive members. Table 30 presents the relevant evidence.

The observers rated the cooperative groups as working together more fre-

Table 30. Differences between Cooperative and Competitive Groups in Coordination of Effort

VARIABLE	PROBLEM TYPE	TOTAL	
		M diff	p
Working together (A)	H.R.	+2.24	.001
Working together (A)	P	+2.68	.001
Degree of coordination (A)	H.R.	+2.62	.001
Degree of coordination (A)	P	+2.57	.001
Group cooperation (C)	H.R.	+1.18	.001

Key: See table 29.

Source: Morton Deutsch, "An Experimental Study of the Effects of Cooperation and Competition upon Group Process," *Human Relations* 2 (1949). Reprinted by permission of the author and the Plenum Publishing Corporation.

quently (A) and as more highly coordinated (A) than the competitive groups. In answer to the question (C), "How cooperatively did the group work together on this problem?" the ratings of cooperating members indicated more working together than did the ratings of competing members.

Communication

The observers noted significantly fewer communication difficulties among the cooperating members than among the competing members, for both the human-relations problems and the puzzles (see table 31). In answer to the question, "Did you find that you had difficulty in getting your ideas across to others?" the ratings of cooperating members expressed significantly less difficulty than did the ratings of the competing members. The same results were obtained in answers to the following question (C): "Did you find that you had difficulty in trying to follow or get the point of what the others were saying?" Thus the competitive subjects experienced more difficulty with respect to the spread of common ideas, both in the roles of communicators and communicatees.

Productivity

Quantitative productivity per unit of time was expected to be greater in the cooperative groups. The evidence given in table 32 indicates that the cooperative groups solved the puzzle problem more rapidly than did the competitive groups and also produced more on the human-relations problems (number of words written in the recommendations were taken as a crude measure of quantity of productivity).

The hypothesis that qualitative productivity would be higher for the cooperative groups was also supported by the observers' ratings of discussion productivity. According to observer ratings, the discussions of the cooperative groups not only came out with more fruitful ideas for handling the problem presented to them; also, their group discussions showed more insight and understanding of the nature of the problem being posed to them. These differences with respect to group productivity and group insight were significant for both kinds of tasks.

Deutsch warned that average individual productivity should not be confused with group productivity. Group productivity ratings referred to the ideas that were agreed upon and accepted as a basis for action by the group. The ratings of average individual productivity showed no significant differences for the cooperative and competitive groups on the human-relations problems. For the puzzles, there was a difference approaching significance favoring cooperative individuals.

Further evidence that the differences in group productivity were not carried over to individual productivity appeared in the members' ratings of their own learning in the discussions and their grades on term papers. The cooperative group members in only three of the five pairs rated themselves as learning more from

Table 31. Differences in Participation Volume, Attentiveness, and Communication Difficulties between Cooperative and Competitive Groups

VARIABLE	PROBLEM TYPE	TOTAL	
		M diff	p
Participation volume* (B)	H.R.	−22.8	†
Participation volume (B)	P	+118.0	.001
Attentiveness (A)	H.R.	+1.04	.01
Attentiveness (A)	P	+1.50	.001
Attentiveness (C)	H.R.	+0.42	‡
Communication difficulties (A)	H.R.	−1.94	.001
Communication difficulties (A)	P	−1.39	.01
Difficulty in communicating to others (C)	H.R.	−0.81	.001
Difficulty in understanding others (C)	H.R.	−0.67	.001

*Participation Volume has the meaning of "total number of participations per 45 minutes." Thus all participation volumes are equaled in terms of a constant time unit.

†The differences for three pairs are in the same direction as the total mean difference; these differences have p values of .007, .06, and .20. The other two pairs go in the opposite direction; these differences have p values of .12 and .73.

‡The differences for three pairs are in the same direction as the total mean difference; these differences have p values of .03, .04, and .72. The other two pairs, in the opposite direction, both have p values of .83.

Key: See table 29.

Source: Morton Deutsch, "An Experimental Study of the Effects of Cooperation and Competition upon Group Process," *Human Relations* 2 (1949). Reprinted by permission of the author and the Plenum Publishing Corporation.

Table 32. Differences between Cooperative and Competitive Groups in Productivity

VARIABLE	PROBLEM TYPE	TOTAL	
		M diff	p
Discussion productivity (A)	H.R.	+1.86	.001
Discussion productivity (A)	P	+1.90	.01
Discussion insight (A)	H.R.	+1.25	.001
Discussion insight (A)	P	+1.72	.02
Time per solution	P	−7.35 minutes	.01
Number of words written in product	H.R.	+299 words	.001
Average individual productivity (A)	H.R.	+0.15	not sig.
Average individual productivity (A)	P	+0.58	.07

Key: See table 29.

Source: Morton Deutsch, "An Experimental Study of the Effects of Cooperation and Competition upon Group Process," *Human Relations* 2 (1949). Reprinted by permission of the author and the Plenum Publishing Corporation.

the discussion of the human-relations problem. Difference in term grades, although in the predicted direction, were not statistically significant.

In summary Deutsch found that, compared with the competitively organized groups, the cooperative groups had the following characteristics:

1. *Stronger individual motivation* to complete the group task and stronger feelings of obligation toward the other members.
2. Greater *division of labor* both in content and frequency of interaction among members and greater coordination of effort.
3. More *effective intermember communication.* More ideas were verbalized, and members were more attentive to one another and more accepting of and affected by each other's ideas. Members also rated themselves as having fewer difficulties in communicating and understanding others.
4. More *friendliness* was expressed in the discussion, and members rated themselves higher on strength of desire to win the respect of one another. Members were also more satisfied with the group and its products.
5. More *group productivity.* Puzzles were solved faster, and the recommendations produced for the human-relations problems were longer and qualitatively better. However, there were no significant differences in the average individual productivity as a result of the two types of group experience, nor were there any clear differences in the amounts of individual learning which occurred during the discussions.

Cooperation versus Self-oriented Needs

When group members are expected to cooperate in a task, any behavior which stems from "self-oriented" needs is in effect competitive behavior, since members compete with each other in their efforts to use the group to satisfy their own ends. In an industrial study, for example, 72 decision-making conferences, averaging 10 members each, were observed and rated on the extent to which member behavior was directed primarily toward the satisfaction of ego-related or "self-oriented" needs without regard to the effect of this behavior on the attainment of the group goal or to the solution of the group's problem. The amount of self-oriented need expressed in the conference was found to be negatively related to satisfaction of members with the meeting, with the decision, and with the chairmanship. Groups exhibiting high frequencies of "self-oriented" behavior were also high in conflict and tended to perceive themselves as less unified. Although conferences of this type met for longer periods of time, they completed fewer of their agenda items than did groups rated low on self-oriented needs (Fouriezos, Hutt, and Guetzkow, 1950; Marquis, Guetzkow, and Heyns, 1951). The differences between these two types of conferences are similar to those found between groups in which cooperation and competition are experimentally controlled.

Games of Cooperation and Conflict

Most of the research on cooperation and conflict has been conducted in the laboratory with two-person games or often one individual playing against a programmed opponent. Since most of these studies are concerned with the reactions of one person to the game strategies of another rather than group behavior, they are marginal to the main focus of this handbook, which is on problem-solving groups. Most studies of helping behavior and social exchange are also marginal in that the focus is on the individual in response to a social situation. For this reason, the next section of this chapter on games, helping behavior, and exchange provides only a brief overview of the research findings in these areas.

The literature on games includes both two-person and n-person games, zero-sum (where one person's winnings are at the expense of another person's losses) and non-zero sum (where all can win) games, games where payoffs are known and unknown, and simulations which involve games (Rapoport and Orwant, 1962). In constructing the games, two types of models are used: (1) two parties through bid and counter bid attempt to reach agreement on terms of future interaction, and (2) actions are taken by each side which influence the other side to continue or change behavior (Patchen, 1970). In resolving their differences of interest, opponents appear to use at least four methods: (1) bargaining, (2) reliance on content-specific norms, (3) reliance on equity norms, and (4) reliance on the norm of mutual responsiveness (Pruitt, 1972). The process of conflict resolution is affected by situational variables which include prior experience, communication opportunity, opponent's strategy, and role (Druckman, 1971b). The most common finding is that cooperation by one subject begets cooperation from the other. In contrast, any moves by one subject which indicate that he is untrustworthy, punative, or not likely to reciprocate positive advances are likely to lead to competition. However, the overall level of cooperation (about one-third of the time) is not as high as one would expect if the "norm of reciprocity" were operating. Nemeth (1970a), after reviewing the literature, concludes that the lack of reciprocity typically found in bargaining games is not because reciprocity is inoperative, but is rather due to the paradigms normally employed for the study of cooperation and competition. He notes that subjects are usually in a position of contrient interdependence with their partners, are given individualistic instructions, and play for imaginary money against a person whom they do not know and whose motives are ambiguous. Additional reviews of the literature are provided by Schelling, 1958; Kelley, 1965; Rapoport, 1968; Harris, 1969a; Vogler, 1969; Marwell and Schmitt, 1971; Hake and Vukelich, 1972; J. Shaw, 1972b.

The following articles provide an introduction to the general literature on two-person and n-person games (research on the Prisoner's Dilemma and some other special games is treated separately): Deutsch, 1958; Loomis, 1959; Deutsch, 1960b; Lieberman, 1960; Minas et al., 1960; L. Solomon, 1960; Lutzker, 1961; Atkinson, 1962; Harsanyi, 1962c; Lieberman, 1962; Scodel, 1962; Shapley, 1962; Shaw, 1962; Joseph and Willis, 1963; Marlowe, 1963; Wilson, 1963; Bixenstine, Chambers, and Wilson, 1964; Brayer, 1964; Lieberman, 1964; Riker and Niemi, 1964; Sermat, 1964; Lefcourt and Ladwig, 1965; Littig, 1965; Thibaut and Faucheux, 1965; Bixenstine and Blundell, 1966; Ells and Sermat, 1966; Gallo, Irwin, and Avery, 1966; Marlowe, Gergen, and Doob, 1966; Swingle, 1966; Todd, Hammond, and Wilkins, 1966; Walton and McKersie, 1966; Wrightsman, 1966; Bixenstine and Douglas, 1967; Chertkoff and Conley, 1967; Deutsch et al., 1967; Eisenman, 1967; Fry, 1967; Hoggatt, 1967; Kelley, Beckman, and Fischer, 1967; Messick, 1967; Messick and McClintock, 1967; Messick and Thorngate, 1967; Morgan and Sawyer, 1967; Murdoch, 1967; Swingle, 1967; Axelrod and May, 1968; Benton et al., 1968; Cook, 1968; Kahan, 1968; Komorita and Brenner, 1968;

Kubička, 1968; Liebert et al., 1968; Murdoch, 1968; Sermat, 1968; Swingle, 1968b; Thibaut, 1968; Cole, 1969; Gahagan and Tedeschi, 1969; McClintock and Nuttin, 1969; Tedeschi et al., 1969; Thibaut and Gruder, 1969; Vincent and Tindell, 1969; Froman and Cohen, 1970; Horai et al., 1970; Kelley et al., 1970; Křivohlavy, 1970a; Lindskold and Tedeschi, 1970; McClintock, Nuttin, and McNeel, 1970; Schmitt and Marwell, 1970; Smith and Leginski, 1970; Teger, 1970; Throop, Holmes, and Donald, 1970; Benton, 1971a, 1971b; Chertkoff and Baird, 1971; Crott, 1971; Gruder, 1971b; Holmes, Throop, and Strickland, 1971; Kennedy, 1971a; Lewicki, 1971; Lewis and Pruitt, 1971; Michener, Griffith, and Palmer, 1971; Organ, 1971; Rubin, 1971; Schmitt and Marwell, 1971; J. I. Shaw, 1971, 1972b; Shubik, 1971a; Starbuck and Grant, 1971; Tedeschi, Bonoma, and Brown, 1971; Abric and Kahan, 1972; Benton, Kelley, and Liebling, 1972; Cole, 1972; Crott, 1972b; Druckman, Zechmeister, and Solomon, 1972; Johnson and Mihal, 1972; Kelley and Grzelak, 1972; Lamm and Rosch, 1972; Lanto and Shute, 1972; Mehrabian and Ksionzky, 1972b; Repp and Wolking, 1972; Rubin and DiMatteo, 1972; Watzke et al., 1972; Wyer and Malinowski, 1972; Yukl, 1972; Ayers, Nacci, and Tedeschi, 1973; Berkowitz, Hylander, and Bakaitis, 1973; Blau and Richardson, 1973; Blumstein, 1973a; Bonoma and Tedeschi, 1973; Crott and Montmann, 1973; England, 1973; Hake, Vukelich, and Kaplan, 1973; Hamner and Harnett, 1973; Harnett, Cummings, and Hamner, 1973; Lewicki and Rubin, 1973; Marma and Deutsch, 1973; Meux, 1973; Michener and Cohen, 1973; Rapoport, Guyer, and Gordon, 1973; Richmond and Weiner, 1973; Rubin, Lewicki, and Dunn, 1973; Yukl, 1973; Bonoma, Tedeschi, and Helm, 1974; Friedland, Arnold, and Thibaut, 1974; Hamner, 1974; Heilman, 1974; Hinton, Hamner, and Pohlen, 1974; McClintock, 1974; Pate et al., 1974; Yukl, 1974a, 1974b.

Deutsch and Krauss (1960) introduced a game in which the players represent the Acme and Bolt trucking companies. They must pass their trucks in opposite directions over the same stretch of road. Each player can block the path of the other to produce a threat. When the game was used in an experiment with 16 pairs of female telephone operators as subjects, players won most when they could not use the threat, least when both could threaten. If only one could threaten, the results were in between. Further research using this game includes Deutsch and Krauss, 1962; Borah, 1963; Gallo, 1966; Krauss, 1966; Krauss and Deutsch, 1966; Shomer, Davis, and Kelley, 1966; Brown, 1968; H. H. Kelley, 1968; Fischer, 1969; Froman and Cohen, 1969; Plon, 1969–1970; Smith and Emmons, 1969; Deutsch and Lewicki, 1970; Deutsch, Canavan, and Rubin, 1971; Cheney, Harford, and Solomon, 1972; Mack, 1972b.

Another bargaining game was introduced by Siegel and Fouraker (1960). Pairs of subjects acted as buyers and sellers for a hypothetical commodity. They were given real payoffs, contingent on their success in bargaining. Variations on this game were used by Pruitt and Drews (1969) and Kahn and Kohls (1972).

Another set of games deal with negotiations between groups in conflict. Usually there is some real-life application, and in some a third party is introduced to help mediate the conflict. Examples of this type of research include Atthowe, 1961; Blake and Mouton, 1961b, 1961d, 1962a; Harsanyi, 1962a, 1962b, 1962c; McGrath and Julian, 1963; Mouton and Blake, 1963; Bartos, 1964; Hornstein, 1965; Harsanyi, 1966; Myers and Kling, 1966; Druckman, 1967; Johnson, 1967; Touzard, 1967; Druckman, 1968; Hermann and Kogan, 1968; Moser, 1968; Deutsch, 1969; Johnson and Lewicki, 1969; Druckman, 1970; Pruitt and Johnson, 1970; Vidmar and McGrath, 1970; Vinacke, Cherulnik, and Lichtman, 1970;

Davis and Triandis, 1971; Druckman, 1971a; Johnson, 1971; Ofshe, 1971; Pruitt, 1971c; Vidmar, 1971; Benton, 1972a; Frey and Adams, 1972; Johnson and Tullar, 1972; Krause, 1972; van den Hove, 1972; Brehmer and Hammond, 1973; Druckman and Zechmeister, 1973; Kohler, Miller, and Klein, 1973; Lamm, 1973; Baker, 1974; Chertkoff and Braden, 1974; Erikson et al., 1974; Greenblat, 1974; Klimoski and Ash, 1974; Rabbie et al., 1974; Short, 1974.

Prisoner's Dilemma Games

The most popular type of laboratory game is called the Prisoner's Dilemma as an indication of the problem faced by two persons who have been arrested and are sent to prison. They know that if one confesses, he will be let free. If both confess, the punishment will be severe. If neither confesses, they will be rewarded, but less than if only one confesses. An example of the payoff matrix used in laboratory game is given in figure 37. Without communication with the other player, each subject must select one of two strategies, cooperation (C) or defection (D), and this determines which of the four outcomes will occur. The payoffs are displayed in the appropriate cell of the matrix with the payoffs for the person choosing the rows listed first. In deciding which strategy to choose, a player will note that he will do better if he chooses D rather than C *regardless* of the other player's choice. If he is the only player to defect, then he gets 10 (in this example), while the other player has 10 taken away. If both defect, they each receive punishment, here −1. However, if both cooperate, both receive a reward, here 5. This, then, is the dilemma: each player separately can do better by defecting, but together they can do better by cooperating. As in the other games, individuals who show that they are willing to cooperate tend to have their cooperation reciprocated. However, unconditional cooperation tends to be exploited (Swingle, 1970; Vincent and Schwerin, 1971; Black and Higbee, 1973; Lindskold and Bennett, 1973; Marwell, Schmitt, and Boyesen, 1973). The effect of the sex of the subject seems to depend on the version of the game and the sex of the other player, since sometimes men are reported to be more cooperative, sometimes women, and sometimes neither (Rapoport and Chammah, 1965b; Pilisuk, Skolnick, and Overstreet, 1968; Lindskold et al., 1969; Halpin and Pilisuk, 1970; Tedeschi, Bonoma, and Novinson, 1970; Gillis and Woods, 1971; Kahn, Hottes, and Davis, 1971; Mack, Auburn, and Knight, 1971; Conrath, 1972; Higbee and Black, 1972; McNeel, McClintock, and Nuttin, 1972; Mack, 1972a; Moore and Mack, 1972; Stevenson and Phillips, 1972; Ajzen and Fishbein, 1973; Bedell and Sistrunk, 1973; Benton, 1973; Johnston, Markey, and Messe, 1973; Miller and Pyke, 1973; Skotko, Langmeyer, and Lundgren, 1973; Slack and Cook, 1973; van de Sande, 1973). Various personality traits have expected effects, with subjects who tend to be

Figure 37. Example of a Prisoner's Dilemma

	C	D
C	(5,5)	(−10,10)
D	(10,−10)	(−1,−1)

Source: Axelrod (1967).

cooperative and trusting in other situations performing in a similar way in the game (Berkowitz, 1968; Podd, Marcia, and Rubin, 1970; Ajzen, 1971; Federico, 1971; Larsen, 1972; Speer, 1972c; Marin, 1973; Nydegger, 1974; Slusher, Roering, and Rose, 1974).

Books and articles which provide reviews of the research on the Prisoner's Dilemma or suggest models or alternative games include Luce and Raiffa, 1958; Shubik, 1963; Pilisuk and Rapoport, 1964; Shubik, 1964; Siegel, Siegel, and Andrews, 1964; Gallo and McClintock, 1965; Rapoport and Chammah, 1965a; Weil, 1966; Plon, 1967; Pruitt, 1967; Rapoport, 1967a; Scheff, 1967; Rapoport and Cole, 1968; Alexander and Weil, 1969; Baldwin, 1969; Harris, 1969a, 1969b; Bonacich, 1970; Emshoff, 1970; Kee and Knox, 1970; Křivohlavý, 1970b; Oskamp, 1970; Shubik, 1970; Umeoka, 1970; Hardin, 1971; Harris, 1971; Oskamp, 1971; Radinsky, 1971; Shubik, 1971b; Swingle and MacLean, 1971; Bonoma, Tedeschi, and Linkskold, 1972; Crott, 1972a; R. J. Harris, 1972; McClintock, 1972; Manz, 1972; Griesinger and Livingston, 1973; Guyer, Fox, and Hamburger, 1973; Hamburger, 1973; Rapoport, Kahan, and Stein, 1973; Hamburger, 1974; Vinacke et al., 1974.

Finally, for those who have a special interest in this area, the following list provides a sample of the variations on this theme: Scodel et al., 1959; Willis and Joseph, 1959; Deutsch, 1960a; Daugherty, 1961; Rapoport et al., 1962; Wilson and Bixenstine, 1962; Bixenstine, Potash, and Wilson, 1963; Schellenberg, 1964; Harrison and McClintock, 1965; Komorita, 1965; Lave, 1965; McClintock, Gallo, and Harrison, 1965; Oskamp and Perlman, 1965; Radlow, 1965; Sampson and Karsush, 1965; Schellenberg, 1965; Bixenstine, Levitt, and Wilson, 1966; Bixenstine and O'Reilly, 1966; Dolbear and Lave, 1966; Evans and Crumbaugh, 1966; McClintock and McNeel, 1966a, 1966b, 1966c; Morehous, 1966; Oskamp and Perlman, 1966; Pylyshyn, Agnew, and Illingworth, 1966; Radlow and Radlow, 1966; Rapoport and Dale, 1966; Rekosh and Feigenbaum, 1966; Arnstein and Feigenbaum, 1967; Crumbaugh and Evans, 1967; Kanouse and Wiest, 1967; Komorita and Mechling, 1967; McClintock and McNeel, 1967; Miller, 1967; Pepitone et al., 1967; Pilisuk et al., 1967; Rapoport, 1967b; Sermat, 1967; Steele and Tedeschi, 1967; Swensson, 1967; Swingle and Coady, 1967; Swinth, 1967; Uejio and Wrightsman, 1967; Ells and Sermat, 1968; Gahagan and Tedeschi, 1968; Guyer, 1968; B. Jones et al., 1968; Komorita, Sheposh, and Braver, 1968; Messick and McClintock, 1968; Morgan and Sawyer, 1968; Pilisuk and Skolnick, 1968; Pruitt, 1968; Radlow, Weidner, and Hurst, 1968; Schelling, 1968; Sibley, Senn, and Epanchin, 1968; Swingle, 1968a; Swingle and Gillis, 1968; Tedeschi, Lesnick, and Gahagan, 1968; Tedeschi, Aranoff, et al., 1968; Tedeschi, Gahagan, et al., 1968; Tedeschi, Horai, et al., 1968; Tedeschi, Steele, et al., 1968; Terhune, 1968; Wilson and Insko, 1968; Wilson and Kayatani, 1968; Berger and Tedeschi, 1969; Bonoma et al., 1969; Dolbear et al., 1969; Gahagan, Long, and Horai, 1969; Gallo, 1969; Gallo, Funk, and Levine, 1969; Gumpert, Deutsch, and Epstein, 1969; Horai and Tedeschi, 1969; Hurst et al., 1969; Komorita and Barnes, 1969; Noland and Catron, 1969; Pruitt, 1969a; Rapoport, 1969; Schoeninger and Wood, 1969; Tedeschi, Hiester, and Gahagan, 1969; Wallace and Rothaus, 1969; W. Wilson, 1969; Worchel, 1969; Wyer, 1969; Abric, 1970; Boyle and Bonacich, 1970; Cederblom and Diers, 1970; Conrath, 1970; Emshoff and Ackoff, 1970; Gallo and Winchell, 1970; Guyer and Rapoport, 1970; Kelley and Stahelski, 1970a, 1970b, 1970c; Kershenbaum and Komorita, 1970; O'Connor, Wrightsman, and Baker, 1970; Orwant and Orwant, 1970; Oskamp and Kleinke, 1970; Pate and Broughton, 1970; Pruitt, 1970; Schlenker et al., 1970; Sermat, 1970; Tedeschi et al., 1970; Wichman, 1970; Bixenstine and Gaebelein, 1971; Burgess, 1971; Gallo and Sheposh, 1971; Kleinke and Pohlen, 1971; Knox and Douglas, 1971; Liebert, Swenson, and Liebert, 1971; Lindskold and Tedeschi, 1971; Lindskold et al., 1971; Messe, Bolt, and Sawyer, 1971; Michelini, 1971; Morrison et al., 1971; Pilisuk, Kiritz, and Clampitt, 1971; Rapoport, Guyer, and Gordon, 1971; Richman, 1971; Schlenker et al., 1971; Stech and McClintock, 1971; Voissem and Sistrunk, 1971; Wahba, 1971a; Wendt and Rüppell, 1971; W. Wilson, 1971; Wyer, 1971; Wyer and Polen, 1971; Baranowski and Summers, 1972; Benton, 1972b; Bonacich, 1972; Bonoma, Tedeschi, and Lindskold, 1972; Fox, 1972; Guyer and Rapoport, 1972; S. Johnson and Johnson, 1972; Mack and Knight, 1972; Marwell and Schmitt, 1972b; Meertens, 1972; Schlenker and Tedeschi, 1972; Scinto, Sistrunk, and Clement, 1972; Sensenig, Reed, and Miller, 1972; Solomon and Kaufmann, 1972; Speer, 1972a, 1972c; Summers et al., 1972; Swingle and Santi, 1972; Wolf, 1972; Yoshino, 1972; Brew, 1973; Capage and Lindskold, 1973; Coombs, 1973; Dion, 1973; Eiser et al., 1973; Fox and Guyer, 1973; Gardin et al., 1973; Gruder and Duslak, 1973; Hogan, Fisher, and Morrison, 1973; Kahan, 1973; Kahan and Goehring, 1973; Knight and Mack, 1973; Komorita, 1973; Lynch, 1973; McClintock et al., 1973; McNeel, 1973; Messe, Dawson, and Lane, 1973; Michener, Lawler, and Bacharach, 1973; Nacci and Tedeschi, 1973; H. D. Schneider, 1973; Sheposh and Gallo, 1973; Wood, Pilisuk, and Uren, 1973; Hogan, Fisher, and Morrison, 1974; Lindskold and Horai, 1974; Mack and Knight, 1974; McNeel, Sweeney, and Bohlin, 1974; Mogby and Pruitt, 1974; Oskamp, 1974; Pate et al., 1974; Vinacke et al., 1974.

Helping Behavior

The widespread publicity in the United States of a murder of a young woman in the street while many people watched but made no attempt to intervene spurred a number of researchers to ask, "When will people help in a crisis?" (Darley and Latané, 1968b). Most of these studies took the form of "field experiments" in which the experimenter or his accomplice gave the appearance of needing help so that passersby on the street or persons in the next room hearing a call for help could be observed to note their reaction under different experimental conditions.

Representative of this research is a study of situational and dispositional variables in helping behavior entitled "From Jerusalem to Jericho" (Darley and Batson, 1973). First the degree of religiosity of 40 theology students was measured by use of several personality scales. Next a field experiment was arranged, based on the parable of the Good Samaritan. Each theology student was asked to give a short talk either on the parable of the Good Samaritan or on another topic to a group which met in another building. It was arranged that some students would be late for the appointment and others would be given ample time. While crossing the campus on the way to the building where the talk was to be held, each student encountered a shabbily dressed person slumped by the side of the road. The experimenters observed that those students who were in a hurry to reach their destination were more likely to pass by without stopping. Neither the assigned topic of his talk nor the religiosity of the student was related to his helping or not. However, if a student did stop to offer help, the character of the helping response was related to his type of religiosity.

If the tendency to drop or break things or appear sick on college campuses and in the community in the interest of science continues, it may become difficult to distinguish a person who is actually in distress from a Ph.D. candidate in psychology. Another example of research on helping behavior which dealt with the variables of race and sex was entitled "The Broken Bag Caper" (Wispe and Freshley, 1971). The experimenters observed 176 black and white 20 to 60-year-old males and females as they were about to enter a supermarket to buy groceries. As they approached the supermarket, a young black or white female accomplice emerged from the store. Her bag of groceries broke, and oranges rolled over the sidewalk. The results showed that (1) significant sex differences occurred in helping behavior for the black but not the white sample, (2) women tended to be less helpful toward women of the same race, (3) with the exception of (2), there were no racial differences in helping behavior, and (4) a significant number of shoppers who saw examples of negative modeling (someone who did not stop to help) helped anyway; and in this the sex of the model was the most important characteristic.

After reviewing the literature on helping behavior, Lück (1970b) concluded that the most important findings were as follows: (1) bystander intervention constitutes an interpersonal relationship which is determined by many personal and situational variables, (2) social norms prescribe altruistic behavior, which is facilitated by a role model and immediate reward, (3) the relationship of dependence between bystander and helped is important, with more help given when the helpless person is very dependent, (4) the number of witnesses influences the decision to help, with less of a tendency to help if others are present and do not help, and (5) the willingness to help differs with the cultural norms in various countries. Additional research indicates that the subject is more likely to help if he feels guilty about some transgression which he has just committed (McMillen, 1970, 1971; McMillen and Austin, 1971; Regan, Williams, and Sparling, 1972; Konečni, 1972; Noel, 1973; Wallington, 1973) or if the person asking for help is ingratiating (Jones et al., 1965; Stires and Jones, 1969; Kipnis and Vanderveer, 1971; Fodor, 1973a, 1973b; Kahn and Young, 1973; Lefebvre, 1973; P. H. Baron, 1974).

Further examples of this type of field or laboratory study include Berkowitz and Daniels, 1964; Berkowitz, Klanderman, and Harris, 1964; Schopler and Bateson, 1965; Schopler and Matthews, 1965; Berkowitz and Connor, 1966; Brehm and Cole, 1966; Goranson and Berkowitz, 1966; Berkowitz and Friedman, 1967; Schopler, 1967; Simon, 1967; Bramel, Taub, and Blum, 1968; Darley and Latané, 1968a; R. E. Feldman, 1968; Frisch and Greenberg 1968; Hornstein, Fisch, and Holmes, 1968; Horowitz, 1968a, 1968b; Jones et al., 1968; Midlarsky, 1968b; Tesser, Gatewood, and Driver, 1968; Aderman and Berkowitz, 1969; Berkowitz, 1969; Epstein and Hornstein, 1969; Greenglass, 1969; Jecker and Landy, 1969; Jones, 1969; Korte, 1969; Latané and Rodin, 1969; McMillen and Reynolds, 1969; Piliavin, Rodin, and Piliavin, 1969; Staub, 1969; Test and Bryan, 1969; Wagner and Wheeler, 1969; Aderman and Berkowitz, 1970; Baron, 1970; Eisenberger et al., 1970; Gaertner, 1970; Isen, 1970; Jones, 1970; Kolb and Boyatzis, 1970; Murdoch and Rosen, 1970; Ross, 1970; Schwartz and Clausen, 1970; Staub, 1970; Tilker, 1970; Wilke and Lanzetta, 1970; Baron, 1971e; Berkowitz, 1971; Borofsky, Stollak, and Messe, 1971; Bickman, 1971; Gaertner and Bickman, 1971; Goodstadt, 1971; Greenberg and Shapiro, 1971; Greenberg, Block, and Silverman, 1971; Gruder and Cook, 1971; Hornstein et al., 1971; Horowitz, 1971; Kazdin and Bryan, 1971; Korte,

1971; Lanzetta and Wilke, 1971; Lerner, Solomon, and Brody, 1971; McMillen and Austin, 1971; Regan, 1971; Ross, 1971; Staub, 1971; Thalhofer, 1971; Wolosin, Sherman, and Mynatt, 1971; Yakimovich and Saltz, 1971; Aderman, 1972; Barocas and Karoly, 1972; Beebe et al., 1972; Bickman, 1972; Bryan, 1972; Campbell, 1972; Clark and Word, 1972; Cohen, 1972; Cotler and Quilty, 1972; Dorris, 1972; Ekstein, 1972; Gergen, Gergen, and Meter, 1972; Graf and Riddell, 1972; Greenberg and Frisch, 1972; M. B. Harris, 1972; Heilman, Hodgson, and Hornstein, 1972; Hodgson, Hornstein, and LaKind, 1972; Hornstein, 1972; Hutte and Van Kreveld, 1972; Isen and Levin, 1972; Kaplan, 1972; Katz, 1972; Langer and Abelson, 1972; Levy et al., 1972; Liebhart, 1972b; Moss and Page, 1972; Piliavin and Piliavin, 1972; Raymond and Unger, 1972; Rosenhan, 1972; Ross and Wilson, 1972; Schapa, 1972; Staub, 1972; Smith, Smythe, and Lien, 1972; Suedfeld, Bochner, and Wnek, 1972; Tessler and Schwartz, 1972; Tipton and Browning, 1972a, 1972b; Walster and Piliavin, 1972; Wispe, 1972; Athanasiou and Greene, 1973; Baker and Reitz, 1973; Baron, 1973a; Berkowitz, 1973; Bickman and Kamzan, 1973; Bickman et al., 1973; Cialdini, Darby, and Vincent, 1973; Darley, Teger, and Lewis, 1973; Diener et al., 1973; Ehlert, Ehlert, and Merrens, 1973; Fischer, 1973; Franklin, 1973; Gaertner, 1973; Gelfand et al., 1973; Gross and Latané, 1973; Harris and Baudin, 1973; Harris and Huang, 1973a, 1973b; Harris and Meyer, 1973; Harris and Robinson, 1973; Kahn and Tice, 1973; Karabenick, Lerner, and Beecher, 1973; Krupat and Epstein, 1973; Lowe and Ritchey, 1973; Masor, Hornstein, and Tobin, 1973; Merrens, 1973; Midlarsky and Midlarsky, 1973; Morgan, 1973; Morris and Rosen, 1973; Penner, Dertke, and Achenbach, 1973; Ross and Braband, 1973; Schellenberg and Blevins, 1973; F. N. Schneider, 1973; Schwartz, 1973; Stokols and Schopler, 1973; Stotland et al., 1973; Thayer, 1973; Weiss, et al., 1973; Bar-Tal and Greenberg, 1974; Bickman, 1974a, 1974b; Blevins and Murphy, 1974; Chaikin et al., 1974; Clark and Word, 1974; Deaux, 1974; Field, 1974; Franklin, 1974; Fish and Kaplan, 1974; Hurley and Allen, 1974; Karpienia and Zippel, 1974; Pliner et al., 1974; Rodin and Slochower, 1974; Roth and Bootzin, 1974; Schiavo, Sherlock, and Wicklund, 1974; Schwartz, 1974; Sherrod and Downs, 1974; Staub and Baer, 1974.

Some studies have been concerned with altruism as a general tendency to be helpful: Lerner and Lichtman, 1968; Midlarsky, 1968a; Schwartz, 1968b; Simmons and Lerner, 1968; Midlarsky and Midlarsky, 1970; Fraser and Fujitomi, 1972; Midlarsky and Bryan, 1972; Midlarsky and Midlarsky, 1972; Underwood, Moore, and Rosenhan, 1972; Anderson and Perlman, 1973; Harris, Liguori, and Stack, 1973; Isen, Horn, and Rosenhan, 1973; Moore, Underwood, and Rosenhan, 1973; Willis and Goethals, 1973; Black, Weinstein, and Tanur, 1974; Lerner and Long, 1974; Long and Lerner, 1974; Rosenhan, Underwood, and Moore, 1974; Tipton and Jenkins, 1974.

Social Exchange

Much of the literature on bargaining games and helping behavior can be seen as a test of hypotheses concerning the process of social exchange in interpersonal behavior. Although it is apparent that some form of social exchange is operating in all forms of social interaction, the topic is included here because its relevance has been particularly apparent with the various gaming tasks.

Major contributions to the social-psychological literature on exchange have been made by Thibaut and Kelley (1959), Homans (1961), Blau (1964), and Parsons (cf. 1968). Blau (1968, p. 452) states that the basic assumptions of the theory of social exchange are that individuals enter into new social relationships because they expect them to be rewarding and that they continue with old relationships because they find them rewarding. A relationship will be rewarding if there is some "profit" in it, that is, if the rewards exceed the costs. Usually there are several "options" open to the individual. He must decide which one will maximize his profit.

When the exchange takes place between two persons, the result is the situation given in the Prisoner's Dilemma; each player finds that in cooperating there is usually a solution which provides a profit for both (Thibaut and Kelley, 1959; p. 106; Shaw, 1971, p. 32).

Although the kinds of social goods which are exchanged are not often categorized in any general way in most of the research on exchange, Parsons (1968) suggests that there are "generalized symbolic media of interchange" that operate within societal systems. The medium of exchange for pattern maintenance (L) is value commitments, for integration (I) it is influence, for goal attainment (G) it is power, and for adaptation (A) it is money. Most of the commodities used for exchange in the experimental literature can be seen as related to one of these four media.

Summaries of the literature on social exchange include Homans, 1963; Adams, 1965; Harari, 1967; Nord, 1968; Gergen, 1969; Meeker, 1971; Wolf and Zahn, 1972; Bierhoff, 1973; Walster, Berscheid, and Walster, 1973.

Research which uses some aspect of exchange theory as a focus includes Blau, 1960a; Rosen, Levinger, and Lippitt, 1960; Gamson, 1961b; Rainio, 1961; Penny and Robertson, 1962; Daniels and Berkowitz, 1963; Gullahorn and Gullahorn, 1963; Longabaugh, 1963; James and Lott, 1964; S. C. Jones, 1966; Kiesler, 1966; Rabinowitz, Kelley, and Rosenblatt, 1966; Rosen, 1966; Wiggins, 1966; Anderson, 1967; Daniels, 1967; Burnstein and Wolosin, 1968; Griffitt, 1968; Rothbart, 1968a, 1968b; Shrauger and Jones, 1968; Taylor, Altman, and Sorrentino, 1968, 1969; Blumstein and Weinstein, 1969; Katz et al., 1969; Leventhal and Bergman, 1969; Leventhal, Weiss, and Long, 1969; Moore and Baron, 1969; Schellenberg and Wright, 1969; Weinstein, DeVaughn, and Wiley, 1969; Worthy, Gary, and Kahn, 1969; Liebert and Fernandez, 1970; McMartin, 1970; Brown and Garland, 1971; Brown, Garland, and Mena, 1971; Lane and Messe, 1971; Lane, Messe, and Phillips, 1971; Liebart and Poulos, 1971; Messe, 1971; Pepitone, 1971; Wahba, 1971b; Crosbie, 1972; Druckman, Solomon, and Zechmeister, 1972; Eiser and Tajfel, 1972; Garland and Brown, 1972; Hinton, 1972; Kahn, 1972; Lane and Messe, 1972; Lefebvre, 1972; Leventhal, Michaels, and Sanford, 1972; Lloyd and Lloyd, 1972; Mikula, 1972a, 1972c, 1972d; Overstreet, 1972; Schmitt and Marwell, 1972b; Singelmann, 1972; Callahan and Messe, 1973; Garrett and Libby, 1973; Greenberg and Leventhal, 1973; Kaplan and Swart, 1973; Leventhal, Weiss, and Buttrick, 1973; Libby and Carlson, 1973; Mikula and Uray, 1973; Nacci, Stapleton, and Tedeschi, 1973a, 1973b; Seligman, Paschall, and Takata, 1973; Taynor and Deaux, 1973; K. Thomas, 1973; Austin and Susmilch, 1974; Austin and Walster, 1974; Burgess and Nielsen, 1974; Cohen, 1974; Lerner, 1974; Messe and Lane, 1974; Mikula, 1974; Zillmann and Bryant, 1974.

The Method of Imposing the Rules

The rules may be imposed upon the group by any of the means described in chapter 2. Like other sets of social norms, however, those for cooperation need not be made explicit in order to introduce them to a group. Cooperation may be achieved simply by reinforcing cooperative behavior in the interaction of a group which is already formed. This has been done with pairs of children seven to twelve years of age where cooperation was developed and extinguished by the positive reinforcement of giving them a jelly bean each time they cooperated in a game (Azrin and Lindsley, 1956).

Stress

An important aspect of the task is the amount of *stress* under which the task must be performed. Groups tend to respond to continuously increasing stress, like *all* living systems, first by a lag in response, then by an overcompensatory response, and finally by a catastrophic collapse of the system (Miller, 1955, p. 528). A representative curve based on animal studies of the effectiveness of individual performance as stress is increased over a period of time is presented in figure 38. After the stress is applied to the individual, there is an initial dip in the curve in the direction of the final collapse which is the alarm reaction. This is followed by a rise of the curve above the level normally maintained by the organism, which constitutes a peak of activity of overcompensation or overdefensiveness. As the stress is increased, more and more defenses are called into play until finally no additional ones are available and the system collapses suddenly into death. There is some evidence that the activity of a family in a crisis brought about by the illness or death of one of its members follows a curve of this sort.

It is also probable that groups may react as individuals do under acute and prolonged stress. In military combat, for example, an acute, intense stress would be disorganizing for individuals with personality problems which made them particularly susceptible, while the same stress would produce reactions of a more temporary nature in a well-adjusted individual. Under prolonged stress, however, even the well-adjusted individuals would begin to feel the strain (Grinker and Spiegel, 1945).

The most common form of stress for a group is a time limit for the completion of the task. In many experiments, like that of Deutsch described above, the time it takes to solve the problem is one of the major dimensions of the task. Often the differences in productivity between groups organized in different ways are only

Figure 38. Performance under Increasing Stress

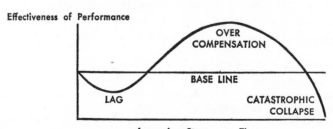

Source: James G. Miller, "Toward a General Theory for the Behavioral Sciences," *American Psychologist* 10 (1955): 528. Copyright 1955 by the American Psychological Association. Reprinted by permission of the author and the publisher.

apparent if the groups are under pressure to complete the task in limited time (Schutz, 1958a).

Too much time can also be used as stress. Members who are incompatible may be able to ignore their differences in the short run but be forced to reveal their underlying differences if they must work together over a long period of time (Schutz, 1958a). The effects of long association are evident in groups of men in arctic weather stations and other isolated outposts (Taylor, Wheeler, and Altman, 1968).

In a study of leadership and crisis, stress was applied by giving some groups a problem without any solution (Hamblin, 1958b). The behavior of leaders in 12 three-man groups with no solution to the problem was compared with that of leaders in a similar set of groups with a solution. All groups were playing a shuffle-board game. Leaders had more influence in the groups in "crisis," but the leader was replaced if he did not appear to have a good solution to the problem.

Stress can also be applied through challenges or threats or punishment if the members do not perform well. Under these conditions, the hostility generated toward the locus of the threat makes it difficult for the group to utilize the resources of its members, and the effectiveness of the group falls off (Frank, 1944; Lanzetta et al., 1954). Threats are, however, often used in an attempt to increase productivity. In a controlled study of mother-child interaction, mothers who were motivated to have their child perform "well" demonstrated more directing, interfering, criticizing, and "structuring a change in activity" behavior that did mothers who had no aspirations for their child in the same play situation (Merrill, 1946).

For optimal performance the amount of stress should neither be so great as to result in collapse of the system or cause the group members to give up the task if they are frustrated in reaching the goal (Barker, Dembo, and Lewin, 1941; Hamblin, 1958a; Ekehammar and Magnusson, 1973) nor so small that the group members are not motivated to perform (Lanzetta and Roby, 1956a, 1956b). A mild stress appears to produce optimal performance (Lanzetta, 1955; Lanzetta and Roby, 1957; Emerson, 1966a, 1966b; Altman and Haythorn, 1967b; Renner and Renner, 1972).

The contrast between the effects of high and low stress is evident in two group experiments in which drugs were used to produce or reduce stress. Groups whose members were given lysergic acid diethylamide became much slower and inefficient in their interpersonal communications (Lennard, Jarvik, and Abramson, 1956). In contrast, members of three-man groups under threat who were given an "anxiety-reducing" medication (Seconal and Benzedrine) showed little anxiety, were elated, unassertive, and happy, but did little with the task (Lanzetta et al., 1956).

Group Behavior under Stress

In the experiment by Lanzetta (1955, p. 49–50):

Twelve groups, each composed of four naval reserve officer trainees, were exposed to three experimental conditions varying along a "stress" dimension. The twelve groups were randomly divided into two classes of six groups each, one class, termed "high motivation," being rewarded with a group prize for the best performing group, the other class, termed "low motivation," being offered no reward. Within each of these classes, each group was exposed to the three experimental stress conditions in a different order, there being six possible orderings. The three experimental conditions were:

non-stress—subjects were given no special instructions; they were given the task materials and told only that we were interested in how groups go about solving problems.

mild stress—a time limit was imposed, and reinforced by the announcement, at intervals, of time remaining.

high stress—a time limit was imposed, the subjects were badgered and belittled by the experimenter and there was a restriction of work space.

At each session the groups worked on a reasoning and mechanical assembly task. An attempt was made to collect extensive data on the social-emotional and problem-solving behavior of the group members. Techniques used were: (a) a continuous on-going recording of behavior, by two observers, in terms of 58 categories, (b) ratings, made by the two observers, of each individual, after each task, for each session, on twelve characteristics, (c) ratings of eleven group characteristics by both observers and participants.

All three independent variables, stress, motivation, and task, affected behavior, but there appeared to be little interaction between them. Quantitative comparisons between them indicated that changes in behavior under stress could be classified into three categories: (a) changes in behavior which would tend to increase interpersonal tension and friction within the groups, (b) changes in behavior which would tend to decrease interpersonal tension and increase integration, (c) changes in problem-solving behavior. There was a decrease in negative social-emotional behavior, in aggression, deflation, dissatisfaction, competition, etc., and in self-oriented behavior, under increased stress. There was an increase in positive group-oriented behavior such as co-operativeness, friendliness, group discussion, and integrating acts under increased stress. These were interpreted as indicating that participants perceived the group as a source of security in the face of the external threat, and thus behavior which would lead to acceptance by the group was facilitated, while behavior which might lead to rejection was depressed.

Analysis of characteristics and behaviors related to performance indicated that the performance of the group was best under mild stress conditions, the relations of performance to stress being curvilinear. Participants did not perceive performance improving, although a similar curvilinear relationship obtained between their ratings of activity, motivation, morale, and interest in job completion. The inconsistency between observers' and participants' ratings could be explained by assuming a linear increase in level of aspiration as stress increased.

There were quite striking behavior differences associated with the two tasks. For the mechanical assembly task there were almost twice as many nonproductive behaviors, over five times as many equalitarian, group-oriented behaviors, and more group discussion regarding the task, than for the reasoning task. The reasoning task showed a greater number of negative social-emotional behaviors, more solidarity-oriented behaviors, and more initiating and insightful behaviors.

These results support the previously reported findings by Carter et al. (1951), that the reasoning task includes more initiating activity with emphasis on making diagnosis, while the mechanical assembly task involves much less behavior devoted to initiating action, but much more to action by the "followers" or "workers."

In conclusion Lanzetta noted that the results of this exploratory study were limited in generality, since the experiment was performed on a selected sample of college males, working in cooperative groups on a limited sample of tasks.

Consequences of Failure or Success and Feedback

One feature that is particularly dependent upon the definition given to it by the members is the degree and kind of "reality" of the task. This, in turn, is partly a matter of the *kind of consequences that are expected to result from action,* and also the amount of feedback that actually comes back from the environment. It is suggested that the less or the slower the feedback, the lower the degree of reality. In turn, the lower the degree of reality, the more the response is determined by internal features and tensions of the individual or group. This, in fact, is what happens in a "projective" test, where stories constructed by a group to describe ambiguous pictures are used to produce diagnostic information about the group (Horwitz and Cartwright, 1953).

A comparison of individual behavior through a range of degrees of "reality" from paper-and-pencil tests, to role playing, to actual behavior incidents (Moldawsky, 1951) indicates only slight correlation among performances in the different situations.

Holding the scoring categories constant, prediction is not found to be justified across the levels. For air corps subjects, a significant increasing trend in profanity was noted from actual behavior, to role playing, to paper-and-pencil test. Using a general measure of distance, role playing was found to be closer to actual behavior than was performance on a paper-and-pencil test (Borgatta, 1951b). However, role playing was still not as involving a task as actual discussion (Borgatta and Bales, 1953a).

Some of the consequences of success are evident in several studies. During the break after the task, members of (air corps) groups who were successful talked more about the task than those who were not successful (Berkowitz and Levy, 1956). The successful groups also tended to raise their level of aspiration for the next problem, while unsuccessful groups lowered their level of aspiration.

Members of groups which continued to experience success had a more favorable attitude toward their group and tended to accept the group's solution to a problem (estimating dots on a card), rather than their own solution (Shelley, 1954). Similar changes in level of aspiration were observed in individual subjects when a simulated "reference group" (tape-recorded responses of four other members) was more or less successful than they were on a task of estimating the number of sounds in a set (Kaiser and Blake, 1955).

Individuals who are successful in a task in a well-defined situation are able to predict their future success in a similar situation (Gerard, 1956). Task success or failure also appears to affect the cohesiveness of the group (Stotland, 1959). In one experiment with groups which were either constantly rewarded or not rewarded, the proportion of ingroup choices increased while groups in which reward was varied did not show a similar trend (Thibaut, 1950). In a similar experiment, subjects who were motivated to succeed liked others who appeared to be doing well. However, highly motivated subjects who did poorly as a group also rated other members as highly attractive, presumably a reflection of greater integration in the face of threat (Berkowitz, Levy, and Harvey, 1957).

Task Completion and Recall

When individual subjects or members of a group perform a number of tasks, some of which are interrupted by the experimenter before the subject (or group) has a chance to complete them, the subjects usually recall more of the interrupted tasks (Horwitz, 1954; Horwitz and Lee, 1954). This happens presumably because when the subject begins the task, a tension is set up which is not reduced unless the task is completed. As a result, the unresolved tension makes the uncompleted tasks easier to recall. However, if the subject works with a partner and the partner completes the interrupted task, the frequency of recall is no greater than it is for tasks which the subject completes himself. This suggests that the subject has identified himself with the group, so that whatever the group does is seen as an extension of himself (Lewis, 1944). This effect varies with the orientation of the subject. Subjects who were told that they were simply helping the experimenter try out some tasks but were not being tested themselves tended to recall the interrupted (partner-completed) tasks. In contrast, subjects who were given less pointed instructions, which seems to imply that they were being tested, tended to recall the tasks which they completed themselves (Lewis and Franklin, 1944).

Summary

The task can be described in terms of six variables:

1. The kind of task (goal)
2. The criteria for task completion
3. The rules (or roles) which must be followed
4. The method of imposing the rules
5. The amount of stress on the members
6. The consequences of failure or success

The task is the most general way of specifying the expectations for group behavior; the task of the group in the broadest sense is to deal with the situation in which it finds itself.

Situational differences in interaction patterns are evident in studies of children's groups where orphanage nursery school children, and children in the third grade at public school are found to be more aggressive on the school playground than in their neighborhoods after school. Intellectual tasks and manual tasks also appear to differ in the types of problem-solving behavior required. The consistency of behavior for different tasks is greater if the tasks require little modification of an individual's central tendencies or require standard behavioral responses which differ only slightly in content.

A solution to the task is more difficult to obtain if the criterion for completion is ambiguous. It is also more difficult if group consensus is required.

Contrasting sets of rules and roles have been imposed on groups by requiring competition versus cooperation, facilitating or interfering with the development of a division of labor, and specifying the channels of communication which can be used. The most efficient groups are those in which the rules are appropriate for the task, although, in general, cooperation results in more individual motivation, division of labor, effective intermember communication, friendliness, and group productivity. When group members expect to cooperate, any behavior which reflects individual "self-oriented" needs tends to disrupt the group. The differences between cooperation and competition have been demonstrated in laboratory games such as the "Prisoner's Dilemma."

A bystander witnessing someone in distress will usually follow the social norm prescribing altruistic behavior, especially if the helpless person is very dependent and others present also try to help. Helping behavior and interaction in bargaining games, like other forms of social behavior, can be seen as a process of social exchange in which individuals enter into new social relationship because they expect them to be rewarding and continue in old relationships because they find them rewarding.

When increasing stress is applied, groups, like individuals, tend to respond by a lag, then overcompensation, and finally collapse. A mild stress results in higher productivity than no stress or extreme stress. Motivation to perform is also higher when the task has a high degree of "reality." Members tend to recall tasks that are incomplete more often than those completed by themselves or a partner.

Chapter 12

COMMUNICATION NETWORK

IN LARGE MILITARY and industrial organizations, a subsegment of the organization often serves as an information-processing center. There the information is collated, displayed, evaluated, and decisions are made which affect the entire operating organization. Frequently some of the members involved are separated physically from each other and communicate by telephone and others devices in restricted networks. The frequency of concern with problems of communication in restricted networks has led to experimentive exploration of the properties of different sorts of networks.

The communication network is a factor in the situation which can be varied independently of the task or of the style of leadership in the group, although it is usually closely associated with it. When a task requires a particular type of communication network for optimum performance, the leader's style tends to place limits on the frequency, duration, and direction of member communications. However, all three variables—task, communication network, and leadership—are similar in that they are ways of manipulating the situation for the group by setting norms for the form and content of interaction.

In addition to its implications for the more general categories of interaction, other aspects of the communication network are discussed in this chapter. These other aspects include the effects of varying amounts of "feedback" and "'noise" in the network, the effects of the amount of participation on changing individual attitudes, the relationship between leader style and the limitations on the amount and distribution of communication, and the extent to which seating position represents an implicit communication network.

Reviews of the literature on communication networks are given by Glanzer and Glaser, 1959, 1961; Guetzkow, 1961; Shaw, 1964; Flament, 1965.

Relative Rates of Communication

Mechanical constrictions on communication, of course, constitute an extreme and obvious case of conditions that prevent the full and free interaction of each member with every other member. At one end of the continuum, subjects who are not allowed to communicate cannot be expected to have much effect on each other (Vinacke, 1957). But even in discussion groups where physical conditions of intercommunication are optimized, spatial location still plays some part. For example, members tend to address more communication to persons seated opposite to them at a table than to those next to them, presumably because of easier eye contact (Steinzor, 1950; Hearn, 1957). However, when the leaderless group is used as a technique for leader selection, seating position has little effect on final leadership ratings received by members (Bass and Klubeck, 1952). Presumably the difficulties of spatial location and interactive contact decrease as the size of the group decreases in a discussion situation. In a situation of this kind, the communication network is probably derived more from the expectations of the members than by other more mechanical considerations.

In free communication situations a gradient of activity rates among members is usually found rather than equal participation (Bales et al., 1951; Stephan and Mishler, 1952). Members who talk most generally also receive the most interaction (Miller and Butler, 1969). This is probably a result, in part, of the tendency for a remark made by one person to be answered by some other, who may then continue to address the person who just spoke. In ad hoc problem-solving groups about half the remarks are addressed to the group as a whole, and about half to particular other members, that is, in pair relationships (Bales et al., 1951). About half the total content is devoted to substantive contributions, while the other half is devoted to positive reactions, negative reactions, and questions. Both of these balances suggest that freely communicating groups devote about as much of their time to feedback (i.e., indications to the sender that the message has been received) as to specific problem-solving attempts. Low participators do not talk to each other as much as high participators talk to each other. The network of communication is thus in effect restricted more or less spontaneously by the members, so that links between low participators tend to drop out as size increases, especially above size seven. It appears to be generally true that status distinctions show a high positive correlation with amount of participation, although status based on popularity is not so highly related as status based on task criteria in task-oriented groups (Bales, 1953; Hurwitz, Zander, and Hymovitch, 1953; Bales and Slater, 1955). In free discussion groups the communication network and the network of interpersonal choice are interdependent, but also each is in some degree independently variable, so that the congruence is seldom perfect.

Centrality and Control

In a series of reports which systematically examine some features of the communication network, Shaw (1954a) found that a measure of centrality proposed by Bavelas did not permit measurement of quantitative differences among individuals in the group. For Bavelas the most central person in the group was the one who needed the least number of communication links to interact with all other group members. Instead of this measure, Shaw proposed a measure which takes into account the number of communication channels available to the individual and to the group, and the number of individuals for which a person is a relayer of information. Independence was found to account reasonably for experimental measures of morale (general satisfaction), number of messages used, and recognition of leadership. In another experiment with four-man groups in three controlled communication conditions, the wheel, the slash, and the circle (Shaw, 1954c; Gilchrist, Shaw, and Walker, 1954; see figure 39), centrality varied inversely with the time required to complete an activity and directly with individual morale, the number of items transmitted, and the probability that a person would be chosen as the leader. The problems used in these experiments are essentially individual problems, such as mathematical problems. The group is said to have completed the problem when each person in the network knows the answer. In general, leadership is more apt to emerge when there are large differences in the degree of centrality (Goldberg, 1955), especially if group members are told to direct all communications to the person in the center (Abrahamson and Smith, 1970). The central persons who have power are more satisfied with their position and are regarded as having high status in the group (Mulder, 1959a, 1960b; Watson, 1965; Watson and Bromberg, 1965; Erbe, 1966).

Similar results were obtained using four-man groups in star, slash, and "comcon" (all channels open) nets, with the additional finding that when the groups met once a day for 10 days all groups solved problems faster, sent fewer messages, and were better satisfied as time passed (Shaw and Rothschild, 1956).

Increasing the amounts of information given to a person has an effect similar to increasing his centrality index. Using a systematic rather than random distribution of information in a net has the effect of allowing the members to reach faster solutions, with fewer errors, and greater satisfaction since they can group the data in their messages (Shaw, 1956). However, in group tasks which require each man to perform a separate function, the most efficient distribution of information is one which permits each individual the most autonomy in reaching his own decision and putting it into effect (Lanzetta and Roby, 1956a).

It is also necessary for the central person in the network to reach a *decision* when the task calls for group participation. If the central person simply collects or transmits information and leaves the decision to some other member, his group will not be as effective (Mulder, 1959b).

The relationship between leader style and communication network is evident in a controlled communication experiment using the wheel, kite, and comcon nets, in which authoritarian (appointed) leadership resulted in better group performance than nonauthoritarian leadership (Shaw, 1955). In the authoritarian situation, morale was lower but evidence in terms of errors indicated that the quality of performance was better. Morale was related to the independence of action per-

Figure 39. Communication Networks Used in Experiments with Three- and Four-Man Groups

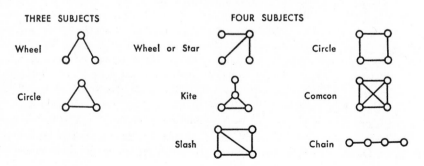

THREE SUBJECTS

Wheel

Circle

FOUR SUBJECTS

Wheel or Star

Kite

Slash

Circle

Comcon

Chain

mitted, while saturation, or the input and output requirements placed upon a position, was related to performance.

Personality versus Position in the Communication Network

Although *behavior* was conceptualized in chapter 1 as a compromise between the tendencies of *personality* and the expectations of *role,* relatively few pieces of evidence have been presented to indicate the results which may be expected from the interaction of personality and role. Some evidence is provided by two studies of communication networks which deal primarily with the area of control.

In the first study 10 four-man groups of college subjects solved three problems in a star communication network. Each group contained one subject who had been previously rated as highly ascendant, one who had been rated as being low on ascendance, and two who were moderately ascendant. The subjects had been previously screened from a larger population by the Guilford-Zimmerman Ascendance Scale; a high-scoring person would be expected to dominate the interaction. In some groups the highly ascendant person occupied the central position, and in other groups the central position was given to the person who was rated lowest on ascendance. In this case, the position in the network appeared to be the dominating factor since, after the first trial, the low ascendants in the center behaved like the highs and the highs in peripheral positions became more passive. In each case, the subject in the center was more satisfied (Berkowitz, 1956b).

In the second experiment 44 previously unacquainted college subjects in three-man groups each received notes which created variations in the centrality and autonomy of each subject. Autonomy in the network was measured by the subject's access to task-relevant information. Each of the subjects had high or low autonomy needs as measured by a paper-and-pencil test. After the experiment, the subjects who had been given positions of high autonomy were the most satisfied, especially when they had high autonomy needs. No differences in satisfaction appeared to accompany differences in centrality. However, a subject perceived another's performance as more valuable if the other person held a position more central than his own. Differences in the relative autonomy of positions seemed to have no effect on the perception of value (Trow, 1957). Here differences in the value of performance were measured by having each subject answer the question "If this were a commercial enterprise, how much do you think X should be paid in comparison with the person filling the position you had?" The subjects holding the more central positions were judged to be those who should receive more pay.

Another experiment reports the result of placing persons of the same personality type in all positions in the network and comparing their performance with that of groups composed of a contrasting personality type (Cohen and Foerst, 1968). Twelve five-man groups were formed of subjects who were repressers (persons who attempt to cope with anxiety through repression, denial, and rationalization), and twelve five-man groups were composed of subjects who were sensitizers (persons who are more maladjusted, with high manifest anxiety). Each group was given 15 trials in a wheel network performing common symbol problems, 15 trials in a completely connected network also performing common symbol problems, and 15 trials in a completely connected network performing story completion problems. The repressers developed appropriate problem-solving systems somewhat earlier, utilized their systems more efficiently, and exhibited significantly greater leadership continuity. Differences between represser and sensitizer groups in times taken to solve problems were significant in the wheel and following a network change, but not significant following a task change.

Communication between High- and Low-Status Members

The studies just mentioned show that positions in the communication network, especially those with one-way and limited connection restrictions, are related to frustration and antagonism on the part of the disadvantaged members and to satisfaction and leadership status for the central members. The disadvantaged members in peripheral positions are especially dissatisfied if the person in the center is of lower status (Johnson, Goodchilds, and Raven, 1972).

When member perceptions of status and possibilities for upward or downward mobility are experimentally established in a restricted network, the amount and kind of written communication initiated differ (Kelley, 1951). Persons who are led to believe that their job status is low are less well satisfied with their jobs and initiate more conjectures about the nature of the jobs at the high-status level. This is interpreted as the result of "phantasy" about upward mobility (Thibaut, 1950). They also initiate more communication with content irrelevant to the task, which is interpreted as a desire to escape from the position. The members who are led to believe they are in a higher status show evidence of constraint in addressing criticism of their job to lower-status members, and constraint in expressing confusion about the job to anyone. Members of control groups where no impression of status differences is established are more free in criticism of other members than are subjects in either of the two status-conscious conditions. The perception of possibility of upward mobility for the lower-status group increases the attractiveness of the job, and the perception of possible downward mobility for the higher-status group decreases the attractiveness. Low status with no possibility of rising and high status with the threat of falling are the variations which are most destructive of interlevel cohesion (Kelley, 1951; A. R. Cohen, 1958).

Proximity and Affection

The communication network as it is defined here refers to the channels of communication among members and subgroups of the group. These channels of communication are evident in residential groups, where spatial location of members relative to each other and probability of contact in the course of daily activity limit in a very tangible way who is likely to interact with whom.

The spatial arrangement of members with respect to each other and the probability of contact are in turn related to members' liking for each other (Festinger, Schachter, and Back, 1950; Wilner, Walkley, and Cook, 1952; Byrne and Buehler, 1955; Byrne, 1961b). In general, the attraction of persons to each other tends to be greater among those who are in spatial locations that promote interaction, and liking tends to decrease, sometimes turning to hostility, as physical distance increases (Merton, 1948; Danielsson, 1949; Lundberg, Hertzler, and Dickson, 1949; Homans, 1950; Sherif, 1951; Maisonneuve, Palmade, and Fourment, 1952; Simon, 1952).

On the other hand, once a subgroup has formed among those persons who are near each other, there is some tendency to symbolize and maintain social separation from other subgroups by maintenance of physical separation (Hughes, 1946). Liking, however, has complex determinants, as does the amount of interactive contact. Neither is a simple function of the other. Particularly in periods of conflict, the two may be "out of joint," since the amount of interaction with deviant members tends to increase in an attempt to influence them, and then to fall off if and when they are given up or rejected (Schachter, 1951). It would appear that some contact is a prerequisite to the rejection or acceptance of a person into another person's sphere of involvement.

The empirical connection between the amount of liking and amount of interaction found in larger groups also appears to some extent in small discussion groups. Pairs of friends spent more time in spontaneous interactions in a pair discussion situation than did pairs of nonfriends, and the members of friendship pairs were more nearly alike in the amounts of interaction initiated to each other (Potashin, 1946). In another study, groups set up to encourage intermember interaction (group-centered) showed a higher average level of liking for each other than leader-centered groups where member-to-member interaction was lower (Bovard, 1951b).

Feedback in Restricted Networks

In a situation where there is one-way communication and the receiver of the information is given no opportunity to "feed back" acknowledgments, questions, or negative reactions to the sender, accuracy and confidence are reduced for both sender and receiver (Leavitt and Mueller, 1951). An initial reaction of hostility on the part of the receiver toward the sender tends to appear. Accuracy can improve with time, but not as rapidly as with feedback, and depends more on the sender than the receiver. An initial period with free feedback appreciably improves subsequent communication without feedback. More time is required with the feedback condition, but with experience the amount of time decreases. Receivers who are permitted to communicate back to a person who has sent them an act of hostility show more postexperimental friendliness to the instigator than those not permitted to communicate (Thibaut and Coules, 1952). Apparently one-way communication prevents not only expressive catharis but also the opportunity for building new understanding and norms by which the members manage their social relationship and their process of communication. From this basic impairment other problems may develop.

Another experiment demonstrates the results of extreme conditions of lack of communication and feedback. Members of 30 six-man groups were given a problem which required closing their eyes and then raising a number of fingers so that the total would equal a number (e.g., six, five, or some smaller number) which the experimenter had previously announced. The subjects were placed in "communication networks" by being seated in a circle, seated at a table with a pair of members on two opposite sides and one member on each of the other sides, or seated in three rows of three, two, and one. To solve a problem requiring a total of five or fewer fingers, the subjects either would have had to have individually decided upon the same method of "cooperating" by having members in certain positions in the "network" raise one finger while others raised no fingers or would have had to reach the solution by chance. Twice as many subjects used a chance type of solution as used a solution based on seating position. Few were able to actually solve the problem using either method (Berg, 1955).

Some Effects of Certain Communication Networks

An experiment by Leavitt (1951; Bavelas, 1950, 1952) provides an example of some of the effects which certain communication networks can have on group performance.

This approach, stemming from the imaginative work of Bavelas (1948), begins by considering persons as self-contained, acting entities, each in a cell, like a phone booth. They can communicate with others according to the manner in which the booths are hooked up to one another. Any one of the possible patterns of linkage of a given number of such units can be selected as a communication network. The experimenter then examines the effects of a given network on task performance and the social-emotional relations of the members occupying each position.

In this specific investigation, 100 male undergraduates serving as subjects were divided into 20 groups of five men each. Each group was composed in one of four types of network, making a total of five groups for each network. These networks are shown in figure 40, with the lines indicating two-way linkages in all cases. The nature of the network for any group was unknown to the subjects at the beginning of the experiment. All a specific individual knew was to whom he could send messages and from whom he could receive them. The idea of the overall network was gradually discovered in the experience of the task. It may be seen that positions differed with respect to how many lines of communication fed in to them, and how far (in terms of number of links) they were from other positions. This notion may be termed *centrality* of position. The most central position is the one closest to all other positions. The researchers hypothesized that if a group were working on a problem which required the collection, pooling, processing, and redistribution of information held by all members, both network efficiency (in making rapid, correct decisions) and behavioral differences for various positions would be related to centrality.

Centrality is a measure of one's closeness to all other group members and hence is a measure of the availability of the information necessary for solving the problem. Availability of information should affect behavior in turn by determining one's role in the group. An individual who can rapidly collect information should see himself and be seen by others in a different way from an individual to whom vital information is

Figure 40. Experimental Communication Networks

Circle   Chain   Y   Wheel

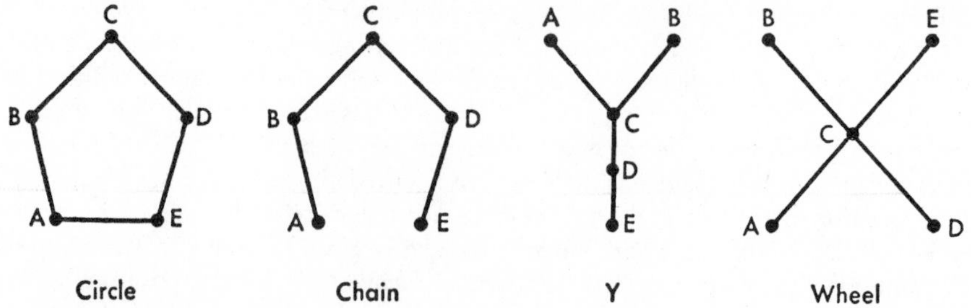

Source: Harold J. Leavitt, "Some Effects of Certain Communication Patterns on Group Performance," *Journal of Abnormal and Social Psychology* 46 (1951): 40. Copyright 1951 by the American Psychological Association. Reprinted by permission of the author and the publisher.

not accessible. Such roles should be different in the extent to which they permit independence of action, in the responsibility they entail, and in the monotony they impose. Finally, differences in independence, in responsibility, and in monotony should affect the speed, the accuracy, the aggressiveness, and the flexibility of behavior.[1]

The problem to be solved by the group members consisted of discovering which of six possible symbols they held in common. For a single trial each member held a card bearing five symbols. The missing (sixth) symbol, which was different for each member, and the common symbol are indicated in figure 41. Communication was restricted to the passing of notes through mail chutes in an arrangement of partitions corresponding to the apparatus in figure 42. There was no other communication between members. When a subject thought he knew the common symbol, he pressed one of six buttons in his cell, lighting a corresponding light in the experimental booth. When all five members had depressed their buttons, the trial was ended.

Information was gathered by recording the number and paths of messages sent, the time required for solution, the number of errors, the answers of post-meeting questionnaires, and the content of the messages themselves

In general, the wheel network operated in the same manner in each of the five groups which employed it. Men on the periphery sent information to the center, where a decision was made and sent back out. The Y also gave the man in the most central position the most decision-making authority. The chain sent information in from both ends to the center, the decision being sent out in both directions. This mode of operation was slower in establishing itself than the Y or wheel, but was consistent when once it was hit upon.

A measure of the fastest single trial of each group indicates that the wheel network at its peak was faster than the circle (see table 33). The number of messages sent by each group during a correct trial was greater for the circle than for other networks. Although more errors were made in the circle than any other network, a greater percentage of these errors were detected and corrected by the group before the trial ended.

On the questionnaires which were administered after the group had completed the full series of 15 trials, subjects were asked if the group had a leader and, if so, in which position. For all networks, the frequency of affirmative responses increased in the order circle, chain, Y, and wheel. The amount of agreement as to the position held by the leader was in the same order. Some networks were more readily perceived by their members than others. Sixteen subjects in the wheel groups reproduced the correct network, while only one circle member recognized the circle network. Satisfaction with the "job in the group" decreased in the order circle, chain, Y, and wheel, with circle members being more satisfied than wheel members. From the analysis of messages sent, it appeared that circle members sent more informational messages and more answers than did members of other networks. They also recognized more of their errors.

The data indicate that persons in the most central positions in the Y, wheel, and chain were more satisfied than anyone in a circle position. Persons in peripheral positions in these networks enjoyed their job less than those in any circle position.

1. Harold J. Leavitt, "Some Effects of Certain Communication Patterns on Group Performance," *Journal of Abnormal and Social Psychology* 46 (1951): 40–41. Copyright 1951 by the American Psychological Association. Reprinted by permission of the author and the publisher.

Figure 41. Symbol Distribution by Trial

| Trial No. | Symbol Missing From: | | | | | Common Symbol |
	White	Red	Brown	Yellow	Blue	
1	△	◇	✳	○	▢	✚
2	◇	○	▢	△	✚	✳
3	✚	✳	▢	△	◇	○
4	▢	◇	△	✳	✚	○
5	○	✳	✚	△	▢	◇
6	△	○	▢	✳	◇	✚
7	▢	✚	○	◇	△	✳
8	◇	✳	▢	✚	○	△
9	✳	◇	▢	△	○	✚
10	✚	○	▢	✳	◇	△
11	○	✚	△	◇	✳	▢
12	✳	○	▢	△	✚	◇
13	△	○	◇	▢	✚	✳
14	▢	◇	✚	✳	△	○
15	✚	○	▢	◇	✳	△

Six Symbols Used: ○ △ ◇ ▢ ✚ ✳

Source: Harold J. Leavitt, "Some Effects of Certain Communication Patterns of Group Performance," *Journal of Abnormal and Social Psychology* 46 (1951): 40. Copyright 1951 by the American Psychological Association. Reprinted by permission of the author and the publisher.

Leavitt grossly characterizes the kinds of differences, in this way: "the circle, one extreme, is active, leaderless, unorganized, erratic and yet is enjoyed by its members. The wheel at the other extreme, is less active, has a distinct leader, is well and stably organized, is less erratic, and yet is unsatisfying to most of its members" (1951, p. 46).

In drawing conclusions from such an experiment, it is necessary to bear in mind the limitations clearly outlined by the author in terms of task and group size. In a task of this sort, self-conception in role and status differentiation are perceptibly related to the amount of information and distributive power a position has relative to another position. Since the task required pooling information from all positions, successful action depended on subordinating individual con-

Figure 42. Apparatus for Communication Network Experiment

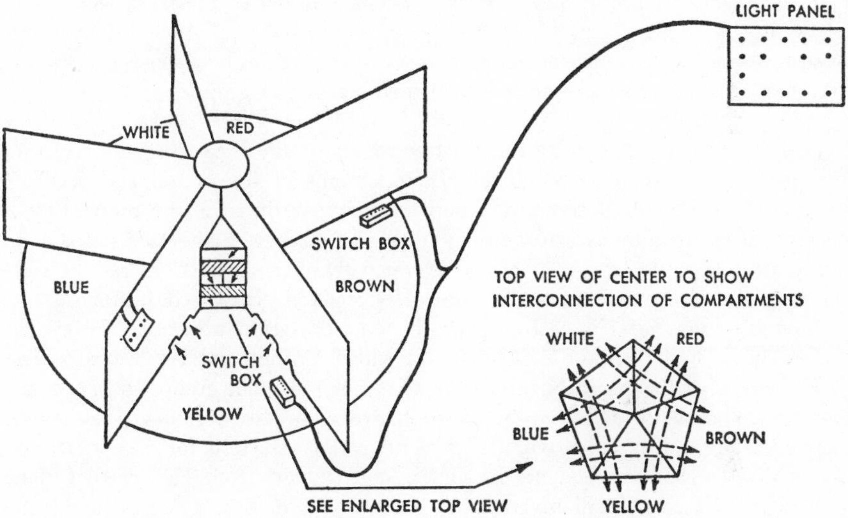

Source: Harold J. Leavitt, "Some Effects of Certain Communication Patterns on Group Performance," *Journal of Abnormal and Social Psychology* 46 (1951): 41. Copyright 1951 by the American Psychological Association. Reprinted by permission of the author and the publisher.

Table 33. Fastest Single Correct Trial for Each Communication Network

FASTEST SINGLE CORRECT TRIAL (IN SECONDS)	COMMUNICATION NETWORKS				
	Circle	Chain	Y	Wheel	Diff.	P
Mean	50.4	53.2	35.4	32.0	Ci-W	<.01
Median	55.0	57.0	32.0	36.0	Ch-W	<.10
Range	44–59	19–87	22–53	20–41	Ci-Y	<.05
					Ch-Y	<.20

Source: Harold J. Leavitt, "Some Effects of Certain Communication Patterns on Group Performance," *Journal of Abnormal and Social Psychology* 46 (1951). Copyright 1951 by the American Psychological Association. Reprinted by permission of the author and the publisher.

tributions in the interest of the group goal. In another task, e.g., one emphasizing other types of contribution, or maximizing opposition, the observed correlation of satisfaction with centrality might not be found. It is clear, however, that differences in accuracy, total activity, leader emergence, and satisfaction are markedly affected by the arrangement of communication channels in the group.

In one repetition of this experiment, the central person became the leader, but other differences were not significant (Hirota, 1953). In another repetition of the experiment with three-man groups, the members in the wheel network used less time to solve the problem of the common symbol than did members in a circle network, although the difference was not statistically significant. However, members in the wheel took longer to solve more complex problems which required simple arithmetical computations (Shaw, 1954b). For an even more complex task, that of the discussion of a human-relations problem, a star network required more time than a slash network, and a slash more than a comcon network (all channels open). No differences in satisfaction or number of messages were found (Shaw, Rothschild, and Strickland, 1957). It is possible that in solving problems requiring some skill the wheel network is more efficient only when the person in the center of the net is the most skillful member of the group.

In a similar experiment (S. L. Smith, 1951), the circle network permitted members to adapt more readily to a change requiring the breaking and relearning of a previously established set. The greater amount of interaction and feedback which characterizes the decentralized network seems to increase the probability of checking gross unanimous errors, to increase adaptability in the face of new demands for relearning, and to increase average member satisfaction, but at some cost in quantity of messages, duplication of effort, and general confusion.

Cultural differences in performance in communication networks are evident in a variation of the Leavitt experiment in which Yoruba and Ibo students from the University of Ibadan in Nigeria were tested in four-man groups in two conditions: wheel network followed by circle network, or circle followed by wheel. Their average number of messages sent, time, and satisfaction for each trial were compared with those of students in similar experiments from Haverford College in the United States, the University of Cape Town in South Africa, and three colleges in the Philippines (Hare, 1969).

The largest differences appeared between the United States groups and the Nigerian groups in the wheel and the United States groups and the Philippines groups in the circle. The students in the United States groups sent fewer messages and took less time to solve the problems in both types of network and tended to give lower ratings on satisfaction when they were not in the center of the wheel. With the exception of the Yoruba in Nigeria, all groups sent fewer messages but took more time to solve the problems in the wheel than in the circle. In all nationality groups the average member was more satisfied in the circle than he was in the noncentral positions in the wheel.

Nigerian groups apparently took longer to solve the problems, especially in the wheel, because they were more likely to interpret the task as one in which each individual should solve the problem for himself rather than cooperate and accept the answer from another group member. Since this was not true at the University of Cape Town in South Africa, it was evident that the difference lay in a "non-European" approach to problem-solving, rather than simply living on the continent of Africa.

In the Philippines the greater number of messages in the circle and the higher level of satisfaction with the task both seemed to reflect a concern for "smooth interpersonal relations," which led group members to continually check the extent of their agreement and understanding and to inhibit the overt expression of negative comment.

Additional research with a focus on differences between wheel and circle networks includes Mohanna and Argyle, 1960; A. M. Cohen, 1961, 1962; Cohen, Bennis, and Wolkon, 1961, 1962; Lawson, 1964a, 1964b; Morrissette, 1966; Davis and Hornseth, 1967; Burgess, 1968b; Vanparijs, 1968; Burgess, 1969.

Additional research with other types of communication networks and variations in task includes Shelly and Gilchrist, 1958; Flament, 1961; Lyle, 1961; Lawson, 1965; Faucheux and Mackenzie, 1966; McConville and Hemphill, 1966; Abric, 1971; Perju-Liiceanu, 1971; Bell, Cheney, and Mayo, 1972; Schneider and Delaney, 1972; Snadowsky, 1974.

Articles which provide mathematical models or other simulations of communication networks include Bavelas, 1959; Leavitt and Knight, 1963; McWhinney, 1964; Morrissette, Pearson, and Switzer, 1965; Burgess, 1968a; Barnes, 1969; Moxley and Moxley, 1974.

Developing a Task Hierarchy

The Leavitt experiment was repeated (Guetzkow and Simon, 1955; Guetzkow and Dill, 1957; Guetzkow, 1960) with a modification of the design which made it possible to study the development of the task hierarchy within each type of communication network. Using the same problem of discovering the common symbol on a set of cards, five-man groups were tested in wheel, circle, and all-channel networks. Between each trial the group members were allowed a two-minute period in which to organize the group. In the wheel, the activity during this two-minute period was centered on discovering the organization which was already present, while in the all-channel and circle networks the members sought to develop an efficient hierarchy. In the circle the members tended to select a three-level hierarchy, and in the all-channel group the members formed either a two- or three-level hierarchy (see figure 43). As soon as the members of a group had worked out a hierarchy, they were able to do better in the task. Fewer task messages and more social-emotional messages were sent after the hierarchy was established. On the first few trials more messages were sent to those subjects who gave good information or who provided the right answer. As these channels began to be used more than others, they were gradually incorporated into the developing communication network. The all-channel networks were the slowest to establish hierarchies because the members had to make a selection from so many channels.

The importance of developing an appropriate decision structure is also evident in two other experiments. In one experiment 13 four-person groups were placed in a wheel network and 13 in a circle network. Each group was given complex problems to solve. The wheel was found to be more effective only when the members had developed a decision structure (Mulder, 1960a). In the other experiment the status of the persons in the positions in the wheels and circles was varied so that the circles had either all first-year college students or all graduate students and the wheels had a graduate student in the center with first-year students in the peripheral positions or vice versa. As a result neither centralization nor decentralization per se resulted in different levels of group efficiency and member satis-

Figure 43. Task Hierarchies in Wheel, Circle, and All-Channel Networks

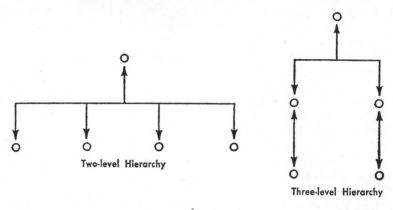

Source: Harold Guetzkow and W. R. Dill, "Factors in the Organizational Development of Task-oriented Groups," *Sociometry* 20 (1957). Reprinted by permission of the authors and the American Sociological Association.

faction, but rather the congruence or incongruence of network structure and previously existing status distinctions among members (Moore, Johnson, and Arnold, 1972).

Noise

The differences between networks become more pronounced as "noise" is introduced into the communication channels. Here *noise* is used to refer to anything which interrupts the messages sent (Heise and Miller, 1951) or makes it difficult to understand and solve the problem, such as the introduction of irrelevant information (Shaw, 1958a).

In one experiment random noise was introduced into one- and two-way telephone circuits connecting three members as a shishing sound that had all frequencies of vibration present at equal intensities. This type of noise in the communication network served to heighten the differences between networks which were related to differences in group task. The group members in each network were given three kinds of problems to solve: (1) a comparatively stereotyped and unimaginative exchange of isolated words, (2) the formation of anagrams from a given word, and (3) sentence construction.

Performance on a task calling for individual mental activity where the products were not highly interdependent but simply additive(making the largest possible number of anagrams out of a given word) was little affected by the type of network or amount of noise (Heise and Miller, 1951). An information collection task (completing a list of words, each subject having part of the list) was performed most rapidly in a network where each member was connected to each other with two-way communication. However, a task requiring assembly plus coordination (completing a sentence in proper order, each subject having part of the words) was performed most rapidly in a centralized network where a central person was furnished two-way communication with each of the two others but no connection was provided between the two peripheral members. A one-way closed chain (no feedback, no centralization) was, in general, prone to error, was inefficient in terms of time and number of messages, and suffered most with the introduction of noise. Members were most satisfied in the central position and felt "left out and unsure of themselves" when in an isolated position with no feedback facilities.

To counteract the effects of "noise" in the information-theory sense, groups repeat the same information several times as a means of reducing error (Christie, Luce, and Macy, 1952; Macy, Christie, and Luce, 1953; Longhurst and Siegel, 1973). Error is further reduced when members' comments are audible and understandable (Marquis, Guetzkow, and Heyns, 1951).

Participation and Attitude Change

In a lecture as opposed to a free discussion, two-way interaction is more or less drastically limited. Although the limitation is accepted by the audience, the results are in some ways similar to forced one-way communication. A whole series of studies shows that if one wishes to change attitudes and the subsequent behavior of a group, discussion and decision where all members participate as directly as possible tend to be more effective than "enlightenment" or "persuasion" by the lecture method, or by an unqualified order from above (see chapter 2).

Job and rate changes in a factory setting are accomplished with less quitting of workers, less aggression toward supervisors, less drop in production, faster recovery, and higher final rate of production if the workers are allowed to participate in the changeover decision (Coch and French, 1948). The effect of workers' participation is especially marked if the decisions are important, the context is relevant, the participation is considered legitimate, and there is no resistance to change (French, Israel, and As, 1960).

The group decision method was also found to be effective in raising the production rate of a group of sewing-machine operators on individual piecework, whereas attention and encouragement from the plant psychologist proved to be ineffective (Bavelas, reported in Maier, 1946). Among college students and housewives, group decision resulted in substantial changes in the consumption of unfamiliar foods, whereas lectures had little or no effect (Klisurich, reported in Lewin, 1947c, and Willerman, 1953). In all of these cases, a change is made to a mode of behavior or performance that presumably is already within the available repertoire of the group members and does not require learning. The mode of behavior can be made the chosen response simply by the development of new group norms to supersede the currently dominant ones. Where learning of new technical content rather than performance or attitude change is required, the results are not so clear. Early studies of the lecture versus discussion in college courses display contradictory reports (Roseborough, 1953). Students participate more in permissive class sections and find them more interesting and enjoyable, but prefer directive classes for exam preparation (Wispe, 1951), although neither method may result in better exam grades (Zeleny, 1940a). Apparently the purposes and values of the members govern to some degree the reactions they will have to a more or less constricted participation procedure (McCurdy and Eber, 1953). Some students seem to learn better under one method, others under the other method (Wispe, 1953).

Constrictions adopted freely by the members in order to accomplish a purpose they value are probably less frustrating than those imposed without choice. Nevertheless, an effective change of norms probably requires knowledge of a new consensus, which can best be achieved by full participation with free feedback.

The Leader's Influence

The attitudes and behavior of the leader apparently can influence the communication network appreciably, even when there are no mechanical constrictions. Indeed, this is one way of looking at the experiments on authoritarian and democratic leadership (Lewin and Lippitt, 1938). Even when there are restrictions, the leader can try to overcome them. When leaders had been instructed to be either authoritarian or democratic in a communication network experiment and were allowed time for organization, the authoritarian leader imposed a structure on a decentralized network and the democratic leader worked to overcome the restrictions of a centralized network (Snadowsky, 1972). In another experiment, leaders in a wheel network who had been chosen by the group continued to act as leaders when the group was changed to a circle network (Cohen and Bennis, 1961).

A "permissive" sort of leadership, which consists mainly in management of the discussion process, without interjection of the leader's opinion (as compared to the nonparticipating "observing" leader), operates to protect minorities from social influence and increases the probability that the single member with the correct answer to the problem will be able to convince the majority (Maier and Solem, 1952; Cohen, 1968). As a result, the minority members who are wrong tend to stay wrong, but the average effect over all groups is definitely to increase the number of right answers through what amounts to a greater error-checking ability.

In a comparison of a "supervisory" type of leader, where the leader is instructed to stay out of the discussion, and a "participatory" type, where the leader injects his opinion as well as tries to insure equal participation for all members, participatory leadership resulted in more group agreement, greater and more permanent influence of the leader on the members, and more interest and enjoyment in the task for both leaders and followers (Preston and Heintz, 1949; Hare, 1953). It appears that members are more satisfied when the leader keeps the communication network balanced and also participates himself. Indeed, in some if not most situations, the leader who expresses no opinions creates an anomalous and frustrating state of affairs. Lack of leadership is used as a therapeutically intended disturbance in some types of group therapy (Bion, 1948a). In business, industry, and government, too, there appears to be a general expectation that the socially designated leader, the conference chairman, should be the sole major behavior leader (Berkowitz, 1953). Leadership sharing by members other than the designated leader tends to result in a decrease in group cohesiveness and satisfaction, except when problems are urgent. This holds when leaders are more or less permissive and even when the secondary leadership is supportive. It seems definitely indicated than the communication network and the gradient of participation set limits on the degree to which new norms can be formed and the degree to which sensitive regulation of the process can take place. The effects of constriction of communication within a given period are in turn dependent upon the values and expectations of the members.

Seating Position

For most of the experiments summarized in this chapter the communication net was *explicitly* imposed by the experimenter. However, communication networks are also *implicit* in the seating arrangements in discussion groups and in other everyday settings, where they have similar effects on patterns of social interaction (Kaminski and Osterkamp, 1962; Patterson, 1968; Casey and Solomon, 1971–1972; Broekmann and Möller, 1973). The overall seating arrangement is directly related to the task. If the task calls for face-to-face interaction in a group discussion, persons usually choose to sit relatively close together (Felipe, 1966) in a circle (Batchelor and Goethals, 1972) or in a semicircle facing the discussion leader (Hendrick, Giesen, and Coy, 1974). If there are only two people, they sit opposite each other (Sommer, 1962).

In a social session when there is no central task and conversations do not have to be heard by all, group members are more likely to turn to the person next to them for informal discussion (Hare and Bales, 1963). This is especially true if one member of the pair is a man and the other a woman (Tyler, Waag, and George, 1972) and in cafeterias or other informal settings, where members of a pair tend to choose seats at right angles at the corner of a table (Sommer, 1959, 1965). When privacy is desirable, as when studying in the library (Sommer, 1967; Desportes and Lesieur, 1971–1972; Eastman and Harper, 1971), eating alone in a restaurant (Barash, 1972), or using a public toilet (Brandeis, 1972), individuals have been observed choosing seats which provide for maximum privacy. If their personal space is invaded, they are likely to retreat (Fry and Willis, 1971; McDowell, 1972; Barash, 1973); individuals will also try to avoid invading another's personal space even if the other person appears to be blocking their way (Barefoot, Hoople, and McClay, 1972).

Since it is customary for formal group leaders to occupy a position at the head of the conference table or in some other clearly identified position, persons who wish to assume leadership in a group will tend to occupy the more central and visible positions, and those who occupy these positions, regardless of personal characteristics, will tend to become leaders (Sommer, 1961; Strodtbeck and Hook, 1961; Howells and Becker, 1962; Hare and Bales, 1963; Lott and Sommer, 1967; Ward, 1968; DeLong, 1970a, 1970b, 1971; Pellegrini, 1971; Rosenthal and DeLong, 1972; DeLong, 1973; Heckel, 1973).

The proximity of seating position is clearly related to attraction (Korner and Misra, 1967). If individuals wish to come closer to someone emotionally, they tend to come closer physically (King, 1964; Rosenfeld, 1965; Cook, 1970; Mehrabian and Diamond, 1971b; Allgeier and Byrne, 1973), but not too close (Boucher, 1972). If they wish to avoid someone, they leave an empty seat (Campbell, Kruskal, and Wallace, 1966; Moore and Feller, 1971) or select a seat which does not face another person (Mehrabian and Diamond, 1971a; Holahan, 1972).

The seat one chooses is only one indicator of the use of personal space. Whether one is seated, standing, or lying down, proximity and other aspects of body position provide nonverbal indicators of all dimensions of social interaction. The literature on personal space has been reviewed by Evans and Howard (1973) and Pedersen and Shears (1973). In a typical experiment the experimenter asks the subjects to come to his office for an interview and then notes how far away the subject stands or sits during the interview. In field observations, observers note how far apart people stand while waiting in queues, talking at parties, or lying on the beach. In general individuals come closer if they have a positive relationship and keep their distance if the relationship is negative or if there are marked status differences. Females usually are comfortable at closer distances than men, and ethnic groups differ in the distance for normal conversation. Examples of research on personal space include Little, 1965; Gottheil, Corey, and Paredes, 1968; Little, 1968; Dosey and Meisels, 1969; Baxter, 1970; Meisels and Canter, 1970; Patterson and Sechrest, 1970; Pellegrini and Empey, 1970; Aiello and Jones, 1971; Byrne, Baskett, and Hodges, 1971; Dabbs, 1971; Holahan and Levinger, 1971; Jones, 1971; Meisels and Dosey, 1971; Aiello and Cooper, 1972; Duke and Nowicki, 1972; Edwards, 1972; Heshka and Nelson, 1972; Karabenick and Meisels, 1972; Knowles, 1972; Nowicki and Duke, 1972; Pedersen and Heaston, 1972; Rawls et al., 1972; Rodgers, 1972; Thayer and Alban, 1972; Bailey, Hartnett, and Glover, 1973; Bauer, 1973; Bowerman, 1973a; Cozby, 1973a; Dabbs, Fuller, and Carr, 1973; Haase and Markey, 1973; Heilweil, 1973; Jones and Aiello, 1973; Leginski and Izzett, 1973; Newman and Pollack, 1973; Pedersen, 1973a, 1973b, 1973c, 1973d; Sewell and Heisler, 1973; Stratton, Tekippe, and Flick, 1973; Tesch, Huston, and Indenbaum, 1973; D. R. Thomas, 1973; Baum, Riess, and O'Hara, 1974; Naus and Eckenrode, 1974; Nesbitt and Steven, 1974; Scherer, 1974; Tedesco and Fromme, 1974.

In common with other animals, people can become attached to a particular area and attempt to defend their territory from invaders (Martindale, 1971; Austin and Bates, 1974; Edney and Jordan-Edney, 1974; Sundstrom and Altman, 1974). In children's groups the defense may involve actual fighting (Esser, 1973); however, adults may defend an area by using personal "markers." For example, a student in a library who wants to have a table to himself may choose a central seat and then place books, sweaters, sandwiches, or other personal "markers" around the table to give the impression that the space is fully occupied (Sommer and Becker, 1969; Becker and Mayo, 1971; Hoppe, Greene, and Kenny, 1972; Becker, 1973). When a person's right to control a territory is legitimized, he is given "jurisdiction" over the territory (Roos, 1968). Territoriality, like other defenses, is more likely to appear in groups of persons who are isolated for a long period of time (Altman and Haythorn, 1967a).

Summary

Although mechanical restrictions on communication and seating position will prevent the free interaction between all members of a discussion group, a gradient of activity rates among members is typical even where "free" communication is allowed. A few individuals receive communications from almost everyone in the group, since low participators do not talk to each other as much as they do to high participators. When communication is restricted, the person in the center of the network tends to become the leader and the most satisfied member. Once status differences are perceived by the members, differences in communication content up and down the status hierarchy may result.

Proximity in the communication network tends to increase intermember attraction. However, if there is no opportunity for "feedback" between members who are close to each other, hostility may appear and efficiency in problem-solving declines. In a comparison of five-man groups in circle, chain, Y, and wheel networks, Leavitt found that the circle, at one extreme, was active, leaderless, unorganized, erratic, and yet enjoyed by its members. The wheel, at the other extreme, was less active, had a distinct leader, was organized, less erratic, and yet unsatisfying to most of its members. Cultural differences in performance are evident, since Nigerian subjects were more likely to try to solve the problem individually while Philippine subjects emphasized smooth interpersonal relations. Given time to organize the group, subjects in an all-channel or circle network will develop either a two- or three-level hierarchy for more efficient problem-solving.

The introduction of "noise" in the communication network is most disruptive when the task requires cooperation and the accurate exchange of information. To counteract the effects of noise, groups use redundant coding as a means of reducing error.

When an individual lectures to a group, the effects may be similar to forced one-way communication. As a result, discussion and decision in a group with full participation and free feedback tend to be more effective in changing attitudes or behavior than the lecture method. In a similar way, the contrasting "authoritarian" and "democratic" leadership styles may be seen as different ways of controlling the communication net. However, the satisfaction of the followers in either situation depends upon their prior expectations for the leader's role.

Group members arrange their seating pattern according to the nature of the task. Leaders are given a central position, and friends sit closer together. Women are usually comfortable at closer distances than men, and ethnic groups differ in the distance for normal conversation. Individuals may defend their "personal space" by placing "markers" in adjacent positions.

Chapter 13

LEADERSHIP

THE LEADERSHIP IN A small group can be varied by selecting an individual with a given set of personality characteristics or by training an individual to perform a given set of behaviors. Variations in leader style will produce the greatest effect on interaction if selection and training are combined. In this chapter the general *traits* of leaders as well as the *functions* of leadership for which an individual might be trained will be summarized. Since leader selection is of particular importance to the armed forces, many of the studies of small group leadership have been made with military personnel. A leaderless group discussion has been used to predict leader potential for a variety of tasks. However, differences in the skills required for leadership in manual and intellectual tasks have led to the development of a number of situational tests and assessment techniques. Many of the effects of differences in the structure, size, and communication network of a group which also place differing demands on the leader have been discussed in some detail in previous chapters and will only be reviewed briefly.

Although in most groups a single individual has the most power and authority and is recognized as the formal leader, the leadership functions may be divided formally or informally among several group members. A common division of labor is that of having a *task leader* who is primarily concerned with task performance and a *social-emotional leader* or best-liked man who is primarily concerned with affectional relationships and member satisfaction.

Books and articles which review leadership theory and research include Browne and Cohn, 1958; Bellows, 1959; Cartwright, 1959; Bass, 1960a, 1961c; Bennis, 1961b; Criswell, 1961; Hemphill, 1961; Petrullo and Bass, 1961; Tannenbaum, Weschler, and Massarik, 1961; Beal, Bohlen, and Raudabaugh, 1962; Hollander, 1964; Hopkins, 1964; Short and Strodtbeck, 1965; Mann, 1966; Gibb, 1968, 1969; Hollander and Julian, 1969; Heald, Romano, and Georgiady, 1970; Kunczik, 1972; Silvi and Trentini, 1972; Stogdill, 1974.

Leadership Traits

The variety of traits which a leader may have is the same as that of any other group member, except that the leader is usually found to have a higher rating on each "good" trait. While correlations between "good" personality traits and leadership are generally positive, they are rarely large. As a result, only a little of the

278

variance in leader behavior can be accounted for in this way (Gibb, 1954). There are indications that certain traits such as intelligence, enthusiasm, dominance, self-confidence, social participation, and equalitarianism are frequently found to characterize leaders (Chevaleva-Ianovskaia and Sylla, 1929; Goodenough, 1930; Partridge, 1934; Zeleny, 1939a; Gibb, 1947; Green, 1948; Stogdill, 1948; Van Dusen, 1948; Martin, Gross, and Darley, 1952; Bass et al., 1953; Borgatta, 1954; Cattell and Stice, 1954; Hollander, 1954; Olmsted, 1957; Titus and Hollander, 1957; Gold, 1958; Bartlett, 1959a; Beer et al., 1959; Borg, 1960; Cattell and Stice, 1960; Showel, 1960; Bass, 1961b; Campbell and Damarin, 1961; Gibb, 1961; Hamblin, Miller, and Wiggins, 1961; Kipnis and Lane, 1962; Newport, 1962; Palmer, 1962a, 1962b; Kirkhart, 1963; McClintock, 1963; Rychlak, 1963; Armilla, 1964; Nelson, 1964b; Poitou, 1964; Rudraswamy, 1964; Dubno, 1965; Gordon and Medland, 1965a; Wolin and Terebinski, 1965; Kanungo, 1966; Megargee, Bogart, and Anderson, 1966; Geis, 1968; Streufert, Streufert, and Castore, 1968; Hacker and Gaitz, 1970; Olson and Smith, 1970; Harrison, Rawls, and Rawls, 1971; Mitchell, 1971; Vertreace and Simmons, 1971; Smith and Cook, 1973; Sorrentino, 1973; Zigon and Cannon, 1974). Usually, however, the relation of the trait to the leadership role is more meaningful if consideration is given to the detailed nature of the role and the characteristics of the followers, as was the case in the experiment in which high- or low-authoritarian leaders were placed in groups with high- or low-authoritarian followers (see chapter 8). (For additional examples see Dubno, 1963; Mulder and Stemerding, 1963; Clifford and Cohn, 1964; Burke, 1965; Geier, 1967; Messe, Aronoff, and Wilson, 1972.)

Although potential leaders tend to have more of all positive attributes than any of the members in their group, they cannot be so extreme that they become deviates. In one college, for example, the well-rounded man and campus leader was usually a "B" student. The "straight-A" man who excelled in nothing else was considered a "grind," who might even be branded as an outcast if he was suspected of being a "curve-wrecker," one who does so well that all the other members of the class receive poor grades by comparison (Davie and Hare, 1956). Or, to take an example which occurs over and over again in research on groups, the person who does most of talking wins most of the decisions and becomes the leader (Terman, 1904; Belyaeff, 1930; Bass, 1949; Strodtbeck, 1951; Bales, 1953; Borgatta, 1954; March, 1956; Lana, Vaughan, and McGinnies, 1960; Jaffee and Lucas, 1969; Lucas and Jaffee, 1969; Wood, 1972a; Hadley and Jacob, 1973; Levin, 1973; Regula and Julian, 1973; B. Schneider, 1973; Stang, 1973), *unless* he talks so much that he antagonizes the other group members. In a similar fashion, leaders of small discussion group of college students were not the most physically attractive members of the groups (Archer, 1973).

Considering total personality as a cluster of traits, a common finding in research, particularly with children's groups, is that there are two basic personality types among leaders. Some are *self-oriented* (authoritarian), rather hostile persons with a driving need to be in the center of the group's activities, while others are *group-oriented* (equalitarian) persons who are able to reduce tension in a group, work toward a group goal, and take a follower role when it is appropriate (Parten, 1933a; Pigors, 1935; Anderson, 1939; Hare, 1957). However, leaders who emerge in leaderless group discussions tend to be more authoritarian in their behavior than leaders who are appointed (Carter et al., 1951). Presumably this occurs because more dominating behavior is required to establish a position of leadership in a group than to maintain one (Hare, 1957). In laboratory groups, leaders who are "elected" gain more acceptance from their followers than those who appear to "take over" (Raven and French, 1958a, 1958b; French and Raven, 1959; Blake and Mouton, 1961b; Goldman and Fraas, 1965; Julian, Hollander, and Regula, 1969; Read, 1974).

A further indication of the behavior of authoritarian leaders in adult groups is reported in a study of 39 three-man air crews in training (Ziller, 1959). Each crew leader was given a chance to throw dice to evade part of the crew's training. Only nine threw the dice, i.e., assumed responsibility for group action. These leaders were less concerned about differing with the opinions of their group members, had higher F Scale scores, and were more highly motivated. Additional references to the personality characteristics of leaders are given in chapters 2, 3, and 8.

Since the *traits* of the effective leader are so closely related to the *functions* he will perform in the group, the most general rule for leader selection would seem to be to select those individuals who have the necessary skills plus a willingness to use them to satisfy the group's needs (Wolman, 1956). The leader should be most effective when the group's needs are clearly defined (Bourricaud, 1955).

Leadership Functions

The group leader functions as a "completer" (Schutz, 1961b); that is, ideally he is the one who has the necessary conception of the purpose of the group, specific problem-solving skills, concern for intermember solidarity, and power and techniques of social control to help the group complete its task when other members fail. Whether or not he fulfills these functions, the leader, through his activity in the group, is a major determinant in establishing the point at which the group will reach equilibrium along each dimension of interaction (Back, 1948). The leadership functions may be concentrated in one person, or they may be distributed among several persons in various combinations (Bjerstedt, 1965). Some of these combinations have been suggested in chapter 6 on member roles.

An indication of the functions which are common to the leader role regardless of the group situation is obtained from Hemphill's (1949) extensive questionnaire study of leadership qualities. In this study each respondent to the questionnaire gave a description of the different groups to which he belonged and also reported his observations of the leaders' behavior. Five functions were identified which were common to leaders of all groups: (1) advance the purpose of the group, (2) administrate, (3) inspire greater activity or set the pace for the group, (4) make the individual member feel secure of his place in the group, (5) act without regard to one's own self-interest. Leader functions which are similar to some or all of those on Hemphill's list also appear in a number of other studies (Stogdill, 1950; Peterson, 1955; Warriner, 1955; Wilson, High, and Comrey, 1955; Stogdill and Coons, 1957; Bartlett, 1959a, 1959b; Berrien, 1961; Greer, 1961; Gross, 1961; Prentice, 1961; Roby, 1961; Lange, 1962; Anderson, 1964; Smith and Tannenbaum, 1965; Wolin and Terebinski, 1965; Anderson, 1966; Burke, 1966; Morris and Hackman, 1969; Lück, 1970a; Butler and Cureton, 1973).

Since the problem of role confusion is present for the leader role as well as for the other roles in the group (see chapter 6), the answer to the question about leader functions will depend upon who is asked. In the armed forces, where status differences are clear-cut, the military rank of the individual determines both his own conception of leadership and the types of leadership others expect of him (Roff, 1950; Campbell, 1953; F. J. Davis, 1954; Halpin, 1954). In the air corps, ratings by the superior officers of airplane commanders were found to have a negative correlation with the commanders' "consideration" score, which was based on his friendship and mutual trust with crew members, and a positive correlation with his "initiating structure" score, which was based on maintaining a formal organization within the crew. In contrast, crew members were most satisfied when their commander was high on "consideration" and low on "initiating structure."

Many military organizations have customs which require social distance between leaders and followers and which place a low value on the "consideration" of commanders for their troops. These customs may have the effect of increasing group effectiveness, not so much because the men will not follow a leader with whom they are too familiar, but rather because a leader who is too close to his men may find it more difficult to reach decisions when he is influenced by his feelings about his men (Fiedler, 1957).

Individuals who differ in personality dimensions also have divergent expectations for the leader. When subjects are ranked on an authoritarian-equalitarian scale, two distinct sets of expectations for leadership are found. Authoritarians accept status-ladened, strongly directive leadership, demand that others adhere to ingroup values, and interact with the leader as a person rather than as a role (Sanford, 1950; Medalia, 1955). A similar dependent state may characterize the emotional atmosphere of a group during the early phases of group formation (Bion, 1949b).

Additional research related to the functions of leaders in small groups and the reactions of groups without a leader includes Marks, 1959; Bennis, 1961a; Bass, 1963; R. M. Anderson, 1964; Ramsoy, 1964; Medow and Zander, 1965; Hoffman and Maier, 1967; Becker et al., 1968; Chow and Billings, 1972.

The Central Person

The "leader," in the usual sense, is only one type of central person who may have the power to control the activity of a group. In a family, for example, a sick child may have more influence on family activity than the father or mother who usually takes the leader role. The variety of emotional relationships which a central person may have with the members of a group is illustrated by Redl's (1942) list of 10 types of persons who provide a basis for group formation. Redl based his work on that of Freud (1922).

Ten Types of Central Person
The central person as an object of identification
    On the basis of love
        Incorporation into conscience—*Patriarchal sovereign*
        Incorporation into the ego ideal—*Leader*
    On the basis of fear
        Identification with the aggressor—*Tyrant*
The central person as the object of drives
    As an object of love drives—*[Idol]*
    As an object of aggressive drives—*[Scapegoat]*
The central person as an ego support
    Providing means for drive satisfaction—*Organizer*
    Dissolving conflict situations through guilt-anxiety assaugement
        Through the technique of the initiatory
            act in the service of drive satisfaction—*Seducer*
            and in the service of drive defense—*Hero*

Through the "infectiousness of the unconflicted
personality constellation over the conflicted
one" in the service of drive satisfaction—*Bad influence*
and in the service of drive defense—*Good example*[1]

Descriptions of the patriarchal sovereign, idol, and organizer in classroom groups are quoted from Redl's article as illustrations of the three major types of central persons, as objects of identification, objects of drives, and ego supports.

The Patriarchal Sovereign

Illustrative example: This group is composed of approximately ten-year-old children, most of whom are just at that point in their development where they most fully represent the end states of "childhood" immediately before the outbreak of preadolescent symptoms. In charge of them is a teacher who fits the following description: "He is an elderly gentleman of stern but not unfriendly exterior, decided but fundamentally mild in his manner. He stands for order and discipline, but they are values so deeply ingrained in him that he hardly thinks of them explicitly, nor does it occur to anyone to doubt them in his presence. He believes in good and thorough work, knows very clearly what he expects and leaves no doubt about it in the minds of his students." The atmosphere of the classroom may be easily described. The children accept his values without question. Their emotions about him are a mixture of love and adoration, with an element of anxiety in all those instances in which they are not quite sure of his approval. As long as they behave according to his code they feel happily secure— sheltered. Thoughts and imaginations which do not comply with his code are suppressed in his presence. The jokes he makes, or acknowledges, are funny. If one youngster is not quite so ready as the others to concentrate his filial adoration upon this type of a teacher, makes unfitting remarks, unruly gestures, or shows lack of submission, the others will experience a deep feeling of moral indignation—even though they may have enjoyed this youngster's jokes a few minutes previously during the recreation period. They all love their teacher and trust him infinitely, but certain thoughts must never enter their minds in his presence. When questioned or doubted by this teacher, tears come more easily than words; behind the happy security felt in his presence there is a nagging fear of its loss which streams into awareness every once in awhile without apparent cause.

Explanation: These youngsters love their teacher, but that is not all that occurs. Their love is of a type which leads to "identification." It would be absurd to say that they want to be like their teacher, but they want to behave so that their teacher will approve of them.

Formula: These children become a group because they incorporate the "superego"—conscience—of the central person, into their own. On the basis of this similarity between them, they develop group emotions toward each other.[2]

The Idol

Imagine a number of women who are in love with a singer or pianist and crowd around him after his performance. Certainly each of them would prefer to be jealous of all others. However, considering their large number and how impossible it is for them to reach the aim of their infatuation, they resign and instead of pulling each other's hair, they act like a uniform group. They bring ovations to their idol in common actions and would be glad to divide his locks among themselves.

1. Fritz Redl, "Group Emotion and Leadership," *Psychiatry* 5 (1942): 583. Copyright 1942 (renewed) by The William Alanson White Psychiatric Foundation, Inc. Reprinted by permission of the author and by special permission of The William Alanson White Psychiatric Foundation, Inc. Since Redl did not name the object of love or aggressive drives, the names *idol* and *scapegoat* have been added.
2. Ibid., pp. 576–577.

The life in the school class furnishes two similar examples for illustration.

Illustrative example, 1: There is a group of sixteen-year-old girls in a class of a girls' high school. In charge of them is a male teacher—young, attractive, but narcissistic enough so that they are not too greatly frightened sexually from the outset. It is known that in some such cases "the whole class falls in love with him." From that moment on, they will act like a group in many ways along the line of Freud's example. Despite their infatuation for him, it would not be surprising if the teacher complained that he had trouble with discipline—that these girls did not obey him or follow his wishes without pressure. It seems that this kind of "being in love" with the central person does not make for "identification" described in *Type 2* [leader].

Illustrative example, 2: In a coeducational class of approximately sixteen-year-old children, there is one especially pretty girl, rather narcissistic. In similar situations one frequently finds a whole cluster of boys loving and adoring her in various ways, but equally unsuccessful insofar as their wish for exclusive possession goes. The girl is equipped with special skills for keeping them all equidistant and yet equally near. Symptoms of dense group formation may sometimes be observed among these boys. They seem very close to each other, and yet their relationship is not genuine friendship. It is on a group emotional basis. This becomes evident when the girl ultimately decides in favor of one of her suitors. The other boys then begin to hate him as their rival, with the exception perhaps of the one or two who may move even closer to the successful colleague and, thus, enjoy some of the satisfactions denied to them *via* the mechanism of *altruistic concession.*

Explanation: There is no doubt that the group emotional symptoms are genuine and that the teacher in *Example 1* and the girl in *Example 2* are playing the role of the central person without whose presence this type of group formative process would not have been evoked. However it is also evident that these central persons could not be called "leaders" by any interpretation of the term—that the other children do not "identify" with them. Nor do they incorporate their central person's standards. The central person remains "outside" but does call out a display of group emotional symptoms in these children.

Formula: The children choose one and the same person as an object of their love, and on the basis of this similarity they develop group emotions between each other.[3]

The Organizer

Illustrative example: In a class of approximately thirteen-year-old boys there are five who find clandestine enjoyment of the cigarette as a symbol of adulthood. And yet, all five are of the type who have decided worries about how they can obtain cigarettes. They have neither the money to buy them, the courage to do so, nor the impudence to steal them from their fathers. Preadolescent revolt against adult concepts of what a good child should be has not progressed far enough. A new boy, for whom smoking is no great problem, enters the class. He neither invites, instigates nor encourages the others in this enterprise. They all know that he can get the desired cigarettes for them if they but ask. In some cases hardly any other factor is involved. The boys neither love nor admire this youngster; on the contrary, he is rather looked down upon as socially inferior. They do not fear him nor does he use any direct or indirect pressure upon them. Yet, by the mere fact that he gets them the cigarettes, they suddenly become a regular "group," held together on the basis of their participation in the same forbidden pleasure.

Explanation: Perhaps this example seems more complicated—less credible—than the others.... Usually, it is coupled with other roles which the central person assumes for the potential group members. Although there are not many clear examples of this type, they cannot be reduced to any of the other types because neither love, hatred, nor identification is involved.

Formula: The central person renders an important service to the ego of the poten-

3. Ibid., pp. 578–579.

tial group members. He does so by providing the means for the satisfaction of common undesirable drives and thus prevents guilt feelings, anxieties, and conflicts which otherwise would be involved in that process for them. On the basis of this service, the latent undesirable drives of these youngsters can manifest openly. Through this common conflict-solution, group emotions develop in the interpersonal situation.[4]

Some of these types of central persons, like the patriarchal sovereign, leader, or tyrant, are found most often among persons who hold the formal "leadership" positions in the group, whereas others, like seducer, hero, or bad influence, are more apt to appear as informal leaders.

Power and Influence

All of the types of central persons have in common the fact that they have influence over other group members. The "dynamics" of power are illustrated by a series of studies conducted in boys' camps (Polansky, Lippitt, and Redl, 1950a; Lippitt, Polansky, and Rosen, 1952). Boys who were rated by their peers as having the most power were the ones who were imitated more often by the others. The high-power boy was actually approached nondirectively and with greater deference, while he was more likely to direct others and to resist the direction of others. The more powerful child was better liked by his associates and more frequently mentioned as a person the others would most want to be like.

The influence of a member in the informal structure will be enhanced if he is placed in a formal position of leadership. In one experiment, five- and six-man groups were given mathematical problems to solve. In some of the groups a person was chosen by the group members to play a leader role, and in other groups a person was selected to be an observer. In neither case did the elected person give his own opinions about the solution of the problem. The subjects recorded their answers to the problem privately both before and after the discussion. In both cases the discussion increased the number of correct answers, but the groups with leaders showed the most improvement. The effectiveness of the leader was especially marked when he made use of the opinion of minority members who were initially correct (Maier and Solem, 1952).

Another experiment indicates that an individual will *try* to exert more influence if he is placed in the leader role. One hundred forty-two airmen were placed in four-man "groups" in which each thought that he was coordinating the activities of the other three men in assembling a jigsaw puzzle. Each subject wrote notes to the other "members" and received fictitious notes in return. Before beginning the task, some of the subjects were told that they were bosses, while others were told that they were clerks. In addition, specific functions of their role and the goal of the group were either made clear or left unspecified. An examination of the notes written by each subject during the experiment indicated that a subject *tried* to exert more control over the other members if he was told that he was "the boss," or if he was given specific directions to do so even though he was only a clerk. The bosses enjoyed the experience more (Gerard, 1957). See also Zander and Forward, 1968; Kipnis, 1972.

Whether the power of a person is based on legitimacy (Janda, 1960; Cohen, Defares, and van Kreveld, 1964), ability to coordinate group activity (Schlesinger, Jackson, and Butman, 1960), skill (Levinger, 1959; Julian, Hollander, and Regula, 1969), or some other factor (Burdick, von Ekartsberg, and Ono, 1959), the more

4. Ibid., pp. 579–580.

he attempts to influence another person, the more he will be successful (Hoffman, Burke, and Maier, 1965; Gray, Richardson, and Mayhew, 1968), especially if the recipient is willing to accept it (French and Snyder, 1959) and his peers do not set counter norms (Stotland, 1959b). If the worker is fairly independent, the supervisor may have to provide continual surveillance to exert his power (Berkowitz and Daniels, 1963). Since surveillance is a cost, the person employing power tries to "maximize subjective expected utility"; that is, the expected rewards for applying power should be greater than the expected costs (Pollard and Mitchell, 1972). The research on the bases of social power (see French and Raven, 1959) is very similar to that on the sources of influence on the formation of group norms reviewed in chapter 2, except that here the focus is on the use of power more to coordinate group productivity than to establish norms.

Subjects will pay more attention and respond more favorably to persons of high power than to persons of low power (Wheeler, 1964; Butler and Miller, 1965), especially if the powerful person seems pleasant and rewarding (Mulder, van Dijk, et al., 1965; Marwell and Schmitt, 1967; Murray, 1967; Schopler et al., 1967; Miller, Butler, and McMartin, 1969; Rubin et al., 1971; Rubin and Lewicki, 1973).

If the powerful person vacates his position or seems incompetent, then the next most powerful person is most likely to try to take over (Mulder et al., 1971; Mulder et al., 1973; Mulder, Veen, Hijzen, and Jansen, 1973). The persons who are low in the power hierarchy tend to have a clearer picture of the roles of those above them than the high-power persons do of the roles of those below (Thomas, Franks, and Calonico, 1972).

The patterns of interaction between persons of high power and other group members and the personality characteristics of persons of high power (such as helpfulness and fairness: Rosen, Levinger, and Lippitt, 1961) are generally the same as those reported for group leaders (Gollob and Rossman, 1973; Archer, 1974. In contrast to the research on leadership, which focuses on the person with the legitimized position of power in a group, studies of power consider the ways in which any group member is able to affect the behavior of another (Nagel, 1968). For a review of the literature on social power see Schopler (1965).

Additional studies which examine different aspects of power in small groups include Back, 1961; W. P. Smith, 1968a; Richardson, Mayhew, and Gray, 1969; Von Broembsen, Mayhew, and Gray, 1969; Bolton, Gray, and Mayhew, 1970; Gray and Mayhew, 1972; Goodstadt and Hjelle, 1973a; Fodor, 1974.

Selection Procedures

In addition to personality and performance tests (Carter and Nixon, 1949b), a frequently used technique for the selection of leaders is the leaderless group discussion. First developed by the German army during World War I (Ansbacher, 1951) this technique was later adopted by the British and American armies and is now used by other organizations. In a series of researches on this subject, Bass and his associates observed college students, officer candidates, and business executives in four- to ten-man groups (Bass, 1949, 1951; Bass and Norton, 1951; Bass and Coates, 1952; Bass and Klubeck, 1952; Bass, Klubeck, and Wurster, 1953; Bass et al., 1953; Bass and Wurster, 1953b; Bass, 1954a, 1954b; Gleason, 1957; Frye and Adams, 1959; Prien and Lee, 1965; S. R. Wilson, 1971). As the candidates discussed a series of problems in a group in which no leader had been appointed, observers recorded the amount of time each member talked and rated each member's behavior on a series of scales which had been found to be valid for identifying leadership potential. A high rating on leadership in an initially leaderless group of this type was found to have a positive correlation with leadership in training performance of army personnel, status of supervisors in an oil company, extracurricular participation of college students, and aptitude of police officers (Bass and White, 1951; Bass and Coates, 1952; Bass and Wurster, 1953b; Wurster and Bass, 1953; Borgatta, 1954; Ames, 1955; Kiessling and Kalish, 1961). Bass concluded, however, that in the case of the oil company supervisors the estimate of leader potential in the "leaderless" groups was not valid, since the rank of each member in the oil company was known to the members and appeared to have a direct influence upon their participation (Bass and Wurster, 1953a).

In a similar study, nominations for the position of leader and "effectiveness" ratings were both made by the same leaderless groups of officer candidates. For this reason the low (.28, .18) but statistically significant correlations between nomination as a leader and effectiveness may have been only a reflection of the consistency of officer candidates' ratings of desirable characteristics (Berkowitz, 1956).

All of the problems that occur in rating and ranking members in any group also occur when using the leaderless group discussion technique. Thus a high ranking on leadership may be a reflection of different personality characteristics of a member (Rim, 1971), a different role played in the group (Burroughs, Rollins and Hopkins, 1972), differential reinforcement of members (Burroughs and Jaffee, 1969; Jaffee, Richards, and McLaughlin, 1970,) or other variables. Often the self-ratings of group members, peer ratings, and observers' ratings are found to be uncorrelated (Kaess, Witryol, and Nolan, 1961; Prien and Culler, 1964; Mitchell, 1970b; B. Schneider, 1970; Stein, 1971). The problems of reliable and valid observation are considered in some detail in appendix 3.

The possibility that one observer may be able to select the leader in an initially leaderless group simply by judging his appearance has also been investigated. In one study 24 college students were asked to judge leadership ability from individual pictures of police officers who had previously participated in four- to six-man problem-solving groups. Although the judges agreed among themselves on what a leader should look like (correlation .80), the average correlation between a judge's ratings and actual leadership performance was less than .18 (Mason, 1957).

Role playing has also been used as an assessment procedure (Tupes, Carp, and Borg, 1958). In a study of 221 army officer candidates, ratings of behavior were made in six role-playing situations. Low but significant correlations were found between role-playing ability and achievement in military academic subjects, military efficiency, and estimated officer effectiveness. Role-playing ability was also correlated with performance in leaderless group discussions and situational tests. Men with high scores were seen by their peers as better adjusted and "all-around" persons.

OSS Construction Test

Leaderless group discussions as well as other group situational tests were combined with life histories, stress interviews, role playing (Symonds, 1947; Bronfenbrenner and Newcomb, 1948), intelligence tests, and personality tests in a week-long assessment program developed by the American OSS (Office of Strategic Services) for the assessment of men who could be used for special missions during World War II. Some indication of the kind of social stress placed on a candidate as part of the selection program is given in the following excerpt,[5] which describes the use of role players in a construction task.

Sometime during the morning of the first day each candidate had an appointment behind the barn. If hearing of the location made the men recall, sometimes with amusement, events in their boyhood when they had kept similar appointments with their fathers, it is safe to assume that even such reollections failed to prepare them for what they would experience on this occasion.

Ostensibly this was a test of the candidate's ability to direct two helpers in building with him a frame structure out of simple wooden materials. Actually the situation was not so benign as it first appeared. To be sure, it was a test of *Leadership,* but more truly it was a test of *Emotional Stability* and frustration tolerance. *Energy* and *Initiative* in carrying out the work and the *Social Relations* of the candidate in relation to his helpers were also rated.

The building materials for this test were wooden poles of two lengths (five and seven feet), wooden blocks with sockets into which the poles could be fitted, and small pegs to hold the poles and blocks together. The blocks were of two sorts, full blocks and half blocks. The full blocks were of octagonal shape with sockets cut into each of the eight sides. Running through the center of each block was a circular hole of the same diameter as that of the poles. The half blocks had sockets in only three sides but attached to and protruding from the opposite long side was a dowel the thickness of a pole which could be inserted through the center hole of a full block. This equipment was a great magnification of the "tinker toy" sets of childhood. With this, each candidate was direced to build a five-foot cube with seven-foot diagonals on the four sides.

When the candidate came to the area where the test was to be conducted the staff member said to him:

"We have a construction problem for you now. We want you to build a structure using the equipment lying around here. Let's see. (*The staff member appears to ponder which of two or three models of different design to use.*) I guess we'll give you this model to copy. (*Staff member picks up the model which is always used from among the others and shows it to the student.*) You see there are short five-foot and long seven-foot poles lying on the ground. (*Staff member points out one of each size.*) The sides of the frame which you are to build are made of five-foot poles, and the diagonals of seven-foot poles. (*Staff member demonstrates this on the model.*) Do you understand?

"Now (*staff member picks up the corner and points to the peg*) you will notice there are holes for pegs like this at each socket, and similar holes in the end of each pole. Be sure, whenever you put a pole into a socket, to cinch it with a peg, because unless that is done all over the structure it will not be stable. (*Staff member then throws the sample corner to the ground.*)

"This is a construction problem, but even more important than that it is a test of leadership. I say that because it is impossible for one man working alone to complete this task in the ten minutes allotted to do it. Therefore we are going to give you two helpers who work here on the estate. You are going to be the supervisor, their boss. You are going to guide them in their work, but as foreman, you will follow more or less a hands-off policy. Let them do the manual labor. You can assume that they have never done such work before and know nothing about it. Any quesions? (*Final pause to amplify any details not understood by the candidate.*)

"All right. It is now ten o'clock. You have just ten minutes in which to do the job. I'll call your two helpers."

5. OSS Assessment Staff, *Assessment of Men: Selection of Personnel for the Office of Strategic Services* (New York: Rinehart, 1948), pp. 102–111. Copyright, 1948, by Holt, Rinehart & Winston, Inc. Reprinted by permission of Holt, Rinehart & Winston.

At this the two assistants, who had been working in the barn, were asked to come out and help the candidate. They complied, but waited for him to take the initiative. These two members of the junior staff traditionally assumed the pseudonyms of Kippy and Buster. Whoever played the part of Kippy acted in a passive sluggish manner. He did nothing at all unless specifically ordered to, but stood around, often getting in the way, either idling with his hands in his pockets or concerned with some insignificant project of his own, such as a minute examination of the small-scale model. Buster, on the other hand, played a different role. He was aggressive, forward in offering impractical suggestions, ready to express dissatisfaction, and quick to criticize what he suspected were the candidate's weakest points.

The two assistants were not permitted, by their secret instructions, to disobey orders, and they were supposed to carry out whatever directions were given to them explicitly. Within the bounds of this ruling, though, it was their function to present the candidate with as many obstructions and annoyances as possible in ten minutes. As it turned out, they succeeded in frustrating the candidates so thoroughly that the construction was never, in the history of S [the OSS testing unit], completed in the allotted time.

At first the assistants appeared cooperative, but if the candidate did not introduce himself and ask their names, Buster would observe that a boss interested in getting along with his men would at least find out their names. If the candidate did not explain in detail what they were to do, referring to the model, Buster would complain that they were receiving inadequate directions and remark that the candidate must be inexperienced. If he were either peremptory or passive, he would be criticized for this. Buster might say that that was a poor trait in a leader, and add that he found it hard to understand how anyone could ever have thought the candidate was worthy of holding an important position in the organization. If the candidate became so incensed at their unmanageableness that he laid a hand on them with the intention of getting them to work faster, the helper who was touched would take great offense. After the work had begun, Buster, or occasionally Kippy, might criticize the candidate's plan of operation and suggest other, often incorrect ways to proceed in order to test the forcefulness of the man's leadership. Kippy, for instance, might attempt to involve the boss in a debate about the relative advantages of the two plans. Or he might get into an argument with the other assistant over alternative methods of building a corner. Again, he might say that the octagonal edges of the corner blocks were the "rolling edges" and that they would not rest firmly enough on the ground to hold the structure. (Actually they would and that was the correct way to build the cube.) The assistants might try to get the leader to lay the blocks down flat, which was incorrect. They might even point to four holes in the ground, suggesting that those must be the places where previous workers had laid the corners flat. Or, in another attempt to divert the candidate from his plan, they might point out to him that the model was mounted on cardboard, and suggest that he search the area for cardboard with which to make the base for the structure so that it would be exactly like the model. If the candidate acceded to their suggestion he wasted time, because he was not directed to build such a base.

Frequently the candidate began to construct the cube incorrectly. When this happened the assistants would follow his orders for a while and then point out the errors, at the same time tearing down the structure if the leader did not stop them. From time to time, if Buster discovered a pole that was not pegged into its socket, he would kick the two pieces apart, saying sharply that no sensible person would expect such a framework to hold together unless it was pegged. It was discouraging to any man to see his cube collapsing before his eyes, but the reactions differed. Some candidates became bitter; others gave up and refused to continue. On the other hand, good leaders would patiently begin again or direct the helpers to stop tearing the pieces apart until they had decided whether the mistakes could be more easily rectified.

Another stratagem used by the two assistants when the work was well under way was to distract the candidate's attention from the job. They asked questions about him— where he came from, what his real name was, how long he had been in the Army, where he got his accent, and so on. They made an effort to break through his cover story if he answered these questions, and often their attempts were successful. If he refused to reply to their queries because of concentration on the job, they accused him of being unsociable. If they noticed anything particularly distinctive about him—for example, a peculiar accent, baldness, a reserved attitude—they burlesqued this trait in order to irritate him further. If he mentioned any special interest, they encouraged him to discuss it. If he became distracted, they continued on that line for a while, and then Buster might suddenly tell the candidate he was neglecting the job. He might accuse him of being "the poorest leader I ever saw around here," and suggest, since he was so obviously inept, that he give up the assignment entirely. If, after a few minutes of such frustrations, the candidate stopped directing the others and began to do the work by himself, or showed any evidence of emotion, Buster would immediately note this reaction and make some caustic comment designed to heighten it.

While Buster was needling the candidate in this way, Kippy was moping about, doing little. If he was given a direction, he complied slowly and clumsily, showing no initiative, stopping as soon as he had completed the specific task. He sometimes went up to the candidate to request permission to leave for a minute "to go get a drink." In general he followed the policy of passive resistance, doing everything possible to sabotage the construction by his inertia.

To illustrate how the helpers turned the conversation in Construction into banter which could be exploited for purposes of personality assessment, a typical protocol is reproduced here.

Staff Member (calling toward the barn):   Can you come out here and help this man for a few minutes?

Buster and Kippy: Sure, we'll be right out.

Staff Member: O.K., Slim, these are your men. They will be your helpers. You have ten minutes.

Slim: Do you men know anything about building this thing?

Buster: Well, I dunno, I've seen people working here. What is it you want done?

Slim: Well, we have got to build a cube like this and we only have a short time in which to do it, so I'll ask you men to pay attention to what I have to say. I'll tell you what to do and you will do it. O.K.?

Buster: Sure, sure, anything you say, Boss.

Slim: Fine. Now we are going to build a cube like this with five-foot poles for the uprights and seven-foot poles for the diagonals, and use the blocks for the corners. So first we must build the corners by putting a half block and a whole block together like this and cinching them with a peg. Do you see how it is done?

Buster: Sure, sure.

Slim: Well, let's get going.

Buster: Well, what is it you want done, exactly: What do I do first?

Slim: Well, first put some corners together—let's see, we need four on the bottom and four topside—yes, we need eight corners. You make eight of these corners and be sure that you pin them like this one.

Buster: You mean we both make eight corners or just one of us?

Slim: You each make four of them.

Buster: Well, if we do that, we will have more than eight because you already have one made there. Do you want eight altogether or nine altogether?

Slim: Well, it doesn't matter. You each make four of these, and hurry.

Buster: O.K., O.K.

Kippy: What cha in, the Navy? Yoo look like one of them curly-headed Navy boys all the girls are after. What cha in, the Navy?

Slim: Er—no. I am not in the Navy. I'm not in anything.

Kippy: Well, you were just talking about "topside" so I thought maybe you were in the Navy. What's the matter with you—you look healthy enough. Are you a draft dodger?

Slim: No, I was deferred for essential work—but that makes no difference. Let's get the work done. Now we have the corners done, let's put them together with the poles.

Kippy: The more I think of it, the more I think you are in the Army. You run this job just like the Army—you know, the right way, the wrong way, and the Army way. I'll bet you are some second lieutenant from Fort Benning.

Slim: That has nothing to do with this job. Let's have less talk and more work.

Kippy: Well, I just thought we could talk while we work—it's more pleasant.

Slim: Well, we can work first and talk afterwards. Now connect those two corners with a five-foot pole.

Buster: Don't you think we ought to clear a place where we can work?

Slim: That's a good idea. Sure, go ahead.

Buster: What kind of work did you do before you came here? Never did any building, I bet. Jeez, I've seen a lot of guys, but no one as dumb as you.

Slim: Well, that may be, but you don't seem to be doing much to help me.

Buster: What—what's that? Who are you talking to, me? Me not being helpful—why, I've done everything you have asked me, haven't I? Now, haven't I? Everything you asked me. Why, I've been about as helpful as anyone could be around here.

Slim: Well, you haven't killed yourself working and we haven't much time, so let's get going.

Buster: Well, I like that. I come out here and do everything you ask me to do. You don't give very good directions. I don't think you know what you are doing anyway. No one else ever complained about me not working. Now I want an apology for what you said about me.

Slim: O.K., O.K., let's forget it. I'll apologize. Let's get going. We haven't much time. You build a square here and you build one over there.

Buster: Who you talking to—him or me?

Kippy: That's right—how do you expect us to know which one you mean? Why don't you give us a number or something—call one of us "number one" and the other "number two"?

Slim: O.K. You are "one" and he is "two."

Buster: Now, wait a minute—just a minute. How do you expect to get along with people if you treat them like that? First we come out here and you don't ask us our names—you call us "you." Then we tell you about it, you give us numbers. How would you like that? How would you like to be called a number? You treat us just like another five-foot pole and then you expect us to break our necks working for you. I can see you never worked much with people.

Slim: I'm sorry, but we do not have much time and I thought—

Kippy: Yes, you thought. Jeez, it doesn't seem to me that you ever did much thinking about anything. First you don't ask our names as any stupid guy would who was courteous. Then you don't know what you did before you came here or whether you are in the Army, Navy, or not, and it's darn sure you don't know anything about building this thing or directing workers. Cripes, man, you stand around here like a ninny arguing when we should be working. What the hell is the matter with you, anyway?

Slim: I'm sorry—what are your names?

Buster: I'm Buster.

Kippy: Mine's Kippy. What is yours?

Slim: You can call me Slim.

Buster: Well, is that your name or isn't it?

Slim: Yes, that is my name.

Kippy: It's not a very good name—Dumbhead would be better.

Slim: Well, I'd like to do as much of this as possible. Will you help me?

Buster: Sure, sure, we'll help you, but it doesn't seem to be much use. What do you want us to do now?

Slim: Well, one of you build a square over there just like this one while the other one puts in the uprights and diagonals on this one.

Kippy: May I ask a question?

Slim: Sure, go ahead.

Kippy: Why build one over there? What are you going to do with it then?

Slim: Well, we'll put it on top—the top of this cube is like the bottom.

Kippy: Well, if that isn't the most stupid thing I ever heard of. Since when do you build the roof of a house and lift it to the top? Why not build it right on top. Listen, when you build a house you build the foundation, then the walls, and then the roof. Isn't that right?

Slim: Well, that is usually the way it's done, but I think we can do this job this way. In fact, I don't think it matters much which way we do it. Either way is O.K., I guess.

Buster: You guess, you guess. What kind of man are you anyway? Why in hell don't you make up your mind and stick to it? Be decisive—didn't they tell you that in OCS?—be decisive—even if you are wrong, be decisive, give an order. What are you—man or mouse?

Kippy: Oh, it's no use talking, Buster, when he doesn't have a bar on his shoulder he doesn't know what to do. Listen, Mac, you're not on Company Street now. You haven't a sergeant to do your work for you. You're all alone and you look pretty silly. Why, you can't even put together a child's toy.

Slim: Now listen to me, you guys, are you going to work for me or aren't you?

Buster: Sure, we want to work for you. We really don't care. We'd as soon work for you as anyone else. We get paid all the same. The trouble is we can't find out what you want done. What exactly do you want?

Slim: Just let's get this thing finished. We haven't much more time. Hey there, you, be careful, you knocked that pole out deliberately.

Kippy: Who, me? Now listen to me, you good-for-nothing, you squirt. If this darned thing had been built right from the beginning the poles wouldn't come out. Weren't you told that you had to pin these things? Why none of it is pinned; look at that, and that, and that! (*Kicks the poles which were not pinned out of position and part of the structure collapses.*)

Slim: Hey—you don't have to knock it all down!

Buster: Well, it wasn't built right. What good was it without pins?

Slim: I told you guys to pin it.

Kippy: I pinned every one you told me about. How did I know you wanted the others pinned? Jeez, they send a boy out here to do a man's job and when he can't do it he starts blaming his helpers. Who is responsible for this—you or me? Cripes, they must really be scraping the bottom of the barrel now.

Staff Member: (*Walking in from sidelines*): All right, Slim. That is all the time we have. The men will take this down.

Buster: Take what down? There's nothing to take down. Never saw anyone get so little done.

It is difficult to say what is the most desirable behavior for a candidate under such trying circumstances. Certainly disparate sorts of solutions were attempted. Some candidates, after they had seen that they were being hindered rather than helped by the assistants, either neglected them or actually discharged them, trying to do as much as they could by themselves. However, this certainly was not the correct procedure according to the directions, because one man could not complete the task in the allotted time, and moreover he had been told he must act as a leader. Others became authoritative or military, attempting to discipline the assistants, but this tended to anger such "sensitive workers" and made them work even more poorly. Still others simply relinquished their authority and followed the directions of the assistants. Some lost their temper or became frustrated easily, and more than one candidate struck an assistant with his fist out of anger.

The best solution, presumably, was one in which the leader first explained what he wished to have done, then delegated specific tasks to each assistant, keeping his eye on both of them, directing them, and keeping them working. At the same time he had to maintain good social relations, treating his helpers like equals, answering their suggestions, justifying his decisions to them, and taking their criticisms lightheartedly. He did well to reply to them with responses calculated not to offend overmuch their delicate sensibilities. It was, of course, hard for the candidate to decide whether he could get more done in the ten-minute period by acting entirely alone or by relying on the dubious cooperation of the helpers. At any rate, the problem was never completed in the allotted time, and usually it was scarcely begun.

An adequate follow-up of the candidiates who were selected by this battery of tests was not possible during World War II, so that the validity of all of the measures is not fully substantiated. In situations in which the criteria for effective leadership are well defined, prediction can be accomplished with far fewer measures. A single half-hour stress interview, for example, may be as valid as a number of more intricate assessment techniques.

Consistency of Leadership Behavior

The assumption of individual consistency in leadership behavior lies behind all leader assessment techniques. Individuals who receive a high rating on leadership behavior in one situation are generally expected to take the leader role in other situations. The consistency is especially high if the social characteristics of the members, group size, and task remain the same even though specific group members may be changed (Terman, 1904; Bell and French, 1950; Jackson, 1953; Blake, Mouton, and Fruchter, 1954; Hollander, 1957; Gellert, 1961; Taylor, Crook, and Dropkin, 1961; Grusky, 1969; Von Broembsen, Mayhew, and Gray, 1969; Gray and Mayhew; 1970; Mayhew and Gray, 1971; Yakobson and Shchur, 1973). Consistency of the dominance structure is also apparent in nonhuman groups (Mazur, 1973). Conversely, consistency will be low if these or other factors are varied (Hemphill et al., 1956; Barnlund, 1962; Bowers, 1963). A change in the personalities of the followers from high authoritarian to low authoritarian results in less authoritarian behavior on the part of the leader regardless of his authoritarian rating (Haythorn et al., 1956a, 1956b), and a change in the communication network may result in another person assuming leadership (Bavelas, 1950).

Once an individual has established himself as the leader in an initially leaderless group situation, it may be difficult to unseat him even if another leader is appointed. In one experiment, 41 six-man teams of unacquainted subjects from an air corps officer candidate school were tested in 12 situational problems requiring team cooperation. After the first six problems, the teams were divided into three groups: 17 teams in which a leader had clearly emerged, 14 with no clear leader, and 10 with two competing leaders. During the final six problems, the effectiveness of the emergent leader was reduced when another subjct was *appointed* leader, but the emergent leader still exhibitd more leader behavior than the other team members. The performance of the appointed leader was not significantly different from his performance as a follower (Borg, 1957). On the other hand, subjects who have had difficulty establishing themselves as the leader in a leaderless group may lose their leader position if the experimenter imposes a task which they did not favor (Katz et al., 1957). Additional evidence of the consistency of leadership behavior is given in chapter 8.

Leadership Training

The effectiveness of the leader can generally be improved by giving him training which fits him specifically for the type of group he has to lead. In experimental training programs, youth leaders have become more democratic, foremen have gained more acceptance from employees in introducing work changes, and college students have improved their discussion leadership techniques (Bavelas, 1942; Maas, 1950; Maier, 1953; Klubeck and Bass, 1954; Barnlund, 1955; Maier and Maier, 1957; Maier and Hoffman, 1960a; Havron and McGrath, 1961; Chemers, 1969; Maier and McRay, 1972; Sheridan et al., 1973). However, not all training programs are as successful. In one study in which foremen were trained in "consideration," a comparison of tests taken before and after the school session showed more consideration, while in actual practice the same foremen were less considerate (Fleishman, 1952). A second program of the same type produced no differences in the foremen's test scores (Harris and Fleishman, 1955). Effects similar to training can be obtained as leaders are given some positive reinforcement while the group is in process, either to increase their participation rate or to direct their activity into some particular content area (Marak, 1964; Zdep and Oakes, 1967; Jaffee and Furr, 1968; Jaffee and Skaja, 1968; Zdep, 1969; Cohen and Jaffee, 1970; Reilly and Jaffee, 1970; Nydegger, 1971; Eaglin, 1973; Butler and Jaffee, 1974).

A number of books have been written over the past 50 years with the aim of helping the individual improve his leadership technique. Only a sample of these appear in the bibliography (Elliott, 1928; Sheffield, 1929; Coyle, 1937; Slavson, 1938; McBurney and Hance, 1939; Lasker, 1949; Gouldner, 1950; Cunningham et al., 1951; Haiman, 1951; Sheffield and Sheffield, 1951; Strauss and Strauss, 1951; Johannot, 1953; Whyte, 1953; Andrews, 1955; Laird and Laird, 1956; Beal, Bohlen and Raudabaugh, 1962).

Authoritarian versus Democratic Leadership

Authoritarian and democratic leadership styles are the two most common types of leadership which have been imposed upon experimental groups (Anderson, 1959). As in any situation, the group will be more effective when the members' expectations about the behavior appropriate for that situation are met. Where group members anticipate a democratic organization, as they do in educational settings, such as children's clubs, discussion groups (Davis, Bates, and Nealey, 1971), or classrooms, the democratic style is usually found to produce the most effective group. In industry or the army, however, where members anticipate forceful leadership from their superiors, a more authoritarian form of leadership results in a more effective group.

The classic experiments in this area by Lewin, Lippitt, and White in 1939–1940, resulted in an increased interest in the scientific study of group dynamics. The first experiment compared the group atmospheres created by authoritarian and democratic leaders, and the second experiment added a laissez-faire leader (Lewin and Lippitt, 1938; Lewin, Lippitt, and White, 1939; Lippitt, 1939, 1940; Lippitt and White, 1952; White and Lippitt, 1960). In the second experiment, which corroborated the findings of the first, four clubs of 11-year-old boys were formed in such a way that they were equated with respect to certain of the personal and sociometric characteristics of their members and degree of interest in the task. All clubs met in the same clubroom setting, two at a time in adjacent meeting spaces, with a common equipment box. Four adults played the roles of "authoritarian," "democratic," and "laissez-faire" leaders in rotation so that, with minor exceptions, each adult played each leader role in each of the groups. The same activities were used in each club by the device of letting the democratic clubs select an activity and then imposing the activity on the authoritarian clubs. In the laissez-faire situation there were a number of potential activities of the same types as those selected by the democratic clubs.

The authoritarian leader determined all policies, techniques, and activities, maintaining his autonomy by remaining aloof from the group except when demonstrating the next step in the activity. In the democratically led groups all policies were determined by group discussion with the leader taking an active role. In the laissez-faire groups the leader did not take an active part, but left the group members free to reach individual or group decisions. During the period of 21 weekly meetings, the leadership style of each club was changed at least once.

Figure 44 illustrates some of the major differences in the patterns of observed behavior of the leaders. The comparison of average percentage of acts in each category is based on four democratic, four authoritarian, and two laissez-faire roles. About 60 percent of all behavior of the authoritarian leaders consisted of orders, disruptive commands, and nonconstructive criticism, compared with only 5 percent for the democratic and laissez-faire leaders.

Some of the major differences between the democratic and laissez-faire leadership roles are found in the next three behavior classifications: guiding suggestions, extending knowledge, and stimulating self-guidance. The democratic leader made more suggestions and stimulated self-guidance, while the laissez-faire leader spent more of his time extending knowledge. In the last three categories, the authoritarian gave more social recognition through social approval, the democratic leader was more jovial, and the laissez-faire leader more matter-of-fact.

During each experimental session four observers made a quantitative running account of social interaction, a minute-by-minute record of group structure, an interpretive running account of significant member interactions, and a continuous stenographic record of all conversation. These data were synchronized at minute intervals so that, when placed side by side, they furnished a continuous picture of the life of the group. In addition, interviews were held with club members, parents, and teachers.

The experimenters also postulated that a fruitful way to discover some of the major differences between the three types of group atmosphere would be to arrange comparable "test episodes" in each club. So at regular intervals the following events took place:

1. Leader arrived late.
2. Leader was called away for an indeterminate time.
3. Stranger ("janitor" or "electrician") arrived while the leader was out and critically attacked work of an individual group member and then of the group as a whole.

Four Group Atmospheres

Some of the major findings, summarized from stenographic records and other case material . . . are as follows: Two distinct types of reaction were shown to the same pattern of authoritarian leadership. All of the data, including the documentary films,

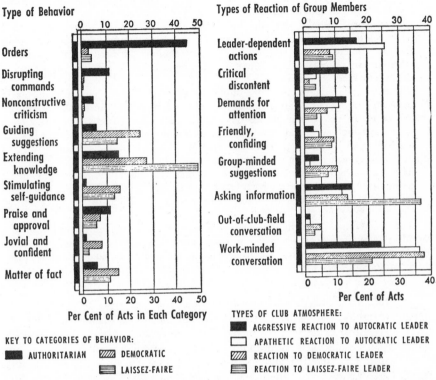

Figure 44. Comparison of Behavior of Average Authoritarian, Democratic, and Laissez-faire Leaders

Type of Behavior

Per Cent of Acts in Each Category

KEY TO CATEGORIES OF BEHAVIOR:
■ AUTHORITARIAN   ▨ DEMOCRATIC
▤ LAISSEZ-FAIRE

Figure 45. Types of Group Reaction to Four Social Atmospheres

Types of Reaction of Group Members

Per Cent of Acts

TYPES OF CLUB ATMOSPHERE:
■ AGGRESSIVE REACTION TO AUTOCRATIC LEADER
☐ APATHETIC REACTION TO AUTOCRATIC LEADER
▨ REACTION TO DEMOCRATIC LEADER
▤ REACTION TO LAISSEZ-FAIRE LEADER

Source: Ronald Lippitt and Ralph K. White, "An Experimental Study of Leadership and Group Life," in Eleanor E. Maccoby et al. (eds.), *Readings in Social Psychology,* 3rd ed. (New York: Holt, Rinehart & Winston, 1958), pp. 499 and 502. Copyright 1947, 1952, © 1958 by Holt, Rinehart & Winston, Inc. Adapted and reprinted by permission of the authors and the publisher.

indicated that three of the clubs responded with a dependent leaning on the adult leader, relatively low levels of frustration tension, and practically no capacity for initiating group action, while the fourth club demonstrated considerable frustration and some degree of channelized aggression toward the authoritarian leader. [This latter pattern is much more comparable to the behavior of the club under authoritarian leadership in a previous experimental study of two clubs (Lippitt, 1940).]

Figure 44 indicates the major differences in the relations which developed between the group members and the adult leaders in the four resultant social atmospheres. In both types of authoritarian atmosphere, the members were markedly more dependent upon the leader than in either the democratic or laissez-faire situations, dependence being somewhat greater in the more passive clubs. All other clubs showed a somewhat greater feeling of discontent in their relations with the adult leader than did the members of the democratic clubs, members of the "aggressive autocracy" being outstanding in their expression of rebellious feelings. There is evidence from other sources that the actual "felt discontent" in the "apathetic autocracies" was somewhat higher than indicated by the conversation which was considerably more restricted than was that of the democratic and laissez-faire club members.

In both types of authoritarian situations the demands for attention from the adult were greater than in the other atmospheres. It seemed clear that getting the attention of the adult represented one of the few paths to more satisfacory social status in the authoritarian situation where all of the "central functions" of group life were in the hands of the dominator.

The category "friendly, confiding" indicates that the members of the democratic and laissez-faire clubs initiated more "personal" and friendly approaches to their adult leaders, and the data on "out-of-club-field conversation" further indicate the more spontaneous exchanging of confidences about other parts of one's life experience in the democratic club atmosphere.

The data on "group-minded suggestions" to the leader show that the members in the democratic atmosphere felt much freer and more inclined to make suggestions on matters of group policy than in the other three group atmospheres. It is clear from other data that the lower level of suggestions in the laissez-faire situation is not because of any feeling of restricted freedom but because of a lack of a cooperative working relationship between the adult and the other group members.

The much greater responsibility of the members of the laissez-faire clubs to get their own information is shown by the fact that about 37 per cent of their behavior toward their leader consisted of asking for information, as compared to about 15 per cent in the other three club situations.

The final category in figure 45, "work-minded conversation," indicates that a considerably larger proportion of the initiated approaches of the club members to their leaders were related to on-going club activity in the democratic and in the apathetic authoritarian situations than in the other two types of social climate.[6]

In figure 46 a comparison is made between the four types of groups in the amount of productivity when the leader was in the room, when he had left the room, and just after he had returned. While the leader was out, both types of authoritarian groups did very little, the democratic group remained about as productive as it was, and the laissez-faire group became more productive. Similar results were obtained when the leader was late. The authors suggest that the high rate of productivity for the laissez-faire group may have resulted from the fact that one of the boys who was a good leader was able to take over the group.

When groups which had previously been led by authoritarian leaders were shifted to a freer democratic or laissez-faire group atmosphere (figure 47), they showed a great burst of horseplay on the first day, an indication of unexpressed group tension. This need to "blow off" disappeared with more meetings in the freer atmosphere.

When the groups were subject to the hostile criticism of a strange adult (e.g., "janitor"), differences in reaction were also noted.

Members of the apathetic authoritarian clubs tended to accept individually and to internalize the unjust criticism or, in one or two cases, they "blew off steam" in aggressive advances toward an out-group [the other club meeting in the adjacent club-room]. In the aggressive authoritarian situation, the frustration was typically channeled

6. Ronald Lippitt and Ralph K. White, "An Experimental Study of Leadership and Group Life," in Eleanor E. Maccoby, Theodore M. Newcomb, and Eugene L. Hartley (eds.), *Readings in Social Psychology,* 3rd ed. (New York: Holt, Rinehart & Winston, 1958), pp. 502–503. Copyright 1947, 1952, © 1958 by Holt, Rinehart & Winston, Inc. Adapted and reprinted by permission of the authors and the publisher.

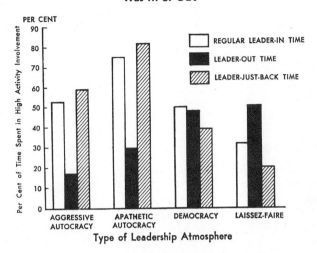

Figure 46. Time Spent in High Activity Involvement by Groups of Four Leadership-Atmosphere Types According to Whether Leader Was In or Out

Source: Ronald Lippitt and Ralph K. White, "An Experimental Study of Leadership and Group Life," in Eleanor E. Maccoby et al. (eds.), *Readings in Social Psychology,* 3rd ed. (New York: Holt, Rinehart & Winston, 1958), p. 503. Copyright 1947, 1952, © 1958 by Holt, Rinehart & Winston, Inc. Adapted and reprinted by permission of the authors and the publisher.

Figure 47. Amount of Horseplay by Group Members under Change in Leadership Type

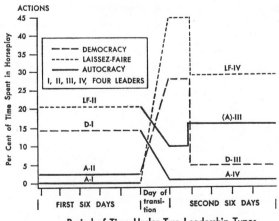

Source: Ronald Lippitt and Ralph K. White, "An Experimental Study of Leadership and Group Life," in Eleanor E. Maccoby et al. (eds.), *Readings in Social Psychology,* 3rd ed. (New York: Holt, Rinehart & Winston, 1958), p. 504. Copyright 1947, 1952, © 1958 by Holt, Rinehart & Winston, Inc. Adapted and reprinted by permission of the authors and the publisher.

in aggression toward the out-group, although in several cases there was some direct reaction to the source of frustration, the hostile stranger. In the democratic atmospheres there was evidence of a greater readiness to unite in rejection of the real source of frustration, the stranger, and to resist out-group aggression.[7]

When the overall productivity ratings of the three types of groups were compared, the authoritarian groups were highest in *quantity,* while the democratic groups were judged to be better in *quality.* This same tendency for authoritarian leadership to result in greater quantitative productivity and democratic leadership to result in higher morale has been noted in other studies (Gibb, 1951; Adams, 1954).

Other Similar Leader Styles

Other variations on the authoritarian-democratic theme use somewhat similar leader roles with discussion groups rather than activity groups (Fox, 1957; Ziller, 1957a; Beran et al., 1958, Ziller, 1958; Anderson, 1959; Page and McGinnies, 1959; Schlesinger, Jackson, and Butman, 1960; Day and Hamblin, 1964; Turk and Wills, 1964; Schneider, 1965; Derbyshire and Foster, 1971; Michener and Tausig, 1971; Myers and Bishop, 1971; Sudolsky and Nathan, 1971; Scontrino, 1972). In general, when leaders who have an active and positive relationship with their discussion groups are contrasted with those who hold negative attitudes, a greater incidence of supportive acts among members is reported for the positively led groups and a greater incidence of opposing acts in the negatively led groups. In addition, there tends to be a greater acceptance on the part of the members of opposing behavior in the negatively led groups, so that opposers receive high popularity ratings and are more highly satisfied with the group decision.

Some of these same effects were observed in a study of the relationship between the behavior of B-29 commanders in the air corps and the attitudes of their crew members. When the leader was considerate, the friendship, willingness, and confidence of the members increased (Christner and Hemphill, 1955).

Experiments have also been performed with discussion groups comparing "participatory" leaders who take part in the discussion and try to insure an equal chance for participation to all group members, and "supervisory" leaders who do not take part but whose job it is to make sure the group finishes the discussion on time. The data indicate that participatory leadership is more effective as a technique for changing opinion. The participatory leader has more influence on the group decision, and the followers are better satisfied with the result of the group decision, apparently because each has had an opportunity to express his opinion though it may not have been accepted by the group (Preston and Heintz, 1949; Hare, 1953; Anderson and Fiedler, 1964).

It can be assumed that the leader who facilitates free discussion among the members will be more effective when the group task requires free discussion among peers. Many tasks, however, require for their successful completion more frequent participation by the more skillful members and a hierarchy of power and influence (Horowitz and Perlmutter, 1955). This is especially evident in studies which contrast groups with leaders and groups without any leaders or without

7. Ibid, pp. 505–506.

leaders chosen by an acceptable method (Whitehorn, 1961; Goldman and Fraas, 1965; Holmes and Cureton, 1970; Clement, 1971; Fraas, 1972a, 1972b; Morozov and Papovyan, 1973).

Teacher-centered versus Learner-centered Classes

In learning situations two contrasting styles have been called "teacher-centered" and "learner-centered." The task-centered, demanding teachers were found to elicit from students hostility, apathy, and other signs of withdrawal, whereas accepting student-supportive teachers decreased anxiety and produced greater interaction and positive feeling among members both in class and outside the classroom (Thelen and Withall, 1949; Perkins, 1950; Bovard, 1951a, 1951b; Flanders, 1951; Perkins, 1951; Bovard, 1952; Di Vesta, 1954; Singer and Goldman, 1954; Gordon, 1955; Wischmeier, 1955; Zimet and Fine, 1955; Bovard, 1956a, 1956b; Costin, 1971). Women appeared to be more affected by these changes in the classroom situation than men (McKeachie, 1958).

Some observers report more learning in the "learner-centered" classes, although some students prefer the more directive classes for examination preparation. Little difference has been found when students from both types of classes are given the same examination (Zeleny, 1940a; Wispe, 1951; Watson 1953; Wispe, 1953; Haigh and Schmidt, 1956; Maloney, 1956; Rasmussen, 1956). In addition, permissive instruction may increase the ambiguity of the teaching situation unless group members have the skills to set and achieve goals (McKeachie, 1954b). The best arrangement is to combine teacher style with the characteristics of the students, since dull, anxious, or dependent students do better with the more directed form of instruction (Calvin, Hoffmann, and Hardin, 1957; Domino, 1971; Dowaliby and Schumer, 1973).

Differences similar to those between "teacher-centered" and "learner-centered" classes have been found between large lecture groups and small discussion groups. In both the "teacher-centered" discussion and the large lecture, a learning situation is created in which one person talks most of the time and has a superior position in the hierarchy of control, while the possibilities for close, intimate relations between members are limited. In contrast, in the "learner-centered" groups and the small discussion groups, all members receive their share of talking time, control is relatively equal, and intimacy prevails.

Additional studies relating teacher style to classroom behavior include Hall, 1970; Malott and Rollofson, 1972; Costin and Grush, 1973; Good, Sikes, and Brophy, 1973; LaBelle and Rust, 1973.

Democratic Leaders in Autocracies

In industrial organizations and the armed services, where members expect the leader to play an autocratic role, attempts to introduce more democratic procedures usually result in member dissatisfaction and low productivity which is similar to that usually associated with autocratic leadership in a democratic culture. In a study of 72 conferences in industry and government, leadership sharing was found to be negatively related to the attractiveness of the group and satisfaction with the conference (Berkowitz, 1953). In this population, the chairman was expected to exert a strong central control over the meetings, and attempts of other members to make frequent proposals for the solution of problems were discouraged. However, if the group had an urgent problem, sharing leadership had no relation to satisfaction, apparently because members were free to deviate from the norms in times of crisis. In other industrial studies high productivity in a shop has been found to be associated with a well-differentiated and authoritative style of leadership (Gekoski, 1952; Kahn and Katz, 1953).

In an air corps study, bomber-crew critiques of training problems were held with different types of leadership (Torrance, 1953b). Crews with critiques which were structured by having a well-defined leader and procedure more frequently showed improvement in a subsequent problem-solving situation than those with less structured critiques. In addition crews with an unstructured, nonauthoritarian leader and those who had no leader assigned but held a "self-critique" did no better than crews receiving no critique.

Similar findings are reported in studies of the smallest autocracy, the doctor and patient in a therapeutic interview. Here progress is found to be associated with high frequencies of directive, interpretive remarks on the part of the therapist (Keet, 1948; Dittman, 1952; Wiener, 1955; Harrow et al., 1967).

Persons who make a successful adjustment to one regime may find that they lose some of their power when the leadership style is changed. In a training school for adolescent boys, two cottages were studied over an eight-month period while the government of one of the cottages was changed from the usual form of an adult-dominated quasi-autocracy to greater self-government. Before the change took place, independent measures of popularity and dominance were obtained for the boys in both cottages. A high positive correlation between rated dominance and sociometric popularity was found in both groups before the period of "democratization," supporting the hypothesis that the openly dominant boy in an autocratic society will be admired because he dares to react in the fashion that others would imitate if it were not for the fear of punishment. When the same measures of popularity and dominance were repeated eight months later, the correlation had dropped until it was not significantly different from zero in the group which had been democratized, while in the control group the correlation had increased. The increase in popularity among the originally least popular boys in the experimental group was more marked than the decrease in popularity among the six most dominant boys (McCandless, 1942). This is perhaps an indication that a change in a group's culture may make originally deviant individuals more popular, but may have less influence on the popularity of leaders since they will tend to adapt their leader style to fit the new customs.

Situational Factors

Leaders can be created in the group by increasing the distance between members in the areas of control or affection, so that more initiating and controlling activity is required to maintain a productive group. When the communication network is arranged so that one person is in the center of the net and receives the greatest number of messages, the central member will tend to become the leader (Leavitt, 1951). Similar effects are obtained by reducing the number of messages which can be sent by the average group member through an increase in group size (Hemphill, 1950). Leaders can also be created by distributing power, prestige, or skill unequally in the group or by giving the group a task which requires a division of labor. In such a situation, the person who provides the control or who has the greatest skill will tend to become the leader. Even in a group in which differences in ability are not a major factor, subjects who appear to be accepted by others will make more attempts to lead (Pepinsky, Hemphill, and Shevitz, 1958).

The variations in the situation which are found in the communication network, the skills and amount of control required, and the amount of stress under which the group must work are all associated with the type of the group task. Variations in the group task call forth different types of leadership (Dubno, 1963; Clifford and Cohn, 1964; Nagata, 1965; Shaw and Blum, 1966; Jaffee, 1968; Ward, 1968; Cohen, Rosner, and Foerst, 1973; Halal, 1974). A more authoritarian, centralized style of leadership is more effective when the task is simple (Rudin, 1964; Katzell et al., 1970) and the stress is high (Torrance, 1961; Korten, 1962; Rosenbaum and Rosenbaum, 1971; Dyson, Fleitas, and Scioli, 1972). In each case the group members will be more satisfied if the leadership style is consistent with their expectations (Zurcher, 1967; Greening, 1973; Stinson and Robertson, 1973; Valenzi and Eldridge, 1973).

Fiedler and his associates report a more complicated relationship between the success of variations in leadership and the type of task (Fiedler, 1968, 1971b). They find that the performance of interacting groups is contingent upon the interaction of leadership style and situational favorableness. "Task-oriented" leaders do well in very favorable or very unfavorable situations, while "relationship-oriented" leaders are more effective in intermediate situations. The "relationship-oriented" leader is one who gives favorable ratings to his "least preferred co-workers" on a scale developed by Fiedler. In style he tends to be permissive, passive, and accepting, while the "task-oriented" leader is managing, controlling, and more active. Thus the task-oriented leader is more effective in favorable situations where the group accepts the leader or the task is highly structured or in very unfavorable situations where a strong, controlling leadership is required (Hutchins and Fiedler, 1960; Fiedler, Meuwese, and Oonk, 1961; Fiedler, 1962; Trentini, 1962; Fiedler, 1964; Burke, 1965; Fiedler, 1966a, 1966b, 1967, 1968; Moran and Klockars, 1968; Shima, 1968a, 1968b; Shirakashi, 1968; Fiedler, O'Brien and Ilgen, 1969; Fishbein, Landy and Hatch, 1969b; Gruenfeld, Rance, and Weissenberg, 1969; Hill, 1969; Shirakashi, 1969; Eagly, 1970; Ninane and Fiedler, 1970; Fiedler, 1971a; Graen, Orris, and Alvares, 1971a, 1971b; Hardy, 1971; Chemers and Skrzypek, 1972; Fiedler, 1972a; Richards and Cuffe, 1972; Shima, 1972; Cammalleri et al., 1973; Hardy, Sack, and Harpine, 1973; Rice and Chemers, 1973; Zanna, 1973).

The fact that some research using the same "least preferred co-worker" measure gives evidence that the relationship-oriented leader is the most effective (Ziller, 1963, 1965b; Jacoby, 1968; Graham, 1973) while other studies report that the task-oriented leader is the most effective (Fiedler, 1961; Sashkin, 1972) can probably be explained by differences in situational favorableness. However, some authors have questioned the validity of the measure (Fishbein, Landy, and Hatch, 1969a; Muller, 1970; Stinson, 1972; Shiflett, 1973b; Evans and Dermer, 1974; Shiflett, 1974). Again, as with other leadership typologies, other variables such as intelligence, birth order, and training also make a difference in the leader's performance (Fiedler and Meuwese, 1963; Chemers, 1970; Mitchell, 1970a; Foa, Mitchell, and Fiedler, 1971; Csoka and Fiedler, 1972; Fiedler, 1972b, 1973; Kerr and Harlan, 1973; Csoka, 1974).

Distributed Leadership

Studies of initially leaderless groups often report that the leadership functions are distributed between a task leader and a social-emotional leader (Bales and Slater, 1955; Slater, 1955; Bales, 1958; Parker, 1958; Criswell, 1961; Philipsen, 1962; Cloyd, 1964a; Burke, 1971; Stein, Geis, and Damarin, 1973) or that the individual who receives the most nominations for leadership is not necessarily the one who is best liked· (Hollander and Webb, 1955; Wilson, 1970). These roles are more visible if there are marked differences in interaction rates between members (Shelley, 1960a, 1960b). A similar distribution of roles appears in organized groups. In the air corps, for example, both in behavior and ideology the educational administrators and deputies showed greater consideration for the enlisted men and less organizing activity than did aircraft commanders (Halpin, 1955a, 1955b; Lundgren, 1972).

When groups do not have a social-emotional leader, the members may be more likely to "scapegoat" one of their members as an attempt at solving social-emotional problems (Gallagher and Burke, 1974).

An exception to this tendency to distribute leader functions has been observed in labor mediations which involve only three persons: the mediator, a representative of management, and a representative of labor. It is the function of the labor mediator to guide the parties toward a settlement by his suggestions and powers of persuasion and thus to provide task leadership. Yet, because of the dispute separating and often alienating the parties, none of them is in a position to serve as the social-emotional leader. As a result the labor mediator must also perform this second type of leadership (Landsberger, 1955a).

Summary

The general functions of the leader role and the traits of the persons who typically become leaders are related to the needs of the small task group. Since the needs of the group depend in turn upon the culture in which the group operates and the personalities of the members, the actual characteristics of the leader role are not the same for all groups.

Different leader styles may be imposed upon groups to create differences in the interaction process. To specify the leader style is, in effect, to give rather explicit directions to *one* group member about the nature of the task and the type of communication network which will be permitted, as well as to set the emotional tone which will pervade the interaction.

Potential leaders usually receive higher ratings than other group members on *traits* such as intelligence, enthusiasm, dominance, self-confidence, and social participation. These traits tend to be found in clusters which have been described as "authoritarian" and "equalitarian." The leaders who emerge in leaderless group discussions tend to be more authoritarian, presumably because more authoritarian behavior is required to establish a position than to maintain one.

Some leaders serve the *functions* of pace setter and coordinator for both task and social-emotional behavior. However, there may be role confusion for the leader if superiors and inferiors or other reference groups have conflicting expectations for his behavior.

Although a single "leader" may be the controlling member in a group, other types of central persons also appear as objects of identification, objects of drives, and ego supports. Redl has described 10 of these types: patriarchal sovereign, leader, tyrant, idol, scapegoat, organizer, seducer, hero, bad influence, and good example. Each of these central persons has power over other group members which will be enhanced if he is placed in a position of formal leadership.

The leaderless group discussion and other forms of situational tests were developed principally in the armed services to select potential leaders. A high leadership rating for a candidate in a situational test has been found to have a positive correlation with performance in organizational activity. Consistency of leadership behavior is especially high between situations which are similar in the social characteristics of members, group size, and task, even if the membership of the group is changed. The effectiveness of the individual possessing the traits of leadership can generally be improved if he is given training for his role.

In the experiments by Lewin, Lippitt, and White contrasting three group atmospheres, members of the authoritarian groups showed more dependency on the leader and more hostile and apathetic behavior between members. In the laissez-faire groups there was little dependency on the leader but greater irritability and aggressiveness among members and dissatisfaction with the task. The democratic group showed less dependency on the leader, more friendliness, and satisfaction with the activities of the club. The autocratic groups surpassed the others in quantity of output, but the products of the democratic groups were judged to be of the best quality.

This same tendency for autocratic leadership to result in greater quantitative productivity and democratic leadership to result in higher morale has been reported in other studies which contrast supervisory and participatory leadership and teacher-centered and learner-centered teachers.

Task-oriented, autocratic leaders are more effective in favorable situations (such as industry) where the group accepts the leader or the task is highly structured, or in very unfavorable situations (such as the armed forces) where strong, controlling leadership is required. Relationship-oriented leaders are more effective in intermediate situations. Similar leader roles can be created in the laboratory by increasing group size and channeling all communication through a central member. Leadership functions may be distributed between a task leader who deals primarily with productivity and a social-emotional leader who deals with interpersonal relationships.

Additional References

Additional studies related to leadership in small groups include Stogdill, Scott, and Jaynes, 1956; Stogdill, 1957; Beran et al., 1958; Utterback, 1958; Manheim, 1963; Short and Strodtbeck, 1963; Binder, Wolin, and Terebinski, 1966a, 1966b; Sashkin and Maier, 1969; Fenelon and Megargee, 1971; Libby, 1971; Shaw and Tremble, 1971; Winter, 1971; Fraas, 1972b; Shchedrovitskii and Nadezhina, 1973.

PERFORMANCE CHARACTERISTICS

In this third part of the book, the literature on social interactions in small groups is reviewed again with emphasis upon the comparative performance characteristics of individuals and groups. In part 1 some of the central tendencies in groups were considered in the chapters on the formation of norms and social control, the interaction process, roles, and interpersonal choice. Then in part 2 some of the variations from these central tendencies were described—variations which resulted from changes in the composition of the group or in the task, communication network, or leadership. Now in the third part of the book these central tendencies and variations in group behavior will be judged against a criterion of productivity.

Chapter 14, in which the productivity of the individual and the small group are compared, is based primarily upon the "together" and "apart" experiments and the child-study literature of the early 1900s. Chapter 15 serves as a summary of the whole book in presenting a comparison of the productivity of groups with different characteristics.

Chapter 14

INDIVIDUAL VERSUS GROUP

SOME OF THE EARLIEST experiments in social psychology compared the behavior of the individual when working alone with his behavior in the presence of others. Much of this early work was done by educators who were interested in finding out if schoolwork or homework could be better performed by the student when working alone or when others in the room were working on the same task (Mayer, 1903; Meumann, 1904; Schmidt, 1904; Burnham, 1905; Moede, 1914). This interest was revived by Floyd Allport in the 1920s (1920, 1924) and has survived to the present day as a focus of social-psychological research. The studies of group problem-solving and the comparison of individuals and groups in the solution of problems which followed the work of Munsterberg (1914) were an offshoot of this main stem. These early "together" and "apart" studies and other researches appearing between 1898 and 1930 are listed in appendix 2. Some of these studies are given in more detail in the present chapter, and others have been included in previous chapters in the text.

The presence of others working on the same task has been found to stimulate some individuals to greater productivity, distract others, and leave others unaffected. Usually one skilled individual is as efficient as a group in problem-solving, unless the problem calls for a variety of skills or a division of labor which can only be provided by a group (Cohen, 1953). The group also excels when the problem requires a judgment about an ambiguous stimulus. Some of the increased accuracy of the group, however, is due only to the fact that a mathematical average is obtained, a process which can take place without group discussion. Since the individual can learn from others or will be influenced to accept the group norm in judging an ambiguous object, the accuracy of the individual is often improved as a by-product of group discussion.

The Four Problem Areas

As indicated in chapter 1, all groups have problems to solve in four areas. Two of these areas, achieving the group's purpose and arranging a satisfying social structure for the members, have received the most attention in research (Barnard, 1938). The other two areas of achieving individual task goals and individual social-emotional goals will not be considered in this chapter. Problems in the first two areas, the group task area and the group social-emotional area, are related to each other in a state of "dynamic balance," so that too much activity in the task area will leave unsolved problems in the social-emotional area. In its attempts to solve the social-emotional problems, the group (or the individual) often swings too far in that direction and the task is left undone. The group then swings back and forth in its activity, tending toward a state of equilibrium (Bales, 1953).

A typical group problem-solving sequence requires both emotional and intellectual participation in the three stages of definition (observation), discussion (hypothesizing), and working through (proposing action) (Alpert and Smith, 1949). Each member must re-examine his view of the problem in the light of the views of the group, a process involving tension and requiring opportunity for interaction followed by release of tension. The process may be obstructed by formalistic participation where tension is concealed through rules of procedure (i.e., much intellect, little emotion), and by anarchic participation where discussion seems to fail to shed new light on the problem and release tension because of lack of verbal skill (i.e., much emotion, little intellect).

In this chapter, those effects on productivity which result from the simultaneous presence of a number of workers will be distinguished from those effects which result from group effort. Some of these effects have only been measured at the end of the decision process; others have been described at various stages of the process. To show the relative importance of these effects, the steps in an "ideal" decision are presented.

Steps in the Decision Process

The steps in the group decision process consist of observing an object or event, comparing it with several possible identifications, considering the associated facts, and, once the nature of the problem is understood, taking appropriate action. This is the same process which has been described earlier as the process by which an individual defines the situation and arrives at an appropriate social act. The process is described by Bales in a more logical framework in the seven steps shown in figure 48.

To these seven steps an eighth step of ACTION can be added to make the social act complete.

These steps in the decision process are given here in more detail than they are usually given in research on productivity. For this reason the process has been collapsed to three stages for the purpose of analysis: (1) observing, (2) formulating hypotheses, (3) proposing action.

Individuals—Together and Apart

Since Tripplett's early study of children winding string with fishing reels in 1898, the "together" and "apart" design has been used again and again to determine the influence of the presence of other persons on individuals who are performing a variety of tasks. The apparatus used by Triplett for his study consisted of two fishing reels whose cranks turned in a circle one and three-fourths inches in diameter. These were arranged on a Y-shaped framework clamped to the top of a heavy table as shown in figure 49.

Figure 48. The Decision Process

1 STATES PRIMARY OBSERVATION:

I OBSERVE A PARTICULAR EVENT, X.

2 MAKES TENTATIVE INDUCTION:

THIS PARTICULAR EVENT, X, MAY BELONG TO THE GENERAL CLASS OF OBJECTS, O.

3 DEDUCES CONDITIONAL PREDICTION:

IF THIS PARTICULAR EVENT, X, DOES BELONG TO THE GENERAL CLASS, O, THEN IT SHOULD BE FOUND ASSOCIATED WITH ANOTHER PARTICULAR EVENT, Y

4 STATES OBSERVATION OF CHECK FACT:

I OBSERVE THE PREDICTED PARTICULAR EVENT, Y.

5 IDENTIFIES OBJECT AS MEMBER OF A CLASS:

I THEREFORE IDENTIFY X-Y AS AN OBJECT WHICH IS A MEMBER OF THE PREDICTED GENERAL CLASS OF OBJECTS, O.

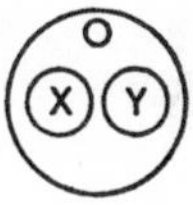

6 STATES MAJOR PREMISE RELATING CLASSES OF OBJECTS:

ALL MEMBERS OF THE GENERAL CLASS OF OBJECTS, O, SHOULD BE TREATED BY WAYS OF THE GENERAL CLASS, W.

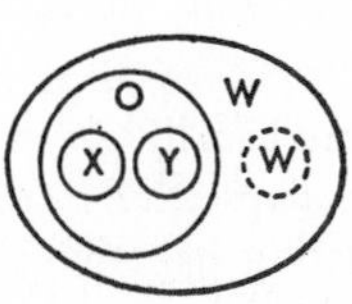

7 PROPOSES SPECIFIC ACTION:

THIS PARTICULAR OBJECT, X-Y, SHOULD THEREFORE BE TREATED IN A PARTICULAR WAY, W.

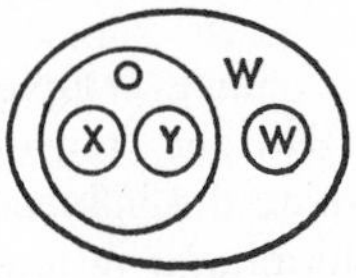

Source: Robert F. Bales, "How People Interact in Conferences," *Scientific American* 192 (March 1955): 35. Copyright © 1955 by Scientific American, Inc. All rights reserved. Reprinted by permission of the author and W. H. Freeman & Co.

Figure 49. Triplett's Competition Machine

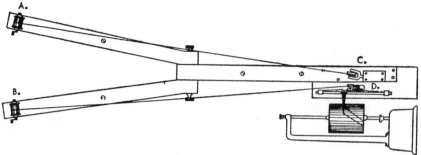

Source: Triplett (1898), p. 519.

The sides of this framework were spread sufficiently far apart to permit two persons to turn the reels side by side. Bands of twisted silk cord ran over the well lacquered axes of the reels and were supported at C and D, two meters distant, by two small pulleys. The records were taken from the course BD, the other course AC being used merely for pacing or competition purposes. The wheel on the side from which the records were taken communciated the movement made to a recorder, the stylus of which traced a curve on the drum of a kymograph. The direction of this curve corresponded to the rate of turning, as the greater the speed the shorter and straighter the resulting line.

The subject taking the experiment was required to practice turning the reel until he had become accustomed to the machine. After a short period of rest the different trials were made with five-minute intervals between to obviate the possible effects of fatigue.

A trial consisted in turning the reel at the highest rate of speed until a small flag sewed to the silk band had made four circuits of the four-meter course. The time of the trial was taken by means of a stopwatch. The direction of the curves made on the drum likewise furnished graphic indications of the difference in time made between trials.

Triplett presented results based upon the records of 40 children who had been tested in two sets of 20. After the usual preliminaries of practice, six trials were made by each of the 20 subjects in the first set in the following order: first a trial alone, followed by a trial in competition, then another alone, and thus alternating through six efforts, giving three trials alone and three in competition. The second set of 20 children, who were about the same age, were given the six trials in the following order: alone, alone, competition, alone, competition, alone.

By this scheme, a trial of either sort, after the first one, by either of the two sets always corresponded to a different type of trial in the second set. Further, when the subjects in the two sets came to their fourth and sixth trials an equal amount of practice had been gained by an equal number of trials of the same kind. In his observations of the trials and examination of the results, Triplett found that all the subjects could be divided into three classes. Some were stimulated to work faster in the competition trials, some were stimulated in such a way that their performance was inhibited, and some appeared to be little affected by the race. As an example of Triplett's results, table 34 gives the data for 20 subjects who were, on the whole, stimulated positively by the trials in competition.

Table 34. Time in Seconds for Subjects Stimulated Positively for Trials Alone and in Competition

NAME & AGE	TRIAL					
	1	2	3	4	5	6
	Alone	Comp.	Alone	Comp.	Alone	Comp.
Violet F., 10	54.4	42.6	45.2	41.0	42.0	46.0
Anna P., 9	67.0	57.0	55.4	50.4	49.0	44.8
Willie H., 12	37.8	38.8	43.0	39.0	37.2	33.4
Bessie V., 11	46.2	41.0	39.0	30.2	33.6	32.4
Howard C., 11	42.0	36.4	39.0	41.0	37.8	34.0
Mary M., 11	48.0	44.8	52.0	44.6	43.8	40.0
Lois P., 11	53.0	45.6	44.0	40.0	40.6	35.8
Inez K., 13	37.0	35.0	35.8	34.0	34.0	32.6
Harvey L., 9	49.0	42.6	39.6	37.6	36.0	35.0
Lora F., 11	40.4	35.0	33.0	35.0	30.2	29.0
Average	47.48	41.88	42.60	39.28	38.42	36.30
Probable Error	6.18	4.45	4.68	3.83	3.74	3.74
Gains		5.60	0.72	3.32	0.86	2.12

Source: Triplett (1898).

Unfortunately for Triplett, two trends are apparent in the data. First, there is a tendency for the average time per trial to decrease from trial 1 through trial 6, presumably due to practice with the task. Second, on trials 3 and 5 about half of the subjects are slower in the alone condition than they were in the preceding competition condition. Thus the second effect, of faster trials under the stimulus of competition, is masked about half of the time by the overall tendency to improve on such trial.

Also, perhaps fortunately for Triplett, this experiment was performed about seven years before the statistician Gauss, alias "student," introduced the *t*-test which could be used to test the differences between means for small samples. The differences between trials alone and in competition are generally not statistically significant. However, Triplett did not know this, and neither did the other social psychologists who followed him with experiments which confirmed the fact that some subjects are stimulated positively by the presence of others while some are not (Shevaleva and Ergolska, 1926; Stotland and Cottrell, 1961; Kenyon and Loy, 1966; Davis et al., 1968; Chapman, 1973).

In general, children seem to find the together situation more stimulating than do adults (Feofanov, 1928). Subjects with low intelligence are less stimulated (Abel, 1938). Under social influence subjects were observed to be more active but less accurate at the beginning of a task such as printing or putting pegs in a board (Sengupta and Sinha, 1926; Anderson, 1929; Dashiell, 1930; Leuba, 1933; Dashiell, 1935). A similar effect was observed when a second subject was added after the first subject was satiated with the task (Burton, 1941). Subjects were less likely to become bored if others were working at the same task (Taylor, Thompson, and Spassoff, 1937). If the subjects think they will do well, they are more likely to work harder and to be pleased with their achievement when an audience is present (d'Amorim and Nuttin, 1972; Good, 1973). On the other hand, subjects who place a high value on socially desirable behavior and are self-conscious are more likely to be affected adversely by an audience (Levin et al., 1960; Taylor and Weinstein, 1974).

The reason for the mixed results of the early together and apart experiments may be explained by more recent research which indicates that the presence of others during a learning experiment has a facilitative effect on the dominant (most likely) response, hindering learning when the dominant response is incorrect and helping learning when the dominant response is correct (Zajonc, 1965a). For example, in an experiment with 45 male and 39 female undergraduates, each subject followed a maze with a stylus either alone or in the presence of others. For one maze the subject had only two choices each time there was a branch in the maze, so that the chance of finding the correct solution was 50 percent or higher; that is, the dominant (or most likely) response would be correct most of the time. On the other maze the subject had to choose between four alternatives at each branching point, so that the dominant (or most likely) response was incorrect and the subject could only be right 25 percent of the time. Under these conditions the subjects who were coactors made fewer errors than those working alone on the maze where dominant responses were likely to be correct. On the maze were dominant responses were likely to be incorrect, subjects performing alone made fewer errors than those coacting (Hunt and Hillery, 1973). In other words, being aroused by the presence of others only helps when it helps to be aroused. (See also Duflos, 1967; Cottrell et al., 1968; Henchy and Glass, 1968; Matlin and Zajonc, 1968; Criddle, 1971; Cohen and Davis, 1973).

The Test Room Studies

From 1927 through the early 1930s, the Western Electric Company carried out a series of researches in a special test room and in other observation rooms in an attempt to measure the effects of certain physical, biological, and social factors upon the productivity of individual workers (Homans, 1941; Haire, 1954; Carey, 1967).

These Western Electric studies have led to a number of research reports by Turner (1933), who, as a Public Health consultant, set up the original test room; by Mayo (1933), who was called in as a psychologist to interview the employees when it was discovered that social factors were more important than physical factors; and by Roethlisberger and Dickson (1939), who made the most extensive report of the research results. Turner's account (1933) of the initial series of test room studies, which took place over a period of two years, provides a detailed illustration of the relative importance of social stimulation in increasing individual productivity.

In April, 1927, six experienced female operators, chosen at random, were removed from the department in which they were working to a small test room in the corner of a regular shop. Their work was the assembly of telephone relays and involved putting together a coil, an armature, contact springs and insulators in a fixture, and securing the parts in position by means of four machine screws. The girls were invited to the office of the Superintendent in charge where the plan and objectives of the study were explained to them. Although shy at this first meeting, they readily consented to take part in the study. They were expressly cautioned to work at a comfortable pace and not to make a race out of the test.

The working equipment in the test room was like that in the regular department except that there was a hole in the bench at the right of each girl's position into which completed relays were dropped. The relay falls through a chute actuating a flapper gate. The opening of the gate closes an electrical circuit which controls a perforating device which in turn records the completion of the relay by punching a hole in a moving tape. This tape moves at the rate of 1/4" per minute and has space for a separate row of holes for each operator. The punched tape furnishes a complete output record for each instant of the day. The tape mechanism also carries a bank of five message register giving a numerical record of the total number of relays completed by each operator.

As we began the test, our objectives were stated in the form of six questions:

1. Do employees actually get tired out?
2. Are rest pauses desirable?
3. Is a shorter working day desirable?
4. What is the attitude of employees toward their work and toward the company?
5. What is the effect of changing the type of working equipment?
6. Why does production fall off in the afternoon?

Disregarding the problems of placement and working equipment, it has been our assumption that the effectiveness of an individual will vary with (a) his bodily status or physiological efficiency (health, skill, endurance); (b) his mental state (contentment and freedom from worry, fear, anger, hate, shame, or other morbid preoccupations); (c) his zest for work (determined by the enjoyment in performing the work, the feeling of justice in his treatment, and the desire for securing reward).[1]

To test these assumptions, certain specific changes having to do with the length of the working day or week, with the introduction of rest periods, and with the sitting position of the operators were made. These are described in table 35.

At the beginning of the study, output records were kept for each girl in her regular department for two weeks without her knowledge. The girls were then moved to the test room where they worked for five weeks before any changes in working conditions were introduced. The intentional changes subsequently introduced have not by any means been the only ones studied.

Differences between Test Room and Shop

In the test room, the group piecework basis of payment paid each girl more nearly in proportion to her individual effort, since she was paid with a group of six instead of 100 or more. The girls in the test room assembled fewer different types of relays. The operators could read their exact output at anytime from the recorder. The test room was not quieter; if anything, it was somewhat noisier than the regular department. New conditions of work provided an element of novelty. The girls realized that the experiment was receiving the attention of company officials, which meant that they were being noticed as individuals.

There has been a fundamental change in supervision. There was no group chief in the test room, but instead a "friendly observer" of the experiment. Discipline was secured through leadership and understanding. The girls were allowed to talk and to leave the bench whenever they liked; they were not compelled to pick up parts from the floor at the time they were dropped. An *esprit de corps* grew up within the group.

The girls were given physical examinations every six weeks. They objected to this at first but later each trip to the hospital became a "party." [2]

Three types of records were kept in the test room in order that changes might be measured in output, the individual, and conditions of work.

1. C. E. Turner, "Test Room Studies in Employee Effectiveness," *American Journal of Public Health* 23 (1933): 577–579. Reprinted by permission of the American Public Health Association.
2. Ibid.

Table 35. Changes in Test Room Conditions

Period Number	Period Name	Duration in Weeks
1.	In regular department	2
2.	Introduction to test room	5
3.	Special group rate	8
4.	Two 5-minute rests	5
5.	Two 10-minute rests	4
6.	Six 5-minute rests	4
7.	15-minute morning lunch; 10-minute afternoon rest*	11
8.	Same as No. 7, but 4:30 stop	7
9.	Same as No. 7, but 4:00 stop	4
10.	Same as No. 7 (check)	12
11.	Same as No. 7, but Saturday morning off	9
12.	Same as No. 3 (no lunch or rests)	12
13.	Same as No. 7, but operators furnish own lunch; company furnishes beverage	31
14.	Same as No. 11	9
15.	Same as No. 13	31
16.	Same as No. 13, except operators changed positions	4
17.	Same as No. 16, except 4:15 stop and Saturday morning off	25
18.	Same as No. 17, except Friday afternoon off	15

*Beginning with Period 7, rest periods were begun at 9:30 in the morning and 2:30 in the afternoon.

Source: C. E. Turner, "Test Room Studies in Employee Effectiveness," *American Journal of Public Health* 23 (1933). Reprinted by permission of the American Public Health Association.

Test Room Results

The first specific problem which the test room sought to study was the effect of rest pauses which were introduced in Period 4. We did learn much concerning rest pauses, but soon found that there was a continually rising output in the test room which was in large measure at least independent of rest pauses. At the end of four years, the individual operators had increased their output from 40 to 62 per cent. The relationship of this increase to rest pauses is shown in figure 50. It will be seen that output rose appreciably in Period 3 before rest periods were introduced. In Period 12, rest periods were entirely eliminated and during 12 weeks, output reached a new height.... With the reintroduction of rest pauses in Period 13, total output rose still further.

We inevitably became more and more concerned with the task of finding the explanations for the remarkably increased output. Was it because of better health or at the expense of health of the workers? Was it due to lessened fatigue? Was it due to changed pay incentive? Was it due to an improved mental state on the part of the worker, to the elimination of unhappy preoccupations, or a greater zest for work?[3]

Although factors such as these *were* shown to be related to productivity, in the judgment of the girls themselves the elements considered to be important in the

3. Ibid., pp. 579–580.

Figure 50. Average Daily Output for Operators 3, 4, and 5

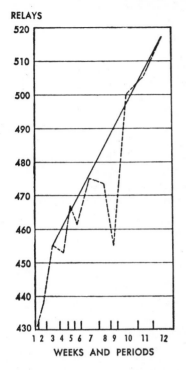

RELAYS

WEEKS AND PERIODS

Solid line shows daily output increase from one full-day period to the next full-day period. Dotted line shows the actual average daily output. The work periods indicated at the bottom of the chart are as follows: (1) regular department (2 weeks), (2) test room (5 weeks), (3) special gang rate (8 weeks), (4) two 5-minute rests (5 weeks), (5) two 10-minute rests (4 weeks), (6) six 5-minute rests (4 weeks), (7) lunch rest (11 weeks), (8) lunch rest and 4:30 stop (7 weeks), (9) lunch rest and 4:00 stop (4 weeks), (10) same as period 7 (12 weeks), (11) lunch rest and Sat. a.m. off (9 weeks), (12) same as No. 3 (12 weeks),

Source: C. E. Turner, "Test Room Studies in Employee Effectiveness," *American Journal of Public Health* 23 (1933). Reprinted by permission of the American Public Health Association.

test room situation were listed in the following order: the small group, the type of supervision, earnings, novelty, interest of the girls in the experiment, the attention given in the test room by officials and investigators.

As a result of his experience with the test room, Turner concluded:

We came to realize that neuromuscular fatigue is not of great importance in light industrial processes and that the mental attitudes of employees are of tremendous importance.[4]

Without intention, Turner and his colleagues had provided a classic demonstration of the positive influence on productivity which results from work in a "together" situation where the subjects are given special attention. Before the experiment was over, the girls had developed from an "initially leaderless group" through the stages in group development described in chapter 4 to become a mutually supportive team which was able to control its own production levels (Hare, 1967).

Social-Emotional Distractions

The quantity and quality of an individual's activity in an intellectual task may be less in the "together" situation (Dashiell, 1935) if some attention of the subject is

4. Ibid., p. 584.

diverted from the task to social-emotional concerns (Allport, 1920, 1924; Anderson, 1929; Hartup, 1964; Neumann, 1969; Innes, 1972; Shrauger, 1972; Thayer and Moore, 1972; Gore and Taylor, 1973; Matova, 1973; Tomasini, 1973; Sasfy and Okun, 1974). On a reasoning task, for example, the presence of a group stimulates more conversational, expansive expression, while the individual alone is more logical (Allport, 1920). This effect may be observed even if the other persons working on the task are not physically present in the room with the subject (Dashiell, 1935). Motor performance may also be impaired by an increasing number of coactors (Martens and Landers, 1972). Of course, as Triplett's experiment demonstrated, the negative effects of social distraction may be overcome by greater motivation to perform in the social situation (Mukerji, 1940), provided that the other persons in the room are having more success. If the others are doing less well, the subject may lower his goals (Hilgard, Sait, and Margaret, 1940).

The negative effects of social distraction are heightened if the other persons present are not doing the same task, but serve as an audience to razz or threaten the subject (Laird, 1923; Coombs and Taylor, 1952). The most intelligent subjects find observation by an audience the most disruptive (Gates, 1924; Anderson, 1929).

In one study on the effects of an audience (Wapner and Alper, 1952), three different kinds of audience were used. A sample of 120 undergraduates of both sexes were asked to select one of two words which more closely fitted a given phrase. Each subject made his choices in a room with a one-way mirror under three variations of audience: (1) no audience other than the experimenter, who was also in the room—the curtain was drawn before the one-way mirror; (2) unseen audience—the mirror was exposed and the subject was told that there were people behind it who could hear and see what was going on in the room, (3) seen audience—lights were turned on behind the mirror so that the subject could see the audience, which consisted of a faculty member and three or four students. For the first half of the 20-minute experimental session, the time that the subject required to select each word was least when there was no audience other than the experimenter, intermediate for the seen audience, and longest for the unseen audience. The unseen condition produced significantly longer decision times than either of the other two conditions. In the second half of the experimental session, no differences appeared and for all subjects there was a general decrease in decision time from the first to the second half. Presumably the unseen audience was the most threatening to the subject because he was unable to estimate either its expectations for his behavior or its penalty for deviation.

The social-emotional distractions created by the presence of others who are working at the same task are not always as subtle. Other members may actively coerce the subject to lower his output to conform to a group norm (F. W. Taylor, 1903).

Observations and Hypotheses

Up to this point in the chapter, individuals have been compared in "together" and "apart" situations primarily with regard to the final outcome of the problem-solving process. However, some studies suggest differences which may occur in the steps of *observation* and *hypothesizing*.

Observation, as we have seen in the discussion of norms and social control, is influenced by the presence of other individuals. Subjects tend to give up their individual standards of judgment in favor of group norms in judgments of phenomena such as line length, light movement, and weight (Allport, 1924; Farnsworth and Behner, 1931; Sherif, 1935; Asch, 1952; Sherif and Sherif, 1956; Kopera, Maier, and Johnson, 1971). As a result, it is difficult to predict what an individual will report as his perception in a group if we know only his perceptual performance when no others are present (de Montmollin, 1955a).

If association and memory may be assumed to be related to the formation of *hypotheses,* then studies in these two areas will provide some information about the second step in the problem-solving process. In studies of word association, the subject in a social situation feels inhibited and restrained (Dashiell, 1935) and as a result makes fewer personal associations and more popular associations (Allport, 1920). However, the frequency of word associations is increased in the presence of others, especially for slow workers.

When a subject uses his memory as a source of hypotheses to apply to a current problem, it might be presumed that the same social distractions which may decrease productivity for an individual would inhibit his memory. As in the other steps of the process, however, the evidence is mixed. The presence of others does interfere with the ability to remembr nonsense syllables (Pessin, 1933; Dashiell, 1935) but has no effect on maze learning (Pessin and Husband, 1933). Information which is learned under adverse conditions may be retained longer than information learned under less stressful conditions (Elkine, 1927; Pessin, 1933).

Although the emphasis here has been on the effect of social stimulation on an individual's efficiency, there are of course more common ways to increase efficiency by providing incentives (Leuba, 1930), training (Marston, 1924), or therapy (Peters and Jones, 1951).

In summary, the presence of other persons may change the content of an individual's activity from personal to group-oriented, it may increase his activity if he is spurred on by the implied competition, or it may depress his activity through distraction, conformity to norms, or group resistance to the task.

A Paradigm for the Analysis of Productivity

In the preceding section the problem-solving behavior of individuals has been compared when the individuals were "alone" and when they were "together," but always with an *individual* task. These two situations are represented by cells C and D in figure 51.

The next set of studies deals with cells A and D, the group working as a group

Figure 51. Paradigm for the Analysis of Productivity

The Relationship of the Individuals:	THE PROBLEM TO BE SOLVED:	
	TOGETHER	APART
Together	A	C
Apart	B	D

versus the individual working as an individual. There is also research on cooperation versus competition in which the individuals are together but with either
group or individual goals—cells A and C. Although persons with a common problem often try to solve it without face-to-face contact, by mail or telephone, there
are few studies which explicitly deal with cell B, although some communication
experiments are relevant here. A comparison of different types of groups in cell A
is the subject matter of chapter 15.

Efficiency of the Group versus the Individual

When pairs or larger groups are compared in the solution of the same types of
problems, the groups are generally found to be more efficient than individuals
(Beasley, 1958; Anderson, 1961; Luchins and Luchins, 1961e; Fox and Lorge,
1962; Lorge and Solomon, 1962; Restle, 1962; Restle and Davis, 1962; Zajonc,
1962a; Sampson, 1963a; Olson and Davis, 1964; Laughlin and Johnson, 1966;
Goldman, McGlynn, and Toledo, 1967; Erdelyi, 1968; Goldman, Dietz, and
McGlynn, 1968; Laughlin et al., 1968; Perju, 1968; Vine and Davis, 1968; J. H.
Davis, 1969b; Luchins and Luchins, 1969; Rotter and Portugal, 1969). The superiority of groups should be especially evident when a division of labor is possible.
For problems similar to those used by the OSS in its assessment of men, such as
crossing a mined road or building a bridge, five-man teams were found to ask more
questions and produce better written and field solutions than individuals, regardless of the method of presenting the problem (e.g., verbal, photograph, or scale
model) (Lorge et al., 1955a, 1955b). The group will be especially efficient if the
members are friends (Husband, 1940). On the other hand, if a task does not lend
itself to a division of labor (e.g., a mathematical problem), pairs take longer to
solve each problem but have more correct answers, presumably because of the
error-checking feature of interaction (Barton, 1926; Watson, 1928; Shaw, 1932;
Klugman, 1944). In another study with a similar type of task three-man groups
were no more effective than individuals in solving problems in symbolic logic
(Moore and Anderson, 1954).

The individual will also be more efficient if the task requires a kind of coordination of the group which some of its members cannot supply because of low motivation, personality conflict, poor communicatin, or other reasons (Thorndike,
1938a; McCurdy and Lambert, 1952). In one experiment college subjects chose
individual problem-solving over paired (Lichtenberg, 1956). On the other hand,
the difficulties in cooperative effort when cooperation is seen as taking too much
time may have unexpected "positive" effects. For example, failure on a non-
creative task (finding combinations to locks) caused more persons working alone
than working cooperatively to lower their estimate of the probability of successfully
completing a second task. This occurred presumably because the subjects working
cooperatively could attribute their difficulty to the possibility that they were not
getting along together, rather than that they did not have the ability (Lichtenberg,
1957).

The differences between groups and individuals on the more manual tasks (jigsaw puzzles) and the more intellectual tasks (arithmetic problems) are in the same
direction as those reported for individuals solving problems together and apart;
that is, there is greater efficiency on manual problems and less on intellectual
problems.

Although the group is usually better than the average individual, it is seldom better than the best individual (Marquart, 1955; Lorge et al., 1958; Steiner and Rajaratnam, 1961; Daval, 1967; Schoner, Rose, and Hoyt, 1974). It is therefore probable that in many cases the apparent superiority of the group results from the presence of *one* superior individual (Taylor and McNemar, 1955; Wiest, Porter, and Ghiselli, 1961). The group effects in any case shoud be greater if the groups are composed of subjects who have made high scores as individuals (Comrey and Staats, 1955; Goldman, 1965, 1966; Laughlin and Branch, 1972). However, in one series of studies, less than half of the variance of paired performance on a pegboard could be predicted from individual scores for college subjects (Comrey, 1953; Comrey and Deskin, 1954a, 1954b). Some of the effects of group interaction can also be attributed to the fact that individual subjects are working in the presence of others rather than *with* them on a common task. In terms of man-hours required the groups are more expensive, since the time for a group solution must be multiplied by the number of members in computing the cost of the product. For this reason the group method would seem to require more accuracy, member satisfaction, or some other result in addition to efficiency in terms of units per hour to justify its use (Davis and Restle, 1963; Zagona, Willis, and MacKinnon, 1966).

One form of generating new ideas in a group is called "brainstorming." Various rules are imposed on the group which are intended to facilitate creativity. Usually group members are not allowed to criticize new ideas, only build upon them or suggest alternatives. Unfortunately for the promoters of brainstorming, individuals are usually found to produce more ideas per person when working alone (Clark, 1958; Taylor, Berry, and Block, 1961; Dunnette, Campbell, and Jaastad, 1963; Milton, 1965; Rosca, 1966; Bouchard and Hare, 1970; Langelar, 1970; Bouchard, 1972a; Dillon, Graham, and Aidells, 1972; Buchanan and Lindgren, 1973; Bouchard, Barsaloux, and Drauden, 1974; Street, 1974). Some of the apparent superiority of brainstorming groups may have resulted from the fact that superior individuals were recruited to take part, since "supergroups" composed of high-performing individuals do better than those composed of individuals who are low performers (Graham and Dillon, 1974).

The ultimate test of the effect of being a good or bad problem solver was made in an experiment in which 263 college students each solved a simple mathematical puzzle (Johnson and Torcivia, 1967). They then solved the puzzle again individually or in one of four pairs: (1) two initially right subjects (RR), (2) one initially right and one initially wrong subject (RW), (3) two initially wrong subjects whose initial answers were the same (WWs), and (4) two initially wrong subjects who had different wrong answers (WWd). The major results indicated that (1) neither WWs nor WWd pairs improved their performance relative to W subjects working independently; (2) performance of the RR subjects did not decrease; and (3) a subject's relative certainty of the correctness of his initial solution was an accurate predictor of performance in RW pairs. Since the WW pairs made no improvement at all, we at last have some evidence to support the common observation that "two wrongs don't make a right."

Twenty Questions

The experiment by Taylor and Faust (1952) using the game Twenty Questions provides a more detailed example of the relative efficiency of the group and the individual. Here, too, groups were found to be more accurate but more costly in terms of man-hours.

To start Twenty Questions, the participants were told only whether the object they were to attempt to identify was animal, vegetable, or mineral. In searching for the object which was the solution to the problem, they asked a series of questions, each of which could be answered yes or no. To find the solution most economically, the subjects had to use a high order of conceptualization, gradually increasing the specificity of the concepts employed until they arrived at the particular object.

A total of 105 students from the elementary course in psychology served as subjects. The subjects were assigned by chance to work in solving the problems either alone, in pairs, or as a member of a group of four. There were 15 individual subjects, 15 groups of two and 15 groups of four. Each individual or group was given four problems a day for four successive days. On the fifth day, all subjects worked alone, each being given four problems.

From a longer list of objects originally constructed, 60 were selected for use as problem topics. Included were 20 animal, 20 vegetable, and 20 mineral objects. Excluded were objects which did not clearly fit in only one of the three categories; e.g., hammer was not included because, with a handle of wood and a head of metal, it would be classed as both vegetable and mineral. Also excluded were objects which could not be expected to be familiar to almost every college student. Examples of objects included are: newspaper, Bob Hope, scissors, camel, dime, rubber band.

With four problems a day for five days, a total of only 20 problems was needed for presentation to any particular subject or group. However, to minimize the possibility that a subject would have any knowledge of what problem object to expect, it was decided to use a total of 60 different objects.[5]

Since the nature of the learning curve was of interest, the order of presentation of the problems was controlled. The problems given on any one day were matched for difficulty with those given on any other day.

All subjects were told that both the number of questions and the time required to reach solution would be recorded, but it was emphasized that the number of questions was the more important score. In presenting each problem, the experimenter stated simply whether the object sought was animal, vegetable, or mineral. Time was measured by means of a stopwatch. A special data sheet was used for groups of two or four to record which subject asked each question. To each question, the experimenter replied "Yes," "No," "Partly," "Sometimes," or "Not in the usual sense of the word." If the question could not be answered in one of these ways or was unclear, the subject was asked to restate it.

The instructions given to groups of two or of four made clear that they might talk freely to each other, reviewing answers to previous questions or suggesting possible questions to ask. It was emphasized that they were not to compete against each other, but were to cooperate as a group to get the answer: they were told that the efficiency of their group would be compared with that of the other groups.

As the name of the game indicates, subjects are traditionally allowed 20 questions in which to obtain the solution. Pretesting showed, however, that with naive subjects this limit results in a rather large proportion of failures. Accordingly, to simplify the

5. Donald W. Taylor and William L. Faust, "Twenty Questions: Efficiency in Problem Solving as a Function of Size of Group," *Journal of Experimental Psychology* 44 (1952): 361. Copyright 1952 by the American Psychological Association. Reprinted by permission of the estate of Donald W. Taylor and the publisher, with special thanks to Ruth S. Taylor.

analysis of the data to be obtained, the number of questions permitted was increased to 30.[6]

The Rate of Learning

When the rates of learning for the subjects in the three experimental conditions are compared,

the data in figure 52 shows that there is rapid improvement in the performance of both individuals and groups. By the fourth day the curves appear already to be flattening out. The score for an individual or single group for one day was the median of the number of questions required to solve each of the four problems on that day. The median was used instead of the mean because there were some failures. Each point plotted in figure 51 is the mean of these median scores on one day for 15 individuals, or for 15 groups of two or of four. In those few cases when an individual or group failed two or more problems on a single day, the median was obtained by treating the failures as though solution had been reached in 31 questions; the number of such cases was too small to affect the results appreciably; after the first day there were no such cases except among individual subjects and even there they were rare.

The mean number of failures per problem on each day by individuals or groups is shown in figure 53. Thus, for example, on the first day the mean number of failures per problem among the 15 groups of four was .08; in other words, about one-twelfth of the problems were failed. The improvement in performance over four days in terms of number of failures per problem is consistent with that shown in figure 52 in terms of number of questions per problem solved.

Figure 52. Number of Questions per Problem as a Function of Days of Practice and Size of Group

Figure 53. Number of Failures per Problem as a Function of Days of Practice and Size of Group

Figure 54. Time per Problem as a Function of Days of Practice and Size of Group

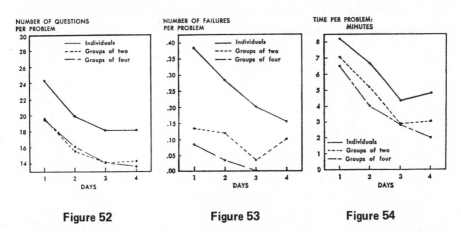

Figure 52　　　　　　Figure 53　　　　　　Figure 54

Source: Donald W. Taylor and W. L. Faust, "Twenty Questions," *Journal of Experimental Psychology* 44 (1952): 362, 362, 363. Copyright 1952 by the American Psychological Association. Reprinted by permission of the estate of Donald W. Taylor and the publisher.

6. Ibid., pp. 361–362.

Figure 54 shows the decrease over four days in the amount of time required per problem. The time required, of course, is somewhat dependent on the number of questions asked, although not entirely so. The score for an individual or single group for one day was the median time required for solution of the four problems. In those few cases where there were two or more failures in one day, the median of the four times was taken simply as obtained; this procedure underestimates somewhat the median time that would have been required to solve all four problems, but as before, the number of such cases was too small to affect the general results appreciably.

Size of Group

The second and major question with which the experiment was concerned involved the relation between efficiency in problem solving and size of group. As is evident in figure 52, there was no significant difference between groups of two and groups of four in terms of the number of questions required to reach solution. The performance of individuals working alone, however, was consistently inferior to that of either size group.[7]

This same tendency holds for the number of failures per problem (figure 53) and the time per problem (figure 54). The individuals were less efficient than the groups, but the groups did not differ in efficiency from each other.

However, if instead of counting the total time elapsed before the solution of the problem, an analysis is made in terms of the number of man-minutes required for solution, the nature of the results obtained changes sharply. The number of man-minutes for a problem will, of course, be equal to the elapsed time multiplied by the number of persons in the group. In terms of man-minutes, the mean of the scores for all four days was 5.06 for individuals, 7.40 for groups of two, and 12.60 for groups of four.[8]

The differences between these means are statistically significant, indicating that the performance of individuals was superior to that of groups of four.

Individual versus Group Practice

The third question which the experiment was intended to answer was whether improvement in individual performance occurs more rapidly with individual practice or with practice as a member of a group. To answer this question, all subjects worked alone on the fifth day. As before, the score for each individual was the median number of questions required to solve the four problems. The mean of these scores for the 15 subjects who had previously worked alone was 20.8; for the 30 who had worked in pairs, 19.3; and for the 60 who had been members of groups of four, 19.1. None of the differences among these means is significant. Nor were any of the differences significant among the corresponding means on the fifth day for number of failures or for time scores. Learning went on as well in groups of two or of four as in individual practice.

[In summary the authors conclude that] group performances were superior to individual performance in terms of number of questions, number of failures, and elapsed time per problem; but the performance of groups of four was not superior to that of groups of two, except in terms of the number of failures to reach solution. The performance of individuals was superior to that of either size group in terms of number of man-minutes required for solution.[9]

7. Ibid., pp. 362–363.
8. Ibid., p. 364.
9. Ibid., p. 365.

Observation: Group versus Individual

Since the group sees only through the eyes of its members, who must reach agreement on what they see if they are to present a single group report, the tendency for the members to converge on a standard or norm is even more marked than it is for the individual in the presence of others. Initially the group members have a larger range of observations or opinions available from which to select the most relevant facts for the solution of the problem. Some of the observations can be eliminated through discussion because they are mutually contradictory (Marston, 1924; Shaw, 1932), while other observations are suppressed by the members if they are uncertain of their own opinions (Gurnee, 1937a). Opinions which are given in the group are generally more carefully and cautiously thought out before they are presented (Bos, 1937). However, because of difficulties in communication or because the opinion is given by a low-status or deviant member, correct ideas are sometimes not accepted (Bos, 1937). For reasons of this sort the *actual* intelligence of a group member may differ from his *effective* intelligence. Some groups can use the contributions of an intelligent but low-status member only after his suggestion has first been rejected and then restated by another member with higher status.

As a result of the factors which enter a group's decision, the group will tend to report fewer but more accurate facts than an individual (Dashiell, 1935; Crannell, Switzer, and Morrissette, 1965; Doise, 1970; Hatfield, 1972), although a single trained judge may be better than a group of untrained subjects (Marston, 1924).

Similar results have been reported when groups and individuals submit written reports on their problem-solving process. Groups were found to underreport and individuals to overreport their thinking and their problem solution (Lorge et al., 1956).

Statistical Pooling

Further evidence of the fact that part of the increased accuracy of a group is due to convergence on a norm is found in studies which compare the mathematical mean of a set of individual judgments with the judgment of a single subject. If the subjects are asked to estimate the number of objects in a bottle or the opinions of a group, the mean judgment will be more reliable than individuals' judgments if the objects or the group members are familiar to them. The mean judgment will be less accurate in those cases where the group judgment is biased because the objects are not familiar or because of some optical illusion (Gordon, 1924; Stroop, 1932; Farnsworth and Williams, 1936; Preston, 1938; Travers, 1941, 1943a, 1943b; Klugman, 1945; Ryack, 1965; Sattler, 1966).

Not only does statistical pooling of opinions tend to increase the accuracy and reliability of the estimate, but it also appears to produce judgments as accurate as those made by the same individuals when they actually arrive at a group judgment (Beran et al., 1958). In a study of the prediction of social and technological events (Kaplan, Skogstad, and Girshick, 1950), 26 subjects made 13 weekly sets of predictions about the outcome of a variety of political, economic, and scientific events to occur within a 20-week period. The predictions were then compared with the actual outcomes. The panel mambers were all of a high education level, 24 having college degrees, and 13 of these with two or more years of graduate training. Nineteen of the subjects were mathematicians, statisticians, or engineers. Half of the panel members were placed in rotation in three kinds of quartets: *independent*—in which the subjects worked alone without discussion; *cooperative*—in which the subjects discussed the questions and then answered individually; *joint*—in which discussion was followed by a collective decision on a single answer for the entire group. The results indicate that predictions by groups are more apt to be correct than predictions by the same persons working separately, but also that the *mean* predictions of the four subjects comprising the independent quartets were virtually as accurate as either those made by the members of the cooperative quartets or those made as group decisions by the joint quartets.

Additional comparisons between pooled data and actual group decisions for different types of tasks give further evidence that the type of task usually makes a difference (Barnlund, 1959; Faust, 1959; Hall, Mouton, and Blake, 1963; Collaros and Anderson, 1969; Bouchard, 1972b; Kanekar and Rosenbaum, 1972; Bouchard, Drauden, and Barsaloux, 1974). Mathematical models have also been proposed to clarify some of the aspects of the pooling process (Thomas and Fink, 1961; Stone, 1963; Tannenbaum and Bachman, 1964; Fienberg and Larntz, 1971).

In addition to "pooling," two other "group effects" of an essentially statistical nature should be considered in the comparison of the individual alone and in co-operation with other group members (Ekman, 1955). The first of these is the *summation effect* where the group productivity is simply the sum of the individual productivities. The second is the *probability effect* where a group may be more effective in that there is a greater chance that someone in the group will find the right answer (Taylor and McNemar, 1955; Lorge and Solomon, 1960; Hoppe, 1962; Tuckman and Lorge, 1962; Hall, Mouton, and Blake, 1963; Shaw and Penrod, 1964; Laughlin and Johnson, 1966).

Accuracy of the Individual after Group Discussion

Since the individual tends to shift his opinion in group discussion in the direction of the group norm (Jenness, 1932a; Gurnee, 1937a; Pawlicki and Gunn, 1967), his opinion taken after discussion will be a more accurate estimate of the "correct" answer, provided that the group decision was close to the true answer (Munsterberg, 1914; Burtt, 1920; Jenness, 1932b; Dashiell, 1935; Thorndike, 1938b; Timmons, 1939, 1942). Actually, the individuals need only be aware of the others' opinions to be able to modify their judgments (Bekhterev and Lange, 1924; Jenness, 1932b; Dashiell, 1935).

The influence of the group may be more apparent if there is someone in the group who can provide a model of good problem-solving (Flanders and Thistlethwaite, 1968; Silverman and Stone, 1972). However, for some groups and some individuals no effect is observed (Hudgins, 1960; Sato, 1963).

The shift in individual opinion, as it is considered here, is only a by-product of group decision and not the main object of discussion, as it is in the experiments which seek to bring about a change in group norms. If improving the accuracy of judgment is the goal, then instruction by an expert may do as well as group discussion by relative novices (Wispe, 1951).

Group Learning

Groups of three persons recall more nonsense words than individuals working separately but in the presence of others, but no differences are reported in the recall of meaningful material between groups of three and two individuals. Presumably here the greater storage capacity of the group gives the group an advantage for recall of disconnected bits of information (Perlmutter and de Montmollin, 1952; Perlmutter, 1953).

In the experiment with nonsense words, 23 three-man groups were asked to learn a list of two syllable nonsense words. Another equivalent list was memorized by the same sets of individuals working separately but in the same room. In the group the members were required to agree on each word before it was adopted to represent the group, and they were not permitted to assign specific parts of the list to specific individuals. On a series of five trials, the average group recalled more words than the average individual, with the group scores in general equal to or better than the best individual scores. The experiment was arranged so that some subjects worked first as a group and others as individuals. Those who worked in a group first were able to do better as individuals on the second trial, possibly by using techniques learned in the group session.

Another interpretation can also be made of the fact that for the individuals who first had experience in the group the best individual score was as high as the group, but that the initial individual learning experience did not seem to effect the subsequent performance as groups. It is possible that both types of initial learning experience improved individual performance, but that the averaging effect of group discussion tended to reduce the effectiveness of the best individuals. The differences between individual and group performance would probably have been greater if the individuals had been tested alone, rather than with the social stimulation of other workers.

Subsequent research with college subjects indicates that two persons in discussion provide a better climate for learning concepts than sets of persons without discussion or in competition (McGlynn and Schick, 1973), although the subjects who learn as individuals may transfer their learning more easily (Lemke, Randle, and Robertshaw, 1969; Beane and Lemke, 1971). Some of the apparent differences in results of group learning experiments may lie in the definitions of "coacting" and "interacting" groups (Foot, 1973).

The Risky Shift

In the 1960s a rash of experiments were conducted on the phenomenon of the "risky shift." It appeared that individuals who would make conservative decisions when they were alone about matters involving risk would shift to more risky decisions when they took part in a group discussion. Ten years later, after a number of competing theories about the phenomenon had been proposed and tested, the evidence suggested that a number of factors were operating, indeed all of the factors which operate in any group decision. However, so much research has now been done on this subject that the "risky shift" provides one of the best-documented examples of the differences between individual and group problem-solving.

Shaw (1971, p. 73) provides a brief history of the interest in group decisions involving risk. He notes that in the late 1950s there was a commonly held belief that group decisions tend to be conservative and mediocre. In contrast, Ziller (1957a) found that decisions made by group-centered decision-making groups were more risky than decisions made by leader-centered groups. A later study by Stoner (1961) made a more direct comparison of individual and group decision-making. He found that decisions made by groups were riskier than prediscussion decisions made by individual members of the group. This research served as the starting point for a series of studies designed to determine the generality of this finding and to explain the processes which produced the effect.

Shaw notes that Wallach, Kogan, and Bem (1962) were taken by surprise by the Stoner findings and apparently experienced some doubt that the risky-shift phenomenon could be reliabley demonstrated. They concucted an experiment with 218 liberal arts university students of both sexes. The students were divided into groups of six, either all males or all females. Before and after group discussion, the students were given an opinion questionnaire with 12 hypothetical situations. The central person in each situation had to choose between two courses of action, one of which was more risky than the other but also more rewarding if successful. For each situation a subject was asked to indicate the lowest probability of success he would accept before recommending that the potentially more rewarding alternative be chosen. The probabilities listed were 1, 3, 5, 7, and 9 chances of success in 10, plus a final category (scored as 10) in which the subject could refuse to recommend the risky alternative no matter how high its likelihood of success.

The situations were designed to cover a wide range of content; as examples, the first three on the list can be summarized as follows:

1. An electrical engineer may stick with his present job at a modest but adequate salary or may take a new job offering considerably more money but no long-term security.
2. A man with a severe heart ailment must seriously curtail his customary way of life if he does not undergo a delicate medical operation which might cure him completely or might prove fatal.
3. A man of moderate means may invest some money he recently inherited in secure "blue chip" low-return securities or in more risky securities that offer the possibility of large gains.

As a result of the group discussions Wallach, Kogan and Bem found that (1) group decisions exhibit greater risk taking than appears in prediscussion individual decisions, (2) private decisions after the discussion exhibit the same increased risk taking, (3) this increase in risk taking endures over a subsequent period of weeks, (4) no shift in risk-taking level occurs over time in the absence of the discussion process, and (5) the degrees of individual risk taking and of judged influence within the group are positively related. Subsequent research tended to confirm these findings (Wallach and Kogan, 1965; Siegel and Zajonc, 1967; Jamieson, 1968; Doise, 1969a), even when the group members could not see each other (Kogan and Wallach, 1967a).

Once the phenomenon of the "risky shift" was well documented, the explanation of the behavior was still open. Various authors sought to account for the presence of the shift in different ways. Some varied the facts of the cases to be discussed, some varied the responsibility of the members for the decisions, some varied the cohesiveness of the group, and some varied the basic values of the members or noted the implicit demands of the experimenter. All these factors make a difference. Articles which support the major findings, review the literature, or provide general observations include Doise, 1969b; Vidmar, 1970; Cartwright, 1971; Clark, 1971; Guerin, 1971-1972; Lewit and Saville, 1971; Mackenzie, 1971; McCauley and Graham, 1971; Pruitt, 1971a, 1971b; Vinokur, 1971b; Castore, 1972; Clark and Willems, 1972; Doise, 1972; Jackson, Hourany, and Vidmar, 1972; Johnson and Davis, 1972; Moscovici and Lecuyer, 1972; Cartwright, 1973;

Payne, 1973; Moscovici and Doise, 1974; Myers, Schreiber, and Viel, 1974; Sims, Harley, and Weiner, 1974.

Facts. Subjects who have more facts or in general know more about the situation are more likely to take a chance. If they are clear about the relative amount of risk involved in choosing each alternative, they can make a more rational decision. Thus one of the effects of group discussion is to provide relevant and persuasive arguments which the individual may not have considered before. Research related to the facts of the case includes Bateson, 1966; Flanders and Thistlethwaite, 1967; Kogan and Wallach, 1967c; Lamm, 1967; Harnett, Cummings, and Hughes, 1968; Ellis, Spencer, and Oldfield-Box, 1969; Vinokur, 1969; Zajonc et al., 1969; Des Jarlais, 1970; Lamm, Trommsdorff, and Kogan, 1970; H. Miller, 1970; Miller and Dion, 1970; St. Jean, 1970; Teger et al., 1970; Wallach and Mabli, 1970; Andrews and Johnson, 1971; Burnstein et al., 1971; Dion and Miller, 1971; Ferguson and Vidmar, 1971; Fraser, 1971; Goodale and Flanders, 1971; Guttentag and Freed, 1971; Johnson and Andrews, 1971 , McCauley, Teger, and Kogan, 1971; Myers and Bishop, 1971; Myers, Wong, and Murdoch, 1971; Silverthorne, 1971; Stokes, 1971; Vinokur, 1971a; Blitz and Dansereau, 1972; Chapko, 1972; Gouge and Fraser, 1972; Lamm, Trommsdorff, and Rost-Schaude, 1972; Lupfer, Jones, and Quin, 1972; McCauley and Kramer, 1972; Moscovici, Doise, and Dulong, 1972; Schönpflug and Schönpflug, 1972; Burnstein and Vinokur, 1973; Burnstein, Vinokur, and Trope, 1973; Fischer and Burdeny, 1973; Gaskell, Thomas, and Farr, 1973; Posavac and Pasko, 1973; Semin and Glendon, 1973; Ebbesen and Bowers, 1974; Myers, Bach, and Schreiber, 1974; Vinokur and Burnstein, 1974.

Responsibility and Majority Opinion. When subjects feel that the responsibility for the decisions has been diffused over the group, the decisions are more risky (Wallach, Kogan, and Bem, 1964; Bem, Wallach, and Kogan, 1965). In some experiments the risk takers do not appear to be the most persuasive persons in the group (Wallach, Kogan, and Burt, 1968), although other research suggests that the risk takers may be more confident of their opinions and have considerable influence, especially when they are in the majority (Burnstein, 1969a). Since risk takers seem to have been a majority in the population from which most experimental groups are drawn, the shift toward risk tends to reflect the influence of majority opinion, especially when the task is ambiguous. Additional evidence is provided by Marquis, 1962; Rettig, 1966a; Kogan and Wallach, 1967b; Hoyt and Stoner, 1968; Pruitt and Teger, 1969; Bell and Jamieson, 1970; Cecil, Chertkoff, and Cummings, 1970; Dion, Miller, and Magnan, 1970; Myers, Murdoch, and Smith, 1970; Castore, Peterson, and Goodrich, 1971; Witte, 1971; Myers and Murdoch, 1972; Roberts and Castore, 1972; Zajonc, Wolosin, and Wolosin, 1972; Bennett, Lindskold, and Bennett, 1973; Gordon, Flanders, and Cranny, 1973; Lamm, Trommsdorff, and Rost-Schaude, 1973; Paicheler and Bouchet, 1973; Bauer and Turner, 1974; Blascovich and Ginsburg, 1974.

Social Approval. Subjects will make more risky decisions if they feel that other group members approve of risk taking (Teger and Pruitt, 1967; Blank, 1968; Madaras and Bem, 1968; Wallach and Wing, 1968) or that the risky choice is more ethical or altruistic (Alker and Kogan, 1968; Horne, 1972; Schroeder, 1973). The effect will be heightened when group members have strong affiliative motives or are highly interdependent (Rettig, 1966b; Weinstein et al., 1968). However, if the other group members seem to approve of taking less risk, then the subjects will be more conservative (Rabow et al., 1966; Stoner, 1968). They will also be more conservative if they are making decisions for another person or group, rather than for themselves (Kogan and Zaleska, 1969). Related research includes Lonegran and McClintock, 1961; Burnstein, 1966; Moscovici and Zavalloni, 1969; Pruitt, 1969b; Swap and Miller, 1969; Horne, 1970; Jellison and Riskind, 1970; Kroger and Briedis, 1970; Lamm and Kogan, 1970; Mackenzie, 1970a; Baron et al., 1971; Clark, Crockett, and Archer, 1971; Dion, Miller, and Magnan, 1971; Fraser, Gouge, and Billig, 1971; Lamm, Schaude, and Trommsdorff, 1971; Lupfer et al., 1971; Teger and Kogan, 1971; Vidmar and Burdeny, 1971; Vroom and Deci, 1971; Willems and Clark, 1971; Zaleska and Kogan, 1971; Blascovich, 1972; Horne and Long, 1972; Kogan, Lamm, and Trommsdorff, 1972; McCauley, 1972; Middleton and Warren, 1972; Baron, Monson, and Baron, 1973; Bennett, Price, and Lindskold, 1973; Brok and Kogan, 1973; Cvetkovich and Baumgardner, 1973; Pilkonis and Zanna, 1973; Schulman, 1973a, 1973b; Baron, Roper, and Baron, 1974; Burnstein, Vinokur, and Pichevin, 1974; Runyan, 1974.

Group Composition. As in the experiments on "social facilitation," some of the group effect in the risky-shift phenomenon may be that the "dominant" or more likely responses are enhanced as a result of making decisions in the presence of others (Zajonc et al., 1970; Myers and Arenson, 1972). However, more obvious effects result from the types of personalities composing the group. As in the Asch experiment on conformity, subjects who are high on autonomy are less likely to be influenced by the group (Wallach, Kogan, and Burt, 1967). In general, subjects tend to behave in a way which is consistent with their personality characteristics (Rim, 1964a, 1964b, 1965; Marquis and Reitz, 1969).

Experimenter Demands. Some of the early results of the risky-shift experiments may have been simply a response to the implicit demands of the experimenter as he defined the situation for the subjects at the beginning of the experiment. In research in which the usual "risk-oriented" instructions are replaced by more neutral instructions, the risky shift seems to disappear (Zajonc et al., 1968; Clark and Willems, 1969; Willems and Clark, 1969).

Researchers who have gone into the field to look for risky shifts at the race track or in the courtroom or those who have attempted to simulate more "real life" conditions in the laboratory report mixed results. The nature of the task and the situation make a difference. See, for example, Flanders, 1970; Raack, 1970; Belovicz and Finch, 1971; Bennett and Lindskold, 1971; Doise, 1971; Peterson and Fulcher, 1971; Pruitt and Teger, 1971; Higbee, 1972; Lambert, 1972; Lamm and Ochsmann, 1972; Malamuth and Feshbach, 1972; Mindock, 1972; Singh and Singh, 1972; Abelson, 1973; Blascovich, Veach, and Ginsburg, 1973; McCauley et al., 1973; Main and Walker, 1973; Reingen, 1973; Walker and Main, 1973; Baron, Baron, and Roper, 1974, Izzett and Leginski, 1974; Yinon, Shoham, and Lewis, 1974.

Finally there are the studies which report negative results or deal with variables which do not fit easily into any of the above groupings. These include Wallach, Kogan, and Burt, 1965; Kogan and Wallach, 1966; Zajonc and Sales, 1966; Rettig and Turoff, 1967; Rettig, 1969; White and Minden, 1969; Lupfer, 1970; Mackenzie, 1970b; Minton and Miller, 1970; Burnstein and Katz, 1971; Carlson and Davis, 1971; Haley and Rule, 1971; Higbee, 1971; Jellison and Riskind, 1971; Marwell, Schmitt, and Shotola, 1971; Bradley, Snyder, and Katahn, 1972; Krauss, Robinson, and Cauthen, 1972; Marwell and Schmitt, 1972a; Rettig, 1972; Schmitt and Marwell, 1972a; Schulman, 1972; Paicheler and Bouchet, 1973; Tracey and

Cross, 1973; Chaubey, 1974; Cooper and Wood, 1974; Davis et al., 1974; Hartnett and Barber, 1974; Myers, 1974.

Summary

The comparison of individual productivity alone, in the presence of others, and in cooperation with others in a group has been a major research interest in social psychology from Triplett's experiment in 1898 to the present. Although it is theoretically possible to break the problem-solving process down into separate steps such as observation, hypothesizing, and proposing action, most researchers have concentrated on a comparison of the end products of the process rather than the process itself.

Following Triplett, later experiments have generally confirmed the generalization that some subjects are stimulated positively by the presence of others, some are stimulated negatively, and some are unaffected. The explanation may lie in the fact that the presence of others has a facilitating effect on the dominant (most likely) response, hindering performance when the dominant response is incorrect and helping performance when the dominant response is correct. The Western Electric researches illustrate the way in which the social influences in a group of girls working on individual tasks can influence productivity.

In the observation and hypothesizing steps of the problem-solving process, subjects tend to be less idiosyncratic when other subjects are working on the same task.

The superiority of the group over the individual with respect to productivity is usually greater on manual problems than on intellectual tasks. The group will lose its superiority in accuracy and efficiency if (1) no division of labor is required, (2) problems of control are too great, or (3) the group develops a standard of productivity which is lower than that of a separate individual. In terms of man-hours an individual is usually more productive.

Because of a tendency to converge on a norm, groups will report fewer but more accurate facts than individuals. However, some increase in accuracy can be obtained by eliminating group discussion and simply pooling the judgments of one individual or of several individuals. As a by-product of group discussion, the individual tends to be more accurate in his own judgment after he has heard the judgments of others.

Groups tend to recall more information than individuals, presumably because of their greater capacity to store information.

Under some conditions individuals make conservative decisions when they are alone but shift to more risky decisions after taking part in group discussion. The "risky shift" phenomena is more likely to occur when the group discussion provides relevant and persuasive arguments, when the responsibility for the decisions has been diffused over the group, when other group members approve risk taking, and when the experimenter seems to desire a risky outcome. A shift toward conservative decisions will occur if the same factors point toward a conservative shift; thus the "risky shift" phenomenon provides a well-documented example of the differences between individual and group problem-solving.

Chapter 15

GROUP VERSUS GROUP

THIS FINAL CHAPTER IS, in effect, a summary of the entire book. In part 1 the central tendencies in group process were observed. Part 2 described the deviations from these central tendencies which could be expected if certain individual or group factors were varied. Now at the end of part 3 we ask the question, Given these central tendencies and these expected deviations, what can be done to make some groups more productive than others?

A general answer is given first in a review of some of the characteristics of productive groups. This raises the question of the criteria for productivity, since groups which are productive in the laboratory may not be productive in the field. Whatever the criteria, productivity in the task area is often achieved only at the expense of member satisfaction in the social-emotional area.

More specific variables related to group productivity are summarized in the last section of the chapter. Here the effects of variations in members' personalities and social characteristics, cohesiveness, group size, task, communication network, and leadership are reviewed. Finally we will consider the effects of using different decision rules and of various forms of feedback and training on the output from problem-solving groups.

General Characteristics of Productive Groups

The most productive groups, like the most productive individuals, are found to be those which can best carry out the steps in the problem-solving process (Lippitt, 1948; Darley, Gross, and Martin, 1952; Cattell, 1953; Gross, Martin, and Darley, 1953; Bjerstedt, 1961; Hoffman, Harburg, and Maier, 1962; C. G. Smith, 1970; Stoller, 1970b; Tallman, 1970; Walter and Miles, 1972). For example, airplane crews which survive when they are forced to bail out of their plane over enemy territory are the ones which are most effective in clarifying an unstructured situation, resuming communication among members, and establishing a goal (Torrance, 1953a, 1954b, 1955a). In general, groups which have a structure suited to their function and have high morale based on a large number of intergroup friendships will be motivated to try harder and be the most productive (French, 1944; Goodacre, 1953; Horwitz and Cartwright, 1953; Horwitz, Exline, and Lee, 1953; Hanhart, 1963; Ramsoy et al., 1963; Shiota, 1965; Poitou and Flament, 1967; Golubeva, 1969; Napier, 1969; Shiflett, 1973a). The motivation of the group is lowered if some members show an indifferent and neglectful attitude toward the task (Rosenthal and Cofer, 1948). This may be expected to occur less often among groups of friends. The organized groups are more productive not only because they have better procedures for solving task and social-emotional problems (Higgin and Bridger, 1964; Fathi, 1968; H. F. Taylor, 1968) but also because the positions of members in the group are relatively stable and less time need be spent in a status struggle (Adams, 1953; Heinicke and Bales, 1953).

The self-perceptions of groups, as revealed in group projective tests, indicate that productive groups tend to be aware of characteristics which make them effective. In another study with airplane crews, crews rated good by instructors perceived in a series of projective sketches more satisfactory outcomes, less leaving the group, more orderly functioning and productivity, more interpersonal harmony, and fewer status differences (Torrance, 1953c).

To help a discussion group increase the accuracy of its self-perception, a non-participating observer has been used who supplies the necessary "feedback." He reports at the end of a discussion his observation on whether or not the group has stayed on the topic, the point reached in discussion, the rate of progress, and the amount of participation. Observations of this type are then used in group self-evaluation (Jenkins, 1948).

Groups which are initially low in productivity can be made more effective, either by increasing the task skill through training (Maier, 1953; Hall, 1957; Maier, 1972), by increasing their motivation by paying more attention to them (Mayo, 1933; Turner, 1933), or by providing other incentives (Berkowitz, 1957a).

The following books and articles provide reviews of the literature on group productivity, suggest basic dimensions for analysis, or high-light aspects of group performance: Cattell and Stice, 1960; McGuire and Tolchin, 1961; Milburn, 1961; Ronning and Horrocks, 1961; Blake, Mouton, and Fruchter, 1962; Borgatta and Glass, 1963; Mulder, 1963; Berrien, 1964; Collins and Guetzkow, 1964; Hoffman, 1965; Ziller, 1965a; Altman, 1966a; Shears and Gunderson, 1966; Owens, 1967; Kelley and Thibaut, 1968; Raven, 1968; Burnand, 1969; Lewis, 1970b; Pheysey and Payne, 1970; Quey, 1971; Zander, 1971; Koile and Gallessich, 1972.

The Criterion for Productivity

The criterion used to predict group productivity may not always be the same for both the experimental and field situation. This is illustrated by a study of crew performance in a test situation as a predictor of field and combat performance. Seventy-one aircraft crews were classified according to combat experience and their actual success in missions and were rated on their effectiveness by their superiors. Although effective combat crews were not found to be different from less effective crews or crews which dropped out of training on some measures made in the test situation, they did differ on others. No differences were found in problem-solving scores, manner of team performance, or the members' perception of their group interaction, but the effective crews were better in use of manpower, completeness of participation, coordination, control, and flexibility. In their stories for the projective test, the successful crews described groups which were better organized and more friendly and had a greater toleration for intermember conflict (Torrance, 1953a, 1955a).

In this case, attempts to predict from some criteria of *productivity* in the test situation (e.g., problem-solving score) to *productivity* in the field would have failed, since in the less stressful laboratory situation the crews which were later to do well in combat did no better on their problem score than those which would prove ineffective.

Although the problem of the criterion of productivity has been raised in the comparison of group with group, it also applies to the comparison of the individual and the group. The tendency of individuals to equal or surpass groups on certain *productivity* criteria in the laboratory may disappear in other situations.

The problems of predicting productivity which result from different ways of measuring a criterion such as performance test, judges' rating, or group self-evaluation have been discussed in chapter 11 on group task.

Satisfaction versus Productivity

Since individuals tend to join groups for three general reasons, either for the prestige of membership, to help the group reach a goal, or because they value the association with the group members (Festinger, Schachter, and Back, 1950), their satisfaction with the group can be the result of success in any of these three areas. Their past experience which has prepared them for participation in the same or similar groups will in turn affect their ability to adjust to, and thereby be satisfied with, the present outcome (Burgess and Cottrell, 1939; Arsenian, 1943).

High productivity in the task area is not always associated with productive intermember relationships, since the former may sometimes be gained only at the expense of the latter (Roy, 1959–1960; Stogdill, 1963). This is especially true in the comparison of various forms of competition with forms of cooperation. For example, in a case study of a group of clothing salesmen in a department store, competition among salesmen for the next customer resulted in morale lower than when a system of cooperative activity was initiated. However, more suits were sold when the salesmen were in competition (Babchuk and Goode, 1951).

In other studies of competition versus cooperation, individuals working together but with individual goals are contrasted with individuals working together with a single group goal (see chapter 14). The competitive groups are generally less efficient and less satisfying to the members (Deutsch, 1949; Mintz, 1951; Stendler, Damrin, and Haines, 1951; Grace, 1954; Willis and Hale, 1963; Zander and Wolfe, 1964; McGlynn, 1972), except in cases where members are asked to cooperate to receive a group score in a task in which it would be more appropriate to rate individual performance. For example, college students who were given group scores for discussion effectiveness rather than individual grades were dissatisfied with their group incentive system (H. C. Smith, 1955).

One element in competition which would appear to be related to member satisfaction is the fact that the members are competing for a high status in the group. Members of groups with a high consensus on status are in general more satisfied with the other members and also with the task performance than members of groups in which the status of the members is uncertain (Heinicke and Bales, 1953). When each member's status is apparent, the contributions of each will be given their appropriate "weight." Groups led by authoritarian leaders show results which are similar to competitive groups, since in these groups all members are in competition for status in the eyes of the leader. Productivity is higher and morale lower than for groups led by democratic leaders (Lewin, Lippitt, and White, 1939; Adams, 1954), although in some research no differences are reported in variations of the two styles (McCurdy and Eber, 1953; see chapter 13 for a discussion of democratic and authoritarian leader styles). In each of these examples, the "productivity" refers to the quantity of the output, since the quality may be higher for the cooperative groups.

This trend only holds in groups in which there is an expectation that the leader will be democratic (Berkowitz, 1953). Also when most of the members of the group attempt to satisfy their "'self-oriented needs" rather than work toward the group goal or the solution of the group's problems, the average member satisfaction with the meeting goes down, along with group productivity (Shaw, 1959b). In the study of 72 decision-making conferences in governmental and industrial organizations, the degree to which these needs were expressed was related to various criteria of satisfaction and accomplishment. A high degree of self-oriented need expression was accompanied by a low level of satisfaction with the decisions reached, with the procedures used to reach the decision, with the chairman's handling of the meeting, and with the meeting as a whole. Members of groups high in self-oriented need expression also tended to perceive themselves as less unified, were rated as having more conflict by the observers, and completed fewer agenda items, although their meetings lasted longer (Fouriezos, Hutt, and Guetzkow, 1950; Marquis, Guetzkow, and Heyns, 1951).

A second study was made by Guetzkow and Gyr (1954) of five- to twenty-man business and government conferences. In these groups, conflict over the task or interpersonal relations also resulted in less consensus. High consensus in all groups was associated with low expression of self-oriented need, high need satisfaction during the meeting, pleasant atmosphere, and orderly activity. In those groups in which there was conflict over the task, higher consensus was achieved if the members used the facts, had an active chairman, and expressed warm interpersonal feelings. Higher consensus was also achieved in those groups in which there was interpersonal conflict if the members avoided some of the conflict by postponing difficult problems, showing little interest in the task, or withdrawing from interpersonal contact.

Additional studies relating member satisfaction to productivity include Heslin and Dunphy, 1964; Shaw and Blum, 1964; Shaw and Caron, 1965; Vos, Doerbecker, and Brinkman, 1969; Matejko, 1973.

Members' Personalities

In selecting members with personality or social characteristics which will result in a productive group, the requirements of the task must be kept in mind. If the group has a purpose which tends to emphasize problems of control (or problems of affection), then it is best to select members who do not have so much internal conflict that they are unable to be effective in this area. This same generalization holds, of course, for the major steps in problem-solving. If the step of observation, hypothesizing, or proposing action is especially important for a particular group, then it would be wise to select members who have the required capacities (Willerman, 1953). Subjects who have high individual scores on intelligence, cognitive complexity, or problem-solving ability reflected in higher levels of education usually form a more productive group than those who are less able (Green, 1950; Scharmann, 1962; Vinacke, 1964; Triandis, Hall, and Ewen, 1965; Friedlander, 1966; Ghiselli, 1966; Lott and Lott, 1966; Stager, 1967; Tuckman, 1967; Laughlin, Branch, and Johnson, 1969; Turney, 1970; Fromkin, Klimoski, and Flanagan,

1972). In addition, an individual can work best with others who are at least equal or better in skill (Rosenberg, Erlick, and Berkowitz, 1955).

Group members with given personality characteristics tend to have more influence upon the patterns of group interaction in newly formed groups than they may be expected to have in groups which have developed a stable culture pattern (Cattell et al., 1953). As groups move through the initial stages of development, members who have problems in one area may impede the progress of the group by forcing other members to continue to work in one problem area for long after the problems in this area have been solved by the majority of the members. Thus, in one instance, the members who were absent most often from a therapy group formed a subgroup which challenged the formal leader and made it difficult for the group to move on to other problems (Herbert and Trist, 1953).

On the other hand, the effectiveness of the group can be increased if some members have personality characteristics which are considered particularly valuable by the group. Since the leader is a key person, the group will be more effective if he closely approximates the group's ideal of a leader (Greer, 1955).

Additional studies of aspects of members' personalities and their relationship to group productivity include Runkel, 1959; Hoffman and Smith, 1960; Shaw, 1960; Hoffman and Maier, 1961a; Roby and Lanzetta, 1961; Moos and Speisman, 1962; Bass and Dunteman, 1963a; Crowell and Scheidel, 1963; Amidjaja and Vinacke, 1965; Beckwith, Iverson, and Reuder, 1965; Denmark, Murgatroyd, and Pepitone, 1965; Zander and Medow, 1965; Klein and Christiansen, 1966; Richmond and Ostlund, 1966; Forward, 1969; O'Brien and Owens, 1969; Shalinsky, 1969; Aronoff, 1970; Torrance, 1971; Bochner and Bochner, 1972; Wood, 1972b; Sorenson, 1973; Ryckman and Sherman, 1974.

Compatibility of Affectional Orientation

A group's ability to handle feelings and emotions is especially important in tasks which require close, intimate relations with others or which arouse member feelings. If the group members have similar personality traits in the area of affection, they should be able to agree more readily on the extent to which they will permit close, intimate relationships within the group. If members differ in that some want close relationships while others prefer to keep at a distance, then the members will be basically incompatible, a condition which should decrease their productivity. Incompatibility in the area of control will have a similar effect (Reddy and Byrnes, 1972).

Compatible groups can be selected fully formed on the basis of past performance, or they can be composed of members who have either chosen each other on an appropriate sociometric criterion or who possess the necessary qualifications as revealed by personality tests.

An experiment by Schutz (1958a, pp. 128–135) using composed groups of college students illustrates the relationship between compatibility and productivity. Schutz sent invitations to every tenth male student at a large university asking him to participate in an experiment to be conducted over a six-week period. When about 100 had accepted, they were called together and given a personality test and other questionnaires. On the basis of the results of the personality test and a consideration of their mathematics and verbal scores on the Scholastic Achievement Test, 12 five-man groups were formed.

Four groups were composed according to "Compatible pattern A," four followed "compatible pattern B," and four followed the "incompatible pattern" (see table 36). Compatible pattern A contained a member who was predicted to be a "focal person," a "main supporting member," and three subjects who were less intelligent and less assertive who would be members. All subjects in this pattern were personal in orientation with a liking for close, intimate relationships. The subjects in compatible pattern B were predicted to play similar roles except that they were all counterpersonal in orientation, persons who liked to keep others at a distance. In the incompatible pattern there were two pairs of a "focal person" and a follower; one pair was personal and the other counterpersonal. The incompatible pattern also contained one neutral person.

Each of these 12 groups was brought to the small group laboratory and run through 14 meetings over a period of six weeks. There were four one-hour meetings a day at 4:00, 5:00, 7:30, and 8:30 P.M., Monday through Friday, and at 10:00 and 11:00 A.M. and 1:00 and 2:00 P.M. on Saturday. Each group met twice a week at the same time (except Saturday), three days apart (e.g., Monday at 5:00 P.M. and Thursday at 5:00).

Table 36. Composition Patterns for Compatible and Incompatible Groups of Personal and Counterpersonal Members

Compatible Group Members (Type A)				
	FP_p	MS_p	M_p	M_p	M_p
Personalness	H	H	H	H	H
Dependence	L,M	L,M	L,M	L,M	L,M
Assertiveness	H	L,M	L,M	L,M	L,M
Intelligence	H	H	L,M	L,M	L,M

Compatible Group Members (Type B)				
	FP_c	MS_c	M_c	M_c	M_c
Personalness	L	L	L	L	L
Dependence	L,M	M,H	M,H	M,H	M,H
Assertiveness	H	L,M	L,M	L,M	L,M
Intelligence	H	H	L,M	L,M	L,M

Incompatible Group Members				
	FP_p	S_p	FP_c	S_c	N
Personalness	H	H	L	L	M
Dependence	L,M	L,M	H	H	M
Assertiveness	H	L,M	H	L,M	L
Intelligence	H	L,M	H	L,M	L,M

	Personal	Counterpersonal	
	Subgroup	Dependent Subgroup	
	Antagonistic		
	Subgroups		

Key: H = roughly highest quarter   FP = focal person
     M = roughly second or third quarter   MS = main supporting member
     L = roughly lowest quarter   M = member
     p = personal   S = supporting member
     c = counterpersonal   N = neutral

Source: William C. Schutz, *FIRO: A Three-Dimensional Theory of Interpersonal Behavior* (New York: Holt, Rinehart & Winston, 1958), p. 129. Copyright © 1958 by William C. Schutz. Adapted and reprinted by permission of the author and the publisher.

Each group was given the sequence of tasks listed in table 37.

Productivity differences were measured by comparison of the scores received on the objective measures assigned to each task. The intercept contests in the eleventh to fourteenth meetings were games played between two teams of different compatibility types. Each team played approximately the same number of contests.

The discussion tasks were administered as follows: The experimenter would read aloud a short (three-paragraph) description of a situation involving a difficult decision, typically based on authority versus friendship, or something similarly related to the personality dimensions. Each subject would then write down what he would do in that situation and the reasons for his decision. Then the group would be allowed 15 to 30 minutes to discuss the problem and come to a "group decision," a purposely ambiguous phrase not specifying unanimity majority, or any other system of decision. Then the members were asked to appoint one member to be spokesman for the group and present the group's decision to the experimenter. The experimenter returned on signal and, before hearing the group's decision, first had the subjects write their own individual postdiscussion decisions.

A typical meeting proceeded as follows: The group would arrive about five minutes before the hour and would go right into the laboratory room. They had all been given a tour of the observation room at the first meeting, so they were fully aware of the observers. Recording apparatus would be turned on in the observation room. The experimenter would watch through the one-way mirror for several minutes, allowing the group time for free discussion. The group was under the impression they were simply waiting for the session to begin. Generally about five minutes were allowed unless there was some especially important interaction occurring.

The experimenter would then greet the group and present the day's activity. He would attempt to be distant and friendly with all groups, trying not to encourage or discourage any single group. After he was assured the instructions were clear, the experimenter would leave the room to return only when summoned at the end of an activity. The experimenter attempted to be with the group only when necessary. After the group's activity was finished, he returned to the room and completed

Table 37. Schedule of Activities of Groups

Meeting	Task
1.	Indoctrination, discussion (choosing a group name), discussion (prison problem)
2.	Building task (the Toy), discussion (cheating problem)
3.	Intercept task (modified chess)
4.	Intercept task, discussion (child rearing)
5.	Free behavior, no task, standings announced, each group told that "all groups were close, they were among lower ones"
6.	Discussion (how to improve groups), concept formation task
7.	Building tasks
8.	Intercept tasks, discussion (traffic problem)
9.	Group projective, concept formation task
10.	Building task, intercept task
11–14.	Intercept contests (pairs of groups)

Source: William C. Schutz, *FIRO: A Three-Dimensional Theory of Interpersonal Behavior* (New York: Holt, Rinehart & Winston, 1958), p. 131. Copyright © 1958 by William C. Schutz. Adapted and reprinted by permission of the author and the publisher.

the hour's work. Usually he would then leave, allowing a few more minutes for free behavior, and then return and dismiss the group.

Conditions of the Experiment

The subjects were selected on the basis of personality tests from the college freshmen volunteers. They had a wide range of backgrounds, with the main differences from a random population probably being higher mean intelligence and higher mean social-economic status. All were from 17 to 23 years old. An attempt was made to balance intelligence between groups. This was done successfully within the limits of scheduling.

All tasks used in the experiment were new to the subjects. There was no indication that any subject had special knowledge that would assist him in the solution of the tasks.

The previous acquaintance of the subjects with each other varied, but on the whole the members of any one of the five-man groups were not well acquainted and certainly no group had ever met as a group prior to the experiment.

There were virtually no restraints put on the groups as to seating arrangements or communication. With regard to leadership, the experimenter never designated a particular member as any type of leader. In some tasks the experimenter named certain roles which had to be filled by men chosen by the group itself. In all cases the group could remove the man they chose from his role at any time.

Motivation was engendered by (1) a talk to all subjects on the importance of the experiment to various industrial, governmental, military, and research activities, (2) a statement at the outset of the experiment that the experimenter wanted only participants who would appear promptly a every meeting and participate fully, (3) a reward of $25 to the "best" group, and several $10 prizes for the "best" individual performance, (4) payment of $1 per hour of meeting for each subject, and (5) payment only if all members attended all meetings.

The nondiscussion tasks given to the groups were:

1. *Game* (Intercept). A modified chess-type game involving the whole group coming to a decision within 30 seconds. One man was chosen coordinator by the group who had complete authority and responsibility for making the decisions.

2. *Concept.* This is the task used by Bruner, Goodnow, and Austin (1956) for individual concept formation studies. It was adapted to the group situation and administered similarly to the intercept task except that (a) there were two coordinators with equal authority, and (b) there was a penalty for total time rather than a time list for individual moves. This served to introduce a new type of decision, that between taking a chance and acting quickly, and being more deliberate.

3. *Toy.* This was a task in which the group was to build a specified structure as fast as possible. The materials used included heavy paper squares and triangles, reinforced with wooden dowels. This was a division-of-labor-type task, requiring the coordination of several different jobs.

Data were collected by questionnaires, observation, and sociometric tests. Throughout the course of the experiment, the following questionnaires were administered:

1. Slater, *Parental Role Preference Questionnaire* (PRP)
2. Blum, *Blacky Projective Test*
3. Blum, *Defense Preference Inventory* (DPI)
4. Schutz, *Fundamental Interpersonal Relations Orientation* (FIRO)

5. *California F Scale* (authoritarianism)
6. Edwards, *Personal Preference Schedule*
7. LaForge and Suczek, *Interpersonal Checklist.*
8. Guilford, *R* (*Rhathmyia*) *and C* (*Cyclothmia*) *Scales*
9. Bales and Couch, *Value Profile*

These questionnaires were administered over the entire 14 meetings so as to spread the work required over a reasonable time period.

Each meeting was observed by two to five trained observers. No category system was used to record the act-by-act sequence behavior, except for a few meetings which involved special projects. The primary observational data were a series of ratings made once or twice a meeting. When there were two activities in one meeting, e.g., a discussion and a building task, one rating was made after each activity. If there was only one activity, only one rating was made per meeting. The ratings were made for a variety of roles commonly noted in group meetings, such as discussion guider, influencer, and promoter of personal feelings. The observer was first asked to decide whether or not any member or members of the group clearly fulfilled the description of the role, and then he was asked to rank all five group members with respect to this role. The weighted sum of all rankings for all meetings was computed for each role for each group member. These ratings were standardized and used as the behavioral data.

In order to obtain the most comparable data, the subjects were given a rating sheet almost identical to that used by the observers. A rating sheet was used at both the fifth and the tenth meetings. In addition the subjects filled out regular sociometric questions regarding "like," "work with," and "influences." These constituted additional sources of data.

Results of the Compatibilty Experiment

Since all the tasks were of different types, it was difficult to combine scores to get an overall productivity measure. It was therefore decided to rank all 12 groups on each task and use the sum of these ranks for the total productivity score.

There were four objective tasks: Toy, Concept, Game, and Game Contest. Where a task occurred more than once (as with Toy and Concept), the ranks were averaged to give a final rank for that task. Thus the final rank was based on one rank for each task (see table 38).

The difference in ranks between the combined "compatibles" and the "incompatibles" is significant beyond the .02 level (Mann-Whitney U-test).

There is virtually no difference in productivity between the "personal-compatibles" (P-Com) and the counterpersonal-compatibles" (CP-Com). The CP-Coms have one "final rank" less, while the P-Coms have two and a half total ranks less; neither difference is significant. The ideal result of the final ranking would have placed the "incompatibles" (Incom) in ranks 9, 10, 11, and 12 and seen the first eight ranks distributed among the compatible groups. Actually, this happened with the one exception of Incom group 5 and P-Com group 1, who ideally should have interchanged ranks 6 and 9.

However, the variations in the ranks make it statistically tenuous to assume that the productivity rank for any group is highly stable. This may mean (1) the number of tests of productivity was inadequate to stabilize performance, (2) the tasks required different abilities of the groups, and thus they performed differentially, or (3) groups are always erratic in their performance.

Table 38. Ranks on Productivity for All Groups on All Tasks

Personal
Compatible Groups

	Toy	Concept	Game	Contest	Total	Final Rank
No. 1	3	8	7	10	28	9
No. 6	1	1	11	1	14	1
No. 9	7.5	4	2	4	17.5	2
No. 12	10	10	1	6.5	27.5	8
Total					87	20
Counterpersonal Compatible Groups						
No. 2	6	6	4	2	18	3
No. 7	2	7	10	3	22	4
No. 8	10	5	5	6.5	26.5	7
No. 11	7.5	2.5	2	11	23	5
Total					89.5	19
Incompatible Groups						
No. 3	10	11.5	8	6.5	36	11
No. 4	12	11.5	9	9	41.5	12
No. 5	4.5	9	6	6.5	26	6
No. 10	4.5	2.5	12	12	31	10
Total					134.5	39

Source: William C. Schutz, *FIRO: A Three-Dimensional Theory of Interpersonal Behavior* (New York: Holt, Rinehart & Winston, 1958), p. 135. Copyright © 1958 by William C. Schutz. Adapted and reprinted by permission of the author and the publisher.

The results of the experiment with college subjects generally confirm the hypothesis that compatible groups are more productive than incompatible groups, although, contrary to the anticipated result, the groups composed of members who were counterpersonal performed as well as those composed of personal members.

Several predictions in the area of interpersonal choice which were supported by a previous experiment with naval recruits (Schutz, 1955) were not confirmed in the experiment with college subjects. In the incompatible group of college subjects, members of subgroups did not prefer to work with each other more, nor did the members of the personal subgroups like each other more as they did in groups composed of naval recruits. Although in the navy experiment a member of a personal subgroup tended to rank the man he liked best higher on competence than an objective measure would justify, the same tendency to overrate performance was not evident in the college groups.

In the college experiment the persons predicted to be focal and main supporting members in each group *did* rank each other highly as easy to work well with in the personal compatible groups, confirming the navy results. This was not true, however, in the college counterpersonal compatible groups. In the personal compatible groups, the person predicted to be focal *appeared* more central to the observers in both experiments.

Social Characteristics

In the selection of productive members by their social characteristics, the major variables have been so apparent that they have received little experimental substantion: Adults are usually more efficient than children, and older children more so than younger children (James, 1956). Single-sex groups are often more efficient than mixed groups because they spend less time on social-emotional activity (South, 1927; Gurnee, 1937b, 1962), and men and women typically do better in the roles for which their culture has trained them. Groups composed of friends are usually more productive than groups of strangers (Husband, 1940; Zeleny, 1947; Goodacre, 1951; Van Zelst, 1952; Orlemans, 1965; Sage, 1969; Weinstein et al., 1972) unless, like the mixed committees, they spend all their time in social-emotional activity (Horsfall and Arensberg, 1949; Scofield, 1960; McGrath, 1962).

The relationship between productivity and duration of membership in a group is illustrated by a study in which one member of a four-man group was placed in another group as a "stranger" and later returned to his own group. In each case, the task of the group was to list the objects which could be seen in a series of Rorschach cards. The production of ideas about the Rorschach card decreased for the experimental subject when he was moved from his initial group to a second four-man group as a stranger, and increased when he returned again. The subject presumably was inhibited in his productivity by the "strangeness" of the social situation in the new group (Nash and Wolfe, 1957).

Additional research illustrating the influence on group productivity of such social factors as social class, occupation, and sex includes Hoffman and Maier, 1961b; Stone, 1971; Back, Bunker, and Dunnagan, 1972; Vandendriessche and Lagrou, 1972; Sperry, 1974.

Cohesiveness

Groups which are highly cohesive tend to work harder regardless of outside supervision (Berkowitz, 1954a, 1954b; Cohen, 1957a; Lodahl and Porter 1961; Cratty and Sage, 1964; Gottheil and Vielhaber, 1966; Samuels and O'Rourke, 1969; Hall, 1971, Landers and Crum, 1971; Martens and Peterson, 1971; D'Augelli, 1973a; Krichevskii, 1973). For example, when 50 six-man work units of five employees and their regular plant supervisor were timed in the task of assembling two factory products, the group attributes of "character," "compactness," and "cohesiveness" were found to be correlated .76, .78, and .88 with a productivity score. In this case, as in other industrial studies, member satisfaction was not related to productivity (Danzig and Galanter, 1955).

Cohesive groups will be especially productive if they are also motivated to do the task well. In an air corps experiment, members of 81 eleven-man B-29 crews were asked to indicate how important they felt the B-29 was for defense as evidence of their own motivation and also to estimate the motivation of other crew members. Cohesiveness of each group was indicated by the extent to which its members liked to spend time with other crew members and their feeling that the members respected each other. Effectiveness was measured by superiors' ratings and the percentage of missions failed. An analysis of the data indicated that in the crews with high cohesiveness, high motivation was related to effectiveness. However, in crews with low cohesiveness, effectiveness was negatively correlated with the discrepancy between actual and perceived motivation, regardless of whether the scores were both high or both low (Berkowitz, 1956a). That is, the crews who were not very friendly would still be effective if members had the same regard for the worth of their job in the air corps.

In some cases cohesiveness in a small ingroup may be generated primarily by antagonism toward some outgroup (Sherif, 1951; Sherif and Sherif, 1953). This intergroup hostility may then make it difficult for members of both groups to join in a new group to arbitrate their differences. This apparently happens between groups of labor and management in some industies. For example, in a study of the interaction process in the mediation of labor-management disputes, it was found that ultimate success of the session could be partially predicted from the parties' states of mind when they embarked upon the session: the more hostile their expressed feelings, the less likelihood of success (Landsberger, 1955b).

Additional research related to cohesiveness includes Bass, 1959; Feldman, 1969; Zander, 1969.

Group Size

To select the appropriate-size group for a given problem, Thelen (1949) has suggested the "principle of the least group size." The group should be just large enough to include individuals with all the relevant skills for problem solution. Since larger groups provide fewer opportunities for each member to speak, require more control, and are generally less friendly, they tend to be less efficient (South, 1927; Hare, 1962; Shaplinskii, 1972; Ball, 1973; see also Walberg, 1969). In addition to these problems, the average number of contributions made by each member decreases as more members are added to the group.

As a simple demonstration of the phenomenon of "diminishing returns," Moede (1927) found that, although a group of eight men could pull harder than a smaller group or a single individual, the decrease in average contribution shown in table 39 became more and more marked as the group size increased. One person could pull 63 kilograms using 100 percent of his capacity, but eight persons were able to use only 49 percent of their average individual capacity in pulling 248 kilograms.

A similar effect with an intellectual task was noted in a study of groups of eight different sizes, ranging from single individuals to groups of 96 members (J. R. Gibb, 1951). As each group discussed one of three types of problems for a half hour, the members called out their contributions, which were recorded on the blackboard. With the increase in the size of the group, the average number of ideas produced by each member decreased.

Task

As noted in the introduction to part 2 of this handbook, the most inclusive way to specify the general outlines of group organization is to designate the task of the group. If a complicated group organization is needed for a difficult task to be performed under stress, then a group is less likely to be highly productive than

Table 39. Pulling Power of Different-sized Groups

	NUMBER OF PERSONS			
	I	2	3	8
Total pull in kilograms	63	118	160	248
Percentage of average individual capacity	100	93	85	49
Marginal pull in kilograms	63	55	42	

Source: Moede (1927).

if there is ample time for a simple task with a simple organization (Kolaja, 1968; Naylor and Dickinson, 1969).

The major effects of changes in task are found in the definition of the situation. More group work can be expected if the group is told that its goal is problem-solving rather than informal discussion (Gouran and Baird, 1972; Reckman and Goethals, 1973). If it is clear that work is the object, then more group productivity is achieved if the members do not spend too much time on individual goals (Zander, Natsoulas, and Thomas, 1960), and are isolated from outside distractions (Altman and Haythorn, 1967b). Whether the problem is solved in the laboratory or a field setting also makes a difference, with less emotionality apparent in the laboratory (O'Rourke, 1963). However, in one experiment subjects who were told that their partner was human did not behave very differently than when they were told that their partner was a machine, except that they thought the human was "more confused" (Hempill and McConville, 1965).

Work is facilitated if there is a clear set of rules which are appropriate to the task and are enforced (Parloff and Handlon, 1964; Schwartz, 1964; O'Brien and Ilgen, 1968; Fry, Hopkins, and Hoge, 1970). The rules may be embodied in a contract on which members agree before the work begins (Ribner, 1974).

Some level of coordination of individual members' activities is necessary even for uncomplicated tasks such as asking blindfolded subjects to show a number of fingers to reach a total called out by the experimenter (Leavitt, 1960; Rapoport, 1960; Zand and Costello, 1963; Schwartz and Philippatos, 1968; Schwartz, Eberle, and Moscato, 1973) or asking sets of subjects without blindfolds to count the number of dots on a card (Thibaut et al., 1960). With a task which requires complex problem-solving or actual production of material, coordination, usually in the form of leadership, is especially important (Lambert, 1967; Sorenson, 1971). Even when the amount of role differentiation and leadership required for a task is at a minmum, a complex task will require more communication between group members and more effort over a longer period of time (Gruen, 1961; Zajonc and Taylor, 1963; Denmark, Murgatroyd, and Pepitone, 1965; Morrissette, Switzer, and Crannell, 1965; Roby and Budrose, 1965; Faucheux and Moscovici, 1968; Streufert, Cafferty, and Cherry, 1972); on the other hand, the more information the group is given, the easier the problem becomes (Shaw and Penrod, 1964; Bower, 1965).

If one member of a group is given special information unknown to the others, he may have a difficult time using it if the others do not expect him to be so well informed. This is demonstrated in an experiment with three-person discussion groups. In some groups a member was given special information about the case under discussion, but the other two members were not informed. In other groups a member was given special information and the group was told that "some of you may have more information than others." Unless the members expected someone to be especially knowledgeable, they reacted negatively to the informed person (Shaw and Penrod, 1962a). On another type of task, group members were more likely to accept the information from the person with special information if it became clear, over a series of trials, that his information led to a correct decision (Shaw, 1961c). What seems to be happening here, and in group decisions generally, is that there is a presumption of equality between members in the "initially leaderless" groups which are used in laboratory experiments. Ordinarily each person is assumed to have the same information and the same degree of skill at the beginning of the task. Assuming this equality, all members are given equal weight in the decision. Thus the group decision is typically the simple average or median of all individual decisions (this point will be developed later in this chapter). Group members resist giving more "weight" to anyone, even though he may in fact have special information or skill, if there is no "visible sign" of this inward state which will allow the other members to defer to his judgment. Conversely, if one person has an obvious ability to find the right answer, the group will follow his lead (Banta and Nelson, 1964).

In the social-psychological literature, group problems which have at first appeared to represent different group tasks have later been discovered to involve the same processes as other problems of the same class. Thus group discussions of moral dilemmas seemed to involve a tendency for members to make a "risky shift" in individual judgments as a result of group discussion. As more research results accumulated, it became evident that the same factors affecting group discussion and attitude change in general were also at work in this particular case (see chapter 14). In a similar way, the task of a jury in reaching a decision about the guilt of a defendant might at first seem to be a unique type of problem. However, studies of simulated juries report that jurors are also subject to the effects of first impressions, majority opinion, social exchange, and other processes which are found in groups judging the number of dots on a card or the personality traits of a group member (Landy and Aronson, 1969; Hoiberg and Stires, 1973; M. Nash, 1973; Nemeth and Sosis, 1973; Sue, Smith, and Caldwell, 1973).

Communication Network

Regardless of the characteristics of the individual members, a number of changes can be made in the communication network of a group which will increase productivity. Feedback from receiver to sender increases the accuracy of the messages transmitted through a communication network (Leavitt and Mueller, 1951), so that groups in which free communication is maximized are generally more accurate in their judgments, although they may take longer to reach a decision. An exception is reported in a study of 31 graduate students at a school of public health from a number of different countries. After noting that some were very vocal while others seldom spoke, the experimenter divided the students into four groups, two quiet and two noisy. Each group was given the task of preparing a public health pamphlet. The quiet groups had difficulty getting organized but performed better at the task, while the noisy groups spent too much time talking and worked too fast (Knutson, 1960). Usually increased participation is associated with increased member satisfaction (Hoffman and Maier, 1959; Harshbarger, 1971). A number of authors have suggested methods of measuring the effectiveness of discussion either by statistical indices or checklists (Findley, 1948; Brandenberg, 1953; Crowell, 1953).

When there is role differentiation, groups which have the fewest communication links between the point at which information is received and the point at which a decision is made should be the most efficient (Roby and Lanzetta, 1956). Groups which are provided with an appropriate organizational pattern or are given time to develop one will be more efficient (Shure et al., 1962; McWhinney, 1963; Morrissette, Switzer, and Crannell, 1965). If newcomers join a group, there is a tendency for a short-run decline in performance while the group reorganizes itself (Trow, 1960). For tasks requiring the individual to spend some time thinking or doing work alone, it is better to allow time for the individual activity rather than to require group members to be in constant communication (Vroom, Grant, and Cotton, 1969; Gustafson et al., 1973).

The mode of communication, whether written, oral, or by other means, will create differences in a group's ability to communicate which may disappear in the long run (Carzo, 1963; Chapanis, et al., 1972).

Leadership

Studies of organizational effectiveness typically report that good leadership is a primary criterion for efficiency (Gekoski, 1952; George, 1962; Maier and Hoffman, 1965). For example, questionnaires were given to 98 workers at a shipyard to isolate factors related to organizational effectiveness (Wilson et al., 1954). A factor analysis of the data indicated four factors: supervisor-subordinate rapport, congenial work group, informal control, and group unity (i.e., the tendency to work for a common purpose). Four somewhat similar variables were reported in a review of industrial research: the supervisor's ability to play a differentiated role, the degree of delegation of authority or closeness of supervision, the quality of supportiveness by employees, and the amount of group cohesiveness (Kahn and Katz, 1953).

Although there is a tendency for groups led by autocratic leaders to produce more but of lower quality than groups led by democratic leaders, there is always higher productivity when a skilled leader is playing the leader role (Maier, 1950; Rock and Hay, 1953; Borgatta, Couch, and Bales, 1954; Ghiselli and Lodahl, 1958; Pryer, Flint, and Bass, 1962; Roby, Nicol, and Farrell, 1963). One aspect of the leader's skill is his ability to differentiate between his most and least preferred co-workers in the amount of skill they possess (Sample and Wilson, 1965; see also discussion of studies by Fiedler and co-workers in chapter 13).

When leadership functions are shared rather than centered in one person, then productivity is increased as more members share the responsibility for the work (Shaw, 1960; Burnstein and Zajonc, 1965a; Lange, 1967S; O'Brien and Owens, 1968; Levine and Katzell, 1971). However, simply dividing the resources among group members or dividing the activities without role differentiation will not have the same effect (Napier, 1969; Shiflett, 1972).

Majority Rule versus Consensus

Since majority rule is so prevalent in Western cultures, it has received the most attention in research (cf. Niemi and Weisberg, 1972). Mathematical models have been devised to compare the likelihood of different decision outcomes under simple majority rule and other versions of majority decision (Taylor, 1970; Fishburn, 1971, 1973, 1974).

Various decision methods have been proposed in the hope of finding more creative methods of decision-making. These include brainstorming (Bouchard, 1969), SPAN, or successive proportional additive numeration (Willis, Hitchcock, and MacKinnon, 1969), and synectics, in which members are asked to identify psychologically with different components of the task (Bouchard, 1972b). Some methods include several others, such as the "method of four states of awareness," which suggests four steps to be used in developing a creative state in a group: (1) taking account of facts by the case method, (2) taking account of an ideal state by a jury panel, (3) taking account of obstacles by role playing, and (4) taking account of solutions by brainstorming (Casse, 1970).

A decision rule of long standing in the non-Western world, especially in villages, is the method of consensus. No votes are taken, but all individual views are considered until a solution can be found which incorporates the concerns of all members and to which all can give their consent. Laboratory studies using versions of this method report that groups produce decisions of higher quality with less emphasis on personal orientations than do groups using a majority rule (Bower, 1965; Hall and Watson, 1970; Holloman and Hendrick, 1972; Knutson, 1972; Kline and Hullinger, 1973). However, one study finds that when a group must select among a number of alternatives of which only one is correct, majority rule will give more reliable decisions in that the decision will be correct more of the time (Smoke and Zajonc, 1962).

A case study of a working party of the Society of Friends (Quakers) in the United States provides an indication of some differences between majority and consensus rules in terms of functional theory (Hare, 1973a). For over 300 years the Quakers have been making group decisions by a method of consensus in which they look for the "sense of the meeting." This process involves the search for a proposal which will encompass the concerns of the individual group members as well as the needs of the group as a whole. In contrast to the typical voting group, which may only make decisions which involve the gathering of new information (adaptation) and the exercise of power (goal attainment), the consensus method is used by a group of people who have a feeling of affection for each other (integration), and above all it involves agreement on common values (pattern maintenance). Thus the consensus method involves all levels of the social system and deals with the complete range of functional needs.

Decision Rules

Observations of different types of groups reaching decisions suggest that group decision behavior is a combination of an individual decision process plus a conflict-resolving process when members do not agree (Clarkson and Tuggle, 1966; Clarkson, 1968). Some of the variations of decision rules include the proposition that "truth wins" no matter how many persons in the group discover the truth; majority rule; and consensus (J. H. Davis, 1973). The various methods can be compared on aspects such as (1) the criterion for when a decision is reached, (2) the number of steps in the decision-making process, and (3) the opportunities for a combination of two or more minorities in opposition to a leading candidate or proposal (Edelstein and Warner, 1971).

In the typical laboratory experiment with initially leaderless groups of persons who are equal in status, explicit decision rules are not usually proposed. However, all groups tend to have implicit rules which govern the decision-making process (Dulong, 1972). Various models of decision making have been compared with actual leaderless groups by simulations using computers or other methods. J. H. Davis et al. find that group members use an equalitarian process (1973). Comparing the decision schemes of majority, plurality, "equiprobability," and highest expected value, they found that the "equiprobability" scheme gave the best fit with their data. In this scheme, each strategy advocated by a member during a discussion has an equal probability of being selected (Davis, Hornik, and Hornseth, 1970). Another study suggests that members try to reach a decision which is "fair" in that most persons in the group reach their own level of aspiration as a result of the decision (Harnett, 1967). Yet another study compares three different models for group decision and finds that the best fit with actual data is obtained with a very simple model which assumes that the group decision is most often the median of the individual decisions (Hare, 1970; see also Hare and Scheiblechner, 1971). This study is presented in some detail below as an example of computer simulation. An overview of other approaches to the simulation of social behavior is given by Abelson (1968) in the *Handbook of Social Psychology*. Some indication of the variety of approaches in current use can be seen in the simulations of Coleman (1961), Gullahorn and Gullahorn (1963), and Coe (1964).

Simulating Interpersonal Behavior[1]

A comprehensive scheme for the simulation of interpersonal behavior in small groups has been outlined by Bales and Stone (1961) in their description of the "Interaction Simulator." The process of simulation would begin after a set of subjects is given a battery of personality and performance tests. Before they come together for a group discussion, the ideal computer simulation would indicate which subject will choose each of the seats around the table, to whom and in what order each will speak, and how the problem-solving will proceed as the group reaches one or more decisions. This simulation would then be compared with the outcome of the actual group discussion. So far relatively little of this scheme has been programmed for the computer, although Bales (1968), Couch (1960), and Stone et al. (1966) have been able to generate theories and methods which bring the task much closer to realization than when it was first proposed.

The present simulation models are concerned with only one aspect of the more general problem, namely the process by which group members pool individual opinions to form a group judgment. These models, which pose different methods of averaging individual judgments, were based on earlier models which used some of the same data to test the simulations (Hare, 1961). In addition to the data from groups composed of American college students used to test the previous simulations, new data were obtained from groups of Austrian college students solving a set of similar problems.

The Process to Be Simulated

The process to be simulated is the formation of a group opinion about a subject, once individual members have formed opinions about the same subject. Since several precomputer studies of group decisions have indicated that the "pooling" of individual opinions may represent accurately the results of group discussion, it is expected that this process will involve some form of averaging such as taking the mean, median, or mode (see Kaplan, Skogstad, and Girshick, 1950; Stone and Kamiya, 1957).

The group to be simulated is a five-man laboratory discussion group of college undergraduates. They are seated at a table with three members along one side, one at each end, and the fourth side open toward the experimenter, who records the interaction rate for each members and monitors the task. In brief, the task consists of giving each of the group members a different question from a questionnaire concerned with value orientations, together with the answer given by an "unknown subject." The group members are told to discuss their information about the unknown subject and then predict his answers to a set of 10 or more questions. After each prediction the unknown subject's actual answer is revealed and is discussed by the group before the members make their next predictions.

1. This section has been adapted from my "Simulating Group Decisions," *Simulation and Games* 1, 4 (December 1970): 361–376, and is reprinted by permission of the publisher, Sage Publications, Inc.

Three Models of Group Decisions

The first model for group decisions assumed that group members took an average of their individual opinions and that this average was best represented by the mean (Hare, 1961). The computer program began with the five individual predictions as inputs. The group decision was simulated by taking the mean of the five predictions. The predictions for the American groups were made on a seven-point scale where −3 represented "strongly disagree," +3 represented "strongly agree," and 0 represented "no opinion." Since group members were required to give some opinion, the compter program provided for an alternative in the case where the mean of the five opinions was actually zero. First the program checked the tendency of the unknown subject to favor responses on the "agree" or "disagree" side of the scale (his "response set") and then recorded an answer of "slightly agree" or "slightly disagree" depending upon his tendency. If the response set was also zero, the program determined whether the majority of the group members thought that the unknown subject would answer on the "agree" side or the "disagree" side of the scale. An answer would be recorded that was in line with the majority opinion.

The members of the Austrian groups used a five-point scale in giving their opinions, ranging from "Entschieden Ja" through "Unentschieden" to "Entschieden Nein." In this case the "undecided" category was allowed, so that it was not necessary to use the response set and majority opinion routines to avoid the midpoint on the scale.

The second model used the mean of the individual opinions as the best estimate of the group decision, but this time members' opinions were given different weights according to their position in the communication network, their interaction weights, or their success with the task. Simulated group members also "learned" more about the unknown subject as the trials progressed by considering the extent to which he had been opinionated in his answers. The routines which simulated the effects of task success and learning were primarily the work of Richardson. In adapting the program for the second model to the five-point scale used by the Austrian groups, the routines used to deal with group guesses of "no opinion" were again eliminated, since the "undecided" category was allowed.

An additional modification in the simulation which had not been tried before with any of the groups was to change the cutting points used to determine the group predictions. This was done to increase the probability of giving a simulated group prediction in the "agree" or "disagree" categories for the American groups (i.e., answers of +2 or −2) and to increase the probability of simulating the most extreme categories for the Austrian groups.

With the second model, the accuracy of the simulation was compared for all groups with and without learning for each of the following conditions: all group members' opinions given the same weight, members given weights according to their seating positions, members weighted according to total interaction using the wider limits for predicting extreme answers.

The third model, which was developed in Vienna, assumes that the majority opinion, or the median, is the best predictor of group decisions. In the case of a five-man group, a majority of three always contains the median. The decision to use both of these possibilities grew out of a discussion between Hare and Scheiblechner as they attempted to find out why the previous simulations failed to predict more of the group decisions. Hare proposed using the majority opinions, Scheiblechner, the median. The program written by Hare is actually the one used in the third model. It begins by finding a majority of three when there is one for each trial. However, when there is no majority, the median is used. In a few cases, in the American groups where the lack of a recorded opinion for some individuals would place the median in the "no opinion" category, a majority of two is used. Using this model in a five-man group it is never necessary to use any of the learning features of model two, nor do the weights assigned the subjects make any difference.

Results

The results of the various simulations for the total of 247 trials with the American groups are given in table 40. The data for the 60 trials of the Austrian sample, which used a different value test and a narrower range of permitted responses, are given in table 41.

With the first model, taking the unweighted mean, 139 trials out of 247 are correctly simulated for the American groups (table 40) and 44 out of 60 for the Austrian groups (table 41). Thus more than half of the decisions are accurately simulated by the simplest model.

When the various starting weights are used as part of the second model, there is no improvement using the seating weights and only slight improvement using interaction weights. The increase is not statistically significant.[2]

The introduction of the wider cutting points for the more extreme answers improves the accuracy of the prediction over model one in all cases, although learning adds to the accuracy for the American groups only. The improvement for the wider cutting points, with and without learning, for the combined American groups is significant at the .05 level.

For seven of the eight types of simulation, the shift from a no-learning to a learning model, which is usually associated with an increase in the accuracy of the prediction of the actual answer, also results in a greater number of gross errors. The most extreme case of this is found in table 40 when the wide cutting points are used. With no learning, there are four simulations which differ by three points from the actual group decision, whereas with learning the number of errors of this size rises to eleven. Thus absolute accuracy is purchased at the price of greater relative error when the simulation is incorrect. This is also true for the American groups when the simulation under model three is compared with that under model one. What is happening here is that the learning routines, the wider cutting points, and the use of the median rather than the mean all have the effect of making a somewhat more extreme prediction, which, if it is right, reduces the discrepancy with the actual groups' guesses to zero, but, if it is wrong, increases the number of large errors.

In the sum, the first model, which used the mean of the individual opinions as a simulation of the group judgment, exactly simulated over half of the trials. The simulation was improved in model two, which also used the mean, when individual opinions were weighted according to their total participation in the discussion, and learning was added. This was especially true when the cutting points were changed so that the mean would represent more extreme opinions.

The best simulation occurred with model three, which used the median of the individual opinions as a simulation of the group decision. With this model, over 75 percent of the trials were accurately simulated.

More Details of Model Two

Although model three produced the most accurate simulation when compared with actual decision-making groups, model two, which used the various weighted means and several learning routines, was the most interesting to program. For this reason it will be presented in more detail, with a general description of the learning

2. Tests of significance were made by comparing the increase in absolute prediction, group by group, under each condition, using a sign test (Siegel, 1956, table D). An increase in the accuracy of the simulation was scored as plus, a decrease was scored as minus, and no change was scored as zero. The probability of the number of minuses, given the total number of groups in which a change was observed, was noted in the table. As a further test the correlation between the simulated and actual group guesses was computed for each group and the average correlations were compared, after using the Z transformation. The results were similar.

Table 40. Total Harvard, Haverford, and Villanova Groups
(25 groups, 247 trials)

Simulation Type		Difference between Simulation and Actual Group Decision				Total
		0	1	2	3	
Mean: unit weights	No Learning	139	85	21	2	247
	Learning	150	70	24	3	
Mean: seating weights	N.L.	138	77	27	5	
	L.	150	64	26	7	
Mean: interaction weights	N.L.	147	77	21	2	
	L.	154	68	18	7	
Mean: wide cutting points (int. wts.)	N.L.	159[a]	70	14	4	
	L.	165[a]	56	15	11	
Majority or median (weights not used)		181[b]	48	12	6	

a. Significant increase over unit weights—no learning, using sign test, $p < .05$.

b. $p < .001$.

Source: A. Paul Hare, "Simulating Group Decisions," *Simulation and Games* 1 (1970). Reprinted by permission of the publisher, Sage Publications, Inc.

Table 41. Vienna Groups: Simulation of Group Decisions
(6 groups X 10 trials = 60 trials)

Simulation Type		Difference between Simulation and Actual Group Decision			Total
		0	1	2	
Mean: unit weights	No Learning	44	16	—	60
	Learning	47	13	—	
Mean: seating weights	N.L.	44	16	—	
	L.	42	17	1	
Mean: interaction weights	N.L.	47	13	—	
	L.	48	11	1	
Mean: wide cutting points (int. wts.)	N.L.	47	13	—	
	L.	47	12	1	
Majority or median (weights not used)		56	4	—	

Source: A. Paul Hare, "Simulating Group Decisions," *Simulation and Games* 1 (1970). Reprinted by permission of the publisher, Sage Publications, Inc.

processes, then a flow chart, and finally a step-by-step account of the simulation of the learning processes with an example of the computations for one group. The present versions of these simulations were written in FORTRAN II and were used on the IBM 1620. Earlier versions were written in machine language for the IBM 650 and in SPS for the IBM 1620. None of the simulations requires very much computer memory or special equipment.

To find the average opinion for a group of five subjects by taking the mean is not difficult with or without a computer. We simply added the five guesses and divided by five. Our problems began to arise when we had to set cutting points so that we would know whether the computed average should represent a more or less extreme opinion, what to do if the average fell in the "nonresponse" category, and how to simulate the various forms of learning which we observed as group members made a series of decisions.

To simulate these learning processes, the following aspects of member performance and subject behavior were incorporated into the program: absolute accuracy and relative accuracy of members' predictions, and opinionatedness and response set of the unknown subject's answers.

Absolute Accuracy of Members. It was expected that the members of the group who were successful in predicting the unknown subject's responses on previous trials would have more influence in the discussion in subsequent trials. Also, the successful members would less readily change their opinions in order to conform to the existing group consensus, for they had achieved a certain amount of security in the group during previous trials and thus were more in a position to lead rather than to follow. In order to simulate this process, the weights of the successful members were increased for the subsequent trials.

It was also expected that the unsuccessful members would have less influence over the group and would more readily change their opinions to conform to the group consensus. This was simulated by decreasing the weights of the members of the group whose individual predictions differed greatly from the unknown subject's responses on the previous trials.

Relative Accuracy of Members. The weights of the members were also changed according to the success of the members relative to the group. Thus the weights were increased for those members who were more accurate than the group decision in predicting the unknown subject's responses. The weights were decreased for those members who were unsuccessful relative to the group's decision.

Uncertain versus Opionated Unknown Subjects. As the groups were observed making actual decisions, it was apparent that the members often took into account whether or not the unkown subject tended to be uncertain or opinionated in his response. If a group was trying to decide between a prediction of "strongly agree" or "agree," it would often choose the "strongly agree" response if the unknown subject's responses had tended to be in the "strongly" or "opinionated" area. In a similar way the group would have less tendency to choose the "strongly agree" or "strongly disagree" response if the unknown subject's responses tended to be in the "slightly" or "uncertain" area. To simulate this learning process, the probability of the group decision falling into the "strongly" or "slightly" areas was increased or decreased according to the trend of the unknown subject's responses toward opinionatedness or uncertainty.

This learning process was also used to combat the tendency of pooling methods to arrive at decisions which cluster around the mean, or uncertain area. If an individual has learned in previous trials that the unknown subject has tended to be rather opinionated, he is more likely to have an individual prediction of either "strongly agree" or "strongly disagree" on succeeding trials. For a given item on the value-orientation test this member may not be able to decide, before the group decision takes

Figure 55. Flow Chart of Group Simulation Program

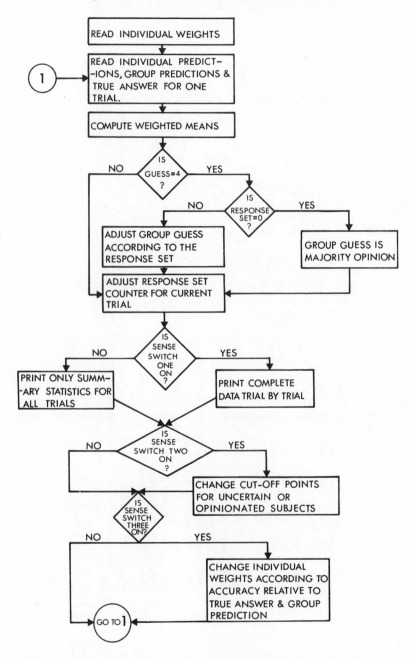

Source: A. Paul Hare, "Simulating Group Decisions," *Simulation and Games* 1 (1970). Reprinted by permission of the publisher, Sage Publications, Inc.

Figure 56. Group No. 22

NO	G1	G2	G3	G4	G5	W1	W2	W3	W4	W5	X	CP	SG	GP	TA
1	1	2	2	1	2	45.0	54.0	38.0	29.0	35.0	1.63	2.50	2	2	1
2	7	6	1	7	7	52.0	56.7	39.9	33.5	36.8	5.65	6.40	6	7	1
3	3	7	6	6	7	46.8	53.6	46.1	30.2	33.1	5.74	6.30	6	6	3
4	7	5	7	7	7	54.1	45.8	43.8	28.7	28.3	6.54	7.00	7	7	5
5	5	2	3	3	5	54.1	52.9	43.8	28.7	28.3	3.54	3.90	3	3	1

Codes:

NO   Number of item on Value Profile
G1   through G5—Guesses made by the five group members
W1   through W5—Weights assigned to the guesses
X   The weighted average guess
CP   The upper cutting point used on that trial
SG   The simulated group decision
GP   The actual group decision
TA   The "true" answer of the unknown subject

Source: A. Paul Hare, "Simulating Group Decisions," *Simulation and Games* 1 (1970). Reprinted by permission of the publisher, Sage Publications, Inc.

place, whether the true response will be in the "agree" or "disagree" category. He may think that the true response is probably either "strongly agree" or "strongly disagree." Since he must make a decision, he decides to guess "strongly disagree." However, if the others in the group feel that the true response is at the "agree" end of the scale, he will be more likely to go along with a group decision of "strongly agree" than of "slightly agree," even though a group decision of "strongly agree" is furthest away from his original prediction.

Response Set of Subject. As in the first model, the response set of the unknown subject was used for the American groups whenever the pooling of individual opinions indicated that the group had no opinion for a given trial. The limits of the no-opinion area were determined empirically in model two and were only one-fifth as wide as those used in Model One. In other respects the use of the response set was the same as before. When the response set was neither positive nor negative, the simulated group decision was taken to be in the direction of the majority opinion for that trial.

Flow Chart

Model two was programmed with the sense switches on the IBM 1620 so that the program could be run with or without each of the previously described modifications. For this version of the simulation, the codes were changed to 1 through 7, with 1 representing "strongly disagree," 4 representing "no opinion," and 7 representing "strongly agree." The flow chart shown on page 351 (figure 55) gives the major steps in the program.

Sample Output and Simulation

A sample of the output for one of the American groups for five trials is given in figure 56.

The computer first reads a lead card giving the starting weights for the series of trials. In this case the starting weights (45.0, 54.0, and so on) are the total number of interactions for each individual over all trials (following the conventions of Bales, 1950). Next a card is read giving the individual predictions. The simulated group decision for the first trial is determined by a set of cutting points which were determined empirically. If the value falls between 3.90 and 4.10, the response set routine is used. On trial 1 for group 22 the mean was 1.63, which was greater than 1.50 but less than 2.50, the cutting points for guesses of "1" and "2." The resulting guess was 2.

Response Set. If the true answer on the trial is in the "agree" area (5, 6, or 7), add one to response set counter. If the true answer is in the "disagree" area (1, 2, or 3), subtract one. If the program refers to the response set because the weighted mean is in the nonresponse area, then the group guess is given as 3, or "slightly disagree," if the response set is negative and 5, or "slightly agree," if the response set is positive.

Majority Opinion. If the response set happens to be zero, the group guess is determined by the majority opinion. If the majority guess on the "disagree" side, the group guess is 3, and if the majority are on the "agree" side the guess is 5.

Uncertain or Opinionated. If the true answer is either "slightly disagree" or "slightly agree," the upper bound 2 is lowered by 0.05 and the upper bound of 5 is raised by 0.05. Thus the weighted mean is more likely to fall into the 3 and 5 areas on the next trial. Also, the upper bound of 1 is lowered by 0.10 and the upper bound of 6 is raised by 0.10, so that the weighted mean is less likely to fall in the "strongly" area on the next trial.

Conversely, if the true answer is in the "strongly" or "opinionated" area, the upper bounds of 5 or 6 are lowered and the upper bounds of 1 and 2 are raised. In this way the probability of simulating an opinionated answer on the next trial is increased. Finally, if the true answer is either "agree" or "disagree," the cutting points are raised and lowered to increase the probability of a middle-of-the-road guess on the next trial. At all times the upper bounds of 3, 4, and 7 remain constant, since the response set is always used when the weighted mean is between 3.90 and 4.10, and the weighted mean can never be higher than 7.

Absolute Accuracy. If an individual's prediction is the same as the true answer, his weight is increased by 10 percent. If his prediction deviates by one, his weight is increased by 5 percent. If the deviation is two, his weight is not changed. If the deviation is three, his weight is *decreased* by 5 percent, and if it is four or more, his weight is *decreased* by 10 percent.

Relative Accuracy. If an individual's prediction is closer to the true answer than the group's decision, his weight is increased by 10 percent. If his prediction is further from the true answer than the group's decision, his weight is decreased by 10 percent. If his prediction is the same as the group's decision, his weight is not changed.

After each trial the computer prints the item number, individual guesses, weights, mean, upper cutting point used, simulated group decision, actual group decision, and true answer. For the first five trials of group 22 the simulation was accurate for trials 1, 3, 4, and 5 and off by one for trial 2. Note that the actual group guess did not agree with the true answer for any of the items. Our goal here was to simulate the group decision, no matter how inaccurate it might be, rather than to find the best way of predicting the true answer. An earlier program was written to simulate a single individual predicting the responses of an unknown subject. This program did better than the average subject, but not as well as the best (Hare, 1961).

Additional research on group productivity covers factors such as the influence of success or failure, status congruency, compatibility, integration, and stress. Examples of this research include Maier, 1946; Thelen, 1948; Levi and Higgins, 1954; Torrance, 1957; Exline and Ziller, 1959; E. E. Smith, 1959; Bass and Dunteman, 1963b; Mulder, 1963; Zander and Medow, 1963; Nelson, 1964a; Nelson and Gunderson, 1964; Burnstein and Zajonc, 1965b; Hammes and Osborne, 1965; Cooper, 1966; Hall and Williams, 1966; Morrissette et al., 1967; Damm, 1968; Lenk, 1968; Poitou, 1968; Streufert, 1969, 1970; Susman, 1970; Altman, Taylor, and Wheeler, 1971; Helus, 1971; Radinsky and Kanekar, 1972; Streufert, 1972; M. B. Jones, 1974.

Training and Feedback

One of the clearest findings in the small group literature is that group productivity will be improved if training is provided for the members, no matter what the task (Pryer and Bass, 1959; Cohen, Whitmyre, and Funk, 1960; Lanzetta and Roby, 1960; Goldberg and Maccoby, 1965; Egerman, 1966; Glaser and Klaus, 1966; Meier and Thurber, 1969; Whalen, 1969; Deloughery, Neuman, and Gebbie, 1972; Leathers, 1972; Gutzmer and Hill, 1973). In some cases the "training" is simply the exposure to the same task on a prior occasion (Loree and Koch, 1960; Meier and Hoffman, 1960b; Faucheux and Moscovici, 1968). Subjects learn quickly and are usually able to do better the second time.

Persons who believe that their skills are inferior to those of others in the group are less likely to use the skills they have. This is demonstrated in an experiment in which college undergraduates were asked to take part in "brainstorming" groups.

In some groups, the subjects were told that all the other members were "experts" in that they had all worked in similar groups before. In a second experimental condition, each subject was told that only one of the others had taken part in this type of group before. In the third condition, no information was given about previous participation. As a result of these instructions, the subjects in the "all experts" condition felt more inhibited than those in the "one expert" condition. Those in the "one expert" condition were in turn more inhibited than the subjects who were given no information. Originality and practicality of ideas varied according to the degree of felt inhibition: the control condition (no information) had the highest originality and practicality scores, followed by the "one expert" condition and then the "all expert" condition (Collaros and Anderson, 1969).

One form of training is to provide individual members or the whole group with some estimate of performance, either while the group is in process or at the end of a session (Spoelders-Claes, 1973). When feedback is provided, group members tend to work harder, especially if they are evaluated by an expert (Berkowitz and Daniels, 1963; Webster, 1969), and become more involved (Bowman and Siegel, 1973). Although subjects look to human observers for evaluation (Zander, Medow, and Efron, 1965), feedback without comment from a TV camera can be equally effective (Weber, 1971, 1972). Feedback provided on an individual basis has been found to be more effective than group feedback (K. H. Smith, 1972a), probably because it can give the individual member a clearer idea of how to change his performance.

The type of reinforcement or feedback also makes a difference (Klaus and Glaser, 1970). Negative feedback can be stressful (Shapiro and Leiderman, 1967).

If group members fail to meet their level of aspiration, they may try harder (Zander and Curtis, 1962; Zander, 1968) or they may not (Dustin, 1966; Fontaine, 1974). The difference in outcome may be explained by an experiment which found that moderate levels of failure produced a greater effort to organize the group than did either low or high failure levels (Streufert, Streufert, and Castore, 1969). Groups which are uncertain about the outcome will also make more effort (Emerson, 1966a, 1966b). When a group does fail, members of the "ingroup" may try to place the blame on members of the "outgroup" (Deschamps, 1972–1973).

Members of groups prefer positive feedback and are more willing to believe it (Jacobs et al., 1974). An indication that the group is effective increases morale (Myers, 1962; Frye, 1966; Streufert and Streufert, 1969). Within the group, members who are successful are highly valued and their opinions are sought (Banta and Nelson, 1964; Jones and Welsh, 1971). Also members who believe they are successful, even though they may not be, will try to exert more influence (Frederickson and Kizziar, 1973). The opposite is also true, since groups which try harder in competition with other groups tend to overevaluate their own group product (Blake and Mouton, 1962b; Ferguson and Kelley, 1964).

Summary

The most productive groups are those which can carry out effectively the major steps in the process of solving task and social-emotional problems for the group and for the individual members. To accomplish this, the group must have a combination of members' personalities and skills, a type of group structure, and group problem-solving experience which is appropriate for the task. In an authoritarian setting the most productive group will tend to be authoritarian, whereas in a more democratic situation the equalitarian group will be more productive.

Predictions about group productivity should be more accurate when the test situation is similar to the field situation in all important respects. Since the amount of stress actually present in the field may be hard to duplicate in the laboratory, the factors which bring success in the laboratory may not be the same as those which lead to success in the field.

Members will be satisfied with the group if it has been able to solve the particular task or social-emotional problem in which they were most interested. However, high productivity in the task area is not always associated with satisfactory relationships in the social-emotional area. In authoritarian groups and competitive groups, high productivity is often gained at the expense of member satisfaction.

The influence of member personality traits on group productivity is illustrated in an experiment that compared five-man groups, in which all subjects either desired close relations with others or preferred to keep their distance, with groups in which some subjects desired close relations and some did not. In a series of group tasks and competitions between groups of opposing types, the "compatible" groups were found to be more productive, presumably because they were able to agree in the social-emotional area and thus free themselves to work on the task.

For the same reason groups tend to be more productive if they are composed of members of the same sex, are cohesive and small, have a communication network with maximum feedback, and have a skilled leader. However, if a complicated group organization is needed for a difficult task to be performed under stress, then a group is less likely to be highly productive than if there is ample time for a simple task with a simple organization.

Decision rules used in groups combine an individual decision process with a conflict resolution process when members do not agree. Some common decision rules include the proposition that "truth wins" no matter how many persons in the group discover the truth; majority rule; and consensus. In laboratory groups, when no rule is specified, members seem to use an "equiprobability" scheme in which each strategy advocated by a member has an equal probability of being selected. Members also try to be fair, allowing most members to reach their own level of aspiration. Resulting decisions are often the median of the individual opinions. Computer simulations can be used to compare different decision processes.

Finally, group productivity will be improved if training or feedback on group performance is provided. This may take the form of simply exposing the group to the same task on a prior occasion. Subjects learn quickly and are usually able to do better the second time.

APPENDIXES

Appendix 1

LABORATORY
EXPERIMENTS

THE FOLLOWING EXPERIMENTS are presented to provide an opportunity to experience directly—as subject and as data gatherer and analyzer—the complexities of small group research and perhaps even the joys of discovery. This appendix may be especially useful to the student or teacher who has not had the opportunity to take part in small group experiments and would like to have a firsthand experience with some of the early research designs.

With each experiment is a simplified set of instructions as well as some suggested ways of analyzing the results. All of this is presented in the form of suggestions for your modification and development. In no case should you feel inhibited about altering aspects of the procedure in order to conduct a different or what you would feel to be more adequate or more interesting experiment. For example, in the Bales experiment you might wish to employ or develop another category system for observation and then compare the results. You might also wish to vary the topics or the circumstances under which the topics are discussed (e.g., the goals or lengths of time of the discussion). In the Asch experiment I have presented several alternative procedures. One could of course vary a great many different aspects of the group, for example, the balance of men versus women, the lengths of the lines or the types of stimulus in general, the group objectives, etc.

Nor should you feel restricted to the hypotheses or ways of analyzing the data. There is a great deal of room for developing your own problems or questions to be put to the material. For example, in the Allport experiment one could analyze the content of the associations generated under the different "together" and "apart" conditions. In all of the experiments one could delve further into the questions of why the group or individual responses occurred as they did. This delving might range from relatively open-ended discussions with the experimental subjects to more structured questionnaires on aspects of individuals' background and experiences.

One final point. There can be some relatively serious moral dilemmas in conducting experimental social research. At the very least, this research often involves withholding information from the experimental subjects. It can even go so far as deceiving the subjects or making them undergo varying degrees of stressful experience. As I indicate in regard to the Asch experiment, my personal preference

359

would be to avoid experimental deception or stress in virtually all circumstances. However, there are no simple answers to these dilemmas, and I encourage you to confront these problems yourself and work out your own solutions.

In conclusion, I feel there is much to be learned through the experimental method, and the frontier of knowledge is not that far away. If you have any vision of becoming a pioneer, you may wish to begin now.

Experiment 1. Allport's Study of Group Influence on Association and Thought

Arrangement of Class.   Divide the class into sets of about six students. At the beginning of the experiment, half of the sets are seated "together" around conference tables, while the students in the other half of the sets are seated "apart" in individual chairs, preferably at some distance from each other and where they cannot see each other. In Allport's original experiment, the students in the "apart" condition were seated in separate classrooms. They were given a signal to begin each trial by a system of buzzers (see Allport, 1920). If your university has a series of experimental rooms which can be used for this purpose, the arrangement would be ideal. Other possibilities include using the booths in a language laboratory or the cubicles in the library.

The reason for having half the class begin in the "together" condition and half the class begin in the "apart" condition is to demonstrate the effects of learning as the experiment progresses. If you have only enough students for one group, you can begin with either condition.

Equipment.   In addition to the small tables for writing in the "together" condition each student will need at least four sheets of paper, a pencil, and one set of instructions. The experimenter needs a watch. If the experimenter's voice cannot be heard by all the students at the same time, he may need a communication system.

Instructions.   After the students have been seated in the "together" and "apart" arrangements, distribute one set of instructions to each student. You can make up your own version, or if you like, you can simply copy my version of the ones used by Allport (1920):

Today you will take part in a "classic" experiment concerned with the influence of the group on association and thought.

There will be four trials; half of the time you will work alone and the other half in the presence of others. In each case the task is an individual one.

You will be given a stimulus word and asked to write down as many words as you can which are associations to this word. You will have three minutes. At the end of the first and second minute you will be asked to draw a line on your paper under the last word you have written to mark the end of each one minute period.

Please wait for the signal from the experimenter before you begin. Then unfold the paper to reveal the first word.

Please do not look ahead at the following words until you are given the signal.

Below these instructions, list by number a stimulus word for each of four trials, leaving about an inch of space between the words:

Trial 1. *Building*

Trial 2. *Laboratory*

Trial 3. *Winter/Summer*

Trial 4. Choose your own word and write it at the top of the page.

Then neatly fold the paper from the bottom five times. Each fold, after the first, should cover the stimulus word for one trial. As a result, each student will receive a piece of paper with the instructions visible and the stimulus words concealed under a series of folds. At the beginning of each trial the student is instructed to unfold the paper to reveal the stimulus word for that trial. Paper folding is not important. The main point is to give each student a set of instructions and four stimulus words. This could be done with five small pieces of paper stapled together or in any other form.

Next the experimenter reads the instructions, which the students follow by reading their own copies. After clarifying any questions, the experimenter signals the start of the first trial. At the end of the first minute he says, "End of the first minute; draw a line and continue to write words which are associations to the stimulus word." At the end of the second minute the experimenter says, "End of second minute; draw a line and continue." At the end of the third minute he says, "Stop writing; this is the end of the trial."

After each trial the students are shifted to new positions. Those who have been "together" during the trial take seats "apart," and those who have been "apart" take seats "together." The experimenter then signals the beginning of a new trial, the students turn over the paper to reveal the new stimulus word, and the trial proceeds as above.

For trial 3, half the students should use the stimulus word *winter* and half the word *summer*. This can be accomplished by crossing out one of the words in turn on each set of instructions before the instructions are given out. Allport thought that it might make a difference if subjects were associating to words which were in "opposition" to each other.

Analysis of the Data. After the last trial the students can all be assembled in one room to code and tabulate their data. First ask them to go over each list of associations and place a check beside every word which was suggested by the surroundings, that is, by objects or persons in the room while the trial was going on. Next ask each subject to count the total number of associations for each minute and the grand total for all three minutes for each trial. Also count the total number of associations suggested by the surroundings for each trial. It is not necessary to count the number of associations suggested by the surroundings for each minute. There are usually so few that only the total for all three minutes is needed for analysis.

At this point, if the class is large and time is short, the experimenter may prefer to collect all the data sheets and tabulate the results himself. Tables can then be prepared to distribute to the class at the next meeting. This method might be used if several different classes are doing the experiment at different times. Then the members of each class would be able to compare their results with other classes.

If the class is small or if ample time is available, there is an advantage in "immediate feedback" by tabulating the results on the blackboard as each student calls out his set of data.

As a sample of the type of data which may be obtained from this version of Allport's experiment I present the results obtained from a class of students attending a summer social science institute on the island of Curaçao in the Netherlands Antilles. In this case the students wrote their associations in the language of their choice, which was usually Dutch or Papiamentu rather than English.

In table 42 I recorded the total number of associations for each person for each trial. Beside each total there is a small graph to indicate the presence of one of two types of trends. Allport had noted that subjects usually have the most associations in the first minute, with a decreasing number for each subsequent minute. If the trend followed this pattern of high, middle, low, I drew a line slanting downward from left to right. The other possibility Allport discussed was an "end spurt" in which the last minute of the trial would have more associations than the second minute. If this was the case I recorded a V-shaped trend line.

Summaries of the raw data in table 42 were then presented in a series of smaller tables. In table 43 I recorded the number of subjects with a decreasing trend (high, middle, low) for the three time periods within each trial. As expected, the decreasing trend predominates. Students who are interested in the theory of probability could compute the number of times each type of trend would appear by chance alone.

Next, table 44 shows the number of subjects whose first trial was as low as or lower than any other trial and whose fourth trial was as high as or higher than any other trial. In this case, barring ties, one would expect any given trial to be the lowest one-fourth of the time and the highest one-fourth of the time. For the 14 subjects who were "together" first the expected number would be 3.50, and for the 11 subjects who were "apart" first the expected value would be 2.75. From table 44 we see that a greater than chance number of subjects had the lowest number of associations on trial 1 and the highest number on trial 4. Trial 1 is low because the subjects are learning the experiment. Because one trial, usually the first, could be noticeably lower than the others, Allport notes that he dropped the lowest trial before analyzing his own data. It would have been better if he had used several pretest runs to familiarize the subjects with the task.

The last trial tends to be high because subjects are associating to a word of their choice. This has the effect of changing the nature of the task in a dramatic way. Thus for comparison one should use only trials 2 and 3, which were not influenced either by "learning" or by a change in the task.

Although the results are not shown in a table, there were no differences in the number of associations to the words *winter* and *summer,* nor did I expect any. It is difficult to see how Allport thought his subjects would even be aware of the fact that half of their colleagues were associating to a word which was in "opposition" to their own.

Table 45 gives the number of subjects whose total for both trials "together" was higher than the total for both trials "apart" and the number whose "together" trial was greater than their "apart" trial for trials 2 and 3 only. We see that if we had used the data for all four trials, overlooking the effect of learning and the change in task on the last trial, the total for trials 1 and 3 would have been lower on the average than the total for trials 2 and 4. Thus if we only had the data for the students who started "together," we would have concluded that the "apart" condition was the most stimulating. Or if we had only had students who started "apart," we would have concluded that the "together" condition was the most stimulating. When we consider only the data for trials 2 and 3, we see that each

Table 42. Total Numbers of Associations for Each Subject for Each Trial

FIRST TRIAL TOGETHER

Subject Number	Trial 1 T*	Trend	Trial 2 A†	Trend	Trial 3 T	Trend	Trial 4 A	Trend	Total Together	Total Apart
1	23		26		21		30		44	56
2	12		9		5		14		17	23
3	8		11		7		17		15	28
4	22		28		33		35		55	63
5	30		23		20		24		50	47
6	11		11		20		25		31	36
7	6		9		13		7		19	15
8	8		20		18		21		26	41
9	20		23		27		20		47	43
10	33		34		35		31		68	65
11	7		7		10		18		17	25
12	19		11		13		29		32	40
13	17		16		13		17		30	33
14	19		19		14		19		33	38

FIRST TRIAL APART

Subject Number	Trial 1 A	Trend	Trial 2 T	Trend	Trial 3 A	Trend	Trial 4 T	Trend	Total Apart	Total Together
15	6		13		8		10		14	23
16	16		17		24		29		40	46
17	21		13		11		15		32	28
18	10		15		15		12		25	27
19	34		18		21		18		55	36
20	14		19		17		13		31	32
21	15		43		21		29		36	72
22	18		17		14		19		32	36
23	19		19		23		25		42	44
24	20		18		20		25		40	43
25	9		14		19		15		28	39

*T = together.
†A = apart.

Table 43. Number of Subjects with Decreasing Trend
(High, Middle, Low) for Three Time Periods
within Each Trial

Subjects	Trial				Number of Subjects
	1	2	3	4	
T first	10	7	5	7	14
A first	6	7	4	5	11

Table 44. Number of Subjects Whose First Trial Was As Low As or Lower
Than Any Other Trial and Whose Fourth Trial Was As High or Higher
(Expected by Chance One-fourth of Time)

Subjects	First Trial Lowest	Fourth Trial Highest	Number of Subjects	Expected
T first	6	10	14	3.50
A first	6	4	11	2.75

Table 45. Number of Subjects Whose Total for Both Trials Together Was
Higher Than Total for Both Trials Apart and Number Whose Together
Trial Was Greater Than Apart Trial for Trials 2 and 3

Subjects	Total Together Higher	Together Higher for Trials 2 & 3	Number of Subjects
T first	4	7	14
A first	9	5*	11

*In addition, one case was equal.

Table 46. Number of Subjects Who Reported Words
Influenced by Surroundings

Subjects	Higher Together	Higher Apart	No Difference
T first	3	1	0
A first	3	0	1

condition was the most stimulating half of the time. This is what we would expect by chance. Thus the data for this particular class do not support Allport's conclusion that the "together" condition was the most stimulating.

Finally, table 46 shows the number of subjects who reported that the number of words influenced by their surroundings was higher in the "together" condition, that it was higher in the "apart" condition, and that it was not different. Although more subjects reported that the surroundings influenced their associations in the "together" condition, the number of subjects is too small to be statistically significant. Allport expected more associations to the surroundings in the "together" condition, since presumably the subjects were more apt to look around the room as they were distracted by the presence of others.

Comments. Unless the experiment is actually carried out in a laboratory setting where the subjects in the "apart" condition are physically isolated from each other, the results may show no differences between the "together" and "apart" conditions. If this proves to be the case, students may wonder what the value of the experiment has been. However, we should recall that Allport found that only *some* of his experimental subjects were stimulated positively. We can still ask the ones who were stimulated positively why this happened. We can also ask the students who were affected negatively why this happened.

Even with inconclusive results there is value in learning about some of the problems and possibilities of the experimental method. Because the individual, rather than the group, is the unit of study in this experiment, it is possible to collect a relatively large amount of data from a single class. One can observe the effects of learning and other trends. One can also observe the effects of small changes in the task. Perhaps most importantly, one can have firsthand experience with a classic experiment from the early days of experimental social psychology.

Experiment 2. Asch's Study of Opinions and Social Pressure

Arrangement of Class. Although it would be possible to produce several sets of materials so that each member of the class could take part in this experiment as one of a set of five to ten students, I suggest that this version of the Asch experiment be used as a class demonstration. The experimenter calls for five to ten volunteers from the class, ideally ones who are not familiar with the Asch experiment. The volunteers come to the front of the class, where they are seated so that class members can see their faces, either in one line or in several lines, with or without tables.

The experimenter takes a position 10 to 15 feet away, facing the subjects. He may have a small table at his side.

Equipment. The experimenter holds pairs of cards (5 by 8 inches or larger). On one card in each pair there are three lines varying in length from 1 to 4 inches, labeled A, B, and C. On the other card is a single unlabeled line which matches one of the other three lines in length. (See sample set in figure 57.) Eight pairs of cards should be enough for the experiment. The single "standard" line should match one of the three lines A, B, and C in random order. It may help to have a small easel or book stand against which to place the pairs of cards for each trial (Asch, 1955).

Instructions. The experimenter instructs the experimental subjects that they are about to take part in an experiment in perception. They will be shown several pairs of cards (show sample pair). On one card there is a single line

Figure 57. Sample Cards for Asch Experiment

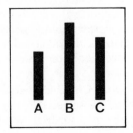

called the standard. On the other card are three lines labeled, A, B, and C. For each trial the task is to select one line from the card with three lines which matches the standard line. To simplify recording the individual opinions, subjects are to call out their answers in turn so that the answers can be recorded by the experimenter, or by his assistant.

At this point subjects can be assigned numbers starting with 1 as they are seated. They are asked to call out their answers in order on each trial.

After answering any questions, the experimenter begins the experiment by showing the first pair of cards and calling for the individual judgments. Over the course of several trials, one or more of the subjects will report a different match- ing line from the majority. After this happens, the experiment can be brought to a close. (A difference of opinion is more likely to occur if some of the sets of three matching lines are very similar in length so that the judgment is difficult to make.)

Analysis of the Data. The main data for analysis are the frequency with which some subjects fail to go along with the majority, their reasons for differing, and their feelings about being different from the majority.

To obtain this information, the experimenter will have to ask some questions of the experimental subjects, such as: "What did you think of the experimental task?" "Were the judgments easy or difficult?" "Did anyone in the majority con- sider giving a different opinion at any time?" "How did you feel about being in the majority?" "How did those who differed from the majority feel?"

Since only a few subjects will be "nonconformists," it should be possible to ask them further questions about the frequency with which they find themselves in opposition to a group and how they usually behave. In each case the answers ob- tained from the subjects can be compared with those recorded by Asch in post- experimental interviews.

Comments. In this version of the Asch experiment I do not instruct all-but- one of the subjects beforehand to give incorrect responses on some trials, thus placing pressure on a single naive subject. I avoid this because I feel it is not con- sistent with the value we place on free and open communication. I feel that the means by which we obtain knowledge about interpersonal behavior should be consistent with the ends. Thus, in this case, I do not feel that I should use subter- fuge by manipulating a majority opinion against a naive subject in order to warn him of the effects of manipulated social opinion. Life itself—or in this case any slightly ambiguous set of stimuli for judgment, such as the number of dots on a card—will provide enough instances in which the individual must stand out against the majority. In the present era there is enough concern about the presence of informers in a group without adding to the paranoia by revealing after the experiment that social psychologists will also use deception when it is felt to be warranted.

Of course, it should be apparent that this type of scruple was not a major concern for Asch or the others who followed him in creating similar experiments. A few years ago I used the "coached majority" version of the experiment myself and thought nothing of it. However, our perceptions of each other are changing. Each time we find a way in which we can treat each other as more human and less like an object, we have an opportunity to enrich our social selves.

Experiment 3. Bales's Observations of Interaction in Conferences

Arrangement of Class. This experiment requires only five persons. I have usually performed the experiment with one group as a demonstration in front of a class, although any number of groups could take part in the experiment. If a small group observation room is available, the class might use this facility. However, an ordinary classroom or lecture hall is all that is needed. The experimenter can draw a diagram of a typical laboratory and observation room on the blackboard (see figure 58) and then arrange the classroom to simulate a laboratory. Place a conference table at the front of the classroom with five chairs, one on each short side and three along the long side away from the class. The class members, who will be the observers, can imagine that there is an observation mirror between the table and themselves.

Equipment. The members of the class who are acting as observers may wish to use paper and pencil to score interaction. If the experimenter would like to have the class use a formal category system for observation, such as Bales's 12 categories, it could be distributed, together with scoring sheets to each member of the class. (See Bales, 1970a.)

Instructions. The experimenter calls for five volunteers from the class. The volunteers are asked to hold a five- to ten-minute discussion on a selected topic while seated at the table in front of the class. Where it is possible without being obvious about it, the experimenter selects three men and two women. The volunteers are asked to leave the classroom while the remainder of the class is told about the observation methods. If a formal category system is to be used, it might be better to explain the use of the system before the five students are asked to leave the room so that they will not become tired of standing in the hall.

While the five subjects are in the hall, the experimenter explains that the center seat on the long side of the table and the two end seats are usually taken by persons who like to talk, while the two seats at the corners of the table are chosen

Figure 58. Laboratory Arrangement for Observing Five Persons with Discussion Task

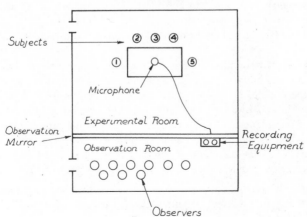

by those who wish to remain silent. Men tend to choose the three high-talking seats and women the two low-talking seats. Since women will also tend to sit together, one of the women may choose a low-talking seat and the other woman sit beside her. There is a sense in which the last person to enter the room has no choice. However, one can ask why he is the last to come into the room. In general, persons enter the room following a "pecking order," with the most dominant individuals first. After the demonstration is over, the subjects can be asked why they chose each seat. If the five subjects are well known to the class, their seating choice can be predicted. (For more detailed predictions, see Hare and Bales, 1963.)

In addition to the differences in interaction rate between central and noncentral seats, the subjects in the low-talking seats tend to respond with short comments to the longer comments of the high-talking subjects. The person who takes the center seat on the long side of the table is likely to be the social-emotional leader. He tends to start the group off and make sure that the discussion is going well. The two subjects at the ends of the table tend to be individualists; they give their own opinions at some length, then withdraw, often leaning back in their chairs when they are not directly involved in the discussion.

Members of the class as observers can be instructed to watch for all of these points, observing all five subjects at once, or sections of the class can be instructed to watch a particular seat. Further, the observers can record who speaks to whom or use a formal category system. (Bales has many detailed suggestions for this type of observation; see Bales, 1970a.)

After the observers have been instructed and a topic of current interest has been chosen for the discussion, the five subjects are called in from the hall with the reminder that they can choose any seat they wish. After the subjects take their seats and the initial reaction of the class concerning the success of the predictions has subsided, the five subjects are given the discussion topic and the discussion begins. After five to ten minutes of discussion the group members will probably come to a natural break in the discussion. At this point the experimenter stops the discussion, and the subjects return to their seats in the class.

Analysis of Data.   Immediately following the discussion the experimenter can review each of the predictions about seating position and type of interaction for the benefit of the five subjects who held the discussion. After each prediction is reviewed, members of the class can be asked whether or not the prediction was verified. Either way, the class can consider why the particular types of observed interaction occurred. The five subjects should be asked to give their opinions, especially whether or not their behavior was "typical" of their behavior in other situations.

If the observers have used formal category systems, these can be presented as interaction matrices or interaction profiles and compared with those of Bales.

If the experimenter is familiar with a category system, he can score the interaction on the blackboard as it goes along. Another possibility is to tape the discussion and have the whole class use a category system as the tape is played back, one act at a time. Unless there is good sound equipment, the tape may be difficult to hear or control. In this case only a few acts might be scored in class, with the complete interaction profile scored outside of class for presentation at a later time.

Comments.   Since this demonstration can be used without any equipment, it is very good for use in a variety of situations. All aspects of group interaction are revealed in a relatively short time.

Experiment 4. Leavitt's Study of the Effects of Certain Communication Networks

Arrangement of Class. The minimum number of persons for the experiment is four. If only four persons are available, I suggest using the wheel communication network. However, it makes a more interesting classroom demonstration to have at least two groups of four, one in the wheel network and one in the circle. If the whole class is to be involved, half of the groups can be in the wheel and half in the circle. When many groups are run at the same time, it helps to have assistants, one assistant for every group if it is possible, otherwise one assistant for every two groups. It is difficult for someone who is not familiar with the experiment to keep track of more than two groups at the same time.

Class members are seated in sets of four around small tables of card-table size. On each table is a set of partitions. Each position is assigned a color (blue, red, black, and green). If there is room and enough tables, an extra table can be placed between each pair of tables to serve as a work space for the experimenter or his assistants.

Equipment. This experiment requires more equipment than any of the others. First you need sets of partitions (see figure 59). Ideally the partitions are high enough so that a seated person cannot easily see over them or around them (24 by 42 inches). However, I have also used small portable models (16 by 24 inches) which will fit into a suitcase. You can use two large rectangles which are slotted to fit together or four squares which are hinged in some way. The material can be almost anything which can stand alone. I have used plywood, sheets of cardboard which are used for bookbinding, and cardboard from boxes. (The bookbinding board and colored paper can be purchased from printers in many countries.)

The partitions should have slots cut in the bottom side for notes and be labeled according to the directions in figure 59. The colors used and the order in which they appear in the network are not important. However, all materials should be consistent.

While you are out shopping, buy enough paper for each of the participants. An ordinary small pad of paper (3 by 5 inches) will last for several experiments. However, you need one pad for each subject. You can give everyone white paper and pens with different colors of ink (preferably matching the colors in the communication network), or you can let everyone use his own pen or pencil (or supply pen or pencil) and use different colors of paper. If colored pads of paper are not available from local stores, a printer may sell the paper by the ream. He would also have a paper cutter to cut the paper into note size. The reason for the colors is to distinguish quickly the notes each person has sent after the notes are collected at the end of the experiment. The colors also help the experimenter or his assistants to check up to see that experimental subjects always write a new note for each message and do not simply pass along or write on the notes received from others.

Next the experimenter needs to cut some stencils to reproduce enough sets of directions and sets of symbols for each group. Since the symbols used are the same for the wheel and the circle, only one set of stencils need be prepared for the symbols. The material for three trials is enough if you wish to conduct the experiment during one class period of about 50 minutes. The contents of the symbol sets and the directions for each network are given in the following figures. The direc-

Figure 59. Partitions for Communication Network Experiment

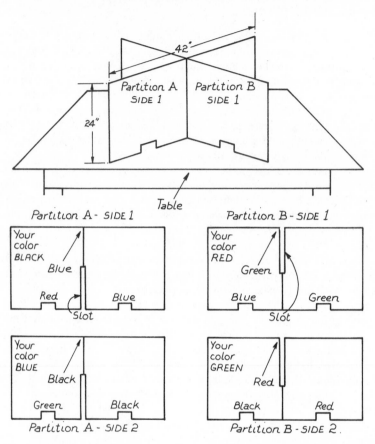

tions and the symbol sets can be cut into sheets of about 3 by 5 inches. (See figures 60–63.)

You will also need a postmeeting questionnaire for each subject (see figure 64). The answer to the question "How did you like your job in the group?" (rated on a 100-point scale from 0 for "Disliked it" to 100 for "Liked it") is the only necessary question. If you do not wish to make up a questionnaire, this question could be written on the blackboard or dictated to the class. The other two questions, concerning the presence of a leader and the direction of communications in the net, are used when many groups are tested at the same time to catch groups in which members go outside the given communication network. Noncentral persons in the wheel may tire of waiting and send messages to the persons on either side of them, or persons in the circle may decide to send messages to persons opposite them to speed things up.

Finally, if a number of groups are being tested at the same time or over a period of time, it may be helpful to have a formal summary sheet to record the results (see figure 65). Here one can record the number of messages sent by each subject, the time and number of correct answers for each trial, and the answers to the questions on the postmeeting questionnaire.

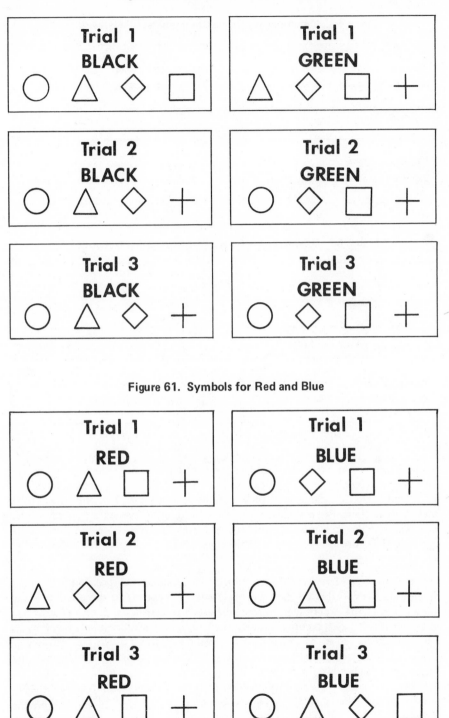

Figure 60. Symbols for Black and Green

Figure 61. Symbols for Red and Blue

Figure 62. Directions for Circle Communication Network

	c
Your color: Red	
Exchange notes with *Blue* and *Black*	

	c
Your color: Blue	
Exchange notes with *Red* and *Green*	

	c
Your color: Black	
Exchange notes with *Red* and *Green*	

	c
Your color: Green	
Exchange notes with *Black* and *Blue*	

Figure 63. Directions for Wheel Communication Network

	w
Your color: Red	
Exchange notes with *Blue*	

	w
Your color: Blue	
Exchange notes with *Red, Green,* and *Black*	

	w
Your color: Black	
Exchange notes with *Blue*	

	w
Your color: Green	
Exchange notes with *Blue*	

To keep all the materials together for a single group, I use large envelopes with odd numbers for wheel groups and even numbers for circle groups. The "kit" for a single group includes sets of directions and symbols, pads of paper, pens, questionnaires, and three small envelopes to collect the messages sent after each trial. The starting and finishing time for each trial is recorded on the front of the envelope. The directions for each subject are stapled on top of the three symbol sets.

Instructions.   Materials for each subject are placed at each position in the communication network before the class begins. If all members of the class are going to take part in the experiment, they can be asked to take seats in any order as they arrive for class. If two groups are being used for a demonstration before the whole class, volunteers can be sought and seated at the beginning of the class session.

As an introduction to the instructions for the experiment, I usually say that the experiment has been performed in different parts of the world with university students and that I am interested in how persons in different cultures solve problems in groups (see Hare, 1969). I then go on to the main part of the instructions:

You will have three problems to solve. They are quite similar. In each case there are five symbols [the symbols are drawn on the blackboard]. We will call the first problem trial 1. For trial 1 each of you has a slip of paper with four of the five sym-

Figure 64. Leavitt Experiment—Questionnaire

1. Did your group have a leader? (please check)   ____ yes ____ no

   If so, what was his color?   1. ____ Blue   2. ____ Red

                                             3. ____ Black   4. ____ Green

2. Draw a picture of the communication network in your group using arrows (⟶) to show the direction of communication. If two persons could both send and receive messages, draw two arrows (⇌).

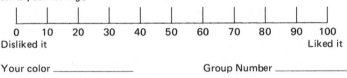

3. How did you like your job in the group? (Place a check on the scale at the point that represents your feeling.)

   | | | | | | | | | | | |
   |0|10|20|30|40|50|60|70|80|90|100|

   Disliked it   Liked it

   Your color _____   Group Number _____

---

bols. One of the symbols is missing from each of your slips of paper. This means that the four members in your group have only one of the five symbols in common. Your task is to discover what the common symbol is. You may communicate with each other only by passing written notes. The trial is over when each of you thinks he has the answer. When you think you have the answer, circle the symbol on the symbol sheet which you believe to be the common symbol. Then raise your hand as a signal to the experimenter that you have the answer. After you have been recognized, put your hand down and continue to work until all members of your group think they have the answer. If one member of the group thinks he has the answer, he may pass it on to the others. After all four of you have raised your hands, the trial is over and the notes will be collected.

Throughout the experiment you will be allowed to communicate with some member or members of the group but not with others. A slip of paper on top of your symbol sheets gives the color of each person or persons you may communicate with. If you are allowed to communicate with the persons on your left and right, pass notes to them through the slots in the partitions. If you are allowed to communicate with the person opposite you, pass notes over the top of the partition.

Please do not talk during the experiment. Communicate only by using written notes. Save all notes you receive, and write a new note for each message you wish to send. Are there any questions?

Usually someone asks a question about what he can write in the notes. The answer is "Anything you want." I attempt to answer the questions in a way that does not reveal the nature of the communication network for each group. At the beginning of the experiment, each person only knows with whom he can communicate. Part of his problem, although he may not realize it, is to discover what the network is and how to use it effectively.

When everyone is ready, the experimenter signals the beginning of the first trial. The experimenter and his assistants note the starting and finishing time for

Figure 65. Leavitt Experiment—Summary Sheet

Group Number _____

MESSAGES SENT:

TRIAL	BLUE	RED	BLACK	GREEN	TOTAL
ONE					
TWO					
THREE					
TOTAL					

TRIAL	TIME (in minutes)	NUMBER OF CORRECT ANSWERS	CORRECT ANSWER
ONE			☐
TWO			+
THREE			◯

QUESTIONNAIRE:

	BLUE	RED	BLACK	GREEN
1. Leader Color				
2.. Correct Communication Network (yes or no)				
3. Satisfaction				

each group. It is not necessary to record the time, since there is a high correlation between number of messages sent and the time used. However, it is an easily gathered item of data, and the presence of the timer provides a mild stress for the group.

As each group finishes, the experimenter notes the time, asks each member to be sure to circle the answer on the symbol sheet for that trial, and to turn in the symbol sheet together with all the messages he has received. Collecting the symbols after each trial provides some insurance that some member of the group will not use the wrong symbol set for a given trial.

When a group is ready, the members can be given the signal to start the next trial. There is no need to have all groups wait to start at the same time. After the third trial the questionnaires are distributed to the members. They are told to fill them out individually.

Analysis of Data. If only one or two groups have been used for the experiment, it is quite possible to process the data immediately and place the results in a table on the blackboard. The messages collected for each trial for a given group can be given to one of the assistants or to a group member to sort. He is asked to sort the messages by color and count all of the messages on each color paper or in each color ink.

While the messages are being sorted, I draw diagrams on the blackboard of the original five-man networks which Leavitt used—wheel, Y, chain, and circle (see Leavitt, 1951). I note that the two extreme versions were the wheel and the circle, the ones we have used in our experiment. I then draw diagrams of the wheel and circle networks for our four-man groups. Class members are asked to determine the minimum number of messages which would need to be sent in the wheel network to complete the task as it has been given (i.e., find the common symbol and make sure that each member of the group has the answer). As class members call out their answers, there are differences of opinion, but the majority usually guess six messages, the correct answer, that is, three messages to Blue, who then finds the answer and sends three messages back to the persons in the spokes of the wheel.

I then ask the class members to calculate the minimum number of messages necessary in the circle network. Once more there is variation in the answers, with eight messages being a typical guess. Few students guess six, the correct answer. I have never seen a group in the circle organize itself to solve the problem in six messages. Usually each person solves the problem for himself and is enjoying the experiment enough not to worry about the added efficiency of an organized network.

By this time the messages for each trial have usually been counted. If ony two groups have been run as a demonstration, the results are now tabulated on the blackboard following the form given in figure 65. Usually fewer messages are sent by each person on each trial as the task is learned. If this is not the case, I inquire of the deviant cases what happened. I compare the number of messages sent with the tables for students of different cultures (see Hare, 1969) to see if the present groups follow a pattern which is more European, African, or Asian. I compare the number of messages sent in the wheel with the number sent in circle. Usually, as expected, fewer messages are sent in the wheel after the first trial. By the third trial the students in the wheel may have arrived at the "ideal" pattern.

Group members tend to adopt one of two strategies to find the common symbol.

Some members will send all their symbols, so that the receiving persons, looking for the common symbol will look for four of a kind. Other members will send only the missing symbol, so that the receiver's problem becomes one of finding the symbol which is missing from among the missing symbols. In both cases the answer is the same. It is not difficult to write computer programs to simulate each of these methods of problem-solving. These programs, together with a program of dummy statements which follow typical patterns for groups in different cultures, make an interesting simulation which can be used as an adjunct to this experiment. Actually, computer simulations could be prepared for all of these experiments.

Next look at the various levels of satisfaction for members in the wheel. Typically the person in the center of the wheel is the most satisfied, the four persons in the circle next (satisfaction scores averaged), and the three noncentral persons in the wheel last (satisfaction scores averaged). There are cultural variations in level of satisfaction which can be noted by comparing the scores with those given by Hare (1969).

Comments. This experiment has many of the attributes of a party game and can be used with your friends if the evening is going slowly. I have used the experiment in a classroom demonstration with students in elementary school, junior high school, high school, college, and graduate school, and I find that students at each educational level are interested and that the results are comparable. Since the basic version of the experiment produces such predictable results, it is a good one to use as a base when introducing some new experimental variation such as social characteristics of members or type of task.

Experiment 5. Leadership and Group Decision

The version of the authoritarian and democratic leadership study initially performed by Lewin, Lippitt, and White (see White and Lippitt, 1960) which I have used for this experiment was first proposed by Preston and Heintz (1949). They called the two contrasting styles "supervisory" and "participatory." In the Preston and Heintz experiment the subjects were college students. The leaders were also students who were given brief instructions on thir leadership style before the experiment began. The task was a group discussion in which the students were to reach some agreement on the desirability of a set of presidential candidates by ranking them in order. I conducted a similar experiment using Boy Scouts as subjects, with a discussion task in which the boys were asked to rank to items of camping equipment on their desirability (Hare, 1953).

Arrangement of Class. The experiment requires two groups of five students as a minimum for a demonstration. However, if the entire class is to be involved, there may be any number of groups of almost any size. In general, the larger the groups, the more dramatic should be the effects of differences in leadership style. For an exact replication of my experiment, use groups of five including the leader. Groups of up to nine members should give similar results. Groups should be seated in a circle or around a table. They need not be in the same room. In this experiment the effects depend on the style of the student leader and not on the way the instructions are given by the experimenter.

Equipment. If all groups can see a blackboard, you can write the list of camping equipment on the board. If this is not possible, you may wish to make a

Figure 66. Forms for Ranking Items of Camping Equipment

First Ranking (1)

Name _____

Group Number _____ Date _____

1. Pack ( )
2. Cook Kit ( )
3. Sleeping bag ( )
4. Flashlight ( )
5. Waterproof Match Box ( )
6. Axe ( )
7. Compass ( )
8. First-Aid Kit ( )
9. Scout Knife ( )
10. Canteen ( )

Final Ranking (3)

Name _____

Group Number _____ Date _____

Name of Group Leader _____

1. Pack ( )
2. Cook Kit ( )
3. Sleeping Bag ( )
4. Flashlight ( )
5. Waterproof Match Box ( )
6. Axe ( )
7. Compass ( )
8. First-Aid Kit ( )
9. Scout Knife ( )
10. Canteen ( )

Group Ranking (2)

Leader _____ Type _____

Group Number _____ Date _____

1. Pack ( )
2. Cook Kit ( )
3. Sleeping Bag ( )
4. Flashlight ( )
5. Waterproof Match Box ( )
6. Axe ( )
7. Compass ( )
8. First-Aid Kit ( )
9. Scout Knife ( )
10. Canteen ( )

Names of Members:

Figure 67. Individual Correlation of Initial, Group, and Final Rankings

Scout Group Ranking Experiment

Name _____ Group Number _____ Date _____

1. Name of Leader

2. Type of leadership: Supervisory _____ Participatory _____

3. Enter raw data here:

Item	(1) Your orig. rank	(2) Your group rank	(3) Your rev'd. rank	(d) Differences 1-3	1-2	2-3	(d²) Squared Differences 1-3	1-2	2-3
1	_____	_____	_____	_____	_____	_____	_____	_____	_____
2	_____	_____	_____	_____	_____	_____	_____	_____	_____
3	_____	_____	_____	_____	_____	_____	_____	_____	_____
4	_____	_____	_____	_____	_____	_____	_____	_____	_____
5	_____	_____	_____	_____	_____	_____	_____	_____	_____
6	_____	_____	_____	_____	_____	_____	_____	_____	_____
7	_____	_____	_____	_____	_____	_____	_____	_____	_____
8	_____	_____	_____	_____	_____	_____	_____	_____	_____
9	_____	_____	_____	_____	_____	_____	_____	_____	_____
10	_____	_____	_____	_____	_____	_____	_____	_____	_____

Σ d² (Sums of squared differences) = _____ _____ _____

4. Correlation, your original ranking and your revised ranking:

$$\rho_{13} = 1 - \frac{\Sigma d^2 \, (13)}{165} = 1 - \frac{}{165} = 1 - (\qquad) = \underline{\hspace{4cm}}$$

5. Correlation, your original ranking and your group's ranking:

$$\rho_{12} = 1 - \frac{\Sigma d^2 \, (12)}{165} = 1 - \frac{}{165} = 1 - (\qquad) = \underline{\hspace{4cm}}.$$

6. Correlation, your group's ranking and your revised ranking:

$$\rho_{23} = 1 - \frac{\Sigma d^2 \, (23)}{165} = 1 - \frac{}{165} = 1 - (\qquad) = \underline{\hspace{4cm}}.$$

Figure 68. Group Correlation of Initial or Final Rankings

Scout Group Ranking Experiment

Ranking (check one): Initial _____ Final _____

Leader _____ Type _____ Group Number _____ Date _____

Item Rated

Rater	I	II	III	IV	V	VI	VIII	IX	X
A	___	___	___	___	___	___	___	___	___
B	___	___	___	___	___	___	___	___	___
C	___	___	___	___	___	___	___	___	___
D	___	___	___	___	___	___	___	___	___
E	___	___	___	___	___	___	___	___	___
F	___	___	___	___	___	___	___	___	___
G	___	___	___	___	___	___	___	___	___
H	___	___	___	___	___	___	___	___	___
I	___	___	___	___	___	___	___	___	___
J	___	___	___	___	___	___	___	___	___

Sum	___	___	___	___	___	___	___	___	___	
MR	___	___	___	___	___	___	___	___	___	AvMR _____
MR²	___	___	___	___	___	___	___	___	___	AvMR² _____

n = number of items = 10; m (number of raters) = _____

1. $AvMR = \dfrac{n+1}{2} = 5.5$

2. SDmr = SD of Mean Ranks

$$= \sqrt{AvMR^2 - (AvMR)^2} = \sqrt{\underline{\quad} - 30.25} = \sqrt{\underline{\quad\quad}} = \underline{\quad\quad}$$

3. $SDn = \sqrt{\dfrac{n^2 - 2}{12}} = \sqrt{\dfrac{99}{12}} = \sqrt{8.25} = 2.87$

4. $t = \dfrac{SDmr}{SDn} = \dfrac{\underline{\quad}}{2.87} = \underline{\quad\quad}$

5. Av r = Average correlation of all the rank orders

$$= \dfrac{mt^2 - 1}{m - 1} = \dfrac{\underline{\quad} - 1}{-1} = \underline{\quad\quad}$$

list of the 10 items on a piece of poster board for each group leader to use. For each individual in the experiment, including the leader, you will need forms for the first and final rankings of the items (see figure 66). For each group you will need a form for the group ranking (also shown in figure 66). If you wish to compute correlations for all individuals as well as for each group, you will need a copy of the form for individual correlation of initial, group, and final rankings for each individual (see figure 67) and two copies of the form for group correlation of initial or final rankings (see figure 68). If you do not want to take time for all the statistics, the individual correlations are probably of more interest. Each member of the class can compute his own correlations by following an example given by the experimenter on the black board.

As a measure of satisfaction with the discussion you will need one short questionnaire for each person involved in the experiment (see figure 69). On three 160-millimeter lines the subjects are asked to indicate their feelings along three continua:

Friendly, enjoyable   . . . . .   Unfriendly, antagonistic

Interested in task   . . . . .   No interest in task

Efficient, productive   . . . . .   Inefficient, unproductive

Instructions.   When I used this experiment with Boy Scouts or young students, I presented the discussion task as a "camping game." Since the way you present the task is not too important, you can make up your own story. However, as a guide I provide the instructions as they were given to the Boy Scouts. During a recreation period the boys were seated around tables in the dining hall or recreation lodge. They were told the following story.

We are going to play a camping game. Let's suppose that three of us are going up to Canada on a camping trip. We put a canoe on top of the car and drive to a point on a series of small lakes where we unload the canoe, put our camping gear in it, and paddle north into unknown country. After winding through the lakes for three or four days, we sight a high mountain which drops right to the lake shore. We decide to climb it, so we hide our canoe in a clump of bushes by the shore. As we make camp that night on the side of the mountain, rain begins to fall. All that night a storm rages with thunder and lightning and torrents of rain. It is so wet the next morning that we decide to turn around and go back down the mountain. At one place the trail is washed out. You and I jump across and make it, but our buddy slips and turns his leg badly. We manage to carry him the rest of the way down, but here we discover that our canoe and the rest of our supplies have been washed away in the storm. Our friend cannot walk, so we decide that I will stay with him and you will go back to the nearest settlement to get help. Since food is scarce, we will keep the few supplies we have left. You will have to live off the land. You may have to hike for three or four days, so you want to travel light. All you know is that civilization is somewhere in a southerly direction. Now suppose that you could take only *one piece of equipment* with you. Which one would it be?

Before the boys were asked actually to rate the pieces of camping equipment on the first rating sheet, they were shown a large poster with each of the items of equipment listed on it and were given the following description of the items:

Figure 69. Postmeeting Questionnaire for Leadership Experiment

Questions about the discussion

Describe the general feeling of your group by placing a mark (/) across the line at the point that describes this feeling:

Friendly, enjoyable	Unfriendly, antagonistic

Interested in task	No interest in task

Efficient, productive	Inefficient, unproductive

Name _____ Group leader _____

Type of group _____ Group number _____

Date _____

Before you decide which piece of equipment to take, let's go down this list of equipment to be sure we all understand what the items are.

1. First the pack. This can be any sort of pack you want—a mountain pack, pack basket, pack board, or official Scout pack. However, the pack is *empty;* there is nothing in it.
2. The cook kit is the regular Scout cook kit. It has a plate, frying pan, cup, pot, knife, fork, and spoon, but there is no food in it. You are going to live off the land.
3. The sleeping bag can be any type you like, a down-filled mountain bag, a Scout bag, anything. The sleeping bag is empty, too. There is nobody in it.
4. The flashlight is of the regular sort—two batteries and a bulb.
5. The waterproof match box is one of those metal ones with a top that screws on tight. It is full of matches.
6. The axe can be any size—probably a hand axe.
7. The compass is one of the small round ones.
8. The first-aid kit has in it the usual things you would expect to find in a first-aid kit—bandages, snake-bit kit, halazone tablets for purifying water, and so forth. The kit is the kind you would carry on your hip.
9. The Scout knife has the usual number of blades—a big one, a little one, a can opener, and a leather punch.
10. The canteen holds about a quart of water and is full of water when you start out.

Are there any questions about the equipment?

At this point the members of each group are told to put their names, group numbers, and the date at the top of the first ranking sheet. Next they are asked to place a "1" in the parentheses beside their first choice on the list, a "2" beside their second choice, and so on until they have ranked each item in the order of its importance for this adventure.

After these slips are collected, the leaders are taken aside for about five minutes of instruction, during which they are told that the way in which they lead the group is the most important part of the experiment. Half of the leaders are given instructions for participatory leadership, and the other half of the leaders are given instructions for supervisory leadership. All leaders hear both sets of instructions so that they are aware of the differences in their leadership style.

The instructions to participatory leaders are as follows:

1. Take part in the discussion yourself.
2. Be sure that each piece of equipment receives a reasonable amount of attention.
3. Be careful that decisions in any case are not overly influenced by extreme prejudice which might be present in one or more members of the group; that is, don't let anyone hog the whole show.
4. Have all the followers represented in the discussion.
5. Pay particular attention to followers who might be backward or shy in offering or defending their opinions. If someone isn't taking part, call him by name and ask him what he thinks.
6. If you get stuck on any item, you can call for a vote and take the majority opinion.
7. The group should come to a decision in 20 minutes.

The instructions to the supervisory leaders are as follows:

1. Do not participate in any of the discussion.
2. Your only responsibility is to see that the group rankings are made within a reasonable time (within 20 minutes).
3. Keep the group on the subject in case the group members begin to talk about something else.

When the leader returns to the group, the followers are informed that they now have 20 minutes for discussion, so that they can decide as a group which of these pieces of equipment is the most important. At the end of the discussion the group ranking form is collected, on which the leader has recorded the group choices and the names of the members as well as the actual time used in discussion. The members are then given a third ranking form with the suggestion that since they have now had a chance to talk over the problem, perhaps they have changed their minds about the order of equipment and perhaps they haven't. Either way, they are asked to record what they *now think* about the order of importance of the equipment. This is not to be simply a record of what the group decided, since that is already known.

After the third ranking is collected, the questionnaires are handed out and the subjects are asked to describe the general feeling in their group by placing a mark across each of the three lines representing different degrees of friendliness, interest, and efficiency.

Analysis of Data.   As noted earlier, the task of computing the correlations between the various rankings can be included as part of the demonstration for college students, although if the experiment is performed with younger groups, the experimenter may be faced with several hours of tabulation. If you are processing data from a large number of subjects, you may wish to use a computer with standard statistical programs.

The correlational data can be assembled in tables similar to those given in my experiment with Boy Scouts (Hare, 1953). A comparison of the individual correlations and of the average correlation of all rank orders for the groups should show the same trends. There should be a greater change in opinion in the group led by participatory leaders. The participatory leaders should also have more influence in their groups (as indicated by higher correlations between their first and final rankings, between their first ranking and the group ranking, and between the group ranking and their final ranking). The followers in the groups led by participatory leaders should find their groups more friendly, interesting, and efficient.

Comments.   Groups usually spend more time discussing the rank order of the first few items than they do as they move farther down the list. Group members can be urged to finish the discussion in 20 minutes without putting too much pressure on them.

If camping is not popular in your area, any list of 10 items can be used for the ranking task. However, you might select the 10 items from a longer list so that the decisions are fairly close. Avoid items which would clearly be ranked first or last by everyone. You could rank as few as five or six items, but the statistical reliability of the correlation will be lower.

These group discussions could also be coded by observers using a formal category system. Since the discussions include all the aspects of a typical problem-solving and decision task, they could provide a basis for computer simulation.

Appendix 2

THE HISTORY AND PRESENT STATE OF SMALL GROUP RESEARCH

IN THIS REVIEW OF the history of small group research I will give special attention to the earliest period from 1898 to 1930, when it was possible to trace the direct influence of one piece of research upon another by following the trail of footnotes backward through the social-psychological literature. Since the terms "small groups" and "group dynamics" were not yet coined, these ancestral social psychologists presumably did not realize that one day they would be seen as the founding fathers of an exciting area in the study of interpersonal behavior. Yet it is of interest to see how many of the big questions had been posed and "contemporary" techniques had been used before 1905.

A second period of 10 years, from 1931 through 1940, is also treated in some detail as the field begins to take shape and some of the now classic studies are performed. After that, the number of articles relevant to small group research written each year begins to grow at an accelerated rate (see table 47), so that it is no longer feasible to give an item-by-item account of the development of the field. (For the years 1954 through 1974 approximately 200 articles were published each

Table 47. Number of Separate Bibliographic References to Small Group Studies, 1890–1953

Period	Number of Years	Items	Items Per Year
1890–1899	10	5	0.5
1900–1909	10	15	1.5
1910–1919	10	13	1.3
1920–1929	10	112	11.2
1930–1939	10	210	21.0
1940–1944	5	156	31.2
1945–1949	5	276	55.2
1950–1953*	4	610	152.5

*Note: Four-year period.

year, bringing the total for the first 75 years to about 6,000 items, using a fairly limited definition of the field.)

Next the main schools during the heyday of small group research in the 1950s will be described. I will conclude with a statement about the present state of the field.

The History of Small Group Research

Since so much of the study of social psychology is relevant for the analysis of interpersonal behavior in small groups, the early history of small group research parallels that of the whole field. This has been summarized by Allport (1954, 1968), who sees the roots of social psychology in the Western tradition, but especially as an American phenomenon. The pragmatic tradition of the United States provided a framework for investigation. However, research in social psychology did not begin to flourish until after World War I, when a series of national emergencies and social disruptions provided special incentive. These were followed by the spread of communism, the depression of the 1930s, the rise of Hitler, the genocide of the Jews, race riots, World War II, and the atomic threat. All branches of science were stimulated, but there was a special challenge to social psychology. Social scientists were led to ask such questions as "How can the value of freedom and individuals' rights be preserved?" and "Can science help?" Their answer to these questions was a burst of creative effort to study leadership, public opinion, rumor, propaganda, prejudice, attitude change, morale, communication, decision-making, race relations, and conflict of values.

A further indication of the place of small group research in social psychology and sociology is given in several published reviews (Cottrell and Gallagher, 1941; Wilson, 1945; Shils, 1948, 1951; Ansbacher, 1951; Faris, 1953).

Within the more narrowly defined field of small group research there are three fairly distinct periods from 1898, when the first identifiable small group study was performed, until the present. The first period was a brief one, lasting from 1898 though 1905. Most of the central ideas and methods in small group research were presented during this period. Two basic questions were being asked. The first was, Does the *group* make any difference for the *individual* as he works on problem-solving tasks, and further, what kinds of problems are solved best by individuals working alone, or side by side, or in groups? Triplett (1898) sought to throw some light on the "dynamogenic factors" which seemed to affect work, especially in bicycle races where the performance of individual bicycle racers seemed to depend on the activity of those next to them on the track. Tripplett asked some small boys to wind pennants along strings of fishing reeds alone and in the company of another boy as a classic "together and apart" experiment. He found that some boys worked faster when stimulated by the presence of another boy, some performed about the same, and some were slower.

A second basic question was, Does *individual* opinion or activity make any difference in the face of *group* pressure to conform to norms? This was a very practical question for Taylor (1903), who was commissioned by the steel industry to help raise individual production. He found that men carrying pig iron or unloading coal from coal cars were much more productive if they were freed from the "group bogey," i.e., the pressures to conform to standards of work set by their fellow workers, which were usually lower than management would wish.

Another theme in the earliest work on small groups was the problem of control, especially as this problem was reflected in leadership. Using data from interviews with members of boys' gangs, Puffer (1905) studied leadership and other aspects of gang behavior, while Terman studied the influence of leaders in experimental groups of school children (1904).

An early interest in the part values play in group life is evident in Cooley's discussions of human nature and the role of the primary group (1902, 1909). Simmel was interested in integrative behavior, especially in groups of different sizes (1902).

Small Group Research in the 1920s and 1930s

Although there were a few articles on small groups published between 1905 and 1920, there was a burst of activity in the early 1920s following World War I. This period of growth lasted from 1920 through the mid-1930s with the primary emphasis on problem-solving behavior. Over 20 "together and apart" studies were published, each concerned with the facilitating effect of a set of co-workers on an individual's performance.

As an aid to visualizing the research during the early years, figure 70 gives a list of the major studies appearing between 1898 and 1930. The influence of early contributions on later work is indicated by the arrows. The criterion of influence most frequently used is that the earlier author is cited by the later author in text or footnote. Only the major connections are indicated, so that with a few exceptions, the authors who are listed in the same column may be assumed to be familiar with the work of those above them. Although Taylor (1903) studied the influence of group norms on productivity, his followers in "Scientific Management" focused only on the individual, so that industrial studies do not appear again until the mid-1930s. Since the Murphys summarized most of the major contributions to experimental social psychology in their 1931 text (revised with Newcomb, 1937), the year 1930 was selected as a cutting point for a detailed analysis of influence.

Representative of the work between 1920 and the early 1930s is Allport's study of the influence of the group upon association and thought (1920). In this experiment, he found that the presence of others would speed free associations for the individual, with efficiency in inverse correlation to the degree to which the task was mechanical in nature. There was also an inverse correlation between an individual's association speed and the amount of group influence on him. In a group more associations were suggested by the surroundings, while alone the individual had more personal associations. For reasoning tasks the presence of the group stimulated more conversational and expansive expression, while the individual alone was more logical.

Some of the experimenters in this period compare groups and individuals in the solution of the same problems and observe the ways in which different types of groups go about the process of gathering information and making group decisions. For example, South (1927) studied "some psychological aspects of committee work." He found that one-sex committees were more efficient than mixed committees. Women were quicker and more accurate in the personal and interesting tasks, while the men were superior on more abstract multiple-choice problems. A definite time limit on a task improved committee efficiency.

It was in the observation of children in school and on the playground that category systems for classifying behavior were first used extensively. The studies of

Figure 70. Major Contributions to Small Group Research, 1898–1930

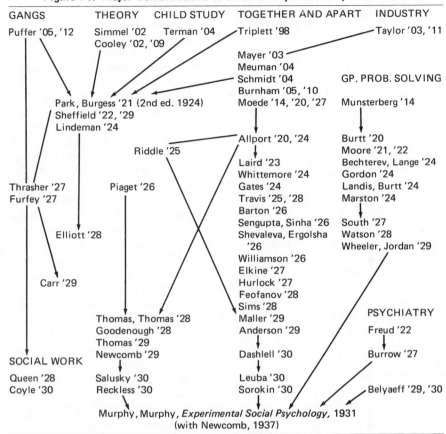

social participation and leadership among preschool children by Parten (1932, 1933a) are representative of this work. She studied the social participation and leadership of nursery school children using a time-sampling technique in which she would record the behavior of each child for one minute out of each hour. She found that social participation was correlated with age and intelligence. She described two types of leaders, the "artful" ones and the "bullies." Green observed friendships and quarrels among preschool children (1933a). She found that girls reached a peak in number of friendships earlier than boys. They also reached a high point of quarrelsomeness earlier and had a smaller ratio of quarrels to friendships. As children grow older, they tend to decrease the number of different companions they have and to increase the frequency of companionship with a few specific children. Quarreling correlated with number of friendships and seemed to be part of friendly interaction at the nursery school level.

Piaget (1926) also developed a category system for the observation of children. His system, together with those of Moreno (1923, translated 1974), who observed "psychodramatic" groups, and Carr (1929), who observed laboratory discussion groups is illustrated in detail in appendix 3.

Major Fields and Emphases, 1931–1940

Since the volume of research between 1931 and 1940 was not yet so great as to be unwieldy, the articles representing the major fields and emphases in small group research during that 10-year period are presented in table 48. It was during this period that most of the contemporary concerns of small group research began to appear, including three of the now classic research projects: Lewin, Lippitt, and White's studies of leadership; Mayo, Turner, Whitehead, Roethlisberger, and Dickson's observations at the Western Electric plant; and Moreno and Jenning's accounts of their sociometric explorations.

The list of authors in table 48 is arranged roughly to follow the same sequence as that in figure 70, which shows the major contributions to small group researcch from 1898 through 1930. Starting at the bottom left of figure 70, we note that group studies in social work were just beginning in the late 1920s with the work of Queen and Coyle. This emphasis in the next 10-year period is represented primarily by the work of Coyle (1937), who had a significant influence on group work. Many of her insights about group process were well ahead of her time. On the applied side of the field, although not limited to group work, is McBurney and Hance's handbook *The Principles and Methods of Discussion* (1939). Here only a few references are made to the handbooks which have been written to guide the practitioner of group dynamics. This is a whole literature in itself.

Next we find that the emphasis on theory which began with Simmel and Cooley and ended with Elliott in the earlier period is continued by Von Wiese and Becker, Wirth, and Znaniecki. All of these theorists were looking at a broad range of forms of social interaction, which included interaction in small groups as well as more general settings.

The early development of category systems for the observation of social interaction which was begun in the child-study literature of the 1920s is also continued during the next 10-year period. By the 1930s at least three different trends were discernible. The majority of the research studies concerned general category systems, but some focused specifically on leadership and others on friendship. Almost all of the research on children at this time was done by women. However, some attention was now turned to category systems to be used with adults in problem-solving groups. This work was done by men.

In the period 1898 through 1930, the mainstream of research was represented by the "together and apart" experiments. Although this theme continues between 1931 and 1940, there is now more emphasis on various aspects of group problem-solving. Some research is concerned with whether or not groups can learn or judge better than individuals, some with the effect of group participation on individual opinion, and some with various aspects of group dynamics, especially the influence of different styles of leadership on group atmosphere.

Although few social psychologists paid attention to the work of Taylor in industry in 1903, there is hardly an introductory student who has not heard of the Western Electric researches completed in the 1930s. Unfortunately a number of texts have since reported variations of the "Hawthorne effect" without going back to the original material to examine it again in the light of current theory. Since much of the original record of these classic researches has been published, it is possible to go over the record in some detail (cf. Hare, 1967).

The concern of psychiatrists for the role of social interaction in mental illness continued during the 1930s; however, it is not until the late 1940s and early 1950s that the interest in group psychotherapy really comes alive.

Table 48. Major Fields and Emphases in the Study of Small Groups, 1931–1940

Fields and Emphases	Author	Pub Date	Content
Group Work	Coyle	1937	Studies in group behavior
Applied (Handbook)	McBurney & Hance	1939	Principles and methods of discussion
Sociology (Theory)	von Wiese & Becker	1932	Systematic sociology
	Wirth	1939	Social interaction, individual and group
	Znaniecki	1939	Social groups as products of participating individuals
Family	Maller	1931	Size of family and personality
	Burgess & Cottrell	1939	Predicting success or failure
Child Study (Social behavior, category system)	Buhler	1931	Social behavior of child
	Goodenough & Anderson	1931	Experimental child study (manual)
	Beaver	1932	Social contacts (category system)
	Greenberg	1932	Competition
	Parten	1932	Social participation
	Washburn	1932	Scheme for grading reactions
	Bott	1933	Method in social studies of children
	Green	1933b	Play and quarreling
	Leuba	1933	Rivalry
	Smith	1933	Method (uses Reckless 1930)
	Thomas	1933	Symposium on observability of social phenomena
	Updegraff & Herbst	1933	Social behavior
	Thomas, Loomis, & Arrington	1933	Observational studies of social behavior
	Dawe	1934	Size of kindergarten group
	Cocherell	1935	Unobserved observer
	Murphy & Murphy	1935	Social situations
	Bernhardt et al.	1937	Use of motion pictures
	Murphy	1937	Social behavior and child personality
	Buhler	1939	Child and his family
	Arrington	1939	Time-sampling studies
	Jersild & Fite	1939	Nursery school and social adjustment
Child Study (Leadership)	Parten	1933a	Leadership, preschool children
	Partridge	1934	Leadership, adolescent boys
	Hanfmann	1935	Social structure, kindergarten
	Anderson	1937	Domination and integration children (pairs)
	Anderson	1939	Domination and integration, children and teachers
Child Study (Friendship)	Mengert	1931	Friendliness (in pairs)
	Green	1933a	Friendships and quarrels
	Hagman	1933	Companionships
	Hardy	1937	Social recognition

Table 48 (continued)

Fields and Emphases	Author	Pub Date	Content
Category Systems of Direct Observation	Wrightstone	1934	Instrument for measuring group discussion
	Newstetter	1937	Group adjustment
	Sanderson	1938	Group description
	Miller	1939	Measuring social interaction
	Lundberg	1940	Problems of classification and measurement
	Chapple	1940	Interaction chronograph
Together and Apart	Pessin	1933	Memorizing
	Pessin & Husband	1933	Maze learning
	Dashiell	1935	Review of literature
	Gurnee	1937b	Maze learning
	May & Doob	1937	Competition and cooperation (Theory)
	Taylor, Thompson, & Spassoff	1937	Boredom
	Abel	1938	Motor performance
	Mukerji	1940	Work
	Husband	1940	Code and jigsaw
Groups Learn or Judge Better?	Shaw	1932	Individual vs. groups in solution of complex problem (offshoot of "together and apart")
	Gurnee	1937a	Collective vs. individual judgments of facts
	Preston	1938	Validity of group judgment
	Thorndike	1938b	Discussion of correctness of group decisions
	Zeleny	1940a	A group learning plan (small discussion groups)
Groups Change Opinion	Jenness	1932a	Summary of group discussions and change of opinions
	Jenness	1932b	Estimate beans in bottle
	Sherif	1935	Perception
	Sherif	1936	Psychology of social norms
	Simpson	1938	Those who influence and are influenced
	Timmons	1939	Discussions of social problems
	Hilgard, Sait, & Margaret	1940	Level of aspiration
Group Dynamics	Lewin & Lippitt	1938	Autocracy vs. democracy
	Lewin, Lippitt, & White	1939	Social climates
	Lippitt	1939	Autocracy vs. democracy
	Lippitt	1940	group atmospheres (thesis)
Industrial	Barnard	1938	Functions of executive
	Mayo	1933	Human problems of industrial civilization
	Turner	1933	Test room
	Whitehead	1938	Industrial worker
	Roethlisberger & Dickson	1939	Management and worker

Table 48 (continued)

Fields and Emphases	Author	Pub Date	Content
Psychiatry	Slavson	1938	Creative group education
	Sullivan	1938	Psychiatry, introduction to interpersonal relations
	Rowland	1939	Friendship in mental hospitals
	Lasswell	1939	Personality, group, culture
Sociometry	Moreno	1934 (revised 1953)	Who shall survive?
	Jennings	1937	Leadership
	Moreno & Jennings	1938	Statistics of configurations
	Richardson	1939	Mental resemblance, husband and wife
	Zeleny	1939a	Group leaders
	Zeleny	1939b	Sociometry of morale
	Zeleny	1940b	Social status
	Moreno, Jennings, & Sargent	1940	Time as qualitative index

The final set of articles listed in table 48, on sociometry, is also related to psychiatry inasmuch as Moreno was a psychiatrist and his whole approach had a therapeutic intent. One should at least read the introduction to Moreno's *Who Shall Survive?*, published in 1934, for a firsthand judgment of the man and his ideas. Some indication of his work, along with that of the other major contributors to the contemporary approach to the study of small groups, is given in the next section on the heyday of small group research.

The Heyday of Small Group Research

The present period of small group research began in the middle 1930s as Hitler was coming into power in Germany and other authoritarian regimes seemed to dominate the world. Even before World War II, scholars whose political views, religion, or ethnic group was not in favor in Eastern or Western Europe began to arrive in the United States. Much of the research in social psychology which was done just prior to, during, or after the war can be seen as an attempt by these social scientists to use their knowledge to promote the theory and practice of democratic forms of group process and to combat the influence of authoritarianism. Two of these men who had the greatest influence on small group research were Moreno, coming from Austria, and Lewin from Germany.

This new interest in small group research began to be recognized in the late 1940s and early 1950s by a number of references in the literature (Hare, 1962, pp. 6–8). For example: "There is a new focusing of interest on the small group in American empirical sociology" (Shils, 1947, p. 27); "The small group has become the focus of considerable interest on the part of social scientists" (Argyle, 1952a, p. 269); "In the past few years the study of small groups as an area of experimentation has been attracting the interest of an increasing number of social scientists" (Roseborough, 1953, p. 275).

Another index of the growth of the field at that time is found in the dates which marked the introduction of terms referring specifically to small group research topics as categories for classification in *Psychological Abstracts*. The subheading "Sociometry" was first used in *Psychological Abstracts* in 1940 with references to research by Moreno, Jennings, and Sargent (1940), Dodd (1940), and Zeleny (1939b). Next the subheading "Group Dynamics" was introduced in 1945 with a reference to the work of Lewin (1944). Finally, the subheading "small group" appeared in 1950 with references to Bales (1950b) and Deutsch (1949a).

The high point of interest in the group dynamics–small groups field was reached in the years 1953 to 1955 with the publication of the first collections of readings (Cartwright and Zander's *Group Dynamics* [1953] and Hare, Borgatta, and Bales's *Small Groups* [1955]), several special issues of journals (*American Sociological Review* [1954] and *Sociometry* [1954]), and numerous special sessions at meetings of psychological and sociological associations.

Three Schools: Sociometry, Group Dynamics, and Small Groups

Three main schools of small group research—sociometry (Moreno), group dynamics (Lewin), and small groups (Bales)—dominated the field from the late 1930s through the early 1960s. Moreno (who died in 1974) was by far the most colorful figure, the most spontaneous in the generation of new ideas, and the most zealous in promoting his own point of view. In brief, Moreno developed his ideas for a "spontaneity theater" (1947b) while he was a medical student in Vienna. During his lunch hour he would sit in a park and watch the children at play. There he would tell stories, which the children would spontaneously act out. His favorite place for storytelling was in the crotch of a tree, where he would sit looking down at the children and directing their action. He went on to establish a "spontaneity theater" in Austria with young actors. Later, when he came to New York City at the time of the depression, he earned his living by engaging actors to act out the news events of the day in a spontaneous performance after he had warmed them up to their roles. This method of recreating social events led to psychodrama, which was widely used in veterans' hospitals at the time of World War II. A group of patients or staff would be asked to act out the parts of significant persons in some crisis event which a patient had experienced so that he might re-enact the event in the hope of greater understanding. The same method led to sociodrama, were incidents in race relations or other social problem areas would be acted out to provide case material for analysis by student groups. Finally the sociometric test, in which individuals were asked whom they would like to have as coparticipants in some social activity so that groups based on personal attraction could be formed, was widely used in the American school system to form reading groups and other educational groups and by the American army to select groups of men as replacements for military units.

Moreno introduced his sociometric ideas in religious terms. He described his major book, *Who Shall Survive?*, as "the new Bible." "It is a bible for social conduct, for human societies," he said. "It has more ideas packed in one book than a whole generation of books" (Moreno, revised edition, 1953, p. 66). Moreno felt that the original creator of the universe had erred by resting on the seventh day. He should have provided man with a release from himself and from society. Fortunately, says Moreno, sociometry provides the missing element. The spontaneous man will survive. Some 30 years after Moreno introduced the ideas, we find the proponents of sensitivity training using role playing and acting out new forms of social relationships in a way which suggests the same concern with release from the authoritarian bonds of society which Moreno felt.

Lewin and Moreno were contemporaries, although Lewin died in 1947, cutting short what was already a very seminal career. Lewin was a practitioner of group dynamics as well as a scientist. With Lippitt, White, Cartwright, Zander, and other colleagues he carried out basic research on the influence of authoritarian and democratic leaders on their groups. This inspired similar research over a period of years (White and Lippitt, 1960) and led to the establishment of a center to teach group dynamics as part of the adult education movement (Bradford, Gibb, and Benne, 1964). (See appendix 4 on sensitivity training.)

In his theoretical approach Lewin placed emphasis on the total situation or "life space" of an actor. Thus he was especially concerned with barriers to movement in the social field. His research was not limited to the group field, but included studies of social influences on children, national characters, minority groups, and adolescents. Deutsch (1954, 1968a) has noted that Lewin first wrote about group dynamics at a time when psychologists commonly denied the existence or reality of "groups." Only "individuals" were real, and to refer to such characteristics of groups as "group atmosphere" and "group goals" was considered nonscientific or mystical. One of Lewin's major contributions was to make the concept of "group" acceptable to psychologists. Through his experimental approach he also opened the door of the laboratory to sociologists, who could now test their theories using the experimental method. However, in later years, members of the group dynamics school have concentrated more on social processes which could occur in any setting than on the dynamics of small groups. Examples of this trend are found in the theories of Festinger on cohesiveness, social comparison, and cognitive dissonance (1954, 1957).

While Lewin had the greatest influence on psychologists doing research on the dynamics of groups, Bales had more influence on sociologists. Bales did not consciously found a social movement as the others did, and for the first 10 years of research in the small groups school there was almost no applied side. Bales and his colleagues were identified by their use of the category system for *Interaction Process Analysis* (Bales, 1950b) and for their laboratory studies of initially leaderless groups of college students using few if any experimental manipulations. They were interested in the process of problem-solving. As a sociologist, Bales was primarily interested in the social system; he only began to consider the individual and his personality as a major variable in the 1960s.

In the late 1950s Bales took over the direction of a course in the group dynamics tradition which was given at Harvard under the title "Social Relations 120." The first version of the course was developed in the Harvard Business School and was based almost entirely on class discussions of human-relations cases. After the course was shifted to the Social Relations Department, gradually more and more sessions were introduced in which the group members would discuss their own process, following techniques which had been developed by Lewin and his colleagues in the group dynamics movement. Since the course was popular, a number of teaching assistants were needed to lead the groups, and gradually a cadre of practitioners was trained who led and reported research on groups in the "Soc Rel 120" format (Mills, 1964; Dunphy, 1964; Slater, 1966; Mann, Gibbard, and Hartman, 1967). At the present time this applied side of the small groups school tends to be limited to academic settings, in contrast to group dynamics and the newer offshoot, sensitivity training, which is widely used in religious, business education, and community settings.

Recent Trends in Research

From the earliest research on small groups to the present, psychologists have dominated the field. Sociologists are next in impact, followed by the applied fields of psychotherapy, education, social work, and business. This dominance has continued during the period 1959–1969, with the major work on cognitive balance in social relationships (Heider, 1958), bargaining (cf. Deutsch and Krauss, 1960), and risk taking (cf. Wallach, Kogan, and Bem, 1962) being contributed by psychologists. The major theme introduced by sociologists is a model of social behavior drawn from economics, in which actors are seen as making exchanges to maximize their social profits at the lowest social cost (Homans, 1961; Blau, 1960a; Siegel and Fouraker, 1960). Most of this research does not focus on the group, but on the actor in a social situation.

Ever since the publications by Sherif (1935), Adorno et al. (1950), and Asch (1951), social psychologists have been been studying the relationship between personality variables (mainly authoritarianism) and conformity (mainly in an experimental situations similar to those used by Sherif and Asch). This type of experiment has dominated the field. During the period 1959–1969 about one-third of the experimental studies of small groups were related directly to the issue of conformity. (For bibliography for 1959–1969, see Hare, 1972.) For all the research in this area, relatively few of the experimenters worked within a general theoretical context which would allow them systematically to relate their results to the results of others.

The next largest area of research includes the sociometric studies of interpersonal choice. In some cases the studies of interpersonal choice are related to the area of social perception, where group members are asked about the perceptions they have about others' liking for them or for others in the group. However, the social perception studies also include perceptions of personality traits and other social characteristics. Social perception ranks below interpersonal attraction and about on a level with studies of interaction process in popularily as a research topic.

The next area, representing about 10 percent of the total output for the years 1959–1969, is leadership. This is a hardy perennial and has been in vogue ever since the earliest days.

Other areas which contained enough research to form a basis for a chapter in this handbook in 1962 have received relatively little attention since then. These areas include roles, personality, social characteristics, group size, and various aspects of group productivity.

In contrast, some special topics which can be approached by simulation, gaming, or simple laboratory experiments have received more attention than some of the older, established areas. Examples of these topics are the helping response, competition and cooperation in games, trust and threat in games, the "risky shift" phenomenon, and the use of personal space.

Summary

The first period in the history of small group research was a brief one lasting from 1898 through 1905, when the major research themes were introduced which would continue until the present. Tripplett tested the hypothesis that the presence of others doing the same task would have a facilitating effect, Taylor was concerned with group pressure to conform to norms in work groups, Puffer with leadership in boys' gangs, and Terman with leadership in groups of school children. Cooley considered the social aspects of human nature and the role of the primary group, and Simmel investigated various forms of social interaction, especially in groups of different sizes.

During the 1920s and 1930s there was a second period of activity following World War I. The major concern was with "together and apart" experiments following Allport's study of the influence of the group on association and thought. Other experiments during this period compared individuals and groups in their solution to the same types of problems or, like South's study of some psychological aspects of committee work, compared groups with different types of membership. Category systems for the analysis of social interaction were developed for the observation of social participation and leadership among school children by Thomas, Goodenough, and Piaget and a few years later by Parten and Green. Category systems were also being used with experimental groups by Carr and with psychodramatic groups by Moreno.

During the period from 1931 to 1940 most of the contemporary concerns of small group research began to appear, including three of the now classic research projects: Lewin, Lippitt, and White's studies of leadership; Mayo et al.'s observations at the Western Electri plant; and Moreno and Jenning's accounts of their sociometric explorations. Identifiable subfields during this period included social work with groups; theory; child study with emphases on category systems, leadership, and friendship; individual and group problem-solving; psychiatry; and sociometry.

The early 1950s were the heyday of small group research. At this time the three main schools of sociometry (Moreno), group dynamics (Lewin), and small groups (Bales) dominated the field. Moreno introduced the spontaneity theater, psychodrama, sociodrama, and the sociometric test for the analysis of group structure. Lewin was concerned about the life space of an actor and barriers to movement in the social field. His experimental studies of leadership popularized the laboratory approach to the study of groups and the training of group members, resulting in the T-group, or sensitivity training, movement. Bales developed a category system for interaction process analysis which was widely used to describe the dynamics of group-problem-solving. In later years the small groups school developed an applied side in the form of self-analtyic groups held in academic settings in which students would learn to analyze their own interaction patterns.

In more recent years psychologists have continued to produce most of the research in the field, but now with more emphasis on the actor in a social situation than on group process. The research topics which attract most of the attention in research are quite similar to those of 1900: conformity, interpersonal choice, social perception, interaction process, and leadership.

Appendix 3

AN OUTLINE OF RESEARCH METHODS

Since the principal emphasis in this text has been on the findings of research rather than the methods by which the results were obtained, only brief descriptions have been given of category systems (chapter 3) and sociometric techniques (chapter 7). As a guide to the literature on methodology, references which are especially relevant for the analysis of behavior in small groups are listed under the following general headings:

1. Research design and experimental method
2. Observation techniques
3. Sociometry
4. Questionnaires
5. Models and simulations
6. Problems with laboratory experiments

The most comprehensive reviews of methodology are found in four sources: Jahoda, Deutsch, and Cook (eds.), *Research Methods in Social Relations* (1951),[1] Festinger and Katz (eds.), *Research Methods in the Behavioral Sciences* (1953), Lindzey (ed.), *Handbook of Social Psychology* (1954), and Lindzey and Aronson (eds.), *Handbook of Social Psychology* (1968). For some indication of the development of research methods in this area, the current texts can be compared with Lindeman's *Social Discovery* (1924), which reviews the methodology of the social sciences prior to 1924.

Research Design and Experimental Method

The following additional references describe some of the general problems in conducting experiments with small groups both in the laboratory and in the field: Miller, 1950; Swanson, 1951a; Whyte, 1951b; Argyle, 1952a, Festinger, 1953b; French, 1953; Grossack, 1953; Rubenstein, 1953; Edwards, 1954; Sherif, 1954a, 1954b; Borgatta and Cottrell, 1957; Taylor and Mitzel, 1957; Myers, 1959;

1. A condensation of this same material appears in Sellitz et al. (1959).

Scharmann, 1959; Golembiewski, 1960; J. A. Davis, Spaeth, and Huson, 1971; Denzin, 1971; Vidmar and Hackman, 1971; Lake, Miles, and Earle, 1973; Petrovskii, 1973. Typical tasks which have been used in research are described by Ray (1955). Additional works giving suggestions for tasks or equipment which can be used in laboratory research include Mucchielli, 1963; Zajonc, 1965b; Sawyer and Friedell, 1966; Durkin, 1968; Coleman, 1969; Driver and Hunsaker, 1972. Some specific experimental designs are suggested by Crutchfield (1951).

Some methods have been proposed for measurement, analysis of data, or classification of results of small group experiments which are broader in focus than any of the types of methods listed below. Works presenting these include Damrin, 1959; J. A. Davis, Spaeth, and Huson, 1961; Johnson, 1965; Brousek, 1967; Heslin and Dunphy, 1968; Clark, Culbert, and Babele, 1969; Sigall and Page, 1972.

Observation Techniques

The chapters in the major references mentioned above which describe observation techniques are by Whyte (1951a), Zander (1951), Heyns and Zander (1953), Peak, (1953), Heyns and Lippitt (1954), and Weick (1968). To collect data, the observer usually uses one of four general approaches:

1. *Recall.* The observer either recalls his own experiences in a group or asks others to do so. If he asks others to recall their observations of behavior, this method of data collection becomes the interview as it has been used with individuals (Puffer, 1905) or with groups (Hare and Davie, 1954; Davie and Hare, 1956). If other untrained observers are asked to write down their impressions of a previous group meeting, the method becomes the questionnaire (Hemphill, 1949). In either event, the data, once recorded, can be processed by methods appropriate for other kinds of observation.

2. *Participant observer.* The observer takes an active part in the life of the group while making his obseravtions. In some cases the other group members do not know that they are being observed. There is usually little time for note taking unless the observer also plays the role of secretary for the group. The participant-observer technique has been used with boys' gangs (Whyte, 1943), on psychiatric wards (Stanton and Schwartz, 1954; Banks, 1956), with discussion groups (Carr, 1929; Koslin et al., 1968), and in studies of rumor transmission (Back et al., 1950). The observer may conduct a "field experiment" by behaving in some predetermined way to note the group's reaction.

3. *Nonparticipant observer.* Most of the observations reported in the child-study literature have been made by nonparticipating adults who stood on the school playground or sat in the classroom (Piaget, 1926; Thomas and Thomas, 1928; Thomas, 1929; Reckless, 1930; Hare, 1957). Nonparticipant observers are also used with laboratory groups of adults, especially in university settings. One study reports that estimates of the relative interaction frequency and speech duration of group members were more accurate when reported by nonparticipant observers than when reported by the group leader (Holmes, 1969).

4. *Unseen observer.* In laboratory experiments the observer is frequently given some place to conceal himself. This may be a simple burlap screen (Lippitt, 1940) or an observation room with a one-way mirror (Bales, 1950b). Some subjects are told that they are being observed, others are not (Cocherell, 1935). Bales and Flanders (1954) suggest a plan for the construction of a small group laboratory and observation room.

Quantity and Quality of Observations

Having decided on his general approach to observation, the observer may attempt to record everything that goes on, he may use a category system, or he may make ratings.

1. *Complete transcript.* The most complete records of group behavior are not made by men, but by machines: sound movies, time-lapse photography (Thelen, 1950; Withall, 1956), television (Nielsen, 1962; Bjerg, 1968; Anderson, Hummel, and Gibson, 1970; Hum, 1970; Landy, 1970; D. Miller, 1970; Robinson, 1970; Stoller, 1970a; Weiss and McKenzie, 1972; Eisler, Hersen, and Agras, 1973; Moore and Lee, 1974), or sound-recording equipment (Psathas, 1961; Metz, 1965). However, detailed transcripts can also be produced by stenographers or by trained observers who alternate with each other in observing a group or an individual over a long period of time (Barker and Wright, 1949; Barker, 1951). In the complete transcript the observer usually uses the most complete category system he has— language. However, a complete language is not a very efficient category system, since so many of the words mean almost the same thing and since there are too many categories to make quantitative analysis of the data possible. Complete transcripts are useful only as a basis for clinical insight or as illustrative material.

2. *Category system.* In a category system the number of words used to describe behavior is reduced and generality of the words is increased. The reduced set of concepts, seldom more than 100, is then used to describe the act-by-act sequence of events in group behavior. The problems of development and use of category systems are elaborated in the paragraphs below.

3. *Ratings.* Summary ratings of certain aspects of group behavior are often made at the end of each session or at some specified intervals during the session. These judgments may be of individual behavior, they may compare or rank group members according to some criterion of behavior, or they may be judgments about the group as a whole (Wrightstone, 1934; Zander, 1948; Wrightstone, 1951; Crowther and Pantleo, 1970).

Category Systems

Five decisions must be made by anyone using a category system. Each of these points is mentioned in chapter 3 and discussed in some detail in the general references on obseravtion methods.

1. *Frame of Reference.* Behavior may be scored primarily by the intent of the actor or by his effect on others. The focus can be on the individual or on the group. Leary (1957) suggests the analysis of data at five levels (public, conscious, and private communication, the unexpressed, and values) through the use of different data-collecting techniques.

2. *Unit Act.* The unit of behavior to be scored may be a sentence, a paragraph, an interaction, or any bit of behavior to which another person may respond.

3. *Sample.* Some observers score continuously (Bales, 1950b); others take short "time samples" at frequent intervals (Arrington, 1939, 1943).

4. *Single of Multiple Code.* If a given unit of behavior appears to have more than one implication (for example, it may contain both work and emotion), some observers score only the dominant characteristic of the act (Bales, 1950b), while others give it two scores (Thelen, 1954).

5. *Recording Devices.* The ultimate objective with any recording device is to prepare the data for machine computation, since hand tabulation is not feasible if any quantity of data is collected. The observer usually records the time that the act took place or the sequence in which it occurred, who initiated the act, who received it, and the content. The devices listed below are ordered from least to most efficient in preparing data for analysis.

    a. Fixed Form. The form can be simply a blank piece of paper on a clipboard, board, or a prepared form (Bales, 1950b; Ferrara, 1973). Acts are usually recorded in sequence. The stenotype machine (Carter et al., 1951) and recording by voice into a portable recorder are in the same class, since these methods preserve only the sequence of acts. Time must be written in if the record is to be compared with a sound transcript unless time is signaled in some other way (Powell and Jackson, 1964).

    b. Moving Tape. When scoring is done on a moving tape, the actual time of the act is preserved. Bales and Gebrands (1948) have developed an Interaction Process Recorder which can be used with interchangeable category systems. Chapple has developed a portable recorder for use with his system. Polygraphs are used to combine categories with other types of behavioral or physiological measures (Boyd and DiMascio, 1954).

    c. Chronograph. Chapple's Interaction Chronograph (Chapple, 1940; Matarazzo, Saslow, and Matarazzo, 1956) is a device which partially processes the data while they are being recorded. More elaborate versions use audio systems, analog computers, or ultrasonic-activity devices (Gurman and Bass, 1961; Zimmer, 1961; Crawford and Nicora, 1964; Nathan, 1965; Pishkin and Foster, 1965; Holmes, 1969). A simpler version records action and silence but does not process the data (Kasl and Mahl, 1956).

    d. Direct Punching. The most direct method is to punch the interactions on IBM cards, one act per card, although this method has two disadvantages. It requires a large permanent installation, and the ordinary punching machines may not operate fast enough to keep pace with a group discussion. The first disadvantage can be avoided by using "mark sense" cards in notebooks which can be carried into the field by observers and later fed to a machine to produce punched cards (Lippitt and Zander, 1943). The second disadvantage can be overcome by recording magnetically on a plastic tape which would then be used to produce punched cards.

Some experimenters have asked the group members to record their own reactions to a discussion on an audience-reaction machine (Thelen and Withall, 1949; Thelen, 1950; Bass et al., 1957) or to recall their reactions when parts of the discussion were played back to them at a later time (Mills, Lichter, and Kassebaum, 1957).

Statistical Analysis of Observational Data

A number of statistical indices and schematic diagrams of participation in discussion have been proposed (Findley, 1948; Pepinsky, Siegel, and Van Atta, 1952; Dickens, 1955; O'Brien, Biglan, and Penna, 1972; Overs and Mooney, 1972). Other statistical problems are discussed by Bales (1950b, 1951a).

Reliability and Validity

Various measures have been used to test interobserver or self-reliability in the use of category systems. Usually the reliability for some categories is higher than it is for others and varies with the topic of discussion (Borgatta and Bales, 1953c; Avery and Bachelis, 1956; Waxler and Mishler, 1966). A statistical test of reliability which could be applied to many systems has been proposed by Schutz (1952a), who actually developed his scheme for use with content analysis. In collecting and analyzing data, the observer using categories and the investigator who uses content analysis share many of the same problems (Berelson, 1952, 1954). The early workers in the child-study field made exhaustive studies of reliability (Thomas, 1932–1933; Thomas, Loomis, and Arrington, 1933).

One of the problems in validity is that the observer, as any other measuring instrument, may affect the field of observation to some extent by his presence. Some of the effects of an observer upon a group are probably similar to the effects of an audience upon performance described in chapter 14.

Additional research bearing on aspects of reliability and validity of observations includes Evans, 1960; Hays, 1960; Trost, 1962; Spaeth, 1965; Gregovich and Sidowski, 1966; Maier and Thurber, 1968; Pierce, 1968.

Early Category Systems

Historically, category systems received a great deal of attention between 1920 and 1930, primarily in the study of the social behavior of children. Thomas and her associates (1929) had an intensive interest in the methodology of repeated samples of behavior (Arrington, 1943). Other interesting early attempts were those of Moreno (1923, translated 1947), Piaget (1926), and Carr (1929, 1930).

Moreno's earliest category system first appeared in his book *The Theatre of Spontaneity,* which was published anonymously in German in 1923. This book described a new kind of "spontaneous" theater, which was the precursor of sociodrama and psychodrama, introduced by Moreno in the 1930s to portray social and psychological problems. The following descriptions are taken from Moreno's translation of his original book on the spontaneity theater.

Notations for Spontaneity States

The condition of the player before beginning of action, the consciousness or zero state, is best expressed by the sign zero (0). The identification of consciousness with the zero state has a practical justification. The player, before he throws himself in a spontaneous creative act, is just conscious of himself and the life situation which contains, however, none of the creative-situational complex which he will be asked to produce any moment. It is a zero state from the point of view of the prospective creative state. If the player has—upon the instruction of the director—presented anxiety, and if he is given the task to pass from it into anger, he has really two tasks: one to produce a new state —anger—and another, to break away from the previous one—anxiety. The transition from anxiety into anger can take place directly by a jump, or indirectly over a zero level, by returning to it. Jumping from one state to another may cause impurities; a hangover from one state may influence and distort the next. As a sign for a spontaneity state, I suggest a vertical drawn pointed angle: $\wedge$. The upward line of the angle portrays the warming up from a zero level to the spontaneity state, the top part of the angle portrays its achievement, the downward line of the angle represents the loss of the stage, its cooling off and return to the zero level. Once this basic sign is accepted all other signs of the spontaneity alphabet develop logically. If one and the same state is repeated immediately after, the sign for it is a double angle with broken inner lines: ᴧ   . If the repetition is continuous, for instance five times, the sign accordingly is ᴧᴧᴧ   . In actuality the player does not return to the zero level, but remains midway, making short pauses. He may be given the task to produce a state of anger for a number of situations in a stretch. He would not produce it as a continuity, but in rhythmic time units. The separation of one unit from another may be hardly noticeable from without, but they are occurring just the same. If a state is not repeated but passes into a new one immediately followed by a jump without a pause, then the sign for it would be the inner lines of the vertically drawn pointed angle, connected by a horizontal line, before they return to a new plane: ⌐ᴧ   . However, if the player is to return from the state to zero and to climb from there anew, then the sign of the self is simply two connected vertical angles: **M**   . For two types of opening states, the opening and the ending tempus at the beginning or at the end of a situation, the sign is an angle reduced in size   ᴧ   , starting and ending tempus amount together to the full duration of the state (½t plus ½t equals t) (see figure 71).[2]

Figure 71. Moreno's Action Diagram

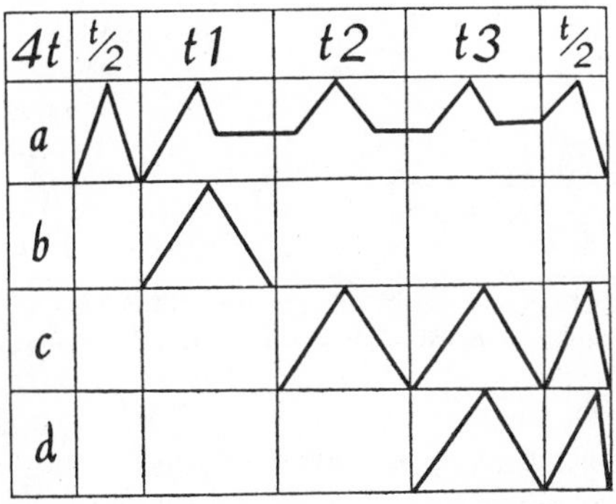

Source: Jacob L. Moreno, *The Theatre of Spontaneity* (Beacon, N.Y.: Beacon House, 1947), p. 98. Reprinted by permission of the publisher.

Piaget's Category System

To collect quantitative data for his study *The Language and Thought of the Child* (1926), Piaget used a system of eight categories. Some of his hypotheses about the functions of language in young children and the typical interaction patterns between children were tested by comparing the frequencies of activity in each of the categories; others were tested by forming indices to represent the ratio of acts in two different categories. These two forms for data analysis have remained the basic ways of handling the data derived from the analysis of interaction. Piaget's eight categories were:

1. Repetition	5. Criticism and derision
2. Monologue	6. Orders and threats
3. Collective monologue	7. Question
4. Adapted information	8. Answer

2. Jacob L. Moreno, *The Theatre of Spontaneity* (Beacon, N.Y.: Beacon House, 1947), pp. 57–58. Reprinted by permission of the publisher.

Figure 72. Interaction of a Six-Year-Old Boy

Number and Text	Category	Remarks

1. Lev puts his pencil down Geo's neck.
   Geo cries out, "Lev!"
   It doesn't matter.
   Lev begins to draw his hat again.
   He shows his work:
	4	

2. I look at things properly. What are you looking at?	4	(This remark belongs to 4 because it is part of a dialogue. It calls forth an answer and then remark 3.)

3. The hat.
   Lev repeats some words which one of
    his companions is learning:
	8	

4. Luloid! celluloid!
   Turning his drawing upside down and
    addressing himself to no one:
	1	

5. I want to see how it looks.
   Ro brings some paper cigarettes.
   He distributees them.
   Lev asks for some:
	2	

6. How about me?
   Lev goes back to his work.
   He points to the little ribs of straw on
   his hat and compares them with the
   drawing.
	7	This is a request, but expressed in interrogative form; it therefore belongs to category 7.

Source: Jean Piaget, *The Language and Thought of the Child* (New York: Harcourt, Brace, 1926), p. 239. Reprinted by permission of Humanities Press, Inc., and Routledge & Kegan Paul Ltd.

His use of the categories is illustrated in an excerpt from his observation of Lev, a six-year-old boy in a French school (see figure 72).

Carr's Interaction Diagram

The last example of an early category system is taken from the work of Carr (1929), who was one of the first to describe the interaction of a small discussion group of college students. Similar small groups of students, unknown to each other until they are brought into the laboratory to solve some discussion problem, have become a standard research population for the social psychologist. Carr formed three-man groups from members of his sociology class and asked them to solve some problem of an immediate practical character, such as how they were to spend some leisure time in the immediate future. One member of the group acted as note taker to record the content of the remarks as they were made by each speaker so that the interaction process could be analyzed later. On pages following are a segment of interaction diagram for one of these discussions, with a key describing notations used, and a table summarizing the number of *initiatives* and *contributions* for each member (see figure 73 and table 49).

Figure 73. Carr's Interaction Diagram

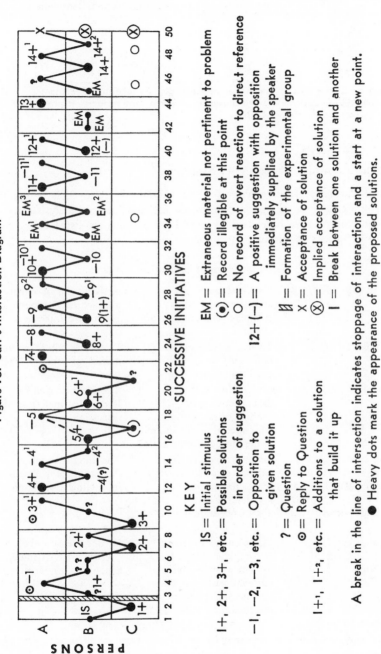

Source: Lowell J. Carr, "Experimental Sociology," *Social Forces* 8 (September 1929): 64. Copyright © The University of North Carolina Press. Reprinted by permission of the publisher.

Table 49. Initiatives and Solutions for a Laboratory Group

	Total Initiatives	Possible Solutions Contributed
Persons		
A	21	5
B	24	6
C	5	3
Total	50	14

Source: Lowell J. Carr, "Experimental Sociology," *Social Forces* 8 (September 1929). Copyright © The University of North Carolina Press. Reprinted by permission of the publisher.

Additional Examples of Category Systems

Each of the many category systems which have been developed is best suited for some particular type of group, type of subject, and level of analysis. Five of these systems which have been used in several experiments are listed below with their major emphases by authors:

Author	Description of categories	Focus
Chapple (1940, 1942, 1953)	Two categories: action and silence. Both frequency and duration are recorded.	Activity rate of clients in a structured business or psychiatric interview.
Bales (1950a, 1950b, 1970a)	Twelve categories: six task and six social-emotional.	Problem-solving in small discussion groups. Widely used in other situations.
Carter et al. (1951a, 1951b)	Seven principal dimensions with subcategories; 53 in all, with special emphasis on leader and follower roles.	The identification of leaders in small leaderless discussion groups.
Freedman, et al. (1951), LaForge et al. (1954), Leary (1955, 1957), Leary and Coffey (1955), LaForge and Suczek (1955)	Sixteen categories in a circular continuum. Two basic dimensions: love-hate and dominance-submission.	The interpersonal dimension of personality in a clinical situation.
Stone et al. (1962), Stone et al. (1966), Dunphy, Stone, and Smith (1965)	The General Inquirer: A computer system for content analysis and retrieval based on the sentence as a unit of information.	Dictionaries can be constructed for content analysis in any area.

Additional category systems are listed by principal focus:

> *Group Classification and Description.* Sanderson, 1938; Lundberg, 1940; Hemphill and Westie, 1950; Jansen, 1952; Borgatta and Cottrell, 1955; Borgatta, Cottrell, and Meyer, 1956; Hemphill, 1956; Roby, 1957; Scharmann, 1966; Betz, 1973.

Discussion Groups. Carr, 1929; Miller, 1939; Hardee and Bernauer, 1948;
Alpert and Smith, 1949; Steinzor, 1949a, 1949b; Di Vesta, Roach, and
Beasley, 1951; Brandenburg and Neal, 1953; Thelen et al., 1954; Matthews and Bendig, 1955; Kuusela, 1956; Miller, 1958–1959; Stock and
Thelen, 1958; Chapple and Miller, 1959; Krug, 1959; Crowell and
Scheidel, 1961; Muller, 1961; Borgatta, 1963a; Hoffman and Maier,
1964; Mills, 1964; Borgatta, 1965; Swanson, 1965; Kingsley, 1967;
Mann, Gibbard, and Hartman, 1967; Katz, 1968; McGuire and Lorch,
1968b; Pollay, 1968; Hays, 1970; Seymour, 1971; Harary and Havelock, 1972; Hare, 1972b; Cannon and Zigon, 1973; Gibbard and Hartman, 1973a; Knight, Langmeyer, and Lundgren, 1973.
Classroom Teaching. Withall, 1949, 1951; Medley and Mitzel, 1958; Emmer
and Peck, 1973.
Child Study. Thomas and Thomas, 1928; Beaver, 1929; Hubbard, 1929;
Thomas, 1929; Goodenough and Anderson, 1931; Thomas, 1932–1933;
Bott, 1933; Smith, 1933; Thomas, Loomis, and Arrington, 1933; Cocherell, 1935; Anderson, 1937a, 1937b, 1939; Arrington, 1939; Buhler,
1939; Arrington, 1943; Barker, Kounin, and Wright, 1943; Swanson,
1950; Biber et al., 1952.
Family. Merrill, 1946; Henry, 1951; Herbst, 1953; Chance, 1957; Foa, 1962;
Borke, 1967.
Counseling and Therapy. Queen, 1928; Porter, 1943; Curran, 1945; Snyder,
1945; Joel and Shapiro, 1949; Ruesch and Prestwood, 1950; Maas, Varon,
and Rosenthal, 1951; Plank, 1951; Gorlow, Hoch, and Telschow, 1952;
Mahl, 1956; Laffal et al., 1957; Rinn, 1966; Heckel and Salzberg, 1967;
McGuire and Lorch, 1968a; Argyris, 1969; Melbin, 1972.
Dramaturgical Approach to Social Interaction. Goffman, 1961; Watson and
Potter, 1962; Gosnell, 1964; Weinstein and Deutschberger, 1964; Ar-
gyle and Kendon, 1967; Burke, 1968; Zicklin, 1968.
Leadership and Social Power. Dodd and Klein, 1962; Ashin, 1968; Knott and
Drost, 1969; Mayhew, Gray, and Richardson, 1969; Tedeschi, Bonoma,
and Brown, 1971; Nebeker and Mitchell, 1973.
Conformity to Group Judgment. Levy, 1960; Crutchfield, 1966; Marino, 1967;
Marino and Parkin, 1969.

Sociometry

General references on the use and analysis of sociometric data are given in
Proctor and Loomis, "Analysis of Sociometric Data" (1951), Lindzey and Borgatta, "Sociometric Measurement" (1954), and Lindzey and Byrne, "Measurement
of Social Choice and Interpersonal Attractiveness" (1968). Many of the references
given in this appendix as well as many others will also be found in these three
works.

Sociometry was developed by Moreno, stemming from his work in Germany
with the spontaneity theater. He early placed an emphasis on the importance of
"liking" relationships and on development of informal structure. Moreno presented more than a technique, in effect, since his major work, *Who Shall Survive?,*
first published in 1934 and revised in 1953, has the overtones of a religious tract

as well as being a methodological work. From Moreno's work have also come two therapeutic techniques; (1) sociodrama, in which members from the audience participate in a spontaneous play to depict some social problems, and (2) psychodrama, in which a person with a problem acts as a central figure in a spontaneous play re-enacting some part of his life (see, for example, Toeman, 1944). Although some other investigators at the same time or earlier than Moreno used something like the sociometric technique in asking group members to reveal interpersonal choices (for example, Newstetter, Feldstein, and Newcomb [1938] asked for liking choices in a camp situation, and Terman [1904] asked grade school students to indicate persons they liked to be like best), Moreno provided the principal impetus for the introduction of sociometric techniques into the scientific literature. References which illustrate sociometric analysis and its relation to other research efforts are given in Moreno, 1941, 1943, 1945, 1947a; Jennings, 1948; Loomis and Pepinsky, 1948; Gurvitch, 1949; Jennings, 1950a, 1950b; Moreno, 1951; Northway, 1952; Jennings, 1953; Moreno, 1953, 1954; Nehnevajsa, 1955c; Bjerstedt, 1956c; Röpcke, 1960; Berlinck, 1961; Krauze, 1964; Nejezchleb, 1967.

Criteria for a Sociometric Test

Moreno's six criteria that define the proper sociometric test are given in chapter 7. (See also Blumberg and DeSoto, 1968.)

A number of investigators ask group members to say whom they like, without specifying a specific criterion. These questions have been called "near-sociometric" (Polansky, Lippitt, and Redl, 1950b).

Gardner and Thompson (1956) have elaborated the sociometric technique by introducing an equal-interval scale which they hope will "permit an inter-comparison of different groups' potentialities for satisfying their members' psychological needs." Their work is based on analysis of four needs which are modifications of Murray's needs. The needs are affiliation, play-mirth, succorance, and achievement recognition.

Sociometric ratings can also be made from data derived from direct observation (James, 1955) or by using other behavioral indices, such as time spent together (Moreno, Jennings, and Sargent, 1940; Fischer, 1953), visiting patterns, work exchange (Loomis, 1941), time spent looking at another person (Murray and McGinley, 1972), or number of words used to describe another person (Lott, Lott, and Crow, 1969). In children's groups, drawings of group activities may provide the basis for sociometric analysis (Hare and Hare, 1956; Lott and Lott, 1970). Ratings based on "group preference" rather than individual preference have also been suggested (Anikeeff, 1957).

Further evidence of the "sociometric status" of an individual may be gained if he is removed from the group and the group is observed in his absence (Florence Moreno, 1942).

Data Analysis

Sociometric data can be analyzed in a number of ways (Proctor and Loomis, 1951):

1. *Sociogram.* A pictorial rendering of choices in which individuals are indicated by circles and their choices by arrows going from one individual to another. Suggestions for the analysis of sociograms are given by Criswell (1943), Bor-

gatta (1951a), Clark and McGuire (1952), Bjerstedt (1952, 1957), Moreno (1953), and Maisonneuve (1962).

2. *Index.* Choices may be formed into indices of liking or disliking, the simplest of which are derived by adding the number of choices received for "like" and "dislike" from all members of the group. This index formation is facilitated if the choices are arrayed in a matrix (see, for example, Zeleny, 1940b, 1941, and Jones, 1959). However, if an index is all that is desired, sociometric questions may be less efficient than rankings. When group members know each other well, it is possible that they can rank each other in more than the two classes "accept" and "not accept" on a given criterion. Thus the sociometric type of question may reveal less information than is actually available (Borgatta, Cottrell, and Mann, 1958). Additional suggestions for indices or sociometric scores have been given by Harary, 1959; Willingham, 1959; Ahtik, 1960; Bass, 1960b; Verhofstad, 1962b; Alexander, 1963; Findley, 1965, 1966; Stassen and Marturano, 1968; Passini and Norman, 1969; Clore and Baldridge, 1970; Hogan and Mankin, 1970; Leik and Nagasawa, 1970; Gustafson and Gaumnitz, 1972; Pattanaik, 1973.

3. *Statistical Analysis.* The data may be analyzed statistically by demonstrating that the choices given or received were more than those which might be received if only chance factors were operating (Leeman, 1952; Nehnevajsa, 1955a, 1955b, 1955d). Additional mathematical and statistical models, some involving computers, include MacRae, 1960; Rapoport and Horvath, 1961; Wright and Evitts, 1961; Nosanchuk, 1963; Wright and Evitts, 1963; Beaton, 1966; Riffenburgh, 1966; Barnes, 1969; Boyle, 1969; J. A. Davis, 1970; Fishburn, 1970; Holland and Leinhardt, 1970; McNeel and Messick, 1970; Rainio, 1970; Byrne, 1971; Farr and Leik, 1971; Foster and Horvath, 1971; Wright, 1971; Hallinan, 1972; Phillips and Conviser, 1972; Rattinger, 1973; Lankford, 1974.

4. *Matrix Algebra.* If the interpersonal choices are placed in a matrix which shows the number of times which choices between individuals are reciprocated, then matrix algebra may be used to derive the number of links which connect members in a group. For example, one may determine the number of members who are directly connected to each other through mutual choice, the number who are connected through one other person, and so forth. (Forsyth and Katz, 1946; Festinger, 1949; Luce and Perry, 1949; Beum and Brundage, 1950; Ross and Harary, 1952; Harary and Ross, 1954, 1957; Ross and Harary, 1959; Bernard, 1973; Peay, 1972).

Reliability and Validity

The reliability and validity of the sociometric tests are discussed in two articles by Mouton, Blake, and Fruchter (1955a, 1955b) which review a large number of sociometric studies. They suggest six conditions to increase the reliability of a sociometric test. These are given in chapter 7.

The validity of the sociometric test has been illustrated by positive correlation between sociometric questions and such criteria as individual productivity and combat effectiveness, training ability, and leadership. A negative relationship has been found between popularity and criteria such as accident-proneness, sickness, and disciplinary offenses. However, high interpersonal attractiveness in groups is not always associated with group productivity, an indication that persons are not always chosen on criteria which are related to task ability.

Articles which comment on the reliability and validity of sociometric tests include Katz and Proctor, 1959; Van Bergen and Koekebakker, 1959; Fiske and Cox, 1960; Borgatta and Sperling, 1963; Tanaka, 1963; Winder and Wiggins, 1964; Gordon and Medland, 1965; Hubbell, 1965; Speal, 1965; Gunderson and Nelson, 1966; Reynolds, 1966; Harper, 1968; Niwa, 1968; Freeberg, 1969; Lorber, 1969; Yanis and Findley, 1969; Lewin, Dubno, and Akula, 1971; Banikiotes, Russell, and Linden, 1972; Mikula, 1972b; Pam, Plutchik, and Conte, 1973; Kaufman and Johnson, 1974.

Problems in the Use of the Test

A number of problems occur in the use of the sociometric test which make the results difficult to interpret. There are too many relationships in large groups to be handled effectively in either a drawing or a matrix, since for groups much larger than a dozen the number of possible combinations and permutations of relationships is so large that the investigator has difficulty in knowing which of these groups are similar and which dissimilar. Formulas which suggest the potential number of relationships in a group have been given by Bossard (1945), Kephart (1950), and R. L. Davis (1954).

The form of the test is so simple and the test is so easy to administer that it can be used indiscriminately; as a result it has been used in a wide variety of situations without a rigorous research design. Since the form is so simple, more attention must be given to the content of the criterion which is used. The extent to which sociometric choices correlate with any other behavioral criteria will depend primarily upon the original criterion of choice used. Lindzey and Borgatta (1954) have organized their review of the literature under a number of headings which suggest the importance of the criterion. Unfortunately, the subjects and the experimenter do not always agree on the interpretation of the criterion (Fybish, 1964).

An index to measure the amount of agreement between the results of sociometric tests based on different criteria has been proposed by Katz and Powell (1953).

The sociometric test is essentially a way of selecting *compatible groups*. For this reason it makes a difference if the basis of compatibility is task or social-emotional. In selecting compatible subgroups from large populations such as a school, an industry, or an army, where individuals do not have the opportunity to know each other well enough to make reliable choices, it may be better to give direct tests of personality as a basis for group composition.

Several articles suggest further applications of the sociometric test in industrial, therapeutic, or military settings (Toeman, 1944; Jacobs, 1945; Smucker, 1949; Van Zelst, 1952; Torrance, 1955b).

Questionnaires

Another data collection technique which is used in the analysis of small group behavior is the questionnaire. The questionnaire is usually given to subjects after each experimental session in the form of a "postmeeting reaction sheet." Several types of questionnaires have been adapted from the study of individual personality and the analysis of interaction process:

1. *Direct Questions.* Subjects describe their reactions to the group in their own words or on checklists (Riley et al., 1954; McGinnies, 1956; Stogdill and Coons, 1957; Gunderson and Nelson, 1965; Ring and Wallston, 1968; Wile, Bron, and Pollack, 1970; Kegan and Rubenstein, 1972; Matheson, 1972; Pedersen, 1973a; Peevers, Blascovich, and Secord, 1973; Sambrooks and MacCulloch, 1973). The average correlation between scales based on questionnaire responses and behavior in groups can be improved severalfold if subjects are first given instruction in making judgments based on ratios. Hamblin (1971a, 1971b) has shown how this can be done.

2. *"Q" Sort.* Subjects select statements which best describe their interaction patterns (Block, 1952; Ruesch, Block, and Bennett, 1953; Kalis and Bennett, 1957; Rinn, 1961).

3. *Projective.* Subjects give their reactions to ambiguous pictures (Henry and Guetzkow, 1951) or to incomplete sentences (Klein and Keill, 1953).

Additional articles which comment on aspects of the use of questionnaires include Schutz, 1961a; Lubin and Harrison, 1964; Rawls, Rawls, and Frye, 1969; McHenry, 1971.

Models and Simulation

Mathematical models of interaction and group structure have been formulated for several theoretical approaches. The models serve to extend theory by generating new hypotheses rather than by analyzing data (Guetzkow, 1958). Articles and books which provide an overview of mathematical models as they are used in the study of small groups include Coleman, 1960; H. Solomon, 1960; Back, 1962; Berger et al., 1962; Criswell, 1962; Criswell, Solomon, and Suppes, 1962; Moore and Anderson, 1962; Abelson, 1967; Bartos, 1967; R. J. Harris, 1972. Additional works treating mathematical models and simulation are listed by principal focus:

Social Interaction, Especially in Two-Person Games. Rapaport, 1947; Simon, 1952; Suppes and Atkinson, 1960; Burke, 1962; Bush, 1962; Coleman, 1962; Estes, 1962; Rosenberg, 1962; McWhinney, 1968; Shelly and Stedry, 1968; Wolf, 1970; Chevrolet and Le Calve, 1973; Hawes and Foley, 1973.

Social Pressure and Persuasion. Simon and Guetzkow, 1955a, 1955b; B. P. Cohen, 1958; Cervin, 1959; Carterette and Wyman, 1962; Flament, 1962; Adler and Loether, 1966; Rabinovich, Hislop, and Derbyshire, 1973.

Voting and Group Decision. Hays and Bush, 1954; Van Dingenen-Donnay, 1966; Garman and Kamien, 1968; Niemi and Weisberg, 1968; Delhees, 1970; G. H. Lewis, 1970a; Muzzy and Moon, 1973.

Structure and Coalitions. Bavelas, 1948; Cartwright and Harary, 1956; J. R. P. French, Jr., 1956; Karlsson, 1962; White, 1962; Flament, 1963; Binder, Wolin, and Terebinski, 1965; Stager, 1966; Holland and Leinhardt, 1971; Mayhew and Gray, 1972; Harary and Schwenk, 1974; Stix, 1974.

Computer Simulations of Interaction and Decisions. Coleman, 1961; Haines, Heider, and Remington, 1961; Hare, 1961; Coe, 1964; Abelson, 1968; Bem, 1968; McGuire and Coleman, 1968; Baldwin, 1969; Groves, 1970; Hare, 1970; Hays, 1970; Joyner and Green, 1970; Penner and Patten, 1970; Hare and Scheiblechner, 1971; Sakoda, 1971.

Problems with Laboratory Experiments

The use of human subjects in scientific experiments can raise ethical problems for the experimenter, especially if the experiment includes some physical or psychological stress. Professional codes of ethics for psychologists and sociologists, who do most of the experimental work in this area, include recommendations concerning the subject's right of privacy and dignity of treatment, and admonitions to the experimenter to avoid causing personal harm to subjects in research and to treat confidential information as such.

Since many laboratory and field experiments involve deception of some kind (Menges, 1973; Newberry, 1973), the social psychologists who conduct the experiments would probably argue that the amount of deception is necessary and justified if the subjects are properly debriefed after the experiment. Some researchers have suggested the use of role playing as an alternative to deception (Mixon, 1971; Holmes and Bennett, 1974). Borgatta, with tongue placed firmly in cheek, has proposed a new model of research which uses only participant observers, no subjects (1967). My own preference is to avoid any form of deceit and look for other ways to gather data to test my hypotheses. For example, in the case of the Asch experiment on conformity (see appendix 1), there are enough real instances of conformity in groups with subjects who have not been coached to provide an adequate demonstration of the process of conformity.

Experimenter Effects

Perhaps the classic example of the results of experimenter effects in the small group literature is in the test room studies of the Western Electric researchers, where a group of working girls responded more to the experimenter and the way the task was presented than to changes in food, fatigue, and other factors which were presumed to influence production (Roethlisberger and Dickson, 1939). However, it was not until the early 1960s that small group researchers began to pay much attention to the possible sources of bias resulting from unintended aspects of the experimental situation, especially from the type of experimenter and his instructions to the group (cf. Mills, 1962).

Experimenter effects for small group research are similar in nature to those for any research with human subjects, and some have been observed with other animals. Rosenthal (1966) has reviewed the literature under two major headings: (1) experimenter effects not influencing subject's behavior (including the experimenter as observer, interpretation of data, and intentional error), and (2) experimenter effects influencing subject's behavior (including biosocial attributes, psychosocial attributes, situational factors, experimenter modeling, experimenter expectancy). (See also Barber and Silver, 1968, Timaeus, 1974.) The experimenter need not even be in the room with the subjects, since his voice alone is enough to produce some of the biasing effects (Adair and Epstein, 1968). Some examples of research designed to test various aspects of the experimenter effect are Back, Hood, and Brehm, 1964; Jourard and Kormann, 1968; Timaeus and Lück, 1968; Bootzin, 1969; Bermant and Starr, 1972; Kähler and Schmid, 1972; Uno, Koivumaki, and Rosenthal, 1972; Adler, 1973; Alexander and Sagatun, 1973; Epstein, Suedfeld, and Silverstein, 1973; Gerson, 1974.

In general, the more neutral the experimenter is, the less likely he is to influence the subjects in an unintended way. However, there are times when the experimenter or observer may have to drop his neutrality and become fully involved in the action. In some cases, there is no room for an "outsider"; in others, such as sensitivity training groups, it has been suggested that unless the researcher takes the role of his subject, he cannot capture the essence of the phenomena being studied (Glass and Frankiel, 1968).

One set of experiments indicates that the experimenter effect is not limited to the laboratory. Rosenthal and his colleagues told teachers in elementary schools that some of their pupils (randomly chosen) had been shown to be "academic bloomers" and should do very well in school that year. When tested later, the pupils had in fact performed better than their peers (Rosenthal and Jacobson, 1966, 1968; Evans and Rosenthal, 1969). Even though the teachers seldom remembered the names of the children who had been identified as "bloomers," they apparently singled them out for sufficient reinforcement to produce increases in IQ scores.

Additional unintended effects in group experiments come from the characteristics and behavior of observers (Gussow, 1964; Oyen, 1972), stooges (Leik, 1965b), and the subjects themselves (Walker, 1971; Kruglanski, 1973).

Appendix 4

SENSITIVITY TRAINING

THE EARLIEST APPLICATIONS of group dynamics in industry, elementary and secondary education, and group therapy involved populations different from that of the college undergraduates who volunteered for most of the social-psychological experiments which form the basis of the social-psychological literature. Thus the application of group dynamics in sensitivity training groups with college students bring the results home in a way that was not so immediate or apparent in other applications. Sensitivity training has not been limited to young adults, but perhaps for them more than others it represented part of a "life style" which appeared as part of the "counter culture" at the time of the Vietnam war. Since some form of sensitivity training is widely used on college campuses as a part of a curriculum in social psychology, a brief outline of research on this type of group is included here together with references to a sample of the recent literature on the subject. This appendix also includes brief references to other applications of group dynamics in therapy, decision-making, and education.

A sensitive article on the "varieties of senstivity training" by Kurt W. Back was included in a special issue of the journal *Sociological Inquiry* on this subject (Back, 1971). For those who may be interested in some comments on aspects of sensitivity training from the point of view of functional theory, I recommend the "Editor's Foreword" (Hare, 1971a). However, Back's article seems more appropriate for this appendix, since it provides a brief overview of the field.[1]

Sensitivity training, or T-groups, has become a part of the common language a bare twenty-five years after the technique was discovered. It has become a symbol of a way of life. It is shown as such in movies and television shows, and mention of T-groups and sensitivity training can be trusted to evoke the right associations. Games are sold for playing T-groups in your own home. In the same way, T-groups have become a target for the opponents of this way of life. According to a recent description of the "forgotten American," ". . . a major share of the villainy is now also attributed to 'the social science centers', to the apostles of sensitivity training, and to what a California lady with some embarrassment called 'nude therapy'" (Schrag, 1969, p. 33).

1. Kurt W. Back, "Varieties of Sensitivity Training," *Sociological Inquiry* 41, 2 (Spring 1971): 133–137. Reprinted by permission of the author and the publisher. An expanded version appears as chapter 8, "Landscape," in Back's *Beyond Words* (New York: Russell Sage Foundation, 1972) (Baltimore: Penguin Books, 1973).

In short, sensitivity training has become something to be talked about, something which certain types of people engage in, an integral part of popular culture.

This recognition of sensitivity training is only a reflection of its indisputable growth. Every weekend innumerable workshops, encounters, and T-groups are conducted by more or less reputable organizations and individuals. Business firms send their executives and employees to various programs, in their own plants as well as at special retreats; college and church groups have programs varying from short demonstrations to training programs lasting several weeks. One can be sure that a sizable part of the population is engaged in sensitivity training at any given time, and those who have been in contact with it constitute something approaching a subculture of the society.

Although all these activities, all these discussions refer to the same core of procedure, we find on closer look a bewildering variety. Sensitivity training can be based on different theories which derive from quite different traditions; it may have different functions, and the aims of the exercise may be quite diverse; it may proceed in different situations and substitute for a variety of interpersonal practices. In each of these ways, theory, function and context, distinct branches of sensitivity can be ascertained. There is some correspondence between the different patterns which emerge. We shall therefore look at each of three kinds of classifications in turn and then try to establish a general taxonomy of sensitivity training.

Theory

The T-group, in its current meaning, was discovered at an intergroup relations workshop in Connecticut, sponsored by the Connecticut Human Relations Commission and the Research Center for Group Dynamics (Lippitt, 1949). Although the discovery itself was almost a chance event, its subsequent use and development was colored by the theory of the leaders of the workshop, a modified social psychological theory, stressing individual participation and group functioning to an almost equal extent. Physically, this group developed—after conducting a more general workshop in group development at Bethel, Maine, the subsequent year—into the National Training Laboratory (NTL). NTL still represents the central power in the whole movement, exerting its primary effort into the improvement of functioning of specific groups, from volunteer civic groups to executives in large corporations.

At the same time, through experience in leadership and team training in World War II and subsequent rehabilitation camps, a group of psychiatrists and psychologists at the Tavistock Institute in London initiated another kind of sensitivity training. Their background was primarily psychiatric with strong psychoanalytic influence. Their distinctive style of thinking led them to view the group as a unit and to apply psychodynamic principles to the group as such. Their consultation typically consists in diagnosing the group process as a unit and treating the group as a patient where sometimes strong intervention may be required. On the other hand, laboratories for strangers conducted by the Tavistock group or groups influenced by them have as their aim improved process; the emphasis is on teaching general principles through interpretation of one's own experiences in a group. The theory is still a modified Freudian, or at least biologically functional theory: the guiding principle sees the group as a functioning unit, and forces analogous to those in the individual can be identified in the disruption and adjustment of the group.

A third orientation started later in the early 1950's, and centered primarily in California. This orientation aims primarily at the enhancement of some capacities presumably inherent in the individual through the medium of group experience. Although group methods are used, the emphasis is on the effect on the individual participant; the name under which they assemble is humanistic psychology—psychology for man. The theory is based on the work of such writers as Reich, Rogers and Maslow: society represses the spontaneous, healthy tendencies of man, his ability to achieve real experiences, and group method, novel ways of encountering the other will make it possible to find this liberation. Here an eclectic choice of all possible theories of human change, from behavior therapy to psychoanalysis, especially the less orthodox varieties like Jung and Reich, and group dynamics is mixed with a strong dose of oriental religion.

The three strains have not been as distinct in their history as an analytic description might indicate. From the beginning there has been an interchange of ideas between Tavistock and NTL (eg., a journal, *Human Relations,* is published jointly by the Research Center for Group Dynamics and Tavistock). On the other hand, the early development of the California encounter group movement was kept within the framework of NTL; some encounter type training is given by NTL under the title of Advanced Human Relations Training. In the early sixties, an independent movement was started, centered at Esalen, and this has little or no formal ties with the other centers.

To understand better the typical approach of the three centers, let us sketch in a simplified way a situation and the way it might be handled in each place. Let us say opposition to the group's leader develops and one of the group members leads a verbal attack on him. The Tavistock approach would deal with the question of why this attack was necessary at this particular moment. An analysis might review the development of the group up to this point, and the actions which led to this particular development. They might even try to find a general rule which would state the conditions leading to an attack of this kind. There would be little interest in the particular person who is leading this attack. The assumption would be that the needs of the group were paramount, and that in the whole configuration somebody would have been pushed into being the leader of the attack in any case.

In a group conducted according to the NTL method, other questions would be raised. They would be directed toward such problems as the needs of the member who made the attack, what the attack revealed about his usual action in group situations, as well as what it revealed about the leader and the other group members by their participation and their nonparticipation. The lessons to be learned would be improved understanding by each person of his actions in a situation of this kind, and of others' interpretation of and reaction to his actions. Presumably he would learn how to handle a situation of this kind more efficiently in the future.

In a personal growth group, there is little emphasis on interpretation. The group would take the conflict as a phenomenon in itself. It would become an occasion to work on, possibly to be driven to an extreme. The two protagonists and perhaps their adherents would be encouraged to express their feelings as strongly as possible, even to the point of engaging in a physical contest. More likely than not, this extreme behavior would lead to an occasion of intimate feeling between all the members involved. In the terms of the leaders of the movement, it would be an encounter.

Function

Sensitivity training groups may differ in the way in which they fit into a person's life or into the needs of a group. One plausible classification of the impact of sensitivity training on individuals is by the depth of the projected experience. The experience may have a temporary superficial effect, or aim at deep, long-range change. A similar distinction may be discerned in the social situation in which the training is beng conducted. Sensitivity training may be an activity in its own right or it may be a part of a larger program used as an adjunct to the other activities. By cross-classifying these two divisions, we obtain four different types of sensitivity training according to its function for the individual and the program which is being conducted.

1. *Deep Effect—Independent Program.* This is the proclaimed function of the encounter groups, special workshops, and weekend laboratories which have prolifer-

ated so much in the last decade. For these groups change would be the proper goal in itself. The basic idea of training becomes different though an experience of this kind would be sufficient for many people today to attend an encounter session. Sessions of this kind are conducted in a variety of settings, springing up in all kinds of environments from the resort-like facilities of the human growth center to the bare classrooms of college campuses. They blossom extremely frequently in religious settings: university religious centers as well as those in city environments encourage sessions and combine them with the traditional retreats. All the technique is directed toward a deep experience which induces a feeling of having been changed. Change is valued for itself. The direcion of possible benefits remains unclear.

2. *Shallow Effect—Independent Program.* These programs shade into the previous category. They do not intend to arouse deep feeling, aiming instead for a variety of experiences. In this way they can be looked at as a variety of entertainment, as re-creating in the original meaning of the word. In some areas of the country today, spending an evening, a weekend, or a week at an encounter center is a popular way to pass one's leisure time. Even the game industry has entered this lucrative market, and several games based on the various sensitivity training techniques are being marketed. In all these instances, too, various elements which sensitivity training has in common with entertainment are stressed: short interpersonal emotional experiences, flirtations, gossiping about one's own and other people's feelings and actions, games of various kinds; pleasant locations and resort facilities may be available.

3. *Deep Effect—Integrated Program.* Sensitivity training may be a planned adjunct to other techniques. The whole regime may be designed to produce intensive changes in the person; sensitivity training in these conditions is used sometimes to produce quick effects which may make people amenable to other methods of change, such as individual psychotherapy. These groups usually bring together people with differing problems, in a kind of medical setting where the patients cooperate to reach some solution for their problems. Sometimes the same techniques are used for the solutions of interpersonal social problems, such as feelings about race. In all these conditions the position of the leader becomes vitally important as he is the person responsible for the conduct of the whole program, not only the sensitivity sessions. Participants, whether patients in a formal sense or not, come to the sessions with a specific aim in mind and for them the technique is subordinate to the goal.

4. *Shallow Effect—Integrated Program.* If the program has a less therapeutic aim it is usually directed toward the teaching of a particular skill. It may be used in instuctional situations, in the training of public officials, in the efforts of promoting the smooth workings of a group or organization. In this use the sessions are planned around the specific problem at hand, and are directed either by experts within the organization or by consulting firms; the proceedings are planned in great detail and the specific aim may relate to persons working better only in the special situation, not in any effort beyond the immediate situation. This limited aim is especially important because participation is frequently not voluntary, but coerced by more or less subtle means, and for success it is important that all members of the organizational unit attend the sessions.

Use

Another way of dividing the different programs is through the different situations in which they are used. They are psychotherapy, personnel management, training of human relations, adaptation of new techniques, and entertainment. Sensitivity training and encounter groups have been started with sponsorship from all these branches. In identifying the different uses to which sensitivity training can be put, we can also discern a common trend and common problems: sensitivity training has filled a void which the traditional ways of dealing with these problems have left. In fulfilling this function, it has tended to neglect specific problems in that field, and a reaction has set in from the traditional disciplines dealing with these problems. We can treat psychotherapy in more detail and then compare the problems in the fields.

Psychotherapy has become a virtual way of life just in those circles which also form the clientele of sensitivity training. The growing acceptance for this service among the "Friends and Supporters of Psychotherapy" (Kadushin, 1969) has had important consequences. Among these are dissatisfaction with psychotherapy because of its long term and uncertain outcome; another is the application of psychotherapy, at least of its outward trappings, to many clients whose troubles are not strong enough to warrant real psychiatric care. However, many people with this background feel a need for an atmosphere equivalent to psychotherapy. For people in this predicament and also more serious patients dissatisfied with their therapy, sensitivity training provides a ready answer. Some psychiatrists have used encounter groups as adjuncts to their own techniques or have integrated sensitivity training with their own process (Burton, 1969). Many other encounter groups are used by patients desiring a quicker breakthrough or by people with a host of personal problems who seek a quiet, intimate discussion. The need here arises not only from any felt deficiencies in the psychiatric professionals, but in addition, from the decline in any previously available non-professional aids—religion or extended family being the most common examples. Although both still exist for a great part of the population, the highly mobile and secular middle-class is likely to rely less on them and to search for substitutes. Sensitivity training is readily at hand for this purpose. However, many psychiatrists have been prompt in showing the limitations of this approach (*American Journal of Psychiatry*, 1969). One indisputable fact is that serious breakdowns have occurred, though rarely, and that most sensitivity training leaders are ill-equipped to handle them. There is some common agreement that individuals who are currently disturbed should not participate in sensitivity training, but little effort has been made to screen applicants to these sessions. A more subtle disturbing effect arises from the fact that the length of the sensitivity workshop is predetermined. The participant is left at some stage of disturbance, insight, or incipient change, to fend for himself as best he can. Sensitivity training leaders do not take any professional responsibility beyond the actual sessions. In addition, the whole approach to sensitivity training is anathema to many practitioners of more traditional procedures (e.g., orthodox psychoanalysts) and is strongly opposed by them.

Sensitivity training can thus be an adjunct to therapy, be used as a substitute for therapy, and extend therapeutic principles over a wider range. It is handicapped by its own flexibility. Not being committed to therapy at all, or to any therapeutic technique, it may give only an appearance of psychotherapy without its substance to a great many clients. Professional therapists can censure sensitivity training, that it plays sometimes dangerously, sometimes successfully, with the important problems of its clients. Similar developments can be seen in other areas of application.

The situation in personnel management is quite similar. In fact, in this field we can find some of the earliest development of the sensitivity training approach. The idea of human relations training grew out of several experiments in management, such as the Westinghouse Study (Roethlisberger and Dickson, 1939) or the Harwood Sudies (French, *et al.*, 1946), and in several places the application of sensitivity training became a natural step. Again, it was the apparent failure of traditional techniques of dealing with workers and employees and impatience with lack of quick success which led to interest in group approaches. It is hard to transform the precepts of any theory of human relations into real life. Sensitivity training implies an immediate experience which gives the almost obvious conclusion that the training will become part of the person. Thus many personnel departments were led to use sensitivity training. Here again the lack of commitment to the specific problem has given difficulties. Sensitivity trainers are often interested in the group action in itself, forgetting the specific aims and problems of the organization with whom they are working. Traditional professionals in the field have been quick to point this out. In many ways, sensitivity training has the same problems here as those of psychotherapy.

Sensitivity training has been used to change interpersonal relations in other fields besides personnel relations. Practically any situation in which dealing with others is important has been included here. Among the practitioners of sensitivity training are organizations like the Peace Corps, poverty agencies, social agencies, and other individuals who meet the public. In all these situations we have a similar problem to that in personnel management itself. Dissatisfaction with the way in which human relations are usually managed leads to the search for new ways of getting people to apply the concepts which have been found valuable. The immediate impact of sensitivity training sessions gives participants the motivation to apply what they have learned. It seems to be, therefore, a natural procedure for implementing a new program of human relations. However, the professionals in the field itself are frequently more skeptical about the eventual success and also about the application of a general technique of emotional impact to the particular problems of the individual program.

In addition, sensitivity training is used as an aid in teaching theory and principles of human relations. In this case an adaptation of the method is made to enable students to live through interpersonal relations while learning the theory. Ideally, the interaction in the sensitivity training group can serve as the basic raw material on which to tie down theories. One class at Harvard, Social Relations 120, has been the model of training of this kind and is discussed in three books by teachers in this course (Mills, 1964; Slater, 1966; Mann, Gibbard, and Hartman, 1967). Some classes have been quite successful in this endeavor, and more and more courses in social psychology use this approach as well as training for professionals outside of academic life.

Finally, there is sensitivity for no purpose or for the most genuine purpose of all, purely for the experience itself. We have mentioned before, in discussing other purposes of sensitivity training that pure action may take over and displace the ostensive purpose of the training. In some training, no such purpose is mentioned at all. The experience of intensive group interaction is a sufficient motive for many people to participate and for others to arrange it. This aim, just to provide new experiences is clearly the most original contribution of sensitivity training to the current scene. This kind of sensitivity training shades into dramatic performing and artistic entertainment. The Living Theater and the Poor Theater (Grotowski, 1969), can be looked at as encounter or drama.

Conclusion

The three ways of classifying sensitivity training, theory, practice, and aims, show some congruence. Sensitivity training for a variety of aims, personnel training, human relations and teaching of group therapy is usually part of another program and not supposed to affect the participants deeply. As an adjunct to psychotherapy, it is intended to have deep effects. Finally, in a situation where we have pure experience, sensitivity training is free-standing, having more or less deep effects depending on the intensity of the method used.

The latter approach, experience for its own sake, seems to be the most favored of the Esalen techniques. "Esalen," or encounter groups have thus become a new middle-class way of recreation. "Esalen was a place where educated middle-class adults came in the summer to try to get out of The Rut and wiggle their fannies a bit" (Wolfe, 1968, p. 119). Many Esalen programs have also a direct tie-in with artistic performances, dance, drama, or music. On the other extreme, the Tavistock theory is used mainly to give a learning experience. Tavistock training selects almost exclusively professionals who need more understanding of theory of interpersonal relations and promises a session of hard work to give it. In between the two, in theory as well as in practice, stands the original National Training Laboratory, the Bethel group. This group, in general, wants training with a purpose; it is engaged in work for personnel departments, for government agencies; it experiments with both the theoretical insight of the Tavistock groups and the almost transcendental experiences of the Esalen type.

The sensitivity training movement thus proceeds along a variety of ways. A common core is more felt than understood. It demonstrates in its existence some of the felt needs of today's society. Its many variations show primarily the varieties of experience which society is not able to give.

Additional Research

Research and comment on sensitivity training:

Books. Trist and Sofer, 1959; Argyris, 1962; Bradford, Gibb and Benne, 1964; Badin, 1965; Schein and Bennis, 1965; Argyris, 1970; Glidewell, 1970; Rogers, 1970; Blank, Gottsegen, and Gottsegen, 1971; Back, 1972; Cooper, 1972c; Coulson, 1972; Lifton, 1972; Solomon and Berzon, 1972; Golembiewski and Blumberg, 1973; Krupar, 1973; Lieberman, Yalom, and Miles, 1973; McLeish, Matheson, and Park, 1973; Saulnier and Simard, 1973; Gillies, 1974.

Articles Which Review the Field and Provide General Comment. Shepard and Bennis, 1956; Cartwright, 1958; Semrad and Arsenian, 1961; Altman, 1963; Whitman, 1964; Flecker, 1967; Loomis, 1968; Gibb and Gibb, 1969; Lake, 1970; Leavitt and Doktor, 1970; Alix and Thomas, 1971; Cohen, 1971; Cooper 1971–1972; Haigh, 1971; Klein and Astrachan, 1971; Koch, 1971; Shumsky, 1971; Lomranz, Lakin, and Schiffman, 1972; Minturn and Lansky, 1972; Weinstein and Pollack, 1972; Barrett-Lennard, 1973; Glass, 1973; S. B. Kiesler, 1973a; Lomranz, Lakin and Schiffman, 1973; Montgomery, 1973.

Sensitivity Training as a Social Movement. Dunnette, 1969; Howard, 1970; Shepard, 1970; Jacobs, 1971; Pages, 1971; Argyris, 1972 Back, 1973.

Research on Sensitivity Training as It Contributes to Personal Growth. Stanley-Jones, 1958; Clark and Culbert, 1965; Harrison, 1965; Kassarjian, 1965; Hampden-Turner, 1966; Schutz and Allen, 1966; Eisenstadt, 1967; Langley, 1967; Lubin and Zuckerman, 1967; P. B. Smith, 1967; Haigh, 1968; Kolb, Winter, and Berlew, 1968; S. B. Shapiro, 1968; Bloomberg, Bloomberg, and Miller, 1969; Buchanan and Schindler-Rainman, 1969; Myers et al., 1969; Snortum and Myers, 1969; Whalen, 1969; Bolman, 1970; Friedlander, 1970; Himber, 1970; Peters, 1970; Solomon, Berzon, and Davis, 1970; Cooper, 1971; Cottle, 1971; Foulds, 1971a; Harrow et al., 1971; Holbert, Cormier, and Friedman, 1971; Meador, 1971; Moscow, 1971; Pollack, 1971; Polsky, 1971; Shapiro and Ross, 1971; P. B. Smith, 1971; Symonds, 1971; Baldwin, 1972; Bare and Mitchell, 1972; Boderman, Freed and Kinnucan, 1972; Cooper, 1972b; Counseling Center Staff, 1972; Gibb, 1972; Insel and Moos, 1972; Lieberman, Yalom, and Miles, 1972; McLeish and Park, 1972; Moscovici, 1972; Nellesen and Svensson, 1972; Pierce and Zarle, 1972; Piercy and Piercy, 1972; Pompilo and Krebs, 1972; Reddy, 1972; Seplowin, 1972; Shapiro and Diamond, 1972; Anderson and Slocum, 1973; Andrews, 1973; Arbes and Hubbell, 1973; Cooper and Bowles, 1973; Diamond and Shapiro, 1973; Edenfield and Myrick, 1973; Eiben and Clack, 1973; Gilligan, 1973; Hurley and Force, 1973; Kaye, 1973; Lundgren, 1973; McIntire, 1973; McLeish and Park, 1973a, 1973b; Peters, 1973; Poland and Jones, 1973; Reddy, 1973; Sisson, Sisson, and Gadza, 1973; Cooper, 1974; Diamond, 1974; Dies and Sadowsky, 1974; Gilligan, 1974; Hoerl, 1974; Kilmann, 1974; Kolb and Boyatzis, 1974; Martin and Fischer, 1974; Rogers and Roethlisberger, 1974; Romano and Quay, 1974; Schwarzel, 1974.

Research with a Focus on Attitude Change. Nadler and Fink, 1970; Koziey, Loken, and Field, 1971; Frye et al., 1972.

The Marathon Group and Its Effects. Bach, 1966, 1967a, 1967b, 1967c; Bindrim, 1969; Dies and Hess, 1970; Foulds, Girona, and Guinan, 1970; Parks and Antenen, 1970; Shepard and Lee, 1970; Sklar et al., 1970; Speer, 1970; Walker and Holbert, 1970; Dies and Hess, 1971; Dinges and Weigel, 1971; Pollack and Stanley, 1971; Weissman, Seldman, and Ritter, 1971; Blank, Wilker, and Grundfest, 1972; Jacobson and Smith, 1972; Treppa and Fricke, 1972; Svensson, 1972; Guinan, Foulds, and Wright, 1973; King, Payne, and McIntire, 1973; Kilmann and Auerbach, 1974; McCardel and Murray, 1974.

Use of Videotape-Feedback and Other Special Techniques. Martin, 1971; Abudabbeh, Prandoni, and Jensen, 1972; Weissman et al., 1972; Archer and Kagan, 1973; Hurst, Delworth, and Garriott, 1973.

Special Applications for Change in Institutions and Societies. Miller, 1966; Doob, Foltz, and Stevens, 1969; Clark, 1970b; Culver and Dunham, 1970; Harvey, Oshry, and Watson, 1970; Heller, 1970; Walton, 1970; Baumgold, 1971; Buchanan, 1971; Delbecq and Van de Ven, 1971; Dimock, 1971; Foa and Donnenwerth, 1971; Wittmer and Ferinden, 1971; Bierman, Carkhuff, and Santilli, 1972; Hjelholt, 1972.

The Trainer and His Skills. Lebo, 1962; Bach, 1967a; Fiebert, 1968; Cooper, 1969; Bolman, 1971, 1973; Frankiel, 1971; Lieberman, 1971–1972; Lobrot, 1971; Burns, 1972; Foulds, 1972a; Luke, 1972; Sampson, 1972; Segal, 1972; Cottle, 1973; O'Day, 1973; J. M. Smith, 1973.

Problems and Ethical Issues. Lakin, 1969, 1970; Cashdan, 1970; Kutash, 1970–1971; Lakin, 1970; Brown, 1971; Eitington, 1971; Lubin and Lubin, 1971; Cooper, 1972a; American Psychological Association, 1973; Johnson, Kavanagh, and Lubin, 1973; Posthuma and Posthuma, 1973.

Research Techniques. Harrison, 1971; Pino, 1971; Trotzer, 1971; Sandler, 1973.

Other applications of research on group dynamics:[2]

Group Therapy. Teirich and Illing, 1958; Kadis and Winick, 1960; Scheidlinger, 1964; Grosz, Stern, and Wright, 1965; Clark, 1970a; Horwitz, 1971; McGee and Williams, 1971; Bugh, 1972; Roback ,1972; Felton and Biggs, 1973.

Decision-making. Mangold, 1960; Phillips, 1965; Baloff and Becker, 1968; Bormann, 1969; Blake and Mouton, 1970; Hall and Williams, 1970; Pyke and Neely, 1970; Danish and Zelenski, 1972; Rittelmeyer, 1972; Pankowski, Schroeder, and Jahns, 1973.

Education. Trow et al., 1950; King, 1960; Pratt, 1960; Beach, 1962; Boyd, 1965; Langmeyer, Schmuck, and Runkel, 1971; Schmuck, Runkel, and Langmeyer, 1971; Heimann and Heimann, 1972.

Industry. Haire, 1959; Blau and Scott, 1962; Dubin et al., 1965; Van Leeuwen and Van Ravenzwaaij, 1968.

Family. Hallenbeck, 1966; Goode, 1972; Pollak, 1972.

Sports. Lenk, 1964; Elias and Dunning, 1966; Koenig, 1966; Lück, 1966; Schafer, 1966; Stone, 1966.

Counseling. Rushlau and Jorgensen, 1966; Shave, 1974.

Nonviolent Action. Hare, 1968a, 1968d.

---

[2] See subject index for additional references.

BIBLIOGRAPHY

No attempt has been made to locate all the books and articles listed here in Psychological Abstracts (*P.A.*) or Sociological Abstracts (*S.A.*), *but abstract numbers have been included in many citations as aids to the reader who may wish further details. Titles of books and articles not originally in English have been translated and put in parentheses. Wherever possible, authors' first names have been given; brackets have occasionally been used to indicate that an author does not customarily use his full first name. Where names of multiple authors are not known, citations including* et al. *appear at the end of the first author's list of works.*

SMALL GROUP
RESEARCH STUDIES

1. Abel, Theodora M.
   1938   "The influence of social facilitation on motor performance at different levels of intelligence." American Journal of Psychology 51: 379–389.
2. Abelson, Robert P.
   1967   "Mathematical models in social psychology." In L. Berkowitz (ed.), Advances in Experimental Social Psychology, vol. 3, pp. 1–54. New York: Academic Press.
3. 1968   "Simulation of social behavior." In G. Lindzey and E. Aronson (eds.), Handbook of Social Psychology, vol. 2, pp. 274–356. Reading, Mass.: Addison-Wesley.
4. 1973   "Comment on 'Group shift to caution at the race track.'" Journal of Experimental Social Psychology 9 (6): 517–521. Reply by McCauley and Stitt, pp. 522–525, and comment by Abelson, pp. 526–527.
5. Aboud, Frances E., Donald M. Taylor, and Robert G. Doumani
   1973   "The effect of contact on the use of role and ethnic stereotypes in person perception." Journal of Social Psychology 89 (2, April): 309–310. P.A. 50:6682.
6. Abraham, Ada
   1973   "A model for exploring intra- and interindividual process in groups." International Journal of Group Psychotherapy 23 (1, January): 3–22. P.A. 51:2959.
7. Abrahams, J.
   1949   "Group psychotherapy: Implications for direction and supervision of mentally ill patients." In T. Muller (ed.), Mental Health in Nursing, pp. 77–83. Washington, D.C.: Catholic University Press.
8. Abrahamson, Mark, and Joan K. Smith
   1970   "Norms, deviance, and spacial location." Journal of Social Psychology 80:95–101.
9. Abric, Jean-Claude
   1970   ("Image of task, image of partner, and cooperation in a play situation.") Cahiers de Psychologie 13 (2): 71–82. P.A. 48:11424.

10.   1971   "Experimental study of group creativity: Task representation, group structure, and performance." European Journal of Social Psychology 1 (3): 311–326. P.A. 48:11423.

11. Abric, Jean-Claude, and J. P. Kahan
       1972   "The effects of representations and behavior in experimental games." European Journal of Social Psychology 2 (2): 129–144. P.A. 49: 9004.

12. Abudabbeh, Nuha, Jogues R. Prandoni, and Diana E. Jensen
       1972   "Application of behavior principles to group therapy techniques with juvenile delinquents." Psychological Reports 31: 375–380.

13. Adair, John G.
       1972   "Demand characteristics or conformity? Suspiciousness of deception and experimenter bias in conformity research." Canadian Journal of Behavioural Science 4 (3, July): 238–248. P.A. 49:2311.

14. Adair, John G., and Joyce Epstein
       1968   "Verbal cues in the mediation of experimenter bias." Psychological Reports 22 (3, pt. 2): 1045–1053. P.A. 42:18726.

15. Adams, Bert N.
       1967   "Interaction Theory and the Social Network." Sociometry 30 (1, March): 64–78.

16. Adams, J. Stacy
       1965   "Inequity in social exchange." In L. Berkowitz (ed.), Advances in Experimental Social Psychology, vol. 2, pp. 267–299. New York: Academic Press.

17. Adams, Stuart
       1953   "Status congruency as a variable in small group performance." Social Forces 32: 16–22. P.A. 28:4111; S.A. 80.

18.   1954   "Social climate and productivity in small military groups." American Sociological Review 19: 421–425. P.A. 30:2618.

19. Adams-Webber, Jack R.
       1973   "The complexity of the target as a factor in interpersonal judgement." Social Behavior and Personality 1 (1): 35–38. P.A. 51:964.

20. Adams-Webber, Jack R., and J. Benjafield
       1973   "The relation between lexical marking and rating extremity in interpersonal judgment." Canadian Journal of Behavioural Science 5 (3, July): 234–241. P.A. 51:7044.

21. Adams-Webber, Jack R., B. Schwenker, and D. Barbeau
       1972   "Personal constructs and the perception of individual differences." Canadian Journal of Behavioural Science 4 (3, July): 218–224. P.A. 49:2312.

22. Aderman, David
       1969   "Effects of anticipating future interaction on the preference for balanced states." Journal of Personality and Social Psychology 11 (3): 214–219. P.A. 43:8270.

23.   1972   "Elation, depression, and helping behavior." Journal of Personality and Social Psychology 24 (1, October): 91–101. P.A. 49:4374.

24. Aderman, David, and Leonard Berkowitz
       1969   "Empathy, outcome, and altruism." Proceedings of the 77th Annual Convention of the American Psychological Association 4 (pt. 1): 379–380. P.A. 43:17332.

25.   1970   "Observational set, empathy, and helping." Journal of Personality and Social Psychology 14 (2): 141–148. P.A. 44:6650.

26. Aderman, David, Sharon S. Brehm, and Lawrence B. Katz
       1974   "Empathic observation of an innocent victim: The just world revisited." Journal of Personality and Social Psychology 29 (3): 342–347.

27. Adler, Franz, and Herman Loether
       1966   "Group discussions as persuasion processes: A mathematical model." Sociologia Internationalis 4 (1): 27–48. S.A. 15:C4798.

28. Adler, Nancy E.
       1973   "Impact of prior sets given experimenters and subjects on the experimenter expectancy effect." Sociometry 36 (1, March): 113–126. P.A. 50:11198.

29. Adorno, T. W., Else Frenkel-Brunswick, Daniel J. Levinson, and R. Nevitt Sanford
    1950   The Authoritarian Personality. New York: Harper. (See also Maccoby, Newcomb, and Hartley, 1958.) P.A. 24:5796.

30. Ahtik, Miroslav
    1960   ("Number marking as a technique in sociometric measurements.") Sociologija 2 (3-4): 103-104. S.A. 15:C8064.

31. Aiello, John R.
    1972   "A test of equilibrium theory: Visual interaction in relation to orientation, distance and sex of interactants." Psychonomic Science 27 (6, June): 335-336. P.A. 49:2313.

32. Aiello, John R., and Ralph E. Cooper
    1972   "Use of personal space as a function of social affect." Proceedings of the 80th Annual Convention of the American Psychological Association 7 (pt. 1): 207-208. P.A. 48:4840.

33. Aiello, John R., and Stanley E. Jones
    1971   "Field study of the proxemic behavior of young school children in three subcultural groups." Journal of Personality and Social Psychology 19 (3): 351-356.

34. Aiken, Edwin G.
    1965   "Interaction process analysis changes accompanying operant conditioning of verbal frequency in small groups." Perceptual and Motor Skills 21 (1): 52-54. P.A. 40:489.

35. Ajzen, Icek
    1971   "Attitudinal vs. normative messages: An investigation of the differential effects of persuasive communications on behavior." Sociometry 34 (2, June): 263-280. P.A. 49:740.

36.   1974   "Effects of information on interpersonal attraction: Similarity versus affective value." Journal of Personality and Social Psychology 29 (3): 374-380.

37. Ajzen, Icek, and Martin Fishbein
    1973   "Attitudinal and normative variables as predictors of specific behavior." Journal of Personality and Social Psychology 27 (1, July): 41-57. P.A. 50:11199.

38.   1974   "Factors influencing intentions and the intention-behavior relation." Human Relations 27 (1, January): 1-15. P.A. 52:12237.

39. Albert, Robert S.
    1953   "Comments on the scientific function of the concept of cohesiveness." American Journal of Sociology 59: 231-234. P.A. 28:4112.

40. Albert, Robert S., and Thomas R. Brigante
    1962   "The psychology of friendship relations: Social factors." Journal of Social Psychology 56 (February): 33-47. P.A. 5G33A.

41. Albert, Rosita
    1973   "Effects of attributions made by a victim on retaliation and transmission of aggression." Proceedings of the 81st Annual Convention of the American Psychological Association 8 (pt. 1): 119-120. P.A. 50:8787.

42. Albert, Stuart
    1973   "Person perception and subjective time: A new problem in attribution." Proceedings of the 81st Annual Convention of the American Psychological Association 8 (pt. 1): 197-198. P.A. 50:8788.

43. Albert, Stuart, and James M. Dabbs, Jr.
    1970   "Physical distance and persuasion." Journal of Personality and Social Psychology 15 (3): 265-270.

44. Aldous, Joan, and Murray A. Straus
    1966   "Social networks and conjugal roles: A test of Bott's hypothesis." Social Forces 44 (4, June): 576-580. P.A. 40:10020.

45. Alexander, C. Norman, Jr.
    1963   "A method for processing sociometric data." Sociometry 26 (2, June): 268-269.

46.   1964   "Consensus and mutual attraction in natural cliques: A study of adolescent drinkers." American Journal of Sociology 69 (4, January):

395–403. P.A. 38:8305; S.A. 12:B1624.

47.   1966   "Ordinal position and sociometric status." Sociometry 29 (1, March): 41–51. S.A. 15:C3471.

48. Alexander, C. Norman, Jr., and Ernest Q. Campbell
      1968   "Balance forces and environmental effects: Factors influencing the cohesiveness of adolescent drinking groups." Social Forces 46 (3, March): 367–374. P.A. 42:12046.

49. Alexander, C. Norman, Jr., and Harrison G. Weil
      1969   "Players, persons, and purposes: Situational meaning and the Prisoner's Dilemma game." Sociometry 32 (2, June): 121–144. S.A. 18: E2905.

50. Alexander, C. Norman, Jr., and Inger Sagatun
      1973   "An attributional analysis of experimental norms." Sociometry 36 (2, June): 127–142. P.A. 51:3005.

51. Alexander, C. Norman, Jr., Lynne G. Zuker, and Charles L. Brody
      1970   "Experimental expectations and autokinetic experiences: Consistency theories and judgemental convergence." Sociometry 33: 108–122.

52. Alfert, Elizabeth
      1958   "Two components of assumed similarity." Journal of Abnormal and Social Psychology 56: 135–138.

53. Alix, Ernest K., and Richard M. Thomas
      1971   "Toward increasing the sociological relevance of sensitivity training." Sociological Inquiry 41 (2, Spring): 233–244.

54. Alker, Henry A., and Nathan Kogan
      1968   "Effects of norm-oriented group discussion on individual verbal risk-taking and conservatism." Human Relations 21 (4, November): 393–405.

55. Alkire, Armand A., Mary E. Collum, Jacques Kaswan, and Leonore R. Love
      1968   "Information exchange and accuracy of verbal communication under social power conditions." Journal of Personality and Social Psychology 9 (4): 301–308. P.A. 42:17155.

56. Allen, Bem P.
      1973   "Perceived trustworthiness of attitudinal and behavioral expressions." Journal of Social Psychology 89 (2, April): 211–218. P.A. 50:6684.

57. Allen, Jon G.
      1974   "When does exchanging personal information constitute 'self-disclosure'?" Psychological Reports 35 (1, pt. 1): 195–198.

58. Allen, Vernon L.
      1965a   "Conformity and the role of deviant." Journal of Personality 33 (4, December): 584–597. P.A. 40:4175.

59.   1965b   "Situational factors in conformity." In L. Berkowitz (ed.), Advances in Experimental Social Psychology, vol. 2, pp. 133–170. New York: Academic Press.

60.   1966   "Effect of knowledge of deception on conformity." Journal of Social Psychology 69 (1, June): 101–106. P.A. 40:10021.

61. Allen, Vernon L., and Barry W. Bragg
      1968   "Effect of social pressure on concept identification." Journal of Educational Psychology 59 (4): 302–308. P.A. 42:15410.

62. Allen, Vernon L., and Richard S. Crutchfield
      1963   "Generalization of experimentally reinforced conformity." Journal of Abnormal and Social Psychology 67 (4): 326–333. P.A. 38:4188.

63. Allen, Vernon L., and John M. Levine
      1968   "Social support, dissent and conformity." Sociometry 31 (2, June): 138–149. P.A. 42:13640; S.A. 17:D6811.

64.   1969   "Consensus and conformity." Journal of Experimental Psychology 5 (4): 389–399. P.A. 44:5094.

65.   1971a   "Social support and conformity: The role of independent assessment of reality." Journal of Experimental Social Psychology 7 (1): 48–58.

66.   1971b   "Social pressure and personal preference." Journal of Experimental Social Psychology 7 (1): 122–124.

67. Allen, Vernon L., and Darren Newtson
    1972   "Development of conformity and independence." Journal of Person-
            ality and Social Psychology 22 (1): 18–30.
68. Allgeier, A. R., and Donn Byrne
    1973   "Attraction toward the opposite sex as a determinant of physical
            proximity." Journal of Social Psychology 90 (2, August): 213–219.
            P.A. 51:965.
69. Allport, Floyd H.
    1920   "The influence of the group upon association and thought." Journal
            of Experimental Psychology 3: 159–182. (See also Hare, Borgatta,
            and Bales, 1955, 1965.)
70.   1924   Social Psychology. Boston: Houghton Mifflin.
71.   1962   "A structuronomic conception of behavior: Individual and collec-
            tive. I. Structural theory and the master problem of social psychol-
            ogy." Journal of Abnormal and Social Psychology 64 (1): 3–30.
72. Allport, Gordon W.
    1954   "The historical background of modern social psychology." In G.
            Lindzey (ed.), Handbook of Social Psychology, pp. 3–56. Cam-
            bridge, Mass.: Addison-Wesley. (See also Lindzey and Aronson,
            1968.) P.A. 29:3774.
73. Alpert, B., and Patricia A. Smith
    1949   "How participation works." Journal of Social Issues 5 (1): 3–13.
            P.A. 23:6123.
74. Altman, Irwin
    1963   "Mainstreams of research on small groups." Public Administration
            Review 23 (4, December): 203–208. S.A. 13:B6752.
75.   1966a   "Aspects of the criterion problem in small group research: I. Behav-
            ioral domains to be studied." Acta Psychologica 25 (2): 101–131.
            P.A. 40:7634.
76.   1966b   "Aspects of the criterion problem in small group research: II. The
            analysis of group tasks." Acta Psychologica 25 (3): 199–221. P.A.
            40:12264.
77.   1973   "Reciprocity of interpersonal exchange." Journal for the Theory of
            Social Behaviour 3 (2): 249–261.
78. Altman, Irwin, and William W. Haythorn
    1965   "Interpersonal exchange in isolation." Sociometry 28 (4, Decem-
            ber): 411–426. P.A. 40:2805.
79.   1967a   "The ecology of isolated groups." Behavioral Science 12 (3, May):
            169–182. S.A. 15:C7232.
80.   1967b   "The effects of social isolation and group composition on perform-
            ance." Human Relations 20 (4, November): 313–340. P.A. 42:8860;
            S.A. 16:D2321.
81. Altman, Irwin, and Elliott McGinnies
    1960   "Interpersonal perception and communication in discussion groups
            of varied attitudinal composition." Journal of Abnormal and Social
            Psychology 60 (3): 390–395. P.A. 35:4806.
82. Altman, Irwin, Dalmas A. Taylor, and Ladd Wheeler
    1971   "Ecological aspects of group behavior in social isolation." Journal of
            Applied Social Psychology 1 (1, January): 76–100. P.A. 47:2817.
83. Altrocchi, John
    1961   "Interpersonal perceptions of repressors and sensitizers and compo-
            nent analysis of assumed dissimilarity scores." Journal of Abnormal
            and Social Psychology 62 (3, May): 528–534.
84. American Journal of Psychiatry
    1969   Groups. 126 (December).
85. American Psychological Association
    1973   "Guidelines for psychologists conducting growth groups." American
            Psychologist 28 (10): 933.
86. Ames, Robert
    1955   "Leaderless group discussion and experience in group leadership."
            California Journal of Education Research 6: 166–169. P.A. 30:
            5841.

87. Amidjaja, Imat R., and W. Edgar Vinacke
    1965   "Achievement, nurturance, and competition in male and female tri-
            ads." Journal of Personality and Social Psychology 2 (3): 447–451.
            P.A. 39:15018.
88. Ancoma, Leonardo, and Rosetta Pareyson
    1971–   ("Contribution to the study of aggression: Dynamics of destructive
    1972   obedience.") Bulletin de Psychologie 24 (5-7): 233–249. P.A. 50:
            8790.
89. Anderson, Alan R.
    1962   "Logic, norms, and roles." In J. H. Criswell, H. Solomon, and P.
            Suppes (eds.), Mathematical Methods in Small Group Processes, pp.
            11–22. Stanford, Calif.: Stanford University Press. S.A. 12:B2397.
90. Anderson, Alan R., Thomas J. Hummel, and Dennis L. Gibson
    1970   "An experimental assessment of video-tape feedback and two pre-
            group orientation procedures in a human relations training labora-
            tory." Comparative Group Studies 1 (2, May): 156–176.
91. Anderson, Carl, and John W. Slocum
    1973   "Personality traits and their impact on T-group training success."
            Training and Development Journal 27 (12, December): 18–25. P.A.
            52:795.
92. Anderson, C. Arnold
    1929   "An experimental study of 'social facilitation' as affected by intelli-
            gence." American Journal of Sociology 34: 874–881.
93. Anderson, Harold H.
    1937a   "An experimental study of dominative and integrative behavior in
            children of pre-school age." Journal of Social Psychology 8: 335–
            345. P.A. 12:560.
94. 1937b   "Domination and integration in the social behavior of young child-
            ren in an experimental play situation." Genetic Psychology Mono-
            graphs 19: 341–408. P.A. 12:559.
95. 1939   "Domination and social integration in the behavior of kindergarten
            children and teachers." Genetic Psychology Monographs 21: 287–
            385. (See also Barker, Kounin, and Wright, 1943.) P.A. 14:514.
96. Anderson, John A., and Daniel Perlman
    1973   "Effects of an adult's preaching and responsibility for hypocritical
            behavior on children's altruism." Proceedings of the 81st Annual
            Convention of the American Psychological Association 8: 291–292.
            P.A. 8792.
97. Anderson, Lynn R.
    1966   "Leader behavior, member attitudes, and task performance of inter-
            cultural discussion groups." Journal of Social Psychology 69 (2,
            August): 305–319. P.A. 40:12282.
98. Anderson, Lynn R., and Fred E. Fiedler
    1964   "The effect of participatory and supervisory leadership on group
            creativity." Journal of Applied Psychology 48 (4): 227–236. P.A.
            39:4903.
99. Anderson, Lynn R., and William J. McGuire
    1965   "Prior reassurance of group consensus as a factor in producing resist-
            ance to persuasion." Sociometry 28 (1, March): 44–56. S.A. 14:
            B9172.
100. Anderson, Norman H.
    1961   "Group performance in an anagram task." Journal of Social Psychol-
            ogy 55 (October): 67–75. P.A. 4GE67A.
101. Anderson, Norman H., and Alfred A. Barrios
    1961   "Primacy effects in personality impression formation." Journal of
            Abnormal and Social Psychology 63 (2): 346–350. P.A. 37:1090.
102. Anderson, Norman H., Rhoda Lindner, and Lola L. Lopes
    1973   "Integration theory applied to judgments of group attractiveness."
            Journal of Personality and Social Psychology 26 (3, June): 400–408.
            P.A. 50:11201.
103. Anderson, Norman H., and Lola L. Lopes
    1974   "Some psycholinguistic aspects of person perception." Memory and
            Cognition 2 (1-A, January): 67–74. P.A. 52:7540.

104. Anderson, Richard C.
      1959   "Learning in discussions: A resume of the authoritarian-democratic studies." Harvard Educational Review 29 (3, Summer): 201–215. P.A. 34:5693; S.A. 1679.
105. Anderson, Ronald E.
      1967   "Status structures in coalition bargaining games." Sociometry 30 (4, December): 393–403. P.A. 42:3890; S.A. 16:D3099.
106. Anderson, Ruth M.
      1964   "Activity preferences and leadership behavior of head nurses: Part I." Nursing Research 13 (3, Summer): 239–243. S.A. 13:B6770.
107. Andrews, I. R., and D. L. Johnson
      1971   "Small group polarization of judgments." Psychonomic Science 24 (4, August): 191–192. P.A. 48:11425.
108. Andrews, John D. W.
      1973   "Interpersonal challenge: A source of growth in laboratory training." Journal of Applied Behavioral Science 9 (4, July): 514–533. P.A. 51:2960.
109. Andrews, R. E.
      1955   Leadership and supervision. U.S. Civil Service Commission, Personnel Management Series No. 9. Washington, D.C.: Government Printing Office.
110. Anger, Hans
      1962   ("Theory building and models in small group research.") Kölner Zeitschrift für Soziologie und Sozialpsychologie 14 (1): 4–18. S.A. 12:A8711.
111.   1966   ("Research on small groups today.") Kölner Zeitschrift für Soziologie und Sozialpsychologie 10 (Supplement): 15–43. S.A. 15:C5568.
112. Anger, Hans, and F. Nachreiner
      1975   ("Group behavior in industry.") In Handwörterbuch der Betriebswirtschaft, 4th ed.
113. Anikeeff, Alexis M.
      1957   "Sociometric empathy." Journal of Social Psychology 45: 283–287.
114. Ansbacher, H[einz] L.
      1951   "The history of the leaderless group discussion technique." Psychological Bulletin 48: 383–391. P.A. 26:5116.
115. Anthony, Susan
      1973   "Anxiety and rumor." Journal of Social Psychology 89 (1, February): 91–98. P.A. 50:2902.
116.   1974   "Immediacy and nonimmediacy: Factors in communicating interpersonal attraction." Journal of Social Psychology 93 (1, June): 141–142. P.A. 52:12238.
117. Appley, Mortimer H., and George Moeller
      1963   "Conforming behavior and personality variables in college women." Journal of Abnormal and Social Psychology 66 (3): 284–290.
118. Arbes, Bill H., and Robert N. Hubbell
      1973   "Packaged impact: A structured communication skills workshop." Journal of Counseling Psychology 20 (4, July): 332–337. P.A. 51: 2961.
119. Arbuthnot, Jack, and Frank Andrasik
      1973   "Situational influences on moral judgment." Proceedings of the 81st Annual Convention of the American Psychological Association 8 (pt. 1): 217–218.
120. Archer, Dane
      1973   "The face of power: Physical attractiveness as a non-verbal predictor of small-group stratification." Proceedings of the 81st Annual Convention of the American Psychological Association 8 (pt. 1): 177–178. P.A. 50:4741.
121.   1974   "Power in groups: Self-concept changes of powerful and powerless group members." Journal of Applied Behavioral Science 10 (2, April): 208–220. P.A. 52:12239.
122. Archer, James, and Norman Kagan
      1973   "Teaching interpersonal relationship skills on campus: A pyramid approach." Journal of Counseling Psychology 20 (6, November):

535-540. P.A. 51:7018.
123. Archibald, W. Peter, and Ronald L. Cohen
    1971   "Self-presentation, embarrassment, and facework as a function of
            self-evaluation, conditions of self-presentation, and feedback from
            others." Journal of Personality and Social Psychology 20 (3): 287-
            297.
124. Argyle, Michael
    1952a   "Methods of studying small social groups." British Journal of Psy-
            chology 43: 269-279. P.A. 27:5793.
125.   1952b   "The concepts of role and status." Sociological Review 44 (3). P.A.
            29:649.
126. Argyle, Michael
    1955   "The study of social behavior." In B. A. Farrell (ed.), Experimental
            Psychology, pp. 46-56. New York: Philosophical Library. P.A. 30:
            2620.
127.   1957a   "Social pressure in public and private situations." Journal of Ab-
            normal and Social Psychology 54: 172-175.
128.   1957b   The Scientific Study of Social Behaviour. London: Methuen. P.A.
            32:2743.
129.   1969   Social Interaction. New York: Atherton.
130.   1972   "Non-verbal communication in human social interaction." In R. A.
            Hinde (ed.), Non-verbal Communication. Cambridge: At the Univer-
            sity Press. P.A. 50:4742.
131. Argyle, Michael, and Janet Dean
    1965   "Eye-contact, distance and affiliation." Sociometry 28 (3, Septem-
            ber): 289-304. P.A. 39:15019.
132. Argyle, Michael, and Adam Kendon
    1967   "The experimental analysis of social performance." In L. Berkowitz
            (ed.), Advances in Experimental Social Psychology, vol. 3, pp. 55-
            98. New York: Academic Press.
133. Argyle, Michael, Mansur Lalljee, and Mark Cook
    1968   "The effects of visibility on interaction in a dyad." Human Relations
            21 (1, February): 3-17. P.A. 42:13641; S.A. 17:D5786.
134. Argyle, Michael, and Victor Lee
    1972   Social Relationships. Bletchley, Bucks.: Open University Press. P.A.
            51:940.
135. Argyris, Chris
    1962   Interpersonal Competence and Organizational Effectiveness. Home-
            wood, Ill.: Dorsey.
136.   1969   "The incompleteness of social psychological theory: Examples from
            small group, cognitive consistency, and attribution research." Ameri-
            can Psychologist 24: 893-908.
137.   1970   Intervention Theory and Method. Reading, Mass.: Addison-Wesley.
138.   1972   "Do personal growth laboratories represent an alternative culture?"
            Journal of Applied Behavioral Science 8 (1): 7-28.
139. Armentrout, David P.
    1972   "We: System." Journal of Psychology 81 (1, May): 59-62. P.A. 48:
            8990.
140. Armentrout, James A.
    1972   "Sociometric classroom popularity and children's reports of parental
            child-rearing behaviors." Psychological Reports 30: 261-262.
141. Armilla, Jose
    1964   "Anxiety in taking the role of the leader." Journal of Abnormal and
            Social Psychology 68 (5, May): 550-552. P.A. 39:4904.
142. Arnstein, Fred, and Kenneth D. Feigenbaum
    1967   "Relationship of three motives to choice in the Prisoner's Dilemma."
            Psychological Reports 20: 751-755.
143. Aronoff, Joel
    1970   "Psychological needs as a determinant in the formation of economic
            structures: A confirmation." Human Relations 23 (2, April): 123-
            138. P.A. 45:2283.

144. Aronoff, Joel, and Lawrence A. Messé
     1971   "Motivational determinants of small-group structure." Journal of
             Personality and Social Psychology 17 (3, March): 319–324. P.A. 46:
             1051.
145. Aronson, Elliot
     1969   "The theory of cognitive dissonance: A current perspective." In L.
             Berkowitz (ed.), Advances in Experimental Social Psychology, vol.
             4, pp. 1–35. New York: Academic Press.
146. 1973   "Dissonance theory: Progress and problems." In L. S. Wrightsman
             and J. C. Brigham (eds.), Contemporary Issues in Social Psychology,
             2nd ed, pp. 310–323. Belmont, Calif.: Brooks Cole.
147. Aronson, Elliot, and Vera Aronson
     1971   "Does a woman's attractiveness influence men's non-sexual reac-
             tions?" Medical Aspects of Human Sexuality 5 (11, November): 12–
             27. P.A. 49:4376.
148. Aronson, Elliot, and J. Merrill Carlsmith
     1968   "Experimentation in social psychology." In G. Lindzey and E. Aron-
             son (eds.), Handbook of Social Psychology, vol. 2, pp. 1–79. Read-
             ing, Mass.: Addison-Wesley.
149. Aronson, Elliot, and J. Mills
     1959   "The effect of severity of initiation on liking for a group." Journal
             of Abnormal and Social Psychology 59: 177–181. (See also Cart-
             wright and Zander, 1960, 1968.) P.A. 34:2853.
150. Aronson, Elliot, and Philip Worchel
     1966   "Similarity versus liking as determinants of interpersonal attractive-
             ness." Psychonomic Science 5 (4): 157–158. P.A. 40:10023.
151. Aronson, H[arriet J.], and Walter Weintraub
     1967   "Verbal productivity as a measure of change in affective status."
             Psychological Reports 20: 483–487.
152. Arrington, Ruth E.
     1939   "Time-sampling studies of child behavior." Psychological Mono-
             graphs 51, No. 2. P.A. 13:6524.
153. 1943   "Time sampling in studies of social behavior: A critical review of
             techniques and results with research suggestions." Psychological Bul-
             letin 40: 81–124. P.A. 17:1630.
154. Arrowood, A. John, and Donald M. Amoroso
     1965   "Social comparison and ordinal position." Journal of Personality
             and Social Psychology 2 (1): 101–104. P.A. 39:12165.
155. Arrowood, A. John, and Judith A. Short
     1973   "Agreement, attraction, and self-esteem." Canadian Journal of Be-
             havioural Science 5 (3, July): 242–252. P.A. 51:7002.
156. Arsenian, Jean M.
     1943   "Young children in an insecure situation." Journal of Abnormal and
             Social Psychology 38: 225–249.
157. Arsenian, John, Elvin V. Semrad, and David Shapiro
     1962   "An analysis of integral functions in small groups." International
             Journal of Group Psychotherapy 12 (4): 421–434. P.A. 38:5956.
158. Asch, Solomon E.
     1946   "Forming impressions of personality." Journal of Abnormal and So-
             cial Psychology 41: 258–290. P.A. 20:4654.
159. 1951   "Effects of group pressure upon the modification and distortion of
             judgments." In H. Guetzkow (ed.), Groups, Leadership, and Men,
             pp. 177–190. Pittsburgh: Carnegie Press. (See also Swanson, New-
             comb, and Hartley, 1952; Cartwright and Zander, 1953, 1960; Mac-
             coby, Newcomb, and Hartley, 1958; Crosbie, 1975.)
160. 1952   Social Psychology. New York: Prentice-Hall. P.A. 27:3409.
161. 1955   "Opinions and social pressure." Scientific American 193 (5): 31–35.
             (See also Hare, Borgatta, and Bales, 1965.) P.A. 30:8022.
162. 1956   "Studies of independence and conformity: I. A minority of one
             against a unanimous majority." Psychological Monographs 70 (9),
             No. 416. P.A. 31:5875.

163.   1961   "Issues in the study of social influences on judgment." In I. A. Berg and B. M. Bass (eds.), Conformity and Deviation, pp. 143-158. New York: Harper. P.A. GE43A.

164. Ashin, G. K.
    1968   ("The problem of leadership in contemporary foreign empirical sociology.") Voprosy Filosofii 22 (5): 161-168. P.A. 43:3934.

165. Ashour, Ahmed S.
    1973   "Coalitional behavior under the condition of risk." Psychological Reports 33 (1, August): 87-96. P.A. 51:7019.

166. Athanasiou, Robert, and Paul Greene
    1973   "Physical attractiveness and helping behavior." Proceedings of the 81st Annual Convention of the American Psychological Association 8: 289-290. P.A. 50:6685.

167. Athanasiou, Robert, and Gary A. Yoshioka
    1973   "The spatial character of friendship formation." Environment and Behavior 5 (1, March): 43-65. P.A. 50:8793.

168. Atkins, Alvin L., and James Bieri
    1968   "Effects of involvement level and contextual stimuli on social judgment." Journal of Personality and Social Psychology 9 (2): 197-204.

169. Atkins, Alvin L., Irma Hilton, William Neigher, and Arthur Bahr
    1972   "Anger, fight, fantasy and catharsis." Proceedings of the 80th Annual Convention of the American Psychological Association 7 (pt. 1): 241-242. P.A. 48:4841.

170. Atkinson, Richard C.
    1962   "Choice behavior and monetary payoff: Strong and weak." In J. H. Criswell, H. Solomon, and P. Suppes (eds.), Mathematical Methods in Small Group Processes, pp. 23-34. Stanford, Calif.: Stanford University Press. S.A. 12:B2398.

171. Atoji, Yoshio
    1961   "Classical form of small group theory: A case of Georg Simmel." Japanese Sociological Review 11 (3-4, May): 1-21. S.A. 11:A6353.

172. Atthowe, John M., Jr.
    1961   "Interpersonal decision making: The resolution of a dyadic conflict." Journal of Abnormal and Social Psychology 62 (1, January): 114-119. P.A. 36:3GE14A; S.A. A1698.

173. Aubert, Vilhelm
    1961   ("Solution of conflicts in pair and triangle.") Tidsskrift for Samfunnsforskning 2 (2, June): 89-102. S.A. 14:B8337.

174. Austin, William, and Charles Susmilch
    1974   "Comment on Lane and Messe's confusing clarification of equity theory." Journal of Personality and Social Psychology 30 (3): 400-404.

175. Austin, William, and Elaine Walster
    1974   "Reactions to confirmations and disconfirmations of expectancies of equity and inequity." Journal of Personality and Social Psychology 30 (2, August): 208-216. P.A. 52:12290.

176. Austin, W. T., and Frederick L. Bates
    1974   "Ethological indicators of dominance and territory in a human captive population." Social Forces 52 (4, June): 447-455. P.A. 52:12225.

177. Avery, Richard, and Warren Bachelis
    1956   "Reliability of scoring in interaction process analysis." Paper presented at meetings of American Sociological Society, Detroit.

178. Axelrod, Robert
    1967   "Conflict of interest: an axiomatic approach." Journal of Conflict Resolution 11 (1): 85-99.

179. Axelrod, Saul, and Jack G. May
    1968   "Effect of increased reward on the two-person non-zero-sum game." Psychological Reports 23: 675-678.

180. Ayers, Lauren, Peter Nacci, and James T. Tedeschi
    1973   "Attraction and reactions to noncontingent promises." Bulletin of

the Psychonomic Society 1 (1-B, January): 75-77. P.A. 50:6686.

181. Azrin, Nathan H., and Ogden R. Lindsley
1956 "The reinforcement of cooperation between children." Journal of Abnormal and Social Psychology 52: 100-102. P.A. 31:2394.

182. Babchuk, Nicholas, and William F. Goode
1951 "Work incentives in a self-determined group." American Sociological Review 16: 679-687. P.A. 27:1491.

183. Bach, George R.
1954 Intensive Group Psychotherapy. New York: Ronald.

184. 1966 "The marathon group: Intensive practice of intimate interaction." Psychological Reports 18: 995-1002.

185. 1967a "Marathon group dynamics: I. Some functions of the professional group facilitator." Psychological Reports 20: 995-999.

186. 1967b "Marathon group dynamics: II. Dimensions of helpfulness: Therapeutic aggression." Psychological Reports 20: 1147-1158.

187. 1967c "Marathon group dynamics: III. Disjunctive contacts." Psychological Reports 20: 1163-1172.

188. Bach, Thomas R.
1973 "Adjustment differences related to pattern of rating of the other." Psychological Reports 32 (1, February): 19-22. P.A. 51:3007.

189. Bachrach, Arthur J., Douglas K. Candland, and Janice T. Gibson
1961 "Group reinforcement of individual response experiments in verbal behavior." In I. A. Berg and B. M. Bass (eds.), Conformity and Deviation, pp. 258-285. New York: Harper. P.A. 36:4GE58B.

190. Back, Kurt W.
1948 "Interpersonal relations in a discussion group." Journal of Social Issues 4: 61-65. P.A. 23:674.

191 1951 "Influence through social communication." Journal of Abnormal and Social Psychology 46: 9-23. (See also Swanson, Newcomb, and Hartley, 1952; Maccoby, Newcomb, and Hartley, 1958.) P.A. 25: 7362.

192. 1961 "Power, influence and pattern of communication." In L. Petrullo and B. M. Bass (eds.), Leadership and Interpersonal Behavior, pp. 137-164. New York: Holt, Rinehart & Winston.

193. 1962 "Can subjects be human and humans be subjects?" In J. H. Criswell, H. Solomon, and P. Suppes (eds.), Mathematical Methods in Small Group Processes, pp. 35-48. Stanford, Calif.: Stanford University Press. S.A. 12:B2399.

194. 1971 "Varieties of sensitivity training." Sociological Inquiry 41 (2, Spring): 133-137.

195. 1972 Beyond Words: The Story of Sensitivity Training and the Encounter Movement. New York: Russell Sage Foundation. P.A. 49:2315.

196. 1973 "The experiential group and society." Journal of Applied Behavioral Science 9 (1): 7-20. P.A. 50:8794.

197. Back, Kurt W., Morton D. Bogdonoff, David M. Shaw, and Robert F. Klein
1963 "An interpretation of experimental conformity through physiological measures." Behavioral Science 8 (1, January): 34-40. S.A. 11: A6354.

198. Back, Kurt W., Stephen Bunker, and Catherine B. Dunnagan
1972 "Barriers to communication and measurement of semantic space." Sociometry 35 (3, September): 347-356. P.A. 49:6786.

199. Back, Kurt W., and Keith E. Davis
1965 "Some personal and situational factors relevant to the consistency and prediction of conforming behavior." Sociometry 28 (3, September): 227-240. P.A. 39:15020.

200. Back, Kurt W., L. Festinger, B. Hymovitch, H. H. Kelley, S. Schachter, and J. W. Thibaut
1950 "The methodology of studying rumor transmission." Human Relations 3: 307-312. P.A. 25:2416.

201. Back, Kurt W., Thomas C. Hood, and Mary L. Brehm
1964 "The subject role in small group experiments." Social Forces 43 (2,

December): 181–187. S.A. 13:B5875.
202. Back, Kurt W., S. R. Wilson, M. D. Bogdonoff, and W. G. Troyer
    1969   "Racial environment, cohesion, conformity and stress." Journal of
            Psychosomatic Research, 13 (1): 27–36. P.A. 44:3537.
203. Backman, Carl W., and Paul F. Secord
    1959   "The effect of perceived liking on interpersonal attraction." Human
            Relations 12 (4, November): 379–384. P.A. 35:6630; S.A. A3284.
204.   1962   "Liking, selective interaction, and misperception in congruent inter-
            personal relations." Sociometry 25 (4, December): 321–335.
205.   1964   "The compromise process and the affect structure of groups." Hu-
            man Relations 17 (1, February): 19–22. P.A. 39:1566; S.A. 12:
            B2400.
206. Backman, Carl W., Paul F. Secord, and Jerry R. Peirce
    1963   "Resistance to change in the self-concept as a function of consensus
            among significant others." Sociometry 26 (1, March): 102–111.
207. Badin, Pierre
    1965   (Problems of Group Life.) Paris: Presses Universitaires de France.
            P.A. 39:12166.
208. Baier, Donald E.
    1947   "Note on 'A review of leadership studies with particular reference to
            military problems.'" Psychological Bulletin 44: 466–467. P.A. 22:
            1145.
209. Bailey, Kent G., John J. Hartnett, and Hilda W. Glover
    1973   "Modeling and personal space behavior in children." Journal of Psy-
            chology 85 (1, September): 143–150. P.A. 51:7003.
210. Baker, Bela O., and Theodore R. Sarbin
    1956   "Differential mediation of social perception as a correlate of social
            adjustment." Sociometry 19: 69–83. P.A. 31:6363; S.A. 4284.
211. Baker, John W., II, and K. Warner Schaie
    1969   "Effects of aggressing 'alone' or 'with another' on physiological and
            psychological arousal." Journal of Personality and Social Psychology
            12 (1): 80–86. P.A. 43:11224.
212. Baker, Keith
    1974   "Experimental analysis of third-party justice behavior." Journal of
            Personality and Social Psychology 30 (2, August): 307–316. P.A.
            52:12292.
213. Baker, Larry D., and H. Joseph Reitz
    1973   "Blindness, situational dependency, and helping behavior." Proceed-
            ings of the 81st Annual Convention of the American Psychological
            Association 8: 803–804. P.A. 50:6687.
214. Baldwin, A., J. Kallhorn, and F. Breese
    1945   "Patterns of parent behavior." Psychological Monographs 58, No.
            268. P.A. 19:3415.
215. Baldwin, Bruce A.
    1972   "Change in interpersonal cognitive complexity as a function of a
            training group experience." Psychological Reports 30: 935–940.
216. Baldwin, John D.
    1969   "Influences detrimental to simulation gaming." American Behavioral
            Scientist 12 (6): 14–20. S.A. 19:E8384.
217. Bale, Richard L.
    1972   "A methodological comment on Page's 'Role of demand awareness
            in the communicator credibility effect.'" Journal of Social Psychol-
            ogy 88 (2, December): 197–201. P.A. 49:9006.
218. Bales, Robert F.
    1945   "Social therapy for a social disorder—compulsive drinking." Journal
            of Social Issues 1 (3): 14–22. P.A. 20:1507.
219.   1950a   "A set of categories for the analysis of small group interaction."
            American Sociological Review 15: 257–263. P.A. 26:4733.
220.   1950b   Interaction Process Analysis: A Method for the Study of Small
            Groups. Cambridge, Mass.: Addison-Wesley. (See also Cartwright and
            Zander, 1953, 1960.) P.A. 24:4553.
221.   1951a   "Some statistical problems in small group research." Journal of

American Statist. Association 46: 311–322. P.A. 26:1863.

222. 1951b "Reply to Keller's comment." American Sociological Review 16: 843.

223. 1952 "Some uniformities of behavior in small social systems." In G. E. Swanson, T. H. Newcomb, and E. L. Hartley (eds.), Readings in Social Psychology, pp. 146–159. New York: Holt. (See also Lazarsfeld and Rosenberg (eds.), The Language of Social Research, pp. 345–358. New York: Free Press, 1955.)

224. 1953 "The equilibrium problem in small groups." In T. Parsons, R. F. Bales, and E. A. Shils, Working Papers in the Theory of Action, pp. 111–161. Glencoe, Ill.: Free Press. (See also Hare, Borgatta, and Bales, 1955, 1965.)

225. 1954 "In conference." Harvard Business Review 32: 44–50.

226. 1955 "How people interact in conferences." Scientific American 192 (3): 31–35. P.A. 29:7061.

227. 1956 "Task status and likeability as a function of talking and listening in decision-making groups." In L. D. White (ed.), The State of the Social Sciences, pp. 148–161. Chicago: University of Chicago Press.

228. 1958 "Task roles and social roles in problem solving groups." In E. E. Maccoby, T. M. Newcomb, and E. L. Hartley (eds.), Readings in Social Psychology, 3rd ed., pp. 437–447. New York: Holt.

229. 1959 "Small-group theory and research." In R. K. Merton, L. Broom, and L. S. Cottrell, Jr. (eds.), Sociology Today: Problems and Prospects, pp. 293–305. New York: Basic Books.

230. 1968 "Interaction process analysis." In D. L. Sills, (ed.), International Encyclopedia of the Social Sciences, vol. 7, pp. 465–471. New York: Macmillan and Free Press.

231. 1970a Personality and Interpersonal Behavior. New York: Holt Rinehart & Winston.

232. 1970b "Perspectives and Theory." Comparative Group Studies 1 (3, August): 315–326.

233. Bales, Robert F., and Edgar F. Borgatta
      1955 "Size of group as a factor in the interaction profile." In A. P. Hare, E. F. Borgatta, and R. F. Bales (eds.), Small Groups: Studies in Social Interaction, pp. 396–413. New York: Knopf. (See also Hare, Borgatta, and Bales, 1965).

234. Bales, Robert F., and Ned A. Flanders
      1954 "Planning an observation room and group laboratory." American Sociological Review 19: 771–781. P.A. 30:2686.

235. Bales, Robert F., and Henry Gerbrands
      1948 "The 'Interaction Recorder': An apparatus and check list for sequential content analysis of social interaction." Human Relations 1: 456–463. P.A. 23:2012.

236. Bales, Robert F., and A. Paul Hare
      1965 "Diagnostic use of the interaction profile." Journal of Social Psychology 67 (December): 239–258.

237. Bales, Robert F., A. Paul Hare, and Edgar F. Borgatta
      1957 "Structure and dynamics of small groups: A review of four variables." In J. B. Gittler (ed.), Review of Sociology: Analysis of a Decade, pp. 391–422. New York: Wiley.

238. Bales, Robert F., and Philip E. Slater
      1955 "Role differentiation." In T. Parsons, R. F. Bales, et al., The Family, Socialization, and Interaction Process, pp. 259–306. Glencoe, Ill.: Free Press.

239. 1957 "Notes on 'Role differentiation in small decision-making groups': Reply to Dr. Wheeler." Sociometry 20: 152–155.

240. Bales, Robert F., and Philip J. Stone
      1961 "The interaction simulator." In Annals of the Computation Laboratory 31: 305–314. Cambridge, Mass.: Harvard University Press.

241. Bales, Robert F., and Fred L. Strodtbeck
      1951 "Phases in group problem solving." Journal of Abnormal and Social Psychology 46: 485–495. (See also Cartwright and Zander, 1953,

1960, 1968.) P.A. 26:3911.
242. Bales, Robert F., Fred L. Strodtbeck, Theodore M. Mills, and Mary E. Rose-borough
    1951   "Channels of communication in small groups." American Sociological Review 16: 461–468. (See also R. F. Bales, Reply to Keller's comment. American Sociological Review 16: 843.) P.A. 27:1035.
243. Ball, Jerry
    1973   "Chabot College: The pentagonal principle for self-oriented classes." Small group behavior 4 (1, February): 64–68.
244. Baloff, Nicholas, and Selwyn W. Becker
    1968   "A model of group adaptation to problem-solving tasks." Organizational Behavior and Human Performance 3 (3): 217–238. P.A. 42: 18727.
245. Bandura, Albert
    1973   Aggression: A Social Learning Analysis. Englewood Cliffs, N. J.: Prentice-Hall. P.A. 51:914.
246. Banghart, Frank W.
    1959   "Group structure, anxiety, and problem-solving efficiency." Journal of Experimental Education 28 (December): 171–175. P.A. 34:7518.
247. Banikiotes, Paul G.
    1971   "Interpersonal attraction, topic importance, and proportion of item agreements." Psychonomic Science 22 (6, March): 353–354. P.A. 47:2819.
248. Banikiotes, Paul G., John M. Russell, and James D. Linden
    1971   "Interpersonal attraction methodology: Oversimplified or related to real interaction?" Proceedings of the 79th Annual Convention of the American Psychological Association 6 (pt. 1): 279–280.
249.   1972   "Interpersonal attraction in simulated and real interactions." Journal of Personality and Social Psychology 23 (1): 1–7.
250. Bankart, C. Peter
    1972   "Attribution of motivation in same-race and different-race stimulus persons." Human Relations 25 (1, February): 35–45. P.A. 49:2316.
251. Banks, E. P.
    1956   "Methodological problems in the study of psychiatric wards." Social Forces 34: 277–280. P.A. 31:4812.
252. Banta, Thomas J., and Mavis Hetherington
    1963   "Relations between needs of friends and fiances." Journal of Abnormal and Social Psychology 66 (4): 401–404. P.A. 37:7941.
253. Banta, Thomas J., and Carnot Nelson
    1964   "Experimental analysis of resource location in problem solving groups." Sociometry 27 (4, December): 488–501. P.A. 39:7632; S.A. 13:B5876.
254. Baranowski, Thomas A., and David D. Summers
    1972   "Perception of response alternatives in a prisoner's dilemma game." Journal of Personality and Social Psychology 21 (1): 35–40.
255. Barash, David P.
    1972   "Human ethology: The snack-bar security syndrome." Psychological Reports 31 (2, October): 577–578. P.A. 49:6787.
256.   1973   "Human ethology: Personal space reiterated." Environment and Behavior 5 (1, March): 67–72. P.A. 50:8795.
257. Barber, James D.
    1966   Power in Committees. Chicago: Rand McNally.
258. Barber, Theodore X., and Maurice J. Silver
    1968   "Fact, fiction, and the experimenter bias effect." Psychological Bulletin Monograph Supplement 70 (pt. 2): 1–29.
259. Bare, Carole E., and Rie R. Mitchell
    1972   "Experimental evaluation of sensitivity training." Journal of Applied Behavioral Science 8 (3): 263–276.
260. Barefoot, John C., Howard Hoople, and David McClay
    1972   "Avoidance of an act which would violate personal space." Psychonomic Science 28 (4, August): 205–206. P.A. 49:4378.

261. Barilari, F., E. Hamuy, R. Ganzarain, and I. Matte
      1958   ("Contribution to the study of sociometric relations: Their effect on
              group influence.") Sociologia 20 (1, March): 18–26. S.A. 12:A8713.
262. Barker, Roger G.
      1942   "The social interrelations of strangers and acquaintances." Sociome-
              try 5: 169–179. P.A. 16:4446.
263. 1951   One Boy's Day: A Specimen Record of Behavior. New York: Har-
              per. P.A. 25:7962.
264. Barker, Roger G., Tamara Dembo, and Kurt Lewin
      1941   "Frustration and regression: An experiment with young children."
              University of Iowa Studies in Child Welfare 18, No. 1.
265. Barker, Roger G., Jacob S. Kounin, and Herbert F. Wright (eds.)
      1943   Child Behavior and Development. New York: McGraw-Hill. P.A. 18:
              1929.
266. Barker, Roger G., and Herbert F. Wright
      1949   "Psychological ecology and the problem of psycho-social develop-
              ment." Child Development 20 (3): 131–143. P.A. 24:4509.
267. Barnard, Chester I.
      1938   The Functions of the Executive. Cambridge, Mass.: Harvard Univer-
              sity Press.
268. Barnes, John A.
      1969   "Graph theory and social networks: A technical comment on con-
              nectedness and connectivity." Sociology 3 (2, May): 215–232. S.A.
              18:E1777.
269. Barnlund, Dean C.
      1955   "Experiments in leadership training for decision-making groups."
              Speech Monographs 22: 1–14. P.A. 30:768.
270. 1959   "A comparative study of individual, majority, and group judgment."
              Journal of Abnormal and Social Psychology 58: 55–60. P.A. 34:700.
271. 1962   "Consistency of emergent leadership in groups with changing tasks
              and members." Speech Monographs 29: 45–52. P.A. 37:1124.
272. Barnlund, Dean C., and Carroll Harland
      1963   "Propinquity and prestige as determinants of communication net-
              works." Sociometry 26 (4): 467–479.
273. Barocas, Ralph, and Leon Gorlow
      1967   "Religious affiliation, religious activities, and conformity." Psycho-
              logical Reports 20: 366.
274. Barocas, Ralph, and Paul Karoly
      1972   "Effects of physical appearance on social responsiveness." Psycho-
              logical Reports 31 (2, October): 495–500. P.A. 49:6789.
275. Baron, Penny H.
      1974   "Self-esteem, ingratiation, and evaluation of unknown others."
              Journal of Personality and Social Psychology 30 (1, July): 104–109.
              P.A. 52:12294.
276. Baron, Penny H., Robert S. Baron, and Gard Roper
      1974   "External validity and the risky shift: Empirical limits and theoreti-
              cal implications. Journal of Personality and Social Psychology 30
              (1, July): 95–103. P.A. 52:12295.
277. Baron, Reuben M., James Jackson, and Barry Fish
      1972   "Long- and short-term determinants of social reinforcer effective-
              ness." Journal of Personality and Social Psychology 24 (1): 122–
              131.
278. Baron, Robert A.
      1970   "Magnitude of model's apparent pain and ability to aid the model as
              determinants of observer reaction time." Psychonomic Science 21
              (4, November): 196–197. P.A. 46:1054.
279. 1971a   "Aggression as a function of magnitude of victim's pain cues, level of
              prior anger arousal, and aggressor-victim similarity." Journal of Per-
              sonality and Social Psychology 18 (1): 48–54.
280. 1971b   "Magnitude of victim's pain cues and level of prior anger arousal as
              determinants of adult aggressive behavior." Journal of Personality

and Social Psychology 17 (3, March): 236–243. P.A. 46:1053.

281.   1971c   "Exposure to an aggressive model and apparent probability of retaliation from the victim as determinants of adult aggressive behavior." Journal of Experimental Social Psychology 7 (3, May): 343–355. P.A. 48:2862.

282.   1971d   "Aggression as a function of audience presence and prior anger arousal." Journal of Experimental Social Psychology 7 (5): 515–523.

283.   1971e   "Behavioral effect of interpersonal attraction: Compliance with requests from liked and disliked others." Psychonomic Science 25 (6, December): 325–326. P.A. 48:8991.

284.   1971f   "Effects of presence of an audience and level of prior anger arousal on adult aggressive behavior." Proceedings of the 79th Annual Convention of the American Psychological Association 6 (pt. 1): 235–236.

285.   1972a   "Aggression as a function of ambient temperature and prior anger arousal." Journal of Personality and Social Psychology 21 (2): 183–189.

286.   1972b   "Reducing the influence of an aggressive model: The restraining effects of peer censure." Journal of Experimental Social Psychology 8 (3): 266–275.

287.   1973a   "The 'foot-in-the-door' phenomenon: Mediating effects of size of first request and sex of requester." Bulletin of the Psychonomic Society 2 (2, August): 113–114. P.A. 51:9026.

288.   1973b   "Threatened retaliation from the victim as an inhibitor of physical aggression." Journal of Research in Personality 7 (2, September): 103–115. P.A. 51:7046.

289.   1974a   "Aggression as a function of victim's pain cues, level of prior anger arousal, and exposure to an aggressive model." Journal of Personality and Social Psychology 29 (1): 117–124.

290.   1974b   "The aggression-inhibiting influence of heightened sexual arousal." Journal of Personality and Social Psychology 30 (3): 318–322.

291. Baron, Robert A., and Rodney L. Ball
    1974   "The aggression-inhibiting influence of nonhostile humor." Journal of Experimental Social Psychology 10 (1): 23–33.

292. Baron, Robert A., and Paul A. Bell
    1973   "Effects of heightened sexual arousal on physical aggression." Proceedings of the 81st Annual Convention of the American Psychological Association 8: 171–172.

293. Baron, Robert A., and Rebecca J. Eggleston
    1972   "Performance on the 'aggression machine': Motivation to help or harm?" Psychonomic Science 26 (6, March): 321–322. P.A. 48: 11426.

294. Baron, Robert A., and Sandra F. Lawton
    1972   "Environmental influences on aggression: The facilitation of modeling effects by high ambient temperatures." Psychonomic Science 26 (2, January): 80–82. P.A. 48:8992.

295. Baron, Robert S., Kenneth L. Dion, Penny H. Baron, and Norman Miller
    1971   "Group consensus and cultural values as determinants of risk taking." Journal of Personality and Social Psychology 20 (3): 446–455.

296. Baron, Robert S., Thomas C. Monson, and Penny H. Baron
    1973   "Conformity pressure as a determinant of risk taking: Replication and extension." Journal of Personality and Social Psychology 28 (3, December): 406–413. P.A. 51:7047.

297. Baron, Robert S., Gard Roper, and Penny H. Baron
    1974   "Group discussion and the stingy shift." Journal of Personality and Social Psychology 30 (4): 538–545.

298. Barr, John A.
    1955   "A multi-question sociometric procedure." Personnel and Guidance Journal 33: 527–530. P.A. 30:2687.

299. Barrett-Lennard, Godfrey T.
    1973   "The intensive group experience: Experiential learning groups in

practice: General process description and guidelines." Canada's Mental Health 73 (January, Supplement). P.A. 51:941.

300. Barron, Frank
      1952   "Some personality correlates of independence of judgment." Journal of Personality 21: 287-297.
301. Barron, Margaret E., and Gilbert K. Krulee
      1948   "Case study of a basic skill training group." Journal of Social Issues 4 (2, Spring): 10-30. P.A. 23:676.
302. Bar-Tal, Daniel, and Martin S. Greenberg
      1974   "Effect of passage of time on reactions to help and harm." Psychological Reports 34 (2, April): 617-618. P.A. 52:12293.
303. Bartlett, Claude J.
      1959a   "Dimensions of leadership behavior in classroom discussion groups." Journal of Educational Psychology 50: 280-284. P.A. 34:7520; P.A. 1KB80B.
304.   1959b   "The relationship between self-ratings and peer ratings on a leadership behavior scale." Personnel Psychology 12: 237-246. P.A. 34: 4165.
305. Barton, K., and R. B. Cattell
      1972   "Real and perceived similarities in personality between spouses: Test of 'likeness' versus 'completeness' theories. Psychological Reports 31 (1, August): 15-18. P.A. 49:4379.
306. Barton, W. A., Jr.
      1926   "The effect of group activity and individual effort in developing ability to solve problems in first-year algebra." Educational Administration and Supervision 12: 512-518.
307. Bartos, Otomar J.
      1964   "A model of negotiation and the recency effect." Sociometry 27 (3, September): 311-326. S.A. 13:B4922.
308.   1967   Simple Models of Group Behavior. New York: Columbia University Press. S.A. 16:D4106.
309. Bass, Alan R., and Fred E. Fiedler
      1961   "Interpersonal prediction scores and their components as predictors of personal adjustment." Journal of Abnormal and Social Psychology 62 (2, March): 442-445.
310. Bass, Bernard M.
      1949   "An analysis of the leaderless group discussion." Journal of Applied Psychology 33: 527-533. P.A. 24:4043.
311.   1951   "Situational tests: II. Leaderless group discussion variables." Educational and Psychological Measurement 11: 196-207. P.A. 26:3041.
312.   1954a   "The leaderless group discussion." Psychological Bulletin 51: 465-492. P.A. 29:3777.
313.   1954b   "The leaderless group discussion as a leadership evaluation instrument." Personnel Psychology 7: 470-477. P.A. 29:7062.
314.   1955   "Authoritarianism or acquiescence." Journal of Abnormal and Social Psychology 51: 616-623. P.A. 31:2534.
315.   1957   "Reply to Messick and Jackson's comments on authoritarianism or acquiescence." Journal of Abnormal and Social Psychology 54: 426-427.
316.   1959   "Effects of motivation on consistency of performance in groups." Educational and Psychological Measurement 19: 247-252. P.A. 34: 4166.
317.   1960a   Leadership, Psychology, and Organizational Behavior. New York: Harper.
318.   1960b   "Measures of average influence and change in agreement of rankings by a group of judges." Sociometry 23 (2, June): 195-202. P.A. 35: 3354; S.A. A2684.
319.   1961a   "Conformity, deviation, and a general theory of interpersonal behavior." In I. A. Berg and B. M. Bass (eds.), Conformity and Deviation, pp. 38-100. New York: Harper. P.A. 36:4GE38B.
320.   1961b   "Some aspects of attempted, successful, and effective leadership." Journal of Applied Psychology 45: 120-122. P.A. 36:3GF20B.

321. 1961c "Some observations about a general theory of leadership and inter-
             personal behavior." In L. Petrullo and B. M. Bass (eds.), Leadership
             and Interpersonal Behavior, pp. 3–9. New York: Holt, Rinehart &
             Winston.
322. 1963   "Amount of participation, coalescence, and profitability of decision
             making discussions." Journal of Abnormal and Social Psychology 67
             (1): 92–94. S.A. 12:B3222.
323. Bass, Bernard M., and Charles H. Coates
      1952   "Forecasting officer potential using the leaderless group discussion."
             Journal of Abnormal and Social Psychology 47: 321–325. P.A. 27:
             2607.
324. Bass, Bernard M., and George Dunteman
      1963a "Behavior in groups as a function of self-interaction and task orien-
             tation." Journal of Abnormal and Social Psychology 66 (5): 419–
             428. P.A. 38:2579; S.A. 12:B2401.
325. 1963b "Biases in the evaluation of one's own group, its allies and oppo-
             nents." Journal of Conflict Resolution 7 (1, March): 16–20. S.A. 14:
             B8339.
326. 1964   "Defensiveness and susceptibility to coercion as a function of self-,
             interaction-, and task-orientation." Journal of Social Psychology 62
             (April): 335–341.
327. Bass, Bernard M., Eugene L. Gaier, F. J. Farese, and Austin W. Flint
      1957   "An objective method for studying behavior in groups." Psychologi-
             cal Reports 3: 265–280. P.A. 32:4059.
328. Bass, Bernard M., and Stanley Klubeck
      1952   "Effects of seating arrangement on leaderless group discussions."
             Journal of Abnormal and Social Psychology 47: 724–727. P.A. 27:
             3410.
329. Bass, Bernard M., Stanley Klubeck, and Cecil R. Wurster
      1953   "Factors influencing reliability and validity of leaderless group dis-
             cussion assessment." Journal of Applied Psychology 37: 26–30. P.A.
             28:671.
330. Bass, Bernard M., Charles R. McGehee, William C. Hawkins, Paul C. Young, and
     Arnold S. Gebel
      1953   "Personality variables related to leaderless group discussion behav-
             ior." Journal of Abnormal and Social Psychology 48: 120–128. P.A.
             28:925.
331. Bass, Bernard M., and Fay-Tyler M. Norton
      1951   "Group size and leaderless discussions." Journal of Applied Psychol-
             ogy 35: 397–400. P.A. 26:6175.
332. Bass, Bernard M., Margaret W. Pryer, Eugene L. Gaier, and Austin W. Flint
      1958   "Interacting effects of control, motivation, group practice, and prob-
             lem difficulty on attempted leadership." Journal of Abnormal and
             Social Psychology 56: 352–358.
333. Bass, Bernard M., and Otey L. White, Jr.
      1951   "Situational tests: III. Observers' rating of leaderless group discus-
             sion participants as indicators of external leadership status." Educa-
             tional and Psychological Measurement 11: 355–361. P.A. 27:5779.
334. Bass, Bernard M., and Cecil R. Wurster
      1953a "Effects of company rank on LGD performance of oil refinery su-
             pervisors." Journal of Applied Psychology 37: 100–104.
335. 1953b "Effects of the nature of the problem on LGD performance." Jour-
             nal of Applied Psychology 37: 96–99. (See also pp. 100–104.) P.A.
             28:1595.
336. Bassett, R. E.
      1944   "Cliques in a student body of stable membership." Sociometry 7:
             290–302. P.A. 19:457.
337. Batchelor, James P., and George R. Goethals
      1972   "Spatial arrangements in freely formed groups." Sociometry 35 (2,
             June): 270–279. P.A. 49:742; S.A. 21:73G4900.
338. Batchelor, Thomas R., and Abraham Tesser
      1971   "Attitude base as a moderator of the attitude similarity-attraction

relationship." Journal of Personality and Social Psychology 19 (2, August): 229-236. P.A. 47:2820.

339. Bates, Alan P.
1952 "Some sociometric aspects of social ranking in a small, face-to-face group." Sociometry 15: 330-341. P.A. 27:7105.

340. Bates, Alan P., and Nicholas Babchuk
1961 "The primary group: A reappraisal." Sociological Quarterly 2 (3, July): 181-191. P.A. 37:1091; S.A. A2711.

341. Bates, Alan P., and Jerry S. Cloyd
1956 "Toward the development of operations for defining group norms and members' roles." Sociometry 19: 26-39. P.A. 31:2736; S.A. 3946.

342. Bates, Frederick L.
1956 "Position, role, and status: A reformulation of concepts." Social Forces 34: 313-321. P.A. 31:4469.

343. 1957 "A conceptual analysis of group structure." Social Forces 36: 103-111.

344. Bateson, Nicholas
1966 "Familiarization, group discussion, and risk taking." Journal of Experimental Social Psychology 2 (2, April): 119-129. P.A. 40:8786.

345. Bath, Kent E., and Daniel L. Daly
1972 "Self-disclosure: Relationships to self-described personality and sex differences." Psychological Reports 31: 623-628.

346. Bauer, Ernest A.
1973 "Personal space: A study of blacks and whites." Sociometry 36 (3, September): 402-408. P.A. 52:2869.

347. Bauer, Richard H., and James H. Turner
1974 "Betting behavior in sexually homogeneous and heterogeneous groups." Psychological Reports 34 (1, February): 251-258. P.A. 52:7520.

348. Baum, Andrew, Marc Riess, and John O'Hara
1974 "Architectural variants of reaction to spatial invasion." Environment and Behavior 6 (1, March): 91-100. P.A. 52:12240.

349. Baum, Andrew, and Stuart Valins
1973 "Residential environments, group size, and crowding." Proceedings of the 81st Annual Convention of the American Psychological Association 8 (pt. 1): 211-212.

350. Baumgold, John
1971 "Developing sensitivity behind bars." Sociological Inquiry 41 (2, Spring): 211-216.

351. Baur, E. Jackson
1960 "Public opinion and the primary group." American Sociological Review 25 (2, April): 208-219. P.A. 35:2104.

352. Bavelas, Alex
1942 "Morale and the training of leaders." In G. Watson (ed.), Civilian Morale, pp. 143-165. New York: Reynal & Hitchcock.

353. 1948 "A mathematical model for group structures." Applied Anthropology 7: 16-30. P.A. 23:1731.

354. 1950 "Communication patterns in task oriented groups." Journal of the Accoustical Society of America 22: 725-730. (See also Cartwright and Zander, 1953, 1960, 1968.) P.A. 27:384.

355. 1952 "Communication patterns in problem-solving groups." In H. von Foerster et al. (eds.), Cybernetics: Circular Causal and Feedback Mechanisms in Biological and Social Systems. New York: Josiah Macy, Jr., Foundation. S.A. 1751.

356. 1959 "Group size, interaction, and structural environment." In B. Schaffner (ed.), Group Processes: Transactions of the Fourth Conference, pp. 133-179. New York: Josiah Macy, Jr., Foundation. P.A. 34: 4284.

357. Bavelas, Alex, Albert H. Hastorf, Alan E. Gross, and W. Richard Kite
1965 "Experiments on the alteration of group structure." Journal of Experimental Social Psychology 1 (1, January): 55-70. (See also

Cartwright and Zander, 1968.) P.A. 39:9988.
358. Baxter, James C.
    1970   "Interpersonal spacing in natural settings." Sociometry 33 (4, De-
            cember): 444–456. P.A. 46:8909.
359. Baxter, James C., and Bettye F. Deanovich
    1970   "Anxiety arousing effects of inappropriate crowding." Journal of
            Consulting and Clinical Psychology 35 (2, October): 174–178. P.A.
            45:4106.
360. Bayes, Marjorie A.
    1972   "Behavioral cues of interpersonal warmth." Journal of Consulting
            and Clinical Psychology 39 (2, October): 333–339. P.A. 49:4381.
361. Beach, Carla M., and Kenneth E. Lloyd
    1965   "Effect of number of prior reinforcements on social convergence."
            Psychonomic Science 3 (4): 149–150. P.A. 39:15021.
362. Beach, Leeroy, and Michael Wertheimer
    1961   "A free response approach to the study of person cognition." Jour-
            nal of Abnormal and Social Psychology 62 (2, March): 367–374.
363. Beach, Leslie R.
    1962   "Use of instructorless small groups in a social psychology course."
            Psychological Reports 10: 209–210.
364. Beal, George M., Joe M. Bohlen, and J. Neil Raudabaugh
    1962   Leadership and Dynamic Group Action. Ames: Iowa State Univer-
            sity Press. P.A. 38:881.
365. Beane, William E., and Elmer A. Lemke
    1971   "Group variables influencing the transfer of conceptual behavior."
            Journal of Educational Psychology 62 (3): 215–218.
366. Beasley, J.
    1958   "Comparison of the performance of individuals and three-member
            groups in a maze learning situation." Perceptual and Motor Skills 8:
            291–294. P.A. 34:746.
367. Beaton, Albert E.
    1966   "An inter-battery factor and analytic approach to clique analysis."
            Sociometry 29 (2, June): 135–145. P.A. 40:10024; S.A. 15:C3472.
368. Beaver, Alma P.
    1929   "A preliminary report on a study of a preschool 'gang.'" In D. S.
            Thomas (ed.), Some New Techniques for Studying Social Behavior,
            pp. 99–117. New York: Columbia University, Teachers College.
369.   1932   "The initiation of social contacts by pre-school children." Child De-
            velopment Monographs No. 7.
370. Bechtel, Robert B., and Howard M. Rosenfeld
    1966   "Expectations of social acceptance and compatibility as related to
            status discrepancy and social motives." Journal of Personality and
            Social Psychology 3 (3): 344–349.
371. Bechterev, W., and M. Lange
    1924   ("The results of the experiments in the field of collective reflex-
            ology.") Zeitschrift für Angewandte Psychologie 24: 305–344.
372. Becker, Franklin D.
    1973   "Study of spatial markers." Journal of Personality and Social Psy-
            chology 26 (3, June): 439–445. P.A. 50:11202.
373. Becker, Franklin D., and Clara Mayo
    1971   "Delineating personal distance and territoriality." Environment and
            Behavior 3 (4, December): 375–381. P.A. 48:2863.
374. Becker, Franklin D., Robert Sommer, Joan Bee, and Bart Oxley
    1973   "College classroom ecology." Sociometry 36 (4): 514–525.
375. Becker, Howard, and Ruth H. Useem
    1942   "Sociological analysis of the dyad." American Sociological Review
            7: 13–26. P.A. 16:3661.
376. Becker, Lee A., and Timothy C. Brock
    1966   "Prospective recipients' estimates of withheld evaluation." Journal
            of Personality and Social Psychology 4 (2): 147–154. P.A. 40:
            11096.

377. Becker, Robert E., Martin Harrow, Boris M. Astrachan, Thomas Detre, and James C. Miller
   1968   "Influence of the leader on the activity level of therapy groups." Journal of Social Psychology 74 (February): 39–51.
378. Becker, Selwyn W., and Jean Carroll
   1962   "Ordinal position and conformity." Journal of Abnormal and Social Psychology 65 (2): 129–131.
379. Becker, Selwyn W., Melvin J. Lerner, and Jean Carroll
   1964   "Conformity as a function of birth order, payoff, and type of group pressure." Journal of Abnormal and Social Psychology 69 (3, September): 318–323. P.A. 39:4852.
380.   1966   "Conformity as a function of birth order and type of group pressure: A verification." Journal of Personality and Social Psychology 3 (2, February): 242–244. P.A. 40:4177; S.A. 15:C3473.
381. Beckwith, Jack, Marvin A. Iverson, and Mary E. Reuder
   1965   "Test anxiety, task relevance of group experience, and change in level of aspiration." Journal of Personality and Social Psychology 1 (6): 579–588.
382. Bedell, Jeffrey, and Frank Sistrunk
   1973   "Power, opportunity costs, and sex in a mixed-motive game." Journal of Personality and Social Psychology 25 (2, February): 219–226. P.A. 50:882.
383. Beebe, Brenda, Kenneth Buback, James McGlone, and Mike Dinoff
   1972   "Simple requesting behavior: Responses toward stereotypes." Psychological Reports 30 (3, June): 788–790. P.A. 49:2317.
384. Beer, M., R. Buckhout, M. W. Horowitz, and S. Levy
   1959   "Some perceived properties of the difference between leaders and non-leaders." Journal of Psychology 47: 49–56.
385. Beier, Ernst G., Ascanio M. Rossi, and Reed L. Garfield
   1961   "Similarity plus dissimilarity of personality: Basis for friendship?" Psychological Reports 8: 3–8. P.A. 36:1GE08B.
386. Beigel, Astrid
   1973   "Resistance to change: Differential effects of favourable and unfavourable initial communications." British Journal of Social and Clinical Psychology 12 (2, June): 153–158. P.A. 51:3009.
387. Bell, Bill D., and Gary G. Stanfield
   1973   "An interactionist appraisal of impression formation: The 'central trait' hypothesis revisited." Kansas Journal of Sociology 9 (1, Spring): 55–68. P.A. 51:3010.
388. Bell, Cecil, John Cheney, and Clara Mayo
   1972   "Structural and subject variation in communication networks." Human Relations 25 (1, February): 1–8. P.A. 49:2318.
389. Bell, Graham B., and R. L. French
   1950   "Consistency of individual leadership position in small groups of varying membership." Journal of Abnormal and Social Psychology 45: 764–767. (See also Hare, Borgatta, and Bales, 1955, 1965.)
390. Bell, Graham B., and Harry E. Hall, Jr.
   1954   "The relationship between leadership and empathy." Journal of Abnormal and Social Psychology 49: 156–157. P.A. 28:7326.
391. Bell, Graham B., and Rhoda Stolper
   1955   "An attempt at validation of the Empathy Test." Journal of Applied Psychology 39: 442–443. P.A. 30:7186.
392. Bell, Paul R., and Bruce D. Jamieson
   1970   "Publicity of initial decisions and the risky shift phenomenon." Journal of Experimental Social Psychology 6 (3, July): 329–345. P.A. 45:622.
393. Bellows, Roger
   1959   Creative Leadership. Englewood Cliffs, N.J.: Prentice-Hall. P.A. 35: 3373.
394. Beloff, Halla
   1958   "Two forms of social conformity: acquiescence and conventional-

ity." Journal of Abnormal and Social Psychology 56: 99–104.

395. Belovicz, Meyer W., and Frederic E. Finch
1971   "Comments on 'The risky shift in group betting.'" Journal of Experimental Social Psychology 7 (1): 81–83.

396. Belyaeff, B. V.
1929   "The problem of the collective and of its experimental-psychological study." Psychologica 2: 179–214; 1930, 3: 488–549.

397. Bem, Daryl J.
1965   "An experimental analysis of self-persuasion." Journal of Experimental Social Psychology 1: 199–218.

398.   1967a   "Self-perception: An alternative interpretation of cognitive dissonance phenomena." Psychological Review 74: 183–200.

399.   1967b   "Reply to Judson Mills." Psychological Review 74 (6): 536. P.A. 42:2500.

400.   1968   "The epistemological status of interpersonal simulations: A reply to Jones, Linder, Kiesler, Zanna, and Brehm." Journal of Experimental Social Psychology 4 (3, July): 270–274. P.A. 43:2539.

401.   1972   "Self-perception theory." In L. Berkowitz (ed.), Advances in Experimental Social Psychology, vol. 6, pp. 1–62. New York: Academic Press.

402. Bem, Daryl J., and H. K. McConnell
1970   "Testing the self-perception explanation of dissonance phenomena: On the salience of premanipulation attitudes." Journal of Personality and Social Psychology 14: 23–31.

403. Bem, Daryl J., Michael A. Wallach, and Nathan Kogan
1965   "Group decision making under risk of aversive consequences." Journal of Personality and Social Psychology 1 (5): 453–460. S.A. 14: B9173.

404. Bender, I. E., and Albert H. Hastorf
1950   "The perception of persons: Forecasting another person's responses in three personality scales." Journal of Abnormal and Social Psychology 45:556–561. P.A. 25:988.

405. Benjamin, Lorna S.
1974   "Structural analysis of social behavior." Psychological Review 81 (5): 392–425.

406. Benlifer, Virginia E., and Sara B. Kiesler
1972   "Psychotherapists' perceptions of adjustment and attraction toward children described as in therapy." Journal of Experimental Research in Personality 6 (2-3, December): 169–177. P.A. 51:967.

407. Benne, Kenneth D., and Grace Levit
1953   "The nature of groups and helping groups improve their operation." Review of Educational Research 23: 289–308. P.A. 28:7327.

408. Benne, Kenneth D., and B. Muntyan
1951   Human Relations in Curriculum Change. New York: Dryden.

409. Benne, Kenneth D., and Paul Sheats
1948   "Functional roles of group members." Journal of Social Issues 4 (2): 41–49. P.A. 23:677.

410. Bennett, Charles R., and Svenn Lindskold
1971   "Procedural artifact in risky-shift research." Proceedings of the 79th Annual Convention of the American Psychological Association 6 (1): 249–250.

411. Bennett, Charles R., Svenn Lindskold, and Russell Bennett
1973   "The effects of group size and discussion time on the risky shift." Journal of Social Psychology 91 (1, October): 137–147. P.A. 51: 10996.

412. Bennett, Edith B.
1955   "Discussion, decision, commitment, and consensus in 'group decision.'" Human Relations 8: 251–274. (See also Maccoby, Newcomb, and Hartley, 1958.)

413. Bennett, Russell, Ronald D. Price, and Svenn Lindskold
1973   "Is the moral revolution an illusion? Decisions for self and others in situations involving values." Proceedings of the 81st Annual Conven-

tion of the American Psychological Association 8 (pt. 1): 311–312.

414. Bennis, Warren G.
    1961a   "Defenses against 'Depressive anxiety' in groups: The case of the absent leader." Merrill-Palmer Quarterly 7 (1, January): 3–30. S.A. A2727.

415.   1961b   "Revisionist theory of leadership." Harvard Business Review 39 (1): 26–36. P.A. 36:3GF26B.

416. Bennis, Warren G., and Dean Peabody
    1962   "The conceptualization of two personality orientations and sociometric choice." Journal of Social Psychology 57 (1, June): 203–215. P.A. 37:3026.

417. Bennis, Warren G., and Herbert A. Shepard
    1956   "A theory of group development." Human Relations 9: 415–437.

418. Benton, Alan A.
    1971a   "Productivity, distributive justice, and bargaining among children." Journal of Personality and Social Psychology 18 (1): 68–78.

419.   1971b   "Some unexpected consequences of jeopardy." Proceedings of the 79th Annual Convention of the American Psychological Association 6 (pt. 1): 223–224. P. A. 46:2889.

420.   1972a   "Accountability and negotiations between group representatives." Proceedings of the 80th Annual Convention of the American Psychological Association 7 (pt. 1): 227–228. P.A. 48:4843.

421.   1972b   "Reactions to various patterns of deceit in a mixed-motive game." Psychonomic Science 29 (6-A, December): 333–336. P.A. 50:883.

422.   1973   "Reactions to demands to win from an opposite sex opponent." Journal of Personality 41 (3, September): 430–442. P.A. 51:5078.

423. Benton, Alan A., Eric R. Gelber, Harold H. Kelley, and Barry A. Liebling
    1968   "Reactions to various degrees of deceit in a mixed-motive relationship." Proceedings of the 76th Annual Convention of the American Psychological Association 3: 401–402.

424.   1969   "Reactions to various degrees of deceit in a mixed-motive relationship." Journal of Personality and Social Psychology 12 (2): 170–180. P.A. 43:12892.

425. Benton, Alan A., Harold H. Kelley, and Barry Liebling
    1972   "Effects of extremity of offers and concession rate on the outcomes of bargaining." Journal of Personality and Social Psychology 24 (1, October): 73–83. P.A. 49:4382.

426. Beran, W., R. S. Albert, P. R. Loiseaux, P. N. Mayfield, and G. Wright
    1958   "Jury behavior as a function of the prestige of the foreman and the nature of leadership." Journal of Public Law 7: 419–449. P.A. 34: 5598.

427. Berelson, Bernard
    1952   Content Analysis in Communication Research. Glencoe, Ill.: Free Press. P.A. 27:7730.

428.   1954   "Content analysis." In G. Lindzey (ed.), Handbook of Social Psychology, pp. 488–522. Cambridge, Mass.: Addison-Wesley. P.A. 29: 3956.

429. Berenda, Ruth W.
    1950   The Influence of the Group on the Judgments of Children. New York: King's Crown Press.

430. Berg, Irwin A.
    1961   "Measuring deviant behavior by means of deviant response sets." In I. A. Berg and B. M. Bass (eds.), Conformity and Deviation, pp. 328–379. New York: Harper. P.A. 36:4GE28B.

431. Berg, Irwin A., and Bernard M. Bass (eds.)
    1961   Conformity and Deviation. New York: Harper P.A. 36:4GE49B.

432. Berg, Jacob
    1955   "Co-operation without communication and observation." Journal of Social Psychology 41: 287–296. P.A. 30:5843.

433. Berger, Charles R.
    1973   "Attributional communication, situational involvement, self-esteem and interpersonal attraction." Journal of Communication 23 (3,

September): 284–305. P.A. 51:10997.

434. Berger, Joseph, Bernard P. Cohen, J. Laurie Snell, and Morris Zelditch, Jr.
    1962   Types of Formalization in Small-Group Research. Boston: Hough-
            ton Mifflin.

435. Berger, Joseph, Bernard P. Cohen, and Morris Zelditch, Jr.
    1972   "Status characteristics and social interaction." American Sociologi-
            cal Review 37 (3, June): 241–255.

436. Berger, Joseph, and M. Hamit Fisek
    1970   "Consistent and inconsistent status characteristics and the determi-
            nation of power and prestige orders." Sociometry 33 (3, Septem-
            ber): 287–304. P.A. 46:6728.

437. Berger, Seymour M.
    1971   "Observer perseverance as related to a model's success: A social com-
            parison analysis." Journal of Personality and Social Psychology 19
            (3, September): 341–350. P.A. 47:2822.

438. Berger, Stephen E., and Kenneth N. Anchor
    1970   "Disclosure process in group interaction." Proceedings of the 78th
            Annual Convention of the American Psychological Association 5
            (pt. 2): 529–530. P.A. 44:18550.

439. Berger, Stephen E., and James T. Tedeschi
    1969   "Aggressive behavior of delinquent, dependent, and 'normal' white
            and black boys in social conflicts." Journal of Experimental Social
            Psychology 5 (3): 352–370.

440. Bergeron, Arthur P., and Mark P. Zanna
    1973   "Group membership and belief similarity as determinants of inter-
            personal attraction in Peru." Journal of Cross-Cultural Psychology 4
            (4, December): 397–411. P.A. 52:7521.

441. Berkowitz, Leonard
    1953   "Sharing leadership in small, decision-making groups." Journal of
            Abnormal and Social Psychology 48: 231–238. (See also Hare,
            Borgatta, and Bales, 1955, 1965.) P.A. 28:2390.

442.   1954a   "Group standards, cohesiveness, and productivity." Human Rela-
            tions 7: 509–519. P.A. 29:5443; S.A. 1484.

443.   1954b   "Studies in group norms: The perception of group attitudes as re-
            lated to criteria of group effectiveness." USAF Personnel Training
            Research Center, Research Bulletin No. AFPTRC-TR-54-62. P.A.
            29:8500.

444.   1956a   "Group norms among bomber crews: Patterns of perceived crew atti-
            tudes, 'actual' crew attitudes, and crew liking related to aircrew
            effectiveness in Far Eastern combat." Sociometry 19: 141–153.

445.   1956b   "Personality and group position." Sociometry 19: 210–222. (See
            also Hare, Borgatta, and Bales, 1965.)

446.   1956c   "Social desirability and frequency of influence attempts as factors in
            leadership choice." Journal of Personality 24: 424–435. P.A. 31:722.

447.   1957a   "Effects of perceived dependency relationships upon conformity to
            group expectations." Journal of Abnormal and Social Psychology
            55: 350–354.

448.   1957b   "Liking for the group and the perceived merit of the group's behav-
            ior." Journal of Abnormal and Social Psychology 54: 353–357.

449.   1960   "Repeated frustrations and expectations in hostility arousal." Jour-
            nal of Abnormal and Social Psychology 60 (3): 422–429. P.A. 35:
            4807.

450. Berkowitz, Leonard (ed.)
    1964–   Advances in Experimental Social Psychology. Vols. 1–4. New York:
    1968   Academic Press.

451. Berkowitz, Leonard
    1965   "Cognitive dissonance and communication preferences." Human Re-
            lations 18 (4, November): 361–372. P.A. 40:4178.

452.   1969   "Resistance to improper dependency relationships." Journal of Ex-
            perimental Social Psychology 5 (3): 283–294. P.A. 44:5067.

453.   1970   "Aggressive humor as a stimulus to aggressive responses." Journal of
            Personality and Social Psychology 16 (4): 710–717.

454.   1971   "The 'weapons effect,' demand characteristics, and the myth of the

compliant subject." Journal of Personality and Social Psychology 20 (3): 332-338.

455.   1973   "Reactance and the unwillingness to help others." Psychological Bulletin 79 (5, May): 310-317. P.A. 50:11203.

456. Berkowitz, Leonard, and Joseph T. Alioto
     1973   "The meaning of an observed event as a determinant of its aggressive consequences." Journal of Personality and Social Psychology 28 (2): 206-217.

457. Berkowitz, Leonard, and William H. Connor
     1966   "Success, failure, and social responsibility." Journal of Personality and Social Psychology 4 (6): 664-669.

458. Berkowitz, Leonard, and Louise R. Daniels
     1963   "Responsibility and dependency." Journal of Abnormal and Social Psychology 66 (5): 429-436. S.A. 12:B2402.

459.   1964   "Affecting the salience of the social responsibility norm: Effects of past help on the response to dependency relationships." Journal of Abnormal and Social Psychology 68 (3, March): 275-281.

460. Berkowitz, Leonard, and Philip Friedman
     1967   "Some social class differences in helping behavior." Journal of Personality and Social Psychology 5 (2): 217-225.

461. Berkowitz, Leonard, and Robert C. Howard
     1959   "Reactions to opinion deviates as affected by affiliation need (n) and group member interdependence." Sociometry 22 (1, March): 81-91. P.A. 34:1151.

462. Berkowitz, Leonard, Sharon B. Klanderman, and Richard Harris
     1964   "Effects of experimenter awareness and sex of subject and experimenter on reactions to dependency relationship." Sociometry 27 (3, September): 327-337.

463. Berkowitz, Leonard, John P. Lepinski, and Eddy J. Angulo
     1969   "Awareness of own anger level and subsequent aggression." Journal of Personality and Social Psychology 11 (3): 293-300. P.A. 43: 8293.

464. Berkowitz, Leonard, and Bernard I. Levy
     1956   "Pride in group performance and group-task motivation." Journal of Abnormal and Social Psychology 53: 300-306. P.A. 32:4028.

465. Berkowitz, Leonard, Bernard I. Levy, and A. R. Harvey
     1957   "Effects of performance evaluations on group integration and motivation." Human Relations 10: 195-208. S.A. A1195.

466. Berkowitz, Leonard, and Richard M. Lundy
     1957   "Personality characteristics related to susceptibility to influence by peers or authority figures." Journal of Personality 25: 306-316. P.A. 32:2660.

467. Berkowitz, Leonard, and Jacqueline R. Macaulay
     1961   "Some effects of differences in status level and status stability." Human Relations 14 (2, May): 135-148. P.A. 36:2GC35B; S.A. 11: A4155.

468. Berkowitz, Norman H.
     1968   "Alternative measures of authoritarianism, response sets, and prediction in a two-person game." Journal of Social Psychology 74 (2, April): 233-242. P.A. 42:10509.

469. Berkowitz, Norman H., Lance Hylander, and Ray Bakaitis
     1973   "Defense, vulnerability, and co-operation in a mixed-motive game." Journal of Personality and Social Psychology 25 (3, March): 401-407. P.A. 50:4745.

470. Berkowitz, Norman H., and George H. Wolkon
     1964   "A forced choice form of the F scale — free of acquiescent response set." Sociometry 27 (1, March): 54-65.

471. Berkun, Mitchell M., and T. Meeland
     1958   "Sociometric effects of race and of combat performance." Sociometry 21: 145-149.

472. Berlew, David E.
     1961   "Interpersonal sensitivity and motive strength." Journal of Abnormal and Social Psychology 63 (2): 390-394.

473. Berlinck, Manoel
  1961   ("Social structure and sociometry.") Sociologia 23 (1, March): 13–
          24. S.A. 14:C0960.
474. Berlyne, D. E.
  1968   "Laughter, humor, and play." In G. Lindzey and E. Aronson (eds.),
          Handbook of Social Psychology, vol. 3, pp. 795–852. Reading,
          Mass.: Addison-Wesley.
475. Berman, John J., and Philip Brickman
  1971   "Standards for attribution of liking: Effects of sex, self-esteem, and
          other's attractiveness." Proceedings of the 79th Annual Convention
          of the American Psychological Association 6 (pt. 1): 271–272.
476. Bermant, Gordon, and Mark Starr
  1972   "Telling people what they are likely to do: Three experiments." Pro-
          ceedings of the 80th Annual Convention of the American Psycho-
          logical Association 7 (pt. 1): 171–172.
477. Bernard, Paul
  1973   ("Sociometric stratification and social networks.") Sociologie et So-
          ciété 5 (1, May): 127–150. S.A. 22:74G6135.
478. Berne, Eric
  1963   The Structure and Dynamics of Organizations and Groups. Philadel-
          phia: Lippincott. P.A. 38:5957.
479.   1964   Games People Play. New York: Grove.
480. Bernhardt, K. S., Dorothy A. Millichamp, Marion W. Charles, and Mary P.
     McFarland
  1937   "An analysis of the social contacts of pre-school children with the
          aid of motion pictures." University of Toronto Studies in Child De-
          velopment No. 10. P.A. 12:2672.
481. Bernstein, A., and H. L. Lennard
  1961   "Communication in the psychotherapy group." Journal of Commu-
          nications 11: 125–218. S.A. 10:A2943.
482. Berrien, F. Kenneth
  1961   "Homeostasis theory of groups: Implications for leadership." In L.
          Petrullo and B. M. Bass (eds.), Leadership and Interpersonal Behav-
          ior, pp. 82–99. New York: Holt, Rhinehart & Winston.
483.   1964   "Homeostasis in groups." In General Systems: Yearbook of the So-
          ciety for General Systems Research, vol. 9, pp. 205–217. Ann
          Arbor: University of Michigan Press. S.A. 14:B9174.
484. Berry, J. W.
  1967   "Independence and conformity in subsistence-level societies." Jour-
          nal of Personality and Social Psychology 7 (4, pt. 1): 415–418. P.A.
          42:3891.
485. Berscheid, Ellen, David Boye, and John M. Darley
  1968   "Effect of forced association upon voluntary choice to associate."
          Journal of Personality and Social Psychology 8 (1): 13–19.
486. Berscheid, Ellen, David Boye, and Elaine Walster
  1968   "Retaliation as a means of restoring equity." Journal of Personality
          and Social Psychology 10 (4): 370–376. P.A. 43:6848.
487. Berscheid, Ellen, Karen Dion, Elaine Walster, and William G. Walster
  1971   "Physical attractiveness and dating choice: A test of the matching
          hypothesis." Journal of Experimental and Social Psychology 7 (2):
          173–189.
488. Berscheid, Ellen, Elaine Walster, and Andrew Barclay
  1969   "Effect of time on tendency to compensate a victim." Psychological
          Reports 25 (2): 431–436. P.A. 44:5068.
489. Betz, Robert L.
  1973   "A proposed typology for group processes." Michigan Personnel and
          Guidance Journal 4 (2, Spring): 18–23. P.A. 52:796.
490. Beum, Corlin O., Jr., and Everett G. Brundage
  1950   "A method for analyzing the sociomatrix." Sociometry 13: 141–
          145. P.A. 27:2634.
491. Bhojak, B. L., and P. Mehta
  1970   "An investigation into the causes responsible for social rejection."

Indian Journal of Social Work 30 (4): 315-324. P.A. 44:16542.

492. Biber, Barbara, Lois B. Murphy, Louise P. Woodcock, and Irma S. Black
 1952   Life and Ways of the Seven-to-Eight Year Old. 2nd ed. New York: Basic Books. P.A. 27:6443.

493. Bickman, Leonard
 1971   "The effect of another bystander's ability to help on bystander intervention in an emergency." Journal of Experimental Social Psychology 7 (3, May): 367-379. P.A. 48:2864.

494.   1972   "Social influence and diffusion of responsibility in an emergency." Journal of Experimental Social Psychology 8 (5, September): 438-445. P.A. 49:6790.

495.   1974a   "Sex and helping behavior." Journal of Social Psychology 93 (1, June): 43-53. P.A. 52:12296.

496.   1974b   "Social roles and uniforms: Clothes make the person." Psychology Today 7 (11, April): 49-51. P.A. 52:7542.

497. Bickman, Leonard, and Mark Kamzan
 1973   "The effect of race and need on helping behavior." Journal of Social Psychology 89 (1, February): 73-77. P.A. 50:2908.

498. Bickman, Leonard, et al.
 1973   "Dormitory density and helping behavior." Environment and Behavior 5 (4, December): 465-490. P.A. 52:7499.

499. Biderman, Albert D.
 1959   "Effects of Communist indoctrination attempts: Some comments based on an Air Force prisoner-of-war study." Social Problems 6:304-313. P.A. 34:4168.

500. Bierhoff, H. W.
 1973   ("Cost and reward: A theory of social behavior.") Zeitschrift für Sozialpsychologie 4 (4): 297-317. P.A. 52:7500.

501. Bieri, James
 1953   "Changes in interpersonal perceptions following social interaction." Journal of Abnormal and Social Psychology 48: 61-66. P.A. 28: 673.

502. Bierman, Ralph, Robert R. Carkhuff, and Muriel Santilli
 1972   "Efficacy of empathic communication training groups for inner city pre-school teachers and family workers." Journal of Applied Behavioral Science 8 (2): 188-202.

503. Bikson, Tora K., and Jacqueline D. Goodchilds
 1973   "Situation, pair, and person as parameters in dyadic communication processes." Proceedings of the 81st Annual Convention of the American Psychological Association 8: 253-254. P.A. 50:4746.

504. Binder, Arnold, Burton R. Wolin, and Stanley J. Terebinski
 1965   "Leadership selection when uncertainty is minimal." Psychonomic Science 3 (8): 367-368. P.A. 40:1529.

505.   1966a   "Leadership in small groups: A resolution of discordance." Journal of Experimental Psychology 71 (5): 783-784. P.A. 40:6596.

506.   1966b   "Learning and extinction of leadership preferences in small groups." Journal of Mathematical Psychology 3 (1): 129-139. P.A. 40:5414.

507. Bindrim, Paul
 1969   "Nudity as a quick grab for intimacy in group therapy." Psychology Today 3 (1, June): 24-28. P.A. 46:1056.

508. Bion, W. R.
 1948a   "Experiences in groups: I." Human Relations 1: 314-320. P.A. 23: 1217.

509.   1948b   "Experiences in groups: II." Human Relations 1: 487-496. P.A. 23: 2175.

510.   1949a   "Experiences in groups: III." Human Relations 2: 13-22. P.A. 23: 3678.

511.   1949b   "Experiences in groups: IV." Human Relations 2: 295-303.

512.   1950a   "Experiences in groups: V." Human Relations 3: 3-14. P.A. 25: 2354.

513.   1950b   "Experiences in groups: VI." Human Relations 3: 395-402. P.A. 25: 6224.

514.   1951   "Experiences in groups: VII." Human Relations 4: 221–227. P.A. 26:6176.
515.   1952   "Group dynamics: A review." International Journal of Psychoanalysis 33: 235–247. P.A. 27:319.
516.   1961   Experiences in Groups: And Other Papers. New York: Basic Books.
517. Birney, Robert C., and John P. Houston
        1961   "The effects of creativity, norm distance, and instructions on social influence." Journal of Personality 29 (3): 294–302. P.A. 37:3027.
518. Bishop, Barbara M.
        1951   "Mother-child interaction and the social behavior of children." Psychological Monographs 65 (11). (Whole No. 328.) (See also Hare, Borgatta, and Bales, 1955, 1965.) P.A. 26:6854.
519. Bixenstine, V. Edwin, and Hazel Blundell
        1966   "Control of choice exerted by structural facotrs in two-person, non-zero-sum games." Journal of Conflict Resolution 10 (4, December): 478–487. S.A. 15:C6374.
520. Bixenstine, V. Edwin, Norman Chambers, and Kellogg V. Wilson
        1964   "Effect of asymmetry in payoff on behavior in a two-person non-zero-sum game." Journal of Conflict Resolution 8 (2, June): 151–159. S.A. 14:C0067.
521. Bixenstine, V. Edwin, and Joan Douglas
        1967   "Effect of psychopathology on group consensus and cooperation choice in a six-person game." Journal of Personality and Social Psychology 5 (1): 32–37.
522. Bixenstine, V. Edwin, and Jacquelyn W. Gaebelein
        1971   "Strategies of 'real' opponents in eliciting cooperative choice in a Prisoner's Dilemma game." Journal of Conflict Resolution 15 (2, June): 157–166. P.A. 48:4844; S.A. 20:F6952.
523. Bixenstine, V. Edwin, Clifford A. Levitt, and Kellogg V. Wilson
        1966   Collaboration among six persons in a Prisoner's Dilemma game." Journal of Conflict Resolution 10 (4, December): 488–496. S.A. 15:C6375.
524. Bixenstine, V. Edwin, and Edmund F. O'Reilly, Jr.
        1966   "Money versus electric shock as payoff in a Prisoner's Dilemma game." Psychological Record 16 (3): 251–264. P.A. 40:11097.
525. Bixenstine, V. Edwin, Herbert M. Potash, and Kellogg V. Wilson
        1963   "Effects of level of cooperative choice by the other player on choices in a Prisoner's Dilemma game, Part I." Journal of Abnormal and Social Psychology 66 (4): 308–313.
526. Bjerg, Kresten
        1968   "Interplay-analysis: A preliminary report on an approach to the problems of interpersonal understanding." Acta Psychologica 28 (3): 201–245. P.A. 43:2530.
527. Bjerstedt, Ake
        1952   "A 'chess-board sociogram' for sociographic representation of choice directions and for the analysis of 'sociometric locomotions.'" Sociometry 15: 244–262. P.A. 27:7129.
528.   1956a   Interpretations of Sociometric Choice Status. Lund, Sweden: Gleerup.
529.   1956b   "The interpretation of sociometric status scores in the classroom." Acta Psychologica 12: 1–14. P.A. 31:3670.
530.   1956c   "The methodology of preferential sociometry." Sociometry Monographs 37.
531.   1957   "Three types of square sociograms and some auxiliary micro-devices." Educational Psychology 3: 175–191.
532.   1958   "A field-force model as a basis for predictions of social behavior." Human Relations 11: 331–340. P.A. 34:1193.
533.   1961   "Preparation, process, and product in small group interaction." Human Relations 14 (2, May): 183–189. P.A. 36:2GE83B; S.A. 11: A4156.
534.   1963   (Sociometric methods.) Uppsala: Almqvist & Wiksell. S.A. 12:B0180.
535.   1965   "The rotation phenomenon in small groups." Educational and Psy-

chological Interactions 4 (January): 1-7. P.A. 39:9989; S.A. 13: B7592.

536. Black, Charlene R., Eugene A. Weinstein, and Judith M. Tanur
    1974   "Self-interest and expectations of altruism in exchange situations." Sociological Quarterly 15 (2, Spring): 242-252. P.A. 52:12241.

537. Black, Harvey
    1969   "Race and sex factors influencing the correct and erroneous perception of emotion." Proceedings of the 77th Annual Convention of the American Psychological Association 4 (pt. 1): 363-364.

538. Black, Harvey, and Virginia B. Angelis
    1974   "Interpersonal attraction: An empirical investigation of platonic and romantic love." Psychological Reports 34 (3, pt. 2): 1243-1246.

539. Black, Terry E., and Kenneth L. Higbee
    1973   "Effects of power, threat, and sex on exploitation." Journal of Personality and Social Psychology 27 (3, September): 382-388. P.A. 51:5026.

540. Blackman, Sheldon, Kenneth M. Goldstein, and Wallace Mandell
    1966   "Deviance and position in the small group." Journal of Social Psychology 70 (December): 287-293.

541. Blake, Brian F., Richard Heslin, and James Rotton
    1970   "Impression formation based on potentially invalid information." Proceedings of the 78th Annual Convention of the American Psychological Association 5 (pt. 1): 413-414.

542. Blake, Brian F., and Abraham Tesser
    1970   "Interpersonal attraction as a function of the other's reward value to the person." Journal of Social Psychology 82: 67-74.

543. Blake, Robert R.
    1953   "The interaction-feeling hypothesis applied to psychotherapy groups." Sociometry 16: 253-265. P.A. 28:4413.

544. Blake, Robert R., and J. W. Brehm
    1954   "The use of tape recording to simulate a group atmosphere." Journal of Abnormal and Social Psychology 49: 311-313. (See also Hare, Borgatta, and Bales, 1955.) P.A. 29:721.

545. Blake, Robert R., H. Helson, and Jane S. Mouton
    1957   "The generality of conformity behavior as a function of factual anchorage, difficulty of task, and amount of social pressure." Journal of Personality 25: 294-305. P.A. 32:2745.

546. Blake, Robert R., and Jane S. Mouton
    1957   "The dynamics of influence and coercion." International Journal of Social Psychiatry 2 (4, Spring): 263-274. P.A. 32:5292; S.A. 15: C5569.

547.   1961a   "Competition, communication, and conformity." In I. A. Berg and B. M. Bass (eds.), Conformity and Deviation, pp. 199-229. New York: Harper. P.A. 4GE99B.

548.   1961b   "Comprehension of own and of out-group positions under intergroup competition." Journal of Conflict Resolution 5 (4): 304-310. P.A. 37:3028.

549.   1961c   "Conformity, resistance, and conversion." In I. A. Berg and B. M. Bass (eds.), Conformity and Deviation, pp. 1-37. New York: Harper. P.A. 36:4GE01B.

550.   1961d   "Loyalty of representatives to ingroup positions during intergroup competition." Sociometry 24 (2, June): 117-183.

551.   1961e   "Perceived characteristics of elected representatives." Journal of Abnormal and Social Psychology 62 (3, May): 693-695. P.A. 4GF93B.

552.   1962a   "Comprehension of points of communality in competing solutions." Sociometry 25 (1, March): 56-63. P.A. 37:1092.

553.   1962b   "Overevaluation of own group's product in intergroup competition." Journal of Abnormal and Social Psychology 64 (3, March): 237-238. P.A. 38:2580; S.A. 11:A5695.

554.   1970   "The fifth achievement." Journal of Applied Behavioral Science 6 (4, October): 413-426. P.A. 46:4821.

555.   1974   "Reactions to intergroup competition under win-lose conditions." In D. A. Kolb, I. M. Rubin, and J. M. McIntyre (eds.), Organizational Psychology: A Book of Readings, 2nd ed. Englewood Cliffs, N.J.: Prentice-Hall. P.A. 52:12242.

556. Blake, Robert R., Jane S. Mouton, and Benjamin Fruchter
    1954   "The consistency of interpersonal behavior judgments made on the basis of short-term interaction in three-man groups." Journal of Abnormal and Social Psychology 49: 573-578. P.A. 29:5444.

557.   1962   "A factor analysis of training group behavior." Journal of Social Psychology 58 (October): 121-130.

558. Blake, Robert R., Clifton C. Rhead, Bryant Wedge, and Jane S. Mouton
    1956   "Housing architecture and social interaction." Sociometry 19: 133-139. P.A. 31:5957.

559. Blanchard, William A., and Carol D. Ganam
    1969   "Complexity of information and accuracy of interpersonal prediction." Psychological Reports 25 (1): 243-251. P.A. 44:3538.

560. Blank, Andrew D.
    1968   "Effects of group and individual conditions on choice behavior." Journal of Personality and Social Psychology 8 (3, pt. 1): 294-298. P.A. 42:8879.

561. Blank, Leonard, Gloria B. Gottsegen, and Monroe G. Gottsegen (eds.)
    1971   Confrontation: Encounters in Self and Interpersonal Awareness. New York: Macmillan. P.A. 47:10765.

562. Blank, Leonard, Paulina Wilker, and Sandra Grundfest
    1972   "The value of intense encounters in interactional and group process training." Comparative Group Studies 3 (1, February): 51-76.

563. Blascovich, Jim
    1972   "Sequence effects on choice shifts involving risk." Journal of Experimental Social Psychology 8 (3, May): 260-265. P.A. 48:11428.

564. Blascovich, Jim, and Gerald P. Ginsburg
    1974   "Emergent norms and choice shifts involving risk." Sociometry 37 (2, June): 205-218. P.A. 52:12297.

565. Blascovich, Jim, Tracy L. Veach, and Gerald P. Ginsburg
    1973   "Blackjack and the risky shift." Sociometry 36 (1, March): 42-55. P.A. 50:11204; S.A. 22:74G6136.

566. Blau, Kim, and James T. Richardson
    1973   "Contract formation and overt power: A reexamination." Social Forces 51 (4, June): 440-447. P.A. 51:943.

567. Blau, Peter M.
    1954a   "Co-operation and competition in a bureaucracy." American Journal of Sociology 59: 530-535. P.A. 29:8501.

568.   1954b   "Patterns of interaction among a group of officials in a government agency." Human Relations 7: 337-348. P.A. 29:3778.

569.   1957   "Formal organization: dimensions of analysis." American Journal of Sociology 63: 58-69.

570.   1960a   "A theory of social integration." American Journal of Sociology 65 (6, May): 545-546. P.A. 35:6331.

571.   1960b   "Patterns of deviation in work groups." Sociometry 23 (3, September): 245-261. P.A. 35:2105; S.A. A2728.

572.   1962   "Patterns of choice in interpersonal relations." American Sociological Review 27 (1, February): 41-55. P.A. 5GE41B.

573.   1964   Exchange of Power in Social Life. New York: Wiley.

574.   1968   "Social exchange." In D. L. Sills (ed.), International Encyclopedia of the Social Sciences, vol. 7, pp. 452-458. New York: Macmillan and Free Press.

575. Blau, Peter M., and W. Richard Scott
    1962   Formal Organizations: A Comparative Approach. San Francisco: Chandler.

576. Bleda, Paul R.
    1974   "Toward a clarification of the role of cognitive and affective processes in the similarity-attraction relationship." Journal of Personality

and Social Psychology 29 (3): 368–373.

577. Bleda, Paul R., Paul A. Bell, and Donn Byrne
     1973   "Prior induced affect and sex differences in attraction." Memory
             and Cognition 1 (4, October): 435–438. P.A. 51:7049.

578. Bleda, Paul R., and Carl H. Castore
     1973   "Social comparison, attraction, and choice of a comparison other."
             Memory and Cognition 1 (4, October): 420–424. P.A. 51:7048.

579. Bledsoe, Joseph C., and R. Gene Wiggins
     1973   "Congruence of adolescents' self-concepts and parents' perceptions
             of adolescents' self-concepts." Journal of Psychology 83 (1, Janu-
             ary): 131–136. P.A. 49:11047.

580. Blevins, Gregory A., and Terrance Murphy
     1974   "Feeling good and helping: Further phonebooth findings." Psycho-
             logical Reports 34 (1): 326.

581. Blitz, Robert, and Donald F. Dansereau
     1972   "The effect of underlying situational characteristics on the risky
             shift phenomenon." Journal of Social Psychology 87 (2, August):
             251–258. P.A. 49:744.

582. Block, Jack
     1952   "The assessment of communication: Role variations as a function of
             interactional context." Journal of Personality 21: 272–286. P.A.
             27:7731.

583. Block, Jack, and Lillian F. Bennett
     1955   "The assessment of communication." Human Relations 8: 317–325.
             P.A. 30:5927.

584. Block, Jeanne, and Jack Block
     1952   "An interpersonal experiment on reactions to authority." Human
             Relations 5: 91–98. P.A. 27:178.

585. Blomfield, O. H.
     1972   "Group: The more primitive psychology? A review of some para-
             digms in group dynamics." Australian and New Zealand Journal of
             Psychiatry 6 (4, December): 238–246. P.A. 50:8800.

586. Bloom, Leonard
     1971   "The formation of friendships among Zambian university students."
             International Journal of Psychology 6 (2): 157–162. P.A. 50:2909.

587. Bloom, Samuel W., Ina Boyd, and Howard B. Kaplan
     1962   "Emotional illness and interaction process: A study of patient
             groups." Social Forces 2 (December): 135–141.

588. Bloomberg, Lawrence I., Paula Bloomberg, and Richard L. Miller
     1969   "The intensive group as a founding experience." Journal of Human-
             istic Psychology 9 (1): 93–99. P.A. 44:6651.

589. Blumberg, Herbert H.
     1969   "On being liked more than you like." Journal of Personality and So-
             cial Psychology 11 (2): 121–128. P.A. 43:8294.

590.   1972   "Communication of interpersonal evaluations." Journal of Personal-
             ity and Social Psychology 23 (2, August): 157–162. P.A. 49:745.

591. Blumberg, Herbert H., and Clinton B. DeSoto
     1968   "Avoiding distortions in soicometric choices." International Journal
             of Sociometry and Sociatry 5 (3-4, September-December): 90–95.
             P.A. 42:15394.

592. Blumer, Herbert
     1953   "Psychological import of the human group." In M. Sherif and M. O.
             Wilson (eds.), Group Relations at the Crossroads, pp. 185–202. New
             York: Harper. P.A. 28:7328.

593. Blumstein, Philip W.
     1973a   "Audience, Machiavellianism, and tactics of identity bargaining." So-
             ciometry 36 (3, September): 346–365. P.A. 52:2882.

594.   1973b   "Subjective probability and normative evaluations." Social Forces
             52 (1, September): 98–107. P.A. 51:5082.

595. Blumstein, Philip W., and Eugene A. Weinstein
     1969   "The redress of distributive injustice." American Journal of Sociol-

ogy 74 (4, January); 408-418. S.A. 17:D8266.

596. Blunden, Dale, Carl Spring, and Lawrence M. Greenberg
      1974   "Validation of the classroom behavior inventory." Journal of Con-
              sulting and Clinical Psychology 42 (1): 84-88.

597. Bochner, Arthur P., and Brenda Bochner
      1972   "A multivariate investigation of Machiavellianism and task structure
              in four-man groups." Speech Monographs 39 (4, November): 277-
              285. P.A. 51:9003.

598. Bodalev, A. A., et al.
      1972   "New data on the problem of social perception: A person's percep-
              tion and conception of another person." Soviet Psychology 11 (1,
              Fall): 85-99. P.A. 49:9011.

599. Boderman, Alvin, Douglas W. Freed, and Mark T. Kinnucan
      1972   "'Touch me, like me': Testing an encounter group assumption."
              Journal of Applied Behavioral Science 8 (5): 527-533.

600. Bogardus, Emory S.
      1954   "Group behavior and groupality." Sociology and Social Research
              38: 401-403. S.A. 2727.

601. Bolman, Lee
      1970   "Laboratory versus lecture in training executives." Journal of Ap-
              plied Behavioral Science 6 (3): 323-335.

602. 1971   "Some effects of trainers on their T groups." Journal of Applied Be-
              havioral Science 7 (3, May-June): 309-325. S.A. 20:F9130.

603. 1973   "Some effects of trainers on their groups: A partial replication."
              Journal of Applied Behavioral Science 9 (4, July): 534-539. P.A.
              51:2962.

604. Bolton, Gaylor M., Louis N. Gray, and Bruce H. Mayhew
      1970   "An experimental examination of a stochastic model of dominance."
              Social Forces 48 (4, June): 511-520. P.A. 47:6665.

605. Bonacich, Phillip
      1970   "Putting the dilemma back into Prisoner's Dilemma." Journal of
              Conflict Resolution 14 (3): 379-387.

606. 1972   "Norms and cohesion as adaptive responses to potential conflict: An
              experimental study." Sociometry 35 (3, September): 357-375. P.A.
              49:6791; S.A. 21:73G4901.

607. Bonacich, Philip, and Gordon H. Lewis
      1973   "Function specialization and sociometric judgment." Sociometry 36
              (1, March): 31-41. P.A. 50:11205; S.A. 22:74G6137.

608. Bond, John R., and W. Edgar Vinacke
      1961   "Coalitions in mixed-sex triads." Sociometry 24 (1, March): 61-75.
              P.A. 36:1GE61B; S.A. A2753.

609. Bond, Michael H.
      1972   "Effect of an impression set on subsequent behavior." Journal of
              Personality and Social Psychology 24 (3, December): 301-305. P.A.
              49:9012.

610. Bond, Michael H., and Donald G. Dutton
      1973   "The effect of interaction anticipation upon the extremity of trait
              ratings." Canadian Journal of Behavioural Science 5 (3, July): 226-
              233. P.A. 51:7051.

611. Bonner, Hubert
      1959   Group Dynamics: Principles and Applications. New York: Ronald.

612. Bonney, Merl E.
      1946   "A sociometric study of the relationship of some factors to mutual
              friendships on the elementary, secondary, and college levels." Socio-
              metry 9: 21-47. P.A. 20:2802.

613. Bonney, Merl E., R. E. Hoblit, and A. H. Dreyer
      1953   "A study of some factors related to sociometric status in a men's
              dormitory." Sociometry 16: 287-301. S.A. 2:478.

614. Bonney, Merl E., and Johnny Powell
      1953   "Differences in social behavior between sociometrically high and so-
              ciometrically low children." Journal of Educational Research 46:
              481-495. P.A. 28:2310.

615. Bonny, Helen L., Martha Cistrunk, Rebecca Makuch, Emily Stevens, and Junotte Tally
     1965   "Some effects of music on verbal interaction in groups." Journal of Music Therapy 2 (2): 61–63. P.A. 40:490.
616. Bonoma, Thomas V., and James T. Tedeschi
     1973   "Some effects of source behavior on target's compliance to threats." Behavioral Science 18 (1, January): 34–41. P.A. 50:8803.
617. Bonoma, Thomas V., James T. Tedeschi, and Bob Helm
     1974   "Some effects of target cooperation and reciprocated promises on conflict resolution." Sociometry 37 (2, June): 251–261. P.A. 52: 12298.
618. Bonoma, Thomas V., James T. Tedeschi, and Svenn Lindskold
     1972   "A note regarding an expected value model of social power." Behavioral Science 17 (2, March): 221–228. P.A. 48:8994.
619. Bonoma, Thomas, et al.
     1969   "Compliance to contingent threats." Proceedings of the 77th Annual Convention of the American Psychological Association 4 (pt. 1): 395–396. P.A. 43:17333.
620. Boomer, Donald S.
     1959   "Subjective certainty and resistance to change." Journal of Abnormal and Social Psychology 58 (May): 323–328. P.A. 34:5698.
621. Booth, Alan
     1972   "Sex and social participation." American Sociological Review 37 (2, April): 183–193. S.A. 20:F9131.
622. Bootzin, Richard R.
     1969   "Induced and stated expectancy in experimenter bias." Proceedings of the 77th Annual Convention of the American Psychological Association 4 (pt. 1): 365–366.
623. Borah, Lee A., Jr.
     1963   "The effects of threat in bargaining: Critical and experimental analysis." Journal of Abnormal and Social Psychology 66 (1): 37–44. P.A. 37:4883.
624. Borden, Richard J., and Stuart P. Taylor
     1973   "The social instigation and control of physical aggression." Journal of Applied Social Psychology 3 (4, October): 354–361. P.A. 52: 7543.
625. Bordow, Allan
     1974   "Aggression and support levels in the dyad: Clarification of a balanced effect." Journal of Social Psychology 93 (2): 299–300.
626. Borg, Walter R.
     1957   "The behavior of emergent and designated leaders in situational tests." Sociometry 20: 95–104.
627.   1960   "Prediction of small group role behavior from personality variables." Journal of Abnormal and Social Psychology 60 (1, January): 112–116. P.A. 34:7528.
628. Borgatta, Edgar F.
     1951a "A diagnostic note on the construction of sociograms and action diagrams." Group Psychotherapy 3: 300–308. P.A. 26:224.
629.   1951b "An analysis of three levels of response: An approach to some relationships among dimensions of personality." Sociometry 14: 267–316.
630.   1954   "Analysis of social interaction and sociometric perception." Sociometry 17: 7–31. P.A. 29:722.
631.   1955   "Analysis of social interaction: Actual, role playing, and projective." Journal of Abnormal and Social Psychology 51: 394–405. P.A. 31: 2682.
632.   1960a "Rankings and self-assessments: Some behavioral characteristics replication studies." Journal of Social Psychology 52 (November): 279–307.
633.   1960b "Role and reference group theory." In L. S. Kogan (ed.), Social Science Theory and Social Work Research. New York: National Association of Social Workers.

456   BIBLIOGRAPHY

634.   1960c   "Small group research: A trend report and bibliography." Current Sociology 9 (3): 173–272. S.A. 11:A4593.
635.   1960d   "The stability of interpersonal judgments in independent situations." Journal of Abnormal and Social Psychology 60 (2, March): 188–194. (See also Hare, Borgatta, and Bales, 1965.) P.A. 34:7529.
636.   1961   "Role-playing specification, personality, and performance." Sociometry 24 (3, September): 218–233. (See also Hare, Borgatta, and Bales, 1965.) P.A. 36:3GE18B; S.A. A3287.
637.   1962   "A systematic study of interaction process scores, peer and self-assessments, personality and other variables." Genetic Psychology Monographs 65: 219–291. P.A. 37:3030.
638.   1963a   "A new systematic interaction observation system: Behavior scores system (BSs System)." Journal of Psychological Studies 14: 24–44.
639.   1963b   "Some task factors in social interaction." Sociology and Social Research 48 (1, October): 5–12. S.A. 12:A9430.
640.   1964a   "A note on the consistency of subject behavior in interaction process analysis." Sociometry 27 (2, June): 222–229. P.A. 39:4853; S.A. 13:B4055.
641.   1964b   "The structure of personality characteristics." Behavioral Science 9: 8–17.
642.   1965   "The analysis of patterns of social interaction." Social Forces 44 (1, September): 27–34. P.A. 40:491.
643.   1967   "Methodological notes on a model new research of small groups." Sociological Quarterly 8 (1, Winter): 133–138. S.A. 15:C7233.
644. Borgatta, Edgar F. (ed.)
        1969   Social Psychology: Readings and Perspective. Chicago: Rand McNally.
645. Borgatta, Edgar F., and Robert F. Bales
        1953a   "Task and accumulation of experience as factors in the interaction of small groups." Sociometry 16: 239–252. P.A. 28:4118.
646.   1953b   "Interaction of individuals in reconstituted groups." Sociometry 16: 302–320. (See also Hare, Borgatta, and Bales, 1955, 1965.) S.A. 479.
647.   1953c   "The consistency of subject behavior and the reliability of scoring in interaction process analysis." American Sociological Review 18: 566–569. (See also Hare, Borgatta, and Bales, 1955, 1965.) P.A. 28: 5846.
648.   1956   "Sociometric status patterns and characteristics of interaction." Journal of Social Psychology 43: 289–297.
649. Borgatta, Edgar F., and Leonard S. Cottrell, Jr.
        1955   "On the classification of groups." Sociometry 18: 665–678. P.A. 32: 1471; S.A. 3438.
650.   1957   "Directions for research in group behavior." American Journal of Sociology 63: 42–48. P.A. 32:5294.
651. Borgatta, Edgar F., Leonard S. Cottrell, Jr., and James H. Mann
        1958   "The spectrum of individual characteristics: An interdimensional analysis." Psychological Reports 4: 279–319.
652. Borgatta, Edgar F., Leonard S. Cottrell, Jr., and Henry J. Meyer
        1956   "On the dimensions of group behavior." Sociometry 19: 223–240. (See also Hare, Borgatta, and Bales, 1965.)
653. Borgatta, Edgar F., Leonard S. Cottrell, Jr., and L. Wilker
        1959   "Initial expectation, group climate, and the assessments of leaders and members." Journal of Social Psychology 49 (May): 285–296. P.A. 34:4171.
654. Borgatta, Edgar F., Arthur S. Couch, and Robert F. Bales
        1954   "Some findings relevant to the great man theory of leadership." American Sociological Review 19: 755–759. (See also Hare, Borgatta, and Bales, 1955, 1965.) P.A. 30:2623.
655. Borgatta, Edgar F., and Betty Crowther
        1965   A Workbook for the Study of Social Interaction Process. Chicago: Rand McNally.

656. Borgatta, Edgar F., and A. E. Eschenbach
1955   "Factor analysis of Rorschach variables and behavior observation."
        Psychological Reports 3: 129–136. P.A. 30:5976.
657. Borgatta, Edgar F., and David C. Glass
1963   "An analysis of some factors in group structures." Journal of Social
        Psychology 59 (2, April): 317–336. P.A. 38:866.
658. Borgatta, Edgar F., and Robert F. Guerrin
1960   "The two-person group: Some notes on theory and research." So-
        ciology and Social Research 45 (1, October): 3–13. P.A. 35:4808;
        S.A. 11:A4594.
659. Borgatta, Edgar F., and John Simpson
1961   "Some formal properties of groups." Journal of Psychological
        Studies 12 (5): 211–223. P.A. 39:9990.
660. Borgatta, Edgar F., and Betty C. Sperling
1963   "A note of the stability of peer judgments in independent situa-
        tions." Journal of Psychological Studies 14 (1): 45–47. P.A. 39:
        9991.
661. Borgatta, Edgar F., and John Stimson
1963   "Sex differences in interaction characteristics." Journal of Social
        Psychology 60 (1, June): 89–100.
662. Borgatta, Marie L.
1958   "The concept of the group: A brief consideration." Sociology and
        Social Research 43: 83–89. P.A. 34:1153.
663. 1961   "Power structure and coalitions in three-person groups." Journal of
        Social Psychology 55 (December): 287–300. P.A. 36:3GE87B.
664. Borgatta, Marie L., and Edgar F. Borgatta
1963   "Coalitions in three-person groups." Journal of Social Psychology
        60 (2, August): 319–326. P.A. 38:4189.
665. Borke, Helene
1967   "The communication of intent: A systematic approach to the obser-
        vation of family interaction." Human Relations 20 (1, February):
        13–28.
666. Borman, Walter C., and William K. Graham
1973   "Polarity and 'accuracy' of ratings and the meaningfulness of per-
        sonality dimensions." Journal of Psychology 84 (1, May): 55–60.
        P.A. 50:6690.
667. Bormann, Ernest G.
1969   Discussion and Group Methods: Theory and Practice. New York:
        Harper & Row. P.A. 44:6652.
668. Borofsky, Gerald L., Gary E. Stollak, and Lawrence A. Messé
1971   "Sex differences in bystander reactions to physical assault." Journal
        of Experimental Social Psychology 7 (3): 313–318.
669. Bos, Maria C.
1937   "Experimental study of productive collaboration." Acta Psycho-
        logica 3: 315–426.
670. Bossard, James H. S.
1945   "Law of family interaction." American Journal of Sociology 50:
        292–294. P.A. 19:1519.
671. Bossman, Larry J., Jr.
1968   "An analysis of interagent residual-influence effects upon members
        of small, decision-making groups." Behavioral Science 13 (3, May):
        220–233. P.A. 42:12048; S.A. 17:D6812.
672. Bott, Elizabeth
1955   "Urban families: Conjugal roles and social networks." Human Rela-
        tions 8: 345–384. P.A. 31:879.
673. 1956   "Urban families: The norms of conjugal roles." Human Relations 9:
        325–341.
674. 1957   Family and Social Network. London: Tavistock.
675. Bott, Helen McM.
1933   Method in Social Studies of Young Children. Toronto: University of
        Toronto Press.

676. Bouchard, Thomas J., Jr.
    1969   "Personality, problem-solving procedure, and performance in small groups." Journal of Applied Psychology Monograph 53, 1 (pt. 2).
677.   1972a   "Training, motivation, and personality as determinants of the effectiveness of brainstorming groups and individuals." Journal of Applied Psychology 56 (4, August): 324–331. P.A. 49:746.
678.   1972b   "A comparison of two group brainstorming procedures." Journal of Applied Psychology 56 (5, October): 418–421. P.A. 49:4384.
679. Bouchard, Thomas J., Jr., Jean Barsaloux, and Gail Drauden
    1974   "Brainstorming procedure, group size, and sex as determinants of the problem-solving effectiveness of groups and individuals." Journal of Applied Psychology 59 (2): 135–138.
680. Bouchard, Thomas J., Jr., Gail Drauden, and Jean Barsaloux
    1974   "A comparison of individual, subgroup, and total group methods of problem solving." Journal of Applied Psychology 59 (2): 226–227.
681. Bouchard, Thomas J., Jr., and Melana Hare
    1970   "Size, performance, and potential in brainstorming groups." Journal of Applied Psychology 54 (1, pt. 1): 51–55. P.A. 44:5069.
682. Boucher, Michael L.
    1972   "Effect of seating distance on interpersonal attraction in an interview situation." Journal of Consulting and Clinical Psychology 38 (1): 15–19.
683. Bouillut, Jean, and Serge Moscovici
    1967   ("Transformation of transmitted messages in terms of subject's interest and image of the recipient.") Bulletin du C.E.R.P. 16 (4): 305–322. P.A. 43:5276.
684. Bourricaud, F.
    1955   ("'Democracy' in small groups.") Cahiers Internationals de Sociologie 19: 104–113. S.A. 2487.
685. Bovard, Everett W., Jr.
    1951a   "Group structure and perception." Journal of Abnormal and Social Psychology 46: 398–405. (See also Cartwright and Zander, 1960.) P.A. 26:2085.
686.   1951b   "The experimental production of interpersonal affect." Journal of Abnormal and Social Psychology 46: 521–528. P.A. 26:3912.
687.   1952   "Clinical insight as a function of group process." Journal of Abnormal and Social Psychology 47: 534–539. P.A. 27:2688.
688.   1953   "Conformity to social norms and attraction to the group." Science 118: 598–599. P.A. 28:5793.
689.   1956a   "Grouping error and interpersonal affect: A correction." Journal of Abnormal and Social Psychology 52: 283–284. P.A. 31:2683.
690.   1956b   "Interaction and attraction to the group." Human Relations 9: 481–489. S.A. 1196.
691. Bowditch, James L., and Donald C. King
    1970   "Relationship between biographical similarity and interpersonal choice." Proceedings of the 78th Annual Convention of the American Psychological Association 5 (pt. 1): 381–382. P.A. 44:18552.
692. Bower, Joseph L.
    1965   "Group decision making: A report of an experimental study." Behavioral Science 10 (3, July): 277–289. P.A. 40:492; S.A. 14: C1882.
693. Bowerman, Charles E., and Barbara R. Day
    1956   "A test of the theory of complementary needs as applied to couples during courtship." American Sociological Review 21: 602–605.
694. Bowerman, William R.
    1973a   "Ambulatory velocity in crowded and uncrowded conditions." Perceptual and Motor Skills 36 (1, February): 107–111. P.A. 50:11206.
695.   1973b   "Attribution of responsibility implied in a notice of acceptance or rejection." Psychological Reports 32 (2, April): 467–472. P.A. 51: 968.
696. Bowers, David G.
    1963   "Self-esteem and the diffusion of leadership style." Journal of Applied Psychology 47 (2): 135–140. P.A. 37:7954.

697. Bowman, Donald D., and Jacob P. Siegel
    1973   "Process and performance: A longitudinal study of the reactions of small task groups to periodic performance feedback." Human Relations 26 (4, August): 433–448. P.A. 51:7020.
698. Boyanowsky, Ehor O.
    1971   "Informational influence, threat of censure, and self-identity as factors in discriminatory behavior." Proceedings of the 79th Annual Convention of the American Psychological Association 6 (pt. 1): 327–328. P.A. 46:2891.
699. Boyd, J. Edwin, and Raymond P. Perry
    1972   "Impression formation as an interpersonal communication phenomenon." Canadian Psychologist 13 (3, July): 207–216. P.A. 49:4385.
700. Boyd, Robert D.
    1965   "The group as a sociopsychological setting for learning." Review of Educational Research 35 (3): 209–217. P.A. 40:1515.
701. Boyd, Richard W., and Alberto DiMascio
    1954   "Social behavior and autonomic physiology: A socio-physiologic study." Journal of Nervous and Mental Diseases 120: 207–212. P.A. 29:7443.
702. Boyle, Richard P.
    1969   "Algebraic systems for normal and hierarchical sociograms." Sociometry 32 (1, March): 99–119. S.A. 18:E1778.
703. Boyle, Richard P., and Phillip Bonacich
    1970   "The development of trust and mistrust in mixed-motive games." Sociometry 33 (2, June): 123–129. S.A. 19:E9546.
704. Bradford, Leland P.
    1964a   "Membership and the learning process." In L. P. Bradford, J. R. Gibb, and K. D. Benne (eds.), T-group Theory and Laboratory Method, pp. 190–215. New York: Wiley.
705.   1964b   "Trainer-intervention: Case episodes." In L. P. Bradford, J. R. Gibb, and K. D. Benne (eds.), T-group Theory and Laboratory Method, pp. 136–167. New York: Wiley.
706. Bradford, Leland P., and John R. P. French, Jr. (eds.)
    1948   "The dynamics of the discussion group." Journal of Social Issues 4 (2).
707. Bradford, Leland P., Jack R. Gibb, and Kenneth D. Benne (eds.)
    1964   T-group Theory and Laboratory Method. New York: Wiley.
708. Bradford, Leland P., and T. Mallinson
    1958   "Group formation and development." In Dynamics of Group Life. Washington, D.C.: National Education Association, National Training Laboratories.
709. Bradley, Larry, C. R. Snyder, and Martin Katahn
    1972   "The effects of subject race and sex and experimenter race upon classroom-related risk-taking behavior." Psychonomic Science 28 (6, September): 362–364. P.A. 49:4386.
710. Bragg, Barry W. E.
    1971   "Resistance of conformity pressure without social support." Proceedings of the 79th Annual Convention of the American Psychological Association 6 (pt. 1): 363–364.
711. Bragg, Barry W. E., and Vernon L. Allen
    1970   "Ordinal position and conformity: A role theory analysis." Sociometry 33 (4): 371–381.
712. Bragg, Barry W. E., and Stephen J. Dooley
    1972   "Generalization of resistance to conformity pressure." Proceedings of the 80th Annual Convention of the American Psychological Association 7 (pt. 1): 167–168.
713. Bramel, Dana
    1969   "Interpersonal attraction, hostility, and perception." In J. Mills (ed.), Experimental Social Psychology, pp. 3–120. New York: Macmillan. P.A. 44:14492.
714. Bramel, Dana, Barry Taub, and Barbara Blum
    1968   "An observer's reaction to the suffering of his enemy." Journal of Personality and Social Psychology 8 (4, pt. 1): 384–392. P.A. 42:

8861.
715. Brandeis, Harry N.
    1972   "The psychology of scatological privacy." Journal of Biological Psychology 14 (2, December): 30-35. P.A. 51:5084.
716. Brandenburg, Earnest
    1953   "Problems in measuring the results of discussion." Journal of Communication 3: 28-33. P.A. 28:7329.
717. Brandenburg, Earnest, and Philip A. Neal
    1953   "Graphic techniques for evaluating discussion and conference procedures." Quarterly Journal of Speech 39: 201-208. P.A. 28:2394.
718. Brandon, Arlene C.
    1965   "Status congruence and expectations." Sociometry 28 (3, September): 272-288. P.A. 39:15023.
719. Brandt, Lewis W., and Elisabeth P. Brandt
    1972   "Second-hand personication: A new model for 'person perception' research." Candian Psychologist 13 (3, July): 217-238. P.A. 49: 4387.
720. Braun, Jean S., and George Daigle
    1973   "Machiavellianism and reputation for manipulativeness in adolescent inpatients." Proceedings of the 81st Annual Convention of the American Psychological Association 8: 379-380. P.A. 50:8805.
721. Brayer, A. Richard
    1964   "An experimental analysis of some variables of minimax theory." Behavioral Science 9 (1, January): 33-44. S.A. 13:B5877.
722. Breed, George
    1972   "The effect of intimacy: Reciprocity or retreat?" British Journal of Social and Clinical Psychology 11 (2, June): 135-142. P.A. 49:6794.
723. Breed, George, and Maynard Porter
    1972   "Eye contact, attitudes, and attitude change among males." Journal of Genetic Psychology 120 (2, June): 211-217. P.A. 48:11429.
724. Breed, George, and Joseph S. Ricci
    1973   "'Touch me, like me': Artifact?" Proceedings of the 81st Annual Convention of the American Psychological Association 8: 153-154. P.A. 50:4747.
725. Breer, Paul E.
    1960   "Predicting interpersonal behavior from personality and role." Ph.D. dissertation. Harvard University.
726. Breer, Paul E., and Edwin A. Locke
    1965   Task Experience as a Source of Attitudes. Homewood, Ill.: Dorsey.
727. Breger, Louis
    1963   "Conformity as a function of the ability to express hostility." Journal of Personality 31: 247-257.
728. Breger, Louis, and Charlotte Ruiz
    1966   "The role of ego-defense in conformity." Journal of Social Psychology 69 (1, June): 73-85. P.A. 40:10025.
729. Brehm, Jack W., and Arthur R. Cohen
    1962   Explorations in Cognitive Dissonance. New York: Wiley.
730. Brehm, Jack W., and Ann H. Cole
    1966   "Effect of a favor which reduces freedom." Journal of Personality and Social Psychology 3 (4): 420-426. P.A. 40:5391.
731. Brehm, Jack W., and Leon Festinger
    1957   "Pressures toward uniformity of performance in groups." Human Relations 10: 85-91. P.A. 32:144; S.A. A1197.
732. Brehm, Jack W., and John Sensenig
    1966   "Social influence as a function of attempted and implied usurpation of choice." Journal of Personality and Social Psychology 4 (6): 703-707.
733. Brehmer, Berndt, and Kenneth R. Hammond
    1970   "Cognitive sources of interpersonal conflict: Analysis of interactions between linear and nonlinear cognitive systems." Umea, Sweden: University of Umea, Psychological Reports No. 31. P.A. 51:2963.

734.   1973   "Cognitive sources of interpersonal conflict: Analysis of interactions between linear and nonlinear cognitive systems." Organizational Behavior and Human Performance 10 (2, October): 290–313. P.A. 51: 10986.

735. Brein, Michael, and David Ryback
    1970   "Stimulus, respondent, and response characteristics of social distance and self-disclosure." Sociology and Social Research 55 (1, October): 17–28. P.A. 47:4701.

736. Brenner, Sten O., and Erland Hjelmquist
    1973   "Verbal interaction in small groups related to personality: A presentation of the VEGA-Project." Göteborg Psychological Reports 3 (7). P.A. 52:818.

737. Brew, J. S.
    1973   "An altruism parameter for Prisoner's Dilemma." Journal of Conflict Resolution 17 (2, June): 351–367. P.A. 51:5028.

738. Brewer, Robert E., and Marilynn B. Brewer
    1968   "Attraction and accuracy of perception in dyads." Journal of Personality and Social Psychology 8 (2, pt. 1): 188–193. P.A. 42:5508.

739. Brickman, Philip, and John J. Berman
    1971   "Effects of performance expectancy and outcome certainty on interest in social comparison." Journal of Experimental Social Psychology 7 (6, November): 600–609. P.A. 48:8995.

740. Brickman, Philip, and Charles Horn
    1973   "Balance theory and interpersonal coping in triads." Journal of Personality and Social Psychology 26 (3, June): 347–355. P.A. 50: 11208.

741. Bridgeman, Winnie
    1972   "Student attraction and productivity as a composite function of reinforcement and expectancy conditions." Journal of Personality and Social Psychology 23 (2, August): 249–258. P.A. 49:747.

742. Briskin, Gerald J.
    1958   "Identification in group therapy." Journal of Abnormal and Social Psychology 56: 195–198.

743. Brock, Timothy C.
    1965   "Communicator-recipient similarity and decision change." Journal of Personality and Social Psychology 1 (6): 650–654.

744.   1969   "On interpreting the effects of transgression upon compliance." Psychological Bulletin 72 (2): 138–145. P.A. 43:15690.

745. Brodbeck, May
    1956   "The role of small groups in mediating the effects of propaganda." Journal of Abnormal and Social Psychology 52: 166–170. P.A. 31: 2870; S.A. 5384.

746. Broekmann, Neil C., and André T. Möller
    1973   "Preferred seating position and distance in various situations." Journal of Counseling Psychology 20 (6, November): 504–508. P.A. 51: 7053.

747. Brok, Albert J., and Nathan Kogan
    1973   "An interpersonal analogue of the 'sealed-fate' effect in risky decision making." Proceedings of the 81st Annual Convention of the American Psychological Association 8: 281–282. P.A. 50:8807.

748. Bronfenbrenner, Urie
    1943   "A constant frame of reference for sociometric research." Sociometry 6: 363–397. P.A. 18:2851.

749.   1944   "A constant frame of reference for sociometric research: Part II. Experiment and inference." Sociometry 7: 40–75. P.A. 18:2852.

750. Bronfenbrenner, Urie, and Theodore M. Newcomb
    1948   "Improvisations: An application of psychodrama in personality diagnosis." Sociatry 1: 367–382. P.A. 22:3935.

751. Bronzo, Anthony F., Jr.
    1968   "Increased zero defects participation through group discussion and public commitment." Psychological Reports 23 (1): 72. P.A. 43:

6837.

752. Brousek, Jan
    1967   ("Apparatus for the study of social interaction in small groups.")
            Psychologia a Patopsychologia Dietata 3 (1): 83-94. P.A. 42:12030.

753. Brown, Bert R.
    1968   "The effects of need to maintain face on interpersonal bargaining."
            Journal of Experimental Social Psychology 4 (1, January): 107-122.
            P.A. 42:7244.

754. Brown, Bert R., and Howard Garland
    1971   "The effects of incompetency, audience acquaintanceship, and anti-
            cipated evaluative feedback on face-saving behavior." Journal of Ex-
            perimental Social Psychology 7 (5, September): 490-502. P.A. 48:
            8996.

755. Brown, Bert R., Howard Garland, and Manuel Mena
    1971   "Effects of another's dependency and expectations of meeting with
            him on the reduction of face-saving behavior." Proceedings of the
            79th Annual Convention of the American Psychological Association
            6 (pt. 1): 299-300.

756. Brown, Bruce L., William J. Strong, and Alvin C. Rencher
    1972   "Manipulation of vocal qualities by speech synthesis: A new way to
            study person perception." Proceedings of the 80th Annual Conven-
            tion of the American Psychological Association 7 (pt. 1): 197-198.

757. Brown, Bruce L., William J. Strong, Alvin C. Rencher, and Bruce L. Smith
    1973   "Fifty-four voices from two: The effects of simultaneous manipula-
            tions of rate, pitch and variance of intonation on ratings of personal-
            ity from speech." Proceedings of the 81st Annual Convention of the
            American Psychological Association 8: 193-194. P.A. 50:4748.

758. Brown, G. A.
    1973   "An exploratory study of interaction amongst British and immigrant
            children." British Journal of Social and Clinical Psychology 12 (2,
            June): 159-162. P.A. 51:2964.

759. Brown, George I.
    1971   "Proceed with caution: On teaching and therapy." Sociological In-
            quiry 41 (2, Spring): 205-209.

760. Brown, James C.
    1952   "An experiment in role-taking." American Sociological Review 17:
            587-597. P.A. 28:791.

761. Brown, Larry T., Terry G. Shaw, and Karen D. Kirkland
    1972   "Affection for people as a function of affection for dogs." Psycho-
            logical Reports 31 (3, December): 957-958. P.A. 50:887.

762. Brown, Marvin, Donald M. Amoroso, Edward E. Ware, Manfred Pruesse, and
    Dennis W. Pilkey
    1973   "Factors affecting viewing time of pornography." Journal of Social
            Psychology 90 (1, June): 125-135. P.A. 51:3016.

763. Brown, Paula, and R. Brown
    1955   "A note on hypotheses in Homans' The Human Group." American
            Sociological Review 20: 83-85. Reply by G. C. Homans, pp. 85-86.

764. Brown, Robert C., Jr., Bob Helm, and James T. Tedeschi
    1973   "Attraction and verbal conditioning." Journal of Social Psychology
            91 (1): 81-85.

765. Brown, Robert C., Jr., Barry R. Schlenker, and James T. Tedeschi
    1972   "Prestige of a harm-doer and subjective estimations of possible
            harm." Journal of Social Psychology 88 (2, December): 223-232.
            P.A. 49:9013.

766. Browne, C[larence] G., and Thomas S. Cohn (eds.)
    1958   The Study of Leadership. Danville, Ill.: Interstate Printers and Pub-
            lishers.

767. Broxton, June A.
    1963   "A test of interpersonal attraction predictions derived from balance
            theory." Journal of Abnormal and Social Psychology 66 (4, April):
            394-397. P.A. 37:7942; S.A. 12:B1627.

768. Bruehl, Dieter, and Diana Solar
    1973   "Systematic variation in the clarity of demand characteristics and task ambiguity in an experiment employing a confederate." Proceedings of the 81st Annual Convention of the American Psychological Association 8: 163–164. P.A. 50:4749.
769. Bruner, Jerome S.
    1950   "Social psychology and group processes." Annual Review of Psychology 1: 119–150.
770. Bruner, Jerome S., Jacqueline J. Goodnow, and G. A. Austin
    1956   A Study of Thinking. New York: Wiley. P.A. 31:582.
771. Bruner, Jerome S., and Renato Tagiuri
    1954   "The perception of people." In G. Lindzey (ed.), Handbook of Social Psychology, pp. 634–654. Cambridge, Mass.: Addison-Wesley.
772. Bruning, James L., and David R. Mettee
    1966   "The effects of various social factors on motivation in a competitive situation." Journal of Social Psychology 70 (December): 295–297.
773. Bruning, James L., David K. Sommer, and Bill R. Jones
    1966   "The motivational effects of cooperation and competition in the means-independent situation." Journal of Social Psychology 68 (2, April): 269–274. P.A. 40:7635.
774. Bruun, Kettil
    1959   "Significance of role and norms in the small group for individual behavior changes while drinking." Quarterly Journal of Studies on Alcohol 20 (1, March): 53–64. S.A. 10:A3242.
775. Bryan, James H.
    1972   "Why children help: A review." Journal of Social Issues 28 (3): 87–104.
776. Bryant, Howard A., D. A. Dobbins, and Bernard M. Bass
    1963   "Group effectiveness, coercion, change, and coalescence among delinquents compared to nondelinquents." Journal of Social Psychology 61 (October): 167–177.
777. Bryson, Jeff B.
    1972   "Relative influence of evaluative sign and evaluative dimensions in impression formation." Psychonomic Science 27 (6, June): 333–334. P.A. 49:2319.
778.   1974   "Factor analysis of impression formation processes." Journal of Personality and Social Psychology 30 (1): 134–143.
779. Buby, Carolyn M., and Louis A. Penner
    1974   "Conformity as a function of response position." Psychological Reports 34 (3, pt. 1): 938.
780. Buchanan, Lyle J., and Henry C. Lindgren
    1973   "Brainstorming in large groups as a facilitator of children's creative responses." Journal of Psychology 83 (1, January): 117–122. P.A. 49:11050.
781. Buchanan, Paul C.
    1971   "Sensitivity, or laboratory, training in industry." Sociological Inquiry 41 (2, Spring): 217–225.
782. Buchanan, Paul C., and Eva Schindler-Rainman
    1969   "Facilitating personal growth." Training and Development Journal 23 (9, September): 28–32. P.A. 48:2866.
783. Buck, Roy C.
    1952   "Acquaintance positions in the group." Sociology and Social Research 37: 33–36. P.A. 27:7385.
784. Buck, Ross W., Robert E. Miller, and William F. Caul
    1974   "Sex, personality, and physiological variables in the communication of affect via facial expression." Journal of Personality and Social Psychology 30 (4): 587–596.
785. Buck, Ross W., and Ross D. Parke
    1972   "Behavioral and physiological response to the presence of a friendly or neutral person in two types of stressful situations." Journal of Personality and Social Psychology 24 (2, November): 143–153. P.A.

49:4388.
786. Buck, Ross W., Virginia J. Savin, Robert E. Miller, and William F. Caul
     1969   "Nonverbal communication of affect in humans." Proceedings of the
             77th Annual Convention of the American Psychological Association
             4 (pt. 1): 367-368.
787.   1972   "Communication of affect through facial expression in humans."
               Journal of Personality and Social Psychology 23 (3): 362-371.
788. Buckley, James J., and T. Edward Westen
     1973   "The symmetric solution to a five-person constant-sum game as a de-
             scription of experimental game outcomes." Journal of Conflict Res-
             olution 17 (4, December): 703-718. P.A. 52:2883.
789. Budman, Simon H.
     1972   "Client's lexical organization and psychotherapist's empathy level."
             Psychological Reports 31 (1, August): 77-78. P.A. 49:4389.
790. Bugental, Daphne E., Jaques W. Kaswan, and Leonore R. Love
     1970   "Perception of contradictory meanings conveyed by verbal and non-
             verbal channels." Journal of Personality and Social Psychology 16
             (4): 647-655.
791. Bugental, Daphne E., and G. F. J. Lehner
     1958   "Accuracy of self-perception and group-perception as related to two
             leadership roles." Journal of Abnormal and Social Psychology 56:
             396-398.
792. Bugh, Vernon G.
     1972   "Group psychotherapy in the mental hospital." Comparative Group
             Studies 1 (February): 99-103.
793. Buhler, Charlotte
     1931   "Social Behavior of the Child." In C. A. Murchison (ed.), A Hand-
             book of Child Psychology, pp. 392-531. Worcester, Mass.: Clark
             University Press.
794.   1939   The Child and His Family. New York: Harper.
795. Bull, Andrew J., et al.
     1972   "Effects of noise and intolerance of ambiguity upon attraction for
             similar and dissimilar others." Journal of Social Psychology 88 (1,
             October): 151-152. P.A. 49:4390.
796. Burchard, Edward M. L., J. Michaels, and B. Kotkov
     1948   "Criteria for the evaluation of group therapy." Psychosomatic Medi-
             cine 10: 257-274.
797. Burchinal, Lee G., Glen R. Hawkes, and Bruce Gardner
     1957   "Personality characteristics and marital satisfaction." Social Forces
             35: 218-222.
798. Burdick, Harry A., Rolf von Ekartsberg, and Hiroshi Ono
     1959   "Two experiments in social power." Psychological Reports 5: 781-
             789. P.A. 34:5699.
799. Burgess, Ernest W., and L. S. Cottrell, Jr.
     1939   Predicting Success or Failure in Marriage. Englewood Cliffs, N.J.:
             Prentice-Hall. P.A. 14:404.
800. Burgess, P. K.
     1971   "Critical note: Aggressive behavior of delinquent, dependent, and
             'normal' white and black boys in social conflicts." Journal of Experi-
             mental Social Psychology 7 (5): 545-550. Rejoinder by Tedeschi
             and Berger, and reply by Burgess.
801. Burgess, Robert L.
     1968a   "An experimental and mathematical analysis of group behavior with-
             in restricted networks." Journal of Experimental Social Psychology
             4 (July): 338-349.
802.   1968b   "Communication networks: An experimental reevaluation." Journal
               of Experimental Social Psychology 4 (3, July): 324-337. P.A. 43:
               2532.
803.   1969   "Communication networks and behavioral consequences." Human
               Relations 22 (2): 137-159. P.A. 44:6673.
804. Burgess, Robert L., and Joyce M. Nielsen
     1974   "An experimental analysis of some structural determinants of equi-

table and inequitable exchange relations." American Sociological Review 39 (3, June): 427–443. P.A. 52:12300.

805. Burgess, Thomas D. G., II, and Richard H. Willis
1973 "Cognitive and affective aspects of balance." Proceedings of the 81st Annual Convention of the American Psychological Association 8: 161–162. P.A. 50:4750.

806. Burhans, David T., Jr.
1973 "Coalition game research: A reexamination." American Journal of Sociology 79 (2): 389–408. S.A. 22:74G8625.

807. Burke, C. J.
1962 "Two-person interactive learning: A progress report." In J. H. Criswell, H. Solomon, and P. Suppes (eds.), Mathematical Methods in Small Group Processes, pp. 49–68. Stanford, Calif.: Stanford University Press. S.A. 12:B2403.

808. Burke, Kenneth
1968 "Dramatism." In D. L. Sills (ed.), International Encyclopedia of the Social Sciences, vol. 7, pp. 445–452. New York: Macmillan and Free Press.

809. Burke, Peter J.
1966 "Authority relations and disruptive behavior in small discussion groups." Sociometry 29 (3, September): 237–250. P.A. 40:13160; S.A. 15:C3474.

810. 1967 "The development of task and social-emotional role differentiation." Sociometry 30 (4, December): 379–392. P.A. 42:3893.

811. 1968 "Role differentiation and the legitimation of task activity." Sociometry 31 (4): 404–411. P.A. 43:3917.

812. 1969 "Scapegoating: An alternative to role differentiation." Sociometry 32 (2): 159–168. P.A. 43:12893.

813. 1971 "Task and social-emotional leadership role performance." Sociometry 34 (1, March): 22–40. P.A. 46:8910.

814. Burke, Richard L., and Warren G. Bennis
1961 "Changes in perception of self and others during human relations training." Human Relations 14 (2, May): 165–182. P.A. 36: 2GE65B.

815. Burke, W. Warner
1965 "Leadership behavior as a function of the leader, the follower, and the situation." Journal of Personality 33 (1, March): 60–81. P.A. 39:10017.

816. Burnand, G.
1969 "A generalisation about group behaviour." Acta Psychologica, 31 (3): 197–231. P.A. 44:14493.

817. Burnham, W. H.
1905 "The hygiene of home study." Pedagogical Seminary 12: 213–230.
818. 1910 "The group as a stimulus to mental activity." Science 31: 761–767.

819. Burns, George W.
1972 "Religious influences on behavior of the group therapist." Psychological Reports 31: 638.

820. Burns, Tom
1955 "The reference of conduct in small groups: Cliques and cabals in occupational milieux." Human Relations 8: 467–486. P.A. 31:882.

821. Burnstein, Eugene
1966 ("The composition of groups and their risk readiness.") Kölner Zeitschrift für Soziologie und Sozialpsychologie 10 (Supplement): 84–91. S.A. 15:C5570.

822. 1969a "An analysis of group decisions involving risk ('the risky shift')." Human Relations 22 (5, October): 381–395.

823. 1969b "Interdependence in groups." In J. Mills (ed.), Experimental Social Psychology, pp. 309–405. New York: Macmillan. P.A. 44:14494.

824. Burnstein, Eugene, and Stuart Katz
1971 "Individual commitment to risky and conservative choices as a determinant of shifts in group decisions." Journal of Personality 39 (4, December): 564–580. P.A. 48:2867.

825. Burnstein, Eugene, and Adie V. McRae
    1962   "Some effects of shared threat and prejudice in racially mixed groups." Journal of Abnormal and Social Psychology 64 (4, April): 257–263. S.A. 11:A6355.
826. Burnstein, Eugene, Harold Miller, Amiram Vinokur, Stuart Katz, and Joan Crowley
    1971   "Risky shift is eminently rational." Journal of Personality and Social Psychology 20 (3): 462–471.
827. Burnstein, Eugene, and Amiram Vinokur
    1973   "Testing two classes of theories about group induced shifts in individual choice." Journal of Experimental Social Psychology 9 (2, March): 123–137. P.A. 50:11209.
828. Burnstein, Eugene, Amiram Vinokur, and Marie-France Pichevin
    1974   "What do differences between own, admired, and attributed choices have to do with group induced shifts in choice?" Journal of Experimental Social Psychology 10 (5): 428–443.
829. Burnstein, Eugene, Amiram Vinokur, and Yaacov Trope
    1973   "Interpersonal comparison versus persuasive argumentation: A more direct test of alternative explanations for group-induced shifts in individual choice." Journal of Experimental Social Psychology 9 (3, May): 236–245. P.A. 51:2965.
830. Burnstein, Eugene, and Robert J. Wolosin
    1968   "The development of status distinctions under conditions of inequity." Journal of Experimental Social Psychology 4 (4, October): 415–430. P.A. 43:3918.
831. Burnstein, Eugene, and Robert B. Zajonc
    1965a   "Individual task performance in a changing social structure." Sociometry 28 (1, March): 16–29. P.A. 39:9992; S.A. 14:B9175.
832.   1965b   "The effect of group success on the reduction of status incongruence in task-oriented groups." Sociometry 28 (4, December): 349–362. P.A. 40:2807; S.A. 14:C1883.
833. Burroughs, Wayne A., and Cabot L. Jaffee
    1969   "Verbal participation and leadership voting behavior in a leaderless group discussion." Psychological Record 19 (4): 605–610. P.A. 44: 10276.
834. Burroughs, Wayne A., Jack B. Rollins, and John J. Hopkins
    1972   "Equality of assigned positions in a leaderless group discussion." Studies in Personnel Psychology 4 (1, Spring): 13–17. P.A. 50:2913.
835. Burroughs, Wayne A., W. Schultz, and S. Autrey
    1973   "Quality of argument, leadership votes, and eye contact in three-person leaderless groups." Journal of Social Psychology 90 (1, June): 89–93. P.A. 51:2966.
836. Burrow, Trigant
    1927   "The group method of analysis." Psychoanalytic Review 14: 268–280. P.A. 2:947.
837. Burton, A.
    1941   "The influence of social factors upon the persistence of satiation in pre-school children." Child Development 12: 121–129.
838. Burton, Arthur (ed.)
    1969   Encounter. San Francisco: Jossey-Bass.
839. Burtt, Harold E.
    1920   "Sex differences in the effect of discussion." Journal of Experimental Psychology 3: 390–395.
840. Bush, Robert R.
    1962   "The application of learning models to interactive behavior." In J. H. Criswell, H. Solomon, and P. Suppes (eds.), Mathematical Methods in Small Group Processes, pp. 69–73. Stanford, Calif.: Stanford University Press. S.A. 12:B2404.
841. Buss, Arnold H., Ann Booker, and Edith Buss
    1972   "Firing a weapon and aggression." Journal of Personality and Social Psychology 22 (3, June): 296–302. P.A. 48:11431.

842. Buss, Arnold H., Robert Plomin, and Charles Carver
    1973   "Delay of frustration and aggression." Psychological Reports 32 (3,
            pt. 2, June): 1074. P.A. 51:2968.
843. Busse, Thomas V., and Craig Love
    1973   "The effect of first names on conflicted decisions: An experimental
            study." Journal of Psychology 84 (2, July): 253-256. P.A. 51:7054.
844. Butler, Donald C., and Norman Miller
    1965   "Power to reward and punish in social interaction." Journal of Ex-
            perimental Social Psychology 1 (4, October): 311-322. P.A. 40:
            4179.
845. Butler, John M.
    1952   "The interaction of client and therapist." Journal of Abnormal and
            Social Psychology 47: 366-378. P.A. 27:2773.
846. Butler, Richard P., and Edward E. Cureton
    1973   "Factor analysis of small group leadership behavior." Journal of So-
            cial Psychology 89 (1, February): 85-89. P.A. 50:2914.
847. Butler, Richard P., and Cabot L. Jaffee
    1974   "Effects of incentive, feedback, and manner of presenting the feed-
            back on leader behavior." Journal of Applied Psychology 59 (3):
            332-336.
848. Byrd, Eugene
    1951   "A study of validity and constancy of choices in a sociometric test."
            Sociometry 14: 175-181. (See also Hare, Borgatta, and Bales, 1955,
            1965.) P.A. 27:4162.
849. Byrne, Donn
    1961a   "Interpersonal attraction and attitude similarity." Journal of Abnor-
            mal and Social Psychology 62 (3, May): 713-715. P.A. 36:4GE13B;
            S.A. A2729.
850.   1961b   "The influence of propinquity and opportunities for interaction on
            classroom relationships." Human Relations 14 (1, February): 63-69.
            (See also Crosbie, 1975.) P.A. 36:2GE63B.
851.   1969   "Attitudes and attraction." In L. Berkowitz (ed.), Advances in Ex-
            perimental Social Psychology, vol. 4, pp. 35-89. New York: Aca-
            demic Press.
852.   1971   "Can Wright be wrong? Let me count the ways." Representative Re-
            search in Social Psychology 2 (2, July): 12-18. P.A. 49:9015.
853. Byrne, Donn, Glen D. Baskett, and Louis A. Hodges
    1971   "Behavioral indicators of interpersonal attraction." Journal of Ap-
            plied Social Psychology 1 (2, April): 137-149. P.A. 47:4703.
854. Byrne, Donn, and J. A. Buehler
    1955   "A note on the influence of propinquity upon acquaintanceships."
            Journal of Abnormal and Social Psychology 51: 147-148. P.A. 30:
            5184.
855. Byrne, Donn, Gerald L. Clore, William Griffitt, John Lamberth, and Herman E.
    Mitchell
    1973a   "When research paradigms converge: Confrontation or integration?"
            Journal of Personality and Social Psychology 28 (3, December):
            313-320. P.A. 51:7056.
856.   1973b   "One more time." Journal of Personality and Social Psychology 28
            (3, December): 323-324. P.A. 51:7055.
857. Byrne, Donn, Charles R. Ervin, and John Lamberth
    1970   "Continuity between the experimental study of attraction and real-
            life computer dating." Journal of Personality and Social Psychology
            16 (1, September): 157-165. P.A. 45:2285.
858. Byrne, Donn, C. Gouaux, William Griffitt, John Lamberth, N. Murakawa, M.
    Prasad, A. Prasad, and M. Ramirez, III
    1971   "The ubiquitous relationship: Attitude similarity and attraction: A
            cross-cultural study." Human Relations 24 (3, June): 201-207. P.A.
            50:888.
859. Byrne, Donn, and William Griffitt
    1966   "A developmental investigation of the law of attraction." Journal of

Personality and Social Psychology 4 (6): 699–702.

860.   1969   "Similarity and awareness of similarity of personality characteristics as determinants of attraction." Journal of Experimental Research in Personality 3 (3): 179–186. P.A. 43:11226.

861.   1973   "Interpersonal attraction." Annual Review of Psychology 24: 317–336. P.A. 50:2915.

862. Byrne, Donn, William Griffitt, W. Hudgins, and Keith Reeves
    1969   "Attitude similarity-dissimilarity and attraction: Generality beyond the college sophomore." Journal of Social Psychology 79 (2): 155–161. P.A. 44:10277.

863. Byrne, Donn, William Griffitt, and Daniel Stefaniak
    1967   "Attraction and similarity of personality characteristics." Journal of Personality and Social Psychology 5 (1): 82–90.

864. Byrne, Donn, Oliver London, and Keith Reeves
    1968   "The effects of physical attractiveness, sex, and attitude similarity on interpersonal attraction." Journal of Personality 36 (2): 259–271. P.A. 42:17136.

865. Byrne, Donn, and Carl McGraw
    1964   "Interpersonal attraction toward Negroes." Human Relations 17 (3, August): 201–213. S.A. 13:B4923.

866. Byrne, Donn, and Don Nelson
    1965   "The effect of topic importance and attitude similarity-dissimilarity on attraction in a multistranger design." Psychonomic Science 3 (10): 449–450. P.A. 40:2808.

867. Calabria, Frank M.
    1963   "Experimentally induced psyche- and socio-process in small groups." Journal of Social Psychology 60 (1, June): 57–69. P.A. 38:4190.

868. Calder, Bobby J.
    1974   "Informational cues and attributions based on role behavior." Journal of Experimental Social Psychology 10 (2): 121–125.

869. Calder, Bobby J., Michael Ross, and Chester A. Insko
    1973   "Attitude change and attitude attribution: Effects of incentive, choice, and consequences." Journal of Personality and Social Psychology 25 (1, January): 84–99. P.A. 50:6691.

870. Caldwell, Michael
    1971   "Coalitions in the triad: Introducing the element of chance into the game structure." Journal of Personality and Social Psychology 20 (3, December): 271–280. P.A. 47:8779.

871. Callahan, Charlene M., and Lawrence A. Messé
    1973   "Conditions affecting attempts to convert fate control to behavior control." Journal of Experimental Social Psychology 9 (6): 481–490.

872. Calvin, Allen D., Frederic K. Hoffman, and Edgar L. Harden
    1957   "The effect of intelligence and social atmosphere on group problem solving behavior." Journal of Social Psychology 45: 61–74.

873. Camilleri, Santo F., and Joseph Berger
    1967   "Decision-making and social influence: A model and an experimental test." Sociometry 30 (4, December): 365–378. P.A. 42: 3914.

874. Cammalleri, Joseph A., Hal W. Hendrick, Wayne C. Pittman, Jr., Harry D. Blout, and Dirk C. Prather
    1973   "Effects of different leadership styles on group accuracy." Journal of Applied Psychology 57 (1): 32–37.

875. Campbell, Donald T.
    1953   A Study of Leadership among Submarine Officers. Columbus: Ohio State University Research Foundation. P.A. 29:8020.

876.   1955   "An error in some demonstrations of the superior social perceptiveness of leaders." Journal of Abnormal and Social Psychology 51: 694–695. P.A. 31:2738.

877.   1961   "Conformity in psychology's theories of acquired behavioral dispositions." In I. A. Berg and B. M. Bass (eds.), Conformity and Deviation, pp. 101–142. New York: Harper. P.A. 36:4GE01C.

878.   1972   "On the genetics of altruism and the counter-hedonic components in human culture." Journal of Social Issues 28 (3): 21–37. P.A. 50: 4751.

879. Campbell, Donald T., and Fred L. Damarin
       1961   "Measuring leadership attitudes through an information test." Journal of Social Psychology 55 (December): 159–176. P.A. 36: 3GF59C.

880. Campbell, Donald T., William H. Kruskal, and William P. Wallace
       1966   "Seating aggregation as an index of attitude." Sociometry 29 (1, March): 1–15.

881. Campbell, Donald T., and Kanwal Mehra
       1958   "Individual differences in evaluations of group discussions as a projective measure of attitudes toward leadership." Journal of Social Psychology 47: 101–106. P.A. 34:2886.

882. Campbell, Donald T., and Bonnie B. Tyler
       1957   "The construct validity of work-group morale measures." Journal of Applied Psychology 41: 91–92.

883. Cannavale, F. J., H. A. Scarr, and A. Pepitone
       1970   "Deindividuation in the small group: Further evidence." Journal of Personality and Social Psychology 16 (1, September): 141–147. P.A. 45:2286.

884. Cannon, John R., and Frank J. Zigon
       1973   "Assessing interpersonal functioning." Journal of Community Psychology 1 (3, July): 297. P.A. 51:5029.

885. Canon, Lance K., and Kenneth Mathews, Jr.
       1971   "Ethnicity, belief, social distance and interpersonal evaluation: A methodological critique." Sociometry 34 (4, December): 515–523. S.A. 21:13G2269.

886. Canter, D., S. West, and R. Wools
       1974   "Judgements of people and their rooms." British Journal of Social and Clinical Psychology 13 (2, June): 113–118. P.A. 52:12302.

887. Cantor, Joanne R., Bella Mody, and Dolf Zillmann
       1974   "Residual emotional arousal as a distractor in persuasion." Journal of Social Psychology 92 (2): 231–244.

888. Capage, James, and Svenn Lindskold
       1973   "Locus of control, sex, target accommodation and attempts at influence." Proceedings of the 81st Annual Convention of the American Psychological Association 8: 297–298. P.A. 50:8809.

889. Caplow, Theodore
       1956   "A theory of coalitions in the triad." American Sociological Review 21: 489–493.

890.   1959   "Further development of a theory of coalitions in the triad." American Journal of Sociology 64: 488–493.

891.   1968   Two against One: Coalitions in Triads. Englewood Cliffs, N.J.: Prentice-Hall. P.A. 43:9630.

892. Carey, Alex
       1967   "The Hawthorne studies: A radical criticism." American Sociological Review 32 (3): 403–416.

893. Carey, Gloria L.
       1958   "Sex differences in problem-solving performance as a function of attitude differences." Journal of Abnormal and Social Psychology 56: 256–260.

894. Carlsmith, J. Merrill, Barry E. Collins, and Robert L. Helmreich
       1966   "Studies in forced compliance: I. The Effect of pressure for compliance on attitude change produced by face-to-face role playing and anonymous essay writing." Journal of Personality and Social Psychology 4 (1): 1–13.

895. Carlsmith, J. Merrill, and Alan E. Gross
       1969   "Some effects of guilt on compliance." Journal of Personality and Social Psychology 11 (3): 232–239.

896. Carlson, Earl R.
       1960   "Clique structure and member satisfaction in groups." Sociometry 23 (4, December): 327–337. P.A. 35:2106; S.A. A2730.

897. Carlson, Julia A., and Clive M. Davis
    1971   "Cultural values and the risky shift: A cross-cultural test in Uganda and the United States." Journal of Personality and Social Psychology 20 (3): 392–399.
898. Carment, D. W.
    1961   "Ascendant-submissive behavior in pairs of human subjects as a function of their emotional responsiveness and opinion strength." Canadian Journal of Psychology 15: 45–51. P.A. 36:1GE45C.
899. Carment, D. W., F. S. Schwartz, and C. G. Miles
    1964   "Participation and opinion change as related to cohesiveness and sex of Ss in two-person groups." Psychological Reports 14 (3): 695–702. P.A. 39:4854.
900. Carr, L. J.
    1929   "Experimental sociology: A preliminary note on theory and method." Social Forces 8: 63–74.
901.   1930   "Experimentation in face-to-face interaction." American Sociological Society Papers 24: 174–176.
902. Carrera, Richard N., and Arthur M. Cohen
    1968   "Discussion patterns of homogeneous groups of repressers and sensitizers following success and failure." Psychological Reports 22 (1): 7–14. P.A. 42:10510.
903. Carter, Launor F.
    1951   "Some research on leadership in small groups." In H. Guetzkow (ed.), Groups, Leadership, and Men: Research in Human Relations, pp. 146–157. Pittsburgh: Carnegie. P.A. 26:792.
904.   1953   "Leadership and small-group behavior." In M. Sherif and M. O. Wilson (eds.), Group Relations at the Crossroads, pp. 257–284. New York: Harper. P.A. 28:7330.
905.   1954   "Recording and evaluating the performance of individuals as members of small groups." Personnel Psychology 7: 477–484. (See also Hare, Borgatta, and Bales, 1955, 1965.) P.A. 29:7065.
906. Carter, Launor F., W. Haythorn, and Margaret Howell
    1950   "A further investigation of the criteria of leadership." Journal of Abnormal and Social Psychology 45: 350–358. (See also Hare, Borgatta, and Bales, 1955.) P.A. 24:5765.
907. Carter, Launor F., W. Haythorn, Beatrice Meirowitz, and J. Lanzetta
    1951a   "A note on a new technique of interaction recording." Journal of Abnormal and Social Psychology 46: 258–260. P.A. 25:7773.
908.   1951b   "The relation of categorizations and ratings in the observation of group behavior." Human Relations 4: 239–254. P.A. 26:6190.
909. Carter, Launor F., W. Haythorn, E. Shriver, and J. Lanzetta
    1951   "The behavior of leaders and other group members." Journal of Abnormal and Social Psychology 46: 589–595. (See also Cartwright and Zander, 1953, 1960, 1968.) P.A. 26:3913.
910. Carter, Launor F., and Mary Nixon
    1949a   "An investigation of the relationship between four criteria of leadership ability for three different tasks." Journal of Psychology 27: 245–261. P.A. 23:2640.
911.   1949b   "Ability, perceptual, personality, and interest factors associated with different criteria of leadership." Journal of Psychology 27: 377–388. P.A. 23:4183.
912. Carter, Lewis F., Richard J. Hill, and S. Dale McLemore
    1967   "Social conformity and attitude change within non-laboratory groups." Sociometry 30 (1, March): 1–13. S.A. 15:C5571.
913. Carter, Thomas N.
    1974   "Group psychological phenomena of a political system as satirized in 'Animal Farm': An application of the theories of W. R. Bion." Human Relations 27 (6): 525–546.
914. Carterette, E. C., and M. J. Wyman
    1962   "Application of a Markov learning model to a simple detection situation involving social pressure." In J. H. Criswell, H. Solomon, and P. Suppes (eds.), Mathematical Methods in Small Group Processes, pp.

74-100. Stanford, Calif.: Stanford University Press. S.A. 12:B2405.
915. Cartwright, Desmond S., and Richard J. Robertson
1961 "Membership in cliques and achievement." American Journal of Sociology 66 (5, March): 441-445.
916. Cartwright, Dorwin
1951 "Achieving change in people: Some applications of group dynamics theory." Human Relations 4: 381-392. P.A. 26:5472.
917. 1952 "Emotional dimensions of group life." In M. L. Reymert (ed.), Feelings and Emotions, pp. 439-447. New York: McGraw-Hill. P.A. 26: 2087.
918. 1957 "Social psychology." Annual Review of Psychology 8: 211-236. P.A. 32:344.
919. 1958 "Some things learned: An evaluative history of the research center for group dynamics." Journal of Social Issues 12 (Supplement): 3-19. S.A. A2653.
920. Cartwright, Dorwin (ed.)
1959 Studies in Social Power. Ann Arbor: University of Michigan. P.A. 34:6701.
921. Cartwright, Dorwin
1968 "The nature of group cohesiveness." In D. Cartwright and A. Zander (eds.), Group Dynamics: Research and Theory, 3rd ed., pp. 91-109. New York: Harper & Row.
922. 1971 "Risk taking by individuals and groups: An assessment of research employing choice dilemmas." Journal of Personality and Social Psychology 20 (3, December): 361-378. P.A. 47:8780.
923. 1973 "Determinants of scientific progress: The case of research on the risky shift." American Psychologist 28 (3, March): 222-231. P.A. 50:11210.
924. Cartwright, Dorwin, and Frank Harary
1956 "Structural balance: A generalization of Heider's theory." Psychological Review 63: 277-293. (See also Cartwright and Zander, 1960.)
925. 1970 "Ambivalence and indifference in generalizations of structural balance." Behavioral Science 15 (6, November): 497-513. P.A. 46: 4823.
926. Cartwright, Dorwin, and Ronald Lippitt
1957 "Group dynamics and the individual." International Journal of Group Psychotherapy 7: 86-102. P.A. 32:2746.
927. Cartwright, Dorwin, and Alvin Zander (eds.)
1968 Group Dynamics: Research and Theory. 3rd ed. (1st ed., 1953; 2nd ed., 1960.) New York: Harper & Row. P.A. 42:12031.
928. Carver, Charles S.
1974 "Facilitation of physical aggression through objective self-awareness." Journal of Experimental Social Psychology 10 (4, July): 365-370. P.A. 52:12303.
929. Carzo, Rocco, Jr.
1963 "Some effects of organization structure on group effectiveness." Administrative Science Quarterly 7 (4, March): 393-424. S.A. 11: A6356.
930. Casey, Nancy A., and Leonard Solomon
1971-
1972 "The effect of seating arrangements of T-Group interaction and sociometric choices." Interpersonal Development 2 (1): 9-20. P.A. 49: 11053.
931. Cashdan, Sheldon
1970 "Sensitivity groups: Problems and promise." Professional Psychology 1 (3): 217-224. P.A. 44:20811.
932. Casse, P.
1970 ("Practicing methods of group animation: The method of four states of awareness.") Revue Belge de Psychologie et de Pédagogie 32 (132, December): 97-108. P.A. 50:889.
933. Castore, Carl H.
1972 "Group discussion and prediscussion assessment of preferences in

the risky shift." Journal of Experimental Social Psychology 8 (2): 161-167.

934. Castore, Carl H., Kevin Peterson, and Thomas A. Goodrich
    1971   "Risky shift: Social value or social choice? An alternative model." Journal of Personality and Social Psychology 20 (3, December): 487-494. P.A. 47:8781.

935. Castore, George F.
    1962   "Number of verbal interrelationships as a determinant of group size." Journal of Abnormal and Social Psychology 64 (6): 456-458. P.A. 38:869.

936. Cattell, Raymond B.
    1948   "Concepts and methods in the measurement of group syntality." Psychological Review 55: 48-63. (See also Hare, Borgatta, and Bales, 1955, 1965.) P.A. 22:2577.

937.   1951a   "Determining syntality dimension as a basis for morale and leadership measurement." In H. Guetzkow (ed.), Groups, Leadership and Men: Research in Human Relations, pp. 16-27. Pittsburgh: Carnegie. P.A. 26:829.

938.   1951b   "New concepts for measuring leadership, in terms of group syntality." Human Relations 4: 161-184. (See also Cartwright and Zander, 1960.)

939.   1953   "On the theory of group learning." Journal of Social Psychology 37: 27-52. P.A. 28:722.

940.   1956   "Second order personality factors in the questionnaire realm." Journal of Consulting Psychology 20: 411-418.

941. Cattell, Raymond B., and Edwin Lawson
    1962   "Sex differences in small group performance." Journal of Social Psychology 58 (1, October): 141-145. P.A. 37:6601.

942. Cattell, Raymond B., D. R. Saunders, and Glen F. Stice
    1953   "The dimensions of syntality in small groups: I. The neonate group." Human Relations 6: 331-356. (See also Hare, Borgatta, and Bales, 1955.) S.A. 240.

943. Cattell, Raymond B., and Glen F. Stice
    1954   "Four formulae for selecting leaders on the basis of personality." Human Relations 7: 493-507. P.A. 29:5450.

944.   1960   The Dimensions of Groups and Their Relations to the Behavior of Members. Champaign, Ill.: Institute for Personality and Ability Testing.

945. Cattell, Raymond B., and L. G. Wispe
    1948   "The dimensions of syntality in small groups." Journal of Social Psychology 28: 57-78. P.A. 23:1720.

946. Cavior, Norman, and Patrick J. Boblett
    1972   "Physical attractiveness of dating versus married couples." Proceedings of the 80th Annual Convention of the American Psychological Association 7 (pt. 1): 175-176.

947. Cecil, Earl A., Jerome M. Chertkoff, and Larry L. Cummings
    1970   "Risk taking in groups as a function of group pressure." Journal of Social Psychology 81: 273-274.

948. Cederblom, Douglas, and Carol Jean Diers
    1970   "Effects of race and strategy in the Prisoner's Dilemma (PD)." Journal of Social Psychology 81 (2): 275-276. P.A. 44:20812.

949. Centers, Richard
    1972   "The completion hypothesis and the compensatory dynamic in intersexual attraction and love." Journal of Psychology 82 (1, September): 111-126. P.A. 49:2321.

950. Centers, Richard, and Arthur C. Granville
    1971   "Reciprocal need gratification in intersexual attraction: A test of the hypotheses of Schutz and Winch." Journal of Personality 39 (1, March): 26-43. P.A. 46:4824.

951. Centers, Richard, Robert William Shomer, and Aroldo Rodrigues
    1970   "A field experiment in interpersonal persuasion using authoritative influence." Journal of Personality 38 (3, September): 392-403.

P.A. 45:4110.
952. Certner, Barry C.
1973   "Exchange of self-disclosures in same-sexed groups of strangers."
Journal of Consulting and Clinical Psychology 40 (2, April): 292–
297. P.A. 50:11211.
953. Cervin, Vladimir B.
1955a   "Experimental investigation of behavior in social situations: I. Behavior under opposition." Canadian Journal of Psychology 9: 107–
116. P.A. 30:2624.
954   1955b   "Experimental investigation of behavior in social situations: II. Individual behavioral effects of change in group attitude from opposition
to cooperation." Canadian Journal of Psychology 9: 155–160. P.A.
30:4336.
955.   1956   "Individual behavior in social situations: Its relation to anxiety, neuroticism, and group solidarity." Journal of Experimental Psychology
51: 161–168. P.A. 31:2686.
956.   1957   "Relationship of ascendant-submissive behavior in dyadic groups of
human subjects to their emotional responsiveness." Journal of Abnormal and Social Psychology 54: 241–249.
957.   1959   "Preliminary test of a mathematical model conceptualizing the persuasion process in debates between two initially disagreeing subjects." Psychological Reports 5: 404.
958. Cervin, Vladimir B., and G. P. Henderson
1961   "Statistical theory of persuasion." Psychological Review 68 (3):
157–166. P.A. 36:2GE57C.
959. Cervin, Vladimir B., Robert C. Joyner, J. Michael Spence, and Rudolph Heinzl
1961   "Relationship of persuasive interaction to change of opinion in
dyadic groups when the original opinions of participants are expressed privately and publicly." Journal of Abnormal and Social Psychology 62 (2, March): 431–432. P.A. 36:4GD31C.
960. Chaikin, Alan L., and Joel Cooper
1973   "Evaluation as a function of correspondence and hedonic relevance."
Journal of Experimental Social Psychology 9 (3, May): 257–264.
P.A. 51:3019.
961. Chaikin, Alan L., and John M. Darley
1973   "Victim or perpetrator? Defensive attribution of responsibility and
the need for order and justice." Journal of Personality and Social
Psychology 25 (2, February): 268–275. P.A. 50:891.
962. Chaikin, Alan L., and Valerian J. Derlega
1974a   "Liking for the norm-breaker in self-disclosure." Journal of Personality 42 (1): 117–129.
963.   1974b   "Variables affecting the appropriateness of self-disclosure." Journal
of Consulting and Clinical Psychology 42 (4, August): 588–593. P.A.
52:12244.
964. Chaikin, Alan L., Valerian J. Derlega, John Yoder, and David Phillips
1974   "The effects of appearance on compliance." Journal of Social Psychology 92 (2): 199–200.
965. Chalmers, Douglas K., William C. Horne, and Milton E. Rosenbaum
1963   "Social agreement and the learning of matching behavior." Journal
of Abnormal and Social Psychology 66 (6): 556–561.
966. Chambliss, William J.
1965   "The selection of friends." Social Forces 43 (3, March): 370–380.
S.A. 13:B7593.
967. Champney, Horace
1941   "The variables of parent behavior." Journal of Abnormal and Social
Psychology 36: 525–542. P.A. 16:797.
968. Chance, Erika
1957   "Methodological problems in the study of parent-child relationships
from treatment interviews." Merrill-Palmer Quarterly 3: 272–283.
969. Chance, June E.
1958   "Adjustment and prediction of others' behavior." Journal of Consulting Psychology 22: 191–194.

970. Chance, June E., and Wilson Meaders
    1960   "Needs and interpersonal perception." Journal of Personality 28: 200-209.

971. Chaney, Marilyn V., and W. Edgar Vinacke
    1960   "Achievement and nurturance in triads varying in power distribution." Journal of Abnormal and Social Psychology 60 (2, March): 175-181.

972. Chapanis, Natalia P., and Alphonse Chapanis
    1964   "Cognitive dissonance: Five years later." Psychological Bulletin 61: 1-22.

973. Chapanis, Alphonse, Robert B. Ochsman, Robert N. Parrish, and Gerald D. Weeks
    1972   "Studies in interactive communication: I. The effects of four communication modes on the behavior of teams during cooperative problem-solving." Human Factors 14 (6, December): 487-509. P.A. 50:892.

974. Chapko, Michael K.
    1972   "Source of increased emphasis of gain in predicted ethical risk taking of groups." Proceedings of the 80th Annual Convention of the American Psychological Association 7 (pt. 1): 219-220. P.A. 48: 4848.

975. Chapman, Antony J.
    1973   "Social facilitation of laughter in children." Journal of Experimental Social Psychology 9 (6): 528-541.

976. Chapman, Loren J., and R. Darrell Bock
    1958   "Components of variance due to acquiescence and content in the F scale measure of authoritarianism." Psychological Bulletin 55: 328-333.

977. Chapman, Loren J., and Donald T. Campbell
    1957a   "An attempt to predict the performance of three-man groups from attitude measures." Journal of Social Psychology 46: 277-286.

978.   1957b   "Response set in the F scale." Journal of Abnormal and Social Psychology 54: 129-132.

979.   1959   "The effect of acquiescence response-set upon relationships among the F scale, ethnocentrism and intelligence." Sociometry 22 (2, June): 153-161. P.A. 34:4175.

980. Chapple, Eliot D.
    1940   "Measuring human relations: An introduction to the study of interaction of individuals." Genetic Psychology Monographs 22: 3-147.

981.   1942   "The measurement of interpersonal behavior." Transactions of the New York Academy of Science 4: 222-233. P.A. 17:223.

982.   1953   "The standard experimental (stress) interview as used in interaction chronograph investigations." Human Organization 12 (2): 23-32. P.A. 29:5503.

983. Chapple, Eliot D., and C. S. Coon
    1942   Principles of Anthropology. New York: Holt. P.A. 16:1989.

984. Chapple, Eliot D., and E. Lindemann
    1942   "Clinical implications of measurements on interaction rates in psychiatric interviews." Applied Anthropology 1: 1-11. P.A. 17:1982.

985. Chapple, Eliot D., and Frank B. Miller
    1959   "Situational interactions — a worthwhile concept? A comment and a rejoinder." Human Organization 18 (3, Fall): 98-99. S.A. A1657.

986. Chase, Lawrence J., and Norbert H. Mills.
    1973   "Status of frustrator as a facilitator of aggression: A brief note." Journal of Psychology 84 (2, July): 225-226. P.A. 51:7004.

987. Chatterjee, Amitava
    1965   "Time phase sequence in the pattern of communication in small groups." Psychological Studies 10 (2): 121-127. P.A. 39:15024.

988. Chaubey, N. P.
    1974   "Effect of age on expectancy of success and on risk-taking behavior." Journal of Personality and Social Psychology 29 (6): 774-778.

989. Chemers, Martin M.
    1969   "Cross-cultural training as a means for improving situational favor-ableness." Human Relations 22 (6): 531-546. P.A. 44:12463.
990.   1970   "The relationship between birth order and leadership style." Journal of Social Psychology 80: 243-244.
991. Chemers, Martin M., and George J. Skrzypek
    1972   "Experimental test of the contingency model of leadership effective-ness." Journal of Personality and Social Psychology 24 (2, Novem-ber): 172-177. P.A. 49:4393.
992. Cheney, John, Thomas Harford, and Leonard Solomon
    1972   "The effects of communicating threats and promise upon the bar-gaining process." Journal of Conflict Resolution 16 (1): 99-107.
993. Cherrington, David J.
    1973   "Satisfaction in competitive conditions." Organizational Behavior and Human Performance 10 (1, August): 47-71. P.A. 51:9004.
994. Cherry, Fran, Herman E. Mitchell, and Don A. Nelson
    1973   "Helping or hurting? The aggression paradigm." Proceedings of the 81st Annual Convention of the American Psychological Association 8: 117-118. P.A. 50:4752.
995. Chertkoff, Jerome M.
    1966   "The effects of probability of future success on coalition forma-tion." Journal of Experimental Social Psychology 2 (3, July): 265-277.
996.   1967   "A revision of Caplow's coalition theory." Journal of Experimental Social Psychology 3 (April): 172-177.
997.   1971   "Coalition formation as a function of differences in resources." Journal of Conflict Resolution 15 (3, September): 371-383. P.A. 48:11432.
998. Chertkoff, Jerome M., and Suzanna L. Baird
    1971   "Applicability of the big lie technique and the last clear chance doc-trine in bargaining." Journal of Personality and Social Psychology 20 (3): 298-303.
999. Chertkoff, Jerome M., and Joseph L. Braden
    1974   "Effects of experience and bargaining restrictions on coalition for-mation." Journal of Personality and Social Psychology 30 (1, July): 169-177. P.A. 52:12245.
1000. Chertkoff, Jerome M., and Melinda Conley
    1967   "Opening offer and frequency of concession as bargaining strate-gies." Journal of Personality and Social Psychology 7 (2, pt. 1): 181-185. P.A. 41:16618.
1001. Chesler, David J., Niel J. Van Steenberg, and Joyce E. Brueckel
    1955   "Effect on morale of infantry team replacement and individual re-placement systems." Sociometry 18: 587-597. S.A. 5:3439.
1002. Chevaleva-Ianovskaia, E., and D. Sylla
    1929   ("A study of leaders among children.") Journal de Psychologie 26: 604-612. P.A. 4:1293.
1003. Chevrolet, D., and G. Le Calve
    1973   ("Formalization of the dynamics of discussions in restricted groups and some conditions which lead to limit behavior.") Mathématiques et Sciences Humaines 41: 13-26. P.A. 50:4753.
1004. Cheyne, James A., and Michael G. Efran
    1972   "The effect of spatial and interpersonal variables on the invasion of group controlled territories." Sociometry 35 (3, September): 477-489. P.A. 49:9018.
1005. Chipman, Abram
    1966   "Conformity as a differential function of social pressure and judg-ment difficulty." Journal of Social Psychology 70 (December): 299-311.
1006. Chittenden, Gertrude E.
    1942   "An experimental study in measuring and modifying assertive be-havior in young children." Society for Research in Child Develop-ment Monograph 7, No. 1. P.A. 17:992.

1007. Chow, Ester Ngan Ling-Ester, and Carmela Billings
 1972 "An experimental study of the effects of style of supervision and group size on productivity." Pacific Sociological Review 15 (1, January): 61–82. S.A. 20:F6953.

1008. Chowdhry, Kamla, and Theodore M. Newcomb
 1952 "The relative abilities of leaders and non-leaders to estimate opinions of their own groups." Journal of Abnormal and Social Psychology 47: 51–57. (See also Hare, Borgatta, and Bales, 1955, 1965.) P.A. 26:6177.

1009. Christian, Walter P.
 1972 "Conditioned attraction toward neutral peers in a task-oriented situation." Representative Research in Social Psychology 3 (2, December): 121–129. P.A. 50:893.

1010. Christie, Lee S., R. Duncan Luce, and Josiah Macy, Jr.
 1952 Communications and Learning in Task Oriented Groups. Cambridge, Mass.: Research Laboratory of Electronics.

1011. Christie, Richard, and Peggy Cook
 1958 "A guide to published literature relating to the authoritarian personality through 1956." Journal of Psychology 45: 171–199. P.A. 33: 9372.

1012. Christie, Richard, Joan Havel, and Bernard Seidenberg
 1958 "Is the F scale irreversible?" Journal of Abnormal and Social Psychology 56: 143–159.

1013. Christner, Charlotte A., and John K. Hemphill
 1955 "Leader behavior of B-29 commanders and changes in crew members' attitudes toward the crew." Sociometry 18: 82–87. S.A. 3: 1488.

1014. Chudnovskii, V. E.
 1971 ("Psychological research studies of conformity abroad.") Voprosy Psikhologii 17 (4, July): 164–174. P.A. 48:8998.

1015. Church, Russell M.
 1962 "The effects of competition on reaction time and palmar skin conductance." Journal of Abnormal and Social Psychology 65 (1): 32–40.

1016. Cialdini, Robert B., Betty L. Darby, and Joyce E. Vincent
 1973 "Transgression and altruism: A case for hedonism." Journal of Experimental Social Psychology 9 (6): 502–526.

1017. Cialdini, Robert B., Alan Levy, C. Peter Herman, and Scott Evenbeck
 1973 "Attitudinal politics: The strategy of moderation." Journal of Personality and Social Psychology 25 (1, January): 100–108. P.A. 50: 6692.

1018. Cieutat, Victor J.
 1959 "Surreptitious modification of verbal behavior during class discussion." Psychological Reports 5: 648. P.A. 34:5702.

1019. 1962 "Sex differences and reinforcement in the conditioning and extinction of conversational behavior." Psychological Reports 10: 467–474.

1020. Clampitt, Richard R., and Don C. Charles
 1956 Sociometric status and supervisory evaluation of institutionalized mentally deficient children." Journal of Social Psychology 44: 223–231.

1021. Clark, Charles H.
 1958 Brainstorming. Garden City, N.Y.: Doubleday.

1022. Clark, James V.
 1970a "Task group therapy (I): Goals and the client system." Human Relations 23 (4): 263–277.

1023. 1970b "Task group therapy (II): Intervention and problems of practice." Human Relations 23 (5): 383–403.

1024. Clark, James V., and Samuel A. Culbert
 1965 "Mutually therapeutic perception and self-awareness in a T-group." Journal of Applied Behavioral Science 1 (2, April-June): 180–194. S.A. 14:C0068.

1025. Clark, James V., Samuel A. Culbert, and H. K. Babele
   1969   "Mutually therapeutic perception and self-awareness under variable conditions." Journal of Applied Behavioral Science 5 (1): 65-72. P.A. 43:15691.
1026. Clark, Rodney A., and Carson McGuire
   1952   "Sociographic analysis of sociometric valuations." Child Development 23: 129-140. P.A. 27:7134.
1027. Clark, Russell D., III
   1971   "Group-induced shift toward risk: A critical appraisal." Psychological Bulletin 76 (4, October): 251-270.
1028. Clark, Russell D., III, Walter H. Crockett, and Richard L. Archer
   1971   "Risk-as-value hypothesis: The relationship between perception of self, others, and the risky shift." Journal of Personality and Social Psychology 20 (3): 425-429.
1029. Clark, Russell D., III, and Edwin P. Willems
   1969   "Where is the risky shift? Dependence on instructions." Journal of Personality and Social Psychology 13 (3): 215-221. P.A. 44:2264.
1030.   1972   "Two interpretations of Brown's hypothesis for the risky shift." Psychological Bulletin 78 (1, July): 62-63. P.A. 49:748.
1031. Clark, Russell D., III, and Larry E. Word
   1972   "Why don't bystanders help? Because of ambiguity?" Journal of Personality and Social Psychology 24 (3, December): 392-400. P.A. 49: 9019.
1032.   1974   "Where is the apathetic bystander? Situational characteristics of the emergency." Journal of Personality and Social Psychology 29 (3): 279-287.
1033. Clarkson, Geoffrey P.
   1968   "Decision making in small groups: A simulation study." Behavioral Sciences 13 (4, July): 288-305. P.A. 42:15396; S.A. 17:D7612.
1034. Clarkson, Geoffrey P., and Francis D. Tuggle
   1966   "Toward a theory of group-decision behavior." Behavioral Science 11 (1, January): 33-42. P.A. 40:4180; S.A. 14:C2797.
1035. Clement, David E.
   1971   "Learning and retention in student-led discussion groups." Journal of Social Psychology 84: 279-286.
1036. Cleveland, Sidney E., and Seymour Fisher
   1957   "Prediction of small group behavior from a body image schema." Human Relations 10: 223-233. S.A. 10:A1198.
1037. Cleveland, Sidney E., and Robert B. Morton
   1962   "Group behavior and body image: A follow-up study." Human Relations 15 (1, February): 77-85. P.A. 37:1094; S.A. 11:A5696.
1038. Clifford, Clare, and Thomas S. Cohn
   1964   "The relationship between leadership and personality attributes perceived by followers." Journal of Social Psychology 64 (1, October): 57-64. P.A. 39:4906.
1039. Cline, Victor B., Jon Atzet, and Elaine Holmes
   1972   "Assessing the validity of verbal and nonverbal cues in accurately judging others." Comparative Group Studies 3 (4, November): 383-394. P.A. 51:973.
1040. Cline, Victor B., and James M. Richards, Jr.
   1960   "Accuracy of interpersonal perception: A general trait?" Journal of Abnormal and Social Psychology 60 (1, January): 1-7. P.A. 34: 7621.
1041.   1961   "The generality of accuracy of interpersonal perception." Journal of Abnormal and Social Psychology 62 (2, March): 446-449. S.A. A2143.
1042. Clore, Gerald L., and Barbara Baldridge
   1968   "Interpersonal attraction: The role of agreement and topic interest." Journal of Personality and Social Psychology 9 (4): 340-346. P.A. 42:17139.
1043.   1970   "The behavior of item weights in attitude-attraction research." Journal of Experimental Social Psychology 6 (2): 177-186. P.A. 43:

16543.

1044. Clore, Gerald L., and Katherine McMillan Jeffery
    1972   "Emotional role playing, attitude change, and attraction toward a disabled person." Journal of Personality and Social Psychology 23 (1): 105–111.

1045. Cloyd, Jerry S.
    1964a   "Functional differentiation and the structure of informal groups." Sociological Quarterly 5 (3, Summer): 243–250. S.A. 13:B4924.

1046.   1964b   "Patterns of role behavior in informal interaction." Sociometry 27 (2, June): 161–173. P.A. 39:4855; S.A. 13:B4056.

1047.   1965   "Small group as social institution." American Sociological Review 30 (3, June): 394–402. S.A. 14:B9176.

1048. Coch, Lester, and John R. P. French, Jr.
    1948   "Overcoming resistance to change." Human Relations 1: 512–532. (See also Cartwright and Zander, 1960, 1968; Maccoby, Newcomb, and Hartley, 1958.) P.A. 23:2436.

1049. Cocherell, D. L.
    1935   "A study of the play of children of pre-school age by an unobserved observer." Genetic Psychology Monographs 17: 377–469.

1050. Codol, Jean P.
    1970   ("Influence of the representation of another person on the activity of members of the experimental group.") Année Psychologique 70 (1): 131–150. P.A. 46:10736.

1051.   1972–   ("Preferential choice and the phenomenon of ideal conformity in it-
    1973   self.") Bulletin de Psychologie 26 (14-16): 807–813. P.A. 51:3020.

1052. Coe, Rodney
    1964   "Conflict, interference, and aggression: Computer simulation of a social process." Behavioral Science 9: 186–197.

1053. Coelho, George V.
    1959   "A guide to literature on friendship: A selective annotated bibliography." Psychological Newsletter 10: 365–394. P.A. 34:2857.

1054. Coffey, Hubert S.
    1952   "Socio and psyche group process: Integrative concepts." Journal of Social Issues 8 (2): 65–74. P.A. 28:2712.

1055. Coffey, Hubert S., Mervin B. Freedman, Timothy F. Leary, and Abel G. Ossorio (eds.)
    1950   "Community service and social research: Group psychotherapy in a church program." Journal of Social Issues 6 (1): 1–65. P.A. 25: 1050, 1117, 1118, 1119.

1056. Cohen, Abraham I.
    1971   "Process in T-groups: Some observations." Journal of Contemporary Psychotherapy 3 (2, Spring): 127–130. P.A. 47:4704.

1057. Cohen, Akiba A., and Randall P. Harrison
    1973   "Intentionality in the use of hand illustrators in face-to-face communication situations." Journal of Personality and Social Psychology 28 (2): 276–279.

1058. Cohen, Arthur M.
    1961   "Changing small group communication networks." Journal of Communication 11: 116–124. P.A. 4GG16C.

1059.   1962   "Changing small-group communication networks." Administrative Science Quarterly 6 (4, March): 443–462. S.A. 11:A5130.

1060. Cohen, Arthur M., and Warren G. Bennis
    1961   "Continuity of leadership in communication networks." Human Relations 14 (4, November): 351–367. P.A. 37:1125.

1061. Cohen, Arthur M., Warren G. Bennis, and George H. Wolkon
    1961   "The effects of continued practice on the behaviors of problem-solving groups." Sociometry 24 (4, December): 416–431. S.A. A3243.

1062.   1962   "The effects of changes in communication networks on the behaviors of problem-solving groups." Sociometry 25 (2, June): 177–196. S.A. 11:A5131.

1063. Cohen, Arthur M., and Joseph R. Foerst, Jr.
    1968   "Organizational behaviors and adaptations to organizational change

of sensitizer and represser problem-solving groups." Journal of Personality and Social Psychology 8 (2, pt. 1): 209–216. P.A. 42:5526.

1064. Cohen, Arthur M., Phillip E. Rosner, and Joseph R. Foerst, Jr.
1973   "Leadership continuity in problem-solving groups: An interactional study." Human Relations 26 (6): 753–774. P.A. 52:2884.

1065. Cohen, Arthur R.
1956   "Experimental effects of ego-defense preference on interpersonal relations." Journal of Abnormal and Social Psychology 52: 19–27. P.A. 31:2539.

1066.   1958   "Upward communication in experimentally created hierarchies." Human Relations 11: 41–53. P.A. 34:2941.

1067.   1962   "A dissonance analysis of the boomerang effect." Journal of Personality 30 (1): 75–88. P.A. 38:8258.

1068. Cohen, Arthur R., Jack W. Brehm, and Bibb Latané
1959   "Choice of strategy and voluntary exposure to information under public and private conditions." Journal of Personality 27 (March): 63–73. P.A. 34:4176.

1069. Cohen, Bernard P.
1958   "A probability model for conformity." Sociometry 21: 69–81.

1070.   1962   "The process of choosing a reference group." In J. H. Criswell, H. Solomon, and P. Suppes (eds.), Mathematical Methods in Small Group Processes, pp. 101–118. Stanford, Calif.: Stanford University Press. S.A. 12:B2406.

1071. Cohen, David, John W. Whitmyre, and Wilmer H. Funk
1960   "Effect of group cohesiveness and training upon creative thinking." Journal of Applied Psychology 44: 319–322. P.A. 35:3356.

1072. Cohen, Donald J., and Ogden R. Lindsley
1964   "Catalysis of controlled leadership in cooperation by human stimulation." Journal of Child Psychology 5 (2): 119–137. P.A. 39:7650.

1073. Cohen, Edwin
1957a   "Stimulus conditions as factors in social change." Sociometry 20: 135–144.

1074.   1957b   "The effect of members' use of a formal group as a reference group upon group effectiveness." Journal of Social Psychology 46: 307–309. P.A. 36:1GE07C.

1075. Cohen, Elizabeth G.
1972   "Interracial interaction disability." Human Relations 25 (1, February): 9–24. P.A. 49:2322.

1076. Cohen, Guido B.
1968   "Communication network and distribution of 'weight' of group members as determinants of group effectiveness." Journal of Experimental Social Psychology 4 (3, July): 302–314. P.A. 43:2533.

1077. Cohen, Guido B., P. B. Defares, and D. van Kreveld
1964   ("The experience of illegitimate use of power.") Nederlands Tijdschrift voor de Psychologie 19 (3): 315–327. P.A. 39:9993.

1078. Cohen, Jerry L., and James H. Davis
1973   "Effects of audience status, evaluation, and time of action on performance with hidden-word problems." Journal of Personality and Social Psychology 27 (1, July): 74–85. P.A. 50:11212.

1079. Cohen, John
1953   "Social thinking." Acta Psychologica 9: 146–158. P.A. 28:2397.

1080. Cohen, Robert, and Edward J. Murray
1972   "Censure of vicarious aggression as an instigation to subsequent aggression." Journal of Consulting and Clinical Psychology 39 (3, December): 473–477. P.A. 50:894.

1081. Cohen, Ronald
1972   "Altruism: Human, cultural, or what?" Journal of Social Issues 28 (3): 39–57. P.A. 50:4754.

1082. Cohen, Ronald L.
1974   "Mastery and justice in laboratory dyads: A revision and extension of equity theory." Journal of Personality and Social Psychology 29 (4, April): 464–474. P.A. 52:7545.

1083. Cohen, Stephen L., and Cabot L. Jaffee
    1970   "The effects of varying the number of conditioned leaders on group problem solving." Psychonomic Science 21 (2, October): 95–96. P.A. 46:1057.
1084. Cohn, Thomas S., Arnold Fisher, and Virgil Brown
    1961   "Leadership and predicting attitudes of others." Journal of Social Psychology 55 (December): 199–206. P.A. 36:3GF99C.
1085. Cohn, Thomas S., William Yee, and Virgil Brown
    1961   "Attitude change and interpersonal attraction." Journal of Social Psychology 55 (December): 207–211. P.A. 36:3GD07C.
1086. Cole, David
    1954   "'Rational argument' and 'prestige-suggestion' as factors influencing judgement." Sociometry 17: 350–354. P.A. 30:5731.
1087. Cole, Steven G.
    1969   "Examination of the power-inversion effect in three-person mixed-motive games." Journal of Personality and Social Psychology 11 (1): 50–58. P.A. 43:8272.
1088.   1971   "Coalition preference as a function of vote commitment in some dictatorial 'political convention' situations." Behavioral Science 16 (5, September): 436–441. P.A. 47:6668.
1089.   1972   "Conflict and cooperation in potentially intense conflict situations." Journal of Personality and Social Psychology 22 (1, April): 31–50. P.A. 48:4849.
1090. Coleman, James S.
    1960   "The mathematical study of small groups." In H. Solomon (ed.), Mathematical Thinking in the Measurement of Behavior, pp. 1–149. New York: Free Press.
1091.   1961   "Analysis of social structure and simulation of social processes with electronic computers." Educational and Psychological Measurement 21: 203–218. P.A. 36:1GA03C.
1092.   1962   "Reward structures and the allocation of effort." In J. H. Criswell, H. Solomon, and P. Suppes (eds.), Mathematical Methods in Small Group Processes, pp. 119–132. Stanford, Calif.: Stanford University Press. S.A. 12:B2407.
1093.   1969   "Games as vehicles for social theory." American Behavioral Scientist 12 (6, July): 2–6. P.A. 45:9840.
1094. Coleman, James S., and John James
    1961   "The equilibrium size distribution of freely-forming groups." Sociometry 24 (1, March): 36–45. P.A. 36:1GE36C; S.A. A2731.
1095. Coleman, Janet F., Robert R. Blake, and Jane S. Mouton
    1958   "Task difficulty and conformity pressures." Journal of Abnormal and Social Psychology 57: 120–122.
1096. Collaros, Panayiota A., and Lynn R. Anderson
    1969   "Effect of perceived expertness upon creativity of members of brainstorming groups." Journal of Applied Psychology 53 (2, pt. 1): 159–163. P.A. 43:8285.
1097. Collins, Barry E., Harry L. Davis, John G. Myers, and Alvin J. Silk
    1964   "An experimental study of reinforcement and participant satisfaction." Journal of Abnormal and Social Psychology 68 (4, April): 463–467.
1098. Collins, Barry E., and Harold Guetzkow
    1964   A Social Psychology of Group Processes for Decision Making. New York: Wiley.
1099. Collins, Barry E., and Michael F. Hoyt
    1972   "Personal responsibility-for-consequences: An integration and extension of the 'forced compliance' literature." Journal of Experimental Social Psychology 8 (6, November): 558–593. P.A. 49:11055.
1100. Collins, Barry E., and Bertram H. Raven
    1968   "Group structure: Attraction, coalitions, communication, and power." In G. Lindzey and E. Aronson (eds.), Handbook of Social Psychology, vol. 4, pp. 102–204. Reading, Mass.: Addison-Wesley.

1101. Combest, Wendy, Katherine Kasten, and Juliet P. Shaffer
1973   "The relationship between personality impression formation and sex: An application of information integration theory." Bulletin of the Psychonomic Society 1 (1-A, January): 2-4. P.A. 50:6695.

1102. Comer, Ronald J., and Jane A. Piliavin
1972   "The effects of physical deviance upon face-to-face interaction: The other side." Journal of Personality and Social Psychology 23 (1): 33-39.

1103. Comrey, Andrew L.
1953   "Group performance in a manual dexterity task." Journal of Applied Psychology 37: 207-210. P.A. 28:3345.

1104. Comrey, Andrew L., and Gerald Deskin
1954a   "Further results on group manual dexterity in men." Journal of Applied Psychology 38: 116-118. P.A. 29:2053.

1105.   1954b   "Group manual dexterity in women." Journal of Applied Psychology 38: 178-180. P.A. 29:3529.

1106. Comrey, Andrew L., and Corolyn K. Staats
1955   "Group performance in a cognitive task." Journal of Applied Psychology 39: 354-356. P.A. 30:6887.

1107. Conlee, Mary C., and Abraham Tesser
1973   "The effects of recipient desire to hear on news transmission." Sociometry 36 (4, December): 588-599. P.A. 52:2885.

1108. Conrad, Dorothy C., and Richard Conrad
1956   "The use of personal pronouns as categories for studying small group interaction." Journal of Abnormal and Social Psychology 52: 277-279. P.A. 31:2689.

1109. Conrath, David W.
1970   "Experience as a factor in experimental gaming behavior." Journal of Conflict Resolution 14 (2, June): 195-202. S.A. 20:F3454.

1110.   1972   "Sex role and 'cooperation' in the game of Chicken." Journal of Conflict Resolution 16 (3, September): 433-443. P.A. 50:895.

1111. Conway, James A.
1967   "Problem solving in small groups as a function of 'open' and 'closed' individual belief systems." Organizational Behavior and Human Performance 2 (4): 394-405. P.A. 42:2484.

1112. Cook, John O.
1968   "Laboratory study of endogenous social change." Psychological Reports 22 (3, pt. 2): 1108. P.A. 42:18728.

1113. Cook, Mark
1970   "Experiments on orientation and proxemics." Human Relations 23 (1): 61-76. P.A. 44:18554.

1114.   1971   Interpersonal Perception. Harmondsworth, Midx., and Baltimore: Penguin. P.A. 50:896.

1115. Cook, Victor J.
1967   "Group decision, social comparison, and persuasion in changing attitudes." Journal of Advertising Research 7 (1, March): 31-37. S.A. 15:C7235.

1116. Cooley, Charles H.
1902   Human Nature and the Social Order. New York: Scribner.

1117.   1909   Social Organization. New York: Scribner.

1118. Coombs, Arthur W., and Charles Taylor
1952   "The effect of the perception of mild degrees of threat on performance." Journal of Abnormal and Social Psychology 47: 420-424.

1119. Coombs, Clyde H.
1973   "A reparameterization of the Prisoner's Dilemma game." Behavioral Science 18 (6, November): 424-428. P.A. 51:7005.

1120. Coombs, Robert H.
1969   "Social participation, self-concept and interpersonal valuation." Sociometry 32 (3): 273-286. P.A. 44:3553.

1121. Coons, W. H., D. L. McEachern, and Helen Annis
1970   "Generalization of verbally conditioned self-acceptance to social interaction in small group discussions." Canadian Journal of Behav-

ioural Science 2 (2): 105-115. P.A. 44:14497.
1122. Cooper, Cary L.
    1969   "The influence of the trainer on participant change in T-groups."
             Human Relations 22 (6, December): 515-530.
1123.   1971   "T-group training and self-actualization." Psychological Reports 28:
                 391-394.
1124.   1971-   "A bibliography of current sensitivity or T-group training research:
        1972   1969-1971." Interpersonal Development 2 (1): 61-64. P.A. 49:
                 11057.
1125.   1972a   "An attempt to assess the psychologically disturbing effects of T-
                 group training." British Journal of Social and Clinical Psychology 11
                 (4, December): 342-345. P.A. 49:9022.
1126.   1972b   "Coping with life stress after sensitivity training." Psychological Re-
                 ports 31 (2, October): 602. P.A. 49:9021.
1127.   1972c   Group Training for Individual and Organizational Development.
                 Basel: Karger. P.A. 51:944.
1128.   1974   "Psychological disturbance following T-groups: Relationship be-
                 tween the Eysenck Personality Inventory and family friends percep-
                 tions." British Journal of Social Work 4 (1, Spring): 39-49. P.A. 52:
                 7502.
1129. Cooper, Cary L., and David Bowles
    1973   "Physical encounter and self-disclosure." Psychological Reports 33
             (2, October): 451-454. P.A. 51:9005.
1130. Cooper, Joel, John M. Darley, and James E. Henderson
    1974   "On the effectiveness of deviant- and conventional-appearing com-
             municators: A field experiment." Journal of Personality and Social
             Psychology 29 (6, June): 752-757. P.A. 52:7547.
1131. Cooper, Joel, and George R. Goethals
    1974   "Unforeseen events and the elimination of cognitive dissonance."
             Journal of Personality and Social Psychology 29 (4, April): 441-
             445. P.A. 52:7546.
1132. Cooper, Joel, and Charles J. Scalise
    1974   "Dissonance produced by deviations from life styles: The interaction
             of Jungian typology and conformity." Journal of Personality and
             Social Psychology 29 (4): 566-571.
1133. Cooper, Joel, Mark P. Zanna, and George R. Goethals
    1974   "Mistreatment of an esteemed other as a consequence affecting dis-
             sonance reduction." Journal of Experimental Social Psychology 10
             (3): 224-233.
1134. Cooper, Michael R., and Michael T. Wood
    1974   "Effects of member participation and commitment in group decision
             making on influence, satisfaction, and decision riskiness." Journal of
             Applied Psychology 59 (2): 127-134.
1135. Cooper, Robert
    1966   "Leader's task relevance and subordinate behavior in industrial work
             groups." Human Relations 19 (1, February): 57-84.
1136. Corfield, Vera K.
    1969   "The role of arousal and cognitive complexity in susceptibility to so-
             cial influence." Journal of Personality 37 (4): 554-566. P.A. 44:
             8369.
1137. Corsini, Raymond J.
    1956   "Understanding and similarity in marriage." Journal of Abnormal
             and Social Psychology 52: 327-332. P.A. 31:4536.
1138.   1957   Methods of Group Psychotherapy. New York: McGraw-Hill.
1139. Corsini, Raymond J., and L. J. Putzey
    1957   "Bibliography of group psychotherapy 1906-1956." Psychodrama
             and Group Psychotherapy Monographs 29. Beacon, N.Y.: Beacon
             House.
1140. Coser, Lewis A.
    1955   "The functions of small-group research." Social Problems 3: 1-6.
             P.A. 30:4338; S.A. 2221.

1141. Costanzo, Philip R.
      1970   "Conformity development as a function of self-blame." Journal of
              Personality and Social Psychology 14 (4): 366–374.
1142. Costanzo, Philip R., Judy F. Grumet, and Sharon S. Brehm
      1974   "The effects of choice and source of constraint on children's attribu-
              tions of preference." Journal of Experimental Social Psychology 10
              (4): 352–364.
1143. Costanzo, Philip R., Harold T. Reitan, and Marvin E. Shaw
      1968   "Conformity as a function of experimentally induced minority and
              majority competence." Psychonomic Science 10 (10): 329–330.
              P.A. 42:10525.
1144. Costin, Frank
      1971   "Empirical test of the 'Teacher-centered' versus 'Student-centered'
              dichotomy." Journal of Educational Psychology 62 (5): 410–412.
1145. Costin, Frank, and Joseph E. Grush
      1973   "Personality correlates of teacher-student behavior in the college
              classroom." Journal of Educational Psychology 65 (1): 35–44.
1146. Cotler, Sheldon, and Robert F. Quilty
      1972   "Help-seeking behavior in a task-oriented dyadic interaction." Jour-
              nal of Social Psychology 86 (1, February): 135–142. P.A. 47:
              10767.
1147. Cottle, Thomas J.
      1971   "The children of nine lives." Sociological Inquiry 41 (2, Spring):
              139–147.
1148. 1973   "Notes on leader disclosure in self-analytic groups." Sociological In-
              quiry 43 (1): 51–65.
1149. Cottrell, Leonard S., Jr.
      1942   "The analysis of situational fields in social psychology." American
              Sociological Review 7: 370–382. (See also Hare, Borgatta, and Bales,
              1955, 1965.) P.A. 16:3671.
1150. Cottrell, Leonard S., Jr., and Ruth Gallagher
      1941   "Developments in social psychology, 1930–1940." Sociometry
              Monographs No. 1. P.A. 15:4736; P.A. 16:1060, 1061.
1151. Cottrell, Nickolas B.
      1963   "Means-interdependence, prior acquaintance, and emotional tension
              during cooperation and subsequent competition." Human Relations
              16 (3, August): 249–262. P.A. 38:5958; S.A. 12:A9432.
1152. Cottrell, Nickolas B., Dennis L. Wack, Gary J. Sekerak, and Robert H. Rittle
      1968   "Social facilitation of dominant responses by the presence of an
              audience and the mere presence of others." Journal of Personality
              and Social Psychology 9 (3): 245–250. P.A. 42:13645.
1153. Couch, Arthur S.
      1960   "Psychological determinants of interpersonal behavior." Ph.D. dis-
              sertation. Harvard University.
1154. Couch, Arthur S., and Launor F. Carter
      1952   "A factorial study of the rated behavior of group members." Paper
              read at Eastern Psychological Association, March.
1155. Couch, Arthur S., and Kenneth H. Keniston
      1960   "Yeasayers and naysayers: Agreeing response set as a personality
              variable." Journal of Abnormal and Social Psychology 60 (2,
              March): 151–174. P.A. 34:7376.
1156. 1961   "Agreeing response set and social desirability." Journal of Abnormal
              and Social Psychology 62 (1, January): 175–179. P.A. 36:3HF75C;
              S.A. A1721.
1157. Couch, Carl J.
      1970   "Dimensions of association in collective behavior episodes." Socio-
              metry 33 (4, December): 457–471. P.A. 46:8911.
1158. Coulson, William R.
      1972   Groups, Gimmicks and Instant Gurus: An Examination of Encoun-
              ter Groups and Their Distortions. New York: Harper & Row. P.A.
              50:4756.

1159. Counseling Center Staff
      1972   "Effects of three types of sensitivity groups on changes in measures
              of self-actualization." Journal of Counseling Psychology 19 (3,
              May): 253-254. P.A. 48:8999.
1160. Cowan, Gloria
      1969   "The Machiavellian: Manipulator or failure in self-presentation?"
              Proceedings of the 77th Annual Convention of the American Psy-
              chological Association 4 (pt. 1): 357-358.
1161. Cowell, Catherine R.
      1972   "Group process as metaphor." Journal of Communication 22 (2,
              June): 113-123. P.A. 49:2324.
1162. Coyle, Grace L.
      1930   Social Process in Organized Groups. New York: R. R. Smith.
1163. Coyle, Grace L. (ed.)
      1937   Studies in Group Behavior. New York: Harper. P.A. 11:2824.
1164. Cozby, Paul C.
      1972   "Self-disclosure, reciprocity and liking." Sociometry 35 (1, March):
              151-160. P.A. 49:750.
1165.   1973a   "Effects of density, activity, and personality on environmental pref-
              erences." Journal of Research in Personality 7 (1, June): 45-60. P.A.
              51:5087.
1166.   1973b   "Self-disclosure: A literature review." Psychological Bulletin 79 (2,
              February): 73-91. P.A. 50:897.
1167. Craig, Kenneth D., Helen Best, and Guenther Reith
      1974   "Social determinants of reports of pain in the absence of painful
              stimulation." Canadian Journal of Behaivoural Science 6 (2, April):
              169-177. P.A. 52:12246.
1168. Craig, Kenneth D., and David J. Crockett
      1968   "Physiological correlates of inflicting pain upon others." Proceedings
              of the 76th Annual Convention of the American Psychological Asso-
              ciation 3: 389-390.
1169. Craig, Kenneth D., and H. Neidermayer
      1974   "Autonomic correlates of pain thresholds influenced by social
              modeling." Journal of Personality and Social Psychology 29 (2):
              246-252.
1170. Crandall, James E.
      1971   "Effects of intolerance of ambiguity upon interpersonal attraction."
              Psychological Reports 28: 550.
1171. Crandall, Rick
      1972   "Effects of preinformation and assumptions concerning future rela-
              tionships in interracial person perception." Journal of Personality
              and Social Psychology 23 (1): 14-20.
1172.   1973   "On the relationship between self-esteem, coping and optimism."
              Psychological Reports 30: 485-486.
1173. Crannell, Clarke W., S. A. Switzer, and Julian O. Morrissette
      1965   "Individual performance in cooperative and independent groups."
              Journal of General Psychology 73 (2): 231-236. P.A. 39:15027.
1174. Crano, William D.
      1970   "Effects of sex, response order, and expertise in conformity: A dis-
              positional approach." Sociometry 33: 239-252.
1175. Crano, William D., and Ralph E. Cooper
      1973   "Examination of Newcomb's extension of structural balance
              theory." Journal of Personality and Social Psychology 27 (3, Sep-
              tember): 344-353. P.A. 51:5056.
1176. Cratty, Bryant J., and Jack N. Sage
      1964   "Effect of primary and secondary group interaction upon improve-
              ment in a complex movement task." Research Quarterly 35 (3, pt.
              1): 265-274. P.A. 39:4856.
1177. Crawford, David E.
      1972   "Dimensions of attribution in the forced-compliance situation." Pro-
              ceedings of the 80th Annual Convention of the American Psycho-
              logical Association 7 (pt. 1): 185-186.

1178. Crawford, Jeffrey L.
    1974   "Task uncertainty decision importance, and group reinforcement as determinants of communication processes in groups." Journal of Personality and Social Psychology 29 (5, May): 619-627. P.A. 52: 12247.
1179. Crawford, Jeffrey L., and Gordon A. Haaland
    1971   "Predecisional process and information seeking in social influence." Proceedings of the 79th Annual Convention of the American Psychological Association 6 (pt. 1): 361-362. P.A. 46:2896.
1180.   1972   "Predecisional information seeking and subsequent conformity in the social influence process." Journal of Personality and Social Psychology 23 (1, July): 112-119. P.A. 48:11433.
1181. Crawford, Jeffrey L., Daniel C. Williams, and Gordon A. Haaland
    1973   "Motivational orientation, sex, and the norm of reciprocity as determinants of communication in dyads." Proceedings of the 81st Annual Convention of the American Psychological Association 8: 249-250. P.A. 50:8814.
1182. Crawford, M. L. J., and B. D. Nicora
    1964   "Measurement of human group activity." Psychological Reports 15: 227-231.
1183. Crawford, Thomas, and Joseph B. Sidowski
    1964   "Monetary incentive and cooperation/competition instructions in a minimal social situation." Psychological Reports 15: 233-234.
1184. Criddle, William D.
    1971   "The physical presence of other individuals as a factor in social facilitation." Psychonomic Science 22 (4, February): 229-230. P.A. 46:8912.
1185. Crisci, Richard, and Howard Kassinove
    1973   "Effect of perceived expertise, strength of advice, and environmental setting on parental compliance." Journal of Social Psychology 89 (2, April): 245-250. P.A. 50:6697.
1186. Criswell, Joan H.
    1939   "Social structure revealed in a sociometric retest." Sociometry 2: 69-75. P.A. 14:1473.
1187.   1943   "Sociometric methods of measuring group preferences." Sociometry 6: 398-408. P.A. 18:2488.
1188.   1949   "Sociometric concepts in personnel administration." Sociometry 12: 287-300.
1189.   1961   "The sociometric study of leadership." In L. Petrullo and B. M. Bass (eds.), Leadership and Interpersonal Behavior, pp. 10-29. New York: Holt, Rinehart & Winston.
1190.   1962   "Introduction." In J. H. Criswell, H. Solomon, and P. Suppes (eds.), Mathematical Methods in Small Group Processes, pp. 1-10. Stanford, Calif.: Stanford University Press. S.A. 12:B2408.
1191. Criswell, Joan H., and Luigi Petrullo
    1957   "Bibliography of unclassified research reports in group psychology." ONR Report ACR-22. Washington, D.C.: Department of the Navy, Office of Naval Research.
1192. Criswell, Joan H., Herbert Solomon, and Patrick Suppes (eds.)
    1962   Mathematical Methods in Small Group Processes. Stanford, Calif.: Stanford University Press. P.A. 38:2581.
1193. Critchlow, Keith F., Robert Herrup, and James M. Dabbs, Jr.
    1968   "Experimenter influence in a conformity situation." Psychological Reports 23 (2): 408-410. P.A. 43:9653.
1194. Crockett, Walter H.
    1955   "Emergent leadership in small, decision-making groups." Journal of Abnormal and Social Psychology 51: 378-383. P.A. 31:2690; S.A. 3440.
1195.   1969   "Balance, agreement, and the object of orientation." Proceedings of the 77th Annual Convention of the American Psychological Association 4 (pt. 1): 431-432. P.A. 43:17336.
1196.   1974   "Balance, agreement, and subjective evaluations of the P-O-X triads."

Journal of Personality and Social Psychology 29 (1): 102–110.

1197. Crockett, Walter H., and Thomas Meidinger
    1956   "Authoritarianism and interpersonal perception." Journal of Abnormal and Social Psychology 53: 378–382. P.A. 32:4030.

1198. Croft, I. J., and T. G. Grygier
    1956   "Social relationships of truants and juvenile delinquents." Human Relations 9: 439–465.

1199. Crombag, Hans F.
    1966   "Cooperation and competition in means interdependent triads: A replication." Journal of Personality and Social Psychology 4 (6, December): 692–695. S.A. 16:D3100.

1200. Cronbach, Lee J.
    1946   "Response sets and test validity." Educational and Psychology Measurement 6: 475–494. P.A. 21:2489.

1201.   1950   "Further evidence on response sets and test design." Educational and Psychological Measurement 10: 3–31. P.A. 25:681.

1202.   1955   "Processes affecting scores on 'understanding of others' and 'assumed similarity.'" Psychological Bulletin 52: 177–193. P.A. 30: 2865.

1203.   1958   "Proposals leading to analytic treatment of social perception scores." In R. Tagiuri and L. Petrullo (eds.), Person Perception and Interpersonal Behavior, pp. 353–379. Stanford, Calif.: Stanford University Press.

1204. Croner, Melvyn D., and Richard H. Willis
    1961   "Perceived differences in task competence and asymmetry of dyadic influence." Journal of Abnormal and Social Psychology 62 (3, May): 705–708. P.A. 36:4GE05C.

1205. Crosbie, Paul V.
    1972   "Social exchange and power compliance: A test of Homans' propositions." Sociometry 35 (1, March): 203–222. (See also Crosbie, 1975.) P.A. 49:751.

1206. Crosbie, Paul V. (ed.)
    1975   Interaction in Small Groups. New York: Macmillan.

1207. Corsbie, Paul V., and Vicki K. Kullberg
    1973   "Minimum resource or balance coalition formation." Sociometry 36 (4, December): 476–493. P.A. 52:2886.

1208. Crott, Helmut W.
    1971   ("An experimental study on negotiation behavior in cooperative games.") Zeitschrift für Sozialpsychologie 2 (1): 61–74. P.A. 47: 2825.

1209.   1972a   ("The influence of structural and situational variables on the behavior in negotiations: I.") Zeitschrift für Sozialpsychologie 3 (2): 134–158. P.A. 49:6797.

1210.   1972b   ("The influence of structural and situational factors on behavior in negotiation situations: II.") Zeitschrift für Sozialpsychologie 3 (3): 227–244. P.A. 50:11213.

1211. Crott, Helmut W., and Volker Montmann
    1973   ("The effect of information concerning opponents' bargaining possibilities on the outcome of a negotiation.") Zeitschrift für Sozialpsychologie 4 (3): 209–219. P.A. 52:819.

1212. Crow, Wayman J.
    1957   "The effect of training upon accuracy and variability in interpersonal perception." Journal of Abnormal and Social Psychology 55: 355–359.

1213. Crow, Wayman J., and Kenneth R. Hammond
    1957   "The generality of accuracy and response sets in interpersonal perception." Journal of Abnormal and Social Psychology 54: 384–390.

1214. Crowell, Laura
    1953   "Problems in measuring participation in discussion." Journal of Communication 3: 17–20. P.A. 28:7331.

1215. Crowell, Laura, Allan Katcher, and S. Frank Miyamoto
    1955   "Self-concepts of communication skill and performance in small

group discussions." Speech Monographs 22: 20–27. P.A. 30:770.

1216. Crowell, Laura, and Thomas M. Scheidel
1961 "Categories for analysis of idea development in discussion groups." Journal of Social Psychology 54 (June): 155–168. P.A. 36:2GE55C.

1217. 1963 "A study of discussant satisfaction in group problem solving." Speech Monographs 30 (1): 56–58. P.A. 37:7943.

1218. Crowne, Douglas P.
1966 "Family orientation, level of aspiration, and interpersonal bargaining." Journal of Personality and Social Psychology 3 (6): 641–645.

1219. Crowne, Douglas P., and Liverant Shephard
1963 "Conformity under varing conditions of personal commitment." Journal of Abnormal and Social Psychology 66 (6): 547–555.

1220. Crowther, Betty
1962 "Note on religious group differences in interaction profiles: A replication study." Psychological Reports 10: 459–464.

1221. Crowther, Betty, and Paul Pantleo
1970 "Measurement of group interaction rate." Psychological Reports 27: 707–712.

1222. Crumbaugh, Charles M., and Gary W. Evans
1967 "Presentation format, other-person strategies, and cooperative behavior in the Prisoner's Dilemma." Psychological Reports 20: 895–902.

1223. Crutchfield, Richard S.
1951 "Assessment of persons through a quasi group-interaction technique." Journal of Abnormal and Social Psychology 46:577–588. P.A. 26:3929.

1224. 1954 "Social psychology and group processes." Annual Review of Psychology 5: 171–202.

1225. 1955 "Conformity and character." American Psychologist 10: 191–198. S.A. 1972.

1226. 1966 "A new technique for measuring individual differences in conformity to group judgment." In A. Anastasi (ed.), Testing Problems in Perspective: 25th Anniversary Volume of Topical Readings from the Invitational Conference on Testing Problems, pp. 539–544. Washington, D.C.: American Council on Education. P.A. 43:9654.

1227. Csoka, Louis S.
1974 "A relationship between leader intelligence and leader rated effectiveness." Journal of Applied Psychology 59 (1): 43–47.

1228. Csoka, Louis S., and Fred E. Fiedler
1972 "Leadership and intelligence: A contingency model analysis." Proceedings of the 80th Annual Convention of the American Psychological Association 7 (pt. 1): 439–440.

1229. Cuceloglu, Dogan
1972 "Facial code in affective communication." Comparative Group Studies 3 (4, November): 395–408.

1230. Culbert, Samuel A.
1970 "Accelerating laboratory learning through a phase progression model for trainer intervention." Journal of Applied Behavioral Science 6 (1): 21–38.

1231. Cull, John
1971 "Conformity behavior in schizophrenics." Journal of Social Psychology 84: 45–49.

1232. Culver, Charles M., and Frances Dunham
1970 "Human relations training with complementary social groups: An experiment in face-to-face interaction." Psychiatry 33 (3, August): 344–351. P.A. 46:4825; S.A. 20:F9132.

1233. Cunningham, Ruth, et al.
1951 Understanding Group Behavior of Boys and Girls. New York: Columbia University, Teachers College. P.A. 25:7069.

1234. Cupchik, Gerald C., and Howard Leventhal
1974 "Consistency between expressive behavior and the evaluation of humorous stimuli: The role of sex and self-observation." Journal of

Personality and Social Psychology 30 (3): 429–442.

1235. Curran, Charles A.
    1945   Personality Factors in Counseling. New York: Grune & Stratton.

1236. Curran, James P.
    1972   "Differential effects of stated preferences and questionnaire role performance on interpersonal attraction in the dating situation." Journal of Psychology 82 (2, November): 313–327. P.A. 49:6798.

1237.   1973a   "Correlates of physical attractiveness and interpersonal attraction in the dating situation." Social Behavior and Personality 1 (2): 153–157. P.A. 51:5088.

1238.   1973b   "Examination of various interpersonal attraction principles in the dating dyad." Journal of Experimental Research in Personality 6 (4, April): 347–356. P.A. 51:3023.

1239. Curry, Timothy J., and Richard M. Emerson
    1970   "Balance theory: A theory of interpersonal attraction?" Sociometry 33 (2, June): 216–238. P.A. 46:6733.

1240. Cvetkovich, George, and Steve R. Baumgardner
    1973   "Attitude polarization: The relative influence of discussion group structure and reference group norms." Journal of Personality and Social Psychology 26 (2, May): 159–165. P.A. 50:11214.

1241. Dabbs, James M., Jr.
    1969   "Similarity of gestures and interpersonal influence." Proceedings of the 77th Annual Convention of the American Psychological Association 4 (pt. 1): 337–338.

1242.   1971   "Physical closeness and negative feelings." Psychonomic Science 23 (2, April): 141–143. P.A. 47:2826.

1243.   1972   "Sex, setting, and reactions to crowding on sidewalks." Proceedings of the 80th Annual Convention of the American Psychological Association 7 (pt. 1): 205–206. P.A. 48:4850.

1244. Dabbs, James M., Jr., James P. H. Fuller, and Timothy S. Carr
    1973   "Personal space when 'cornered': College students and prison inmates." Proceedings of the 81st Annual Convention of the American Psychological Association 8: 213–214. P.A. 50:8815.

1245. Dabbs, James M., Jr., and Robert L. Helmreich
    1972   "Fear, anxiety, and affiliation following a role-played accident." Journal of Social Psychology 86 (2, April): 269–278. P.A. 48: 2869.

1246. Dahlke, H. Otto
    1953   "Determinants of sociometric relations among children in the elementary school." Sociometry 16: 327–338. P.A. 29:1487.

1247. Damm, John
    1968   "Effects of interpersonal contexts on relationships between goal setting behavior and achievement motivation." Human Relations 21 (3, August): 213–226.

1248. d'Amorim, Maria A., and Joseph R. Nuttin
    1972   ("The perception of one's own successes and failures in function of the outcomes of a partner: The influence of task involvement and level of aspiration in male and female subjects.") Psychologica Belgica 12 (1): 9–31. P.A. 49:11058.

1249. Damrin, Dora E.
    1959   "The Russell Sage Social Relations Test: A technique for measuring group problem solving skills in elementary school children." Journal of Experimental Education 28 (September): 85–99. P.A. 34:7538.

1250. Daniell, Robert J., and Philip Lewis
    1972   "Stability of eye contact and physical distance across a series of structured interviews." Journal of Consulting and Clinical Psychology 39 (1, August): 172. P.A. 49:2325.

1251. Daniels, Louise R., and Leonard Berkowitz
    1963   "Liking and response to dependency relationships." Human Relations 16 (2, May): 141–148. S.A. 12:A8715.

1252. Daniels, Victor
  1967   "Communication, incentive, and structural variables in interpersonal exchange and negotiation." Journal of Experimental Social Psychology 3 (January): 47–74.
1253. Danielsson, B.
  1949   "Some attraction and repulsion patterns among Jibaro Indians." Sociometry 12: 83–105.
1254. Danish, Steven J., and Joseph F. Zelenski
  1972   "Structured group interaction." Journal of College Student Personnel 13 (1, January): 53–56. P.A. 48:4851.
1255. Dannick, Lionel I.
  1973   "Influence of an anonymous stranger on a routine decision to act or not to act: An experiment in conformity." Sociological Quarterly 14 (1, Winter): 127–134. P.A. 50:4762.
1256. Danzig, Elliott R., and E. H. Galanter
  1955   "The dynamics and structure of small industrial work groups." Institute Report No. 7, Institute for Research in Human Relations, Philadelphia.
1257. Darley, John G., N. Gross, and W. E. Martin
  1951   "Studies of group behavior: The stability, change, and interrelations of psychometric and sociometric variables." Journal of Abnormal and Social Psychology 46: 565–576. P.A. 26:3915.
1258.   1952   "Studies of group behavior: Factors associated with the productivity of groups." Journal of Applied Psychology 36: 396–403. P.A. 27:6472.
1259. Darley, John M.
  1966   "Fear and social comparison as determinants of conformity behavior." Journal of Personality and Social Psychology 4 (1): 73–78.
1260. Darley, John M., and C. Daniel Batson
  1973   "'From Jerusalem to Jericho': A study of situational and dispositional variables in helping behavior." Journal of Personality and Social Psychology 27 (1, July): 100–108. P.A. 50:11215.
1261. Darley, John M., and Ellen Berscheid
  1967   "Increased liking as a result of the anticipation of personal contact." Human Relations 20 (1, February): 29–40.
1262. Darley, John M., and Bibb Latané
  1968a   "Bystander intervention in emergencies: Diffusion of responsibility." Journal of Personality and Social Psychology 8 (4, pt. 1): 377–383. P.A. 42:8862.
1263.   1968b   "When will people help in a crisis?" Psychology Today 2 (7, December): 54–57, 70–71. P.A. 46:10741.
1264. Darley, John M., T. Moriarty, Susan Darley, and Ellen Berscheid
  1974   "Increased conformity to a fellow deviant as a function of prior deviation." Journal of Experimental Social Psychology 10 (3): 211–223.
1265. Darley, John M., Allan I. Teger, and Lawrence D. Lewis
  1973   "Do groups always inhibit individuals' responses to potential emergencies?" Journal of Personality and Social Psychology 26 (3, June): 395–399. P.A. 50:11216.
1266. Dashiell, John F.
  1930   "An experimental analysis of some group effects." Journal of Abnormal and Social Psychology 25: 190–199.
1267.   1935   "Experimental studies of the influence of social situations on the behavior of individual human adults." In C. Murchison (ed.), A Handbook of Social Psychology, pp. 1097–1158. Worcester, Mass.: Clark University Press.
1268. D'Augelli, Anthony R.
  1973a   "Group composition using interpersonal skills: An analogue study on the effects of members' interpersonal skills on peer ratings and group cohesiveness." Journal of Counseling Psychology 20 (6, November): 531–534. P.A. 51:7021.

1269.   1973b   "The assessment of interpersonal skills: A comparison of observer, peer, and self ratings." Journal of Community Psychology 1 (2, April): 177-179. P.A. 52:821.

1270. Daugherty, B. N.
       1961   "Situational determinants of affective reactions to persons." Psychological Record 11: 139-144. P.A. 36:3GE39D.

1271. Dauler, Sue A.
       1966   "Durability of influence effects in the social influence experiment." Journal of the Scientific Laboratories of Denison University 47 (5-9): 41-48. P.A. 42:2501.

1272. Daval, R.
       1967   ("Psychosociology of decision: Individual decisions and collective decision.") Bulletin de Psychologie 20 (23-24): 1460-1469. P.A. 42: 2485.

1273. Daves, Walter F., and Patricia W. Swaffer
       1971   "Effect of room size on critical interpersonal distance." Perceptual and Motor Skills 33 (3, pt. 1, December): 926. P.A. 48:856.

1274. David, Kenneth H.
       1972   "Generalization of operant conditioning of verbal output in three-man discussion groups." Journal of Social Psychology 87 (2, August): 243-249. P.A. 49:752.

1275. Davie, James S., and A. Paul Hare
       1956   "Button-down collar culture: A study of undergraduate life at a men's college." Human Organization 14 (4): 13-20. P.A. 31:5091.

1276. Davis, Deborah, and Thomas M. Ostrom
       1973   "Trait implication in impression formation." Proceedings of the 81st Annual Convention of the American Psychological Association 8: 195-196. P.A. 50:8816.

1277. Davis, Earl E., and Harry C. Triandis
       1971   "An experimental study of black-white negotiations." Journal of Applied Social Psychology 1 (3, July): 240-262. P.A. 48:2870.

1278. Davis, F. James
       1954   "Conceptions of official leader roles in the Air Force." Social Forces 32: 253-258. P.A. 29:3786.

1279. Davis, Fred
       1964   "Deviance disavowal: The management of strained interaction by the visibly handicapped." In H. S. Becker (ed.), The Other Side, pp. 119-138. New York: Free Press. S.A. 12:B3224.

1280. Davis, James A.
       1961   "Compositional effects, role systems, and the survival of small discussion groups." Public Opinion Quarterly 25 (4, Winter): 574-584. (See also Hare, Borgatta, and Bales, 1965.) P.A. 38:870; S.A. 11: A4157.

1281.   1963   "Structural balance, mechanical solidarity, and interpersonal relations." American Journal of Sociology 68 (4, January): 444-462.

1282.   1970   "Clustering and hierarchy in interpersonal relations: Testing two graph theoretical models." American Sociological Review 35 (5, October): 843-851. S.A. 19:E8387.

1283. Davis, James A., Ruth U. Gebhard, Carolyn Huson, and Joe L. Spaeth
       1961   Great Books and Small Groups. New York: Free Press.

1284. Davis, James A., Joe L. Spaeth, and Carolyn Huson
       1961   "A technique for analyzing the effects of group composition." American Sociological Review 26 (2, April): 215-225. P.A. 36: 1GE15D.

1285.   1971   "A technique for analyzing the effects of group composition." Revista Mexicana de Sociología 33 (2, April-June): 411-428. S.A. 21: 73G2270.

1286. Davis, James H.
       1969a   Group Performance. New York: Addison-Wesley.

1287.   1969b   "Individual-group problem solving, subject preference, and problem type." Journal of Personality and Social Psychology 13 (4): 362-374.

1288.   1973   "Group decision and social interaction: A theory of social decision schemes." Psychological Review 80 (2, March): 97–125. P.A. 50: 900.

1289. Davis, James H., Peter A. Bates, and Stanley M. Nealey
       1971   "Long-term groups and complex problem solving." Organizational Behavior and Human Performance 6 (1, January): 28–35. P.A. 46: 1060.

1290. Davis, James H., Morgan H. Carey, Paul N. Foxman, and David B. Tarr
       1968   "Verbalization, experimenter presence, and problem solving." Journal of Personality and Social Psychology 8 (3): 299–302.

1291. Davis, James H., Jerry L. Cohen, John Hornik, and A. Kent Rissman
       1973   "Dyadic decision as a function of the frequency distributions describing the preferences of members' constituencies." Journal of Personality and Social Psychology 26 (2, May): 178–195. P.A. 50: 11217.

1292. Davis, James H., John Hornik, and John P. Hornseth
       1970   "Group decision schemes and strategy preferences in a sequential response task." Journal of Personality and Social Psychology 15 (4): 397–408. P.A. 44:20815.

1293. Davis, James H., and John P. Hornseth
       1967   "Discussion patterns and word problems." Sociometry 30 (1, March): 91–103. S.A. 15:C5573.

1294. Davis, James H., Ruth Kalb, and John P. Hornseth
       1966   "Stability of impression formation and implications for emergent group structure." Sociometry 29 (2, June): 104–120. P.A. 40: 10027; S.A. 15:C3475.

1295. Davis, James H., Norbert Kerr, Mario Sussmann, and A. Kent Rissman
       1974   "Social decision schemes under risk." Journal of Personality and Social Psychology 30 (2, August): 248–271. P.A. 52:12248.

1296. Davis, James H., and Frank Restle
       1963   "The analysis of problems and prediction of group problem solving." Journal of Abnormal and Social Psychology 66 (2, February): 103–116. S.A. 12:B0181.

1297. Davis, James W.
       1967   "Variations in verbal behavior in dyads as a function of varied reinforcing conditions." Speech Monographs 34 (4): 443–447. P.A. 42: 3895.

1298. Davis, Jay M., and Amerigo Farina
       1970   "Humor appreciation as social communication." Journal of Personality and Social Psychology 15 (2): 175–178.

1299. Davis, John D., and Adrian E. Skinner
       1974   "Reciprocity of self-disclosure in interviews: Modeling or social change?" Journal of Personality and Social Psychology 29 (6, June): 779–784. P.A. 52:7522.

1300. Davis, Junius A., and Charles F. Warnath
       1957   "Reliability, validity, and stability of a sociometric rating scale." Journal of Social Psychology 45: 111–121.

1301. Davis, Keith E., and Edward E. Jones
       1960   "Changes in interpersonal perception as a means of reducing cognitive dissonance." Journal of Abnormal and Social Psychology 61 (3): 402–410.

1302. Davis, Murray S.
       1973   Intimate Relations. New York: Free Press. P.A. 51:7006.

1303. Davis, R. L.
       1954   "Structures of dominance relations." Bulletin of Mathematics and Biophysics 16: 131–140.

1304. Davis, William L., and E. Jerry Phares
       1967   "Internal-external control as a determinant of information-seeking in a social influence situation." Journal of Personality 35 (4): 547–561. P.A. 42:18729.

1305. Davitz, Joel R.
       1955   "Social perception and sociometric choice." Journal of Abnormal

and Social Psychology 50: 173–176. P.A. 30:685; S.A. 1973.
1306. Davol, Stephen H.
    1959   "An empirical test of structural balance in sociometric triads." Journal of Abnormal and Social Psychology 59: 393–398. P.A. 34:5765.
1307. Dawe, Helen C.
    1934   "The influence of the size of kindergarten group upon performance." Child Development 5: 295–303.
1308. Day, Robert C., and Robert L. Hamblin
    1964   "Some effects of close and punitive styles of supervision." American Journal of Sociology 69 (5, March): 499–510. S.A. 12:B2409.
1309. Dayhaw, Lawrence T., and Charles E. McInnis
    1970   "The effect of peer rating treatments on group morale." Canadian Psychologist 11 (3): 281–288. P.A. 44:20816.
1310. Dean, John P., and Alex Rosen
    1955   A Manual of Intergroup Relations. Chicago: University of Chicago Press. P.A. 30:2707.
1311. Deaux, Kay K.
    1972   "To err is humanizing: But sex makes a difference." Representative Research in Social Psychology 3 (1, May): 20–28. P.A. 49:9025.
1312.   1974   "Anonymous altruism: Extending the lost letter technique." Journal of Social Psychology 92 (1): 61–66.
1313. Deaux, Kay K., and Cynthia Coppess
    1971   "Partner preferences for cooperative and competitive tasks: The effect of self-esteem." Psychological Record 21 (2, Spring): 265–268. P.A. 47:2827.
1314. de Charms, Richard
    1957   "Affiliation motivation and productivity in small groups." Journal of Abnormal and Social Psychology 55: 222–226.
1315. de Charms, Richard, and Edward J. Wilkins
    1963   "Some effects of verbal expression of hostility." Journal of Abnormal and Social Psychology 66 (5): 462–470.
1316. Deci, Edward L., Carl Benware, and David Landy
    1973   "Money talks: So does output in attributing motivation." Proceedings of the 81st Annual Convention of the American Psychological Association 8: 245–246. P.A. 50:6701.
1317. Deets, Lee E.
    1955–   "The small group: An eclectic bibliography." Autonomous Groups
    1956   Bulletin 11 (2 and 3): 11–16. P.A. 32:5301.
1318. De la Haye, Anne M.
    1972–   ("Continuance of communication and image of a partner.") Bulletin
    1973   de Psychologie 26 (14-16): 780–788. P.A. 51:2945.
1319. DeLamater, John, Charles G. McClintock, and Gordon Becker
    1965   "Conceptual orientations of contemporary small group theory." Psychological Bulletin 64 (6): 402–412. P.A. 40:2809.
1320. Delbecq, André L., and Andrew H. Van de Ven
    1971   "A group process model for problem identification and program planning." Journal of Applied Behavioral Science 7 (4, July-August): 466–492. S.A. 20:F9133.
1321. DeLeon, Patrick H., Jean L. DeLeon, and Joseph A. Sheflin
    1970   "A validation study of self-disclosure." Proceedings of the 78th Annual Convention of the American Psychological Association 5 (pt. 1): 473–474.
1322. Delhees, Karl H.
    1970   "Conceptions of group decision and group conflict applied to vector space: A research model." Acta Psychologica 34 (4, December): 440–450. P.A. 46:1061.
1323. Delia, Jesse G., and Walter H. Crockett
    1973   "Social schemas, cognitive complexity, and the learning of social structures." Journal of Personality 41 (3): 413–429.
1324. Delin, Peter S., and Kee Poo-Kong
    1974   "The measurement of mutual conformity in a dyadic situation." British Journal of Social and Clinical Psychology 13 (2, June): 211–

213. P.A. 52:12249.

1325. DeLong, Alton J.
1970a "Dominance-territorial relations in a small group." Environment and Behavior 2 (2, September): 170-191. P.A. 48:4852.
1326. 1970b "Seating position and perceived characteristics of members of a small group." Cornell Journal of Social Relations 5 (2, Fall): 134-152. S.A. 21:73G0552.
1327. 1971 "Dominance-territorial criteria and small group structure." Comparative Group Studies 2 (3, August): 235-266. P.A. 48:2871.
1328. 1973 "Territorial stability and hierarchical formation." Small Group Behavior 4 (1, February): 55-63. P.A. 50:4763.
1329. Deloughery, Grace W., Betty M. Neuman, and Kristine M. Gebbie
1972 "Mental health consultation as a means of improving problem-solving ability in work groups." Comparative Group Studies 3 (1, February): 89-97.
1330. De Monchaux, Cecily, and Sylvia Shimmin
1955 "Some problems in experimental group psychology: Considerations arising from cross-cultural experiments on threat and rejection." Human Relations 8: 53-60. P.A. 30:822; S.A. 1756.
1331. de Montmollin, Germaine
1955a ("Group effects on perceptive structuration.") Année Psychologique 55: 1-25. P.A. 31:737.
1332. 1955b ("Group effects on perceptive structuration. II.") Année Psychologique 55: 329-348. P.A. 31:738.
1333. 1958 ("Processes in social influence.") Année Psychologique 58: 427-447. P.A. 34:2860.
1334. 1959 ("Effect of age on group behavior.") Année Psychologique 59: 93-106. P.A. 34:5705.
1335. 1960 ("Reflections on the study and utilization of small groups.") Bulletin du C.E.R.P. 9: 110-121. P.A. 35:3357.
1336. 1965 ("The influence of others' responses on perceptual judgments.") Année Psychologique 65 (2): 377-395. P.A. 40:8787.
1337. 1966a ("Social influence and perceptive judgment: The effect of information scattering on individual change.") Année Psychologique 66 (1): 111-129. P.A. 40:12266.
1338. 1966b ("The idea of group cohesion.") Bulletin de Psychologie 19 (19-20): 1206-1211. P.A. 40:10028.
1339. 1971 ("Subjective probabilities in friendship relations.") Année Psychologique 71 (2): 439-449. P.A. 49:11059.
1340. Dengerink, H. A., and P. G. Levendusky
1972 "Effects of massive retaliation and balance of power on aggression." Journal of Experimental Research in Personality 6 (2-3, December): 230-236. P.A. 51:916.
1341. Denmark, Florence, Dorothy Murgatroyd, and Albert Pepitone
1965 "Effect of differential valuation on group level of aspiration, decision time, and productivity." Journal of Social Psychology 67 (2, December): 201-209. P.A. 40:5392.
1342. Denner, Bruce
1969 "Refusal to communicate: Preliminary study of a classical interpersonal tactic." Perceptual and Motor Skills 29 (3, December): 835-842. P.A. 46:4826.
1343. Dentler, Robert A.
1961 "Political concern and opinion change in ten work groups." Journal of Educational Sociology 35 (1, September): 27-31. S.A. A3802.
1344. Denzin, Norman K.
1971 "The logic of naturalistic inquiry." Social Forces 50 (2): 166-182.
1345. Derbyshire, Robert L., and Barbara B. Foster
1971 "Small groups: A study of leadership style and its effects on communication among medical students." Comparative Group Studies 2 (3, August): 267-292.
1346. Derlega, Valerian J., Marian S. Harris, and Alan L. Chaikin
1973 "Self-disclosure reciprocity, liking and the deviant." Journal of Ex-

perimental Social Psychology 9 (4, July): 277–284. P.A. 51:2970.

1347. Derlega, Valerian J., James Walmer, and Gail Furman
    1973   "Mutual disclosure in social interactions." Journal of Social Psychology 90 (1, June): 159–160. P.A. 51:3024.

1348. Dertke, Max C., Louis A. Penner, Harold L. Hawkins, and Conchita Suarez
    1973   "The inhibitory effects of an observer on instrumental aggression." Bulletin of the Psychonomic Society 1 (2, February): 112–114. P.A. 50:6702.

1349. Deschamps, Jean C.
    1972–   ("Imputation of responsibility for failure (or success) and social
    1973   categorization.") Bulletin de Psychologie 26 (14-16): 794–806. P.A. 51:2946.

1350. Des Jarlais, Don
    1970   "Shifts to risk and reward." Psychological Reports 26 (1, February): 119–122. P.A. 45:2289.

1351. Desor, J. A.
    1972   "Toward a psychological theory of crowding." Journal of Personality and Social Psychology 21 (1): 79–83.

1352. De Soto, Clinton B., Nancy M. Henley, and Marvin London
    1968   "Balance and the grouping schema." Journal of Personality and Social Psychology 8 (1, pt. 1): 1–7. P.A. 42:5509.

1353. De Soto, Clinton B., James L. Kuethe, and Richard Wunderlich
    1960   "Social perception and self-perception of high and low authoritarians." Journal of Social Psychology 52 (August): 149–155. P.A. 35: 6333.

1354. Desportes, Jean P., and Liliane Lesieur
    1971–   ("The maximization of interindividual distances: Study in a natural
    1972   situation of a behavior avoiding the presence of others.") Bulletin de Psychologie 25 (5-7): 312–314. P.A. 50:8820.

1355. Deutsch, Morton
    1949a   "A theory of cooperation and competition." Human Relations 2: 129–152. (See also Cartwright and Zander, 1968.) P.A. 24:137.

1356.   1949b   "An experimental study of the effects of cooperation and competition upon group process." Human Relations 2: 199–231. (See also Cartwright and Zander 1953, 1960, 1968.) P.A. 24:4051.

1357.   1954   "Field theory in social psychology." In G. Lindzey (ed.), Handbook of Social Psychology, pp. 181–222. Cambridge, Mass.: Addison-Wesley.

1358.   1958   "Trust and suspicion." Journal of Conflict Resolution 2 (4, December): 265–279. S.A. A3244.

1359.   1959   "Some factors affecting membership motivation and achievement motivation in a group." Human Relations 12: 81–95. P.A. 34:5706; S.A. A2732.

1360.   1960a   "The effect of motivational orientation upon trust and suspicion." Human Relations 13 (2, May): 123–139. P.A. 35:6334; S.A. A3820.

1361.   1960b   "Trust, trustworthiness, and the F scale." Journal of Abnormal and Social Psychology 61 (1): 138–140. P.A. 35:2107.

1362.   1961   "The interpretation of praise and criticism as a function of their social context." Journal of Abnormal and Social Psychology 62 (2, March): 391–400. P.A. 4GE91D; S.A. A2208.

1363.   1968a   "Field theory in social psychology." In G. Lindzey and E. Aronson (eds.), Handbook of Social Psychology, vol. 1, pp. 412–487. Reading, Mass.: Addison-Wesley.

1364.   1968b   "Group behavior." In D. L. Sills (ed.), International Encyclopedia of the Social Sciences, vol. 6, pp. 265–276. New York: Macmillan and Free Press.

1365.   1969   "Socially relevant science: Reflections on some studies of interpersonal conflict." American Psychologist 24 (12): 1076–1092. P.A. 44:10278.

1366. Deutsch, Morton, Donnah Canavan, and Jeffery Rubin
    1971   "The effects of size of conflict and sex of experimenter upon interpersonal bargaining." Journal of Experimental Social Psychology 7

(2, March): 258–267. P.A. 46:4827.

1367. Deutsch, Morton, Yakov Epstein, Donnah Canavan, and Peter Gumpert
    1967   "Strategies of inducing cooperation: An experimental study." Journal of Conflict Resolution 11 (3, September): 345–360. S.A. 16: D0606.

1368. Deutsch, Morton, and Harold B. Gerard
    1955   "A study of normative and informational social influences upon individual judgement." Journal of Abnormal and Social Psychology 51: 629–636. (See also Cartwright and Zander, 1960; Crosbie, 1975.) P.A. 31:2366.

1369. Deutsch, Morton, and Robert M. Krauss
    1960   "The effect of threat upon interpersonal bargaining." Journal of Abnormal and Social Psychology 61 (2): 181–189.

1370.   1962   "Studies of interpersonal bargaining." Journal of Conflict Resolution 6 (1): 52–76.

1371. Deutsch, Morton, and Roy J. Lewicki
    1970   "'Locking-in' effects during a game of Chicken." Journal of Conflict Resolution 14 (3): 367–378.

1372. Deutsch, Morton, and Leonard Solomon
    1959   "Reactions to evaluations by others as influenced by self-evaluations." Sociometry 22 (2, June): 93–112. P.A. 34:4179.

1373. Deutschberger, Paul
    1947   "The 'tele'-factor: Horizon and awareness." Sociometry 10: 242–249. P.A. 23:1223.

1374. Deutscher, Verda, and Irwin Deutscher
    1955   "Cohesion in a small group: A case study." Social Forces 33: 336–341. S.A. 2488.

1375. Dewey, John
    1933   How We Think. Lexington, Mass.: Heath.

1376. Diab, Lutfy N.
    1968   "Conformity and deviation: Two processes or one?" Psychological Reports 22: 1134–1136.

1377. Diamond, Michael J.
    1974   "From Skinner to Satori? Toward a social learning analysis of encounter group behavior change." Journal of Applied Behavioral Science 10 (2, April): 133–148. P.A. 52:12250.

1378. Diamond, Michael J., and Jerrold L. Shapiro
    1973   "Changes in locus of control as a function of encounter group experiences: A study and replication." Journal of Abnormal Psychology 82 (3): 514–518.

1379. Dickenberger, Dorothee, and Gisla Grabitz-Gniech
    1972   "Restrictive conditions for the occurrence of psychological reactance: Interpersonal attraction, need for social approval, and a delay factor." European Journal of Social Psychology 2 (2): 177–198. P.A. 49:9027.

1380. Dickens, M.
    1955   "A statistical formula to quantify the 'spread of participation' in group discussion." Speech Monographs 22: 28–30. P.A. 30:772.

1381. Dicks, Henry V.
    1944   Psychological Foundations of the Wehrmacht. London: War Offices.

1382. Diener, Edward, Karen L. Westford, John Dineen, and Scott C. Fraser
    1973   "Beat the pacifist: The deindividuating effects of anonymity and group presence." Proceedings of the 81st Annual Convention of the American Psychological Association 8: 221–222. P.A. 50:8821.

1383. Diener, Edward, Karen L. Westford, Scott C. Fraser, and Arthur L. Beaman
    1973   "Selected demographic variables in altruism." Psychological Reports 33 (1, August): 226. P.A. 51:7058.

1384. Dies, Robert R., and Allen K. Hess
    1970   "Self-disclosure, time perspective and semantic-differential changes. Marathon and short-term group psychotherapy." Comparative Group Studies 1 (4, November): 387–395.

1385.   1971   "An experimental investigation of cohesiveness in marathon and conventional group psychotherapy." Journal of Abnormal Psychology 77 (3): 258–262.

1386. Dies, Robert R., and Richard Sadowsky
1974   "A brief encounter group experience and social relationships in a dormitory." Journal of Counseling Psychology 21 (2, March): 112–115. P.A. 52:7523.

1387. Diggins, Dean
1974   "The role of social and nonsocial traits in interpersonal attraction." Journal of Personality 42 (3): 345–359.

1388. Dillon, Peter C., William K. Graham, and Andrea L. Aidells
1972   "Brainstorming on a 'hot' problem: Effects of training and practice on individual and group performance." Journal of Applied Psychology 56 (6, December): 487–490. P.A. 49:9028.

1389. Dimock, Hedley G.
1971   "Sensitivity training as a method of increasing on-the-job effectiveness." Sociological Inquiry 41 (2, Spring): 227–231.

1390. Dinges, Norman G., and Richard G. Weigel
1971   "The marathon group. A review of practice and research." Comparative Group Studies 2 (4, November): 339–458.

1391. Dion, Karen K.
1972   "Physical attractiveness and evaluation of children's transgressions." Journal of Personality and Social Psychology 24 (2, November): 207–213. P.A. 49:4397.

1392. Dion, Karen K., and Ellen Berscheid
1974   "Physical attractiveness and peer perception among children." Sociometry 37 (1): 1–12.

1393. Dion, Karen K., Ellen Berscheid, and Elaine Walster
1972   "What is beautiful is good." Journal of Personality and Social Psychology 24 (3): 285–290.

1394. Dion, Kenneth L.
1973   "Cohesiveness as a determinant of ingroup-outgroup bias." Journal of Personality and Social Psychology 28 (2, November): 163–171. P.A. 52:822.

1395. Dion, Kenneth L., and Karen K. Dion
1973   "Correlates of romantic love." Journal of Consulting and Clinical Psychology 41 (1, August): 51–56. P.A. 51:11000.

1396. Dion, Kenneth L., and Patricia A. Mathewson
1973   "Contrast, anxiety, and attraction in response to changes in another's esteem." Proceedings of the 81st Annual Convention of the American Psychological Association 8: 203–204. P.A. 50:4765.

1397. Dion, Kenneth L., and Norman Miller
1971   "An analysis of the familiarization explanation of the risky-shift." Journal of Experimental Social Psychology 7 (5, September): 524–533. P.A. 48:9001.

1398. Dion, Kenneth L., Norman Miller, and Mary Ann Magnan
1970   "Cohesiveness and social responsibility as determinants of group risk taking." Proceedings of the 78th Annual Convention of the American Psychological Association 5 (pt. 1): 335–336. P.A. 44:18556.

1399.   1971   "Cohesiveness and social responsibility as determinants of group risk taking." Journal of Personality and Social Psychology 20 (3, December): 400–406. P.A. 47:8782.

1400. Dittes, James E.
1959   "Attractiveness of group as function of self-esteem and acceptance by group." Journal of Abnormal and Social Psychology 59: 77–82. P.A. 34:4180.

1401. Dittes, James E., and H. H. Kelley
1956   "Effects of different conditions of acceptance upon conformity to group norms." Journal of Abnormal and Social Psychology 53: 100–107. (See also Hare, Borgatta, and Bales, 1965.) P.A. 32:1443.

1402. Dittmann, Allen T.
1952   "The interpersonal process in psychotherapy: Development of a research method." Journal of Abnormal and Social Psychology 47:

236–244. P.A. 27:2778.

1403. Dittmann, Allen T., and Lynn G. Llewellyn
    1969   "Body movement and speech rhythm in social conversation." Journal of Personality and Social Psychology 11 (2): 98–106. P.A. 43: 8286.

1404. Di Vesta, Francis J.
    1954   "Instructor-centered and student-centered approaches in teaching a human relations course." Journal of Applied Psychology 38: 329–335. P.A. 29:6161.

1405.   1959   "Effects of confidence and motivation on susceptibility to informational social influence." Journal of Abnormal and Social Psychology 59: 204–209.

1406. Di Vesta, Francis J., and Landon Cox
    1960   "Some dispositional correlates of conformity behavior." Journal of Social Psychology 22 (November): 259–268. P.A. 35:4813.

1407. Di Vesta, Francis J., and Jack C. Merwin
    1960   "The effects of need-oriented communications on attitude change." Journal of Abnormal and Social Psychology 60 (January): 80–85. P.A. 34:7539.

1408. Di Vesta, Francis J., James H. L. Roach, and William Beasley
    1951   "Rating conference participation in a human relations training program." Journal of Applied Psychology 35: 386–391. P.A. 26:6578.

1409. Dmitruk, Victor M., Robert W. Collins, and Dennis L. Clinger
    1973   "The 'Barnum effect' and acceptance of negative personal evaluation." Journal of Consulting and Clinical Psychology 41 (2, October): 192–194. P.A. 51:7059.

1410. Dodd, Stuart C.
    1935   "A social distance test in the Near East." American Journal of Sociology 41: 194–204.

1411.   1940   "The interrelation matrix." Sociometry 3: 91–101. P.A. 14:3308.

1412.   1955   "The transact model." Sociometry 18: 688–703. P.A. 32:1444.

1413. Dodd, Stuart C., and Peter G. Garabedian
    1961   "The logistic law of interaction when people pair off 'at will.'" Journal of Social Psychology 53 (February): 143–158. P.A. 35:6335.

1414. Dodd, Stuart C., and Louise B. Klein
    1962   "The concord index for social influence." Pacific Sociological Review 5 (1, Spring): 60–64. S.A. 11:A5141.

1415. Doherty, Edmund G., and Paul F. Secord
    1971   "Change of roommate and interpersonal congruency." Representative Research in Social Psychology 2 (2, July): 70–75. P.A. 49:9030.

1416. Doise, Willem
    1969a   "Intergroup relations and polarization of individual and collective judgments." Journal of Personality and Social Psychology 12 (2): 136–143. P.A. 43:12894.

1417.   1969b   ("Collective judgment and risk in small groups.") Psychologie Française 14 (2, June): 87–95. S.A. 20:F6012.

1418.   1970   ("The importance of a principal dimension in collective judgments.") Année Psychologique 70 (1): 151–159. P.A. 46:10743.

1419.   1971   "An apparent exception to the extremization of collective judgments." European Journal of Social Psychology 1 (4): 511–518. P.A. 48:9002; S.A. 22:74G6139.

1420. Doise, Willem, and Serge Moscovici
    1969–   ("Acceptance and rejection of the deviant within groups of differing
    1970   cohesiveness.") Bulletin de Psychologie 23 (9-10): 522–525. P.A. 46:2898.

1421. Dolbear, F. Trenery, Jr., and Lester B. Lave
    1966   "Risk orientation as a predictor in the Prisoner's Dilemma." Journal of Conflict Resolution 10 (4, December): 506–515. S.A. 15:C6377.

1422. Dolbear, F. Trenery, Jr., Lester B. Lave, G. Bowman, A. Lieberman, E. Prescott, F. Rueter, and R. Sherman
    1969   "Collusion in the Prisoner's Dilemma: Number of strategies." Journal of Conflict Resolution 13 (2, June): 252–261.

1423. Doll, Richard E., and E. K. Eric Gunderson
    1970   "Influence of group size on perceived compatibility and achievement in an extreme environment." Proceedings of the 78th Annual Convention of the American Psychological Association 5 (2): 601–602.

1424. Domino, George
    1971   "Interactive effects of achievement orientation and teaching style on academic achievement." Journal of Educational Psychology 62 (5): 427–431.

1425. Donnay, Jean M.
    1972   ("Affiliation: Its dynamic substratum and its behavioral and intellectual implications.") Psychologica Belgica 12 (2): 175–187. P.A. 49:6800.

1426. Donnenwerth, Gregory V., and Uriel G. Foa
    1974   "Effect of resource class on retaliation to injustice in interpersonal exchange." Journal of Personality and Social Psychology 29 (6, June): 785–793. P.A. 52:7548.

1427. Donnerstein, Edward, and Marcia Donnerstein
    1973   "Variables in interracial aggression: Potential ingroup censure." Journal of Personality and Social Psychology 27 (1, July): 143–150. P.A. 50:11218.

1428. Doob, Anthony N.
    1970   "Catharsis and aggression: The effect of hurting one's enemy." Journal of Experimental Research in Personality 4 (4, October): 291–296. P.A. 45:6192.

1429. Doob, Anthony N., and Barbara P. Ecker
    1970   "Stigma and compliance." Journal of Personality and Social Psychology 14 (4): 302–304.

1430. Doob, Anthony N., and Hershi M. Kirshenbaum
    1973   "The effects on arousal of frustration and aggressive films." Journal of Experimental Social Psychology 9 (1, January): 57–64. P.A. 50: 2920.

1431. Doob, Leonard W., William J. Foltz, and Robert B. Stevens
    1969   "The Fermeda Workshop: A different approach to border conflicts in eastern Africa." Journal of Psychology 73 (2): 249–266. P.A. 44: 8355.

1432. Dornbusch, Sanford M., Albert H. Hastorf, Stephen A. Richardson, Robert E. Muzzy, and Rebecca S. Vreeland
    1965   "The perceiver and the perceived: Their relative influence on the categories of interpersonal cognition." Journal of Personality and Social Psychology 1 (5): 434–440.

1433. Dorris, J. William
    1972   "Reactions to unconditional cooperation: A field study emphasizing variables neglected in laboratory research." Journal of Personality and Social Psychology 22 (3, June): 387–397. P.A. 48:11435.

1434. Dosey, Michael A., and Murray Meisels
    1969   "Personal space and self-protection." Journal of Personality and Social Psychology 11 (2): 93–97.

1435. Doster, Joseph A., and Samuel J. Brooks
    1974   "Interviewer disclosure modeling, information revealed, and interviewee verbal behavior." Journal of Consulting and Clinical Psychology 42 (3, June): 420–426. P.A. 52:12251.

1436. Dove, John L., and William T. McReynolds
    1972   "Effects of modeling and model-observer similarity in imitation and generalization of aggressive verbal behavior." Psychological Reports 31 (2, October): 599–601. P.A. 49:9031.

1437. Dowaliby, Fred J., and Harry Schumer
    1973   "Teacher-centered versus student-centered mode of college classroom instruction as related to manifest anxiety." Journal of Educational Psychology 64 (2): 125–132.

1438. Dowdle, Michael D.
    1973   "Differences in attributions of personality as a function of the type of interaction between actor and observer." Proceedings of the 81st

Annual Convention of the American Psychological Association 8: 349-350. P.A. 50:4766.

1439. Downing, J.
1958   "Cohesiveness, perception, and values." Human Relations 11: 157-166. S.A. A1699.

1440. Draughon, Margaret
1973   "Duplication of facial expressions: Conditions affecting task and possible clinical usefulness." Journal of Personality 41 (1, March): 140-150. P.A. 50:4768.

1441. Driscoll, Richard, Keith E. Davis, and Milton E. Lipetz
1972   "Parental interference and romantic love: The Romeo and Juliet effect." Journal of Personality and Social Psychology 24 (1, October): 1-10. P.A. 49:4399.

1442. Driver, Michael J., and Phillip L. Hunsaker
1972   "The Luna I Moon Colony: A programmed simulation for the analysis of individual and group decision making." Psychological Reports 31 (3, December): 879-888. P.A. 50:905.

1443. Drost, Bruce A., and Paul D. Knott
1971   "Effects of status of attacker and intensity of attack on the intensity of counter-aggression." Journal of Personality 39: 450-459.

1444. Druckman, Daniel
1967   "Dogmatism, prenegotiation experience, and simulated group representation as determinants of dyadic behavior in a bargaining situation." Journal of Personality and Social Psychology 6 (3): 279-290.

1445.   1968   "Prenegotiation experience and dyadic conflict resolution in a bargaining situation." Journal of Experimental Social Psychology 4 (4, October): 367-383. P.A. 43:3921.

1446.   1970   "Position change in cognitive conflict as a function of the cue-criterion relationship and the initial conflict." Psychonomic Science 20 (2): 91-93. P.A. 44:20818.

1447.   1971a   "On the effects of group representation." Journal of Personality and Social Psychology 18 (2, May): 273-274. P.A. 46:4828.

1448.   1971b   "The influence of the situation in interparty conflict." Journal of Conflict Resolution 15 (4, December): 523-554. P.A. 48:9003.

1449. Druckman, Daniel, Daniel Solomon, and Kathleen Zechmeister
1972   "Effects of representational role obligations on the process of children's distribution of resources." Sociometry 35 (3, September): 387-410. P.A. 49:6801.

1450. Druckman, Daniel, and Kathleen Zechmeister
1973   "Conflict of interest and value dissensus: Propositions in the sociology of conflict." Human Relations 26 (4, August): 449-466. P.A. 51:7008.

1451. Druckman, Daniel, Kathleen Zechmeister, and Daniel Solomon
1972   "Determinants of bargaining behavior in a bilaterial monopoly situation: Opponent's concession rate and relative defensibility." Behavioral Science 17 (5, November): 514-531. P.A. 50:11219; S.A. 22: 74G6140.

1452. Dubin, Robert, George C. Homans, Floyd C. Mann, and Delbert C. Miller
1965   Leadership and Productivity: Some Facts of Industrial Life. San Francisco: Chandler.

1453. Dubno, Peter
1963   "Decision time characteristics of leaders and group problem solving behavior." Journal of Social Psychology 59 (2, April): 259-282. P.A. 38:883.

1454.   1965   "Leadership, group effectiveness, and speed of decision." Journal of Social Psychology 65 (2, April): 351-360. P.A. 39:15075.

1455.   1968   "Group congruency patterns and leadership characteristics." Personnel Psychology 21 (3): 335-344. P.A. 43:3922.

1456. Duck, Steven W.
1972   "Friendship, similarity and the Reptest." Psychological Reports 31 (1, August): 231-234. P.A. 49:6802.

1457.   1973a   "Personality similarity and friendship choice: Similarity of what, when?" Journal of Personality 41 (4): 542-558.

1458.   1973b   "Similarity and perceived similarity of personal constructs as influences on friendship choice." British Journal of Social and Clinical Psychology 12 (1, February): 1-6. P.A. 50:2921.

1459. Duck, Steven W., and Christopher Spencer
         1972   "Personal constructs and friendship formation." Journal of Personality and Social Psychology 23 (1, July): 40-45. P.A. 48:11437.

1460. Duflos, André
         1967   ("Do collective tasks facilitate dominant responses to the detriment of unusual responses?") Bulletin du C.E.R.P. 16 (4): 323-336. P.A. 43:5263.

1461. Duke, Marshall P., and Stephen Nowicki
         1972   "A new measure and social-learning model for interpersonal distance." Journal of Experimental Research in personality 6 (2-3, December): 119-132. P.A. 51:976.

1462. Dulong, Renaud
         1972   ("Cognitive aspects of the collective decision: Predicision.") Bulletin du C.E.R.P. 21 (2-3, April): 1-65. P.A. 52:823.

1463. Duncan, Starkey, Jr.
         1970   "Floor apportionment in a dyad." Proceedings of the 78th Annual Convention of the American Psychological Association 5 (pt. 1): 383-384. P.A. 44:18557.

1464.   1972   "Some signals and rules for taking speaking turns in conversations." Journal of Personality and Social Psychology 23 (2, August): 283-292. P.A. 49:754.

1465. Duncan, Starkey, Jr., and George Niederehe
         1974   "On signalling that it's your turn to speak." Journal of Experimental Social Psychology 10 (3): 234-247.

1466. Dunn, Robert E., and Morton Goldman
         1966   "Competition and noncompetition in relationship to satisfaction and feelings toward own-group and non-group members." Journal of Social Psychology 68 (2, April): 299-311. P.A. 40:7637.

1467. Dunnette, Marvin D.
         1969   "People feeling: Joy, more joy, and the 'slough of despond.'" Journal of Applied Behavioral Science 5 (1, January-March): 25-44. P.A. 43:15695. S.A. 18:E1779.

1468. Dunnette, Marvin D., John Campbell, and Kay Jaastad
         1963   "The effect of group participation on brainstorming effectiveness for 2 industrial samples." Journal of Applied Psychology 47 (1): 30-37. P.A. 37:7944.

1469. Dunphy, Dexter C.
         1963   "The social structure of urban adolescent peer groups." Sociometry 26 (2, June): 230-246.

1470.   1964   "Social change in self-analytic groups." Ph.D. dissertation. Harvard University. S.A. 14:C1884.

1471. Dunphy, Dexter C., Philip J. Stone, and Marshall S. Smith
         1965   "The general inquirer: Further developments in a computer system for content analysis of verbal data in the social sciences." Behavioral Science 10: 468-480.

1472. Dupuis, A. M.
         1959   "Group dynamics: Philosophical presuppositions." Journal of Social Psychology 50 (November): 247-260. P.A. 35:4814.

1473. Durkin, James E.
         1968   "Dyadic permeability in a noncognitive interpersonal reaction-time task." Proceedings of the 76th Annual Convention of the American Psychological Association 3: 413-414.

1474. Dustin, David S.
         1966   "Member reactions to team performance." Journal of Social Psychology 69 (2, August): 237-243. P.A. 40:12267.

1475. Dustin, David S., and Henry P. Davis
         1970   "Evaluative bias in group and individual competition." Journal of

Social Psychology 80 (1): 103–108. P.A. 44:12464.

1476. Dustin, David S., and Charles T. Polihronakis
    1970   "Team bias in a card contest." Psychological Reports 27 (2, October): 558. P.A. 45:6193.

1477. Dutton, Donald G.
    1972   "Effect of feedback parameters on congruency versus positivity effects in reactions to personal evaluations." Journal of Personality and Social Psychology 24 (3, December): 366–371. P.A. 49:9032.

1478.   1973   "Attribution of cause for opinion change and liking for audience members." Journal of Personality and Social Psychology 26 (2, May): 208–216. P.A. 50:11220.

1479. Dutton, Donald G., and Arthur P. Aron
    1974   "Some evidence for heightened sexual attraction under conditions of high anxiety." Journal of Personality and Social Psychology 30 (4): 510–517.

1480. Dutton, Donald G., and A. John Arrowood
    1971   "Situational factors in evaluation congruency and interpersonal attraction." Journal of Personality and Social Psychology 18 (2): 222–229.

1481. Duval, Shelley, and Robert A. Wicklund
    1973   "Effects of objective self-awareness on attribution of causality." Journal of Experimental Social Psychology 9 (1, January): 17–31. P.A. 50: 2922.

1482. Dymond, Rosalind F.
    1949   "A scale for the measurement of empathic ability." Journal of Consulting Psychology 13: 127–133. (See also Hare, Borgatta, and Bales, 1955, 1965.) P.A. 23:4497.

1483.   1950   "Personality and empathy." Journal of Consulting Psychology 14: 343–350. P.A. 25:4352.

1484. Dymond, Rosalind F., Anne S. Hughes, and Virginia L. Raabe
    1952   "Measurable changes in empathy with age." Journal of Consulting Psychology 16: 202–206. P.A. 27:5021.

1485. Dymond, Rosalind F., J. Seeman, and D. L. Grummon
    1956   "Patterns of perceived interpersonal relations." Sociometry 19: 166–177.

1486. Dyson, James W., Danial W. Fleitas, and Frank P. Scioli, Jr.
    1972   "The interaction of leadership, personality, and decisional environments." Journal of Social Psychology 86: 29–33.

1487. D'Zurilla, Thomas J.
    1966   "Persuasion and praise as techniques for modifying verbal behavior in a 'real-life' group setting." Journal of Abnormal Psychology 71 (5): 369–376. P.A. 40:13151.

1488. Eaglin, Ronald G.
    1973   "The effect of verbal reinforcement on leader behavior." Journal of College Student Personnel 14 (1, January): 71–76. P.A. 50: 6704.

1489. Eagly, Alice H.
    1970   "Leadership style and role differentiation as determinants of group effectiveness." Journal of Personality 38 (4, December): 509–524. P.A. 46:1062.

1490. Eagly, Alice H., and Barbara A. Acksen
    1971   "The effect of expecting to be evaluated on change toward favorable and unfavorable information about oneself." Sociometry 34 (4): 411–422.

1491. Eastman, Charles M., and Joel Harper
    1971   "A study of proxemic behavior: Toward a predictive model." Environment and Behavior 3 (4, December): 418–437. P.A. 48:2873.

1492. Ebbesen, Ebbe B., and Richard J. Bowers
    1974   "Proportion of risky to conservative arguments in a group discussion and choice shift." Journal of Personality and Social Psychology 29 (3): 316–327.

1493. Edelstein, J. David, and Malcolm Warner
    1971   "Voting and allied systems in group decision-making: Their relation-
            ship to innovation, competition and conflict resolution." Human Re-
            lations 24 (2): 179–188.
1494. Edenfield, William H., and Robert D. Myrick
    1973   "The effect of group sensitivity experience on learning facilitative
            verbal responses." Small Group Behavior 4 (2, May): 249–256. P.A.
            51:7024.
1495. Edmonds, Vernon H.
    1964   "Logical error as a function of group consensus: An experimental
            study of the effect of erroneous group consensus upon the logical
            judgments of graduate students." Social Forces 43 (1, October): 33–
            38. P.A. 39:4857; S.A. 13:B4925.
1496. Edney, Julian J.
    1972   "Place and space: The effects of experience with a physical locale."
            Journal of Experimental Social Psychology 8 (2): 124–135.
1497. Edney, Julian J., and Nancy L. Jordan-Edney
    1974   "Territorial spacing on a beach." Sociometry 37 (1): 92–104.
1498. Edwards, Allen L.
    1954   "Experiments: Their planning and execution." In G. Lindzey (ed.),
            Handbook of Social Psychology, pp. 259–288. Cambridge, Mass.:
            Addison-Wesley. P.A. 29:3840.
1499.   1961   "Social desirability or acquiescence in the MMPI?" Journal of Ab-
            normal and Social Psychology 63 (2): 351–359.
1500. Edwards, Allen L., and Jerold N. Walker
    1961a   "A note on the Couch and Keniston measure of agreement response
            set." Journal of Abnormal and Social Psychology 62 (1, January):
            173–174. P.A. 36:3HF73E; S.A. A1722.
1501.   1961b   "Social desirability and agreement response set." Journal of Abnor-
            mal and Social Psychology 62 (1, January): 180–183. P.A. 36:
            3HF80E; S.A. A1723.
1502. Edwards, Bill E., and Jettie M. McWilliams
    1974   "Perceiver sex and expressor sex as related to cognitive perception."
            Journal of Psychology 86 (2, March): 203–207. P.A. 52:12306.
1503. Edwards, D. J.
    1972   "Approaching the unfamiliar: A study of human interaction dist-
            ances." Journal of Behavioral Science 1 (4): 249–250. P.A. 50:907.
1504. Effrat, Andrew
    1968   "Editor's introduction." (Applications of Parsonian theory.) Socio-
            logical Inquiry 38 (Spring): 97–103.
1505. Efran, Jay S.
    1968   "Looking for approval: Effects on visual behavior of approbation
            from persons differing in importance." Journal of Personality and
            Social Psychology 10 (1): 21–25. P.A. 43:787.
1506. Efran, Jay S., and E. Robert Boylin
    1967   "Social desirability and willingness to participate in a group discus-
            sion." Psychological Reports 20: 402.
1507. Efran, Jay S., and Andrew Broughton
    1966   "Effect of expectancies for social approval on visual behavior." Jour-
            nal of Personality and Social Psychology 4 (1): 103–107. P.A. 40:
            10029.
1508. Efran, Michael G., and James A. Cheyne
    1973   "Shared space: The co-operative control of spatial areas by two in-
            teracting individuals." Canadian Journal of Behavioural Science 5 (3,
            July): 201–210. P.A. 51:7025.
1509.   1974   "Affective concomitants of the invasion of shared space: Behavioral,
            physiological, and verbal indicators." Journal of Personality and So-
            cial Psychology 29 (2): 219–226.
1510. Egerman, Karl
    1966   "Effects of team arrangement on team performance: A learning-
            theoretic analysis." Journal of Personality and Social Psychology 3
            (5, May): 541–550. P.A. 40:7638; S.A. 15:C4084.

1511. Ehlert, Jeff, Nuala Ehlert, and Matthew Merrens
    1973   "The influence of ideological affiliation on helping behavior." Journal of Social Psychology 89 (2, April): 315-316. P.A. 50:6705.
1512. Ehrlich, Howard J.
    1969   "Affective style as a variable in person perception." Journal of Personality 37: 522-539.
1513. Ehrlich, Howard J., and David B. Graeven
    1971   "Reciprocal self-disclosure in a dyad." Journal of Experimental Social Psychology 7 (4, July): 389-400. P.A. 48:2874.
1514. Ehrlich, Howard J., James W. Rinehart, and John C. Howell
    1962   "The study of role conflict: Explorations in methodology." Sociometry 25 (1): 85-97. P.A. 37:1095.
1515. Eiben, Ray, and R. James Clack
    1973   "Impact of a participatory group experience on counselors in training." Small Group Behavior 4 (4, November): 486-495.
1516. Eibl-Eibesfeldt, Irenäus
    1968   ("Ethology of human greeting behavior.") Zeitschrift für Tierpsychologie 25 (6): 727-744. P.A. 43:3935.
1517. Eifermann, Rivka R.
    1970   "Cooperativeness and egalitarianism in kibbutz children's games." Human Relations 23 (6): 579-587.
1518. Eisenberger, Robert, Carl Carlson, David M. Kuhlman, and Daniel C. Williams
    1970   "More help for those who try harder." Psychological Reports 27 (2, October): 451-454. P.A. 45:8101.
1519. Eisenman, Richard L.
    1967   "A profit-sharing interpretation of Shapley value for N-person games." Behavioral Science 12 (September): 396-398.
1520. Eisenstadt, Jeanne W.
    1967   "An investigation of factors which influence response to laboratory training." Journal of Applied Behavioral Science 3 (4): 575-578. P.A. 42:13646.
1521.   1970   "Interpersonal orientation, coping style, and two dimensions of sociometric choice." Human Relations 23 (6, December): 515-531. P.A. 48:858.
1522. Eiser, J. Richard, Carl N. Aiyeola, Sally M. Bailey, and Elaine J. Gaskell
    1973   "Attributions of intention to a simulated partner in a mixed-motive game." British Journal of Social and Clinical Psychology 12 (3, September): 241-247. P.A. 51:5091.
1523. Eiser, J. Richard, and Alistair J. Smith
    1972   "Preference for accuracy and positivity in the description of oneself by another." European Journal of Social Psychology 2 (2): 199-201. P.A. 50:2923.
1524. Eiser, J. Richard, and Wolfgang Stroebe
    1972   Categorization and Social Judgement. London: Academic Press. P.A. 50:6707.
1525. Eiser, J. Richard, and Henri Tajfel
    1972   "Acquisition of information in dyadic interaction." Journal of Personality and Social Psychology 23 (3): 340-345.
1526. Eiser, J. Richard, and Sarah J. Taylor
    1972   "Favouritism as a function of assumed similarity and anticipated interaction." European Journal of Social Psychology 2 (4): 453-454. P.A. 50:6706.
1527. Eisler, Richard M., Michel Hersen, and W. Stewart Agras
    1973   "Videotape: A method for the controlled observation of nonverbal interpersonal behavior." Behavior Therapy 4 (3, May): 420-425. P.A. 51:946.
1528. Eisman, Bernice
    1959   "Some operational measures of cohesiveness and their interrelations." Human Relations 12 (2, May): 183-189. P.A. 34:7543; S.A. A2733.
1529. Eister, Allan W.
    1957   "Basic continuities in the study of small groups." In H. Becker and

A. Boskoff (eds.), Modern Sociological Theory, pp. 305–339. New York: Dryden.

1530. Eitington, Julius E.
1971   "Assessing laboratory training using psychology of learning concepts." Training and Development Journal 25 (2, February): 2–7. P.A. 49:4401.

1531. Ekehammar, Bo, and David Magnusson
1973   "A method to study stressful situations." Journal of Personality and Social Psychology 27 (2, August): 176–179. P.A. 51:3028.

1532. Ekman, Gosta
1955   "The four effects of cooperation." Journal of Social Psychology 41: 149–162. P.A. 30:580.

1533. Ekman, Paul, and Wallace V. Friesen
1974   "Detecting deception from the body or face." Journal of Personality and Social Psychology 29 (3): 288–298.

1534. Ekstein, Rudolf
1972   "Psychoanalysis and education for the facilitation of positive human qualities." Journal of Social Issues 28 (3): 71–85. P.A. 50:4770.

1535. Elias, Norbert, and Eric Dunning
1966   ("On the dynamics of sports groups.") Kölner Zeitschrift für Soziologie and Sozialpsychologie 10 (Supplement): 118–134. S.A. 15: C5575.

1536. Elkine, D.
1927   ("The influence of the group on memory functions.") Journal de Psychologie 24: 827–830. P.A. 3:92.

1537. Elliott, H. S.
1928   The Process of Group Thinking. New York: Association Press.

1538. Ellis, Desmond P., Paul Weinir, and Louie Miller, III
1971   "Does the trigger pull the finger? An experimental test of weapons as aggression-eliciting stimuli." Sociometry 34 (4, December): 453–465. P.A. 48:859.

1539. Ellis, Haydn D., Christopher P. Spencer, and Hilary Oldfield-Box
1969   "Matched groups and the risky shift phenomenon: A defence of the extreme member hypothesis." British Journal of Social and Clinical Psychology 8 (4): 333–339: P.A. 47:6675.

1540. Ellison, Craig W., and Ira J. Firestone
1974   "Development of interpersonal trust as a function of self-esteem, target status, and target style." Journal of Personality and Social Psychology 29 (5, May): 655–663. P.A. 52:12307.

1541. Ells, Jerry G., and Vello Sermat
1966   "Cooperation and the variation of payoff in non-zero-sum games." Psychonomic Science 5 (4): 149–150. P.A. 40:10030.

1542.   1968   "Motivational determinants of choice in Chicken and Prisoner's Dilemma." Journal of Conflict Resolution 12 (3): 374–380. P.A. 43: 14227.

1543. Ellsworth, Phoebe C., and J. Merrill Carlsmith
1968   "Effects of eye contact and verbal content on affective response to a dyadic interaction." Journal of Personality and Social Psychology 10 (1): 15–20. P.A. 43:798.

1544.   1973   "Eye contact and gaze aversion in an aggressive encounter." Journal of Personality and Social Psychology 28 (2): 280–292.

1545. Ellsworth, Phoebe C., J. Merrill Carlsmith, and Alexander Henson
1972   "The stare as a stimulus to flight in human subjects: A series of field experiments." Journal of Personality and Social Psychology 21 (3): 302–311.

1546. Ellsworth, Phoebe C., and Linda M. Ludwig
1972   "Visual behavior in social interaction." Journal of Communication 22 (4, December): 375–403. P.A. 50:4771.

1547. Elms, Alan C., and Irving L. Janis
1965   "Counter-norm attitudes induced by consonant vs. dissonant conditions of role playing." Journal of Experimental Research Personality 1: 50–60.

1548. Emerson, Richard M.
    1954   "Deviation and rejection: An experimental replication." American Sociological Review 19: 688–693. P.A. 30:2631.
1549.   1964   "Power-dependence relations: Two experiments." Sociometry 27 (3, September): 282–298. S.A. 13:B4926.
1550.   1966a   "Mount Everest: A case study of communication feedback and sustained group goal-striving." Sociometry 29 (3, September): 213–227. P.A. 40:13152; S.A. 15:C3476.
1551.   1966b   ("Mount Everest: A case study of communication backflow and the maintenance of the goal orientation of groups.") Kölner Zeitschrift für Soziologie und Sozialpsychologie 10 (Supplement): 135–167. S.A. 15:C5576.
1552.   1968   "Role theory and diminishing utility in group problem solving." Pacific Sociological Review 11 (2, Fall): 110–115. S.A. 17:D8267.
1553. Emmer, Edmund T., and Robert F. Peck
    1973   "Dimensions of classroom behavior." Journal of Educational Psychology 64 (2): 223–240.
1554. Emshoff, James R.
    1970   "A computer simulation model of the Prisoner's Dilemma." Behavioral Science 15 (4, July): 304–317. S.A. 19:F0467.
1555. Emshoff, James R., and Russell L. Ackoff
    1970   "Explanatory models of interactive choice behavior." Journal of Conflict Resolution 14 (1, March): 77–89. P.A. 46:2901.
1556. Endleman, Shalom
    1963   "Comparison of the sociometric structure of two college classes." International Journal of Sociometry and Sociatry 3 (3-4, September-December): 72–76. S.A. 13:B6753.
1557. Endler, Norman S.
    1960   "Social conformity in perception of the autokinetic effect." Journal of Abnormal and Social Psychology 61 (3): 489–490. P.A. 36:2GE89E.
1558.   1961   "Conformity analyzed and related to personality." Journal of Social Psychology 53 (April): 271–283. P.A. 36:1GE71E.
1559.   1965   "The effects of verbal reinforcement on conformity and deviant behavior." Journal of Social Psychology 66 (1, June): 147–154. P.A. 39:15031.
1560.   1966   "Conformity as a function of different reinforcement schedules." Journal of Personality and Social Psychology 4 (2): 175–180. P.A. 40:11099.
1561.   1973   "Source and type of prior experience as antecedents of conformity." Journal of Social Psychology 90 (1, June): 161–162. P.A. 51:2973.
1562. Endler, Norman S., and Susan Hartley
    1973   "Relative competence, reinforcement and conformity." European Journal of Social Psychology 3 (1): 63–72. P.A. 52:824; S.A. 22:74G8626.
1563. Endler, Norman S., and Elizabeth Hoy
    1967   "Conformity as related to reinforcement and social pressure." Journal of Personality and Social Psychology 7 (2, pt. 1): 197–202. P.A. 41:16644.
1564. Endler, Norman S., and C. J. Marino
    1972   "The effects of source and type of prior experience on subsequent conforming behavior." Journal of Social Psychology 88 (1, October): 21–29. P.A. 49:4402.
1565. Endler, Norman S., David L. Wiesenthal, and Sheldon H. Geller
    1972   "The generalization of the effects of agreement and correctness on relative competence mediating conformity." Canadian Journal of Behavioural Science 4 (4, October): 322–329. P.A. 49:6804.
1566. Eng, Erling W.
    1954   "An approach to the prediction of sociometric choice." Sociometry 17: 329–339. P.A. 30:5875.
1567. England, J. Lynn
    1973   "Mathematical models of two-party negotiations." Behavioral Sci-

ence 18 (3, May): 189-197. P.A. 51:2974.

1568. Enoch, J. Rex, and S. Dale McLemore
1967   "On the meaning of group cohesion." Southwestern Social Science Quarterly 48 (2, September): 174-182. S.A. 16:D2322.

1569. Eoyang, Carson K.
1974   "Effects of group size and privacy in residential crowding." Journal of Personality and Social Psychology 30 (3): 389-392.

1570. Epstein, Yakov M., and Harvey A. Hornstein
1969   "Penalty and interpersonal attraction as factors influencing the decision to help another person." Journal of Experimental Social Psychology 5 (3): 272-282. P.A. 47:5070.

1571. Epstein, Yakov M., Peter Suedfeld, and Stanley J. Silverstein
1973   "The experimental contract: Subjects' expectations of and reactions to some behaviors of experimenters." American Psychologist 28 (3, March): 212-221. P.A. 50:11222.

1572. Erbe, William
1966   "Accessibility and informal social relationships among American graduate students." Sociometry 29 (3, September): 251-264.

1573. Erdélyi, Rozalia
1968   ("Group solving of thinking problems.") Studia Universitatis Babes-Bolvai 13: 21-26. P.A. 47:10768.

1574. Erikson, Bonnie, et al.
1974   "Functions of a third party in the resolution of conflict: The role of a judge in pretrial conferences." Journal of Personality and Social Psychology 30 (2, August): 293-306. P.A. 52:12227.

1575. Esser, Aristide H.
1973   "Cottage Fourteen. Dominance and territoriality in a group of institutionalized boys." Small Group Behavior 4 (2, May): 131-146.

1576. Estes, William K.
1962   "Theoretical treatments of differential rewards in multiple-choice learning and two-person interactions." In J. H. Criswell, H. Solomon, and P. Suppes (eds.), Mathematical Methods in Small Group Processes, pp. 133-149. Stanford, Calif.: Stanford University Press. S.A. 12:B2410.

1577. Eswara, H. S.
1972   "Assimilation and contrast as factors in interpersonal perception." Journal of the Indian Academy of Applied Psychology 9 (2): 45-47. P.A. 51:7061.

1578. Ettinger, Ronald F., C. J. Marino, Norman S. Endler, Sheldon H. Geller, and Taras Natziuk
1971   "Effects of agreement and correctness on relative competence and conformity." Journal of Personality and Social Psychology 19 (2): 204-212.

1579. Ettinger, Ronald F., Stephen Nowicki, Jr., and Don A. Nelson
1970   "Interpersonal attraction and the approval motive." Journal of Experimental Research in Personality 4 (2): 95-99. P.A. 44:10279.

1580. Evans, Gloria C.
1960   "Validity of ascendance measurements in group interaction." Psychological Reports 7: 114. P.A. 35:3374.

1581. Evans, Gary W., and Charles M. Crumbaugh
1966   "Effects of Prisoner's Dilemma format on cooperative behavior." Journal of Personality and Social Psychology 3 (4): 486-488. P.A. 40:5393.

1582. Evans, Gary W., and Roger B. Howard
1973   "Personal space." Psychological Bulletin 80 (4, October): 334-344. P.A. 51:5092.

1583. Evans, James F.
1974   "Motivational effects of being promised an opportunity to engage in social comparison." Psychological Reports 34 (1, February): 175-181: P.A. 52:7550.

1584. Evans, James F., and Arieh Bonder
1973   "A possible relationship between rivalry and impending social com-

parison." Proceedings of the 81st Annual Convention of the American Psychological Association 8: 333–334. P.A. 50:8824.

1585. Evans, John T.
    1950   "Objective measurements of the therapeutic group process." Ph.D. dissertation. Harvard University.

1586. Evans, Judith T., and Robert Rosenthal
    1969   "Interpersonal self-fulfilling prophecies: Further extrapolations from the laboratory to the classroom." Proceedings of the 77th Annual Convention of the American Psychological Association 4 (pt. 1): 371–372.

1587. Evans, Martin G., and Jerry Dermer
    1974   "What does the least preferred co-worker scale really measure?: A cognitive interpretation." Journal of Applied Psychology 59 (2): 202–206.

1588. Ex, J., and J. Schouten
    1968   "Experience of real similarity, sympathy and person perception." Acta Psychologica 28 (1): 92–96. P.A. 42:10511.

1589. Exline, Ralph V.
    1957   "Group climate as a factor in the relevance and accuracy of social perception." Journal of Abnormal and Social Psychology 55: 382–388.

1590.   1960a   "Effects of sex, norms, and affiliation motivation upon accuracy of perception of interpersonal perferences." Journal of Personality 28: 397–412. P.A. 35:4815.

1591.   1960b   "Interrelations among two dimensions of sociometric status, group congeniality and accuracy of social perception." Sociometry 23 (1, March): 85–101. P.A. 35:2109.

1592.   1962a   "Effects of need for affiliation, sex, and the sight of others upon initial communications in problem-solving groups." Journal of Personality 30 (4): 541–556. P.A. 39:1567.

1593.   1962b   "Need affiliation and initial communication behavior in problem-solving groups characterized by low interpersonal visibility." Psychological Reports 10 (1): 79–89. P.A. 37:1097.

1594.   1963   "Explorations in the process of person perception: Visual interaction in relation to competition, sex, and need for affiliation." Journal of Personality 31 (March): 1–20.

1595. Exline, Ralph V., E. Gottheil, A. Paredes, and W. Winklemeier
    1968   "Gaze direction as a factor in the accurate judgment of nonverbal expressions of affect." Proceedings of the 76th Annual Convention of the American Psychological Association 3: 415–416.

1596. Exline, Ralph V., and Robert C. Ziller
    1959   "Status congruency and interpersonal conflict in decision-making groups." Human Relations 12 (2, May): 147–161. P.A. 34:7544; S.A. A2734.

1597. Eysenck, H. J.
    1954   The Psychology of Politics. London: Routledge & Kegan Paul. P.A. 30:909.

1598. Falk, Hans S.
    1969   "Thinking styles and individualism: The problem of human autonomy." Bulletin of the Menninger Clinic, 33 (3): 133–145. P.A. 43: 17337.

1599. Fancher, Raymond E.
    1969   "Group and individual accuracy in person perception." Journal of Consulting and Clinical Psychology 33 (1): 127. P.A. 43:11228.

1600. Farina, Amerigo, Jon G. Allen, and B. Brigid Saul
    1968   "The role of the stigmatized person in affecting social relationships." Journal of Personality 36 (2): 169–182. P.A. 42:17141.

1601. Farina, Amerigo, Barry Chapnick, Jason Chapnick, and Rafaello Msiti
    1972   "Political views and interpersonal behavior." Journal of Personality and Social Psychology 22 (3, June): 273–278. P.A. 48: 11438.

1602. Farina, Amerigo, Mark Sherman, and Jon G. Allen
       1968   "Role of physical abnormalities in interpersonal perception and be-
               havior." Journal of Abnormal Psychology 73 (6): 590–593. P.A. 43:
               3947.
1603. Faris, Robert E. L.
       1953   "Development of small-group research movement." In M. Sherif and
               M. O. Wilson (eds.), Group Relations at the Crossroads, pp. 155–
               184. New York: Harper. P.A. 28:7335.
1604. Farnsworth, Paul R., and Alice Behner
       1931   "A note on the attitude of social conformity." Journal of Social Psy-
               chology 2: 126–128.
1605. Farnsworth, Paul R., and M. F. Williams
       1936   "The accuracy of the median and mean of a group of judgments."
               Journal of Social Psychology 2: 237–239.
1606. Faroqi, M. A.
       1973   "Motivation and morale in a co-operative group." In T. E. Shanmu-
               gam (ed.), Researches in Personality and Social Problems. Madras:
               University of Madras. P.A. 50:11223.
1607. Farr, Grant, and Robert K. Leik
       1971   "Computer simulation of interpersonal choice." Comparative Group
               Studies 2 (2, May): 125–148. P.A. 48:2875.
1608. Fathi, Asghar
       1965   "Effects of latent positions on interaction." Sociology and Social
               Research 49 (2, January): 190–200. S.A. 13:B7594.
1609. 1968   "Expressive behavior and social integration in small groups: A com-
               parative analysis." Pacific Sociological Review 11 (1, Spring): 29–
               37. S.A. 17:D5788.
1610. Faucheux, Claude, and Kenneth D. Mackenzie
       1966   "Task dependency of organizational centrality: Its behavioral conse-
               quences." Journal of Experimental Social Psychology 2 (4, Octo-
               ber): 361–375.
1611. Faucheux, Claude, and Serge Moscovici
       1967   ("The style of behavior of a minority and its influence on majority
               responses.") Bulletin du C.E.R.P. 16 (4): 337–361. P.A. 43:5277.
1612. 1968   "Studies on group creativity: III. Noise and complexity in the infer-
               ential processes." Human Relations 21 (1, February): 29–40. P.A.
               42:13647; S.A. 17:D5789.
1613. Faucheux, Claude, and John Thibaut
       1964   ("The clinical and experimental approach to the genesis of contract-
               ual norms in different conditions of conflict and threat.") Bulletin
               d'Études et Recherches Psychologiques 13 (4): 225–243. P.A. 40:
               1516.
1614. Faunce, Dale, and J. Allan Beegle
       1948   "Cleavages in a relatively homogeneous group of rural youth: An
               experiment in the use of sociometry in attaining and measuring inte-
               gration." Sociometry 11: 207–216. P.A. 24:611.
1615. Fauquier, William, and W. Edgar Vinacke
       1964   "Communication and opinion as a function of member attractive-
               ness and opinion discrepancy." Journal of Social Psychology 63 (2,
               August): 295–308. P.A. 39:4858.
1616. Faust, William L.
       1959   "Group versus individual problem-solving." Journal of Abnormal
               and Social Psychology 59 (July): 68–72. P.A. 34:4185.
1617. Feather, Norman T.
       1964   "A structural balance model of communication effects." Psychologi-
               cal Review 71 (4): 291–313.
1618. 1965   "A structural balance analysis of evaluative behavior." Human Rela-
               tions 18 (2, May): 171–185. P.A. 39:15032.
1619. 1966   "The prediction of interpersonal attraction: Effects of sign and
               strength of relations in different structures." Human Relations 19
               (2, May): 213–237. P.A. 40:11100; S.A. 15:C4085.
1620. 1967a   "A structural balance approach to the analysis of communication

effects." In L. Berkowitz (ed.), Advances in Experimental Social Psychology, vol. 3, pp. 100–165. New York: Academic Press.

1621.   1967b   "Effects of institutional affiliation and attitude discrepancy on evaluation of communications and interpersonal attraction." Human Relations 20 (2, May): 101–120.

1622. Feather, Norman T., and D. J. Armstrong
        1967   "Effects of variations in source attitude, receiver attitude and communication stand on reactions to source and contents of communications." Journal of Personality 35 (3): 435–455. P.A. 42:2503.

1623. Federico, Pat-Anthony
        1971   "Sanction assignment in a dyad as a function of aggression and outcome quality." Journal of Social Psychology 85: 127–136.

1624. Feldman, Marvin J., and Marvin Goldfried
        1962   "Validity of group judgment as a factor affecting independent and conformity behavior." Journal of Social Psychology 58 (2, December): 289–294. P.A. 37:6604.

1625. Feldman, Robert S., and Karl E. Scheibe
        1972   "Determinants of dissent in a psychological experiment." Journal of Personality 40 (3, September): 331–348. P.A. 49:4403.

1626. Feldman, Ronald A.
        1968   "Interrelationships among three bases of group integration." Sociometry 31 (1, March): 30–46. P.A. 42:8876; S.A. 16:D4107.

1627.   1969   "Group integration and intense interpersonal disliking." Human Relations 22 (5, October): 405–413.

1628. Feldman, Roy E.
        1968   "Response to compatriot and foreigner who seek assistance." Journal of Personality and Social Psychology 10 (3): 202–214. P.A. 43: 3923.

1629. Feldstein, Stanley
        1968   "Interspeaker influence in conversational interaction." Psychological Reports 22 (3, pt. 1): 826–828. P.A. 42:13682.

1630. Felipe, Abraham I.
        1970   "Evaluative versus descriptive consistency in trait inferences." Journal of Personality and Social Psychology 16 (4): 627–638.

1631. Felipe, Nancy
        1966   "Interpersonal distance and small group interaction." Cornell Journal of Social Relations 1 (1, Spring): 59–64. S.A. 14:C2798.

1632. Felker, Donald W.
        1972   "Social stereotyping of male and female body types with differing facial expressions by elementary age boys and girls." Journal of Psychology 82 (1, September): 151–154. P.A. 49:2327.

1633. Felton, Gary S., and Barbara E. Biggs
        1973   "Psychotherapy and responsibility. Teaching internalization behavior to black low achievers through group therapy." Small Group Behavior 4 (2, May): 147–155.

1634. Fenelon, James R., and Edwin I. Megargee
        1971   "Influence of race on the manifestation of leadership." Journal of Applied Psychology 55 (4, August): 353–358. P.A. 47:2828.

1635. Fenigstein, Allan, and Arnold H. Buss
        1974   "Association and affect as determinants of displaced aggression." Journal of Research in Personality 7 (4, March): 306–313. P.A. 52: 7551.

1636. Feofanov, M. P.
        1928   ("The question of investigating the structural characteristics of a group.") Zhurnal Psikhologii, Pedologii i Psikhotekhniki 1: 107–120. P.A. 3:4117.

1637. Ferguson, Charles K., and Harold H. Kelley
        1964   "Significant factors in over-evaluation of own-group's product." Journal of Abnormal and Social Psychology 69 (2, August): 223–228. P.A. 39:4859; S.A. 14:B8342.

1638. Ferguson, Duncan A., and Neil Vidmar
        1971   "Effects of group discussion on estimates of culturally appropriate

risk levels." Journal of Personality and Social Psychology 20 (3): 436-445.

1639. Ferneau, Ernest W., Jr.
1968   "Note on 'facilitative distortion.'" Psychological Reports 22 (3, pt. 1): 982. P.A. 42:13648.

1640. Ferrara, Joseph W.
1973   "A verbal interaction recording technique for studying individuals in small groups." Journal of Social Psychology 90 (2, August): 207-212. P.A. 51:947.

1641. Fertig, Elaine S., and Clara Mayo
1969   "Impression formation as a function of trait consistency and cognitive complexity." Proceedings of the 77th Annual Convention of the American Psychological Association 4 (pt. 1): 345-346.

1642. Feshbach, Norma D.
1967   "Nonconformity to experimentally induced group norms of high-status versus low-status members." Journal of Personality and Social Psychology 6 (1): 55-63.

1643. Fessenden, S. A.
1953   "An index of cohesiveness-morale based on the analysis of sociometric choice distribution." Sociometry 16: 321-326. P.A. 29:667.

1644. Festinger, Leon
1947   "The role of group belongingness in a voting situation." Human Relations 1: 154-180. P.A. 22:2609.

1645.   1949   "The analysis of sociograms using matrix algebra." Human Relations 2: 153-158. P.A. 24:20.

1646.   1950a   "Informal social communication." Psychological Review 57: 271-292. (See also Cartwright and Zander, 1953, 1960.) P.A. 25:4528.

1647.   1950b   "Laboratory experiments: The role of group belongingness." In J. G. Miller (ed.), Experiments in Social Process, pp. 31-46. New York: McGraw-Hill. P.A. 25:1715.

1648.   1951a   "Architecture and group membership." Journal of Social Issues 7 (2): 152-163. (See also Cartwright and Zander, 1953.)

1649.   1951b   "Informal communications in small groups." In H. Guetzkow (ed.), Groups, Leadership and Men: Research in Human Relations, pp. 28-43. Pittsburgh: Carnegie. P.A. 26:797.

1650.   1953a   "An analysis of compliant behavior." In M. Sherif and M. O. Wilson (eds.), Group Relations at the Crossroads, pp. 232-256. New York: Harper. P.A. 28:7336.

1651.   1953b   "Laboratory experiments." In L. Festinger and D. Katz (eds.), Research Methods in the Behavioral Sciences, pp. 136-172. New York: Dryden. P.A. 28:3542.

1652.   1954   "Theory of social comparison processes." Human Relations 7: 117-140. (See also Hare, Borgatta, and Bales, 1955, 1965.) P.A. 29: 2305.

1653.   1955   "Social psychology and group processes." Annual Review of Psychology 6: 187-216.

1654.   1957   A Theory of Cognitive Dissonance. Evanston, Ill.: Row, Peterson. P.A. 32:347. (2nd ed., 1962. Stanford, Calif.: Stanford University Press.) P.A. 5GD91F.

1655. Festinger, Leon, and Elliot Aronson
1960   "The arousal and reduction of dissonance in social contexts." In D. Cartwright and A. Zander (eds.), Group Dynamics: Research and Theory, pp. 214-231. Evanston Ill.: Row, Peterson. (See also Cartwright and Zander, 1968.)

1656. Festinger, Leon, and James M. Carlsmith
1959   "Cognitive consequences of forced compliance." Journal of Abnormal and Social Psychology 58: 203-210. P.A. 34:1158.

1657. Festinger, Leon, D. Cartwright, Kathleen Barber, Juliet Fleischl, Josephine Gottsdanker, Annette Keysen, and Gloria Leavitt
1948   "A study of rumor: Its origin and spread." Human Relations 1: 464-486. P.A. 23:2201.

1658. Festinger, Leon, H. B. Gerard, B. Hymovitch, H. H. Kelley, and B. Raven
      1952   "The influence process in the presence of extreme deviates." Human
              Relations 5: 327-346. P.A. 27:7114; S.A. 123.
1659. Festinger, Leon, and H. A. Hutte
      1954   "An experimental investigation of the effect of unstable interper-
              sonal relations in a group." Journal of Abnormal and Social Psychol-
              ogy 49: 513-522. P.A. 29:5454.
1660. Festinger, Leon, and D. Katz (eds.)
      1953   Research Methods in the Behavioral Sciences. New York: Dryden.
              P.A. 28:3542.
1661. Festinger, Leon, A. Pepitone, and T. Newcomb
      1952   "Some consequences of de-individuation in a group." Journal of Ab-
              normal and Social Psychology 47: 382-389. (See also Hare, Bor-
              gatta, and Bales, 1955.) P.A. 27:2609.
1662. Festinger, Leon, S. Schachter, and K. Back
      1950   Social Pressures in Informal Groups: A Study of Human Factors in
              Housing. New York: Harper. (See also Cartwright and Zander, 1953,
              1960, 1968.) P.A. 25:2994.
1663. Festinger, Leon, and J. Thibaut
      1951   "Interpersonal communication in small groups." Journal of Abnor-
              mal and Social Psychology 46: 92-99. P.A. 25:7370.
1664. Festinger, Leon, Jane Torrey, and B. Willerman
      1954   "Self-evaluation as a function of attraction to the group." Human
              Relations 7: 161-174. S.A. 763.
1665. Fiebert, Martin S.
      1968   "Sensitivity training: An analysis of trainer intervention and group
              process." Psychological Reports 22 (3, pt. 1): 829-838. P.A. 42:
              13649.
1666. Fiebert, Martin S., and Paula D. Fiebert
      1969   "A conceptual guide to friendship formation." Perceptual and Motor
              Skills 28 (2): 383-390. P.A. 43:15696.
1667. Fiedler, Fred E.
      1953a   "Assumed similarity measures as predictors of team effectiveness in
              surveying." University of Illinois, College of Education, Technical
              Report 6: 1-20. P.A. 28:4127.
1668. 1953b   "The psychological-distance dimension in interpersonal relations."
               Journal of Personality 22: 142-150. P.A. 28:4128.
1669. 1954a   "Assumed similarity measures as predictors of team effectiveness."
               Journal of Abnormal and Social Psychology 49: 381-388. (See also
               Hare, Borgatta, and Bales, 1955, 1965.) P.A. 28:4127.
1670. 1954b   "The influence of leader-keyman relations on combat crew effective-
               ness." Urbana: University of Illinois, Group Effectiveness Research
               Laboratory. P.A. 29:3790.
1671. 1955   "The influence of leader-keyman relations on combat crew effective-
               ness." Journal of Abnormal and Social Psychology 51: 227-235.
               P.A. 30:5346.
1672. 1957   "A note on leadership theory: The effect of social barriers between
               leaders and followers." Sociometry 20: 87-94.
1673. 1958   Leader Attitudes and Group Effectiveness. Urbana: University of
               Illinois Press. P.A. 32:1446.
1674. 1960   "The Leader's psychological distance and group effectiveness." In
               D. Cartwright and A. Zander (eds.), Group Dynamics: Research and
               Theory, pp. 586-606. Evanston, Ill.: Row, Peterson.
1675. 1961   "Leadership and leadership effectiveness traits: A reconceptualiza-
               tion of the leadership trait problem." In L. Petrullo and B. M. Bass
               (eds.), Leadership and Interpersonal Behavior, pp. 179-186. New
               York: Holt, Rinehart & Winston.
1676. 1962   "Leader attitudes, group climate, and group creativity." Journal of
               Abnormal and Social Psychology 65 (5, November): 308-318. S.A.
               12:A9433.
1677. 1964   "Contingency model of leadership effectiveness." In L. Berkowitz

(ed.), Advances in Experimental Social Psychology, vol. 1, pp. 149–190. New York: Academic Press. S.A. 13:B6771.

1678. 1966a   "The effect of leadership and cultural heterogeneity on group performance: A test of the contingency model." Journal of Experimental Social Psychology 2 (3, July): 237–264. P.A. 40:13161.

1679. 1966b   ("A model of leader effectiveness.") Bulletin d'Etudes et Recherches Psychologiques 14 (3): 179–202. P.A. 40:5415.

1680. 1967   A Theory of Leadership Effectiveness. New York: McGraw-Hill.

1681. 1968   "Personality and situational determinants of leadership effectiveness." In D. Cartwright and A. Zander (eds.), Group Dynamics: Research and Theory, 3rd ed., pp. 362–380. New York: Harper & Row.

1682. 1971a   "Note on the methodology of the Graen, Orris, and Alvares studies testing the contingency model." Journal of Applied Psychology 55 (3, June): 202–204. P.A. 46:8916.

1683. 1971b   "Validation and extension of the contingency model of leadership effectiveness: A review of empirical findings." Psychological Bulletin 76 (2, August): 128–148. P.A. 47:2829.

1684. 1972a   "Personality, motivational systems, and behavior of high and low LPC persons." Human Relations 25 (5, November): 391–412. P.A. 50:908.

1685. 1972b   "Predicting the effects of leadership training and experience from the contingency model." Journal of Applied Psychology 56 (2): 114–119.

1686. 1973   "Predicting the effects of leadership training and experience from the contingency model: A clarification." Journal of Applied Psychology 57 (2): 110–113.

1687. Fiedler, Fred E., Walter Hartmann, and Stanley A. Rudin
      1952   "The relationship of interpersonal perception to effectiveness in basketball teams." University of Illinois, College of Education, Technical Report No. 3. P.A. 27:339.

1688. Fiedler, Fred E., Edwin B. Hutchins, and Joan S. Dodge
      1959   "Quasi-therapeutic relations in small college and military groups." Psychological Monographs 73, No. 3. (Whole No. 473.)

1689. Fiedler, Fred E., and Willem A. T. Meuwese
      1963   "Leader's contribution to task performance in cohesive and uncohesive groups." Journal of Abnormal and Social Psychology 67 (1): 83–87. P.A. 38:884; S.A. 12:B3232.

1690. Fiedler, Fred E., Willem A. T. Meuwese, and Sophie Oonk
      1961   "An exploratory study of group creativity in laboratory tasks." Acta Psychologica 18: 100–119. P.A. 36:2GE00F.

1691. Fiedler, Fred E., Gordon E. O'Brien, and Daniel R. Ilgen
      1969   "The effect of leadership style upon the performance and adjustment of volunteer teams operating in stressful foreign environment." Human Relations 22 (6, December): 503–514.

1692. Fiedler, Fred E., Willard G. Warrington, and Francis J. Blaisdell
      1952   "Unconscious attitudes as correlates of sociometric choice in social group." Journal of Abnormal and Social Psychology 47: 790–796. P.A. 27:5054.

1693. Field, Mildred
      1974   "Power and dependency: Legitimation of dependency conditions." Journal of Social Psychology 92 (1): 31–37.

1694. Fienberg, Stephen E., and F. Kinley Larntz
      1971   "Some models for individual-group comparisons and group behavior." Psychometrika 36 (4, December): 349–367. P.A. 47:10769.

1695. Finch, Kaye, Henry C. Rickard, and Warner Wilson
      1970   "Personality variables and sexual status in observer performance." Psychological Reports 26 (2): 676–678. P.A. 44:20819.

1696. Findley, Warren G.
      1948   "A statistical index of participation in discussion." Journal of Educational Psychology 39: 47–51. P.A. 22:3414.

1697. 1965   "Group vs. individual sociometric relations." Journal of Psychology (Lahore) 2 (2): 25–32. P.A. 40:1517.

1698.   1966   "Group vs. individual sociometric relations." International Journal
                    of Sociometry and Sociatry 5 (1-2, March-June): 60–66. S.A. 16:
                    D1443.

1699. Firestone, Ira J., Kalman J. Kaplan, and J. Curtis Russell
         1973   "Anxiety, fear, and affiliation with similar-state versus dissimilar-
                    state others: Misery sometimes loves nonmiserable company." Jour-
                    nal of Personality and Social Psychology 26 (3, June): 409–414.
                    P.A. 50:11224.

1700. Fischer, Claude S.
         1969   "The effect of threats in an incomplete information game." Sociom-
                    etry 32 (3): 301–314. P.A. 44:3554; S.A. 18:E5680.

1701. Fischer, Donald G., and Terry C. Burdeny
         1973   "Individual shifts and the group-shift phenomenon." Proceedings of
                    the 81st Annual Convention of the American Psychological Associa-
                    tion 8: 285–286. P.A. 50:8828.

1702. Fischer, Edward H.
         1973   "Consistency among humanitarian and helping attitudes." Social
                    Forces 52 (2): 157–168.

1703. Fischer, P. H.
         1953   "An analysis of the primary group." Sociometry 16: 272–276. P.A.
                    28:4129.

1704. Fisek, M. Hamit, and Richard Ofshe
         1970   "The process of status evolution." Sociometry 33 (3, September):
                    327–346. P.A. 46:6735; S.A. 19:F0468.

1705. Fish, Barry, and Kalman J. Kaplan
         1974   "Does a 'foot-in-the-door' get you in or out?" Psychological Reports
                    34 (1, February): 35–42. P.A. 52:7524.

1706. Fishbein, Martin
         1963   "The perception of non-members: A test of Merton's reference
                    group theory." Sociometry 26 (3, September): 271–286. P.A. 38:
                    5960.

1707.   1965   "Prediction of interpersonal preferences and group member satisfac-
                    tion from estimated attitudes." Journal of Personality and Social
                    Psychology 1 (6): 663–667. S.A. 14:B9177.

1708. Fishbein, Martin, and Icek Ajzen
         1973   "Attribution of responsibility: A theoretical note." Journal of Ex-
                    perimental Social Psychology 9 (2, March): 148–153. P.A. 50:
                    11225.

1709. Fishbein, Martin, Eva Landy, and Grace Hatch
         1969a   "A consideration of two assumptions underlying Fiedler's contin-
                    gency model for prediction of leadership effectiveness." American
                    Journal of Psychology 82 (4): 457–473. P.A. 44:12465.

1710.   1969b   "Some determinants of an individual's esteem for his least preferred
                    co-worker: An attitudinal analysis." Human Relations 22 (2, April):
                  · 173–188.

1711. Fishburn, Peter C.
         1970   "The irrationality of transitivity in social choice." Behavioral Sci-
                    ence 15 (2): 119–123. P.A. 44:10280.

1712.   1971   "A comparative analysis of group decision methods." Behavioral
                    Science 16 (6, November): 538–544. P.A. 47:8785; S.A. 20:F8108.

1713.   1973   "Voter concordance, simple majorities, and group decision meth-
                    ods." Behavioral Science 18: 364–376.

1714.   1974   "Simple voting systems and majority rule." Behavioral Science 19
                    (3): 166–176.

1715. Fisher, Seymour, and Ardie Lubin
         1958   "Distance as a determinant of influence in a two-person serial inter-
                    action situation." Journal of Abnormal and Social Psychology 56:
                    230–238. P.A. 36:1GE30F.

1716. Fishman, Daniel B.
         1966   "Need and expectancy as determinants of affiliative behavior in
                    small groups." Journal of Personality and Social Psychology 4 (2,
                    August): 155–164. P.A. 40:11101; S.A. 16:D1444.

1717. Fiske, Donald W., and John A. Cox, Jr.
    1960   "The consistency of ratings by peers." Journal of Applied Psychology 44 (February): 11–17. P.A. 34:7545.
1718. Fjeld, Stanton P.
    1965   "A longitudinal study of sociometric choice and the communication of values." Journal of Social Psychology 66 (2, August): 297–306. P.A. 39:15033.
1719. Flament, Claude
    1958a   ("Rational and genetic views of the changes of opinion by social influence.") Psychologie Française 3 (July): 186–196. P.A. 34:2890.
1720.   1958b   ("Social influence and perception.") Année Psychologique 58: 377–400. P.A. 34:2861.
1721.   1959   ("Ambiguity of stimulus, uncertainty of response, and the process of social influence.") Année Psychologique 59: 73–92. P.A. 34:5711.
1722.   1961   ("Processes of social influence and communication nets.") Psychologie Française 6: 115–125. P.A. 4GG15F.
1723.   1962   ("Bayes' theorem and the process of social influence.") In J. H. Criswell, H. Solomon, and P. Suppes (eds.), Mathematical Methods in Small Group Processes, pp. 150–165. Stanford, Calif.: Stanford University Press. S.A. 12:B2411.
1724.   1963   Applications of Graph Theory to Group Structure. Englewood Cliffs, N.J.: Prentice-Hall.
1725.   1965   (Networks of Communication and Group Structure.) Paris: Dunod. S.A. 16:C9754.
1726. Flament, Claude, and Erika Apfelbaum
    1966   "Elementary processes of communication and structuration in a small group." Journal of Experimental Social Psychology 2 (4, October): 376–386.
1727. Flanders, James P.
    1968   "A review of research on imitative behavior." Psychological Bulletin 69 (5): 316–337. P.A. 42:10527.
1728.   1970   "Does the risky shift generalize to a task with demonstrably nontrivial decision consequences?" Proceedings of the 78th Annual Convention of the American Psychological Association 5 (pt. 1): 331–332. P.A. 44:18560.
1729. Flanders, James P., and Donald L. Thistlethwaite
    1967   "Effects of familiarization and group discussion upon risk taking." Journal of Personality and Social Psychology 5 (1): 91–97.
1730.   1968   "Effects of vicarious reinforcement, verbalization, and task difficulty upon imitation." Proceedings of the 76th Annual Convention of the American Psychological Association 3: 395–396.
1731. Flanders, Ned A.
    1951   "Personal-social anxiety as a factor in experimental learning situations." Journal of Educational Research 45: 100–110. P.A. 26: 5096.
1732. Flanders, Ned A., and Sulo Havumaki
    1960a   "Group compliance to dominative teacher influence." Human Relations 13 (1, February): 67–82. P.A. 35:7013; S.A. A3519.
1733.   1960b   "The effect of teacher-pupil contacts involving praise on the sociometric choices of students." Journal of Educational Psychology 51: 65–68. P.A. 35:2679.
1734. Flecker, R.
    1967   "Group centred learnings: A growing field and its problems." Australian Psychologist 2 (1): 31–39. P.A. 42:3896.
1735. Fleishman, Edwin A.
    1952   "The leadership role of the foreman in industry." Ohio State University, Engineering Experimental Station News 24: 27–35.
1736. Foa, Edna R., Jim L. Turner, and Uriel G. Foa
    1972   "Response generalization in aggression." Human Relations 25 (4, September): 337–350. P.A. 49:6807.
1737. Foa, Uriel G.
    1958a   "Behavior, norms, and social rewards in a dyad." Behavioral Science

3: 323-334. P.A. 34:1159.

1738. 1958b "Empathy or behavioral transparency?" Journal of Abnormal and Social Psychology 56: 62-66.

1739. 1958c "The contiguity principle in the structure of interpersonal relations." Human Relations 11: 229-238.

1740. 1962 "The structure of interpersonal behavior in the dyad." In J. H. Criswell, H. Solomon, and P. Suppes (eds.), Mathematical Methods in Small Group Processes, pp. 166-179. Stanford, Calif.: Stanford University Press. S.A. 12:B2412.

1741. Foa, Uriel G., and Gregory V. Donnenwerth
1971 "Love poverty in modern culture and sensitivity training." Sociological Inquiry 41 (2, Spring): 149-159.

1742. Foa, Uriel G., Terence R. Mitchell, and Fred E. Fiedler
1971 "Differentiation matching." Behavioral Science 16 (2, March): 130-142. P.A. 46:4832.

1743. Fodor, Eugene M.
1973a "Disparagement by a subordinate, ingratiation, and the use of power." Journal of Psychology 84 (1, May): 181-186. P.A. 50: 6710.

1744. 1973b "Group stress, ingratiation, and the use of power." Journal of Social Psychology 91 (2, December): 345-346. P.A. 52:825.

1745. 1974 "Disparagement by a subordinate as an influence on the use of power." Journal of Applied Psychology 59 (5): 652-655.

1746. Fontaine, Gary
1974 "Social comparison and some determinants of expected personal control and expected performance in a novel task situation." Journal of Personality and Social Psychology 29 (4, April): 487-496. P.A. 52:7552.

1747. Foot, Hugh C.
1973 "Group learning and performance: A reclassification." British Journal of Social and Clinical Psychology 12 (1, February): 7-17. P.A. 50:2925.

1748. Ford, LeRoy H., Jr., and Michael I. Singer
1968 "Projection of self-attributes onto similar and dissimilar others." Journal of Social Psychology 74 (2, April): 265-273. P.A. 42: 10512.

1749. Forsyth, Elaine, and Leo Katz
1946 "A matrix approach to the analysis of sociometric data: Preliminary report." Sociometry 9: 340-347. P.A. 21:2362.

1750. Forward, John R.
1969 "Group achievement motivation and individual motives to achieve success and to avoid failure." Journal of Personality 37: 297-309.

1751. Foster, Caxton C., and William J. Horvath
1971 "A study of a large sociogram, III: Reciprocal choice probabilities as a measure of social distance." Behavioral Science 16 (5, September): 429-435. S.A. 20:F8109.

1752. Foster, Robert J.
1961 "Acquiescent response set as a measure of acquiescence." Journal of Abnormal and Social Psychology 63 (1): 115-160.

1753. Foulds, Melvin L.
1971a "Changes in locus of internal-external control: A growth group experience." Comparative Group Studies 2 (3, August): 293-300. P.A. 48:7099.

1754. 1971b "Measured changes in self-actualization as a result of a growth group experience." Psychotherapy: Theory, Research and Practice 8 (4, Winter): 338-341. P.A. 50:910.

1755. 1972a "The experiential-Gestalt growth group experience." Journal of College Student Personnel 13 (1, January): 48-52. P.A. 48:4858.

1756. 1972b "The growth center model. Proactive programs of a university counseling service." Comparative Group Studies 3 (1, February): 77-88.

1757. 1973 "Effects of a personal growth on ratings of self and others." Small Group Behavior 4 (4, November): 508-512.

1758. Foulds, Melvin L., Ricardo Girona, and James F. Guinan
    1970   "Changes in ratings of self and others as a result of a marathon group." Comparative Group Studies 1 (4, November): 349–355. P.A. 47: 6671.

1759. Foulkes, S. H.
    1950   "Group therapy: A short survey and orientation with particular reference to group analysis." British Journal of Medical Psychology 25: 199–205.

1760. Fouriezos, Nicholas T., Max L. Hutt, and Harold Guetzkow
    1950   "Measurement of self-oriented needs in discussion groups." Journal of Abnormal and Social Psychology 45: 682–690. P.A. 25:2359. (See also Cartwright and Zander, 1953.)

1761. Fox, David J., and Irving Lorge
    1962   "The relative quality of decisions written by individuals and by groups as the available time for problem solving is increased." Journal of Social Psychology 57 (1, June): 227–242. P.A. 37:3032.

1762. Fox, John
    1972   "The learning of strategies in a simple, two-person zero-sum game without saddlepoint." Behavioral Science 17 (3, May): 300–308. P.A. 48:11439.

1763. Fox, John, and Melvin Guyer
    1973   "Equivalence and stooge strategies in zero-sum games." Journal of Conflict Resolution 17 (3, September): 513–533. P.A. 51:9029.

1764. Fox, J. B., and J. F. Scott
    1943   Absenteeism: Management's Problem. Boston: Harvard University, Graduate School of Business Administration. P.A. 18:1832.

1765. Fox, J. W.
    1967   "The concepts of image and adoption in relation to interpersonal behavior." Journal of Communication 17 (2): 147–151. P.A. 41: 16622.

1766. Fox, William F.
    1957   "Group reaction to two types of conference leadership." Human Relations 10: 279–289. S.A. 10:A1340.

1767. Fraas, Louis A.
    1972a   "Differential effects of reward and punishment on group performance by normal and psychotic males." Psychological Reports 30: 399–403.

1768.   1972b   "Leadership selection and group performance: An expanded replication." Journal of Social Psychology 87 (2, August): 317–318. P.A. 49:756.

1769. Frager, Robert
    1970   "Conformity and anticonformity in Japan." Journal of Personality and Social Psychology 15 (3): 203–210.

1770. Franck, Barbara M.
    1972   "Phases of development of a multinational training group." Comparative Group Studies 3 (1, February): 3–50. P.A. 49:2328.

1771. Frank, Frederic, and Lynn R. Anderson
    1971   "Effects of task and group size upon group productivity and member satisfaction." Sociometry 34 (1, March): 135–149. P.A. 46: 8918; S.A. 20:F8110.

1772. Frank, Harold H., and Carol Wolman
    1973   "Gender deviancy in male peer groups." Proceedings of the 81st Annual Convention of the American Psychological Association 8: 1063–1064. P.A. 50:4773.

1773. Frank, Jerome D.
    1944   "Experimental studies of personal pressure and resistance: I. Experimental production of resistance." Journal of General Psychology 30: 23–64. P.A. 18:2473, 2474, 2475.

1774. Frank, Jerome D., Joseph Margolin, Helen T. Nash, Anthony R. Stone, Edith Varon, and E. Ascher
    1952   "Two behavior patterns in therapeutic groups and their apparent motivation." Human Relations 5: 289–317. P.A. 27:3577.

1775. Frankel, A. Steven
    1969   "Attitudes toward a group as a function of self-esteem, group
            achievement level, and success or failure on a group-relevant task."
            Proceedings of the 77th Annual Convention of the American Psy-
            chological Association 4 (pt. 1): 351-352. P.A. 43:17338.
1776. Frankiel, Harry H.
    1971   "Mutually perceived therapeutic relationships in T groups: The co-
            trainer puzzle." Journal of Applied Behavioral Science 7 (4, July-
            August): 449-465. S.A. 20:F9134.
1777. Franklin, Billy J.
    1971   "Attitude similarity-dissimilarity, dogmatism, and interpersonal
            attraction." Psychology 8 (1, February): 4-11. P.A. 46:4833.
1778.   1973   "The effects of status on the honesty and verbal responses of
                others." Journal of Social Psychology 91 (2): 347-348.
1779.   1974   "Victim characteristics and helping behavior in a rural southern set-
                ting." Journal of Social Psychology 93 (1, June): 93-100. P.A. 52:
                12308.
1780. Fraser, Colin
    1971   "Group risk-taking and group polarization." European Journal of
            Social Psychology 1 (4): 493-510. P.A. 48:9006. S.A. 22:74G6141.
1781. Fraser, Colin, Celia Gouge, and Michael Billig
    1971   "Risky shifts, cautious shifts, and group polarization." European
            Journal of Social Psychology 1 (1): 7-30. P.A. 48:7100; S.A. 22:
            74G6142.
1782. Fraser, Scott C., and Irene Fujitomi
    1972   "Perceived prior compliance, psychological reactance and altruistic
            contributions." Proceedings of the 80th Annual Convention of the
            American Psychological Association 7 (pt. 1): 247-248. P.A. 48:
            4859.
1783. Frauenfelder, Kenneth J.
    1974   "A cognitive determinant of favorability of impression." Journal of
            Social Psychology 94 (1): 71-81.
1784. Frederickson, William A., and Gary Kizziar
    1973   "Accurate, deceptive, and no prior feedback about decisionmaking
            acumen as an influencer of group decisionmaking." Journal of Ap-
            plied Social Psychology 3 (3, July): 232-239. P.A. 52:2888.
1785. Frederiksen, Norman
    1972   "Toward a taxonomy of situations." American Psychologist 27 (2,
            February): 114-123. P.A. 48:9007.
1786. Freeberg, Norman E.
    1969   "Relevance of rater-ratee acquaintance in the validity and reliability
            of ratings." Journal of Applied Psychology 53 (6): 518-524. P.A.
            44:5071.
1787. Freedman, Jonathan L.
    1971   "The crowd: Maybe not so madding after all." Psychology Today 5
            (4, September): 58-61. P.A. 47:8786.
1788. Freedman, Jonathan L., Simon Klevansky, and Paul R. Ehrlich
    1971   "The effect of crowding on human task performance." Journal of
            Applied Social Psychology 1 (1, January): 7-25. P.A. 47:2830.
1789. Freedman, Jonathan L., Alan S. Levy, Roberta W. Buchanan, and Judy Price
    1972   "Crowding and human aggressiveness." Journal of Experimental So-
            cial Psychology 8 (6, November): 528-548. P.A. 49:11066.
1790. Freedman, Mervin B., Timothy F. Leary, Abel B. Ossorio, and Hubert S. Coffey
    1951   "The interpersonal dimension of personality." Journal of Personality
            20: 143-161. P.A. 27:993.
1791. Freedman, Norbert, Thomas Blass, Arthur Rifkin, and Frederic Quitkin
    1973   "Body movements and the verbal encoding of aggressive affect."
            Journal of Personality and Social Psychology 26 (1, April): 72-85.
            P.A. 50:4775.
1792. Freedman, Norbert, James O'Hanlon, Philip Oltman, and Herman A. Witkin
    1972   "The imprint of psychological differentiation on kinetic behavior in
            varying communicative contexts." Journal of Abnormal Psychology

79 (3, June): 239-258. P.A. 49:2329.

1793. Freese, Lee
    1974   "Conditions for status equality in informal task groups." Sociometry 37 (2, June): 174-188. P.A. 52:12309.

1794. Freese, Lee, and Bernard P. Cohen
    1973   "Eliminating status generalization." Sociometry 36 (2, June): 177-193. S.A. 22:74G6143.

1795. French, Elizabeth G.
    1956   "Motivation as a variable in work-partner selection." Journal of Abnormal and Social Psychology 53: 96-99.

1796. French, Elizabeth G., and Irene Chadwick
    1956   "Some characteristics of affiliation motivation." Journal of Abnormal and Social Psychology 52: 296-300. P.A. 31:5093.

1797. French, John R. P., Jr.
    1941   "The disruption and cohesion of groups." Journal of Abnormal and Social Psychology 36: 361-377. (See also Cartwright and Zander, 1953.) P.A. 15:5253.

1798.   1944   "Organized and unorganized groups under fear and frustration." University of Iowa Studies in Child Welfare 20 (409): 231-308. P.A. 19:3427.

1799.   1950   "Field experiments: Changing group productivity." In J. G. Miller (ed.), Experiments in Social Process: A Symposium on Social Psychology, pp. 79-96. New York: McGraw-Hill. P.A. 25:1716.

1800.   1951   "Group Productivity." In H. Guetzkow (ed.), Groups, Leadership and Men: Research in Human Relations, pp. 44-45. Pittsburgh: Carnegie. P.A. 26:798.

1801.   1953   "Experiments in field settings." In L. Festinger and D. Katz (eds), Research Methods in the Behavioral Sciences, pp. 98-135. New York: Dryden. P.A. 28:3542.

1802.   1956   "A formal theory of social power." Psychological Review 63: 181-194. (See also Cartwright and Zander, 1960, 1968.) P.A. 31:4473.

1803. French, John R. P., Jr., Joachim Israel, and Dagfinn As
    1960   "An experiment on participation in a Norwegian factory." Human Relations 13 (1, February): 3-19. P.A. 35:7259; S.A. 10:A3410.

1804. French, John R. P., Jr., Arthur Kornhauser, and Alfred Marrow
    1946   "Conflict and cooperation in industry." Journal of Social Issues 2 (February).

1805. French, John R. P., Jr., H. William Morrison, and George Levinger
    1960   "Coercive power and forces affecting conformity." Journal of Abnormal and Social Psychology 61 (1): 93-101. P.A. 35:2110.

1806. French, John R. P., Jr., and Bertram Raven
    1959   "The bases of social power." In D. Cartwright (ed.), Studies in Social Power, pp. 150-167. Ann Arbor: University of Michigan. (See also Cartwright and Zander, 1960, 1968.) P.A. 34:7546.

1807. French, John R. P., Jr., and Richard Snyder
    1959   "Leadership and interpersonal power." In D. Cartwright (ed.), Studies in Social Power, pp. 118-149. Ann Arbor: University of Michigan. P.A. 34:7547.

1808. French, John R. P., Jr., and A. Zander
    1949   "The group dynamics approach." In A. Kornhouser (ed.), Psychology of Labor Management Relations, pp. 71-80. New York: American Book - Stratford Press.

1809. French, Robert L.
    1955   "Social psychology and group processes." Annual Review of Psychology 7: 63-94. P.A. 30:5849.

1810. French, Robert L., and I. N. Mensh
    1948   "Some relationships between interpersonal judgements and sociometric status in a college group." Sociometry 11: 335-345.

1811. Freud, Sigmund
    1949   Group Psychology and the Analysis of the Ego. New York: Liveright. (1st ed., 1922. London: Hogarth.)

1812.   1950   "Libidinal types." In Collected Papers, vol. 5, pp. 247-251. London: Hogarth.

1813. Frey, Dieter, Martin Irle, and Martin Kumpf
    1973   ("Attribution or the reduction of cognitive dissonance?") Zeitschrift
            für Sozialpsychologie 4 (4): 366–377. P.A. 52:7553.
1814. Frey, Jerry D., and Darren Newtson
    1973   "Differential attribution in an unequal power situation: Biased infer-
            ence or biased input?" Proceedings of the 81st Annual Convention
            of the American Psychological Association 8: 125–126. P.A. 50:
            4776.
1815. Frey, Robert L., Jr., and J. Stacy Adams
    1972   "The negotiator's dilemma: Simultaneous in-group and out-group
            conflict." Journal of Experimental Social Psychology 8 (4, July):
            331–346. P.A. 49:758.
1816. Friedell, Morris F.
    1968   "Laboratory experiment in retaliation." Journal of Conflict Resolu-
            tion 12 (3): 357–373. P.A. 43:14228.
1817. Friedland, Nehemia, Susan E. Arnold, and John Thibaut
    1974   "Motivational bases in mixed-motive interactions: The effects of
            comparison levels." Journal of Experimental Social Psychology 10
            (2): 188–199.
1818. Friedland, Seymour J., Walter H. Crockett, and James D. Laird
    1973   "The effects of role and sex on the perception of others." Journal of
            Social Psychology 91 (2): 273–283.
1819. Friedlander, Frank
    1966   "Performance and interactional dimensions of organizational work
            groups." Journal of Applied Psychology 50 (3): 257–265. P.A. 40:
            8788.
1820.   1970   "The primacy of trust as a facilitator of further group accomplish-
            ment." Journal of Applied Behavioral Science 6 (4, October-Decem-
            ber): 387–400. P.A. 46:4834; S.A. 20:F3455.
1821. Frijda, Nico H.
    1969   "Recognition of emotion." In L. Berkowitz (ed.), Advances in Ex-
            perimental Social Psychology, vol. 4, pp. 167–223. New York: Aca-
            demic Press.
1822. Frisch, David M., and Martin S. Greenberg
    1968   "Reciprocity and intentionality in the giving of help." Proceedings
            of the 76th Annual Convention of the American Psychological Asso-
            ciation 3: 383–384.
1823. Frisch, James E., and Sheldon Zedeck
    1972   "Status, interest, and proximity as factors in interaction and com-
            munication channels." Journal of Psychology 82 (2, November):
            259–267. P.A. 49:6808.
1824. Froman, Lewis A., Jr., and Michael D. Cohen
    1969   "Threats and bargaining efficiency." Behavioral Science 14 (2,
            March): 147–153. S.A. 18:E2906.
1825.   1970   "Compromise and logroll: Comparing the efficiency of two bargain-
            ing processes." Behavioral Science 15: 180–183.
1826. Fromkin, Howard L., Richard J. Klimoski, and Michael F. Flanagan
    1972   "Race and competence as determinants of acceptance of newcomers
            in success and failure work groups." Organizational Behavior and
            Human Performance 7 (1, February): 25–42. P.A. 47:10770.
1827. Fromm, Erich
    1947   Man for Himself. New York: Rinehart. P.A. 22:1441.
1828. Fromme, Donald K., and Carol K. Schmidt
    1972   "Affective role enactment and expressive behavior." Journal of Per-
            sonality and Social Psychology 24 (3, December): 413–419. P.A.
            49:9036.
1829. Fry, Anna M., and Frank N. Willis
    1971   "Invasion of personal space as a function of the age of the invader."
            Psychological Record 21 (3, Summer): 385–389. P.A. 47:8787.
1830. Fry, Charles L.
    1967   "A developmental examination of performance in a tacit coordina-
            tion game situation." Journal of Personality and Social Psychology
            5 (3): 277–281.

1831. Fry, Charles L., J. Roy Hopkins, and Peyton Hoge
    1970   "Triads in minimal social situations." Journal of Social Psychology
            80 (1): 37-42. P.A. 44:12466.
1832. Fry, Christopher
    1950   "Comedy." Adelphi 27 (1): 27-29.
1833. Frye, Roland L.
    1966   "The effect of orientation and feedback of success and effectiveness
            on the attractiveness and esteem of the group." Journal of Social
            Psychology 70 (December): 205-211.
1834. Frye, Roland L., and Henry E. Adams
    1959   "Effect of the volunteer variable on leaderless group discussion ex-
            periments." Psychological Reports 5: 184. P.A. 34:2762.
1835. Frye, Roland L., and Bernard M. Bass
    1963   "Behavior in a group related to tested social acquiescence." Journal
            of Social Psychology 61 (December): 263-266.
1836. Frye, Roland L., Jean Spruill, and Thomas M. Stritch
    1964   "Effect of group size on public and private coalescence, efficiency
            and change." Journal of Social Psychology 62 (1, February): 131-
            139. P.A. 39:1569.
1837. Frye, Roland L., and Thomas M. Stritch
    1964   "Effect of timed vs. non-timed discussion upon measures of influ-
            ence and change in small groups." Journal of Social Psychology 63
            (1, June): 139-143. P.A. 39:1568.
1838. Frye, Roland L., Robert N. Vidulich, Barbara Meierhoefer, and Sylvia A. Joure
    1972   "Differential T-group behaviors of high and low dogmatic partici-
            pants." Journal of Psychology 81 (2, July): 301-309. P.A. 49:759.
1839. Fthenakis, Wassilios
    1967   ("The formation of judgments in small groups under particular con-
            sideration of the developmental and ethnopsychological aspect.")
            Zeitschrift für Experimentelle und Angewandte Psychologie 14 (3):
            351-393. P.A. 42:5512.
1840. Fugita, Stephen S.
    1974   "Effects of anxiety and approval on visual interaction." Journal of
            Personality and Social Psychology 29 (4, April): 586-592. P.A. 52:
            7525.
1841. Furfey, Paul H.
    1927   "Some factors influencing the selection of boys' chums." Journal of
            Applied Psychology 11: 47-51. P.A. 1:2062.
1842. Furuhata, Yasuyoshi
    1965   ("An experimental study of cooperation and competition: On group
            participation, group cohesiveness and group productivity.") Japanese
            Journal of Educational Psychology 13 (4): 1-13. P.A. 40:6588.
1843.   1968   ("The interrelations of the group productivity, group cohesiveness
            and group participation.") Japanese Journal of Educational Psychol-
            ogy 16 (1): 26-31. P.A. 42:13650.
1844. Fybish, Ira
    1964   "A study of the difficulties encountered in negative criteria for so-
            ciometric testing." International Journal of Sociometry and Sociatry
            4 (1-2): 37-42. S.A. 13:B6754a.

1845. Gaebelein, Jacquelyn W.
    1973a   "Instigative aggression in females." Psychological Reports 33 (2, Oc-
            tober): 619-622. P.A. 51:8996.
1846.   1973b   "Third-party instigation of aggression: An experimental approach."
            Journal of Personality and Social Psychology 27 (3, September):
            389-395. P.A. 51:5032.
1847. Gaebelein, Jacquelyn W., and William M. Hay
    1974   "Third party instigation of aggression as a function of attack and
            vulnerability." Journal of Research in Personality 7 (4, March): 324-
            333. P.A. 52:7554.
1848. Gaertner, Samuel L.
    1970   "A 'call' for help: Helping behavior extended to black and white

victims by New York City Liberal and Conservative party members."
Proceedings of the 78th Annual Convention of the American Psychological Association 5 (pt. 1): 441-442. P.A. 44:18561.

1849.   1973   "Helping behavior and racial discrimination among liberals and conservatives." Journal of Personality and Social Psychology 25 (3, March): 335-341. P.A. 50:4777.

1850. Gaertner, Samuel L., and Leonard Bickman
        1971   "Effects of race on the elicitation of helping behavior: The wrong number technique." Journal of Personality and Social Psychology 20 (2, November): 218-222. P.A. 47:6672.

1851. Gage, N[athaniel] L.
        1953   "Accuracy of social perception and effectiveness in interpersonal relationships." Journal of Personality 22: 128-141.

1852, Gage, N[athaniel] L., and B. B. Chatterjee
        1960   "The psychological meaning of acquiescence: Further evidence." Journal of Abnormal and Social Psychology 60 (2, March): 280-283. P.A. 34:7548.

1853. Gage, N[athaniel] L., and Lee Cronbach
        1955   "Conceptual and methodological problems in interpersonal perception." Psychological Review 62: 411-422. (See also Hare, Borgatta, and Bales, 1965.) P.A. 30:5876.

1854. Gage, N[athaniel] L., and Ralph V. Exline
        1953   "Social perception and effectiveness in discussion groups." Human Relations 6: 381-396. S.A. 2:242.

1855. Gage, N[athaniel] L., George S. Leavitt, and George C. Stone
        1956   "The intermediary key in the analysis of interpersonal perception." Psychological Bulletin 53: 258-266.

1856.   1957   "The psychological meaning of acquiescence set for authoritarianism." Journal of Abnormal and Social Psychology 55: 98-103.

1857. Gahagan, James P., Harold Long, and Joann Horai
        1969   "Race of experimenter and reactions to threats by black preadolescents." Proceedings of the 77th Annual Convention of the American Psychological Association 4 (pt. 1): 397-398.

1858. Gahagan, James P., and James T. Tedeschi
        1968   "Strategy and the credibility of promises in the Prisoner's Dilemma game." Journal of Conflict Resolution 12 (2): 224-233.

1859.   1969   "Shifts of power in a mixed-motive game." Journal of Social Psychology 77 (2): 241-252. P.A. 43:9632.

1860. Galejs, Irma
        1974   "Social interaction of preschool children." Home Economics Research Journal 2 (3, March): 153-159. P.A. 52:12228.

1861. Gallagher, James, and Peter J. Burke
        1974   "Scapegoating and leader behavior." Social Forces 52 (4, June): 481-488. P.A. 52:12252.

1862. Gallo, Philip S., Jr.
        1966   "Effects of increased incentives upon the use of threat in bargaining." Journal of Personality and Social Psychology 4 (1, July): 14-20. S.A. 15:C5577.

1863.   1969   "Personality impression formation in a maximizing difference game." Journal of Conflict Resolution 13 (1, March): 118-122.

1864. Gallo, Philip S., Jr., Sandra G. Funk, and Joseph R. Levine
        1969   "Reward size, method of presentation, and number of alternatives in a Prisoner's Dilemma game." Journal of Personality and Social Psychology 13 (3): 239-244.

1865. Gallo, Philip S., Jr., Roberta Irwin, and Gerald Avery
        1966   "The effects of score feedback and strategy of the other on cooperative behavior in a Maximizing Differences game." Psychonomic Science 5 (10): 401-402. P.A. 40:12268.

1866. Gallo, Philip S., Jr., and Charles G. McClintock
        1962   "Behavioral, attitudinal, and perceptual differences between leaders and non-leaders in situations of group support and non-support." Journal of Social Psychology 56 (February): 121-133. P.A. 5GF21G.

1867.   1965   "Cooperative and competitive behavior in mixed-motive games."
                  Journal of Conflict Resolution 9 (1, March): 68–78. S.A. 14:C1885.

1868. Gallo, Philip S., Jr., and John Sheposh
          1971   "Effects of incentive magnitude on cooperation in the Prisoner's
                  Dilemma game: A reply to Gumpert, Deutsch, and Epstein." Journal
                  of Personality and Social Psychology 19 (1, July): 42–46. P.A. 46:
                  8919.

1869. Gallo, Philip S., Jr., Shirley Smith, and Sandra Mumford
          1973   "Effects of deceiving subjects upon experimental results." Journal
                  of Social Psychology 89 (1, February): 99–107. P.A. 50:2927.

1870. Gallo, Philip S., Jr., and Jim D. Winchell
          1970   "Matrix indices, large rewards, and cooperative behavior in a Prison-
                  er's Dilemma game." Journal of Social Psychology 81 (2): 235–241.
                  P.A. 44:20820.

1871. Gamson, William A.
          1961a   "A theory of coalition formation." American Sociological Review
                  26 (3, June): 373–382. (See also Hare, Borgatta, and Bales, 1965;
                  Crosbie, 1975.)

1872.   1961b   "An experimental test of a theory of coalition formation." Ameri-
                  can Sociological Review 26 (4, August): 565–573. P.A. 36:3GE65G.

1873.   1964   "Experimental studies of coalition formation." In L. Berkowitz
                  (ed.), Advances in Experimental Social Psychology, vol. 1, pp. 81–
                  110. New York: Academic Press. S.A. 13:B6755.

1874. Garai, Josef E.
          1964   "Support of judgmental independence or conformity in situations of
                  exposure to strong group pressure." Psychology 1 (3): 21–25. P.A.
                  39:4860.

1875. Gardin, Hershel, Kalman J. Kaplan, Ira J. Firestone, and Gloria A. Cowan
          1973   "Proxemic effects on cooperation, attitude, and approach-avoidance
                  in a Prisoner's Dilemma game." Journal of Personality and Social
                  Psychology 27 (1, July): 13–18. P.A. 50:11228.

1876. Gardiner, James C.
          1972   "The effects of expected and perceived receiver response on source
                  attitudes." Journal of Communication 22 (3, September): 289–299.
                  P.A. 50:914.

1877. Gardner, Eric F., and George G. Thompson
          1956   Social Relations and Morale in Small Groups. New York: Appleton-
                  Century-Crofts. P.A. 30:8184.

1878. Gardner, G.
          1956   "Functional leadership and popularity in small groups." Human Re-
                  lations 9: 491–509. S.A. A1341.

1879. Garland, Howard, and Bert R. Brown
          1972   "Face-saving as affected by subjects' sex, audiences' sex and audi-
                  ence expertise." Sociometry 35 (2, June): 280–289. P.A. 49:760.

1880. Garman, Mark B., and Morton I. Kamien
          1968   "The paradox of voting: Probability calculations." Behavioral Sci-
                  ence 13 (4, July): 306–316. P.A. 42:15399.

1881. Garrett, James, and William L. Libby, Jr.
          1973   "Role of intentionality in mediating responses to inequity in the
                  dyad." Journal of Personality and Social Psychology 28 (1, Octo-
                  ber): 21–27. P.A. 51:11001.

1882. Gartner, Dorothy, and Marvin A. Iverson
          1967   "Some effects of upward mobile status in established and ad hoc
                  groups." Journal of Personality and Social Psychology 5 (4): 390–
                  397.

1883. Gaskell, George D., Ewart A. C. Thomas, and Robert M. Farr
          1973   "Effect of pretesting on measures of individual risk preferences."
                  Journal of Personality and Social Psychology 25 (2, February): 192–
                  198. P.A. 50:915.

1884. Gates, Georgina S.
          1924   "The effect of an audience upon performance." Journal of Abnor-
                  mal and Social Psychology 18: 334–342.

1885. Gatton, Michael J., and Don A. Nelson
       1973   "Interpersonal attraction in a role-played interaction." Psychological
               Reports 32 (2, April): 627-634. P.A. 51:920.
1886. Gatton, Michael J., and John D. Tyler
       1974   "Nonverbal interview behavior and dependency." Journal of Social
               Psychology 93 (2): 303-304.
1887. Gebel, Arnold S.
       1954   "Self-perception and leaderless group discussion status." Journal of
               Social Psychology 40: 309-318. P.A. 29:7070.
1888. Geen, Russell G.
       1970   "Perceived suffering of the victim as an inhibitor of attack-induced
               aggression." Journal of Social Psychology 81 (2): 208-215. P.A.
               44:20821.
1889. Geen, Russell G., and Roger Pigg
       1973   "Interpretation of arousal and its effects on motivation." Journal of
               Social Psychology 90 (1, June): 115-123. P.A. 51:2977.
1890. Geen, Russell G., John J. Rakosky, and Roger Pigg
       1972   "Awareness of arousal and its relation to aggression." British Journal
               of Social and Clinical Psychology 11 (2, June): 115-121. P.A. 49:
               6810.
1891. Geen, Russell G., and David Stonner
       1972   "The context of observed violence: Inhibition of aggression through
               displays of unsuccessful retaliation." Psychonomic Science 27 (6,
               June): 243-244. P.A. 49:2330.
1892. 1973   "Context effects in observed violence." Journal of Personality and
               Social Psychology 25 (1, January): 145-150. P.A. 50:8833.
1893. Geen, Russell G., David Stonner, and David R. Kelley
       1974   "Aggression anxiety and cognitive appraisal of aggression-threat
               stimuli." Journal of Personality and Social Psychology 29 (2): 196-
               200.
1894. Geer, James H., and Lynn Jarmecky
       1973   "The effect of being responsible for reducing another's pain on sub-
               ject's response and arousal." Journal of Personality and Social Psy-
               chology 26 (2): 232-237.
1895. Geier, John G.
       1967   "A trait approach to the study of leadership in small groups." Jour-
               nal of Communication 17 (4): 316-323. P.A. 42:7261.
1896. Geis, Florence
       1968   "Machiavellianism in a semireal world." Proceedings of the 76th An-
               nual Convention of the American Psychological Association 3: 407-
               408.
1897. Geis, Florence, and Vilnis Viksne
       1972   "Touching: Physical contact and level of arousal." Proceedings of
               the 80th Annual Convention of the American Psychological Associa-
               tion 7 (pt. 1): 179-180.
1898. Gekoski, Norman
       1952   "Predicting group productivity." Personnel Psychology 5: 281-292.
               P.A. 27:6817.
1899. Gelfand, Donna M., Donald P. Hartmann, Patrice Walder, and Brent Page
       1973   "Who reports shoplifters? A field-experimental study." Journal of
               Personality and Social Psychology 25 (2, February): 276-285. P.A.
               50:916.
1900. Geller, Sheldon H., and Norman S. Endler
       1973   "The effects of subject roles, demand characteristics, and suspicion
               on conformity." Canadian Journal of Behavioural Science 5 (1, Jan-
               uary): 46-54. P.A. 50:4778.
1901. Geller, Sheldon H., Norman S. Endler, and David L. Wiesenthal
       1973   "Conformity as a function of task generalization and relative com-
               petence." European Journal of Social Psychology 3 (1): 53-62. P.A.
               52:826.
1902. Gellert, Elizabeth
       1961   "Stability and fluctuation in the power relationships of young child-

ren." Journal of Abnormal and Social Psychology 62 (1, January): 8-15. S.A. A1700.

1903. Genthner, Robert W., and Stuart P. Taylor
    1973   "Physical aggression as a function of racial prejudice and the race of the target." Journal of Personality and Social Psychology 27 (2, August): 207-210. P.A. 51:3029.

1904. Gentry, William D.
    1972   "Biracial aggression: I. Effect of verbal attack and sex of victim." Journal of Social Psychology 88 (1, October): 75-82. P.A. 49: 4405.

1905. Gentry, William D., Ernest Harburg, and Louise Hauenstein
    1973   "Effects of anger expression/inhibition and guilt on elevated diastolic blood pressure in high/low stress and black/white females." Proceedings of the 81st Annual Convention of the American Psychological Association 8: 115-116.

1906. George, Clay E.
    1962   "Some determinants of small-group effectiveness." HumRRO Research Memorandum, Subtask Unifect No. 26. P.A. 37:6606.

1907. Gerard, Harold B.
    1953   "The effect of different dimensions of disagreement on the communication process in small groups." Human Relations 6: 249-271. P.A. 28:2404.

1908.   1954   "The anchorage of opinions in face-to-face groups." Human Relations 7: 313-325. P.A. 29:3792.

1909.   1956   "Some factors affecting an individual's estimate of his probable success in a group situation." Journal of Abnormal and Social Psychology 52: 235-239. P.A. 31:2696; S.A. 5290.

1910.   1957   "Some effects of status, role clarity, and group goal clarity upon the individual's relations to group process." Journal of Personality 25: 475-488.

1911.   1961a   "Disagreement with others, their credibility, and experienced stress." Journal of Abnormal and Social Psychology 62 (3, May): 559-564. P.A. 36:4GE59G.

1912.   1961b   "Some determinants of self-evaluation." Journal of Abnormal and Social Psychology 62 (2, March): 288-293. P.A. 4GE88G.

1913.   1964   "Conformity and commitment to the group." Journal of Abnormal and Social Psychology 68 (2, February): 209-211. P.A. 38:5961; S.A. 13:B6756.

1914. Gerard, Harold B., Duane Green, Michael F. Hoyt, and Edward S. Conolley
    1972   "Influence of affect on exposure-frequency estimates." Proceedings of the 80th Annual Convention of the American Psychological Association 7 (pt. 1): 173-174.

1915.   1973   "Influence of affect on exposure-frequency estimates." Journal of Personality and Social Psychology 28 (1, October): 151-154. P.A. 51:11002.

1916. Gerard, Harold B., and Michael F. Hoyt
    1974   "Distinctiveness of social categorization and attitude toward ingroup members." Journal of Personality and Social Psychology 29 (6, June): 836-842. P.A. 52:7555.

1917. Gerard, Harold B., and Grover C. Mathewson
    1966   "The effect of severity of initiation on liking for a group: A replication." Journal of Experimental Social Psychology 2 (3, July): 278-287. P.A. 40:13154.

1918. Gerard, Harold B., and Norman Miller
    1967   "Group dynamics." Annual Review of Psychology 18: 287-332. P.A. 42:3897.

1919. Gerard, Harold B., and Jacob M. Rabbie
    1961   "Fear and social comparison." Journal of Abnormal and Social Psychology 62 (3, May): 586-592. P.A. 36:4GE86G.

1920. Gerard, Harold B., and George B. Rotter
    1961   "Time perspective, consistency of attitude, and social influence." Journal of Abnormal and Social Psychology 62 (3, May): 565-572.

P.A. 36:4GE65G; S.A. A2736.

1921. Gerard, Harold B., Roland A. Wilhelmy, and Edward S. Conolley
    1968   "Conformity and group size." Journal of Personality and Social Psychology 8 (1, pt. 1): 79–82. P.A. 42:5531.

1922. Gergen, Kenneth J.
    1965   "The effects of interaction goals and personalistic feedback on the presentation of self." Journal of Personality and Social Psychology 1 (5): 413–424.

1923.   1969   The Psychology of Behavior Exchange. Reading, Mass.: Addison-Wesley.

1924. Gergen, Kenneth J., and Raymond A. Bauer
    1967   "Interactive effects of self-esteem and task difficulty on social conformity." Journal of Personality and Social Psychology 6 (1): 16–22.

1925. Gergen, Kenneth J., Mary M. Gergen, and William H. Barton
    1973   "Deviance in the dark." Psychology Today 7 (5, October): 129–133. P.A. 51:10990.

1926. Gergen, Kenneth J., Mary M. Gergen, and Kenneth Meter
    1972   "Individual orientations to prosocial behavior." Journal of Social Issues 28 (3): 105–130. P.A. 50:4779.

1927. Gergen, Kenneth J., and Margaret G. Taylor
    1969   "Social expectancy and self-presentation in a status hierarchy." Journal of Experimental Social Psychology 5 (1): 79–92. P.A. 43: 8287.

1928. Gergen, Kenneth J., and Barbara Wishnov
    1965   "Others' self-evaluations and interaction anticipation as determinants of self-presentation." Journal of Personality and Social Psychology 2 (3): 348–358. P.A. 39:15036.

1929. Gerson, Allan R.
    1974   "Subject's satisfaction with a task as a function of E's communication style and S's dependency." Psychological Reports 34 (2, April): 463–466. P.A. 52:12253.

1930. Getzels, Jacob W., and Egon G. Guba
    1955   "Role conflict and personality." Journal of Personality 24: 74–85. P.A. 30:5758.

1931. Ghiselli, Edwin E.
    1966   "Psychological properties of groups and group learning." Psychological Reports 19 (1): 17–18. P.A. 40:12269.

1932. Ghiselli, Edwin E., and Thomas M. Lodahl
    1958   "Patterns of managerial traits and group effectiveness." Journal of Abnormal and Social Psychology 57: 61–66.

1933. Gibb, Cecil A.
    1947   "The principles and traits of leadership." Journal of Abnormal and Social Psychology 42: 267–284. (See also Hare, Borgatta, and Bales, 1955, 1965.) P.A. 22:1149.

1934.   1950   "The sociometry of leadership in temporary groups." Sociometry 13: 226–243. (See also Hare, Borgatta, and Bales, 1955, 1965.)

1935.   1951   "An experimental approach to the study of leadership." Occupational Psychology 25: 233–248. P.A. 26:5475.

1936.   1954   "Leadership." In G. Lindzey (ed.), Handbook of Social Psychology, pp. 877–920. Cambridge, Mass.: Addison-Wesley. P.A. 29:3793. (See also Lindzey and Aronson, 1968.)

1937.   1969   Leadership: Selected Readings. Baltimore: Penguin. P.A. 44:586.

1938. Gibb, Jack R.
    1951   "The effects of group size and of threat reduction upon creativity in a problem-solving situation." American Psychologist 6: 324.

1939.   1961   "Defense level and influence potential in small groups." In L. Petrullo and B. M. Bass (eds.), Leadership and Interpersonal Behavior, pp. 66–81. New York: Holt, Rinehart & Winston.

1940.   1972   "Tori Theory: Nonverbal Behavior and the Experience of Community." Comparative Group Studies 3 (4, November): 461–472.

1941. Gibb, Jack R., and Lorraine M. Gibb
    1969   "Leaderless groups: Growth-centered values and potentialities." In
            H. A. Otto and J. Mann (eds.), Ways of Growth: Approaches to Ex-
            panding Awareness, pp. 101-114. New York: Viking. P.A. 44:
            2268.
1942. Gibbard, Graham S., and John J. Hartman
    1973a   "Relationship patterns in self-analytic groups: A clinical and empiri-
            cal study." Behavioral Science 18 (5, September): 335-353. P.A.
            51:10991.
1943.   1973b   "The oedipal paradigm in group development: A clinical and empiri-
            cal study." Small Group Behavior 4 (3, August): 305-354. P.A. 51:
            5057.
1944. Giedt, F. Harold
    1956   "Factor analysis of roles patients take in therapy groups." Journal of
            Social Psychology 44: 165-171.
1945. Giesen, Martin, and Clyde Hendrick
    1974   "Effects of false positive and negative arousal feedback on persua-
            sion." Journal of Personality and Social Psychology 30 (4): 449-
            457.
1946. Gilchrist, Jack C.
    1952   "The formation of social groups under conditions of success and fail-
            ure." Journal of Abnormal and Social Psychology 47: 174-187. P.A.
            27:2613.
1947.   1959   "Social psychology and group processes." Annual Review of Psy-
            chology 10: 233-264. P.A. 34:1162.
1948. Gilchrist, Jack C., Marvin E. Shaw, and L. C. Walker
    1954   "Some effects of unequal distribution of information in a wheel
            group structure." Journal of Abnormal and Social Psychology 49:
            554-556. P.A. 29:5621.
1949. Gillespie, David F.
    1972   "The seminar as a social system and symbolic interaction." Com-
            parative Groups Studies 3 (3, August): 241-248.
1950. Gillies, Jerry
    1974   My Needs, Your Needs, Our Needs. Garden City, N.Y.: Doubleday.
            P.A. 52:2890.
1951. Gilligan, John F.
    1973   "Personality characteristics of selectors and non-selectors on sensi-
            tivity training." Journal of Counseling Psychology 20 (3, May): 265-
            268. P.A. 50:11229.
1952.   1974   "Sensitivity training and self-actualization." Psychological Reports
            34 (1): 319-325.
1953. Gillis, John S., and George T. Woods
    1971   "The 16 PF as an indicator of performance in the Prisoner's Di-
            lemma game." Journal of Conflict Resolution 15 (3, September):
            393-402. P.A. 48:2876.
1954. Gilmore, J. Barnard
    1971   "Implications for a theory of contagion from an experiment invok-
            ing model self-censure." Journal of Social Psychology 85 (2, Decem-
            ber): 195-208. P.A. 47:8788.
1955. Gitin, Sharon R.
    1970   "A dimensional analysis of manual expression." Journal of Person-
            ality and Social Psychology 15 (3): 271-277.
1956. Gitter, A. George, Harvey Black, and David Mostofsky
    1972a   "Race and sex in the communication of emotion." Journal of Social
            Psychology 88 (2, December): 273-276. P.A. 49:9037.
1957.   1972b   "Race and sex in the perception of emotion." Journal of Social
            Issues 28 (4): 63-78. P.A. 50:4780.
1958. Gitter, A. George, Nicholas J. Kozel, and David I. Mostofsky
    1972   "Perception of emotion: The role of race, sex, and presentation
            mode." Journal of Social Psychology 88 (2, December): 213-222.
            P.A. 49:9038.

1959. Gitter, A. George, David Mostofsky, and Michael Guichard
   1972 "Some parameters in the perception of gaze." Journal of Social Psychology 88 (1, October): 115-121. P.A. 49:6812.

1960. Gittler, Joseph B. (ed.)
   1957 Review of Sociology: Analysis of a decade. New York: Wiley. P.A. 32:348.

1961. Glad, Donald D., W. Lynn Smith, and Virginia M. Glad
   1957 "Behaviour factor reactions to leader emphases upon feelings or social expressions." International Journal of Social Psychiatry 3 (2, Autumn): 129-132. S.A. 15:C5595.

1962. Gladstone, Roy
   1969 "Authoritarianism, social status, transgression, and punitiveness." Proceedings of the 77th Annual Convention of the American Psychological Association 4 (pt. 1): 287-288. P.A. 43:17339.

1963. Glanzer, Murray, and Robert Glaser
   1959 "Techniques for the study of group structure and behavior: I. Analysis of structure." Psychological Bulletin 56 (5, September): 317-332. P.A. 34:4227.

1964. 1961 "Techniques for the study of group structure and behavior: II. Empirical studies of the effects of structure in small groups." Psychological Bulletin 58 (1, January): 1-27. (See also Hare, Borgatta, and Bales, 1965.) P.A. 36:1GE01G.

1965. Glaser, Robert, and David J. Klaus
   1966 "A reinforcement analysis of group performance." Psychological Monographs: General and Applied 80 (13). P.A. 40:12270.

1966. Glass, David C.
   1964 "Changes in liking as a means of reducing cognitive discrepancies between self-esteem and aggression." Journal of Personality 32: 531-549.

1967. Glass, John F.
   1973 "The presentation of self and the encounter culture: Notes on the sociology of T-groups." Small Group Behavior 4 (4, November): 449-458.

1968. Glass, John F., and Harry H. Frankiel
   1968 "The influence of subjects on the researcher: A problem in observing social interaction." Pacific Sociological Review 11 (2, Fall): 75-80. S.A. 17:D8268.

1969. Gleason, Walter J.
   1957 "Predicting army leadership ability by modified leaderless group discussion." Journal of Applied Psychology 41: 231-235.

1970. Glick, Oren W., and Jay Jackson
   1970 "Effects of normative similarity on group formation among college freshmen." Pacific Sociological Review 13 (4, Fall): 263-269. S.A. 19:E9549.

1971. Glidewell, John C.
   1970 Choice Points: Essays on the Emotional Problems of Living with People. Cambridge, Mass.: MIT Press. P.A. 48:2877.

1972. Glinski, Richard J., Bernice C. Glinski, and Gerald T. Slatin
   1970 "Nonnaivety contamination in conformity experiments: Sources, effects, and implications for control." Journal of Personality and Social Psychology 16 (3): 478-485.

1973. Gnagey, William J.
   1960 "Effects on classmates of a deviant student's power and response to a teacher-exerted control technique." Journal of Educational Psychology 51: 1-8. P.A. 35:2113.

1974. Godwin, William F., and Frank Restle
   1974 "The road to agreement: Subgroup pressures in small group consensus processes." Journal of Personality and Social Psychology 30 (4): 500-509.

1975. Goethals, George R.
   1972 "Consensus and modality in the attribution process: The role of

similarity and information." Journal of Personality and Social Psychology 21 (1, January): 84–92. P.A. 47:8789.

1976. Goethals, George R., and Joel Cooper
      1972   "Role of intention and postbehavioral consequence in the arousal of cognitive dissonance." Journal of Personality and Social Psychology 23 (3): 293–301.

1977. Goethals, George R., and R. Eric Nelson
      1973   "Similarity in the influence process: The belief-value distinction." Journal of Personality and Social Psychology 25 (1, January): 117–122. P.A. 50:6713.

1978. Goffman, Erving
      1961   Encounters: Two Studies in the Sociology of Interaction. Indianapolis: Bobbs-Merrill. P.A. 37:6607.

1979.   1963   Behavior in Public Places. Glencoe, Ill.: Free Press.
1980.   1969   Strategic Interaction. Philadelphia: University of Pennsylvania Press. P.A. 47:6674.

1981. Goffman, Irwin
      1957   "Alienation from interaction." Human Relations 10: 47–60.

1982. Gold, Joel A., Richard M. Ryckman, and William C. Rodda
      1973   "Differential responsiveness of dissonance manipulations by open- and closed-minded subjects in a forced-compliance situation." Journal of Social Psychology 90 (1, June): 73–83. P.A. 51:3030.

1983. Gold, Martin
      1958   "Power in the classroom." Sociometry 21: 50–60. (See also Cartwright and Zander, 1968.)

1984. Gold, Steven, Patrick De Leon, and Clifford Swensen
      1966   "Behavioral validation of a dominance-submission scale." Psychological Reports 19: 735–739.

1985. Goldberg, Gordon N., Charles A. Kiesler, and Barry E. Collins
      1969   "Visual behavior and face-to-face distance during interaction." Sociometry 32 (1, March): 43–53. P.A. 43:9633.

1986. Goldberg, Moses H., and Eleanor E. Maccoby
      1965   "Children's acquisition of skill in performing a group task under two conditions of group formation." Journal of Personality and Social Psychology 2 (6): 898–902. P.A. 40:2811.

1987. Goldberg, Solomon C.
      1954   "Three situational determinants of conformity to social norms." Journal of Abnormal and Social Psychology 49: 325–329. P.A. 29: 3796.

1988.   1955   "Influence and leadership as a function of group structure." Journal of Abnormal and Social Psychology 51: 119–122. P.A. 30:4345; S.A. 2489.

1989. Goldberg, Solomon C., and Ardie Lubin
      1958   "Influence as a function of perceived judgement error." Human Relations 11: 275–281. P.A. 34:1163.

1990. Goldman, Morton
      1965   "A comparison of individual and group performance for varying combinations of initial ability." Journal of Personality and Social Psychology 1 (3): 210–216. P.A. 39:9996.

1991.   1966   "A comparison of group and individual performance where subjects have varying tendencies to solve problems." Journal of Personality and Social Psychology 3 (5): 604–607. P.A. 40:7640.

1992.   1971   "Group performance related to size and initial ability of group members." Psychological Reports 28: 551–557.

1993. Goldman, Morton, Merlyn E. Bolen, and Randall B. Martin
      1961   "Some conditions under which groups operate and how this affects their performance." Journal of Social Psychology 54 (June): 47–56. P.A. 36:2GF47G.

1994. Goldman, Morton, Dona M. Dietz, and Ana McGlynn
      1968   "Comparison of individual and group performance related to heterogeneous-wrong responses, size, and patterns of interaction." Psychological Reports 23 (2): 459–465. P.A. 43:9634.

1995. Goldman, Morton, and Louis A. Fraas
      1965   "The effects of leader selection on group performance." Sociometry 28 (1, March): 82-88. P.A. 39:10019.
1996. Goldman, Morton, Bernard J. Haberlein, and Gloria J. Feder
      1965   "Conformity and resistance to group pressure." Sociometry 28 (2, June): 220-226. P.A. 39:12172.
1997. Goldman, Morton, John G. Kretschmann, and Nelle Westergard
      1972   "Feelings toward a frustrating agent as affected by replies to correction." Journal of Social Psychology 88 (2, December): 301-302. P.A. 49:9039.
1998. Goldman, Morton, Ana McGlynn, and Ann Toledo
      1967   "Comparison of individual and group performance of size three and five with various initially right and wrong tendencies." Journal of Personality and Social Psychology 7 (2, pt. 1): 222-226. P.A. 41: 16624.
1999. Goldman-Eisler, Frieda
      1951   "The measurement of time sequences in conversational behavior." British Journal of Psychology (General Section) 42: 355-362. P.A. 26:5548.
2000. Goldstein, Joel W., and Howard M. Rosenfeld
      1969   "Insecurity and preference for persons similar to oneself." Journal of Personality 37: 253-268.
2001. Goldstone, Sanford, William K. Boardman, William T. Lhamon, Fred L. Fason, and Clarence Jernigan
      1963   "Sociometric status and apparent duration." Journal of Social Psychology 61 (December): 303-310.
2002. Golembiewski, Robert T.
      1960   "O and M and the small group." Public Administration Review 20 (4, Autumn): 205-212. S.A. A1701.
2003.   1962   The Small Group. Chicago: University of Chicago Press. P.A. 37: 1100.
2004. Golembiewski, Robert T., and Arthur Blumberg (eds.)
      1970   Sensitivity Training and the Laboratory Approach: Readings about Concepts and Applications. Itasca, Ill.: Peacock. P.A. 45:6194. (2nd ed., 1973. P.A. 51:5033.)
2005. Gollob, Harry F., and Gregory W. Fischer
      1973   "Some relationships between social inference, cognitive balance, and change in impression." Journal of Personality and Social Psychology 26 (1, April): 16-22. P.A. 50:4781.
2006. Gollob, Harry F., and Andrew M. Lugg
      1973   "Effects of instruction and stimulus presentation on the occurrence of averaging responses in impression formation." Journal of Experimental Psychology 98 (1, April): 217-219. P.A. 50:8835.
2007. Gollob, Harry F., and Betty B. Rossman
      1973   "Judgments of an actor's 'power and ability to influence others.'" Journal of Experimental Social Psychology 9 (5, September): 391-406. P.A. 51:9031.
2008. Gollob, Harry F., Betty B. Rossman, and Robert P. Abelson
      1973   "Social inference as a function of the number of instances and consistency of information presented." Journal of Personality and Social Psychology 27 (1, July): 19-33. P.A. 50:11230.
2009. Golubeva, N. V.
      1969   ("An experiment with small groups.") Voprosy Psikhologii 15 (3): 144-149. P.A. 44:3539.
2010. Good, Kenneth J.
      1973   "Social facilitation: Effects of performance anticipation, evaluation, and response competition on free associations." Journal of Personality and Social Psychology 28 (2): 270-275.
2011. Good, Lawrence R., and Katherine C. Good
      1972a   "On perceiving probability of marital success." Psychological Reports 31 (1, August): 300-302. P.A. 49:4406.
2012.   1972b   "Role of vindication motivation in the attitude similarity-attraction

relationship." Psychological Reports 31 (3, December): 769–770. P.A. 50:918.

2013.   1972c   "Attitude similarity and evaluation of potential counselors." Psychological Reports 31 (3, December): 963–966. P.A. 50:919.

2014.   1973   "Fear of appearing incompetent and attraction toward agreeing and disagreeing strangers." Psychological Reports 33 (2, October): 673–674. P.A. 51:9032.

2015. Good, Lawrence R., and Don A. Nelson
         1971   "Effects of person-group and intragroup attitude similarity on perceived group attractiveness and cohesiveness." Psychonomic Science 25 (4, November): 215–217. P.A. 48:11441.

2016.   1973   "Effects of person-group and intragroup attitude similarity on perceived group attractiveness and cohesiveness: II." Psychological Reports 33 (2, October): 551–560. P.A. 51:9033.

2017. Good, Thomas L., J. Neville Sikes, and Jere E. Brophy
         1973   "Effects of teacher sex and student sex on classroom interaction." Journal of Educational Psychology 65 (1): 74–87.

2018. Goodacre, Daniel M.
         1951   "The use of a sociometric test as a predictor of combat unit effectiveness." Sociometry 14: 148–152. P.A. 27:4618.

2019.   1953   "Group characteristics of good and poor performing combat units." Sociometry 16: 168–178. P.A. 28:5026.

2020. Goodale, James G., and James P. Flanders
         1971   "Predicting and explaining risky and cautious shifts with situational stimuli." Proceedings of the 79th Annual Convention of the American Psychological Association 6 (pt. 1): 253–254.

2021. Goodchilds, Jacqueline D.
         1959   "Effects of being witty on position in the social structure of a small group." Sociometry 22 (3, September): 261–272. P.A. 34:7553.

2022. Goodchilds, Jacqueline D., and Ewart E. Smith
         1964   "The wit and his group." Human Relations 17 (1, February): 23–31. P.A. 39:1570; S.A. 12:B2413.

2023. Goode, William J.
         1972   "Social change and family renewal." In Families of the Future. Ames: Iowa State University Press. P.A. 49:11068.

2024. Goodenough, Florence L.
         1928   "Measuring behavior traits by means of repeated short samples." Journal of Juvenile Research 12:230–235.

2025.   1930   "Interrelationships in the behavior of young children." Child Development 1: 29–48.

2026. Goodenough, Florence L., and J. E. Anderson
         1931   Experimental Child Study. New York: Appleton-Century-Crofts.

2027. Goodkin, Robert
         1966   "Changes in conformity behavior on a perceptual task following verbal reinforcement and punishment." Journal of Psychology 62 (1): 99–110. P.A. 40:6589.

2028. Goodnow, Robert E., and R. Tagiuri
         1952   "Religious ethnocentricism and its recognition among adolescent boys." Journal of Abnormal and Social Psychology 47: 316–320. P.A. 27:2582.

2029. Goodstadt, Barry E., and Larry A. Hjelle
         1973a   "Power to the powerless: Locus of control and the use of power." Journal of Personality and Social Psychology 27 (2): 190–196.

2030.   1973b   "Use of power and the attractive other." Proceedings of the 81st Annual Convention of the American Psychological Association 8: 155–156. P.A. 50:4782.

2031. Goodstadt, Michael S.
         1971   "Helping and refusal to help: A test of balance and reactance theories." Journal of Experimental Social Psychology 7 (6): 610–622.

2032. Goranson, Richard E., and Leonard Berkowitz
         1966   "Reciprocity and responsibility reactions to prior help." Journal of Personality and Social Psychology 3 (2): 227–232. P.A. 40:4181.

2033. Gorden, Raymond L.
    1952   "Interaction between attitude and the definition of the situation in the expression of opinion." American Sociological Review 17: 50-58. (See also Cartwright and Zander, 1953.) P.A. 27:3419.
2034. Gordon, Kate
    1924   "Group judgments in the field of lifted weights." Journal of Experimental Psychology 7: 398-400.
2035. Gordon, Leonard V., and Francis F. Medland
    1965a   "Leadership aspiration and leadership ability." Psychological Reports 17: 388-390.
2036.   1965b   "The cross-group stability of peer ratings of leadership potential." Personnel Psychology 18 (2): 173-177. P.A. 39:15076.
2037. Gordon, Robert A., James F. Short, Jr., Desmond S. Cartwright, and Fred L. Strodtbeck
    1963   "Values and gang delinquency: A study of street-corner groups." American Journal of Sociology 69 (2, September): 109-128.
2038. Gordon, Stewart M., James P. Flanders, and Charles J. Cranny
    1973   "Inside the black box: A content analysis of group discussions involving risk." Proceedings of the 81st Annual Convention of the American Psychological Association 8: 283-284. P.A. 50:8837.
2039. Gordon, Thomas
    1955   Group-Centered Leadership: A Way of Releasing the Creative Power of Groups. Boston: Houghton Mifflin. P.A. 30:2644.
2040. Gore, William V., and Dalmas A. Taylor
    1973   "The nature of the audience as it effects social inhibition." Representative Research in Social Psychology 4 (2, June): 18-27. P.A. 51:3031.
2041. Gorfein, David S.
    1961   "Conformity behavior and the 'authoritarian personality.'" Journal of Social Psychology 53 (February): 121-125. P.A. 35:6480.
2042.   1964a   "Scaling theory and group influence: A re-examination." Journal of Social Psychology 62 (2, April): 303-308. P.A. 39:4862.
2043.   1964b   "The effects of a nonunanimous majority on attitude change." Journal of Social Psychology 63 (2, August): 333-338. P.A. 39:4863.
2044. Gorlow, Leon, Erasmus L. Hoch, and Earl F. Telschow
    1952   The Nature of Nondirective Group Psychotherapy. New York: Columbia University, Teachers College.
2045. Gormly, John, Anne Gormly, and Charles Johnson
    1971   "Interpersonal attraction: Competence motivation and reinforcement theory." Journal of Personality and Social Psychology 19 (3, September): 375-380. P.A. 47:2831.
2046.   1972   "Consistency of sociobehavioral responses to interpersonal disagreement." Journal of Personality and Social Psychology 24 (2, November): 221-224. P.A. 49:4407.
2047. Goslin, David A.
    1962   "Accuracy of self perception and social acceptance." Sociometry 25 (3, September): 283-296. P.A. 37:3033; S.A. 11:A5133.
2048. Gosnell, Douglas E.
    1964   "Some similarities and dissimilarities between the dramaturgical approaches of J. L. Moreno and Erving Goffman." International Journal of Sociometry and Sociatry 4 (3-4): 94-106. S.A. 14: B8343.
2049. Gottheil, Edward
    1955   "Changes in social perceptions contingent upon competing or cooperating." Sociometry 18: 132-137. P.A. 30:4346.
2050. Gottheil, Edward, Jeffrey Corey, and Alfonso Paredes
    1968   "Psychological and physical dimensions of personal space." Journal of Psychology 69 (1): 7-9. P.A. 42:12035.
2051. Gottheil, Edward, and David P. Vielhaber
    1966   "Interaction of leader and squad attributes related to performance of military squads." Journal of Social Psychology 68 (1, February): 113-127. P.A. 40:5416.

2052. Gouaux, Charles
    1971   "Induced affective states and interpersonal attraction." Journal of
            Personality and Social Psychology 20 (1): 37–43.
2053. Gouaux, Charles, and John Lamberth
    1970   "The effect on interpersonal attraction of successive and simultane-
            ous presentation of strangers." Psychonomic Science 21 (6, Decem-
            ber): 337–338. P.A. 46:2903.
2054. Gouaux, Charles, John Lamberth, and Gustav Friedrich
    1972   "Affect and interpersonal attraction: A comparison of trait and state
            measures." Journal of Personality and Social Psychology 24 (1, Oc-
            tober): 53–58. P.A. 49:4408.
2055. Gouge, Celia, and Colin Fraser
    1972   "A further demonstration of group polarization." European Journal
            of Social Psychology 2 (1): 95–97. P.A. 49:2331.
2056. Gouldner, Alvin W. (ed.)
    1950   Studies in Leadership. New York: Harper. P.A. 28:2997.
2057. Gouldner, Alvin W., William J. Goode, and Bruno Bettelheim
    1967   "Review symposium (of Philip Slater: Microcosm)." American So-
            ciological Review 32 (1, February): 121–127. S.A. 15:C4799.
2058. Gouran, Dennis S., and John E. Baird
    1972   "An analysis of distributional and sequential structure in problem-
            solving and informal group discussions." Speech Monographs 39 (1,
            March): 16–22. P.A. 50:11231.
2059. Grace, Harry A.
    1951   "The effects of different degrees of knowledge about an audience on
            the content of communication." Journal of Social Psychology 34:
            31–40. P.A. 27:3510.
2060.   1952a   "The effects of different degrees of knowledge about an audience on
            the content of communication: The male audience." Journal of So-
            cial Psychology 36: 83–88.
2061.   1952b   "The effects of different degrees of knowledge about an audience on
            the content of communication: The comparison of male and female
            audiences." Journal of Social Psychology 36: 89–96.
2062.   1954   "Conformance and performance." Journal of Social Psychology 40:
            333–335. P.A. 29:7073.
2063. Graen, George, James B. Orris, and Kenneth M. Alvares
    1971a   "Contingency model of leadership effectiveness: Some experimental
            results." Journal of Applied Psychology 55 (3, June): 196–201. P.A.
            46:8922.
2064.   1971b   "Contingency model of leadership effectiveness: Some methodologi-
            cal issues." Journal of Applied Psychology 55 (3, June): 205–210.
            P.A. 46:8923.
2065. Graf, Richard G., and Duane Green
    1971   "The equity restoring components of retaliation." Journal of Per-
            sonality 39 (4, December): 581–590. P.A. 48:2878.
2066. Graf, Richard G., and Jeanne C. Riddell
    1972   "Helping behavior as a function of interpersonal perception." Jour-
            nal of Social Psychology 86: 227–231.
2067. Graham, D.
    1962   "Experimental studies of social influence in simple judgment situa-
            tions." Journal of Social Psychology 56 (April): 245–269. P.A. 37:
            1101.
2068. Graham, Gerald H.
    1971   "Interpersonal attraction as a basis of informal organization." Acad-
            emy of Management Journal 14 (4, December): 483–495. P.A. 48:
            2879.
2069. Graham, William K.
    1973   "Leader behavior, esteem for the least preferred co-worker, and
            group performance." Journal of Social Psychology 90 (1): 59–66.
2070. Graham, William K., and Peter C. Dillon
    1974   "Creative supergroups: Group performance as a function of individ-
            ual performance on brainstorming tasks." Journal of Social Psychol-

ogy 93 (1): 101-105.

2071. Grant, Malcolm J.
        1973   "Attribution of responsibility and estimated frequency of suffering as factors affecting evaluation of a victim." Proceedings of the 81st Annual Convention of the American Psychological Association 8: 151-152. P.A. 50:4783.

2072. Gratton, Carolyn
        1970   "Selected subject bibliography on friendship." Humanitas 6 (2, Fall): 249-257. P.A. 46:2905.

2073. Gray, Louis N., and Bruce H. Mayhew, Jr.
        1970   "The stability of power structures in small groups: A regression analysis." Pacific Sociological Review 13 (2, Spring): 110-120. S.A. 19: E7003.

2074.   1972   "Proactive differentiation, sequence restraint, and the asymmetry of power: A multidimensional analysis." Human Relations 25 (3, July): 199-214. P.A. 49:6813.

2075. Gray, Louis N., James T. Richardson, and Bruce H. Mayhew, Jr.
        1968   "Influence attempts and effective power: a re-examination of an unsubstantiated hypothesis." Sociometry 31 (3, September): 245-258. P.A. 43:800; S.A. 17:D8269.

2076. Grebstein, Lawrence C.
        1967   "Defensive behavior in an interpersonal situation." Journal of Consulting Psychology 31 (5): 529-535. P.A. 41:16625.

2077. Green, Duane
        1974   "Dissonance and self-perception analysis of 'forced compliance': When two theories make competing predictions." Journal of Personality and Social Psychology 29 (6, June): 819-828. P.A. 52:7556.

2078. Green, Elise H.
        1933a   "Friendships and quarrels among pre-school children." Child Development 4: 237-252.

2079.   1933b   "Group play and quarreling among pre-school children." Child Development 4: 302-307. P.A. 8:2828.

2080. Green, G. H.
        1948   "Insight and group adjustment." Journal of Abnormal and Social Psychology 43: 49-61. P.A. 22:3416.

2081. Green, James A.
        1972   "Attitudinal and situational determinants of intended behavior toward blacks." Journal of Personality and Social Psychology 22 (1, April): 13-17. P.A. 48:4862.

2082. Green, Norman E.
        1950   "Verbal intelligence and effectiveness of participation in group discussion." Journal of Educational Psychology 41: 440-445. P.A. 25: 5227.

2083. Green, Robert A., and Edward J. Murray
        1973   "Instigation to aggression as a function of self-disclosure and threat to self-esteem." Journal of Consulting and Clinical Psychology 40 (3, June): 440-443. P.A. 50:11232.

2084. Greenberg, Jerald, and Gerald S. Leventhal
        1973   "Violating equity to prevent group failure." Proceedings of the 81st Annual Convention of the American Psychological Association 8: 215-216. P.A. 50:8838.

2085. Greenberg, Martin S.
        1967   "Role playing: An alternative to deception?" Journal of Personality and Social Psychology 7 (2, pt. 1): 152-157. P.A. 41:16626.

2086. Greenberg, Martin S., and David M. Frisch
        1972   "Effect of intentionality on willingness to reciprocate a favor." Journal of Experimental Social Psychology 8 (2): 99-111.

2087. Greenberg, Martin S., and Solomon P. Shapiro
        1971   "Indebtedness: An adverse aspect of asking for and receiving help." Sociometry 34 (2, June): 290-301. P.A. 49:763.

2088. Greenberg, Martin S., Myron W. Block, and Michael A. Silverman
        1971   "Determinants of helping behavior: Person's rewards versus other's

costs." Journal of Personality 39: 79–93.

2089. Greenberg, Pearl J.
    1932   "Competition in children: An experimental study." American Journal of Psychology 44: 221–248. P.A. 6:2940.

2090. Greenberger, Ellen, and Annemette Sorensen
    1971   "Interpersonal choices among junior high school faculty." Sociology of Education 44 (2, Spring): 198–216. S.A. 20:F8111.

2091. Greenblat, Cathy S.
    1974   "Sociological theory and the 'multiple reality' game." Simulation and Games 5 (1, March): 3–21. P.A. 52:12312.

2092. Greenglass, Esther R.
    1969   "Effects of prior help and hindrance on willingness to help another: Reciprocity or social responsibility." Journal of Personality and Social Psychology 11 (3): 224–231.

2093. Greening, Thomas C.
    1973   "When a group rejects its leader." Small Group Behavior 4 (2, May): 245–248. P.A. 51:7009.

2094. Greenwell, J., and H. A. Dengerink
    1973   "The role of perceived versus actual attack in human physical aggression." Journal of Personality and Social Psychology 26 (1, April): 66–71. P.A. 50:4784.

2095. Greer, F. Loyal
    1955   "Small group effectiveness." Report No. 6. Philadelphia: Institute for Research in Human Relations.

2096.   1961   "Leader indulgence and group performance." Psychological Monographs 75, No. 12 (Whole No. 516.) P.A. 5GF35G.

2097. Greer, F. Loyal, Eugene H. Galanter, and Peter G. Nordlie
    1954   "Interpersonal knowledge and individual and group effectiveness." Journal of Abnormal and Social Psychology 49: 411–414. P.A. 29: 3797.

2098. Gregovich, Robert P., and Joseph B. Sidowski
    1966   "Verbal reports of strategies in a two-person interaction: A note." Psychological Reports 19: 641–642.

2099. Griesinger, Donald W., and James W. Livingston, Jr.
    1973   "Toward a model of interpersonal motivation in experimental games." Behavioral Science 18 (3, May): 173–188. P.A. 51:2978; S.A. 22:74G8628.

2100. Griffitt, William B.
    1966   "Interpersonal attraction as a function of self-concept and personality similarity-dissimilarity." Journal of Personality and Social Psychology 4 (5): 581–584.

2101.   1968   "Anticipated reinforcement and attraction." Psychonomic Science 11 (10): 355. P.A. 42:17145.

2102.   1970   "Environmental effects on interpersonal affective behavior: Ambient effective temperature and attraction." Journal of Personality and Social Psychology 15 (3): 240–244. P.A. 44:16547.

2103. Griffitt, William B., Donn Byrne, and Michael H. Bond
    1971   "Proportion of positive adjectives and personal relevance of adjectival descriptions as determinants of attraction." Journal of Experimental Social Psychology 7 (1, January): 111–121. P.A. 46:1070.

2104. Griffitt, William B., James May, and Russell Veitch
    1974   "Sexual stimulation and interpersonal behavior: Heterosexual evaluative responses, visual behavior, and physical proximity." Journal of Personality and Social Psychology 30 (3): 367–377.

2105. Griffitt, William B., and Paul Nelson
    1970   "Short-term temporal stability of interpersonal attraction." Psychonomic Science 18 (2): 119–120. P.A. 44:6654.

2106. Griffitt, William B., and Russell Veitch
    1971   "Hot and crowded: Influence of population density and temperature on interpersonal affective behavior." Journal of Personality and Social Psychology 17 (1, January): 92–98. P.A. 45:9845.

2107.   1974   "Preacquaintance attitude similarity and attraction revisited: Ten days in a fall-out shelter." Sociometry 37 (2, June): 163-173. P.A. 52:12313.

2108. Grinker, Roy R., and John P. Spiegel
    1945   Men under Stress. Philadelphia: Blakiston. P.A. 20:2372.

2109. Gronlund, Norman E.
    1955a "Sociometric status and sociometric perception." Sociometry 18: 122-128. P.A. 30:4348; S.A. 2223.

2110.   1955b "The relative stability of classroom social status with unweighted and weighted sociometric choices." Journal of Educational Psychology 46: 345-354. P.A. 30:7645.

2111.   1956a "Generality of teachers' sociometric perceptions: Relative judgment accuracy on several sociometric criteria." Journal of Educational Psychology 47: 25-31. P.A. 31:6556.

2112.   1956b "The general ability to judge sociometric status: Elementary student teachers' sociometric perceptions of classmates and pupils." Journal of Educational Psychology 47: 147-157.

2113. Gross, Alan E., and Julie G. Latané
    1973 "Some effects of receiving and giving help." Proceedings of the 81st Annual Convention of the American Psychological Association 8: 287-288. P.A. 50:8839.

2114. Gross, Edward
    1953 "Some functional consequences of primary controls in formal work organizations." American Sociological Review 18: 368-373. P.A. 28:5028.

2115.   1954 "Primary functions of the small group." American Journal of Sociology 60: 24-30. P.A. 30:780.

2116.   1956 "Symbiosis and consensus as integrative factors in small groups." American Sociological Review 21: 174-179. P.A. 31:2698; S.A. 2924.

2117.   1961 "Dimensions of leadership." Personnel 40: 213-218. P.A. 36: 3GF13G.

2118. Gross, David E., Harold H. Kelley, Arie W. Kruglanski, and Michael E. Patch
    1972 "Contingency of consequences and type of incentive in interdependent escape." Journal of Experimental Social Psychology 8 (4, July): 360-377. P.A. 49:764.

2119. Gross, Neal, Alexander W. McEachern, and Ward S. Mason
    1958 "Role conflict and its resolution." In E. E. Maccoby, T. M. Newcomb, and E. L. Hartley (eds.), Readings in Social Psychology, 3rd ed., pp. 447-459. New York: Holt.

2120. Gross, Neal, and William E. Martin
    1952 "On group cohesiveness." American Journal of Sociology 57: 546-554. Comment by S. Schachter, pp. 554-562, and rejoinder by N. Gross and W. E. Martin, pp. 562-564. P.A. 27:1883.

2121. Gross, Neal, William E. Martin, and John G. Darley
    1953 "Studies of group behavior: Leadership structures in small organized groups." Journal of Abnormal and Social Psychology 48: 429-432. P.A. 28:2408; S.A. 82.

2122. Gross, Neal, Ward S. Mason, and Alexander W. McEachern
    1958 Explorations in Role Analysis: Studies of the School Superintendency Role. New York: Wiley.

2123. Grossack, Martin M.
    1953 "Controlling interaction in small group research." Journal of Psychology 35: 241-244. P.A. 28:726.

2124.   1954 "Some effects of cooperation and competition upon small group behavior." Journal of Abnormal and Social Psychology 49: 341-348. P.A. 29:3798.

2125. Grosser, Daniel, Norman Polansky, and Ronald Lippitt
    1951 "A laboratory study of behavioral contagion." Human Relations 4: 115-142. (See also D. F. Sullivan (ed.), Readings in Group Work, pp. 284-317. New York: Association Press, 1952.) P.A. 26:1418.

2126. Grosz, Hanus J., Herbert Stern, and Carl S. Wright
    1965 "Interactions in therapy groups as a function of differences among

therapists and group size." Psychological Reports 17: 827–834.

2127. Grotowski, Jergy
    1969   Towards a Poor Theater. New York: Simon & Schuster.

2128. Grove, L. G.
    1965   "Attitude convergence in small groups." Journal of Communication
             15 (4): 226–238. P.A. 40:4182.

2129. Groves, Patricia H.
    1970   "A computer simulation of interaction in decision making." Behav-
             ioral Science 15: 277–285.

2130. Gruber, Sigmund
    1952   "Task-orientation in the preschool child and its implications for
             early school adjustment." Ph.D. dissertation. Harvard University.

2131. Gruder, Charles L.
    1971a   "Determinants of social comparison choices." Journal of Experi-
             mental Social Psychology 7 (5, September): 473–489. P.A. 48:9008.

2132.   1971b   "Relationships with opponent and partner in mixed motive bargain-
             ing." Journal of Conflict Resolution 15 (3, September): 403–416.
             P.A. 48:2880.

2133. Gruder, Charles L., and Thomas D. Cook
    1971   "Sex, dependency, and helping." Journal of Personality and Social
             Psychology 19 (3, September): 290–294. P.A. 47:2832.

2134. Gruder, Charles L., and Robert J. Duslak
    1973   "Elicitation of cooperation by retaliatory and non-retaliatory strate-
             gies in a mixed-motive game." Journal of Conflict Resolution 17 (1,
             March): 162–174. P.A. 51:950.

2135. Gruen, Walter
    1961   "Some factors in the etiology of social interaction and group forma-
             tion." Journal of Social Psychology 54 (June): 57–73. P.A. 36:
             2GE57G.

2136.   1962   "Tolerance for idiosyncratic roles in group cohesion." Psychological
             Reports 11 (2): 462. P.A. 37:7945.

2137.   1965   "A contribution toward understanding of cohesiveness in small
             groups." Psychological Reports 17 (1): 311–322. P.A. 40:1521.

2138. Gruen, Walter, and Ralph Bierman
    1960   "Determinants for verbal communication among strangers." Psy-
             chological Reports 7: 463–469. P.A. 35:2157.

2139. Gruenfeld, Leopold W., David E. Rance, and Peter Weissenberg
    1969   "The behavior of task-oriented (low LPC) and socially-oriented (high
             LPC) leaders under several conditions of social support." Journal of
             Social Psychology 79 (1, October): 99–107. P.A. 44:6676.

2140. Grundy, Dominick, and Stephen F. Wilson
    1973   "Diagnosis and planning of a community residence: A sociometric
             study." Small Group Behavior 4 (2, May): 206–226.

2141. Grusky, Oscar
    1957   "A case for the theory of familial role differentiation in small
             groups." Social Forces 35: 209–217. P.A. 32:2751; S.A. 4683.

2142.   1969   "Effects of inside versus outside succession on communication pat-
             terns." Proceedings of the 77th Annual Convention of the American
             Psychological Association 4 (pt. 1): 451–452.

2143. Gubar, George
    1966   "Recognition of human facial expressions judged live in a laboratory
             setting." Journal of Personality and Social Psychology 4 (1): 108–
             111. P.A. 40:10031.

2144. Guerin, Chr. L.
    1971–   ("Effect of the group on the judgments and attitudes of individu-
    1972   als.") Bulletin de Psychologie 25 (13: 705–713. P.A. 50:8840.

2145. Guetzkow, Harold (ed.)
    1951   Groups, Leadership and Men: Research in Human Relations. Pitts-
             burgh: Carnegie. P.A. 26:803.

2146. Guetzkow, Harold
    1958   "Building models about small groups." In R. Young (ed.), Ap-
             proaches to the Study of Political Science, pp. 265–281. Evanston,

Ill.: Northwestern University Press.

2147. 1960 "Differentiation of roles in task-oriented groups." In D. Cartwright and A. Zander (eds.), Group Dynamics: Research and Theory, pp. 683–704. Evanston, Ill.: Row, Peterson. (See also Cartwright and Zander, 1968.)

2148. 1961 "Organizational leadership in task-oriented groups." In L. Petrullo and B. M. Bass (eds.), Leadership and Interpersonal Behavior, pp. 187–200. New York: Holt, Rinehart & Winston.

2149. Guetzkow, Harold, and William R. Dill
1957 "Factors in the organizational development of task-oriented groups." Sociometry 20: 175–204. P.A. 33:1023.

2150. Guetzkow, Harold, and John Gyr
1954 "An analysis of conflict in decision-making groups." Human Relations 7: 367–382. P.A. 29:3799.

2151. Guetzkow, Harold, and Herbert A. Simon
1955 "The impact of certain communication nets upon organization and performance in task-oriented groups." Management Science 1: 233–250.

2152. Guinan, James F., Melvin L. Foulds, and James C. Wright
1973 "Do the changes last? A six-month follow-up of a marathon group." Small Group Behavior 4 (2, May): 177–180.

2153. Gullahorn, John T., and Jeanne E. Gullahorn
1963 "A computer model of elementary behavior." Behavioral Science 8: 354–362.

2154. Gumpert, Peter, Morton Deutsch, and Yakov Epstein
1969 "Effect of incentive magnitude on cooperation in the Prisoner's Dilemma game." Journal of Personality and Social Psychology 11 (1): 66–69. P.A. 43:8275.

2155. Gumpert, Peter, John W. Thibaut, and Emir H. Shuford
1961 "Effect of personality and status experience upon the valuation of unobtained statuses." Journal of Abnormal and Social Psychology 63 (1): 47–52. P.A. 36:4GE47G.

2156. Gunderson, E. K. Eric, and Paul D. Nelson
1965 "Measurement of group effectiveness in natural isolated groups." Journal of Social Psychology 66 (2, August): 241–249. P.A. 39: 15037. (See also P.A. 38:5962.)

2157. 1966 "Criterion measures for extremely isolated groups." Personnel Psychology 19 (1): 67–80. P.A. 40:8789.

2158. Gurman, Ernest B., and Bernard M. Bass
1961 "Objective compared with subjective measures of the same behavior in groups." Journal of Abnormal and Social Psychology 63 (2): 368–374. P.A. 37:1102.

2159. Gurnee, Herbert
1937a "A comparison of collective and individual judgments of facts." Journal of Experimental Psychology 21: 106–112.

2160. 1937b "Maze learning in the collective situation." Journal of Psychology 3: 437–443.

2161. 1962 "Group learning." Psychological Monographs 76, No. 13. (Whole No. 532.)

2162. 1968 "Learning under competitive and collaborative sets." Journal of Experimental Social Psychology 4 (January): 26–34.

2163. Gurvitch, Georges
1949 "Microsociology and sociometry." Sociometry 12: 1–31. P.A. 26: 4720.

2164. Gurwitz, Sharon B.
1973 "Effects of alternatives and prior support on maintaining causal attributions." Proceedings of the 81st Annual Convention of the American Psychological Association 8 (1): 243–244.

2165. Gussow, Zachary
1964 "The observer-observed relationship as information about structure in small-group research." Psychiatry 27 (3, August): 230–247. P.A. 39:4864; S.A. 13:B4927.

2166. Gustafson, David H., Ramesh K. Shukla, Andre Delbecq, and G. William Walster
1973   "A comparative study of differences in subjective likelihood esti-mates made by individuals, interacting groups, Delphi groups, and nominal groups." Organizational Behavior and Human Performance 9 (2, April): 280-291. P.A. 50:11234.

2167. Gustafson, David P.
1973   "Task commitment and role differentiation." Human Relations 26 (5): 667-679. P.A. 52:828.

2168. Gustafson, David P., and Jack E. Gaumnitz
1972   "Consensus rankings in small groups: Self-rankings included and ex-cluded." Sociometry 35 (4, December): 610-618. P.A. 50:921; S.A. 22:74G6144.

2169. Guthe, C. E.
1945   "Manual for the study of food habits: Report of the Committee on Food Habits." Bulletin of the National Research Council No. 111. P.A. 19:3326.

2170. Gutman, Gloria M., and Robert E. Knox
1972   "Balance, agreement, and attraction in pleasantness, tension, and consistency ratings of hypothetical social situations." Journal of Per-sonality and Social Psychology 24 (3, December): 351-357. P.A. 49:9041.

2171. Gutman, Gloria M., Robert E. Knox, and Thomas F. Storm
1974   "Developmental study of balance, agreement, and attraction effects in the ratings of hypothetical social situations." Journal of Person-ality and Social Psychology 29 (2): 201-211.

2172. Guttentag, Marcia, and Ruth Freed
1971   "The effect on risk taking of sex of group members, group homo-geneity, and problem content." Journal of Social Psychology 83 (2, April): 305-306. P.A. 46:2906.

2173. Gutzmer, Willard E., and William Fawcett Hill
1973   "Evaluation of the effectiveness of the Learning Thru Discussion method." Small Group Behavior 4 (1, February): 5-34.

2174. Guyer, Melvin
1968   "Response-department parameter changes in the Prisoner's Dilemma game." Behavioral Science 13 (3, May): 205-219. P.A. 42:12036; S.A. 17:D6814.

2175. Guyer, Melvin, John Fox, and Henry Hamburger
1973   "Format effects in the Prisoner's Dilemma game." Journal of Con-flict Resolution 17 (4, December): 719-744. P.A. 52:2891.

2176. Guyer, Melvin, and Anatol Rapoport
1970   "Threat in a two-person game." Journal of Experimental Social Psy-chology 6 (1): 11-25. P.A. 44:14502.

2177.   1972   "2 × 2 games played once." Journal of Conflict Resolution 16 (3, September): 409-431. P.A. 50:922.

2178. Guze, Samuel B., and Ivan N. Mensh
1959   "An analysis of some features of the interview with the interaction chronograph." Journal of Abnormal and Social Psychology 58: 269-271.

2179. Gyr, John
1951   "Analysis of committee member behavior in four cultures." Human Relations 4: 193-202. P.A. 26:1419.

2180. Haaland, Gordon A.
1968   "Information-seeking behavior and sources of influence in conform-ity." Behavioral Science 13 (3): 238-239. P.A. 42:12037.

2181. Haan, Norma, and Norman Livson
1973   "Sex differences in the eyes of expert personality assessors: Blind spots?" Journal of Personality Assessment 37 (5, October): 486-492. P.A. 51:5097.

2182. Haas, Kurt
1969   "Obedience to harmful orders: Do we have a phenomenon?" Psy-

chology 6 (2): 2-5. P.A. 43:14229.

2183. Haase, Richard F., and Martin J. Markey
1973   "A methodological note on the study of personal space." Journal of
Consulting and Clinical Psychology 40 (1, February): 122-125. P.A.
50:923.

2184. Hacker, Sally, and Charles Gaitz
1970   "Interaction and performance correlates of Machiavellianism." Sociological Quarterly 11 (1, Winter): 94-102. S.A. 18:E5681.

2185. Hackman, J. Richard
1968   "Effects of task characteristics on group products." Journal of Experimental Social Psychology 4 (2): 162-187. P.A. 42:13654.

2186. Hackman, J. Richard, and Neil Vidmar
1970   "Effects of size and task type on group performance and member
reactions." Sociometry 33 (1, March): 37-54. P.A. 46:8924; S.A.
19:E8388.

2187. Hadley, Trevor R., and Theodore Jacob
1973   "Relationship among measures of family power." Journal of Personality and Social Psychology 27 (1, July): 6-12. P.A. 50:11235.

2188. Hage, Jerald, and Gerald Marwell
1968   "Toward the development of an empirically based theory of role relationships." Sociometry 31 (2): 200-212. P.A. 42:13678.

2189. Hagman, Elizabeth P.
1933   "The companionships of preschool children." University of Iowa
Studies in Child Welfare 7 (4). (New series No. 255.)

2190. Hagstrom, Warren O., and Hanan C. Selvin
1965   "Two dimensions of cohesiveness in small groups." Sociometry 28
(1, March): 30-43. P.A. 39:9997; S.A. 14:B9179.

2191. Haigh, Gerard V.
1968   "A personal growth crisis in laboratory training." Journal of Applied
Behavioral Science 4 (4, October-December): 437-452. S.A. 18:
E0901.

2192.   1971   "Response to Koch's assumptions about group process." Journal of
Humanistic Psychology 11 (2, Fall): 129-132. P.A. 48:2881.

2193. Haigh, Gerard V., and W. Schmidt
1956   "The learning of subject matter in teacher-centered and group-centered classes." Journal of Educational Psychology 47: 295-301.

2194. Haiman, Franklyn S.
1951   Group Leadership and Democratic Action. Boston: Houghton
Mifflin. P.A. 27:1043.

2195. Haines, Donald B., and W. J. McKeachie
1967   "Cooperative versus competitive discussion methods in teaching introductory psychology." Journal of Educational Psychology 58 (6):
386-390.

2196. Haines, G. F., F. Heider, and D. Remington
1961   "The computer as a small-group member." Administrative Science
Quarterly 6 (3, December): 360-374. S.A. 10:A3245.

2197. Haire, Mason
1954   "Industrial social psychology." In G. Lindzey (ed.), Handbook of
Social Psychology, pp. 1104-1123. Cambridge, Mass.: Addison-
Wesley.

2198. Haire, Mason (ed.)
1959   Modern Organization Theory. New York: Wiley.

2199. Hájek, P., and S. Kratochvil
1973   ("Social influencibility and hypnotic susceptibility.") Ceskoslovenska Psychologie 17 (4): 368-374. P.A. 52:7526.

2200. Hake, Don F., and Ron Vukelich
1972   "A classification and review of cooperation procedures." Journal of
the Experimental Analysis of Behavior 18 (2, September): 333-343.
P.A. 49:4409.

2201. Hake, Don F., Ron Vukelich, and Sheldon J. Kaplan
1973   "Audit responses: Responses maintained by access to existing self
or coactor scores during non-social parallel work, and cooperation

procedures." Journal of the Experimental Analysis of Behavior 19 (3, May): 409-423. P.A. 50:11236.

2202. Halal, William E.
    1974   "Toward a general theory of leadership." Human Relations 27 (4): 401-416.

2203. Haley, Hugh J., and Brendan G. Rule
    1971   "Group composition effects of risk taking." Journal of Personality 39 (1, March): 150-161. P.A. 46:4836.

2204. Hall, Douglas T.
    1970   "The effect of teacher-student congruence upon student learning in college classes." Journal of Educational Psychology 61 (3): 205-213.

2205. Hall, Edward T.
    1959   The Silent Language. Garden City, N.Y.: Doubleday.
2206.   1966   The Hidden Dimension. Garden City, N.Y.: Doubleday.

2207. Hall, Ernest J., Jane S. Mouton, and Robert R. Blake
    1963   "Group problem solving effectiveness under conditions of pooling vs. interaction." Journal of Social Psychology 59 (1, February): 147-157. P.A. 38:872.

2208. Hall, Jay
    1971   "Decisions, decisions, decisions." Psychology Today 5 (6, November): 51-54, 86-88. P.A. 47:10772.

2209. Hall, Jay, and W. H. Watson
    1970   "The effects of a normative intervention on group decision-making performance." Human Relations 23 (4, August): 299-317. P.A. 45: 8104.

2210. Hall, Jay, and Martha S. Williams
    1966   "A comparison of decision-making performances in established and ad hoc groups." Journal of Personality and Social Psychology 3 (2, February): 214-222. P.A. 40:4183; S.A. 15:C3478.
2211.   1970   "Group dynamics training and improved decision making." Journal of Applied Behavioral Science 6 (1, January-March): 39-68. S.A. 19:F0470.
2212.   1971   "Personality and group encounter style: A multivariate analysis of traits and preferences." Journal of Personality and Social Psychology 18 (2): 163-172.

2213. Hall, Robert L.
    1955   "Social influence on the aircraft commander's role." American Sociological Review 20: 292-299. P.A. 30:8498.
2214.   1957   "Group performance under feedback that confounds responses of group members." Sociometry 20: 297-305.
2215.   1962   "Two-alternative learning in interdependent dyads." In J. H. Criswell, H. Solomon, and P. Suppes (eds.), Mathematical Methods in Small Group Processes, pp. 180-192. Stanford, Calif.: Stanford University Press. S.A. 12:B2414.

2216. Hallenbeck, Phyllis N.
    1966   "An analysis of power dynamics in marriage." Journal of Marriage and the Family 28 (2): 200-203. P.A. 40:7642.

2217. Hallinan, Maureen
    1972   "Comment on Holland and Leinhardt." American Journal of Sociology 77 (6, May): 1201-1205. S.A. 21:73G2271.

2218. Halpern, Howard M.
    1955   "Empathy, similarity, and self-satisfaction." Journal of Consulting Psychology 19: 449-452.

2219. Halpin, Andrew W.
    1954   "The leadership behavior and combat performance of airplane commanders." Journal of Abnormal and Social Psychology 49: 19-22. P.A. 28:8211.
2220.   1955a   "The leader behavior and leadership ideology of educational administrators and aircraft commanders." Harvard Educational Review 25: 18-32. P.A. 30:2646.
2221.   1955b   "The leadership ideology of aircraft commanders." Journal of Ap-

plied Psychology 39: 82–84. P.A. 30:1740.

2222. Halpin, Stanley M., and Marc Pilisuk
    1970   "Prediction and choice in the Prisoner's Dilemma." Behavioral Science 15 (2): 141–153.

2223. Halverson, Charles F., Jr.
    1970   "Interpersonal perception: Cognitive complexity and trait implication." Journal of Consulting and Clinical Psychology 34 (1): 86–90.

2224. Hamblin, Robert L.
    1958a   "Group integration during a crisis." Human Relations 11: 67–76. S.A. A1702.

2225.   1958b   "Leadership and crisis." Sociometry 21: 322–335. (See also Cartwright and Zander, 1960.) P.A. 34:1166.

2226.   1971a   "Mathematical experimentation and sociological theory: A critical analysis." Sociometry 34 (4): 423–452.

2227.   1971b   "Ratio measurement for the social sciences." Social Forces 50 (2): 191–206.

2228. Hamblin, Robert L., and L. Keith Miller
    1961   "Variation of interaction profiles and group size." Sociological Quarterly 2: 105–117. P.A. 36:3GE05H.

2229. Hamblin, Robert L., L. Keith Miller, and James A. Wiggins
    1961   "Group morale and competence of the leader." Sociometry 24 (3, September): 295–311. P.A. 36:3GF95H; S.A. A3422.

2230. Hamburger, Henry
    1973   "N-person Prisoner's Dilemma." Journal of Mathematical Sociology 3 (1): 27–48. P.A. 52:2892.

2231.   1974   "Take some: A format and family of games." Behavioral Science 19 (1): 28–34.

2232. Hamid, Paul N., and Brian R. Flay
    1974   "Changes in locus of control as a function of value modification." British Journal of Social and Clinical Psychology 13 (2, June): 143–150. P.A. 52:12316.

2233. Hamilton, David L., and Roger D. Fallot
    1974   "Information salience as a weighting factor in impression formation." Journal of Personality and Social Psychology 30 (4): 444–448.

2234. Hamilton, David L., and Mark P. Zanna
    1972   "Differential weighting of favorable and unfavorable attributes in impressions of personality." Journal of Experimental Research in Personality 6 (2-3, December): 204–212. P.A. 51:983.

2235.   1974   "Context effects in impression formation: Changes in connotative meaning." Journal of Personality and Social Psychology 29 (5, May): 649–654. P.A. 52:12317.

2236. Hammes, John A., and R. Travis Osborne
    1965   "Survival research in group isolation studies." Journal of Applied Psychology 49 (6): 418–421. P.A. 40:2812.

2237. Hammond, Kenneth R., Marilyn Wilkins, and Frederick J. Todd
    1966   "A research paradigm for the study of interpersonal learning." Psychological Bulletin 65 (4): 221–232.

2238. Hammond, Leo K., and Morton Goldman
    1961   "Competition and non-competition and its relationship to individual and group productivity." Sociometry 24 (1, March): 46–60. P.A. 36:1GE46H; S.A. A2737.

2239. Hamner, W. Clay
    1974   "Effects of bargaining strategy and pressure to reach agreement in a stalemated negotiation." Journal of Personality and Social Psychology 30 (4): 458–467.

2240. Hamner, W. Clay, and D. L. Harnett
    1973   "Effects of information of the opponent's reward structure on bargaining behavior." Proceedings of the 81st Annual Convention of the American Psychological Association 8: 139–140. P.A. 50:6716.

2241. Hampden-Turner, Charles M.
    1966   "An existential 'learning theory' and the integration of T-group re-

search." Journal of Applied Behavioral Sciences 2 (4, October-December): 367–386. S.A. 16:C8895.

2242. Hanfmann, Eugenia P.
 1935   "Social structure of a group of kindergarten children." American Journal of Orthopsychiatry 5: 407–410.

2243. Hanhart, Dieter
 1963   ("Test of group productivity and contributions for experimental group research.") Schweizerische Zeitschrift für Psychologie und Ihre Anwendungen 22 (1): 29–42. S.A. 14:B9180.

2244. Hanno, Mildred S., and Lawrence E. Jones
 1973   "Effects of a change in reference person on the multidimensional structure and evaluations of trait adjectives." Journal of Personality and Social Psychology 28 (3, December): 368–375. P.A. 51:7065.

2245. Hansen, Donald A.
 1965   "Personal and positional influence in formal groups: Propositions and theory for research on family vulnerability to stress." Social Forces 44 (2, December): 202–210. P.A. 40:2813.

2246. Harari, Herbert
 1967   "An experimental evaluation of Heider's balance theory with respect to situational and predispositional variables." Journal of Social Psychology 73 (2, December): 177–189. P.A. 42:3899.

2247. Harary, Frank
 1959   "Status and contrastatus." Sociometry 22 (1, March): 23–43.

2248. Harary, Frank, and Ronald Havelock
 1972   "Anatomy of a communication arc." Human Relations 25 (5, November): 413–426. P.A. 50:926.

2249. Harary, Frank, and I. C. Ross
 1954   "The number of complete cycles in a communication network." Journal of Social Psychology 40: 329–332. P.A. 29:7209.

2250.   1957   "A procedure for clique detection using the group matrix." Sociometry 20: 205–215.

2251. Harary, Frank, and Allen J. Schwenk
 1974   "Efficiency of dissemination of information in one-way and two-way communication networks." Behavioral Science 19 (2): 133–135.

2252. Hardee, Melvene D., and Margaret Bernauer
 1948   "A method of evaluating group discussion." Occupations 27: 90–94. P.A. 23:4245.

2253. Hardin, Russell
 1971   "Collective action as an agreeable n-prisoners' dilemma." Behavioral Science 16: 472–481.

2254. Hardy, Kenneth R.
 1957   "Determinants of conformity and attitude change." Journal of Abnormal and Social Psychology 54: 289–294.

2255. Hardy, Martha C.
 1937   "Social recognition at the elementary school age." Journal of Social Psychology 8: 365–384. P.A. 12:575.

2256. Hardy, Robert C.
 1971   "Effect of leadership style on the performance of small classroom groups: A test of the contingency model." Journal of Personality and Social Psychology 19 (3, September): 367–374. P.A. 47:2834.

2257.   1973   "A developmental study of relationships between birth order and leadership style for two distinctly different American groups." Journal of Social Psychology 87: 147–148.

2258. Hardy, Robert C., Stanley Sack, and Frances Harpine
 1973   "An experimental test of the contingency model on small classroom groups." Journal of Psychology 85 (1, September): 3–16. P.A. 51: 7028.

2259. Hare, A. Paul
 1952   "A study of interaction and consensus in different sized groups." American Sociological Review 17: 261–267. (See also Cartwright

and Zander, 1953. See also Phillips, Duke, and DeVault (eds.), Psychology at Work in the Elementary Classroom. New York: Harper, 1960.) P.A. 27:4153.

2260. 1953 "Small group discussions with participatory and supervisory leadership." Journal of Abnormal and Social Psychology 48: 273-275. (See also Hare, Borgatta, and Bales, 1955, 1965. See also Phillips, Duke, and DeVault (eds.), Psychology at Work in the Elementary Classroom. New York: Harper, 1960.) P.A. 28:2410.

2261. 1957 "Situational differences in leader behavior." Journal of Abnormal and Social Psychology 55: 132-135.

2262. 1958 "Areas for research in small groups." Sociology and Social Research 42: 430-435.

2263. 1960a "Interview responses: Personality or conformity?" Public Opinion Quarterly 24: 679-685. S.A. A2145.

2264. 1960b "The dimensions of social interaction." Behavioral Science 5 (July): 211-215. P.A. 35:6339; S.A. A2738.

2265. 1961 "Computer simulation of interaction in small groups." Behavioral Science 6 (3, July): 261-265. S.A. 11:A4595.

2266. 1962 Handbook of Small Group Research. New York: Free Press.

2267. 1963 "A review of small group research for group therapists." International Journal of Group Psychotherapy 13: 476-484.

2268. 1964 "Interpersonal relations in the small group." In R.E.L. Faris (ed.), Handbook of Modern Sociology, pp. 217-271. Chicago: Rand McNally.

2269. 1967 "Small group development in the relay assembly testroom." Sociological Inquiry 37 (2, Spring): 169-182. S.A. 16:D0609.

2270. 1968a "Nonviolent action from a social-psychological perspective." Sociological Inquiry 38 (1, Winter): 5-12. (See also Hare and Blumberg (eds.), Nonviolent Direct Action. Washington, D.C.: Corpus Books, 1968.)

2271. 1968b "Phases in the development of the Bicol Development Planning Board." In S. Wells and A. P. Hare (eds.), Studies in Regional Development, pp. 29-64. Bicol Development Planning Board (Philippines).

2272. 1968c "Role structure." In D. L. Sills (ed.), International Encyclopedia of the Social Sciences, vol. 6, pp. 283-288. New York: Macmillan and Free Press.

2273. 1968d "Social-psychological analyses of nonviolence." In A. P. Hare and H. H. Blumberg (eds.), Nonviolent Direct Action, pp. 1-30. Washington, D.C.: Corpus Books. (See also W. Moss (ed.), Violence. Williamsburg, Va.: College of William and Mary, 1968.)

2274. 1969 "Cultural differences in performance in communication networks in Africa, the United States, and the Philippines." Sociology and Social Research 54 (1): 25-41.

2275. 1970 "Simulating group decisions." Simulation and Games 1 (4, December): 361-376.

2276. 1971a "Editor's foreword (Sensitivity training)." Sociological Inquiry 41 (2, Spring): 125-132.

2277. 1971b "The conditional personality test: A cross-cultural analysis." Journal of Social Psychology 83: 141-142.

2278. 1972a "Bibliography of small group research: 1959-1969." Sociometry 35 (1, March): 1-150. P.A. 49:2334.

2279. 1972b "Four dimensions of interpersonal behavior." Psychological Reports 30 (2, April): 499-512. P.A. 50:2933.

2280. 1973a "Group decision by consensus: Reaching unity in the Society of Friends." Sociological Inquiry 43 (1): 75-84.

2281. 1973b "Theories of group development and categories for interaction analysis." Small Group Behavior 4 (3, August): 259-304. P.A. 51:5034.

2282. Hare, A. Paul, and Robert F. Bales
1963 "Seating position and small group interaction." Sociometry 26 (4, December): 480-486. (See also Hare, Borgatta, and Bales, 1965.)

P.A. 38:5989; S.A. 12:A9434.

2283. Hare, A. Paul, Edgar F. Borgatta, and Robert F. Bales (eds.)
   1955   Small Groups: Studies in Social Interaction. (Rev. Ed., 1965.) New York: Knopf. P.A. 39:15038.

2284. Hare, A. Paul, and James S. Davie
   1954   "The group interview: Its use in a study of undergraduate culture." Sociology and Social Research 39: 81-87. P.A. 29:6198.

2285. Hare, A. Paul, and Andrew Effrat
   1969   "Content and process of interaction in 'Lord of the Flies.'" Report No. 8. Haverford, Pa.: Haverford College, Nonviolent Action Research Project.

2286. Hare, A. Paul, and Rachel T. Hare
   1948   "Family friendship within the community." Sociometry 11: 329-334.

2287.   1956   "The Draw-a-Group Test." Journal of Genetic Psychology 89: 51-59.

2288. Hare, A. Paul, and Dean Peabody
   1971   "Attitude content and agreement set in autonomy-authoritarianism items for United States, African, and Philippine University students." Journal of Social Psychology 83: 23-31.

2289. Hare, A. Paul, and Hartmann Scheiblechner
   1971   "Computer simulation of small group decisions: Model three." Behavioral Science 16 (4, July): 399-403. S.A. 20:F6013.

2290. Hare, A. Paul, Nancy Waxler, George Saslow, and Joseph D. Matarazzo
   1960   "Simultaneous recording of Bales and Chapple interaction measures during initial psychiatric interviews." Journal of Consulting Psychology 24 (2): 193.

2291. Harnack, R. Victor
   1953   "Problems in measuring discussion process." Journal of Communication 3: 13-16. P.A. 28:7341.

2292.   1955   "An experimental study of the effects of training in the recognition and formulation of goals upon intra-group cooperation." Speech Monographs 22: 31-38. P.A. 30:781.

2293.   1963   "A study of the effect of an organized minority upon a discussion group." Journal of Communication 13 (1): 12-24. P.A. 37:7946.

2294. Harnett, Donald L.
   1967   "A level of aspiration model for group decision making." Journal of Personality and Social Psychology 5 (1): 58-66.

2295. Harnett, Donald L., Larry L. Cummings, and W. Clay Hamner
   1973   "Personality, bargaining style and payoff in bilateral monopoly bargaining among European managers." Sociometry 36 (3, September): 325-345. P.A. 52:2893.

2296. Harnett, Donald L., Larry L. Cummings, and G. David Hughes
   1968   "The influence of risk taking propensity on bargaining behavior." Behavioral Science 13 (2, March): 91-101. S.A. 17:D5790.

2297. Harper, D. G.
   1968   "The reliability of measures of sociometric acceptance and rejection." Sociometry 31 (2): 219-227. P.A. 42:13679.

2298. Harper, Frank F. B., and Read D. Tuddenham
   1964   "The sociometric composition of the group as a determinant of yielding to a distorted norm." Journal of Psychology 58 (2): 307-311. P.A. 39:4865.

2299. Harrell, W. Andrew
   1973   "The effects of an aggressive model on the magnitude of extinction-induced aggression." Journal of Social Psychology 90 (2): 311-315.

2300. Harrell, W. Andrew, and David R. Schmitt
   1973   "Effects of a minimal audience on physical aggression." Psychological Reports 32 (2, April): 651-657. P.A. 51:3032.

2301. Harris, Edwin F., and E. A. Fleishman
   1955   "Human relations training and the stability of leadership patterns." Journal of Applied Psychology 39: 20-25. P.A. 30:1741.

2302. Harris, Mary B.
1972 "The effects of performing one altruistic act on the likelihood of performing another." Journal of Social Psychology 88 (1, October): 65–73. P.A. 49:4410.

2303. 1973 "Field studies of modeled aggression." Journal of Social Psychology 89 (1, February): 131–139. P.A. 50:2934.

2304. Harris, Mary B., and Hortensia Baudin
1973 "The language of altruism: The effects of language, dress, and ethnic group." Journal of Social Psychology 91 (1): 37–41.

2305. Harris, Mary B., and Lily C. Huang
1973a "Competence and helping." Journal of Social Psychology 89 (2, April): 203–210. P.A. 50:6717.

2306. 1973b "Helping and the attribution process." Journal of Social Psychology 90 (2, August): 291–297. P.A. 51:984.

2307. 1974 "Aggression and the attribution process." Journal of Social Psychology 92 (2): 209–216.

2308. Harris, Mary B., Ralph A. Liguori, and Andrew Joniak
1973 "Aggression, altruism, and models." Journal of Social Psychology 91 (2): 343–344.

2309. Harris, Mary B., Ralph A. Liguori, and Conrad Stack
1973 "Favors, bribes, and altruism." Journal of Social Psychology 89 (1, February): 47–54. P.A. 50:2935.

2310. Harris, Mary B., and Fred W. Meyer
1973 "Dependency, threat, and helping." Journal of Social Psychology 90 (2, August): 239–242. P.A. 51:985.

2311. Harris, Richard J.
1969a "A geometric classification system for 2 × 2 interval-symmetric games." Behavioral Science 14 (2, March): 138–146. S.A. 18:E2907.

2312. 1969b "Note on 'Optimal policies for the Prisoner's Dilemma.'" Psychological Review 76 (4, July): 363–375.

2313. 1971 "Interval-scale classification system for all 2 × 2 games." Proceedings of the 79th Annual Convention of the American Psychological Association 6 (pt. 1): 219–220.

2314. 1972 "An interval-scale classification system for all 2 × 2 games." Behavioral Science 17 (4, July): 371–383. P.A. 49:765; S.A. 21:73G4902.

2315. Harris, Victor A., and Carol E. Robinson
1973 "Bystander intervention: Group size and victim status." Bulletin of the Psychonomic Society 2 (1, July): 8–10. P.A. 51:7066.

2316. Harrison, Albert A., and Charles G. McClintock
1965 "Previous experience within the dyad and cooperative game behavior." Journal of Personality and Social Psychology 1 (6): 671–675. P.A. 39:12173.

2317. Harrison, C. Wade, James R. Rawls, and Donna J. Rawls
1971 "Differences between leaders and nonleaders in six-to-eleven-year-old children." Journal of Social Psychology 84: 269–272.

2318. Harrison, Murelle G., Lawrence A. Messé, and Gary E. Stollak
1971 "Effects of racial composition and group size on interaction patterns in preschool children." Proceedings of the 79th Annual Convention of the American Psychological Association 6 (pt. 1): 325–326.

2319. Harrison, Roger
1965 "Group composition models for laboratory design." Journal of Applied Behavioral Science 1 (4, December): 409–432. S.A. 14:C1886.

2320. 1971 "Research on human relations training: Design and interpretation." Journal of Applied Behavioral Science 7 (1, January): 71–85. P.A. 46:8925.

2321. Harrison, Roger, and Bernard Lubin
1965 "Personal style, group composition, and learning." Journal of Applied Behavioral Science 1 (3, July-September): 286–301. P.A. 40: 2814; S.A. 14:C0069.

2322. Harrocks, John E., and Mae E. Buker
1951 "A study of the friendship fluctuations of pre-adolescents." Journal

of Genetic Psychology 78: 131–144.

2323. Harrocks, John E., and George G. Thompson
    1946   "A study of the friendship fluctuations of rural boys and girls."
            Journal of Genetic Psychology 69: 189–198.

2324. Harrow, Martin, Boris M. Astrachan, Robert E. Becker, James C. Miller, and
    Arthur H. Schwartz
    1967   "Influence of the psychotherapist on the emotional climate in group
            therapy." Human Relations 20 (1, February): 49–64.

2325. Harrow, Martin, Boris M. Astrachan, Gary J. Tucker, Edward B. Klein, and
    James C. Miller
    1971   "The T-group and study group laboratory experiences." Journal of
            Social Psychology 85 (2, December): 225–237. P.A. 47:8790.

2326. Harsanyi, John C.
    1962a   "Bargaining in ignorance of the opponent's utility function." Jour-
            nal of Conflict Resolution 6 (1): 29–38.

2327.   1962b   "Measurement of social power, opportunity costs, and the theory
            of two-person bargaining games." Behavioral Science 7 (1, January):
            67–80. P.A. 37:1104.

2328.   1962c   "Measurement of social power in n-person reciprocal power situa-
            tions." Behavioral Science 7 (1, January): 81–91. P.A. 37:1103.

2329.   1966   "Bargaining model for social status in informal groups and formal
            organizations." Behavioral Science 11: 357–369.

2330. Harshbarger, Dwight
    1971   "An investigation of a structural model of a small group problem
            solving." Human Relations 24 (1): 43–63.

2331. Hart, Joe W.
    1961   "Bibliography of sociometric cleavage." Journal of Psychological
            Studies 12 (4): 137–142. P.A. 39:9998.

2332. Hart, Roland J.
    1973   "Evaluations of self and others and aggression." Proceedings of the
            81st Annual Convention of the American Psychological Association
            8: 233–234. P.A. 50:4787.

2333. Hartley, Ruth E., L. K. Frank, and R. M. Goldenson
    1952   Understanding Children's Play. New York: Columbia University
            Press. P.A. 27:269.

2334. Hartnett, John J. and Robert M. Barber
    1974   "Fear of failure in group risk-taking." British Journal of Social and
            Clinical Psychology 13 (2, June): 125–129. P.A. 52:12255.

2335. Hartup, Willard W.
    1964   "Friendship status and the effectiveness of peers reinforcing agents."
            Journal of Experimental Child Psychology 1 (2): 154–162. P.A. 39:
            4866.

2336. Harvey, Jerry B., Barry I. Oshry, and Goodwin Watson
    1970   "A design for a laboratory exploring issues of organization." Jour-
            nal of Applied Behavioral Science 6 (4, October): 401–411. P.A.
            46:4837.

2337. Harvey, John H., Robert M. Arkin, James M. Gleason, and Shawn Johnston
    1974   "Effect of expected and observed outcome of an action on the dif-
            ferential causal attributions of actor and observer." Journal of Per-
            sonality 42 (1): 62–77. P.A. 52:7557.

2338. Harvey, John H., and David R. Kelley
    1973   "Effects of attitude similarity and success-failure upon attitude to-
            ward other persons." Journal of Social Psychology 90 (1, June):
            105–114. P.A. 51:3033.

2339. Harvey, O. J.
    1953   "An experimental approach to the study of status reactions in in-
            formal groups." American Sociological Review 18: 357–367. P.A.
            28:4136; S.A. 83.

2340.   1956   "An experimental investigation of negative and positive relations
            between small groups through judgmental indices." Sociometry 19:
            201–209. P.A. 32:1451.

2341.   1960   "Reciprocal influence of the group and three types of leaders in an unstructured situation." Sociometry 23 (1, March): 57-68. P.A. 35: 2143.

2342. 1964 "Some cognitive determinants of influencibility." Sociometry 27 (2, June): 208-221. P.A. 39:4867.

2343. Harvey, O. J., and Conrad Consalvi
1960 "Status and conformity to pressures in informal groups." Journal of Abnormal and Social Psychology 60 (2, March): 182-187. (See also Crosbie, 1975.) P.A. 34:7558.

2344. Harvey, O. J., David E. Hunt, and Harold M. Schroder
1961 Conceptual Systems and Personality Organization. New York: Wiley.

2345. Harvey, O. J., Harold H. Kelley, and Martin M. Shapiro
1957 "Reactions to unfavorable evaluations of the self made by other persons." Journal of Personality 25: 393-411.

2346. Harvey, O. J., and Jeanne Rutherford
1958 "Gradual and absolute approaches to attitude change." Sociometry 21: 61-68.

2347. Hass, R. Glen, and Darwyn E. Linder
1972 "Counterargument availability and the effects of message structure on persuasion." Journal of Personality and Social Psychology 23 (2, August): 219-233. P.A. 49:766.

2348. Hastorf, Albert H., I. E. Bender, and D. J. Weintraub
1955 "The influence of response patterns on the 'refined empathy score.'" Journal of Abnormal and Social Psychology 51: 341-343. P.A. 30: 4349.

2349. Hatfield, Frederick C.
1972 "Effect of prior experience, access to information and level of performance on individual and group performance ratings." Perceptual and Motor Skills 35 (1, August): 19-26. P.A. 49:4411.

2350. Hautaluoma, Jacob E., and William A. Scott
1973 "Values and sociometric choices of incarcerated juveniles." Journal of Social Psychology 91 (2): 229-237.

2351. Hautaluoma, Jacob E., and Helene Spungin
1974 "Effects of initiation severity and interest on group attitudes." Journal of Social Psychology 93 (2): 245-259.

2352. Havron, M. Dean, and Joseph E. McGrath
1961 "The contribution of the leader to the effectiveness of small military groups." In L. Petrullo and B. M. Bass (eds.), Leadership and Interpersonal Behavior, pp. 167-178. New York: Holt, Rinehart & Winston.

2353. Hawes, Leonard C., and Joseph M. Foley
1973 "A Markov analysis of interview communication." Speech Monographs 40 (3, August): 210-219. P.A. 52:829.

2354. Hawkins, Charles H.
1962 "Interaction rates of jurors aligned in factions." American Sociological Review 27 (5, October): 689-691.

2355. Hawkins, Nancy E., and Merle E. Meyer
1965 "Social values and conformity." Psychonomic Science 2 (2): 31-32. P.A. 39:7634.

2356. Hayes, Donald P., and Leo Meltzer
1972 "Interpersonal judgments based on talkativeness: I. Fact or artifact?" Sociometry 35 (4, December): 538-561. P.A. 50:928.

2357. Hayes, Donald P., Leo Meltzer, and Gary D. Bouma
1968 "Activity as a determinant of interpersonal perception." Proceedings of the 76th Annual Convention of the American Psychological Association 3: 417-418.

2358. Hayes, Donald P., Leo Meltzer, and Signe Lundberg
1968 "Information distribution, interdependence, and activity levels." Sociometry 31 (2, June): 162-179. S.A. 17:D6815.

2359. Hayes, Donald P., and Sally Sievers
1972 "A sociolinguistic investigation of the 'dimensions' of interpersonal behavior." Journal of Personality and Social Psychology 24 (2, November): 254-261. P.A. 49:4412.

2360. Hays, Daniel G.
    1970   "Computer representation of social behavior transcripts." Proceedings of the 78th Annual Convention of the American Psychological Association 5 (pt. 1): 491–492.
2361. Hays, David G., and Robert R. Bush
    1954   "A study of group action." American Sociological Review 19: 693–701. P.A. 30:2647.
2362. Hays, William L.
    1960   "Psychological dimensionality and the distribution of rank order agreement among judges." Sociometry 23 (3, September): 262–272. P.A. 35:2098; S.A. A2694.
2363. Haythorn, William
    1953   "The influence of individual members on the characteristics of small groups." Journal of Abnormal and Social Psychology 48: 276–284. (See also Hare, Borgatta, and Bales, 1955, 1965.) P.A. 28:2412.
2364.   1968   "The composition of groups: A review of the literature." Acta Psychologica 28 (2): 97–128. P.A. 42:13680.
2365. Haythorn, William, Arthur S. Couch, Donald Haefner, Peter Langham, and Launor F. Carter
    1956a   "The behavior of authoritarian and equalitarian personalities in groups." Human Relations 9: 57–74. P.A. 31:5887. S.A. 3661.
2366.   1956b   "The effects of varying combinations of authoritarian and equalitarian leaders and followers." Journal of Abnormal and Social Psychology 53: 210–219. (See also Maccoby, Newcomb, and Hartley, 1958.) P.A. 32:2752.
2367. Heald, James E., Louis G. Romano, and Nicholas P. Georgiady (eds.)
    1970   Selected Readings on General Supervision. New York: Macmillan.
2368. Hearn, Gordon
    1957   "Leadership and the spatial factor in small groups." Journal of Abnormal and Social Psychology 54: 269–272.
2369. Heber, Rick F., and Mary E. Heber
    1957   "The effect of group failure and success on social status." Journal of Educational Psychology 48: 129–134.
2370. Heckel, Robert V.
    1963   "Comment on Oakes: 'Reinforcement of Bales' categories in group discussion." Psychological Reports 13: 301–302.
2371.   1973   "Leadership and voluntary seating choice." Psychological Reports 32 (1, February): 141–142. P.A. 51:3034.
2372. Heckel, Robert V., and Herman C. Salzberg
    1967   "Predicting verbal behavioral change in group therapy using a screening scale." Psychological Reports 20: 403–406.
2373. Heider, Fritz
    1958   The Psychology of Interpersonal Relations. New York: Wiley.
2374. Heilbrun, Alfred B., Jr.
    1968   "Influence of observer and target sex in judgments of sex-typed attributes." Perceptual and Motor Skills 27 (3, pt. 2): 1194. P.A. 43:9661.
2375. Heilman, Madeline E.
    1974   "Threats and promises: Reputational consequences and transfer of credibility." Journal of Experimental Social Psychology 10 (4, July): 310–324. P.A. 52:12319.
2376. Heilman, Madeline E., Susan A. Hodgson, and Harvey A. Hornstein
    1972   "Effects of magnitude and rectifiability of harm and information value on the reporting of accidental harm-doing." Journal of Personality and Social Psychology 23 (2, August): 211–218. P.A. 49: 767.
2377. Heilweil, Martin
    1973   "The influence of dormitory architecture on resident behavior." Environment and Behavior 5 (4, December): 377–412. P.A. 52:7507.
2378. Heimann, Robert A., and Hope M. Heimann
    1972   "Nonverbal communication and counselor education." Comparative Group Studies 3 (4, November): 443–460.

2379. Heinicke, Christoph M., and Robert F. Bales
        1953   "Developmental trends in the structure of small groups." Sociom-
                etry 16: 7-38. P.A. 28:692.
2380. Heise, George A., and George A. Miller
        1951   "Problem solving by small groups using various communication
                nets." Journal of Abnormal and Social Psychology 46: 327-336.
                (See also Hare, Borgatta, and Bales, 1955.) P.A. 26:2148.
2381. Heiss, Jerold S.
        1962   "Degree of intimacy and male-female interaction." Sociometry 25
                (2, June): 197-208. P.A. 37:3034.
2382.   1963   "The dyad views the newcomber: A study of perception." Human
                Relations 16 (3, August): 241-248. S.A. 12:A9435.
2383. Heller, Frank A.
        1970   "Group feed-back analysis as a change agent." Human Relations 23
                (4): 319-333.
2384. Heller, Jack F., Michael S. Pallak, and James M. Picek
        1973   "The interactive effects of intent and threat on boomerang attitude
                change." Journal of Personality and Social Psychology 26 (2, May):
                273-279. P.A. 50:11238.
2385. Helm, Bob, Thomas V. Bonoma, and James T. Tedeschi
        1971   "Counter-aggression as a function of physical aggression: Reciproc-
                ity for harm done." Proceedings of the 79th Annual Convention of
                the American Psychological Association 6 (pt. 1): 237-238. P.A. 46:
                2908.
2386. Helm, Bob, Robert C. Brown, and James T. Tedeschi
        1972   "Esteem and the effectiveness of a verbal reinforcer." Journal of
                Social Psychology 87 (2, August): 293-300. P.A. 49:768.
2387. Helmreich, Robert L., Elliot Aronson, and James LeFan
        1970   "To err is humanizing—sometimes: Effects of self-esteem, compe-
                tence, and a pratfall on interpersonal attraction." Journal of Person-
                ality and Social Psychology 16 (2): 259-264.
2388. Helmreich, Robert L., Roger Bakeman, and Larry Scherwitz
        1973   "The study of small groups." Annual Review of Psychology 24:
                337-354. P.A. 50:2936.
2389. Helmreich, Robert L., and Barry E. Collins
        1967   "Situational determinants of affiliative preference under stress."
                Journal of Personality and Social Psychology 6 (1): 79-85.
2390. Helson, Harry, Robert R. Blake, Jane S. Mouton, and J. A. Olmstead
        1956   "Attitudes as adjustments to stimulus, background, and residual
                factors." Journal of Abnormal and Social Psychology 52: 314-322.
                P.A. 31:4475.
2391. Helus, Z.
        1971   ("Analysis of a group emergence of creative activity.") Ceskos-
                lovenska Psychologie 15 (5): 487-491. P.A. 49:6816.
2392. Hemphill, John K.
        1949   "Situational factors in leadership." Ohio State University Education-
                al Research Monographs 32. P.A. 24:5770.
2393.   1950   "Relations between the size of the group and the behavior of 'super-
                ior' leaders." Journal of Social Psychology 32: 11-22. P.A. 25:
                3759.
2394.   1956   "Group dimensions: A manual for their measurement." Ohio State
                University Bureau of Business Research Monographs 87. P.A. 31:
                7657.
2395.   1961   "Why people attempt to lead." In L. Petrullo and B. M. Bass (eds.),
                Leadership and Interpersonal Behavior, pp. 201-215. New York:
                Holt, Rinehart & Winston.
2396. Hemphill, John K., and Carolyn B. McConville
        1965   "The effect of 'human' vs. 'machine' set on group problem-solving
                procedures." Journal of Social Psychology 67 (October): 45-60.
2397. Hemphill, John K., Pauline N. Pepinsky, R. N. Shevitz, W. E. Jaynes, and
        Charlotte A. Christner
        1956   "The relation between possession of task-relevant information and

attempts to lead." Psychological Monographs 70 (7): No. 414. P.A. 31:4467.

2398. Hemphill, John K., and Charles M. Westie
1950   "The measurement of group dimensions." Journal of Psychology 29: 325-342. P.A. 24:5789.

2399. Henchy, Thomas, and David C. Glass
1968   "Evaluation apprehension and the social facilitation of dominant and subordinate responses." Journal of Personality and Social Psychology 10 (4): 446-454. P.A. 43:6839.

2400. Hendrick, Clyde
1968   "Averaging vs summation in impression formation." Perceptual and Motor Skills 27 (3, pt. 2): 1295-1302. P.A. 43:9662.

2401. Hendrick, Clyde, V. Edwin Bixenstine, and Gayle Hawkins
1971   "Race versus belief similarity as determinants of attraction: A search for a fair test." Journal of Personality and Social Psychology 17 (3, March): 250-258. P.A. 46:1072.

2402. Hendrick, Clyde, and Steven R. Brown
1971   "Introversion, extraversion, and interpersonal attraction." Journal of Personality and Social Psychology 20 (1): 31-36.

2403. Hendrick, Clyde, Martin Giesen, and Sharon Coy
1974   "The social ecology of free seating arrangements in a small group interaction context." Sociometry 37 (2, June): 262-274. P.A. 52: 12256.

2404. Hendrick, Clyde, and Gayle Hawkins
1969   "Race and belief similarity as determinants of attraction." Perceptual and Motor Skills 29 (3, December): 710. P.A. 46:4839.

2405. Hendrick, Clyde, and Horace A. Page
1970   "Self-esteem, attitude similarity, and attraction." Journal of Personality 38: 588-601.

2406. Hendrick, Clyde, and Donna K. Rumenik
1973   "Race versus belief about race as determinants of attraction: Belief prejudice and two kinds of race prejudice." Journal of Research in Personality 7 (2, September): 148-164. P.A. 51:7067.

2407. Hendrick, Clyde, and B. A. Seyfried
1974   "Salience of similarity awareness and attraction: A comparison of balance vs reinforcement predictions." Memory and Cognition 2 (1-A, January): 1-4. P.A. 52:7558.

2408. Hendrick, Clyde, C. Scully Stikes, and Edward J. Murray
1972   "Race versus belief similarity as determinants of attraction in a live interaction setting." Journal of Experimental Research in Personality 6 (2-3, December): 162-168. P.A. 51:986.

2409 Hendrick, Clyde, C. Scully Stikes, Edward J. Murray, and Carol Puthoff
1973   "Race vs. belief as determinants of attraction in a group interaction context." Memory and Cognition 1 (1, January): 41-46. P.A. 50: 6719.

2410. Hendrick, Clyde, and Stuart P. Taylor
1971   "Effects of belief similarity and aggression on attraction and counteraggression." Journal of Personality and Social Psychology 17 (3): 342-349.

2411. Henley, Nancy M.
1973   "Status and sex: Some touching observations." Bulletin of the Psychonomic Society 2 (2, August): 91-93. P.A. 51:9007.

2412. Henry, Jules
1951   "Family structure and the transmission of neurotic behavior." American Journal of Orthopsychiatry 21: 800-818. P.A. 26:5681.

2413. Henry, Norman R., Art W. Rousseau, and Robert S. Schlottmann
1974   "Singular vs combined effects of frustration and insult on aggressive behavior." Psychological Reports 35 (1, pt. 1): 327-335.

2414. Henry, William E., and Harold Guetzkow
1951   "Group projection sketches for the study of small groups." Journal of Social Psychology 33: 77-102. P.A. 26:917.

2415. Hepburn, John R.
1973 "Violent behavior in interpersonal relationships." Sociological Quarterly 14 (3, Summer): 419–429. P.A. 51:9008.

2416. Herbert, Eleonore L., and E. L. Trist
1953 "The institution of an absent leader by a students' discussion group." Human Relations 6: 215–248. P.A. 28:2415; S.A. 84.

2417. Herbst, P. G.
1952 "The measurement of family relationships." Human Relations 5: 3–35. P.A. 27:371.

2418. 1953 "Analysis and measurement of a situation: The child in the family." Human Relations 6: 113–140. P.A. 28:2462.

2419. 1971 "Interpersonal distance regulation and affect control on merchant ships." European Journal of Social Psychology 1 (1): 47–58. P.A. 48:7103. S.A. 22:74G6145.

2420. Herman, Simon N., and Erling O. Schild
1961 "The stranger-group in a cross-cultural situation." Sociometry 24 (2, June): 165–176.

2421. Hermann, Margaret G., and Nathan Kogan
1968 "Negotiation in leader and delegate groups." Journal of Conflict Resolution 12 (3, September): 332–344. P.A. 14231; S.A. 18: E0902.

2422. Hermann, Theo
1971 "'Prescriptive' and 'proscriptive' conformity as a result of childhood training." European Journal of Social Psychology 1 (1): 140. P.A. 48:7104.

2423. Heshka, Stanley, and Yona Nelson
1972 "Interpersonal speaking distance as a function of age, sex, and relationship." Sociometry 35 (4, December): 491–498. P.A. 50:930.

2424. Heslin, Richard
1964 "Predicting group task effectiveness from member characteristics." Psychological Bulletin 62 (4): 248–256. P.A. 39:4869.

2425. Heslin, Richard, and Jack Collins
1970 "Other-directed observers and the information value of a person's deviation from role expectation." Proceedings of the 78th Annual Convention of the American Psychological Association 5 (pt. 1): 411–412.

2426. Heslin, Richard, and Dexter Dunphy
1964 "Three dimensions of member satisfaction in small groups." Human Relations 17 (2, May): 99–112. P.A. 39:4868; S.A. 13:B4057.

2427. 1968 "System for cross-classification of small group studies." Psychological Reports 23 (3, pt. 2): 1295–1304. P.A. 43:8276.

2428. Hewitt, David
1972 "Conceptual complexity, environment complexity, communication salience and attitude change." European Journal of Social Psychology 2 (3): 285–305. P.A. 50:4790.

2429. Hewitt, Jay
1969 "Interpersonal attraction as a function of the accuracy of personal evaluations." Psychonomic Science 17 (2): 95–96. P.A. 44:3540.

2430. 1971 "Interpersonal attraction as a function of the type of favorable and unfavorable evaluation." Psychonomic Science 22 (4, February): 197–198. P.A. 46:8926.

2431. 1972 "Integration of information about others." Psychological Reports 30 (3, June): 1007–1010. P.A. 49:2336.

2432. Hewitt, Jay, and Betty J. Chung
1969 "Observed benevolence and hostility as determinants of interpersonal attraction." Psychonomic Science 17 (2): 82. P.A. 44:3541.

2433. Hewitt, Jay, and Morton Goldman
1974 "Self-esteem, need for approval, and reactions to personal evaluations." Journal of Experimental Social Psychology 10 (3): 201–210.

2434. Hewitt, Jay, and Marty Kraft
1973 "Effects of an encounter group experience on self-perception and

interpersonal relations." Journal of Consulting and Clinical Psychology 40 (1, February): 162. P.A. 50:931.

2435. Heyns, Roger W.
1958   "Social psychology and group processes." Annual Review of Psychology 9: 419–452. P.A. 32:4035.

2436. Heyns, Roger W., and Ronald Lippitt
1954   "Systematic observational techniques." In G. Lindzey (ed.), Handbook of Social Psychology, pp. 370–404. Cambridge, Mass.: Addison-Wesley. P.A. 29:3847.

2437. Heyns, Roger W., and Alvin Zander
1953   "Observation of group behavior." In L. Festinger and D. Katz (eds.), Research Methods in the Behavioral Sciences, pp. 381–418. New York: Dryden. P.A. 30:3542.

2438. Hicks, David J., and Richard G. Lathrop
1968   "Some dimensions of justified aggression." Proceedings of the 76th Annual Convention of the American Psychological Association 3: 425–426.

2439. Hicks, Jack M.
1962   "The influence of group flattery upon self evaluation." Journal of Social Psychology 58 (1): 147–151. P.A. 37:6608.

2440. Hicks, Jack M., Richard A. Monty, and Thomas I. Myers
1966   "Group consensus and judgmental accuracy: Extension of the Asch effect." Psychonomic Science 5 (4): 159–160. P.A. 40:10032.

2441. Higbee, Kenneth L.
1971   "Expression of 'Walter Mitty-ness' in actual behavior." Journal of Personality and Social Psychology 20 (3): 416–422.

2442.   1972   "Group risk taking in military decisions." Journal of Social Psychology 88 (1, October): 55–64. P.A. 49:4414.

2443. Higbee, Kenneth L., and Terry E. Black
1972   "Exploitative behavior in a dyad." Proceedings of the 80th Annual Convention of the American Psychological Association 7 (pt. 1): 233–234. P.A. 48:4864.

2444. Higgin, Gurth, and Harold Bridger
1964   "The psychodynamics of an inter-group experience." Human Relations 17 (4, November): 391–446. P.A. 39:7635.

2445. Hilgard, Ernest R., E. M. Sait, and G. Ann Margaret
1940   "Level of aspiration as affected by relative standing in an experimental social group." Journal of Experimental Psychology 27: 411–421. P.A. 15:143.

2446. Hilkevitch, Rhea R.
1960   "Social interactional processes: A quantitative study." Psychological Reports 7: 195–201. P.A. 35:2114.

2447. Hill, Reuben L.
1951   "Review of current research on marriage and the family." American Sociological Review 16: 694–701. P.A. 27:3491.

2448. Hill, Walter
1969   "A situational approach to leadership effectiveness." Journal of Applied Psychology 53 (6): 513–517.

2449. Hill, William Fawcett, and LeRoy Gruner
1973   "A study of development in open and closed groups." Small Group Behavior 4 (3, August): 355–381.

2450. Himber, Charlotte
1970   "Evaluating sensitivity training for teen-agers." Journal of Applied Behavioral Science 6 (3, July-September): 307–322. S.A. 20:F3456.

2451. Himmelfarb, Samuel
1969   "Combination of cues of varying validities in the perception of persons." Proceedings of the 77th Annual Convention of the American Psychological Association 4 (pt. 1): 405–406. P.A. 43:17340.

2452.   1973   "General test of a differential weighted averaging model of impression formation." Journal of Experimental Social Psychology 9 (5, September): 379–390. P.A. 51:9036.

2453. Hinckley, Barbara
      1972   "Coalitions in Congress: Size and ideological distance." Midwest
                Journal of Political Science 16 (2, May): 197-207. S.A. 22:
                74G6146.
2454. Hinton, Bernard L.
      1972   "The experimental extension of equity theory to interpersonal and
                group interaction situations." Organizational Behavior and Human
                Performance 8 (3, December): 434-449. P.A. 49:11072.
2455. Hinton, Bernard L., W. Clay Hamner, and Michael F. Pohlen
      1974   "The influence of reward magnitude, opening bid and concession
                rate on profit earned in a managerial negotiation game." Behavioral
                Science 19 (3, May): 197-203. P.A. 52:12257.
2456. Hirota, Kimiyoshi
      1953   ("Group problem solving and communication.") Japanese Journal of
                Psychology 24: 105-113. P.A. 29:674.
2457. Hites, R. W., and D. T. Campbell
      1950   "A test of the ability of fraternity leaders to estimate group opin-
                ion." Journal of Social Psychology 32: 95-100. P.A. 25:3971.
2458. Hjelholt, Gunnar
      1972   "Group training in understanding society: The mini-society." Inter-
                personal Development 3 (1-4): 140-151. P.A. 51:9009.
2459. Hjelle, Larry A.
      1968   "Accuracy of personality and social judgments as functions of famil-
                iarity." Psychological Reports 22 (1): 311-319. P.A. 42:10514.
2460. Hobson, G. N., K. T. Strongman, D. Bull, and G. Craig
      1973   "Anxiety and gaze aversion in dyadic encounters." British Journal
                of Social and Clinical Psychology 12 (2, June): 122-129. P.A. 51:
                2979.
2461. Hochbaum, Godfrey M.
      1954   "The relation between group members' self-confidence and their re-
                actions to group pressures to uniformity." American Sociological
                Review 19: 678-687. P.A. 30:2649.
2462. Hochberg, Julian, and Ruth E. Galper
      1974   "Attribution of intention as a function of physiognomy." Memory
                and Cognition 2 (1-A, January): 39-42. P.A. 52:7559.
2463. Hodges, Bert H.
      1974   "Effect of valence on relative weighting in impression formation."
                Journal of Personality and Social Psychology 30 (3): 378-381.
2464. Hodges, Louis A., and Donn Byrne
      1972   "Verbal dogmatism as a potentiator of intolerance." Journal of Per-
                sonality and Social Psychology 21 (3, March): 312-317. P.A. 48:
                2859.
2465. Hodgson, Susan A., Harvey A. Hornstein, and Elizabeth LaKind
      1972   "Socially mediated Zeigarnik effects as a function of sentiment, val-
                ence, and desire for goal attainment." Journal of Experimental
                Social Psychology 8 (5, September): 446-456. P.A. 49:6817.
2466. Hoerl, Richard T.
      1974   "Encounter groups: Their effect on rigidity." Human Relations 27
                (5): 431-438.
2467. Hoffman, Joyce M., and John Arsenian
      1965   "An examination of some models applied to group structure and
                process." International Journal of Group Psychotherapy 15 (2):
                131-153. P.A. 39:15041.
2468. Hoffman, L. Richard
      1958   "Similarity of personality: A basis for interpersonal attraction?" So-
                ciometry 21: 300-308. P.A. 34:1169.
2469.   1959   "Homogeneity of member personality and its effect on group prob-
                lem-solving." Journal of Abnormal and Social Psychology 58: 27-
                32. P.A. 34:954.
2470.   1962   "A note on ratings versus choices as measures of group attraction."
                Sociometry 25 (3, September): 313-320. P.A. 37:3035; S.A. 11:

A5134.
2471.   1965   "Group problem solving." In L. Berkowitz (ed.), Advances in Experimental Social Psychology, vol. 2, pp. 99-127. New York:
Academic Press.
2472. Hoffman, L. Richard, Ronald J. Burke, and Norman R. F. Maier
1965   "Participation, influence, and satisfaction among members of problem-solving groups." Psychological Reports 16: 661-667.
2473. Hoffman, L. Richard, Ernest Harburg, and Norman R. F. Maier
1962   "Differences and disagreement as factors in creative group problem
solving." Journal of Abnormal and Social Psychology 64 (3): 206-
214. P.A. 38:2585.
2474. Hoffman, L. Richard, and Norman R. F. Maier
1959   "The use of group decision to resolve a problem of fairness." Personnel Psychology 12: 545-559. P.A. 34:5721.
2475.   1961a   "Quality and acceptance of problem solutions by members of homogeneous and heterogeneous groups." Journal of Abnormal and Social Psychology 62 (2, March): 401-407. P.A. 36:4GE01H; S.A.
A2209.
2476.   1961b   "Sex differences, sex composition, and group problem solving."
Journal of Abnormal and Social Psychology 63 (2, September):
453-456. S.A. 11:A4158.
2477.   1964   "Valence in the adoption of solutions by problem-solving groups:
Concept, method, and results." Journal of Abnormal and Social Psychology 69 (3, September): 264-271. S.A. 14:B8344.
2478.   1966   "An experimental reexamination of the similarity-attraction hypothesis." Journal of Personality and Social Psychology 3 (2): 145-
152. P.A. 40:4184.
2479.   1967   "Valence in the adoption of solutions by problem-solving groups:
II. Quality and acceptance as goals of leaders and members." Journal
of Personality and Social Psychology 6 (2): 175-182.
2480. Hoffman, L. Richard, and Clagett G. Smith
1960   "Some factors affecting the behavior of members of problem solving
groups." Sociometry 23 (3, September): 273-291. P.A. 35:1726;
S.A. A2739.
2481. Hoffman, Martin L.
1957   "Conformity as a defense mechanism and a form of resistance to
genuine group influence." Journal of Personality 25: 412-424.
2482. Hoffman, Paul J., Leon Festinger, and Douglas H. Lawrence
1954   "Tendencies toward group comparability in competitive bargaining."
Human Relations 7: 141-159. P.A. 29:2311.
2483. Hofstetter, C. Richard
1972   "The promise of participation for learning, comprehension, and the
acquisition of democratic values." Comparative Group Studies 3 (2,
May): 225-245. P.A. 49:9042.
2484. Hogan, H. Wayne, and C. Boyd Loadholt
1972   "Cognitive consistency and class identification: Study of social perception." Perceptual and Motor Skills 35 (1, August): 329-330. P.A.
49:4415.
2485. Hogan, James L., Roger H. Fisher, and Bruce J. Morrison
1973   "Accuracy of perception and cooperative game behavior." Perceptual and Motor Skills 37 (2, October): 391-398. P.A. 51:9037.
2486.   1974   "Social feedback and cooperative game behavior." Psychological
Reports 34 (3, pt. 2): 1075-1082.
2487. Hogan, Robert, and Donald Mankin
1970   "Determinants of interpersonal attraction: A clarification." Psychological Reports 26 (1, February): 235-238. P.A. 45:4118.
2488. Hoggatt, Austin C.
1967   "Measuring the cooperativeness of behavior in quantity variation
duopoly games." Behavioral Science 12 (2, March): 109-121. S.A.
15:C6379.
2489. Hoiberg, Bruce C., and Lloyd K. Stires
1973   "Effects of pretrial publicity and juror traits on the guilt attributions

of simulated jurors." Proceedings of the 81st Annual Convention of the American Psychological Association 8 (pt. 1): 269-270.

2490. Holahan, Charles
    1972   "Seating patterns and patient behavior in an experimental dayroom." Journal of Abnormal Psychology 80 (2): 115-124.

2491. Holahan, Charles, and George Levinger
    1971   "Psychological versus spatial determinants of social schema distance: A methodological note." Journal of Abnormal Psychology 78 (2, October): 232-236. P.A. 47:8791.

2492. Holbert, William M., William H. Cormier, and Martin I. Friedman
    1971   "The semantic differential in sensitivity training: An exploratory study." Comparative Group Studies 2 (1, February): 36-42. P.A. 47:4715.

2493. Holland, Paul W., and Samuel Leinhardt
    1970   "A method for detecting structure in sociometric data." American Journal of Sociology 76 (3): 492-513.

2494.   1971   "Transitivity in structural models of small groups." Comparative Group Studies 2 (2, May): 107-124. P.A. 48:2882.

2495. Hollander, Edwin P.
    1954   "Authoritarianism and leadership choice in a military setting." Journal of Abnormal and Social Psychology 49: 365-370.

2496.   1956   "The friendship factor in peer nominations." Personnel Psychology 9: 435-447. P.A. 32:2780.

2497.   1957   "The reliability of peer nominations under various conditions of administration." Journal of Applied Psychology 41: 85-90.

2498.   1958   "Conformity, status, and idiosyncrasy credit." Psychological Review 65: 117-127.

2499.   1959   "Some points of reinterpretation regarding social conformity." Sociological Review 7: 159-168. P.A. 36:3GE59H.

2500.   1960a   "Competence and conformity in the acceptance of influence." Journal of Abnormal and Social Psychology 61 (3, November): 365-370. P.A. 36:2GE65H; S.A. A1703.

2501.   1960b   "Reconsidering the issue of conformity in personality." In H. P. David and J. C. Brengelmann (eds.), Perspectives in Personality Research, pp. 210-225. New York: Springer. P.A. 35:2116.

2502.   1961a   "Emergent leadership and social influence." In L. Petrullo and B. M. Bass (eds.), Leadership and Interpersonal Behavior, pp. 30-47. New York: Holt, Rinehart & Winston.

2503.   1961b   "Some effects of perceived status on responses to innovative behavior." Journal of Abnormal and Social Psychology 63 (2): 247-250.

2504.   1964   Leaders, Groups, and Influence. New York: Oxford University Press. P.A. 39:7651; S.A. 17:D4868.

2505. Hollander, Edwin P., and James W. Julian
    1969   "Contemporary trends in the analysis of leadership processes." Psychological Bulletin 71 (5): 387-397. P.A. 43:11231.

2506. Hollander, Edwin P., James W. Julian, and Gordon A. Haaland
    1965   "Conformity process and prior group support." Journal of Personality and Social Psychology 2 (6): 852-858. P.A. 40:2815.

2507. Hollander, Edwin P., and Wilse B. Webb
    1955   "Leadership, followership, and friendship: An analysis of peer nominations." Journal of Abnormal and Social Psychology 50: 163-167. (See also Maccoby, Newcomb, and Hartley, 1958.) P.A. 30:782; S.A. 1977.

2508. Hollander, Edwin P., and David L. Wiesenthal
    1969   "Compliance as a function of confirmation or disconfirmation of an expected monetary reward." Proceedings of the 77th Annual Convention of the American Psychological Association 4 (pt. 1): 359-360.

2509. Hollander, Edwin P., and Richard H. Willis
    1967   "Some current issues in the psychology of conformity and nonconformity." Psychological Bulletin 68 (1): 62-76.

2510. Hollingshead, August B.
      1949   Elmtown's Youth. New York: Wiley. P.A. 23:4697.
2511. Holloman, Charles R., and Hal W. Hendrick
      1971   "Problem solving in different sized groups." Personnel Psychology
               24 (3, Fall): 489-500. P.A. 51:9010.
2512.   1972   "Adequacy of group decisions as a function of the decision-making
               process." Academy of Management Journal 15 (2, June): 175-184.
               P.A. 49:2338.
2513. Holmes, Davis S., and David H. Bennett
      1974   "Experiments to answer questions raised by the use of deception in
               psychological research: I. Role playing as an alternative to decep-
               tion: II. Effectiveness of debriefing after a deception: III. Effect of
               informed consent on deception." Journal of Personality and Social
               Psychology 29 (3): 358-367.
2514. Holmes, Douglas S., and Leonard Berkowitz
      1961   "Some contrast effects in social perception." Journal of Abnormal
               and Social Psychology 62 (1, January): 150-152. P.A. 36:3GE50H;
               S.A. A1726.
2515. Holmes, John G., Warren F. Throop, and Lloyd H. Strickland
      1971   "The effects of prenegotiation expectations on the distributive bar-
               gaining process." Journal of Experimental Social Psychology 7 (6,
               November): 582-599. P.A. 48:9011.
2516. Holmes, J. Steven
      1967   "Relation of depression and verbal interaction in group therapy."
               Psychological Reports 20: 1039-1042.
2517.   1969   "Comparison of group leader and non-participant observer judg-
               ments of certain objective interaction variables." Psychological Re-
               ports 24 (2): 655-659. P.A. 43:15698.
2518. Holmes, J. Steven, and Edward E. Cureton
      1970   "Group therapy interaction with and without the leader." Journal
               of Social Psychology 81: 127-128.
2519. Holstein, Carolyn M., Joel W. Goldstein, and Daryl J. Bem
      1971   "The importance of expressive behavior, involvement, sex, and need-
               approval in inducing liking." Journal of Experimental Social Psy-
               chology 7 (5, September): 534-544. P.A. 48:9012.
2520. Homans, George C.
      1941   "The Western Electric researches." In National Research Council,
               Fatigue of Workers: Its Relation to Industrial Production. New
               York: Reinhold. (See also Swanson, Newcomb, and Hartley, 1952;
               Maccoby, Newcomb, and Hartley, 1958.)
2521.   1946   "The Western Electric researches." In S. D. Hoslett (ed.), Human
               Factors in Management, pp. 152-185. Parkville, Mo.: Park College
               Press.
2522.   1947   "A conceptual scheme for the study of social organization." Ameri-
               can Sociological Review 12: 13-26. P.A. 21:2719.
2523.   1950   The Human Group. New York: Harcourt, Brace. P.A. 25:3002.
2524.   1953   "Status among clerical workers." Human Organization 12 (1): 5-10.
               (See also Crosbie, 1975.) P.A. 29:6371.
2525.   1954   "The cash posters: A study of a group of working girls." American
               Sociological Review 19: 724-733. P.A. 30:3526.
2526.   1958   "Social behavior as exchange." American Journal of Sociology 63:
               597-606. (See also Hare, Borgatta, and Bales, 1965.)
2527.   1961   Social Behavior: Its Elementary Forms. New York: Harcourt, Brace.
               P.A. 36:4GA04H. (Rev. ed., 1974. New York: Harcourt Brace Jo-
               vanovich. P.A. 52:800.)
2528.   1963   "Small groups." In B. Berelson (ed.), The Behavioral Sciences To-
               day, pp. 165-175. New York: Basic Books. S.A. 12:B3225.
2529.   1968   "The study of groups." In D. L. Sills (ed.), International Encyclo-
               pedia of the Social Sciences, vol. 6, pp. 259-265. New York: Mac-
               millan and Free Press.
2530. Hood, Thomas C., and Kurt W. Back
      1971   "Self-disclosure and the volunteer: A source of bias in laboratory

experiments." Journal of Personality and Social Psychology 17 (2, February): 130–136. P.A. 45:8106.

2531. Hood, William R., and Muzafer Sherif
1962 "Verbal report and judgment of an unstructured stimulus." Journal of Psychology 54 (1): 121–130. P.A. 37:3036.

2532. Hopkins, Terence K.
1964 The Exercise of Influence in Small Groups. Totowa, N.J.: Bedminster.

2533. Hoppe, Ronald A.
1962 "Memorizing by individuals and groups: A test of the pooling-of-ability model." Journal of Abnormal and Social Psychology 65 (1): 64–67. P.A. 38:4192.

2534. Hoppe, Ronald A., Michael S. Greene, and Jack W. Kenny
1972 "Territorial markers: Additional findings." Journal of Social Psychology 88 (2, December): 305–306. P.A. 49:9043.

2535. Horai, Joann, Irving Haber, James T. Tedeschi, and R. Bob Smith, III
1970 "It's not what you say, it's how you do it: A study of threats and promises." Proceedings of the 78th Annual Convention of the American Psychological Association 5 (pt. 1): 393–394. P.A. 44:18564.

2536. Horai, Joann, and James T. Tedeschi
1969 "Effects of credibility and magnitude of punishment on compliance to threats." Journal of Personality and Social Psychology 12 (2): 164–169.

2537. Horne, William C.
1970 "Group influence on ethical risk taking: The inadequacy of two hypotheses." Journal of Social Psychology 80: 237–238.

2538. 1972 "Risk-taking and ethical risk-taking: No relationship." Psychological Reports 30 (2, April): 492. P.A. 50:2938.

2539. Horne, William C., and Gary Long
1972 "Effect of group discussion on universalistic-particularistic orientation." Journal of Experimental Social Psychology 8 (3): 236–246.

2540. Horney, Karen
1945 Our Inner Conflicts. New York: Norton. P.A. 20:442.

2541. Hornstein, Harvey A.
1965 "The effects of different magnitudes of threat upon interpersonal bargaining." Journal of Experimental Social Psychology 1 (3, August): 282–293.

2542. 1972 "Promotive tension: The basis of prosocial behavior from a Lewinian perspective." Journal of Social Issues 28 (3): 191–218. P.A. 50: 4792.

2543. Hornstein, Harvey A., Elisha Fisch, and Michael Holmes
1968 "Influence of a model's feeling about his behavior and his relevance as a comparison other on observers' helping behavior." Journal of Personality and Social Psychology 10 (3): 222–226. P.A. 43:3925.

2544. Hornstein, Harvey A., Hugo N. Masor, Kenneth Sole, and Madeline Heilman
1971 "Effects of sentiment and completion of a helping act on observer helping: A case for socially mediated Zeigarnik effects." Journal of Personality and Social Psychology 17 (1): 107–112.

2545. Horowitz, Herbert
1969 "The effect of interpersonal focusing on imitation and opposition learning." Journal of Social Psychology 77 (1): 55–67. P.A. 43: 6831.

2546. Horowitz, Irwin A.
1968a "Effect of choice and locus of dependence on helping behavior." Journal of Personality and Social Psychology 8 (4, pt. 1): 373–376. P.A. 42:8866.

2547. 1968b "Social responsibility as a function of repression-sensitization and social exchange." Journal of Social Psychology 75 (1, June): 135–146. P.A. 42:13656.

2548. 1971 "The effect of group norms on bystander intervention." Journal of Social Psychology 83 (2, April): 265–273. P.A. 46:2909.

2549. 1972 "Attitude change as a function of perceived arousal." Journal of

Social Psychology 87 (1, June): 117-126. P.A. 48:8983.
2550. Horowitz, Irwin A., and Bertram H. Rothschild
1970   "Conformity as a function of deception and role playing." Journal
of Personality and Social Psychology 14 (3): 224-226.
2551. Horowitz, Milton W., Joseph Lyons, and Howard V. Perlmutter
1951   "Induction of forces in discussion groups." Human Relations 4: 57-
76. P.A. 25:8004.
2552. Horowitz, Milton W., and Howard V. Perlmutter
1953   "The concept of the social group." Journal of Social Psychology 37:
69-95. P.A. 28:694.
2553.   1955   "The discussion group and democratic behavior." Journal of Social
Psychology 41: 231-246. P.A. 30:5852; S.A. 3667.
2554. Horrocks, John E., and Murray Benimoff
1966   "Stability of adolescent's nominee status, over a one-year period, as
a friend by their peers." Adolescence 1 (3, Fall): 224-229. S.A. 16:
D1445.
2555.   1967   "Isolation from the peer group during adolescence." Adolescence 2
(5): 41-52. P.A. 42:3900.
2556. Horsfall, A. B., and C. M. Arensberg
1949   "Teamwork and productivity in a shoe factory." Human Organization 8 (1): 13-25. P.A. 23:6500.
2557. Horsfall, Robert B., and Nancy M. Henley
1969   "Mixed social structures: Strain and probability ratings." Psychonomic Science 15 (4): 186-187. P.A. 43:12896.
2558. Horvath, William J.
1965   "A mathematical model of participation in small group discussions."
Behavioral Science 10 (2, April): 164-166. S.A. 14:B8346.
2559.   1969   "Comment on the paper by Kadane, Lewis, and Ramage: 'Horvath's
theory of participation in group discussions.'" Sociometry 32 (3):
362-364. P.A. 44:3542.
2560. Horwitz, Leonard
1971   "Group-centered interventions in therapy groups." Comparative
Group Studies 2 (3, August): 311-331.
2561. Horwitz, Murray
1953   "The conceptual status of group dynamics." Review of Educational
Research 23: 309-328. P.A. 28:7345.
2562.   1954   "The recall of interrupted group tasks: An experimental study of
individual motivation in relation to group goals." Human Relations
7: 3-38. (See also Cartwright and Zander, 1953, 1960, 1968.) S.A.
486.
2563. Horwitz, Murray, and Dorwin Cartwright
1953   "A projective method for the diagnosis of group properties." Human
Relations 6: 397-410. P.A. 28:5860.
2564. Horwitz, Murray, Ralph V. Exline, and F. J. Lee
1953   Motivational Effects of Alternative Decision-Making Processes in
Groups. Urbana: University of Illinois, Bureau of Educational Research.
2565. Horwitz, Murray, David C. Glass, Seymour Giniger, and Alfred Cohn
1966   "The effect of frustrating acts upon the expectation of openness."
Human Relations 19 (2, May): 179-198. P.A. 40:11104.
2566. Horwitz, Murray, and F. G. Lee
1954   "Effects of decision making by group members on recall of finished
and unfinished tasks." Journal of Abnormal and Social Psychology
49: 201-210. P.A. 29:676.
2567. Hoshino, Kikuzo
1969   ("The ability to identify the affective meanings of facial expressions
at successive age levels.") Japanese Journal of Educational Psychology 17 (2): 90-101. P.A. 44:16551.
2568. House, William C.
1974   "Actual and perceived differences in male and female expectancies
and minimal goal levels as a function of competition." Journal of
Personality 42 (3): 493-509.

2569. Hovland, Carl I.
    1959   "Reconciling conflicting results derived from experimental and sur-
            vey studies of attitude change." American Psychologist 14 (Janu-
            ary): 8-17. P.A. 34:2893.
2570. Hovland, Carl I., and Irving L. Janis (eds.)
    1959   Personality and Persuasibility. New Haven, Conn.: Yale University
            Press. P.A. 34:7155.
2571. Hovland, Carl I., Irving L. Janis, and H. H. Kelley
    1953   Communication and Persuasion: Psychological Studies of Opinion
            Change. New Haven, Conn.: Yale University Press. P.A. 28:5952.
2572. Howard, Jane
    1970   Please Touch: A Guided Tour of the Human Potential Movement.
            New York: McGraw-Hill. P.A. 45:8107.
2573. Howells, Lloyd T., and Selwyn W. Becker
    1962   "Seating arrangement and leadership emergence." Journal of Abnor-
            mal and Social Psychology 64 (2): 148-150. P.A. 38:2596.
2574. Hoyt, George C., and James A. Stoner
    1968   "Leadership and group decisions involving risk." Journal of Experi-
            mental Social Psychology 4 (3, July): 275-284. P.A. 43:2525.
2575. Hrabal, V.
    1967   ("Perceptions of dyadic relations concerning social emotions in a
            high school class.") Ceskoslovenska Psychologie 11 (6): 563-576.
            P.A. 43:5266.
2576. Hubbard, Ruth M.
    1929   "A method of studying spontaneous group formation." In D. S.
            Thomas (ed.), Some New Techniques for Studying Social Behavior,
            pp. 76-85. New York: Columbia University, Teachers College.
2577. Hubbell, Charles H.
    1965   "An input-output approach to clique identification." Sociometry
            28 (4, December): 377-399. P.A. 40:2817; S.A. 14:C1887.
2578. Hudgins, Bryce B.
    1960   "Effects of group experience on individual problem solving." Jour-
            nal of Educational Psychology 51 (February): 37-42. P.A. 35:1727;
            34:7560.
2579. Huff, Frederick W., and Thomas P. Piantianida
    1968   "The effect of group size on group information transmitted." Psy-
            chonomic Science 11 (10): 365-366. P.A. 42:17156.
2580. Hughes, Everett C.
    1946   "The knitting of racial groups in industry." American Sociological
            Review 11: 512-519.
2581. Hum, Sterling P. C.
    1970   "Use of focused video-tape feedback in high school counseling."
            Comparative Group Studies 1 (2, May): 101-127.
2582. Hunt, J[oseph] McV., and R. L. Solomon
    1942   "The stability and some correlates of group-status in a summer camp
            group of young boys." American Journal of Psychology 55: 33-45.
            P.A. 16:1997.
2583. Hunt, Peter J., and Joseph M. Hillery
    1973   "Social facilitation in a coaction setting: An examination of the
            effects over learning trials." Journal of Experimental Social Psy-
            chology 9 (6, November): 563-571. P.A. 52:801.
2584. Hunt, Raymond G., and Vonda Synnerdahl
    1959   "Social influence among kindergarten children." Sociology and So-
            cial Research 43 (3, January-February): 171-174. S.A. 10:A1199.
2585. Hunyady, György
    1970   ("Interpersonal relation and sociometric method.") Pszichologiai
            Tanulmanyok 12: 135-149. P.A. 46:4840.
2586. Hurley, Dennis, and Bem P. Allen
    1974   "The effect of the number of people present in a non-emergency sit-
            uation." Journal of Social Psychology 92 (1): 27-29.
2587. Hurley, John R., and Elizabeth J. Force
    1973   "T-group gains in acceptance of self and others." International Jour-

nal of Group Psychotherapy 23 (2, April): 166–176. P.A. 52:831.

2588. Hurlock, Elizabeth B.
1927   "The use of group rivalry as an incentive." Journal of Abnormal and Social Psychology 22: 278–290.

2589. Hurst, James C., Ursula Delworth, and Robert Garriott
1973   "Encountertapes: Evaluation of a leaderless group procedure." Small Group Behavior 4 (4, November): 476–485.

2590. Hurst, Paul M., Robert Radlow, Nicholas C. Chubb, and Sallyann K. Bagley
1969   "Drug effects upon choice behavior in mixed motive games." Behavioral Science 14 (6, November): 443–452.

2591. Hurwitz, Jacob I., Alvin Zander, and Bernard Hymovitch
1953   "Some effects of power on the relations among group members." In D. Cartwright and A. Zander (eds.), Group Dynamics: Research and Theory, pp. 483–492. Evanston, Ill.: Row, Peterson. (See also Cartwright and Zander, 1960, 1968.)

2592. Husband, R. W.
1940   "Cooperative versus solitary problem solution." Journal of Social Psychology 11: 405–409. P.A. 14:4936.

2593. Huston, Ted L.
1973   "Ambiguity of acceptance, social desirability, and dating choice." Journal of Experimental Social Psychology 9 (1, January): 32–42. P.A. 50:2940.

2594. Hutchins, Edwin B., and Fred E. Fiedler
1960   "Task-oriented and quasi-therapeutic role functions of the leader in small military groups." Sociometry 23 (4, December): 393–406. P.A. 35:2144; S.A. A2898.

2595. Hutte, Herman A., and David Van Kreveld
1972   "The perception of door-knocks in terms of authority and urgency." European Journal of Social Psychology 2 (1): 98–99. P.A. 49:771.

2596. Ingham, Alan G., George Levinger, James Graves, and Vaughn Peckham
1974   "The Ringelmann effect: Studies of group size and group performance." Journal of Experimental Social Psychology 10 (4, July): 371–384. P.A. 52:12258.

2597. Ingils, C. R.
1968   "Group dynamics: Boon or bane?" Personnel and Guidance Journal 46 (8): 744–748. P.A. 42:15400.

2598. Innes, John M.
1972   "The effect of presence of co-workers and evaluative feedback on performance of a simple reaction time task." European Journal of Social Psychology 2 (4): 466–470. P.A. 50:6722.

2599.   1973   "The influence of attitude on the learning of balanced and unbalanced social structures." European Journal of Social Psychology 3 (1): 91–94. P.A. 52:802.

2600. Insel, Paul, and Rudolf Moos
1972   "An experimental investigation of process and outcome in an encounter group." Human Relations 25 (5, November): 441–447. P.A. 50:934.

2601. Insko, Chester A., Marilyn Rall, and John Schopler
1972   "Role of inconsistency in mediating awareness of interaction processes." Journal of Personality and Social Psychology 24 (1, October): 102–107. P.A. 49:4416.

2602. Insko, Chester A., Elaine Songer, and William McGarvey
1974   "Balance, positivity, and agreement in the Jordan paradigm: A defense of balance theory." Journal of Experimental Social Psychology 10 (1): 53–83.

2603. Insko, Chester A., Vaida D. Thompson, Wolfgang Stroebe, Karen F. Shaud, Berna E. Pinner, and Bruce D. Layton
1973   "Implied evaluation and the similarity-attraction effect." Journal of Personality and Social Psychology 25 (3, March): 297–308. P.A. 50: 4794.

2604. Insko, Chester A., and Christopher Wetzel
　　　1974　"Preacquaintance attraction as an interactive function of the propor-
　　　　　　tion and number of similar attitudes." Representative Research in
　　　　　　Social Psychology 5 (1, January): 27-33. P.A. 52:7560.
2605. Irle, Martin
　　　1963　(Social Systems: A Critical Analysis of the Theory of Formal and In-
　　　　　　formal Organizations.) Göttingen: Hogrefe. P.A. 39:1572.
2606.　1971　("Behavior in organized groups.") In C. F. Graumann (ed.), Hand-
　　　　　　buch der Psychologie, vol. 7, pt. 2, Sozialpsychologie. Göttingen.
2607. Iscoe, Ira, Martha Williams, and Jerry Harvey
　　　1964　"Age, intelligence, and sex as variables in the conformity behavior of
　　　　　　Negro and white children." Child Development 35 (2): 451-460.
　　　　　　P.A. 39:4870.
2608. Isen, Alice M.
　　　1970　"Success, failure, attention, and reaction to others: The warm glow
　　　　　　of success." Journal of Personality and Social Psychology 15 (4):
　　　　　　294-301.
2609. Isen, Alice M., Nancy Horn, and D. L. Rosenhan
　　　1973　"Effects of success and failure on children's generosity." Journal of
　　　　　　Personality and Social Psychology 27 (2, August): 239-247. P.A.
　　　　　　51:3036.
2610. Isen, Alice M., and Paula F. Levin
　　　1972　"Effect of feeling good on helping: Cookies and kindness." Journal
　　　　　　of Personality and Social Psychology 21 (3, March): 384-388. P.A.
　　　　　　48:2883.
2611. Israel, Joachim
　　　1956　Self-Evaluation and Rejection in Groups: Three Experimental Stud-
　　　　　　ies and a Conceptual Outline. Stockholm: Almqvist & Wiksell. P.A.
　　　　　　31:5891.
2612. Iwao, Sumiko
　　　1963　"Internal versus external criticism of group standards." Sociometry
　　　　　　26 (4, December): 410-421. P.A. 38:5964; S.A. A9437.
2613. Iwashita, Toyohiko
　　　1961　("A basic study of the mechanisms of interpersonal feeling and of its
　　　　　　perception: Part I.") Japanese Journal of Psychology 32: 84-96. P.A.
　　　　　　36:3GE84I.
2614. Izard, Carroll E.
　　　1960a　"Personality similarity and friendship." Journal of Abnormal and
　　　　　　Social Psychology 61 (1): 47-51. P.A. 35:2117.
2615.　1960b　"Personality similarity, positive affect, and interpersonal attraction."
　　　　　　Journal of Abnormal and Social Psychology 61 (3): 484-485. P.A.
　　　　　　36:2GE84I.
2616.　1963a　"Personality profile similarity as a function of group membership."
　　　　　　Journal of Abnormal and Social Psychology 67 (4): 404-408. P.A.
　　　　　　38:4193.
2617.　1963b　"Personality similarity and friendship: A follow-up study." Journal
　　　　　　of Abnormal and Social Psychology 66 (6): 598-600.
2618. Izzett, Richard R., and Walter Leginski
　　　1972　"Impression formation as a function of self versus other as source of
　　　　　　the information." Journal of Social Psychology 87 (2, August): 229-
　　　　　　233. P.A. 49:772.
2619.　1974　"Group discussion and the influence of defendant characteristics in
　　　　　　a simulated jury setting." Journal of Social Psychology 93 (2): 271-
　　　　　　279.

2620. Jackson, Douglas N.
　　　1972　"A model for inferential accuracy." Canadian Psychologist 13 (3,
　　　　　　July): 185-195. P.A. 49:4417.
2621. Jackson, Douglas N., Larry Hourany, and Neil J. Vidmar
　　　1972　"A four-dimensional interpretation of risk taking." Journal of Per-
　　　　　　sonality 40 (3): 483-501.

2622. Jackson, Douglas N., and Samuel J. Messick
      1957   "A note on 'ethnocentrism' and acquiescent response sets." Journal
              of Abnormal and Social Psychology 54: 132-135.
2623. Jackson, Douglas N., Samuel J. Messick, and Charles M. Solley
      1957   "How 'rigid' is the 'authoritarian'?" Journal of Abnormal and Social
              Psychology 54: 137-140.
2624. Jackson, Jay M.
      1953   "The effect of changing the leadership of small work groups." Hu-
              man Relations 6: 25-44. P.A. 28:2419.
2625.   1959a "A space for conceptualizing person-group relationships." Human
              Relations 12: 3-15. P.A. 34:7562; S.A. A2740.
2626.   1959b "Reference group processes in a formal organization." Sociometry
              22: 307-327. (See also Cartwright and Zander, 1960.)
2627. Jackson, Jay M., and Charles McGehee
      1965   "Group structure and role behavior." Annals of the American Acad-
              emy of Political and Social Science 361 (September): 130-140. S.A.
              14:C0070.
2628. Jackson, Jay M., and Herbert D. Saltzstein
      1958   "The effect of person-group relationships on conformity processes."
              Journal of Abnormal and Social Psychology 57: 17-24.
2629. Jackson, Lee A., and Guillermo F. Mascaro
      1971   "Interpersonal attraction as a function of attitude similarity dissimi-
              larity and attitude extremity." Psychonomic Science 23 (2, April):
              187-188. P.A. 47:2836.
2630. Jackson, Russell H., and Harold B. Pepinsky
      1972   "Interviewer activity and status effects upon revealingness in the ini-
              tial interview." Journal of Clinical Psychology 28 (3, July): 400-
              404. P.A. 51:2980.
2631. Jackson, Russell H., Arthur N. Wiens, Thomas S. Manaugh, and Joseph D.
      Matarazzo
      1972   "Speech behavior under conditions of differential saliency in inter-
              view content." Journal of Clinical Psychology 28 (3, July): 318-
              327. P.A. 51:2981.
2632. Jackson, W. M.
      1944   "Interaction in a college fraternity." Applied Anthropology 3: 16-
              21. P.A. 19:2671.
2633. Jacobs, Alfred, Marion Jacobs, Norman Cavior, and John Burke
      1974   "Anonymous feedback: Credibility and desirability of structured
              emotional and behavioral feedback delivered in groups." Journal of
              Counseling Psychology 21 (2, March): 106-111. P.A. 52:7527.
2634. Jacobs, J. H.
      1945   "The application of sociometry to industry." Sociometry 8: 181-
              198. P.A. 20:287.
2635. Jacobs, Larry, Ellen Berscheid, and Elaine Walster
      1971   "Self esteem and attraction." Journal of Personality and Social Psy-
              chology 17 (1): 84-91.
2636. Jacobs, Marion, Alfred Jacobs, Garry Feldman, and Norman Cavior
      1973a   "Feedback: II. The 'credibility gap': Delivery of positive and nega-
              tive and emotional and behavioral feedback in groups." Journal of
              Consulting and Clinical Psychology 41 (2, October): 215-223. P.A.
              51:7029.
2637. Jacobs, Marion, Alfred Jacobs, Margaret Gatz, and Todd Schaible
      1973b   "Credibility and desirability of positive and negative structured feed-
              back in groups." Journal of Consulting and Clinical Psychology 40
              (2, April): 244-252. P.A. 50:11241.
2738. Jacobs, Robert C., and Donald T. Campbell
      1961   "The perpetuation of an arbitrary tradition through several genera-
              tions of a laboratory microculture." Journal of Abnormal and Social
              Psychology 62 (3, May): 649-658. (See also Hare, Borgatta, and
              Bales, 1965.)
2639. Jacobs, Ruth H.
      1971   "Emotive and control groups as mutated new American utopian

communities." Journal of Applied Behavioral Science 7 (2, March): 234-251. P.A. 49:6820.

2640. Jacobson, Eugene, W. W. Charters, Jr., and Seymour Lieberman
      1951   "The use of the role concept in the study of complex organizations." Journal of Social Issues 7 (3): 18-27.

2641. Jacobson, Edward A., and Stephen J. Smith
      1972   "Effect of weekend encounter group experience upon interpersonal orientations." Journal of Consulting and Clinical Psychology 38 (3, June): 403-410. P.A. 48:11443.

2642. Jacoby, Jacob
      1968   "Creative ability of task-oriented versus person-oriented leaders." Journal of Creative Behavior 2 (4): 249-253. P.A. 43:14232.

2643.   1969   "Accuracy of person perception as a function of dogmatism." Proceedings of the 77th Annual Convention of the American Psychological Association 4 (pt. 1): 347-348.

2644.   1971   "Interpersonal perceptual accuracy as a function of dogmatism." Journal of Experimental Social Psychology 7 (2): 221-236.

2645. Jaffee, Cabot L.
      1968   "Leadership attempting: Why and when?" Psychological Reports 23 (3, pt. 1): 939-946. P.A. 43:9636.

2646. Jaffee, Cabot L., and Richard Furr
      1968   "Number of reinforcements, conditioned leadership, and expectancy of reward." Journal of Social Psychology 76 (October): 49-53.

2647. Jaffee, Cabot L., and Richard L. Lucas
      1969   "Effects of rates of talking and correctness of decisions on leader choice in small groups." Journal of Social Psychology 79 (2): 247-254. P.A. 44:10282.

2648. Jaffee, Cabot L., Steven A. Richards, and Gerald W. McLaughlin
      1970   "Leadership selection under differing feedback conditions." Psychonomic Science 20 (6, September): 349-350. P.A. 46:1075.

2649. Jaffee, Cabot L., and N. W. Skaja
      1968   "Conditioned leadership in a two-person interaction." Psychological Reports 23: 135-140.

2650. Jahoda, Marie
      1956   "Psychological issues in civil liberties." American Psychologist 11: 234-240.

2651.   1959   "Conformity and independence." Human Relations 12 (2, May): 99-120. P.A. 34:7563.

2652. Jahoda, Marie, M. Deutsch, and S. W. Cook (eds.)
      1951   Research Methods in Social Relations. New York: Dryden. P.A. 27: 2637.

2653. Jakobovits, Leon A., and Robert Hogenraad
      1967   "Some suggestive evidence on the operation of semantic generation and satiation in group discussions." Psychological Reports 20: 1247-1250.

2654. James, Bernard J.
      1955   "Methodological problems in the application of sociometry under 'uncontrolled' conditions." Sociometry 18: 111-121. P.A. 30: 4398.

2655. James, Gale, and Albert J. Lott
      1964   "Reward frequency and the formation of positive attitudes toward group members." Journal of Social Psychology 62 (1, February): 111-115. P.A. 39:1573.

2656. James, John
      1950   "Some elements in a theory of small groups." State College of Washington, Research Studies 18: 144-152.

2657.   1951a   "A preliminary study of the size determinant in small group interaction." American Sociological Review 16: 474-477. P.A. 27:1045.

2658.   1951b   "Clique organization in a small industrial plant." State College of Washington, Research Studies 19: 125-130.

2659.   1953   "The distribution of free-forming small group size." American Sociological Review 18: 569-570.

2660.   1956   "Verbal behavior in problem-solving small groups without formally designated leaders." State College of Washington, Research Studies 24: 125–133. S.A. 2925.

2661. Jamieson, Bruce D.
    1968   "The 'risky-shift' phenomenon with a heterogeneous sample." Psychological Reports 23 (1): 203–206. P.A. 43:6840.

2662. Jamous, Haroun
    1962   ("Relation to the stimulus level of involvement, and process of experimental influence.")Revue Française de Sociologie 3 (1,January-March): 20–36. S.A. 11:A7193.

2663. Janda, Kenneth F.
    1960   "Towards the explication of the concept of leadership in terms of the concept of power." Human Relations 13 (4, November): 345–363. P.A. 36:1GF45J; S.A. A3784.

2664. Janis, Irving L., and B. T. King
    1954   "The influence of role playing on opinion change." Journal of Abnormal and Social Psychology 49: 211–218. (See also Maccoby, Newcomb, and Hartley, 1958.) P.A. 29:677.

2665. Janney, Fred, Sharon Mallory, Richard Rossitto, and John Simon
    1969   "Conformity as a function of race and age." Psychological Reports 25: 591–597.

2666. Janofsky, A. Irene
    1971   "Affective self-disclosure in telephone versus face to face interviews." Journal of Humanistic Psychology 11 (1, Spring): 93–103. P.A. 47:4717.

2667. Janoušek, J.
    1971   ("Structure and typology of a group problem situation.") Ceskoslovenska Psychologie 15 (5): 492–495. P.A. 49:6821.

2668. Jansen, Luther T.
    1952   "Measuring family solidarity." American Sociological Review 17: 727–733. P.A. 28:808.

2669. Jaques, Elliott
    1948   "Interpretive group discussion as a method of facilitating social change." Human Relations 1: 533–549. P.A. 23:2207.

2670. Jastrebske, Ellen M., and Brendan G. Rule
    1970   "Effects of group variance and advocated position on conformity." Journal of Personality 38 (4, December): 550–559. P.A. 46:1076.

2671. Jecker, Jon, and David Landy
    1969   "Liking a person as a function of doing him a favour." Human Relations 22 (4, August): 371–378.

2672. Jellison, Jerald M., and Deborah Davis
    1973   "Relationships between perceived ability and attitude extremity." Journal of Personality and Social Psychology 27 (3, September): 430–436. P.A. 51:7069.

2673. Jellison, Jerald M., and William John Ickes
    1974   "The power of the glance: Desire to see and be seen in cooperative and competitive situations." Journal of Experimental Social Psychology 10 (5): 444–450.

2674. Jellison, Jerald M., and Judson Mills
    1967   "Effect of similarity and fortune of the other on attraction." Journal of Personality and Social Psychology 5 (4): 459–463.

2675. Jellison, Jerald M., and John Riskind
    1970   "A social comparison of abilities interpretation of risk-taking behavior." Journal of Personality and Social Psychology 15 (4): 375–390. P.A. 44:20823.

2676.   1971   "Attribution of risk to others as a function of their ability." Journal of Personality and Social Psychology 20 (3): 413–415.

2677. Jellison, Jerald M., and Paul T. Zeisset
    1969   "Attraction as a function of the commonality and desirability of a trait shared with another." Journal of Personality and Social Psychology 11 (2): 115–120.

2678. Jenkins, David H.
       1948   "Feedback and group self-evaluation." Journal of Social Issues 4
                 (2): 50–60. P.A. 23:686.
2679. Jenkins, David H., and Ronald Lippitt
       1951   Interpersonal Perceptions of Teachers, Students, and Parents. Wash-
                 ington, D.C.: National Education Association. P.A. 26:4175.
2680. Jenness, Arthur
       1932a   "Social influences in the change of opinion." Journal of Abnormal
                 and Social Psychology 27: 29–34.
2681. 1932b   "The role of discussion in changing opinion regarding a matter of
                 fact." Journal of Abnormal and Social Psychology 27: 279–296.
2682. Jennings, Helen H.
       1937   "Structure of leadership-development and sphere of influence." So-
                 ciometry 1: 99–143.
2683. 1941   "Individual differences in the social atom." Sociometry 4: 269–277.
                 (See also Hare, Borgatta, and Bales, 1955, 1965.) P.A. 16:1080.
2684. 1942   "Experimental evidence on the social atom at two time points." So-
                 ciometry 5: 135–145. P.A. 16:4460.
2685. 1943   "A sociometric study of emotional and social expansiveness." In R.
                 G. Barker, J. S. Kounin, and H. F. Wright (eds.), Child Behavior and
                 Development, pp. 527–543. New York: McGraw-Hill. P.A. 17:
                 2520.
2686. 1947a   "Leadership and sociometric choice." Sociometry 10: 32–49. P.A.
                 22:254.
2687. 1947b   "Sociometric differentiation of the psychegroup and the socio-
                 group." Sociometry 10: 71–79.
2688. 1948   Sociometry in Group Relations: A Work Guide for Teachers. Wash-
                 ington, D.C.: American Council of Education.
2689. 1950a   Leadership and Isolation. 2nd ed. New York: Longmans, Green.
                 (See also Barker, Kounin, and Wright, 1943; Cartwright and Zander,
                 1953; Maccoby, Newcomb, and Hartley, 1958.) P.A. 24:5772.
2690. 1950b   "Sociometric grouping in relation to child development." In C.
                 Tryon (ed.), Fostering Mental Health in Our Schools. Wahsington,
                 D.C.: National Education Association, Association for Supervision
                 and Curriculum Development.
2691. 1953   "Sociometric structure in personality and group formation." In M.
                 Sherif and M. O. Wilson (eds.), Group Relations at the Crossroads,
                 pp. 332–365. New York: Harper. P.A. 28:7347.
2692. Jensen, E. M., E. P. Reese, and T. W. Reese
       1950   "The subitizing and counting of visually presented fields of dots."
                 Journal of Psychology 30: 363–392. P.A. 25:2830.
2693. Jersild, Arthur T., and Mary D. Fite
       1939   "The influence of nursery school experience on children's social
                 adjustments." Child Development Monographs No. 25. P.A. 13:
                 3892.
2694. Joel, Walther, and D. Shapiro
       1949   "A genotypical approach to the analysis of personal interaction."
                 Journal of Psychology 28: 9–17. P.A. 24:657.
2695. Joesting, Joan, and Robert Joesting
       1972   "Sex differences in group belongingness as influenced by instructor's
                 sex." Psychological Reports 31 (3, December): 717–718. P.A. 50:
                 935.
2696. Johannot, H.
       1953   (The Individual and the Group: Interpersonal Relations, Leadership,
                 and Teamwork.) Neuchâtel: Delachaux & Niestle.
2697. Johnsen, Tom B.
       1970   "Balance tendencies in sociometric group structures." Scandinavian
                 Journal of Psychology 11 (2): 80–88. P.A. 45:8108.
2698. Johnson, Charles D., and James H. Davis
       1972   "An equiprobability model of risk-taking." Organizational Behavior
                 and Human Performance 8 (1, August): 159–175. P.A. 49:773.

2699. Johnson, Charles D., John Gormly, and Anne Gormly
    1973   "Disagreements and self-esteem: Support for the competence-rein-
            forcement model of attraction." Journal of Research in Personality
            7 (2, September): 165–172. P.A. 51:7071.
2700. Johnson, Daniel L., and I. Robert Andrews
    1971   "Risky-shift phenomenon tested with consumer products as stimul."
            Journal of Personality and Social Psychology 20 (3): 382–385. P.A.
            47:8792.
2701. Johnson, David W.
    1967   "Use of role reversal in intergroup competition." Journal of Person-
            ality and Social Psychology 7 (2, pt. 1): 135–141. P.A. 41:16629.
2702.   1970   "Efficacy of role reversal: Warmth of interaction, accuracy of under-
            standing, and the proposal of compromises." Proceedings of the
            78th Annual Convention of the American Psychological Association
            5 (pt. 1): 385–386. P.A. 44:18565.
2703.   1971   "Role reversal: A summary and review of the research." Internation-
            al Journal of Group Tensions 1 (4, October): 318–334. P.A. 49:
            2341.
2704. Johnson, David W., and Stephen Johnson
    1972   "The effects of attitude similarity, expectation of goal facilitation,
            and actual goal facilitation on interpersonal attraction." Journal of
            Experimental Social Psychology 8 (3): 197–206.
2705. Johnson, David W., Jack A. Kavanagh, and Bernard Lubin
    1973   "T-groups, tests, and tension." Small Group Behavior 4 (1, Febru-
            ary): 81–88.
2706. Johnson, David W., and Roy J. Lewicki
    1969   "The initiation of superordinate goals." Journal of Applied Behav-
            ioral Science 5 (1): 9–24. P.A. 43:15700; S.A. 18:E1780.
2707. Johnson, David W., and M. Patricia Noonan
    1972   "Effects of acceptance and reciprocation of self-disclosures on the
            development of trust." Journal of Counseling Psychology 19 (5,
            September): 411–416. P.A. 49:2340.
2708. Johnson, Donald M.
    1955   The Psychology of Thought and Judgment. New York: Harper. P.A.
            29:6894.
2709. Johnson, Douglas F., and William L. Mihal
    1972   "Sex differences in interpersonal conflict." Psychonomic Science 28
            (6, September): 357–360. P.A. 49:4419.
2710. Johnson, Douglas F., and William L. Tullar
    1972   "Style of third-party intervention, face-saving and bargaining behav-
            ior." Journal of Experimental Social Psychology 8 (4, July): 319–
            330. P.A. 49:774.
2711. Johnson, Eugene B., Jacqueline D. Goodchilds, and Bertram H. Raven
    1972   "Male and female differences in response to status congruency-in-
            congruency and status ambiguity in a restricted communication net-
            work." Proceedings of the 80th Annual Convention of the American
            Psychological Association 7 (pt. 1): 215–216.
2712. Johnson, Homer H., and Ivan D. Steiner
    1968   "The effects of source on responses to negative information about
            one's self." Journal of Social Psychology 74 (2, April): 215–224.
            P.A. 42:10515.
2713. Johnson, Homer H., and James M. Torcivia
    1967   "Group and individual performance on a single-stage task as a func-
            tion of distribution of individual performance." Journal of Experi-
            mental Social Psychology 3 (July): 266–273.
2714. Johnson, M. Clemens
    1965   "Computer search for group differences." Educational and Psycho-
            logical Measurement 25 (1): 239–243. P.A. 39:12174.
2715. Johnson, Martha J., and Abraham Tesser
    1972   "Some interactive effects of evaluative similarity, structural similar-
            ity and type of interpersonal situation on interpersonal attraction."
            Journal of Experimental Research in Personality 6 (2-3, December):

154–161. P.A. 51:987.

2716. Johnson, Michael P., and William L. Ewens
 1969 "Power relations and affective style as determinants of confidence in impression formation." Proceedings of the 77th Annual Convention of the American Psychological Association 4 (pt. 1): 349–350.

2717. 1971 "Power relations and affective style as determinants of confidence in impression formation in a game situation." Journal of Experimental Social Psychology 7 (1): 98–110.

2718. Johnson, Richard E., Mary C. Conlee, and Abraham Tesser
 1974 "Effects of similarity of fate on bad news transmission: A reexamination." Journal of Personality and Social Psychology 29 (5, May): 644–648. P.A. 52:12259.

2719. Johnson, Ronald W., and Joan MacDonnell
 1974 "The relationship between conformity and male and female attitudes toward women." Journal of Social Psychology 94 (1): 155–156.

2720. Johnson, Stephen, and David W. Johnson
 1972 "The effects of other's actions, attitude similarity, and race on attraction towards others." Human Relations 25 (2, April): 121–130. P.A. 49:6822.

2721. Johnston, Mary, Cathleen Markey, and Lawrence A. Messé
 1973 "Sex difference in labeling effects on behavior in the Prisoner's Dilemma game." Proceedings of the 81st Annual Convention of the American Psychological Association 8: 323–324. P.A. 50:8847.

2722. Johnston, Shawn, and Richard Centers
 1973 "Cognitive systemization and interpersonal attraction." Journal of Social Psychology 90 (1, June): 95–103. P.A. 51:2982.

2723. Jones, Brooks, Matthew Steele, James Gahagan, and James Tedeschi
 1968 "Matrix values and cooperative behavior in the Prisoner's Dilemma game." Journal of Personality and Social Psychology 8 (2): 148–153.

2724. Jones, Cathaleene, and Elliot Aronson
 1973 "Attribution of fault to a rape victim as a function of respectability of the victim." Journal of Personality and Social Psychology 26 (3, June): 415–419. P.A. 50:11242.

2725. Jones, Edward E.
 1965 "Conformity as a tactic of ingratiation." Science 149 (Whole No. 3680): 144–150. P.A. 39:15077.

2726. Jones, Edward E., and Keith E. Davis
 1965 "From acts to dispositions." In L. Berkowitz (ed.), Advances in Experimental Social Psychology, vol. 2, pp. 220–266. New York: Academic Press.

2727. Jones, Edward E., Keith E. Davis, and Kenneth J. Gergen
 1961 "Role playing variations and their informational value for person perception." Journal of Abnormal and Social Psychology 63 (2): 302–310.

2728. Jones, Edward E., and R. deCharms
 1957 "Changes in social perception as a function of the personal relevance of behavior." Sociometry 20: 75–85. (See also Maccoby, Newcomb, and Hartley, 1958.) P.A. 32:352.

2729. Jones, Edward E., Kenneth J. Gergen, Peter Gumpert, and John W. Thibaut
 1965 "Some conditions affecting the use of ingratiation to influence performance evaluation." Journal of Personality and Social Psychology 1: 613–625. (See also Cartwright and Zander, 1968.)

2730. Jones, Edward E., and Eric M. Gordon
 1972 "Timing of self-disclosure and its effects on personal attraction." Journal of Personality and Social Psychology 24 (3, December): 358–365. P.A. 49:9044.

2731. Jones, Edward E., Stephen L. Hester, Amerigo Farina, and Keith E. Davis
 1959 "Reactions to unfavorable personal evaluations as a function of the evaluator's perceived adjustment." Journal of Abnormal and Social Psychology 59 (November): 363–370. P.A. 34:5724.

2732. Jones, Edward E., Lloyd K. Stires, Kelly G. Shaver, and Victor A. Harris
    1968   "Evaluation of an ingratiator by target persons and bystanders."
            Journal of Personality 36 (3): 349-385. P.A. 43:3948.
2733. Jones, Edward E., and Gary A. Wein
    1972   "Attude similarity, expectancy violation, and attraction." Journal of
            Experimental Social Psychology 8 (3): 222-235.
2734. Jones, Edward E., H. Herbert Wells, and Richard Torrey
    1958   "Some effects of feedback from the experimenter on conformity be-
            havior." Journal of Abnormal and Social Psychology 57: 207-213.
2735. Jones, Francis D., and Henry N. Peters
    1952   "An experimental evaluation of group psychotherapy." Journal of
            Abnormal and Social Psychology 47: 345-353. P.A. 27:2785.
2736. Jones, James A.
    1959   "An index of consensus on rankings in small groups." American So-
            ciological Review 24: 533-537.
2737. Jones, Lawrence E., and Forrest W. Young
    1972   "Structure of a social environment: Longitudinal individual differ-
            ences scaling of an intact group." Journal of Personality and Social
            Psychology 24 (1, October): 108-121. P.A. 49:4420.
2738. Jones, Marshall B.
    1974   "Regressing group on individual effectiveness." Organizational Be-
            havior and Human Performance 11 (3, June): 426-451. P.A. 52:
            12260.
2739. Jones, Russell A.
    1969   "Choice, degree of dependence, and possibility of future dependence
            as determinants of helping behavior." Proceedings of the 77th Annu-
            al Convention of the American Psychological Association 4 (pt. 1):
            381-382. P.A. 43:17342.
2740.   1970   "Volunteering to help: The effects of choice, dependence and antici-
            pated dependence." Journal of Personality and Social Psychology 14
            (2): 121-129. P.A. 44:6656.
2741. Jones, Russell A., et al.
    1968   "Internal states or external stimuli: Observers' attitude judgments
            and the dissonance-theory–self-persuasion controversy." Journal of
            Experimental Social Psychology 4 (3, July): 247-269. P.A. 43:
            2544.
2742. Jones, Robert G., and Edward E. Jones
    1964   "Optimum conformity as an ingratiation tactic." Journal of Person-
            ality 32: 436-458.
2743. Jones, Robert G., and James B. Welsh
    1971   "Ability attribution and impression formation in a strategic game:
            A limiting case of the primacy effect." Journal of Personality and
            Social Psychology 20 (2, November): 166-175. P.A. 47:6676.
2744. Jones, Stanley E.
    1971   "A comparative proxemics analysis of dyadic interaction in selected
            subcultures of New York City." Journal of Social Psychology 84:
            35-44.
2745. Jones, Stanley E., and John R. Aiello
    1973   "Proxemic behavior of black and white first-, third-, and fifth-grade
            children." Journal of Personality and Social Psychology 25 (1, Janu-
            ary): 21-27. P.A. 50:6726.
2746. Jones, Stephen C.
    1966   "Some determinants of interpersonal evaluating behavior." Journal
            of Personality and Social Psychology 3 (4): 397-403. P.A. 40:5396.
2747.   1968a   "Certainty of self-appraisal and reactions to evaluations from
            others." Sociometry 31 (4): 395-403. P.A. 43:3949.
2748.   1968b   "Expectation, performance, and the anticipation of self-revealing
            events." Journal of Social Psychology 74 (2, April): 189-197. P.A.
            42:10529.
2749.   1968c   "Some effects of interpersonal evaluations on group process and so-
            cial perception." Sociometry 31 (2): 150-161. P.A. 42:13657; S.A.
            17:D6816.

2750. 1973 "Self- and interpersonal evaluations: Esteem theories versus consistency theories." Psychological Bulletin 79 (3, March): 185-199. P.A. 50:937.

2751. 1974 "The psychology of interpersonal attraction." In C. Nemeth, Social Psychology: Classic and Contemporary Integrations. Chicago: Rand McNally. P.A. 52:12261.

2752. Jones, Stephen C., Dennis A. Knurek, and Dennis T. Regan
    1973 "Variables affecting reactions to social acceptance and rejection." Journal of Social Psychology 90 (2, August): 269-284. P.A. 51: 990.

2753. Jones, Stephen C., and Deborah Panitch
    1971 "The self-fulfilling prophecy and interpersonal attraction." Journal of Experimental Social Psychology 7 (3): 356-366.

2754. Jones, Stephen C., and Harvey A. Pines
    1968 "Self-revealing events and interpersonal evaluations." Journal of Personality and Social Psychology 8 (3, pt. 1): 277-281. P.A. 42: 8867.

2755. Jones, Stephen C., and Dennis T. Regan
    1974 "Ability evaluation through social comparison." Journal of Experimental Social Psychology 10 (2): 133-146.

2756. Jones, Stephen C., and J. Sidney Shrauger
    1968 "Locus of control and interpersonal evaluations." Journal of Consulting and Clinical Psychology 32 (6): 664-668. P.A. 43:3950.

2757. 1970 "Reputation and self-evaluation as determinants of attractiveness." Sociometry 33: 276-286.

2758. Jones, Stephen C., and Ronna Tager
    1972 "Exposure to others, need for social approval, and reactions to agreement and disagreement from others." Journal of Social Psychology 86: 111-120.

2759. Jones, Stephen C., and Victor H. Vroom
    1964 "Division of labor and performance under cooperative and competitive conditions." Journal of Abnormal and Social Psychology 68 (3, March): 313-320. P.A. 38:8307; S.A. 13:B6758.

2760. Jordan, Nehemiah
    1966 "Perceived discrepancy in attitude intensity between the actors A and B in ABX situations and its effect upon affect." Journal of Psychology 63 (2): 299-308. P.A. 40:10034.

2761. Jordan, Nehemiah, B. T. Jensen, and S. J. Terebinsky
    1963 "The development of cooperation among three-man crews in a simulated man-machine information processing system." Journal of Social Psychology 59 (1, February): 175-184. P.A. 38:752.

2762. Joseph, Myron L., and Richard H. Willis
    1963 "An experimental analog to two-party bargaining." Behavioral Science 8 (2): 117-127. S.A. 11:A6357.

2763. Jourard, Sidney M.
    1964 The Transparent Self: Self-Disclosure and Well-Being. New York: Van Nostrand.

2764. 1971 Self-Disclosure: An Experimental Analysis of the Transparent Self. New York: Wiley. P.A. 48:7107.

2765. Jourard, Sidney M., and Leo A. Kormann
    1968 "Getting to know the experimenter, and its effect on psychological test performance." Journal of Humanistic Psychology 8 (2): 155-159. P.A. 43:9637.

2766. Jourard, Sidney M., and Jaquelyn L. Resnick
    1970 "Some effects of self-disclosure among college women." Journal of Humanistic Psychology 10 (1, Spring): 84-93. P.A. 46:6747.

2767. Jovick, Robert L.
    1972 "Cohesiveness-conformity relationship and conformity instrumentality." Psychological Reports 30 (2, April): 404-406. P.A. 50:2941.

2768. Joyner, Robert C., and Christopher J. Green
    1970 "Demonstration of computer-augmented group problem solving." Behavioral Science 15: 452-462.

2769. Julian, James W., Doyle W. Bishop, and Fred E. Fiedler
      1966   "Quasi-therapeutic effects of intergroup competition." Journal of
              Personality and Social Psychology 3 (3): 321–327. P.A. 40:5397.
2770. Julian, James W., Edwin P. Hollander, and C. Robert Regula
      1969   "Endorsement of the group spokesman and a function of his source
              of authority, competence, and success." Journal of Personality and
              Social Psychology 11 (1): 42–49.
2771. Julian, James W., and Richard K. Kimball
      1970   "Effects of task orientation and level of prior agreement on willing-
              ness to agree." Psychonomic Science 21 (4, November): 213–215.
              P.A. 46:1077.
2772. Julian, James W., and Franklyn A. Perry
      1967   "Cooperation contrasted with intra-group competition." Sociometry
              30 (1, March): 79–90. S.A. 15:C5578.
2773. Julian, James W., C. Robert Regula, and Edwin P. Hollander
      1968   "Effects of prior agreement by others on task confidence and con-
              formity." Journal of Personality and Social Psychology 9 (2, pt. 1):
              171–178. P.A. 42:12050.
2774. Julian, James W., and Ivan D. Steiner
      1961   "Perceived acceptance as a determinant of conformity behavior."
              Journal of Social Psychology 55 (December): 191–198. P.A. 36:
              3GE91J.

2775. Kadane, Joseph B., and Gordon H. Lewis
      1969   "The distribution of participation in group discussions: An empirical
              and theoretical reappraisal." American Sociological Review 34 (5,
              October): 710–723. Comment, pp. 723–724. S.A. 18:E4568.
2776. Kadane, Joseph B., Gordon H. Lewis, and John G. Ramage
      1969a   "Horvath's theory of participation in group discussions." Sociom-
              etry 32 (3, September): 348–361. Comment, pp. 362–364. P.A. 44:
              3543; S.A. 18:E5682.
2777.   1969b   "Rejoinder to Horvath." Sociometry 32 (4): 505–506. P.A. 44:
              6657.
2778. Kadis, Asya L., and Charles Winick
      1960   "The role of the deviant in the therapy group." International Jour-
              nal of Social Psychiatry 6 (3 and 4, Autumn): 277–287. S.A. 15:
              C6380.
2779. Kadushin, C.
      1969   Why People Go to Psychiatrists. New York: Atherton.
2780. Kaess, Walter A., Sam L. Witryol, and Richard E. Nolan
      1961   "Reliability, sex differences, and validity in the leaderless group dis-
              cussion technique." Journal of Applied Psychology 45: 345–350.
              P.A. 5GF45K.
2781. Kagan, Jerome, and P. H. Mussen
      1956   "Dependency themes on the TAT and group conformity." Journal
              of Consulting Psychology 20: 29–32. P.A. 31:3042.
2782. Kahan, James P.
      1968   "Effects of level of aspiration in an experimental bargaining situa-
              tion." Journal of Personality and Social Psychology 8 (2): 154–159.
2783.   1973   "Noninteraction in an anonymous three-person Prisoner's Dilemma
              game." Behavioral Science 18: 124–127.
2784. Kahan, James P., and Dwight J. Goehring
      1973   "Responsiveness in two-person zero-sum games." Behavioral Science
              18 (1, January): 27–33. P.A. 50:8848.
2785. Kähler, Harro D., and Rudolf Schmid
      1972   "A study on the resistance of observation systems of observers' ex-
              pectancies." European Journal of Social Psychology 2 (3): 245–254.
              P.A. 50:4798.
2786. Kahn, Arnold S.
      1972   "Reactions to generosity or stinginess from an intelligent or stupid
              work partner: A test of equity theory in a direct exchange relation-
              ship." Journal of Personality and Social Psychology 21 (1): 116–123.

2787. Kahn, Arnold S., and Sheldon Alexander
1971 "Effects of social status and attitude similarity on behavior in dyads." Psychological Reports 29 (1, August): 91-102. P.A. 47: 2837.

2788. Kahn, Arnold S., Joe Hottes, and William L. Davis
1971 "Cooperation and optimal responding in the Prisoner's Dilemma game: Effects of sex and physical attractiveness." Journal of Personality and Social Psychology 17 (3, March): 267-279. P.A. 46:1078.

2789. Kahn, Arnold S., and John W. Kohls
1972 "Determinants of toughness in dyadic bargaining." Sociometry 35 (2, June): 305-315. P.A. 49:775; S.A. 21:73G4903.

2790. Kahn, Arnold S., and Thomas E. Tice
1973 "Returning a favor and retaliating harm: The effects of stated intentions and actual behavior." Journal of Experimental Social Psychology 9 (1, January): 43-56. P.A. 50:2942.

2791. Kahn, Arnold S., and Douglas L. Young
1973 "Ingratiation in a free social situation." Sociometry 36 (4): 579-587.

2792. Kahn, Michael H., and Kjell E. Rudestam
1971 "The relationship between liking and perceived self-disclosure in small groups." Journal of Psychology 78 (1, May): 81-85. P.A. 46: 4841.

2793. Kahn, Robert L., and Daniel Katz
1953 "Leadership practices in relation to productivity and morale." In D. Cartwright and A. Zander (eds.), Group Dynamics: Research and Theory, pp. 612-628. Evanston, Ill.: Row, Peterson. (See also Cartwright and Zander, 1960.)

2794. Kaiser, Richard L., and Robert R. Blake
1955 "Aspiration and performance in a simulated group atmosphere." Journal of Social Psychology 42: 193-202. P.A. 31:759.

2795. Kalin, Rudolf, and David Marlowe
1968 "The effects of intergroup competition, personal drinking habits, and frustration on intragroup cooperation." Proceedings of the 76th Annual Convention of the American Psychological Association 3: 405-406.

2796. Kalis, Betty L., and Lillian F. Bennett
1957 "The assessment of communication: The relation of clinical improvement to measured changes in communicative behavior." Journal of Consulting Psychology 21: 10-14.

2797. Kaminski, Gerhard, and Ute Osterkamp
1962 ("Investigations on the topology of areas of social activity.") Zeitschrift für Experimentelle und Angewandte Psychologie 9 (3): 417-451. P.A. 37:6610.

2798. Kane, Thomas R., Phoebe Doerge, and James T. Tedeschi
1973 "When is intentional harm-doing perceived as aggressive? A naive reappraisal of the Berkowitz aggression paradigm." Proceedings of the 81st Annual Convention of the American Psychological Association 8: 113-114.

2799. Kane, Thomas R., and James T. Tedeschi
1973 "Impressions created by conforming and independent persons." Journal of Social Psychology 91 (1): 109-116.

2800. Kanekar, Suresh, and Milton E. Rosenbaum
1972 "Group performance on a multiple-solution task as a function of available time." Psychonomic Science 27 (6, June): 331-332. P.A. 49:2342.

2801. Kanfer, Federick H., Bernard M. Bass, and Irvin Guyett
1963 "Dyadic speech patterns, orientation, and social reinforcement." Journal of Consulting Psychology 27 (3): 199-205.

2802. Kanfer, Frederick H., Jeanne S. Phillips, Joseph D. Matarazzo, and George Saslow
1960 "Experimental modification of interviewer content in standardized interviews." Journal of Consulting Psychology 24 (6): 528-536.

2803. Kangas, Jon A.
    1971   "Group members' self-disclosure. A function of preceding self-disclosure by leader or other group member." Comparative Group Studies 2 (1, February): 65–70.
2804. Kanin, Eugene, and Karen R. Davidson
    1972   "Some evidence bearing on the aim-inhibition hypothesis of love." Sociological Quarterly 13 (2, Spring): 210–217. P.A. 49:11075.
2805. Kanouse, David E., and William M. Wiest
    1967   "Some factors affecting choice in Prisoner's Dilemma." Journal of Conflict Resolution 11 (2, June): 206–213. S.A. 16:C8896.
2806. Kanungo, R.
    1966   "Sociometric ratings and perceived interpersonal behavior." Journal of Social Psychology 68 (2, April): 253–268. P.A. 40:7651.
2807. Kaplan, A., A. L. Skogstad, and M. A. Girshick
    1950   "The prediction of social and technological events." Public Opinion Quarterly 14: 93–110. P.A. 26:5477.
2808. Kaplan, Howard B., Neil R. Burch, Tom D. Bedner, and John D. Trenda
    1965   "Physiologic (GSR) activity and perceptions of social behavior in positive, negative and neutral pairs." Journal of Nervous and Mental Disease 140 (6): 457–463. P.A. 40:2818.
2809. Kaplan, John
    1972   "A legal look at prosocial behavior: What can happen for failing to help or trying to help someone." Journal of Social Issues 28 (3): 219–226. P.A. 50:4796.
2810. Kaplan, Kalman J., and Reuben M. Baron
    1974   "An integrative balance notation for the attractive-persuasiveness relationship in persuasive communication versus forced compliance." Human Relations 27 (3): 287–301.
2811. Kaplan, Martin F.
    1971   "Response hierarchy, information reception, and the process of person perception." Human Relations 24 (3, June): 189–199. P.A. 50:939.
2812.   1972a   "Interpersonal attraction as a function of relatedness of similar and dissimilar attitudes." Journal of Experimental Research in Personality 6 (1, March): 17–21. P.A. 50:11243.
2813.   1972b   "The modifying effect of stimulus information on the consistency of individual differences in impression formation." Journal of Experimental Research in Personality 6 (2-3, December): 213–219. P.A. 51:991.
2814.   1973   "Stimulus inconsistency and response dispositions in forming judgments of other persons." Journal of Personality and Social Psychology 25 (1, January): 58–64. P.A. 50:6728.
2815. Kaplan, Martin F., and Norman H. Anderson
    1973a   "Information integration theory and reinforcement theory as approaches to interpersonal attraction." Journal of Personality and Social Psychology 28 (3, December): 301–312. P.A. 51:7074.
2816.   1973b   "Comment on 'When research paradigms converge: Confrontation or integration?'" Journal of Personality and Social Psychology 28 (3, December): 321–322. P.A. 51:7073.
2817. Kaplan, Martin F., and Paul V. Olczak
    1970   "Attitude similarity and direct reinforcement as determinants of attraction." Journal of Experimental Research in Personality 4 (3): 186–189. P.A. 44:16553.
2818.   1971   "Attraction toward another as a function of similarity and commonality of attitudes." Psychological Reports 28: 515–521.
2819. Kaplan, Robert M., and Roy D. Goldman
    1973   "Interracial perception among black, white and Mexican-American high school students." Journal of Personality and Social Psychology 28 (3, December): 383–389. P.A. 51:7075.
2820. Kaplan, Robert M., and Steven G. Swart
    1973   "Reward characteristics in appraisal of achievement behavior." Representative Research in Social Psychology 4 (2, June): 11–17. P.A.

51:3041.

2821. Kaplan, S., and M. Roman
    1963   "Phases of development in an adult therapy group." International
        Journal of Group Psychotherapy 13: 10-26.

2822. Karabenick, Stuart A.
    1972   "Effect of sex of competitor on the performance of females follow-
        ing success." Proceedings of the 80th Annual Convention of the
        American Psychological Association 7 (pt. 1): 275-276.

2823. Karabenick, Stuart A., Richard M. Lerner, and Michael D. Beecher
    1973   "Relation of political affiliation to helping behavior on election day,
        November 7, 1972." Journal of Social Psychology 91 (2): 223-227.

2824. Karabenick, Stuart A., and Murray Meisels
    1972   "Effects of performance evaluation on interpersonal distance." Jour-
        nal of Personality 40 (2, June): 275-286. P.A. 49:2345.

2825. Karlsson, Georg
    1962   "Some aspects of power in small groups." In J. H. Criswell, H. Solo-
        mon, and P. Suppes (eds.), Mathematical Methods in Small Group
        Processes, pp. 193-202. Stanford, Calif.: Stanford University Press.
        S.A. 12:B2415.

2826. Karpienia, Joseph, and Bert Zippel
    1974   "Ethnicity and helping behavior." Journal of Social Psychology 94
        (1): 31-32.

2827. Karson, Samuel, and Kenneth B. Pool
    1958   "Second-order factors in personality measurement." Journal of Con-
        sulting Psychology 22: 299-303.

2828. Kasl, Stanislav V., and George F. Mahl
    1956   "A simple device for obtaining certain verbal activity measures dur-
        ing interviews." Journal of Abnormal and Social Psychology 53:
        388-390.

2829. Kassarjian, Harold H.
    1965   "Social character and sensitivity training." Journal of Applied Be-
        havioral Science 1 (4): 433-440. P.A. 40:5398.

2830. Kassarjian, Waltraud M., and Harold H. Kassarjian
    1962   "Conformity of judgment in a group situation." Psychological Re-
        ports 10 (2): 491-494. P.A. 37:3037.

2831. Kassebaum, Gene G.
    1958   "Value orientations and interpersonal behavior: An experimental
        study." Ph.D. dissertation. Harvard University.

2832. Kassebaum, Gene G., Arthur S. Couch, and Philip E. Slater
    1959   "The factorial dimensions of the MMPI." Journal of Consulting Psy-
        chology 23: 226-236.

2833. Kates, Solis L.
    1959   "First-impression formation and authoritarianism." Human Rela-
        tions 12 (3, August): 277-286. S.A. A2776.

2834. Katz, Daniel
    1951   "Social psychology and group processes." Annual Review of Psy-
        chology 2: 137-172. P.A. 25:3760.

2835. Katz, Elihu, Peter M. Blau, Morton L. Brown, and Fred L. Strodtbeck
    1957   "Leadership stability and social change: An experiment with small
        groups." Sociometry 20: 36-50. P.A. 32:376.

2836. Katz, Elihu, Michael Gurevitch, Tsiyona Peled, and Brenda Danet
    1969   "Doctor-patient exchanges: A diagnostic approach to organizations
        and professions." Human Relations 22 (4, August): 309-324.

2837. Katz, Elihu, William L. Libby, Jr., and Fred L. Strodtbeck
    1964   "Status mobility and reactions to deviance and subsequent conform-
        ity." Sociometry 27 (3, September): 245-260. S.A. 13:B4928.

2838. Katz, Evelyn W.
    1968   "A quantitative procedure for classifying descriptions of interperson-
        al behavior." Perceptual and Motor Skills 26 (3, pt. 2): 1227-1235.
        P.A. 42:18735.

2839. Katz, Irwin, and Lawrence Benjamin
    1960   "Effects of white authoritarianism in biracial work groups." Journal

of Abnormal and Social Psychology 61 (3, November): 448–456. P.A. 36:26D48K; S.A. A1727.

2840. Katz, Irwin, and Melvin Cohen
1962   "The effects of training Negroes upon cooperative problem solving in biracial teams." Journal of Abnormal and Social Psychology 64 (5): 319–325.

2841. Katz, Irwin, David C. Glass, and Sheldon Cohen
1973   "Ambivalence, guilt, and the scapegoating of minority group victims." Journal of Experimental Social Psychology 9 (5, September): 423–436. P.A. 51:9039.

2842. Katz, Irwin, Judith Goldston, and Lawrence Benjamin
1958   "Behavior and productivity in bi-racial work groups." Human Relations 11: 123–141. S.A. 10:A1704.

2843. Katz, Joseph
1972   "Altruism and sympathy: Their history in philosophy and some implication for psychology." Journal of Social Issues 28 (3): 59–69. P.A. 50:4797.

2844. Katz, Leo, and James H. Powell
1953   "A proposed index of the conformity of one sociometric measurement to another." Psychometrika 18: 249–256. P.A. 28:4174.

2845.   1955   "Measurement of the tendency toward reciprocation of choice." Sociometry 18: 659–665.

2846. Katz, Leo, and Charles H. Proctor
1959   "The concept of configuration of interpersonal relations in a group as a time-dependent stochastic process." Psychometrika 24 (December): 317–327. P.A. 34:7567.

2847. Katzell, Raymond A., Charles E. Miller, Naomi G. Rotter, and Theodore G. Venet
1970   "Effects of leadership and other inputs on group processes and outputs." Journal of Social Psychology 80 (2): 157–169. P.A. 44: 14505.

2848. Kauffmann, Duane R., and Ivan D. Steiner
1968   "Some variables affecting the use of conformity as an ingratiation technique." Journal of Experimental Social Psychology 4 (4): 400–414. P.A. 43:3936.

2849. Kaufman, E. L., M. W. Lord, T. W. Reese, and J. Volkmann
1949   "The discrimination of visual number." American Journal of Psychology 62: 498–525. P.A. 24:3568.

2850. Kaufman, Gary G., and James C. Johnson
1974   "Scaling peer ratings: An examination of the differential validities of positive and negative nominations." Journal of Applied Psychology 59 (3, June): 302–306. P.A. 52:12322.

2851. Kaufmann, Harry
1967   "Similarity and cooperation received as determinants of cooperation rendered." Psychonomic Science 9 (2): 73–74. P.A. 42:2488.

2852. Kaufmann, Harry, and Seymour Feshbach
1963   "The influence of anti-aggressive communications upon the response to provocation." Journal of Personality 31 (3): 428–444. P.A. 39: 12176.

2853. Kaufmann, Harry, and Linda Zener
1967   "Perceived similarity and liking as functions of manipulated similarity and subjective social favorability." Psychonomic Science 9 (2): 75–76. P.A. 42:2489.

2854. Kaye, J. D.
1973   "Group interaction and interpersonal learning." Small Group Behavior 4 (4, November): 424–448.

2855. Kazdin, Alan E., and James H. Bryan
1971   "Competence and volunteering." Journal of Experimental Social Psychology 7 (1, January): 87–97. P.A. 46:1079.

2856. Keasey, Charles B., and C. Tomlinson-Keasey
1973   "Petition signing in a naturalistic setting." Journal of Social Psychology 89 (2, April): 313–314. P.A. 50:6729.

2857. Keating, John P., and Timothy C. Brock
 1974   "Acceptance of persuasion and the inhibition of counter-argumenta-
         tion under various distraction tasks." Journal of Experimental Social
         Psychology 10 (4, July): 301-309. P.A. 52:12323.
2858. Kee, Herbert W., and Robert E. Knox
 1970   "Conceptual and methodological considerations in the study of trust
         and suspicion." Journal of Conflict Resolution 14 (3): 357-366.
2859. Keedy, T. C., Jr.
 1956   "Factors in the cohesiveness of small groups." Sociology and Social
         Research 40: 329-332. P.A. 31:5893; S.A. 4296.
2860. Keet, Charles D.
 1948   "Two verbal techniques in a miniature counseling situation." Psy-
         chological Monographs 62 (294). P.A. 24:3225.
2861. Kegan, Daniel L., and Albert H. Rubenstein
 1972   "Measures of trust and openness." Comparative Group Studies 3 (2,
         May): 179-201. P.A. 49:9046.
2862. Keller, Joseph B.
 1951   "Comment on 'Channels of communications in small groups.'"
         American Sociological Review 16: 842-843. (See also Bales, Strodt-
         beck, Mills, and Roseborough, 1951.)
2863. Kelley, E. W.
 1968   "Techniques of studying coalition formation." Midwest Journal of
         Political Science 12 (1, February): 62-84. S.A. 17:D4869.
2864. Kelley, Harold H.
 1950   "The warm-cold variable in first impressions of persons." Journal of
         Personality 18: 431-439. P.A. 25:4486.
2865.   1951   "Communication in experimentally created hierarchies." Human Re-
         lations 4: 39-56. (See also Cartwright and Zander, 1953, 1960.) P.A.
         25:8302.
2866.   1955   "Salience of membership and resistance to change of group-anchored
         attitudes." Human Relations 8: 275-290. P.A. 30:5858. S.A. 3141.
2867.   1965   "Experimental studies of threats in interpersonal negotiations."
         Journal of Conflict Resolution 9 (1): 79-105.
2868.   1967   "Attribution theory in social psychology." In D. Levine (ed.), Ne-
         braska Symposium on Motivation: 1967. Lincoln: University of
         Nebraska Press.
2869.   1968   "Interpersonal accommodation." American Psychologist 23 (6):
         399-410. P.A. 43:2526.
2870.   1971   Causal Schemata and the Attribution Process. New York: General
         Learning Press.
2871. Kelley, Harold H., and A. John Arrowood
 1960   "Coalitions in the triad: Critique and experiment." Sociometry 23
         (3, September): 231-244. (See also Hare, Borgatta, and Bales,
         1965.) P.A. 35:2118; S.A. A2741.
2872. Kelley, Harold H., Linda L. Beckman, and Claude S. Fischer
 1967   "Negotiating the division of a reward under incomplete informa-
         tion." Journal of Experimental Social Psychology 3 (October): 361-
         398.
2873. Kelley, Harold H., and Janusz Grzelak
 1972   "Conflict between individual and common interest in an N-person
         relationship." Journal of Personality and Social Psychology 21 (2):
         190-197.
2874. Kelley, Harold H., and Thomas W. Lamb
 1957   "Certainty of judgment and resistance to social influence." Journal
         of Abnormal and Social Psychology 55: 137-139.
2875. Kelley, Harold H., and Kenneth Ring
 1961   "Some effects of 'suspicious' versus 'trusting' training schedules."
         Journal of Abnormal and Social Psychology 63 (2): 294-301.
2876. Kelley, Harold H., and Martin M. Shapiro
 1954   "An experiment on conformity to group norms where conformity is
         detrimental to group achievement." American Sociological Review
         19: 667-678.

2877. Kelley, Harold H., G. H. Shure, M. Deutsch, C. Faucheux, J. T. Lanzetta, S.
Moscovici, J. M. Nuttin, Jr., J. M. Rabbie, and J. W. Thibaut
    1970   "A comparative experimental study of negotiation behavior." Jour-
            nal of Personality and Social Psychology 16 (3, November): 411–
            438. P.A. 45:4121.
2878. Kelley, Harold H., and Anthony J. Stahelski
    1970a   "Errors in perception of intentions in a mixed-motive game." Jour-
            nal of Experimental Social Psychology 6 (4): 379–400.
2879.   1970b   "The inference of intentions from moves in the Prisoner's Dilemma
            game." Journal of Experimental Social Psychology 6 (4): 401–419.
2880.   1970c   "Social interaction basis of cooperators' and competitors' beliefs
            about others." Journal of Personality and Social Psychology 16 (1):
            66–91.
2881. Kelley, Harold H., and John W. Thibaut
    1954   "Experimental studies of group problem solving and process." In G.
            Lindzey, Handbook of Social Psychology, pp. 735–785. Cambridge,
            Mass.: Addison-Wesley. P.A. 29:3804.
2882.   1968   "Group problem solving." In G. Lindzey and E. Aronson (eds.),
            Handbook of Social Psychology, vol. 4, pp. 1–101. Reading Mass.:
            Addison-Wesley.
2883. Kelley, Harold H., and Edmund H. Volkhart
    1952   "The resistance to change of group-anchored attitudes." American
            Sociological Review 17: 453–465. P.A. 27:6475.
2884. Kelley, Harold H., and Christine L. Woodruff
    1956   "Members' reactions to apparent group approval of a counternorm
            communication." Journal of Abnormal and Social Psychology 52:
            67–74. S.A. 4396.
2885. Kelly, G[eorge] A.
    1955   The Psychology of Personal Constructs. New York: Norton. P.A.
            30:4524.
2886. Kelly, Richard T., Harve E. Rawson, and Roger L. Terry
    1973   "Interaction effects of achievement need and situational press on
            performance." Journal of Social Psychology 89 (1, February): 141–
            145. P.A. 50:2943.
2887. Kelly, Roy W., and Hollis F. Ware
    1947   "An experiment in group dynamics." Advanced Management 12:
            116–119. P.A. 22:2356.
2888. Kelman, Herbert C.
    1950   "Effects of success and failure on 'suggestibility' in the autokinetic
            situation." Journal of Abnormal and Social Psychology 45: 267–
            285. P.A. 24:5702.
2889.   1958   "Compliance, identification, and internalization: Three processes of
            attitude change." Journal of Conflict Resolution 2: 51–60.
2890. Kelman, Herbert C., and Morris B. Parloff
    1957   "Interrelations among three criteria of improvement in group
            therapy: Comfort, effectiveness, and self-awareness." Journal of Ab-
            normal and Social Psychology 54: 281–288.
2891. Keltner, John W.
    1960   "Communication in discussion and group processes: Some research
            trends of the decade 1950–1959. Part I." Journal of Communication
            10: 195–204. P.A. 35:3379.
2892.   1961   "Communication in discussion and group processes: Some research
            trends of the decade 1950–1959. Part II." Journal of Communica-
            tion 11: 27–33. P.A. 36:1GG27K.
2893. Kelvin, Peter
    1973   "A social-psychological examination of privacy." British Journal of
            Social and Clinical Psychology 12 (3, September): 248–261. P.A.
            51:5035.
2894. Kendon, Adam, and Mark Cook
    1969   "The consistency of gaze patterns in social interaction." British
            Journal of Psychology 60 (4): 481–494. P.A. 44:5073.

2895. Kenkel, William F.
1957   "Influence differentiation in family decision making." Sociology and Social Research 42: 18-25.

2896.   1961   "Husband-wife interaction in decision making and decision choices." Journal of Social Psychology 54 (August): 255-262.

2897. Kennedy, John L.
1971a   "Simulation study of competition in an 'open world.'" Journal of Applied Psychology 55 (1, February): 42-45. P.A. 46:1081.

2898.   1971b   "The system approach: A preliminary exploratory study of the relation between team composition and financial performance in business games." Journal of Applied Psychology 55 (1, February): 46-49. P.A. 46:1082.

2899. Kenny, Charles T., and Dixie Fletcher
1973   "Effects of beardedness on person perception." Perceptual and Motor Skills 37 (2, October): 413-414. P.A. 51:9011.

2900. Kent, R. N., and Joseph E. McGrath
1969   "Task and group characteristics as factors influencing group performance." Journal of Experimental Social Psychology 5 (4): 429-440. P.A. 44:5074.

2901. Kenyon, Gerald S., and John W. Loy
1966   ("Social influence on achievement in four psycho-motor tasks.") Kölner Zeitschrift für Soziologie und Sozialpsychologie 10 (Supplement): 192-202. S.A. 15:C5579.

2902. Kephart, William M.
1950   "A quantitative analysis of intragroup relationships." American Journal of Sociology 60: 544-549. P.A. 25:288.

2903. Kerckhoff, Alan C., and Frank D. Bean
1967   "Role-related factors in person perception among engaged couples." Sociometry 30 (2, June): 176-186.

2904. Kerlinger, Fred N.
1958   "On authoritarianism and acquiescence: An added note to Bass and Messick and Jackson." Journal of Abnormal and Social Psychology 56: 141-142.

2905. Kerr, Steven, and Anne Harlan
1973   "Predicting the effects of leadership training and experience from the contingency model: Some remaining problems." Journal of Applied Psychology 57 (2): 114-117.

2906. Kershenbaum, Brenda R., and S. S. Komorita
1970   "Temptation to defect in the Prisoner's Dilemma game." Journal of Personality and Social Psychology 16 (1, September): 110-113. P.A. 45:2294.

2907. Khan, Taswir A.
1965   "Experiment study of group influence upon individual judgement." Journal of Psychology (Lahore) 2 (2): 133-144. P.A. 40:1522.

2908. Khol, Timothy A., and Shirley A. Nickols
1971   "Conformity and repression-sensitization." Journal of Social Psychology 84: 251-256.

2909. Kidd, Jerry S.
1958   "Social influence phenomena in a task-oriented group situation." Journal of Abnormal and Social Psychology 56: 13-17.

2910. Kidd, Jerry S., and D. T. Campbell
1955   "Conformity to groups as a function of group success." Journal of Abnormal and Social Psychology 51: 390-393. P.A. 31:2703. S.A. 3442.

2911. Kiesler, Charles A.
1963   "Attraction to the group and conformity to group norms." Journal of Personality 31 (4): 559-569. P.A. 38:8308.

2912.   1969   "Group pressure and conformity." In J. Mills (ed.), Experimental Social Psychology, pp. 235-306. New York: Macmillan. P.A. 44:14506.

2913.   1971   The Psychology of Commitment: Experiments Linking Behavior to

Belief. New York: Academic Press.

2914. Kiesler, Charles A., and Lee H. Corbin
      1965   "Commitment, attraction, and conformity." Journal of Personality
              and Social Psychology 2 (6): 890–895. P.A. 40:2819.

2915. Kiesler, Charles A., and James de Salvo
      1967   "The group as an influencing agent in a forced compliance para-
              digm." Journal of Experimental Social Psychology 3 (April): 160–
              171.

2916. Kiesler, Charles A., and Gordon N. Goldberg
      1968   "Multi-dimensional approach to the experimental study of interper-
              sonal attraction: Effect of a blunder on the attractiveness of a com-
              petent other." Psychological Reports 22 (3, pt. 1): 693–705. P.A.
              42:13659.

2917. Kiesler, Charles A., Sara B. Kiesler, and Michael S. Pallak
      1967   "The effect of commitment to future interaction on reactions to
              norm violations." Journal of Personality 35 (4): 585–599. P.A. 42:
              18736.

2918. Kiesler, Charles A., Mark Zanna, and James de Salvo
      1966   "Deviation and conformity: Opinion change as a function of com-
              mitment, attraction, and presence of a deviate." Journal of Personal-
              ity and Social Psychology 3 (4, April): 458–467. S.A. 15:C4086.

2919. Kiesler, Sara B.
      1966   "The effect of perceived role requirements on reactions to favor-
              doing." Journal of Experimental Social Psychology 2 (2, April):
              198–210. P.A. 40:8790.

2920.   1973a   "Emotion in groups." Journal of Humanistic Psychology 13 (3,
              Summer): 19–31. P.A. 52:803.

2921.   1973b   "Preference for predictability or unpredictability as a mediator of
              reactions to norm violations." Journal of Personality and Social Psy-
              chology 27 (3): 354–359.

2922. Kiesler, Sara B., and Roberta L. Baral
      1970   "The search for a romantic partner: The effects of self-esteem and
              physical attractiveness on romantic behavior." In K. J. Gergen and
              D. Marlowe (eds.), Personality and Social Behavior. Reading, Mass.:
              Addison-Wesley. (See also Crosbie, 1975.)

2923. Kiessling, Ralph J., and Richard A. Kalish
      1961   "Correlates of success in leaderless group discussion." Journal of
              Social Psychology 54 (August): 359–365. P.A. 36:3GE59K.

2924. Kilham, Wesley, and Leon Mann
      1974   "Level of destructive obedience as a function of transmitter and
              executant roles in the Milgram obedience paradigm." Journal of Per-
              sonality and Social Psychology 29 (5, May): 696–702. P.A. 52:
              12325.

2925. Killian, Lewis M.
      1952   "The significance of multiple-group membership in disaster." Ameri-
              can Journal of Sociology 57: 309–314. (See also Cartwright and
              Zander, 1953; Maccoby, Newcomb, and Hartley, 1958.) P.A. 26:
              5526.

2926. Kilmann, Peter R., and Stephen M. Auerbach
      1974   "Effects of marathon group therapy on trait and state anxiety."
              Journal of Consulting and Clinical Psychology 42 (4): 607–612.

2927. Kilmann, Ralph H.
      1974   "The effect of interpersonal values on laboratory training: An em-
              pirical investigation." Human Relations 27 (3): 247–265.

2928. Kilty, Keith M.
      1972   "Attitudinal affect and behavioral intentions." Journal of Social
              Psychology 86 (2, April): 251–256. P.A. 48:2860.

2929. Kimball, Richard K., and Edwin P. Hollander
      1974   "Independence in the presence of an experienced but deviate group
              member." Journal of Social Psychology 93 (2): 281–292.

2930. Kimberly, James C., and Paul V. Crosbie
      1967   "An experimental test of a reward-cost formulation of status incon-

sistency." Journal of Experimental Social Psychology 3 (October): 399–415.

2931. King, Charles E.
1960 "The applicability of small group knowledge to the classroom situation." Sociology and Social Research 45 (1, October): 18–23.

2932. 1962 The Sociology of Small Groups. New York: Pageant. S.A. 12: B0182.

2933. King, Mark, David C. Payne, and Walter G. McIntire
1973 "The impact of marathon and prolonged sensitivity training on self-acceptance." Small Group Behavior 4 (4, November): 414–423.

2934. King, Maurice G.
1964 "Structural balance, tension, and segregation in a university group." Human Relations 17 (3, August): 221–225. P.A. 39:4871; S.A. 13: B4929.

2935. King, Ronald, and Gary Easthope
1973 "Social class and friendship choice in school." Research in Education 9 (May): 16–24. P.A. 51:5062.

2936. Kingdon, Donald R.
1974 "Team or group development: The development of dyadic relationships." Human Relations 27 (2): 169–177.

2937. Kingsley, Leonard
1967 "Process analysis of a leaderless countertransference group." Psychological Reports 20: 555–562.

2938. Kinney, Elva E.
1953 "A study of peer group social acceptability at the fifth-grade level in a public school." Journal of Educational Research 47: 57–64. P.A. 28:4884.

2939. Kinoshita, T.
1964 "The effects of group cohesiveness and importance of the tasks upon conformity behavior." Japanese Journal of Psychology 34 (4): 181–198. P.A. 39:7636.

2940. Kipnis, David
1958 "The effects of leadership style and leadership power upon the inducement of an attitude change." Journal of Abnormal and Social Psychology 57: 173–180.

2941. 1972 "Does power corrupt?" Journal of Personality and Social Psychology 24 (1): 33–41.

2942. Kipnis, David, and William P. Lane
1962 "Self-confidence and leadership." Journal of Applied Psychology 46 (4): 291–295. P.A. 37:3052.

2943. Kipnis, David, and Richard Vanderveer
1971 "Ingratiation and the use of power." Journal of Personality and Social Psychology 17 (3): 280–286.

2944. Kipnis, Dorothy M.
1957 "Interaction between members of bomber crews as a determinant of sociometric choice." Human Relations 10: 263–270. S.A. A1351.

2945. Kirkhart, Robert O.
1963 "Minority group identification and group leadership." Journal of Social Psychology 59 (1, February): 111–117. P.A. 38:886.

2946. Kirkpatrick, Clifford, and Charles Hobart
1954 "Disagreement, disagreement estimate, and non-empathetic imputations for intimacy groups varying from favorite date to married." American Sociological Review 19: 10–19. P.A. 29:3915.

2947. Kirscht, John P., Thomas M. Lodahl, and Mason Haire
1959 "Some factors in the selection of leaders by members of small groups." Journal of Abnormal and Social Psychology 58: 406–408. (See also Cartwright and Zander, 1960.)

2948. Kirtley, Donald
1968 "Conformity and prejudice in authoritarians of opposing political ideologies." Journal of Psychology 70 (2): 199–204. P.A. 43:3951.

2949. Klaus, David J., and Robert Glaser
1970 "Reinforcement determinants of team proficiency." Organizational

580   BIBLIOGRAPHY

Behavior and Human Performance 5 (1): 33–67. P.A. 44:8357.
2050. Kleck, Robert E.
    1966   "Emotional arousal in interactions with stigmatized persons." Psychological Reports 19: 1226.
2951.   1968   "Physical stigma and nonverbal cues emitted in face to face interaction." Human Relations 21 (1, February): 19–28. P.A. 42:13660; S.A. 17:D5791.
2952.   1969   "Physical stigma and task oriented interactions." Human Relations 22 (1, February): 53–60.
2953. Kleck, Robert E., et al.
    1968   "Effects of stigmatizing conditions on the use of personal space." Psychological Reports 23 (1): 111–118. P.A. 43:6832.
2954. Kleck, Robert E., and William Nuessle
    1968   "Congruence between the indicative and communicative functions of eye contact in interpersonal relations." British Journal of Social and Clinical Psychology 7 (4): 241–246. P.A. 43:15701.
2955. Kleck, Robert E., Hiroshi Ono, and Albert Hastorf
    1966   "The effects of deviance upon face-to-face interaction." Human Relations 19 (4, November): 425–436.
2956. Klein, Armin, and Norman Keill
    1953   "The experiencing of group psychotherapy." Sociatry 5: 205–221. P.A. 28:4440.
2957. Klein, Edward B., and Boris M. Astrachan
    1971   "Learning in groups: A comparison of study groups and T groups." Journal of Applied Behavioral Science 7 (6): 659–683.
2958. Klein, Josephine
    1956   The Study of Groups. London: Routledge & Kegan Paul.
2959.   1961   Working with Groups. London: Hutchinson.
2960. Klein, Michael, and Gerd Christiansen
    1966   ("Group composition, group structure, and effectiveness of basketball teams.") Kölner Zeitschrift für Soziologie und Sozialpsychologie 10 (Supplement): 180–191. S.A. 15:C5580.
2961. Kleiner, Robert J.
    1960   "The effects of threat reduction upon interpersonal attractiveness." Journal of Personality 28: 145–155. P.A. 35:2119.
2962. Kleinke, Chris L.
    1972   "Interpersonal attraction as it relates to gaze and distance between people." Representative Research in Social Psychology 3 (2, December): 105–120. P.A. 50:2944.
2963. Kleinke, Chris L., Armando A. Bustos, Frederick B. Meeker, and Richard A. Staneski
    1973   "Effects of self-attributed and other-attributed gaze on interpersonal evaluations between males and females." Journal of Experimental Social Psychology 9 (2, March): 154–163. P.A. 50:11244.
2964. Kleinke, Chris L., Frederick B. Meeker, and Carl La Fong
    1974   "Effects of gaze, touch, and use of name on evaluation of 'engaged' couples." Journal of Research in Personality 7 (4, March): 368–373. P.A. 52:7562.
2965. Kleinke, Chris L., and Paul D. Pohlen
    1971   "Affective and emotional responses as a function of other person's gaze and cooperativeness in a two-person game." Journal of Personality and Social Psychology 17 (3, March): 308–313. P.A. 46:1083.
2966. Kleinke, Chris L., Richard A. Staneski, and Pam Weaver
    1972   "Evaluation of a person who uses another's name in ingratiating and noningratiating situations." Journal of Experimental Social Psychology 8 (5, September): 457–466. P.A. 49:6825.
2967. Klimoski, Richard J., and Ronald A. Ash
    1974   "Accountability and negotiator behavior." Organizational Behavior and Human Performance 11 (3, June): 409–425. P.A. 52:12262.
2968. Kline, John A., and James L. Hullinger
    1973   "Redundancy, self orientation, and group consensus." Speech Monographs 40 (1, March): 72–74. P.A. 52:833.

2969. Klubeck, Stanley, and Bernard M. Bass
    1954   "Differential effects of training on persons of different leadership status." Human Relations 7: 59–72. S.A. 2:487.
2970. Klugman, Samuel F.
    1944   "Cooperative versus individual efficiency in problem-solving." Journal of Educational Psychology 35: 91–100. P.A. 18:2859.
2971.   1945   "Group judgements for familiar and unfamiliar materials." Journal of General Psychology 32: 103–110. P.A. 19:1649.
2972. Knapp, Deanne E., and David Knapp
    1966   "Effect of position on group verbal conditioning." Journal of Social Psychology 69 (1, June): 95–99. P.A. 40:10052.
2973. Knapp, Mark L., Roderick P. Hart, Gustav W. Friedrich, and Gary M. Shulman
    1973   "The rhetoric of goodbye: Verbal and nonverbal correlates of human leave-taking." Speech Monographs 40 (3, August): 182–198. P.A. 52:834.
2974. Knapp, Robert H.
    1964a   "Perceptual interpretation of the social diad: I. Judgments of acceptance." Journal of Social Psychology 63 (June): 169–177.
2975.   1964b   "Perceptual interpretation of the social diad: II. Character of relationship." Journal of Social Psychology 64 (October): 89–100.
2976. Knecht, Laura, Daniel Lippman, and Walter Swap
    1973   "Similarity, attraction, and self-disclosure." Proceedings of the 81st Annual Convention of the American Psychological Association 8 (pt. 1): 205–206.
2977. Knight, David J., Daniel Langmeyer, and David C. Lundgren
    1973   "Eye-contact, distance, and affiliation: The role of observer bias." Sociometry 36 (3, September): 390–401. P.A. 52:2871.
2978. Knight, George P., and David Mack
    1973   "Race and behavior in the Prisoner's Dilemma game." Psychological Record 23 (1, Winter): 61–64. P.A. 50:2945.
2979. Kniveton, Bromley H.
    1973a   "Social class and imitation of aggressive adult and peer models." Journal of Social Psychology 89 (2, April): 311–312. P.A. 50: 6730.
2980.   1973b   "The effect of rehearsal delay on long-term imitation of filmed aggression." British Journal of Psychology 64 (2, May): 259–265. P.A. 51:5037.
2981. Kniveton, Bromley H., and Geoffrey M. Stephenson
    1973   "An examination of individual susceptibility to the influence of aggressive film models." British Journal of Psychiatry 122 (566, January): 53–56. P.A. 50:2946.
2982. Knott, Paul D.
    1970   "A further methodological study of the measurement of interpersonal aggression." Psychological Reports 26 (3, June): 807–809. P.A. 45:627.
2983. Knott, Paul D., and Bruce A. Drost
    1969   "A measure of interpersonal dominance." Behavior Research Methods and Instrumentation 1 (4): 139–140. P.A. 43:9638.
2984.   1971   "Effects of varying intensity of attack and fear arousal on the intensity of counter aggression." Journal of Personality 39: 27–37.
2985. Knott, Paul D., Lane Lasater, and Rich Shuman
    1974   "Aggression-guilt and conditionability for aggressiveness." Journal of Personality 42 (2): 332–344.
2986. Knowles, Eric S.
    1972   "Boundaries around social space: Dyadic responses to an invader." Environment and Behavior 4 (4, December): 437–445. P.A. 50: 2947.
2987.   1973   "Boundaries around group interaction: The effect of group size and member status on boundary permeability." Journal of Personality and Social Psychology 26 (3, June): 327–331. P.A. 50:11245.
2988. Knowles, Malcolm S., and Hulda F. Knowles
    1972   Introduction to Group Dynamics. Rev. ed. New York: Association

Press. P.A. 50:4802.
2989. Knox, Robert E., and Ronald L. Douglas
      1971   "Trivial incentives, marginal comprehension, and dubious generaliza-
              tions from Prisoner's Dilemma studies." Journal of Personality and
              Social Psychology 20 (2, November): 160-165. P.A. 47:6678.
2990. Knutson, Andie L.
      1960   "Quiet and vocal groups." Sociometry 23 (1, March): 36-49. P.A.
              35:2120.
2991. Knutson, Thomas J.
      1972   "An experimental study of the effects of orientation behavior on
              small group consensus." Speech Monographs 39 (3, August): 159-
              165. P.A. 51:11005.
2992. Koch, Sigmund
      1971   "The image of man implicit in encounter group theory." Journal of
              Humanistic Psychology 11 (2, Fall): 109-128. P.A. 48:2885.
2993. Koenig, Fredrick
      1972   "Sex attribution to hypothetical persons described by adjective trait
              lists." Perceptual and Motor Skills 35 (1, August): 15-18. P.A. 49:
              4423.
2994. Koenig, René
      1966   ("The group in sports and research on small groups.") Kölner Zeits-
              chrift für Soziologie und Sozialpsychologie 10 (Supplement): 5-10.
              S.A. 15:C5581.
2995. Kogan, Nathan, Helmut Lamm, and Gisela Trommsdorff
      1972   "Negotiation constraints in the risk-taking domain: Effects of being
              observed by partners of higher or lower status." Journal of Personal-
              ity and Social Psychology 23 (2, August): 143-156. P.A. 49:777.
2996. Kogan, Nathan, and R. Tagiuri
      1958a   "Interpersonal preference and cognitive organization." Journal of
              Abnormal and Social Psychology 56: 113-116.
2997.   1958b   "On visibility of choice and awareness of being chosen." Psychologi-
              cal Reports 4: 83-86.
2998. Kogan, Nathan, and Michael A. Wallach
      1966   "Modification of a judgmental style through group interaction."
              Journal of Personality and Social Psychology 4 (2): 165-174. P.A.
              40:11105.
2999.   1967a   "Effects of physical separation of group members upon group risk-
              taking." Human Relations 20 (1, February): 41-48. S.A. 15:C6381.
3000.   1967b   ("Risk-taking behavior in small decision groups.") Bulletin du
              C.E.R.P. 16 (4): 363-375. P.A. 43:5280.
3001.   1967c   "Risky-shift phenomenon in small decision-making groups: A test of
              the information-exchange hypothesis." Journal of Experimental So-
              cial Psychology 3 (January): 75-84.
3002. Kogan, Nathan, and Maryla Zaleska
      1969   "Level of risk selected by individuals and groups when deciding for
              self and for others." Proceedings of the 77th Annual Convention of
              the American Psychological Association 4 (pt. 1): 423-424.
3003. Kohler, Adam T., James C. Miller, and Edward B. Klein
      1973   "Some effects of intergroup experience on study group phenomena."
              Human Relations 26 (3): 293-305. P.A. 51:9012.
3004. Kohn, Paul M., and G. W. Mercer
      1973   "Authoritarianism, rebelliousness, permissiveness about drugs, and
              person perception." Proceedings of the 81st Annual Convention of
              the American Psychological Association 8: 309-310. P.A. 50:4803.
3005. Koile, Earl A., and June Gallessich
      1972   "Beyond the group's mythology." Journal of Psychology 81 (1,
              May): 129-138. P.A. 48:9017.
3006. Kolaja, Jiri
      1968   "Two processes: A new framework for the theory of participation in
              decision making." Behavioral Science 13 (January): 66-70.
3007. Kolb, David A., and Richard E. Boyatzis
      1970   "On the dynamics of the helping relationship." Journal of Applied

Behavioral Science 6 (3): 267–289. (See also Kolb, Rubin, and Mc-Intyre (eds.), Organizational Psychology: A Book of Readings, 1974.) P.A. 52:12265.

3008.   1974   "Goal-setting and self-directed behavior change." In D. A. Kolb, I. M. Rubin, and J. M. McIntyre (eds.), Organizational Psychology: A Book of Readings, 2nd ed. Englewood Cliffs, N.J.: Prentice-Hall.

3009. Kolb, David A., Sara K. Winter, and David E. Berlew
        1968   "Self-directed change: Two studies." Journal of Applied Behavioral Science 4 (4, October-December): 453–472. S.A. 18:E0903.

3010. Kolominskiy, Y. L.
        1971   ("Social-psychological problems of interrelationships in small groups and organized groups.") Voprosy Psikhologii 17 (6, November): 101–111. P.A. 48:7109.

3011.   1972   "Sociopsychological problems in small groups and collectives." Soviet Psychology 11 (1, Fall): 46–64. P.A. 49:9047.

3012. Komorita, Samuel S.
        1965   "Cooperative choice in a Prisoner's Dilemma game." Journal of Personality and Social Psychology 2 (5): 741–745.

3013.   1973   "Concession-making and conflict resolution." Journal of Conflict Resolution 17 (4, December): 745–762. P.A. 52:2894.

3014.   1974   "A weighted probability model of coalition formation." Psychological Review 81 (3, May): 242–256.

3015. Komorita, Samuel S., and Marc Barnes
        1969   "Effects of pressures to reach agreement in bargaining." Journal of Personality and Social Psychology 13 (3): 245–252. P.A. 44: 2265.

3016. Komorita, Samuel S., and Arline R. Brenner
        1968   "Bargaining and concession making under bilateral monopoly." Journal of Personality and Social Psychology 9 (1): 15–20.

3017. Komorita, Samuel S., and Jerome M. Chertkoff
        1973   "A bargaining theory of coalition formation." Psychological Review 80 (3, May): 149–162. P.A. 50:8850.

3018. Komorita, Samuel S., and John Mechling
        1967   "Betrayal and reconciliation in a two-person game." Journal of Personality and Social Psychology 6 (3): 349–353.

3019. Komorita, Samuel S., J. P. Sheposh, and S. L. Braver
        1968   "Power, the use of power, and cooperative choice in a two-person game." Journal of Personality and Social Psychology 8 (2): 134–142.

3020. Konečni, Vladimir J.
        1972   "Some effects of guilt on compliance: A field replication." Journal of Personality and Social Psychology 23 (1, July): 30–32. P.A. 48: 11445.

3021. Konečni, Vladimir J., and Anthony N. Doob
        1972   "Catharsis through desplacement of aggression." Journal of Personality and Social Psychology 23 (3, September): 379–387. P.A. 49: 2347.

3022. Kopera, Anthony A., Richard A. Maier, and James E. Johnson
        1971   "Perception of physical attractiveness: The influence of group interaction and group coaction on ratings of the attractiveness of photographs of women." Proceedings of the 79th Annual Convention of the American Psychological Association 6 (pt. 1): 317–318.

3023. Korner, Ija N., and R. K. Misra
        1967   "Perception of human relationship as a function of inter-individual distance." Journal of Psychological Researches 11 (3): 129–132. P.A. 42:13661.

3024. Korte, Charles
        1969   "Group effects on help-giving in an emergency." Proceedings of the 77th Annual Convention of the American Psychological Association 4 (pt. 1): 383–384.

3025.   1971   "Effects of individual responsibility and group communication on help-giving in an emergency." Human Relations 24 (2): 149–159.

3026. Korten, David C.
    1962   "Situational determinants of leadership structure." Journal of Con-
            flict Resolution 6 (3, September): 222-235. S.A. 12:A8723.
3027. Koslin, Bertram L., Robert N. Haarlow, Marvin Karlins, and Richard Pargament
    1968   "Predicting group status from members' cognitions." Sociometry 31
            (1, March): 64-75. P.A. 42:8877; S.A. 16:D4108.
3028. Kotkov, Benjamin
    1950   "A bibliography for the student of group therapy." Journal of Clini-
            cal Psychology 6: 77-91. P.A. 25:377.
3029. Koulack, David, and David Cumming
    1973   "Acceptance and rejection as a function of ethnicity and belief in-
            tensity." Journal of Social Psychology 91 (2): 207-213.
3030. Koziey, Paul W., Joel O. Loken, and James A. Field
    1971   "T-group influence on feelings of alienation." Journal of Applied
            Behavioral Science 7 (6): 724-731.
3031. Kozman, Hilda C.
    1951   Group Process in Physical Education. New York: Harper.
3032. Krain, Mark
    1973   "Communication as a process of dyadic organization and develop-
            ment." Journal of Communication 23 (4, December): 392-408. P.A.
            52:2895.
3033. Krause, Merton S.
    1972   "Strategies in argument." Journal of Psychology 81 (2, July): 269-
            279. P.A. 49:778.
3034. Krauss, Herbert H., Ira E. Robinson, and Nelson E. Cauthen
    1972   "Variables that influence ethical risk taking among convicts." Pro-
            ceedings of the 80th Annual Convention of the American Psycho-
            logical Association 7 (pt. 1): 225-226.
3035. Krauss, Robert M.
    1966   "Structural and attitudinal factors in interpersonal bargaining."
            Journal of Experimental Social Psychology 2 (1, January): 42-55.
3036. Krauss, Robert M., and Morton Deutsch
    1966   "Communication in interpersonal bargaining." Journal of Personal-
            ity and Social Psychology 4 (5): 572-577.
3037. Krauze, Ted K.
    1964   "Sociometry and sociodrama." International Journal of Sociometry
            and Sociatry 4 (3-4, September-December): 107-115. S.A. 14:
            B8347.
3038. Krebs, Allen M.
    1958   "Two determinants of conformity: Age of independence training
            and n achievement." Journal of Abnormal and Social Psychology
            56: 130-131.
3039. Krech, David, and R. S. Crutchfield
    1948   Theory and Problems of Social Psychology. New York: McGraw-
            Hill. P.A. 23:1723.
3040. Krichevskii, R. L.
    1973   ("The problem of cohesiveness in small groups in non-Soviet social
            psychology.") Voprosy Psikhologii 19 (3, May): 174-184. P.A. 51:
            7030.
3041. Krieger, Margery H., and William S. Kogan
    1964   "A study of group processes in the small therapeutic group." Inter-
            national Journal of Group Psychotherapy 14 (2): 178-188. P.A.
            39:8112.
3042. Křivohlavý, Jaro
    1970a   ("Experimental research into the effectiveness of promises.") Psy-
            chologia a Patopsychologia Dietata 5 (2): 119-130. P.A. 45:8109.
3043.   1970b   ("Interpersonal relations in asymmetric situations.") Ceskoslovenska
            Psychologie 14 (6): 544-567. P.A. 50:945.
3044. Kroger, Rolf O., and Irene Briedis
    1970   "Effects of risk and caution norms on group decision making." Hu-
            man Relations 23 (3, June): 181-190. P.A. 45:8111.

3045. Krug, Robert E.
    1959   "The development of group scores in the prediction of group performance." Personnel Psychology 12: 267-295. P.A. 34:4229.
3046. Kruglanski, Arie W.
    1969   "Incentives in interdependent escape as affecting the degree of group incoordination." Journal of Experimental Social Psychology 5 (4): 454-466. P.A. 44:5075.
3047.   1973   "Much ado about the 'volunteer artifacts.'" Journal of Personality and Social Psychology 28 (3, December): 348-354. P.A. 51:7010.
3048. Kruglanski, Arie W., and Menashe Cohen
    1973   "Attributed freedom and personal causation." Journal of Personality and Social Psychology 26 (2, May): 245-250. P.A. 50:11247.
3049. Krupar, Karen R.
    1973   Communication Games: Participant's Manual. New York: Free Press. P.A. 51:952.
3050. Krupat, Edward
    1974   "Context as a determinant of perceived threat: The role of prior experience." Journal of Personality and Social Psychology 29 (6): 731-736.
3051. Krupat, Edward, and Yakov Epstein
    1973   "'I'm too busy': The effects of overload and diffusion of responsibility on working and helping." Proceedings of the 81st Annual Convention of the American Psychological Association 8 (pt. 1): 293-294.
3052. Kubička, Luděk
    1968   "The psychological background of adolescents' behavior in a two-person nonzero sum game." Behavioral Science 13 (November): 455-466.
3053. Kunczik, Michael
    1972   (Leadership: Theories and Findings.) Düsseldorf and Vienna: Econ Verlag.
3054. Kutash, Samuel B.
    1970-   "Values and dangers in group process experiences." Group Process
    1971   3 (2, Winter): 7-11. P.A. 49:2348.
3055. Kutner, David H., Jr.
    1973   "Overcrowding: Human responses to density and visual exposure." Human Relations 26 (1, February): 31-50. P.A. 50:11248.
3056. Kuusela, Ruth
    1956   "Systematic observation methods in the study of small groups." Acta Psychologica 12: 25-46. P.A. 31:2745.
3057. Kuusinen, Jorma, and Lars Nystedt
    1972   "Individual versus provided constructs, cognitive complexity, and extremity of ratings in person perception." University of Stockholm, Reports from the Psychological Laboratories 365 (October). P.A. 50:6731.

3058. LaBelle, Thomas J., and Val D. Rust
    1973   "Control mechanics and their justifications in preschool classrooms." Small Group Behavior 4 (1, February): 35-46.
3059. Laffal, Julius, Irwin G. Sarason, Lane Ameen, and Aaron Stern
    1957   "Individuals in groups: A behaviour rating technique." International Journal of Social Psychiatry 2 (4, Spring): 254-262. S.A. 15: C5582.
3060. LaForge, [Gene] Rolfe, T. F. Leary, H. Naboisek, H. S. Coffey, and M. B. Freedman
    1954   "The interpersonal dimensions of personality: II. An objective study of repression." Journal of Personality 23: 131-153. P.A. 29: 5313.
3061. LaForge, [Gene] Rolfe, and R. F. Suczek
    1955   "The interpersonal dimension of personality: III. An interpersonal check list." Journal of Personality 24: 94-112. P.A. 30:5990.

3062. La Gaipa, John J.
    1972   "Perception of friendship rewards and affiliation arousal." Psycho-
             nomic Science 28 (2, July): 69–71. P.A. 50:2948.
3063. Lagrou, Leo
    1968   ("Evaluation of partiality in group discussions by content analysis.")
             Psychologica Belgica 8 (1): 59–85. P.A. 44:8358.
3064. Laing, James D., and Richard J. Morrison
    1974   "Sequential games of status." Behavioral Science 19 (3, May): 177–
             196. P.A. 52:12266.
3065. Laird, Donald A.
    1923   "Changes in motor control and individual variations under the influ-
             ence of 'razzing.'" Journal of Experimental Psychology 6: 236–246.
3066. Laird, Donald A., and Eleanor C. Laird
    1956   The New Psychology of Leadership. New York: McGraw-Hill.
3067. Lake, Dale G., Matthew B. Miles, and Ralph B. Earle
    1973   Measuring Human Behavior: Tools for the Assessment of Social
             Functioning. New York: Columbia University, Teachers College.
             P.A. 50:11250.
3068. Lake, Richard
    1970   "The varieties of communicative experience." Comparative Group
             Studies 1 (3, August): 305–314.
3069. Lakin, Martin
    1969   "Some ethical issues in sensitivity training." American Psychologist
             24 (10): 923–928. P.A. 44:8359.
3070. 1970   "Group sensitivity training and encounter: Uses and abuses of a
             method." Counseling Psychologist 2 (2): 66–70. P.A. 46:1084.
3071. Lalljee, Mansur, and Mark Cook
    1973   "Uncertainty in first encounters." Journal of Personality and Social
             Psychology 26 (1, April): 137–141. P.A. 50:4804.
3072. Lambert, Roger
    1957   ("Structure of influence in small work groups.") Psychologie Fran-
             çaise 2 (October): 213–226. P.A. 34:2865.
3073. 1960   ("Cooperation and competition in small groups.") Revue Française
             de Sociologie 1 (1, January-March): 61–72. S.A. 11:A5135.
3074. 1967   ("The process of influence and productivity in small work groups.")
             Bulletin du C.E.R.P. 16 (4): 377–392. P.A. 43:5267.
3075. 1971   ("Allocentric activity and egocentric activity as determinants of the
             influence exerted in small work groups.") Bulletin du C.E.R.P. 20
             (2, April): 81–91. P.A. 50:946.
3076. 1972   "Risky shift in relation to choice of metric." Journal of Experi-
             mental Social Psychology 8 (4, July): 315–318. P.A. 49:779.
3077. Lamberth, John, and Donn Byrne
    1971   "Similarity-attraction or demand characteristics?" Personality: An
             International Journal 2 (2, Summer): 77–91. P.A. 47:6679.
3078. Lamberth, John, Charles Gouaux, and Wayne Padd
    1973   "The affective eliciting and reducing properties of attraction stim-
             uli." Social Behavior and Personality 1 (2): 93–107. P.A. 51:5101.
3079. Lamm, Helmut
    1967   "Will an observer advise higher risk taking after hearing a discussion
             of the decision problem?" Journal of Personality and Social Psychol-
             ogy 6 (4): 467–471.
3080. 1973   "Intragroup effects on intergroup negotiation." European Journal
             of Social Psychology 3 (2): 179–192. P.A. 52:2896.
3081. Lamm, Helmut, and Nathan Kogan
    1970   "Risk taking in the context of intergroup negotiation." Journal of
             Experimental Social Psychology 6 (3, July): 351–363. P.A. 45:629.
3082. Lamm, Helmut, and Randolph Ochsmann
    1972   "Factors limiting the generality of the risky-shift phenomenon."
             European Journal of Social Psychology 2 (4): 455–458. P.A. 50:
             6732.
3083. Lamm, Helmut, and Ekkehard Rosch
    1972   "Information and competitiveness of incentive structure as factors in

two-person negotiation." European Journal of Social Psychology 2 (4): 459–462. P.A. 50:6733.

3084. Lamm, Helmut, Edith Schaude, and Gisela Trommsdorff
      1971   "Risky shift as a function of group members' value of risk and need for approval." Journal of Personality and Social Psychology 20 (3): 430–435.

3085. Lamm, Helmut, Gisela Trommsdorff, and Nathan Kogan
      1970   "Pessimism-optimism and risk taking in individual and group contexts." Journal of Personality and Social Psychology 15 (4): 366–374. P.A. 44:20824.

3086. Lamm, Helmut, Gisela Trommsdorff, and Edith Rost-Schaude
      1972   "Self-image, perception of peers' risk acceptance and risky shift." European Journal of Social Psychology 2 (3): 255–272. P.A. 50: 4805.

3087.   1973   "Group-induced extremization: Review of evidence and a minority-change explanation." Psychological Reports 33 (2, October): 471–484. P.A. 51:9041.

3088. Lammers, C. J.
      1967   "Stratification in a small group." Human Relations 20 (3): 283–299. P.A. 42:2498.

3089. Lana, Robert E.
      1964   "Existing familiarity and order of presentation of persuasive communications." Psychological Reports 15 (2): 607–610. P.A. 39:4872.

3090. Lana, Robert E., Willard Vaughan, and Elliott McGinnies
      1960   "Leadership and friendship status as factors in discussion group interaction." Journal of Social Psychology 52 (August): 127–134. P.A. 35:6341.

3091. Landau, Jeffrey S., Leslie E. Packer, and Jeffrey C. Levy
      1973   "Sex and environmental determinants of aggression." Proceedings of the 81st Annual Convention of the American Psychological Association 8: 175–176. P.A. 50:4806.

3092. Landecker, Werner S.
      1970   "Status congruence, class crystallization, and social cleavage." Sociology and Social Research 54 (3, April): 343–355. P.A. 47:4722.

3093. Landers, Daniel M., and Thomas F. Crum
      1971   "The effect of team success and formal structure on inter-personal relations and cohesiveness of baseball teams." International Journal of Sport Psychology 2 (2): 88–96. P.A. 49:2349.

3094. Landis, M. H., and H. E. Burtt
      1924   "A study of conversations." Journal of Comparative Psychology 4: 81–89.

3095. Landsberger, Harry A.
      1955a   "Interaction process analysis of professional behavior: A study of labor mediators in twelve labor-management disputes." American Sociological Review 20: 566–575. P.A. 31:1864.

3096.   1955b   "Interaction process analysis of the mediation of labor-management disputes." Journal of Abnormal and Social Psychology 51: 552–558. (See also Hare, Borgatta, and Bales, 1965.) P.A. 31:3918.

3097. Landy, David, and Elliot Aronson
      1968   "Liking for an evaluator as a function of his discernment." Journal of Personality and Social Psychology 9 (2, pt. 1): 133–141. P.A. 42:12038.

3098.   1969   "The influence of the character of the criminal and his victim on the decisions of simulated jurors." Journal of Experimental Social Psychology 5 (2): 141–152.

3099. Landy, David, and Harold Sigall
      1974   "Beauty is talent: Task evaluation as a function of the performer's physical attractiveness." Journal of Personality and Social Psychology 29 (3): 299–304.

3100. Landy, Eugene E.
      1970   "Attitude and attitude change toward interaction as a function of participation versus observation." Comparative Group Studies 1 (2,

May): 129-155.

3101. Lane, Irving M., and Lawrence A. Messé
1971   "Equity and the distribution of rewards." Journal of Personality and Social Psychology 20 (1, October): 1-17. P.A. 47:6680.

3102.   1972   "Distribution of insufficient, sufficient, and over-sufficient rewards: A clarification of equity theory." Journal of Personality and Social Psychology 21 (2, February): 228-233. P.A. 48:867.

3103. Lane, Irving M., Lawrence A. Messé, and James L. Phillips
1971   "Differential inputs as a determinant in the selection of a distributor of rewards." Psychonomic Science 22 (4, February): 228-229. P.A. 46:8929.

3104. Lange, Alfred, and A. Van de Nes
1973   "Frustration and instrumentality of aggression." European Journal of Social Psychology 3 (2): 159-177. P.A. 52:2897.

3105. Lange, Carl J.
1962   "Leadership in small military units: Some recent research findings." In F. Geldard (ed.), Defence Psychology, pp. 286-301. London: Pergamon. P.A. 37:4891.

3106. Lange, Lydia
1967   ("The influence of role-division and function-delegation on group productivity during problem solving.") Zeitschrift für Psychologie 174 (1-2): 68-95. P.A. 42:10530.

3107. Langelar, J. W.
1970   ("Is brainstorming really effective?") Mens en Onderneming 24 (3, May): 194-201. P.A. 45:4123.

3108. Langer, Ellen J., and Robert P. Abelson
1972   "The semantics of asking a favor: How to succeed in getting help without really dying." Journal of Personality and Social Psychology 24 (1, October): 26-32. P.A. 49:4425.

3109. Langley, C. W.
1967   "The viability of self-analytic groups." Australian Psychologist 2 (1): 23-31. P.A. 42:3902.

3110. Langmeyer, Daniel, Richard Schmuck, and Philip Runkel
1971   "Technology for organizational training in schools." Sociological Inquiry 41 (2, Spring): 193-205.

3111. Lankford, Philip M.
1974   "Comparative analysis of clique identification methods." Sociometry 37 (2): 287-305.

3112. Lansing, Frank W.
1957   "Selected factors of group interaction and their relation with leadership performance." International Journal of Sociometry and Sociatry 1 (4, December): 170-174. S.A. 12:B0183.

3113. Lanto, Sandra, and Gerald H. Shure
1972   "Effects of size of payoff and real versus imaginary rewards on pre-bargaining perceptions." Proceedings of the 80th Annual Convention of the American Psychological Association 7 (pt. 1): 231-232.

3114. Lanzetta, John T.
1955   "Group behavior under stress." Human Relations 8: 29-52. P.A. 30:783; S.A. 3:1765.

3115. Lanzetta, John T., Don Haefner, Peter Langham, and Howard Axelrod
1954   "Some effects of situational threat on group behavior." Journal of Abnormal and Social Psychology 49: 445-453. P.A. 29:3813.

3116. Lanzetta, John T., and Robert E. Kleck
1970   "Encoding and decoding of nonverbal affect in humans." Journal of Personality and Social Psychology 16 (1): 12-19.

3117. Lanzetta, John T., and Thornton B. Roby
1956a   "Effects of work-group structure and certain task variables on group performance." Journal of Abnormal and Social Psychology 53: 307-314. P.A. 32:4038.

3118.   1956b   "Group performance as a function of work-distribution patterns and task load." Sociometry 19: 95-104. P.A. 31:5895; S.A. 4295.

3119.   1957   "Group learning and communication as a function of task and structure 'demands.'" Journal of Abnormal and Social Psychology 55: 121-131.

3120. 1960 "The relationship between certain group process variables and group problem-solving efficiency." Journal of Social Psychology 52 (August): 135-148. P.A. 35:6342.

3121. Lanzetta, John T., G. R. Wendt, Peter Langham, and Don Haefner
1956 "The effects of an 'anxiety-reducing' medication on group behavior under threat." Journal of Abnormal and Social Psychology 52 (1, January): 103-108. P.A. 31:2706.

3122. Lanzetta, John T., and Henk Wilke
1971 "The obligation to help: The effect of levels of prior help on subsequent helping behavior." European Journal of Social Psychology 1 (1): 97-106. P.A. 48:7111.

3123. Larsen, Knud S.
1971 "Dogmatism and sociometric status as determinants of interaction in a small group." Psychological Reports 29 (2, October): 449-450. P.A. 47:8793.

3124. 1972 "Attributed power, response strategies and non-zero sum game behavior." Psychological Reports 30 (3, June): 821-822. P.A. 49: 2350.

3125. Larsen, Knud S., Stephen Blades, Susan Goldschmidt, Patti Turner, and Dale Webber
1973 "Social cost, belief incongruence, and race: Experiments in choice behavior." Proceedings of the 81st Annual Convention of the American Psychological Association 8: 229-230. P.A. 50:4807.

3126. Larsen, Knud S., Don Coleman, Jim Forbes, and Robert Johnson
1972 "Is the subject's personality or the experimental situation a better predictor of a subject's willingness to administer shock to a victim?" Journal of Personality and Social Psychology 22 (3, June): 287-295. P.A. 48:11447.

3127. Larsen, Knud S., and Katherine J. Larsen
1969 "Leadership, group activity and sociometric choice in service sororities and fraternities." Perceptual and Motor Skills 28 (2): 539-542. P.A. 43:15702.

3128. Lasker, B.
1949 Democracy through Discussion. New York: Wilson.

3129. Lasswell, Harold D.
1939 "Person, personality, group, culture." Psychiatry 2: 533-561. P.A. 14:2514.

3130. Latané, Bibb, and John M. Darley
1968 "Group inhibition of bystander intervention in emergencies." Journal of Personality and Social Psychology 10 (3): 215-221. P.A. 43: 3938.

3131. Latané, Bibb, and Judith Rodin
1969 "A lady in distress: Inhibiting effects of friends and strangers on bystander intervention." Journal of Experimental Social Psychology 5 (2): 189-202.

3132. Laughlin, Patrick R., and Laurence G. Branch
1972 "Individual versus tetradic performance on a complementary task as a function of initial ability level." Organizational Behavior and Human Performance 8 (2, October): 201-216. P.A. 49:6826.

3133. Laughlin, Patrick R., Laurence G. Branch, and Homer H. Johnson
1969 "Individual versus triadic performance on a unidimensional complementary task as a function of initial ability level." Journal of Personality and Social Psychology 12 (2): 144-150. P.A. 43:12897.

3134. Laughlin, Patrick R., and Mary A. Doherty
1967 "Discussion versus memory in cooperative group concept attainment." Journal of Educational Psychology 58 (2): 123-128.

3135. Laughlin, Patrick R., and Homer H. Johnson
1966 "Group and individual performance on a complementary task as a function of initial ability level." Journal of Experimental Social Psychology 2 (4, October): 407-414.

3136. Laughlin, Patrick R., Richard P. McGlynn, Jon A. Anderson, and Everett S. Jacobson
    1968   "Concept attainment by individuals versus cooperative pairs as a function of memory, sex, and concept rule." Journal of Personality and Social Psychology 8 (4): 410–417.

3137. Lave, Lester B.
    1965   "Factors affecting co-operation in the Prisoner's Dilemma." Behavioral Science 10: 26–38.

3138. Lawless, Walter, and Stephen Nowicki, Jr.
    1972   "Role of self-disclosure in interpersonal attraction." Journal of Consulting and Clinical Psychology 38 (2): 300.

3139. Lawlor, Monica
    1955   "An investigation concerned with changes of preference which are observed after group discussion." Journal of Social Psychology 42: 323–332. P.A. 31:763.

3140. Lawrence, Lois C., and Patricia C. Smith
    1955   "Group decision and employee participation." Journal of Applied Psychology 39: 334–337. P.A. 30:7847.

3141. Lawson, Edwin D.
    1964a   "Reinforced and non-reinforced four-man communication nets." Psychological Reports 14: 287–296.

3142.   1964b   "Reinforcement in group problem-solving with arithmetic problems." Psychological Reports 14: 703–710. P.A. 39:4873.

3143.   1965   "Change in communication nets, performance, and morale." Human Relations 18 (2, May): 139–147. P.A. 39:15043; S.A. 14:B9181.

3144. Lawson, Edwin D., and Ross Stagner
    1957   "Group pressure, attitude change, and autonomic involvement." Journal of Social Psychology 45: 299–312.

3145. Lay, Clarry H.
    1972   "Expected base rates and trait covariations in person perception." Canadian Psychologist 13 (3, July): 196–206. P.A. 49:4426.

3146. Lay, Clarry H., Bryan F. Burron, and Douglas N. Jackson
    1973   "Base rates and informational value in impression formation." Journal of Personality and Social Psychology 28 (3, December): 390–395. P.A. 51:7078.

3147. Layton, Bruce D., and Chester A. Insko
    1974   "Anticipated interaction and the similarity-attraction effect." Sociometry 37 (2, June): 149–162. P.A. 52:12327.

3148. Leach, Chris
    1974   "The importance of instructions in assessing sequential effects in impression formation." British Journal of Social and Clinical Psychology 13 (2, June): 151–156. P.A. 52:12328.

3149. Leader, Gerald C.
    1973   "Interpersonally skillful bank officers view their behavior." Journal of Applied Behavioral Science 9 (4, July): 484–497. P.A. 51:2983.

3150. League, Betty Jo, and Douglas N. Jackson
    1964   "Conformity, veridicality, and self-esteem." Journal of Abnormal and Social Psychology 68 (1, January): 113–115.

3151. Leary, Timothy
    1955   "The theory and measurement methodology of interpersonal communication." Psychiatry 18: 147–161. P.A. 30:2694.

3152.   1957   Interpersonal Diagnosis of Personality. New York: Ronald. P.A. 31: 2556.

3153. Leary, Timothy, and Hubert S. Coffey
    1955   "Interpersonal diagnosis: Some problems of methodology and validation." Journal of Abnormal and Social Psychology 50: 110–124. P.A. 29:7241.

3154. Leathers, Dale G.
    1972   "Quality of group communication as a determinant of group product." Speech Monographs 39 (3, August): 166–173. P.A. 51:11007.

3155. Leavitt, Harold J.
    1951   "Some effects of certain communication patterns on group perform-

ance." Journal of Abnormal and Social Psychology 46: 38-50. (See also Swanson, Newcomb, and Hartley, 1952; Maccoby, Newcomb, and Hartley, 1958; Crosbie, 1975.) P.A. 25:7439.

3156. 1960 "Task ordering and organizational development in the common target game." Behavioral Science 5 (July): 233-239. P.A. 35:745.

3157. Leavitt, Harold J., and Robert Doktor
    1970 "Personal growth, laboratory training, science and all that: A shot at a cognitive clarification." Journal of Applied Behavioral Science 6 (2): 173-179.

3158. Leavitt, Harold J., Herbert Hax, and James H. Roche
    1955 "'Authoritarianism' and agreement with things authoritative." Journal of Psychology 40: 215-221. P.A. 30:6916.

3159. Leavitt, Harold J., and Kenneth E. Knight
    1963 "Most 'efficient' solutions to communication networks: Empirical versus analytical search." Sociometry 26 (2, June): 260-267. S.A. 11:A7195.

3160. Leavitt, Harold J., and Ronald A. H. Mueller
    1951 "Some effects of feedback on communication." Human Relations 4: 401-410. (See also Hare, Borgatta, and Bales, 1955, 1965.) P.A. 26:5551.

3161. Lebo, Dell
    1962 "Setting and maintaining an effective emotional atmosphere." Adult Leadership 11 (2): 34-36, 60-62. P.A. 37:6611.

3162. Le Compte, William F., and Howard M. Rosenfeld
    1971 "Effects of minimal eye contact in the instruction period on impressions of the experimenter." Journal of Experimental Social Psychology 7 (2): 211-220.

3163. Leeman, Cavin P.
    1952 "Patterns of sociometric choice in small groups: A mathematical model and related experimentation." Sociometry 15: 220-243. P.A. 27:7137.

3164. Leet-Pellegrini, Helena, and Jeffrey Z. Rubin
    1974 "The effects of six bases of power upon compliance, identification, and internalization." Bulletin of the Psychonomic Society 3 (1B, January): 68-70. P.A. 52:2873.

3165. Lefcourt, Herbert M., and Gordon W. Ladwig
    1965 "The effect of reference group upon Negroes' task persistence in a biracial competitive game." Journal of Personality and Social Psychology 1 (6): 668-671. P.A. 39:12180.

3166. Lefebvre, Luc M.
    1972 "Reciprocity and altruism as social exchange rules in a judge-performer relation." Psychologica Belgica 12 (2): 207-220. P.A. 49: 9052.

3167. 1973 "The ingratiation correlates of the Machiavel." Psychologica Belgica 13 (2): 149-164. P.A. 51:7031.

3168. Legant, Patricia, and David R. Mettee
    1973 "Turning the other cheek versus getting even: Vengeance, equity, and attraction." Journal of Personality and Social Psychology 25 (2, February): 243-253. P.A. 50:947.

3169. Leginski, Walter, and Richard R. Izzett
    1973 "Linguistic styles as indices for interpersonal distance." Journal of Social Psychology 91 (2): 291-304.

3170. Leik, Robert K.
    1963 "Instrumentality and emotionality in family interaction." Sociometry 26 (2, June): 131-145. P.A. 38:4195.

3171. 1965a "Type of group and the probability of initiating acts." Sociometry 28 (1, March): 57-65. P.A. 39:10001; S.A. 14:B9182.

3172. 1965b "'Irrelevant' aspects of stooge behavior: Implications for leadership studies and experimental methodology." Sociometry 28 (3, September): 259-271.

3173. 1967 "The distribution of acts in small groups." Sociometry 30 (3, September): 280-299. P.A. 41:16632; S.A. 16:C9755.

3174. Leik, Robert K., and Timothy J. Curry
    1971   "On integrating small group concepts and models." Pacific Socio-
            logical Review 14 (1, January): 38-52. S.A. 19:F0471.
3175. Leik, Robert K., and Richard Nagasawa
    1970   "A sociometric basis for measuring social status and social struc-
            ture." Sociometry 33: 55-78.
3176. Leinhardt, Samuel
    1973   "The development of transitive structure in children's interpersonal
            relations." Behavioral Science 18 (4, July): 260-271. P.A. 51:2951.
3177. Leith, William R., and Max R. Uhlemann
    1972   "The shaping group approach to stuttering. A pilot study." Com-
            parative Group Studies 3 (3, August): 175-199.
3178. Lemann, Thomas B., and Richard L. Solomon
    1952   "Group characteristics as revealed in sociometric patterns and per-
            sonality ratings." Sociometry 15: 7-90. P.A. 27:7138.
3179. Lemineur, R., and E. Meurice
    1972   ("Relationships between empathy and sociometric status.") Journal
            de Psychologie Normale et Pathologique 3 (July): 327-332. P.A. 50:
            8855.
3180. Lemke, Elmer A., Kenneth Randle, and C. Stuart Robertshaw
    1969   "Effects of degree of initial acquisition, group size, and general men-
            tal ability on concept learning and transfer." Journal of Educational
            Psychology 60 (1): 75-78.
3181. Lemon, Nigel, and Neil Warren
    1974   "Salience, centrality and self-relevance of traits in construing
            others." British Journal of Social and Clinical Psychology 13 (2,
            June): 119-124. P.A. 52:12329.
3182. Lenk, Hans
    1964   ("Conflict and achievement in high-performance sports teams: So-
            ciometric structures of competitive eight-oar crews in rowing.")
            Soziale Welt 15 (4): 307-343. S.A. 14:B9183.
3183.   1968   ("Abandonment of value ties by West German oarsmen under stress
            feigned by sociodrama.") Soziale Welt 19 (1): 66-73. S.A. 18:
            E1781.
3184. Lennard, Henry L., and Arnold Bernstein (with Helen C. Hendin and Erdman
    B. Palmore)
    1960   The Anatomy of Psychotherapy: Systems of Communication and
            Expectation. New York: Columbia University Press.
3185. Lennard, Henry L., M. E. Jarvik, and H. A. Abramson
    1956   "Lysergic acid diethylamide (LSD-25): XII. A preliminary statement
            of its effects upon interpersonal communication." Journal of Psy-
            chology 41: 185-198.
3186. Leon, Manuel, Gregg C. Oden, and Norman H. Anderson
    1973   "Functional measurement of social values." Journal of Personality
            and Social Psychology 27 (3, September): 301-310. P.A. 51:5103.
3187. Leonard, Russell L., Jr.
    1973   "Self-concept as a factor in the similarity-attraction paradigm."
            Proceedings of the 81st Annual Convention of the American Psycho-
            logical Association 8: 199-200. P.A. 50:8856.
3188. Leppaluoto, Jean R.
    1972   "Resistance to persuasion as a function of time and issue familiar-
            ity." Proceedings of the 80th Annual Convention of the American
            Psychological Association 7 (pt. 1): 169-170.
3189. Lepper, Mark R.
    1973   "Dissonance, self-perception, and honesty in children." Journal of
            Personality and Social Psychology 25 (1, January): 65-74. P.A. 50:
            6734.
3190. Lerea, Louis, and Alvin Goldberg
    1961   "The effects of socialization upon group behavior." Speech Mono-
            graphs 28: 60-64. P.A. 36:3GE60L.
3191. Lerner, Melvin J.
    1965   "The effect of responsibility and choice on a partner's attractiveness

following failure." Journal of Personality 33 (2, June): 178–187. P.A. 40:2821.

3192.   1971   "Justified self-interest and the responsibility for suffering." Journal of Human Relations 19 (4): 550–559. P.A. 49:9054.

3193.   1974   "The justice motive: 'Equity' and 'parity' among children." Journal of Personality and Social Psychology 29 (4, April): 539–550. P.A. 52:7563.

3194. Lerner, Melvin J., and Elaine Agar
   1972   "The consequences of perceived similarity: Attraction and rejection, approach and avoidance." Journal of Experimental Research in Personality 6 (1, March): 69–75. P.A. 50:11251.

3195. Lerner, Melvin J., and Selwyn Becker
   1962   "Interpersonal choice as a function of ascribed similarity and definition of the situation." Human Relations 15 (1, February): 27–34. P.A. 37:1106; S.A. 11:A5697.

3196. Lerner, Melvin J., Ronald C. Dillehay, and William C. Sherer
   1967   "Similarity and attraction in social contexts." Journal of Personality and Social Psychology 5 (4): 481–486.

3197. Lerner, Melvin J., and Rosemary R. Lichtman
   1968   "Effects of perceived norms on attitudes and altruistic behavior toward a dependent other." Journal of Personality and Social Psychology 9 (3): 226–232. P.A. 42:13662.

3198. Lerner, Melvin J., and Gary T. Long
   1974   "Deserving, the 'personal contract,' and altruistic behavior by children." Journal of Personality and Social Psychology 29 (4): 551–556.

3199. Lerner, Richard M., and Tanes Moore
   1974   "Sex and status effects on perception of physical attractiveness." Psychological Reports 34 (3, pt. 2): 1047–1050.

3200. Lerner, Richard M., Henry Solomon, and Sherl Brody
   1971   "Helping behavior at a busstop." Psychological Reports 28 (1, February): 200. P.A. 46:4842.

3201. Leuba, Clarence J.
   1930   "A preliminary experiment to quantify an incentive and its effects." Journal of Abnormal and Social Psychology 25: 275–288.

3202.   1933   "An experimental study of rivalry in young children." Journal of Comparative Psychology 16: 367–378.

3203. Leventhal, D. B., K. M. Shemberg, and S. Kaye Van Schoelandt
   1968   "Effects of sex-role adjustment upon the expression of aggression." Journal of Personality and Social Psychology 8 (4, pt. 1): 393–396. P.A. 42:8869.

3204. Leventhal, Gerald S., and James Bergman
   1969   "Self-depriving behavior as a response to unprofitable inequity." Journal of Experimental Social Psychology 5 (2): 153–171.

3205. Leventhal, Gerald S., James W. Michaels, and Charles Sanford
   1972   "Inequity and interpersonal conflict: Reward allocation and secrecy about reward as methods of preventing conflict." Journal of Personality and Social Psychology 23 (1, July): 88–102. P.A. 48:11448.

3206. Leventhal, Gerald S., Thomas Weiss, and Richard Buttrick
   1973   "Attribution of value, equity, and the prevention of waste in reward allocation." Journal of Personality and Social Psychology 27 (2, August): 276–286. P.A. 51:3043.

3207. Leventhal, Gerald S., Thomas Weiss, and Gary Long
   1969   "Equity, reciprocity, and reallocating rewards in the dyad." Journal of Personality and Social Psychology 13 (4): 300–305. P.A. 44: 3544.

3208. Levi, Mario, and A. C. Higgins
   1954   "A comparison of two methods of conducting critiques." USAF Personnel Training Research Center, Research Bulletin No. AFPTRC-TR-54-108.

3209. Levi, Mario, E. Paul Torrance, and Gilbert O. Pletts
   1954   "Sociometric studies of combat air crews in survival training." Sociometry 17: 304–328. P.A. 30:5859; S.A. 1496.

3210. Levin, Fredrica M., and Kenneth J. Gergen
    1969   "Revealingness, ingratiation, and the disclosure of self." Proceedings of the 77th Annual Convention of the American Psychological Association 4 (pt. 1): 447-448. P.A. 43:17345.
3211. Levin, Harry, Alfred L. Baldwin, Mary Gallwey, and Allan Pavio
    1960   "Audience stress, personality, and speech." Journal of Abnormal and Social Psychology 61 (3, November): 469-473. S.A. A1705.
3212. Levin, Irwin P., Linda L. Wall, Jeanette M. Dolezal, and Kent L. Norman
    1973   "Differential weighting of positive and negative traits in impression formation as a function of prior exposure." Journal of Experimental Psychology 97 (1, January): 114-115. P.A. 49:11093.
3213. Levin, Joseph
    1973   "Bifactor analysis of a multitrait-multimethod matrix of leadership criteria in small groups." Journal of Social Psychology 89 (2, April): 295-299. P.A. 50:6735.
3214. Levine, Edward L., and Raymond A. Katzell
    1971   "Effects of variations in control structure on group performance and satisfaction: A laboratory study." Proceedings of the 79th Annual Convention of the American Psychological Association 6 (pt. 1): 475-476.
3215. Levine, Jacob, and John Butler
    1952   "Lecture vs. group decision in changing behavior." Journal of Applied Psychology 36: 29-33. (See also Cartwright and Zander, 1953.) P.A. 26:6908.
3216. Levine, Jacob, Julius Laffal, Martin Berkowitz, James Lindemann, and John Drevdahl
    1954   "Conforming behavior of psychiatric and medical patients." Journal of Abnormal and Social Psychology 49: 251-255. P.A. 29:1305.
3217. Levine, John M., Candice J. Ranelli, and Ronald S. Valle
    1974   "Self-evaluation and reaction to a shifting other." Journal of Personality and Social Psychology 29 (5, May): 637-643. P.A. 52: 12331.
3218. Levine, John M., Leonard Saxe, and Hobart Harris
    1973   "Amount of initial disagreement as a determinant of reaction to a shifting attitudinal deviate." Proceedings of the 81st Annual Convention of the American Psychological Association 8: 157-158. P.A. 50:4808.
3219. Levine, Ned
    1971   "Emotional factors in group development." Human Relations 24 (1, February): 65-89. P.A. 46:10756.
3220. Levinger, George
    1959   "The development of perceptions and behavior in newly formed social power relationships." In D. Cartwright (ed.), Studies in Social Power, pp. 83-98. Ann Arbor: University of Michigan. P.A. 34: 7573.
3221.   1964   "Task and social behavior in marriage." Sociometry 27 (4, December): 433-448. P.A. 39:7637.
3222.   1972   "Little sand box and big quarry: Comment on Byrne's paradigmatic spade for research on interpersonal attraction." Representative Research in Social Psychology 3 (1, May): 3-19. P.A. 49:9055.
3223. Levinger, George, David J. Senn, and Bruce W. Jorgensen
    1970   "Progress toward permanence in courtship: A test of the Kerckhoff-Davis hypotheses." Sociometry 33 (4, December): 427-443. P.A. 46:8930.
3224. Levinson, Daniel J.
    1959   "Role, personality, and social structure in the organizational setting." Journal of Abnormal and Social Psychology 58: 170-180.
3225. Levitt, Lynn, and Wayne Viney
    1973   "Inhibition of aggression against the physically disabled." Perceptual and Motor Skills 36 (1, February): 255-258. P.A. 50:11252.
3226. Levy, D. M.
    1955   "Oppositional syndromes and oppositional behavior." In P. H. Hoch

and J. Zubin (eds.), Psychopathology of Childhood, pp. 204-226.
New York: Grune & Stratton.

3227. Levy, Leo
1960   "Studies in conformity behavior: A methodological note." Journal
of Psychology 50: 39-41. P.A. 35:6343.

3228. Levy, Leon H.
1964   "Group variance and group attractiveness." Journal of Abnormal
and Social Psychology 68 (6, June): 661-664. P.A. 39:1576; S.A.
14:B8348.

3229. Levy, Peter, Diane Lundgren, Marc Ansel, David Fell, Betty Fink, and Joseph
E. McGrath
1972   "Bystander effect in a demand-without-threat situation." Journal of
Personality and Social Psychology 24 (2, November): 166-171. P.A.
49:4427.

3230. Levy, Stephen J., and Alvin L. Atkins
1971   "An empirical investigation of disclosing behavior in a verbal encounter group." Proceedings of the 79th Annual Convention of the
American Psychological Association 6 (pt. 1): 297-298.

3231. Lewicki, Roy J.
1971   "Effects of exploitative and cooperative relationships on subsequent
interpersonal relations." Proceedings of the 79th Annual Convention
of the American Psychological Association 6 (pt. 1): 225-226.

3232. Lewicki, Roy J., and Jeffrey Z. Rubin
1973   "Effects of variations in the informational clarity of threats and
promises upon interpersonal bargaining." Proceedings of the 81st
Annual Convention of the American Psychological Association 8:
137-138. P.A. 50:8857.

3233. Lewin, Arie Y., Peter Dubno, and William G. Akula
1971   "Face-to-face interaction in the peer-nomination process." Journal
of Applied Psychology 55 (5, October): 495-497. P.A. 47:6681.

3234. Lewin, Kurt
1943   "Forces behind food habits and methods of change." Bulletin of the
National Research Council 108: 35-65. (See also Cartwright and
Zander, 1953.)

3235.   1944   "Constructs in psychology and psychological ecology." University of
Iowa Studies in Child Welfare 20 (409): 1-49. P.A. 19:3432.

3236.   1947a   "Frontiers in group dynamics: Concept, method and reality in social
science: social equilibria and social change." Human Relations 1: 5-
41. (See also Hare, Borgatta, and Bales, 1955.) P.A. 22:256.

3237.   1947b   "Frontiers in group dynamics: 2. Channels of group life; social planning and action research." Human Relations 1: 143-153. P.A. 22:
2610.

3238.   1947c   "Group decision and social change." In T. M. Newcomb and E. L.
Hartley (eds.), Readings in Social Psychology, pp. 330-344. New
York: Holt. (See also Maccoby, Newcomb, and Hartley, 1958.)

3239.   1948   Resolving Social Conflicts: Selected Papers on Group Dynamics.
New York: Harper. P.A. 22:4891.

3240.   1951   Field Theory in Social Science. New York: Harper. P.A. 25:6769.

3241. Lewin, Kurt, and Ronald Lippitt
1938   "An experimental approach to the study of autocracy and democracy: A preliminary note." Sociometry 1: 292-300. (See also Hare,
Borgatta, and Bales, 1955, 1965.)

3242. Lewin, Kurt, Ronald Lippitt, and Ralph K. White
1939   "Patterns of aggressive behavior in experimentally created 'social
climates.'" Journal of Social Psychology 10: 271-299. (See also
Gouldner, 1950.)

3243. Lewis, Gordon H.
1970a   "Bales' Monte Carlo model of small group discussions." Sociometry
33 (1, March): 20-36. S.A. 19:E8391.

3244.   1970b   "The assumption of stationary parameters in theories of group discussion." Behavioral Science 15: 269-273.

3245.   1971   "The accuracy of alternative stochastic models of participation in group discussion." Journal of Mathematical Sociology 1 (2, July): 263-276. P.A. 47:10779; S.A. 21:73G5648.

3246.   1972   "Role differentiation." American Sociological Review 37 (4, August): 424-434.

3247. Lewis, Helen B.
    1944   "An experimental study of the role of the ego in work: I. The role of the ego in cooperative work." Journal of Experimental Psychology 34: 113-126. P.A. 18:2739.

3248. Lewis, Helen B., and M. Franklin
    1944   "An experimental study of the role of the ego in work: II. The significance of task orientation in work." Journal of Experimental Psychology 34: 195-215. P.A. 18:3083.

3249. Lewis, Robert A.
    1973a   "A longitudinal test of a developmental framework for premarital dyadic formation." Journal of Marriage and the Family 35 (1, February): 16-25. S.A. 22:74G6147.

3250.   1973b   "Social reaction and the formation of dyads: An interactionist approach to mate selection." Sociometry 36 (3): 409-418.

3251. Lewis, Steven A., Charles J. Langan, and Edwin P. Hollander
    1972   "Expectation of future interaction and the choice of less desirable alternatives in conformity." Sociometry 35 (3, September): 440-447. P.A. 49:6828.

3252. Lewis, Steven A., and Dean G. Pruitt
    1971   "Orientation, aspiration level, and communication freedom in integrative bargaining." Proceedings of the 79th Annual Convention of the American Psychological Association 6 (pt. 1): 221-222.

3253. Lewis, Steven A., and John Sample
    1970   "Motivation as a component in alliance attitude formation." Proceedings of the 78th Annual Convention of the American Psychological Association 5 (pt. 1): 399-400. P.A. 44:18567.

3254. Lewit, David W., and Margaret R. Saville
    1971   "Can groups be conservative? The case of realism." Proceedings of the 79th Annual Convention of the American Psychological Association 6 (pt. 1): 251-252.

3255. Leyens, Jacques P.
    1972   "The role of a positive model, a frustrating situation and aggressive context on imitation." European Journal of Social Psychology 2 (1): 5-17. P.A. 49:781.

3256. Leyens, Jacques P., and Steve Picus
    1973   "Identification with the winner of a fight and name mediation: Their differential effects upon subsequent aggressive behavior." British Journal of Social and Clinical Psychology 12 (4, November): 374-377. P.A. 52:806.

3257. Libby, Roger W., and John E. Carlson
    1973   "Exchange as concept, conceptual framework or theory?: The case of Goode's application of exchange to the family." Journal of Comparative Family Studies 4 (2, Fall): 159-170. P.A. 52:7510.

3258. Libby, William L., Jr.
    1970   "Eye contact and direction of looking as stable individual differences." Journal of Experimental Research in Personality 4 (4, October): 303-312. P.A. 45:6198.

3259.   1971   "Sociometric task leadership and the perception of deviance and subsequent conformity, as functions of personality." Genetic Psychology Monographs 84 (2, November): 245-273. P.A. 49:782.

3260. Libby, William L., Jr., and Donna Yaklevich
    1973   "Personality determinants of eye contact and direction of gaze aversion." Journal of Personality and Social Psychology 27 (2, August): 197-206. P.A. 51:2984.

3261. Libo, Lester M.
    1953   Measuring Group Cohesiveness. Ann Arbor: University of Michigan, Research Center for Group Dynamics, Institute for Social Research. P.A. 28:8654.

3262. Lichtenberg, P.
1955 "Emotional maturity as manifested in ideational interaction." Journal of Abnormal and Social Psychology 51: 298–301. P.A. 30: 4353.
3263. 1956 "Time perspective and the initiation of cooperation." Journal of Social Psychology 43: 247–260.
3264. 1957 "Reactions to success and failure during the individual and cooperative effort." Journal of Social Psychology 46: 31–34. P.A. 34: 2866.
3265. Lichtenstein, Edward, Robert P. Quinn, and Gerald L. Hover
1961 "Dogmatism and acquiescent response set." Journal of Abnormal and Social Psychology 63 (3): 636–638.
3266. Lidman, Robert I.
1969 "Contagion of aggression and the number of reinforcements given by a model to an instigator." Psychonomic Science 16 (2): 69–70. P.A. 43:17347.
3267. Lieberman, Bernhardt
1960 "Human behavior in a strictly determined 3 X 3 matrix game." Behavioral Science 5 (4, October): 317–322. P.A. 35:1743; S.A. A3246.
3268. 1962 "Experimental studies of conflict in some two-person and three-person games." In J. H. Criswell, H. Solomon, and P. Suppes (eds.), Mathematical Methods in Small Group Processes, pp. 203–220. Stanford, Calif.: Stanford University Press. S.A. 12:B2416.
3269. 1964 "i-Trust: A notion of trust in three-person games and international affairs." Journal of Conflict Resolution 8 (3): 271–286.
3270. Lieberman, Morton A.
1971– "Encounter leaders: Their behavior and impact." Interpersonal Development 2 (1): 21–49. P.A. 49:11095.
1972
3271. Lieberman, Morton A., Irvin D. Yalom, and Matthew B. Miles
1972 "The impact of encounter groups on participants: Some preliminary findings." Journal of Applied Behavioral Science 8 (1): 29–50.
3272. 1973 Encounter Groups: First Facts. New York: Basic Books.
3273. Liebert, Diane E., Sharon A. Swenson, and Robert M. Liebert
1971 "Risk taken by the opponent and experience of subject as determinants of imitation in a competitive situation." Perceptual and Motor Skills 32 (3, June): 719–722. P.A. 47:2839.
3274. Liebert, Robert M., and Luis E. Fernandez
1970 "Effects of single and multiple modeling cues on establishing norms for sharing." Proceedings of the 78th Annual Convention of the American Psychological Association 5 (pt. 1): 437–438.
3275. Liebert, Robert M., and Rita W. Poulos
1971 "Eliciting the 'norm of giving': Effects of modeling and presence of witness on children's sharing behavior." Proceedings of the 79th Annual Convention of the American Psychological Association 6 (pt. 1): 345–346.
3276. Liebert, Robert M., William P. Smith, J. H. Hill, and Miriam Keiffer
1968 "The effects of information and magnitude of initial offer on interpersonal negotiation." Journal of Experimental Social Psychology 4 (4, October): 431–441. P.A. 43:3926.
3277. Liebhart, Ernst H.
1972a ("Attribution and dissonance: Critical remarks and a critical experiment.") Zeitschrift für Sozialpsychologie 3: 277–286.
3278. 1972b "Empathy and emergency helping: The effects of personality, self-concern, and acquaintance." Journal of Experimental Social Psychology 8 (5, September): 404–411. P.A. 49:6829.
3279. Liebling, Barry A., and Phillip Shaver
1973 "Social facilitation and social comparison process." Proceedings of the 81st Annual Convention of the American Psychological Association 8: 327–328. P.A. 50:4809.
3280. Liebowitz, Bernard
1972 "A method for the analysis of the thematic structure of T groups."

Journal of Applied Behavioral Science 8 (2, March-April): 149-173. S.A. 21:73G3960.

3281. Lietaer, G.
1965- ("The level of performance of a peer as a factor affecting the percep-
1966 tion of own successes and failures: An experimental approach.")
Psychologica Belgica 6: 87-102. P.A. 43:789.

3282. Lifton, Robert J.
1956 "'Thought reform' of Western civilians in Chinese Communist pris-
ons." Psychiatry 19: 173-195.

3283. 1961 Thought Reform and the Psychology of Totalism: A Study of
"Brainwashing" in China. New York: Norton. London: Gollancz,
1962. P.A. 35:4801.

3284. Lifton, Walter M.
1961 Working with Groups: Group Process and Individual Growth. New
York: Wiley.

3285. 1972 Groups: Facilitating Individual Growth and Societal Change. New
York: Wiley.

3286. Linde, Thomas F., and C. H. Patterson
1964 "Influence of orthopedic disability on conformity behavior." Journal of Abnormal and Social Psychology 68 (1, January): 115-118.

3287. Lindeman, Eduard C.
1924 Social Discovery. New York: Republic.

3288. Lindgren, Henry C., and Jacqueline Robinson
1953 "An evaluation of Dymond's test of insight and empathy." Journal
of Consulting Psychology 17: 172-176. P.A. 28:2650.

3289. Lindsay, J. S. B.
1972 "On the number in a group." Human Relations 25 (1, February):
47-64. P.A. 49:2351.

3290. Lindskold, Svenn, and Russell Bennett
1973 "Attributing trust and conciliatory intent from coercive power capa-
bility." Journal of Personality and Social Psychology 28 (2): 180-
186.

3291. Lindskold, Svenn, and Joann Horai
1974 "Effects of target's disclosure of intent on exercise of influence in
conflict." Psychological Reports 34 (2, April): 623-629. P.A. 52:
12332.

3292. Lindskold, Svenn, Brian Maclean, Noel Novinson, and Charles Phillips
1969 "Prior announcement of compliance or defiance and the reactions of
a threatening source." Proceedings of the 77th Annual Convention
of the American Psychological Association 4 (pt. 1): 399-400. P.A.
43:17348.

3293. Lindskold Svenn, Ronald Price, Mark Rubinstein, Russell Bennett, and Sue
Foster
1974 "The perception of individual and group stability." Journal of Social
Psychology 93 (2): 211-218.

3294. Lindskold, Svenn, and James T. Tedeschi
1970 "Self-confidence, prior success, and the use of power in social conflicts." Proceedings of the 78th Annual Convention of the American
Psychological Association 5 (pt. 1): 425-426. P.A. 44:18568.

3295. 1971 "Reward power and attraction in interpersonal conflict." Psychonomic Science 22 (4, February): 211-213. P.A. 46:8931.

3296. Lindskold, Svenn, James T. Tedeschi, Thomas V. Bonoma, and Barry R.
Schlenker
1971 "Reward power and bilateral communication in conflict resolution."
Psychonomic Science 23 (6, June): 415-416. P.A. 48:9019.

3297. Lindzey, Gardner (ed.)
1954 Handbook of Social Psychology. Cambridge, Mass.: Addison-Wesley.
P.A. 29:3817.

3298. Lindzey, Gardner, and Elliot Aronson (eds.)
1968 The Handbook of Social Psychology. 2nd ed. Reading, Mass.: Addison-Wesley.

3299. Lindzey, Gardner, and Edgar F. Borgatta
    1954   "Sociometric measurement." In G. Lindzey (ed.), Handbook of Social Psychology, pp. 405-448. Cambridge, Mass.: Addison-Wesley. P.A. 29:3850.

3300. Lindzey, Gardner, and Donn Byrne
    1968   "Measurement of social choice and interpersonal attractiveness." In G. Lindzey and E. Aronson (eds.), Handbook of Social Psychology, vol. 2, pp. 452-525, Reading, Mass.: Addison-Wesley.

3301. Lindzey, Gardner, and Henry W. Riecken
    1951   "Inducing frustration in adult subjects." Journal of Consulting Psychology 15: 18-23. P.A. 26:6388.

3302. Lindzey, Gardner, and J. A. Urdan
    1954   "Personality and social choice." Sociometry 17: 47-63. P.A. 29: 731.

3303. Linton, Harriet B.
    1954   "Autokinetic judgment as a measure of influence." Journal of Abnormal and Social Psychology 49: 464-466. P.A. 29:3571.

3304. Lippitt, Ronald
    1939   "Field theory and experiment in social psychology: Autocratic and democratic group atmospheres." American Journal of Sociology 45: 26-49.

3305.   1940   "An experimental study of the effect of democratic and authoritarian group atmospheres." University of Iowa Studies in Child Welfare 16: 43--195. (See also Barker, Kounin, and Wright, 1943.) P.A. 14:3655.

3306.   1948   "A program of experimentation on group functioning and group productivity." In W. Dennis, R. Lippitt, et al., Current Trends in Social Psychology, pp. 14-49. Pittsburgh: University of Pittsburgh Press. P.A. 23:5432.

3307.   1949   Training in Community Relations: A Research Exploration toward New Group Skills. New York: Harper. P.A. 24:551.

3308. Lippitt, Ronald, Norman Polansky, and Sidney Rosen
    1952   "The dynamics of power: A field study of social influence in groups of children." Human Relations 5: 37-64. (See also Cartwright and Zander, 1953, 1968; Maccoby, Newcomb, and Hartley, 1958.) P.A. 27:278.

3309. Lippitt, Ronald, Jeanne Watson, and Bruce Westley
    1958   The Dynamics of Planned Change: A Comparative Study of Principles and Techniques. New York: Harcourt, Brace.

3310. Lippitt, Ronald, and Ralph K. White
    1952   "An experimental study of leadership and group life." In G. E. Swanson, T. M. Newcomb, and E. L. Hartley (eds.), Readings in Social Psychology, pp. 340-355. New York: Holt. (See also Maccoby, Newcomb, and Hartley, 1958.)

3311. Lippitt, Ronald, and Alvin Zander
    1943   "Observation and interview methods for the leadership training study." Mimeo. New York: Boy Scouts of America.

3312. Lippitt, Rosemary
    1941   "Popularity among preschool children." Child Development 12: 305-332. P.A. 16:1746.

3313. Lipsitt, Lewis P., and T. R. Vallance
    1955   "The expression of telenomic trends in private and in group-related problem situations." Journal of Personality 23: 381-390. P.A. 30: 2661.

3314. Littig, Lawrence W.
    1965   "Behavior in certain zero-sum, two-person games." Journal of Social Psychology 66 (June): 113-125.

3315. Little, Kenneth B.
    1965   "Personal space." Journal of Experimental Social Psychology 1 (3, August): 237-247. P.A. 40:1524.

3316.   1968   "Cultural variations in social schemata." Journal of Personality and

Social Psychology 10 (1): 1-7.

3317. Lloyd, Kathryn, and Cliff Lloyd
1972 "Reciprocity, equivalence, normative behavior and the existence of social prices." Journal of Mathematical Sociology 2 (2, July): 249–265. P.A. 51:7033.

3318. Lobrot, Michel
1971 ("The self-regulation of T-groups.") Gruppendynamik 2 (June): 166–183. P.A. 48:11451.

3319. Lodahl, Thomas M., and Lyman W. Porter
1961 "Psychometric score patterns, social characteristics, and productivity of small industrial work groups." Journal of Applied Psychology 45: 73–79. P.A. 36:3LH73L.

3320. Loehlin, John C.
1965 "'Interpersonal' experiments with a computer model of personality." Journal of Personality and Social Psychology 2 (4): 580–584.

3321. Loether, Herman J.
1960 "Propinquity and homogeneity as factors in the choice of best buddies in the Air Force." Pacific Sociological Review 3: 8–22. P.A. 36:3LH08L.

3322. Lombardo, John P., Robert F. Weiss, and William Buchanan
1972 "Reinforcing and attracting functions of yielding." Journal of Personality and Social Psychology 21 (3, March): 359–368. P.A. 48: 2887.

3323. Lombardo, John P., Robert F. Weiss, and Mark H. Stich
1973 "Effectance reduction through speaking in reply and its relation to attraction." Journal of Personality and Social Psychology 28 (3, December): 325–332. P.A. 51:7079.

3324. Lomranz, Jacob, Martin Lakin, and Harold Schiffman
1972 "Variants of sensitivity training and encounter: Diversity or fragmentation?" Journal of Applied Behavioral Science 8 (4, July): 399–420. P.A. 49:6830.

3325. 1973 "A three-valued typology for sensitivity training and encounter groups." Human Relations 26 (3): 339–358. P.A. 51:8997.

3326. London, Harvey, Dennis McSeveney, and Richard Tropper
1971 "Confidence, overconfidence and persuasion." Human Relations 24 (5, October): 359–369. P.A. 50:951.

3327. London, Harvey, Philip J. Meldman, and A. Van C. Lanckton
1970a "The jury method: How the persuader persuades." Public Opinion Quarterly 34 (2, Summer): 171–183. S.A. 19:E8392.

3328. 1970b "The jury method: Some correlates of persuading." Human Relations 23 (2): 115–121.

3329. London, Perry, and Howard Lim
1964 "Yielding reason to social pressure: Task complexity and expectation in conformity." Journal of Personality 32 (1): 75–89. P.A. 39: 4875.

3330. Lonegran, Brendan G., and Charles G. McClintock
1961 "Effects of group membership on risk-taking behavior." Psychological Reports 8: 447–455. P.A. 36:2GE47L.

3331. Long, Gary T., and Melvin J. Lerner
1974 "Deserving, the 'personal contract,' and altruistic behavior by children." Journal of Personality and Social Psychology 29 (4, April): 551–556. P.A. 52:7565.

3332. Long, Huey B.
1970 "Relationships of selected personal and social variables in conforming judgement." Journal of Social Psychology 81: 177–182.

3333. Longabaugh, Richard
1963 "A category system for coding interpersonal behavior as social exchange." Sociometry 26 (3, September): 319–344.

3334. 1966 "The structure of interpersonal behavior." Sociometry 29 (4, December): 441–460.

3335. Longhurst, Thomas M., and Gerald M. Siegel
1973 "Effects of communication failure on speaker and listener behavior."

Journal of Speech and Hearing Research 16 (1, March): 128-140. P.A. 51:953.

3336. Loo, Chalsa M.
1972   "The effects of spatial density on the social behavior of children." Journal of Applied Social Psychology 2 (4, October): 372-381. P.A. 50:2952.

3337. Loomis, Charles P.
1941   "Informal groupings in a Spanish-American village." Sociometry 4: 36-51. P.A. 15:3515.

3338.   1968   "Wanted: A model for understanding and predicting change in natural and therapeutic groups and systems which are Gemeinschaft-like." Group Psychotherapy 21 (2-3): 131-136. P.A. 45:4125.

3339. Loomis, Charles P., and J. Allan Beegle
1948   "A topological analysis of social systems." Sociometry 11: 147-191. P.A. 24:569.

3340. Loomis, Charles P., and Harold B. Pepinsky
1948   "Sociometry, 1937-1947: Theory and methods." Sociometry 11: 262-283. P.A. 24:570.

3341. Loomis, James L.
1959   "Communication, the development of trust, and co-operative behavior." Human Relations 12 (4, November): 305-315. P.A. 35: 6363.

3342. Loomis, Ross J., and Bernard Spilka
1972   "Social desirability and conformity in a group test situation." Psychological Reports 30 (1, February): 199-203. P.A. 48:7113.

3343. Loprieno, M., F. Emili, and R. Esposito
1967   ("Relationships between evaluation of self and others: Sociometric role.") Securitas 52 (9): 97-112. P.A. 42:17149.

3344. Lorber, Neil M.
1969   "The reliability and validity of sociometric measures." American Sociologist 4 (3, August): 243-244. S.A. 18:E0904.

3345. Loree, M. Ray, and Margaret B. Koch
1960   "Use of verbal reinforcement in developing group discussion skills." Journal of Educational Psychology 51: 164-168. P.A. 35:3875.

3346. Lorge, Irving, David Fox, Joel Davitz, and Marlin Brenner
1958   "A survey of studies contrasting the quality of group performance and individual performance, 1920-1957." Psychological Bulletin 55: 337-372.

3347. Lorge, Irving, and Herbert Solomon
1960   "Group and individual performance in problem solving related to previous exposure to problem, level of aspiration, and group size." Behavioral Science 5 (1, January): 28-38. P.A. 34:7577; S.A. A2743.

3348.   1962   "Group and individual behavior in free-recall verbal learning." In J. H. Criswell, H. Solomon, and P. Suppes (eds.), Mathematical Methods in Small Group Processes, pp. 221-231. Stanford, Calif.: Stanford University Press. S.A. 12:B2417.

3349. Lorge, Irving, Jacob Tuckman, Louis Aikman, Joseph Spiegel, and Gilda Moss
1955a   "Solutions by teams and by individuals to a field problem at different levels of reality." Journal of Educational Psychology 46: 17-24. P.A. 29:8413.

3350.   1955b   "Problem-solving by teams and by individuals in a field setting." Journal of Education Psychology 55: 160-166. P.A. 30:588.

3351.   1956   "The adequacy of written reports in problem solving by teams and by individuals." Journal of Social Psychology 43: 65-74. P.A. 31: 2512.

3352. Lorr, Maurice, and Richard L. Jenkins
1953   "Three factors in parent behavior." Journal of Consulting Psychology 17: 306-308. P.A. 28:4087.

3353. Lorr, Maurice, and Douglas M. McNair
1963   "An interpersonal behavior circle." Journal of Abnormal and Social Psychology 67 (1): 68-75.

3354.   1965   "Expansion of the interpersonal behavior circle." Journal of Personality and Social Psychology 2 (6): 823–830.
3355. Lorr, Maurice, and Antanas Suziedelis
1969   "Modes of interpersonal behaviour." British Journal of Social and
Clinical Psychology 8 (2): 124–132. P.A. 43:15703.
3356. Lorr, Maurice, Antanas Suziedelis, and John F. Kinnane
1969   "Characteristic response modes to interpersonal situations." Multivariate Behavioral Research 4 (4): 445–458. P.A. 44:10286.
3357. Lott, Albert J., Joseph F. Aponte, Bernice E. Lott, and W. Hugh McGinley
1969   "The effect of delayed reward on the development of positive attitudes toward persons." Journal of Experimental Social Psychology
5 (1): 101–113.
3358. Lott, Albert J., Mary A. Bright, Philip Weinstein, and Bernice E. Lott
1970   "Liking for persons as a function of incentive and drive during acquisition." Journal of Personality and Social Psychology 14 (1): 66–76.
3359. Lott, Albert J., and Bernice E. Lott
1961   "Group cohesiveness, communication level, and conformity." Journal of Abnormal and Social Psychology 62 (2, March): 408–412.
P.A. 36:4GE08L; S.A. A2210.
3360.   1965   "Group cohesiveness as interpersonal attraction: A review of relationships with antecedent and consequent variables." Psychological
Bulletin 64 (4): 259–309. P.A. 39:15044.
3361.   1966   "Group cohesiveness and individual learning." Journal of Educational Psychology 57 (2): 61–73. P.A. 40:5400.
3362.   1969   "Liked and disliked persons as reinforcing stimuli." Journal of Personality and Social Psychology 11 (2): 129–137. P.A. 43:8288.
3363.   1970   "Some indirect measures of interpersonal attraction among children." Journal of Educational Psychology 61 (2): 124–135.
3364. Lott, Albert J., Bernice E. Lott, and Terry Crow
1969   "Use of descriptive words in measuring liking for persons." Proceedings of the 77th Annual Convention of the American Psychological
Association 4 (pt. 1): 407–408.
3365. Lott, Albert J., Bernice E. Lott, and Gail M. Matthews
1969   "Interpersonal attraction among children as a function of vicarious
reward." Journal of Educational Psychology 60 (4, pt. 1): 274–283.
P.A. 43:15704.
3366. Lott, Albert J., Bernice E. Lott, Thomas Reed, and Terry Crow
1970   "Personality-trait descriptions of differentially liked persons." Journal of Personality and Social Psychology 16 (2): 284–290.
3367. Lott, Bernice E.
1961   "Group cohesiveness: A learning phenomenon." Journal of Social
Psychology 55 (December): 275–286. P.A. 36:3GE75L.
3368. Lott, Bernice E., and Albert J. Lott
1960   "The formation of positive attitudes toward group members." Journal of Abnormal and Social Psychology 61 (2): 297–300. P.A. 35:
4819; S.A. A1200.
3369. Lott, Dale F., and Robert Sommer
1967   "Seating arrangements and status." Journal of Personality and Social
Psychology 7 (1): 90–95.
3370. Louis-Guérin, Christiane
1972–   ("Perception of others: Mode of integration of information.") Bulle-
1973   tin de Psychologie 26 (14-16): 814–830. P.A. 51:3044.
3371. Lowe, Charles A., and Joel W. Goldstein
1970   "Reciprocal liking and attributions of ability: Mediating effects of
perceived intent and personal involvement." Journal of Personality
and Social Psychology 16 (2): 291–297.
3372. Lowe, Roland, and James Murphy
1972   "Communication patterns in engaged couples." Psychological Reports 31 (2, October): 655–658. P.A. 49:9056.
3373. Lowe, Roland, and Gary Ritchey
1973   "Relation to altruism to age, social class, and ethnic identity." Psychological Reports 33 (2, October): 567–572. P.A. 51:9043.

3374. Lubin, Bernard, and Roger L. Harrison
     1964   "Predicting small group behavior with the self-disclosure inventory."
             Psychological Reports 15: 77-78.
3375. Lubin, Bernard, and Alice W. Lubin
     1971   "Laboratory training stress compared with college examination
             stress." Journal of Applied Behavioral Science 7 (4, July-August):
             502-507. S.A. 20:F9135.
3376. Lubin, Bernard, and Marvin Zuckerman
     1967   "Affective and perceptual-cognitive patterns in sensitivity training
             groups." Psychological Reports 21 (2): 365-376. P.A. 42:5533.
3377. Lucas, Carol
     1965   "Task performance and group structure as a function of personality
             and feedback." Journal of Social Psychology 66 (2, August): 257-
             270. P.A. 39:15045.
3378. Lucas, Richard L., and Cabot L. Jaffee
     1969   "Effects of high-rate talkers on group voting behavior in the leader-
             less-group problem-solving situation." Psychological Reports 25 (2):
             471-477. P.A. 44:5096.
3379. Luce, R. Duncan, and Albert D. Perry
     1949   "A method of matrix analysis of group structure." Psychometrika
             14: 95-116. P.A. 24:889.
3380. Luce, R. Duncan, and Howard Raiffa
     1958   Games and Decisions: Introduction and Critical Survey. New York:
             Wiley.
3381. Luchins, Abraham S.
     1945   "Social influences on perception of complex drawings." Journal of
             Social Psychology 21: 257-273. P.A. 19:2294.
3382. 1947   "Group structures in group psychotherapy." Journal of Clinical Psy-
             chology 3: 269-273. P.A. 22:318.
3383. 1955   "A variational approach to social influences on perception." Journal
             of Social Psychology 42: 113-119. P.A. 30:6694.
3384. Luchins, Abraham S., and Edith H. Luchins
     1955a   "On conformity with true and false communications." Journal of
             Social Psychology 42: 283-303. P.A. 31:974.
3385. 1955b   "Previous experience with ambiguous and non-ambiguous percep-
             tual stimuli under various social influences." Journal of Social Psy-
             chology 42: 249-270. P.A. 31:975.
3386. 1956   "Discovering the source of contradictory communications." Journal
             of Social Psychology 44: 49-63.
3387. 1961a   "On conformity with judgements of a majority or an authority."
             Journal of Social Psychology 53 (April): 303-316. P.A. 36:1GE03L.
3388. 1961b   "Social influences on judgement of changing evidence." Journal of
             Social Psychology 54 (June): 13-36. P.A. 36:2GE13L.
3389. 1961c   "Social influences on impressions of personality." Journal of Social
             Psychology 54 (June): 111-125. P.A. 36:2GE11L.
3390. 1961d   "Intentional and unintentional models in social learning." Journal of
             Social Psychology 54 (August): 321-335. P.A. 36:3GF21L.
3391. 1961e   "Einstellung effect in social learning." Journal of Social Psychology
             55 (October): 59-66. P.A. 36:4GE59L.
3392. 1963a   "Social influences on judgments of descriptions of people." Journal
             of Social Psychology 60 (August): 231-249.
3393. 1963b   "Focusing on the object of judgment in the social situation." Jour-
             nal of Social Psychology 60 (August): 273-287.
3394. 1963c   "The role of understanding in social influences on judgment." Jour-
             nal of Social Psychology 61 (October): 133-150.
3395. 1963d   "Effects of order of evidence on social influences on judgment."
             Journal of Social Psychology 61 (December): 345-363.
3396. 1966   "Consequences for agreeing with another's wrong judgments." Jour-
             nal of Social Psychology 68 (2, April): 275-290. P.A. 40:7644.
3397. 1968   "Motivation to tell the truth vs. social influences." Journal of Social
             Psychology 76 (1, October): 97-105. P.A. 43:2535.
3398. 1969   "Einstellung effect and group problem solving." Journal of Social

Psychology 77 (1): 78–89. P.A. 43:6842.

3399.   1971   "Wertheimer's seminars revisited: Social influence and power." Albany: State University of New York, Psychology Department. P.A. 47:6682.

3400. Lucito, Lenard F.
1964   "Independence-conformity behavior as a function of intellect: Bright and dull children." Exceptional Children 31 (1): 1–13. P.A. 39:4876.

3401. Lück, Helmut E.
1966   ("Bibliography of selected literature on small group research.") Kölner Zeitschrift für Soziologie und Sozialpsychologie 10 (Supplement): 273–280. S.A. 15:C5583.

3402.   1970a   ("Some determinants and dimensions in leader behavior.") Gruppendynamik 1 (February): 63–69. P.A. 46:4843.

3403.   1970b   ("Experimental studies in bystander behavior.") Gruppendynamik 4 (October): 380–394. P.A. 47:2842.

3404. Luft, Joseph
1970   Group Processes: An Introduction to Group Dynamics. Palo Alto, Calif.: National Press Books. P.A. 49:2353.

3405. Luke, Robert A., Jr.
1972   "The internal normative structure of sensitivity training groups." Journal of Applied Behavioral Science 8 (4, July): 421–437. P.A. 49:6831.

3406. Lumsden, Ernest A., Jr.
1970   "Person perception as a function of the deviation of the visual axes of the object-person." Journal of Social Psychology 80: 71–78.

3407. Lundberg, George A.
1940   "Some problems of group classification and measurement." American Sociological Review 5: 351–360.

3408. Lundberg, George A., Virginia B. Hertzler, and Lenore Dickson
1949   "Attraction patterns in a university." Sociometry 12: 158–169.

3409. Lundberg, George A., and Mary Steele
1938   "Social attraction patterns in a village." Sociometry 1: 375–419.

3410. Lundgren, David C.
1971   "Trainer style and patterns of group development." Journal of Applied Behavioral Science 7 (6, November–December): 689–709. S.A. 21:73G3961.

3411.   1973   "Attitudinal and behavioral correlates of emergent status in training groups." Journal of Social Psychology 90 (1, June): 141–153. P.A. 51:2985.

3412. Lundgren, David C., and Dodd H. Bogart
1974   "Group size, member dissatisfaction, and group radicalism." Human Relations 27 (4): 339–355.

3413. Lundgren, Earl F.
1972   "The effects of differential rank on maintaining stability in the dyad." Journal of Social Psychology 87: 273–278.

3414. Lundy, Richard M.
1956a   "Assimilative projection and accuracy of prediction in interpersonal relations." Journal of Abnormal and Social Psychology 52: 33–38. P.A. 31:2560.

3415.   1956b   "Self-perceptions and descriptions of opposite sex sociometric choices." Sociometry 19: 272–277. P.A. 32:1367.

3416.   1958   "Self-perceptions regarding masculinity-femininity and descriptions of same and opposite sex sociometric choices." Sociometry 21: 238–246.

3417.   1959   "The relationship of changes in assimilative projection to accepting and rejecting interpersonal groups and to the order of the groups." Journal of Social Psychology 50 (November): 327–333. P.A. 35: 4993.

3418. Lundy, Richard M., Walter Katkovsky, Rue L. Cromwell, and Donald J. Shoemaker
1955   "Self-acceptability and descriptions of sociometric choices." Journal

of Abnormal and Social Psychology 51: 260–262. P.A. 30:4356.
3419. Lupfer, Michael
1970   "The effects of risk-taking tendencies and incentive conditions on the performance of investment groups." Journal of Social Psychology 82: 135–136.
3420. Lupfer, Michael, Mark Jones, and Cecilia Quin
1972   "Group risk taking as a function of three types of monetary incentive." Journal of Psychology 80 (2, March): 273–282. P.A. 48: 4871.
3421. Lupfer, Michael, Mark Jones, Lionel Spaulding, and Richard Archer
1971   "Risk-taking in cooperative and competitive dyads." Journal of Conflict Resolution 15 (3, September): 385–392. P.A. 48:2888.
3422. Lutzker, Daniel R.
1961   "Sex role, cooperation and competition in a two-person, non-zero sum game." Journal of Conflict Resolution 5: 366–368. P.A. 37: 3038.
3423. Lyle, Jack
1961   "Communication, group atmosphere, productivity, and morale in small task groups." Human Relations 14 (4, November): 369–379.
3424. Lynch, Gerald W.
1973   "Cooperation and competition among police." Proceedings of the 81st Annual Convention of the American Psychological Association 8: 385–386. P.A. 50:6737.
3425. Lynch, Steve, William A. Watts, Charles Galloway, and Spyros Tryphonopoulos
1973   "Appropriateness of anxiety and drive for affiliation." Journal of Research in Personality 7 (1, June): 71–77. P.A. 51:5106.

3426. Maas, Henry S.
1950   "Personal and group factors in leaders' social perception." Journal of Abnormal and Social Psychology 45: 54–63. P.A. 24:4547.
3427.   1954a   "Evaluating the individual member in the group." In National Conference of Social Work, Group Work and Community Organization, 1953–1954, pp. 36–44. New York: Columbia University Press. P.A. 29:5464.
3428.   1954b   "The role of members in clubs of lower-class and middle-class adolescents." Child Development 25: 241–251. P.A. 29:7013.
3429. Maas, Henry S., Edith Varon, and David Rosenthal
1951   "A technique for studying the social behavior of schizophrenics." Journal of Abnormal and Social Psychology 46: 119–123. P.A. 25: 7583.
3430. Macaranas, Eduarda A., and Joel M. Savell
1973   "An experimental examination of two types of explanation for the prior-agreement/conformity relationship." Representative Research in Social Psychology 4 (2, June): 75–84. P.A. 51:3045.
3431. Macbride, Philip D., and Read D. Tuddenham
1965   "The influence of self-confidence upon resistance of perceptual judgments to group pressure." Journal of Psychology 60 (1): 9–23. P.A. 39:15047.
3432. Maccoby, Eleanor E., Theodore M. Newcomb, and Eugene L. Hartley (eds.)
1958   Readings in Social Psychology. 3rd ed. New York: Holt.
3433. MacDonald, A. P., Jr., Richard G. Games, and Oscar G. Mink
1972   "Film-mediated facilitation of self-disclosure and attraction to sensitivity training." Psychological Reports 30 (3, June): 847–857. P.A. 49:2354.
3434. MacDonald, A. P., Jr., Vicki S. Kessel, and James B. Fuller
1972   "Self-disclosure and two kinds of trust." Psychological Reports 30: 143–148.
3435. MacDonald, W. Scott, and Chester W. Oden, Jr.
1973   "Effects of extreme crowding on the performance of five married couples during twelve weeks of intensive training." Proceedings of the 81st Annual Convention of the American Psychological Association 8: 209–210. P.A. 50:8859.

3436. Mack, David
    1972a   "'Leader': An unbiased mixed-motive game?" Psychologische Beit-
             rage 14 (2): 244–252. P.A. 49:6832.
3437.   1972b   "Personality, payoff information, and behavior in a two-person bar-
                  gaining game." Acta Psychologica 36 (2, April): 125–144. P.A. 49:
                  785.
3438. Mack, David, Paula N. Auburn, and George P. Knight
    1971   "Sex role identification and behavior in a reiterated Prisoner's Di-
            lemma game." Psychonomic Science 24 (6, September): 280–282.
            P.A. 48:9022.
3439. Mack, David, and George P. Knight
    1972   "Information on the nature of the game as a determinant of behav-
            ior in the Prisoner's Dilemma." Psychonomic Science 27 (2, April):
            99–100. P.A. 48:11452.
3440.   1974   "Identification of other players' characteristics in the reiterated Pris-
                 oner's Dilemma." Psychological Record 24 (1, Winter): 93–100. P.A.
                 52:7566.
3441. Mackenzie, Kenneth D.
    1970a   "Risk as a value and risky shift." Organizational Behavior and Hu-
             man Performance 5 (2): 125–134. P.A. 44:20826.
3442.   1970b   "The effects of status upon group risk taking." Organizational Be-
                  havior and Human Performance 5 (6, November): 517–541. P.A.
                  45:8114.
3443.   1971   "An analysis of risky shift experiments." Organizational Behavior
                 and Human Performance 6 (3, May): 283–303. P.A. 46:8933.
3444. MacNeil, M. K., and Dorothy Pace
    1973   "Differential adoption of norms by high-status and low-status mem-
            bers of informal groups." Perceptual and Motor Skills 36 (3, pt. 2,
            June): 1275–1283. P.A. 51:9044.
3445. MacRae, Duncan, Jr.
    1960   "Direct factor analysis of sociometric data." Sociometry 23 (4, De-
            cember): 360–371. P.A. 35:2122; S.A. A2688.
3446. Macy, Josiah, Jr., Lee S. Christie, and R. Duncan Luce
    1953   "Coding noise in a task-oriented group." Journal of Abnormal and
            Social Psychology 48: 401–409. P.A. 28:2544.
3447. Madaras, George R., and Daryl J. Bem
    1968   "Risk and conservatism in group decision-making." Journal of Ex-
            perimental Social Psychology 4 (3, July): 350–365. P.A. 43:2527.
3448. Madden, Joseph M.
    1960   "Personal preferences and conformity." Journal of Social Psychol-
            ogy 52 (November): 269–277. P.A. 35:4820.
3449. Maddock, Richard C., and Charles T. Kenny
    1973   "Impression formation as a function of age, sex, and race." Journal
            of Social Psychology 89 (2, April): 233–243. P.A. 50:6739.
3450. Maehr, Martin L., Josef Mensing, and Samuel Nafzger
    1962   "Concept of self and the reaction of others." Sociometry 25 (4, De-
            cember): 353–357.
3451. Mahl, George F.
    1956   "Disturbances and silences in the patient's speech in psychotherapy."
            Journal of Abnormal and Social Psychology 53: 1–15.
3452. Mahler, Irwin
    1962   "Yeasayers and naysayers: A validating study." Journal of Abnormal
            and Social Psychology 64 (4): 317–318.
3453. Maier, Norman R. F.
    1946   Psychology in Industry. Boston: Houghton Mifflin. P.A. 20:3287.
3454.   1950   "The quality of group decisions as influenced by the discussion
                 leader." Human Relations 3: 155–174. P.A. 25:2364.
3455.   1953   "An experimental test of the effect of training on discussion leader-
                 ship." Human Relations 6: 161–173. P.A. 28:2426.
3456.   1970   "Male versus female discussion leaders." Personnel Psychology 23 (4,
                 Winter): 455–461. P.A. 46:6753.
3457.   1972   "Effects of training on decision-making." Psychological Reports 30:

159-164.

3458. Maier, Norman R. F., and L. Richard Hoffman
    1960a   "Using trained 'developmental' discussion leaders to improve further
             the quality of group decisions." Journal of Applied Psychology 44:
             247-251. P.A. 35:3363.

3459. 1960b   "Quality of first and second solutions in group problem solving."
                Journal of Applied Psychology 44: 278-283. P.A. 35:3362.

3460. 1962   "Group decision in England and the United States." Personal Psy-
               chology 15 (2): 75-87. P.A. 37:3054.

3461. 1964   "Financial incentives and group decision in motivating change."
               Journal of Social Psychology 64 (December): 369-378.

3462. 1965   "Acceptance and quality of solutions as related to leader's attitudes
               toward disagreement in group problem-solving." Journal of Applied
               Behavioral Science 1 (4): 373-386. P.A. 40:5417.

3463. Maier, Norman R. F., and Richard A. Maier
    1957   "An experimental test of the effects of 'developmental' vs. 'free' dis-
            cussions on the quality of group decisions." Journal of Applied Psy-
            chology 41: 320-323.

3464. Maier, Norman R. F., and Ellen P. McRay
    1972   "Increasing innovation in change situations through leadership
            skills." Psychological Reports 31 (2, October): 343-354. P.A. 49:
            6833.

3465. Maier, Norman R. F., and Allen R. Solem
    1952   "The contribution of a discussion leader to the quality of group
            thinking: The effective use of minority opinions." Human Relations
            5: 277-288. (See also Cartwright and Zander, 1953.) P.A. 27:3432.

3466. Maier, Norman R. F., and James A. Thurber
    1968   "Accuracy of judgments of deception when an interview is watched,
            heard, and read." Personnel Psychology 21 (1): 23-30. P.A. 42:
            15402.

3467. 1969   "Limitations of procedures for improving group problem solving."
               Psychological Reports 25 (2): 639-656. P.A. 44:5077.

3468. Main, Eleanor C., and Thomas G. Walker
    1973   "Choice shifts and extreme behavior: Judicial review in the federal
            courts." Journal of Social Psychology 91 (2, December): 215-221.
            P.A. 52:807.

3469. Maisonneuve, Jean
    1954   "A contribution to the sociometry of mutual choices." Sociometry
            17: 33-46. P.A. 29:732.

3470. 1962   ("The elaboration of individual sociograms and dyadic analysis.")
               Psychologie Française 7 (2): 156-160. P.A. 37:4884.

3471. Maisonneuve, Jean, G. Palmade, and Claude Fourment
    1952   "Selective choices and propinquity." Sociometry 15: 135-140. P.A.
            27:7390.

3472. Malamuth, Neil M., and Seymour Feshbach
    1972   "Risky shift in a naturalistic setting." Journal of Personality 40 (1,
            March): 38-49. P.A. 48:11453.

3473. Malefijt, Annemarie
    1968   "Dutch joking patterns." Transactions of the New York Academy
            of Sciences 30 (8): 1181-1186. P.A. 43:6833.

3474. Maller, J. B.
    1929   "Cooperation and competition: An experimental study in motiva-
            tion." Columbia University, Teachers College, Contributions to Edu-
            cation No. 384.

3475. 1931   "Size of family and personality of offspring." Journal of Social Psy-
               chology 2: 3-27.

3476. Malof, Milton, and Albert J. Lott
    1962   "Ethnocentrism and the acceptance of Negro support in a group
            pressure situation." Journal of Abnormal and Social Psychology 65
            (4): 254-258.

3477. Maloney, R. M.
    1956   "Group learning through group discussion: A group discussion

implementation analysis." Journal of Social Psychology 43: 3-9.

3478. Malott, Richard W., and Robert L. Rollofson
1972   "An empirical evaluation of student-led discussions." Psychological Reports 30: 531-535.

3479. Malpass, Leslie F., and Eugene D. Fitzpatrick
1959   "Social facilitation as a factor in reaction to humor." Journal of Social Psychology 50 (November): 295-303. P.A. 35:4754.

3480. Mandelbaum, David G.
1952   Soldier Groups and Negro Soldiers. Berkeley and Los Angeles: University of California Press. P.A. 27:2647.

3481. Mangan, G. L., D. Quartermain, and G. Vaughan
1959   "Relationship between Taylor MAS scores and group conformity." Perceptual and Motor Skills 9 (September): 207-209. P.A. 34: 5731.

3482.   1960   "Taylor MAS and group conformity pressure." Journal of Abnormal and Social Psychology 61 (1): 146-147.

3483. Mangold, Werner
1960   ("Objective and method of group discussion studies.") Frankfurter Beiträge zur Soziologie, No. 9. Frankfurt am Main: Europäische Verlagsanstalt. S.A. 15:C4800.

3484. Manheim, Henry L.
1963   "Experimental demonstration of relationships between group characteristics and pattern of intergroup interaction." Pacific Sociological Review 6: 25-29. P.A. 38:4196.

3485. Manis, Melvin
1955   "Social interaction and the self concept." Journal of Abnormal and Social Psychology 51: 362-370. P.A. 31:2708.

3486. Manis, Melvin, S. Douglas Cornell, and Jeffrey C. Moore
1974   "Transmission of attitude relevant information through a communication chain." Journal of Personality and Social Psychology 30 (1, July): 81-94. P.A. 52:12334.

3487. Mann, James
1953   "Group therapy with adults." American Journal of Orthopsychiatry 23: 332-337.

3488. Mann, John H.
1958   "The influence of racial group composition on sociometric choices and perceptions." Journal of Social Psychology 48: 137-146.

3489.   1959   "The effect of inter-racial contact on sociometric choices and perceptions." Journal of Social Psychology 50 (August): 143-152. P.A. 35:3364.

3490.   1960   "The differential nature of prejudice reduction." Journal of Social Psychology 52 (November): 339-343. P.A. 35:4804.

3491. Mann, John H., and Edgar F. Borgatta
1959   "Personality and behavior correlates of changes produced by role playing experience." Psychological Reports 5: 505-526.

3492. Mann, John H., and Carola H. Mann
1959a   "Insight as a measure of adjustment in three kinds of group experience." Journal of Consulting Psychology 23 (1): 91.

3493.   1959b   "The importance of group task in producing group-member personality and behavior changes." Human Relations 12: 75-80. P.A. 34: 5732; S.A. A2744.

3494.   1960   "The relative effectiveness of role playing and task oriented group experience in producing personality and behavior change." Journal of Social Psychology 51 (May): 313-317. P.A. 34:7584.

3495. Mann, Philip A.
1971   "Effects of anxiety and defensive style on some aspects of friendship." Journal of Personality and Social Psychology 18 (1, April): 55-61. P.A. 46:2917.

3496. Mann, Richard D.
1959   "A review of the relationships between personality and performance in small groups." Psychological Bulletin 56 (4, July): 241-270. P.A. 34:4194.

3497.   1961   "Dimensions of individual performance in small groups under task and social-emotional conditions." Journal of Abnormal and Social Psychology 62 (3, May): 674–682. P.A. 4GE74M; S.A. A2745.

3498.   1966   "The development of the member-trainer relationships in self-analytic groups." Human Relations 19 (1, February): 85–115.

3499. Mann, Richard D., Graham S. Gibbard, and John J. Hartman
         1967   Interpersonal Styles and Group Development. New York: Wiley. S.A. 18:E0905.

3500. Mannheim, Bilha F.
         1966   "Reference groups, membership groups and the self image." Sociometry 29 (3, September): 265–279. P.A. 40:13156.

3501. Manz, Wolfgang
         1972   ("A simple apparatus for two-person matrix games.") Zeitschrift für Experimentelle und Angewandte Psychologie 19 (1): 130–140. P.A. 49:786.

3502. Marak, George E.
         1964   "The evolution of leadership structure." Sociometry 27 (2, June): 174–182. (See also Crosbie, 1975.) P.A. 39:4908.

3503. March, James G.
         1953   "Husband-wife interaction over political issues." Public Opinion Quarterly 17: 461–470.

3504.   1956   "Influence measurement in experimental and semi-experimental groups." Sociometry 19: 260–271.

3505.   1962   "Theory of organizational decision-making." In A. Ranney (ed.), Essays on the Behavioral Study of Politics, pp. 191–208. Urbana: University of Illinois Press. (See also Hare, Borgatta, and Bales, 1965.)

3506. March, James G., and Edward A. Feigenbaum
         1960   "Latent motives, group discussion, and the 'quality' of group decisions in a non-objective decision problem." Sociometry 23 (1, March): 50–56. P.A. 35:2124.

3507. Marcus, Philip M.
         1960   "Expressive and instrumental groups: Toward a theory of group structure." American Journal of Sociology 66 (1, July): 54–59.

3508. Margolin, Joseph B.
         1952   "The use of an interaction matrix to validate patterns of group behavior." Human Relations 5: 407–416. P.A. 27:6880.

3509. Marin, Gerardo
         1973   ("Behavioral interchange and the Dogmatism and Machiavellianism scales.") Revista Latinoamericana de Psicologia 5 (3): 257–262. P.A. 52:835.

3510. Marino, Charles J., Jr.
         1967   "Theoretical origins of a modification of the Asch test." Papers in Psychology 1 (2): 77–81. P.A. 42:3905.

3511. Marino, Charles J., Jr., and C. J. Parkin
         1969   "A modification of the Asch experiment." Journal of Social Psychology 77 (1): 91–95. P.A. 43:6843.

3512. Markel, Norman N., Layne D. Prebor, and John F. Brandt
         1972   "Biosocial factors in dyadic communication." Journal of Personality and Social Psychology 23 (1): 11–13.

3513. Markey, Vicki K.
         1973   "Psychological need relationships in dyadic attraction and rejection." Psychological Reports 32 (1, February): 111–123. P.A. 51:2986.

3514. Marks, John B.
         1959   "Interests and group formation." Human Relations 12 (4, November): 385–390. P.A. 35:6358.

3515. Marlatt, G. Alan
         1970   "A comparison of vicarious and direct reinforcement control of verbal behavior in an interview setting." Journal of Personality and Social Psychology 16 (4, December): 695–703. P.A. 45:4126.

3516. Marlowe, David
         1963   "Psychological needs and cooperation: Competition in a two-person

game." Psychological Reports 13: 364.

3517. Marlowe, David, and Kenneth J. Gergen
       1968   "Personality and social interaction." In G. Lindzey and E. Aronson
               (eds.), Handbook of Social Psychology, vol. 3, pp. 590–665. Read-
               ing, Mass.: Addison-Wesley.

3518. Marlowe, David, Kenneth J. Gergen, and Anthony N. Doob
       1966   "Opponent's personality, expectation of social interaction, and in-
               terpersonal bargaining." Journal of Personality and Social Psychol-
               ogy 3 (2): 206–213. P.A. 40:4187.

3519. Marma, Victor J., and Karl W. Deutsch
       1973   "Survival in unfair conflict: Odds, resources, and random walk
               models." Behavioral Science 18: 313–334.

3520. Marquart, Dorothy I.
       1955   "Group problem solving." Journal of Social Psychology 41: 103–
               113. P.A. 30:589.

3521. Marquis, Donald G.
       1962   "Individual responsibility and group decisions involving risk." In-
               dustrial Management Review 3 (2, Spring): 8–23. S.A. 14:C0963.

3522. Marquis, Donald G., Harold Guetzkow, and R. W. Heyns
       1951   "A social psychological study of the decision-making conference."
               In H. Guetzkow (ed.), Groups, Leadership, and Men: Research in
               Human Relations, pp. 55–67. Pittsburgh: Carnegie. P.A. 26:814.

3523. Marquis, Donald G., and H. Joseph Reitz
       1969   "Effect of uncertainty on risk taking in individual and group deci-
               sions." Behavioral Science 14 (4, July): 281–289. S.A. 18:E5683.

3524. Marquis, Peggy C.
       1973   "Experimenter-subject interaction as a function of authoritarianism
               and response set." Journal of Personality and Social Psychology 25
               (2, February): 289–296. P.A. 50:956.

3525. Marriott, R.
       1949   "Size of working group and output." Occupational Psychology
               (London) 23: 47–57. P.A. 23:3956.

3526. Marsden, Edith N.
       1966   "Values as determinants of friendship choice." Connecticut College
               Psychology Journal 3: 3–13. P.A. 40:8791.

3527. Marston, Albert R., and Edward M. Levine
       1964   "Interaction patterns in a college population." Journal of Social
               Psychology 62 (1, February): 149–154. P.A. 39:1577.

3528. Marston, W. M.
       1924   "Studies in testimony." Journal of Criminal Law and Criminology
               15: 5–31.

3529. Martens, Rainer, and Daniel M. Landers
       1972   "Evaluation potential as a determinant of coaction effects." Journal
               of Experimental Social Psychology 8 (4, July): 347–359. P.A. 49:
               787.

3530. Martens, Rainer, and James A. Peterson
       1971   "Group cohesiveness as a determinant of success and member satis-
               faction in team performance." International Review of Sport Sociol-
               ogy 6: 49–61. S.A. 22:74G8631.

3531. Martin, J. David
       1970   "Suspicion and the experimental confederate: A study of role and
               credibility." Sociometry 33 (2, June): 178–192. S.A. 19:E9552.

3532. Martin, J. David, J. Sherwood Williams, and Louis N. Gray
       1974   "Norm formation and subsequent divergence: Replication and varia-
               tion." Journal of Social Psychology 93 (2): 261–269.

3533. Martin, Roger D.
       1971   "Videotape self-confrontation in human relations training." Journal
               of Counseling Psychology 18 (4, July): 341–347. P.A. 46:10758.

3534. 1974   "Friendship choices and residence hall proximity among freshmen
               and upper year students." Psychological Reports 34 (1, February):
               118. P.A. 52:7529.

3535. Martin, Roger D., and Donald G. Fischer
1974   "Encounter-group experience and personality change." Psychological Reports 35 (1, pt. 1): 91-96.

3536. Martin, William E., John G. Darley, and Neal Gross
1952   "Studies of group behavior: II. Methodological problems in the study of interrelationships of group members." Educational and Psychological Measurement 12: 533-553. P.A. 27:6486.

3537. Martin, William E., Neal Gross, and John G. Darley
1952   "Studies of group behavior: Leaders, followers, and isolates in small organized groups." Journal of Abnormal and Social Psychology 47: 838-842. P.A. 27:5065; S.A. 127.

3538. Martindale, David A.
1971   "Territorial dominance behavior in dyadic verbal interactions." Proceedings of the 79th Annual Convention of the American Psychological Association 6 (pt. 1): 305-306. P.A. 46:2918.

3539. Marwell, Gerald
1963   "Visibility in small groups." Journal of Social Psychology 61 (2, December): 311-325. P.A. 38:8309.

3540.   1966   "Types of past experience with potential work partners: Their effects on partner choice." Human Relations 19 (4, November): 437-447.

3541.   1968   "Role allocation and differentiation through time in medium-sized groups." Journal of Social Psychology 74 (2, April): 225-231. P.A. 42:10517.

3542. Marwell, Gerald, and Jerald Hage
1970   "The organization of role-relationships: A systematic description." American Sociological Review 35 (5): 884-900.

3543. Marwell, Gerald, and David R. Schmitt
1967   "Dimensions of compliance-gaining behavior: An empirical analysis." Sociometry 30 (4, December): 350-364. S.A. 16:D3101.

3544.   1971   "Some notes on the concept and experimental study of cooperation." Journal for the Theory of Social Behaviour 1 (2, October): 153-164. S.A. 21:73G3962.

3545.   1972a   "Cooperation and interpersonal risk: Cross-cultural and cross-procedural generalization." Journal of Experimental Social Psychology 8 (6, November): 594-599. P.A. 49:11099.

3546.   1972b   "Cooperation in a three-person Prisoner's Dilemma." Journal of Personality and Social Psychology 21 (3, March): 376-383. P.A. 48:2889.

3547. Marwell, Gerald, David R. Schmitt, and Bjorn Boyesen
1973   "Pacifist strategy and cooperation under interpersonal risk." Journal of Personality and Social Psychology 28 (1, October): 12-20. P.A. 51:11008.

3548. Marwell, Gerald, David R. Schmitt, and Robert Shotola
1970   "Sex differences in a cooperative task." Behavioral Science 15: 184-186.

3549.   1971   "Cooperation and interpersonal risk." Journal of Personality and Social Psychology 18 (1, April): 9-32. P.A. 46:2919.

3550. Mascaro, Guillermo F.
1970   "Interpersonal attraction and uncertainty reduction as functions of judgmental similarity." Perceptual and Motor Skills 30 (1, February): 71-75. P.A. 46:8934.

3551. Mascaro, Guillermo F., and William Graves
1973   "Contrast effects of background factors on the similarity-attraction relationship." Journal of Personality and Social Psychology 25 (3, March): 346-350. P.A. 50:4812.

3552. Mascaro, Guillermo F., and Lee A. Jackson
1971   "Interpersonal attraction as a function of attitude similarity-dissimilarity and desire for certainty." Psychological Reports 28: 856-858.

3553. Maselli, Mary D., and John Altrocchi
1969   "Attribution of intent." Psychological Bulletin 71 (6): 445-454.

P.A. 43:11233.

3554. Maslach, Christina
1972 "Social and personal bases of individuation." Proceedings of the 80th Annual Convention of the American Psychological Association 7 (pt. 1): 213–214. P.A. 48:4872.

3555. 1974 "Social and personal bases of individuation." Journal of Personality and Social Psychology 29 (3): 411–425.

3556. Masling, Joseph, F. Loyal Greer, and Robert Gilmore
1955 "Status, authoritarianism, and sociometric choice." Journal of Social Psychology 41: 297–310. P.A. 30:5914.

3557. Mason, Donald J.
1957 "Judgements of leadership based upon physiognomic cues." Journal of Abnormal and Social Psychology 54: 273–274.

3558. Masor, Hugo N., Harvey A. Hornstein, and Thomas A. Tobin
1973 "Modeling, motivational interdependence, and helping." Journal of Personality and Social Psychology 28 (2): 236–248.

3559. Matarazzo, Joseph D., and George Saslow
1961 "Difference in interview interaction behavior among normal and deviant groups." In I. A. Berg and B. M. Bass (eds.), Conformity and Deviation, pp. 286–327. New York: Harper. P.A. 36:4GE86M.

3560. Matarazzo, Joseph D., George Saslow, and Samuel B. Guze
1956 "Stability of interaction patterns during interviews: A replication." Journal of Consulting Psychology 20: 267–274.

3561. Matarazzo, Joseph D., George Saslow, and A. Paul Hare
1958 "Factor analysis of interview interaction behavior." Journal of Consulting Psychology 22: 419–429.

3562. Matarazzo, Joseph D., George Saslow, and Ruth G. Matarazzo
1956 "The interaction chronograph as an instrument for objective measurement of interaction patterns during interviews." Journal of Psychology 41: 347–367.

3563. Matarazzo, Joseph D., George Saslow, Ruth G. Matarazzo, and Jeanne S. Phillips
1958 "Stability and modifiability of personality patterns manifested during a standardized interview." In P.A. Hoch and J. Zubin (eds.), Psychopathology of Communication. New York: Grune & Stratton.

3564. Matarazzo, Joseph D., Arthur N. Wiens, and George Saslow
1964 "Studies in interview speech behavior." In L. Krasner and L. P. Ullmann (eds.), Research in Behavior Modification: New Developments and Their Clinical Implications, pp. 179–210. New York: Holt, Rinehart & Winston.

3565. Matarazzo, Joseph D., Arthur N. Wiens, George Saslow, Richard M. Dunham, and Robert M. Voas
1964 "Speech durations of astronaut and ground communicator." Science 143 (Whole No. 3602): 148–150. P.A. 38:8319.

3566. Matarazzo, Ruth G., Joseph D. Matarazzo, George Saslow, and Jeanne S. Phillips
1958 "Psychological test and organismic correlates of interview interaction patterns." Journal of Abnormal and Social Psychology 56: 329–338.

3567. Matejko, Alexander
1962 ("The small group.") Studia Socjologiczne 5: 5–34. S.A. 16:C9756.

3568. 1973 "Institutional conditions of scientific inquiry: Survey of research teams in Poland." Small Group Behavior 4 (1, February): 89–126.

3569. Matheson, W.
1972 "An independent validation of Bales' concept of 'social psychological space.'" Alberta Journal of Educational Research 18 (3, September): 174–179. P.A. 49:9061.

3570. Matlin, Margaret W., and Robert B. Zajonc
1968 "Social facilitation of word associations." Journal of Personality and Social Psychology 10 (4): 455–460. P.A. 43:6844.

3571. Matova, M. A.
1973 ("Complex investigation of mental states in humans engaged in indi-

vidual and group activity.") Voprosy Psikhologii 19 (4, July): 42–52. P.A. 51:7034.

3572. Matthews, J., and A. W. Bendig
    1955   "The index of agreement: A possible criterion for measuring the outcome of group discussion." Speech Monographs 22: 39–42. P.A. 30:791.

3573. Mattmüller-Frick, Felix
    1971   ("Group education.") Praxis der Kinderpsychologie und Kinderpsychiatrie 20 (4, May): 135–141. P.A. 48:2890.

3574. Mattsson, Patrik O.
    1960   "Communicated anxiety in a two-person situation." Journal of Consulting Psychology 24 (6): 488–495. P.A. 36:1GE88M.

3575. Maucorps, Paul-H, and René Bassoul
    1960   ("Empathies and knowledge of others.") Monographies Françaises de Psychologie 3. P.A. 36:1GE93M.

3576. Mausner, Bernard
    1953   "Studies in social interaction: III. Effect of variation in one partner's prestige on the interaction of observer pairs." Journal of Applied Psychology 37: 391–393.

3577.   1954a   "The effect of one partner's success in a relevant task on the interaction of observer pairs." Journal of Abnormal and Social Psychology 49: 557–560. P.A. 29:5466.

3578.   1954b   "The effect of prior reinforcement on the interaction of observer pairs." Journal of Abnormal and Social Psychology 49: 65–68. P.A. 28:7352.

3579.   1955   "Studies in social interaction: I. A conceptual scheme." Journal of Social Psychology 41: 259–270. P.A. 30:5861.

3580. Mausner, Bernard, and Barbara L. Bloch
    1957   "A study of the additivity of variables affecting social interaction." Journal of Abnormal and Social Psychology 54: 250–256.

3581. Mausner, Bernard, and Judith Graham
    1970   "Field dependence and prior reinforcement as determinants of social interaction in judgment." Journal of Personality and Social Psychology 16 (3, November): 486–493. P.A. 45:4127.

3582. May, Mark A., and Leonard W. Doob
    1937   "Competition and cooperation." Social Science Research Council Bulletin No. 25.

3583. Mayer, A.
    1903   ("On the schoolchild's work alone and in the group.") Archiv für die Gesamte Psychologie 1: 276–416.

3584. Mayhew, Bruce H., Jr., and Louis N. Gray
    1971   "The structure of dominance relations in triadic interaction systems: A stochastic process." Comparative Group Studies 2 (2, May): 161–190. P.A. 48:2892.

3585.   1972   "Growth and decay of structure in interaction: Stochastic models of dominance and related asymmetric structures." Comparative Group Studies 3 (2, May): 131–160. P.A. 49:9062.

3586. Mayhew, Bruce H., Jr., Louis N. Gray, and James T. Richardson
    1969   "Behavioral measurement of operating power structures: Characterizations of asymmetrical interaction." Sociometry 32 (4): 474–489. P.A. 44:6658.

3587. Mayo, Elton
    1933   The Human Problems of an Industrial Civilization. New York: Macmillan.

3588. Mayo, Elton, and G. F. F. Lombard
    1944   Team Work and Labor Turnover in the Aircraft Industry of Southern California. Boston: Harvard University, Graduate School of Business Administration. P.A. 19:2036.

3589. Mazur, Allan
    1968   "A nonrational approach to theories of conflict and coalitions." Journal of Conflict Resolution 12 (2): 196–205.

3590.   1973   "A cross-species comparison of status in small established groups."

American Sociological Review 38 (5, October): 513-530. S.A. 22: 74G8632.

3591. McBurney, J. H., and K. G. Hance
1939   The Principles and Methods of Discussion. New York: Harper. P.A. 14:1996.

3592. McCall, James, and Gordon Rae
1973   "Inferential sets and person perception: A partial replication and extension." Perceptual and Motor Skills 37 (2, October): 479-482. P.A. 51:9045.

3593. McCandless, Boyd R.
1942   "Changing relationships between dominance and social acceptability during group democratization." American Journal of Orthopsychiatry 12: 529-535. P.A. 16:4821.

3594. McCardel, Janet, and Edward J. Murray
1974   "Nonspecific factors in weekend encounter groups." Journal of Consulting and Clinical Psychology 42 (3): 337-345.

3595. McCauley, Clark R.
1972   "Extremity shifts, risk shifts and attitude shifts after group discussion." European Journal of Social Psychology 2 (4): 417-436. P.A. 50:6740.

3596. McCauley, Clark R., and Norma Graham
1971   "Influence of values in risky decision making: A formalization." Representative Research in Social Psychology 2 (2, July): 3-11. P.A. 49:9063.

3597. McCauley, Clark R., and Lenore Kramer
1972   "Strategy differences between group and individual gambling." Journal of Experimental Social Psychology 8 (6, November): 518-527. P.A. 49:11101.

3598. McCauley, Clark R., Christopher L. Stitt, Kathryn Woods, and Diana Lipton
1973   "Group shift to caution at the race track." Journal of Experimental Social Psychology 9 (1, January): 80-86. P.A. 50:2956.

3599. McCauley, Clark R., Allan I. Teger, and Nathan Kogan
1971   "Effect of the pretest in the risky-shift paradigm." Journal of Personality and Social Psychology 20 (3, December): 379-381. P.A. 47:8794.

3600. McClintock, Charles G.
1963   "Group support and the behavior of leaders and nonleaders." Journal of Abnormal and Social Psychology 67 (2): 105-113. P.A. 38: 2597.

3601.   1965   "Group support, satisfaction, and the behaviour profiles of group members." British Journal of Social and Clinical Psychology 4 (3): 169-174. P.A. 40:1525.

3602.   1972   "Social motivation: A set of propositions." Behavioral Science 17 (5, September): 438-455. P.A. 49:4430.

3603.   1974   "Development of social motives in Anglo-American and Mexican-American children." Journal of Personality and Social Psychology 29 (3): 348-354.

3604. McClintock, Charles G., Philip Gallo, and Albert A. Harrison
1965   "Some effects of variations in other strategy upon game behavior." Journal of Personality and Social Psychology 1 (4): 319-325.

3605. McClintock, Charles G., and Steven P. McNeel
1966a   "Cross cultural comparisons of interpersonal motives." Sociometry 29 (4, December): 406-427.

3606.   1966b   "Reward and score feedback as determinants of cooperative and competitive game behavior." Journal of Personality and Social Psychology 4 (6): 606-613.

3607.   1966c   "Reward level and game playing behavior." Journal of Conflict Resolution 10 (1, March): 98-102. S.A. 15:C4801.

3608.   1967   "Prior dyadic experience and monetary reward as determinants of cooperative and competitive game behavior." Journal of Personality and Social Psychology 5 (3): 282-294.

3609. McClintock, Charles G., David M. Messick, David M. Kuhlman, and Frances T. Campos
      1973   "Motivational bases of choice in three-choice decomposed games."
               Journal of Experimental Social Psychology 9 (6): 572-590.
3610. McClintock, Charles G., and Josef M. Nuttin, Jr.
      1969   "Development of competitive game behavior in children across two
               cultures." Journal of Experimental Social Psychology 5 (2): 203-
               218.
3611. McClintock, Charles G., Josef M. Nuttin, Jr., and Steven P. McNeel
      1970   "Sociometric choice, visual presence, and game-playing behavior."
               Behavioral Science 15 (2, March): 124-131. P.A. 44:10287; S.A.
               19:E9553.
3612. McConville, Carolyn B., and John K. Hemphill
      1966   "Some effects of communication restraints on problem-solving be-
               havior." Journal of Social Psychology 69 (2, August): 265-276. P.A.
               40:12273.
3613. McCranie, Edward W., and James C. Kimberly
      1973   "Rank inconsistency, conflicting expectations and injustice." Soci-
               ometry 36 (2, June): 152-176. P.A. 51:2988.
3614. McCurdy, Harold G., and Herbert W. Eber
      1953   "Democratic versus authoritarian: A further investigation of group
               problem-solving." Journal of Personality 22: 258-269. P.A. 28:
               5820.
3615. McCurdy, Harold G., and Wallace E. Lambert
      1952   "The efficiency of small human groups in the solution of problems
               requiring genuine co-operation." Journal of Personality 20: 478-
               494. P.A. 27:3430.
3616. McDaniel, James W., Edgar O'Neal, and Ellen S. Fox
      1971   "Magnitude of retaliation as a function of the similarity of avail-
               able responses to those employed by attacker." Psychonomic Sci-
               ence 22 (4, February): 215-217. P.A. 46:8935.
3617. McDavid, John W., Jr.
      1959   "Personality and situational determinants of conformity." Journal
               of Abnormal and Social Psychology 58: 241-246. P.A. 34:1174.
3618. McDavid, John W., Jr., and Frank Sistrunk
      1964   "Personality correlates of two kinds of conforming behavior." Jour-
               nal of Personality 32 (3): 420-435. P.A. 39:7638.
3619. McDowell, Kenneth V.
      1972   "Violations of personal space." Canadian Journal of Behavioural Sci-
               ence 4 (3, July): 210-217. P.A. 49:2357.
3620. 1973   "Accommodations of verbal and nonverbal behaviors as a function
               of the manipulation of interaction distance and eye contact." Pro-
               ceedings of the 81st Annual Convention of the American Psychologi-
               cal Association 8: 207-208. P.A. 50:4813.
3621. McGee, Richard K.
      1962a   "The relationship between response style and personality variables:
               I. The measurement of response acquiescence." Journal of Abnormal
               and Social Psychology 64 (3): 229-233.
3622. 1962b   "The relationship between response style and personality variables:
               II. The prediction of independent conformity behavior." Journal of
               Abnormal and Social Psychology 65 (5): 347-351.
3623. McGee, Thomas F., and Meyer Williams
      1971   "Time-limited and time-unlimited group psychotherapy: A com-
               parison with schizophrenic patients." Comparative Group Studies
               2 (1, February): 71-84.
3624. McGhee, Paul E.
      1973   "Birth order and social facilitation of humor." Psychological Re-
               ports 33 (1, August): 105-106. P.A. 51:7080.
3625. McGinley, Hugh, and Pat McGinley
      1972   "Attraction toward a stranger as a function of direct and vicarious
               reinforcement." Journal of Experimental Research in Personality 6

(1, March): 60–68. P.A. 50:11254.
3626. McGinnies, Elliott M.
1956   "A method for matching anonymous questionnaire data with group discussion material." Journal of Abnormal and Social Psychology 52: 139–140.
3627. McGinnies, Elliott M., and Irwin Altman
1959   "Discussion as a function of attitudes and content of a persuasive communication." Journal of Applied Psychology 43 (February): 53–59. P.A. 34:4293.
3628. McGinnies, Elliott M., and Willard Vaughan
1957   "Some biographical determiners of participation in group discussion." Journal of Applied Psychology 41: 179–185.
3629. McGlynn, Richard P.
1972   "Four-person group concept attainment as a function of interaction format." Journal of Social Psychology 86 (1, February): 89–94. P.A. 47:10781.
3630. McGlynn, Richard P., and Connie Schick
1973   "Dyadic concept attainment as a function of interaction format, memory requirements, and sex." Journal of Educational Psychology 65 (3): 335–340.
3631. McGrath, Joseph E.
1957   "A framework for integration of small group research studies." Arlington, Va.: Psychological Research Associates.
3632.   1962   "The influence of positive interpersonal relations on adjustment and effectiveness in rifle teams." Journal of Abnormal and Social Psychology 65 (6): 365–375.
3633.   1963a   "A descriptive model for the study of interpersonal relations in small groups." Journal of Psychological Studies 14 (3): 89–116. P.A. 39: 10003.
3634.   1963b   "Systems of information in small group research studies." Human Relations 16 (3, August): 263–277. P.A. 38:5965; S.A. 12:A9438.
3635. McGrath, Joseph E., and Irwin Altman
1966   Small Group Research: A Synthesis and Critique of the Field. New York: Holt, Rinehart & Winston.
3636. McGrath, Joseph E., and James W. Julian
1963   "Interaction process and task outcome in experimentally created negotiation groups." Journal of Psychological Studies 14 (3): 117–138. P.A. 39:10004.
3637. McGrew, John M.
1969   "The cognitive consistency of left and right authoritarians: A test of Rokeach's 'belief congruency' hypothesis." Journal of Social Psychology 79 (2): 227–234. P.A. 44:10288.
3638. McGuire, Frederick, and Sidney Tolchin
1961   "Group adjustment at the South Pole." Journal of Mental Science 107: 954–960. P.A. 36:4GE54M.
3639. McGuire, John M.
1973   "Aggression and sociometric status with preschool children." Sociometry 36 (4): 542–549.
3640. McGuire, Michael T., and Roger Coleman
1968   "A model for the study of dyadic communication: II. Research approach, research and discussion." Journal of Nervous and Mental Disease 146 (3): 230–238. P.A. 43:5283.
3641. McGuire, Michael T., and Stephen Lorch
1968a   "A model for the study of dyadic communication: I. Orientation and model." Journal of Nervous and Mental Disease 146 (3): 221–229. P.A. 43:5284.
3642.   1968b   "Natural language conversation modes." Journal of Nervous and Mental Disease 146 (3): 239–248. P.A. 43:5285.
3643. McGuire, William J.
1964   "Inducing resistance to persuasion: Some contemporary approaches." In L. Berkowitz (ed.), Advances in Experimental Social Psychology, vol. 1, pp. 191–229. New York: Academic Press.

3644. McHenry, Robert
      1971   "New methods of assessing the accuracy of interpersonal percep-
              tion." Journal for the Theory of Social Behaviour 1 (2): 109-119.
3645. McIntire, Walter G.
      1973   "The impact of T-group experience on level of self-actualization."
              Small Group Behavior 4 (4, November): 459-465.
3646. McKeachie, W[ilbert] J.
      1954a   "Individual conformity to attitudes of classroom groups." Journal of
              Abnormal and Social Psychology 49: 282-289. P.A. 29:688.
3647.   1954b   "Student centered versus instructor centered instruction." Journal
              of Educational Psychology 45: 143-150. P.A. 29:2974.
3648.   1958   "Students, groups, and teaching methods." American Psychologist
              13: 580-584. P.A. 34:303.
3649. McKenna, Helen V., Peter R. Hofstaetter, and James P. O'Connor
      1956   "The concepts of the ideal self and of the friend." Journal of Person-
              ality 24: 262-271. P.A. 31:620.
3650. McKillip, Jack, and Emil J. Posavac
      1972   "Attribution of responsibility for an accident: Effects of similarity
              to the victim and severity of consequences." Proceedings of the 80th
              Annual Convention of the American Psychological Association 7
              (pt. 1): 181-182.
3651. McLaughlin, David, and Jay Hewitt
      1972   "Need for approval and perceived openness." Journal of Experi-
              mental Research in Personality 6 (2-3, December): 255-258. P.A.
              51:995.
3652. McLeish, John, Wayne Matheson, and James Park
      1973   The Psychology of the Learning Group. London: Hutchinson.
3653. McLeish, John, and James Park
      1972   "Outcomes associated with direct and vicarious experience in train-
              ing groups: I. Personality changes." British Journal of Social and
              Clinical Psychology 11 (4, December): 333-341. P.A. 49:9064.
3654.   1973a   "Outcomes associated with direct and vicarious experience in train-
              ing groups: II. Attitudes, dogmatism." British Journal of Social and
              Clinical Psychology 12 (4, November): 353-358. P.A. 52:808.
3655.   1973b   "Outcomes associated with direct and vicarious experience in train-
              ing groups: III. Intended learning outcomes." British Journal of So-
              cial and Clinical Psychology 12 (4, November): 359-373. P.A. 52:
              809.
3656. McLeod, Jack M., Kendall O. Price, and Ernest Harburg
      1966   "Socialization, liking and yielding of opinions in imbalanced situa-
              tions." Sociometry 29 (3, September): 197-212. P.A. 40:13157;
              S.A. 15:C3479.
3657. McMartin, James A.
      1970   "Two tests of an averaging model of social influence." Journal of
              Personality and Social Psychology 15 (4): 317-325.
3658. McMartin, James A., and Jerry I. Shaw
      1972   "Effects of ability level and outcome severity on the degree of re-
              sponsibility assigned for a happy accident." Proceedings of the 80th
              Annual Convention of the American Psychological Association 7
              (pt. 1): 183-184.
3659. McMillan, John J., and J. Silverberg
      1955   "Sociometric choice patterns in hospital ward groups with varying
              degrees of interpersonal disturbances." Journal of Abnormal and So-
              cial Psychology 50: 168-172. P.A. 30:788.
3660. McMillen, David L.
      1970   "Transgression, fate control, and compliant behavior." Psychonomic
              Science 21 (2, October): 1⌐3-104. P.A. 46:1086.
3661.   1971   "Transgression, self-image, and compliant behavior." Journal of Per-
              sonality and Social Psychology 20 (2, November): 176-179. P.A.
              47:6686.
3662. McMillen, David L., and James B. Austin
      1971   "Effect of positive feedback on compliance following transgression."

Psychonomic Science 24 (2, July): 59–61. P.A. 48:9023.

3663. McMillen, David L., and Joyce E. Reynolds
1969   "Self-esteem and the effectiveness of reconcilation techniques following an argument." Psychonomic Science 17 (4): 208–209. P.A. 44:5078.

3664. McNeel, Steven P.
1973   "Training cooperation in the Prisoner's Dilemma." Journal of Experimental Social Psychology 9 (4, July): 335–348. P.A. 51:5063.

3665. McNeel, Steven P., Charles G. McClintock, and Josef M. Nuttin, Jr.
1972   "Effects of sex role in a two-person mixed-motive game." Journal of Personality and Social Psychology 24 (3, December): 372–380. P.A. 49:9065.

3666. McNeel, Steven P., and David M. Messick
1970   "A Bayesian analysis of subjective probabilities of interpersonal relationships." Acta Psychologica 34 (2-3, December): 311–321. P.A. 46:1087.

3667. McNeel, Steven P., James D. Sweeney, and Peter C. Bohlin
1974   "Cooperation and competitive goals: A social-comparison analysis." Psychological Reports 34 (3, pt. 1): 887–894.

3668. McWhinney, William H.
1963   "Isolating organizational dynamics in a small group experiment." Sociometry 26 (3, September): 354–372. P.A. 38:5966; S.A. 12: A9439.

3669.   1964   "Simulating the communication network experiments." Behavioral Science 9: 80–84.

3670.   1968   "Synthesizing a social interaction model." Sociometry 31 (3): 229–244. P.A. 43:790.

3671. Mead, George H.
1950   Mind, Self, and Society from the Standpoint of a Social Behaviorist. Chicago: University of Chicago Press.

3672. Meade, Robert D., and William A. Barnard
1973   "Conformity and anticonformity among Americans and Chinese." Journal of Social Psychology 89 (1): 15–24.

3673. Meador, Betty D.
1971   "Individual process in a basic encounter group." Journal of Counseling Psychology 18 (1, January): 70–76. P.A. 45:8115.

3674. Means, John R., and Max Weiss
1971   "Gestural behavior of the courtroom witness." Journal of Forensic Psychology 3 (1, December): 12–20. P.A. 49:9066.

3675. Medalia, Nahum Z.
1955   "Authoritarianism, leader acceptance, and group cohesion." Journal of Abnormal and Social Psychology 51: 207–213. P.A. 30:4359.

3676. Medley, Donald M., and H. E. Mitzel
1958   "A technique for measuring classroom behavior." Journal of Educational Psychology 49: 86–92.

3677. Medow, Herman, and Alvin Zander
1965   "Aspirations for the group chosen by central and peripheral members." Journal of Personality and Social Psychology 1 (3, March): 224–228. P.A. 39:10005; S.A. 13:B7596.

3678. Meeker, Barbara F.
1971   "Decisions and exchange." American Sociological Review 36 (3, June): 485–495.

3679. Meertens, R. W.
1972   "Meaningfulness of scales and extremity of ratings: A replication." Nederlands Tijdschrift voor de Psychologie en haar Grensgebieden 27 (5, May): 273–276. P.A. 49:6835.

3680. Megargee, Edwin I., Patricia Bogart, and Betty J. Anderson
1966   "Prediction of leadership in a simulated industrial task." Journal of Applied Psychology 50 (4): 292–295. P.A. 40:11112.

3681. Mehlman, Benjamin
1962   "Similarity in friendships." Journal of Social Psychology 57 (June): 195–202.

3682. Mehrabian, Albert
    1968a   "Inference of attitudes from the posture, orientation, and distance of a communicator." Journal of Consulting and Clinical Psychology 32 (3): 296-308. P.A. 42:13684.
3683.   1968b   "Relationship of attitude to seated posture, orientation, and distance." Journal of Personality and Social Psychology 10 (1): 26-30. P.A. 43:791.
3684.   1969   "Significance of posture and position in the communication of attitude and status relationships." Psychological Bulletin 71 (5): 359-372. P.A. 43:11234.
3685.   1970a   "A semantic space for nonverbal behavior." Journal of Consulting and Clinical Psychology 35 (2): 248-257.
3686.   1970b   "Some determinants of affiliation and conformity." Psychological Reports 27 (1, August): 19-29. P.A. 45:6199.
3687.   1971a   Silent Messages. Belmont, Calif.: Wadsworth. P.A. 49:4431.
3688.   1971b   "Verbal and nonverbal interaction of strangers in a waiting situation." Journal of Experimental Research in Personality 5 (2, June): 127-138. P.A. 48:869.
3689. Mehrabian, Albert, and Shirley G. Diamond
    1971a   "Effects of furniture arrangement, props, and personality on social interaction." Journal of Personality and Social Psychology 20 (1, October): 18-30. P.A. 47:6687.
3690.   1971b   "Seating arrangement and conversation." Sociometry 34 (2, June): 281-289. P.A. 49:788; S.A. 20:F8112.
3691. Mehrabian, Albert, and Sheldon Ksionzky
    1970   "Models for affiliative and conformity behavior." Psychological Bulletin 74 (2): 110-126. P.A. 44:20827.
3692.   1971   "Factors of interpersonal behavior and judgment in social groups." Psychological Reports 28 (2, April): 483-492. P.A. 46:6756.
3693.   1972a   "Categories of social behavior." Comparative Group Studies 3 (4, November): 425-436. P.A. 51:955.
3694.   1972b   "Some determiners of social interaction." Sociometry 35 (4, December): 588-609. P.A. 50:957.
3695. Mehrabian, Albert, and Martin Williams
    1969   "Nonverbal concomitants of perceived and intended persuasiveness." Journal of Personality and Social Psychology 13 (1): 37-58.
3696. Meisels, Murray, and Francis M. Canter
    1970   "Personal space and personality characteristics: A non-confirmation." Psychological Reports 27: 287-290.
3697. Meisels, Murray, and Michael A. Dosey
    1971   "Personal space, anger-arousal, and psychological defense." Journal of Personality 39: 333-344.
3698. Meister, Albert
    1961   ("Organized participation and spontaneous participation: Some studies on small groups in the United States.") L'Année Sociologique, pp. 131-161. S.A. 12:B0858.
3699. Melbin, Murray
    1972   Alone and with Others: A Grammer of Interpersonal Behavior. New York: Harper & Row.
3700. Mellinger, Glen D.
    1956   "Interpersonal trust as a factor in communication." Journal of Abnormal and Social Psychology 52: 304-309. P.A. 31:5178.
3701. Meltzer, Leo, William N. Morris, and Donald P. Hayes
    1971   "Interruption outcomes and vocal amplitude: Explorations in social psychophysics." Journal of Personality and Social Psychology 18 (3, June): 392-402. P.A. 46:6757.
3702. Meltzer, Leo, and Nancy F. Russo
    1970   "Interpersonal evaluation as a function of social attention." Journal of Social Psychology 81: 79-86.
3703. Mengert, Ida G.
    1931   "A preliminary study of the reactions of two-year-old children to each other when paired in a semi-controlled situation." Journal of

Genetic Psychology 39: 393–398. P.A. 6:463.

3704. Menges, Robert J.
1973   "Openness and honesty versus coercion and deception in psychological research." American Psychologist 28 (12): 1030–1034.

3705. Merei, Ferenc
1949   "Group leadership and institutionalization." Human Relations 2: 23–39. (See also Swanson, Newcomb, and Hartley, 1952; Maccoby, Newcomb, and Hartley, 1958.) P.A. 23:3684.

3706.   1971   "The pair and the group: Experiments in group dynamics with children." Comparative Group Studies 2 (1, February): 17–24.

3707. Merrens, Matthew R.
1973   "Nonemergency helping behavior in various sized communities." Journal of Social Psychology 90 (2, August): 327–328. P.A. 51: 933.

3708. Merrick, Richard, and Stuart P. Taylor
1970   "Aggression as a function of vulnerability to attack." Psychonomic Science 20 (4, August): 203–204. P.A. 45:2297.

3709. Merrill, Barbara
1946   "A measurement of mother-child interaction." Journal of Abnormal and Social Psychology 41: 37–49. P.A. 20:2006.

3710. Mertesdorf, Frank, Helmut E. Lück, and Ernst Timaeus
1969   "Heartrate in an Asch-type conformity situation." Perceptual and Motor Skills 29 (2): 565–566. P.A. 44:3545.

3711. Merton, Robert K.
1948   "The social psychology of housing." In W. Dennis, R. Lippitt, et al., Current Trends in Social Psychology, pp. 163–217. Pittsburgh: University of Pittsburgh Press. P.A. 23:5482.

3712. Messé, Lawrence A.
1971   "Equity in bilateral bargaining." Journal of Personality and Social Psychology 17 (3, March): 287–291. P.A. 46:1089.

3713. Messé, Lawrence A., Joel Aronoff, and John P. Wilson
1972   "Motivation as a mediator of the mechanisms underlying role assignments in small groups." Journal of Personality and Social Psychology 24 (1, October): 84–90. P.A. 49:4432.

3714. Messé, Lawrence A., Martin Bolt, and Jack Sawyer
1971   "Nonstructural determinants of behavior in the replicated Prisoner's Dilemma game." Psychonomic Science 25 (4, November): 238–240. P.A. 48:11455.

3715. Messé, Lawrence A., Jack E. Dawson, and Irving M. Lane
1973   "Equity as a mediator of the effect of reward level on behavior in the Prisoner's Dilemma game." Journal of Personality and Social Psychology 26 (1, April): 60–65. P.A. 50:4814.

3716. Messé, Lawrence A., and Irving M. Lane
1974   "Rediscovering the need for multiple operations: A reply to Austin and Susmilch." Journal of Personality and Social Psychology 30 (3): 405–408.

3717. Messick, David M.
1967   "Interdependent decision strategies in zero-sum games: A computer-controlled study." Behavioral Science 12 (1, January): 33–48. S.A. 15:C5884.

3718. Messick, David M., and Charles G. McClintock
1967   "Measures of homogeneity in two-person, two-choice games." Behavioral Science 12 (6, November): 474–479. S.A. 16:D1447.

3719.   1968   "Motivational bases of choice in experimental games." Journal of Experimental Social Psychology 4 (January): 1–25.

3720. Messick, David M., and Glenn Reeder
1972   "Perceived motivation, role variations, and the attribution of personal characteristics." Journal of Experimental Social Psychology 8 (5, September): 482–491. P.A. 49:6836.

3721. Messick, David M., and Warren B. Thorngate
1967   "Relative gain maximization in experimental games." Journal of Experimental Social Psychology 3 (January): 85–101.

3722. Messick, Samuel J., and D. N. Jackson
       1957   "Authoritarianism or acquiescence in Bass's data." Journal of Ab-
               normal and Social Psychology 54: 424–426.
3723. Mettee, David R.
       1971a   "Changes in liking as a function of the magnitude and effect of se-
               quential evaluations." Journal of Experimental Social Psychology 7
               (2, March): 157–172. P.A. 46:4844.
3724. 1971b   "The true discerner as a potent source of positive affect." Journal of
               experimental Social Psychology 7 (3): 292–303.
3725. Mettee, David R., and John Riskind
       1974   "Size of defeat and liking for superior and similar ability competi-
               tors." Journal of Experimental Social Psychology 10 (4, July): 333–
               351. P.A. 52:12337.
3726. Mettee, David R., Shelley E. Taylor, and Stuart Fisher
       1971   "The effect of being shunned upon the desire to affiliate." Psycho-
               nomic Sciences 23 (6, June): 429–431. P.A. 48:9024.
3727. Metz, A. Stafford
       1965   "A comparison of the use of the sound recording and the written
               transcript in the coding of verbal interaction." Journal of Social
               Psychology 65: 325–335.
3728. Meumann, E.
       1904   ("Home and school work.") Die Deutsche Schule 8: 278–303, 337–
               359, 416–431.
3729. Meunier, Clement, and Brendan G. Rule
       1967   "Anxiety, confidence, and conformity." Journal of Personality 35
               (3): 498–504. P.A. 42:2505.
3730. Meux, Eleanor P.
       1973   "Concern for the common good in an N-person game." Journal of
               Personality and Social Psychology 28 (3, December): 414–418.
               P.A. 51:7082.
3731. Meyer, Timothy P.
       1972a   "Effects of viewing justified and unjustified real film violence on ag-
               gressive behavior." Journal of Personality and Social Psychology 23
               (1): 21–29.
3732. 1972b   "The effects of sexually arousing and violent films on aggressive be-
               havior." Journal of Sex Research 8 (4, November): 324–331. P.A.
               50:960.
3733. Meyer, William J., and Mary A. Barbour
       1968   "Generality of individual and group social attractiveness over several
               rating situations." Journal of Genetic Psychology 113 (1): 101–108.
               P.A. 43:792.
3734. Meyer, William J., and George G. Thompson
       1956   "Sex differences in the distribution of teacher approval and dis-
               approval among sixth-grade children." Journal of Educational Psy-
               chology 47: 385–396.
3735. Meyers, C[harles] E.
       1944   "The effect of conflicting authority on the child." University of
               Iowa Studies in Child Welfare 20: 31–98. P.A. 19:3531.
3736. Mezei, Louis
       1971   "Perceived social pressure as an explanation of shifts in the relative
               influence of race and belief on prejudice across social interactions."
               Journal of Personality and Social Psychology 19 (1, July): 69–81.
               P.A. 46:8936.
3737. Michelini, Ronald L.
       1971   "Effects of prior interaction, contact, strategy, and expectation of
               meeting on game behavior and sentiment." Journal of Conflict Reso-
               lution 15 (1, March): 97–103. P.A. 48:2893.
3738. Michener, H. Andrew, and Eugene D. Cohen
       1973   "Effects of punishment magnitude in the bilateral threat situa-
               tion: Evidence for the deterrence hypothesis." Journal of Person-
               ality and Social Psychology 26 (3, June): 427–438. P.A. 50:
               11256.

3739. Michener, H. Andrew, James Griffith, and Robert L. Palmer
     1971   "Threat potential and rule enforceability as sources of normative emergence in a bargaining situation." Journal of Personality and Social Psychology 20 (2, November): 230-239. P.A. 47:6688.
3740. Michener, H. Andrew, and Edward J. Lawler
     1971   "Revolutionary coalition strength and collective failure as determinants of status reallocation." Journal of Experimental Social Psychology 7 (4, July): 448-460. P.A. 48:2894.
3741. Michener, H. Andrew, Edward J. Lawler, and Samuel B. Bacharach
     1973   "Perception of power in conflict situations." Journal of Personality and Social Psychology 28 (2): 155-162.
3742. Michener, H. Andrew, and Morgan Lyons
     1972   "Perceived support and upward mobility as determinants of revolutionary coalitional behavior." Journal of Experimental Social Psychology 8 (2): 180-195. (See also Crosbie, 1975.)
3743. Michener, H. Andrew, and Margaret Schwertfeger
     1972   "Liking as a determinant of power tactic preference." Sociometry 35 (1, March): 190-202. P.A. 49:789.
3744. Michener, H. Andrew, and Mark Tausig
     1971   "Usurpation and perceived support as determinants of the endorsement accorded formal leaders." Journal of Personality and Social Psychology 18 (3): 364-372.
3745. Michener, H. Andrew, and Richard A. Zeller
     1972   "The effects of coalition strength on the formation of contractual norms." Sociometry 35 (2, June): 290-304. P.A. 49:790; S.A. 21: 73G4904.
3746. Middleton, Marino A., and Lawrence Warren
     1972   "Risk-taking effects on group decision making." Journal of Psychology 82 (2, November): 189-196. P.A. 49:6838.
3747. Midlarsky, Elizabeth S.
     1968a   "Aiding responses: An analysis and review." Merrill-Palmer Quarterly 14 (3): 229-260. P.A. 43:5300.
3748.   1968b   "Some antecedents of aiding under stress." Proceedings of the 76th Annual Convention of the American Psychological Association 3: 385-386.
3749. Midlarsky, Elizabeth S., and James H. Bryan
     1972   "Affect expressions and children's imitative altruism." Journal of Experimental Research in Personality 6 (2-3, December): 195-203. P.A. 51:997.
3750. Midlarsky, Elizabeth S., and Manus I. Midlarsky
     1970   "Aiding under stress: The effects of competence, status, and cost to the aider." Proceedings of the 78th Annual Convention of the American Psychological Association 5 (pt. 1): 439-440. P.A. 44:18569.
3751.   1973   "Some determinants of aiding under experimentally-induced stress." Journal of Personality 41 (3, September): 305-327. P.A. 51:5108.
3752. Midlarsky, Manus I., and Elizabeth S. Midlarsky
     1972   "Additive and interactive status effects on altruistic behavior." Proceedings of the 80th Annual Convention of the American Psychological Association 7 (pt. 1): 245-246. P.A. 48:4873.
3753. Mikula, Gerold
     1972a   ("Equity distribution behavior in same-sex dyads: A comparative study between Austrian and American students.") Psychologie und Praxis 16 (3, July): 97-106. P.A. 52:836.
3754.   1972b   ("Studies concerning the reliability of sociometric data.") Zeitschrift für Sozialpsychologie 3 (1): 51-54. P.A. 48:11456.
3755.   1972c   ("Profit sharing in dyads with varying performance ratios.") Zeitschrift für Sozialpsychologie 3 (2): 126-133. P.A. 49:6840.
3756.   1972d   ("The importance of achievement in sharing profits: An investigation with sexually heterogeneous dyads.") Psychologische Beitrage 14 (2): 283-291. P.A. 49:6839.
3757.   1974   "Nationality, performance, and sex as determinants of reward allocation." Journal of Personality and Social Psychology 29 (4, April):

435-440. P.A. 52:7568.

3758. Mikula, Gerold, and Hans Uray
　　1973　("Neglecting individual performances in the allocation of reward in social work settings.") Zeitschrift für Sozialpsychologie 4 (2): 136-144. P.A. 52:837.

3759. Mikula, Gerold, and H. Walter
　　1969　("Observations of group-dynamic developments in a four-man expedition team.") Psychologie und Praxis 13 (4): 145-155. P.A. 44: 12471.

3760. Milburn, Thomas W.
　　1961　"Space crews: Psychology, and American society." Journal of Social Issues 17 (2): 24-28. S.A. 11:A4159.

3761. Milgram, Stanley
　　1963　"Behavioral study of obedience." Journal of Abnormal and Social Psychology 67 (4): 371-378. (See also Crosbie, 1975.)

3762.　1964　"Group pressure and action against a person." Journal of Abnormal and Social Psychology 69 (2, August): 137-143. P.A. 39:4878; S.A. 14:B8349.

3763.　1965a　"Liberating effects of group pressure." Journal of Personality and Social Psychology 1 (2, February): 127-134. P.A. 39:7639; S.A. 13:B6759.

3764.　1965b　"Some conditions of obedience and disobedience to authority." Human Relations 18 (1, February): 57-75. S.A. 13:B6760.

3765.　1966　("Some conditions for obedience to authority and refusal thereof.") Zeitschrift für Experimentelle und Angewandte Psychologie 13 (3): 433-463. P.A. 40:13162.

3766. Milgram, Stanley, Leonard Bickman, and Lawrence Berkowitz
　　1969　"Note on the drawing power of crowds of different size." Journal of Personality and Social Psychology 13 (2): 79-82. P.A. 44:589.

3767. Miller, Arthur G.
　　1972　"Effect of attitude similarity-dissimilarity on the utilization of additional stimulus inputs in judgments of interpersonal attraction." Psychonomic Science 26 (4, February): 199-203. P.A. 48:11457.

3768. Miller, Arthur G., Barry Gillen, Charles Schenker, and Shirley Radlove
　　1973　"The perception of obedience to authority." Proceedings of the 81st Annual Convention of the American Psychological Association 8: 127-128. P.A. 50:4816.

3769.　1974　"The prediction and perception of obedience to authority." Journal of Personality 42 (1, March): 23-42. P.A. 52:7569.

3770. Miller, David
　　1970　"The effects of immediate and delayed audio- and video-taped feedback on group counseling." Comparative Group Studies 1 (1, February): 19-46.

3771. Miller, Delbert C.
　　1939　"An experiment in the measurement of social interaction in group discussion." American Sociological Review 4: 341-351. P.A. 14: 455.

3772. Miller, Derek H.
　　1966　"Staff training in the penal system: The use of small groups." Human Relations 19 (2, May): 151-163.

3773. Miller, Frank B.
　　1958-　"'Situational interactions': A worthwhile concept?" Human Organi-
　　1959　zation 17 (4, Winter): 37-47. S.A. A1128.

3774.　1967　"Humor in a Chippewa tribal council." Ethnology 6 (3, July): 263-271. S.A. 16:D0610.

3775. Miller, G. H., and S. W. Pyke
　　1973　"Sex, matrix variations, and perceived personality effects in mixed-motive games." Journal of Conflict Resolution 17 (2, June): 335-349. P.A. 51:5039.

3776. Miller, Gerald R., and William R. Tiffany
　　1963　"The effects of group pressure on judgments of speech sounds." Journal of Speech and Hearing Research 6 (2): 149-156. P.A.

38:875.

3777. Miller, Harold
    1970   "Is the risky shift the result of a rational group decision?" Proceedings of the 78th Annual Convention of the American Psychological Association 5 (pt. 1): 333-334. P.A. 44:18570.

3778. Miller, Harold, and Dennis Geller
    1972   "Structural balance in dyads." Journal of Personality and Social Psychology 21 (2): 135-138.

3779. Miller, James G. (ed.)
    1950   Experiments in Social Process. New York: McGraw-Hill. P.A. 25: 1699.

3780. Miller, James G.
    1955   "Toward a general theory for the behavioral sciences." American Psychologist 10: 513-531. P.A. 30:3687.

3781.   1971   "Living systems: The group." Behavioral Science 16 (4, July): 302-398. S.A. 20:F6015.

3782. Miller, K. M., and J. B. Biggs
    1958   "Attitude change through undirected group discussion." Journal of Educational Psychology 49: 224-228.

3783. Miller, L. Keith, and Robert L. Hamblin
    1963   "Interdependence, differential rewarding, and productivity." American Sociological Review 28 (5, October): 768-778. P.A. 38:5967; S.A. 12:A8716.

3784. Miller, Norman
    1968   "Contrast effects between communicators." Journal of Experimental Social Psychology 4 (April): 188-198.

3785. Miller, Norman, and Donald C. Butler
    1969   "Social power and communication in small groups." Behavioral Science 14 (1, January): 11-18. P.A. 43:6845; S.A. 18:E1782.

3786. Miller, Norman, Donald C. Butler, and James A. McMartin
    1969   "The ineffectiveness of punishment power in group interaction." Sociometry 32 (1, March): 24-42. P.A. 43:9657; S.A. 18:E1783.

3787. Miller, Norman, Donald T. Campbell, Helen Twedt, and Edward J. O'Connell
    1966   "Similarity, contrast, and complementarity in friendship choice." Journal of Personality and Social Psychology 3 (1): 3-12. P.A. 40: 2822.

3788. Miller, Norman, and Kenneth L. Dion
    1970   "An analysis of the familiarization explanation of the risky shift." Proceedings of the 78th Annual Convention of the American Psychological Association 5 (pt. 1): 337-338.

3789. Miller, Norman, and Burton H. Levy
    1967   "Defaming and agreeing with the communicator as a function of emotional arousal, communication extremity, and evaluative set." Sociometry 30 (2, June): 158-175.

3790. Miller, Ralph R.
    1967   "No play: A means of conflict resolution." Journal of Personality and Social Psychology 6 (2): 150-156.

3791. Miller, Tiiu-Imbi, and Patrick McC. Miller
    1973   "Some fantasy correlates of experimentally aroused aggression." British Journal of Social and Clinical Psychology 12 (4, November): 378-383. P.A. 52:810.

3792. Mills, Judson
    1967   "Comments on Bem's 'Self-perception: An alternative interpretation of cognitive dissonance phenomena.'" Psychological Review 74 (6): 535. P.A. 42:2506.

3793.   1971   "Effect on opinion change of the communicator's liking for the audience he addressed." Psychonomic Science 25 (6, December): 335-337. P.A. 48:8985.

3794. Mills, Judson, and Ronald Egger
    1972   "Effect on derogation of a victim of choosing to reduce his distress." Journal of Personality and Social Psychology 23 (3): 405-408.

3795. Mills, Judson, and John Harvey
  1972   "Opinion change as a function of when information about the com-
          municator is received and whether he is attractive or expert." Jour-
          nal of Personality and Social Psychology 21 (1): 52–55.
3796. Mills, Judson, and Charles E. Kimble
  1973   "Opinion change as a function of perceived similarity of the com-
          municator and subjectivity of the issue." Bulletin of the Psycho-
          nomic Society 2 (1, July): 35–36. P.A. 51:7083.
3797. Mills, Judson, and Paul M. Mintz
  1972   "Effect of unexplained arousal on affiliation." Journal of Personal-
          ity and Social Psychology 24 (1): 11–13.
3798. Mills, Judson, and Edgar O'Neal
  1971   "Anticipated choice, attention, and halo effect." Psychonomic Sci-
          ence 22 (4, February): 231–233. P.A. 46:8937.
3799. Mills, Theodore M.
  1951   "A method of content analysis for the study of small groups." Ph.D.
          dissertation. Harvard University.
3800.   1953   "Power relations in three-person groups." American Sociological Re-
          view 18: 351–357. (See also Cartwright and Zander, 1953, 1960.)
          P.A. 28:4145; S.A. 89.
3801.   1954   "The coalition pattern in three-person groups." American Socio-
          logical Review 19: 657–667. P.A. 30:2668.
3802.   1956   "Developmental process in three-person groups." Human Relations
          9: 343–354. P.A. 32:2764; S.A. 5022.
3803.   1962   "A sleeper variable in small group research: The experimenter."
          Pacific Sociological Review 5 (1): 21–28. P.A. 37:4885.
3804.   1964   Group Transformation. Englewood Cliffs, N.J.: Prentice-Hall.
3805.   1967   The Sociology of Small Groups. Englewood Cliffs, N.J.: Prentice-
          Hall.
3806. Mills, Theodore M., Hope Lichter, and Gene Kassebaum
  1957   "Frankness and consensus." Mimeo. Cambridge, Mass.: Harvard Uni-
          versity, Laboratory of Social Relations.
3807. Mills, Theodore M., and Stan Rosenberg (eds.)
  1970   Readings on the Sociology of Small Groups. Englewood Cliffs, N.J.:
          Prentice-Hall. P.A. 46:8938; S.A. 20:F6954.
3808. Mills, Theodore M., et al.
  1957   "Group structure and the newcomer: An experimental study of
          group expansion." University of Oslo Institute of Sociology, Studies
          in Society No. 1. S.A. 4685.
3809. Milton, G. A.
  1965   "Enthusiasm vs. effectiveness in group and individual problem-solv-
          ing." Psychological Reports 16: 1197–1201.
3810. Minas, J. Sayer, Alvin Scodel, David Marlow, and Harve Rawson
  1960   "Some descriptive aspects of two-person non-zero-sum games, II."
          Journal of Conflict Resolution 4 (2, June): 193–197. S.A. 11:
          A4596.
3811. Mindock, Richard
  1972   "Risk taking as a function of an individual's impression of the power
          situation." Psychological Reports 31 (2, October): 471–474. P.A.
          49: 6841.
3812. Minton, Henry L., and Arthur G. Miller
  1970   "Group risk taking and internal-external control of group members."
          Psychological Reports 26 (2): 431–436. P.A. 44:20828.
3813. Minturn, Eric B., and Leonard M. Lansky
  1972   "The trainerless laboratory." Journal of Applied Behavioral Sciences
          8 (3): 277–286.
3814. Mintz, Alexander
  1951   "Non-adaptive group behavior." Journal of Abnormal and Social
          Psychology 46: 150–159. (See also Swanson, Newcomb, and Hart-
          ley, 1952; Maccoby, Newcomb, and Hartley, 1958.) P.A. 25:8008.
3815. Mintz, Paul M., and Judson Mills
  1971   "Effects of arousal and information about its source upon attitude

change." Journal of Experimental Social Psychology 7 (6, November): 561–570. P.A. 48:8986.

3816. Mirels, Herbert, and Judson Mills
     1964   "Perception of the pleasantness and competence of a partner." Journal of Abnormal and Social Psychology 68 (4, April): 456–459.

3817. Misovich, Stephen, John J. Colby, and Kenneth Welch
     1973   "Similarity as determinant of social influence in affective judgments." Psychological Reports 33 (3): 803–810.

3818. Misra, Sasi
     1973   "Instability in self-evaluation, conformity, and affiliation." Journal of Personality 41 (3): 361–375.

3819. Mitchell, James V., Jr.
     1956   "The factor analysis of a 'Guess-Who' questionnaire designed to identify significant behavior patterns in children." Journal of Personality 24: 376–386. P.A. 31:1059.

3820. Mitchell, Terence R.
     1970a   "Leader complexity and leadership style." Journal of Personality and Social Psychology 16 (1): 166–174.

3821.   1970b   "The construct validity of three dimensions of leadership research." Journal of Social Psychology 80: 89–94.

3822.   1971   "Cognitive complexity and group performance." Journal of Social Psychology 86 (1, February): 35–43. P.A. 47:10782.

3823. Mitchell, Terence R., and Uriel G. Foa
     1969   "Diffusion of the effect of cultural training of the leader in the structure of heterocultural task groups." Australian Journal of Psychology 21 (1): 31–43. P.A. 43:14235.

3824. Mithaug, Dennis E.
     1973   "The development of procedures for identifying competitive behavior in children." Journal of Experimental Child Psychology 16 (1, August): 76–90. P.A. 51:3049.

3825. Mitnick, Leonard L., and Elliott McGinnies
     1958   "Influencing ethnocentrism in small discussion groups through a film communication." Journal of Abnormal and Social Psychology 56: 82–90.

3826. Mixon, Don
     1971   "Behaviour analysis treating subjects as actors rather than organisms." Journal for the Theory of Social Behaviour 1 (1, April): 19–31. P.A. 51:7011.

3827. Miyamoto, S. Frank, and Sanford M. Dornbusch
     1956   "A test of interactionist hypotheses of self-conception." American Journal of Sociology 61: 399–403. (See also Hare, Borgatta, and Bales, 1965.) P.A. 31:2562; S.A. 3430.

3828. Modigliani, Andre
     1971   "Embarrassment, facework, and eye contact: Testing a theory of embarrassment." Journal of Personality and Social Psychology 17 (1, January): 15–24. P.A. 45:9853.

3829. Moede, W.
     1914   ("Emulation, its structure and extent.") Zeitschrift für Pädagogische Psychologie 15: 353–368, 369–393.

3830.   1920   (Experimental Group Psychology.) Leipzig: Hirzel.

3831.   1927   ("Guidelines for a psychology of achievement.") Industrielle Psychotechnik 4: 193–209.

3832. Moeller, George [O., Jr.], and M. H. Applezweig
     1957   "A motivational factor in conformity." Journal of Abnormal and Social Psychology 55: 114–120.

3833. Moerk, Ernst L.
     1972   "Effects of personality structure on individual activities in a group and on group processes." Human Relations 25 (6, December): 505–513. P.A. 52:7530.

3834. Mogby, Robert B., and Dean G. Pruitt
     1974   "Effects of a threatener's enforcement costs on threat credibility and compliance." Journal of Personality and Social Psychology 29

(2): 173–180.

3835. Mohanna, A. I., and Michael Argyle
    1960   "A cross-cultural study of structured groups with unpopular central members." Journal of Abnormal and Social Psychology 60 (1, January): 139–140. P.A. 34:7589.

3836. Moldawsky, Stanley
    1951   "An empirical validation of a rigidity scale against a criterion of rigidity in an interpersonal situation." Sociometry 14: 153–174. P.A. 27:4111.

3837. Montgomery, L. June
    1973   "The sensitivity movement: Questions to be researched." Small Group Behavior 4 (4, November): 387–406.

3838. Montgomery, Robert L.
    1971   "Status, conformity, and resistance to compliance in natural groups." Journal of Social Psychology 84 (2, August): 197–206. P.A. 47:2845.

3839. Moore, Bert S., Bill Underwood, and D. L. Rosenhan
    1973   "Affect and altruism." Developmental Psychology 8 (1, January): 99–104. P.A. 49:11108.

3840. Moore, Henry T.
    1921   "The comparative influence of majority and expert opinion." American Journal of Psychology 32: 16–20.

3841.   1922   "Further data concerning sex differences." Journal of Abnormal and Social Psychology 17: 210–214.

3842. Moore, James C., Jr.
    1968   "Status and influence in small group interactions." Sociometry 31 (1, March): 47–63. P.A. 42:8880; S.A. 16:D4109.

3843. Moore, James C., Jr., Eugene B. Johnson, and Martha S. Arnold
    1972   "Status congruence and equity in restricted communication networks." Sociometry 35 (4, December): 519–537. P.A. 50:962; S.A. 22:74G6148.

3844. Moore, James C., Jr., and Edward Krupat
    1971   "Relationships between source status, authoritarianism and conformity in a social influence setting." Sociometry 34 (1, March): 122–134. S.A. 20:F8113.

3845. Moore, Larry F., and Alec J. Lee
    1974   "Comparability of interviewer, group, and individual interview ratings." Journal of Applied Psychology 59 (2): 163–167.

3846. Moore, Loretta M., and Reuben M. Baron
    1969   "Effects of wage inequities on work attitudes and performance." Proceedings of the 77th Annual Convention of the American Psychological Association 4 (pt. 1): 361–362.

3847. Moore, Michael F., and David Mack
    1972   "Dominance-ascendance and behavior in the reiterated Prisoner's Dilemma game." Acta Psychologica 36 (6, December): 480–491. P.A. 50:11257.

3848. Moore, Omar K., and Alan R. Anderson
    1962   "Some puzzling aspects of social interaction." Review of Metaphysics 15: 409–433. P.A. 37:4886. (See also Criswell, Solomon, and Suppes, 1962, pp. 232–249. S.A. 12:B2418.)

3849. Moore, Omar K., and Scarvia B. Anderson
    1954   "Search Behavior in individual and group problem solving." American Sociological Review 19: 702–714. P.A. 30:2436.

3850. Moore, Robert J., and Erika E. Feller
    1971   "Seating preferences: Preliminary investigation." Psychological Reports 29: 1073–1074.

3851. Moos, Rudolf H., and Joseph C. Speisman
    1962   "Group compatibility and productivity." Journal of Abnormal and Social Psychology 65 (3, September): 190–196. S.A. 11:A7196.

3852. Moran, Gary
    1965   "Group cohesion and conformity behavior." Psychological Reports 17 (2): 465–466. P.A. 40:1526.

3853.   1966   "Dyadic attraction and orientational consensus." Journal of Personality and Social Psychology 4 (1): 94–99. P.A. 40:10037.

3854. Moran, Gary, and Alan J. Klockars
          1968   "Favorability of group atmosphere and group dimensionality." Psychological Reports 22 (1): 3–6. P.A. 42:10532.

3855. Morehous, L. G.
          1966   "One-play, two-play, five-play, and ten-play runs of Prisoner's Dilemma." Journal of Conflict Resolution 10 (3): 354–362.

3856. Moreno, Florence B.
          1942   Sociometric status of children in a nursery school group." Sociometry 5: 295–411. P.A. 17:1760.

3857. Moreno, Jacob L.
          1941   "Foundations of sociometry, an introduction." Sociometry 4: 15–35. P.A. 15:3521.

3858.   1943   "Sociometry and the cultural order." Sociometry 6: 299–344. P.A. 18:2186.

3859.   1945   Group Psychotherapy. Beacon, N.Y.: Beacon House. P.A. 20:1927.
3860.   1947a   "Contributions of sociometry to research methodology in sociology." American Sociological Review 12: 287–292. (See also Hare, Borgatta, and Bales, 1955, 1965.) P.A. 22:268.

3861.   1947b   The Theatre of Spontaneity, Beacon, N.Y.: Beacon House. P.A. 23:186.

3862.   1951   Sociometry, Experimental Method and the Science of Society. Beacon, N.Y.: Beacon House. P.A. 25:8009.

3863.   1953   Who Shall Survive? Rev. ed. Beacon, N.Y.: Beacon House. (See also Swanson, Newcomb, and Hartley, 1952.) P.A. 28:4178.

3864.   1954   "Old and new trends in sociometry: Turning points in small group research." Sociometry 17: 179–193. P.A. 29:3851.

3865.   1964   "Discussion of J. D. Sutherland's address, recent advances in the understanding of small groups, their disorders and treatment." International Journal of Sociometry and Sociatry 4 (1-2, March-June): 56–59. S.A. 13:B6761.

3866. Moreno, Jacob L., and Helen H. Jennings
          1938   "Statistics of social configurations." Sociometry 1: 342–374.

3867.   1944   "Sociometric methods of grouping and regrouping: With reference to authoritative and democratic methods of grouping." Sociometry 7: 397–414. P.A. 19:1748.

3868. Moreno, Jacob L., Helen H. Jennings, and J. Sargent
          1940   "Time as a qualitative index to interpersonal relations." Sociometry 3: 62–80. P.A. 14:3663.

3869. Moreno, Jacob L., et al.
          1960   The Sociometry Reader. New York: Free Press. P.A. 36:1GE73M.

3870. Morgan, Wesley G.
          1973   "Situational specificity in altruistic behavior." Representative Research in Social Psychology 4 (2, June): 56–66. P.A. 51:3052.

3871. Morgan, William R., and Jack Sawyer
          1967   "Bargaining, expectations, and the preference for equality over equity." Journal of Personality and Social Psychology 6 (2): 139–149.

3872.   1968   "How presumed disadvantage hurts cooperation." Proceedings of the 76th Annual Convention of the American Psychological Association 3: 403–404.

3873. Moriarty, Thomas
          1974   "Role of stigma in the experience of deviance." Journal of Personality and Social Psychology 29 (6): 849–855.

3874. Morozov, Y. I., and S. S. Papovyan
          1973   ("The operational definition of 'leadership' in social psychology.") Voprosy Psikhologii 19 (1, January): 59–68. P.A. 51:7035.

3875. Morris, Charles G.
          1966   "Task effects on group interaction." Journal of Personality and Social Psychology 4 (5, November): 545–554. S.A. 16:D2323.

3876.   1970   "Changes in group interaction during problem solving." Journal of

Social Psychology 81 (2): 157–165. P.A. 44:20830.

3877. Morris, Charles G., and J. Richard Hackman
    1969   "Behavioral Correlates of perceived leadership." Journal of Personality and Social Psychology 13 (4): 350–361. P.A. 44:3546.

3878. Morris, Sheridan C., III, and Sidney Rosen
    1973   "Effects of felt adequacy and opportunity to reciprocate on help seeking." Journal of Experimental Social Psychology 9 (3): 265–276.

3879. Morris, William N.
    1971   "Manipulated amplitude and interruption outcomes." Journal of Personality and Social Psychology 20 (3, December): 319–331. P.A. 47:8795.

3880. Morrison, Bruce J., Michael Enzle, Toni Henry, Diana Dunway, Michael Griffin, Kenneth Kneisel, and John Gimperling
    1971   "The effect of electrical shock and warning on cooperation in a non-zero-sum game." Journal of Conflict Resolution 15 (1, March): 105–108. P.A. 48:2897.

3881. Morrissette, Julian O.
    1966   "Group performance as a function of task difficulty and size and structure of group: II." Journal of Personality and Social Psychology 3 (3, March): 357–359. S.A. 15:C3481.

3882. Morrissette, Julian O., John Jahnke, and Keith Baker
    1966   "Structural balance: A test of the completeness hypothesis." Behavioral Science 11 (2, March): 121–125. S.A. 15:3482.

3883. Morrissette, Julian O., John Jahnke, Keith Baker, and Nicholas Rohrman
    1967   "Degree of structural balance and group effectiveness." Organizational Behavior and Human Performance 2 (4): 383–393. P.A. 42: 2499.

3884. Morrissette, Julian O., William H. Pearson, and S. A. Switzer
    1965   "A mathematically defined task for the study of group performance." Human Relations 18 (2, May): 187–192. P.A. 39:15050; S.A. 14:B9184.

3885. Morrissette, Julian O., S.A. Switzer, and Clarke W. Crannell
    1965   "Group performance as a function of size, structure, and task difficulty." Journal of Personality and Social Psychology 2 (3): 451–455. P.A. 39:15051.

3886. Morsbach, Helmut
    1973   "Aspects of nonverbal communication in Japan." Journal of Nervous and Mental Disease 157 (4, October): 262–277. P.A. 51:5064.

3887. Moscovici, Fela
    1972   ("Sensitivity training: A study of perceptions.") Arquivos Brasileiros de Psicologia Aplicada 24 (1, January): 63–72. P.A. 49:2360.

3888. Moscovici, Serge, and Willem Doise
    1974   "Decision making in groups." In C. Nemeth, Social Psychology: Classic and Contemporary Integrations. Chicago: Rand McNally. P.A. 52:12269.

3889. Moscovici, Serge, Willem Doise, and Renaud Dulong
    1972   "Studies in group decision: II. Differences of positions, differences of opinion and group polarization." European Journal of Social Psychology 2 (4): 385–399. P.A. 50:6741; S.A. 22:74G6151.

3890. Moscovici, Serge, E. Lage, and M. Naffrechoux
    1969   "Influence of a consistent minority on the responses of a majority in a color perception task." Sociometry 32 (4): 365–380. P.A. 44: 6678.

3891. Moscovici, Serge, and Roger Lecuyer
    1972   "Studies in group decision: I. Social space, patterns of communication and group consensus." European Journal of Social Psychology 2 (3): 221–244. P.A. 50:4818; S.A. 22:74G6149.

3892. Moscovici, Serge, and Patricia Nève
    1971   "Studies in social influence: I. Those absent are in the right: Convergence and polarization of answers in the course of a social interaction." European Journal of Social Psychology 1 (2): 201–214.

S.A. 22:74G6150.
3893. Moscovici, Serge, and Marisa Zavalloni
1969   "The group as a polarizer of attitudes." Journal of Personality and Social Psychology 12 (2): 125-135.
3894. Moscovici, Serge, Marisa Zavalloni, and Christiane Louis-Guerin
1972   "Studies on polarization of judgments: I. Group effects on person perception." European Journal of Social Psychology 2 (1): 87-91. P.A. 49:2362; S.A. 22:74G6161.
3895. Moscovici, Serge, Marisa Zavalloni, and Monique Weinberger
1972   "Studies on polarization of judgments: II. Person perception, ego involvement and group interaction." European Journal of Social Psychology 2 (1): 92-94. P.A. 49:2361.
3896. Moscow, David
1971   "T-group training in the Netherlands: An evaluation and cross-cultural comparison." Journal of Applied Behavioral Science 7 (4, July-August): 427-448. S.A. 20:F9136.
3897. Moser, Ulrich
1968   ("On the psychology of mutual understanding.") Psyche (Stuttgart) 22 (1): 50-66. P.A. 42:10518.
3898. Mosher, Donald L.
1967   "The learning of congruent and noncongruent social structures." Journal of Social Psychology 73 (2, December): 285-290. P.A. 42: 3912.
3899. Moss, Martin K., and Frank Andrasik
1973   "Belief similarity and interracial attraction." Journal of Personality 41 (2, June): 192-205. P.A. 51:3053.
3900. Moss, Martin K., and Richard A. Page
1972   "Reinforcement and helping behavior." Journal of Applied Social Psychology 2 (4, October): 360-371. P.A. 50:2959.
3901. Motz, Annabelle B.
1952   "The role conception inventory: A tool for research in social psychology." American Sociological Review 17: 465-471. P.A. 27: 6489.
3902. Mouton, Jane S., and Robert R. Blake
1962   "The influence of competitively vested interests on judgments." Journal of Conflict Resolution 6 (2): 149-153.
3903.   1963   "Influence of partially vested interests on judgment." Journal of Abnormal and Social Psychology 66 (3): 276-278. P.A. 37:7948.
3904. Mouton, Jane S., Robert R. Blake, and B. Fruchter
1955a   "The reliability of sociometric measures." Sociometry 18: 7-48. P.A. 30:5884.
3905.   1955b   "The validity of sociometric responses." Sociometry 18: 181-206. S.A. 3142.
3906. Mouton, Jane S., Robert R. Blake, and Joseph A. Olmstead
1956   "The relationship between frequency of yielding and the disclosure of personal identity." Journal of Personality 24: 339-347. P.A. 31: 771.
3907. Moxley, Robert L., and Nancy F. Moxley
1974   "Determining point-centrality in uncontrived social networks." Sociometry 37 (1): 122-130.
3908. Mucchielli, Roger
1963   (Sociometric Models and Formation of Small Groups: An Active Method of Formation through Communication and Cooperation.) Paris: Presses Universitaires de France. P.A. 38:10091.
3909. Mudd, Samuel A.
1968   "Group sanction severity as a function of degree of behavior deviation and relevance of norm." Journal of Personality and Social Psychology 8 (3, pt. 1): 258-260. P.A. 42:8870.
3910. Mugny, Gabriel, Blaise Pierrehumbert, and Rosita Zubel
1972-   ("Style of interaction as a factor of social influence.") Bulletin de
1973   Psychologie 26 (14-16): 789-793. P.A. 51:2952.

3911. Mukerji, N. P.
    1940   "An investigation of ability in work in groups and in isolation." British Journal of Psychology 30: 352-356. P.A. 14:3781.
3912. Mulder, Mauk
    1959a   "Power and satisfaction in task-oriented groups." Acta Psychologica 16: 178-225. P.A. 34:5737.
3913.   1959b   "Group-structure and group-performance." Acta Psychologica 16: 356-402. P.A. 34:5736.
3914.   1960a   "Communication structure, decision structure and group performance." Sociometry 23 (1, March): 1-14. P.A. 35:2125.
3915.   1960b   "The power variable in communication experiments." Human Relations 13 (3, August): 241-257. P.A. 35:2126.
3916.   1963   Group Structure, Motivation and Group Performance. The Hague: Mouton.
3917. Mulder, Mauk, and Ad Stemerding
    1963   "Threat, attraction to group, and need for strong leadership." Human Relations 16 (4, November): 317-334.
3918. Mulder, Mauk, Rob van Dijk, et al.
    1965   "Non-instrumental liking tendencies toward powerful group-members." Acta Psychologica 22 (4): 367-386. P.A. 39:15080.
3919. Mulder, Mauk, Peter Veen, Dolf Hartsuiker, and Ton Westerduin
    1971   "Cognitive processes in power equalization." European Journal of Social Psychology 1 (1): 107-130. P.A. 48:7115; S.A. 22:74G6152.
3920. Mulder, Mauk, Peter Veen, Theo Hijzen, and Peggy Jansen
    1973   "On power equalization: A behavioral example of power-distance reduction." Journal of Personality and Social Psychology 26 (2, May): 151-158. P.A. 50:11258.
3921. Mulder, Mauk, Peter Veen, Claes Rodenburg, Jos Frenken, and Harry Tielens
    1973   "The power distance reduction hypothesis on a level of reality." Journal of Experimental Social Psychology 9 (2, March): 87-96. P.A. 50:11259.
3922. Muller, Heinz A.
    1961   ("The use of Bales' categories of interactions in experiments with team work.") Psychologische Rundschau 12: 251-263. P.A. 36: 4GE51M.
3923. Muller, Helgaard P.
    1970   "Relationship between time-span of discretion, leadership behavior, and Fiedler's LPC scores." Journal of Applied Psychology 54 (2): 140-144.
3924. Mumford, Enid M.
    1959   "Social behavior in small groups." Sociological Review 7: 135-157. P.A. 36:3GE35M.
3925. Muney, Barbara F., and Morton Deutsch
    1968   "The effects of role-reversal during the discussion of opposing viewpoints." Journal of Conflict Resolution 12 (3, September): 345-356. P.A. 43:14236; S.A. 18:E0906.
3926. Munroe, Robert L., and Ruth H. Munroe
    1972   "Obedience among children in an East African society." Journal of Cross-Cultural Psychology 3 (4, December): 395-399. P.A. 50: 4819.
3927. Munson, Paul, and Charles A. Kiesler
    1974   "The role of attributions by others in the acceptance of persuasive communications." Journal of Personality 42 (3): 453-466.
3928. Munsterberg, H.
    1914   (Fundamentals of Psychotechnics.) Leipzig: Barth.
3929. Murdoch, Peter
    1967   "Development of contractual norms in a dyad." Journal of Personality and Social Psychology 6 (2): 206-211.
3930.   1968   "Exploitation-accommodations and social responsibility in a bargaining game." Journal of Personality 36 (3): 440-453. P.A. 43: 3953.

3931. Murdoch, Peter, and Dean Rosen
    1970   "Norm formation in an interdependent dyad." Sociometry 33 (3, September): 264-275. P.A. 46:6759; S.A. 19:F0472.
3932. Murphy, Gardner, Lois B. Murphy, and Theodore M. Newcomb
    1937   Experimental Social Psychology. New York: Harper.
3933. Murphy, Lois B.
    1937   Social Behavior and Child Personality: An Exploratory Study of Some Roots of Sympathy. New York: Columbia University.
3934. Murphy, Lois B., and Gardner Murphy
    1935   "The influence of social situations upon the behavior of children." In C. Murchison (ed.), A Handbook of Social Psychology, pp. 1034-1096. Worcester, Mass.: Clark University Press.
3935. Murray, Robert P., and Hugh McGinley
    1972   "Looking as a measure of attraction." Journal of Applied Social Psychology 2 (3, July): 267-274. P.A. 49:6843.
3936. Murray, Victor V.
    1957   "Interaction patterns and felt own power in a simulated work situation." Canadian Review of Sociology and Anthropology 4 (4, November): 219-241. S.A. 17:D5792.
3937. Murstein, Bernard I.
    1957   "Some comments on the measurement of projection and empathy." Journal of Consulting Psychology 21: 81-82.
3938.   1970   "Self and ideal self discrepancy and the choice of marital partner." Proceedings of the 78th Annual Convention of the American Psychological Association 5 (pt. 1): 459-460.
3939.   1972   "Physical attractiveness and marital choice." Journal of Personality and Social Psychology 22 (1): 8-12.
3940. Murstein, Bernard I., and Gary D. Beck
    1972   "Person perception, marriage adjustment, and social desirability." Journal of Consulting and Clinical Psychology 39 (3, December): 396-403. P.A. 50:964.
3941. Mussen, Paul H., and Jerome Kagan
    1958   "Group conformity and perceptions of parents." Child Development 29: 57-60. P.A. 33:8095.
3942. Mussen, Paul H., and Lyman W. Porter
    1959   "Personal motivations and self-conceptions associated with effectiveness and ineffectiveness in emergent groups." Journal of Abnormal and Social Psychology 59: 23-27. P.A. 34:4198.
3943. Muzzy, Robert E., and John J. Moon
    1973   "Modifications of Bales' Monte Carlo model." Simulation and Games 4 (3, September): 295-314. P.A. 52:7531.
3944. Myers, Albert E.
    1962   "Team competition, success, and the adjustment of group members." Journal of Abnormal and Social Psychology 65 (5): 325-332. S.A. 12:A9440.
3945.   1966   "Performance factors contributing to the acquisition of a psychological advantage in competition." Human Relations 19 (3, August): 283-295. S.A. 15:C4803.
3946. Myers, Albert E., and Frederick R. Kling
    1966   "Experience as an 'instructional set' in negotiation." Journal of Social Psychology 68 (2, April): 331-345. P.A. 40:7646.
3947. Myers, Albert E., and Gene E. Myers
    1972   "Discussion of papers on nonverbal communication." Comparative Group Studies 3 (4, November): 487-496.
3948. Myers, David G.
    1974   "Interpersonal comparison processes in choice dilemma responding." Journal of Psychology 86 (2, March): 287-292. P.A. 52:2339.
3949. Myers, David G., and Sidney J. Arenson
    1968   "Stimulus factors in conformity." Journal of Social Psychology 76 (1, October): 37-41. P.A. 43:2536.
3950.   1972   "Enhancement of dominant risk tendencies in group discussion." Psychological Reports 30 (2, April): 615-623. P.A. 50:2960.

3951. Myers, David G., Paul J. Bach, and F. Barry Schreiber
1974 "Normative and informational effects of group interaction." Sociometry 37 (2, June): 275-286. P.A. 52:12340.

3952. Myers, David G., and George D. Bishop
1971 "Enhancement of dominant attitudes in group discussion." Journal of Personality and Social Psychology 20 (3, December): 386-391. P.A. 47:8796.

3953. Myers, David G., and Peter J. Murdoch
1972 "Is risky shift due to disproportionate influence by extreme group members?" British Journal of Social and Clinical Psychology 11 (2, June): 109-114. P.A. 49:6844.

3954. Myers, David G., Peter J. Murdoch, and Gene F. Smith
1970 "Responsibility diffusion and drive enhancement effects on risky shift." Journal of Personality 38 (3, September): 418-425. P.A. 45:4130.

3955. Myers, David G., F. Barry Schreiber, and Donald J. Viel
1974 "Effects of discussion on opinions concerning illegal behavior." Journal of Social Psychology 92 (1): 77-84.

3956. Myers, David G., David W. Wong, and Peter J. Murdoch
1971 "Discussion arguments, information about others' responses, and risky shift." Psychonomic Science 24 (2, July): 81-83. P.A. 48: 9025.

3957. Myers, Gail E., Michele T. Myers, Alvin Goldberg, and Charles E. Welch
1969 "Effect of feedback on interpersonal sensitivity in laboratory training groups." Journal of Applied Behavioral Science 5 (2): 175-185. P.A. 44:10289.

3958. Myers, Jerome L.
1959 "The statistical analysis of some group experiments." Journal of General Psychology 61: 205-210. P.A. 35:746.

3959. Nacci, Peter, Richard E. Stapleton, and James T. Tedeschi
1973a "Frequency and value of benefits as determinants of reciprocity behavior." Psychological Record 23 (1, Winter): 121-128. P.A. 50: 2961.

3960. 1973b "An empirical restatement of the reciprocity norms." Journal of Social Psychology 91 (2): 263-271.

3961. Nacci, Peter, and James T. Tedeschi
1973 "Trust and reactions to threats." Bulletin of the Psychonomic Society 1 (6-A, June): 421-422. P.A. 51:5111.

3962. Nadler, Eugene B.
1959 "Yielding, authoritarianism, and authoritarian ideology regarding groups." Journal of Abnormal and Social Psychology 58: 408-410.

3963. Nadler, Eugene B., and Stephen L. Fink
1970 "Impact of laboratory training on sociopolitical ideology." Journal of Applied Behavioral Science 6 (1): 79-92.

3964. Nagata, Yoshiaki
1965 "The effects of task structure upon group organization process in terms of the relevance of the individual's goal oriented activities." Japanese Journal of Psychology 36 (2): 56-66. P.A. 39:15052.

3965. 1966 "Effects of task structure on the process of group organization in terms of the difficulty of the task: I." Psychological Reports 18 (2): 566. P.A. 40:8793.

3966. Nagel, Jack H.
1968 "Some questions about the concept of power." Behavioral Science 13 (2, March): 129-137. P.A. 42:10519.

3967. Nahemow, Lucille, and Ruth Bennett
1967 "Conformity, persuasibility and counternormative persuasion." Sociometry 30 (1, March): 14-25. S.A. 15:C5585.

3968. Nahinsky, Irwin D.
1969 "A group interaction stochastic model based on balance theoretical considerations." Behavioral Science 14 (4, July): 289-302. P.A. 44:2269; S.A. 18:E5684.

3969. Napier, Herman S.
    1969   "Group learning: Note on undivided vs. equally divided task information." Psychological Reports 24 (3): 847–848. P.A. 44:590.
3970. Napier, Rodney W., and Matti K. Gershenfeld
    1973   Groups: Theory and Experience. Boston: Houghton Mifflin. P.A. 50:11260.
3971. Nash, Dennison J., and Alvin W. Wolfe
    1957   "The stranger in laboratory culture." American Sociological Review 22 (4, August): 400–405. S.A. 4677.
3972. Nash, Michael
    1973   "Unanimity in criminal jury verdicts." Journal of Forensic Psychology 5 (December): 5–13. P.A. 52:7532.
3973. Nash, Roy
    1973   "Clique formation among primary and secondary school children." British Journal of Sociology 24 (3, September): 303–313. P.A. 51: 8999.
3974. Nathan, Peter E.
    1965   "Operant evaluation of change in dyadic relationship intensity." Proceedings of the 73rd Annual Convention of the American Psychological Association: 245–246. P.A. 39:15053.
3975. Naus, Peter J., and John J. Eckenrode
    1974   "Age differences and degree of acquaintance as determinants of interpersonal distance." Journal of Social Psychology 93 (1, June): 133–134. P.A. 52:12270.
3976. Naver, Isabelle, and Robert Helmreich
    1971   "Prior social setting, type of arousal, and birth order as determinants of affiliative preference for a working situation." Representative Research in Social Psychology 2 (2, July): 32–42. P.A. 49:9068.
3977. Naylor, James C., and Terry L. Dickinson
    1969   "Task structure, work structure, and team performance." Journal of Applied Psychology 53 (3, pt. 1): 167–177. P.A. 43:11236.
3978. Nebeker, Delbert M., and Terrence R. Mitchell
    1973   "Expectancy theory predictions of leader behavior." Proceedings of the 81st Annual Convention of the American Psychological Association 8 (2): 575–576.
3979. Neely, J. J., R. V. Heckel, and H. M. Leichtman
    1973   "The effect of race of model and response consequences to the model on imitation in children." Journal of Social Psychology 89 (2, April): 225–231. P.A. 50:6742.
3980. Nehnevajsa, Jiri
    1955a   "Chance expectancy and intergroup choice." Sociometry 18: 153–163. P.A. 30:4400.
3981.   1955b   "Probability in sociometric analysis." Sociometry 18: 678–688.
3982.   1955c   ("The sociometric analysis of groups.") Kölner Zeitschrift für Soziologie und Sozialpsychologie 7: 119–140. S.A. 2493.
3983.   1955d   ("The sociometric analysis of groups.") Kölner Zeitschrift für Soziologie und Sozialpsychologie 7: 280–302. S.A. 2730.
3984. Nejezchleb, Ivo
    1967   ("Comments on methodological problems of sociometry.") Sociologicky Casopis 3 (4): 455–463. S.A. 18:E2908.
3985. Nellesen, Lothar, and Axel Svensson
    1972   ("A factor analytical description of the T-group.") Gruppendynamik Forschung und Praxis 3 (1, March): 92–110. P.A. 50:965.
3986. Nelson, Don A., and Barry L. Meadow
    1971   "Attitude similarity, interpersonal attraction, actual success, as the evaluative perception of that success." Proceedings of the 79th Annual Convention of the American Psychological Association 6 (pt. 1): 283–284.
3987. Nelson, Paul D.
    1964a   "Compatibility among work associates in isolated groups." USN MNRU Reports No. 64-13. P.A. 39:7641.
3988.   1964b   "Similarities and differences among leaders and followers." Journal

of Social Psychology 63 (1, June): 161–167. P.A. 39:1590.

3989.   1964c   "Structural change in small isolated groups." USN MNRU Reports
                  No. 64-24. P.A. 39:7642.
3990. Nelson, Paul D., and E. K. E. Gunderson
         1964   ("Analysis of dimensions of adjustment in small groups.") Bulletin des
                  Études Recherches Psychologiques 13 (2): 111–126. P.A. 39:7640.
3991. Nelson, Stephen D.
         1973   "Objective power, subjective power, and causal attribution in social
                  interaction." Proceedings of the 81st Annual Convention of the
                  American Psychological Association 8: 325–326. P.A. 50:6743.
3992. Nemeth, Charlan
         1970a   "Bargaining and reciprocity." Psychological Bulletin 74 (5, Novem-
                  ber): 297–308. P.A. 45:4131.
3993.   1970b   "Effects of free versus contrained behavior on attraction between
                  people." Journal of Personality and Social Psychology 15 (4): 302–
                  311.
3994. Nemeth, Charlan, and Jack Markowski
         1972   "Conformity and discrepancy of position." Sociometry 35 (4, De-
                  cember): 562–575. P.A. 50:966.
3996. Nemeth, Charlan, and Ruth H. Sosis
         1973   "A simulated jury study: Characteristics of the defendant and the
                  jurors." Journal of Social Psychology 90 (2): 221–229.
3996. Nemeth, Charlan, and Joel Wachtler
         1973   "Consistency and modification of judgment." Journal of Experi-
                  mental Social Psychology 9 (1, January): 65–79. P.A. 50:2962.
3997. Nesbitt, Paul D., and Girard Steven
         1974   "Personal space and stimulus intensity at a Southern California
                  amusement park." Sociometry 37 (1): 105–115.
3998. Neumann, Joseph
         1969   "Influence of group size upon individual anagram solutions." Psy-
                  chological Reports 24 (3): 721–722. P.A. 44:592.
3999. Neuringer, Charles, and Lowell W. Wandke
         1966   "Interpersonal conflicts in persons of high self-concept and low self-
                  concept." Journal of Social Psychology 68 (2, April): 313–322. P.A.
                  40:7647.
4000. Nevill, Dorothy
         1974   "Experimental manipulation of dependency motivation and its
                  effects on eye contact and measures of field dependency." Journal
                  of Personality and Social Psychology 29 (1, January): 72–79. P.A.
                  52:839.
4001. Newberry, Benjamin H.
         1973   "Truth telling in subjects with information about experiments: Who
                  is being deceived?" Journal of Personality and Social Psychology 25
                  (3, March): 369–374. P.A. 50:4820.
4002. Newcomb, Theodore M.
         1929   "The consistency of certain extrovert-introvert behavior patterns in
                  51 problem boys." Columbia University, Teachers College, Contribu-
                  tions to Education 382.
4003.   1943   Personality and Social Change. New York: Dryden. P.A. 17:3460.
4004.   1950   "Role behaviors in the study of individual personality and of
                  groups." Journal of Personality 18: 273–289. P.A. 25:2912.
4005.   1953a   "An approach to the study of communicative acts." Psychological
                  Review 60: 393–404. (See also Hare, Borgatta, and Bales, 1955,
                  1965.) P.A. 28:5963.
4006.   1953b   "Social psychology and group processes." Annual Review of Psy-
                  chology 4: 183–214. P.A. 27:6478.
4007.   1956   "The prediction of interpersonal attraction." American Psychologist
                  11: 575–586. (See also Crosbie, 1975.) P.A. 31:7607.
4008.   1960   "Varieties of interpersonal attraction." In D. Cartwright and A.
                  Zander (eds.), Group Dynamics: Research and Theory, pp. 104–119.
                  Evanston, Ill.: Row, Peterson. (See also Peatman and Hartley (eds.),
                  Festchrift for Gardner Murphy. New York: Harper, 1960.)

4009.　1961　The Acquaintance Process. New York: Holt, Rinehart & Winston. P.A. 36:1GE03N.

4010.　1963　"Stabilities underlying changes in interpersonal attraction." Journal of Abnormal and Social Psychology 66 (4, April): 376–386. (See also Cartwright and Zander, 1968.) P.A. 37:7949; S.A. 12:B1631.

4011. Newman, Robert C., and Donald Pollack
　　　　1973　"Proxemics in deviant adolescents." Journal of Consulting and Clinical Psychology 40 (1, February): 6–8. P.A. 50:968.

4012. Newport, Gene
　　　　1962　"A study of attitudes and leader behavior." Personnel Administration 25 (5): 42–46. P.A. 38:5981.

4013. Newstetter, Wilber I.
　　　　1937　"An experiment in the defining and measuring of group adjustment." American Sociological Review 2: 230–236. P.A. 11:4245.

4014. Newstetter, Wilber I., M. J. Feldstein, and Theodore M. Newcomb
　　　　1938　Group Adjustment: A Study in Experimental Sociology. Cleveland: Western Reserve University, School of Applied Social Sciences.

4015. Newtson, Darren
　　　　1973　"Attribution and the unit of perception of ongoing behavior." Journal of Personality and Social Psychology 28 (1): 28–38.

4016.　1974　"Dispositional inference from effects of actions: Effects chosen and effects forgone." Journal of Experimental Social Psychology 10 (5): 489–496.

4017. Nichols, Keturah A., and B. G. Champness
　　　　1971　"Eye gaze and GSR." Journal of Experimental Social Psychology 7 (6): 623–626.

4018. Nidorf, Louis J.
　　　　1968　"Information-seeking strategies in person perception." Perceptual and Motor Skills 26 (2): 355–365. P.A. 42:12039.

4019. Nidorf, Louis J., and Walter H. Crockett
　　　　1964　"Some factors affecting the amount of information sought about others." Journal of Abnormal and Social Psychology 69 (1, July): 98–101. S.A. 14:B8351.

4020. Nielsen, Gerhard
　　　　1962　Studies in Self-Confrontation: Viewing a Sound Motion Picture of Self and Another Person in a Stressful Dyadic Interaction. Copenhagen: Munksgaard. P.A. 37:6613.

4021. Niemi, Richard G., and Herbert F. Weisberg
　　　　1968　"A mathematical solution for the probability of the paradox of voting." Behavioral Science 13 (4, July): 317–323. P.A. 42:15404.

4022. Niemi, Richard G., and Herbert F. Weisberg (eds.)
　　　　1972　Probability Models of Collective Decision Making. Columbus Ohio: Merrill.

4023. Ninane, Paul, and Fred E. Fiedler
　　　　1970　"Member reactions to success and failure of task groups." Human Relations 23 (1): 3–13. P.A. 44:18571.

4024. Nisbett, Richard E., Craig Caputo, Patricia Legant, and Jeanne Marecek
　　　　1973　"Behavior as seen by the actor and as seen by the observer." Journal of Personality and Social Psychology 27 (2, August): 154–164. P.A. 51:3056.

4025. Nitz, Lawrence H., and James L. Phillips
　　　　1969　"The effects of divisibility of payoff on confederative behavior." Journal of Conflict Resolution 13 (3, September): 381–387.

4026. Niwa, Takaaki
　　　　1968　"A methodological study on the group cohesiveness of sport group based on sociometry." International Review of Sport Sociology 3: 57–71. S.A. 21:73G3963.

4027. Nobler, Hindy
　　　　1972　"Group therapy with male homosexuals." Comparative Group Studies 3 (2, May): 161–178.

4028. Noel, Richard C.
　　　　1973　"Transgression-compliance: A failure to confirm." Journal of Per-

sonality and Social Psychology 27 (2, August): 151–153. P.A. 51: 3057.

4029. Noland, Sarah J., and David W. Catron
1969   "Cooperative behavior among high school students on the Prisoner's Dilemma game." Psychological Reports 24: 711–718.

4030. Nord, Walter R.
1968   "Social exchange theory: An integrative approach to social conformity." Psychological Bulletin 71 (3): 174–208. P.A. 43:8278.

4031. Norfleet, Bobbie
1948   "Interpersonal relations and group productivity." Journal of Social Issues 4 (2): 66–69. P.A. 23:690.

4032. Norrison, W. F., and D. W. Carment
1968   "Participation and opinion change in two-person groups as related to amount of peer group support." British Journal of Social and Clinical Psychology 7 (3): 176–183. P.A. 43:805.

4033. Northway, Mary L.
1952   A Primer of Sociometry. Toronto: University of Toronto Press. P.A. 27:5083.

4034.   1968   "What is sociometry?" Group Psychotherapy 21 (2-3): 110–112. P.A. 45:4133.

4035. Nosanchuk, Terrance A.
1963   "A comparison of several sociometric partitioning techniques." Sociometry 26 (1, March): 112–124.

4036. Nosanchuk, Terrance A., and Jack Lightstone
1974   "Canned laughter and public and private conformity." Journal of Personality and Social Psychology 29 (1): 153–156.

4037. Nottingham, Jack A.
1970   "Attitude extremity and the process of judging others as related to information-seeking behavior." Proceedings of the 78th Annual Convention of the American Psychological Association 5 (1): 409–410.

4038. Novak, David W., and Melvin J. Lerner
1968   "Rejection as a consequence of perceived similarity." Journal of Personality and Social Psychology 9 (2, pt. 1): 147–152. P.A. 42: 12040.

4039. Nowak, I.
1963   "Need for similarity with friends as a personality trait." Polish Sociological Bulletin 1 (7): 69–78. S.A. 12:B1633.

4040. Nowicki, Stephen, and Marshall P. Duke
1972   "Use of comfortable interpersonal distance scale in high school students: Replication." Psychological Reports 30 (1, February): 182. P.A. 48:7116.

4041. Nowicki, Stephen, Don A. Nelson, and Ronald F. Ettinger
1974   "The role of need for social approval in initial attraction." Journal of Social Psychology 94 (1): 149–150.

4042. Numakami, Yasuko
1972   ("The boomerang effect via failure of persuasion: I.") Japanese Journal of Experimental Social Psychology 11 (2, March): 85–91. P.A. 52:12272.

4043. Nunn, Clyde Z.
1971   "Peer popularity, misperceptions, and academic achievement." Journal of Social Psychology 84: 243–250.

4044. Nurmi, Raimo
1966   "Judging weight under group pressure." Scandinavian Journal of Psychology 7 (1): 31–33. P.A. 40:6591; S.A. 17:D5793.

4045.   1970   "Conformity with group in a serial judgment situation." Annales Universitatis Turkuensis 115. P.A. 49:6848.

4046. Nydegger, Rudy V.
1971   "Leadership status and verbal behavior in small groups as a function of schedule of reinforcement and level of information-processing complexity." Proceedings of the 79th Annual Convention of the American Psychological Association 6 (pt. 1): 293–294. P.A. 46: 2921.

4047.   1974   "Information processing complexity and gaming behavior: The Prisoner's Dilemma." Behavioral Science 19 (3): 204-210.

4048. Oakes, William F.
       1962a   "Effectiveness of signal light reinforcers given various meanings on participation in group discussion." Psychological Reports 11 (2): 469-470. P.A. 37:7951.
4049.   1962b   "Reinforcement of Bales' categories in group discussion." Psychological Reports 11 (2): 427-435. P.A. 37:7950.
4050. Oakes, William F., Arnold E. Droge, and Barbara August
       1960   "Reinforcement effects on participation in group discussion." Psychological Reports 7: 503-514. P.A. 35:2128.
4051. Obitz, Frederick W., and L. Jerome Oziel
       1972   "Varied information levels and accuracy of person perception." Psychological Reports 31 (2, October): 571-576. P.A. 49:6849.
4052. O'Brien, Gordon E.
       1970   "Group structure and productivity." Australian Military Forces Research Report No. 7-70 (August). P.A. 46:4845.
4053. O'Brien, Gordon E., Anthony Biglan, and Judith Penna
       1972   "Measurement of the distribution of potential influence and participation in groups and organizations." Journal of Applied Psychology 56 (1): 11-18.
4054. O'Brien, Gordon E., and Daniel Ilgen
       1968   "Effects of organizational structure, leadership style, and member compatibility upon small group creativity." Proceedings of the 76th Annual Convention of the American Psychological Association 3: 555-556.
4055. O'Brien, Gordon E., and A. G. Owens
       1968   "Member intelligence and group productivity." Australian Military Forces Research Report 6-68. P.A. 44:3547.
4056.   1969   "Effects of organizational structure on correlations between member abilities and group productivity." Journal of Applied Psychology 53 (6): 525-530.
4057. O'Connell, Edward J., Jr.
       1965   "The effect of cooperative and competitive set on the learning of imitation and nonimitation." Journal of Experimental Social Psychology 1 (2, May): 172-183.
4058. O'Connell, Walter E.
       1960   "The adaptive functions of wit and humor." Journal of Abnormal and Social Psychology 61 (2): 263-270.
4059. O'Connor, John, Lawrence S. Wrightsman, and Norma Baker
       1970   "Nature of rationality in the Prisoner's Dilemma game." Proceedings of the 78th Annual Convention of the American Psychological Association 5 (pt. 1): 435-436.
4060. O'Connor, William F.
       1963   "A methodological note on the Cline and Richards' studies on accuracy of interpersonal perception." Journal of Abnormal and Social Psychology 66 (2): 194-195.
4061. O'Day, Rory
       1973   "Training style: A content-analytic assessment." Human Relations 26 (5): 599-637.
4062. O'Dell, Jerry W.
       1968   "Group size and emotional interaction." Journal of Personality and Social Psychology 8 (1, pt. 1): 75-78. P.A. 42:5534.
4063. Oerter, Rolf
       1963   ("The suggestive effect of group members with extreme status upon the group.") Psychologische Rundschau 14 (4): 275-285. P.A. 38: 5969.
4064. Oeser, O. A., and Frank Harary
       1962   "A mathematical model for structural role theory. Part I." Human Relations 15 (2, May): 89-109. P.A. 37:3040.
4065.   1964   "A mathematical model for structural role theory. Part II." Human

Relations 17 (1, February): 3–17.

4066. Oeser, O. A., and Gordon O'Brien
    1967   "A mathematical model for structural role theory. Part III." Human
            Relations 20 (1, February): 83–97.

4067. Ofshe, Richard J.
    1971   "The effectiveness of pacifist strategies: A theoretical approach."
            Journal of Conflict Resolution 15 (2, June): 261–269. P.A. 48:
            4875.

4068. Ofshe, Richard J. (ed.)
    1973   Interpersonal Behavior in Small Groups. Englewood Cliffs, N.J.:
            Prentice-Hall. P.A. 51:935.

4069. Ofshe, Richard J., and S. Lynne Ofshe
    1969   "Social choice and utility in coalition formation." Sociometry 32 (3,
            September): 330–347. P.A. 44:3548; S.A. 18:E5685.

4070.   1970   "Choice behavior in coalition games." Behavioral Science 15 (4,
            July): 337–349. S.A. 19:F0473.

4071. Ofshe, S. Lynne, and Richard J. Ofshe
    1970   Utility and Choice in Social Interaction. Englewood Cliffs, N.J.:
            Prentice-Hall.

4072. Ogawa, Dennis M.
    1971   "Small-group communication stereotypes of black Americans."
            Journal of Black Studies 1 (3, March): 273–281. S.A. 21:73G1498.

4073. Ogawa, Dennis M., and Terry A. Welden
    1972   "Cross-cultural analysis of feedback behavior within Japanese Ameri-
            can and Caucasian American small groups." Journal of Communica-
            tion 22 (2, June): 189–195. P.A. 49:4434.

4074. Ohashi, Masao, et al.
    1971   ("Studies on the information-processing in the process of impression
            formation of personality: I. On variables affecting the predictability
            of the averaging model.") University of Nagoya, Bulletin of the
            Faculty of Education 18 (March): 43–60. P.A. 51:9046.

4075. O'Leary, Charles J., and Morton Goldman
    1969   "Comparison of several patterns of communication." Journal of Ap-
            plied Psychology 53 (6): 451–455.

4076. O'Leary, M. R., and H. A. Dengerink
    1973   "Aggression as a function of the intensity and pattern of attack."
            Journal of Research in Personality 7 (1, June): 61–70. P.A. 51:5113.

4077. Olesker, Wendy, and Lawrence Balter
    1972   "Sex and empathy." Journal of Counseling Psychology 19 (6, No-
            vember): 559–562. P.A. 49:6850.

4078. Olmstead, Joseph A., and Robert R. Blake
    1955   "The use of simulated groups to produce modifications in judg-
            ment." Journal of Personality 23: 335–345. P.A. 30:840.

4079. Olmsted, Donald W.
    1957   "Inter-group similarities of role correlates." Sociometry 20: 8–20.

4080.   1962   "A developmental model of the social group." Sociological Quarter-
            ly 3: 195–207. P.A. 37:3041.

4081. Olmsted, Michael S.
    1952   "Small group interaction as a function of group norms." Ph.D. dis-
            sertation. Harvard University.

4082.   1954   "Orientation and role in the small group." American Sociological
            Review 19: 741–751. S.A. 1505.

4083.   1959   The Small Group. New York: Random House.

4084. Olson, John T., and David H. Smith
    1970   "Leadership roles in a psychiatrically deviant adolescent collectiv-
            ity." Psychological Reports 27: 499–510.

4085. Olson, Philip, and James H. Davis
    1964   "Divisible tasks and pooling performance in groups." Psychological
            Reports 15 (2): 511–517. P.A. 39:4881.

4086. O'Neal, Edgar, and Laura Kaufman
    1972   "The influence of attack, arousal, and information about one's
            arousal upon interpersonal aggression." Psychonomic Science 26

(4, February): 211-214. P.A. 48:11458.

4087. O'Neal, Edgar, and Judson Mills
    1969   "The influence of anticipated choice on the halo effect." Journal of Experimental Social Psychology 5 (3): 347-351.

4088. Oppenheim, A. N.
    1955   "Social status and clique formation among grammar school boys." British Journal of Sociology 6: 228-245.

4089. Orcutt, James D.
    1973   "Societal reaction and the response to deviation in small groups." Social Forces 52 (2): 259-267.

4090. O'Reilly, Charles A., and Karlene H. Roberts
    1974   "Information filtration in organizations: Three experiments." Organizational Behavior and Human Performance 11 (2, April): 253-265. P.A. 52:7533.

4091. Organ, Dennis W.
    1971   "Some variables affecting boundry role behavior." Sociometry 34 (4): 524-537.

4092. Orlemans, J. W.
    1965-   ("The level of aspiration for the group in positive and negative socio-
    1966   metric groups.") Psychologica Belgica 6: 103-122. P.A. 43:793.

4093. O'Rourke, John F.
    1963   "Field and laboratory: The decision-making behavior of family groups in two experimental conditions." Sociometry 26 (4, December): 422-435. P.A. 38:5970; S.A. 12:A9441.

4094. Orpen, Christopher, and Raymond Bush
    1974   "The lack of congruence between self-concept and public image." Journal of Social Psychology 93 (1, June): 145-146. P.A. 52:12273.

4095. Ort, Robert S.
    1950   "A study of role-conflicts as related to happiness in marriage." Journal of Abnormal and Social Psychology 45: 691-699. P.A. 25:2409.

4096. Orwant, Carol J., and Jack E. Orwant
    1970   "A comparison of interpreted and abstract versions of mixed-motive games." Journal of Conflict Resolution 14 (1, March): 91-97. P.A. 46:2923.

4097. Osgood, Charles E.
    1970   "Speculation on the structure of interpersonal intentions." Behavioral Science 15: 237-254.

4098. Oskamp, Stuart
    1970   "Comparison of strategy effects in the Prisoner's Dilemma and other mixed-motive games." Proceedings of the 78th Annual Convention of the American Psychological Association 5 (pt. 1): 433-434.

4099.   1971   "Effects of programmed strategies on cooperation in the Prisoner's Dilemma and other mixed-motive games." Journal of Conflict Resolution 15 (2, June): 225-259. P.A. 48:4877.

4100.   1974   "Comparison of sequential and simultaneous responding, matrix, and strategy variables in a Prisoner's Dilemma game." Journal of Conflict Resolution 18 (1, March): 107-115.

4101. Oskamp, Stuart, and Chris Kleinke
    1970   "Amount of reward as a variable in the Prisoner's Dilemma game." Journal of Personality and Social Psychology 16 (1, September): 133-140. P.A. 45:2300.

4102. Oskamp, Stuart, and Daniel Perlman
    1965   "Factors affecting cooperation in a Prisoner's Dilemma game." Journal of Conflict Resolution 9 (3): 359-374.

4103.   1966   "Effects of friendship and disliking on cooperation in a mixed-motive game." Journal of Conflict Resolution 10 (2, June): 221-226. S.A. 15:C4804.

4104. OSS Assessment Staff
    1948   Assessment of Men. New York: Rinehart. P.A. 22:3668.

4105. Ostlund, Leonard A.
    1953   "Group integration in a case discussion course." Journal of Educational Psychology 44: 463-474.

4106. O'Toole, Richard, and Robert Dubin
1968 "Baby feeding and body sway: An experiment in George Herbert Mead's 'taking the role of the other.'" Journal of Personality and Social Psychology 10 (1): 59-65. P.A. 43:822.

4107. Overs, Robert P., and Terence Mooney
1972 "An outline of interaction patterns and spatial arrangements for empirical study." Wisconsin Sociologist 9 (2-3, Spring): 79-95. P.A. 49:4435.

4108. Overstreet, R. E.
1972 "Social exchange in a three-person game." Journal of Conflict Resolution 16 (1, March): 109-123. P.A. 48:11459; S.A. 21:73G3964.

4109. Owens, A. G.
1967 "The assessment of performance in small Antarctic groups: Part III. Factor analysis of Leary Interpersonal Checklist items." Australian Military Forces Research Report 10-67. P.A. 42:7254.

4110. Owens, William A.
1947 "Item form and 'false-positive' responses on a neurotic inventory." Journal of Clinical Psychology 3: 264-269. P.A. 22:306.

4111. Oyen, Else
1972 "The impact of prolonged observation on the role of the 'neutral observer' in small groups." Acta Sociologica 15 (3): 254-266. S.A. 21:73G4905.

4112. Page, Monte M.
1972a "Demand characteristics and the verbal operant conditioning experiment." Journal of Personality and Social Psychology 23 (3, September): 372-378. P.A. 49:2366.

4113. 1972b "Statistical tests of significance and the significance of psychological data: A reply to Bale." Journal of Social Psychology 88 (2, December): 203-206. P.A. 49:9072.

4114. Page, Richard H., and Elliott McGinnies
1959 "Comparison of two styles of leadership in small group discussion." Journal of Applied Psychology 43 (August): 240-245. P.A. 34:5738.

4115. Pages, Max
1971 "Bethel culture, 1969: Impressions of an immigrant." Journal of Applied Behavioral Science 7 (3, May-June): 267-284. S.A. 20:F9137.

4116. Paicheler, Genevieve, and Jean Bouchet
1973 "Attitude polarization, familiarization and group process." European Journal of Social Psychology 3 (1): 83-90. P.A. 52:840; S.A. 22:74G8633.

4117. Pallak, Michael S., and Jack F. Heller
1971 "Interactive effects of commitment to future interaction and threat to attitudinal freedom." Journal of Personality and Social Psychology 17 (3): 325-331.

4118. Pallak, Michael S., Margaret Mueller, Kathleen Dollar, and Judith Pallak
1972 "Effect of commitment on responsiveness to an extreme consonant communication." Journal of Personality and Social Psychology 23 (3): 429-436.

4119. Palmer, George, J., Jr.
1962a "Task ability and effective leadership." Psychological Reports 10: 836-866. P.A. 37:4892.

4120. 1962b "Task ability and successful and effective leadership." Psychological Reports 11 (3): 813-816. P.A. 38:2598.

4121. Palmer, John, and Donn Byrne
1970 "Attraction toward dominant and submissive strangers: Similarity versus complementarity." Journal of Experimental Research in Personality 4 (2): 108-115. P.A. 44:10293.

4122. Palmore, Erdman, Henry L. Lennard, and Helen Hendin
1959 "Similarities of therapist and patient verbal behavior in psychotherapy." Sociometry 22 (1, March): 12-22.

4123. Pam, Alvin, Robert Plutchik, and Hope Conte
    1973   "Love: A psychometric approach." Proceedings of the 81st Annual
            Convention of the American Psychological Association 8: 159–160.
            P.A. 50:4822.
4124. Pankowski, Mary L., Wayne L. Schroeder, and Irwin Jahns
    1973   "The relationship between group process training group problem
            solving." Adult Education 24 (1, Fall): 20–42. P.A. 51:9015.
4125. Panyard, Christine M.
    1973   "Self-disclosure between friends: A validity study." Journal of
            Counseling Psychology 20 (1, January): 66–68. P.A. 50:971.
4126. Park, Peter
    1967   "Measurement of the pattern variables." Sociometry 30 (2, June):
            187–198.
4127. Park, Robert E., and Ernest W. Burgess
    1924   Introduction to the Science of Sociology. Chicago: University of
            Chicago Press.
4128. Parke, Ross D., William Ewall, and Ronald G. Slaby
    1972   "Hostile and helpful verbalizations as regulators of nonverbal aggres-
            sion." Journal of Personality and Social Psychology 23 (2, August):
            243–248. P.A. 49:793.
4129. Parker, James H.
    1968   "The interaction of Negroes and whites in an integrated church set-
            ting." Social Forces 46 (3, March): 359–366. P.A. 42:12042.
4130. Parker, Seymour
    1958   "Leadership patterns in a psychiatric ward." Human Relations 11:
            287–301. S.A. A2391.
4131. Parks, James C., and W. W. Antenen
    1970   "A modified marathon with voluntarily institutionalized alcoholics:
            An interaction process analysis." Comparative Group Studies 1 (4,
            November): 357–371.
4132. Parloff, Morris B., and Joseph H. Handlon
    1964   "The influence of criticalness on creative problem-solving in dyads."
            Psychiatry 27 (1, February): 17–27. S.A. 12:B3227.
4133. Parrott, George L., and Georgetta Coleman
    1971   "Sexual appeal: In black and white." Proceedings of the 79th An-
            nual Convention of the American Psychological Association 6 (pt.
            1): 321–322.
4134. Parsons, Talcott
    1961   "An outline of the social system." In T. Parsons et al. (eds.), Theo-
            ries of Society, pp. 30–79. New York: Free Press.
4135.   1968a   "On the concept of value-commitments." Sociological Inquiry 38
            (2): 135–160.
4136.   1968b   "Social interaction." In D. L. Sills (ed.), International Encyclopedia
            of the Social Sciences, vol. 7, pp. 429–441. New York: Macmillan
            and Free Press.
4137. Parsons, Talcott, Robert F. Bales, and Edward A. Shils
    1953   Working Papers in the Theory of Action. Glencoe, Ill.: Free
            Press.
4138. Parsons, Talcott, Robert F. Bales, et al.
    1955   Family, Socialization, and Interaction Process. Glencoe, Ill.: Free
            Press.
4139. Parten, Mildred B.
    1932   "Social participation among preschool children." Journal of Ab-
            normal and Social Psychology 27: 243–269.
4140.   1933a   "Leadership among preschool children." Journal of Abnormal and
            Social Psychology 27: 430–440.
4141.   1933b   "Social play among preschool children." Journal of Abnormal and
            Social Psychology 28: 136–147. (See also Barker, Kounin, and
            Wright, 1943.)
4142. Partridge, E. D.
    1934   "Leadership among adolescent boys." Columbia University, Teach-
            ers College, Contributions to Education No. 608.

4143. Passini, Frank T., and Warren T. Norman
       1969   "Ratee relevance in peer nominations." Journal of Applied Psychol-
               ogy 53 (3): 185–187.
4144. Pasternack, Thomas L., and Martha Van Landingham
       1972   "A comparison of the self-disclosure behavior of female undergradu-
               ates and married women." Journal of Psychology 82 (2, November):
               233–240. P.A. 49:6852.
4145. Patchen, Martin
       1970   "Models of cooperation and conflict: A critical review." Journal of
               Conflict Resolution 14 (3): 389–407.
4146. Pate, James L., and Elizabeth Broughton
       1970   "Game-playing behavior as a function of incentive." Psychological
               Reports 27 (1, August): 36. P.A. 45:6200.
4147. Pate, James L., Elizabeth D. Broughton, Lorraine K. Hallman, and N. Lynn
       Letterman
       1974   "Learning in two-person, zero-sum games." Psychological Reports
               34 (2, April): 503–510. P.A. 52:12233.
4148. Pattanaik, Prasanta K.
       1973   "Group choice with lexicographic individual orderings." Behavioral
               Science 18 (2, March): 118–123. P.A. 50:8867.
4149. Patterson, G. R., and D. Anderson
       1964   "Peers as social reinforcers." Child Development 35 (3): 951–960.
               P.A. 39:4882.
4150. Patterson, Miles L.
       1968   "Spatial factors in social interaction." Human Relations 21 (4):
               351–361. P.A. 43:14237.
4151.   1973a   "Compensation in nonverbal immediacy behaviors: A review." So-
               ciometry 36 (2, June): 237–252. P.A. 51:2990.
4152.   1973b   "Stability of nonverbal immediacy behaviors." Journal of Experi-
               mental Social Psychology 9 (2): 97–109.
4153. Patterson, Miles L. and Lee B. Sechrest
       1970   "Interpersonal distance and impression formation." Journal of Per-
               sonality 38: 161–166.
4154. Patterson, Miles L., Sherry Mullens, and Jeanne Romano
       1971   "Compensatory reactions to spatial intrusion." Sociometry 34 (1,
               March): 114–121. P.A. 46:8941.
4155. Pawlicki, Robert, and Walter Gunn
       1967   "Individual and group performance." Psychological Reports 21 (2):
               341–344. P.A. 42:5536.
4156. Payne, John W.
       1973   "Alternative approaches to decision making under risk: Moments
               versus risk dimensions." Psychological Bulletin 80 (6, December):
               439–453.
4157. Peabody, Dean
       1961   "Attitude content and agreement set in scales of authoritarianism,
               dogmatism, anti-Semitism, and economic conservatism." Journal of
               Abnormal and Social Psychology 63 (1): 1–11.
4158.   1970a   "Evaluative and descriptive aspects in personality perception: A re-
               appraisal." Journal of Personality and Social Psychology 16 (4):
               639–646.
4159.   1970b   "Symmetry and asymmetry in interpersonal relations: With impli-
               cations for the concept of projection." Journal of Personality 38
               (3, September): 426–434. P.A. 45:4134.
4160. Peak, Helen
       1953   "Problems of objective observation." In L. Festinger and D. Katz
               (eds.), Research Methods in the Behavioral Sciences, pp. 243–299.
               New York: Dryden. P.A. 28:3542.
4161. Pearce, W. Barnett, and Stewart M. Sharp
       1973   "Self-disclosing communication." Journal of Communication 23
               (4, December): 409–425. P.A. 52:2899.
4162. Pearce, W. Barnett, and Bernie Wiebe
       1973   "Relationship with and self-disclosure to friends." Perceptual and

Motor Skills 37 (2, October): 610. P.A. 51:9016.

4163. Peay, Edmund R.
1974   "Hierarchical clique structures." Sociometry 37 (1): 54–65.

4164. Pedersen, Darhl M.
1973a   "Development of a personal space measure." Psychological Reports 32 (2, April): 527–535. P.A. 51:998.

4165.   1973b   "Personality and demographic correlates of simulated personal space." Journal of Psychology 85 (1, September): 101–108. P.A. 51:7013.

4166.   1973c   "Relationships among self, other, and consensual personal space." Perceptual and Motor Skills 36 (3, pt. 1, June): 732–734. P.A. 51: 2955.

4167.   1973d   "Prediction of behavioral personal space from simulated personal space." Perceptual and Motor Skills 37 (3, December): 803–813. P.A. 52:2874.

4168. Pedersen, Darhl M., and Anne B. Heaston
1972   "The effects of sex of subject, sex of approaching person, and angle of approach upon personal space." Journal of Psychology 82 (2, November): 276–286. P.A. 49:6853.

4169. Pedersen, Darhl M., and Kenneth L. Higbee
1969   "Self-disclosure and relationship to the target person." Merrill-Palmer Quarterly 15 (2): 213–220. P.A. 44:8362.

4170. Pedersen, Darhl M., and Loyda M. Shears
1973   "A review of personal space research in the framework of general system theory." Psychological Bulletin 80 (5, November): 367–388. P.A. 51:9047.

4171. Peele, Stanton, and Stanley J. Morse
1972   "'The thrill of the chase': A study of achievement motivation and dating behavior." Proceedings of the 80th Annual Convention of the American Psychological Association 7 (pt. 1): 177–178.

4172. Peevers, Barbara H., Jim Blascovich, and Paul F. Secord
1973   "Assessment of interpersonal causality." Proceedings of the 81st Annual Convention of the American Psychological Association 8: 145–146. P.A. 50:4823.

4173. Peevers, Barbara H., and Paul F. Secord
1973   "Developmental changes in attribution of descriptive concepts to persons." Journal of Personality and Social Psychology 27 (1, July): 120–128. P.A. 50:11263.

4174. Pellegrin, Roland J.
1953   "The achievement of high status and leadership in the small group." Social Forces 32: 10–16. P.A. 28:4147; S.A. 90.

4175. Pellegrini, Robert J.
1971   "Some effects of seating position on social perception." Psychological Reports 28: 887–893.

4176.   1973   "Impressions of the male personality as a function of beardedness." Psychology 10 (1, February): 29–33. P.A. 51:999.

4177. Pellegrini, Robert J., and John Empey
1970   "Interpersonal spatial orientation in dyads." Journal of Psychology 76 (1, September): 67–70. P.A. 45:2301.

4178. Pellegrini, Robert J., Robert A. Hicks, and Lance Gordon
1970   "The effect of an approval-seeking induction on eye-contact in dyads." British Journal of Social and Clinical Psychology 9 (4, December): 373–374. P.A. 45:8116.

4179. Penner, Donald D., and Richard L. Patten
1970   "Comment on 'The epistemological status of interpersonal simulations.'" Representative Research in Social Psychology 1 (1): 62–66. P.A. 48:872.

4180. Penner, Louis A.
1971   "Interpersonal attraction toward a black person as a function of value importance." Personality: An International Journal 2 (2, Summer): 175–187. P.A. 47:6694.

4181. Penner, Louis A., Max C. Dertke, and Carole J. Achenbach
    1973   "The 'flash' system: A field study of altruism." Journal of Applied Social Psychology 3 (4, October): 362–370. P.A. 52:7571.

4182. Penner, Louis A., and Harold L. Hawkins
    1971   "The effects of visual contact and aggressor identification on interpersonal aggression." Psychonomic Science 24 (6, September): 261–263. P.A. 48:9027.

4183. Penny, R., and L. Robertson
    1962   "The Homans sentiment/interaction hypothesis." Psychological Reports 11 (1): 257–258. P.A. 37:4887.

4184. Pentony, P.
    1970   "Persons as teams: An analogy." Comparative Group Studies 1 (3, August): 211–268.

4185. Pepinsky, Harold B., Laurence Siegel, and Ellis L. Van Atta
    1952   "The criterion in counseling: A group participation scale." Journal of Abnormal and Social Psychology 47: 415–419. P.A. 27:2791.

4186. Pepinsky, Pauline N.
    1961   "Social exceptions that prove the rule." In I. A. Berg and B. M. Bass (eds.), Conformity and Deviation, pp. 380–411. New York: Harper. P.A. 4GE80P.

4187. Pepinsky, Pauline N., John K. Hemphill, and Reuben N. Shevitz
    1958   "Attempts to lead, group productivity, and morale under conditions of acceptance and rejection." Journal of Abnormal and Social Psychology 57: 47–54.

4188. Pepitone, Albert
    1950   "Motivational effects in social perception." Human Relations 3: 57–76. P.A. 25:2367.

4189.   1971   "The role of justice in interdependent decision making." Journal of Experimental Social Psychology 7 (1, January): 144–156. P.A. 46:1091.

4190. Pepitone, Albert, and Robert Kleiner
    1957   "The effects of threat and frustration on group cohesiveness." Journal of Abnormal and Social Psychology 54: 192–199.

4191. Pepitone, Albert, and George Reichling
    1955   "Group cohesiveness and the expression of hostility." Human Relations 8: 327–337. (See also Cartwright and Zander, 1960.) P.A. 30: 5868; S.A. 3143.

4192. Pepitone, Albert, and Janet Sherberg
    1957   "Intentionality, responsibility, and interpersonal attraction." Journal of Personality 25: 757–766.

4193. Pepitone, Albert, et al.
    1967   "The role of self-esteem in competitive choice behavior." International Journal of Psychology 2 (3): 147–159. P.A. 43:5302.

4194. Peri, Giovanni
    1966   ("Study of some aspects of interpersonal valuation.") Archivio di Psicologia, Neurologia e Psichiatria 27 (6): 519–551. P.A. 42:10533.

4195. Perju, A.
    1968   ("Small group research into small group and individual problem solving.") Revista de Psihologie 14 (4): 451–462. S.A. 18:E4569.

4196. Perju-Liiceanu, Aurora
    1971   ("Group performance: Experimental investigations on task and task-communication relationship.") Revista de Psihologie 17 (1): 41–51. P.A. 51:11010.

4197. Perkins, Hugh V., Jr.
    1950   "The effects of climate and curriculum on group learning." Journal of Educational Research 44: 269–286. P.A. 25:7655.

4198.   1951   "Climate influences group learning." Journal of Educational Research 45: 115–119. P.A. 26:5076.

4199. Perlmutter, Howard V.
    1953   "Group memory of meaningful material." Journal of Psychology 35: 361–370. P.A. 28:511.

646   BIBLIOGRAPHY

4200.   1954   "Impressions of influential members of discussion groups." Journal
                of Psychology 38: 223-234. P.A. 29:3821.
4201. Perlmutter, Howard V., and Germaine DeMontmollin
        1952   "Group learning of nonsense syllables." Journal of Abnormal and
                Social Psychology 47: 762-769. (See also Hare, Borgatta, and Bales,
                1955.) P.A. 27:4966.
4202. Perloe, Sidney I.
        1970   "Authoritarianism, antinomianism, and affiliation among college
                students." Proceedings of the 78th Annual Convention of the Ameri-
                can Psychological Association 5 (pt. 1): 325-326.
4203. Perry, Raymond P., and J. Edwin Boyd
        1972   "Communicating impressions of people: A methodological study of
                person perception." Journal of Social Psychology 86: 95-103.
4204.   1974a   "Language differences and message length as determinants in com-
                municating personality judgments between people." Journal of
                Social Psychology 94 (1): 83-94.
4205.   1974b   "The effect of message length, motivation, and object person infor-
                mation on communicating personality impressions." Journal of So-
                cial Psychology 92 (1): 115-125.
4206. Pessin, Joseph
        1933   "The comparative effects of social and mechanical stimulation on
                memorizing." American Journal of Psychology 45: 263-270.
4207. Pessin, Joseph, and Richard W. Husband
        1933   "Effects of social stimulation on human maze learning." Journal of
                Abnormal and Social Psychology 28: 148--154.
4208. Peters, David R.
        1970   "Self-ideal congruence as a function of human relations training."
                Journal of Psychology 76 (2, November): 199-207. P.A. 45:4135.
4209.   1973   "Identification and personal learning in T-groups." Human Relations
                26 (1, February): 1-21. P.A. 50:11264.
4210. Peters, George R., and Carroll E. Kennedy
        1970   "Close friendships in the college community." Journal of College
                Students Personnel 11 (6, November): 449-456. P.A. 45:8117.
4211. Peters, Henry N., and Francis D. Jones
        1951   "Evaluation of group psychotherapy by means of performance
                tests." Journal of Consulting Psychology 15: 363-367. P.A. 26:
                7149.
4212. Petersen, Robert J., S. S. Komorita, and Herbert C. Quay
        1964   "Determinants of sociometric choices." Journal of Social Psychol-
                ogy 62 (1, February): 65-75. P.A. 39:1579.
4213. Peterson, David E., Herbert D. Saltzstein, and Christopher Ebbe
        1967   "Sequential effects in social influence." Journal of Personality and
                Social Psychology 6 (2): 169-174.
4214. Peterson, Gerald L.
        1973   "Evaluation and immediacy in attitude inference." Psychological Re-
                ports 33 (2, October): 643-646. P.A. 51:9048.
4215. Peterson, O. F.
        1955   "Leadership and group behavior." USAF, ATC Instructors Journal
                6: 48-54. P.A. 30:2670.
4216. Peterson, Robert A., and David G. Fulcher
        1971   "Risky shift in marketing decision making: A nonconfirmation."
                Psychological Reports 29 (3, pt. 2, December): 1135-1138. P.A. 48:
                873.
4217. Petrovskii, A. V.
        1973   ("Experimental development of a social-psychological concept of
                group activity.") Voprosy Psikhologii 19 (5, September): 3-17. P.A.
                52:7512.
4218. Petrullo, Luigi, and Bernard M. Bass (eds.)
        1961   Leadership and Interpersonal Behavior. New York: Holt, Rinehart &
                Winston. P.A. 36:1GF82P.
4219. Phares, E. Jerry, and Kenneth G. Wilson
        1971   "Internal-external control, interpersonal attraction, and empathy."

Psychological Reports 28: 543-549.

4220. Phelps, Richard E., and Merle E. Meyer
    1966   "Personality and conformity, and sex differences." Psychological
            Reports 18: 730.

4221. Pheysey, Diana C., and Roy L. Payne
    1970   "The Hemphill group dimensions description questionnaire: A Brit-
            ish industrial application." Human Relations 23 (5): 473-497.

4222. Philips, E. L., Shirley Shenker, and Paula Revitz
    1951   "The assimilation of the new child into the group." Psychiatry 14:
            319-325. P.A. 26:2067.

4223. Philipsen, H.
    1962   ("A simple dichotomy: Factors outside the small group and leader-
            ship.") Sociologische Gids 9 (5, September-October): 252-272. S.A.
            17:D4870.

4224. Phillips, Beeman N., and Louis A. D'Amico
    1956   "Effects of cooperation and competition on the cohesiveness of
            small face-to-face groups." Journal of Educational Psychology 47:
            65-70. P.A. 31:7614.

4225. Phillips, David P., and Richard H. Conviser
    1972   "Measuring the structure and boundary properties of groups: Some
            uses of information theory." Sociometry 35 (2, June): 235-254.
            S.A. 21:73G4906.

4226. Phillips, G. M.
    1965   "'PERT' as a logical adjunct to the discussion process." Journal of
            Communication 15 (2): 89-99. P.A. 39:15056.

4227. Phillips, Jeanne S., Joseph D. Matarazzo, Ruth G. Matarazzo, and George
    Saslow
    1957   "Observer reliability of interaction patterns during interviews." Jour-
            nal of Consulting Psychology 21: 269-275.

4228. Phillips, Jeanne S., Ruth G. Matarazzo, Joseph D. Matarazzo, George Saslow,
    and Frederick H. Kanfer
    1961   "Relationships between descriptive content and interaction behavior
            in interviews." Journal of Consulting Psychology 25 (3): 260-
            266.

4229. Philp, Alice J.
    1940   "Strangers and friends as competitors and cooperators." Journal of
            Genetic Psychology 57: 249-258. P.A. 15:2423.

4230. Philp, Hugh, and Dexter Dunphy
    1959   "Developmental trends in small groups." Sociometry 22: (2, June):
            162-174. P.A. 34:4200.

4231. Paiget, Jean
    1926   The Language and Thought of the Child. New York: Harcourt,
            Brace.

4232.   1932   The Moral Judgement of the Child. New York: Harcourt, Brace.
4233. Pierce, Douglas R.
    1968   "Perceptual distortion cues to the dynamics of social interaction."
            Sociometry 31 (4): 412-419. P.A. 43:3941.

4234. Pierce, Richard M., and Thomas H. Zarle
    1972   "Differential referral to significant others as a function of interper-
            sonal effectiveness." Journal of Clinical Psychology 28 (2, April):
            230-232. P.A. 50:8869.

4235. Pierce, Robert A.
    1970   "Need similarity and complementarity as determinants of friendship
            choice." Journal of Psychology 76 (2, November): 231-238. P.A.
            45:4136.

4236. Pierce, William D.
    1971   "Anxiety about the act of communicating and perceived empathy."
            Psychotherapy: Theory, Research and Practice 8 (2, Summer): 120-
            123. P.A. 49:11111.

4237. Piercy, Fred P., and Susan K. Piercy
    1972   "Interpersonal attraction as a function of propinquity in two sensi-
            tivity groups." Psychology 9 (1, February): 27-30. P.A. 49:4438.

4238. Pigg, Roger, and Russell G. Geen
     1971   "Self-directed aggression and similarity between frustrator and ag-
               gressor." Journal of Abnormal Psychology 78 (3, December): 241–
               244. P.A. 47:8797.
4239. Pigors, Paul
     1935   Leadership or Domination. Boston: Houghton Mifflin.
4240. Piliavin, Irving M., Judith Rodin, and Jane A. Piliavin
     1969   "Good Samaritanism: An underground phenomenon?" Journal of
               Personality and Social Psychology 13 (4): 289-299. P.A. 44:3549.
4241. Piliavin, Jane A., and Irving M. Piliavin
     1972   "Effect of blood on reactions to a victim." Journal of Personality
               and Social Psychology 23 (3, September): 353-361. P.A. 49:2367.
4242. Pilisuk, Marc
     1962   "Cognitive balance and self-relevant attitudes." Journal of Abnormal
               and Social Psychology 65 (2): 95-103.
4243. Pilisuk, Marc, Stewart Kiritz, and Stuart Clampitt
     1971   "Undoing deadlocks of distrust: Hip Berkeley students and the
               ROTC." Journal of Conflict Resolution 15 (1, March): 81-95. P.A.
               48:2901.
4244. Pilisuk, Marc, and Anatol Rapoport
     1964   "Stepwise disarmament and sudden destruction in a two-person
               game: A research tool." Journal of Conflict Resolution 8 (1, March):
               36-49. S.A. 14:C0072.
4245. Pilisuk, Marc, and Paul Skolnick
     1968   "Inducing trust: A test of the Osgood proposal." Journal of Person-
               ality and Social Psychology 8 (2, pt. 1): 121-133. P.A. 42:5521.
4246. Pilisuk, Marc, Paul Skolnick, and Edward Overstreet
     1968   "Predicting cooperation from the two sexes in a conflict simulation."
               Journal of Personality and Social Psychology 10 (1): 35-43.
4247. Pilisuk, Marc, Paul Skolnick, Kenneth Thomas, and Reuben Chapman
     1967   "Boredom vs. cognitive reappraisal in the development of coopera-
               tive strategy." Journal of Conflict Resolution 11 (1): 110-116.
4248. Pilkonis, Paul A., and Mark P. Zanna
     1973   "The choice-shift phenomenon in groups: Replication and exten-
               sion." Representative Research in Social Psychology 4 (2, June):
               36-47. P.A. 51:2992.
4249. Pino, Christopher J.
     1971   "Relation of a trainability index to T-group outcomes." Journal of
               Applied Psychology 55 (5): 439-442.
4250. Pintner, R., G. Forlano, and H. Freedman
     1937   "Personality and attitudinal similarity among classroom friends."
               Journal of Applied Psychology 21: 48-65.
4251. Pisano, Richard, and Stuart P. Taylor
     1971   "Reduction of physical aggression: The effects of four strategies."
               Journal of Personality and Social Psychology 19 (2, August): 237-
               242. P.A. 47:828.
4252. Pishkin, Vladimir, and J. A. Foster
     1965   "Apparatus for group concept identification and verbal interaction."
               Journal of Clinical Psychology 21 (1): 104-108. P.A. 39:12182.
4253. Pitkänen, Lea
     1973   "An aggression machine: I. The intensity of aggressive defence
               aroused by aggressive offence." Scandinavian Journal of Psychology
               14 (1): 56-64. P.A. 50:11265.
4254. Plank, Robert
     1951   "An analysis of a group therapy experiment." Human Organization
               10 (3): 5-21, (4): 26-36. P.A. 26:7037.
4255. Pleck, Joseph H.
     1972   "Self-referent accuracy in self-analytic groups." Journal of Social
               Psychology 88 (2, December): 289-296. P.A. 49:9076.
4256. Pliner, Patricia, Heather Hart, Joanne Kohl, and Dory Saari
     1974   "Compliance without pressure: Some further data on the foot-in-
               the-door technique." Journal of Experimental Social Psychology 10

(1): 17-22.

4257. Plon, Michel
1967   ("Theoretical and experimental problems posed by the use of 'games' in the study of interpersonal conflicts.") Bulletin du C.E.R.P. 16 (4): 393-433. P.A. 43:5268.

4258.   1969-   ("Regarding the controversy over the effects of threat in negotia-
         1970   tions.") Bulletin de Psychologie 23 (4-5): 268-282. P.A. 46:1092.

4259. Podd, Marvin H., James E. Marcia, and Barry M. Rubin
1970   "The effects of ego identity and partner perception on a Prisoner's Dilemma game." Journal of Social Psychology 82: 117-126.

4260. Poe, Charles A., and David H. Mills
1972   "Interpersonal attraction, popularity, similarity of personal needs, and psychological awareness." Journal of Psychology 81 (1, May): 139-149. P.A. 48:9028.

4261. Poitou, Jean-Pierre
1964   ("Perception of the individual contributions to group work in a hier-archised social structure.") Psychologie Française 9 (4): 304-315. P.A. 39:10007.

4262.   1968   ("Evaluation of one's own performance and the performance of others in a social situation: II.") Année Psychologique 68 (1): 115-120. P.A. 43:5304.

4263.   1969   ("Effects of the social norm of solidarity in a group hierarchy.") Année Psychologique 69 (1): 127-132. P.A. 44:6660.

4264. Poitou, Jean-Pierre, and Claude Flament
1967   ("Social structure and task structure.") Année Psychologique 67 (2): 493-512. P.A. 43:11238.

4265. Poland, Willis D., and John E. Jones
1973   "Personal orientations and perceived benefit from a human relations laboratory." Small Group Behavior 4 (4, November): 496-502.

4266. Polansky, Norman A., Ronald Lippitt, and Fritz Redl
1950a   "An investigation of behavioral contagion in groups." Human Rela-tions 3: 319-348. P.A. 25:6121.

4267.   1950b   "The use of near-sociometric data in research on group treatment processes." Sociometry 13: 39-62.

4268. Pollack, Donald, and Gerald Stanley
1971   "Coping and marathon sensitivity training." Psychological Reports 29: 379-385.

4269. Pollack, Herbert B.
1971   "Change in homogeneous and heterogeneous sensitivity training groups." Journal of Consulting and Clinical Psychology 37 (1, Au-gust): 60-66. P.A. 47:829.

4270. Pollak, Otto
1972   "Family functions in transition." In Families of the Future. Ames: Iowa State University Press. P.A. 49:11113.

4271. Pollard, William E., and Terence R. Mitchell
1972   "Decision theory analysis of social power." Psychological Bulletin 78 (6, December): 433-446. P.A. 49:9077.

4272. Pollay, Richard W.
1968   "The measurement of role differentiation." Sociometry 31 (1): 120-124. P.A. 42:8878.

4273. Pollis, Nicholas P.
1967   "Relative stability of scales formed in individual, togetherness and group situations." British Journal of Social and Clinical Psychology 6 (4): 249-255. P.A. 42:7269.

4274.   1968   "Reference group re-examined." British Journal of Sociology 19 (3): 300-307. P.A. 43:12475.

4275. Pollis, Nicholas P., and Joseph A. Cammalleri
1968   "Social conditions and differential resistance to majority pressure." Journal of Psychology 70 (1): 69-76. P.A. 43:823.

4276. Pollis, Nicholas P., and Robert L. Montgomery
1966   "Conformity and resistance to compliance." Journal of Psychology 63 (1): 35-41. P.A. 40:10039.

4277.   1968   "Individual judgmental stability and the natural group." Journal of
                 Social Psychology 74 (1, February): 75–81. P.A. 42:8871.
4278. Polsky, Howard W.
         1971   "Notes on personal feedback in sensitivity training." Sociological
                 Inquiry 41 (2, Spring): 175–182.
4279. Pompilo, Peter T., and Richard Krebs
         1972   "A time-limited group experience with a religious teaching order."
                 Journal of Religion and Health 11 (2, April): 139–152. P.A. 48:
                 9029.
4280. Porter, Donald E.
         1963   "Some effects of information distribution and group size on group
                 problem solving." Industrial Management Review 4 (2, April): 1–18.
                 S.A. 14:C0964.
4281. Porter, E[lias] H., Jr.
         1943   "The development and evaluation of a measure of counseling inter-
                 view procedures." Educational and Psychological Measurement 3:
                 105–126, 215–238. P.A. 18:1901, 2599.
4282. Posavac, Emil J.
         1971   "Need for approval as a moderator of interpersonal attraction based
                 on attitude similarity." Journal of Social Psychology 85: 141–142.
4283. Posavac, Emil J., and Jack McKillip
         1973   "Effects of similarity and endorsement frequency on attraction and
                 expected agreement." Journal of Experimental Research in Person-
                 ality 6 (4, April): 357–362. P.A. 51:3061.
4284. Posavac, Emil J., and Stanley J. Pasko
         1973   "Risk-taking and the set-size effect in interpersonal attraction."
                 Journal of Social Psychology 90 (1, June): 137–140. P.A. 51:2993.
4285.   1974   "Attraction, personality similarity, and popularity of the personality
                 of a stimulus person." Journal of Social Psychology 92 (2): 269–
                 275.
4286. Posthuma, Allan B., and Barbara W. Posthuma
         1973   "Some observations on encounter group casualities." Journal of Ap-
                 plied Behavioral Science 9 (5, September): 595–608. P.A. 51:9000.
4287. Potashin, Reva
         1946   "A sociometric study of children's friendships." Sociometry 9: 48–
                 70. P.A. 20:2953.
4288. Potter, David A.
         1973   "Personalism and interpersonal attraction." Journal of Personality
                 and Social Psychology 28 (2): 192–198.
4289. Powdermaker, Florence, and Jerome D. Frank
         1948   "Group psychotherapy with neurotics." American Journal of Psy-
                 chiatry 105: 449–455.
4290. Powell, Evan R., and Charles S. Wilson
         1969   "Peer concept and sociometric analysis of a small group." Psycho-
                 logical Reports 25 (2): 452–454. P.A. 44:5097.
4291. Powell, John P., and Paul Jackson
         1964   "A note on a simplified technique for recording group interaction."
                 Human Relations 17 (3, August): 289–291. P.A. 39:4884; S.A. 13:
                 B4930.
4292. Powell, Reed M., et al.
         1956   "An experimental study of role taking, group status, and group for-
                 mation." Sociology and Social Research 40: 159–165. P.A. 31:
                 2714; S.A. 3146.
4293. Powell, Reed M., and L. LaFave
         1958   "Some determinants of role-taking accuracy." Sociology and Social
                 Research 42: 319–326.
4294. Powers, Patrick C., and Russell G. Geen
         1972   "Effects of the behavior and the perceived arousal of a model on in-
                 strumental aggression." Journal of Personality and Social Psychology
                 23 (2, August): 175–183. P.A. 49:794.
4295. Pratt, Grace K.
         1960   "Group dynamics in the evaluation of classes." Journal of Educa-

tional Sociology 34 (3, November): 106–108. S.A. A3532.

4296. Precker, Joseph A.
1952 "Similarity of valuings as a factor in selection of peers and near-authority figures." Journal of Abnormal and Social Psychology 47: 406–414. P.A. 27:2626.

4297. 1953 "The automorphic process in the attribution of values." Journal of Personality 21: 356–363. P.A. 28:2434.

4298. Prentice, W[illiam] C. H.
1961 "Understanding leadership." Harvard Business Review 39 (5): 143–151. P.A. 37:4893.

4299. Preston, Malcolm G.
1938 "Note on the reliability and the validity of the group judgment." Journal of Experimental Psychology 22: 462–471.

4300. Preston, Malcolm G., and Roy K. Heintz
1949 "Effects of participatory versus supervisory leadership on group judgment." Journal of Abnormal and Social Psychology 44: 345–355. (See also Cartwright and Zander, 1953.) P.A. 24:1129.

4301. Price, Kendall O., Ernest Harburg, and Jack M. McLeod
1965 "Positive and negative affect as a function of perceived discrepancy in ABX situations." Human Relations 18 (1, February): 87–100.

4302. Price, Kendall O., Ernest Harburg, and Theodore M. Newcomb
1966 "Psychological balance in situations of negative interpersonal attitudes." Journal of Personality and Social Psychology 3 (3): 265–270. P.A. 40:5405.

4303. Price, Richard H., and Dennis L. Bouffard
1974 "Behavioral appropriateness and situational constraint as dimensions of social behavior." Journal of Personality and Social Psychology 30 (4): 579–586.

4304. Prien, Erich P., and Allan R. Culler
1964 "Leaderless group discussion participation and inter-observer agreements." Journal of Social Psychology 62 (2, April): 321–328. P.A. 39:4885.

4305. Prien, Erich P., and Robert J. Lee
1965 "Peer ratings and leaderless group discussions for evaluation of classroom performance." Psychological Reports 16: 59–64.

4306. Priest, Robert F., and Jack Sawyer
1967 "Proximity and peership: Bases of balance in interpersonal attraction." American Journal of Sociology 72 (6, May): 633–649. S.A. 15:C8067.

4307. Prock, William R., and Karl E. Weick
1970 "Programmed interaction: Verbalization in a simulated social interaction." Proceedings of the 78th Annual Convention of the American Psychological Association 5 (pt. 1): 489–490. P.A. 44:18572.

4308. Proctor, Charles H., and Charles P. Loomis
1951 "Analysis of sociometric data." In M. Jahoda, M. Deutsch, and S. E. Cook (eds.), Research Methods in Social Relations: With Especial Reference to Prejudice, pp. 561–585. New York: Dryden.

4309. Pruitt, Dean G.
1967 "Reward structure and cooperation: The decomposed Prisoner's Dilemma game." Journal of Personality and Social Psychology 7 (1): 21–27.

4310. 1968 "Reciprocity and credit building in a laboratory dyad." Journal of Personality and Social Psychology 8 (2, pt. 1): 143–147. P.A. 42: 5522.

4311. 1969a "Stability and sudden change in interpersonal and international affairs." Journal of Conflict Resolution 13 (1): 18–38. P.A. 44: 16560.

4312. 1969b "'Walter Mitty' effect in individual and group risk taking." Proceedings of the 77th Annual Convention of the American Psychological Association 4 (pt. 1): 425–426. P.A. 43:17351.

4313. 1970 "Motivational processes in the decomposed Prisoner's Dilemma game." Journal of Personality and Social Psychology 14 (3):

227-238.

4314.   1971a   "Choice shifts in group discussion: An introductory review." Journal of Personality and Social Psychology 20 (3, December): 339-360. P.A. 47:8798.

4315.   1971b   "Conclusions: Toward an understanding of choice shifts in group discussion." Journal of Personality and Social Psychology 20 (3, December): 495-510. P.A. 47:8799.

4316.   1971c   "Indirect communication and the search of agreement in negotiation." Journal of Applied Social Psychology 1 (3, July): 205-239. P.A. 48:2902.

4317.   1972   "Methods for resolving differences of interest: A theoretical analysis." Journal of Social Issues 28 (1): 133-154. P.A. 48:11460.

4318. Pruitt, Dean G., and Julie L. Drews
       1969   "The effect of time pressure, time elapsed, and the opponent's concession rate on behavior in negotiation." Journal of Experimental Social Psychology 5 (1): 43-60. P.A. 43:8290.

4319. Pruitt, Dean G., and Douglas F. Johnson
       1970   "Mediation as an aid to face saving in negotiation." Journal of Personality and Social Psychology 14 (3): 239-246. P.A. 44:8364.

4320. Pruitt, Dean G., and Allan I. Teger
       1969   "The risky shift in group betting." Journal of Experimental Social Psychology 5 (2): 115-126.

4321.   1971   "Reply to Belovicz and Finch's comments on 'The risky shift in group betting.'" Journal of Experimental Social Psychology 7 (1): 84-86.

4322. Pryer, Margaret W., and Bernard M. Bass
       1959   "Some effects of feedback on behavior in groups." Sociometry 22 (1, March): 56-63. P.A. 34:1182.

4323. Pryer, Margaret W., Austin W. Flint, and Bernard M. Bass
       1962   "Group effectiveness and consistency of leadership." Sociometry 25 (4, December): 391-397. P.A. 38:4204; S.A. 11:A6358.

4324. Psathas, George
       1960a   "Interaction process analysis of two psychotherapy groups." International Journal of Group Psychotherapy 10: 430-445.

4325.   1960b   "Phase movement and equilibrium tendencies in interaction process in psychotherapy groups." Sociometry 23 (2, June): 177-194. P.A. 35:2380; S.A. A3118.

4326.   1961   "Alternative methods for scoring interaction process analysis." Journal of Social Psychology 53 (February): 97-103. P.A. 35:6347.

4327. Psathas, George, and Ronald Hardert
       1966   "Trainer interventions and normative patterns in the T group." Journal of Applied Behavioral Science 2 (2, April-June): 149-169. S.A. 14:C2799.

4328. Psathas, George, and Sheldon Stryker
       1965   "Bargaining behavior and orientations in coalition formation." Sociometry 28 (2, June): 124-144. S.A. 14:B9185.

4329. Puffer, J. A.
       1905   "Boys' gangs." Pedagogical Seminary 12: 175-212.

4330.   1912   The Boy and His Gang. Boston: Houghton Mifflin.

4331. Purcell, Kenneth, John A. Modrick, and Roy Yamahiro
       1960   "Item vs. trait accuracy in interpersonal perception." Journal of General Psychology 62 (April): 285-292. P.A. 34:7596.

4332. Pyke, Sandra W., and Cathie A. Neely
       1970   "Evaluation of a group communication training program." Journal of Communication 20 (3, September): 291-304. P.A. 45: 6203.

4333. Pylyshyn, Z., N. Agnew, and J. Illingworth
       1966   "Comparison of individuals and pairs as participants in a mixed-motive game." Journal of Conflict Resolution 10 (2, June): 211-220. S.A. 15:C4805.

4334. Pyron, Bernard
       1965   "Accuracy of interpersonal perception as a function of consistency

of information." Journal of Personality and Social Psychology 1 (2): 111–117.

4335. Quade, A. E.
    1955   "The relationship between marital adjustment and certain interactional patterns in problem solving situations." Ph.D. dissertation. Ohio State University.

4336. Queen, Stuart A.
    1928   "Social interaction in the interview: An experiment." Social Forces 6: 545–558.

4337. Quereshi, Mohammed Y., Anne H. Leggio, and Frederick W. Widlak
    1974   "Some biosocial determinants of interpersonal perception." Journal of Social Psychology 93 (2): 229–244.

4338. Query, Joy M.
    1968   "The influence of group pressures on the judgments of children and adolescents: A comparative study." Adolescence 3 (10): 153–160. P.A. 42:17159.

4339. Quey, Richard L.
    1971   "Functions and dynamics of work groups." American Psychologist 26 (12, December): 1077–1084.

4340. Raack, R. C.
    1970   "When plans fail: Small group behavior and decision-making in the conspiracy of 1808 in Germany." Journal of Conflict Resolution 14 (1, March): 3–20. P.A. 46:2924; S.A. 20:F3457.

4341. Rabbie, Jacob M., Frits Benoist, Henk Oosterbaan, and Lieuwe Visser
    1974   "Differential power and effects of expected competitive and cooperative intergroup interaction on intragroup and outgroup attitudes." Journal of Personality and Social Psychology 30 (1, July): 46–56. P.A. 52:12275.

4342. Rabinovich, Harry, Donald H. Hislop, and Robert L. Derbyshire
    1973   "A vector model of small group behavior." Small Group Behavior 4 (2, May): 163–176. P.A. 51:7036.

4343. Rabinowitz, Larry, Harold H. Kelley, and Robert M. Rosenblatt
    1966   "Effects of different types of interdependence and response conditions in the minimal social situation." Journal of Experimental Social Psychology 2 (2, April): 169–197. P.A. 40:8794.

4344. Rabinowitz, William
    1956   "A note on the social perceptions of authoritarians and non-authoritarians." Journal of Abnormal and Social Psychology 53: 384–386. P.A. 32:4045.

4345.   1957   "Anality, aggression, and acquiescence." Journal of Abnormal and Social Psychology 54: 140–142.

4346. Rabow, Jerome, Floyd J. Fowler, Jr., David L. Braadford, Margaret A. Hoefeller, and Yuriko Shibuya
    1966   "The role of social norms and leadership in risk-taking." Sociometry 29 (1, March): 16–27. P.A. 40:6592; S.A. 15:C3483.

4347. Radinsky, Thomas L.
    1971   "Exposing an individual to two types of Prisoner's Dilemma game matrix formats." Psychonomic Science 24 (2, July): 62–64. P.A. 48:9031.

4348. Radinsky, Thomas L., and Suresh Kanekar
    1972   "The influence of interpersonal comparisons of outcomes under conditions of free responding." Psychonomic Science 29 (4-A, November): 201–202. P.A. 49:11117.

4349. Radke, Marian J., and P. Klisurich
    1947   "Experiments in changing food habits." Journal of American Dietetics Association 23: 403–409.

4350. Radloff, Roland W.
    1961   "Opinion evaluation and affiliation." Journal of Abnormal and Social Psychology 62 (3, May): 578–585. (See also Cartwright and Zander, 1968.) P.A. 4GE78R.

4351. Radlow, Robert
    1965   "An experimental study of 'cooperation' in the Prisoner's Dilemma game." Journal of Conflict Resolution 9 (2, June): 221–227. S.A. 14:C1888.
4352. Radlow, Robert, and Marianna Radlow
    1966   "Unenforced commitments in 'cooperative' and 'non-cooperative' non-constant-sum games." Journal of Conflict Resolution 10 (4, December): 497–505. S.A. 15:C6383.
4353. Radlow, Robert, Marianna F. Weidner, and Paul M. Hurst
    1968   "The effect of incentive magnitude and 'motivational orientation' upon choice behavior in a two-person nonzero-sum game." Journal of Social Psychology 74 (April): 199–208.
4354. Rainio, Kullervo
    1961   "Stochastic process of social contacts." Scandinavian Journal of Psychology 2: 113–128. P.A. 36:3GE13R.
4355.   1970   "The conceptual representation of choice behavior and social interaction." Quality and Quantity 4 (1, June): 165–191. P.A. 48:9032.
4356. Rake, Johan M.
    1970   "Friendship: A fundamental description of its subjective dimension." Humanitas 6 (2, Fall): 161–176. P.A. 46:2925.
4357. Ramey, J. W.
    1958   "The relationship of peer group rating to certain individual perceptions in personality." Journal of Experimental Psychology 27 (December): 143–149. P.A. 34:2783.
4358. Ramsoy, Odd
    1963   ("Coordination with minimal communication.") Tidsskrift for Samfunnsforskning 4 (4): 241–253. S.A. 14:C0074.
4359.   1964   ("Rank and acceptance: The relation between the rank of the person making a suggestion and its fate.") Tidsskrift for Samfunnsforskning 5 (4): 205–220. S.A. 14:C0965.
4360. Ramsoy, Odd, Erling H. Albreschtsen, Unni Husabo, and Magne Stromnes
    1963   ("Group atmosphere and task-solving: An experimental approach.") Tidsskrift for Samfunnsforskning 4 (3): 129–149. S.A. 14:C0073.
4361. Ramuz-Nienhuis, Wilhelmina, and Annie Van Bergen
    1960   "Relations between some components of attraction-to-group." Human Relations 13 (3, August): 271–277. P.A. 35:2129; S.A. A3804.
4362. Rapoport, Amnon
    1969   "Effects of payoff information in multistage mixed-motive games." Behavioral Science 14 (3, May): 204–215.
4363. Rapoport, Amnon, and Nancy Cole
    1968   "Experimental studies of interdependent mixed motive games." Behavioral Science 13 (3, May): 189–204. S.A. 17:D6817.
4364. Rapoport, Amnon, James P. Kahan, and William E. Stein
    1973   "Decisions of timing in conflict situations of incomplete information." Behavioral Science 18 (4, July): 272–287. P.A. 51:3063.
4365. Rapoport, Anatol
    1947   "Mathematical theory of motivation interactions of two individuals." Bulletin of Mathematical Biophysics 9: 17–28, 41–61. P.A. 22: 4353, 4354.
4366.   1959   "A logical task as a research tool in organization theory." In M. Haire (ed.), Modern Organization Theory, pp. 91–114. New York: Wiley. S.A. 13:B4931.
4367.   1960   "Some self-organization parameters in three-person groups." General Systems 5: 129–143. S.A. 13:B6762.
4368.   1967a   "A note on the 'index of cooperation' For Prisoner's Dilemma." Journal of Conflict Resolution 11 (1): 100–103.
4369.   1967b   "Exploiter, leader, hero, and martyr." Behavioral Science 12 (2, March): 81–84. S.A. 15:C6384.
4370.   1968   "Prospects for experimental games." Journal of Conflict Resolution 12 (4): 461–470.
4371. Rapoport, Anatol, and Albert M. Chammah
    1965a   Prisoner's Dilemma. Ann Arbor: University of Michigan Press.

4372.   1965b   "Sex differences in factors contributing to level of cooperation in the Prisoner's Dilemma game." Journal of Personality and Social Psychology 2 (6): 831-838.

4373. Rapoport, Anatol, Albert M. Chammah, John Dwyer, and John Gyr
       1962   "Three-person non-zero-sum nonnegotiable games." Behavioral Science 7 (1, January): 38-58. P.A. 37:1110.

4374. Rapoport, Anatol, and Phillip S. Dale
       1966   "The 'end' and 'start' effects in iterated Prisoner's Dilemma." Journal of Conflict Resolution 10 (3): 363-366.

4375. Rapoport, Anatol, Melvin Guyer, and David Gordon
       1971   "A comparison of performance of Danish and American students in a 'threat game.'" Behavioral Science 16 (5, September): 456-466. S.A. 20:F8114.

4376.   1973   "Threat games: A comparison of performance of Danish and American subjects." In H. R. Alker, K. W. Deutsch, and A. H. Stoetzel (eds.), Mathematical Approaches to Politics. San Francisco: Jossey-Bass. P.A. 51:9017.

4377. Rapoport, Anatol, and William J. Horvath
       1961   "A study of a large sociogram." Behavioral Science 6 (4, October): 279-291. P.A. 4GE79R; S.A. 11:A4597.

4378. Rapoport, Anatol, and Carol Orwant
       1962   "Experimental games: A review." Behavioral Science 7 (1, January): 1-37. P.A. 37:1109.

4379. Rapoport, Rhona, and Robert N. Rapoport
       1964   "New light on the honeymoon." Human Relations 17 (1, February): 33-56.

4380. Rapoport, Rhona, and I. Rosow
       1957   "An approach to family relationships and role performance." Human Relations 10: 209-221.

4381. Rappoport, Leon H.
       1965   "Interpersonal conflict in cooperative and uncertain situations." Journal of Experimental Social Psychology 1 (4, October): 323-333. P.A. 40:4188.

4382. Rasmussen, Glen R.
       1956   "An evaluation of a student-centered and instructor-centered method of conducting a graduate course in education." Journal of Educational Psychology 47: 449-461.

4383. Rasmussen, Glen R., and A. Zander
       1954   "Group membership and self-evaluation." Human Relations 7: 239-251. S.A. 774.

4384. Rath, R., and S. K. Misra
       1963   "Change of attitudes as a function of size of discussion-groups." Journal of Social Psychology 59 (April): 247-257.

4385. Rattinger, Hans
       1973   ("A simple method and a FORTRAN program for the detection of cliques.") Zeitschrift für Sozialpsychologie 4 (1): 5-14. P.A. 52: 812.

4386. Raush, Harold L.
       1965   "Interaction sequences." Journal of Personality and Social Psychology 2 (4): 487-499.

4387. Raush, Harold L., Allen T. Dittmann, and Thaddeus J. Taylor
       1959   "Person, setting, and change in social interaction." Human Relations 12 (4, November): 361-378.

4388. Raush, Harold L., Irwin Farbman, and Lynn G. Llewellyn
       1960   "Person, setting, and change in social interaction. II: A normal-control study." Human Relations 13 (4, November): 305-332.

4389. Raven, Bertram H.
       1959a   "Social influence on opinions and the communication of related content." Journal of Abnormal and Social Psychology 58: 119-128. P.A. 34:1183.

4390.   1959b   "The dynamics of groups." Review of Educational Research 29 (October): 332-343. P.A. 34:5741.

4391.   1965   Bibliography of Small Group Research. 3rd ed. University of California, Los Angeles, Technical Report No. 15.
4392.   1968   "Group performance." In D. L. Sills (ed.), International Encyclopedia of the Social Sciences, vol. 6, pp. 288–293. New York: Macmillan and Free Press.
4393.   Raven, Bertram H., and H. Todd Eachus
         1963   "Cooperation and competition in means-interdependent triads." Journal of Abnormal and Social Psychology 67 (4): 307–316. P.A. 38:4197.
4394.   Raven, Bertram H., and Martin Fishbein
         1961   "Acceptance of punishment and change in belief." Journal of Abnormal and Social Psychology 63 (2, September): 411–416. S.A. 11:A4159a.
4395.   Raven, Bertram H., and J. R. P. French, Jr.
         1958a   "Group support, legitimate power, and social influence." Journal of Personality 26: 400–409.
4396.   1958b   "Legitimate power, coercive power, and observability in social influence." Sociometry 21: 83–97.
4397.   Raven, Bertram H., and Jan Rietsema
         1957   "The effects of varied clarity of group goal and group path upon the individual and his relation to his group." Human Relations 10: 29–45. (See also Cartwright and Zander, 1960.) P.A. 32:1461; S.A. A1201.
4398.   Raven, Bertram H., and Jerry I. Shaw
         1970   "Interdependence and group problem-solving in the triad." Journal of Personality and Social Psychology 14 (2): 157–165. P.A. 44: 6661.
4399.   Rawls, James R., Donna J. Rawls, and Roland L. Frye
         1969   "Membership satisfaction as it is related to certain dimensions of interaction in a T-group." Journal of Social Psychology 78 (2): 243–248. P.A. 44:6662.
4400.   Rawls, James R., Ronald E. Trego, Charles N. McGaffesy, and Donna J. Rawls
         1972   "Personal space as a predictor of performance under close working conditions." Journal of Social Psychology 86: 261–267.
4401.   Ray, William S.
         1951   A Laboratory Manual for Social Psychology. New York: American Book. P.A. 27:1053.
4402.   1955   "Complex tasks for use in human problem-solving research." Psychological Bulletin 52: 134–149. P.A. 30:2437.
4403.   Raymond, Beth J., and Rhoda K. Unger
         1972   "'The apparel oft proclaims the man': Cooperation with deviant and conventional youths." Journal of Social Psychology 87 (1, June): 75–82. P.A. 48:9033.
4404.   Read, Peter B.
         1974   "Source of authority and the legitimation of leadership in small groups." Sociometry 37 (2, June): 189–204. P.A. 52:12342.
4405.   Reckless, Walter C.
         1930   "Case studies built around observations of individual foster-children in the playroom of a receiving home." American Sociological Society Papers 24: 170–173.
4406.   Reckman, Richard F., and George R. Goethals
         1973   "Deviancy and group orientation as determinants of group composition preferences." Sociometry 36 (3, September): 419–423. P.A. 52:2900.
4407.   Reddy, W. Brendan
         1972   "On affection, group composition, and self-actualization in sensitivity training." Journal of Consulting and Clinical Psychology 38 (2): 211–214.
4408.   1973   "The impact of sensitivity training on self-actualization: A one-year follow-up." Small Group Behavior 4 (4, November): 407–413.
4409.   Reddy, W. Brendan, and Anne Byrnes
         1972   "Effects of interpersonal group composition on the problem-solving

behavior of middle managers." Journal of Applied Psychology 56 (6): 516-517.

4410. Redl, Fritz
    1942   "Group emotion and leadership." Psychiatry 5: 573-596. (See also D. F. Sullivan (ed.), Readings in Group Work. New York: Association Press, 1952. See also Hare, Borgatta, and Bales, 1955, 1965.) P.A. 17:2085.

4411.   1948   "Resistance in therapy groups." Human Relations 1: 307-313. P.A. 23:1313.

4412. Reed, Thomas R.
    1972   "Connotative meaning of social interaction concepts: An investigation of factor structure and the effects of imagined contexts." Journal of Personality and Social Psychology 24 (3, December): 306-312. P.A. 49:9082.

4413. Reese, Hayne W.
    1961   "Relationships between self-acceptance and sociometric choices." Journal of Abnormal and Social Psychology 62 (2, March): 472-474. S.A. A2242.

4414. Regan, Dennis T.
    1971   "Effects of a favor and liking on compliance." Journal of Experimental Social Psychology 7 (6, November): 627-639. P.A. 48: 9034.

4415. Regan, Dennis T., Ellen Straus, and Russell Fazio
    1974   "Liking and the attribution process." Journal of Experimental Social Psychology 10 (4, July): 385-397. P.A. 52:12343.

4416. Regan, Dennis T., Margo Williams, and Sondra Sparling
    1972   "Voluntary expiation of guilt: A field experiment." Journal of Personality and Social Psychology 24 (1, October): 42-45. P.A. 49: 6854.

4417. Regula, C. Robert, and James W. Julian
    1973   "The impact of quality and frequency of task contributions on perceived ability." Journal of Social Psychology 89 (1, February): 115-122. P.A. 50:2967.

4418. Reid, David W., and Edward E. Ware
    1972   "Affective style and impression formation: Reliability, validity and some inconsistencies." Journal of Personality 40 (3, September): 436-450. P.A. 49:6855.

4419. Reilly, Mary St. Anne, William D. Commins, and Edward C. Stefic
    1960   "The complementarity of personality needs in friendship choice." Journal of Abnormal and Social Psychology 61 (2): 292-294. P.A. 35:4822; S.A. A1202.

4420. Reilly, Richard R., and Cabot L. Jaffee
    1970   "Influences of some task-irrelevant factors on leader selection." Psychological Record 20 (4, Fall): 535-539. P.A. 46: 1094.

4421. Reingen, Peter H.
    1973   "Risk-taking by individuals and informal groups with the use of industrial product purchasing situations as stimuli." Journal of Psychology 85 (2, November): 339-345. P.A. 51:11011.

4422. Reisman, David, Robert J. Potter, and Jeanne Watson
    1960   "Sociability, permisiveness, and equality: A preliminary formulation." Psychiatry 23 (4, November): 323-340. S.A. A2213. (See also "The vanishing host." Human Organization 19 (1): 17-27. S.A. A2212.)

4423. Reisman, John M., and Tom Yamokoski
    1974   "Psychotherapy and friendship: An analysis of the communications of friends." Journal of Counseling Psychology 21 (4, July): 269-273. P.A. 52:12277.

4424. Reisman, Stephen R., and John Schopler
    1973   "An analysis of the attribution process and an application to determinants of responsibility." Journal of Personality and Social Psychology 25 (3, March): 361-368. P.A. 50:4825.

4425. Reitan, Harold T., and Marvin E. Shaw
1964 "Group membership, sex-composition of the group, and conformity behavior." Journal of Social Psychology 64 (1, October): 45-51. P.A. 39:4887.

4426. Reitz, Willard E., and Nancy Robinson
1969 "Effect of social desirability on interpersonal attraction." Proceedings of the 77th Annual Convention of the American Psychological Association 4 (pt. 1): 339-340. P.A. 43:17354.

4427. Reker, Gary T.
1974 "Interpersonal conceptual structures of emotionally disturbed and normal boys." Journal of Abnormal Psychology 83 (4): 380-386.

4428. Rekosh, Jerold H., and Kenneth Feigenbaum
1966 "The necessity of mutual trust for cooperative behavior in a two-person game." Journal of Social Psychology 69 (1, June): 149-154. P.A. 40:10041.

4429. Renner, John, and Vivian Renner
1972 "Effects of stress on group versus individual problem solving." Psychological Reports 30 (2, April): 487-491. P.A. 50:2968.

4430. Repp, Alan C., and William D. Wolking
1972 "Human preference for nonconflict vs. conflict situations." Psychonomic Science 29 (6-B, December): 394-396. P.A. 50:974.

4431. Restle, Frank
1962 "Speed and accuracy of cognitive achievement in small groups." In J. H. Criswell, H. Solomon, and P. Suppes (eds.), Mathematical Methods in Small Group Processes, pp. 250-262. Stanford, Calif.: Stanford University Press. S.A. 12:B2420.

4432. Restle, Frank, and James H. Davis
1962 "Success and speed of problem solving by individuals and groups." Psychological Review 69 (6): 520-536.

4433. Rettig, Salomon
1966a "Group discussion and predicted ethical risk taking." Journal of Personality and Social Psychology 3 (6, June): 629-633. P.A. 40:7648; S.A. 15:C4806.

4434. 1966b "Ethical risk taking in group and individual conditions." Journal of Personality and Social Psychology 4 (6): 648-654.

4435. 1969 "Locus of control in predictive judgments of unethical behavior." Proceedings of the 77th Annual Convention of the American Psychological Association 4 (pt. 1): 427-428.

4436. 1972 "Trust and locus of control in predictive judgments of unethical behavior." Proceedings of the 80th Annual Convention of the American Psychological Association 7 (pt. 1): 221-222.

4437. Rettig, Salomon, and Stuart J. Turoff
1967 "Exposure to group discussion and predicted ethical risk taking." Journal of Personality and Social Psychology 7 (2): 177-180.

4438. Reynolds, Herbert H.
1966 "Efficacy of sociometric ratings in predicting leadership success." Psychological Reports 19: 35-40.

4439. Reynolds, Paul Davidson
1971 "Comment on 'The distribution of participation in group discussions' as related to group size." American Sociological Review 36 (4, August): 704-706. P.A. 47:8800; S.A. 20:F4687.

4440. Reynolds, Paul D., and Mustafa H. Fisek
1972 "Development of influence hierarchies in small discussion groups: Alternatives for measuring temporal change." Behavioral Science 17 (6, November): 542-548. P.A. 50:11266; S.A. 22:74G6154.

4441. Rhine, Ramon J.
1960 "The effect of peer group influence upon concept-attitude development and change." Journal of Social Psychology 51 (February): 173-179. P.A. 34:7600; P.A. 36:3GE73R.

4442. Rhine, W. Ray
1973 "Adaptation to a click-counting task and its use in the simulated group." Psychological Reports 32 (3, pt. 2, June): 1239-1241. P.A.

51:2994.

4443. Ribner, Neil G.
1974   "Effects of an explicit group contract on self-disclosure and group cohesiveness." Journal of Counseling Psychology 21 (2, March): 116-120. P.A. 52:7536.

4444. Rice, A. K.
1951   "The use of unrecognized cultural mechanisms in an expanding machine shop." Human Relations 4: 143-160. P.A. 26:1744.

4445.   1969   "Individual, group and intergroup processes." Human Relations 22 (6, December): 565-584.

4446. Rice, Robert W., and Martin M. Chemers
1973   "Predicting the emergence of leaders using Fiedler's contingency model of leadership effectiveness." Journal of Applied Psychology 57 (3): 281-287.

4447. Rich, J. M.
1952   "Measuring supervisory training: The sociometric approach." Personnel 29: 78-84. P.A. 27:3066.

4448. Richards, Steven A., and James U. Cuffe
1972   "Behavioral correlates of leadership effectiveness in interacting and counteracting groups." Journal of Applied Psychology 56 (5, October): 377-381. P.A. 49:4441.

4449. Richardson, Helen M.
1939   "Studies of mental resemblance between husbands and wives and between friends." Psychological Bulletin 36: 104-120.

4450.   1940   "Community of values as a factor in friendships of college and adult women." Journal of Social Psychology 11: 303-312. P.A. 14:5132.

4451. Richardson, James T., John R. Dugan, Louis N. Gray, and Bruce H. Mayhew, Jr.
1973   "Expert power: A behavioral interpretation." Sociometry 36 (3, September): 302-324. P.A. 52:2901.

4452. Richardson, James T., Bruce H. Mayhew, Jr., and Louis N. Gray
1969   "Differentiation, restraint, and the asymmetry of power." Human Relations 22 (3, June): 263-274. P.A. 44:6663.

4453. Richardson, L. P.
1973   "Polarization in impression formation as a function of affect and range dispersion." Bulletin of the Psychonomic Society 1 (5-A, May): 289-290. P.A. 51:1001.

4454. Richardson, Stephen A., and Patricia Emerson
1970   "Race and physical handicap in children's preference for other children: A replication in a southern city." Human Relations 23 (1): 31-36. P.A. 44:18574.

4455. Richey, Marjorie H., Harold W. Richey, and Gregory Thieman
1972   "Negative salience in impression of character: Effects of new information on established relationships." Psychonomic Science 28 (2, July): 65-67. P.A. 50:2969.

4456. Richman, Joel
1971   "Concept of cooperation in the Prisoner's Dilemma and other tasks: Some need structure correlates." Proceedings of the 79th Annual Convention of the American Psychological Association 6 (pt. 1): 227-228.

4457. Richmond, Bert O., Robert L. Mason, and Harry G. Padgett
1972   "Self-concept and perception of others." Journal of Humanistic Psychology 12 (2, Fall): 103-111. P.A. 49:9083.

4458. Richmond, Bert O., and Gerald P. Weiner
1973   "Cooperation and competition among young children as a function of ethnic grouping, grade, sex, and reward condition." Journal of Educational Psychology 64 (3, June): 329-334. P.A. 50:11267.

4459. Richmond, Robert D., and Leonard A. Ostlund
1966   "Relationship between academic preference and group discussion performance." Journal of Human Relations 14 (2): 207-216. P.A. 40:11109.

4460. Rickard, Henry C., and Edwin O. Timmons
1961   "Manipulating verbal behavior in groups: A comparison of three

intervention techniques." Psychological Reports 9: 729–736.

4461. Riddle, Ethel M.
1925   "Aggressive behavior in a small social group." Archives of Psychology 12, No. 78. (See also Hare, Borgatta, and Bales, 1955, 1965.)

4462. Riecken, Henry W.
1952   "Some problems of consensus development." Rural Sociology 17: 245–252.

4463.   1958   "The effect of talkativeness on ability to influence group solutions to problems." Sociometry 21: 309–321. (See also Crosbie, 1975.) P.A. 34:1184.

4464.   1960   "Social psychology." Annual Review of Psychology 11: 479–510.

4465. Riecken, Henry W., and George C. Homans
1954   "Psychological aspects of social structure." In G. Lindzey (ed.), Handbook of Social Psychology, pp. 786–832. Cambridge, Mass.: Addison-Wesley. P.A. 29:3824.

4466. Riffenburgh, Robert H.
1966   "A method of sociometric identification of the basis of multiple measurements." Sociometry 29 (3, September): 280–290.

4467. Riker, William H., and Richard G. Niemi
1964   "Anonymity and rationality in the essential three-person game." Human Relations 17 (2, May): 131–140. S.A. 13:B4059.

4468. Riley, Matilda W., and R. Cohn
1958   "Control networks in informal groups." Sociometry 21: 30–49.

4469. Riley, Matilda W., Richard Cohn, Jackson Toby, and John W. Riley, Jr.
1954   "Interpersonal orientations in small groups: A consideration of the questionnaire approach." American Sociological Review 19: 715–724. S.A. 1509.

4470. Rim, Yeshayahu
1964a   ("The intolerance of ambiguity and risk taking.") Schweizerische Zeitschrift für Psychologie und Ihre Anwendungen 23 (3): 253–259. P.A. 39:4888.

4471.   1964b   "Social attitudes and risk-taking." Human Relations 17 (3, August): 259–265. S.A. 13:B4932.

4472.   1965   ("Inner-directedness and decisions involving a risk.") Zeitschrift für Experimentelle und Angewandte Psychologie 12 (3): 493–501. P.A. 40:4189.

4473   1971   ("Values in leaderless group discussions.") Archivio di Psicologia, Neurologia e Psichiatria 32 (1-2, January): 131–136. P.A. 49:9084.

4474. Ring, Kenneth, Dorothea Braginsky, and Benjamin Braginsky
1966   "Performance styles in interpersonal relations: A typology." Psychological Reports 18 (1): 203–220. P.A. 40:6593.

4475. Ring, Kenneth, Dorothea Braginsky, Lawrence Levine, and Benjamin Braginsky
1967   "Performance styles in interpersonal behavior: An experimental validation of a typology." Journal of Experimental Social Psychology 3 (April): 140–159.

4476. Ring, Kenneth, and Kenneth Wallston
1968   "A test to measure performance styles in interpersonal relations." Psychological Reports 22 (1): 147–154. P.A. 42:10520.

4477. Rinn, John L.
1961   "Q methodology: An application to group phenomena." Educational and Psychological Measurement 21: 315–329. P.A. 36:2GE15R.

4478.   1966   "Dimensions of group interaction: The cooperative analysis of idiosyncratic descriptions of training groups." Educational and Psychological Measurement 26 (2): 343–362. P.A. 40:13158.

4479. Rioch, Margaret J.
1970   "The work of Wilfred Bion on groups." Psychiatry (Washington, D.C.) 33 (1, February): 56–66. P.A. 45:633.

4480. Rittelmeyer, Christian
1972   ("The SPAN-Technique: A method to improve participation in group decisions.") Soziale Welt 23 (3): 284–292. S.A. 22:74G6155.

4481. Roback, Howard B.
1972   "Experimental comparison of outcomes in insight- and non-insight-

oriented therapy groups." Journal of Consulting and Clinical Psychology 38 (3): 411-417.

4482. Roberts, Bertram H., and Fred L. Strodtbeck
1953 "Interaction process differences between groups of paranoid schizophrenic and depressed patients." International Journal of Group Psychotherapy 3: 29-41. P.A. 28:4670.

4483. Roberts, John C., and Carl H. Castore
1972 "The effects of conformity, information, and confidence upon subjects' willingness to take risk following a group discussion." Organizational Behavior and Human Performance 8 (3, December): 384-394. P.A. 49:11119.

4484. Roberts, John M.
1951 Three Navaho Households: A Comparative Study in Small Group Culture. Cambridge, Mass.: Peabody Museum of American Archeology and Ethnology. P.A. 27:1101.

4485. Robinson, K. F.
1941 "An experimental study of the effects of group discussion upon the social attitudes of college students." Speech Monographs 8: 34-57. P.A. 16:1611.

4486. Robinson, Margaret B.
1970 "A study of the effects of focused video-tape feedback in group counseling." Comparative Group Studies 1 (1, February): 47-75.

4487. Robson, Reginald A. H.
1971 "The effects of different group sex compositions on support rates and coalition formation." Canadian Review of Sociology and Anthropology 8 (4, November): 244-262. S.A. 20:F6957.

4488. Roby, Thornton B.
1957 "On the measurement and description of groups." Behavioral Science 2: 119-129. P.A. 32:5324.

4489. 1961 "The executive function in small groups." In L. Petrullo and B. M. Bass (eds.), Leadership and Interpersonal Behavior, pp. 118-136. New York: Holt, Rinehart & Winston.

4490. 1962 "Subtask phasing in small groups." In J. H. Criswell, H. Solomon, and P. Suppes (eds.), Mathematical Methods in Small Group Processes, pp. 263-281. Stanford, Calif.: Stanford University Press. S.A. 12:B2421.

4491. Roby, Thornton B., and C. R. Budrose
1965 "Pattern recognition in groups: Laboratory and simulation studies." Journal of Personality and Social Psychology 2 (5): 648-653. P.A. 40:2823.

4492. Roby, Thornton B., and John T. Lanzetta
1956 "Work group structure, communication, and group performance." Sociometry 19: 105-113. P.A. 31:5903; S.A. 4297.

4493. 1958 "Considerations in the analysis of group tasks." Psychological Bulletin 55: 88-101.

4494. 1961 "A study of an 'assembly effect' in small group task performance." Journal of Social Psychology 53 (February): 53-68.

4495. Roby, Thornton B., Elizabeth H. Nicol, and Francis M. Farrell
1963 "Group problem solving under two types of executive structure." Journal of Abnormal and Social Psychology 67 (6, December): 550-556. P.A. 38:5968; S.A. 13:B6763.

4496. Roby, Thornton B., and Jeffrey Z. Rubin
1973 "An exploratory study of competitive temporal judgment." Behavioral Science 18 (1, January): 42-51. P.A. 50:8871.

4497. Rock, Milton L., and Edward N. Hay
1953 "Investigation of the use of tests as a predictor of leadership and group effectiveness in a job evaluation situation." Journal of Social Psychology 38: 109-119. P.A. 28:5831.

4498. Rodgers, David A.
1959 "Relationship between real similarity and assumed similarity with favorability controlled." Journal of Abnormal and Social Psychology 59 (November): 431-433. P.A. 34:5744.

4499. Rodgers, Janet A.
    1972   "Relationship between sociability and personal space preference at two different times of day." Perceptual and Motor Skills 35 (2, October): 519-526. P.A. 49:6857.
4500. Rodin, Judith, and Joyce Slochower
    1974   "Fat chance for a favor: Obese-normal differences in compliance and incidental learning." Journal of Personality and Social Psychology 29 (4, April): 557-565. P.A. 52:7573.
4501. Rodrigues, Aroldo
    1965   "On the differential effects of some parameters of balance." Journal of Psychology 61 (2): 241-250. P.A. 40:5406.
4502.   1967   "Effects of balance, positivity, and agreement in triadic social relations." Journal of Personality and Social Psychology 5 (4): 472-476.
4503.   1968   "The biasing effect of agreement in balanced and imbalanced triads." Journal of Personality 36 (1): 138-153. P.A. 42:15406.
4504. Roethlisberger, Fritz J., and William J. Dickson
    1939   Management and the Worker. Cambridge, Mass.: Harvard University Press. P.A. 14:509.
4505. Roff, Merrill
    1949   "A factorial study of the Fels parent behavior scales." Child Development 20:29-44.
4506.   1950   "A study of combat leadership in the Air Force by means of a rating scale: Group differences." Journal of Psychology 30: 229-239. P.A. 25:1303.
4507. Rogers, Carl R.
    1941   Counselling and Psychotherapy. Boston: Houghton Mifflin. P.A. 17: 2749.
4508.   1970   Carl Rogers on Encounter Groups. New York: Harper & Row. P.A. 49:797.
4509. Rogers, Carl R., and Fritz J. Roethlisberger
    1974   "Barriers and gateways to communication." In D. A. Kolb, I. M. Rubin, and J. M. McIntyre (eds.), Organizational Psychology: A Book of Readings, 2nd ed. Englewood Cliffs, N.J.: Prentice-Hall. P.A. 52:12278.
4510. Rohde, David W.
    1972   "Policy goals and opinion coalitions in the Supreme Court." Midwest Journal of Political Science 16 (2, May): 208-224. S.A. 22: 74G6156.
4511. Rohner, Ronald P.
    1974   "Proxemics and stress: An empirical study of the relationship between living space and roommate turnover." Human Relations 27 (7): 697-702.
4512. Rohrer, John H., S. H. Baron, E. L. Hoffman, and D. V. Swander
    1954   "The stability of autokinetic judgments." Journal of Abnormal and Social Psychology 49: 595-597. P.A. 29:5480.
4513. Rohrer, John H., and Muzafer Sherif
    1951   Social Psychology at the Crossroads: The University of Oklahoma Lectures in Social Psychology. New York: Harper P.A. 26:817.
4514. Roistacher, Richard C.
    1974   "A microeconomic model of sociometric choice." Sociometry 37 (2, June): 219-238. P.A. 52:12344.
4515. Rokeach, Milton
    1961   "Authority, authoritarianism, and conformity." In I. A. Berg and B. M. Bass (eds.), Conformity and Deviation, pp. 230-257. New York: Harper.
4516. Rokeach, Milton, and Ray Cochrane
    1972   "Self-confrontation and confrontation with another as determinants of long-term value change." Journal of Applied Social Psychology 2 (4, October): 283-292. P.A. 50:2971.
4517. Rolla, E. H., and J. M. de Rolla
    1964   ("Verbal and nonverbal signals in group dynamics.") Acta Psiquia-

tríca y Psicológica de America Latina 10 (4): 315-320. P.A. 39: 15058.

4518. Romano, John L., and Alan T. Quay
1974   "Follow-up of community college C-group participants." Journal of College Student Personnel 15 (4, July): 278-283. P.A. 52:12234.

4519. Ronning, Royce R., and John E. Horrocks
1961   "A method for estimating effectiveness of groups in a 'group' teaching situation." Educational and Psychological Measurement 21: 331-347. P.A. 36:2GE31R.

4520. Roos, Philip D.
1968   "Jurisdiction: An ecological concept." Human Relations 21 (1, February): 75-84. P.A. 42:13667.

4521. Röpcke, J.
1960   ("Sociometric knowledge as group diagnosis.") Mens en Maatschappij 35 (2, March-April): 81-95. S.A. A1131.

4522. Rosca, A.
1966   ("The creativity of thought in groups.") Revue Roumaine des Sciences Sociales: Série de Psychologie 10 (1): 45-58. P.A. 41:16636.

4523. Roseborough, Mary E.
1953   "Experimental studies of small groups." Psychological Bulletin 50: 275-303. P.A. 28:2438.

4524. Rosen, Bernard C.
1955a   "Conflicting group membership: A study of parent-peer group cross pressures." American Sociological Review 20: 155-161. S.A. 1769.

4525.   1955b   "The reference group approach to the parental factor in attitude and behavior formation." Social Forces 34: 137-144. P.A. 31:781.

4526. Rosen, Sidney
1966   "The comparative roles of informational and material commodities in interpersonal transactions." Journal of Experimental Social Psychology 2 (2, April): 211-226. P.A. 40:8795.

4527. Rosen, Sidney, and Karen S. Helgerson
1969   "Empathic avoidance of a victim's condition as a function of perceived similarity and causal locus." Proceedings of the 77th Annual Convention of the American Psychological Association 4 (pt. 1): 393-394.

4528. Rosen, Sidney, Robert D. Johnson, Martha J. Johnson, and Abraham Tesser
1973   "Interactive effects of new valence and attraction on communicator behavior." Journal of Personality and Social Psychology 28 (3, December): 298-300. P.A. 51:7037.

4529. Rosen, Sidney, George Levinger, and Ronald Lippitt
1960   "Desired change in self and others as a function of resource ownership." Human Relations 13 (3, August): 187-193. P.A. 35:2130.

4530.   1961   "Perceived sources of social power." Journal of Abnormal and Social Psychology 62 (2, March): 439-441. P.A. 4GF39R.

4531. Rosen, Sidney, and Abraham Tesser
1970   "On reluctance to communicate undesirable information: The MUM effect." Sociometry 33: 253-263.

4532.   1972   "Fear of negative evaluation and the reluctance to transmit bad news." Journal of Communication 22 (2, June): 124-141. P.A. 49: 2369.

4533. Rosenbaum, Leonard L., and William B. Rosenbaum
1971   "Morale and productivity consequences of group leadership style, stress, and type of task." Journal of Applied Psychology 55 (4, August): 343-348. P.A. 47:2848.

4534. Rosenbaum, Milton E.
1956   "The effect of stimulus and background factors on the volunteering response." Journal of Abnormal and Social Psychology 53: 118-121. P.A. 32:1463.

4535.   1959   "Social perception and the motivational structure of interpersonal relations." Journal of Abnormal and Social Psychology 59: 130-133.

4536. Rosenbaum, Milton E., and Robert R. Blake
1955   "Volunteering as a function of field structure." Journal of Abnormal

and Social Psychology 50: 193–196. P.A. 30:799; S.A. 1981.

4537. Rosenberg, Leon A.
    1961   "Group size, prior experience, and conformity." Journal of Abnormal and Social Psychology 63 (2, September): 436–437. P.A. 37: 1111; S.A. 11:A4160.

4538.   1963   "Conformity as a function of confidence in self and confidence in partner." Human Relations 16 (2, May): 131–140. S.A. 12:A8717.

4539. Rosenberg, Milton J.
    1965   "When dissonance fails: On eliminating evaluation apprehension from attitude measurement." Journal of Personality and Social Psychology 1: 28–42.

4540. Rosenberg, Seymour
    1959   "The maintenance of a learned response in controlled interpersonal conditions." Sociometry 22 (2, June): 124–138. P.A. 34:4204.

4541.   1960   "Cooperative behaviors in dyads as a function of reinforcement parameters." Journal of Abnormal and Social Psychology 60 (3): 318–333. P.A. 35:4823.

4542.   1962   "Two-person interactions in a continuous-response task." In J. H. Criswell, H. Solomon, and P. Suppes (eds.), Mathematical Methods in Small Group Processes, pp. 282–304. Stanford, Calif.: Stanford University Press. S.A. 12:B2422.

4543. Rosenberg, Seymour, Dwight E. Erlick, and Leonard Berkowitz
    1955   "Some effects of varying combinations of group members on group performance measures and leadership behaviors." Journal of Abnormal and Social Psychology 51: 195–203. P.A. 30:4372; S.A. 2731.

4544. Rosenberg, Seymour, Carnot Nelson, and P. S. Vivekananthan
    1968   "A multidimensional approach to the structure of personality impressions." Journal of Personality and Social Psychology 9 (4): 283–294. P.A. 42:17150.

4545. Rosenberg, Seymour, and Karen Olshan
    1970   "Evaluative and descriptive aspects in personality perception." Journal of Personality and Social Psychology 16 (4): 619–626.

4546. Rosenblood, Lorne K., and Jeffrey H. Goldstein
    1969   "Similarity, intelligence, and affiliation." Proceedings of the 77th Annual Convention of the American Psychological Association 4 (pt. 1): 341–342.

4547. Rosenfeld, Howard M.
    1965   "Effect of an approval-seeking induction on interpersonal proximity." Psychological Reports 17 (1): 120–122. P.A. 40:1527.

4548.   1966a   "Instrumental affiliative functions of facial and gestural expressions." Journal of Personality and Social Psychology 4 (1): 65–72. P.A. 40:10042.

4549.   1966b   "Approval-seeking and approval-inducing functions of verbal and nonverbal responses in the dyad." Journal of Personality and Social Psychology 4 (6): 597–605.

4550. Rosenfeld, Howard M., and Samuel S. Franklin
    1966   "Arousal of need for affiliation in women." Journal of Personality and Social Psychology 3 (2): 245–248. P.A. 40:4190.

4551. Rosenfeld, Howard M., and Dennis J. Nauman
    1969   "Effects of dogmatism on the development of informal relationships among women." Journal of Personality 37: 497–511.

4552. Rosenfeld, Howard M., and Virginia L. Sullwold
    1969   "Optimal informational discrepancies for persistent communication." Behavioral Science 14 (4): 303–315. P.A. 44:2270.

4553. Rosenhan, David L.
    1972   "Learning theory and prosocial behavior." Journal of Social Issues 28 (3): 151–163. P.A. 50:4829.

4554. Rosenhan, David L., Daniel de Wilde, and Stuart McDougal
    1963   "Pressure to conform and logical problem solving." Psychological Reports 13: 227–230.

4555. Rosenhan, David L., Bill Underwood, and Bert Moore
    1974   "Affect moderates self-gratification and altruism." Journal of Per-

sonality and Social Psychology 30 (4): 546–552.

4556. Rosenthal, Bernard G., and Alton J. DeLong
1972 "Complementary leadership and spatial arrangement of group members." Group Psychotherapy and Psychodrama 25 (1-2): 34–52. P.A. 49:4442.

4557. Rosenthal, David, and Charles N. Cofer
1948 "The effect on group performance of an indifferent and neglectful attitude shown by one group member." Journal of Experimental Psychology 38: 568–577. P.A. 23:1728.

4558. Rosenthal, Paul I., and Kalman J. Kaplan
1973 "Effects of evaluative versus descriptive trait inconsistency on acceptance, impact and attitude change." Proceedings of the 81st Annual Convention of the American Psychological Association 8: 365–366. P.A. 50:8872.

4559. Rosenthal, Robert
1966 Experimenter Effects in Behavioral Research. New York: Appleton-Century-Crofts.

4560. Rosenthal, Robert, and Lenore Jacobson
1966 "Teacher's expectancies: Determinants of pupils' IQ gains." Psychological Reports 19: 115–118. (See also Crosbie, 1975.)

4561. 1968 Pygmalion in the Classroom: Teacher Expectation and Pupils' Intellectual Development. New York: Holt, Rinehart & Winston.

4562. Rosenthal, Ted L., Cecil Rogers, and Kathleen Durning
1972 "Sequence of extreme belief-incongruent versus neutral information in social perception." Australian Journal of Psychology 24 (3, December): 267–273. P.A. 50:8873.

4563. Rosner, Stanley
1957 "Consistency in response to group pressures." Journal of Abnormal and Social Psychology 55: 145–146.

4564. Rosnow, Ralph L., Barry E. Goodstadt, Jerry M. Suls, and George A. Gitter
1973 "More on the social psychology of the experiment: When compliance turns to self-defense." Journal of Personality and Social Psychology 27 (3, September): 337–343. P.A. 51:5067.

4565. Rosnow, Ralph L., Howard Wainer, and Robert L. Arms
1970 "Personality and group impression formation as a function of the amount of overlap in evaluative meaning of the stimulus elements." Sociometry 33 (4): 472–484.

4566. Rosow, Irving
1957 "Issues in the concept of need-complementarity." Sociometry 20: 216–233.

4567. Ross, Abraham S.
1970 "The effect of observing a helpful model on helping behavior." Journal of Social Psychology 81: 131–132.

4568. 1971 "Effect of increased responsibility on bystander intervention: The presence of children." Journal of Personality and Social Psychology 19 (3, September): 306–310. P.A. 47:2849.

4569. Ross, Abraham S., and Janinne Braband
1973 "Effect of increased responsibility on bystander intervention: II: The cue value of a blind person." Journal of Personality and Social Psychology 25 (2, February): 254–258. P.A. 50:977.

4570. Ross, Abraham S., and Pauline Wilson
1972 "The effects of utility of information and intent on interpersonal esteem." Journal of Social Psychology 87 (1, June): 83–88. P.A. 48:9035.

4571. Ross, Ian C., and Frank Harary
1952 "On the determination of redundancies in sociometric chains." Psychometrica 17: 195–208. P.A. 29:4749.

4572. 1959 "A description of strengthening and weakening members of a group." Sociometry 22 (2, June): 139–147. P.A. 34:4206.

4573. Ross, Joel A.
1973 "Influence of expert and peer upon Negro mothers of low socioeconomic status." Journal of Social Psychology 89 (1, February): 79–

84. P.A. 50:2973.

4574. Ross, Michael, Bruce Layton, Bonnie Erickson, and John Schopler
1973 "Affect, facial regard, and reactions to crowding." Journal of Personality and Social Psychology 28 (1): 69-76.

4575. Ross, Shirley, and James Walters
1973 "Perceptions of a sample of university men concerning women." Journal of Genetic Psychology 122 (2, June): 329-336. P.A. 51: 1002.

4576. Rossel, Robert D.
1970 "Fantasy in interracial groups." Sociological Quarterly 11 (1, Winter): 50-66. S.A. 18:E5686.

4577. Roth, Susan, and Richard R. Bootzin
1974 "Effects of experimentally induced expectancies of external control: An investigation of learned helplessness." Journal of Personality and Social Psychology 29 (2): 253-264.

4578. Rothbart, Myron
1968a "Effects of motivation, equity, and compliance on the use of reward and punishment." Journal of Personality and Social Psychology 9 (4): 353-362. P.A. 42:17151.

4579. 1968b "Factors influencing the use of reward and punishment by subjects attempting behavior modification." Proceedings of the 76th Annual Convention of the American Psychological Association 3: 393-394.

4580. Rotter, George S.
1967 "An experimental evaluation of group attractiveness as a determinant of conformity." Human Relations 20 (3, August): 273-282. P.A. 42:2507; S.A. 16:D0611.

4581. Rotter, George S., and Stephen M. Portugal
1969 "Group and individual effects in problem solving." Journal of Applied Psychology 53 (4): 338-341.

4582. Rotter, Julian B.
1954 Social Learning in Clinical Psychology. New York: Prentice-Hall.

4583. Rowland, H.
1938 "Interaction processes in the State Mental Hospital." Psychiatry 1: 323-337.

4584. 1939 "Friendship patterns in a mental hospital." Psychiatry 2: 363-373.

4585. Roy, Donald F.
1959- "'Banana time': Job satisfaction and informal interaction." Human
1960 Organization 18 (4, Winter): 158-168. S.A. A2382.

4586. Rubenstein, Albert H.
1953 "Problems in the measurement of interpersonal communication in an ongoing situation." Sociometry 16: 78-100. P.A. 28:870.

4587. Rubin, Jeffrey Z.
1971 "The nature and success of influence attempts in a four-party bargaining relationship." Journal of Experimental Social Psychology 7 (1): 17-35.

4588. Rubin, Jeffrey Z., and Maryanne R. DiMatteo
1972 "Factors affecting the magnitude of subjective utility parameters in a tacit bargaining game." Journal of Experimental Social Psychology 8 (5, September): 412-426. P.A. 49:6861.

4589. Rubin, Jeffrey Z., and Roy J. Lewicki
1973 "A three-factor experimental analysis of promises and threats." Journal of Applied Social Psychology 3 (3, July): 240-257. P.A. 52:2902.

4590. Rubin, Jeffrey Z., Roy J. Lewicki, and Lynne Dunn
1973 "The perception of promisors and threateners." Proceedings of the 81st Annual Convention of the American Psychological Association 8: 141-142. P.A. 50:8874.

4591. Rubin, Jeffrey Z., Carol T. Mowbray, Lora-Jean Collett, and Roy J. Lewicki
1971 "Perception of attempts at interpersonal influence." Proceedings of the 79th Annual Convention of the American Psychological Association 6 (pt. 1): 391-392.

4592. Rubin, Zick
    1970   "Measurement of romantic love." Journal of Personality and Social Psychology 16 (2, October): 265-273. P.A. 45:2302.

4593.   1973   Liking and Loving: An Invitation to Social Psychology. New York: Holt, Rinehart & Winston. P.A. 50:11269.

4594. Ruble, Thomas L.
    1973   "Effects of actor and observer roles on attributions of causality in situations of success and failure." Journal of Social Psychology 90 (1, June): 41-44. P.A. 51:3066.

4595. Rudin, Stanley A.
    1964   "Leadership as psychophysiological activation of group members: A case experimental study." Psychological Reports 15 (2): 577-578. P.A. 39:4909.

4596. Rudraswamy, V.
    1964   "An investigation of the relationships between perceptions of status and leadership attempts." Journal of the Indian Academy of Applied Psychology 1 (1): 12-19. P.A. 39:1593.

4597. Ruesch, Jurgen, Jack Block, and Lillian Bennett
    1953   "The assessment of communication: I. A method for the analysis of social interaction." Journal of Psychology 35: 59-80. P.A. 27: 6491.

4598. Ruesch, Jurgen, and Weldon Kees
    1972   Nonverbal Communication: Notes on the Visual Perception of Human Relations. Berkeley and Los Angeles: University of California Press. P.A. 49:11121.

4599. Ruesch, Jurgen, and A. Rodney Prestwood
    1950   "Interaction processes and personal codification." Journal of Personality 18: 391-430. P.A. 25:4631.

4600. Rule, Brendan G.
    1964   "Group effects on deviant behavior." Psychological Reports 15 (2): 611-614. P.A. 39:4889.

4601. Rule, Brendan G., and Pieter Duker
    1973   "Effects of intentions and consequences on children's evaluations of aggressors." Journal of Personality and Social Psychology 27 (2): 184-189.

4602. Rule, Brendan G., and Lynn S. Hewitt
    1971   "Effects of thwarting on cardiac response and physical aggression." Journal of Personality and Social Psychology 19 (2, August): 181-187. P.A. 47:2851.

4603. Rule, Brendan G., and John Renner
    1965   "Distance, group dispersion and opinion change." Psychological Reports 17: 777-778.

4604.   1968   "Involvement and group effects on opinion change." Journal of Social Psychology 76 (December): 189-198.

4605. Rule, Brendan G., and Mark L. Sandilands
    1969   "Test anxiety, confidence, commitment, and conformity." Journal of Personality 37: 460-467.

4606. Rump, E. E., and P. S. Delin
    1973   "Differential accuracy in the status-height phenomenon and an experimenter effect." Journal of Personality and Social Psychology 28 (3, December): 343-347. P.A. 51:7087.

4607. Runcie, John F.
    1973   "Group formation: Theoretical and empirical approaches." Small Group Behavior 4 (2, May): 181-205. P.A. 51:7038.

4608. Runkel, Philip J.
    1956   "Cognitive similarity in facilitating communication." Sociometry 19: 178-191.

4609.   1959   "The social-psychological basis of human relations." Review of Educational Research 29: 317-331. P.A. 34:5746.

4610. Runkel, Philip J., Marilyn Lawrence, Shirley Oldfield, Mimi Rider, and Candee Clark
    1971   "Stages of group development: An empirical test of Tuckman's

hypothesis." Journal of Applied Behavioral Science 7 (2, March-April): 180-193. S.A. 20:F9139.

4611. Runyan, David L.
1974   "The group risky-shift effect as a function of emotional bonds, actual consequences, and extent of responsibility." Journal of Personality and Social Psychology 29 (5, May): 670-676. P.A. 52: 12345.

4612. Rushlau, Perry J., and Gary Q. Jorgensen
1966   "Interpersonal relationships: A review." Regional Rehabilitation Research Institute Bulletin 1 (July). S.A. 15:C6385.

4613. Rustin, Michael
1971   "Structural and unconscious implications of the dyad and triad: An essay in theoretical integration, Durkheim, Simmel, Freud." Sociological Review 19 (2, May): 179-201. S.A. 20:F4689.

4614. Rutter, D. R., Ian E. Morley, and Jane C. Graham
1972   "Visual interaction in a group of introverts and extraverts." European Journal of Social Psychology 2 (4): 371-384. P.A. 50:6749.

4615. Ryack, Bernard L.
1965   "A comparison of individual and group learning of nonsense syllables." Journal of Personality and Social Psychology 2 (2): 296-299.

4616. Ryan, E. Dean, and W. L. Lakie
1965   "Competitive and noncompetitive performance in relation to achievement motive and manifest anxiety." Journal of Personality and Social Psychology 1 (4): 342-345.

4617. Rychlak, Joseph F.
1960   "A sociopsychological theory of performance in competitive situations." Human Relations 13 (2, May): 157-166. S.A. A3806.

4618.   1963   "Personality correlates of leadership among first level managers." Psychological Reports 12 (1): 43-52. P.A. 38:2600.

4619.   1965   "The similarity, compatibility, or incompatibility of needs in interpersonal selection." Journal of Personality and Social Psychology 2 (3): 334-340. P.A. 39:15059.

4620. Ryckman, Richard M., and William C. Rodda
1972   "Conformity in college men and women as a function of locus of control and prior group support." Journal of Social Psychology 86: 313-314.

4621. Ryckman, Richard M., and Martin F. Sherman
1974   "Locus of control and perceived ability level as determinants of partner and opponent choice." Journal of Social Psychology 94 (1): 103-110.

4622. Ryckman, Richard M., Martin F. Sherman, and Gary D. Burgess
1973   "Locus of control and self-disclosure of public and private information by college men and women: A brief note." Journal of Psychology 84 (2, July): 317-318. P.A. 51:9019.

4623. Rywick, Thomas, and Michael Gaffney
1972   "Imagined vs. real aversive stimulation." Perceptual and Motor Skills 35 (3, December): 742. P.A. 49:11122.

4624. Sabath, Gerald
1964   "The effect of disruption and individual status on person perception and group attraction." Journal of Social Psychology 64 (1, October): 119-130. P.A. 39:4890.

4625. Sacks, Elinor L.
1952   "Intelligence scores as a function of experimentally established social relationships between child and examiner." Journal of Abnormal and Social Psychology 47: 354-358. P.A. 27:2761.

4626. Sader, Manfred
1972   ("Psychological comments on the theory of group dynamics.") Gruppendynamik (Forschung und Praxis) 1 (March): 111-122. P.A. 50:2975.

4627. Sadler, Orin, and Abraham Tesser
1973   "Some effects of salience and time upon interpersonal hostility and

attraction during social isolation." Sociometry 36 (1, March): 99–
122. P.A. 50:11270.

4628. Saegert, Susan, Walter Swap, and R. B. Zajonc
1973   "Exposure, context, and interpersonal attraction." Journal of Personality and Social Psychology 25 (2, February): 234–242. P.A. 50:
979.

4629. Sage, John N.
1969   "Effects of incentives and primary and secondary group interaction
on learning a complex maze." Perceptual and Motor Skills 29 (1):
71–74. P.A. 44:2271.

4630. Sagi, Philip C., Donald W. Olmsted, and Frank Atelsek
1955   "Predicting maintenance of membership in small groups." Journal of
Abnormal and Social Psychology 51: 308–311. P.A. 30:4373; S.A.
2732.

4631. Saiyadain, Mirza S., and David A. Summers
1973   "The effects of influence conditions and discrepancy upon authoritarian conformity." Bulletin of the Psychonomic Society 1 (5-B,
May): 357–358. P.A. 51:3067.

4632. Sakoda, James M.
1952   "Factor analysis of OSS situational tests." Journal of Abnormal and
Social Psychology 47: 843–852. P.A. 27:5160.

4633.   1971   "The checkerboard model of social interaction." Journal of Mathematical Sociology 1 (1, January): 119–132. S.A. 20:F4688.

4634. Sales, Stephen M.
1971   "Need for stimulation as a factor in social behavior." Journal of Personality and Social Psychology 19 (1, July): 124–134. P.A. 46:
8946.

4635. Saltzstein, Herbert D., Alene Klausner, and R. Steven Schiavo
1974   "Social influence on perceptual judgments and responses." Journal
of Social Psychology 94 (1): 123–135.

4636. Salusky, A. S.
1930   "Collective behavior of children at a preschool age." Journal of Social Psychology 1: 367–378.

4637. Salzberg, Herman C.
1961   "Manipulation of verbal behavior in a group psychotherapeutic
setting." Psychological Reports 9: 183–186.

4638. Sambrooks, Jean E., and M. J. MacCulloch
1973   "A modification of the sexual orientation method and an automated
technique for presentation and scoring." British Journal of Social
and Clinical Psychology 12 (2, June): 163–174. P.A. 51:2995.

4639. Samelson, Franz
1957   "Conforming behavior under two conditions of conflict in the cognitive field." Journal of Abnormal and Social Psychology 55: 181–
187.

4640.   1964   "Agreement set and anticontent attitudes in the F scale: A reinterpretation." Journal of Abnormal and Social Psychology 68 (3):
338–342.

4641. Sample, John A., and Thurlow R. Wilson
1965   "Leader behavior, group productivity, and rating of least preferred
co-worker." Journal of Personality and Social Psychology 1 (3,
March): 266–290. P.A. 39:10020; S.A. 13:B7604.

4642. Sampson, Edward E.
1962   "Birth order, need achievement, and conformity." Journal of Abnormal and Social Psychology 64 (2): 155–159.

4643.   1963a   "Individual and group performance under reward and fine." Journal
of Social Psychology 61 (October): 111–125.

4644.   1963b   "Status congruence and cognitive consistency." Sociometry 26 (2,
June): 146–162.

4645.   1969   "Studies of status congruence." In L. Berkowitz (ed.), Advances in
Experimental Social Psychology, vol. 4, pp. 225–270. New York:
Academic Press.

4646.   1972   "Leader orientation and T-group effectiveness." Journal of Applied

Behavioral Science 8 (5): 564-575.

4647. Sampson, Edward E., and Arlene C. Brandon
1964   "The effects of role and opinion deviation on small group behavior." Sociometry 27 (3, September): 261-281. P.A. 39:4891; S.A. 13: B4933.

4648. Sampson, Edward E., and Francena T. Hancock
1967   "An examination of the relationship between ordinal position, personality, and conformity: An extension, replication, and partial verification." Journal of Personality and Social Psychology 5 (4): 398-407.

4649. Sampson, Edward E., and Chester A. Insko
1964   "Cognitive consistency and performance in the autokinetic situation." Journal of Abnormal and Social Psychology 68 (2, February): 184-192.

4650. Sampson, Edward E., and Marcelle Karsush
1965   "Age, sex, class, and race differences in response to a two-person non-zero sum game." Journal of Conflict Resolution 9 (2, June): 212-220. S.A. 14:C1889.

4651. Samuel, William
1973   "On clarifying some interpretations of social comparison theory." Journal of Experimental Social Psychology 9 (5, September): 450-465. P.A. 51:9050.

4652. Samuels, Frederick
1970   "The intra-and-inter-competitive group." Sociological Quarterly 11 (3, Summer): 391-396. S.A. 19:E9555.

4653. Samuels, Frederick, and John F. O'Rourke
1969   "The ambiguity of negative social-emotional behavior as an index of group cohesion." Canadian Review of Sociology and Anthropology 6 (1, February): 47-53. S.A. 18:E2909.

4654. Sanderson, Dwight
1938   "Group description." Social Forces 16: 309-319.

4655. Sandler, Georgette B.
1973   "Improving participant observation: The T group as an answer." Journal of Applied Behavioral Science 9 (1): 51-61. P.A. 51:957.

4656. Sanford, Fillmore H.
1950   Authoritarianism and Leadership. Philadelphia: Institute for Research in Human Relations. (See also Swanson, Newcomb, and Hartley, 1952.) P.A. 26:818.

4657. Sappenfield, Bert R.
1969   "Stereotypical perception of a personality trait in personal acquaintances." Proceedings of the 77th Annual Convention of the American Psychological Association 4 (pt. 1): 409-410.

4658. Saral, Tulsi B.
1972   "Cross-cultural generality of communication via facial expressions." Comparative Group Studies 3 (4, November): 473-486.

4659. Sarbin, Theodore R.
1954   "Role Theory." In G. Lindzey (ed.), Handbook of Social Psychology, pp. 223-258. Cambridge, Mass.: Addison-Wesley.

4660. Sarbin, Theodore R., and Vernon L. Allen
1968a   "Increasing participation in a natural group setting: A preliminary report." Psychological Record 18 (1): 1-7. P.A. 42:8882.

4661.   1968b   "Role theory." In G. Lindzey and E. Aronson (eds.), Handbook of Social Psychology, vol. 1, pp. 488-567. Reading, Mass.: Addison-Wesley.

4662. Sarbin, Theodore R., and Donal S. Jones
1955   "An experimental analysis of role behavior." Journal of Abnormal and Social Psychology 51: 236-241. (See also Maccoby, Newcomb, and Hartley, 1958.) P.A. 30:4374.

4663. Sasfy, Joseph, and Morris Okun
1974   "Form of evaluation and audience expertness as joint determinants of audience effects." Journal of Experimental Social Psychology 10 (5): 461-467.

4664. Sashkin, Marshall
1972 "Leadership style and group decision effectiveness: Correlational and behavioral tests of Fiedler's contingency model." Organizational Behavior and Human Performance 8 (3, December): 347-362. P.A. 49:11123.

4665. Sashkin, Marshall, and Norman R. Maier
1971 "Sex effects in delegation." Personnel Psychology 24 (3, Fall): 471-476. P.A. 51:9020.

4666. Saslow, George, D. W. Goodrich, and Marvin Stein
1956 "Study of therapist behavior in diagnostic interviews by means of the interaction chronograph." Journal of Clinical Psychology 12: 133-139. P.A. 31:4665.

4667. Saslow, George, Joseph D. Matarazzo, and Samuel B. Guze
1955 "The stability of interaction chronograph patterns in psychiatric interviews." Journal of Consulting Psychology 19: 417-430. P.A. 30:7176.

4668. Saslow, George, Joseph D. Matarazzo, Jeanne S. Phillips, and Ruth G. Matarazzo
1957 "Test-retest stability of interaction patterns during interviews conducted one week apart." Journal of Abnormal and Social Psychology 54: 295-302.

4669. Sato, Yasumasa
1963 "Comparison of group judgments made by blind and sighted subjects." Perceptual and Motor Skills 17 (3): 654. P.A. 38:5971.

4670. Sattler, Howard E.
1966 "Effect of group variability on pooled group decisions." Psychological Reports 18 (3): 676-678. P.A. 40:10043.

4671. Saulnier, Leda, and Teresa Simard
1973 Personal Growth and Interpersonal Relations. Englewood Cliffs, N.J.: Prentice-Hall. P.A. 50:11271.

4672. Savell, Joel M., and Gary W. Healey
1969 "Private and public conformity after being agreed and disagreed with." Sociometry 32 (3): 315-329. P.A. 44:3555.

4673. Savell, Joel M., and Jeanne M. Luttrell
1972 "Some effects of race and belief under different conditions of belief similarity-dissimilarity." Proceedings of the 80th Annual Convention of the American Psychological Association 7 (pt. 1): 281-282. P.A. 49:11124.

4674. Savicki, Victor
1972 "Outcomes of nonreciprocal self-disclosure strategies." Journal of Personality and Social Psychology 23 (2, August): 271-276. P.A. 49:801.

4675. Savitsky, Jeffrey C., Carroll E. Izard, William E. Kotsch, and Lo Christy
1974 "Aggressor's response to the victim's facial expression of emotion." Journal of Research in Personality 7 (4, March): 346-357. P.A. 52: 7575.

4676. Sawyer, Jack, and Morris F. Friedell
1965 "The interaction screen: An operational model for experimentation on interpersonal behavior." Behavioral Science 10: 446-460.

4677. Sbandi, Pio, and Ann Vogl
1973 ("The three-dimensional group model of R. F. Bales.") Gruppendynamik (Forschung und Praxis) 3 (June): 181-192. P.A. 51:2996.

4678. Schachter, Stanley
1951 "Deviation, rejection, and communication." Journal of Abnormal and Social Psychology 46: 190-207. (See also Cartwright and Zander, 1960, 1968; Crosbie, 1975.) P.A. 25:8043.

4679. 1952 "Comment on 'On group cohesiveness.'" American Journal of Sociology 57: 554-562.

4680. 1959 The Psychology of Affiliation: Experimental Studies of the Sources of Gregariousness. Stanford, Calif.: Stanford University Press. (See also Crosbie, 1975.)

4681. 1964 "Birth order and sociometric choice." Journal of Abnormal and

Social Psychology 68 (4, April): 453-456. S.A. 13:B7597.

4682. Schachter, Stanley, N. Ellertson, Dorothy McBride, and Doris Gregory
1951   "An experimental study of cohesiveness and productivity." Human Relations 4: 229-238. (See also Cartwright and Zander, 1960, 1968.) P.A. 26:6188.

4683. Schachter, Stanley, and R. Hall
1952   "Group-derived restraints and audience persuasion." Human Relations 5: 397-406. P.A. 27:7178.

4684. Schachter, Stanley, J. Nuttin, Cecily De Monchaux, P. H. Maucorps, D. Osmer, H. Duijker, R. Rommetveit, and J. Israel
1954   "Cross-cultural experiments on threat and rejection." Human Relations 7: 403-439. S.A. 1511.

4685. Schafer, Walter E.
1966   ("The social structure of sports groups.") Kölner Zeitschrift für Soziologie und Sozialpsychologie 10 (Supplement): 107-117. S.A. 15:C5586.

4686. Schaffner, Bertram (ed.)
1957   Group Processes: Transactions of the Third Conference. New York: Josiah Macy, Jr., Foundation.

4687. Schanck, Richard L.
1932   "A study of a community and its groups and institutions conceived of as behavior of individuals." Psychological Monographs 43 (2).

4688. Schapa, Eric
1972   "Cost, dependency, and helping." Journal of Personality and Social Psychology 21 (1): 74-78.

4689. Scharff, William H., and Robert S. Schlottmann
1973   "The effects of verbal reports of violence on aggression." Journal of Psychology 84 (2, July): 283-290. P.A. 51:9001.

4690. Scharmann, Theodor
1959   ("On methods of experimental group research.") In Report on the 22nd Congress of the German Society for Psychology in Heidelberg, pp. 259-262. Göttingen: Verlag fuer Psychologie. S.A. 12:B0185.

4691. 1962   ("Experimental interaction analysis of small groups.") Kölner Zeitschrift für Soziologie und Sozialpsychologie 14 (1, January): 139-154. P.A. 38:877; S.A. 12:A8718.

4692. 1966   ("The method of 'gruppenfertigung': Formation of laboratory groups.") Kölner Zeitschrift für Soziologie und Sozialpsychologie 10 (Supplement): 66-83. S.A. 15:C5587.

4693. 1972   (Teamwork in Business.) Bern and Stuttgart: UTB 154.

4694. Scheff, Thomas J.
1967   "A theory of social coordination applicable to mixed-motive games." Sociometry 30 (3, September): 215-234.

4695. Scheiblechner, Hartmann
1971   "The separation of individual- and system-influences on behavior in social contexts." Acta Psychologica 35 (6, December): 442-460. P.A. 48:11463.

4696. 1972   "Personality and system influences on behavior in groups: Frequency models." Acta Psychologica 36 (4, September): 322-336. P.A. 49:11127.

4697. Scheidlinger, Saul
1952   Psychoanalysis and Group Behavior: A Study in Freudian Group Psychology. New York: Norton. (See also Cartwright and Zander, 1953.) P.A. 27:1887.

4698. 1964   "Identification, the sense of belonging and of identity in small groups." International Journal of Group Psychotherapy 14 (3): 291-306. P.A. 39:7643.

4699. Scheier, Michael F., Allan Fenigstein, and Arnold H. Buss
1974   "Self-awareness and physical aggression." Journal of Experimental Social Psychology 10 (3): 264-273.

4700. Schein, Edgar H.
1956   "The Chinese indoctrination program for prisoners of war: A study of attempted 'brainwashing.'" Psychiatry 19: 149-172. (See also

Maccoby, Newcomb, and Hartley, 1958.)

4701.   1960   "Interpersonal communication, group solidarity, and social influ-
               ence." Sociometry 23 (2, June): 148-161. P.A. 35:2161; S.A.
               A2746.
4702. Schein, Edgar H., and Warren G. Bennis
      1965   Personal and Organizational Change through Group Methods. New
               York: Wiley.
4703. Schein, Edgar H., Inge Schneier, and Curtis H. Barker
      1961   Coercive Persuasion. New York: Norton. P.A. 36:3GG20S.
4704. Schellenberg, James A.
      1959   "Group size as a factor in success of academic discussion groups."
               Journal of Educational Sociology 33: 73079. P.A. 35:2704.
4705.   1964   "Distributive justice and collaboration in non-zero-sum games."
               Journal of Conflict Resolution 8 (2, June): 147-150. S.A. 14:
               C0075.
4706.   1965   "Dependence and cooperation." Sociometry 28 (2, June): 158-172.
4707. Schellenberg, James A., and Gregory A. Blevins
      1973   "Feeling good and helping: How quickly does the smile of Dame
               Fortune fade?" Psychological Reports 33 (1, August): 72-74. P.A.
               51:7088.
4708. Schellenberg, James A., and Mary U. Wright
      1969   "Imagined disengagement and cooperation: A study of expectations
               of social behavior." Journal of Social Psychology 79 (October): 79-
               87.
4709. Schelling, Thomas C.
      1958   "The strategy of conflict: Prospectus for a reorientation of game
               theory." Journal of Conflict Resolution 2 (3, September): 203-
               264. S.A. A3426.
4710.   1968   "Game theory and the study of ethical systems." Journal of Conflict
               Resolution 12 (1): 34-44. P.A. 43:5271.
4711. Scherer, Klaus R.
      1971   "Attribution of personality from voice: A cross-cultural study on
               interpersonal perception." Proceedings of the 79th Annual Conven-
               tion of the American Psychological Association 6 (pt. 1): 351-352.
4712.   1972   "Judging personality from voice: A cross-cultural approach to an old
               issue in interpersonal perception." Journal of Personality 40 (2,
               June): 191-210. P.A. 49:2372.
4713. Scherer, Klaus R., Robert Rosenthal, and Judy Koivumaki
      1972   "Mediating interpersonal expectancies via vocal cues: Differential
               speech intensity as a means of social influence." European Journal
               of Social Psychology 2 (2): 163-176. P.A. 49:9086.
4714. Scherer, Shawn E.
      1974   "Proxemic behavior of primary school children as a function of their
               socioeconomic class and subculture." Journal of Personality and So-
               cial Psychology 29 (6, June): 800-805. P.A. 52:7514.
4715. Scherer, Shawn E., and Myra R. Schiff
      1973   "Perceived intimacy, physical distance and eye contact." Perceptual
               and Motor Skills 36 (3, pt. 1, June): 835-841. P.A. 51:3068.
4716. Scherwitz, Larry, and Robert Helmreich
      1973   "Interactive effects of eye contact and verbal content on interper-
               sonal dyads." Journal of Personality and Social Psychology 25 (1,
               January): 6-14. P.A. 50:6752.
4717. Schettino, Andrew P., and Willa B. Baldwin
      1974   "Attraction as a function of similarity of perceptual judgments."
               Bulletin of the Psychonomic Society 3 (5-A, May): 350-352. P.A.
               52:12279.
4718. Schiavo, R. Steven
      1973   "Locus of control and judgments about another's accident." Psycho-
               logical Reports 32 (2, April): 483-488. P.A. 51:1003.
4719. Schiavo, R. Steven, Barbara Sherlock, and Gail Wicklund
      1974   "Effect of attire on obtaining directions." Psychological Reports 34
               (1, February): 245-246. P.A. 52:7577.

4720. Schiff, Herbert
    1954   "Judgemental response sets in the perception of sociometric status."
            Sociometry 17: 207-227. P.A. 29:5482; S.A. 4:1982.
4721. Schiff, William
    1973   "Social-event perception and stimulus pooling in deaf and hearing
            observers." American Journal of Psychology 86 (1, March): 61-78.
            P.A. 51:5115.
4722. Schiffenbauer, Allen
    1974a   "Effect of observer's emotional state on judgments of the emotional
            state of others." Journal of Personality and Social Psychology 30
            (1, July): 31-35. P.A. 52:12346.
4723.   1974b   "When will people use facial information to attribute emotion? The
            effect of judge's emotional state and intensity of facial expression on
            attribution of emotion." Representative Research in Social Psychol-
            ogy 5 (1, January): 47-53. P.A. 52:7578.
4724. Schindler, R.
    1958   "Bifocal group therapy." In J. Masserman and J. L. Moreno (eds.),
            Progress in Psychotherapy, vol. 3, pp. 176-186. New York: Grune &
            Stratton. P.A. 34:6123.
4725. Schlenker, Barry R., Thomas Bonoma, James T. Tedeschi, and William P.
    Pivnick
    1970   "Compliance to threats as a function of the wording of the threat
            and the exploitativeness of the threatener." Sociometry 33 (4): 394-
            408.
4726. Schlenker, Barry R., Robert Brown, and James T. Tedeschi
    1971   "Subjective probability of receiving harm as a function of attraction
            and harm delivered." Proceedings of the 79th Annual Convention of
            the American Psychological Association 6 (pt. 1): 285-286.
4727. Schlenker, Barry R., Bob Helm, and James T. Tedeschi
    1973   "The effects of personality and situational variables on behavioral
            trust." Journal of Personality and Social Psychology 25 (3): 419-
            427.
4728. Schlenker, Barry R., and Patricia A. Schlenker
    1973   "Reactions after delivering an inconsistent but favorable interperson-
            al evaluation." Proceedings of the 81st Annual Convention of the
            American Psychological Association 8: 109-110. P.A. 50:8876.
4729. Schlenker, Barry R., and James T. Tedeschi
    1972   "Interpersonal attraction and the exercise of coercive and reward
            power." Human Relations 25 (5, November): 427-439. P.A. 50:982.
4730. Schlenker, Barry R., et al.
    1971   "The effects of referent and reward power upon social conflict."
            Psychonomic Science 24 (6, September): 268-270. P.A. 48:9036.
4731. Schlesinger, Lawrence, Jay M. Jackson, and Jean Butman
    1960   "Leader-member interaction in management committees." Journal
            of Abnormal and Social Psychology 61 (3, November): 360-364.
            P.A. 36:2CF60S; S.A. A1861.
4732. Schmidt, Charles F., and Irwin P. Levin
    1972   "Test of an averaging model of person preference: Effect of con-
            text." Journal of Personality and Social Psychology 23 (2, August):
            277-282. P.A. 49:802.
4733. Schmidt, F.
    1904   ("Experimental studies of the schoolchild's homework.") Archive
            für die Gesamte Psychologie 3: 33-152.
4734. Schmitt, David R.
    1964   "The invocation of moral obligation." Sociometry 27 (3, Septem-
            ber): 299-310. P.A. 39:4892.
4735. Schmitt, David R., and Gerald Marwell
    1968   "Stimulus control in the experimental study of cooperation." Jour-
            nal of the Experimental Analysis of Behavior 11 (5): 571-574. P.A.
            43:5272.
4736.   1970   "Reward and punishment as influence techniques for the achieve-
            ment of cooperation under inequity." Human Relations 23 (1): 37-

45. P.A. 44:18577.

4737. 1971 "Taking and the disruption of cooperation." Journal of the Experimental Analysis of Behavior 15 (3, May): 405-412. P.A. 46:6763.

4738. 1972a "Experimental use of points or money as reinforcers: Does what is risked make a difference?" Psychological Reports 31 (2, October): 425-426. P.A. 49:9087.

4739. 1972b "Withdrawal and reward reallocation as responses to inequity." Journal of Experimental Social Psychology 8 (3, May): 207-221. P.A. 48:11464.

4740. Schmitt, Raymond L.
1967 "Applied Homans: Rank, interaction, and conformity in an informal group." Sociological Inquiry 37 (2, Spring): 183-190. S.A. 16: D0612.

4741. Schmuck, Richard, Philip Runkel, and Daniel Langmeyer
1971 "Theory to guide organizational training in schools." Sociological Inquiry 41 (2, Spring): 183-191.

4742. Schneider, Benjamin
1970 "Relationships between various criteria of leadership in small groups." Journal of Social Psychology 82: 253-261.

4743. 1973 "Answering questions and questioning answers: A reply to Levin." Journal of Social Psychology 89 (2, April): 301-302. P.A. 50: 6754.

4744. Schneider, David J.
1969 "Tactical self-presentation after success and failure." Journal of Personality and Social Psychology 13 (3): 262-268. P.A. 44:2272.

4745. Schneider, David J., Andrew C. Eustis, John Manzolati, Robert S. Miller, and Joseph Gordon
1971 "Effects of visual contact on verbal self-presentation." Proceedings of the 79th Annual Convention of the American Psychological Association 6 (pt. 1): 303-304.

4746. Schneider, Eliezer
1965 "Theoretical problem of leadership and group atmosphere." Psychological Reports 16 (2): 416. P.A. 39:10021.

4747. Schneider, Frank N.
1973 "When will a stranger lend a helping hand?" Journal of Social Psychology 90 (2, August): 335-336. P.A. 51:1004.

4748. Schneider, Frank W.
1970 "Conforming behavior of black and white children." Journal of Personality and Social Psychology 16 (3): 466-471.

4749. Schneider, Frank W., and James G. Dalenay
1972 "Effect of individual achievement motivation on group problem-solving efficiency." Journal of Social Psychology 86 (2, April): 291-298. P.A. 48:2905.

4750. Schneider, Hans D.
1973 ("The effects of the partner's strategy and amount of risk on playing behavior and reward in a modification of the Prisoner's Dilemma game.") Zeitschrift für Sozialpsychologie 4 (3): 220-230. P.A. 52: 841.

4751. Schneider, Leonard I.
1955 "A proposed conceptual integration of group dynamics and group therapy." Journal of Social Psychology 42: 173-191. P.A. 31: 1151.

4752. Schoeninger, D. W., and W. D. Wood
1969 "Comparison of married and ad hoc mixed-sex dyads negotiating the division of a reward." Journal of Experimental Social Psychology 5 (4): 483-499. P.A. 44:5086.

4753. Schonbar, Rosalea A.
1945 "The interaction of observer-pairs in judging visual extent and movement: The formation of social norms in 'structured' situations." Archives of Psychology No. 299. P.A. 20:1017.

4754. Schoner, Bertram, Gerald L. Rose, and G. C. Hoyt
1974 "Quality of decisions: Individuals versus real and synthetic groups."

Journal of Applied Psychology 59 (4): 424-432.

4755. Schönpflug, Ute
    1972   ("Expectations in chance and achievement control and their influ-
            ence on group formation.") Zeitschrift für Sozialpsychologie 3 (3):
            177-226. P.A. 50:11272.

4756. Schönpflug, Ute, and Wolfgang Schönpflug
    1972   "Scaling of attitude items under stress: Responses shift or change of
            personal preference scale?" European Journal of Social Psychology
            2 (2): 145-162. P.A. 49:9088.

4757. Schopler, John
    1965   "Social power." In L. Berkowitz (ed.), Advances in Experimental
            Social Psychology, vol. 2, pp. 177-214. New York: Academic Press.

4758.   1967   "An investigation of sex differences on the influence of depend-
            ence." Sociometry 30 (1, March): 50-63.

4759. Schopler, John, and Nicholas Bateson
    1962   "A dependence interpretation of the effects of a severe initiation."
            Journal of Personality 30 (4): 633-649. P.A. 39:1580.

4760.   1965   "The power of dependence." Journal of Personality and Social Psy-
            chology 2 (2): 247-254.

4761. Schopler, John, and John S. Compere
    1971   "Effects of being kind or harsh to another on liking." Journal of Per-
            sonality and Social Psychology 20 (2, November): 155-159. P.A.
            47:6696.

4762. Schopler, John, Charles L. Gruder, Mickay Miller, and Mark O. Rousseau
    1967   "The endurance of change induced by a reward and a coercive power
            figure." Human Relations 20 (3, August): 301-309.

4763. Schopler, John, and Bruce Layton
    1972   "Determinants of the self-attribution of having influenced another
            person." Journal of Personality and Social Psychology 22 (3): 326-
            332.

4764. Schopler, John, and Marjorie W. Matthews
    1965   "The influence of the perceived causal locus of partner's dependence
            on the use of interpersonal power." Journal of Personality and
            Social Psychology 2 (4): 609-612. P.A. 40:497.

4765. Schopler, John, and Vaida D. Thompson
    1968   "Role of attribution processes in mediating amount of reciprocity
            for a favor." Journal of Personality and Social Psychology 10 (3):
            243-250. P.A. 43:3955.

4766. Schrag, P.
    1969   "The forgotten American." Harpers 252 (August): 27-39.

4767. Schroder, Harold M., and O. J. Harvey
    1963   "Conceptual organization and group structure." In O. J. Harvey
            (ed.), Motivation and Social Interaction, pp. 134-166. New York:
            Ronald.

4768. Schroder, Harold M., and David E. Hunt
    1958   "Dispositional effects upon conformity at different levels of discrep-
            ancy." Journal of Personality 26: 243-258. P.A. 34:4208.

4769. Schroeder, Harold E.
    1973   "The risky shift as a general choice shift." Journal of Personality
            and Social Psychology 27 (2, August): 297-300. P.A. 51:3069.

4770. Schubert, Glendon
    1964   "The power of organized minorities in a small group." Administra-
            tive Science Quarterly 9 (2, September): 133-153. S.A. 13:B4934.

4771. Schuck, John, and Kim Pisor
    1974   "Evaluating an aggression experiment by the use of simulating sub-
            jects." Journal of Personality and Social Psychology 29 (2): 181-
            186.

4772. Schuham, Anthony I.
    1972   "Activity, talking time, and spontaneous agreement in disturbed and
            normal family interaction." Journal of Abnormal Psychology 79 (1):
            68-75.

4773. Schulberg, Herbert C.
    1961   "Authoritarianism, tendency to agree and interpersonal perception."
            Journal of Abnormal and Social Psychology 63 (1): 101-108.

4774. Schulman, Gary I.
    1967   "Asch conformity studies: Conformity to the experimenter and/or
            to the groups?" Sociometry 30 (1, March): 26-40. S.A. 15:C5588.

4775. Schulman, Michael
    1972   "Prediction versus admiration of unethical risk." Proceedings of the
            80th Annual Convention of the American Psychological Association
            7 (pt. 1): 223-224.

4776.   1973a   "Group structure and locus of control in predictive risk judgments."
                Proceedings of the 81st Annual Convention of the American Psycho-
                logical Association 8: 279-280. P.A. 50:8877.

4777.   1973b   "The prediction vs. the admiration of unethical risk." Journal of
                Social Psychology 89 (2, April): 307-308. P.A. 50:6755.

4778. Schultz, Duane P.
    1965   "Group behavior in a simulated-escape situation." Journal of Psy-
            chology 61 (1): 69-72. P.A. 40:5408.

4779. Schutz, William C.
    1952a   "Reliability, continuity, and content analysis." Psychological Re-
            view 59: 119-127.

4780.   1952b   "Some theoretical considerations for group behavior." In Sympo-
                sium on Techniques for the Measurement of Group Performance, pp.
                27-36. Washington, D.C.: U. S. Government Research and Develop-
                ment Board.

4781.   1955   "What makes groups productive?" Human Relations 8: 429-465.
                P.A. 31:786; S.A. 3145.

4782.   1958a   FIRO: A Three-Dimensional Theory of Interpersonal Behavior. New
                York: Holt, Rinehart.

4783.   1958b   "The interpersonal underworld." Harvard Business Review 36 (4):
                123-135.

4784.   1961a   "On group composition." Journal of Abnormal and Social Psychol-
                ogy 62 (2, March): 275-281. P.A. 4GE75S; S.A. A2214.

4785.   1961b   "The ego, FIRO theory and the leader as a completer." In L.
                Petrullo and B. M. Bass (eds.), Leadership and Interpersonal Behav-
                ior, pp. 48-65. New York: Holt, Rinehart & Winston.

4786.   1968   "Interaction and personality." In D. L. Sills (ed.), International
                Encyclopedia of the Social Sciences, vol. 7, pp. 458-465. New York:
                Macmillan and Free Press.

4787. Schutz, William C., and Vernon L. Allen
    1966   "The effects of a T-group laboratory on interpersonal behavior."
            Journal of Applied Behavioral Science 2 (3, September): 265-286.
            S.A. 15:C3484.

4788. Schwanenberg, Enno
    1973   "Aggression, imitation and authority." European Journal of Social
            Psychology 3 (2): 205-207. P.A. 52:2903.

4789. Schwartz, M.
    1964   "The reciprocities multiplier: An empirical evaluation." Administra-
            tive Science Quarterly 9 (3): 264-277. P.A. 39:7652.

4790. Schwartz, Shalom H.
    1968a   "Awareness of consequences and the influence of moral norms on
            interpersonal behavior." Sociometry 31 (4): 355-369. P.A. 43:3956.

4791.   1968b   "Words, deeds and the perception of consequences and responsibil-
                ity in action situations." Journal of Personality and Social Psychol-
                ogy 10 (3): 232-242. P.A. 43:3929.

4792.   1973   "Normative explanations of helping behavior: A critique, proposal,
                and empirical test." Journal of Experimental Social Psychology 9
                (4, July): 349-364. P.A. 51:5116.

4793.   1974   "Awareness of interpersonal consequences, responsibility denial, and
                volunteering." Journal of Personality and Social Psychology 30 (1,
                July): 57-63. P.A. 52:12347.

4794. Schwartz, Shalom H., and Geraldine T. Clausen
    1970   "Responsibility, norms, and helping in an emergency." Journal of
            Personality and Social Psychology 16 (2, October): 299–310. P.A.
            45:2303.
4795. Schwartz, Theodore M., Robert A. Eberle, and Donald R. Moscato
    1973   "Effects of awareness of individual group membership on group
            problem-solving under constrained communication." Psychological
            Reports 33 (3): 823–827.
4796. Schwartz, Theodore M., and George C. Philippatos
    1968   "Effect of training in components of complex problems on group
            problem-solving efficiency under constrained communication." Psy-
            chological Reports 23 (2): 651–657. P.A. 43:9643.
4797. Schwärzel, Wiltrud
    1974   ("Nonverbal interaction training: A new market for utilization of
            training?") Gruppendynamik (Forschung und Praxis) 5 (1, Febru-
            ary): 25–38. P.A. 52:7515.
4798. Scinto, Daniel L., Frank Sistrunk, and David E. Clement
    1972   "Effect of the magnitude of reward upon cooperative game behav-
            ior." Journal of Social Psychology 86 (1, February): 155–156. P.A.
            47:10786.
4799. Scioli, Frank P., Jr.
    1971   "Conformity in small groups: The relationship between political atti-
            tude and overt behavior." Comparative Group Studies 2 (1, Febru-
            ary): 53–64.
4800. Scodel, Alvin
    1962   "Induced collaboration in some non-zero-sum games." Journal of
            Conflict resolution 6 (4): 335–340.
4801. Scodel, Alvin, and Maria L. Freedman
    1956   "Additional observations on the social perceptions of authoritarians
            and non-authoritarians." Journal of Abnormal and Social Psychol-
            ogy 52: 92–95. P.A. 31:2571; S.A. 4288.
4802. Scodel, Alvin, J. Sayer Minas, Philburn Ratoosh, and Milton Lipetz
    1959   "Some descriptive aspects of two-person non-zero-sum games." Jour-
            nal of Conflict Resolution 3 (2, June): 114–119. S.A. A3247.
4803. Scodel, Alvin, and P. Mussen
    1953   "Social perceptions of authoritarians and non-authoritarians." Jour-
            nal of Abnormal and Social Psychology 48: 181–184. P.A. 28:
            2443.
4804. Scofield, Robert W.
    1960   "Task productivity of groups of friends and non-friends." Psycho-
            logical Reports 6: 459–460. P.A. 35:6349.
4805. Scontrino, M. Peter
    1972   "The effects of fulfilling and violating group members' expectations
            about leadership style." Organizational Behavior and Human Per-
            formance 8 (1, August): 118–138. P.A. 49:803.
4806. Scott, William C.
    1973   "The linear relationship between interpersonal attraction and simi-
            larity: An analysis of the 'unique stranger' technique." Journal of
            Social Psychology 91 (1): 117–125.
4807. Seaborne, A. E. M.
    1962   "Group influence on the perception of ambiguous stimuli." British
            Journal of Psychology 53 (3): 287–298. P.A. 37:3042.
4808. Sears, David O.
    1967   "Social anxiety, opinion structure, and opinion change." Journal of
            Personality and Social Psychology 7 (2): 142–151.
4809. Seashore, Stanley E.
    1954   Group Cohesiveness in the Industrial Work Group. Ann Arbor: Uni-
            versity of Michigan. S.A. 3150.
4810. Secord, Paul F., and Carl W. Backman
    1964   "Interpersonal congruency, perceived similarity, and friendship." So-
            ciometry 27 (2, June): 115–127. S.A. 13:B4060.
4811.   1974   Social Psychology. 2nd ed. New York: McGraw-Hill. P.A. 51:9002.

4812. Seeman, Melvin
      1953   "Role conflict and ambivalence in leadership." American Sociologi-
              cal Review 18: 373–380. P.A. 28:4151; S.A. 92.
4813. Segal, Richard L.
      1972   "Work with patient chairmen in task groups in a psychiatric hospi-
              tal." Comparative Group Studies 3 (1, February): 105–115.
4814. Seidman, Dennis, Stanley B. Bensen, Irwin Miller, and Tor Meeland
      1957   "Influence of a partner on tolerance for a self-administered electric
              shock." Journal of Abnormal and Social Psychology 54: 210–212.
4815. Seligman, Clive, Nancy Paschall, and Glenn Takata
      1973   "Attribution of responsibility for a chance event as a function of
              physical attractiveness of target persons outcome and likelihood of
              event." Proceedings of the 81st Annual Convention of the American
              Psychological Association 8: 147–148. P.A. 50:4835.
4816. Selltiz, Claire, Marie Jahoda, Morton Deutsch, and S. W. Cook
      1959   Research Methods in Social Relations. Rev. one-vol. ed. New York:
              Holt.
4817. Semin, Gün R., and A. Ian Glendon
      1973   "Polarization and the established group." British Journal of Social
              and Clinical Psychology 12 (2, June): 113–121. P.A. 51:7040.
4818. Semrad, Elvin V., and John Arsenian
      1961   "The use of group processes in teaching group dynamics." In W. G.
              Bennis, K. D. Benne, and R. Chin (eds.), The Planning of Change,
              pp. 737–743. New York: Holt, Rinehart, & Winston.
4819. Sengupta, N. N., and C. P. N. Sinha
      1926   "Mental work in isolation and in group." Indian Journal of Psychol-
              ogy 1: 106–110.
4820. Senn, David J.
      1971   "Attraction as a function of similarity-dissimilarity in task perform-
              ance." Journal of Personality and Social Psychology 18 (1, April):
              120–123. P.A. 46:2932.
4821. Sensenig, John, Thomas E. Reed, and Jerome S. Miller
      1972   "Cooperation in the Prisoner's Dilemma as a function of interper-
              sonal distance." Psychonomic Science 26 (2, January): 105–106.
              P.A. 48:9037.
4822. Seplowin, Virginia M.
      1972   "A study of perceptions before and after a managerial development
              course." Comparative Group Studies 3 (3, August): 135–158.
4823. Sereno, Kenneth K., and C. David Mortensen
      1969   "The effects of ego-involved attitudes on conflict negotiation in
              dyads." Speech Monographs 36 (1): 8–12. P.A. 43:9644.
4824. Sermat, Vello
      1964   "Cooperative behavior in a mixed-motive game." Journal of Social
              Psychology 62 (April): 217–239.
4825.   1967   "The effect of an initial cooperative or competitive treatment upon
              a subject's response to conditional cooperation." Behavioral Science
              12 (July): 301–313.
4826.   1968   "Dominance-submissiveness and competition in a mixed-motive
              game." British Journal of Social and Clinical Psychology 7 (1): 35–
              44. P.A. 42:8872.
4827.   1970   "Is game behavior related to behavior in other interpersonal situa-
              tions?" Journal of Personality and Social Psychology 16 (1, Septem-
              ber): 92–109. P.A. 45:2304.
4828. Sermat, Vello, and Michael Smyth
      1973   "Content analysis of verbal communication in the development of
              relationship: Conditions influencing self-disclosure." Journal of
              Personality and Social Psychology 26 (3, June): 332–346. P.A. 50:
              11274.
4829. Sewell, Alan F.
      1973   "Personal perception as a function of the personal consequences and
              immediacy of a decision." Journal of Psychology 85 (1, September):
              157–164. P.A. 51:7089.

4830. Sewell, Alan F., and James T. Heisler
    1973   "Personality correlates of proximity preferences." Journal of Psychology 85 (1, September): 151–155. P.A. 51:7015.
4831. Sewell, W., P. Mussen, and C. Harris
    1955   "Relationships among child training practices." American Sociological Review 20: 137–148. P.A. 31:691.
4832. Seyfried, B. A., and Clyde Hendrick
    1973a   "Need similarity and complementarity in interpersonal attraction." Sociometry 36 (2, June): 207–220. P.A. 51:2997.
4833.   1973b   "When do opposites attract? When they are opposite in sex and sex-role attitudes." Journal of Personality and Social Psychology 25 (1, January): 15–20. P.A. 50:6756.
4834. Seymour, George E.
    1971   "The concurrent validity of unobtrusive measures of conflict in small isolated groups." Journal of Clinical Psychology 27 (4, October): 431–435. P.A. 47:8803.
4835. Shalinsky, William
    1969   "Group composition as a factor in assembly effects." Human Relations 22 (5, October): 457–464.
4836. Shannon, John, and Bernard Guerney, Jr.
    1973   "Interpersonal effects of interpersonal behavior." Journal of Personality and Social Psychology 26 (1, April): 142–150. P.A. 50:4836.
4837. Shapira, Ariella, and Jacob Lomranz
    1972   "Cooperative and competitive behavior of rural Arab children in Israel." Journal of Cross-Cultural Psychology 3 (4, December): 353–359. P.A. 50:4837.
4838. Shapiro, David, and P. Herbert Leiderman
    1967   "Arousal correlates of task role and group setting." Journal of Personality and Social Psychology 5 (1): 103–107.
4839. Shapiro, Jeffrey G.
    1968a   "Responsivity to facial and linguistic cues." Journal of Communication 18 (1): 11–17. P.A. 42:10535.
4840.   1968b   "Variability in the communication of affect." Journal of Social Psychology 76 (2, December): 181–188. P.A. 43:3957.
4841.   1972   "Variability and usefulness of facial and body cues." Comparative Group Studies 3 (4, November): 437–442. P.A. 51:958.
4842. Shapiro, Jerrold L., and Michael J. Diamond
    1972   "Increases in hypnotizability as a function of encounter group training: Some confirming evidence." Journal of Abnormal Psychology 79 (1, February): 112–115. P.A. 48:2906.
4843. Shapiro, Jerrold L., and Robert R. Ross
    1971   "Sensitivity training for staff in an institution for adolescent offenders." Journal of Applied Behavioral Science 7 (6): 710–723.
4844. Shapiro, Kenneth J., and Irving E. Alexander
    1969   "Extraversion-introversion, affiliation, and anxiety." Journal of Personality 37: 387–406.
4845. Shapiro, Stewart B.
    1968   "Some aspects of a theory of interpersonal contracts." Psychological Reports 22 (1): 171–183. P.A. 42:10521.
4846. Shapley, L. S.
    1962   "Simple games: An outline of the descriptive theory." Behavioral Science 7 (1, January): 59–66. P.A. 37:1112.
4847. Shaplinskii, V. V.
    1972   ("Experimental study of the parameters of small groups.") Voprosy Psikhologii 5 (September): 66–76. P.A. 50:2980.
4848. Shave, David W.
    1974   The Therapeutic Listener. Huntington, N.Y.: Robert E. Krieger. P.A. 52:12280.
4849. Shaw, David M.
    1960   "Size of share in task and motivation in work groups." Sociometry 23 (2, June): 203–208. P.A. 35:4100; S.A. A2747.

4850. Shaw, Jerry I.
    1971 "Situational factors contributing to a psychological advantage in competitive negotiations." Journal of Personality and Social Psychology 19 (2, August): 251–260. P.A. 47:2853.
4851. 1972a "Reactions to victims and defendants of varying degrees of attractiveness." Psychonomic Science 27 (6, June): 329–330. P.A. 49: 2373.
4852. 1972b "Reward size and game playing behavior." Scandinavian Journal of Psychology 13 (2): 121–132. P.A. 49:804.
4853. Shaw, Jerry I., and Paul Skolnick
    1970 "Attribution of responsibility for a happy accident." Proceedings of the 78th Annual Convention of the American Psychological Association 5 (pt. 1): 469–470.
4854. Shaw, Marjorie E.
    1932 "A comparison of individuals and small groups in the rational solution of complex problems." American Journal of Psychology 44: 491–504. (See also Swanson, Newcomb, and Hartley, 1952; Maccoby, Newcomb, and Hartley, 1958.)
4855. Shaw, Marvin E.
    1954a "Group structure and the behavior of individuals in small groups." Journal of Psychology 38: 139–149. P.A. 29:3829.
4856. 1954b "Some effects of problem complexity upon problem solution efficiency different communication nets." Journal of Experimental Psychology 48: 211–217. P.A. 29:5645.
4857. 1954c "Some effects of unequal distribution of information upon group performance in various communication nets." Journal of Abnormal and Social Psychology 49: 547–553. P.A. 29:5646.
4858. 1955 "A comparison of two types of leadership in various communication nets." Journal of Abnormal and Social Psychology 50: 127–134. P.A. 29:7098.
4859. 1956 "Random versus systematic distribution of information in communication nets." Journal of Personality 25: 59–69.
4860. 1958a "Some effects of irrelevant information upon problem-solving by small groups." Journal of Social Psychology 47: 33–37. P.A. 34: 2871.
4861. 1958b "Some motivational factors in cooperation and competition." Journal of Personality 26: 155–169. P.A. 34:3895.
4862. 1959a "Acceptance of authority, group structure, and the effectiveness of small groups." Journal of Personality 27 (June): 196–210. P.A. 34: 4209.
4863. 1959b "Some effects of individually prominent behavior upon group effectiveness and member satisfaction." Journal of Abnormal and Social Psychology 59: 382–386. P.A. 34:5749.
4864. 1960 "A note concerning homogeneity of membership and group problem solving." Journal of Abnormal and Social Psychology 60 (3): 448–450. P.A. 35:4824.
4865. 1961a "A serial position effect in social influence on group decisions." Journal of Social Psychology 54 (June): 83–91. P.A. 36:2GE83S.
4866. 1961b "Group dynamics." Annual Review of Psychology 12: 129–156.
4867. 1961c "Some factors influencing the use of information in small groups." Psychological Reports 8: 187–198. P.A. 36:1GE87S.
4868. 1962 "Implicit conversion of fate control in dyadic interaction." Psychological Reports 10: 758. P.A. 37:4888.
4869. 1963 "Some effects of varying amounts of information exclusively possessed by a group member upon his behavior in the group." Journal of General Psychology 68 (1): 71–79. P.A. 38:2589.
4870. 1964 "Communication networks." In L. Berkowitz (ed.), Advances in Experimental Social Psychology, vol. 1, pp. 111–147. New York: Academic Press.
4871. 1971 Group Dynamics: The Psychology of Small Group Behavior. New York: McGraw-Hill.

4872. Shaw, Marvin E., and J. Michael Blum
    1964   "Effects of the group's knowledge of member satisfaction upon group performance." Psychonomic Science 1 (1): 15-16. P.A. 38: 10096.
4873.   1965   "Group performance as function of task difficulty and the group's awareness of member satisfaction." Journal of Applied Psychology 49 (3): 151-154. P.A. 39:12185.
4874.   1966   "Effects of leadership style upon group performance as a function of task structure." Journal of Personality and Social Psychology 3 (2): 238-242. P.A. 40:4194.
4875. Shaw, Marvin E., and George R. Breed
    1970   "Effects of attribution of responsibility for negative events on behavior in small groups." Sociometry 33 (4, December): 382-393. P.A. 46:8947.
4876.   1971   "Some effects of attribution of responsibility upon the effectiveness of small problem-solving groups." Psychonomic Science 22 (4, February): 207-209. P.A. 46:8948.
4877. Shaw, Marvin E., and Paul Caron
    1965   "Group effectiveness as a function of the group's knowledge of member dissatisfaction." Psychonomic Science 2 (10): 299-300. P.A. 39:12184.
4878. Shaw, Marvin E., and Philip R. Costanzo
    1970   Theories of Social Psychology. New York: McGraw-Hill.
4879. Shaw, Marvin E., Fred A. Floyd, and Norris E. Gwin
    1971   "Perceived locus of motivation as a determinant of attribution of responsibility." Representative Research in Social Psychology 2 (2, July): 43-51. P.A. 49:9089.
4880. Shaw, Marvin E., and Jack C. Gilchrist
    1955   "Repetitive task failure and sociometric choice." Journal of Abnormal and Social Psychology 50: 29-32. P.A. 29:7099; S.A. 1983.
4881.   1956   "Intra-group communication and leader choice." Journal of Social Psychology 43: 133-138. P.A. 31:2721.
4882. Shaw, Marvin E., and William T. Penrod, Jr.
    1962a   "Does more information available to a group improve group performance?" Sociometry 25 (4, December): 377-390. P.A. 38: 4199; S.A. 11:A6359.
4883.   1962b   "Validity of information, attempted influence, and quality of group decisions." Psychological Reports 10 (1): 19-23. P.A. 37: 1113.
4884.   1964   "Group effectiveness as a function of amount of 'legitimate' information." Journal of Social Psychology 62 (2, April): 241-246. P.A. 39:4894.
4885. Shaw, Marvin E., and Gerard H. Rothschild
    1956   "Some effects of prolonged experience in communication nets." Journal of Applied Psychology 40: 281-286.
4886. Shaw, Marvin E., Gerard H. Rothschild, and John F. Strickland
    1957   "Decision process in communication nets." Journal of Abnormal and Social Psychology 54: 323-330.
4887. Shaw, Marvin E., and Orin W. Sadler
    1965   "Interaction patterns in heterosexual dyads varying in degree of intimacy." Journal of Social Psychology 66 (2, August): 345-351. P.A. 39:15062.
4888. Shaw, Marvin E., and Lilly M. Shaw
    1962   "Some effects of sociometric grouping upon learning in a second grade classroom." Journal of Social Psychology 57 (2, August): 453-458. P.A. 37:4889.
4889. Shaw, Marvin E., and Trueman R. Tremble, Jr.
    1971   "Effects of attribution of responsibility for a negative event to a group member upon group process as a function of the structure of the event." Sociometry 34 (4, December): 504-514. P.A. 48:877; S.A. 21:73G2273.

4890. Shchedrovitskii, G. P., and R. G. Nadezhina
    1973   ("Two types of leadership relations in children's group activity.")
            Voprosy Psikhologii 19 (5, September): 74-84. P.A. 52:7537.
4891. Shears, Loyda M.
    1967   "Patterns of coalition formation in two games played by male
            tetrads." Behavioral Science 12 (2, March): 130-137. S.A. 15:
            C6387.
4892. Shears, Loyda M., and E. K. Eric Gunderson
    1966   "Stable attitude factors in natural isolated groups." Journal of So-
            cial Psychology 70 (December): 199-204.
4893. Sheffield, Alfred D.
    1922   Joining in Public Discussion. New York: Doran.
4894.   1929   Training for Group Experience. New York: Inquiry.
4895. Sheffield, Alfred D., and Ada E. Sheffield
    1951   The Mind of a 'Member.' New York: Exposition Press. P.A. 26:
            1427.
4896. Shelley, Harry P.
    1954   "Level of aspiration phenomena in small groups." Journal of Social
            Psychology 40: 149-164. P.A. 29:5484.
4897.   1956   "Response set and the California attitude scales." Educational and
            Psychological Measurement 16: 63-67. P.A. 31:5919.
4898.   1960a   "Focused leadership and cohesiveness in small groups." Sociometry
            23 (2, June): 209-216. P.A. 35:2131; S.A. A2748.
4899.   1960b   "Status consensus, leadership, and satisfaction with the group."
            Journal of Social Psychology 51 (February): 157-164. P.A. 34:
            7605; P.A. 36:3GF57S. S.A. 11:A5699.
4900. Shelly, Maynard W., and Jack C. Gilchrist
    1958   "Some effects of communication requirements in group structures."
            Journal of Social Psychology 48: 37-44. P.A. 34:5750.
4901. Shelly, Maynard W., and Andrew C. Stedry
    1968   "Toward the design of a group: A preliminary model." Psychologi-
            cal Reports 22 (3, pt. 2): 1177-1189. P.A. 42:18743.
4902. Shepard, Herbert A.
    1970   "Personal growth laboratories: Toward an alternative culture."
            Journal of Applied Behavioral Science 6 (3): 259-266.
4903. Shepard, Herbert A., and Warren G. Bennis
    1956   "A theory of training by group methods." Human Relations 9: 403-
            413.
4904. Shepard, Martin, and Marjorie Lee
    1970   Marathon 16. New York: Putnam's. P.A. 47:2854.
4905. Shepherd, Clovis R.
    1964   Small Groups: Some Sociological Perspectives. Chandler Publications
            in Anthropology and Sociology. San Francisco: Chandler. S.A.
            14:C0966.
4906. Shepherd, Clovis R., and Irwin R. Weschler
    1955   "The relation between three interpersonal variables and communica-
            tion effectiveness: A pilot study." Sociometry 18: 103-110. P.A.
            30:4376.
4907. Shepherd, J. W.
    1972   "The effects of variations in evaluativeness of traits on the relation
            between stimulus affect and cognitive complexity." Journal of So-
            cial Psychology 88 (2, December): 233-239. P.A. 9091.
4908. Sheposh, J. P., and P. S. Gallo, Jr.
    1973   "Asymmetry of payoff structure and cooperative behavior in the
            Prisoner's Dilemma game." Journal of Conflict Resolution 17 (2,
            June): 321-333. P.A. 51:5044.
4909. Sheras, Peter L., Joel Cooper, and Mark P. Zanna
    1973   "On the irreversibility of cognitive dissonance." Proceedings of the
            81st Annual Convention of the American Psychological Association
            8: 275-276. P.A. 50:8880.
4910. Sheridan, Charles L., and Richard G. King, Jr.
    1972   "Obedience to authority with an authentic victim." Proceedings of

the 80th Annual Convention of the American Psychological Association 7 (pt. 1): 165–166. P.A. 48:4881.

4911. Sheridan, Kathleen, et al.
    1973   "A training program for small-group leaders: I. Overview." Journal of Community Psychology 1 (1, January): 3–7. P.A. 52:12281.

4912. Sherif, Carolyn W.
    1973   "Social distance as categorization of intergroup interaction." Journal of Personality and Social Psychology 25 (3, March): 327–334. P.A. 50:4838.

4913. Sherif, Carolyn W., Merrilea Kelly, H. Lewis Rodgers, Jr., Gian Sarup, and Bennett I. Tittler
    1973   "Personal involvement, social judgment, and action." Journal of Personality and Social Psychology 27 (3, September): 311–328. P.A. 51:5117.

4914. Sherif, Muzafer
    1935   "A study of some social factors in perception." Archives of Psychology 27, No. 187.

4915.   1936   The Psychology of Social Norms. New York: Harper. (See also Swanson, Newcomb, and Hartley, 1952; Maccoby, Newcomb, and Hartley, 1958.)

4916.   1951   "A preliminary study of inter-group relations." In J. H. Rohrer and M. Sherif (eds.), Social Psychology at the Crossroads: The University of Oklahoma Lectures in Social Psychology, pp. 388–424. New York: Harper. P.A. 26:834. (See also Roff, 1950.)

4917.   1954a   "Integrating field work and laboratory in small group research." American Sociological Review 19: 759–771. P.A. 30:2699.

4918.   1954b   "Sociocultural influences in small group research." Sociology and Social Research 39: 1–10. S.A. 2733.

4919.   1956   "Experiments in group conflict." Scientific American 195 (5): 54–58.

4920.   1957   "Towards integrating psychological and sociological approaches in small group research." In M. Sherif and M. O. Wilson (eds.), Emerging Problems in Social Psychology. Norman, Okla.: University Book Exchange.

4921.   1958   "Superordinate goals in the reduction of intergroup conflict." American Journal of Sociology 63: 349–356.

4922.   1961   "Conformity-deviation, norms, and group relations." In I. A. Berg and B. M. Bass (eds.), Conformity and Deviation, pp. 159–198. New York: Harper. P.A. 36:4GE59S.

4923. Sherif, Muzafer, and H. Cantril
    1947   The Psychology of Ego-Involvements. New York: Wiley. P.A. 21:3335.

4924. Sherif, Muzafer, and O. J. Harvey
    1952   "A study in ego functioning: Elimination of stable anchorages in individual and group situations." Sociometry 15: 272–305. P.A. 27:7125.

4925. Sherif, Muzafer, O. J. Harvey, B. Jack White, William R. Hood, and Carolyn W. Sherif
    1961   Intergroup Conflict and Cooperation: The Robbers Cave Experiment. Norman, Okla.: University Book Exchange.

4926. Sherif, Muzafer, and Carl I. Hovland
    1961   Social Judgment. New Haven, Conn.: Yale University Press.

4927. Sherif, Muzafer, and Carolyn W. Sherif
    1953   Groups in Harmony and Tension. New York: Harper. P.A. 28:2446.

4928.   1956   An Outline of Social Psychology. Rev. ed. Chap. 9. New York: Harper. P.A. 31:2722.

4929.   1964   Reference Groups: Exploration into Conformity and Deviation of Adolescents. New York: Harper & Row.

4930.   1968   "Group formation." In D. L. Sills (ed.), International Encyclopedia of the Social Sciences, vol. 6, pp. 276–283. New York: Macmillan and Free Press.

4931. Sherif, Muzafer, B. Jack White, and O. J. Harvey
    1955   "Status in experimentally produced groups." American Journal of Sociology 60: 370–379. (See also Crosbie, 1975.) P.A. 30:800; S.A. 1512.

4932. Sherman, Mark, Robert Sprafkin, and Kenneth Higgins
    1974   "Perceived efficacy and interpersonal impact of impression management among psychiatric patients." Journal of Abnormal Psychology 83 (4): 440–445.

4933. Sherrod, Drury R., and Robin Downs
    1974   "Environmental determinants of altruism: The effects of stimulus overload and perceived control on helping." Journal of Experimental Social Psychology 10 (5): 468–479.

4934. Sherwood, Clarence E., and William S. Walker
    1960   "Role differentiation in real groups: An extrapolation of a laboratory small-group research finding." Sociology and Social Research 45 (1, October): 14–17. P.A. 35:4825. S.A. 11:A4598.

4935. Sherwood, John J.
    1965   "Self identity and retreat referent others." Sociometry 28 (1, March): 66–81. P.A. 39:10008.

4936.   1967   "Increased self evaluation as a function of ambiguous evaluations by referent others." Sociometry 30 (4, December): 404–409. S.A. 16: D3102.

4937. Sherwood, Michael
    1964   "Bion's 'Experiences in Groups': A critical evaluation." Human Relations 17 (2, May): 113–129. P.A. 39:4895; S.A. 13:B4061.

4938. Shevaleva E., and O. Ergolska
    1926   ("Children's collectives in the light of experimental reflexology.") Bekhterev 40th Anniversary Commemorative Volume, pp. 147–182. P.A. 1:2486.

4939. Shichor, David
    1970   "Nonconformity patterns of different types of leaders in small groups." Comparative Group Studies 1 (3, August): 269–274.

4940. Shiflett, Samuel C.
    1972   "Group performance as a function of task difficulty and organizational interdependence." Organizational Behavior and Human Performance 7 (3, June): 442–456. P.A. 49:805.

4941.   1973a   "Performance effectiveness and efficiency under different dyadic work strategies." Journal of Applied Psychology 57 (3): 257–263.

4942.   1973b   "The contingency model of leadership effectiveness: Some implications of its statistical and methodological properties." Behavioral Science 18: 429–440.

4943.   1974   "Stereotyping and esteem for one's least preferred co-worker." Journal of Social Psychology 93 (1): 55–65. P.A. 52:12348.

4944. Shils, Edward A.
    1947   "The present situation in American sociology." Pilot Papers 2 (2): 8–36.

4945.   1948   The Present Situation in American Sociology. Glencoe, Ill.: Free Press. P.A. 23:1729.

4946.   1950   "Primary groups in the American army." In R. K. Merton and P. F. Lazarsfeld (eds.), Continuities in Social Research: Studies in the Scope and Method of "The American Soldier," pp. 16–39. Glencoe, Ill.: Free Press.

4947.   1951   "The study of the primary group." In D. Lerner and H. D. Laswell (eds.), The Policy Sciences, pp. 44–69. Stanford, Calif.: Stanford University Press.

4948. Shils, Edward A., and Morris Janowitz
    1948   "Cohesion and disintegration of the Wehrmacht in World War II." Public Opinion Quarterly 12: 280–315. P.A. 23:136.

4949. Shima, Hisahiro
    1968a   ("The effects of the leader's modes of interpersonal cognition upon the enforcement of the group norm.") Japanese Journal of Educational and Social Psychology 8 (1): 87–103. P.A. 44:5087.

4950.   1968b   "The relationship between the leader's modes of interpersonal cogni-
                  tion and the performance of the group." Japanese Psychological Re-
                  search 10 (1): 13–30. P.A. 44:2273.
4951.   1972   ("The effects of the cognitive structure of the leader upon the per-
                  formance of the group.") Japanese Journal of Experimental Social
                  Psychology 11 (2, March): 99–108. P.A. 52:12283.
4952. Shinotsuka, Hiromi
         1972   ("Process analysis of behavior in a three-person mutual-choice game:
                  I.") Japanese Journal of Psychology 42 (6, February): 296–309.
                  P.A. 49:806.
4953. Shiota, Y.
         1965   "A study of buzz group: Group structure and productivity." Bulle-
                  tin of the Faculty of Education (U. Nagoya) 12: 70–71. P.A. 40:2825.
4954. Shirakashi, S.
         1968   ("An experimental study of leadership effectiveness in a small
                  group: A test of the contingency model.") Japanese Journal of Edu-
                  cational and Social Psychology 8 (1): 123–141. P.A. 44:5088.
4955.   1969   ("An experimental study of leadership effectiveness in a small
                  group: II. A test of the contingency model in a coacting group.")
                  Japanese Journal of Education and Social Psychology 8 (2): 249–
                  267. P.A. 44:5089.
4956. Shoemaker, Donald J., Donald R. South, and Jay Lowe
         1973   "Facial stereotypes of deviants and judgments of guilt or innocence."
                  Social Forces 51 (4, June): 427–433. P.A. 51:1005.
4957. Shomer, Robert W., Alice H. Davis, and Harold H. Kelley
         1966   "Threats and the development of coordination: Further studies of
                  the Deutsch and Krauss trucking game." Journal of Personality and
                  Social Psychology 4 (2): 119–126.
4958. Short, James F., Jr., and Fred L. Strodtbeck
         1963   "The response of gang leaders to status threats: An observation on
                  group process and delinquent behavior." American Journal of Soci-
                  ology 68 (5, March): 571–579. (See also Crosbie, 1975.) S.A. 11:
                  A5700.
4959.   1965   Group Process and Gang Delinquency. Chicago: University of Chi-
                  cago Press.
4960. Short, John A.
         1974   "Effects of medium of communication on experimental negotia-
                  tion." Human Relations 27 (3): 225–234.
4961. Showel, Morris
         1960   "Interpersonal knowledge and rated leader potential." Journal of
                  Abnormal and Social Psychology 61 (1): 87–92. P.A. 35:2145; S.A.
                  A1349.
4962. Shrader, Elizabeth G., and David W. Lewit
         1962   "Structural Factors in cognitive balancing behavior." Human Rela-
                  tions 15 (3, August): 265–276. P.A. 37:6616.
4963. Shrauger, J. Sidney
         1972   "Self-esteem and reactions to being observed by others." Journal of
                  Personality and Social Psychology 23 (2): 192–200.
4964. Shrauger, J. Sidney, and Stephen C. Jones
         1968   "Social validation and interpersonal evaluations." Journal of Experi-
                  mental Social Psychology 4 (3, July): 315–323. P.A. 43:2551.
4965. Shubik, Martin
         1963   "Some reflections on the design of game theoretic models for the
                  study of negotiation and threats." Journal of Conflict Resolution 7
                  (1): 1–12.
4966.   1964   Game Theory and Related Approaches to Social Behavior. New
                  York: Wiley.
4967.   1970   "Game theory, behavior and the paradox of the Prisoner's Dilemma:
                  Three solutions." Journal of Conflict Resolution 14 (2, June): 181–
                  194. S.A. 20:F3458.
4968.   1971a   "Games of status." Behavioral Science 16 (2, March): 117–129. P.A.
                  46:4849.

4969.   1971b   "The dollar auction game: A paradox in noncooperative behavior and escalation." Journal of Conflict Resolution 15 (1, March): 109-111. P.A. 48:2907.

4970. Shubkin, V. N., Y. D. Karpov, and G. M. Kochetov
        1968   ("Quantitative evaluations in studies of groups.") Soviet Sociology 7 (2, Fall): 32-48. S.A. 17:D9289.

4971. Shumsky, Marshall E.
        1971   "A sociolinguistic approach to encounter groups." Sociological Inquiry 41 (2, Spring): 161-174.

4972. Shure, Gerald H., Miles S. Rogers, Ida M. Larson, and Jack Tassone
        1962   "Group planning and task effectiveness." Sociometry 25 (3, September): 263-282. P.A. 37:3044; S.A. 11:A5140.

4973. Sibley, Sally A., Sara K. Senn, and Alexis Epanchin
        1968   "Race and sex of adolescents and cooperation in a mixed-motive game." Psychonomic Science 13 (2): 123-124. P.A. 43:6834.

4974. Sidowski, Joseph B., and Manuel Smith
        1961   "Sex and game instruction variables in a minimal social situation." Psychological Reports 8: 393-397. P.A. 36:2GE93S.

4975. Siegel, Alberta E., and Sidney Siegel
        1957   "Reference groups, membership groups, and attitude change." Journal of Abnormal and Social Psychology 55: 360-364. (See also Cartwright and Zander, 1960.)

4976. Siegel, Sheldon, and Robert B. Zajonc
        1967   "Group risk taking in professional decisions." Sociometry 30 (4, December): 339-349.

4977. Siegel, Sidney
        1956   Nonparametric Statistics for the Behavioral Sciences. New York: McGraw-Hill.

4978. Siegel, Sidney, and Lawrence E. Fouraker
        1960   Bargaining and Group Decision Making: Experiments in Bilateral Monopoly. New York: McGraw-Hill. P.A. 35:1746.

4979. Siegel, Sidney, Alberta E. Siegel, and J. M. Andrews
        1964   Choice Strategy and Utility. New York: McGraw-Hill.

4980. Siegman, Aron W., Thomas Blass, and Benjamin Pope
        1971   ("Verbal signs of interpersonal imbalance in conversation.") Bulletin du C.E.R.P. 20 (1, January): 1-4. P.A. 48:11465.

4981. Siegman, Aron W., and Benjamin Pope (eds.)
        1972   Studies in Dyadic Communication. New York: Pergamon. P.A. 49: 9092.

4982. Sigall, Harold, and Elliot Aronson
        1967   "Opinion change in the gain-loss model of interpersonal attraction." Journal of Experimental Social Psychology 3 (April): 178-188.

4983.   1969   "Liking for an evaluator as a function of her physical attractiveness and nature of the evaluations." Journal of Experimental Social Psychology 5 (1): 93-100.

4984. Sigall, Harold, and David Landy
        1973   "Radiating beauty: Effects of having a physically attractive partner on person perception." Journal of Personality and Social Psychology 28 (2): 218-224.

4985. Sigall, Harold, and Nancy Ostrove
        1973   "Effects of the physical attractiveness of the defendant and nature of the crime on juridic judgment." Proceedings of the 81st Annual Convention of the American Psychological Association 8: 267-268. P.A. 50:8881.

4986. Sigall, Harold, and Richard Page
        1972   "Reducing attenuation in the expression of interpersonal affect via the bogus pipeline." Sociometry 35 (4, December): 629-642. P.A. 50:983.

4987. Sigall, Harold, Richard Page, and Ann C. Brown
        1971   "Effort expenditure as a function of evaluation and evaluator attractiveness." Representative Research in Social Psychology 2 (2, July): 19-25. (See also 1969 Proceedings of the 77th Annual Convention

of the American Psychological Association 4 (pt. 1): 355–356.) P.A. 49:9093.

4988. Sills, David L. (ed.)
1968   International Encyclopedia of the Social Sciences. New York: Macmillan and Free Press.

4989. Silver, Albert W., and Darlene W. Mood
1971   "Group homogeneity, conformity, and flexibility of interpersonal perceptions." Comparative Group Studies 2 (1, February): 25–36.

4990. Silverman, Alan F., Mark E. Pressman, and Helmut W. Bartel
1973   "Self-esteem and tactile communication." Journal of Humanistic Psychology 13 (2, Spring): 73–77. P.A. 51:11013.

4991. Silverman, Bernie I.
1974   "Consequences, racial discrimination, and the principle of belief congruence." Journal of Social Psychology 29 (4, April): 497–508. P.A. 52:7579.

4992. Silverman, Irwin W., and Judith M. Stone
1972   "Modifying cognitive functioning through participation in a problem-solving group." Journal of Educational Psychology 63 (6): 603–608.

4993. Silverman, Ronald E., and Sidney Shrauger
1971   "Locus of control and correlates of attraction towards others." Journal of Social Psychology 84: 207–218.

4994. Silverthorne, Colin P.
1971   "Information input and the group shift phenomenon in risk taking." Journal of Personality and Social Psychology 20 (3, December): 456–461. P.A. 47:8804.

4995. Silverthorne, Colin P., Gordon Chelune, and Andrew Imada
1974   "The effects of competition and cooperation on level of prejudice." Journal of Social Psychology 92 (2): 293–301.

4996. Silvi, Sergio, and Giancarlo Trentini
1972   ("Bibliographical contribution to the study of leadership.") Archivio di Psicologia, Neurologia e Psichiatria 33 (1, January): 54–120. P.A. 52:7516.

4997. Simard, Lise M., and Donald M. Taylor
1973   "The potential for bicultural communication in a dyadic situation." Canadian Journal of Behavioural Science 5 (3, July): 211–225. P.A. 51:7041.

4998. Simkins, Lawrence D.
1971   "Modification of duration of peer interactions in emotionally disturbed children." Journal of Social Psychology 84: 287–299.

4999. Simkins, Lawrence D., and Jack West
1965   "Modification of verbal interactions in triad groups: Preliminary report." Psychological Reports 16: 684.

5000.   1966   "Reinforcement of duration of talking in triad groups." Psychological Reports 18 (1): 231–236. P.A. 40:6594.

5001. Simmel, Georg
1902–   "The number of members as determining the sociological form of
1903   the group." American Journal of Sociology 8: 1–46, 158–196.

5002.   1955   Conflict. Translated by K. H. Wolff. The Web of Group-Affiliations. Translated by R. Bendix. Glencoe, Ill.: Free Press. P.A. 29:5485.

5003. Simmons, Carolyn H., and Melvin J. Lerner
1968   "Altruism as a search for justice." Journal of Personality and Social Psychology 9 (3): 216–225. P.A. 42:13668.

5004. Simon, Herbert A.
1952   "A formal theory of interaction of social groups." American Sociological Review 17: 202–211. (See also Hare, Borgatta, and Bales, 1955.) P.A. 27:5084.

5005. Simon, Herbert A., and Harold Guetzkow
1955a   "A model of short- and long-run mechanisms involved in pressures toward uniformity in groups." Psychological Review 62: 56–68. P.A. 29:8523.

5006.   1955b   "Mechanisms involved in group pressures on deviate-members." British Journal of Statistical Psychology 8: 93–100. P.A. 31:834.

5007. Simon, Walter B.
1967 "Helping transactions: Classificatory and semantic considerations." Psychiatry 30 (3): 249–261. P.A. 42:2495.

5008. Simpson, Ray H.
1938 "A study of those who influence and of those who are influenced in discussion." Columbia University, Teachers College, Contributions to Education No. 748.

5009. Simpson, W. E., and Sally J. Crandall
1972 "The perception of smiles." Psychonomic Science 29 (4-A, November): 197–200. P.A. 49:11128.

5010. Sims, Thomas K., Cecelia Harley, and Elliot A. Weiner
1974 "Risk in decision making across college students' major fields." Psychological Reports 34 (1): 145–146.

5011. Sims, V. M.
1928 "The relative influence of two types of motivation on improvement." Journal of Educational Psychology 19: 480–484.

5012. Singelmann, Peter
1972 "Exchange as symbolic interaction: Convergences between two theoretical perspectives." American Sociological Review 37 (4, August): 414–424.

5013. Singer, Jerome E., Lenore S. Radloff, and David M. Wark
1963 "Renegades, heretics, and changes in sentiment." Sociometry 26 (2, June): 178–189. P.A. 38:4200; S.A. 11:A7198.

5014. Singer, Jerome L., and G. D. Goldman
1954 "Experimentally contrasted social atmospheres in group psychotherapy with chronic schizophrenics." Journal of Social Psychology 40: 23–37.

5015. Singh, Agya J.
1971 "A study of effect of excursion on sociometric choices." Manas 18 (1, May): 45–50. P.A. 48:9038.

5016. Singh, Narayan P., and Kiran Singh
1972 "Risk-taking among agricultural and business entrepreneurs of Delhi." Psychologia: An International Journal of Psychology in the Orient 15 (3, September): 175–180. P.A. 50:2985.

5017. Singh, Ramadhar
1973 "Attraction as a function of similarity in attitudes and personality characteristics." Journal of Social Psychology 91 (1): 87–95.

5018. Sigh, Ramadhar, Donn Byrne, Naim C. Gupta, and Merrilee Clouser
1974 "Informational set size as a determinant of interpersonal judgment in a between-subjects design." Representative Research in Social Psychology 5 (1, January): 17–26. P.A. 52:7580.

5019. Sinha, Jai B.
1968 "The n-Ach/n-Cooperation under limited/unlimited resource conditions." Journal of Experimental Social Psychology 4 (2, April): 233–246. P.A. 42:13669.

5020. Sisson, P. J., C. J. Sisson, and G. M. Gadza
1973 "Extended group counseling with psychiatry residents. An interaction process analysis." Small Group Behavior 4 (4, November): 466–475.

5021. Sistrunk, Francis, and John W. McDavid
1965 "Achievement motivation, affiliation motivation, and task difficulty as determinants of social conformity." Journal of Social Psychology 66 (1, June): 41–50. P.A. 39:15064.

5022. Sistrunk, Frank
1969 "Conditioning and extinction of conforming behavior." Psychonomic Science 17 (4): 255–256. P.A. 44:5098.

5023. 1973 "Two processes of conformity demonstrated by interactions of commitment, set, and personality." Journal of Social Psychology 89 (1, February): 63–72. P.A. 50:2986.

5024. Sistrunk, Frank, David E. Clement, and Jerome D. Ulman
1972 "Effect of reinforcement magnitude on nonconformity." Journal of

Social Psychology 86: 11–22.

5025. Sklar, Alan D., Irvin D. Yalom, Alyosha Zim, and Gary L. Newell
1970   "Time-extended group therapy: A controlled study." Comparative Group Studies 1 (4, November): 373–386.

5026. Skolnick, Paul
1971   "Reactions to personal evaluations: A failure to replicate." Journal of Personality and Social Psychology 18 (1, April): 62–67. P.A. 46: 2933.

5027. Skotko, Vincent P., Daniel Langmeyer, and David C. Lundgren
1973   "Effect of sex of experimenter and sex of subject on defection level in the Prisoner's Dilemma." Proceedings of the 81st Annual Convention of the American Psychological Association 8: 321–322. P.A. 50:8882.

5028. Slack, Barbara D., and John O. Cook
1973   "Authoritarian behavior in a conflict situation." Journal of Personality and Social Psychology 25 (1, January): 130–136. P.A. 50:6757.

5029. Slater, Philip E.
1955   "Role differentiation in small groups." American Sociological Review 20: 300–310. (See also Hare, Borgatta, and Bales, 1955, 1965.) P.A. 30:8179.

5030.   1958   "Contrasting correlates of group size." Sociometry 21: 129–139.

5031.   1966   Microcosm: Structural, Psychological and Religious Evolution in Groups. New York: Wiley. S.A. 15:C4808.

5032. Slater, Philip E., and Robert F. Bales
1957   "Experimental groups—social session." Unpublished data.

5033. Slater, Philip E., K. Morimoto, and R. W. Hyde
1958   Social Interaction in Experimentally Induced Psychotic-like States. Paper read at American Sociological Society Meetings, Seattle, Washington.

5034. Slavson, Samuel R.
1938   Creative Group Education. New York: Association Press.

5035. Slavson, Samuel R. (ed.)
1947   The Practice of Group Therapy. New York: International University Press.

5036. Sloan, Lloyd R., and Thomas M. Ostrom
1974   "Amount of information and interpersonal judgment." Journal of Personality and Social Psychology 29 (1, January): 23–29. P.A. 52: 842.

5037. Slusher, E. Allen, Kenneth J. Roering, and Gerald L. Rose
1974   "The effects of commitment to future interaction in single plays of three games." Behavioral Science 19 (2): 119–132.

5038. Small, Donald O., and Donald T. Campbell
1960   "The effect of acquiescence response-set upon the relationship of the F scale and conformity." Sociometry 23 (1, March): 69–71.

5039. Smart, Reginald G.
1965   "Social-group membership, leadership, and birth order." Journal of Social Psychology 67 (December): 221–225.

5040. Smelser, William T.
1961   "Dominance as a factor in achievement and perception in cooperative problem solving interactions." Journal of Abnormal and Social Psychology 62 (3, May): 535–542. P.A. 36:4CN35S.

5041. Smith, Alexander B., Alexander Bassin, and Abraham Froehlich
1962   "Interaction process and equilibrium in a therapy group of adult offenders." Journal of Social Psychology 56 (April): 141–147. P.A. 37:1114.

5042. Smith, Anthony J.
1960a   "A developmental study of group processes." Journal of Genetic Psychology 97: 29–39. P.A. 35:6350.

5043.   1960b   "The attribution of similarity: The influence of success and failure." Journal of Abnormal and Social Psychology 61 (3): 419–423.

5044. Smith, Anthony J., Jack Jaffe, and Donald G. Livingston
1955   "Consonance of interpersonal perception and individual effective-

ness." Human Relations 8: 385-397. P.A. 31:790; S.A. 3144.

5045. Smith, Anthony J., Harrison E. Madden, and Ronald Sobol
1957 "Productivity and recall in cooperative and competitive discussion groups." Journal of Psychology 43: 193-204.

5046. Smith, Bruce
1966 "Modal behavior change and the cognitive strain model." In J. L. Philbrick (ed.), Contemporary Studies in Social Psychology and Behavior Change: Selected Academic Readings, pp. 213-223. New York: Associated Educational Services. P.A. 42:702.

5047. Smith, Carole R., Lev Williams, and Richard H. Willis
1967 "Race, sex, and belief as determinants of friendship acceptance." Journal of Personality and Social Psychology 5 (2): 127-137.

5048. Smith, Carroll E.
1936 "A study of autonomic excitation resulting from the interaction of individual and group opinion." Journal of Abnormal and Social Psychology 31: 138-164.

5049. 1964 "The effect of anxiety on the performance and attitudes of authoritarians in a small group situation." Journal of Psychology 58 (1): 191-203. P.A. 39:4896.

5050. Smith, Clagett G.
1970 "Age of R and D groups: A reconsideration." Human Relations 23 (2, April): 81-96. P.A. 45:2306.

5051. Smith, Clagett G., and Arnold S. Tannenbaum
1965 "Some implications of leadership and control for effectiveness in a voluntary association." Human Relations 18 (3, August): 265-272. P.A. 40:503.

5052. Smith, David H., and John T. Olson
1970 "Sociometric status in a psychiatrically deviant adolescent collectivity." Psychological Reports 27: 483-497.

5053. Smith, Edward W.
1972 "Postural and gestural communication of A and B 'therapist types' during dyadic interviews." Journal of Consulting and Clinical Psychology 39 (1, August): 29-36. P.A. 49:2377.

5054. Smith, Ewart E.
1957 "The effects of clear and unclear role expectations on group productivity and defensiveness." Journal of Abnormal and Social Psychology 55: 213-217.

5055. 1959 "Individual versus group goal conflict." Journal of Abnormal and Social Psychology 58: 134-137. P.A. 34:728.

5056. Smith, Ewart E., and Jacqueline D. Goodchilds
1963 "The wit in large and small established groups." Psychological Reports 13 (1): 273-274. P.A. 38:5972.

5057. Smith, Gene F., and Peter Murdoch
1970 "Performance of informed versus noninformed triads and quartets in the 'minimal social situation.'" Journal of Personality and Social Psychology 15 (4): 391-396.

5058. Smith, Harvey L., and Jean Thrasher
1963 "Roles, cliques and sanctions: Dimensions of patient society." International Journal of Social Psychiatry 9 (3, Summer): 184-191. S.A. 15:C7238.

5059. Smith, Henry C.
1955 "Team work in the college class." Journal of Educational Psychology 46: 274-286. P.A. 30:6282.

5060. Smith, Herman W.
1973 "Some developmental interpersonal dynamics through childhood." American Sociological Review 38 (5, October): 543-552. S.A. 22: 74G8634.

5061. Smith, Jackie M.
1973 Leading Groups in Personal Growth. Richmond: John Knox. P.A. 52:813.

5062. Smith, James E., and Joel M. Savell
1972 "Effects of prior agreement and disagreement by a peer on suscepti-

bility to influence by the same or a different peer." Representative Research in Social Psychology 3 (1, May): 61–72. P.A. 49:9095.

5063. Smith, Kay H.
1961   "Ego strength and perceived competence as conformity variables." Journal of Abnormal and Social Psychology 62 (1, January): 169–171. P.A. 36:3GE69S.

5064.   1970   "Conformity as related to masculinity, self, and other descriptions, suspicion, and artistic preference by sex groups." Journal of Social Psychology 80: 79–88.

5065.   1972a   "Changes in group structure through individual and group feedback." Journal of Personality and Social Psychology 24 (3, December): 425–428. P.A. 49:9096.

5066.   1972b   "The effect of varying reward systems on cooperative game behavior." Journal of Psychology 80 (1, January): 29–35. P.A. 47:10787.

5067. Smith, Kay H., Darhl M. Pedersen, and Robert E. Lewis
1966   "Dimensions of interpersonal perception in a meaningful ongoing group." Perceptual and Motor Skills 22 (3): 867–880. P.A. 40: 11110.

5068. Smith, M.
1933   "A method of analyzing the interaction of children." Journal of Juvenile Research 17: 78–88. P.A. 7:4786.

5069.   1944   "Some factors in the friendship selections of high school students." Sociometry 7: 303–310. P.A. 19:494.

5067. Smith, M. Brewster
1952   "Social psychology and group processes." Annual Review of Psychology 3: 175–204.

5071. Smith, Peter B.
1963   "Differentiation between sociometric rankings: A test of four theories." Human Relations 16 (4, November): 335–350. S.A. 12: B1635.

5072.   1967   "The use of T-groups in effecting individual and organisational change." Psychological Scene 1: 16–18. P.A. 42:17161.

5073.   1971   "Correlations among some tests of T-group learning." Journal of Applied Behavioral Science 7 (4, July-August): 508–511. S.A. 20: F9140.

5074.   1972   "The skills of social interaction." In P.C. Dodwell (ed.), New Horizons in Psychology 2. Harmondsworth, Midx., and Baltimore: Penguin. P.A. 50:4839.

5075. Smith, Robert J., and Patrick E. Cook
1973   "Leadership in dyadic groups as a function of dominance and incentives." Sociometry 36 (4): 561–568.

5076. Smith, Ronald E.
1972   "Social anxiety as a moderator variable in the attitude similarity-attraction relationship." Journal of Experimental Research in Personality 6 (1, March): 22–28. P.A. 50:11277.

5077. Smith, Ronald E., and Arnold L. Campbell
1973   "Social anxiety and strain toward symmetry in dyadic attraction." Journal of Personality and Social Psychology 28 (1): 101–107.

5078. Smith, Ronald E., Lisa Smythe, and Douglas Lien
1972   "Inhibition of helping behavior by a similar or dissimilar nonreactive fellow bystander." Journal of Personality and Social Psychology 23 (3): 414–419.

5079. Smith, Seward, and William W. Haythorn
1972   "Effects of compatibility, crowding, group size, and leadership seniority on stress, anxiety, hostility, and annoyance in isolated groups." Journal of Personality and Social Psychology 22 (1, April): 67–79. P.A. 48:4882.

5080. Smith, Sidney L.
1951   "Communication pattern and the adaptability of task-oriented groups: An experimental study." Cited in A. Bavelas, "Communication patterns in task-oriented groups," in D. Lerner and H. Lasswell (eds.), The Policy Sciences: Recent Developments in Scope and

Method, pp. 193-202. Stanford, Calif.: Stanford University Press.

5081. Smith, Stanley A.
1965 "Conformity in cooperative and competitive groups." Journal of Social Psychology 65 (2, April): 337-350. P.A. 39:15065.

5082. Smith, William M.
1966 "Observations over the lifetime of a small isolated group: Structure, danger, boredom, and vision." Psychological Reports 19: 475-514.

5083. Smith, William P.
1968a "Precision of control and the use of power in the triad." Human Relations 21 (3, August): 295-310.

5084. 1968b "Reward structure and information in the development of cooperation." Journal of Experimental Social Psychology 4 (2, April): 199-223. P.A. 42:13670.

5085. Smith, William P., and Timothy D. Emmons
1969 "Outcome information and competitiveness in interpersonal bargaining." Journal of Conflict Resolution 13 (2): 262-270. P.A. 43: 16565.

5086. Smith, William P., and Walter A. Leginski
1970 "Magnitude and precision of punitive power in bargaining strategy." Journal of Experimental Social Psychology 6 (1): 57-76. P.A. 44: 14512.

5087. Smoke, William H., and Robert B. Zajonc
1962 "On the reliability of group judgments and decisions." In J. H. Criswell, H. Solomon, and P. Suppes (eds.), Mathematical Methods in Small Group Processes, pp. 322-333. Stanford, Calif.: Stanford University Press. S.A. 12:B2423.

5088. Smucker, O.
1949 "Near-sociometric analysis as a basis for guidance." Sociometry 12: 326-340.

5089. Snadowsky, Alvin M.
1972 "Communication network research: An examination of controversies." Human Relations 25 (4): 283-306.

5090. 1974 "Member satisfaction in stable communication networks." Sociometry 37 (1): 38-53.

5091. Snoek, J. Diedrick
1962 "Some effects of rejection upon attraction to a group." Journal of Abnormal and Social Psychology 64 (3): 175-182. P.A. 38:2590.

5092. Snortum, John R., and Hector F. Myers
1969 "Intensity of T-group relationships as a function of interaction." Proceedings of the 77th Annual Convention of the American Psychological Association 4 (pt. 1): 455-456. P.A. 43:17355.

5093. Snyder, Eloise C.
1958 "The Supreme Court as a small group." Social Forces 36: 232-238.

5094. Snyder, Mark
1974 "Self-monitoring of expressive behavior." Journal of Personality and Social Psychology 30 (4): 526-537.

5095. Snyder, William U.
1945 "An investigation of the nature of non-directive psychotherapy." Journal of Genetic Psychology 33: 193-223.

5096. Soares, Louise M., and Anthony T. Soares
1971 "Interpersonal perceptions of disadvantaged children." Proceedings of the 79th Annual Convention of the American Psychological Association 6 (pt. 1): 261-262.

5097. Solar, Diana, and Albert Mehrabian
1973 "Impressions based on contradictory information as a function of affiliative tendency and cognitive style." Journal of Experimental Research in Personality 6 (4, April): 339-346. P.A. 51:3071.

5098. Solomon, Adrian
1963 "Authoritarian attitude changes and group homogeneity." Journal of Social Psychology 59 (February): 129-135.

5099. Solomon, Herbert (ed.)
      1960   Mathematical Thinking in the Measurement of Behavior: Small
              Groups, Utility, Factor Analysis. New York: Free Press.
5100. Solomon, Lawrence N., and Betty Berzon (eds.)
      1972   New Perspectives on Encounter Groups. San Francisco: Jossey-Bass.
              P.A. 49:9097.
5101. Solomon, Lawrence N., Betty Berzon, and David P. Davis
      1970   "A personal growth program for self-directed groups." Journal of
              Applied Behavioral Science 6 (4, October-December): 427-452.
              S.A. 20:F3459.
5102. Solomon, Leonard
      1960   "The influence of some types of power relationships and game
              strategies upon the development of interpersonal trust." Journal
              of Abnormal and Social Psychology 61 (2): 223-230. S.A. A1203.
5103. Solomon, Leonard, and Edward Klein
      1963   "The relationships between agreeing response set and social desira-
              bility." Journal of Abnormal and Social Psychology 66 (2): 176-
              179.
5104. Solomon, Linda Z., and Harry Kaufmann
      1972   "The effects of reward structure and partner's cooperation upon
              strategy." Psychonomic Science 26 (2, January): 87-88. P.A. 48:
              9039.
5105. Sommer, Robert
      1959   "Studies in personal space." Sociometry 22 (3, September): 247-
              260. P.A. 34:7606.
5106.   1961   "Leadership and group geography." Sociometry 24 (1, March): 99-
              110. P.A. 36:1GF99S. S.A. A2749.
5107.   1962   "The distance for comfortable conversation: A further study."
              Sociometry 25 (1, March): 111-116. P.A. 37:1115; S.A. 11:A4599.
5108.   1965   "Further studies of small group ecology." Sociometry 28 (4, Decem-
              ber): 337-348. P.A. 40:2826; S.A. 14:C1891.
5109.   1967   "Sociofugal space." American Journal of Sociology 72 (6, May):
              654-660.
5110. Sommer, Robert, and Franklin D. Becker
      1969   "Territorial defense and the good neighbor." Journal of Personality
              and Social Psychology 11 (2): 85-92.
5111. Sorenson, James R.
      1971   "Task demands, group interaction and group performance." Sociom-
              etry 34 (4, December): 483-495. P.A. 48:878; S.A. 21:73G2275.
5112.   1973   "Group member traits, group process, and group performance." Hu-
              man Relations 26 (5): 639-655. P.A. 52:843.
5113. Sorokin, Pitirim A., Mamie Tanquist, Mildred Parten, and Mrs. C. C. Zimmer-
      man
      1930   "An experimental study of efficiency of work under various speci-
              fied conditions." American Journal of Sociology 35: 765-782.
5114. Sorrentino, Richard M.
      1973   "An extension of theory of achievement motivation to the study of
              emergent leadership." Journal of Personality and Social Psychology
              26 (3, June): 356-368. P.A. 50:11278.
5115. Sorrentino, Richard M., and Robert G. Boutilier
      1974   "Evaluation of a victim as a function of fate similarity/dissimilar-
              ity." Journal of Experimental Social Psychology 10 (1): 84-93.
5116. Sosis, Ruth H.
      1974   "Internal-external control and the perception of responsibility of
              another for an accident." Journal of Personality and Social Psychol-
              ogy 30 (3): 393-399.
5117. Sote, Gbade A., and Lawrence R. Good
      1974   "Similarity of self-disclosure and interpersonal attraction." Psycho-
              logical Reports 34 (2, April): 491-494. P.A. 52:12349.
5118. Soucar, Emil, and Joseph DuCette
      1972   "A reexamination of the vigilance hypothesis in person perception."
              Journal of Social Psychology 88 (1, October): 31-36. P.A. 49:4448.

5119. Sousa-Poza, Joaquin F., Ernest Shulman, and Robert Rohrberg
 1973 "Field dependence and self-disclosure." Perceptual and Motor Skills 36 (3, pt. 1, June): 735-738. P.A. 51:2998.

5120. South, Earl B.
 1927 "Some psychological aspects of committee work." Journal of Applied Psychology 11: 348-368, 437-464. P.A. 2:2885.

5121. Southall, Aidan
 1959 "An operational theory of role." Human Relations 12: 17-34.

5122. Spaeth, Harold J.
 1965 "Unidimensionality and item invariance in judicial scaling." Behavioral Science 10 (3, July): 290-304. P.A. 40:500.

5123. Spaulding, Charles B.
 1966 "Relative attachment of students to groups and organizations." Sociology and Social Research 50 (4): 421-435. P.A. 40:12278.

5124. Speal, Gerald K.
 1965 "The sociometry of lunch-taking in an economic group." Group Psychotherapy 18 (4): 247-251. P.A. 40:5409.

5125. Speer, David C.
 1970 "Effects of marathon group therapy: Short-term MMPI changes." Comparative Group Studies 1 (4, November): 397-404.

5126. 1972a "Marital dysfunctionality and two-person non-zero-sum game behavior: Cumulative monadic measures." Journal of Personality and Social Psychology 21 (1): 18-24.

5127. 1972b "Nonverbal communication of affective information: Some laboratory findings pertaining to an interactional process." Comparative Group Studies 3 (4, November): 409-423.

5128. 1972c "Variations of the Prisoner's Dilemma game as measures of marital interaction: Sequential dyadic measures." Journal of Abnormal Psychology 80 (3): 287-293.

5129. Spence, Janet T., and Robert Helmreich
 1972 "Who likes competent women? Competence, sex role, congruence of interests, and subjects' attitudes toward women as determinants of interpersonal attraction." Journal of Applied Social Psychology 2 (3, July): 197-213. P.A. 49:9099.

5130. Speroff, B. J.
 1955 "Job satisfaction and interpersonal desirability values." Sociometry 18: 69-72. P.A. 30:6392.

5131. Sperry, Len
 1974 "Effects of expectation, social class, and experience on in-service teacher behavior in small groups." Journal of Applied Psychology 59 (2): 244-246.

5132. Spiegel, John P.
 1957 "The resolution of role conflict within the family." Psychiatry 20: 1-16.

5133. Spitzer, Stephan P.
 1964 "Consensual states and communicative behavior." Sociometry 27 (4, December): 510-515. P.A. 39:7645.

5134. Spivey, Jan, and Warner Wilson
 1973 "Attractiveness as a result of having certain personality traits." Bulletin of the Psychonomic Society 1 (4, April): 229-230. P.A. 50: 11279.

5135. Spoelders-Claes, Rita
 1973 "The effect of varying feedback on the effectiveness of a small group on a physical task." Psychologica Belgica 13 (1): 61-68. P.A. 51: 2999.

5136. Squier, Roger W., Jr.
 1971 "The effect of feedback information and behavior consistency on accuracy of social prediction." Journal of Social Psychology 83: 255-264.

5137. Srivastava, P. K.
 1968 "Personality types and social persuasibility." Journal of Psychological Researches 12 (1): 12-16. P.A. 43:5288.

5138. Stager, Paul
      1966   "Note on use of information concepts in the assessment of group
              structure." Perceptual and Motor Skills 23 (1): 238-242. P.A. 40:
              12279.
5139. 1967   "Conceptual level as a composition variable in small-group decision
              making." Journal of Personality and Social Psychology 5 (2): 152-
              161.
5140. Stalling, Richard B.
      1970   "Personality similarity and evaluative meaning as conditioners of
              attraction." Journal of Personality and Social Psychology 14 (1):
              77-82. P.A. 44:5091.
5141. Stang, David J.
      1973   "Effect of interaction rate on ratings of leadership and liking." Jour-
              nal of Personality and Social Psychology 27 (3, September): 405-
              408. P.A. 51:5045.
5142. Stanley-Jones, D.
      1958   "Dynamics of groups of normal people." International Journal of
              Social Psychiatry 4 (2, Autumn): 140-145. S.A. 15:C5589.
5143. Stanton, A. H., and M. S. Schwartz
      1954   The Mental Hospital. New York: Basic Books. P.A. 29:4248.
5144. Stapert, John C., and Gerald L. Clore
      1969   "Attraction and disagreement-produced arousal." Journal of Person-
              ality and Social Psychology 13 (1): 64-69. P.A. 43:17356.
5145. Stapleton, Richard E., Peter Nacci, and James T. Tedeschi
      1973   "Interpersonal attraction and the reciprocation of benefits." Journal
              of Personality and Social Psychology 28 (2): 199-205.
5146. Starbuck, William H., and Dorothy F. Grant
      1971   "Bargaining strategies with asymmetric initiation and termination."
              Journal of Applied Social Psychology 1 (4, October): 344-363. P.A.
              48:7122.
5147. Starkweather, John A.
      1956   "Content-free speech as a source of information about the speaker."
              Journal of Abnormal and Social Psychology 52: 394-402. P.A. 31:
              4629.
5148. Stassen, Maurice, and Edna M. Marturano
      1968   ("The influence of the limitation and the weighting of the choices
              and the rejections on the sociometric status.") Revista de Psicologia
              Normal e Patalógica 14 (3-4, July): 135-146. P.A. 45:6206.
5149. Staub, Ervin
      1969   "Effects of variation in permissibility of movement on children help-
              ing another child in distress." Proceedings of the 77th Annual Con-
              vention of the American Psychological Association 4 (pt. 1): 385-
              386.
5150. 1970   "A child in distress: The influence of age and number of witnesses
              on children's attempts to help." Journal of Personality and Social
              Psychology 14 (2): 130-140.
5151. 1971   "Helping a person in distress: The influence of implicit and explicit
              'rules' of conduct on children and adults." Journal of Personality
              and Social Psychology 17 (2): 137-144.
5152. 1972   "Instigation to goodness: The role of social norms and interpersonal
              influence." Journal of Social Issues 28 (3): 131-150. P.A. 50:4840.
5153. Staub, Ervin, and Robert S. Baer
      1974   "Stimulus characteristics of a sufferer and difficulty of escape as
              determinants of helping." Journal of Personality and Social Psychol-
              ogy 30 (2, August): 279-284. P.A. 52:12350.
5154. Stebbins, Robert A.
      1967   "A note on the concept of role distance." American Journal of So-
              ciology 73 (2): 247-250. P.A. 42:3910.
5155. Stech, Frank J., and Charles G. McClintock
      1971   "Cooperative and competitive price bidding in a duopoly game."
              Behavioral Science 16 (6, November): 545-557. P.A. 47:8806; S.A.
              20:F8115.

5156. Steele, Claude M., and Thomas M. Ostrom
    1974   "Perspective-mediated attitude change: When is indirect persuasion more effective than direct persuasion?" Journal of Personality and Social Psychology 29 (6, June): 737–741. P.A. 52:7581.
5157. Steele, Matthew W., and James T. Tedeschi
    1967   "Matrix indices and strategy choices in mixed-motive games." Journal of Conflict Resolution 11 (2, June): 198–205. S.A. 16:C8897.
5158. Stein, R. Timothy
    1971   "Accuracy in perceiving emergent leadership in small groups." Proceedings of the 79th Annual Convention of the American Psychological Association 6 (pt. 1): 295–296.
5159. Stein, R. Timothy, F. L. Geis, and Fred Damarin
    1973   "Perception of emergent leadership hierarchies in task groups." Journal of Personality and Social Psychology 28 (1): 77–87.
5160. Steiner, Ivan D.
    1955   "Interpersonal behavior as influenced by accuracy of social perception." Psychological Review 62: 268–274. P.A. 30:2673.
5161.   1959   "Human interaction and interpersonal perception." Sociometry 22 (3, September): 230–235. P.A. 34:7609.
5162.   1960   "Sex differences in the resolution of A-B-X conflicts." Journal of Personality 28: 118–128. P.A. 36:3GE18S.
5163.   1964   "Group dynamics." In P. R. Farnsworth et al. (eds.), Annual Review of Psychology, vol. 15, pp. 421–446. P.A. 39:7646.
5164.   1966   "Models for inferring relationships between group size and potential group productivity." Behavioral Science 11: 273–283.
5165.   1974   "Whatever happens to the group in social psychology?" Journal of Experimental Social Psychology 10 (1): 94–108.
5166. Steiner, Ivan D., James Anderson, and Rosemary Hays
    1967   "Immediate and delayed reactions to interpersonal disagreements: Some effects of the type of issue and order of response." Journal of Experimental Social Psychology 3 (April): 206–219.
5167. Steiner, Ivan D., and Joan S. Dodge
    1956   "Interpersonal perception and role structure as determinants of group and individual efficiency." Human Relations 9: 467–480. S.A. 1204.
5168.   1957   "A comparison of two techniques employed in the study of interpersonal perception." Sociometry 20: 1–7. P.A. 32:381.
5169. Steiner, Ivan D., and William L. Field
    1960   "Role assignment and interpersonal influence." Journal of Abnormal and Social Psychology 61 (2): 239–245. P.A. 35:5009; S.A. A1205.
5170. Steiner, Ivan D., and Homer H. Johnson
    1963   "Authoritarianism and conformity." Sociometry 26 (1, March): 21–34.
5171. Steiner, Ivan D., and Colin G. McDiarmid
    1957   "Two kinds of assumed similarity between opposites." Journal of Abnormal and Social Psychology 55: 140–142.
5172. Steiner, Ivan D., and Stanley C. Peters
    1958   "Conformity and the A-B-X model." Journal of Personality 26: 229–242. P.A. 34:4212.
5173. Steiner, Ivan D., and Nageswari Rajaratnam
    1961   "A model for the comparison of individual and group performance scores." Behavioral Science 6 (2, April): 142–147. P.A. 36:1AE42S; S.A. A3249.
5174. Steiner, Ivan D., and Evan D. Rogers
    1963   "Alternative responses to dissonance." Journal of Abnormal and Social Psychology 66 (2, February): 128–136. P.A. 37:6618; S.A. 12: B0186.
5175. Steiner, Ivan D., and Joseph S. Vannoy
    1966   "Personality correlates of two types of conformity behavior." Journal of Personality and Social Psychology 4 (3): 307–315.
5176. Steinmann, Anne, David J. Fox, and Ruth Farkas
    1968   "Male and female perceptions of male sex roles." Proceedings of the

76th Annual Convention of the American Psychological Association 3: 421-422.

5177. Steinzor, Bernard
    1949a   "The development and evaluation of a measure of social interaction: Part I. The development and reliability." Human Relations 2: 103-122. P.A. 24:152.

5178   1949b   "The development and evaluation of a measure of social interaction: Part II." Human Relations 2: 319-347.

5179.   1950   "The spatial factor in face to face discussion groups." Journal of Abnormal and Social Psychology 45: 552-555. (See also Hare, Borgatta, and Bales, 1955.) P.A. 25:1007.

5180. Stendler, Celia, Dora Damrin, and Aleyne C. Haines
    1951   "Studies in cooperation and competition: I. The effects of working for group and individual rewards on the social climate of children's groups." Journal of Genetic Psychology 79: 173-197. P.A. 26:5454.

5181. Stephan, Cookie
    1973   "Attribution of intention and perception of attitude as a function of liking and similarity." Sociometry 36 (4): 463-475.

5182. Stephan, Frederick F.
    1952   "The relative rate of communication between members of small groups." American Sociological Review 17: 482-486. P.A. 27: 6519.

5183. Stephan, Frederick F., and Elliot G. Mishler
    1952   "The distribution of participation in small groups: An exponential approximation." American Sociological Review 17: 598-608. (See also Hare, Borgatta, and Bales, 1955, 1965.) P.A. 28:711.

5184. Stephenson, Geoffrey M., and Geoffrey T. Fielding
    1971   "An experimental study of the contagion of leaving behavior in small gatherings." Journal of Social Psychology 84: 81-91.

5185. Stern, Herbert, and Hanus J. Grosz
    1966   "Verbal interactions in group psychotherapy between patients with similar and with dissimilar personalities." Psychological Reports 19: 1111-1114.

5186. Stevens, Stig R.
    1953   ("Social intelligence as a function of role expectancy.") Nordisk Psykologi 5: 203-207. P.A. 29:5488.

5187. Stevenson, Marguerite B., and James L. Phillips
    1972   "Entrapment in 2 x 2 games with force vulnerable equilibria." Behavioral Science 17 (4, July): 361-370. P.A. 49:807.

5188. Stewart, Robert A., S. Jane Tutton, and Richard E. Steele
    1973   "Stereotyping and personality: I. Sex differences in perception of female physiques." Perceptual and Motor Skills 36 (3, pt. 1, June): 811-814. P.A. 51:3074.

5189. Stimpson, David V., and Bernard M. Bass
    1964   "Dyadic behavior of self-, interaction-, and task-oriented subjects in a test situation." Journal of Abnormal and Social Psychology 68 (5, May): 558-562. P.A. 39:4898.

5190. Stimson, John
    1960   "Some religious-ethnic differences in interaction rates." Psychological Reports 7: 345-356. P.A. 35:2132.

5191. Stinson, John E.
    1972   "'Least preferred coworker' as a measure of leadership style." Psychological Reports 30: 930.

5192. Stinson, John E., and John H. Robertson
    1973   "Follower-maturity and preference for leader-behavior style." Psychological Reports 32 (1, February): 247-250. P.A. 51:3000.

5193. Stires, Lloyd K., and Edward E. Jones
    1969   "Modesty versus self-enhancement as alternative forms of ingratiation." Journal of Experimental Social Psychology 5 (2): 172-188.

5194. Stirn, H.
    1952   (The Informal Work Group.) Dortmund.

5195.   1955   ("The 'small group' in German sociology.") Kölner Zeitschrift für

Soziologie und Socialpsychologie 7: 532–557. S.A. 2927.

5196.   1970   ("The work group.") In A. Mayer and B. Herwig (eds.), Handbuch der Psychologie, vol. 9, Betriebspsychologie, pp. 494–520. Göttingen.

5197. Stix, Allen H.
    1974   "An improved measure of structural balance." Human Relations 27 (5): 439–455.

5198. St. Jean, Richard
    1970   "Reformulation of the value hypothesis in group risk taking." Proceedings of the 78th Annual Convention of the American Psychological Association 5 (pt. 1): 339–340. P.A. 44:18579.

5199. Stock, Dorothy, and Herbert A. Thelen
    1958   Emotional Dynamics and Group Culture: Experimental Studies of Individual and Group Behavior. New York: New York University Press.

5200. Stock, Dorothy, and Roy M. Whitman
    1957   "Patient's and therapist's apperceptions of an episode in group therapy." Human Relations 10: 367–383. S.A. 10:A2053.

5201. Stock, Dorothy, Roy M. Whitman, and Morton A. Lieberman
    1958   "The deviant member in therapy groups." Human Relations 11: 341–372. S.A. 10:A2628.

5202. Stogdill, Ralph M.
    1948   "Personal factors associated with leadership: A survey of the literature." Journal of Psychology 25: 35–71. P.A. 22:3001.

5203.   1950   "Leadership, membership and organization." Psychological Bulletin 47: 1–14. (See also Cartwright and Zander, 1953.) P.A. 24: 4552.

5204.   1957   "Leadership and structures of personal interaction." Ohio State University, Bureau of Business Research, Monograph No. 84.

5205.   1959   Individual Behavior and Group Achievement: A Theory: The Experimental Evidence. New York: Oxford University Press.

5206.   1963   "Team achievement under high motivation." Ohio State University, Bureau of Business Research, Monograph No. R-113. S.A. 13: B7598.

5207.   1974   Handbook of Leadership: A Survey of Theory and Research. New York: Free Press. P.A. 52:2876.

5208. Stogdill, Ralph M., and A. E. Coons (eds.)
    1957   "Leader behavior: Its description and measurement." Ohio State University, Bureau of Business Research, Monograph No. 88. P.A. 32:1466.

5209. Stogdill, Ralph M., Ellis L. Scott, and William E. Jaynes
    1956   "Leadership and role expectations." Ohio State University, Bureau of Business Research, Monograph No. 86. P.A. 32:2171.

5210. Stokes, Joseph P.
    1971   "Effects of familiarization and knowledge of others' odds choices on shifts to risk and caution." Journal of Personality and Social Psychology 20 (3, December): 407–412. P.A. 47:8807.

5211. Stokols, Daniel
    1972   "On the distinction between density and crowding: Some implications for future research." Psychological Review 79 (3, May): 275–277. P.A. 48:9041.

5212. Stokols, Daniel, Marilyn Rall, Berna Pinner, and John Schopler
    1973   "Physical, social, and personal determinants of the perception of crowding." Environment and Behavior 5 (1, March): 87–115. P.A. 50:8883.

5213. Stokols, Daniel, and John Schopler
    1973   "Reactions to victims under conditions of situational detachment: The effect of responsibility, severity, and expected future interaction." Journal of Personality and Social Psychology 25 (2, February): 199–209. P.A. 50:986.

5214. Stoller, Frederick H.
    1970a   "Therapeutic concepts reconsidered in light of video tape experi-

ence." Comparative Group Studies 1 (1, February): 5–17.

5215. 1970b "Psychotherapy and the time grain: Pace in progress." Comparative Group Studies 1 (4, November): 411–418.

5216. Stone, Anthony R.
1969 "The interdisciplinary research team." Journal of Applied Behavioral Science 5 (3): 351–365. P.A. 44:10296.

5217. Stone, G. C., N. L. Gage, and G. S. Leavitt
1957 "Two kinds of accuracy in predicting another's responses." Journal of Social Psychology 45: 245–254.

5218. Stone, Gregory P.
1966 ("Conceptual problems in research on small groups.") Kölner Zeitschrift für Soziologie und Sozialpsychologie 10 (Supplement): 44–65. S.A. 15:C5590.

5219. Stone, LeRoy A.
1963 "Use of a multiple regression model with group decision-making." Human Relations 16 (2, May): 183–188. S.A. 12:A8719.

5220. Stone, Lewis J., and Jack E. Hokanson
1969 "Arousal reduction via self-punitive behavior." Journal of Personality and Social Psychology 12 (1): 72–79. P.A. 43:11240.

5221. Stone, Phil, and Joe Kamiya
1957 "Judgement of consensus during group discussion." Journal of Abnormal and Social Psychology 55: 171–175.

5222. Stone, Philip J.
1960 "Changes in muscle tonus during social interaction." Ph.D. dissertation. Harvard University.

5223. Stone, Philip J., Robert F. Bales, J. Zvi Namenwirth, and Daniel M. Ogilvie
1962 "The General Inquirer: A computer system for content analysis and retrieval based on the sentence as a unit of information." Behavioral Science 7: 484–498.

5224. Stone, Philip J., Dexter C. Dunphy, Marshall S. Smith, Daniel M. Ogilvie, with associates
1966 The General Inquirer: A Computer Approach to Content Analysis. Cambridge, Mass.: MIT Press.

5225. Stone, Thomas H.
1971 "Effects of mode of organization and feedback level on creative task groups." Journal of Applied Psychology 53 (4): 324–330.

5226. Stone, William F.
1967 "Autokinetic norms: An experimental analysis." Journal of Personality and Social Psychology 5 (1): 76–81.

5227. 1973 "Patterns of conformity in couples varying in intimacy." Journal of Personality and Social Psychology 27 (3, September): 413–418. P.A. 51:5046.

5228. Stoner, James A. F.
1961 "A comparison of individual and group decisions involving risk." M.S. thesis. Massachusetts Institute of Technology. (Cited in Wallach, Kogan, and Bem, 1962.)

5229. 1968 "Risky and cautious shifts in group decisions: The influence of widely held values." Journal of Experimental Social Psychology 4 (4, October): 442–459. P.A. 43:3942.

5230. Storms, Michael D.
1973 "Videotape and the attribution process: Reversing actors' and observers' points of view." Journal of Personality and Social Psychology 27 (2, August): 165–175. P.A. 51:3075.

5231. Stotland, Ezra
1959a "Determinants of attraction to groups." Journal of Social Psychology 49: 71–80. P.A. 35:4827.

5232. 1959b "Peer groups and reaction to power figures." In D. Cartwright (ed.), Studies in Social Power, pp. 53–68. Ann Arbor: University of Michigan. P.A. 34:7611.

5233. 1969 "Exploratory investigations of empathy." In L. Berkowitz (ed.), Advances in Experimental Social Psychology, vol. 4, pp. 271–314. New York: Academic Press.

5234. Stotland, Ezra, and Nickolas B. Cottrell
      1961   "Self-esteem, group interaction, and group influence on perform-
              ance." Journal of Personality 29 (3): 273–284. P.A. 37:3045.
5235.   1962   "Similarity of performance as influenced by interaction, self-esteem,
              and birth order." Journal of Abnormal and Social Psychology 64
              (3): 183–191. P.A. 38:2591.
5236. Stotland, Ezra, Nickolas B. Cottrell, and Gordon Laing
      1960   "Group interaction and perceived similarity of members." Journal of
              Abnormal and Social Psychology 61 (3): 335–340. P.A. 36:2GE35S;
              S.A. A1706.
5237. Stotland, Ezra, Thomas Reed, Solveig Thomson, and Arnold Katz
      1973   "Social schemata of American college students." Human Relations
              26 (2, April): 171–188. P.A. 51:3076.
5238. Stotland, Ezra, Stanley Thorley, Edwin Thomas, Arthur R. Cohen, and Alvin
      Zander
      1957   "The effects of group expectations and self-esteem upon self-evalua-
              tion." Journal of Abnormal and Social Psychology 54: 55–63.
5239. Stotland, Ezra, and James A. Walsh
      1963   "Birth order and an experimental study of empathy." Journal of Ab-
              normal and Social Psychology 66 (6): 610–614.
5240. Stotland, Ezra, Alvin Zander, and Thomas Natsoulas
      1961   "Generalization of interpersonal similarity." Journal of Abnormal
              and Social Psychology 62 (2, March): 250–256.
5241. Stouffer, Samuel A., et al.
      1949   The American Soldier. Princeton, N.J.: Princeton University Press.
5242. Stoute, Argyle
      1950   "Implementation of group interpersonal relationships through psy-
              chotherapy." Journal of Psychology 30: 145–156.
5243. Strassberg, Donald S., and Burton I. Klinger
      1972   "The effect on pain tolerance of social pressure within the labora-
              tory setting." Journal of Social Psychology 88 (1, October): 123–
              130. P.A. 49:6864.
5244. Strassberg, Donald S., and Emily Wiggen
      1973   "Conformity as a function of age in preadolescents." Journal of
              Social Psychology 91 (1): 61–66.
5245. Stratton, Lois O., Dennis J. Tekippe, and Grad L. Flick
      1973   "Personal space and self-concept." Sociometry 36 (3): 424–429.
5246. Strauss, B., and Frances Strauss
      1951   New Ways to Better Meetings. New York: Viking. P.A. 26:219.
5247. Street, Warren R.
      1974   "Brainstorming by individuals, coacting and interacting groups."
              Journal of Applied Psychology 59 (4): 433–436.
5248. Streufert, Siegfried
      1965   "Communicator importance and interpersonal attitudes toward con-
              forming and deviant group members." Journal of Personality and So-
              cial Psychology 2 (2): 242–246. P.A. 39:15066.
5249.   1966   "Conceptual structure, communicator importance, and interpersonal
              attitudes toward conforming and deviant group members." Journal
              of Personality and Social Psychology 4 (1): 100–103. P.A. 40:
              10045; S.A. 15:C5591.
5250.   1969   "Increasing failure and response rate in complex decision making."
              Journal of Experimental Social Psychology 5 (3): 310–323.
5251.   1970   "Complexity and complex decision making: Convergences between
              differentiation and integration approaches to the prediction of task
              performance." Journal of Experimental Social Psychology 6 (4):
              494–509.
5252.   1972   "Success and response rate in complex decision making." Journal of
              Experimental Social Psychology 8 (5, September): 389–403. P.A.
              49:6865.
5253. Streufert, Siegfried, Ronnie G. Bushinsky, and Carl H. Castore
      1967   "Conceptual structure and social choice: A replication under modi-
              fied conditions." Psychonomic Science 9 (4): 227–228. P.A. 42:703.

5254. Streufert, Siegfried, Thomas Cafferty, and Frances Cherry
 1972   "Information load, group organization, and communication fre-
         quency." Psychonomic Science 27 (6, June): 348-350. P.A. 49:
         2383.

5255. Streufert, Siegfried, and Carl H. Castore
 1971   "Information search and the effects of failure: A test of complexity
         theory." Journal of Experimental Social Psychology 7 (1, January):
         125-143. P.A. 46:1097.

5256. Streufert, Siegfried, and Susan C. Streufert
 1969   "Effects of conceptual structure, failure, and success on attribution
         of causality and interpersonal attitudes." Journal of Personality and
         Social Psychology 11 (2): 138-147.

5257. Streufert, Siegfried, Susan C. Streufert, and Carl H. Castore
 1968   "Leadership in negotiations and the complexity of conceptual struc-
         ture." Journal of Applied Psychology 52 (3): 218-223. P.A. 42:
         12051.

5258. 1969   "Complexity, increasing failure, and decision making." Journal of
               Experimental Research in Personality 3 (4): 293-300. P.A. 43:
               14242.

5259. Stricker, Lawrence J., Samuel Messick, and Douglas N. Jackson
 1967   "Suspicion of deception: Implications for conformity research."
         Journal of Personality and Social Psychology 5 (4): 379-389.

5260. 1970   "Conformity, anticonformity, and independence: Their dimension-
               ality and generality." Journal of Personality and Social Psychology
               16 (3): 494-507.

5261. Strickland, Bonnie R., and Douglas P. Crowne
 1962   "Conformity under conditions of simulated group pressure as a func-
         tion of the need for social approval." Journal of Social Psychology
         58 (1, October): 171-181. P.A. 37:6619.

5262. Strickland, Lloyd H., Edward E. Jones, and William P. Smith
 1960   "Effects of group support on the evaluation of an antagonist." Jour-
         nal of Abnormal and Social Psychology 61 (1): 73-81. S.A. A1206.

5263. Strickland, Lloyd H., and Bernard S. Lacome
 1968   "Coalition formation in continuous, episodic and terminal situa-
         tions." Psychological Reports 23 (3, pt. 1): 915-921. P.A. 43:
         9646.

5264. Strodtbeck, Fred L.
 1950   "A study of husband-wife interaction in three cultures." Ph.D. dis-
         sertation. Harvard University.

5265. 1951   "Husband-wife interaction over revealed differences." American So-
               ciological Review 16: 468-473. (See also Hare, Borgatta, and Bales,
               1955, 1965; Crosbie, 1975.) P.A. 27:1142.

5266. 1954a   "The family as a three-person group." American Sociological Review
               19: 23-29. (See also Hare, Borgatta, and Bales, 1955.) P.A. 3949.

5267. 1954b   "A case for the study of small groups." American Sociological Re-
               view 19: 651-657. P.A. 30:2701.

5268. 1956   "Sociology of small groups, 1944-55." In H. L. Zetterberg (ed.),
               Sociology in the United States of America: A Trend Report. Paris:
               UNESCO.

5269. Strodtbeck, Fred L., and A. Paul Hare
 1954   "Bibliography of small group research: From 1900 through 1953."
         Sociometry 17: 107-178. P.A. 29:3831.

5270. Strodtbeck, Fred L., and L. Harmon Hook
 1961   "The social dimensions of a twelve-man jury table." Sociometry 24
         (4, December): 397-415. P.A. 37:1116; S.A. A3579.

5271. Strodtbeck, Fred L., Rita M. James, and C. Hawkins
 1957   "Social status in jury deliberations." American Sociological Review
         22: 713-719. (See also Maccoby, Newcomb, and Hartley, 1958;
         Crosbie, 1975.) S.A. 5302.

5272. Strodtbeck, Fred L., and Richard D. Mann
 1956   "Sex role differentiation in jury deliberations." Sociometry 19:
         3-11. (See also Hare, Borgatta, and Bales, 1965.) S.A. 6:3950.

5273. Stroebe, Wolfgang, Chester A. Insko, Vaida D. Thompson, and Bruce D. Layton
    1971   "Effects of physical attractiveness, attitude similarity, and sex on various aspects of interpersonal attraction." Journal of Personality and Social Psychology 18 (1, April): 79-91. P.A. 46:2934.

5274. Strongman, K. T., and B. G. Champness
    1968   "Dominance hierarchies and conflict in eye contact." Acta Psychologica 28 (4): 376-386. P.A. 43:6835.

5275. Stroop, J. R.
    1932   "Is the judgement of the group better than that of the average member of the group?" Journal of Experimental Psychology 15: 550-562.

5276. Strupp, Hans H.
    1955a   "An objective comparison of Rogerian and psychoanalytic techniques." Journal of Consulting Psychology 19: 1-7.

5277.   1955b   "Psychotherapeutic technique, professional affiliation, and experience level." Journal of Consulting Psychology 19: 97-102.

5278.   1955c   "The effect of the psychotherapist's personal analysis upon his techniques." Journal of Consulting Psychology 19: 197-204. P.A. 30: 2994.

5279.   1958   "The performance of psychoanalytic and client-centered therapists in an initial interview." Journal of Consulting Psychology 22: 265-274.

5280. Stryker, Sheldon, and George Psathas
    1960   "Research on coalitions in the triad: Findings, problems and strategy." Sociometry 23 (3, September): 217-230. P.A. 35:2133; S.A. A2750.

5281. Suchman, J. Richard
    1956   "Social sensitivity in the small task-oriented group." Journal of Abnormal and Social Psychology 52: 75-83. P.A. 31:2724.

5282. Sudnow, David (ed.)
    1972   Studies in Social Interaction. New York: Free Press. P.A. 49:9100.

5283. Sudolsky, Mitchell, and Ronald Nathan
    1971   "A replication in questionnaire form of an experiment by Lippitt, Lewin, and White concerning conditions of leadership and social climates in groups." Cornell Journal of Social Relations 6 (2, Fall): 188-196. S.A. 21:73G2276.

5284. Sue, Stanley, Ronald E. Smith, and Cathy Caldwell
    1973   "Effects of inadmissible evidence on the decisions of simulated jurors: A moral dilemma." Proceedings of the 81st Annual Convention of the American Psychological Association 8 (pt. 1): 263-264.

5285. Suedfeld, Peter, Stephen Bochner, and Deanna Wnek
    1972   "Helper-sufferer similarity and specific request for help: Bystander intervention during a peace demonstration." Journal of Applied Social Psychology 2 (1, January): 17-23. P.A. 48:9042.

5286. Sullivan, Harry S.
    1938   "Psychiatry: Introduction to the study of interpersonal relations." Psychiatry 1: 121-134.

5287.   1954   The Interpersonal Theory of Psychiatry. New York: Norton.

5288. Summers, David A.
    1968   "Conflict, compromise, and belief change in a decision-making task." Journal of Conflict Resolution 12 (2): 215-221. P.A. 43:5289.

5289. Summers, David A., Stephen Peirce, Dale Olen, and Thomas Baranowski
    1972   "Strategy detection in the Prisoner's Dilemma game." Journal of Social Psychology 88 (1, October): 131-138. P.A. 49:6866.

5290. Summers, David A., J. Dale Taliaferro, and Donna J. Fletcher
    1970   "Judgment policy and interpersonal learning." Behavioral Science 15 (6, November): 514-521. P.A. 46:4853.

5291. Sundstrom, Eric, and Irwin Altman
    1974   "Field study of territorial behavior and dominance." Journal of Personality and Social Psychology 30 (1, July): 115-124. P.A. 52: 12235.

5292. Suppes, Patrick, and Richard C. Atkinson
    1960   Markov Learning Models for Multi-Person Interactions. Stanford, Calif.: Stanford University Press.

5293. Suppes, Patrick, and Franklin Krasne
    1961   "Applications of stimulus sampling theory to situations involving social pressure." Psychological Review 68 (1): 46-59. P.A. 37: 3046.

5294. Suppes, Patrick, and Madeleine Schlag-Rey
    1962   "Analysis of social conformity in terms of generalized conditioning models." In J. H. Criswell, H. Solomon, and P. Suppes (eds.), Mathematical Methods in Small Group Processes, pp. 334-361. Stanford, Calif.: Stanford University Press. S.A. 12:B2424.

5295. Susman, Gerald I.
    1970   "The impact of automation on work group autonomy and task specialization." Human Relations 23 (6): 567-577.

5296. Sutherland, Anne E., and Chester A. Insko
    1973   "Attraction and interestingness of anticipated interaction." Journal of Personality 41 (2, June): 234-243. P.A. 51:3078.

5297. Sutherland, Richard L.
    1972   "An anatomy of loving." Journal of Religion and Health 11 (2, April): 167-174. P.A. 48:9043.

5298. Sutton-Smith, Brian, and B. G. Rosenberg
    1968   "Sibling consensus on power tactics." Journal of Genetic Psychology 112 (1): 63-72. P.A. 42:10537.

5299. Svensson, Axel
    1972   ("The marathon method according to Bach and Stoller.") Gruppendynamik (Forschung und Praxis) 4 (3, December): 407-422. P.A. 50:4842.

5300. Swanson, Guy E.
    1950   "The development of an instrument for rating child-parent relationships." Social Forces 29: 84-90. P.A. 25:4991.

5301.   1951a   "Some problems of laboratory experiments with small populations." American Sociological Review 16: 349-358. P.A. 27:1077.

5302.   1951b   "Some effects of member object-relationships on small groups." Human Relations 4: 355-380. P.A. 26:5486.

5303.   1965   "On explanations of social interaction." Sociometry 28 (2, June): 101-123. S.A. 14:B9186.

5304.   1968   "Symbolic interaction." In D. L. Sills (ed.), International Encyclopedia of the Social Sciences, vol. 7, pp. 441-445. New York: Macmillan and Free Press.

5305.   1974   "The primary process of groups, its systematics and representation." Journal for the Theory of Social Behaviour 4 (1): 53-69.

5306. Swanson, Guy E., Theodore M. Newcomb, and Eugene L. Hartley (eds.)
    1952   Readings in Social Psychology. Rev. ed. New York: Holt. P.A. 27: 4160.

5307. Swap, Walter C., and Harold Miller
    1969   "Risky shift and social exchange in dyads." Psychonomic Science 17 (4): 249-250. P.A. 44:5099.

5308. Swensson, Richard G.
    1967   "Cooperation in the Prisoner's Dilemma game I: The effects of asymmetric payoff information and explicit communication." Behavioral Science 12 (July): 314-322.

5309. Swingle, Paul G.
    1966   "Effects of the emotional relationship between protagonists in a two-person game." Journal of Personality and Social Psychology 4 (3, September): 270-279. S.A. 16:D1449.

5310.   1967   "The effects of the win-loss difference upon cooperative responding in a 'dangerous' game." Journal of Conflict Resolution 11 (2, June): 214-222. S.A. 16:C8898.

5311.   1968a   "Effects of prior exposure to cooperative treatment upon subject's responding in the Prisoner's Dilemma." Journal of Personality and Social Psychology 10 (1): 44-52.

5312.   1968b   "Illusory power in a dangerous game." Canadian Journal of Psychology 22 (3): 176-185. P.A. 42:15407.
5313.   1970   "Exploitative behavior in non-zero-sum games." Journal of Personality and Social Psychology 16 (1, September): 121-132. P.A. 45: 2308.
5314. Swingle, Paul G., and Henry Coady
         1967   "Effects of the partner's abrupt strategy change upon subject's responding in the Prisoner's Dilemma." Journal of Personality and Social Psychology 5 (3): 357-363.
5315. Swingle, Paul G., and John S. Gillis
         1968   "Effects of the emotional relationship between protagonists in the Prisoner's Dilemma." Journal of Personality and Social Psychology 8 (2, pt. 1): 160-165. P.A. 42:5525.
5316. Swingle, Paul G., and Brian MacLean
         1971   "The effect of illusory power in non-zero-sum games." Journal of Conflict Resolution 15 (4): 513-522.
5317. Swingle, Paul G., and Angelo Santi
         1972   "Communication in non-zero-sum games." Journal of Personality and Social Psychology 23 (1, July): 54-63. P.A. 48:11467.
5318. Swinth, Robert L.
         1967   "The establishment of the trust relationship." Journal of Conflict Resolution 11 (3): 335-344.
5319. Swinth, Robert L., and Francis D. Tuggle
         1971   "A complete dyadic process model of four man group problem solving." Organizational Behavior and Human Performance 6 (5, September): 517-549. P.A. 47:8808.
5320. Switkin, Linda R., and Malcolm D. Gynther
         1974   "Trust, activism, and interpersonal perception in black and white college students." Journal of Social Psychology 94 (1): 153-154.
5321. Symonds, Carolyn
         1971   "A nude touchy-feely group." Journal of Sex Research 7 (2, May): 126-133. Discussion, pp. 134-137. S.A. 22:74G8635.
5322. Symonds, Percival M.
         1947   "Role playing as a diagnostic procedure in the selection of leaders." Sociatry 1: 43-50. P.A. 21:3720.
5323. Szmatka, Jacek
         1974   ("Conceptual models in the theory of social role.") Studia Socjologiczne 1 (52): 73-97. P.A. 52:12236.

5324. Taft, Ronald
         1955   "The ability to judge people." Psychological Bulletin 52: 1-23.
5325.   1966   "Accuracy of empathic judgments of acquaintances and strangers." Journal of Personality and Social Psychology 3 (5): 600-604.
5326. Tagiuri, Renato
         1952   "Relational analysis: An extension of sociometric method with emphasis upon sociometric perception." Sociometry 15: 91-104. (See also Hare, Borgatta, and Bales, 1955, 1965.) P.A. 27:7144.
5327.   1957   "The perception of feelings among members of small groups." Journal of Social Psychology 46: 219-227. P.A. 34:2873.
5328.   1968   "Person perception." In G. Lindzey and E. Aronson (eds.), Handbook of Social Psychology, vol. 3, pp. 395-449. Reading, Mass.: Addison-Wesley.
5329. Tagiuri, Renato, and Rosalind Barnett
         1968   "Perception of values and self-presentation." Proceedings of the 76th Annual Convention of the American Psychological Association 3: 419-420.
5330. Tagiuri, Renato, Robert R. Blake, and Jerome S. Bruner
         1953   "Some determinants of the perception of positive and negative feelings in others." Journal of Abnormal and Social Psychology 48: 585-592. P.A. 28:5838; S.A. 249.
5331. Tagiuri, Renato, Jerome S. Bruner, and Robert R. Blake
         1958   "On the relations between feelings and perception of feelings among

members of small groups." In E. E. Maccoby, T. M. Newcomb, and E. L. Hartley (eds.), Readings in Social Psychology, 3rd ed., pp. 110–116. New York: Holt.

5332. Tagiuri, Renato, Jerome S. Bruner, and Nathan Kogan
    1955   "Estimating the chance expectancies of dyadic relationships within a group." Psychological Bulletin 52: 122–131. P.A. 30:2702.

5333. Tagiuri, Renato, and Nathan Kogan
    1957   "The visibility of interpersonal preferences." Human Relations 10: 385–390. P.A. 34:2874; S.A. A1707.

5334.   1960   "Personal preference and the attribution of influence in small groups." Journal of Personality 28: 257–265. P.A. 35:2135.

5335. Tagiuri, Renato, Nathan Kogan, and Jerome S. Bruner
    1955   "The transparency of interpersonal choice." Sociometry 18: 624–635. P.A. 32:1497; S.A. 3435.

5336. Tagiuri, Renato, Nathan Kogan, and Lewis M. K. Long
    1959   ("Differentiation of sociometric choices and status relations in a group.") Bulletin du C.E.R.P. 8 (January-June): 101–104. P.A. 34: 4213.

5337. Tagiuri, Renato, and Luigi Petrullo (eds.)
    1958   Person Perception and Interpersonal Behavior. Stanford, Calif.: Stanford University Press.

5338. Takahashi, Susumu
    1970   "Analysis of weighted averaging model on integration of informations in personality impression formation." Japanese Psychological Research 12 (4, December): 154–162. P.A. 49:6868.

5339.   1971   "Effect of inter-relatedness of informations on context effect in personality impression formation." Japanese Psychological Research 13 (4, December): 167–175. P.A. 49:6869.

5340. Takala, Martti, Toivo A. Pihkanen, and Touko Markkanen
    1957   "The effects of distilled and brewed beverages: A physiological, neurological, and psychological study." Finnish Foundation for Alcohol Studies. Vol. 4. P.A. 31:4890.

5341. Talland, George A.
    1954   "The assessment of group opinion by leaders, and their influence on its formation." Journal of Abnormal and Social Psychology 89: 431–434. P.A. 29:3832.

5342.   1955   "Task and interaction process: Some characteristics of therapeutic group discussion." Journal of Abnormal and Social Psychology 50: 105–109. (See also Hare, Borgatta, and Bales, 1955, 1965.) P.A. 29:7396.

5343.   1957a   "Rate of speaking as a group norm." Human Organization 15 (4): 8–10.

5344.   1957b   "Role and status structure in therapy groups." Journal of Clinical Psychology 13: 27–33.

5345.   1958   "Sex differences in self assessment." Journal of Social Psychology 48: 25–35. P.A. 34:5752.

5346. Talland, George A., and David H. Clark
    1954   "Evaluation of topics in therapy group discussion." Journal of Clinical Psychology 10: 131–137. P.A. 29:1015.

5347. Tallman, Irving
    1970   "The family as a small problem solving group." Journal of Marriage and the Family 32 (1, February): 94–104. S.A. 19:E7005.

5348. Tanaka, Kumajiro
    1963   "A psychological study on the affiliation-repulsion tendencies among group members." Japanese Psychological Research 5 (1): 28–42. P.A. 38:5973.

5349. Tannenbaum, Arnold S.
    1962   "Reactions of members of voluntary groups: A logarithmic function of size of group." Psychological Reports 10 (1): 113–114. P.A. 37: 1117.

5350. Tannenbaum, Arnold S., and Jerald G. Bachman
    1964   "Structural versus individual effects." American Journal of Sociol-

ogy 69 (6, May): 585–595. S.A. 12:B3229.

5351. Tannenbaum, Robert J., Irving R. Weschler, and Fred Massarik
  1961   Leadership and Organization: A Behavioral Science Approach. New York: McGraw-Hill. P.A. 36:1GF56T.

5352. Tarantino, Santo J.
  1973   "Interpersonal perception in male and female dyads." Perceptual and Motor Skills 36 (3, pt. 2, June): 1046. P.A. 51:9052.

5353. Taves, E. H.
  1941   "Two mechanisms for the perception of visual numerousness." Archives of Psychology 37, No. 265. P.A. 16:2594.

5354. Taylor, Dalmas A.
  1968   "The development of interpersonal relationships: Social penetration processes." Journal of Social Psychology 75 (1, June): 79–90. P.A. 42:13671.

5355. Taylor, Dalmas A., Irwin Altman, and Richard Sorrentino
  1968   "Interpersonal exchange as a function of reward/cost and situational factors: Expectancy confirmation-disconfirmation." Proceedings of the 76th Annual Convention of the American Psychological Association 3: 409–410.

5356.   1969   "Interpersonal exchange as a function of rewards and costs and situational factors: Expectancy confirmation-disconfirmation." Journal of Experimental Social Psychology 5 (3): 324–339. P.A. 44:5092.

5357. Taylor, Dalmas A., Ladd Wheeler, and Irwin Altman
  1968   "Stress relations in socially isolated groups." Journal of Personality and Social Psychology 9 (4): 369–376. P.A. 42:17152.

5358.   1973   "Self-disclosure in isolated groups." Journal of Personality and Social Psychology 26 (1, April): 39–47. P.A. 50:4843.

5359. Taylor, Donald W., P. C. Berry, and C. H. Block
  1961   ("Does group effort aid or inhibit creative thought in 'brainstorming'?") Travail Humain 24: 1–20. P.A. 36:1GE01T.

5360. Taylor, Donald W., and William L. Faust
  1952   "Twenty Questions: Efficiency in problem solving as a function of size of group." Journal of Experimental Psychology 44: 360–368. (See also Hare, Borgatta, and Bales, 1955, 1965.) P.A. 27:4994.

5361. Taylor, Donald W., and Olga W. McNemar
  1955   "Problem solving and thinking." Annual Review of Psychology 6: 455–482. P.A. 29:5286.

5362. Taylor, F. Kräupl
  1954   "The three-dimensional basis of emotional interactions in small groups. I." Human Relations 7: 441–471. P.A. 29:5489; S.A. 1514.

5363.   1955   "The three-dimensional basis of emotional interactions in small groups. II." Human Relations 8: 3–28. P.A. 30:806; S.A. 1774.

5364.   1957   "Display of dyadic emotions." Human Relations 10: 257–262. S.A. 1207.

5365. Taylor, Frederick W.
  1903   "Group management." Transactions of the American Society of Mechanical Engineers 24: 1337–1480.

5366.   1911   The Principles of Scientific Management. New York: Harper.

5367. Taylor, Howard F.
  1967   "Balance and change in the two-person group." Sociometry 30 (3, September): 262–279. P.A. 41:16639.

5368.   1968   "Balance, tension, and tension release in the two person group." Human Relations 21 (1, February): 59–74. P.A. 42:13672; S.A. 17:D5795.

5369. Taylor, James B.
  1961a   "The 'yeasayer' and social desirability: A comment on the Couch and Kenniston paper." Journal of Abnormal and Social Psychology 62 (1, January): 172. P.A. 36:3HF72T; S.A. A1738.

5370.   1961b   "What do attitude scales measure: The problem of social desirability." Journal of Abnormal and Social Psychology 62 (2, March): 386–390. S.A. A2152.

5371. Taylor, James H., Claude E. Thompson, and Dimiter Spassoff
   1937   "The effect of conditions of work and various suggested attitudes on production and reported feelings of tiredness and boredom." Journal of Applied Psychology 21: 431-450.
5372. Taylor, M., and Harold E. Mitzel
   1957   "Research tools: Observing and recording group behavior." Review of Educational Research 27: 476-486.
5373. Taylor, Marvin, Robert Crook, and Stanley Dropkin
   1961   "Assessing emerging leadership behavior in small discussion groups." Journal of Educational Psychology 52: 12-18. P.A. 36:2GF12T.
5374. Taylor, Michael
   1970   "The problem of salience in the theory of collective decision-making." Behavioral Science 15 (5, September): 415-430. S.A. 20: F3460.
5375. Taylor, Minna, and Eugene A. Weinstein
   1974   "Criticism, witnesses and the maintenance of interaction." Social Forces 52 (4, June): 473-480. P.A. 52:12353.
5376. Taylor, Shelley E., and L. Rowell Huesmann
   1974   "Replication report. Expectancy confirmed again: A computer investigation of expectancy theory." Journal of Experimental Social Psychology 10 (5): 497-501.
5377. Taylor, Shelley E., and David R. Mettee
   1971   "When similarity breeds contempt." Journal of Personality and Social Psychology 20 (1, October): 75-81. P.A. 47:6700.
5378. Taylor, Stuart P., and Richard Pisano
   1971   "Physical aggression as a function of frustration and physical attack." Journal of Social Psychology 84 (2, August): 261-267. P.A. 47:835.
5379. Taynor, Janet, and Kay Deaux
   1973   "When women are more deserving than men: Equity, attribution, and perceived sex differences." Journal of Personality and Social Psychology 28 (3, December): 360-367. P.A. 51:7092.
5380. Tear, Daniel G., and George M. Guthrie
   1955   "The relationship of cooperation to the sharpening-leveling continuum." Journal of Social Psychology 42: 203-208. P.A. 31:794.
5381. Tedeschi, James T.
   1972   The Social Influence Processes. Chicago: Aldine-Atherton. P.A. 49: 9101.
5382. Tedeschi, James T., Daniel Aranoff, James Gahagan, and Douglas Hiester
   1968   "The partial reinforcement effect and the Prisoner's Dilemma." Journal of Social Psychology 75 (August): 209-215.
5383. Tedeschi, James T., and Thomas V. Bonoma
   1969   "Effects of retaliation on the behavior of a threatening source." Proceedings of the 77th Annual Convention of the American Psychological Association 4 (pt. 1): 401-402. P.A. 43:17358.
5384. Tedeschi, James T., Thomas V. Bonoma, and Robert C. Brown
   1971   "A paradigm for the study of coercive power." Journal of Conflict Resolution 15 (2, June): 197-224. S.A. 20:F6958.
5385. Tedeschi, James T., Thomas V. Bonoma, and Noel Novinson
   1970   "Behavior of a threatener: Retaliation vs. fixed opportunity costs." Journal of Conflict Resolution 14 (1, March): 69-76. P.A. 46: 2936.
5386. Tedeschi, James T., James P. Gahagan, Daniel Aranoff, and Matthew W. Steele
   1968   "Realism and optimism in the Prisoner's Dilemma game." Journal of Social Psychology 75 (August): 191-197.
5387. Tedeschi, James T., Douglas S. Hiester, and James P. Gahagan
   1969   "Trust and the Prisoner's Dilemma game." Journal of Social Psychology 79 (1, October): 43-50. P.A. 44:6666.
5388. Tedeschi, James T., Joann Horai, Svenn Lindskold, and Thomas Faley
   1970   "The effects of opportunity costs and target compliance on the behavior of a threatening source." Journal of Experimental Social Psychology 6 (2): 205-213. P.A. 44:16567.

5389. Tedeschi, James T., Joann Horai, Svenn Lindskold, and James P. Gahagan
    1968   "The effects of threat upon prevarication and compliance in social conflict." Proceedings of the 76th Annual Convention of the American Psychological Association 3: 399-400.
5390. Tedeschi, James T., Stuart Lesnick, and James P. Gahagan
    1968   "Feedback and 'washout' effects in the Prisoner's Dilemma game." Journal of Personality and Social Psychology 10 (1): 31-34.
5391. Tedeschi, James T., Svenn Lindskold, Joann Horai, and James P. Gahagan
    1969   "Social power and the credibility of promises." Journal of Personality and Social Psychology 13 (3): 253-261. P.A. 44:2274.
5392. Tedeschi, James T., R. Bob Smith, III, and Robert C. Brown, Jr.
    1974   "A reinterpretation of research on aggression." Psychological Bulletin 81 (9): 540-562.
5393. Tedeschi, James T., Matthew W. Steele, James P. Gahagan, and Daniel Aranoff
    1968   "Intentions, predictions, and patterns of strategy choices in a Prisoner's Dilemma game." Journal of Social Psychology 75 (August): 199-207.
5394. Tedesco, John F., and Donald K. Fromme
    1974   "Cooperation, competition and personal space." Sociometry 37 (1): 116-121.
5395. Teger, Allan I.
    1970   "The effect of early cooperation on the escalation of conflict." Journal of Experimental Social Psychology 6 (2): 187-204. P.A. 44:16568.
5396. Teger, Allan I., and Nathan Kogan
    1971   "Effect of a reciprocal decision rule on decisions for another person." Proceedings of the 79th Annual Convention of the American Psychological Association 6 (pt. 1): 247-248.
5397. Teger, Allan I., and Dean G. Pruitt
    1967   "Components of group risk taking." Journal of Experimental Social Psychology 3 (April): 189-205.
5398. Teger, Allan I., Dean G. Pruitt, Richard St. Jean, and Gordon A. Haaland
    1970   "A reexamination of the familiarization hypothesis in group risk taking." Journal of Experimental Social Psychology 6 (3, July): 346-350. P.A. 45:635.
5399. Teichman, Yona
    1973   "Emotional arousal and affiliation." Journal of Experimental Social Psychology 9 (6): 591-605.
5400.   1974   "Predisposition for anxiety and affiliation." Journal of Personality and Social Psychology 29 (3): 405-410.
5401. Teirich, H. R., and Hans A. Illing
    1958   "Sociometry in groups." International Journal of Social Psychiatry 4 (1, Summer): 55-59. Discussion, pp. 60-61. S.A. 15:C5592.
5402. Terauds, Anita, Irwin Altman, and Joseph E. McGrath
    1960   A Bibliography of Small Group Research. Arlington, Va.: Human Sciences Research.
5403. Terhune, Kenneth W.
    1968   "Motives, situation, and interpersonal conflict within Prisoner's Dilemma." Journal of Personality and Social Psychology 8 (3, pt. 2, March). P.A. 42:8873.
5404. Terman, Lewis M.
    1904   "A preliminary study of the psychology and pedagogy of leadership." Pedagogical Seminary 11: 413-451. (See also Hare, Borgatta, and Bales, 1955, 1965.)
5405. Terry, Roger L., Norma L. Carey, and Timothy D. Hutson
    1973   "A dependence interpretation of the effects of performance expectancies." Journal of Social Psychology 89 (2, April): 219-224. P.A. 50:6760.
5406. Terry, Roger L., and William G. Snider
    1972   "Veridicality of interpersonal perceptions based upon physiognomic cues." Journal of Psychology 81 (2, July): 205-208. P.A. 50: 2988.

5407. Tesch, Frederick E., Ted L. Huston, and Eugene A. Indenbaum
    1973   "Attitude similarity, attraction, and physical proximity in a dynamic space." Journal of Applied Social Psychology 3 (1, January): 63-72. P.A. 51:3079.
5408. Tesser, Abraham
    1969   "Trait similarity and trait evaluation as correlates of attraction." Psychonomic Science 15 (6): 319-320. P.A. 43:17359.
5409.   1971   "Evaluative and structural similarity of attitudes as determinants of interpersonal attraction." Journal of Personality and Social Psychology 18 (1, April): 92-96. P.A. 46:2938.
5410.   1972   "Attitude similarity and intercorrelations as determinants of interpersonal attraction." Journal of Experimental Research in Personality 6 (2-3, December): 142-153. P.A. 51:1008.
5411. Tesser, Abraham, and Mary C. Conlee
    1973   "Recipient emotionality as a determinant of the transmission of bad news." Proceedings of the 81st Annual Convention of the American Psychological Association 8: 247-248. P.A. 50:4844.
5412. Tesser, Abraham, Robert Gatewood, and Michael Driver
    1968   "Some determinants of gratitude." Journal of Personality and Social Psychology 9 (3): 233-236. P.A. 42:13673.
5413. Tesser, Abraham, and Sidney Rosen
    1972   "Similarity of objective fate as a determinant of the reluctance to transmit unpleasant information: The mum effect." Journal of Personality and Social Psychology 23 (1): 46-53.
5414. Tesser, Abraham, Sidney Rosen, and Thomas R. Batchelor
    1972a   "On the reluctance to communicate bad news (the mum effect): A role play extension." Journal of Psychology 40 (1): 88-103.
5415.   1972b   "Some message variables and the MUM effect." Journal of Communication 22 (3, September): 239-256. P.A. 50:991.
5416. Tesser, Abraham, Sidney Rosen, and Mary C. Conlee
    1972   "News valence and available recipient as determinants of news transmission." Sociometry 35 (4, December): 619-628. P.A. 50:992.
5417. Tessler, Richard C., and Shalom H. Schwartz
    1972   "Help seeking self-esteem, and achievement motivation: An attributional analysis." Journal of Personality and Social Psychology 21 (3, March): 318-326. P.A. 48:2908.
5418. Test, Mary A., and James H. Bryan
    1969   "The effects of dependency, models, and reciprocity upon subsequent helping behavior." Journal of Social Psychology 78 (2): 205-212. P.A. 44:6667.
5419. Tewes, Uwe
    1973   ("Some conditions for discrimination of the emotional status of perceived facial expressions.") Zeitschrift für Experimentelle und Angewandte Psychologie 20 (2): 317-346. P.A. 51:3080.
5420. Thalhofer, Nancy N.
    1971   "Responsibility, reparation, and self-protection as reasons for three types of helping." Journal of Personality and Social Psychology 19 (2, August): 144-151. P.A. 47:2855.
5421. Thayer, Robert E., and Louis E. Moore
    1972   "Reported activation and verbal learning as a function of group size (social facilitation) and anxiety-inducing instructions." Journal of Social Psychology 88 (2, December): 277-287. P.A. 49:9102.
5422. Thayer, Stephen
    1973   "Lend me your ears: Racial and sexual factors in helping the deaf." Journal of Personality and Social Psychology 28 (1, October): 8-11. P.A. 51:11015.
5423. Thayer, Stephen, and Lewis Alban
    1972   "A field experiment on the effect of political and cultural factors on the use of personal space." Journal of Social Psychology 88 (2, December): 267-272. P.A. 49:9103.
5424. Thayer, Stephen, and William Schiff
    1969   "Stimulus factors in observer judgment of social interaction: Facial

expression and motion pattern." American Journal of Psychology 82 (1): 73-85. P.A. 43:15706.

5425.　1974　"Observer judgment of social interaction: Eye contact and relationship inferences." Journal of Personality and Social Psychology 30 (1, July): 110-114. P.A. 52:12354.

5426. Thelen, Herbert A.
　　　　1948　"Engineering research in curriculum building." Journal of Educational Research 41: 579-596. (See also Benne and Muntyan, 1951.)

5427.　1949　"Groups dynamics in instruction: Principle of least group size." School Review 57: 139-148.

5428.　1950　"Educational dynamics: Theory and research." Journal of Social Issues 6 (2). P.A. 25:3376.

5429.　1954　Dynamics of Groups at Work. Chicago: University of Chicago Press.

5430.　1956　"Emotionality and work in groups." In L. D. White (ed.), The State of the Social Sciences, pp. 184-200. Chicago: University of Chicago Press.

5431. Thelen, Herbert A., and Watson Dickerman
　　　　1962　"The growth of a group." In W. G. Bennis, K. D. Benne, and R. Chin (eds.), The Planning of Change, pp. 340-347. New York: Holt, Rinehart & Winston.

5432. Thelen, Herbert A., Dorothy Stock, et al.
　　　　1954　Methods for Studying Work and Emotionality in Group Operation. Chicago: University of Chicago, Human Dynamics Laboratory.

5433. Thelen, Herbert A., and John Withall
　　　　1949　"Three frames of reference: The description of climate." Human Relations 2: 159-176. P.A. 24:148.

5434. Theodorson, George A.
　　　　1953　"Elements in the progressive development of small groups." Social Forces 31: 311-320. S.A. 250.

5435.　1957　"The relationship between leadership and popularity roles in small groups." American Sociological Review 22: 58-67. P.A. 32:366; S.A. 3951.

5436.　1962　"The function of hostility in small groups." Journal of Social Psychology 56 (February): 57-66. P.A. 5GC57T.

5437. Thibaut, John W.
　　　　1950　"An experimental study of the cohesiveness of underprivileged groups." Human Relations 3: 251-278. (See also Cartwright and Zander, 1953.) P.A. 25:2369.

5438.　1968　"The development of contractual norms in bargaining: Replication and variation." Journal of Conflict Resolution 12 (1): 102-112. P.A. 43:5290.

5439. Thibaut, John W., and John Coules
　　　　1952　"The role of communication in the reduction of interpersonal hostility." Journal of Abnormal and Social Psychology 47: 770-777. P.A. 27:5076.

5440. Thibaut, John W., and Claude Faucheux
　　　　1965　"The development of contractual norms in a bargaining situation under two types of stress." Journal of Experimental Social Psychology 1 (1, January): 89-102. P.A. 39:10009.

5441. Thibaut, John W., and Charles L. Gruder
　　　　1969　"Formation of contractual agreements between parties of unequal power." Journal of Personality and Social Psychology 11 (1): 59-65. P.A. 43:8281.

5442. Thibaut, John W., and Harold H. Kelley
　　　　1959　The Social Psychology of Groups. New York: Wiley. P.A. 34: 4214.

5443. Thibaut, John W., and Henry W. Riecken
　　　　1955a　"Authoritarianism, status, and the communication of aggression." Human Relations 8: 95-120. P.A. 30:4380.

5444.　1955b　"Some determinants and consequences of the perception of social causality." Journal of Personality 24: 113-133. (See also Maccoby, Newcomb, and Hartley, 1958.) P.A. 30:7025.

5445. Thibaut, John W., and Lloyd H. Strickland
    1956   "Psychological set and social conformity." Journal of Personality
            25: 115-129.
5446. Thibaut, John W., Lloyd H. Strickland, David Mundy, and Elizabeth F. Goding
    1960   "Communication, task demands, and group effectiveness." Journal
            of Personality 28: 156-166. P.A. 35:2136.
5447. Thomas, Darwin L., David D. Franks, and James M. Calonico
    1972   "Role-taking and power in social psychology." American Sociologi-
            cal Review 37 (5, October): 605-614.
5448. Thomas, David R.
    1973   "Interaction distances in same-sex and mixed-sex groups." Perceptu-
            al and Motor Skills 36 (1, February): 15-18. P.A. 50:11280.
5449. Thomas, Dorothy S. (ed.)
    1929   Some New Techniques for Studying Social Behavior. New York:
            Columbia University, Teachers College. (See also Child Develop-
            ment Monographs No. 1.)
5450. Thomas, Dorothy S.
    1932-   "A symposium on the observability of social phenomena with re-
    1933   spect to statistical analysis. I. An attempt to develop precise meas-
            urements in the social behavior field." Sociologus 8: 436-456. II.
            Sociologus 9: 1-24.
5451. Thomas, Dorothy S., Alice M. Loomis, and Ruth E. Arrington
    1933   Observational Studies of Social Behavior, vol. 1, Social Behavior
            Patterns. New Haven, Conn.: Yale University, Institute of Human
            Relations.
5452. Thomas, Edwin J.
    1957   "Effects of facilitative role interdependence on group functioning."
            Human Relations 10: 347-366. (See also Cartwright and Zander,
            1960.) P.A. 34:2875; S.A. A1708.
5453. Thomas, Edwin J., and Clinton F. Fink
    1961   "Models of group problem solving." Journal of Abnormal and So-
            cial Psychology 63 (1, July): 53-56. P.A. 36:4GE53T; S.A. A3250.
5454.   1963   "Effects of group size." Psychological Bulletin 60 (4): 371-384.
            (See also Hare, Borgatta, and Bales, 1965.) P.A. 38:878.
5455. Thomas, Kerry
    1973   "Situational determinants of equitable behavior." Human Relations
            26 (5): 551-566. P.A. 52:845.
5456. Thomas, William I., and Dorothy S. Thomas
    1928   The Child in America: Behavior Problems and Programs. New York:
            Knopf.
5457. Thompson, Diane D.
    1972   "Attributions of ability from patterns of performance under com-
            petitive and cooperative conditions." Journal of Personality and So-
            cial Psychology 23 (3): 302-308.
5458. Thompson, Diana F., and Leo Meltzer
    1964   "Communication of emotional intent by facial expression." Journal
            of Abnormal and Social Psychology 68 (2, February): 129-135.
5459. Thompson, Robert J., and Ralph H. Kolstoe
    1974   "Physical aggression as a function of strength of frustration and in-
            strumentality of aggression." Journal of Research in Personality 7
            (4, March): 314-323. P.A. 52:7583.
5460. Thompson, W. R., and Rhoda Nishimura
    1952   "Some determinants of friendship." Journal of Personality 20: 305-
            314. P.A. 27:2630.
5461. Thompson, Vaida D., Wolfgang Stroebe, and John Schopler
    1971   "Some situational determinants of the motives attributed to the per-
            son who performs a helping act." Journal of Personality 39: 460-
            472.
5462. Thorndike, Robert L.
    1938a   "On what type of task will a group do well?" Journal of Abnormal
            and Social Psychology 33: 409-413.
5463.   1938b   "The effect of discussion upon the correctness of group decisions,

when the factor of majority influence is allowed for." Journal of Social Psychology 9: 343–362.

5464. Thorpe, J. G.
1955 "A study of some factors in friendship formation." Sociometry 18: 207–214. P.A. 30:7026.

5465. Thrasher, Frederic M.
1927 The Gang. Chicago: University of Chicago Press. (See also Hare, Borgatta, and Bales, 1965.)

5466. Thrasher, James D.
1954 "Interpersonal relations and gradations of stimulus structure as factors in judgemental variation: An experimental approach." Sociometry 17: 228–241. S.A. 1986.

5467. Throop, Warren F., John G. Holmes, and Marjorie N. Donald
1970 "Need for social approval as a predictor of the strategic and outcome aspects of bargaining behaviour in assymmetric power situations: An interactionist approach." Canadian Journal of Behavioural Science 2 (3): 191–198. P.A. 44:20833.

5468. Tiger, Lionel
1969 Men in Groups. New York: Random House.

5469. 1972 "Comment on 'Sex and Social Participation.'" American Sociological Review 37 (5, October): 634–637. Reply, p. 637. S.A. 21: 73G3965.

5470. Tilker, Harvey A.
1970 "Socially responsible behavior as a function of observer responsibility and victim feedback." Journal of Personality and Social Psychology 14 (2): 95–100. P.A. 44:6668.

5471. Timaeus, Ernst
1967 ("Instructions as variables: A methodical-experimental contribution to the so-called conformist behavior.") In F. Merz (ed.), Bericht über den 25. Kongress der Deutschen Gesellschaft für Psychologie Münster 1966, pp. 602–607. Göttingen: Hogrefe. P.A. 43:17360.

5472. 1974 (Experiment and Psychology on the Social Psychology of Psychological Experiments.) Göttingen: Hogrefe.

5473. Timaeus, Ernst, and Helmut E. Lück
1968 "Experimenter expectancy and social facilitation I. Aggression under coaction." Psychological Reports 23: 456–458.

5474. Timmons, W. M.
1939 "Decisions and attitudes as outcomes of the discussion of a social problem." Columbia University, Teachers College, Contributions to Education No. 777. P.A. 14:479.

5475. 1942 "Can the product superiority of discussors be attributed to averaging or majority influences?" Journal of Social Psychology 15: 23–32. P.A. 16:3225.

5476. Tipton, Robert M., and Sharon Browning
1972a "Altruism: Reward or punishment?" Journal of Psychology 80 (2, March): 319–322. P.A. 48:4887.

5477. 1972b "The influence of age and obesity on helping behavior." British Journal of Social and Clinical Psychology 11 (4, December): 404–406. P.A. 49:9104.

5478. Tipton, Robert M., and Larry Jenkins
1974 "Altruism as a function of response cost to the benefactor." Journal of Psychology 86 (2, March): 209–216. P.A. 52:12355.

5479. Titley, Robert W., and Wayne Viney
1969 "Expression of aggression toward the physically handicapped." Perceptual and Motor Skills 29 (1): 51–56. P.A. 44:2266.

5480. Titus, H. Edwin, and Edwin P. Hollander
1957 "The California F scale in psychological research: 1950–1955." Psychological Bulletin 54: 47–64. P.A. 32:2688.

5481. Todd, Frederick J., Kenneth R. Hammond, and Marilyn M. Wilkins
1966 "Differential effects of ambiguous and exact feedback on two-person conflict and compromise." Journal of Conflict Resolution 10 (1, March): 88–97. S.A. 15:C4809.

5482. Todd, Frederick J., and Leon Rappoport
    1964   "A cognitive structure approach to person perception: A comparison of two models." Journal of Abnormal and Social Psychology 68 (5, May): 469–478.

5483. Toder, Nancy L., and James E. Marcia
    1973   "Ego identity status and response to conformity pressure in college women." Journal of Personality and Social Psychology 26 (2, May): 287–294. P.A. 50:11281.

5484. Toeman, Zerka
    1944   "Role analysis and audience structure: With special emphasis on problems of military adjustment." Sociometry 7: 205–221. (See also Psychodrama Monographs 1945, No. 12.) P.A. 19:499.

5485. Tognoli, Jerome, and Robert Keisner
    1972   "Gain and loss of esteem as determinants of interpersonal attraction: A replication and extension." Journal of Personality and Social Psychology 23 (2, August): 201–204. P.A. 49:809.

5486. Tomasini, Jerry
    1973   "Effect of peer-induced anxiety on a problem-solving task." Psychological Reports 33 (2, October): 355–358. P.A. 51:9053.

5487. Tomeh, Aida K.
    1970   "Birth order and friendship associations." Journal of Marriage and the Family 32 (3, August): 360–369. P.A. 46:6768.

5488. Tomeković, Tomislav
    1970   "An evaluation of some theories related to human choice." Studia Psychologica 12 (2): 89–98. P.A. 45:6209.

5489. Torrance, E. Paul
    1953a   "Crew performance in a test situation as a predictor of field and combat performance." HFORL Report No. 33, ARDC. Bolling Air Force Base, Washington, D.C.

5490.   1953b   "Methods of conducting critiques of group problem-solving performance." Journal of Applied Psychology 37: 394–398. (See also Hare, Borgatta, and Bales, 1955, 1965.) P.A. 29:708.

5491. Torrance, E. Paul
    1953c   "Perception of group functioning as a predictor of group performance." Washington State College, Research Studies 21: 262–265.

5492.   1954a   "Some consequences of power differences on decision making in permanent and temporary three-man groups." Washington State College, Research Studies 22: 130–140. (See also Hare, Borgatta, and Bales, 1955, 1965.) P.A. 30:2676.

5493.   1954b   "The behavior of small groups under the stress of conditions of 'survival.'" American Sociological Review 19: 751–755. P.A. 30: 2675.

5494.   1955a   "Perception of group functioning as a predictor of group performance." Journal of Social Psychology 42: 271–282. P.A. 31:799.

5495.   1955b   "Sociometric techniques for diagnosing group ills." Sociometry 18: 597–612. P.A. 32:1498; S.A. 3445.

5496.   1957   "Group decision-making and disagreement." Social Forces 35: 314–318. P.A. 32:5328; S.A. 5024.

5497.   1959   "The influence of experienced members of small groups on the behavior of the inexperienced." Journal of Social Psychology 49 (May): 249–257. P.A. 34:4216.

5498.   1961   "A theory of leadership and interpersonal behavior under stress." In L. Petrullo and B. M. Bass (eds.), Leadership and Interpersonal Behavior, pp. 100–117. New York: Holt, Rinehart & Winston.

5499.   1971   "Freedom-control orientation and need for structure in group creativity." Sciences de l'Art 8 (1): 61–64. P.A. 51:5072.

5500. Torrance, E. Paul, and Nicholas C. Aliotti
    1965   "Accuracy, task effectiveness, and emergence of a social-emotional resolver as a function of one- and two-expert groups." Journal of Psychology 61 (2): 161–170. P.A. 40:5418.

5501. Torrance, E. Paul, and R. Mason
    1956   "The indigenous leader in changing attitudes and behavior." Inter-

national Journal of Sociometry 1: 23-28. P.A. 31:7632.

5502. Touhey, John C.
        1972a   "Comparison of two dimensions of attitude similarity on hetero-
                 sexual attraction." Journal of Personality and Social Psychology
                 23 (1): 8-10.

5503.   1972b   "Role perception and the relative influence of the perceiver and the
                 perceived." Journal of Social Psychology 87 (2, August): 213-217.
                 P.A. 49:810.

5504.   1972c   "Attribution of person concepts by role accessibility and interaction
                 outcomes." Journal of Social Psychology 87 (2, August): 269-272.
                 P.A. 49:811.

5505.   1973a   "Attitude similarity and attraction: The predictability of a stranger's
                 attitudes." Journal of Social Psychology 90 (2, August): 251-257.
                 P.A. 51:1009.

5506.   1973b   "Individual differences in attitude change following two acts of
                 forced compliance." Journal of Personality and Social Psychology
                 27 (1, July): 96-99. P.A. 50:11282.

5507. Touzard, Hubert
        1967   ("Experimental study of some psycho-sociological aspects of media-
                 tion in two negotiation tasks.") Psychologie Française 12 (4): 317-
                 326. P.A. 42:18749.

5508. Tracey, James J., and Herbert J. Cross
        1973   "Antecedents of shift in moral judgement." Journal of Personality
                 and Social Psychology 26 (2): 238-244.

5509. Trapp, E. Philip
        1955   "Leadership and popularity as a function of behavioral predictions."
                 Journal of Abnormal and Social Psychology 51: 452-457. P.A. 31:
                 2726.

5510. Travers, Robert M. W.
        1941   "A study in judging the opinions of groups." Archives of Psychology
                 47, No. 266. P.A. 16:2787.

5511.   1943a   "A study of the ability to judge group-knowledge." American Jour-
                 nal of Psychology 56: 54-65. P.A. 17:2091.

5512.   1943b   "The general ability to judge group-knowledge." American Journal
                 of Psychology 56: 95-99. P.A. 17:2092.

5513. Travis, Lee E.
        1925   "The effect of a small audience upon eye-hand coordination." Jour-
                 nal of Abnormal and Social Psychology 20: 142-146.

5514.   1928   "The influence of the group upon the stutterer's speed in free asso-
                 ciation." Journal of Abnormal and Social Psychology 23: 45-51.
                 P.A. 2:3572.

5515. Traylor, Gary
        1973   "Joking in a bush camp." Human Relations 26 (4, August): 479-
                 486. P.A. 51:7042.

5516. Treadwell, Yvonne
        1967   "Bibliography of empirical studies of wit and humor." Psychological
                 Reports 20: 1079-1083.

5517. Trentini, G.
        1962   ("Assumed similarity of leaders.") Archivio di Psicologia, Neurologia
                 e Psichiatria 23 (6): 537-565. P.A. 37:6627.

5518. Treppa, Jerry A., and Lawrence Fricke
        1972   "Effects of a marathon group experience." Journal of Counseling
                 Psychology 19 (5, September): 466-467. P.A. 49:2386.

5519. Triandis, Harry C.
        1960a   "Cognitive similarity and communication in a dyad." Human Rela-
                 tions 13 (2, May): 175-183. P.A. 35:6368; S.A. A3807.

5520.   1960b   "Some determinants of interpersonal communication." Hu-
                 man Relations 13 (3, August): 279-287. P.A. 35:2166; S.A.
                 A3808.

5521. Triandis, Harry C., Eleanor R. Hall, and Robert B. Ewen
        1965   "Member heterogeneity and dyadic creativity." Human Rela-
                 tions 18 (1, February): 33-55. P.A. 39:10010; S.A. 13:36764.

5522. Triandis, Harry C., and Roy S. Malpass
       1971   "Studies of black and white interaction in job settings." Journal of
               Applied Social Psychology 1 (2, April): 101-117. P.A. 47:4727.
5523. Triandis, Harry C., Vasso Vassiliou, and Erich K. Thomanek
       1966   "Social status as a determinant of respect and friendship accept-
               ance." Sociometry 29 (4, December): 396-405.
5524. Triandis, Harry C., David E. Weldon, and Jack M. Feldman
       1974   "Level of abstraction of disagreements as a determinant of inter-
               personal perception." Journal of Cross-Cultural Psychology 5 (1,
               March): 59-79. P.A. 52:7584.
5525. Trickett, Edison J.
       1971   "The interaction of achievement motivation, task difficulty, and
               confidence-enhancing information in producing conformity behav-
               ior." Journal of Social Psychology 84: 233-242.
5526. Trickett, Edison J., and Rudolph H. Moos
       1973   "Social environment of junior high and high school classrooms."
               Journal of Educational Psychology 65 (1): 93-102.
5527. Triplett, Norman
       1898   "The dynamogenic factors in pacemaking and competition." Amer-
               ican Journal of Psychology 9: 507-533.
5528. Trist, E. L., and K. W. Bamforth
       1951   "Some social and psychological consequences of the longwall
               method of coal-getting." Human Relations 4: 3-38. P.A. 25:8304.
5529. Trist, E. L., and H. Murray
       1960   ("Progressive adaptation of team work organization.") Bulletin du
               C.E.R.P. 9: 153-164. P.A. 35:3371.
5530. Trist, E. L., and C. Sofer
       1959   Exploration in Group Relations. Leicester: Leicester University
               Press.
5531. Trope, Yaacov
       1974   "Inferential processes in the forced compliance situation: A Baye-
               sian analysis." Journal of Experimental Social Psychology 10 (1):
               1-16.
5532. Trost, Jan
       1962   "Measurement of emotions in different groups." Acta Sociologica 6
               (3): 215-227. S.A. 13:B5880.
5533. 1965   "Coalitions in triads." Acta Sociologica 8 (3): 226-243. S.A. 14:
               C2800.
5534. Trotzer, James P.
       1971   "Process comparison of encounter groups and discussion groups
               using videotape excerpts." Journal of Counseling Psychology 18 (4,
               July): 358-361. P.A. 46:10773.
5535. Trow, Donald B.
       1957   "Autonomy and job satisfaction in task-oriented groups." Journal
               of Abnormal and social Psychology 54: 204-209.
5536. 1960   "Membership succession and team performance." Human Relations
               13 (3, August): 259-269. P.A. 35:2137; S.A. A3809.
5537. Trow, W. Clark, Alvin F. Zander, William C. Morse, and David M. Jenkins
       1950   "Psychology of group behavior: The class as a group." Journal of
               Educational Psychology 41: 322-338. P.A. 25:3377.
5538. Truax, Charles B., Hal Altmann, and Joe Whittmer
       1973   "Self-disclosure as a function of personal adjustment and the facili-
               tative conditions offered by the target person." Journal of Com-
               munity Psychology 1 (3, July): 319-322. P.A. 51:5073.
5539. Tubbs, Stewart L., and Sylvia Moss
       1974   Human Communication: An Interpersonal Perspective. New York:
               Random House. P.A. 52:846.
5540. Tucker, Don M.
       1973   "Some relationships between individual and group development."
               Human Development 16 (4): 249-272. P.A. 51:11016.
5541. Tucker, James, and S. Thomas Friedman
       1972   "Population density and group size." American Journal of Sociology

77 (4): 742-749.

5542. Tuckman, Bruce W.
    1964   "Personality structure, group composition, and group functioning."
            Sociometry 27 (4, December): 469-487. P.A. 39:7648.

5543.   1965   "Developmental sequence in small groups." Psychological Bulletin
                 63 (6): 384-399. P.A. 39:12187.

5544.   1966   "Interpersonal probing and revealing and systems of integrative com-
                 plexity." Journal of Personality and Social Psychology 3 (6): 655-
                 664.

5545.   1967   "Group composition and group performance of structured and un-
                 structured tasks." Journal of Experimental Social Psychology 3
                 (January): 25-40.

5546. Tuckman, Jacob, and Irving Lorge
    1962   "Individual ability as a determinant of group superiority." Human
            Relations 15 (1, February): 45-51.

5547. Tuddenham, Read D.
    1958a   "The influence of a distorted group norm upon individual judg-
            ment." Journal of Psychology 46: 227-241. P.A. 34:2877.

5548.   1958b   "The influence of an avowedly distorted norm upon individual judg-
                 ment." Journal of Psychology 46 (October): 329-338. P.A. 34:
                 2878.

5549.   1959   "Correlates of yielding to a distorted group norm." Journal of Per-
                 sonality 27: 272-284.

5550.   1961a   "The influence of a distorted group norm upon judgments of adults
                 and children." Journal of Psychology 52: 231-239. P.A. 36:
                 2GE31T.

5551.   1961b   "The influence upon judgment of apparent discrepancy between self
                 and others." Journal of Social Psychology 53 (February): 69-79.
                 P.A. 35:6351.

5552. Tuddenham, Read D., and Philip D. McBride
    1959   "The yielding experiment from the subject's point of view." Journal
            of Personality 27: 259-271.

5553. Tuddenham, Read D., Philip D. McBride, and V. Zahn
    1958   "The influence of sex composition of the group upon yielding to a
            distorted norm." Journal of Psychology 48: 243-251. P.A. 34:
            2879.

5554. Tulane Studies in Social Welfare
    1957   The Use of Group Methods in Social Welfare Settings. New Orleans:
            Tulane University School of Social Work.

5555. Tupes, Ernest C., A. Carp, and Walter R. Borg
    1958   "Performance in role-playing situations as related to leadership and
            personality measures." Sociometry 21: 165-179. P.A. 33:1111.

5556. Turk, Herman
    1961a   "Instrumental and expressive ratings reconsidered." Sociometry 24
            (1, March): 76-81. P.A. 36:1GE76T.

5557.   1961b   "Instrumental values and the popularity of instrumental leaders."
                 Social Forces 39 (3, March): 252-260. P.A. 36:1GF52T.

5558.   1963a   "Norms, persons, and sentiments." Sociometry 26 (2, June): 163-
                 177. P.A. 38:4202; S.A. 11:A7200.

5559.   1963b   "Social cohesion through variant values: Evidence from medical role
                 relations." American Sociological Review 28 (1): 28-37. P.A. 37:
                 7952.

5560. Turk, Herman, Eugene L. Hartley, and David M. Shaw
    1962   "The expectation of social influence." Journal of Social Psychology
            58 (1, October): 23-29. P.A. 37:6620.

5561. Turk, Herman, and G. Robert Wills
    1964   "Authority and interaction." Sociometry 27 (1, March): 1-18. S.A.
            12:B2425.

5562. Turk, Theresa, and Herman Turk
    1962   "Group interaction in a formal setting: The case of the triad."
            Sociometry 25 (1, March): 48-55. P.A. 37:1118; S.A. 11:
            A4600.

5563. Turner, C. E.
      1933   "Test room studies in employee effectiveness." American Journal of
              Public Health 23: 577–584. (See also Hare, Borgatta, and Bales,
              1955, 1965.)
5564. Turner, Charles W., and Lynn S. Simons
      1974   "Effects of subject sophistication and evaluation apprehension on
              aggressive responses to weapons." Journal of Personality and Social
              Psychology 30 (3): 341–348.
5565. Turner, Ralph H.
      1956   "Role-taking, role standpoint, and reference-group behavior." Amer-
              ican Journal of Sociology 61: 316–328.
5566. Turney, John R.
      1970   "The cognitive complexity of group members, group structure, and
              group effectiveness." Cornell Journal of Social Relations 5 (2, Fall):
              152–165. P.A. 46:8949; S.A. 21:73G0553.
5567. Tyler, Ann I., Wayne L. Waag, and Clay E. George
      1972   "Determinants of the ecology of the dyad: The effects of age and
              sex." Journal of Psychology 81 (1, May): 117–120. P.A. 48:9046.
5568. Tyler, Fred T.
      1951   "A factor analysis of fifteen MMPI scales." Journal of Consulting
              Psychology 15: 451–456. P.A. 26:7015.

5569. Uejio, Clifford K., and Lawrence S. Wrightsman
      1967   "Ethnic-group differences in the relationship of trusting attitudes
              to cooperative behavior." Psychological Reports 20: 563–571.
5570. Uesugi, Thomas K., and W. Edgar Vinacke
      1963   "Strategy in a feminine game." Sociometry 26 (1, March): 75–88.
              P.A. 38:2592; S.A. 11:A6360.
5571. Ulehla, Z. Joseph, and Darrell K. Adams
      1973   "Detection theory and expectations for social reinforcers: An appli-
              cation to aggression." Psychological Review 80 (6, November): 439–
              445. P.A. 51:10994.
5572. Umeoka, Yoshitaka
      1970   "A 2 × 2 non-constant-sum game with a coordination problem."
              Journal of Conflict Resolution 14 (1): 99–100.
5573. Underwood, Bill, Bert S. Moore, and David L. Rosenhan
      1972   "Effect of mood on children's giving." Proceedings of the 80th An-
              nual Convention of the American Psychological Association 7 (pt.
              1): 243–244.
5574. Uno, Yoshiyasu, Judith H. Koivumaki, and Robert Rosenthal
      1972   "Unintended experimenter behavior as evaluated by Japanese and
              American observers." Journal of Social Psychology 88 (1, October):
              91–106. P.A. 49:6873.
5575. Updegraff, Ruth, and Edithe K. Herbst
      1933   "An experimental study of the social behavior stimulated in young
              children by certain play materials." Journal of Genetic Psychology
              42: 372–390.
5576. Upmeyer, Arnold, and Wilfried K. Schreiber
      1972   "Effects of agreement and disagreement in groups on recognition
              memory performance and confidence." European Journal of Social
              Psychology 2 (2): 109–128. P.A. 49:9105.
5577. Utterback, William E.
      1958   "The influence of style of moderation on the outcomes of discus-
              sion." Quarterly Journal of Speech 44: 149–152. P.A. 35:747.

5578. Valenzi, Enzo, and Larry Eldridge
      1973   "Leader behavior, situational variables and satisfaction and effec-
              tiveness." Proceedings of the 81st Annual Convention of the Amer-
              ican Psychological Association 8 (2): 573–574.
5579. Valins, Stuart, and Andrew Baum
      1973   "Residential group size, social interaction, and crowding." Environ-
              ment and Behavior 5 (4, December): 421–439. P.A. 52:7517.

5580. Van Bergen, Annie, and J. Koekebakker
    1959   "'Group cohesiveness' in laboratory experiments." Acta Psychologica 16: 81-98. P.A. 34:5753.
5581. Vandendriessche, Filip, and Leo Lagrou
    1972   "The formulation of opinions in homogeneous and heterogeneous discussion groups." International Review of Applied Psychology 21 (2, October): 123-132. P.A. 49:11134.
5582. van den Hove, D.
    1972   ("Conflict, mediation and observation: Theoretical analysis.") Revue de Psychologie et des Sciences de l'Education 7 (3): 279-308. P.A. 50:8886.
5583. van de Sande, J. P.
    1973   ("An investigation of the behavioral differences between men and women with regard to game theory.") Nederlands Tijdschrift voor de Psychologie en haar Grensgebieden 28 (5, October): 327-341. P.A. 51:7017.
5584. Van Dingenen-Donnay, A.
    1966   ("Mathematical analysis of decision schemes in small groups.") Revue de l'Institut de Sociologie 3: 563-602. S.A. 16:D0613.
5585. Van Dusen, A. C.
    1948   "Measuring leadership ability." Personnel Psychology 1: 67-79. P.A. 22:3919.
5586. Van Kreveld, David, and Jean Pierre Poitou
    1972   "Is there a position bias in the learning of influence structures?" European Journal of Social Psychology 2 (1): 75-85. S.A. 22: 74G6160.
5587. Van Leeuwen, J. A., and J. F. Van Ravenzwaaij
    1968   ("The laboratory method of training in human relationships with respect to changes in organizations.") Mens en Onderneming 22 (1): 1-11. P.A. 42:8874.
5588. Vanparijs, Maurice
    1968   ("Communication networks and communication structures.") Psychologica Belgica 8 (1): 87-97. P.A. 44:8374.
5589. Van Zelst, Raymond H.
    1952   "An interpersonal relations technique for industry." Personnel 29: 68-76. P.A. 27:3069.
5590. Vaughan, Graham M., and G. L. Mangan
    1963   "Conformity to group pressure in relation to the value of the task material." Journal of Abnormal and Social Psychology 66 (2, February): 179-183. P.A. 37:6621; S.A. 12:B0188.
5591. Vaughan, Graham M., and A. J. Taylor
    1966   "Clinical anxiety and conformity." Perceptual and Motor Skills 22 (3): 719-722. P.A. 40:11111.
5592. Vaughan, Graham M., and Kenneth D. White
    1966   "Conformity and authoritarianism reexamined." Journal of Personality and Social Psychology 3 (3): 363-366.
5593. Veitch, Russell, and William Griffitt
    1973   "Attitude commitment: Its impact on the similarity-attraction relationship." Bulletin of the Psychonomic Society 1 (5-A, May): 295-297. P.A. 51:936.
5594. Verba, Sidney
    1961   Small Groups and Political Behavior: A Study of Leadership. Princeton, N.J.: Princeton University Press. P.A. 38:879.
5595. Verhofstad, O.
    1962a   ("A study of some aspects of self-concept among members of a small group.") Gawein 11 (2): 145-164. P.A. 37:7953.
5596.   1962b   ("A comparison of three sociometric methods.") Tijdschrift voor Sociale Wetenschappen 7 (1, January): 17-36. S.A. 13:B6766.
5597.   1962c   ("Psychogroup and socio-group.") Tijdschrift voor Sociale Wetenschappen 7 (2): 111-123. S.A. 13:B6765.
5598. Vernon, David T. A.
    1974   "Modeling and birth order in responses to painful stimuli." Journal

of Personality and Social Psychology 29 (6): 794-799.

5599. Vernon, Glen M., and Robert L. Stewart
1957   "Empathy as a process in the dating situation." American Sociological Review 22: 48-52.

5600. Verplanck, William S.
1955   "The control of the content of conversation: Reinforcement of statements of opinion." Journal of Abnormal and Social Psychology 51: 668-676. P.A. 31:2940.

5601.   1956   "The operant conditioning of human motor behavior." Psychological Bulletin 53: 70-83.

5602. Vertreace, Walter C., and Carolyn H. Simmons
1971   "Attempted leadership in the leaderless group discussion as a function of motivation and ego involvement." Journal of Personality and Social Psychology 19 (3, September): 285-289. P.A. 47:2857.

5603. Vesprani, George J.
1969   "Personality correlates of accurate empathy in a college companion program." Journal of Consulting and Clinical Psychology 33 (6): 722-727.

5604. Videbeck, Richard
1960   "Self-conception and the reaction of others." Sociometry 23 (4, December): 351-359. S.A. A2790.

5605. Videbeck, Richard, and Alan P. Bates
1959   "An experimental study of conformity to role expectations." Sociometry 22 (1, March): 1-11. P.A. 34:1188.

5606. Vidmar, Neil
1970   "Group composition and the risky shift." Journal of Experimental Social Psychology 6 (2): 153-166.

5607.   1971   "Effects of representational roles and mediators on negotiation effectiveness." Journal of Personality and Social Psychology 17 (1): 48-58.

5608.   1974   "Effects of group discussion on category width judgments." Journal of Personality and Social Psychology 29 (2): 187-195.

5609. Vidmar, Neil, and Terry C. Burdeny
1971   "Effects of group size and item type in the 'group shift' effect." Canadian Journal of Behavioural Science 3 (4, October): 393-407. P.A. 47:8810.

5610. Vidmar, Neil, and Linda D. Crinklaw
1974   "Attributing responsibility for an accident: A methodological and conceptual critique." Canadian Journal of Behavioural Science 6 (2, April): 112-130. P.A. 52:12287.

5611. Vidmar, Neil, and J. Richard Hackman
1971   "Interlaboratory generalizability of small group research: An experimental study." Journal of Social Psychology 83 (1, February): 129-139. P.A. 45:8121.

5612. Vidmar, Neil, and Joseph E. McGrath
1970   "Forces affecting success in negotiation groups." Behavioral Science 15 (2, March): 154-163. P.A. 44:10298; S.A. 19:E9556.

5613. Vidulich, Robert N., and Gerald A. Bayley
1966   "A general field experimental technique for studying social influence." Journal of Social Psychology 69 (2, August): 253-263. P.A. 40:12280.

5614. Vidulich, Robert N., and Ivan P. Kaiman
1961   "The effects of information source status and dogmatism upon conformity behavior." Journal of Abnormal and Social Psychology 63 (3): 639-642. P.A. 37:1119.

5615. Vidulich, Robert N., and Fred P. Stabene
1965   "Source certainty as a variable in conformity behavior." Journal of Social Psychology 66 (August): 323-330.

5616. Vinacke, W. Edgar
1957   "Some variables in buzz sessions." Journal of Social Psychology 45: 25-33.

5617.   1959   "Sex roles in a three-person game." Sociometry 22 (4, December):

343-359.

5618.   1964   "Intra-group power relations, strategy, and decisions in inter-triad competition." Sociometry 27 (1, March): 25-39. P.A. 38:8310; S.A. 12:B0860.

5619. Vinacke, W. Edgar, and Abe Arkoff
         1957   "An experimental study of coalitions in the triad." American Sociological Review 22: 406-414.

5620. Vinacke, W. Edgar, Paul D. Cherulnik, and Cary M. Lichtman
         1970   "Strategy in intratriad and intertriad interaction." Journal of Social Psychology 81 (2): 183-198. P.A. 44:20834.

5621. Vinacke, W. Edgar, Doris C. Crowell, Dora Dien, and Vera Young
         1966   "The effect of information about strategy on a three-person game." Behavioral Science 11 (3, May): 180-189. S.A. 15:C4088.

5622. Vinacke, W. Edgar, Robert Mogy, William Powers, Charles Langan, and Robert Beck
         1974   "Accommodative strategy and communication in a three-person matrix game." Journal of Personality and Social Psychology 29 (4, April): 509-525. P.A. 52:7538.

5623. Vincent, Jack E., and Edward W. Schwerin
         1971   "Ratios of force and escalation in a game situation." Journal of Conflict Resolution 15 (4): 489-511.

5624. Vincent, Jack E., and James O. Tindell
         1969   "Alternative cooperative strategies in a bargaining game." Journal of Conflict Resolution 13 (4, December): 494-510.

5625. Vine, Armand D., and James H. Davis
         1968   "Group problem solving, task divisibility, and prior social organization." Proceedings of the 76th Annual Convention of the American Psychological Association 3: 411-412.

5626. Vine, Ian
         1971   "Judgement of direction of gaze: An interpretation of discrepant results." British Journal of Social and Clinical Psychology 10 (4, December): 320-331. P.A. 48:881.

5627. Vingoe, F. J.
         1973   "Comment on H. B. Gibson's report on the validity of the Eysenck Personality Inventory Extraversion, degree of acquaintanceship, and mean peer-ratings." British Journal of Social and Clinical Psychology 12 (3, September): 268-274. P.A. 51:5122.

5628. Vinokur, Amiram
         1969   "Distribution of initial risk levels and group decisions involving risk." Journal of Personality and Social Psychology 13 (3): 207-214.

5629.   1971a   "Cognitive and affective processes influencing risk taking in groups: An expected utility approach." Journal of Personality and Social Psychology 20 (3, December): 472-486. P.A. 47:8811.

5630.   1971b   "Review and theoretical analysis of the effects of group processes upon individual and group decisions involving risk." Psychological Bulletin 76 (4, October): 231-250.

5631. Vinokur, Amiram, and Eugene Burnstein
         1974   "Effects of partially shared persuasive arguments on group-induced shifts: A group-problem solving approach." Journal of Personality and Social Psychology 29 (3): 305-315.

5632. Vitz, Paul C., and W. Richard Kite
         1970   "Factors affecting conflict and negotiation within an alliance." Journal of Experimental Social Psychology 6 (2): 233-247.

5633. Vockell, Edward L., and J. William Asher
         1972   "Dating frequency among high school seniors." Psychological Reports 31 (2, October): 381-382. P.A. 49:6874.

5634. Vogler, Roger E.
         1968   "Possibility of artifact in studies of cooperation." Psychological Reports 23 (1): 9-10. P.A. 43:6836.

5635.   1969   "On the definition of cooperation." Psychological Reports 25 (1): 281-282. P.A. 44:3550.

5636. Voicu, Maria
1971   ("A study of verbal activism in children in the 1st–4th forms.")
Revista de Psihologie 17 (1): 53–65. P.A. 51:11017.
5637. Voissem, Norman H., and Frank Sistrunk
1971   "Communication schedule and cooperative game behavior." Journal
of Personality and Social Psychology 19 (2): 160–167.
5638. Von Broembsen, Maximilian H., Bruce H. Mayhew, Jr., and Louis N. Gray
1969   "The stability of power structures in short-term simulations." Pacific
Sociological Review 12 (2, Fall): 118–129. S.A. 18:E2910.
5639. von Cranach, Mario L.
1960   ("Experiments toward formation of judgment in structured
groups.") Zeitschrift für Experimentelle und Angewandte Psychologie 7: 427–450. P.A. 35:4828.
5640. Vondracek, Fred W., and Marilyn J. Marshall
1971   "Self-disclosure and interpersonal trust: An exploratory study."
Psychological Reports 28 (1, February): 235–240. P.A. 46:4855.
5641. von Sivers, Erik
1963   ("Structural shapes assumed by the smallest group in modern society.") Sociology International 1 (2): 129–148. S.A. 13:B4935.
5642. von Wiese, Leopold, and H. Becker
1932   Systematic Sociology: On the Basis of the Beziehungslehre and
Gebildelehre. New York: Wiley.
5643. Vos, Koos, and Wim Brinkman
1967   ("Success and cohesion in sports groups.") Sociologische Gids 14
(1, January-February): 30–40. S.A. 18:E1785.
5644. Vos, Koos, Carl Doerbecker, and Wim Brinkman
1969   ("Success and cohesion in small groups, a replication.") Mens en
Maatschappij 44 (6, November-December): 493–509. S.A. 21:
73G1499.
5645. Vraa, Calvin W.
1971   "Influence of need for inclusion on group participation." Psychological Reports 28 (1, February): 271–274. P.A. 46:4856.
5646. Vraa, Calvin W., and Mary C. Gerszewski
1972   "Personality characteristics and level of genuineness in group interaction." Psychological Reports 31 (2, October): 383–386. P.A. 49:
6875.
5647. Vreeland, F. M.
1942   "Social relations in the college fraternity." Sociometry 5: 151–
162. P.A. 16:4481.
5648. Vroom, Victor H.
1959   "Some personality determinants of the effects of participation."
Journal of Abnormal and Social Psychology 59 (November): 322–
327. P.A. 34:5640.
5649. Vroom, Victor H., and Edward L. Deci
1971   "Leadership, social value, and the risky shift." Representative Research in Social Psychology 2 (1, January): 33–41. P.A. 46:8950.
5650. Vroom, Victor H., Lester D. Grant, and Timothy S. Cotton
1969   "The consequences of social interaction in group problem solving."
Organizational Behavior and Human Performance 4 (1): 77–95. P.A.
43:8283.

5651. Waag, Wayne L., and Charles G. Halcomb
1972   "Team size and decision rule in the performance of simulated moni-
toring teams." Human Factors 14 (4, August): 309–314. P.A. 49:
2389.
5652. Wagner, Carl
1966   "Expectation and attractiveness of group membership as functions
of task difficulty and magnitude of reward." Psychological Reports
18 (2): 471–482. P.A. 40:8798.
5653. Wagner, Carl, and Ladd Wheeler
1969   "Model, need, and cost effects in helping behavior." Journal of Personality and Social Psychology 12 (2): 111–116.

5654. Wagner, Mervyn K.
 1966 "Reinforcement of verbal productivity in group therapy." Psychological Reports 19: 1217-1218.
5655. Wagner, Peggy J., and Marvin E. Shaw
 1973 "Effects of the subject's awareness of the nature of the experiment upon conformity behavior." Bulletin of the Psychonomic Society 1 (4, April): 235-237. P.A. 50:11283.
5656. Wagoner, Robert, and Hanus J. Grosz
 1971 "MMPI and EPPS profiles of high and low verbal interactors in therapy groups." Psychological Reports 28: 951-955.
5657. Wahba, Mahmoud A.
 1971a "Effects of game structure, range of pay-off and strategy of the other on cooperation in mixed-motive games." Psychological Reports 28 (3, June): 683-689. P.A. 46:10775.
5658. 1971b "Equity theory as a predictor of payoff apportionment among partners in coalition formations." Psychonomic Science 24 (4, August): 177-179. P.A. 48:11472.
5659. 1972a "Coalition formation under conditions of uncertainty." Journal of Social Psychology 88 (1, October): 43-54. P.A. 49:4452.
5660. 1972b "Expectancy model of coalition formations." Psychological Reports 30 (2, April): 671-677. P.A. 50:2992.
5661. 1972c "Preferences among alternative forms of equity: The apportionment of coalition reward in the males and the females." Journal of Social Psychology 87 (1, June): 107-115. P.A. 48:9047.
5662. Wahba, Mahmoud A., and Sidney I. Lirtzman
 1972 "A theory of organizational coalition formations." Human Relations 25 (6, December): 515-527. P.A. 50:2991.
5663. Wahrman, Ralph
 1970 "High status, deviance and sanctions." Sociometry 33 (4): 485-504.
5664. 1972 "Status, deviance, and sanctions: A critical review." Comparative Group Studies 3 (2, May): 203-223. P.A. 49:9107.
5665. Wahrman, Ralph, and Meredith D. Pugh
 1972 "Competence and conformity: Another look at Hollander's study." Sociometry 35 (3, September): 376-386. P.A. 49:6877; S.A. 21: 73G4907.
5666. 1974 "Sex, nonconformity and influence." Sociometry 37 (1): 137-147.
5667. Wainerman, Catalina H.
 1969 ("Styles of 'taking the floor': A study of verbal habits.") Revista Interamericana de Psicologia 3 (4): 259-272. P.A. 44:16569.
5668. Waisman, Morton M.
 1964 "Sociometric perception and self-other attitudes." International Journal of Sociometry and Sociatry 4 (1-2, March-June): 43-50. S.A. 13:B6767.
5669. Wakil, S. Parvez
 1973a "Campus dating: An exploratory study of cross-cultural relevance." Journal of Comparative Family Studies 4 (2, Fall): 286-294. P.A. 52:7518.
5670. 1973b "Campus mate selection preferences: A cross-national comparison." Social Forces 51 (4, June): 471-476. P.A. 51:1010.
5671. Walberg, Herbert J.
 1969 "Class size and the social environment of learning." Human Relations 22 (5, October): 465-475.
5672. Waldman, David M., and Robert A. Baron
 1971 "Aggression as a function of exposure and similarity to a nonaggressive model." Psychonomic Science 23 (6, June): 381-383. P.A. 48:9048.
5673. Walker, Martha, and William Holbert
 1970 "Perceived acceptance and helpfulness in a marathon group." Psychological Reports 27 (1, August): 83-90. P.A. 45:6211.
5674. Walker, Michael B.
 1973 "Caplow's theory of coalitions in the triad reconsidered." Journal of

Personality and Social Psychology 27 (3, September): 409–412. P.A. 51:5074.

5675. Walker, Ronald E.
1971   "The behavior of experimental subjects." In W. A. Hunt (ed.), Human Behavior and Its Control. Cambridge, Mass.: Schenkman, P.A. 50:6761.

5676. Walker, Thomas G.
1973   "Behavior of temporary members in small groups." Journal of Applied Psychology 58 (1, August): 144–146. P.A. 51:9022.

5677. Walker, Thomas G., and Eleanor C. Main
1973   "Choice shifts in political decisionmaking: Federal judges and civil liberties cases." Journal of Applied Social Psychology 3 (1, January): 39–48. P.A. 51:3083.

5678. Wallace, Donnel, and Paul Rothaus
1969   "Communication, group loyalty, and trust in the PD game." Journal of Conflict Resolution 13 (3, September): 370–380.

5679. Wallace, John
1966   "Role reward and dissonance reduction." Journal of Personality and Social Psychology 3: 305–312.

5680. Wallach, Michael A., and Nathan Kogan
1965   "The roles of information, discussion, and consensus in group risk taking." Journal of Experimental Social Psychology 1 (1, January): 1–19.

5681. Wallach, Michael A., Nathan Kogan, and Daryl J. Bem
1962   "Group influence on individual risk taking." Journal of Abnormal and Social Psychology 65 (2, August): 75–86. (See also Cartwright and Zander, 1968.) S.A. 11:A7201.

5682.   1964   "Diffusion of responsibility and level of risk taking in groups." Journal of Abnormal and Social Psychology 68 (3, March): 263–274. S.A. 13:B6768.

5683. Wallach, Michael A., Nathan Kogan, and Roger B. Burt
1965   "Can group members recognize the effects of group discussion upon risk taking?" Journal of Experimental Social Psychology 1 (4, October): 379–395. P.A. 40:4191.

5684.   1967   "Group risk taking and field dependence-independence of group members." Sociometry 30 (4, December): 323–338. P.A. 42:3911; S.A. 16:D3104.

5685.   1968   "Are risk takers more persuasive than conservatives in group discussion?" Journal of Experimental Social Psychology 4 (January): 76–88.

5686. Wallach, Michael A., and Jerome Mabli
1970   "Information versus conformity in the effects of group discussion on risk taking." Journal of Personality and Social Psychology 14 (2): 149–156. P.A. 44:6682.

5687. Wallach, Michael A., and Cliff W. Wing, Jr.
1968   "Is risk a value?" Journal of Personality and Social Psychology 9 (1): 101–106. P.A. 42:10522.

5688. Wallen, Richard
1943   "Individuals' estimates of group opinion." Journal of Social Psychology 17: 269–274. P.A. 17:3896.

5689. Wallington, Sue A.
1973   "Consequences of transgression: Self-punishment and depression." Journal of Personality and Social Psychology 28 (1, October): 1–7. P.A. 51:11018.

5690. Walster, Elaine
1970   "The effect of self-esteem on liking for dates of various social desirabilities." Journal of Experimental Social Psychology 6 (2): 248–253.

5691. Walster, Elaine, and Ellen Berscheid
1971   "Adrenaline makes the heart grow fonder." Psychology Today 5 (1, June): 47–50. P.A. 47:2859.

5692. Walster, Elaine, Ellen Berscheid, and G. William Walster
      1973   "New directions in equity research." Journal of Personality and So-
              cial Psychology 25 (2, February): 151-176. P.A. 50:995.
5693. Walster, Elaine, and Jane A. Piliavin
      1972   "Equity and the innocent bystander." Journal of Social Issues 28
              (3): 165-189. P.A. 50:4845.
5694. Walster, Elaine, Bill Walster, Darcy Abrahams, and Zita Brown
      1966   "The effect on liking of underrating or overrating another." Journal
              of Experimental Social Psychology 2 (1, January): 70-84.
5695. Walster, Elaine, G. William Walster, Jane A. Piliavin, and Lynn Schmidt
      1973   "'Playing hard to get': Understanding an elusive phenomenon."
              Journal of Personality and Social Psychology 26 (1, April): 113-
              121. P.A. 50:4846.
5696. Walter, Gordon A., and Raymond E. Miles
      1972   "Essential elements for improving task-group membership behav-
              iors." Proceedings of the 80th Annual Convention of the American
              Psychological Association 7 (pt. 1): 461-462. P.A. 48:7124.
5697. Walters, Richard H., William E. Marshall, and J. Richard Shooter
      1960   "Anxiety, isolation, and susceptibility to social influence." Journal
              of Personality 28: 518-529. P.A. 35:4829.
5698. Walters, Richard H., and Ross D. Parke
      1964   "Social motivation, dependency, and susceptibility to social influ-
              ence." In L. Berkowitz (ed.), Advances in Experimental Social
              Psychology, vol. 1, pp. 231-276. New York: Academic Press.
5699. Walters, Richard H., and Michael J. Quinn
      1960   "The effects of social and sensory deprivation on autokinetic judg-
              ments." Journal of Personality 28: 210-219.
5700. Walton, Richard E.
      1970   "A problem-solving workshop on border conflicts in eastern Africa."
              Journal of Applied Behavioral Science 6 (4, October): 453-496. P.A.
              46:4857.
5701. Walton, Richard E., and Robert B. McKersie
      1966   "Behavioral dilemmas in mixed-motive decision making." Behavioral
              Science 11 (5, September): 370-384. S.A. 15:C4802.
5702. Walum, Laurel R.
      1968   "Group perception of threat of non-members." Sociometry 31:
              278-284.
5703. Wankel, Leonard M.
      1972   "Competition in motor performance: An experimental analysis of
              motivational components." Journal of Experimental Social Psychol-
              ogy 8 (5): 427-437.
5704. Wapner, Seymour, and Thelma G. Alper
      1952   "The effect of an audience on behavior in a choice situation." Jour-
              nal of Abnormal and Social Psychology 47: 222-229. P.A. 27:
              2633.
5705. Ward, Charles D.
      1968   "Seating arrangement and leadership emergence in small discussion
              groups." Journal of Social Psychology 74 (1, February): 83-90.
              P.A. 42:8883.
5706.   1970   Laboratory Manual in Experimental Social Psychology. New York:
                      Holt, Rinehart & Winston.
5707. Warr, Peter
      1974   "Inference magnitude, range, and elevative direction as factors
              affecting relative importance of cues.in impression formation." Jour-
              nal of Personality and Social Psychology 30 (2, August): 191-197.
              P.A. 52:12357.
5708. Warriner, Charles K.
      1955   "Leadership in the small group." American Journal of Sociology 60:
              361-369. P.A. 30:809; S.A. 1519.
5709. Warwick, Charles E.
      1964   "Relationship of scholastic aspriation and group cohesiveness to the

academic achievement of male freshmen at Cornell University." Human Relations 17 (2, May): 155-168.

5710. Washburn, Ruth W.
1932   "A scheme for grading the reactions of children in a new social situation." Journal of Genetic Psychology 40: 84-99.

5711. Watson, David L.
1965   "Effects of certain social power structures on communication in task-oriented groups." Sociometry 28 (3, September): 322-336. P.A. 39:15069.

5712.   1971   "Reinforcement theory of personality and social system: Dominance and position in a group power structure." Journal of Personality and Social Psychology 20 (2, November): 180-185. P.A. 47:6702.

5713. Watson, David L., and Barbara Bromberg
1965   "Power, communication, and position satisfaction in task-oriented groups." Journal of Personality and Social Psychology 2 (6): 859-864. P.A. 40:2830.

5714. Watson, Goodwin B.
1928   "Do groups think more efficiently than individuals?" Journal of Abnormal and Social Psychology 23: 328-336.

5715.   1953   "An evaluation of small group work in a large class." Journal of Educational Psychology 44: 385-408.

5716. Watson, Jeanne
1958   "A formal analysis of sociable interaction." Sociometry 21: 269-280. P.A. 34:1190.

5717. Watson, Jeanne, and Robert J. Potter
1962   "An analytic unit for the study of interaction." Human Relations 15 (3, August): 245-264. P.A. 37:6622; S.A. 12:A7961.

5718. Watson, Sharon G.
1972   "Judgment of emotion from facial and contextual cue combinations." Journal of Personality and Social Psychology 24 (3, December): 334-342. P.A. 49:9108.

5719. Watzke, G. D., J. M. Dana, R. H. Doktor, and F. D. Rubenstein
1972'   "An experimental study of individual vs. group interest." Acta Sociologica 15 (4): 366-370. S.A. 21:73G4908.

5720. Waxler, Nancy E., and Elliot G. Mishler
1966   "Scoring and reliability problems in interaction process analysis: A methodological note." Sociometry 29 (1, March): 28-40. S.A. 15: C3486.

5721. Weber, R. Jack
1971   "Effects of videotape feedback on task group behavior." Proceedings of the 79th Annual Convention of the American Psychological Association 6 (pt. 2): 499-500.

5722.   1972   "Effects of process feedback, consultation, and knowledge of results on perceptions of group process." Proceedings of the 80th Annual Convention of the American Psychological Association 7 (pt. 1): 459-460.

5723. Weber, Louis C.
1950   "A study of peer acceptance among delinquent girls." Sociometry 13: 363-381. P.A. 28:6329.

5724. Webster, Murray, Jr.
1969   "Source of evaluations and expectations for performance." Sociometry 32 (3): 243-258. P.A. 44:3551.

5725. Weick, Karl E.
1968   "Systematic observational methods." In G. Lindzey and E. Aronson (eds.), Handbook of Social Psychology, vol. 2, pp. 357-451. Reading, Mass.: Addison-Wesley.

5726. Weick, Karl E., and David P. Gilfillan
1971   "Fate of arbitrary traditions in a laboratory micro-culture." Journal of Personality and Social Psychology 17 (2, February): 179-191. P.A. 45:9864.

5727. Weick, Karl E., and Donald D. Penner
1969   "Discrepant membership as an occasion for effective cooperation."

Sociometry 32 (4): 413-424. P.A. 44:6670.

5728. Weil, Roman L., Jr.
    1966   "The N-person Prisoner's Dilemma: Some theory and a computer-oriented approach." Behavioral Science 11: 227-236.

5729. Weiler, John, and Eugene Weinstein
    1972   "Honesty, fabrication, and the enhancement of credibility." Sociometry 35 (2, June): 316-331. P.A. 49:815.

5730. Weiner, Bernard
    1966   "Achievement motivation and task recall in competitive situations." Journal of Personality and Social Psychology 3 (6): 693-696.

5731. Weiner, Harold, and Elliott McGinnies
    1961   "Authoritarianism, conformity, and confidence in a perceptual judgement situation." Journal of Social Psychology 55 (October): 77-84. P.A. 36:3GE77W.

5732. Weinstein, Alan G., and Robert L. Holzbach
    1972   "Effects of financial inducement on performance under two task structures." Proceedings of the 80th Annual Convention of the American Psychological Association 7 (pt. 1): 217-218.

5733.   1973   "Impact of individual differences, reward distribution, and task structure on productivity in a simulated work environment." Journal of Applied Psychology 58 (3, December): 296-301. P.A. 52:7539.

5734. Weinstein, Eugene A., Lawrence S. Beckhouse, Philip W. Blumstein, and Robert B. Stein
    1968   "Interpersonal strategies under conditions of gain or loss." Journal of Personality 36 (4): 616-634. P.A. 43:6846.

5735. Weinstein, Eugene A., and Susan E. Crowdus
    1968   "The effects of positive and negative information on person perception." Human Relations 21 (4, November): 383-391.

5736. Weinstein, Eugene A., and Paul Deutschberger
    1963   "Some dimensions of altercasting." Sociometry 26 (4, December): 454-466.

5737.   1964   "Tasks, bargains, and identities in social interaction." Social Forces 42 (4, May): 451-455. P.A. 39:4899.

5738. Weinstein, Eugene A., William L. DeVaughn, and Mary Glen Wiley
    1969   "Obligation and the flow of deference in exchange." Sociometry 32 (1, March): 1-12. S.A. 18:E1786.

5739. Weinstein, Eugene A., Kenneth A. Feldman, Norman Goodman, and Martin Markowitz
    1972   "Empathy and communication efficiency." Journal of Social Psychology 88 (2, December): 247-254. P.A. 49:9109.

5740. Weinstein, Eugene A., Mary G. Wiley, and William L. DeVaughn
    1966   "Role and interpersonal style as components of social interaction." Social Forces 45 (2, December): 210-216.

5741. Weinstein, Malcolm S., and Herbert B. Pollack
    1972   "The use of exercises in sensitivity training: A survey." Comparative Group Studies 3 (4, November): 497-512. P.A. 51:961.

5742. Weiss, Mark H., and Donald H. McKenzie
    1972   "The effects of videotape focused feedback on facilitative genuineness in interracial encounters." Comparative Group Studies 3 (2, May): 247-259.

5743. Weiss, Robert F., Jenny L. Boyer, John P. Lombardo, and Mark H. Stich
    1973   "Altruistic drive and altruistic reinforcement." Journal of Personality and Social Psychology 25 (3, March): 390-400. P.A. 50: 4847.

5744. Weiss, Robert F., John P. Lombardo, Don R. Warren, and Kathryn A. Kelley
    1971   "Reinforcing effects of speaking in reply." Journal of Personality and Social Psychology 20 (2, November): 186-199. P.A. 47: 6703.

5745. Weiss, Robert F., Mary J. Williams, and Catherine R. Miller
    1972   "Disagreement-induced drive in conversation: A Social analog of intermittent shock in escape conditioning." Psychonomic Science 29 (6-A, December): 342-344. P.A. 50:998.

5746. Weiss, Robert L.
    1966   "Some determinants of emitted reinforcing behavior: Listener rein-
            forcement and birth order." Journal of Personality and Social Psy-
            chology 3 (4): 489–492. P.A. 40:5412.
5747. Weissbach, Theodore A.
    1973   "Scope and autonomy in prison work groups." Journal of Social
            Psychology 90 (1): 85–88.
5748. Weissman, Herbert N., Marcel L. Goldschmid, Robert Gordon, and Helene
    Feinberg
    1972   "Changes in self-regard, creativity and interpersonal behavior as a
            function of audio-tape encounter-group experiences." Psychological
            Reports 31: 975–981.
5749. Weissman, Herbert N., Martin Seldman, and Kenneth Ritter
    1971   "Changes in awareness of impact upon others as a function of en-
            counter and marathon group experiences." Psychological Reports 28
            (2, April): 651–661. P.A. 46:6770.
5750. Weitz, Shirley
    1972   "Attitude, voice, and behavior: A repressed affect model of inter-
            racial interaction." Journal of Personality and Social Psychology 24
            (1, October): 14–21. P.A. 49:4456.
5751. Welkowitz, Joan, and Stanley Feldstein
    1969   "Dyadic interaction and induced differences in perceived similar-
            ity." Proceedings of the 77th Annual Convention of the American
            Psychological Association 4 (pt. 1): 343–344.
5752.   1970   "Relation of experimentally manipulated interpersonal perception
            and psychological differentiation to the temporal patterning of con-
            versation." Proceedings of the 78th Annual Convention of the Amer-
            ican Psychological Association 5 (pt. 1): 387–388. P.A. 44:18582.
5753. Welkowitz, Joan, and Marta Kuc
    1973   "Interrelationships among warmth, genuineness, empathy, and tem-
            poral speech patterns in interpersonal interaction." Journal of Con-
            sulting and Clinical Psychology 41 (3, December): 472–473. P.A.
            51:9023.
5754. Weller, Leonard
    1963   "The effects of anxiety on cohesiveness and rejection." Human
            Relations 16 (2, May): 189–198. P.A. 38:5974; S.A. 12:A8720.
5755.   1964   "The relationship of birth order to cohesiveness." Journal of Social
            Psychology 63 (2, August): 249–254. P.A. 39:4900.
5756. Wells, William D., Guy Weinert, and Marilyn Rubel
    1956   "Conformity pressure and authoritarian personality." Journal of
            Psychology 42: 133–136.
5757. Wendt, D., and H. Rüppell
    1971   ("Learning strategies in a two-person zero-sum-game.") Zeitschrift
            für Psychologie 179 (3): 381–388. P.A. 50:1001.
5758. Weschler, Irving R., Robert Tannenbaum, and Eugene Talbot
    1952   "A new management tool: The multi-relational sociometric survey."
            Personnel 29: 85–94. P.A. 27:3073.
5759. Weschsler, David
    1971   "Concept of collective intelligence." American Psychologist 26 (10,
            October): 904–907. P.A. 48:882.
5760. Whalen, Carol
    1969   "Effects of a model and instructions on group verbal behaviors."
            Journal of Consulting and Clinical Psychology 33 (5): 509–521.
            P.A. 44:2276.
5761. Wheeler, David, and Howard Jordan
    1929   "Change of individual opinion to accord with group opinion." Jour-
            nal of Abnormal and Social Psychology 24: 203–206.
5762. Wheeler, D. K.
    1957   "Notes on 'Role differentiation in small decision-making groups.'"
            Sociometry 20: 145–151. P.A. 33:3562.
5763. Wheeler, Ladd S.
    1964   "Information seeking as a power strategy." Journal of Social Psy-

chology 62 (1, February): 125-130. P.A. 39:1595.

5764. Wheeler, Ladd S., and A. John Arrowood
  1966   "Restraints against imitation and their reduction." Journal of Experimental Social Psychology 2 (3, July): 288-300. P.A. 40:13159.

5765. Wheeler, Ladd S., and Lewis Levine
  1967   "Observer-model similarity in the contagion of aggression." Sociometry 30 (1, March): 41-49. S.A. 15:C5593.

5766. Wheeler, Ladd S., Kelly G. Shaver, Russell A. Jones, George R. Goethals, Joel Cooper, James E. Robinson, Charles L. Gruder, and Kent W. Butzine
  1969   "Factors determining choice of a comparison other." Journal of Experimental Social Psychology 5 (2): 219-232.

5767. Wheeler, Ronald, and Frank L. Ryan
  1973   "Effects of cooperative and competitive classroom environments on the attitudes and achievement of elementary school students engaged in social studies inquiry activities." Journal of Educational Psychology 65 (3): 402-407.

5768. Wheeler, William M., Kenneth B. Little, and George F. J. Lehner
  1951   "The internal structure of the MMPI." Journal of Consulting Psychology 15: 134-141. P.A. 26:6307.

5769. White, Harrison
  1962   "Chance models of systems of casual groups." Sociometry 25 (2, June): 153-172. Comment by James Coleman, pp. 172-176. S.A. 11:A5142.

5770. White, J. H., J. R. Hegarty, and N. A. Beasley
  1970   "Eye contact and observer bias: A research note." British Journal of Psychology 61 (2): 271-273. P.A. 44:14515.

5771. White, Ralph K., and Ronald Lippitt
  1960   Autocracy and Democracy. New York: Harper. P.A. 35:750.

5772. White, William F., and Nicklaus J. Minden
  1969   "Risky-shift phenomenon in moral attitudes of high school boys and girls." Psychological Reports 25: 515-518.

5773. Whitehead, Thomas N.
  1938   The Industrial Worker. Cambridge, Mass.: Harvard University Press.

5774. Whitehorn, John C.
  1961   "Alienation and leadership." Psychiatry 24 (2, Supplement, May): 1-6. S.A. A3424.

5775. Whitman, Roy M.
  1964   "Psychodynamic principles underlying T-group processes." In L. P. Bradford, J. R. Gibb, and K. Benne (eds.), T-Group Theory and Laboratory Methods, pp. 310-335. New York: Wiley.

5776. Whitmyre, John W., James C. Diggory, and David Cohen
  1961   "The effects of personal liking, perceived ability, and value of prize on choice of partners for a competition." Journal of Abnormal and Social Psychology 63 (1, July): 198-200. P.A. 4GE98W; S.A. A3310.

5777. Whittaker, James K.
  1970   "Models of group development: Implications for social group work practice." Social Service Review 44 (3, September): 308-322. S.A. 20:F4691.

5778. Whittaker, James O.
  1964   "Parameters of social influence in the autokinetic situation." Sociometry 27 (1, March): 88-95. P.A. 38:8311.

5779.   1965   "Sex differences and susceptibility to interpersonal persuasion." Journal of Social Psychology 66 (1, June): 91-94. P.A. 39:15070.

5780. Whittemore, Irving C.
  1924   "The influence of competition on performance: An experimental study." Journal of Abnormal and Social Psychology 19: 236-253.

5781. Whyte, William F.
  1943   Street Corner Society: The Social Structure of an Italian Slum. Chicago: University of Chicago Press. (See also Gouldner, 1950; Crosbie, 1975.) P.A. 18:2198.

5782.   1949   "The social structure of the restaurant." American Journal of Sociology 54: 302-310. P.A. 23:2457.

5783.   1951a   "Observational field-work methods." In M. Jahoda, M. Deutsch, and S. W. Cook (eds.), Research Methods in Social Relations: With Especial Reference to Prejudice, pp. 493-513. New York: Dryden.

5784.   1951b   "Small groups and large organizations." In J. H. Rohrer and M. Sherif (eds.), Social Psychology at the Crossroads: The University of Oklahoma Lectures in Social Psychology, pp. 297-312. New York: Harper.

5785.   1953   "Leadership and group participation." Cornell University, New York State School of Industrial and Labor Relations, Bulletin 24.

5786. Wichman, Harvey
    1970   "Effects of isolation and communication on cooperation in a two-person game." Journal of Personality and Social Psychology 16 (1, September): 114-120. P.A. 45:2309.

5787. Wiebe, Bernhard, and John D. Williams
    1972   "Self-disclosure to parents by high school seniors." Psychological Reports 31 (3, December): 690. P.A. 50:1004.

5788. Weiner, Daniel J.
    1970   "Failure of personality variables to mediate interpersonal attraction." Psychological Reports 26 (3, June): 784-786. P.A. 45:639.

5789. Wiener, Morton
    1955   "The effects of two experimental counseling techniques on performances impaired by induced stress." Journal of Abnormal and Social Psychology 51: 565-572. P.A. 31:2996.

5790.   1959   "Some correlates of conformity responses." Journal of Social Psychology 49 (May): 215-221. P.A. 34:4219.

5791. Wiener, Morton, Janeth T. Carpenter, and B. Carpenter
    1957   "Some determinants of conformity behavior." Journal of Social Psychology 45: 289-297.

5792. Wiener, Morton, Shannon Devoe, Stuart Rubinow, and Jesse Geller
    1972   "Nonverbal behavior and nonverbal communication." Psychological Review 79 (3, May): 185-214.

5793. Wiesenthal, David L.
    1974   "Some effects of the confirmation and disconfirmation of an expected monetary reward on compliance." Journal of Social Psychology 92 (1): 39-52.

5794. Wiesenthal, David L., Norman S. Endler, and Sheldon H. Geller
    1973   "Effects of prior group agreement and task correctness on relative competence mediating conformity." European Journal of Social Psychology 3 (2): 193-203. P.A. 52:2907.

5795. Wiest, William M., Lyman W. Porter, and Edwin E. Ghiselli
    1961   "Relationship between individual proficiency and team performance and efficiency." Journal of Applied Psychology 45 (6): 435-440. P.A. 37:1120.

5796. Wiggins, James A.
    1965   "Interaction structure, frustration, and the extensiveness and intensity of aggression." Sociometry 28 (1, March): 89-99. P.A. 39: 10011.

5797.   1966   "Status differentiation, external consequences, and alternative reward distributions." Sociometry 29 (2, June): 89-103. P.A. 40: 10046; S.A. 15:C3487.

5798. Wiggins, James A., Forrest Dill, and Richard D. Schwartz
    1965   "On 'status-liability.'" Sociometry 28 (2, June): 197-209. (See also Cartwright and Zander, 1968.)

5799. Wiggins, Nancy, Stuart Itkin, and Gerald Clore
    1973   "Gain and loss of esteem in a non-verbal behavioral context." Proceedings of the 81st Annual Convention of the American Psychological Association 8: 201-202. P.A. 50:8891.

5800. Wile, Daniel B., Gary D. Bron, and Herbert B. Pollack
    1970   "The group therapy questionnaire: An instrument for study of leadership in small groups." Psychological Reports 27: 263-273.

5801. Wiley, Mary G.
    1973   "Sex roles in games." Sociometry 36 (4, December): 526-541. P.A.
            52:2908.
5802. Wilhelmy, Roland A., and Birt L. Duncan
    1974   "Cognitive reversibility in dissonance reduction." Journal of Person-
            ality and Social Psychology 29 (6): 806-811. P.A. 52:7585.
5803. Wilke, Henk, and John T. Lanzetta
    1970   "The obligation to help: The effects of amount of prior help on
            subsequent helping behavior." Journal of Experimental Social Psy-
            chology 6 (4, October): 488-493. P.A. 45:6212.
5804. Wilke, Henk, Roel Meertens, and Theo Steur
    1973   "Uncertainty and power inversion in coalition formation: Again
            strength is weakness." British Journal of Social and Clinical Psy-
            chology 12 (1, February): 38-45. P.A. 50:2995.
5805. Wilke, Henk, and Mauk Mulder
    1971   "Coalition formation on the gameboard." European Journal of
            Social Psychology 1 (3): 339-355. P.A. 48:11475.
5806. Wilkins, Greg, Franz Epting, and Hani Van de Riet
    1972   "Relationship between repression-sensitization and interpersonal
            cognitive complexity." Journal of Consulting and Clinical Psychol-
            ogy 39 (3, December): 448-450. P.A. 50:1005.
5807. Wilkins, Judy L., William H. Scharff, and Robert S. Schlottmann
    1974   "Personality type, reports of violence, and aggressive behavior."
            Journal of Personality and Social Psychology 30 (2, August): 243-
            247. P.A. 52:12358.
5808. Willard, Don, and Fred L. Strodtbeck
    1972   "Latency of verbal response and participation in small groups."
            Sociometry 35 (1, March): 161-175. P.A. 49:816; S.A. 21:
            73G2277.
5809. Willems, Edwin P., and Russell D. Clark, III
    1969   "Dependence of the risky shift on instructions: A replication."
            Psychological Reports 25: 811-814.
5810.   1971   "Shift toward risk and heterogeneity of groups." Journal of Ex-
            perimental Social Psychology 7 (3, May): 304-312. P.A. 48:2909.
5811. Willerman, Ben
    1943   "Group decision and request as means of changing food habits." In
            K. Lewin (ed.), Forces behind Food Habits and Methods of Change.
            Bulletin of National Research Council 108: 35-65.
5812.   1953   "The relation of motivation and skill to active and passive partici-
            pation in the group." Journal of Applied Psychology 37: 387-390.
            P.A. 29:715.
5813. Willerman, Ben, and L. Swanson
    1952   "An ecological determinant of differential amounts of sociometric
            choices within college sororities." Sociometry 15: 326-329. P.A.
            27:7394.
5814. Williams, Christene B.
    1968   "Dissonance following aggressive behavior with and without social
            support and choice." Psychological Reports 23: 1343-1350.
5815. Williams, Daniel C.
    1973   "Consistency between and within indices of aptitude, diligence and
            performance in the attribution of motivation and ability." Pro-
            ceedings of the 81st Annual Convention of the American Psycho-
            logical Association 8: 241-242. P.A. 50:8892.
5816. Williams, Harold L., and James F. Lawrence
    1954   "Comparison of the Rorschach and MMPI by means of factor analy-
            sis." Journal of Consulting Psychology 18: 193-197. P.A. 29:
            2484.
5817. Williams, Robin M., Jr
    1947   The Reduction of Intergroup Tensions. New York: Social Science
            Research Council Bulletin No. 57. P.A. 22:688.
5818. Williams, Ruth M., and Marion L. Mattson
    1942   "The effect of social groupings upon the language of pre-school

children." Child Development 13: 233-245. P.A. 17:2539.

5819. Williams, Stanley B., and Harold J. Leavitt
      1947   "Group opinion as a predictor of military leadership." Journal of
              Consulting Psychology 11: 283-291. P.A. 22:2347.

5820. Williamson, E. G.
      1926   "Allport's experiments in 'social facilitation.'" Psychological Mono-
              graphs 35, No. 163: 138-143.

5821. Willingham, Warren W.
      1959   "On deriving standard scores for peer nominations with subgroups
              of unequal size." Psychological Reports 5: 397-403.

5822. Willis, Joe E., James D. Hitchcock, and William J. MacKinnon
      1969   "SPAN decision making in established groups." Journal of Social
              Psychology 78 (2): 185-203. P.A. 44:6671.

5823. Willis, Judith A., and George R. Goethals
      1973   "Social responsibility and threat to behavioral freedom as determin-
              ants of altruistic behavior." Journal of Personality 41 (3, Septem-
              ber): 376-384. P.A. 51:5123.

5824. Willis, Richard H.
      1961   "Social influence and conformity: Some research perspectives."
              Acta Sociologica 5 (2): 100-114. S.A. A2139.

5825.   1962   "Coalitions in the tetrad." Sociometry 25 (4, December): 358-376.
              P.A. 38:4203; S.A. 11:A6361.

5826.   1963   "Two dimensions of conformity-nonconformity." Sociometry 26
              (4, December): 499-512. S.A. 12:A9443.

5827.   1965a   "Conformity, independence, and anticonformity." Human Relations
              18 (4, November): 373-388. P.A. 40:4192.

5828.   1965b   "Social influence, information processing, and net conformity in
              dyads." Psychological Reports 17 (1): 147-156. P.A. 40:1528.

5829.   1965c   "The phenomenology of shifting agreement and disagreement in
              dyads." Journal of Personality 33 (2, June): 188-199. P.A. 40:
              2831.

5830.   1969   "Coalitions in the triad: Additive case." Psychonomic Science 17
              (6): 347-348. P.A. 44:6672.

5831. Willis, Richard H., and Thomas D. Burgess, II
      1974   "Cognitive and affective balance in sociometric dyads." Journal of
              Personality and Social Psychology 29 (1, January): 145-152. P.A.
              52:847.

5832. Willis, Richard H., and John F. Hale
      1963   "Dyadic interaction as a function of amount of feedback and in-
              structional orientation." Human Relations 16 (2, May): 149-160.
              S.A. 12:A8721.

5833. Willis, Richard H., and Edwin P. Hollander
      1964   "An experimental study of three response modes in social influence
              situations." Journal of Abnormal and Social Psychology 69 (2, Au-
              gust): 150-156. P.A. 39:4901.

5834. Willis, Richard H., and Myron L. Joseph
      1959   "Bargaining behavior. I. 'Prominence' as a predictor of the outcome
              of games of agreement." Journal of Conflict Resolution 3 (2): 102-
              113.

5835. Wilner, Daniel M., Rosabelle P. Walkley, and Stuart W. Cook
      1952   "Residential proximity and intergroup relations in public housing
              projects." Journal of Social Issues 8 (1): 45-69.

5836. Wilson, Atholl L.
      1963   "An optimal strategy for repeated N-person games." Behavioral
              Science 8 (4, October): 312-316. S.A. 12:A8712.

5837. Wilson, Dennis T.
      1965   "Ability evaluation, postdecision dissonance, and co-worker attrac-
              tiveness." Journal of Personality and Social Psychology 1 (5): 486-
              489. P.A. 39:10012.

5838. Wilson, Kellogg V., and V. Edwin Bixenstine
      1962   "Forms of social control in two-person, two-choice games." Behav-
              ioral Science 7 (1, January): 92-102. P.A. 37:1121; S.A. 11:A5143.

5839. Wilson, Logan
        1945   "Sociography of groups." In G. Gurvitch and W. E. Moore (eds.), Twentieth Century Sociology, pp. 139-171. New York: Philosophical Library.
5840. Wilson, Robert C., W. S. High, Helen P. Beem, and A. L. Comrey
        1954   "A factor-analytic study of supervisory and group behavior." Journal of Applied Psychology 38: 89-92. P.A. 29:3180.
5841. Wilson, Robert C., Wallace S. High, and Andrew L. Comrey
        1955   "An iterative analysis of supervisory and group dimensions." Journal of Applied Psychology 39: 85-91. P.A. 30:1756.
5842. Wilson, Ronald S.
        1960   "Personality patterns, source of attractiveness, and conformity." Journal of Personality 28: 186-199. P.A. 35:2138.
5843. Wilson, Stephen R.
        1969   "The effect of the laboratory situation on experimental discussion groups." Sociometry 32 (2): 220-236. P.A. 43:12901; S.A. 18: E2911.
5844.   1970   "Some factors influencing instrumental and expressive ratings in task-oriented groups." Pacific Sociological Review 13 (2, Spring): 127-131. S.A. 19:E7006.
5845.   1971   "Leadership, participation, and self-orientation in observed and non-observed groups." Journal of Applied Psychology 55 (5, October): 433-438. P.A. 47:6704.
5846. Wilson, Stephen R., and Larry A. Benner
        1971   "The effects of self-esteem and situation upon comparison choices during ability evaluation." Sociometry 34 (3, September): 381-397. P.A. 49:2390.
5847. Wilson, Warner
        1969   "Cooperation and the cooperativeness of the other player." Journal of Conflict Resolution 13 (1, March): 110-117.
5848.   1971   "Reciprocation and other techniques for inducing cooperation in the Prisoner's Dilemma game." Journal of Conflict Resolution 15 (2): 167-195.
5849. Wilson, Warner, and Chester Insko
        1968   "Recency effects in face-to-face interaction." Journal of Personality and Social Psychology 9 (1): 21-23.
5850. Wilson, Warner, and Myra Kayatani
        1968   "Intergroup attitudes and strategies in games between opponents of the same or of a different race." Journal of Personality and Social Psychology 9 (1): 24-30. P.A. 42:10523.
5851. Wilson, Warner, and Norman Miller
        1961   "Shifts in evaluations of participants following intergroup competition." Journal of Abnormal and Social Psychology 63 (2): 428-431. P.A. 37:1122.
5852. Wilson, Wayne
        1973   "Secrecy and written dialogue." Psychological Reports 32 (2, April): 419-425. P.A. 51:962.
5853. Winch, Robert F.
        1955   "The theory of complementary needs in mate-selection: Final results on the test of the general hypothesis." American Sociological Review 20: 552-554. P.A. 31:937.
5854.   1957   "Comment on 'A test of the theory of complementary needs as applied to couples during courtship,' by Bowerman and Day." American Sociological Review 22: 336.
5855.   1958   Mate Selection: A Study of Complementary Needs. New York: Harper.
5856. Winch, Robert F., T. Ktsanes, and Virginia Ktsanes
        1954   "The theory of complementary needs in mate selection: An analytic and descriptive study." American Sociological Review 19: 241-249. P.A. 30:2795.
5857.   1955   "Empirical elaboration of the theory of complementary needs in mate selection." Journal of Abnormal and Social Psychology 51:

508-513. P.A. 31:2863.

5858. Winder, C. L., and Jerry S. Wiggins
       1964   "Social reputation and social behavior: A further validation of the
               Peer Nomination Inventory." Journal of Abnormal and Social Psy-
               chology 68 (6, June): 681-684. P.A. 39:1588.
5859. Winslow, Charles N.
       1937   "A study of the extent of agreement between friends' opinions and
               their ability to estimate the opinions of each other." Journal of So-
               cial Psychology 8: 433-442.
5860. Winter, Gibson
       1952   "Value-orientations as factors in the organization of small groups."
               Ph.D. dissertation. Harvard University.
5861. Winter, Sara K.
       1971   "Black man's bluff." Psychology Today 5 (4, September): 39-43,
               78-81. P.A. 47:8812.
5862. Wirth, Louis
       1939   "Social interaction: The problem of the individual and the group."
               American Journal of Sociology 44: 965-979. P.A. 13:4795.
5863. Wischmeier, Richard R.
       1955   "Group-centered and leader-centered leadership: An experimental
               study." Speech Monographs 22: 43-48. P.A. 30:811.
5864. Wish, Myron, Susan J. Kaplan, and Morton Deutsch
       1973   "Dimensions of interpersonal relations: Preliminary results." Pro-
               ceedings of the 81st Annual Convention of the American Psycho-
               logical Association 8: 179-180. P.A. 50:4848.
5865. Wispé, Lauren G.
       1951   "Evaluating section teaching methods in the introductory course."
               Journal of Educational Research 45: 161-186. P.A. 26:6521.
5866.   1953   "Teaching methods research." American Psychologist 8: 147-149.
               P.A. 28:1503.
5867.   1955   "A sociometric analysis of conflicting role-expectations." American
               Journal of Sociology 61: 134-137. P.A. 31:806.
5868.   1972   "Positive forms of social behavior: An overview." Journal of Social
               Issues 28 (3): 1-19. P.A. 50:4849.
5869. Wispé, Lauren G., and Harold B. Freshley
       1971   "Race, sex, and sympathetic helping behavior: The broken bag
               caper." Journal of Personality and Social Psychology 17 (1, Janu-
               ary): 59-65. P.A. 45:9867.
5870. Withall, John
       1949   "The development of a technique for the measurement of social-
               emotional climate in classrooms." Journal of Experimental Educa-
               tion 17: 347-361. P.A. 24:1456.
5871.   1951   "The development of the climate index." Journal of Educational
               Research 45: 93-100. P.A. 26:5084.
5872.   1956   "An objective measurement of a teacher's classroom interaction."
               Journal of Educational Psychology 47: 203-212.
5873. Witt, Robert E., and Subrata K. Sen
       1972   "Conformity influence in small groups: A probabilistic measure."
               Journal of Social Psychology 86 (1, February): 45-54. P.A. 47:
               10788.
5874. Witte, E. H.
       1971   ("The 'risky-shift' phenomenon: A critical examination of existing
               hypotheses.") Psychologie und Praxis 15 (3, July): 104-117. P.A.
               48:883.
5875. Wittmer, Joe, and Fred Ferinden
       1971   "The effects of group counseling on the attitude and GPA of de-
               prived Negro underachievers: With a profile of the counselor's activ-
               ity." Comparative Group Studies 2 (1, February): 43-52.
5876. Wolf, Edith
       1972-   ("The joint influence of cognitive and emotional tendencies among
       1973   cooperating groups.") Zeitschrift für Psychologie 180-181 (1):
               15-40. P.A. 51:9024.

5877. Wolf, Gerrit
    1970   "A model of conversation." Comparative Group Studies 1 (3, August): 275-304.
5878.   1972   "Behavioral processes in different minimal social situations." Comparative Group Studies 3 (3, August): 221-239.
5879. Wolf, Gerrit, and Larry Zahn
    1972   "Exchange in games and communication." Organizational Behavior and Human Performance 7 (1, February): 142-187. P.A. 47:10789.
5880. Wolf, Irvin S., and James F. Zolman
    1959   "Social influence: Self-confidence and prestige determinants." Psychological Record 9: 71-79. P.A. 34:2898.
5881. Wolfe, Donald M.
    1959   "Power and authority in the family." In D Cartwright (ed.), Studies in Social Power, pp. 99-107. University of Michigan, Institute for Social Research, Research Center for Group Dynamics. (See also Crosbie, 1975.)
5882. Wolfe, Tom
    1968   The Electric Kool-Aid Acid Test. New York: Farrar, Straus & Giroux.
5883. Wolff, Kurt H.
    1950   The Sociology of Georg Simmel. Glencoe, Ill.: Free Press.
5884. Wolin, Burton R., and Stanley J. Terebinski
    1965   "Leadership in small groups: A mathematical approach." Journal of Experimental Psychology 69 (2): 126-134. P.A. 39:7653.
5885. Wolman, Benjamin B.
    1956   "Leadership and group dynamics." Journal of Social Psychology 43: 11-25. P.A. 31:2731.
5886.   1960   "Impact of failure on group cohesiveness." Journal of Social Psychology 51 (May): 409-418. P.A. 34:7614; S.A. 11:A5701.
5887. Wolosin, Robert J., Steven J. Sherman, and Clifford R. Mynatt
    1971   "When self-interest and altruism conflict: Diffusion of responsibility and victim retribution." Proceedings of the 79th Annual Convention of the American Psychological Association 6 (pt. 1): 339-340. P.A. 46:2939.
5888.   1972   "Perceived social influence in a conformity situation." Journal of Personality and Social Psychology 23 (2, August): 184-191. P.A. 49:817.
5889. Wolosin, Robert J., Steven J. Sherman, and Amnon Till
    1973   "Effects of cooperation and competition on responsibility attribution after success and failure." Journal of Experimental Social Psychology 9 (3, May): 220-235. P.A. 51:3093.
5890. Wood, Donald, Marc Pilisuk, and Emmanuel Uren
    1973   "The martyr's personality: An experimental investigation." Journal of Personality and Social Psychology 25 (2, February): 177-186. P.A. 50:1006.
5891. Wood, Michael T.
    1972a   "Effects of decision processes and task situations on influence perceptions." Organizational Behavior and Human Performance 7 (3, June): 417-427. P.A. 49:818.
5892.   1972b   "Participation, influence, and satisfaction in group decision making." Journal of Vocational Behavior 2 (4, October): 389-399. P.A. 50:6764.
5893. Woods, Thomas L.
    1972   "Parents preparation groups." Comparative Group Studies 3 (3, August): 201-211.
5894. Woodyard, Howard D.
    1972   "An interpersonal simulation of the Jecker conflict experiment: A test of Bem's theory." Journal of Psychology 82 (2, November): 201-207. P.A. 49:6878.
5895. Woodyard, Howard D., and David A. Hines
    1973   "Accurate compared to inaccurate self-disclosure." Journal of Humanistic Psychology 13 (3, Summer): 61-67. P.A. 52:848.

5896. Worchel, Philip
    1969   "Temptation and threat in non-zero-sum games." Journal of Conflict Resolution 13 (1, March): 103–109. S.A. 18:E4570.
5897. Worchel, Stephen
    1974   "The effect of three types of arbitrary thwarting on the instigation to aggression." Journal of Personality 42 (2): 300–318.
5898. Worchel, Stephen, and Virginia A. Andreoli
    1974   "Attribution of causality as a means of restoring behavioral freedom." Journal of Personality and Social Psychology 29 (2): 237–245.
5899. Worchel, Stephen, Chester A. Insko, Virginia A. Andreoli, and David Drachman
    1974   "Attribution of attitude as a function of behavioral direction and freedom: Reactance in the eye of the observer." Journal of Experimental Social Psychology 10 (5): 399–414.
5900. Word, Carl O., Mark P. Zanna, and Joel Cooper
    1974   "The nonverbal mediation of self-fulfilling prophecies in interracial interaction." Journal of Experimental Social Psychology 10 (2): 109–120.
5901. Workie, Abaineh
    1974   "The relative productivity of cooperation and competition." Journal of Social Psychology 92 (2): 225–230.
5902. Worthy, Morgan, Albert L. Gary, and Gay M. Kahn
    1969   "Self-disclosure as an exchange process." Journal of Personality and Social Psychology 13 (1): 59–63. P.A. 43:17362.
5903. Wortman, Camille B., Philip R. Costanzo, and Thomas R. Witt
    1973   "Effect of anticipated performance on the attributions of causality to self and others." Journal of Personality and Social Psychology 27 (3, September): 372–381. P.A. 51:5125.
5904. Wortman, Camille B., and Darwyn E. Linder
    1973   "Attribution of responsibility for an outcome as a function of its likelihood." Proceedings of the 81st Annual Convention of the American Psychological Association 8: 149–150. P.A. 50:4850.
5905. Wrench, David, and Kirk Endicott
    1965   "Denial of affect and conformity." Journal of Personality and Social Psychology 1 (5): 484–486. P.A. 39:10013.
5906. Wright, Benjamin, and Mary A. Evitts
    1961   "Direct factor analysis in sociometry." Sociometry 24 (1, March): 82–98. P.A. 36:1GE82W; S.A. A2697.
5907. Wright, Benjamin, and Sue Evitts
    1963   "Multiple regression in the explanation of social structure." Journal of Social Psychology 61 (1, October): 87–98.
5908. Wright, Jack M., and Morgan Worthy
    1971   "Volunteering as group spokesman as a function of task effectiveness, leader success, and task similarity." Psychological Reports 28: 911–917.
5909. Wright, M. E.
    1943   "The influence of frustration upon the social relations of young children." Character and Personality 12: 111–112. P.A. 18:1952.
5910. Wright, Paul H.
    1966   "Attitude change under direct and indirect interpersonal influence." Human Relations 19 (2, May): 199–211. S.A. 15:C4089.
5911.   1968   "Need similarity, need complementarity and the place of personality in interpersonal attraction." Journal of Experimental Research in Personality 3 (2): 126–135. P.A. 43:9649.
5912.   1969   "A model and a technique for studies of friendship." Journal of Experimental Social Psychology 5 (3): 295–309. P.A. 44:5093.
5913.   1971   "Byrne's paradigmatic approach to the study of attraction: Misgivings and alternatives." Representative Research in Social Psychology 2 (1, January): 66–70. P.A. 46:8952.
5914. Wright, Paul H., and Katherine D. Wright
    1972   "Attitude similarity and three 'anticipated rewards' as predictors of attraction to a hypothetical stranger." Representative Research in

Social Psychology 3 (2, December): 131-140. P.A. 50:1007.

5915. Wrightsman, Lawrence S., Jr.
1960 "Effects of waiting with others on changes in level of felt anxiety." Journal of Abnormal and Social Psychology 61 (2): 216-222. P.A. 35:5012.

5916. 1966 "Personality and attitudinal correlates of trusting and trustworthy behaviors in a two-person game." Journal of Personality and Social Psychology 4 (3, September): 328-332. S.A. 16:D1450.

5917. Wrightstone, J. Wayne
1934 "An instrument for measuring group discussion and planning." Journal of Educational Research 27: 641-650. P.A. 8:4309.

5918. 1951 "Measuring the social climate of a classroom." Journal of Educational Research 44: 341-351. P.A. 25:8287.

5919. Wuebben, Paul L.
1973 "A critique of Sarnoff and Zimbardo's psychoanalytic alternative to a social comparison theory of emotions." Journal of Psychology 84 (1, May): 145-157. P.A. 50:6765.

5920. Wurster, C. R., and Bernard M. Bass
1953 "Situational tests: IV. Validity of leaderless group discussions among strangers." Educational and Psychological Measurement 13: 122-132. P.A. 28:717.

5921. Wyatt, S., L. Frost, and F. G. L. Stock
1934 Incentives in Repetitive Work. Medical Research Council, Industrial Health Research Board, Report No. 69. London: H. M. Stationery Office.

5922. Wyer, Robert S., Jr.
1966 "Effects of incentive to perform well, group attraction, and group acceptance on conformity in a judgmental task." Journal of Personality and Social Psychology 4 (1): 21-26. P.A. 40:10049.

5923. 1969 "Prediction of behavior in two-person games." Journal of Personality and Social Psychology 13 (3): 222-238. P.A. 44:2267.

5924. 1971 "Effects of outcome matrix and partner's behavior in two-person games." Journal of Experimental Social Psychology 7 (2, March): 190-210. P.A. 46:4859.

5925. 1972 "Test of a subjective probability model of social evaluation processes." Journal of Personality and Social Psychology 22 (3): 279-286.

5926. 1973 "Effects of information inconsistency and grammatical context on evaluation of persons." Journal of Personality and Social Psychology 25 (1, January): 45-49. P.A. 50:6766.

5927. 1974 "Changes in meaning and halo effects in personality impression formation." Journal of Personality and Social Psychology 29 (6, June): 829-835. P.A. 52:7586.

5928. Wyer, Robert S., Jr., and John D. Lyon
1970 "A test of cognitive balance theory implications for social inference processes." Journal of Personality and Social Psychology 16 (4, December): 598-618. P.A. 45:4142.

5929. Wyer, Robert S., Jr., and Christine Malinowski
1972 "Effects of sex and achievement level upon individualism and competitiveness in social interaction." Journal of Experimental Social Psychology 8 (4, July): 303-314. P.A. 49:819.

5930. Wyer, Robert S., Jr., and Steven J. Polen
1971 "Some effects of fate control upon the tendency to benefit an exploitative other." Journal of Personality and Social Psychology 20 (1, October): 44-54. P.A. 47:6705.

5931. Yablonsky, Lewis
1953 "An operational theory of roles." Sociometry 16: 349-354. P.A. 29:718.

5932. Yakimovich, Dorothy, and Eli Saltz
1971 "Helping behavior: The cry for help." Psychonomic Sicence 23 (6, June): 427-428. P.A. 48:9051.

5933. Yakobson, S. G., and V. G. Shchur
    1973   ("Individual differences in children in the performance of a leader-
            ship function in teamwork.") Voprosy Psikhologii 19 (3, May):
            92–103. P.A. 51:5076.
5934. Yalom, Irvin D., and Kenneth Rand
    1966   "Compatibility and cohesiveness in therapy groups." Archives of
            General Psychiatry 15 (3): 267–275. P.A. 40:12281.
5935. Yang, Kuo-Shu, and Pen-Hua L. Yang
    1973   "The effects of anxiety and threat on the learning of balanced and
            unbalanced social structures." Journal of Personality and Social
            Psychology 26 (2): 201–207.
5936. Yanis, Martin, and Warren G. Findley
    1969   "Use of an interaction index to quantify subgroup acceptance."
            Proceedings of the 77th Annual Convention of the American Psy-
            chological Association 4 (pt. 1): 171–172. P.A. 43:17363.
5937. Yin, Robert K., and Herbert D. Saltzstein
    1968   "Transfer of social influence effects on psychophysical judgments."
            Journal of Psychology 68 (2): 313–319. P.A. 42:8884.
5938. Yinon, Yoel, Varda Shoham, and Tirtza Lewis
    1974   "Risky-shift in a real vs. role-played situation." Journal of Social
            Psychology 93 (1): 137–138.
5939. Yoshino, Kinuko
    1972   ("Models of choice behavior in two-person non-zero-sum games with
            response-dependent payoff matrices.") Japanese Journal of Psychol-
            ogy 43 (1, April): 31–40. P.A. 49:6879.
5940. Young, Richard D., and Margaret Frye
    1966   "Some are laughing; some are not: Why?" Psychological Reports 18
            (3): 747–754. P.A. 40:10050.
5941. Yuker, Harold E.
    1955   "Group atmosphere and memory." Journal of Abnormal and Social
            Psychology 51: 17–23. S.A. 2495.
5942. Yukl, Gary A.
    1972   "Effect of opponent concessions on a bargainer's perception and
            concessions." Proceedings of the 80th Annual Convention of the
            American Psychological Association 7 (pt. 1): 229–230.
5943.   1973   "The effects of the opponent's initial offer and concession magni-
            tude on bargaining outcomes." Proceedings of the 81st Annual Con-
            vention of the American Psychological Association 8: 143–144. P.A.
            50:4851.
5944.   1974a   "Effects of situational variables and opponent concessions on a bar-
            gainer's perception, aspirations, and concessions." Journal of Per-
            sonality and Social Psychology 29 (2): 227–236.
5945.   1974b   "Effects of the opponent's initial offer, concession magnitude, and
            concession frequency on bargaining behavior." Journal of Person-
            ality and Social Psychology 30 (3): 323–335.

5946. Zabrack, Merle, and Norman Miller
    1972   "Group aggression: The effects of friendship ties and anonymity."
            Proceedings of the 80th Annual Convention of the American Psy-
            chological Association 7 (pt. 1): 211–212.
5947. Zadny, Jerry, and Harold B. Gerard
    1974   "Attributed intentions and informational selectivity." Journal of
            Experimental Social Psychology 10 (1): 34–52.
5948. Zagona, Salvatore V., Joe E. Willis, and William J. MacKinnon
    1966   "Group effectiveness in creative problem-solving tasks: An examina-
            tion of relevant variables." Journal of Psychology 62 (1): 111–137.
            P.A. 40:6595.
5949. Zajonc, Robert B.
    1960   "The concepts of balance, congruity, and dissonance." Public Opin-
            ion Quarterly 24 (2): 280–296.
5950.   1962a   "The effects of feedback and probability on group success on indi-
            vidual and group performance." Human Relations 15 (2, May): 149–

161. P.A. 37:3049; S.A. 11:A5702.

5951. 1962b "A note on group judgements and group size." Human Relations 15 (2, May): 177-180. P.A. 37:3050; S.A. 11:A5703.

5952. 1965a "Social Facilitation." Science 149: 269-274. (See also Cartwright and Zander, 1968.)

5953. 1965b "The requirements and design of a standard group task." Journal of Experimental and Social Psychology 1 (1, January): 71-88. P.A. 39:10014.

5954. 1968 "Cognitive theories and social psychology. In G. Lindzey and E. Aronson (eds.), Handbook of Social Psychology, 2nd ed., vol. 1, pp. 320-411. Reading, Mass.: Addison-Wesley.

5955. Zajonc, Robert B., and Stephen M. Sales
1966 "Social facilitation of dominant and subordinate responses." Journal of Experimental Social Psychology 2 (2, April): 160-168. P.A. 40: 8799.

5956. Zajonc, Robert B., and Steven J. Sherman
1967 "Structural balance and the induction of relations." Journal of Personality 35 (4): 635-650. P.A. 42:18747.

5957. Zajonc, Robert B., and James J. Taylor
1963 "The effect of two methods of varying group task difficulty on individual and group performance." Human Relations 16 (4, November): 359-368. P.A. 38:5976; S.A. 12:B1637.

5958. Zajonc, Robert B., Robert J. Wolosin, and Myrna A. Wolosin
1972 "Group risk-taking under various group decision schemes." Journal of Experimental Social Psychology 8 (1, January): 16-30. P.A. 48: 2910.

5959. Zajonc, Robert B., Robert J. Wolosin, Myrna A. Wolosin, and Wallace D. Loh
1970 "Social facilitation and imitation in group risk-taking." Journal of Experimental Social Psychology 6 (1): 26-46. P.A. 44:14517.

5960. Zajonc, Robert B., Robert J. Wolosin, Myrna A. Wolosin, and Steven J. Sherman
1968 "Individual and group risk-taking in a two-choice situation." Journal of Experimental Social Psychology 4 (January): 89-106.

5961. 1969 "Group risk-taking in a two-choice situation: Replication, extension, and a model." Journal of Experimental Social Psychology 5 (2): 127-140.

5962. Zaleska, Maryla, and Nathan Kogan
1971 "Level of risk selected by individuals and groups when deciding for self and for others." Sociometry 34 (2, June): 198-213. P.A. 49: 820.

5963. Zand, Dale E., and Timothy W. Costello
1963 "Effect of problem variation on group problem-solving efficiency under constrained communication." Psychological Reports 13: 219-224.

5964. Zander, Alvin
1948 "The WP club: An objective case study of a group." Human Relations 1: 321-332. P.A. 23:1258.

5965. 1951 "Systematic observation of small face-to-face groups." In M. Jahoda, M. Deutsch, and S. W. Cook (eds.), Research Methods in Social Relations: With Especial Reference to Prejudice, pp. 515-538. New York: Dryden.

5966. 1958 "Group membership and individual security." Human Relations 11: 99-111. S.A. A1741.

5967. 1968 "Group aspirations." In D. Cartwright and A. Zander (eds.), Group Dynamics: Research and Theory, 3rd ed, pp. 418-429. New York: Harper & Row.

5968. 1969 "Students' criteria of satisfaction in a classroom committee project." Human Relations 22 (3, June): 195-207.

5969. 1971 Motives and Goals in Groups. New York: Academic Press.

5970. Zander, Alvin, and A. R. Cohen
1955 "Attributed social power and group acceptance: A classroom experimental demonstration." Journal of Abnormal and Social Psychology

51: 490-492. P.A. 31:2733; S.A. 3446.

5971. Zander, Alvin, and Theodore Curtis
1962   "Effects of social power on aspiration setting and striving." Journal of Abnormal and Social Psychology 64 (1): 63-74. P.A. 37:3051.

5972.   1965   "Social support and rejection of organizational standards." Journal of Educational Psychology 56 (2): 87-95. P.A. 39:10015.

5973. Zander, Alvin, and John Forward
1968   "Position in group, achievement motivation, and group aspirations." Journal of Personality and Social Psychology 8 (3, pt. 1): 282-288. P.A. 42:8875.

5974. Zander, Alvin, Richard Fuller, and Warwick Armstrong
1972   "Attributed pride or shame in group and self." Journal of Personality and Social Psychology 23 (3): 346-352.

5975. Zander, Alvin, and Arnold Havelin
1960   "Social comparison and interpersonal attraction." Human Relations 13 (1, February): 21-32. P.A. 35:6353; S.A. A3311.

5976. Zander, Alvin, and Herman Medow
1963   "Individual and group levels of aspiration." Human Relations 16 (1, February): 89-105. P.A. 38:2594.

5977.   1965   "Strength of group and desire for attainable group aspirations." Journal of Personality 33 (1, March): 122-139. P.A. 39:10016.

5978. Zander, Alvin, Herman Medow, and Ronald Efron
1965   "Observers' expectations as determinants of group aspirations." Human Relations 18 (3, August): 273-287. P.A. 40:502; S.A. 14: C2802.

5979. Zander, Alvin, Thomas Natsoulas, and Edwin J. Thomas
1960   "Personal goals and the group's goals for the member." Human Relations 13 (4, November): 333-344. P.A. 36:1GE33Z; S.A. A3810.

5980. Zander, Alvin, Ezra Stotland, and Donald Wolfe
1960   "Unity of group, identification with group, and self-esteem of members." Journal of Personality 28: 463-478. P.A. 35:4831.

5981. Zander, Alvin, and Donald Wolfe
1964   "Administrative rewards and coordination among committee members." Administrative Science Quarterly 9 (1, June): 50-69. S.A. 12:B3230.

5982. Zander, Alvin, and David Wulff
1966   "Members' test anxiety and competence: Determinants of a group's aspriations." Journal of Personality 34 (1): 55-70. P.A. 40:8800.

5983. Zanna, Mark P.
1973   "On inferring one's beliefs from one's behavior in a low-choice setting." Journal of Personality and Social Psychology 26 (3, June): 386-394. P.A. 50:11287.

5984. Zanna, Mark P., Mark R. Lepper, and Robert P. Abelson
1973   "Attentional mechanisms in children's devaluation of a forbidden activity in a forced-compliance situation." Journal of Personality and Social Psychology 28 (3, December): 355-359. P.A. 51:7093.

5985. Zavala, Albert, and James J. Paley (eds.)
1972   Personal Appearance Identification. Springfield, Ill.: Charles C. Thomas. P.A. 51:3095.

5986. Zdep, Stanley M.
1969   "Intra group reinforcement and its effects on leadership behavior." Organizational Behavior and Human Performance 4 (3): 284-298. P.A. 43:17364.

5987. Zdep, Stanley M., and William F. Oakes
1967   "Reinforcement of leadership behavior in group discussion." Journal of Experimental Social Psychology 3 (July): 310-320.

5988. Zeff, Leon H., and Marvin A. Iverson
1966   "Opinion conformity in groups under status threat." Journal of Personality and Social Psychology 3 (4): 383-389. P.A. 40:5413.

5989. Zeisel, Hans
1963   "What determines the amount of argument per juror?" American Sociological Review 28 (2, April): 279. S.A. 11:A6362.

5990. Zeleny, Leslie D.
    1939a "Characteristics of group leaders." Sociology and Social Research 24: 140–149. P.A. 14:1519.
5991.   1939b "Sociometry of morale." American Sociological Review 4: 799–808. P.A. 14:2026.
5992.   1940a "Experimental appraisal of a group learning plan." Journal of Educational Research 34: 37–42. P.A. 14:6242.
5993.   1940b "Measurement of social status." American Journal of Sociology 45: 576–582. P.A. 14:1518.
5994.   1941 "Measurement of sociation." American Sociological Review 6: 173–188. P.A. 15:3085.
5995.   1947 "Selection of compatible flying partners." American Journal of Sociology 52: 424–431. P.A. 21:2447.
5996. Zellner, Miriam, and George Levinger
    1971 "Liking and self-evaluation: Comfort and respect as sources of attraction." Representative Research in Social Psychology 2 (1, January): 58–65. P.A. 46:8955.
5997. Zemore, Robert W., and Timothy J. Greenough
    1973 "Reduction of ego threat following attributive projection." Proceedings of the 81st Annual Convention of the American Psychological Association 8: 343–344. P.A. 50:8893.
5998. Zentner, Henry
    1955 "Primary group affiliation and institutional group morale." Sociology and Social Research 40: 31–34. S.A. 2928.
5999. Zicklin, Gilbert
    1968 "A conversation concerning face-to-face interaction." Psychiatry 31 (3): 236–249. P.A. 44:2277.
6000. Zigon, Frank J., and John R. Cannon
    1974 "Processes and outcomes of group discussions as related to leader behaviors." Journal of Educational Research 67 (5, January): 199–201. P.A. 52:2909.
6001. Ziller, Robert C.
    1955 "Scales of judgement: A determinant of the accuracy of group decisions." Human Relations 8: 153–164. S.A. 1987.
6002.   1957a "Four techniques of group decision making under uncertainty." Journal of Applied Psychology 41: 384–388.
6003.   1957b "Group size: A determinant of the quality and stability of group decisions." Sociometry 20: 165–173.
6004.   1958 "Communication restraints, group flexibility, and group confidence." Journal of Applied Psychology 42: 346–352.
6005.   1959 "Leader acceptance of responsibility for group action under conditions of uncertainty and risk." Journal of Psychology 47: 57–66. P.A. 34:4221.
6006.   1962 "The newcomer's acceptance in open and closed groups." Personnel Administration 25 (5): 24–31. P.A. 38:5977.
6007.   1963 "Leader assumed dissimilarity as a measure of prejudical congnitive style." Journal of Applied Psychology 47 (5): 339–342. P.A. 38:4207.
6008.   1965a "Toward a theory of open and closed groups." Psychological Bulletin 64 (3): 164–182. P.A. 39:15072.
6009.   1965b "The leader's perception of the marginal member." Personnel Administration 28 (2): 6–11. P.A. 39:10022.
6010.   1973 The Social Self. New York: Pergamon.
6011. Ziller, Robert C., and Richard D. Behringer
    1959 "Group persuasion by the most knowledgeable member under conditions of incubation and varying group size." Journal of Applied Psychology 43 (December): 402–406. P.A. 34:7617.
6012.   1960 "Assimilation of the knowledgeable newcomer under conditions of group success and failure." Journal of Abnormal and Social Psychology 60 (2, March): 288–291. P.A. 34:7618.
6013.   1961 "A longitudinal study of the assimilation of the new child in the group." Human Relations 14 (2, May): 121–133.

6014.   1965   "Motivational and perceptual effects in orientation toward a new-comer." Journal of Social Psychology 66 (1, June): 79–90. P.A. 39: 15073.

6015. Ziller, Robert C., Richard D. Behringer, and Jacqueline D. Goodchilds
    1960   "The minority newcomer in open and closed groups." Journal of Psychology 50: 75–84. P.A. 35:6354.

6016. Ziller, Robert C., Richard D. Behringer, and Mathilda J. Jansen
    1961   "The newcomer in open and closed groups." Journal of Applied Psychology 45: 55–58. P.A. 36:2GE55Z.

6017. Ziller, Robert C., and Ralph V. Exline
    1958   "Some consequences of age heterogeneity in decision-making groups." Sociometry 21: 198–211. P.A. 33:10123.

6018. Zillmann, Dolf
    1971   "Excitation transfer in communication-mediated aggressive behavior." Journal of Experimental Social Psychology 7 (4, July): 419–434. P.A. 48:2911.

6019.   1972   "Rhetorical elicitation of agreement in persuasion." Journal of Personality and Social Psychology 21 (2, February): 159–165. P.A. 48: 2861.

6020. Zillmann, Dolf, and Jennings Bryant
    1974   "Retaliatory equity as a factor in humor appreciation." Journal of Experimental Social Psychology 10 (5): 480–488.

6021. Zillmann, Dolf, and Joanne R. Cantor
    1972   "Directionality of transitory dominance as a communication variable affecting humor appreciation." Journal of Personality and Social Psychology 24 (2, November): 191–198. P.A. 49:4460.

6022. Zillmann, Dolf, Aaron H. Katcher, and Barry Milavsky
    1972   "Excitation transfer from physical exercise to subsequent aggressive behavior." Journal of Experimental Social Psychology 8 (3): 247–259.

6023. Zimbardo, Philip G.
    1960   "Involvement and communication discrepancy as determinants of opinion conformity." Journal of Abnormal and Social Psychology 60 (1, January): 86–94. P.A. 34:7619.

6024. Zimbardo, Philip G., and Robert Formica
    1963   "Emotional comparison and self-esteem as determinants of affiliation." Journal of Personality 31: 141–162.

6025. Zimet, Carl N., and Harold J. Fine
    1955   "Personality changes with a group therapeutic experience in a human relations seminar." Journal of Abnormal and Social Psychology 51: 68–73. P.A. 30:4715.

6026. Zimet, Carl N., and Carol Schneider
    1969   "Effects of group size on interaction in small groups." Journal of Social Psychology 77 (2): 177–187. P.A. 43:9650.

6027. Zimmer, Herbert
    1956   "Motivational factors in dyadic interaction." Journal of Personality 24: 251–261.

6028.   1961   "Preparing psychophysiologic analog information for the digital computer." Behavioral Science 6 (2, April): 161–164. S.A. A3190.

6029. Zipf, Shelia G.
    1960   "Resistance and conformity under reward and punishment." Journal of Abnormal and Social Psychology 61 (1): 102–109. P.A. 35:2140.

6030. Zlutnick, Steven, and Irwin Altman
    1972   "Crowding and human behavior." In J. F. Wohlwill and D. H. Carson (eds.), Environment and the Social Sciences: Perspectives and Applications. Washington, D.C.: American Psychological Association. P.A. 50:11197.

6031. Znamierowski, Czeslaw
    1960   ("The situation of a partner in a two-person independent group.") Przeglad Socjologiczny 14 (1): 41–56. S.A. 13:B6769.

6032. Znaniecki, Florian
    1939   "Social groups as products of participating individuals." American

Journal of Sociology 44: 799–812. P.A. 13:4798.
6033. Zolman, James F., Irvin S. Wolf, and Seymour Fisher
    1960   "Distance and conformity in continuous social influence interactions." Journal of Social Psychology 52 (November): 251–257. P.A. 35:4832.
6034. Zuckerman, Miron
    1972   "Personality and situational factors in the process of inferring attitudes from behavior." Psychological Reports 31 (1, August): 283–289. P.A. 49:4461.
6035. Zurcher, Louis A., Jr.
    1967   "The leader and the lost: A case study of indigenous leadership in a poverty program community action committee." Genetic Psychology Monographs 76 (1): 23–93. P.A. 41:16640.
6036.   1970   "The 'friendly' poker game: A study of an ephemeral role." Social Forces 49 (2, December): 173–185. S.A. 19:F0474. (See also Proceedings of the Southwestern Sociological Association, 1969, 19 (April): 50–54. S.A. 18:E4571.)
6037. Zych, Kenneth, and Brian Bolton
    1972   "Galvanic skin responses and cognitive attitudes toward disabled persons." Rehabilitation Psychology 19 (4, Winter): 172–173. P.A. 51:3096.

INDEXES

Authors' names are not always consistently cited in research literature. Various publications use various combinations of given names and/or initials. Where it seems clear that different combinations have been used to name the same author, all references are here listed under one name, with variations of initials indicated by parentheses. Where it is not clear that similar initials signify the same author, the different names are listed separately.

AUTHOR INDEX

Koivumaki, J. H., 59, 410
Kolaja, J., 342
Kolb, D. A., 251, 418
Kolominskiy, Ya. L., 18
Kolstoe, R. H., 49
Komorita, S. S., 154, 228, 246, 249, 250
Konečni, V. J., 49, 251
Kopera, A. A., 317
Kormann, L. A., 410
Korner, I. N., 275
Korte, C., 251
Korten, D. C., 301
Koslin, B. L., 397
Kotkov, B., 53
Koulack, D., 165
Kounin, J. S., 405
Kozel, N. J., 116
Koziey, P. W., 419
Kozman, H. C., 18
Kraft, M., 126
Krain, M., 112
Kramer, L., 327
Krasne, F., 58
Kratochvil, S., 26
Krause, M. S., 248
Krauss, H. H., 328
Krauss, R. M., 247, 394
Krauze, T. K., 406
Krebs, A. M., 27
Krebs, R., 418
Krech, D., 214
Kretschmann, J. G., 49
Krichevskii, R. L., 340
Krieger, M. H., 141
Křivohlavý, J., 247, 249
Kroger, R. O., 328
Krug, R. E., 405
Kruglanski, A. W., 123, 238, 411
Krulee, G. K., 112
Krupar, K. R., 418
Krupat, E., 34, 50, 252
Kruskal, W. H., 275
Ksionsky, S., 30, 83, 177, 247
Ktsanes, T., 164
Ktsanes, V., 164
Kubička, L., 247
Kuc, M., 87
Kuethe, J. L., 186
Kullberg, V. K., 228
Kumpf, M., 39
Kunczik, M., 278
Kutash, S. B., 419
Kutner, D. H., Jr., 229
Kuusela, R., 405
Kuusinen, J., 118

LaBelle, T. J., 299
Lacome, B. S., 228
Ladwig, G. W., 246
LaFave, L., 203

Laffal, J., 405
LaFong, C., 178
LaForge, (G.) R., 404
La Gaipa, J. J., 176
Lage, E., 59
Lagrou, L., 147, 340
Laing, G., 125
Laing, J. D., 228
Laird, D. A., 293, 316, 387
Laird, E. C., 293
Laird, J. D., 116
Lake, D. G., 397
Lake, R., 418
Lakie, W. L., 239
Lakin, M., 418, 419
LaKind, E., 252
Lalljee, M., 84, 87
Lamb, T. W., 28
Lambert, R., 58, 198, 238, 328, 342
Lambert, W. E., 318
Lamberth, J., 156, 164, 166
Lamm, H., 247, 248, 327, 328
Lammers, C. J., 167
Lana, R. E., 50, 279
Lanckton, A. Van C., 25, 28
Landau, J. S., 48
Landecker, W. S., 142
Landers, D, M., 316, 340
Landis, M. H., 129, 202, 387
Landsberger, H. A., 64, 89, 302, 341
Landy, D., 119, 123, 156, 205, 251, 343
Landy, E., 301
Landy, E. E., 398
Lane, I. M., 250, 253
Lane, W. P., 279
Langan, C. J., 30
Lange, A., 49
Lange, C. J., 280
Lange, L., 344
Lange, M., 324, 387
Langelar, J. W., 319
Langer, E. J., 252
Langley, C. W., 418
Langmeyer, D., 248, 405, 419
Lankford, P. M., 407
Lansing, F. W., 167, 208
Lansky, L. M., 418
Lanto, S., 247
Lanzetta, J. T., 50, 93, 234, 235, 251, 252, 255, 262, 334, 343, 354
Larntz, F. K., 324
Larsen, K. J., 168
Larsen, K. S., 49, 165,

167, 168, 208, 249
Lasater, L., 48
Lasker, B., 293
Lasswell, H. D., 18, 391
Latané, B., 25, 39, 250, 251
Latané, J. G., 252
Lathrop, R. G., 50
Laughlin, P. R., 238, 318, 319, 324, 333
Lave, L. B., 249
Lawler, E. J., 228, 250
Lawless, W., 122
Lawlor, M., 53
Lawrence, D., 135
Lawrence, J. F., 182
Lawrence, L. C., 53
Lawson, E. (D.), 31, 201, 271
Lawton, S. F., 49
Lay, C. H., 115, 117
Layton, B. D., 124, 166
Leach, C., 114
Leader, G. C., 184
League, B. J., 26
Leary, T., 70, 182, 398, 404
Leathers, D. G., 354
Leavitt, G. S., 27, 117, 119
Leavitt, H. J., 27, 163, 170, 265, 266-270, 271, 300, 342, 343, 375, 418
Lebo, D., 419
Le Calve, G., 409
Le Compte, W. F., 84
Lecuyer, R., 326
Lee, A. J., 398
Lee, F. J., 167, 257, 330
Lee, M., 419
Lee, R. J., 285
Lee, V., 18
Leeman, C. P., 156, 407
Leet-Pellegrini, H., 57
LeFan, J., 170
Lefcourt, H. M., 246
Lefebvre, L. M., 251, 253
Legant, P., 49
Leggio, A. H., 116
Leginski, W. (A.), 116, 247, 276, 328
Lehner, G. F. J., 167, 182
Leichtman, H. M., 34
Leiderman, P. H., 355
Leik, R. K., 18, 82, 86, 142, 407, 411
Leinhardt, S., 178, 407, 409
Leith, W. R., 53
Lemann, T. B., 126, 167, 169
Lemineur, R., 167, 208
Lemke, E. A., 325

SUBJECT INDEX